MANAGERIAL ACCOUNTING

3rd Edition

CHARLES E. DAVIS | ELIZABETH DAVIS

WILEY

EDITORIAL DIRECTOR Michael McDonald
EDITORIAL MANAGER Karen Staudinger
EXECUTIVE EDITOR Zoe Craig
DEVELOPMENT EDITOR Courtney Jordan
ASSOCIATE MARKETING DIRECTOR Carolyn Wells
PRODUCT DESIGNER Matt Origoni
MEDIA SPECIALIST Elena Saccaro
SENIOR CONTENT MANAGER Dorothy Sinclair
SENIOR PRODUCTION EDITOR Valerie Vargas
PHOTO EDITOR MaryAnn Price
COVER DESIGN Maureen Eide
EDITORIAL ASSISTANT Anna Durkin and Iana Robitaille
MARKETING ASSISTANT Ashley Migliaro
COVER CREDIT Courtney Keating/Getty Images, Inc.

This book was set in Sabon Roman by Aptara®, Inc. and printed and bound by LSC Communications. The cover was printed by LSC Communications.

This book is printed on acid free paper. ∞

EPUB: 9781119234173

The inside back cover will contain printing identification and country of origin if omitted from this page. In addition, if the ISBN on the back cover differs from the ISBN on this page, the one on the back cover is correct.

Printed in the United States of America

10 9 8 7 6 5 4 3 2

Brief Contents

Author Biographies

Charles E. Davis, Professor of Accounting at Baylor University, joined the accounting faculty at Baylor in 1991 after receiving his Ph.D. in accounting from the University of North Carolina at Chapel Hill. He also holds an MBA from University of Richmond and a BBA in accounting from The College of William and Mary, and is a CMA, CGMA, and CPA (Virginia).

Prior to pursing his Ph.D., Professor Davis worked for Reynolds Metals Company, Coopers & Lybrand, and Investors Savings Bank, all in Richmond, Virginia. It was while working in various cost accounting positions at Reynolds Metals that Professor Davis developed his appreciation for managerial accounting.

Professor Davis's research has been published in a number of journals including *Accounting Horizons, Advances in Accounting, Advances in Accounting Behavioral Research, Advances in Accounting Education,* and *Issues in Accounting Education.* He has received The Institute of Management Accountants' Lybrand Gold Medal and three Certificates of Merit for his publications in *Management Accounting* and *Strategic Finance*. Professor Davis currently serves on the Editorial Board of *Strategic Finance* and is a former member of the Editorial Board of *Issues in Accounting Education.*

Elizabeth Davis, President at Furman University, began her academic career as a member of the accounting faculty at Baylor University in 1992 after receiving her Ph.D. in accounting from Duke University. She also holds a BBA in accounting from Baylor University and is a CPA (Louisiana, inactive).

Prior to pursuing her graduate studies, Dr. Davis worked as an auditor for Arthur Andersen & Co. in New Orleans, Louisiana. While in public practice, she specialized in the audits of financial institutions and real estate.

Dr. Davis's research has been published in a number of journals including *Organizational Behavior and Human Decision Processes, Advances in Accounting, Advances in Accounting Behavioral Research, Advances in Accounting Education, Issues in Accounting Education, Journal of Accounting Case Research,* and *Today's CPA.* She has received The Institute of Management Accountants' Lybrand Gold Medal and a Certificate of Merit for her publications in *Management Accounting and Strategic Finance.*

Preface

Today's business environment is a complex assortment of relationships, all of which are necessary for an organization's success in the marketplace. These relationships can involve external parties such as suppliers and customers, or internal parties such as employees. And all of these relationships rely on some form of managerial accounting information to support decision-making activities.

Non-accounting business majors frequently ask, "Why do I need to take accounting? I'm not going to do accounting; I'll hire an accountant to do that for me." What these students fail to understand is that a working knowledge of accounting is essential to success in business, even when the accounting "work" is left to the trained accountants. Decision makers at all levels in the organization must know what accounting information to ask for and must know how to interpret that information before reaching a conclusion about a course of action. For instance, how can a marketing manager decide on a price for a product without fully understanding the product's cost to manufacture? How can a plant manager determine how to reward employees' performance without understanding their ability to control costs and quality?

Those of us teaching introductory accounting courses may be partly to blame for this misconception. Often we place too much emphasis on the "accounting" and not enough emphasis on the "business." We are more concerned with students getting the "right" answer rather than understanding what to *do* with that right answer. Realizing that most students in an introductory managerial accounting course are not going to major in accounting, this book seeks to position managerial accounting in a broader context of business decision making.

This book does not attempt to be all things for all people. Instead, it is targeted to a typical university sophomore with limited business knowledge, both in terms of theoretical education and practical experience. While the nature of the book may be suitable for other audiences, we anticipate that the majority of students using this book have very little business foundation on which to build. Limited knowledge of business topics is assumed, though we anticipate that students have completed an introductory financial accounting course. Therefore, our overriding objective is to lay a firm foundation of basic managerial accounting on which new concepts in areas of finance, marketing, and management can be built.

The vision of this book is to provide an easy-to-use learning system for introductory managerial accounting students. Our expectation is that this learning system will:

1. facilitate students' learning of introductory managerial accounting concepts,
2. improve students' understanding of how to use these concepts as support for management decisions, and
3. improve students' retention of these concepts for use in subsequent business and accounting courses.

DISTINGUISHING FEATURES

BUSINESS DECISION-MAKING CONTEXT

Business Organizations, Supply Chain Players, Key Decisions

To really understand how managerial accounting information supports business decision-making activities, students need a **CONTEXT** in which to place those decisions. Davis and Davis *Managerial Accounting* creates this context by using C&C Sports, a fictitious manufacturer of sports apparel, and its supply chain partners to illustrate and explain concepts. The story of C&C begins in the business decision posed at the start of each chapter, carries throughout units in the chapter, and is applied in a new continuing case problem at the end of each chapter.

Business Decision and Context

Martin Keck, vice president for sales at Universal Sports Exchange, was talking with his sales team at the monthly sales meeting. "As you know, the company missed its sales target last year. We were expecting to sell 10% more jerseys than we did. And we all saw the effect that the lower sales level had on our bottom line. When we miss our sales targets, it affects what everyone else in the company can accomplish because they count on us to generate revenue."

Sarah Yardley, one of the company's top salespeople, had been listening intently as Martin discussed the concept of cost behavior. "I think I understand all this talk about cost behavior," she said, "but I'm still not sure how it plays into my decisions."

"Sarah," Martin replied, "we have to use our knowledge of cost behaviors to *predict* what effect our decisions will have on the bottom line. We know when it is advantageous to, say, initiate a new advertising campaign instead of reducing prices, but to persuade the president and the CFO, we need to have more convincing data, and that includes the financial impact of our decisions. In fact, I'll be meeting with the president and CFO next week to discuss the relative merits of a $50,000 advertising campaign and a 10% reduction in sales price. You can be sure that I'll know the expected financial impact of each alternative before I walk into the meeting."

© alarik/Shutterstock

Business Organizations: Students better understand the decision-making process by understanding the context of decisions made by managers across all departments and divisions in the organization.

SUPPLY CHAIN KEY PLAYERS

END CUSTOMER

UNIVERSAL SPORTS EXCHANGE

Vice President of Sales, Martin Keck

Top Salesperson, Sarah Yardley

C&C SPORTS

DURABLE ZIPPER COMPANY

BRADLEY TEXTILE MILLS

CENTEX YARNS

Supply Chain Key Players: Decisions often are made with other **manufacturing and retail companies.** Illustrating decisions in this context allows students to better understand the **supply chain** concept and the reality that companies must work with their supply chain partners to achieve maximum results.

"I'll be meeting with the president and CFO next week to discuss the relative merits of a ... 10% ... sure ... of each ... meeting."

Key Decision: Each chapter is framed with a decision that key players must address. The decision is highlighted in quotes in the opening of the chapter. Discussions, examples, and illustrations in the chapter address the topics associated with the business decision. A **Wrap Up** at the end of the chapter applies topics addressed in the chapter to the key decision.

BUSINESS DECISION AND CONTEXT Wrap Up

Martin Keck now knows how to present the financial implications of the $50,000 advertising campaign and a 10% price reduction.

The advertising campaign represents a $50,000 increase in fixed expenses. Since nothing else is changing, Martin determined that Universal will need to sell at least 12,500 additional jerseys to cover the additional fixed expense ($50,000 ÷ $4 contribution margin). That's a 24% increase in sales volume just to earn the same net income that Universal earns without the

BUSINESS DECISION-MAKING CONTEXT

Temporal Order

The order of the chapters in the book is designed around the context of a story that places business decisions in temporal order rather than the more traditional grouping of "Planning/Controlling," "Decision Making," and "Evaluating" sections. With this ordering of topics, students learn about managerial accounting and how to use managerial accounting to support decision making. Key players in the story include:

Centex Yarns, Yarn Manufacturer

© itaesem/iStockphoto

Bradley Textile Mills, Fabric Manufacturer

© petekarici/iStockphoto

Durable Zipper Company, Zipper Manufacturer

© aopsan/iStockphoto

C&C Sports, Team Uniform Manufacturer

© jsnyderdesign/iStockphoto

Universal Sports Exchange, Retail

© Tischenko Irina/Shutterstock

The ordering of the chapters is based on the following story line:

- C&C Sports is introduced. **(Topic Focus 1)**
- Universal Sports Exchange, a retailer in C&C Sports' supply chain, explores the need for cost behavior information to estimate and predict financial results. **(Chapters 2 and 3)**
- C&C Sports develops product costs for its three products using job order costing. **(Chapter 4)**
- Bradley Textile Mills develops product costs for its fabric using process costing. **(Topic Focus 2)**
- Bradley Textile Mills managers are engaged in a discussion of how increasing production will decrease the fixed cost per unit of yard of material. **(Topic Focus 3)**
- C&C Sports plans for the coming year by developing standards and a master budget once desired production volume is determined. **(Chapter 5)**
- C&C Sports recognizes the need to evaluate its performance using a flexible budget and variance analysis. It finds that results for direct materials and direct labor are in line with standards, but overhead costs differ from expectations. This finding leads to the need to better understand the company's cost drivers. **(Chapter 6)**
- Durable Zipper Company's accountant is overwhelmed by the volume of entries needed to record product costs. She looks to a standard cost system to help reduce the recording volume. **(Topic Focus 4)**
- C&C Sports explores the use of activity-based costing (ABC) in response to its earlier performance evaluation. Management discusses overhead pools and how those resources are consumed by the organization. The resulting product costs yield a picture of product profitability that is different from management's assumptions using traditional job order costing. Management also explores other nonfinancial performance metrics. **(Chapter 7)**
- Bradley Textile Mills' managers evaluate the profitability of the company's customers and explore the need to price certain extra services based on the ABC results to increase profitability. **(Topic Focus 5)**
- C&C Sports' management team meets to discuss the vice presidents' various areas of responsibility. Each vice president faces a different decision whose costs are not as obvious as it first seems. **(Chapter 8)**
- C&C Sports seeks to expand its product line to increase profitability. The company's managers use capital budgeting techniques to assess the viability of investing in equipment to produce baseball. **(Chapter 9)**
- Centex Yarns' Nylon Fibers division has shown a loss for the past three years. The division's vice president must determine how much the division is contributing to the company's financial health. **(Chapter 10)**
- C&C Sports' management recognizes that performance evaluation needs to be expanded to include the relation between financial and nonfinancial measures. A balanced scorecard is developed for the company. **(Chapter 11)**

DISTINGUISHING FEATURES

LEARNING DESIGN: CONCEPTS AND PRACTICE

Students stay **ENGAGED** as they read manageable units of content in each chapter that are written in a conversational style. Students **INTERACT** more with managerial accounting topics as they work through practice questions and exercises at the end of each unit. Students gain **CONFIDENCE** when they review practice exercise solutions before they move on to another topic. Frequent, **ACTIVE** demonstrations, exercises, and explorations replace the traditional passive reading of lengthy chapters.

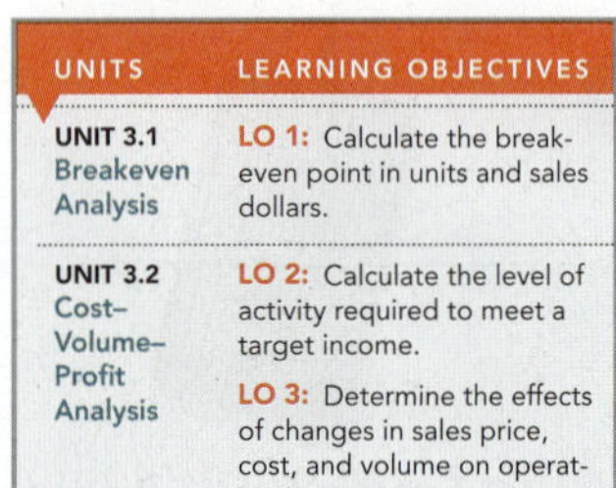

With active learning units, students analyze topics before moving to a new topic.

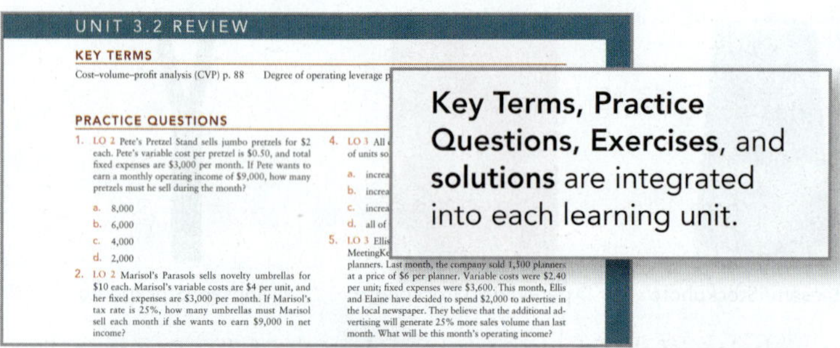

Key Terms, Practice Questions, Exercises, and solutions are integrated into each learning unit.

With Lightboard technology, students can watch the author solve problems in an easy-to-follow, step-by-step format.

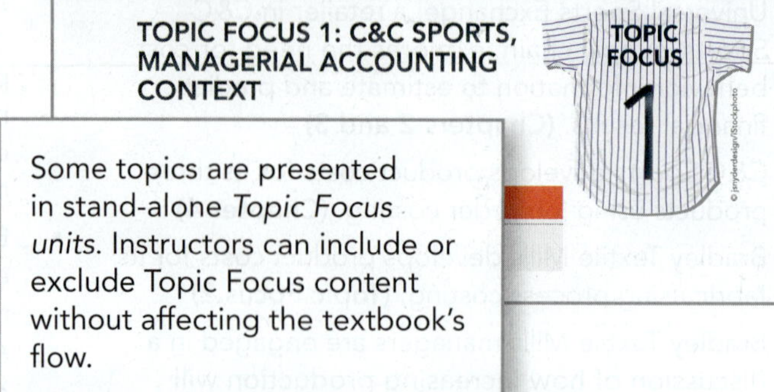

Some topics are presented in stand-alone *Topic Focus* units. Instructors can include or exclude Topic Focus content without affecting the textbook's flow.

ASSESSMENT

An extensive amount of comprehensive homework exercises, problems, and cases for all units are also provided at the end of each chapter. All are assignable in WileyPLUS.

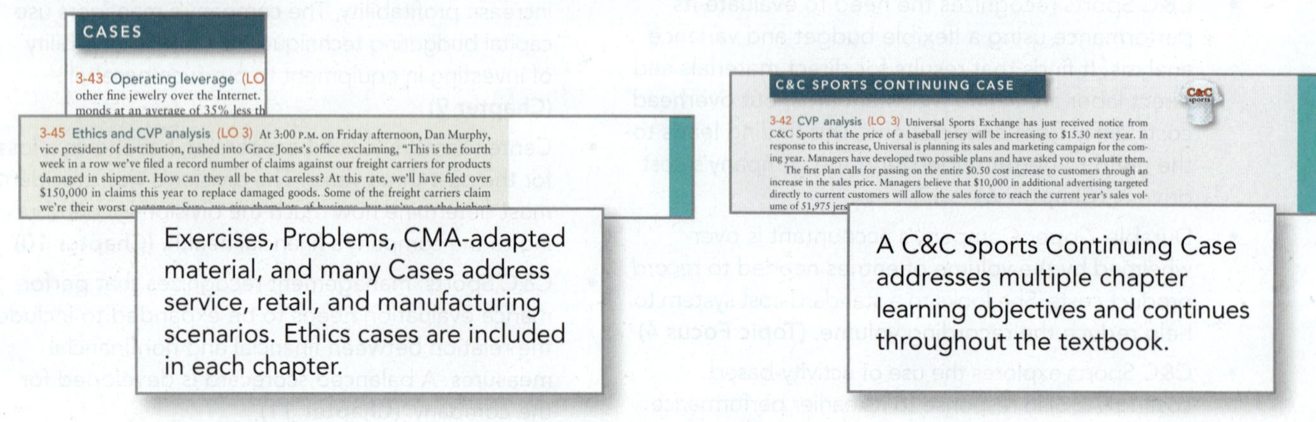

Exercises, Problems, CMA-adapted material, and many Cases address service, retail, and manufacturing scenarios. Ethics cases are included in each chapter.

A C&C Sports Continuing Case addresses multiple chapter learning objectives and continues throughout the textbook.

REAL-WORLD FOCUS

Business decision-making context is also illustrated through the examples of real-world companies discussed in Reality Check boxes, *WileyPLUS* videos, and homework problems.

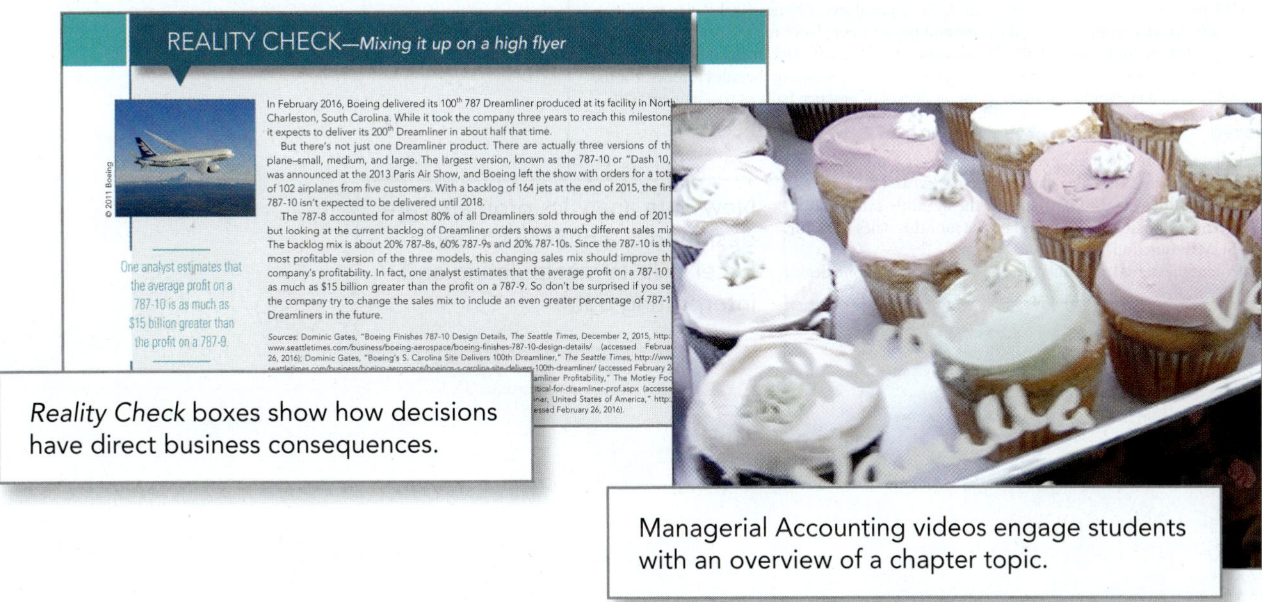

REALITY CHECK—*Mixing it up on a high flyer*

In February 2016, Boeing delivered its 100th 787 Dreamliner produced at its facility in Nort Charleston, South Carolina. While it took the company three years to reach this milestone it expects to deliver its 200th Dreamliner in about half that time.

But there's not just one Dreamliner product. There are actually three versions of th plane–small, medium, and large. The largest version, known as the 787-10 or "Dash 10, was announced at the 2013 Paris Air Show, and Boeing left the show with orders for a tota of 102 airplanes from five customers. With a backlog of 164 jets at the end of 2015, the firs 787-10 isn't expected to be delivered until 2018.

The 787-8 accounted for almost 80% of all Dreamliners sold through the end of 201 but looking at the current backlog of Dreamliner orders shows a much different sales mi The backlog mix is about 20% 787-8s, 60% 787-9s and 20% 787-10s. Since the 787-10 is th most profitable version of the three models, this changing sales mix should improve th company's profitability. In fact, one analyst estimates that the average profit on a 787-10 as much as $15 billion greater than the profit on a 787-9. So don't be surprised if you se the company try to change the sales mix to include an even greater percentage of 787-1 Dreamliners in the future.

One analyst estimates that the average profit on a 787-10 is as much as $15 billion greater than the profit on a 787-9.

Sources: Dominic Gates, "Boeing Finishes 787-10 Design Details, *The Seattle Times*, December 2, 2015, http: www.seattletimes.com/business/boeing-aerospace/boeing-finishes-787-10-design-details/ (accessed Februa 26, 2016); Dominic Gates, "Boeing's S. Carolina Site Delivers 100th Dreamliner," *The Seattle Times*, http://www seattletimes.com/business/boeing-aerospace/boeings-s-carolina-site-delivers-100th-dreamliner/ (accessed February 2 amliner Profitability," The Motley Foo itical-for-dreamliner-prof.aspx (accesse ner, United States of America," http: essed February 26, 2016).

Reality Check boxes show how decisions have direct business consequences.

Managerial Accounting videos engage students with an overview of a chapter topic.

CRITICAL THINKING

Students are asked to think critically in all learning units and homework problems.

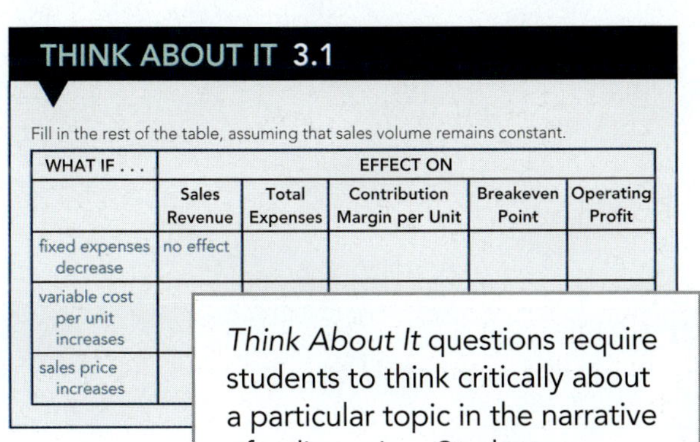

THINK ABOUT IT 3.1

Fill in the rest of the table, assuming that sales volume remains constant.

WHAT IF . . .	EFFECT ON				
	Sales Revenue	Total Expenses	Contribution Margin per Unit	Breakeven Point	Operating Profit
fixed expenses decrease	no effect				
variable cost per unit increases					
sales price increases					

Think About It questions require students to think critically about a particular topic in the narrative of a discussion. Students can evaluate their understanding with a solution that appears later in the discussion.

WATCH OUT!

When volume changes, total sales revenue, total variable expenses, and t bution margin a Students typica total sales rever get to change t expenses. The s start with contri per unit × sales sure to capture in total sales an expenses.

Concepts that students frequently find confusing or for which errors often occur are highlighted in *Watch Out!* boxes. Students' critical thinking is developed by helping them avoid common mistakes and eliminate bad habits.

38. Assume a sales price per unit of $25, variable cost per unit $15, and total fixed costs of $18,000. Wha the breakeven point in units?
    a. 720 units
    b. 1,200 units
    c. 1,800 units
    d. None of these answer choices is correct.

$18,000 ÷ ($25 − $15) = 1,800

Ans: c, LO: 1, Bloom: AP, Unit 3-1, Difficulty: Easy, Min: 3, AACSB: Analytic, AICPA FN: Decision Modeling, AICPA PC: Problem Solving and Decision Making, IMA: Decision Analysis

Test Bank and Homework questions address many learning outcomes that develop critical thinking skills.

DATA ANALYSIS PROBLEMS

ANALYTICS PROBLEM

3-46 Multiproduct CVP analysis using data analytics and Excel (LO 5) Greer Golf Supplies is an online store that sells two types of golf balls: practice balls and tournament balls. The golf balls are sold in plastic sleeves containing three golf balls. Practice balls sell for $4 per sleeve; tournament balls sell for $12 per sleeve. Owner Carl Rider purchases the golf balls directly from the manufacturer and pays $1 per sleeve for the practice balls and $4 per sleeve for the tournament balls. Fixed costs total $14,000 per month and include Carl's salary, website hosting, and accounting and legal fees. When preparing the sales forecast for the year, Carl assumed he would sell twice as many sleeves of practice balls as tournament balls.

Required

a. Calculate the annual breakeven point for Greer Golf Supplies.
b. Carl has gathered the sales data for the past year. Use Excel's C
prepare a 100% stacked bar chart of the monthly sales mix bas
data. You will first need to calculate the monthly sales total for
the SUMIF function.
c. Calculate the actual sales mix for the year. Round to one decim

New data analytics problems are designed to enhance students' Excel skills in manipulating and interpreting data.

NEW to the Third Edition

Informed by feedback from instructors and students, the Third Edition expands our emphasis on business decision making, practice, context, and a commitment to accuracy.

LIGHTBOARD TECHNOLOGY VIDEOS

NEW Lightboard Technology Videos provide students with over 70 new videos that allow them to watch the author solve problems.

Improved Test Bank includes new and refreshed multiple-choice questions and problems.

NEW Data Analytics Problems included in Chapters 2-11 use "big" (relatively speaking) data sets to enhance students' Excel skills in manipulating and interpreting data to make decisions.

Revised and Updated Reality Check Problems help students apply concepts through real-world business decisions.

Supplements

Instructor

In addition to the support instructors receive from *WileyPLUS* and the **Wiley Faculty Network**, we offer the following useful supplements.

Textbook website

On this website, www.wiley.com/college/davis, instructors will find electronic versions of the solutions manual, instructor's manual, test bank, computerized test bank, and other resources.

Solutions Manual

The solutions manual contains complete solutions, prepared by the authors, for each question, exercise, problem, and case in the textbook.

Instructor's Manual

The instructor's manual, prepared by the authors, contains unit and chapter summaries organized by learning objective, additional readings and critical thinking exercises, recommended instructional cases, and detailed notes to accompany the PowerPoint slides in each chapter.

Test Bank and Computerized Test Bank

The test bank allows instructors to tailor examinations according to study objectives and learning outcomes, including AACSB and AICPA professional standards. New multiple-choice questions and problems were added to the third edition.

PowerPoint Slides

This supplement includes PowerPoint slides prepared by the authors for each learning unit.

Student

Textbook Website

On this website students will find Excel Templates, PowerPoint slides, quizzes, and other resources.

WileyPLUS

Additional student online supplements are available in *WileyPLUS*. Here, students will find the following useful study and practice tools and more:

Study Guide

Contains a chapter outline with problems, multiple-choice questions, solutions, and more.

Excel Working Papers

Templates that help students correctly format their textbook accounting answers.

Managerial Accounting Videos Series

A series of videos that provide a real-world context and overview for chapter topics.

Lightboard Solution Videos

Author Charles Davis walks you through over 70 similar end-of-chapter homework exercises by recording himself behind an LED powered glass chalkboard. His writing glows in front of you.

Narrated PowerPoints Slides

PowerPoint slides prepared by the authors for each learning unit guide students through topics with voice-narrated and animated illustrations and examples.

The Development Story

Reviewed and Tested by over 200 Professors and 350 Students!

Managerial Accounting, Third Edition, is the result of incredibly extensive instructor and student involvement, every step of the way, from creation to development and execution.

Class Tests Dating back to the initial class tests of the first edition manuscript in 2007, over 40 instructors and 350 students have class tested chapters from this book. Their feedback was overwhelmingly supportive and enthusiastic, with over 93% of all instructors stating that the Davis and Davis student-focused learning design met their course goals. They offered valuable suggestions that can only come from use in the classroom, and their comments factored into each decision that was made to produce the final textbook and accompanying *WileyPLUS* course.

Developmental Reviews A team of development editors, including line editors and designers, worked closely with the authors to hone their distinctive learning design, test the explanation of concepts in the classroom, and confirm that the pedagogy is consistent and adds value to the learning process.

The Preliminary Edition To market test the first edition before its full release, we created a preliminary edition for evaluation, testing, and adoption.

Instructor Focus Groups Over 50 professors participated in live and virtual focus groups throughout the development process to provide invaluable feedback on the Davis and Davis solution and how it could help them better achieve their course goals.

Student Focus Groups Students participated in a variety of focus groups to provide feedback on the text design and share insights into their preferred learning style.

Faculty Reviewers More than 200 professors across the United States reviewed the manuscript at various stages to ensure the content was clear and precise and facilitated student engagement and understanding.

Reviewers, Focus Group Participants, and Class Testers:

We thank the following reviewers who provided valuable feedback:

Nishat Abbasi, *Metropolitan State College—Denver*
Wagdy Abdallah, *Seton Hall University*
Mohamed Abo-Hebeish, *California State University—Dominguez Hills*
Jim Aitken, *Central Michigan University*
Natalie Allen, *Texas A&M University*
Vernon Allen, *Central Florida Community College*
Nicolaou Andreas, *Bowling Green State University*
Melody Ashenfelter, *Southwestern Oklahoma State University*
Kristen Ball, *Dodge City Community College*
John Bedient, *Albion College*
Sarah Bee, *Seattle University*
Sharon Bell, *University of North Carolina—Pembroke*
Linda Benz, *Jefferson Community and Technical College*
Carol Bishop, *Georgia Southwestern State University*
David Bland, *Cape Fear Community College*
Benoit Boyer, *Sacred Heart University*
Bruce Bradford, *Fairfield University*
Roger Brannan, *University of Minnesota—Duluth*
Thomas Branton, *Alvin Community College*
Ann Brooks, *University of New Mexico—Albuquerque*
Myra Bruegger, *Southeastern Community College—Burlington*
Don Brunner, *Spokane Falls Community College*
Marci Butterfield, *University of Utah*
Don Campbell, *Brigham Young University—Idaho*
Michael Cerullo, *Southwest Missouri State University*
Linda Chase, *Baldwin Wallace College*
Bea Chiang, *The College of New Jersey*
Carolyn Christesen, *Westchester Community College*
Stanley Chu, *Borough of Manhattan Community College*
Anna Cianci, *Wake Forest University*
Cheryl Clark, *Point Park University*
Rob Clarke, *Brigham Young University—Idaho*
Antoinette Clegg, *Delta College*
Curtis Clements, *Abilene Christian University*
Jacklyn Collins, *University of Miami*
Mark Comstock, *Missouri Southern State University*
Martha Cranford, *Central Piedmont Community College*
Sue Cullers, *Tarleton State University*

Mai Dao, *University of Toledo*
Alan Davis, *Community College of Philadelphia*
David Dearman, *University of Arkansas—Little Rock*
Stephen Delvecchio, *Central Missouri State University*
Rosemond Desir, *Colorado State University*
Sandy Devona, *Northern Illinois University*
Jim Dodd, *Drake University*
Patricia Doherty, *Boston University*
Carleton Donchess, *Bridgewater State College*
David Doyon, *Southern New Hampshire University*
Andrea Drake, *Louisiana Tech University*
Rick Dunie, *University of Utah*
Reed Easton, *Seton Hall University*
Ahmed Ebrahim, *State University of New York—New Paltz*
Gene Elrod, *University of North Texas*
Kim Everett, *East Carolina University*
Robert Fahnestock, *University of West Florida*
Brian Fink, *Danville Area Community College*
Melissa Force, *Walsh College*
Don Foster, *Tacoma Community College*
Amy Fredin, *St. Cloud State University*
Peter Frischmann, *Idaho State University—Pocatello*
Mohamed Gaber, *State University of New York—Plattsburgh*
Catherine Gaharan, *Midwestern State University*
Clyde Galbraith, *West Chester University*
Mike Gilbert, *Ivy Tech Community College*
Jackson Gillespie, *University of Delaware*
Julie Gittelman, *Salisbury State University*
Connie Groer, *Frostburg State University*
Lillian Grose, *Delgado Community College*
Sanjay Gupta, *Valdosta State University*
Laurie Hagberg, *Trident Technical College*
Becky Hancock, *El Paso Community College*
Heidi Hansel, *Kirkwood Community College*
Julie Hansen, *Mesa College*
Rhonda Harbeson, *Lone Star College—CyFair*
Sara Harris, *Arapahoe Community College*
Martin Hart, *Manchester Community College*
Michael Haselkorn, *Bentley University*
Jeanne Haser-Lafond, *Rhode Island College*
Sueann Hely, *West Kentucky Community College*
Liliana Hickman-Riggs, *Richland College*
Lyle Hicks, *Danville Area Community College*
Mary Hollars, *Vincennes University*
Bambi Hora, *University of Central Oklahoma*
Carol Hutchinson, *Asheville-Buncombe Tech*
Laura Ilcisin, *University of Nebraska—Omaha*
Marianne James, *California State University—Los Angeles*
Cathy Jeppson, *California State University—Northridge*
Gene Johnson, *Clark College*
George Joseph, *University of Massachusetts—Lowell*
John Karayan, *Woodbury University*
J. Howard Keller, *Indiana University–Purdue University Indianapolis*
Zafar Khan, *Eastern Michigan University*
Michael Kilgore, *Georgia Institute of Technology*
Larry Killough, *Virginia Tech University—Blacksburg*
Tom Klammer, *University of North Texas*
Frank Klaus, *Cleveland State University*
Nazi Knox, *Angelo State University*
Janice Kraft, *Northwest College*
Joseph Krupka, *Georgia Southwestern State University*
Anthony Kurek, *Eastern Michigan University*
Wikil Kwak, *University of Nebraska—Omaha*
Kelly LaLonde, *Northern Essex Community College*
Kate Lancaster, *Cal Poly San Luis Obispo*
Doug Larson, *Salem State College*
Mark Lawrence, *University of North Alabama*
Jason Lee, *State University of New York—Plattsburgh*
Bruce Leung, *City College of San Francisco*
William Link, *University of Missouri—St. Louis*
May Lo, *Western New England College*
Dennis Lopez, *University of Texas—San Antonio*
D. Jordan Lowe, *Arizona State University—West*
James Lukawitz, *University of Memphis*
Cathy Lumbattis, *Southern Illinois University—Carbondale*
Suneel Maheshwari, *Marshall University*
Lois Mahoney, *Eastern Michigan University*
Sue Marcum, *American University*
Christian Mastilak, *Xavier University*
Lizbeth Matz, *University of Pittsburgh—Bradford*
Richard Mayer, *Bemidji State University*
Mark McCarthy, *DePaul University*
Britton McKay, *Georgia Southern University*
Terri Meta, *Seminole Community College*
Tammy Metzke, *Milwaukee Area Community College*
Mike Meyer, *University of Notre Dame*
Pam Meyer, *University of Louisiana—Lafayette*
James Miller, *Gannon University*
Linda Miller, *Northeast Community College*
Susan Minke, *Indiana University—Purdue University Fort Wayne*
Lowell Mooney, *Georgia Southern University*
David Morris, *North Georgia College*
Dennis Mullen, *City College of San Francisco*
Greg Nelson, *Idaho State University—Pocatello*
Mary Beth Nelson, *North Shore Community College*
Bruce Neumann, *University of Colorado—Denver*

Richard Newmark, *University of Northern Colorado*
Joseph Nicassio, *Westmoreland County Community College*
Chris O'Byrne, *Cuyamaca College*
Rod Oglesby, *Drury University*
Janet O'Tousa, *University of Notre Dame*
Jack Paul, *Lehigh University*
Sandra Pelfrey, *Oakland University*
Valerie Peterson, *Bryant University*
Yvonne Phang, *Borough of Manhattan Community College*
Robert Picard, *Idaho State University—Pocatello*
Chuck Pier, *Angelo State University*
John Plouffe, *California State University—Los Angeles*
Sharon Polansky, *Texas A&M University—Corpus Christi*
Laura Prosser, *Black Hills State University*
Monsurur Rahman, *Indiana University of Pennsylvania*
Tom Ramsey, *Wake Forest University*
Vasant Raval, *Creighton University*
Anita Reed, *Texas A&M University—Corpus Christi*
Barbara Reider, *University of Montana*
Laura Rickett, *Kent State University*
Jane Romal, *State University of New York—Brockport*
Jorge Romero, *Towson University*
Kristen Rosacker, *University of Wisconsin—LaCrosse*
Joan Ryan, *Clackamas Community College*
Angela Sandberg, *Jacksonville State University*
Christine Schalow, *University of Wisconsin—Stevens Point*
David Schestag, *Lorain County Community College*
Tony Scott, *Norwalk Community College*
Ann Selk, *University of Wisconsin—Green Bay*
Margaret Shackell-Dowell, *Cornell University*
David Shapiro, *The City University of New York—John Jay College of Criminal Justice*
Shiv Sharma, *Robert Morris University*
Dee Ann Shepherd, *Abilene Christian University*
Mehdi Sheikholeslami, *Bemidji State University*
Jeff Shields, *University of Southern Maine*
Carl Shultz, *Rider University*
Lakshmy Sivarantnam, *Kansas City Community College*
Michael Slaubaugh, *Indiana University—Purdue University Fort Wayne*
David Smith, *Missouri Southern State University*
Sondra Smith, *West Gate University*
Talitha Smith, *Auburn University*
Walter Smith, *Siena College*
Hakjoon Song, *Temple University*
Liga Spoge, *Drexel University*
John Stancil, *Florida Southern College*
Frank Stangota, *Rutgers University*
Christine Stinson, *Ferrum College*
Scott Stovall, *Abilene Christian University*
Holly Sudano, *Florida State University*
John Surdick, *Xavier University*
Dana Sweat, *Tallahassee Community College*
Karen Tabak, *Maryville University—St. Louis*
Kim Tan, *California State University—Stanislaus*
Linda Tarrago, *Hillsborough Community College*
Barbara Thomas, *Illinois Central College*
Dorothy Thompson, *North Central Texas College*
Michael Tyler, *Barry University—Miami Shores*
Eric Typpo, *University of the Pacific*
Joan Van Hise, *Fairfield University*
Johnny Van Horn, *Arkansas State University*
Ram Venkataraman, *Southern Methodist University*
John Virchick, *Chapman University*
Ron Vogel, *College of Eastern Utah*
Anne Warrington, *Michigan Technical University*
Leo Welsh, *University of Texas—Austin*
Anne Wessely, *St. Louis Community College—Meramec*
Stephen Wheeler, *University of the Pacific*
Lourdes White, *University of Baltimore*
Stephen Woehrle, *Minnesota State University—Mankato*
Emily Wright, *MacMurray College*
Jia Wu, *University of Massachusetts—Dartmouth*
Lee Yao, *Loyola University of New Orleans*
Austin Zekeri, *North Greenville University*
Thomas Zeller, *Loyola University—Chicago*

Second Edition

Ervin Black, *Brigham Young University*
Steve Buchheit, *Texas Tech University*
Jacklyn Collins, *University of Miami*
Nancy Coulmas, *Bloomsburg University*
Rafik Elias, *California State University*
Amanda Farmer, *University of Georgia*
Amy Fredin, *St. Cloud State*
Richard Green, *Texas A&M University—San Antonio*
Sanjay Gupta, *Valdosta State University*
Kevin Jones, *Drexel University*
Mark Judd, *University of San Diego*
Barbara Lamberton, *University of Hartford*
Linxiao Liu, *University of West Georgia*
Dennis McCrory, *Ivy Tech Community College*
Mahmoud Nourayi, *Loyola Marymount University*

Rosemary Nurre, *College of San Mateo*
Glen Owen, *Allan Hancock College*
Antonio Rodriguez, *Texas A&M International University*
P. N. Saksena, *Indiana University—South Bend*
Ali Sedaghat, *Loyola University—Maryland*
Jamie Seitz, *University of Southern Indiana*
Karen Tabak, *Maryville University*
Terry Tranter, *University of Minnesota*
Michael Tyler, *Barry University*
Charles Wain, *Babson College*

Third Edition

Kelvie A. Crabb, *University of Kansas*
Corinne Frad, *Muscatine Community College*
Mary Anne Gaffney, *Temple University*
Justin Goss, *UCLA*
Barbara Lamberton, *University of Hartford*
Linxiao Liu, *University of West Georgia*
Kate Mooney, *St. Cloud University*
Barbara Rice, *Gateway Community and Technical College*
Lily Sieux, *Golden Gate University*
Amy Stahl, *Central Ohio Technical College*

Media Contributors and Accuracy Checkers

We sincerely thank the following individuals for their hard work and skill in preparing and accuracy checking the content that accompanies this textbook.

Kyle Anderson, *Clemson University*
Ellen Bartley, *St. Joseph's College*
LuAnn Bean, *Florida Institute of Technology*
Debby Bloom, *York Technical College*
Jack Borke, *University of Wisconsin—Platteville*
James Emig, *Villanova University*
Larry Falcotto, *Emporia State University*
Tony Falgiani, *Western Illinois University*
Heidi Hansel, *Kirkwood Community College*
Cathy Larson, *Middlesex Community College*
Jill Misuraca, *University of Tampa*
Patricia Mounce, *University of Central Arkansas*
Barbara Muller, *Arizona State University*
Laura Prosser, *Black Hills State University*
Lynn Stallworth, *Appalachian State University*
Holly Sudano, *Florida State University*
Michelle Suminski, *Macomb Community College*
Diane Tanner, *University of North Florida*
Dick Wasson, *Southwestern College*

Acknowledgments

A project of this magnitude cannot be completed solely by the authors listed on the book's cover. We want to thank our colleagues at Baylor University who have supported our early work on this project, particularly Scott Bryant, who assisted in classroom testing the book's early drafts for several semesters, and Gia Chevis, who read the entire manuscript and provided helpful comments. Our students also deserve thanks for persevering through early drafts and numerous typographical errors. Dr. Lorynn Divita, associate professor of fashion merchandising at Baylor University, provided us with a crash course on the textile industry, helping us to understand C&C Sports' supply chain. A special thanks is due to Bill Sturgeon, Armando DeLeon, and all the other employees of Southland Athletic Manufacturing Company in Terrell, Texas, for showing us their operations.

We were fortunate to have an extraordinary team from John Wiley & Sons to guide us through the process of bringing this textbook and *WileyPLUS* course to publication. We are grateful for the assistance and guidance provided by Editorial Director, Mike McDonald, Senior Marketing Manager Carolyn Wells, Editorial Manager Karen Staudinger, Development Editor Courtney Jordan, Product Designer Matt Origoni, Senior Content Manager Dorothy Sinclair, Senior Production Editor Valerie Vargas, Senior Designer Wendy Lai, Editorial Assistants Iana Robitaille and Anna Durkin, and

Marketing Assistant Ashley Migliaro. Thank you to Amy Scholz, Susan Elbe, George Hoffman, Tim Stookesberry, and Steve Smith for their support and leadership in the Wiley's Global Education Division.

In the course of developing *Managerial Accounting*, we have benefited greatly from the input of manuscript reviewers, accuracy checkers, supplement authors, focus group participants, and class testers.

Dedication

To our C&C, Chad and Claire.

To our parents, Charles and Marilyn Boozer (in memory) and Cedric and Shirley Davis.

Contents

© Tischenko Irina/Shutterstock

ACCOUNTING AS A TOOL FOR MANAGEMENT

UNITS	LEARNING OBJECTIVES
UNIT 1.1 What Is Managerial Accounting?	**LO 1:** Define managerial accounting. **LO 2:** Describe the differences between managerial and financial accounting. **LO 3:** List and describe the four functions of managers.
UNIT 1.2 Different Strategies, Different Information	**LO 4:** Explain how the selection of a particular business strategy determines the information that managers need to run an organization effectively.
UNIT 1.3 Ethical Considerations in Managerial Accounting	**LO 5:** Discuss the importance of ethical behavior in managerial accounting.

© wavebreakmedia/Shutterstock

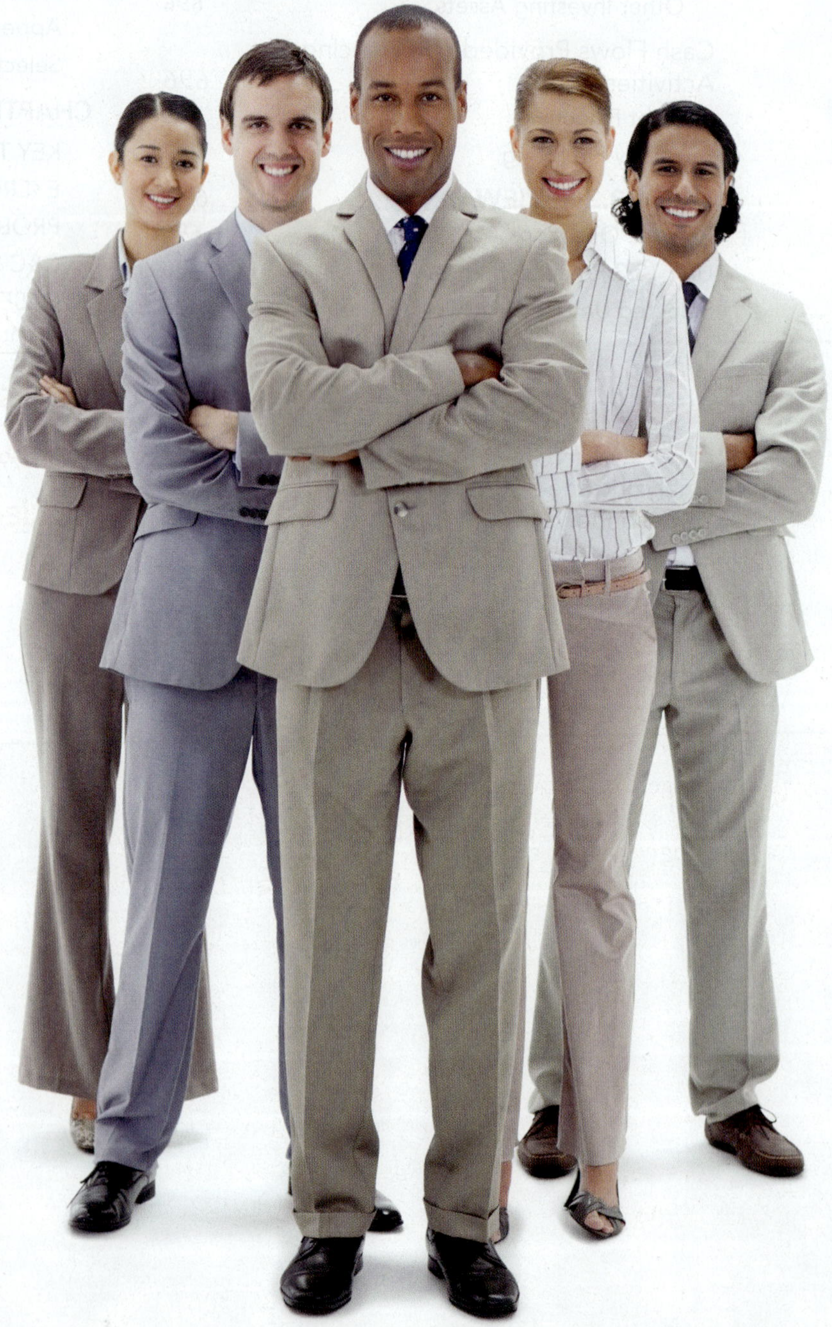

UNIT 1.1

What Is Managerial Accounting?

GUIDED UNIT PREPARATION

Answering the following questions while you read this unit will guide your understanding of the key concepts found in the unit. The questions are linked to the learning objectives at the beginning of the chapter.

LO 1
1. Define managerial accounting in your own words.

LO 2
2. Who are the primary users of financial accounting information?
3. Who are the primary users of managerial accounting information?
4. Compare and contrast managerial and financial accounting information.

LO 3
5. What are the four functions of management? How does management carry out each function?

What do a marketing manager, a human resources manager, and a production manager have in common? A large part of their job is decision making. To make the best decisions possible, these managers need a wealth of good information. Much of that information will be the product of a managerial accounting system.

Watch the ***What is Managerial Accounting?*** *and the Pizza Hut* ***Managerial Accounting Today*** *videos in WileyPLUS for an introduction to managerial accounting.*

Definition of Managerial Accounting

You may be wondering, "What is managerial accounting? Is it accounting done by managers? Is it managers' accountability for their actions?" The Institute of Management Accountants (IMA®), the leading worldwide professional organization for management accountants and finance professionals, first defined managerial accounting in 1981 as "the process of identification, measurement, accumulation, analysis, preparation, interpretation, and communication of financial information used by management to plan, evaluate, and control within an organization and to assure appropriate use of and accountability for its resources."[1] However, in recognition of the increasingly strategic role that managerial accounting plays in today's organizations, the IMA issued the following revised definition in December 2008.

> Management accounting is a profession that involves partnering in management decision making, devising planning and performance management systems, and providing expertise in financial reporting and control to assist management in the formulation and implementation of an organization's strategy.[2]

What does this formal definition really mean? Simply put, **managerial accounting** is the generation and analysis of relevant information to support managers' strategic decision-making activities. In this context, relevant information is information that will make a difference in the decision (see Exhibit 1-1). Managerial accounting adds value to the organization by helping managers do their jobs more efficiently and effectively. In a recent article, Peter Brewer discusses how management accounting adds value to the organization "by providing leadership, by supporting a company's strategic management efforts, by creating operational alignment throughout an organization, and by facilitating continuous learning and improvement."[3]

EXHIBIT 1-1

Managerial accounting.

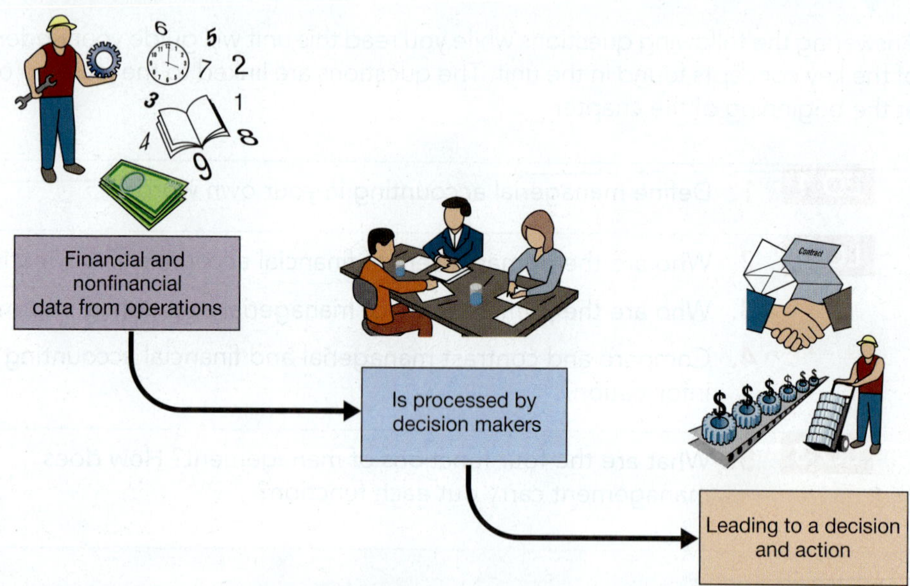

Comparison of Managerial and Financial Accounting

If you have completed a financial accounting course, you are familiar with many of its concepts. If you have not already taken a financial accounting course, you may have read about financial accounting issues in publications such as *The Wall Street Journal* or *Bloomberg Businessweek*. If you have a little knowledge of financial accounting, it will be useful to compare and contrast what you know about financial accounting to managerial accounting. Exhibit 1-2 summarizes the differences between managerial accounting and financial accounting.

EXHIBIT 1-2

Comparison of managerial and financial accounting.

	Managerial Accounting	Financial Accounting
Primary users	Internal—managers and decision makers	External—investors and creditors
Mandated rules	None	Generally accepted accounting principles (GAAP)
Reporting unit	Organizational segments such as divisions, locations, and product lines	Organization as a whole
Time horizon	Past results and projected future results	Past results
Timing of information	As needed, even if information is not exact	After the end of an accounting period

Internal versus External Users

When most people think about accounting, they think about financial statements such as those contained in corporate annual reports. The purpose of such statements is to communicate information about the financial health of a company to external users—people outside the company such as creditors and current or potential investors. The information contained in financial statements benefits those external users who otherwise would have no access to financial or operating information about a company.

Managerial accounting, on the other hand, benefits internal users. It includes reports and information prepared for a range of decision makers within the organization. These reports come in a variety of formats, each designed to provide the ultimate decision maker with the appropriate information.

The information provided by managerial accountants is *not* disseminated to the general public. To do so would be to provide competitors with vital information about corporate strategies and capabilities. Imagine what could happen if Samsung were to report publicly what it cost the company to produce a 55-inch 4K ultra-high-definition television. If Samsung's cost was higher than Sony's, Sony's sales manager could start and win a price war simply by setting Sony's price lower than Samsung's cost. Sony would still make money on the televisions it sold, but at the lower price, Samsung would lose money.

Lack of Mandated Rules

All public companies that are traded on a United States stock exchange and governed by the Securities and Exchange Commission (SEC) must prepare financial statements following **generally accepted accounting principles (GAAP)**. Many other nonpublic companies prepare GAAP-based financial statements at the request of creditors. GAAP "rules" govern how transactions are valued and recorded and how information about them is presented. Since external users of financial statements have no way to verify the reported information, GAAP provides a level of protection or assurance that the reports will follow certain standards. Managerial accounting, on the other hand, has no comparable set of rules governing what information must be provided to decision makers or how that information is presented. Since internal users have access to all of the underlying data, they can create reports that suit their particular decision-making needs. In fact, managerial accounting is completely optional—a company does not have to prepare managerial accounting reports. However, a company is unlikely to be successful in the long run without adequate managerial accounting information to support decision makers.

Consider the case of a family-run lumber mill that borrowed $2 million from the bank to modernize its operations, but then had trouble generating enough cash to repay the loan. The bank brought in consultants to improve the mill's profitability. In talking with the lumber mill's president and accountant, the consultants realized that the company had not prepared basic managerial accounting information such as the cost of producing a particular size of lumber. The product that managers thought was most profitable (because the company could sell all it could produce) was actually being sold at a loss. Unfortunately, the mill was not able to return to profitability and was eventually sold to satisfy the bank's loan.

Focus on Operating Segments

GAAP-based financial statements present a picture of the financial health of the company as a whole. Think about how inventory is reported on the balance sheet. If the company is a merchandising firm, inventory is just one number. But does Macy's department store have only one kind of inventory? Of course not. The store sells men's clothes, women's clothes, shoes, and many other items. In each of those categories Macy's carries different styles, colors, and sizes. How could a manager know how well a certain item sells by looking at one number on a balance sheet? It would be impossible.

Macy's inventory decision is just one example of the decisions managers face. Because most managerial decisions are made at an operating-segment level, managerial accounting information must focus on smaller units of the company. Decision makers need to know about product lines, manufacturing plants, business segments, and operating divisions.

Focus on the Future

Financial accounting exists to report the results of operations. The basic financial statements always report on transactions and events that have already occurred. Thus, the information contained in these financial statements is historical in nature. Managerial accounting, too, reports historical information, often with the purpose of comparing actual results to budgeted results. But managerial accounting helps managers to make decisions that will affect the company's future by projecting the results of certain decisions. That does not mean that managerial accountants don't use historical amounts in developing future projections, but it does mean that they can and will estimate the future results of certain decisions. That is the only way to evaluate whether a decision will have a positive or negative effect on the company.

Suppose Panera Bread is trying to decide whether to open a new restaurant in Greenville, South Carolina. Before making a decision, managers will project the new restaurant's sales and profits. While they might look at the historical performance of their other restaurants in the Greenville area, ultimately it is their future projections rather than past performance that will determine whether they open a new store.

Emphasis on Timeliness

Suppose you have been thinking about opening a business. One day, you just happen to drive by what looks like the perfect location. You call the real estate broker who listed the property to get details and are offered what appears to be an attractive price if you purchase the property within 48 hours. You might like to do a lot of detailed research and analysis first, but time will not allow you that luxury. You have only two days to get all your information together. So you do the best you can and then decide whether to purchase the building.

Because of the nature of many business decisions, managerial accountants place more emphasis on the timely delivery of information than on the delivery of information that is precise to the penny. Financial accountants, in contrast, record transaction amounts to the penny, and it often takes weeks or even months after the end of the period to gather all of the necessary information to prepare accurate reports for external users.

Time-limited windows of opportunity often arise in business. Decision makers might have a long list of information they would find helpful, and they might want that information to be very accurate. But sometimes they might need to sacrifice precision for timeliness and make a decision without all the information they want. After all, receiving highly accurate information after the deadline has passed would be of no help. J. David Flanery, Papa John's International, Inc.'s then senior vice president, CFO, and treasurer, told students at the 8th Annual

IMA Student Leadership Conference that "Most decisions are made without 100% certainty, so you've just got to trust your gut. . . . There is a range of possible answers. . . . So you've got to go with a decision and move ahead—and have confidence in your own judgment to do that."[4]

The Manager's Role

Have you ever been in a group of people who are trying to decide which restaurant to go to? Often in this type of situation, everyone is waiting for someone else to make the decision. As a result, nothing gets done. The same is true in business. Someone with authority must take responsibility for making decisions and directing operations. That person is a manager. Managers are found throughout the organization, from the lower operational levels up to the chief executive officer's suite.

Managerial accounting is designed to assist managers with four general activities: planning, controlling, evaluating, and decision making (see Exhibit 1-3). While this list may appear to imply a linear relationship between the four activities, in practice that is not the case. Frequent feedback from all four activities creates more of a circular decision-making process.

	Planning	Controlling	Evaluating	Decision Making
What is it?	Strategic: deciding on long-term direction of corporation Operational: deciding how to implement long-term strategy	Monitoring day-to-day operations to ensure that processes operate as required	Comparing actual results to planned results for the period	Choosing a course of action
Who does it?	Strategic: upper management Operational: upper and middle management	Managers and workers	Managers	Managers and workers
When is it done?	Strategic: annually, focusing on a 5- to 10-year period Operational: monthly, quarterly, or annually, focusing on no more than the next 12 months	In real time, hourly, daily—the sooner the better	Weekly, monthly, quarterly, annually	As needed
Examples	Preparing the annual operating budget that allocates resources	Checking a sample of products to determine whether they are in compliance with customer specifications	Reviewing the regional sales history for the year during the regional sales manager's annual performance appraisal	Dropping a slow-selling product from the catalog

EXHIBIT 1-3 *The role of managers.*

Planning

Managers participate in both short-term and long-term planning activities. **Long-term planning**, often referred to as strategic planning, establishes the direction in which an organization wishes to go. Managers must decide where the company is currently and where they want it to be in the future. Typical questions asked during the strategic planning process include: "Who are we?"; "What do we do?"; "What value do we deliver to our customers?" "Why do we do what we do?" and "Where do we want to go?" Many organizations prepare a formal strategic plan that documents the answers to these questions and provides direction for a five- to ten-year period.

Once a strategy has been established for the organization as a whole, managers begin to develop plans for achieving that strategy. **Short-term planning** or **operational planning** translates the long-term strategy into a short-term plan to be completed within the next year. One of the primary products of this planning stage will likely be a budget that specifies how resources will be spent to achieve the organization's goals. Managerial accountants provide much of the information that is used to prepare the budget.

Consider the case of San Francisco–based Design Within Reach, Inc., a retailer of modern design furniture and accessories (http://www.dwr.com/). When founder Rob Forbes experienced difficulty acquiring modern design furniture for his home, he decided that there had to be a better way to buy furniture. His company has adopted a strategy of accessibility, selling its products through multiple channels including a catalog, a sales force, a website, and retail showrooms. Design Within Reach delivers value to customers by maintaining its inventory in a single warehouse and shipping the majority of orders within 24 to 48 hours. Compared to what can be a three- to six-month wait for delivery at many other dealers, its service is exceptional.

Strategically, Design Within Reach aimed to become the country's leading provider of modern design furniture and accessories. To accomplish this goal, the company opened 66 studios, two DWR: Tools for Living stores, two outlets, and one fulfillment center between 2000 and 2008. Unfortunately, a fast expansion coupled with a weakened economy created financial difficulties for the company, and the company voluntarily delisted itself on the Nasdaq stock exchange in July 2009. By early 2010, company managers decided to close the Tools for Living stores, though the product line was still available through other outlets. Herman Miller purchased the company in 2014, and today Design Within Reach operates 32 studios, one outlet, and one warehouse. Though the fundamental strategy has not changed, managers continue to look for more focused ways to implement the strategy.[5]

Controlling and Evaluating

After plans have been put in place and the organization has begun to move toward its goals, managers become involved in **controlling** activities. One purpose of controlling activities is to monitor day-to-day operations to ensure that processes are operating as expected. If something appears out of line, corrective action should be taken before the problem becomes worse. For instance, Kellogg's monitors how much Raisin Bran® goes into each cereal box. If the box is supposed to have 20 ounces of cereal, the company doesn't want to overfill it with 23 ounces or underfill it with only 19 ounces. Without controlling activities, an organization will not be able to track its performance in implementing the strategic plan.

Managers can perform controlling activities in real time as operations are occurring, or they may choose to perform them once an hour or once a day. The frequency will be based on the potential consequences of the process being out of control. All other things held equal, the more frequent the controlling activity, the faster an out-of-control process can be corrected. And generally, the faster the process is corrected, the better the results.

Besides production processes, managers also monitor individual employees' actions, though less frequently than they do process control. Managers want to motivate employees to help the organization achieve its strategic plan and must assess how well they have performed relative to expectations. This task is an **evaluating** activity. Once operations have been completed (say, at the end of a job or a period), managers review the information and compare actual results to planned results. The results of this evaluation may lead to changes in business processes, or even in strategy. To help managers with their evaluations, managerial accountants often perform variance analysis and prepare performance reports. The information they prepare is used by managers as the basis for evaluating employees and awarding bonuses.

THINK ABOUT IT 1.1

Companies that buy online advertising often pay search engine sites based on the number of times that web surfers "click" on the company's hyperlink. This practice has given rise to "click fraud" in which the company's competitors erode the advertising budget or websites increase their advertising revenues through false clicking on such links. As a manager, how could you use controlling activities to determine whether your company is a victim of "click fraud"?[6]

Decision Making

Decision making is at the forefront of managerial activity. A human resource manager must select the best health care plan for the company's employees. A sales manager must decide whether to pay the sales staff a salary or a commission. An advertising manager must choose the campaign that will deliver the best message to potential customers. An operations manager must select the best piece of equipment. Managers face such choices on a daily basis. Before making a decision, they need information about the available alternatives. Managerial accountants provide much of that information.

Management in Action

Let's look at a real-world example of the four managerial functions in action. GLK Foods, LLC (http://www.glkfoods.com) traces its roots in Bear Creek, Wisconsin, back to 1900. Annual sauerkraut production at its plants is now more than 125,000 tons, making the company the world's largest sauerkraut producer, with over 85% of the market in the northern hemisphere. How do managers at GLK Foods plan, control, evaluate, and make decisions?

One of the planning activities that occupies managers is inventory planning. To produce 125,000 tons of sauerkraut, the company must obtain 170,000 tons of raw cabbage. That means planning cabbage purchases, production schedules, and inventory levels. Inputs to the planning process include projected sales forecasts, projected cabbage supply and prices, and anticipated manufacturing capacity. The outcome of this planning process includes a production schedule

The managers at GLK Foods must use their sales forecast to determine how much cabbage to buy to meet anticipated demand. Then they use actual orders from customers to schedule production.

Courtesy of GLK Foods

and an operating budget. One thing that makes the planning process a challenge is that all the cabbage used in production for the entire year is harvested between September and November. After the harvest is over, no more cabbage can be purchased to cover unexpected increases in demand.

Once the plan is in place and sauerkraut production has begun, managers control and evaluate production. They monitor actual production rates and output, checking them against the plan to ensure that the desired inventory levels will be there when needed. If a machine breaks down, causing production to slip behind schedule, managers might ask employees to work overtime or shift to another production line for a time. At the end of the month, they compare actual production to the plan, evaluate the results, and make any necessary changes to the plan for the next month.

Throughout this process, decision making takes place almost automatically, as managers decide what to do based on their controlling and evaluating activities. Sometimes managers face unexpected events and must evaluate their alternatives for responding. One such event occurred when studies suggesting that sauerkraut might serve as a preventative for avian or bird flu surfaced in the media in 2005. According to Ryan Downs, co-owner of GLK Foods, same-store sales rose 15% after the studies were made public. Since the stories broke just before the end of the cabbage harvest, GLK was able to adjust its plan, purchasing all the cabbage its farmers could deliver to cover the anticipated increase in demand for the coming year. The company purchased about 20% more cabbage than originally planned. To meet the increased demand, managers ramped up production schedules from 40 to 50 hours a week.

The Managerial Accountant's Role

Just as managers in different areas of the organization use managerial accounting information to make decisions, a variety of accounting personnel provide this information. Managerial accounting information can be provided by a controller, a plant accountant, a cost accountant, a financial analyst, a budget or cost analyst, a general accountant, or even a chief financial officer. And these accountants aren't necessarily located in the accounting department. Some organizations prefer to locate accounting personnel within the operating units, where they can learn about the business processes they are supporting.

To understand what functions preparers of managerial accounting information perform, the IMA conducted two studies, *The Practice Analysis of Management Accounting* (1995) and *Counting More, Counting Less: Transformations in the Management Accounting Profession* (1999). The authors of these studies found that preparers of managerial accounting information are no longer solely number crunchers but active participants in the decision-making process. Across the organization, their skill at analyzing and interpreting financial and operating data is becoming more valuable. These accounting personnel reported that the time they spend analyzing information and making decisions has increased, and they expect it to continue to increase. They are also spending more time doing strategic planning and internal consulting and less time preparing standard financial reports than in the past. Exhibit 1-4 shows the reported changes in their work.[7]

EXHIBIT 1-4

The changing nature of management accountants' work.

Change in the Nature of Management Accountants' Work, 1995–1999

More Time
Same Time
Less Time
Percent of Respondents
0
20
40
60
80
100
Collect & Compile
Prepare Standardized Reports
Interpret Information
Involved in Decisions
Type of Work

Anticipated Change in the Nature of Management Accountants' Work, 2000–2003

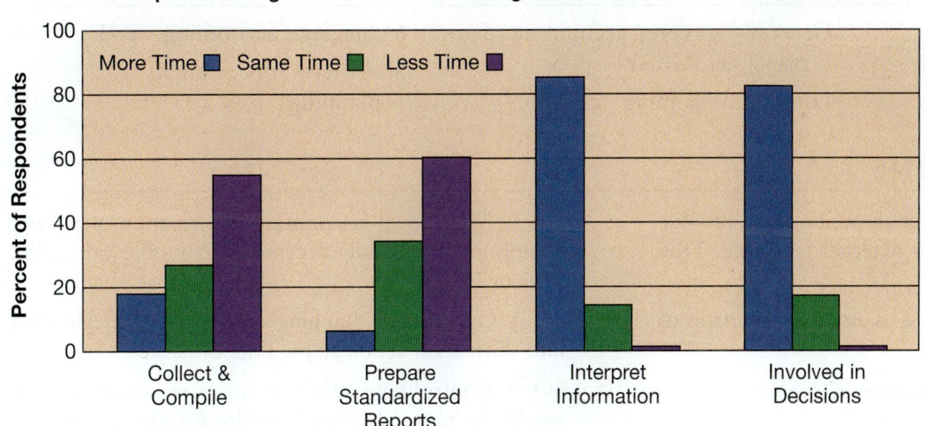

Source: Gary Siegel and James E. Sorensen, *Counting More, Counting Less: Transformations in the Management Accounting Profession* (Institute of Management Accountants, 1999); Montvale, NJ.

REALITY CHECK—*Taking a sales route detour can be a good thing*

© IgorDutina/iStockphoto

What would you do if a customer backed out of an order for 500 pounds of raw peanuts? In Phillip L. Lance's case, he roasted them and peddled them on the streets of Charlotte, NC. And that's how Lance, Inc. started in 1913. From those humble beginnings, Lance, Inc. developed a vast direct-store delivery route system and grew into a leader in the snack food industry.

Almost 100 years later, after a two-year drop in sales and net income, managers developed plans to revamp the company's sales route system with the goal of removing unprofitable, low-volume customers so that salespeople could spend more time servicing profitable customers. By the end of 2009, the company had reduced the number of direct-store delivery routes by 33% while increasing the average sales per stop and average sales per route. Without a program of strategic planning, control, and evaluation, managers would not have recognized the need to realign the sales routes, nor would they have been able to measure the results of their decisions.

In 2010, Lance and Snyder's of Hanover agreed to a "merger of equals," creating an even stronger national snack foods company. Snyder's-Lance continued the Lance model of direct-store delivery routes and now supports approximately 3,100 routes. While many of these routes once had been company-owned, most of the routes now are serviced by independent business operators. The company re-engineers the routes when sales volume increases.

With these routes accounting for 71% of net sales revenue in 2014, early indications are promising.

Time will tell if the company's decision to divest its routes was a good move. But with these routes accounting for 71% of net sales revenue in 2014, early indications are promising.

Sources: Gillian Wee, "Lance Reshuffles Its Snack Strategy," *The Charlotte Observer*, March 20, 2005, 1D; Lance, Inc., 2003 Annual Report; Lance, Inc., 2003 Form 10-K; Lance, Inc., 2009 Form 10-K; Snyder's-Lance, Inc., 2011 Form 10-K; Snyder's-Lance, Inc., 2014 Form 10-K; http://northcarolinahistory.org/encyclopedia/lance-incorporated/ (accessed June 28, 2016) Snyder's-Lance 2011 Annual Report.

UNIT 1.1 REVIEW

KEY TERMS

Controlling p. 8
Decision making p. 9
Evaluating p. 9
Generally accepted accounting principles (GAAP) p. 5
Long-term planning p. 7
Managerial accounting p. 3
Short-term (operational) planning p. 8

PRACTICE QUESTIONS

1. LO 1 The goal of management accounting is to provide accurate financial records for external reporting. True or False?
2. LO 2 Which of the following is *not* characteristic of managerial accounting?
   a. Providing information to internal users
   b. Focusing on historical cost information
   c. Focusing on operating segments
   d. Emphasizing the timeliness of information
3. LO 2 Managerial accounting information need *not* comply with generally accepted accounting principles. True or False?
4. LO 3 Operational planning converts a strategic plan into short-term action steps. True or False?
5. LO 3 Controlling activities compare actual annual results to planned annual results for the purpose of awarding managers' bonuses. True or False?

UNIT 1.1 PRACTICE EXERCISE

Marcie Scott owns several laundromats in Morrisville. Identify each of the following actions she performs as a planning, controlling, evaluating, or decision-making activity.

	PLANNING	CONTROLLING	EVALUATING	DECISION MAKING
1. Marcie prepares a budget for the next year.				
2. Marcie chooses to replace the 10-year-old washing machines with the latest model.				
3. Marcie looks at her income statement for the last month to see how well the business performed.				
4. Marcie checks the change machine to make sure that it dispenses four, and only four, quarters for each dollar bill inserted.				

SELECTED UNIT 1.1 ANSWERS

Think About It 1.1

You could compare the actual click-through volume to historical or planned click-through volume. If the additional click-throughs are legitimate, the company should see a corresponding increase in sales volume. If actual click-through volume is higher than historical or planned volume—particularly if there is not a corresponding increase in sales volume—your company may be a victim of "click fraud."

Practice Questions

1. False
2. B
3. True
4. True
5. False

Unit 1.1 Practice Exercise

1. Planning: Marcie is determining the resources required to operate next year.
2. Decision making: Marcie is deciding to take action.
3. Evaluating: Marcie is evaluating operations by comparing actual results against expectations.
4. Controlling: Marcie is monitoring daily operations to ensure that processes are operating as expected.

UNIT 1.2

Different Strategies, Different Information

GUIDED UNIT PREPARATION

Answering the following questions while you read this unit will guide your understanding of the key concepts found in the unit. The questions are linked to the learning objectives presented at the beginning of the chapter.

LO 4

1. How does information assist in achieving corporate strategy?
2. How does corporate strategy influence the selection of information used in decision-making activities?

Have you ever heard the saying "If you don't know where you're going, you'll probably end up somewhere else"? Well, that adage certainly applies to business. Companies that want to be successful have to know what they want to accomplish and how they are going to achieve it. That is, they must have goals and a strategy for achieving those goals. Without goals and a strategy, a company will flounder and may even be forced out of business. Managerial accounting information is an invaluable tool that provides feedback about how well the organization is implementing its strategy and achieving its goals.

Matching Accounting Information to an Organization's Strategy

In his book *Competitive Advantage*, management strategy expert Michael Porter argues that one important characteristic of effective management is a set of clear strategic priorities. But if those priorities are to be realized, the organization must develop supporting business processes and information systems. Managers must also realize that as strategies change, so must the accounting information that is used to monitor their achievement.

Product Differentiation versus Low-Cost Production

Porter developed a strategic framework in which the firm has two ways to develop a competitive advantage: product differentiation and low-cost production.[8] If the company follows a strategy of product differentiation, it will seek ways to set its products apart from those of its competitors in terms of quality, design, or service. If it chooses to follow a low-cost production strategy, the company will set itself apart from competitors in terms of a lower sales price.

Monitoring these two strategies requires different accounting information. For the product differentiation strategy, companies will want information on

REALITY CHECK—*What's the price tag for a new strategy?*

© Joe_Potato/iStockphoto

Strategic planning lies at the heart of successful organizations, whether for-profit or not-for-profit. Articulating the strategic direction of the organization allows managers to translate that strategy into an operating plan and then take action.

Sometimes organizations change their strategic direction, as J. C. Penney did when it rolled out its new Fair and Square™ pricing strategy on February 1, 2012. In an attempt to revitalize the company, new CEO Ron Johnson devised the new pricing strategy that offered three price points. "Everyday prices" promised consumers a fair price every day of the year and were set at an average 40% markdown of previous listed prices. "Month-long prices" were specific month-long sales promotions. Finally, "best prices" were clearance prices that were announced on the first and third Fridays of each month.

Why is this new strategy a challenge? J. C. Penney's customers were accustomed to frequent sales—the company had featured 590 unique promotions in the previous year. And customers were used to not paying the list price—almost 75% of the company's revenue had been from products sold at 50% or more off the original ticket price.

While early results of the new strategy were promising, implementing the new strategy has been costly on several fronts.

While early results of the new strategy were promising, implementing the new strategy has been costly on several fronts. Sales revenue declined dramatically in 2012, and after three straight quarters of losses, the company's stock price was down 62% and its credit rating was at "junk" status. As a result, Johnson eliminated one of the price levels and labeling periodic sales as "clearance" prices.

But this change was too little too late. The company's board of directors fired Johnson in April 2013 and brought back former CEO Mike Ullman. Ullman quickly reinstated the company's previous promotional pricing model, but the pricing woes were far from resolved. The company faced a class action lawsuit for marking up prices just so it could mark them down, which it settled for $50 million in November 2015.

Sources: J. C. Penney Company, Inc. 2011 Annual Report; Anne D'Innocenzio, "JC Penney CEO Tries to Change the Way We Shop," *U.S. News and World Report*, November 17, 2012, http://www.usnews.com/news/us/articles/2012/11/17/jc-penney-ceo-tries-to-change-the-way-we-shop (accessed June 28, 2016); Gail Hoffer, "JCP Teaches a 'Fair and Square' Lesson on Pricing, Marketing and Image," RetailingToday.com, July 27, 2012, http://www.retailingtoday.com/article/jcp-teaches-%E2%80%98fair-and-square%E2%80%99-lesson-pricing-marketing-and-image (accessed November 26, 2012); Susanna Kim, "J.C. Penney Returns to Coupons and Marks Up Prices," abcnews.go.com, June 5, 2013, http://abcnews.go.com/Business/jc-penney-admits-marking-prices-order-customers-discounted/story?id=19323843 (accessed June 11, 2013); Hiroko Tabuchi, "J.C. Penney Settles Shoppers' Suit Over False Advertising," *The Wall Street Journal*, November 11, 2015, http://www.nytimes.com/2015/11/12/business/jc-penney-settles-shoppers-suit-over-false-advertising.html?_r=0 (accessed February 2, 2016); Brad Tuttle, "The Price is Righter," *Time*, February 13, 2012, http://www.time.com/time/magazine/article/0,9171,2105961,00.html?pcd=pw-ml (accessed November 26, 2012).

quality, such as defect rates, percentage of on-time deliveries, and customer satisfaction. For a low-cost production strategy, managers will be more interested in monitoring the production process. That doesn't mean, however, that other kinds of information should be neglected. A company that focuses on product differentiation must monitor product costs because, if too much money is spent on quality, the sales price will be too high to be competitive. Likewise, even a low-cost producer must monitor product quality because consumers demand a certain level of quality. Either way, managers must monitor external information, such as competitor actions, to evaluate the likelihood of successfully implementing the strategy.

Market Share: Build, Hold, Harvest, or Divest

Strategies can also be classified based on a firm's approach to market share growth,[9] or the trade-off between short-term earnings and market share. There are four such strategies: build, hold, harvest, and divest. Under a build strategy, a company aims to increase its market share and competitive position relative to others in the industry, even at the expense of short-term earnings and cash flows. Under a hold strategy, a company seeks to maintain its current market share and generate a reasonable return on investment. A harvest strategy focuses on short-term profits and cash, even at the expense of market share. A divest strategy is appropriate when a company desires to exit a particular market.

Companies that want to build market share need information about sales volumes, sales growth, market share growth, sales from new customers, and customer satisfaction. Managers who understand the firm's strategy won't worry when cash balances decrease over the short term. However, they will need to monitor those cash balances to know when to borrow money in order to avoid a cash crisis. Useful information for monitoring a hold strategy would include percentage of sales from repeat customers, market share, return on investment, and gross margin. To monitor a harvest strategy, managers will want to know about gross margin and cash sales.

Monitoring Strategic Performance

Information can be provided to managers who are monitoring strategic progress using several tools and management philosophies. Many of these are relatively new to managerial accounting; some of the more common are introduced here.[10]

The Balanced Scorecard

One tool that managerial accountants have developed to assist in monitoring organizational performance is the **balanced scorecard**. Developed in the early 1990s by David Norton and Robert Kaplan, the balanced scorecard is a collection of performance measures that track an organization's progress toward achieving its goals.[11] The selection of performance measures to be included on the scorecard is driven by the organization's strategy. The balanced scorecard is then used to communicate the corporate strategy throughout the organization.

Historically, firms have measured their performance through financial measures, such as stock price and sales revenue. While the balanced scorecard uses some financial performance measures, it places equal emphasis on nonfinancial performance measures, such as customer satisfaction, on-time delivery percentage, and employee turnover. These measures are grouped into four categories: financial, customer, internal business processes, and learning and growth (see Exhibit 1-5). We will explore the balanced scorecard in more detail in Chapter 11. What is important to understand at this point is that managers should not be limited to what financial results or projections imply. Instead, financial data should be balanced by customer and operational data, and all data should be evaluated based on the company's strategy.

In a recent survey of global business executives, Bain & Company found that almost 40% of the firms represented were using a balanced scorecard.[12] Although the balanced scorecard was originally developed to measure the performance of for-profit organizations, it has also been applied to nonprofit organizations, governmental units, and service organizations. Among the organizations that use balanced scorecards are BMW Financial Services, Duke University Hospitals, DuPont, General Electric, Hilton Hotels, Royal Canadian Mounted Police, Philips Electronics, UPS, and Walt Disney World Company.

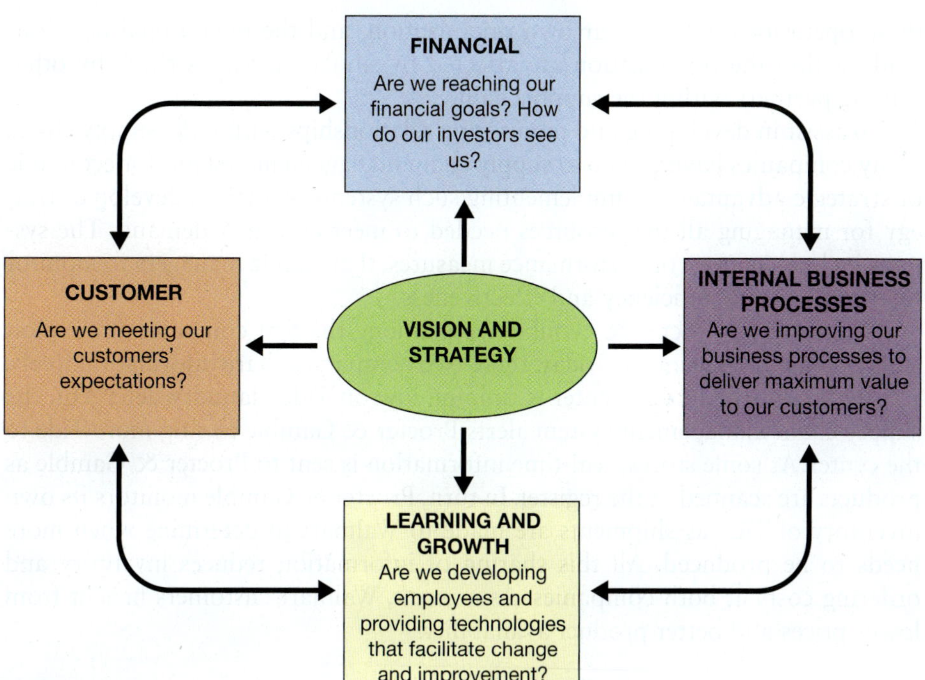

EXHIBIT 1-5 *The balanced scorecard.*

Supply Chain Management

Organizations operate within an interdependent system of suppliers and customers that is called a **supply chain**. A supply chain is a network of facilities that procure raw materials, transform them into intermediate goods and then into final products, and deliver the final products to customers through a distribution system.[13] The supply chain's goal is to get the right product to the right location, in the right quantities, at the right time, and at the right cost. A simple supply chain may include as few as three trading partners—one supplier, one company, and one customer. A more complex supply chain might include hundreds of trading partners including multiple raw materials producers, manufacturers, service providers, distributors, retailers, and end users.

The Supply Chain Council (supply-chain.org) describes supply chains with its Supply Chain Operations Reference (SCOR®) model. This model includes the four major operational categories—plan, source, make, and deliver—shown in Exhibit 1-6. Notice that all trading partners within the supply chain carry out

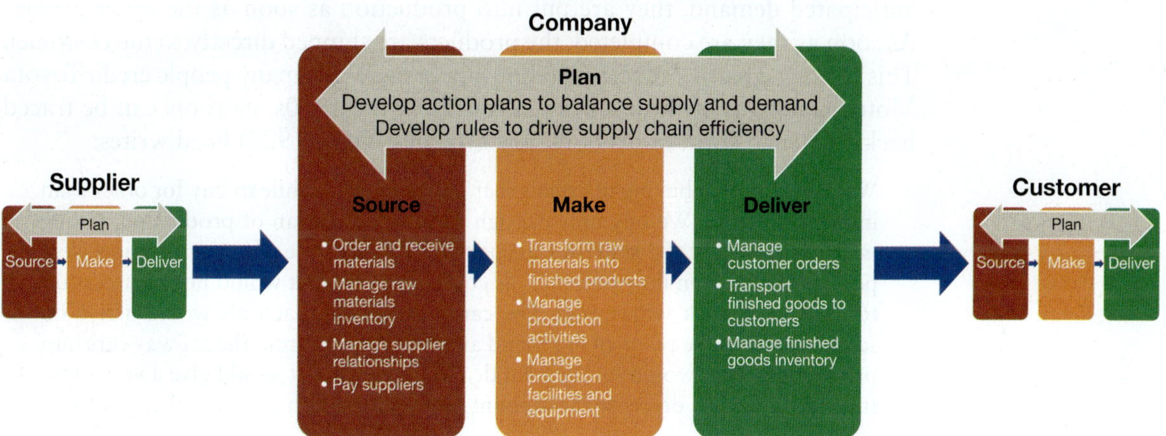

Source: Adapted from Michael Hugos, *Essentials of Supply Chain Management*, John Wiley & Sons, 2003.

EXHIBIT 1-6 *Typical supply chain operations.*

these operations within their own organization, and the operational decisions made within the organization are affected by similar decisions made by other trading partners within the supply chain.

To assist in developing and monitoring relationships within the supply chain, many companies have turned to supply chain management systems for economic or strategic advantage. In implementing such systems, managers develop a strategy for managing all the resources needed to meet customer demand. The systems include metrics, or performance measures, that enable managers to monitor the supply chain's efficiency and effectiveness.

Walmart and Procter & Gamble were among the first companies to exploit supply chain management. Today, these two companies share information freely. If a Walmart distribution center is running low on Tide® laundry detergent, the supply chain management system alerts Procter & Gamble to ship more Tide to the center. At some stores, real-time information is sent to Procter & Gamble as products are scanned at the register. In turn, Procter & Gamble monitors its own inventory of Tide as shipments are made to Walmart to determine when more needs to be produced. All this sharing of information reduces inventory and ordering costs at both companies. As a result, Walmart customers benefit from lower prices and better product availability.

THINK ABOUT IT 1.2

ProFlowers.com is an Internet florist. One of its print advertisements estimates that for a traditional florist, the time between flowers being cut in the field and reaching the customer averages from 8 to 12 days. ProFlowers claims that its average time from field to customer is only 1 to 3 days. How do you think ProFlowers has been able to eliminate so much time from the delivery cycle?

Just-In-Time (JIT) Inventory

Just-in-time inventory management **(JIT)** is an inventory strategy that focuses on reducing waste and inefficiency by ordering inventory items so that they arrive just when they are needed. Since goods are produced to customer order, not to anticipated demand, they are put into production as soon as the order arrives. As soon as they are completed, the products are shipped directly to the customer. This strategy greatly reduces warehousing costs. While many people credit Toyota Motor Company with development of JIT in the 1950s, its roots can be traced back to Henry Ford. In his book *My Life and Work* (1922) Ford writes:

> We have found in buying materials that it is not worth while to buy for other than immediate needs. We buy only enough to fit into the plan of production, taking into consideration the state of transportation at the time. If transportation were perfect and an even flow of materials could be assured, it would not be necessary to carry any stock whatsoever. The carloads of raw materials would arrive on schedule and in the planned order and amounts, and go from the railway cars into production. That would save a great deal of money, for it would give a very rapid turnover and thus decrease the amount of money tied up in materials. (p. 143)

Traditionally, inventory managers stockpiled large amounts of inventory as a buffer against unexpected problems in delivery, manufacturing, or distribution. As a consumer, that strategy works for you—products are available when you want

REALITY CHECK—*A supply chain touchdown*

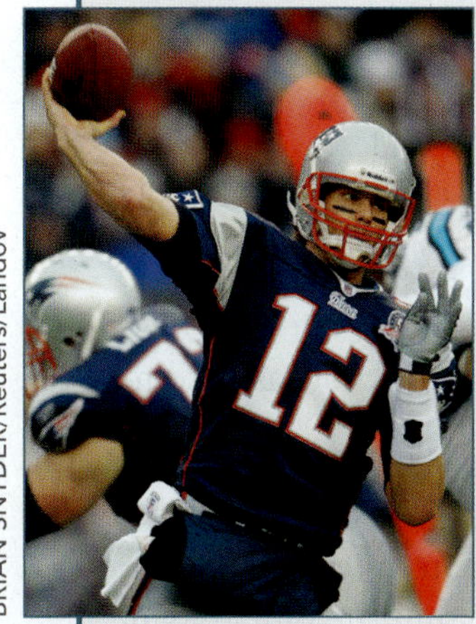

BRIAN SNYDER/Reuters/Landov

Retail sales can be a very tricky business, particularly when you are selling NFL jersey replicas. One season-ending injury or an unexpected march to the Super Bowl can turn demand upside down, leaving a retailer with too much or too little inventory on hand. Reebok Apparel faces just this situation each year.

In the past, Reebok Apparel's supply chain created problems for the company—problems that translated into lost dollars when sales were missed or too much money was invested in inventory that didn't sell. To solve these problems, Reebok made several changes in its supply chain. Previously, Reebok had contracted with manufacturers in Vietnam, Korea, and Central America for blank team jerseys. The blanks were shipped to a Reebok facility in Indiana for customization with players' names and numbers. This process was 50% more costly than if the original manufacturers produced the entire jersey. So managers asked the foreign manufacturers to retool and complete the entire jersey. Reebok then shared the resulting cost savings with retail customers.

Another change managers made was to begin ordering extra blank jerseys for popular teams, to keep on hand for unexpected surges in demand. This practice paid off in 2002, when the New England Patriots' starting quarterback, Drew Bledsoe, was injured early in the season and replaced with future Super Bowl MVP Tom Brady. Without the blank Patriots jerseys on hand, Reebok would not have been able to meet customer demand for Tom Brady jerseys.

This model allows Reebok to do a better job of ordering raw materials and blank jerseys to meet unexpected demand.

Reebok now uses a sales forecasting model that includes previous years' demand by player, historical team demand, and previous team records. This model allows Reebok to do a better job of ordering raw materials and blank jerseys to meet unexpected demand. In 2004, the company was able to ship 150,000 Ben Roethlisberger jerseys after he unexpectedly led the Pittsburgh Steelers on a winning streak, even though the original forecast had predicted demand at only about 1,200.

Source: Anne Field, "When Delaying Decisions Is Good," June 2005 *Supply Chain Strategy Newsletter*, Harvard Business Review Press, Vol. 1, no. 4, pp. 5–7.

them. For a company, it is an expensive strategy. More inventory space is needed, meaning more rent and/or property costs like taxes and insurance are incurred. Having funds tied up in inventory means cash isn't as readily available for other investments. Just-in-time inventory systems eliminate that extra inventory. Some companies have found they can reduce inventory levels by as much as 50 to 60 percent without affecting their ability to meet customer demand for the final product. Besides reducing inventory levels, managers have also reworked manufacturing processes to eliminate unnecessary steps and enhance efficiency. The end result is a shorter production cycle and reduced financial investment in inventory.

Just-in-time inventory systems take time and effort to implement, and there is no guarantee that the final system will work for everyone. In a typical JIT system, products are completed in small batches in response to customer requests. To make these smaller production runs successful, companies must often rearrange the layout of equipment on the factory floor and work with employees to develop more efficient setup procedures. A quality program is also a must because no safety stock is available in the event that several units are found to be defective.

Shoemaker Allen-Edmonds tried JIT in 1991, but had to back off after discovering the company did not have the clout to force leather suppliers to make small, weekly deliveries.[14] Managers were also unsuccessful in developing an appropriate culture among workers, many of whom had been put on salary in lieu of compensation by the finished piece. A second try in 2004 was successful, however. The company now produces to customer orders rather than maintaining an inventory. As a result of its new lean manufacturing system, Allen-Edmonds achieved a 30% increase in productivity, a 15% reduction in direct labor and overhead costs, and a 100% on-time delivery rate.[15]

Enterprise Resource Planning (ERP) Systems

When businesses first began to computerize their operations, functional areas such as marketing and production created automated systems to meet their own needs. The problem was that each area developed its own system, without considering the needs of other areas for the same information. The result was often a collection of mismatched or even redundant systems that could not easily communicate across departments.

Today, many companies use **enterprise resource planning (ERP)** systems such as SAP and Oracle to accumulate data and provide information to decision makers on a companywide basis. The goal of an ERP system is to integrate all data from the company's many business processes into a single information system. The result is a system that can easily share production data with the accounting department and sales data with the production department. Now, when a salesperson enters an order, she can easily see the customer's credit status and the number of units on hand to fulfill the order—information that would require at least two different systems in a non-ERP environment.

UNIT 1.2 REVIEW

KEY TERMS

Balanced scorecard p. 16

Enterprise resource planning (ERP) p. 20

Just-in-time inventory (JIT) p. 18

Supply chain p. 17

PRACTICE QUESTIONS

1. LO 4 A company whose strategy is to build market share would be *least* interested in knowing its
   a. market share.
   b. percentage of sales from new customers.
   c. short-term profits.
   d. number of units sold.
2. LO 4 Which of the following is *not* an area of focus on a balanced scorecard?
   a. Financial
   b. Internal business processes
   c. Customer
   d. Suppliers
3. LO 4 Which of the following would be considered part of Nike's supply chain?
   a. Finish Line, an athletic shoe retailer
   b. Athletic shoe manufacturer in China that makes Nike shoes
   c. Marine transportation company that ships shoes from China to the United States
   d. All of the above are in Nike's supply chain
4. LO 4 A company that utilizes a just-in-time inventory system will not report any inventory on the balance sheet. True or False?

UNIT 1.2 PRACTICE EXERCISE

For each of the following scenarios, indicate the management tool being implemented.

	JIT	ERP	SUPPLY CHAIN MANAGEMENT	BALANCED SCORECARD
1. A company replaces its accounting information system, marketing information system, sales information system, and production information system with a single, integrated software solution.				
2. A company begins to evaluate its performance using metrics such as customer satisfaction, training hours per employee, and average cycle time in addition to traditional financial measures, such as earnings per share.				
3. A company requires its suppliers to deliver components in orders of 25 every two hours rather than in orders of 2,000 once every month.				
4. A company decides to implement a system of regional distribution centers to better meet the delivery needs of customers.				

SELECTED UNIT 1.2 ANSWERS

Think About It 1.2

ProFlowers.com gets its flowers directly from the grower and ships them directly to the customer. The typical floral supply chain includes an importer, a wholesaler, and a florist between the fields and the customer. Since ProFlowers shipments don't have to go through as many hands, the time they take to reach the customer decreases, and the flowers arrive fresher.

Practice Questions

1. C
2. D
3. D
4. False

Unit 1.2 Practice Exercise

1. Enterprise resource planning (ERP)
2. Balanced scorecard
3. Just-in-time inventory management
4. Supply chain management

UNIT 1.3

Ethical Considerations in Managerial Accounting

GUIDED UNIT PREPARATION

Answering the following questions while you read this unit will guide your understanding of the key concepts found in the unit. The questions are linked to the learning objectives presented at the beginning of the chapter.

LO 5

1. Why is it important for an organization to have a code of conduct?
2. How can an employee's unethical behavior affect an organization?

"Accountant Arrested for Sham Audits." "Madoff Aide Allegedly Got Fake Trading 'Tickets'." "Former CEO Bennett Is Indicted in Refco Collapse." "U.S. Probes Possible Fraud by Pharmacies." "How Some Doctors Turn a $79 Profit from a $30 Test." "Boeing Could Avoid Prosecution, Pay Up to $500 Million to U.S." "Volkswagen Blames 'Chain of Mistakes' for Emissions Scandal." As these headlines from *The Wall Street Journal* attest, one doesn't have to look long or hard to find unethical behavior in business or to see its dramatic effects on companies and individuals. The names Enron, WorldCom, and Adelphia will forever be linked to fatal lapses in ethical behavior. In 2002, Congress passed the Sarbanes–Oxley Act, a reaction against and an intended deterrent to unethical business practices.

Exactly what is **ethical behavior**? Basically, it is knowing right from wrong and conducting yourself accordingly, so that your decisions are consistent with your own value system and the values of those affected by your decisions. The Institute of Business Ethics (http://www.ibe.org.uk) poses three simple tests of an ethical business decision: (1) "Do I mind others knowing what I have done?" (2) "Who does my decision affect or hurt?" and (3) "Would my decision be considered fair by those affected?"

Ethical business behavior is not the same as mere compliance with the law. It is doing the *right* thing, not just doing what you are *required* to do. In ethical behavior, the spirit of the law is more important than the letter of the law, and moral values and codes are more important than rules and policies. Of course, that doesn't mean that you can ignore company rules and policies.

As an employee of an organization, you will be directed by your firm's **code of conduct**, which is based on a set of core values that are meant to guide employees' behavior. Some companies require employees to review the code of conduct annually and sign an acknowledgment that they understand and will adhere to it. Exhibit 1-7 lists the typical components of a code of conduct.

EXHIBIT 1-7

Typical components of a code of conduct.

Compliance, Integrity and Anticorruption

- Accuracy of corporate finances and financial reporting
- Employee records and expense reports
- Bribes
- Political contributions

Conflicts of Interest

- Gifts and gratuities
- Political activity
- Outside employment
- Family members
- Disclosure of financial interests

Employee, Client and Vendor Information

- Maintaining records and information
- Privacy and confidentiality
- Disclosure of information

Employment Practices

- Workplace harassment
- Equal opportunity
- Diversity
- Fair treatment of staff
- Work-family balance
- Discrimination
- Fair labor practices
- Illegal drugs and alcohol
- Use of organization property and resources
- Proper exercise of authority
- Employee volunteer activities
- Romantic relationships with coworkers
- Incentives and recognition systems

Environmental Issues

- Commitment to sustainability
- Employee health and safety

Ethics and Compliance Resources

- Ethics advice helpline
- Reporting procedures
- Anonymous/confidential reporting hotline
- Summary of investigations process
- Anti-retaliation policy and protections for reporters
- Accountability and discipline for violators
- Ombuds program

Internet, social networking and social media

- Internet and social network use at work
- Prohibited sites and content
- Policies regarding posts about company, work products or coworkers
- Online relationships between managers and their reports

Relationships with third parties

- Procurement
- Negotiating contracts

Source: Ethics Resource Center Common Code Provisions website, https://www.ethics.org/eci/research/free-toolkit/code-provisions (accessed June 28, 2016). Courtesy of ECIconnects

In the 2011 *National Business Ethics Survey*, 82% of respondents indicated that their employers had a written code of conduct—up from 67% in the 1994 survey.[16] One company that displays its code of conduct on its corporate website is Google. The value that Google places on ethical behavior is easy to see: "Don't be evil . . . is about doing the right thing more generally—following the law, acting honorably and treating each other with respect" (https://abc.xyz/investor/other/google-code-of-conduct.html).

Section 406 of the Sarbanes–Oxley Act now requires that all publicly traded companies disclose whether the "principal executive officer, principal financial officer, principal accounting officer or controller, or persons performing similar functions" are subject to a corporate code of ethics. The code must be published in the annual report or on the corporate website, or provided without charge upon request to any individual. In addition, companies must disclose all instances in which these codes have been waived for a particular individual, as well as all changes to the code. A company that does not have a written code of ethics is required to publish a disclosure explaining why no code has been adopted.

If you are a member of a professional organization, you will be directed by that organization's code of professional conduct. One such organization is the Institute of Management Accountants (IMA), the leading professional organization for managerial accountants, which offers the Certified Management Accountant (CMA®) designation. Exhibit 1-8 provides the current version of the IMA's Statement of Ethical Professional Practice. The result of a three-year revision process that culminated in 2005, it is consistent with the Sarbanes–Oxley Act of 2002 and incorporates the principles of the International Federation of Accountants, of which the IMA is a member.[17] The IMA's statement is just one example of a professional code of conduct, however. Other organizations, such as the American Institute of Certified Public Accountants, the American Marketing Association, the Financial Executives Institute, the Financial Planning Association, and the Society for Human Resource Management, have similar codes of conduct.

EXHIBIT 1-8

IMA Statement of Ethical Professional Practice.

IMA STATEMENT OF ETHICAL PROFESSIONAL PRACTICE

Members of IMA shall behave ethically. A commitment to ethical professional practice includes: overarching principles that express our values, and standards that guide our conduct.

PRINCIPLES

IMA's overarching ethical principles include: Honesty, Fairness, Objectivity, and Responsibility. Members shall act in accordance with these principles and shall encourage others within their organizations to adhere to them.

STANDARDS

A member's failure to comply with the following standards may result in disciplinary action.

I. COMPETENCE

Each member has a responsibility to:

1. Maintain an appropriate level of professional expertise by continually developing knowledge and skills.
2. Perform professional duties in accordance with relevant laws, regulations, and technical standards.
3. Provide decision support information and recommendations that are accurate, clear, concise, and timely.
4. Recognize and communicate professional limitations or other constraints that would preclude responsible judgment or successful performance of an activity.

II. CONFIDENTIALITY

Each member has a responsibility to:

1. Keep information confidential except when disclosure is authorized or legally required.
2. Inform all relevant parties regarding appropriate use of confidential information. Monitor subordinates' activities to ensure compliance.
3. Refrain from using confidential information for unethical or illegal advantage.

III. INTEGRITY

Each member has a responsibility to:

1. Mitigate actual conflicts of interest. Regularly communicate with business associates to avoid apparent conflicts of interest. Advise all parties of any potential conflicts.
2. Refrain from engaging in any conduct that would prejudice carrying out duties ethically.
3. Abstain from engaging in or supporting any activity that might discredit the profession.

EXHIBIT 1-8

(continued)

IV. CREDIBILITY

Each member has a responsibility to:

1. Communicate information fairly and objectively.
2. Disclose all relevant information that could reasonably be expected to influence an intended user's understanding of the reports, analyses, or recommendations.
3. Disclose delays or deficiencies in information, timeliness, processing, or internal controls in conformance with organization policy and/or applicable law.

RESOLUTION OF ETHICAL CONFLICT

In applying the Standards of Ethical Professional Practice, you may encounter problems identifying unethical behavior or resolving an ethical conflict. When faced with ethical issues, you should follow your organization's established policies on the resolution of such conflict. If these policies do not resolve the ethical conflict, you should consider the following courses of action:

1. Discuss the issue with your immediate supervisor except when it appears that the supervisor is involved. In that case, present the issue to the next level. If you cannot achieve a satisfactory resolution, submit the issue to the next management level. If your immediate superior is the chief executive officer or equivalent, the acceptable reviewing authority may be a group such as the audit committee, executive committee, board of directors, board of trustees, or owners. Contact with levels above the immediate superior should be initiated only with your superior's knowledge, assuming he or she is not involved. Communication of such problems to authorities or individuals not employed or engaged by the organization is not considered appropriate, unless you believe there is a clear violation of the law.
2. Clarify relevant ethical issues by initiating a confidential discussion with an IMA Ethics Counselor or other impartial advisor to obtain a better understanding of possible courses of action.
3. Consult your own attorney as to legal obligations and rights concerning the ethical conflict.

Source: *IMA Statement of Ethical Professional Practice*, available online at http://www.imanet.org/docs/default-source/press_releases/statement-of-ethical-professional-practice_2-2-12.pdf?sfvrsn=2 (accessed January 29, 2016). Courtesy of Institute of Management Accountants

Unfortunately, it takes more than a code of ethics to promote ethical business behavior. In *Politics, Book IV*, Aristotle cautioned, "But we must remember that good laws, if they are not obeyed, do not constitute good government. Hence there are two parts of good government; one is the actual obedience of citizens to the laws, the other part is the goodness of the laws which they obey." Enron had a code of ethics that specified the desired behavior, but top managers chose to ignore it. The result was catastrophic for thousands of innocent employees and shareholders.

A key component of a positive ethical environment, in fact, is the "tone at the top," or management's commitment to ethical behavior. If employees are to act ethically, managers must not only "talk the talk," but "walk the walk." Employees who witness managers engaging in unethical behavior will assume that while the company may have a corporate code of ethics, it doesn't really matter. In the 2011 *National Business Ethics Survey*, only 62% of the respondents had confidence in their company's senior management. And 34% of the respondents believed that their manager did not exhibit ethical behavior, up from 24% in 2009. As Ira Lipman, chairman and president of Guardsmark, LLC, commented in an October 12, 2005, press release, "The leadership of corporate America should see ethics as one of their top responsibilities, and as an integral part of their stewardship and service to shareholders and customers."[18]

THINK ABOUT IT 1.3

You work for an interior design firm. The company has an agreement with several up-and-coming artists in the area to buy their paintings and resell them to clients. The difference between the purchase price and the resale price is split between the artist and the company. You have noticed recently that a designer is telling the artists that he is purchasing a painting for his personal collection, so that the artists do not expect an additional payment for its resale. The designer then sells the painting to a client, and the company keeps the entire profit. The designer says his practice is good for the company (it receives a higher profit) and good for the artists (their work is being sold). Do you regard the designer's behavior as ethical? Why or why not? If you believe it is unethical, what are the next steps you should take?

Based on Amy Joyce, "But It Was Only a Few Pens, Officer," *The Washington Post*, November 10, 2002.

What is the current state of ethical behavior in business? The Ethics Resource Center (http://www.ethics.org) repeats the *National Business Ethics Survey* periodically to determine the answer to this question. Exhibit 1-9 compares the results from recent surveys. Observed incidences of unethical behavior reported in the survey reached an all-time low in 2013, with only 41% of respondents having observed such behavior. Of those in the 2013 survey who witnessed unethical behavior, only 63% reported it—down from 65% in 2011.

EXHIBIT 1-9

National Business Ethics Survey results, 2003–2013.

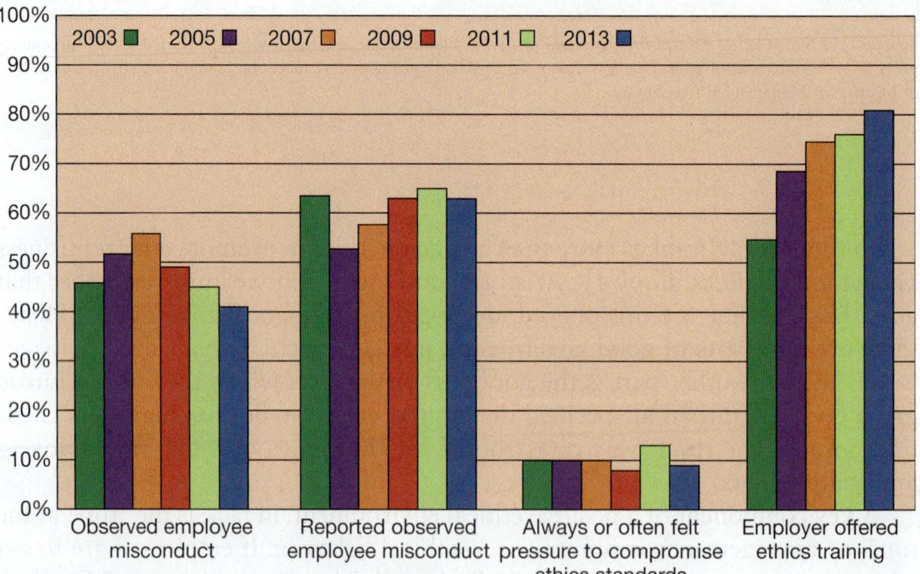

Sources: Ethics Resource Center, *National Business Ethics Survey: How Employees View Ethics in Their Organizations 1994–2005* (Arlington, VA: Ethics Resource Center, 2005) and Ethics Resource Center, *National Business Ethics Survey: An Inside View of Private Sector Ethics*, 2007 (Arlington, VA: Ethics Resource Center, 2007); Ethics Resource Center, *2009 National Business Ethics Survey: Ethics in the Recession* (Arlington, VA: Ethics Resource Center, 2009); Ethics Resource Center, *2011 National Business Ethics Survey: Workplace Ethics in Transition* (Arlington, VA: Ethics Resource Center, 2011); Ethics Resource Center, *National Business Ethics Survey of the U.S. Workforce* (Arlington, VA: Ethics Resource Center, 2014).

You may wonder what kind of unethical conduct employees observe. Based on the 2013 survey, the top five observed unethical behaviors are abusive or intimidating behavior (18%), lying to employees (17%), conflict of interest (12%), violating company policies related to Internet use (12%), and discriminating against

REALITY CHECK—*Blowing the whistle*

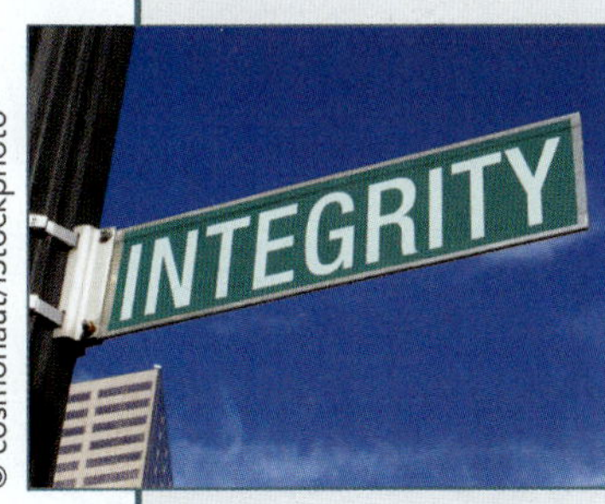

© cosmonaut/iStockphoto

Whistleblowers were elevated to a new status when *Time* named Sherron Watkins of Enron, Cynthia Cooper of WorldCom, and Coleen Rowley of the FBI as its 2002 Persons of the Year. The Securities and Exchange Commission receives approximately 4,000 tips annually through its whistleblower program. But what does it take to "blow the whistle" on your employer, and what could happen if you do?

The Corporate and Criminal Fraud Accountability Act of 2002, part of the Sarbanes–Oxley Act (Section 806), was passed to protect whistleblowers in publicly traded companies against retaliation. According to an August 1, 2005, *USA Today* article, hundreds of whistleblowers have filed complaints of retaliation under the act. But while they may have thought their jobs were protected under the act, only some of them have actually returned to work. Others have settled their complaints out of court or are still waiting to be reinstated.

Linda Kimble, an agent with Hertz, and Schott Bechtel, a vice president of Competitive Technologies, are two employees who have returned to the office after being fired. Both were out of work for at least 18 months while their claims were being investigated. Others, such as David Welch, former CFO of the Bank of Floyd, and David Windhauser, former controller of Trane, have not fared as well. Windhauser was out of work for several months before he secured a temporary job that eventually became a full-time position, at a 25% cut in pay. He eventually agreed to an out-of-court settlement with Trane. Welch was not rehired by the Bank of Floyd, even though the bank was ordered to reinstate him, and he remained unemployed until 2007, when he changed professions and joined the Franklin University faculty. While the law requires reinstatement, there is no penalty for a company's failure to comply.

As you may have gathered from these stories, whistleblowing is not for the faint-hearted.

As you may have gathered from these stories, whistleblowing is not for the faint-hearted. Many whistleblowers become the target of personal and professional attacks—the *2013 National Business Ethics Survey* found 21% of whistleblowers experienced some form of retaliation at work. If you find yourself thinking of blowing the whistle on unethical or illegal activity, Professor Brian Martin recommends that you take the following actions: document the problem, know the context, propose solutions, and get advice and support.

Sources: *2013 National Business Ethics Survey*: Ethics Resource Center, Brian Martin, *The Whistleblower's Handbook: How to Be an Effective Resister* (Charlbury, UK: Jon Carpenter Publishing, 1999); Jayne O'Donnell, "Blowing the Whistle Can Lead to Harsh Aftermath, Despite Law," *USA Today*, August 1, 2005, 1B; Stephen Taub, "Five Years Out of Work," *CFO.com*, http://cfo.com/printable/article.cfm/9210493/ (accessed June 28, 2016); Curtis Verschoor, "To Blow the Whistle or Not Is a Tough Decision," *Strategic Finance*, 87 (October 2005): 21–22; "With the Whistleblower Provision, No One Wins," *Banking Wire*, 13 (August 8, 2005): 8; "The Age of the Whistleblower," *The Economist*, December 5, 2015, http://www.economist.com/news/business/21679455-life-getting-better-those-who-expose-wrongdoing-companies-continue-fight (accessed February 10, 2016).

employees (12%). A troubling finding is that 60% of misconduct involved managers, and 24% involved senior-level managers. This high rate of managerial misconduct brings into question the "tone at the top."

Clearly, failing to follow a corporate code of ethics can lead to serious consequences. But what happens in companies that demonstrate a commitment to ethical behavior? At least one researcher has found a positive financial impact from corporate ethical behavior. In a 1998 study of the 500 largest U.S. companies (based on their 1996 sales revenue), those companies that openly committed themselves to ethical standards in their annual reports experienced better financial performance than those that failed to make a public commitment.[19]

UNIT 1.3 REVIEW

KEY TERMS

Code of conduct p. 22

Ethical behavior p. 22

PRACTICE QUESTIONS

1. LO 5 Which of the following is not a typical component of a code of conduct?
   a. Fair employment practices
   b. Salary scales
   c. Conflicts of interest
   d. Privacy
2. LO 5 Ethical behavior is governed by laws and rules. True or False?
3. LO 5 If an organization has a published code of conduct, its employees will not become involved in unethical behavior. True or False?

UNIT 1.3 PRACTICE EXERCISE

Darlene Matthews is president of a regional chain of doughnut shops. During a recent interview, a candidate for the chief financial officer's position asked to see the company's code of conduct. Darlene responded, "This isn't a Fortune 500 company, so we don't need a code of conduct. Besides, I interview all employees and hire only good people." Do you think Darlene's position is justified? Why or why not?

SELECTED UNIT 1.3 ANSWERS

Think About It 1.3

The designer is misrepresenting his intentions to the artists. While his actions may ultimately increase the popularity of their works, he is cheating the artists out of some of their income. The designer is showing a lack of integrity, as well as a lack of credibility (because he isn't accurately disclosing all the information to the artists). You should discuss the matter with him.

If your discussion does not resolve the matter, you should refer it to your supervisor. If a resolution still cannot be reached, continue to the next level of management. You may wish to confer confidentially with an impartial adviser. You may also wish to speak with your attorney concerning any legal implications of your actions.

While these general steps may apply in any ethical conflict, your actions should also be guided by the company's corporate code of conduct, if one exists. In addition, if you belong to a professional organization, then you are bound by its code of professional ethics, which may specify the steps to follow in resolving an ethical conflict.

Practice Questions

1. B
2. False
3. False

Unit 1.3 Practice Exercise

Darlene is incorrect in her assumption. Firms of all sizes benefit from a code of conduct. The code of conduct communicates the organization's core values to its employees and guides their behavior. Darlene's conviction that she hires only "good" people doesn't mean that those people are "good." Even "good" people may not always recognize that a particular action is inconsistent with the organization's core values if those values have not been communicated to them explicitly.

CHAPTER SUMMARY

In this chapter you learned some important terms and techniques that will be relevant throughout the rest of this book. Specifically, you should be able to meet the learning objectives set out at the beginning of the chapter:

1. ***Define managerial accounting. (Unit 1.1)***

   There are several formal definitions of managerial accounting. A simple one is "the generation of relevant information to support management's decision-making activities."

2. ***Describe the differences between managerial and financial accounting. (Unit 1.1)***

   Managerial accounting's primary users are managers and decision makers within an organization, whereas financial accounting is aimed primarily at external users. Unlike GAAP that guides financial accounting, there are no mandated rules in managerial accounting. Managerial accounting reports focus on operating segments, while financial accounting statements report results for the organization as a whole. Managerial accounting is concerned more with projecting future results than reporting past results. Managerial accounting information is prepared to take advantage of a window of opportunity, even if some accuracy must be sacrificed. Financial accounting information is balanced to the penny and is delivered after the end of the accounting period.

3. ***List and describe the four functions of managers. (Unit 1.1)***

   Planning means setting a direction for the organization. Long-term, or strategic, planning provides direction for a five- to ten-year period. Short-term, or operational, planning provides more detailed guidance for the coming year; it translates the company's strategy into action steps. Controlling is the monitoring of day-to-day operations to identify any problems that require corrective action. Evaluating is the process of comparing a particular period's actual results to planned results, for the purpose of assessing managerial performance. Decision making means choosing between alternative courses of action.

4. ***Explain how the selection of a particular business strategy determines the information that managers need to run an organization effectively. (Unit 1.2)***

   To run a business effectively, managers need information that shows how well operations are meeting the organization's strategic goals. For instance, if the organization's strategy is to be a low-cost producer, information about product costs and cost variances will be more useful to managers than information about research and development.

5. ***Discuss the importance of ethical behavior in managerial accounting. (Unit 1.3)***

   Ethical behavior means knowing right from wrong and then doing the right thing. Many companies and most professional organizations have codes of conduct to guide employees' actions. Acting unethically can lead to illegal activity and ultimately to the destruction of the firm. Furthermore, research has shown that a public commitment to ethical behavior can lead to superior financial performance.

KEY TERMS

Balanced scorecard (Unit 1.2)
Code of conduct (Unit 1.3)
Controlling (Unit 1.1)
Decision making (Unit 1.1)

Enterprise resource planning (ERP) (Unit 1.2)

Ethical behavior (Unit 1.3)

Evaluating (Unit 1.1)

Generally accepted accounting principles (GAAP) (Unit 1.1)

Just-in-time inventory (JIT) (Unit 1.2)

Long-term planning (Unit 1.1)

Managerial accounting (Unit 1.1)

Short-term (operational) planning (Unit 1.1)

Supply chain (Unit 1.2)

EXERCISES

1-1 Understanding how managers use managerial accounting information (LO 1) Managerial accounting information is not just for accountants. All areas within an organization can use the information to support decision making. Choose a position in an organization that is appealing to you and identify several decisions that you might be asked to make in that position. What kind of managerial accounting information would you need to make those decisions?

1-2 Discriminating between managerial and financial accounting (LO 2) In each of the following situations, identify whether the setting is primarily financial accounting or managerial accounting.

a. Volkswagen has experienced a decline in U.S. sales, which dropped 18% in 2005 and 24% between 2002 and 2004. Then chief executive, Bernd Pischetsrieder, believed the biggest problem at Volkswagen was the cost incurred to produce a car, which was not competitive with other automakers. The company tried to get German workers to agree to pay cuts to reduce the cost. (*Source*: Stephen Power, "Once Hot Volkswagen Attempts to Reverse U.S. Sales Decline," *The Wall Street Journal*, September 8, 2005.)

b. In reporting a 2.1% drop in quarterly income from the previous year's second quarter, Oracle Corp. noted that a weaker dollar affected revenue in its database segment. A weaker dollar makes Oracle's products more expensive overseas and lowers the company's revenue after currency conversion. (*Source*: David P. Hamilton, "Oracle Profit Slips 2.1% on Costs Tied to PeopleSoft Acquisition," *The Wall Street Journal*, December 16, 2005.)

c. Cerner is a developer of information technology for the health care industry. As the company incurs expenses to develop a software package, it capitalizes those costs as an asset. Beginning in the year after the software is released, it then amortizes those costs over a five-year period. Normal practice in the software industry is to amortize these costs over a three-year period. (*Source*: Jesse Eisinger, "Cerner's Growth Has Been Healthy, But Its Accounting Could Be Ailing," *The Wall Street Journal*, December 14, 2005.)

d. BNSF Railway was experiencing an increase in demand for information technology resources even though, overall, the company's business wasn't growing. In an effort to understand the technology group's operations, Chief Information Officer Jeff Campbell developed a balanced scorecard for the IT group. Among the measures he tracked were monthly performance against operating budget, percentage of projects delivered on time, employee absenteeism, and internal rate of return on IT projects. Now everyone in the company understands how much it costs to provide the technology support for a particular business application. (*Source*: Meredith Levinson, "Why You Keep Score," CIO.com, July 19, 2007, http://www.cio.com/article/124652/CASE_STUDY_3_Why_You_Keep_Score.)

1-3 Classifying managerial functions (LO 3) Classify each of the following activities as planning, controlling, evaluating, or decision making.

a. A corporate chef prepares a menu and shopping list for the upcoming board of directors meeting.
b. The human resources manager reviews the monthly payroll report and identifies departments that paid overtime to workers.
c. The production supervisor notices that the pressure in a sauerkraut fermenting vat is too high and opens the release valve to lower the pressure.
d. The marketing director considers whether to offer a $0.50 coupon or a $0.75 coupon through a direct mail campaign.
e. At the end of the coupon campaign, the marketing director determines the number of coupons redeemed and the additional unit sales achieved through the campaign.
f. The sales manager prepares the sales forecast for the coming year.
g. The divisional vice president determines which employees should receive a performance bonus.

1-4 Meeting managers' need for information (LO 4) For each of the following managers, identify the information that would be useful for monitoring strategic performance.

a. The store manager of a Wendy's in Austin, Texas
b. The regional manager for all Wendy's restaurants in the state of Texas
c. Wendy's executive vice president of operations

1-5 Understanding a supply chain (LO 4) Choose a company you are familiar with and diagram its supply chain. For each entity in the supply chain, identify one or two specific decisions that might affect other members of the supply chain.

1-6 Constructing a balanced scorecard (LO 4) For each of the following measures that could be incorporated into a balanced scorecard, identify which of the four balanced scorecard perspectives it would most likely belong to.

a. Training hours per employee
b. Average time to answer a customer complaint
c. Gross profit
d. Number of new products in development
e. Number of defective units produced
f. Percentage of orders delivered on or before due date
g. Employee turnover
h. Number of new customers
i. Market share
j. Return on investment

1-7 Applying the IMA's Statement of Ethical Professional Practice (LO 5) (Adapted from M. Elizabeth Haywood and Donald E. Wygal, "Corporate Greed vs. IMA's Ethics Code," *Strategic Finance*, November 2004, 45–49).

The IMA's Statement of Ethical Professional Practice was designed to help finance professionals "to link ethical perspectives directly to their ongoing workplace responsibilities." Unfortunately, some individuals may choose to act unethically and perhaps cause great harm to other individuals and organizations. In each of the following examples, determine which of the four standards of ethical conduct has been violated. Some examples may violate more than one standard.

a. Douglas Faneuil was a Merrill Lynch brokerage assistant who was involved in Martha Stewart's sale of ImClone stock. During the investigation, he lied to federal investigators, saying that there was a standing order to sell the stock if the share price fell below $60. In return for lying, Mr. Faneuil reportedly received money, airplane tickets, and an extra week's vacation.

b. The day after Sam Waksal, ImClone's CEO, learned that the Food and Drug Administration was not going to review ImClone's application for approval of a new cancer drug, family members sold $10 million in ImClone stock. Mr. Waksal reportedly shared the information about the failed review with his family.
c. Scott Sullivan, WorldCom's chief financial officer, recorded billions of dollars of operating expenses as capital assets. Depreciating these "assets" over time inflated the company's profits and hid the expenses from the company's auditors.
d. Adelphia co-signed loans of $3 billion with its founders, the Rigas family, who used the proceeds of the loans to purchase shares of Adelphia stock and other personal items. The family did not disclose the loans to the board of directors. When the company's auditors discovered the loans and asked the Rigases to report them to the board, the family refused. The auditors did not report the issue to Adelphia's audit committee.

PROBLEMS

1-8 Using managerial accounting information (LO 1, 3, 4) John Dough's bakery in Waxahachie, Texas, specializes in chocolate chip cookies. While John's business does not yet have a national presence, like Mrs. Fields, he does have a strong statewide reputation. Recently, John has been receiving some out-of-state orders through the company's website. He is beginning to think about the potential for growing his out-of-state business.

Required

a. How can managerial accounting information be useful to John as he thinks about growing his out-of-state business?
b. What decisions might John need to make if he decides to grow his out-of-state business?
c. What managerial accounting information might John find useful as he decides how to grow his out-of-state business?

1-9 Corporate codes of conduct (LO 5) Use the Internet to find a corporate code of conduct. Compare the code you find to the list of typical components of a code of conduct in Exhibit 1-7. Does the code you examined cover all the components? If not, which components are missing? What business problems could result from the omission of those components?

CASES

1-10 Management activities (LO 3) After working for three different companies in ten years, Martin Long decided that he just wasn't cut out to be someone else's employee. For the next four years, he saved 25% of his salary and then opened his own graphic design firm. He intends to target small- and medium-sized businesses that need graphic design services for their letterhead, brochures, and packaging but who cannot afford to employ a full-time graphic artist.

Martin plans to build customer relationships based on his design skills and advertising expertise. Companies can hire him for design work only or for creating a comprehensive print strategy that includes the design and production of print materials. Martin will outsource the production of his print materials to a local printing company.

Required

a. Diagram a supply chain that shows how brochures would be created for a company that cannot make them in house. Be sure to identify Martin's place in the supply chain.
b. Assume that Martin will operate his business out of his home. Identify the costs he will incur in the first year to get the business up and running.
c. Will Martin need to engage in planning, controlling, and evaluating even though he is a sole proprietor with no employees? If so, identify several specific activities he might perform. If not, explain why Martin will not need to perform these activities.
d. Martin probably will not make a lot of money in the first few months of owning his business. What other measures will signal that his business is becoming successful?

1-11 Making ethical decisions (LO 5) Charlie Anderson recently began a new job as the office manager for a prominent medical clinic. He has just received a bill from Med-Count, one of the labs that performs tests for the clinic. In reviewing the bill, Charlie notices that the lab has charged the clinic $25 for a complete blood count test. The clinic, however, bills patients or their insurance companies $90 for the test, and that is the amount that most insurance companies will pay on the patient's behalf. Thus, the clinic is earning a $65 profit on each blood test it orders. After a bit more investigation, Charlie finds similar profit margins on a number of other lab tests. He is concerned about the billing practice and suspects the clinic may have selected the lab based on its low cost rather than on the lab's qualifications and the accuracy of its test results. He also wonders if the tests' profit potential is driving doctors to order unnecessary tests.

Required

Read Opinion 8.09 of the American Medical Association's Code of Medical Ethics (http://www.ama-assn.org/ama/pub/physician-resources/medical-ethics/code-medical-ethics/opinion809.page?). Based on this opinion, do you believe that the clinic's billing for lab tests is an acceptable business practice? Discuss your reasoning.

ENDNOTES

1. Institute of Management Accountants, *Statement on Management Accounting No. 1A, Definition of Management Accounting* (Colorado Springs, CO: Shepard's/McGraw-Hill, 1981), 4.
2. Institute of Management Accountants, *Statement on Management Accounting, Definition of Management Accounting* (Montvale, NJ: Institute of Management Accountants, 2008), 1.
3. Peter C. Brewer, "Redefining Management Accounting: Promoting the Four Pillars of Our Profession," *Strategic Finance*, 89, no. 9 (March 2008): 28.
4. "Leading by Example: A CFO's Role in Company Growth," http://www.imanet.org/newsletter/campus/dflanery.asp (accessed January 18, 2008; site now discontinued).
5. This section on Design Within Reach, Inc. adapted from the company's 2004 Annual Report; 2007 Form 10-K; 2008 Form 10-K; dwrpress.com/about-dwr/ (accessed November 18, 2012; site now discontinued); Belinda Lanks, "Herman Miller Buys DWR for $154 Million. What Does That Mean for Chairs?" *BloombergBusiness*, July 21, 2014, http://www.bloomberg.com/bw/articles/2014-07-21/herman-miller-buys-dwr-for-154-million-dot-what-does-that-mean-for-chairs (accessed February 8, 2016); Louise Lee, "Design Within Reach," *BusinessWeek*, June 6, 2005, 78; Julie Sloane, "Designing," *FSB: Fortune Small Business*, November 2003, 92; Reuters, "Design Within Reach Announces Voluntary Delisting from Nasdaq," http://www.reuters.com/

article/idUS213688+25-Jun-2009+BW20090625 (accessed February 12, 2016); Stephanie Schomer, "Design Within Reach Will Close Its Tools for Living Stores," FastCompany.com, March 24, 2010, http://http://www.fastcompany.com/1596073/design-within-reach-will-close-its-tools-living-stores (accessed June 24, 2016).

6. To learn more about click fraud, read Brian Grow, Ben Elgin, and Moira Herbst, "Click Fraud: The Dark Side of Online Advertising," *BusinessWeek*, October 2, 2006, available online at http://www.bloomberg.com/news/articles/2006-10-01/click-fraud (accessed November 20, 2012).
7. To learn more about management accountants' role in planning, see Jeffrey C. Thomson, "Anatomy of a Plan: Better Practices for Management Accountants," *Strategic Finance,* 89, no. 4 (October 2007): 21–28.
8. See Michael Porter's books *Competitive Strategy* and *Competitive Advantage,* both published by The Free Press.
9. Anil K. Gupta and V. Govindarajan, "Business Unit Strategy, Managerial Characteristics, and Business Unit Effectiveness at Strategy Implementation," *Academy of Management Journal,* 27 (1984): 25–41.
10. Consulting firm Bain & Company conducts a survey of executives to explore the most popular management tools. Results of their surveys can be found on their website at http://bain.com/management_tools/home.asp.
11. Robert S. Kaplan and David Norton, "The Balanced Scorecard—Measures That Drive Performance," *Harvard Business Review,* 70 (January–February 1992): 71–79.
12. Darrell K. Rigby "Management Tools for 2015: An Executive's Guide," Bain & Company, http://www.bain.com/Images/BAIN_GUIDE_Management_Tools_2015_executives_guide.pdf (accessed February 11, 2016).
13. Hau L. Lee and Corey Billington, "The Evolution of Supply-Chain-Management Models and Practice at Hewlett-Packard," *Interfaces,* 25 (September–October 1995): 42–63.
14. Barbara Marsh, "Allen-Edmonds Shoe Tries 'Just-in-Time' Production—But Company Painfully Finds Approach Isn't Perfect Fit for Small Concerns," *The Wall Street Journal,* March 4, 1993.
15. "Allen-Edmonds Serves Customers Better with Lean Manufacturing System," Allen-Edmonds Shoe Corporation Press Release, March 1, 2005, http://www.businesswire.com/news/home/20050301005087/en/Allen-Edmonds-Serves-Customers-Lean-Manufacturing-System (accessed November 19, 2012).
16. Available online at http://berkleycenter.georgetown.edu/publications/2011-national-business-ethics-survey-workplace-ethics-in-transition.
17. See Curtis Verschoor, "Do The Right Thing: IMA Issues New Ethics Guidance," *Strategic Finance,* 87, no. 5 (November 2005): 43–46, to learn more about the revision effort.
18. "Survey Documents State of Ethics in the Workplace," Ethics Resource Center Press Release, October 17, 2005, http://www.globalethics.org/newsline/2005/10/17/survey-documents-state-of-ethics-in-the-workplace/ (accessed on November 19, 2012; site now discontinued).
19. Curtis Verschoor, "A Study of the Link between a Corporation's Financial Performance and Its Commitment to Ethics," *Journal of Business Ethics,* 17 (October 1998): 1509–1516.

TOPIC FOCUS 1: C&C SPORTS, MANAGERIAL ACCOUNTING CONTEXT

FOCUS	LEARNING OBJECTIVE
TOPIC FOCUS 1	**LO 1:** Describe the business environment of C&C Sports.

TOPIC FOCUS 1—GUIDED UNIT PREPARATION

Answering the following questions while you read this unit will guide your understanding of the key concepts found in the unit. The questions are linked to the learning objective presented above.

LO 1

1. What is C&C Sports' strategy?
2. What are C&C Sports' greatest financial challenges?
3. How might C&C Sports' managers generate additional cash flow?
4. What are the potential threats to C&C Sports' future success?
5. If you wanted to purchase baseball jerseys, baseball pants, or letter award jackets, what would you look for in a supplier?

Business decisions are always made within the context of a specific organization. To help you understand how to use managerial accounting information in making business decisions, we will focus throughout this book on a hypothetical company called C&C Sports, a manufacturer of athletic uniforms. By focusing on a single company, we hope to help you understand how managerial decisions unfold within the organization. Although C&C Sports is fictitious, its story is based on that of a similar real-world company.

C&C's History

C&C Sports is located in Brownsville, Texas, where it has been run by the Douglas family since 1928. The company began as a small sewing operation that supplied clothing to workers on the Gateway International Bridge. As Brownsville grew and workers came and went, the Douglases began to look for a market niche to guide the company's future growth. Recognizing the increasing number of youth participating in organized sports, the family decided to manufacture baseball uniforms. Today, President George Douglas heads the third generation of leadership at the company, and several other relatives hold key management positions. Exhibit T1-1 shows C&C Sports' current organization chart.

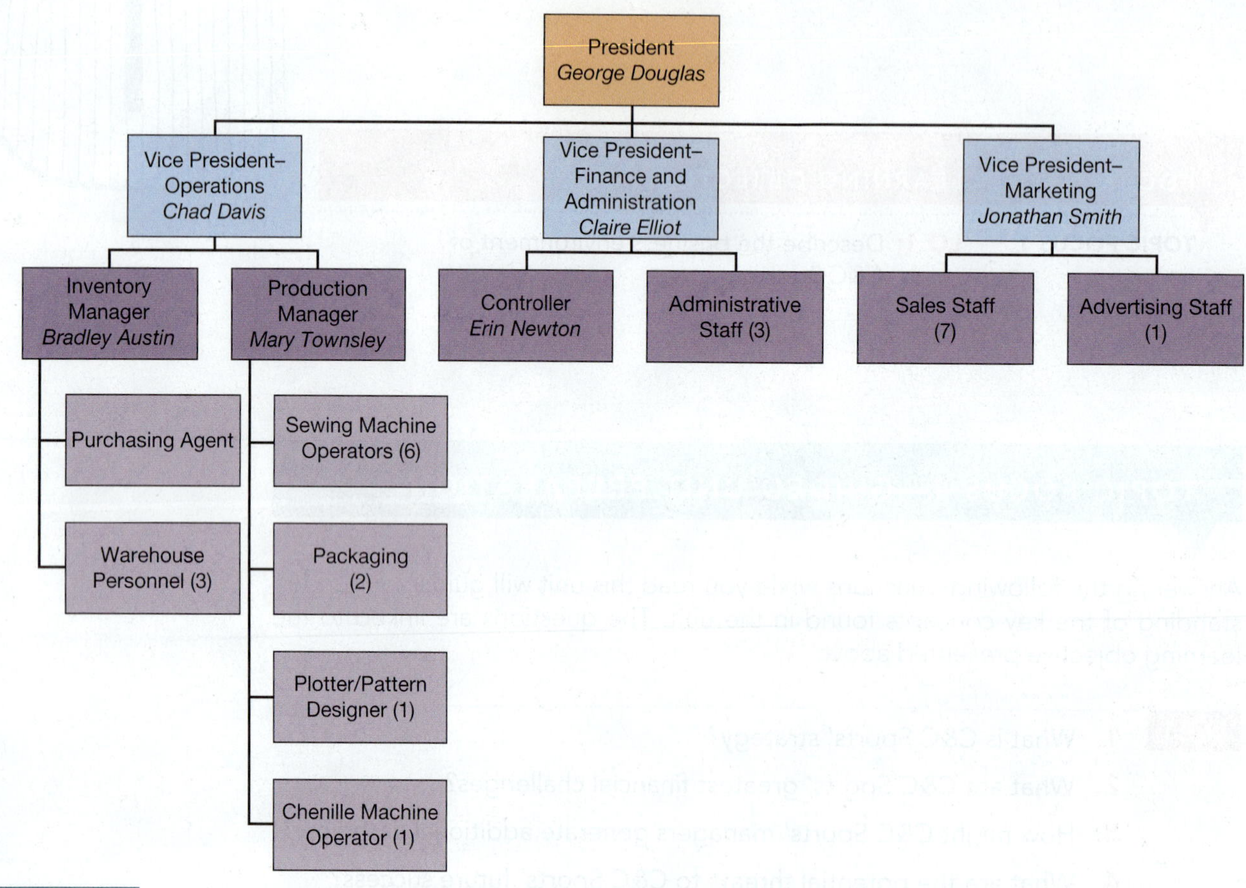

EXHIBIT T1-1 *C&C Sports' organization chart.*

The family has made a conscious decision not to follow the textile industry's trend of transferring manufacturing operations to China and other foreign countries that offer cheap labor. They have chosen to remain a domestic producer and to focus instead on quick delivery and fast customer response within a local market—the state of Texas. The company manufactures three products: baseball jerseys, baseball pants, and letter award jackets.

Exhibit T1-2 illustrates C&C Sports' supply chain. Notice that it begins with Bruin Polymers, Inc., which makes polyester pellets. Neff Fiber Manufacturing melts the polyester pellets and pushes them through an extruder to create the

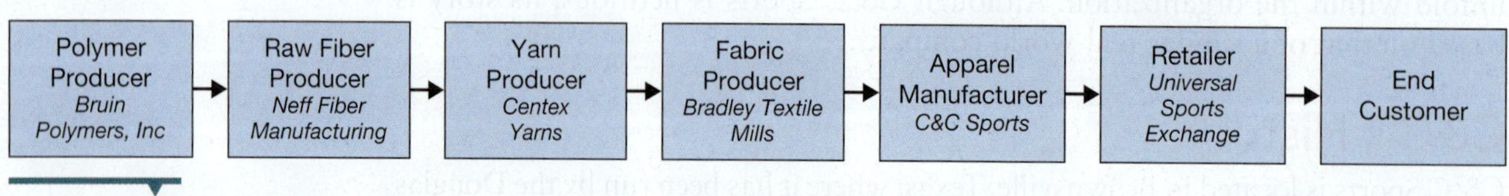

EXHIBIT T1-2 *C&C Sports' supply chain.*

raw fiber, called partially oriented yarn. Centex Yarns converts the raw fiber into finished yarn by covering, twisting, texturizing, and coloring it. Bradley Textile Mills then uses the finished yarn to weave the fabric that C&C Sports buys. C&C Sports manufactures the uniforms and sells them to retailers such as Universal Sports Exchange, which resell them to the end customer.

While Exhibit T1-2 shows the major links in the supply chain, a number of other firms play a role as well. For instance, transportation companies provide shipping services between C&C Sports and Universal Sports Exchange. And providers of other items, such as buttons and thread, supply C&C's need for production materials.

A Brief Look at C&C's Resources

If C&C is to remain successful, it must generate sufficient resources to continue operating. To date, the company has enjoyed moderate financial success. Its latest financial statements are presented in Exhibits T1-3, T1-4, and T1-5.

EXHIBIT T1-3

C&C Sports' income statement.

C&C SPORTS
Income Statements
for the Years Ended December 31

	2016	2015	2014
Sales	$5,237,000	$4,654,000	$4,668,400
Cost of goods sold	3,876,432	3,464,440	3,514,630
Gross profit	1,360,568	1,189,560	1,153,770
Selling and administrative expense	1,160,566	1,067,721	1,043,437
Operating income	200,002	121,839	110,333
Interest expense	41,715	43,210	45,698
Income before taxes	158,287	78,629	64,635
Tax expense (30%)	47,486	23,589	19,390
Net income	$ 110,801	$ 55,040	$ 45,245

Although details of conducting an analysis of C&C's financial statements are presented in Chapter 12, a brief look at some important trends and indicators will help you understand the company's resource position. The availability of resources such as cash and inventory will determine how C&C is able to respond to changes in the business environment to take advantage of opportunities that arise.

Let's first take a look at the Statement of Cash Flows because the ability to generate cash can make or break a small business. The first section of the statement shows that in the last three years C&C has not been able to generate cash from operations. Income has been increasing, but accounts receivable and inventories have been increasing, too. In fact, the changes in all of the working capital accounts (current assets and current liabilities) have created a drain on cash.

C&C doesn't have any investing activities, which is not unusual for a small business. The other source of cash flow is financing activities, and you can see that each year, C&C has paid off more debt than it has borrowed. It appears that C&C may be trading long-term debt for short-term debt, as evidenced by the repaying of long-term debt and the increase in short-term debt. This is a good strategy only if the terms of the short-term debt are better than what the company can currently get on long-term debt. Since cash from operations and cash from financing activities are decreasing, the cash balance is decreasing. This trend can't continue into the future, so management needs to find a way to increase cash, preferably from operating activities.

EXHIBIT T1-4

C&C Sports' balance sheets.

C&C SPORTS Balance Sheets As of December 31	2016		2015	
Cash		$ 7,752		$ 22,114
Accounts receivable, net		623,713		583,429
Raw materials	$186,955		$168,428	
Work in process	6,137		6,991	
Finished goods	447,280		371,690	
Total inventories		640,372		547,109
Prepaid expenses		24,388		8,164
Total current assets		1,296,225		1,160,816
Machinery and equipment, net		532,858		600,647
Other assets		41,704		35,812
Total assets		$1,870,787		$1,797,275
Accounts payable		441,602		$ 445,014
Accrued liabilities		86,749		115,626
Short-term debt		125,000		110,000
Current maturities of long-term debt		20,000		20,000
Total current liabilities		673,351		690,640
Long-term debt		280,000		300,000
Total liabilities		953,351		990,640
Common stock		210,000		210,000
Retained earnings		707,436		596,635
Total stockholders' equity		917,436		806,635
Total liabilities and stockholders' equity		$1,870,787		$1,797,275

Now let's consider some key relationships on the income statement. You can see that sales decreased from 2014 to 2015 and increased from 2015 to 2016, yet net income increased every year. C&C was able to generate increasing income, even when sales declined, because expenses as a percentage of sales were reduced. The following table shows various income statement accounts as a percentage of sales. Cost of goods sold as a percentage of sales decreased each year, resulting in a higher gross profit percentage. Selling and administrative expense increased as a percentage of sales from 2014 to 2015 and decreased from 2015 to 2016.

	December 31, 2016	December 31, 2015	December 31, 2014
Sales	100.00%	100.00%	100.00%
Cost of goods sold	74.02%	74.44%	75.29%
Gross profit	25.98%	25.56%	24.71%
Selling & administrative expense	22.16%	22.94%	22.35%
Operating income	3.82%	2.62%	2.36%
Net income	2.12%	1.18%	0.97%

C&C SPORTS Statements of Cash Flows for the Years Ended December 31	2016	2015	2014
Cash flows from operating activities			
Net income	$110,801	$55,040	$ 45,245
Adjustments to reconcile net income to cash provided by operating activities			
Depreciation	67,789	66,912	70,626
Changes in operating assets and liabilities			
Accounts receivable	(40,284)	(31,466)	(21,993)
Inventories	(93,263)	(98,510)	(105,411)
Prepaid expenses/other assets	(22,116)	(14,507)	(22,116)
Accounts payable	(3,412)	9,651	8,197
Accrued liabilities	(28,877)	(8,318)	1,098
Net cash used by operating activities	(9,362)	(21,198)	(24,354)
Net cash provided by investing activities	0	0	0
Cash flows used by financing activities			
Short-term borrowing	15,000	10,000	10,000
Repayment of long-term debt	(20,000)	(20,000)	(20,000)
Net cash used by financing activities	(5,000)	(10,000)	(10,000)
Increase/(Decrease) in cash	(14,362)	(31,198)	(34,354)
Cash at beginning of period	22,114	53,312	87,666
Cash at end of period	$ 7,752	$22,114	$ 53,312

EXHIBIT T1-5

C&C Sports' statement of cash flows.

The operating income percentage is low when compared to other apparel manufacturers. IBISWorld, a company that provides market analyses by industry, estimates that companies in this industry have an average 7.5% profit margin, as shown in Exhibit T1-6.[1] In the industry, smaller firms tend to lack economies of scale in production, have a higher cost of capital, and have higher administrative costs than larger firms. This is true of C&C Sports and is the primary reason that C&C's costs runs higher as a percentage of sales than that of other apparel manufacturers.

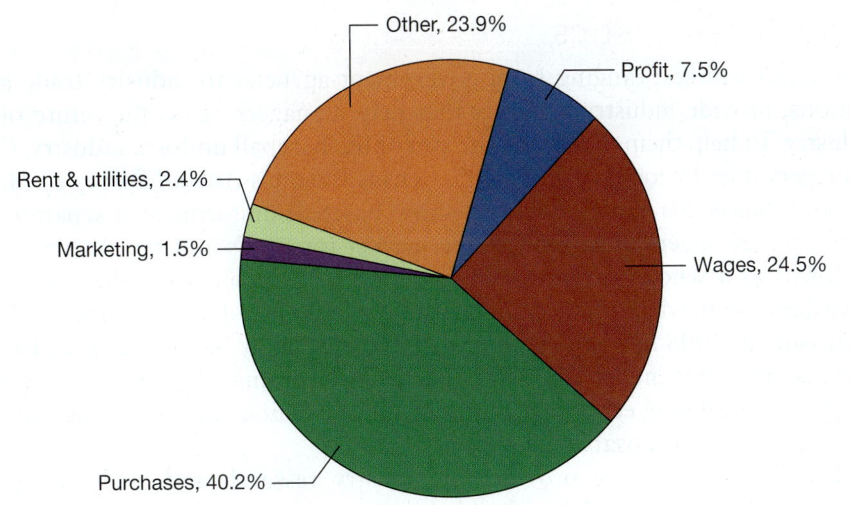

EXHIBIT T1-6

Average cost structure for costume and team uniform manufacturing in the United States, 2015.

Analyzing the composition of the balance sheet will help you understand the funding sources of assets and what kinds of assets C&C holds. The table below shows selected balance sheet accounts as a percentage of total assets. First look at the liabilities and stockholders' equity section. Notice that in 2015, stockholders' equity funded about 45% of assets, and liabilities funded the other 55%. By 2016, stockholders' equity funded 49% and liabilities funded the remaining 51%. C&C Sports is decreasing its reliance on debt as a source of funding assets.

	December 31, 2016	December 31, 2015
Accounts receivable, net	33.34%	32.46%
Total inventories	34.23%	30.44%
Total current assets	69.29%	64.59%
Machinery and equipment, net	28.48%	33.42%
Total assets	100.00%	100.00%
Total current liabilities	35.99%	38.43%
Long-term debt	14.97%	16.69%
Total stockholders' equity	49.04%	44.88%
Total liabilities and stockholders' equity	100.00%	100.00%

Notice that most of C&C's assets are current assets and that the relative percentage increased from 2015 to 2016. Accounts receivable represents sales not yet collected and is much higher than that of other apparel manufacturers. For example, in 2014 Under Armour, Inc. had accounts receivable that were approximately 13.4% of total assets. C&C's inventory balance increased not only in absolute size (dollars) but also in relative size. This increase could indicate that C&C is experiencing a buildup in inventory that could be caused by overproduction or obsolete inventory. Or it could indicate that the company is building up an inventory buffer in anticipation of sales growth. C&C's inventory as a percentage of assets is not out of line with others in the industry.

Industry Statistics

Numerous sources, ranging from government agencies to industry trade associations, provide industry statistics that help managers assess the future of the industry. To help them determine the size of the baseball uniform industry, C&C managers start by looking at the U.S. Census Bureau's *Annual Survey of Manufactures*. Since this survey does not show baseball uniforms as a separate category, the managers must look at the market for men's and boys' team sports uniforms as a whole. As shown in Exhibit T1-7, shipments of these uniforms have been somewhat cyclical—increasing to 2003 and then falling to 2006, increasing to 2008 and then falling to 2011, and finally increasing to 2014. The decrease in shipments in 2009 was particularly dramatic, possibly a result of the general declining economic conditions in the United States and the resulting lower consumer disposable incomes.

IBISWorld, a leading provider of industry research and analysis reports, estimates that men's and boys' team sports uniforms account for 11.5% of

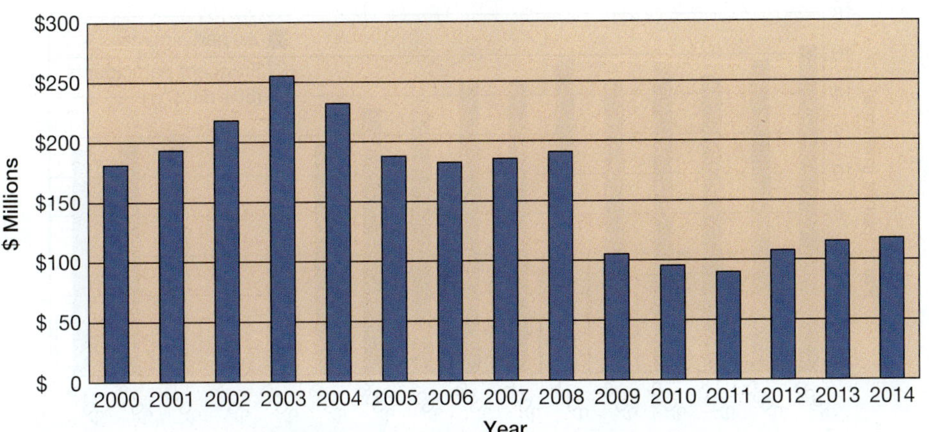

Sources: U.S. Census Bureau, *Annual Survey of Manufactures Value of Product Shipments: 2001*; U.S. Census Bureau, *Annual Survey of Manufactures Value of Product Shipments: 2004*; U.S. Census Bureau, *Annual Survey of Manufactures Value of Product Shipments: 2006*; U.S. Census Bureau, *Annual Survey of Manufactures Value of Product Shipments: 2008*; U.S. Census Bureau, *Annual Survey of Manufactures Value of Product Shipments: 2010*; U.S. Census Bureau, *Annual Survey of Manufactures Value of Shipments: 2011*; U.S. Census Bureau, *Annual Survey of Manufactures Value of Shipments: 2014*.

EXHIBIT T1-7

Value of U.S. men's and boys' team sports uniform shipments.

the $1.1 billion costume and team uniform manufacturing industry (NAICS 31529). The market for team uniforms has been steady for the past five years, and there is little projected growth in the coming years. IBISWorld reports that manufacturers of these uniforms have largely moved manufacturing from the United States to countries that offer lower wage rates. Imports satisfied 78.3% of total U.S. demand in 2015, although this level is expected to decrease in the next few years as U.S. manufacturers increase domestic production levels. A bright spot for the team uniform industry is that many of the new high-tech specialty fabrics used in uniforms are produced primarily in the United States, which supports a healthy niche of domestic manufacturers that produce custom team uniforms using these materials.[2]

Consumers are willing to pay a higher price for a uniform that is durable and of high quality. Firms that provide a high level of customer service by producing special orders and making timely deliveries can establish a competitive advantage. While the majority of uniforms are sold through retail outlets, Internet sales are growing and becoming a more important sales channel.

While we have been examining the overall market for athletic uniforms, C&C managers need to understand the size of the potential market for baseball uniforms to evaluate the company's future prospects. Perhaps the most important factor in assessing the market for baseball uniforms is the number of people playing baseball, and trade associations such as the Sports and Fitness Industry Association (SFIA) are a good source for this type of specific information. SFIA reports that in 2012, baseball was the second most popular team sport in the United States, based on total number of participants.[3]

According to statistics reported by the Sports Business Research Network (SBRnet) and shown in Exhibit T1-8, the number of people playing baseball has been in gradual decline since 2004.[4] This decline has also been reflected in Little League Baseball[5] and high school baseball.[6] SBRnet also reports that 53% of baseball players in 2014 were between the ages of 7 and 17, and 49% of the players lived in a household with income of at least $75,000. The vast majority of players (78.6%) are male, and there has been recent growth in the number of people who are playing baseball 50 or more days each year.

EXHIBIT T1-8

U.S. participants in team baseball 7 years of age or older, at least once per year.

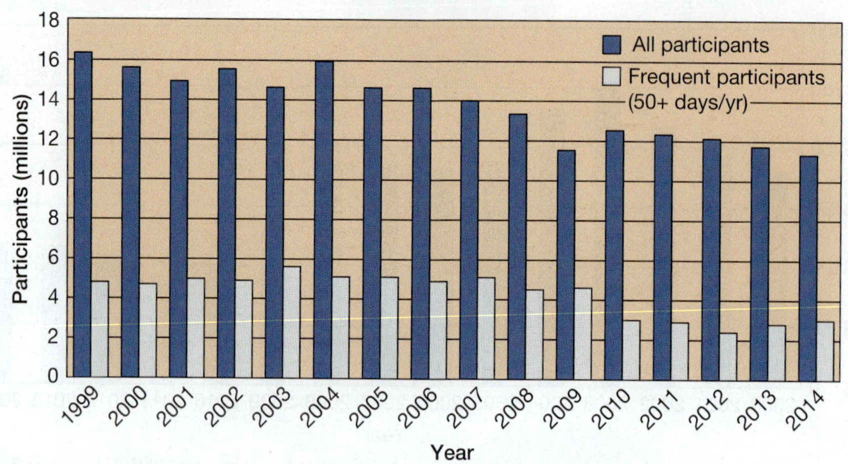

Source: Sports Business Research Network, *Baseball: Participation by Total vs. Frequent*

TOPIC FOCUS SUMMARY

Describe the business environment of C&C Sports.

C&C Sports is a manufacturer of baseball jerseys, baseball pants, and letter award jackets. Located in Brownsville, Texas, the company is a domestic manufacturer that competes in a local market (Texas). C&C Sports focuses on quick delivery and fast customer response time.

Recently, C&C Sports has experienced a decrease in available cash and an increase in inventory. Sales revenue has been increasing at a faster rate than expenses, generating a higher level of profits. Approximately half of C&C's asset base is financed through debt and half through equity.

The industry faces increasing pressure from imports, particularly from China, which creates a need to compete on price. However, customers in this market are willing to pay higher prices for goods that are durable and of high quality. The Internet is becoming an increasingly important sales channel.

ENDNOTES

1. Max Oston, IBIS*World* Industry Report 31529: *Costume & Team Uniform Manufacturing in the US*, September 2015.
2. Max Oston, IBIS*World* Industry Report 31529: *Costume & Team Uniform Manufacturing in the US*, September 2015.
3. The Sports and Fitness Industry Association, *2013 Sports, Fitness and Leisure Activities Topline Participation Report.*
4. Sports Business Research Network, *Baseball: Participation by Total vs. Frequent* (accessed February 22, 2016).
5. Marc Fisher, "Baseball is struggling to hook kids—and risks losing fans to other sports," *The Washington Post*, April 5, 2015, https://www.washingtonpost.com/sports/nationals/baseballs-trouble-with-the-youth-curve–and-what-that-means-for-the-game/2015/04/05/2da36dca-d7e8-11e4-8103-fa84725dbf9d_story.html (accessed February 16, 2016).
6. The National Federation of State High School Associations, "2014–15 High School Athletics Participation Survey," http://www.nfhs.org/ParticipationStatistics/PDF/2014-15_Participation_Survey_Results.pdf (accessed February 22, 2016).

© Tischenko Irina/Shutterstock

COST BEHAVIOR AND COST ESTIMATION

UNITS	LEARNING OBJECTIVES
UNIT 2.1 Cost Behavior Patterns	**LO 1:** Identify basic cost behavior patterns and explain how changes in activity level affect total cost and unit cost.
UNIT 2.2 Cost Estimation	**LO 2:** Estimate a cost equation from a set of cost data and predict future total cost from that equation.
UNIT 2.3 Contribution Margin Analysis	**LO 3:** Prepare a contribution format income statement.

Photodisc/Getty Images

Business Decision and Context

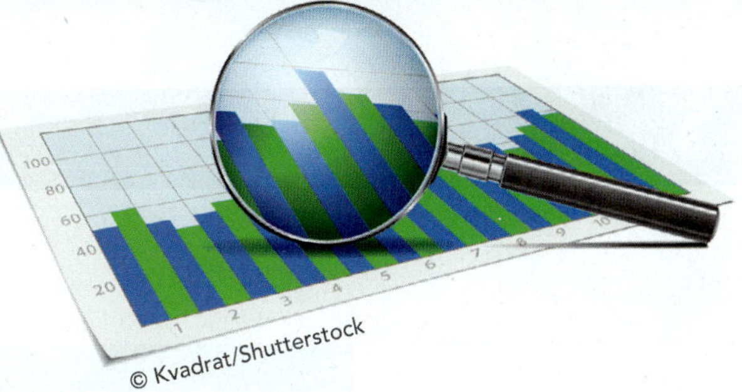

© Kvadrat/Shutterstock

Martin Keck, vice president for sales at Universal Sports Exchange, one of C&C Sports' customers, was reviewing the latest corporate income statement prior to meeting with Judy Elmore, the company's chief financial officer.

"I don't understand these numbers," Martin thought. "We fell short of our projected sales volume of jerseys by 10%, so I was anticipating net income to be 10% lower than expected as well. But that's not what the numbers are showing. How can I use this information to help me plan for the coming year? I just placed an order for jerseys with C&C Sports last week thinking I knew what we needed, and now I'm not so sure I did the right thing."

Martin's thoughts were interrupted by the telephone's ringing. He answered, and heard **Jonathan Smith, C&C Sports' vice president for marketing**, on the other end.

"Hi, Martin," Jonathan said. "I'm calling to check on your last order of jerseys—it's smaller than I expected."

"I was just thinking about that order, Jonathan," said Martin. "I told our purchasing manager to cut the order this month because we sold 10% fewer jerseys than we expected last year. That means we have leftover jerseys in inventory, and we don't need as many as we originally thought we would."

> "I told our purchasing manager to cut the order this month because we sold 10% fewer jerseys than we expected last year. That means we have leftover jerseys in inventory, and we don't need as many as we originally thought we would."

"Ouch," commented Jonathan. "That had to hurt Universal's bottom line last year."

"It did," replied Martin. "Although for the life of me I can't figure out how much money we lost from the lower sales volume."

Martin faces a problem that is common in companies that rely on financial statements prepared according to GAAP to make business decisions. GAAP-based income statements categorize expenses based on business function—product, selling, or administrative. To predict what the company's income might have been under certain scenarios, we need to know how those costs behave—that is, how they change with changes in the company's activity level.

SUPPLY CHAIN KEY PLAYERS

- END CUSTOMER
- UNIVERSAL SPORTS EXCHANGE
  - Vice President of Sales: Martin Keck
- C&C SPORTS
  - Vice President for Marketing: Jonathan Smith
- DURABLE ZIPPER COMPANY
- BRADLEY TEXTILE MILLS
- CENTEX YARNS
- NEFF FIBER MANUFACTURING
- BRUIN POLYMERS, INC.

UNIT 2.1

Cost Behavior Patterns

GUIDED UNIT PREPARATION

Answering the following questions while you read this unit will guide your understanding of the key concepts found in the unit. The questions are linked to the learning objectives presented at the beginning of the chapter.

LO 1

1. Why is it important for managers to understand cost behavior patterns?
2. What is a variable cost? If the activity level increases, what happens to the total cost incurred? Give three examples of a variable cost.
3. What is a fixed cost? If the activity level increases, what happens to the total cost incurred? Give three examples of a fixed cost.
4. Distinguish between committed and discretionary fixed costs.
5. What is a mixed cost? If the activity level increases, what happens to the total cost incurred? Give three examples of a mixed cost.
6. What is a step cost? If the activity level increases, what happens to the total cost incurred? Give three examples of a step cost.

In evaluating a business decision, it is important to understand how the costs associated with a given course of action will change over a range of activity levels. When managers talk about **cost behavior,** they are referring to the way in which total costs change in response to changes in the level of activity. This unit introduces four common cost behavior patterns that serve as the foundation for cost–volume–profit analysis (Chapter 3), and you'll learn how to use these cost behavior patterns to estimate total cost.

Variable Costs

Let's assume that you are planning a party. The caterer has presented a menu based on the number of guests attending. For each guest that attends, the caterer will charge \$10 for food and beverages. If you have 10 guests, you will be charged \$100 (10 guests × \$10 per guest); if you have 100 guests, you will be charged \$1,000 (100 guests × \$10 per guest).

This hypothetical catering plan is an everyday example of a variable cost. Any total cost that varies in proportion to a business activity is a **variable cost**. The **activity** can be any repetitive event that serves as a measure of output or usage, such as units sold, units produced, minutes talked, or miles driven. As the level of activity increases, the total cost increases by the same proportion. Conversely, as the level of activity decreases, the total cost decreases by the same proportion.

So a 10% increase in volume results in a 10% increase in total variable cost, and a 10% decrease in volume results in a 10% decrease in total variable cost.

Variable costs have two main characteristics:

- The total cost varies in proportion to changes in the level of activity.
- The cost per unit remains constant, regardless of the level of activity.

These characteristics are illustrated in Exhibit 2-1, representing your hypothetical party catering plan. As the number of guests you invite increases, so does your catering bill. Notice that if you have no guests, the total cost is $0. This pattern is true of all variable costs: If there is no activity, no cost is incurred. But while the total bill changes with the number of guests invited, the cost per guest remains constant at $10 per guest. Notice that the slope of the total cost line equals the cost per guest, $10.

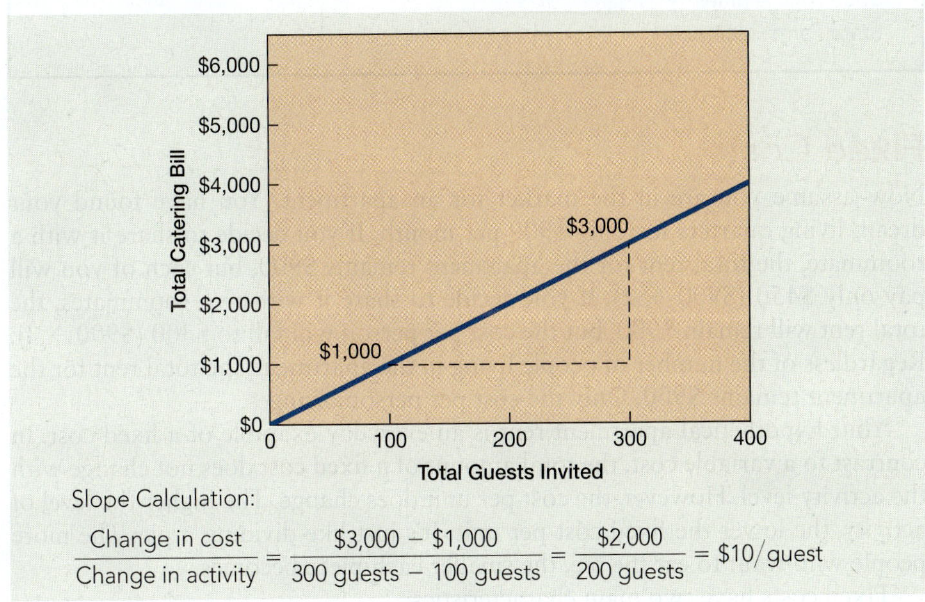

$$\frac{\text{Change in cost}}{\text{Change in activity}} = \frac{\$3{,}000 - \$1{,}000}{300 \text{ guests} - 100 \text{ guests}} = \frac{\$2{,}000}{200 \text{ guests}} = \$10/\text{guest}$$

EXHIBIT 2-1

Variable cost of catering.

The following table illustrates the relationship between guests invited, cost per guest at various levels of activity, and total cost.

Guests Invited	Cost per Guest	Total Cost
1	$10	$ 10
10	$10	$ 100
50	$10	$ 500
100	$10	$1,000
200	$10	$2,000
300	$10	$3,000

Total variable cost is easy to estimate if you know the cost per unit of activity. Suppose you have invited 237 guests to your party. How much is your catering bill going to be? The answer is $2,370:

237 guests × $10 per guest = $2,370

THINK ABOUT IT 2.1

For each of the following companies, identify at least one cost that you think is variable. What is the unit of activity that makes that cost variable?

	Variable Cost	*Unit of Activity*
Starbucks	*coffee, cups, cream, cup lids*	*cups of coffee sold*
Honda Motor Co.		
UPS		
Amazon.com		
Dell		
Hilton Hotels		
Southwest Airlines		
State Farm Insurance		

Fixed Costs

Now assume you are in the market for an apartment. You have found your dream living quarters for only $900 per month. If you decide to share it with a roommate, the total rent for the apartment remains $900, but each of you will pay only $450 ($900 ÷ 2). If you decide to share it with two roommates, the total rent will remain $900, but the cost per person will fall to $300 ($900 ÷ 3). Regardless of the number of people living in the apartment, the total rent for the apartment remains $900. Only the cost per person changes.

Your hypothetical apartment rent is an everyday example of a fixed cost. In contrast to a variable cost, the total amount of a **fixed cost** does not change with the activity level. However, the cost per unit does change. The higher the level of activity, the lower the fixed cost per unit. It's just like dividing a pie: The more people who want to eat the pie, the smaller each piece becomes.

Fixed costs have two main characteristics:

- The total cost remains fixed, regardless of changes in the level of activity.
- The cost per unit varies inversely with changes in the level of activity.

Exhibit 2-2 illustrates these characteristics. As the number of roommates increases, the total rent remains constant. But while the total rent remains constant as the number of roommates changes, the cost per person varies.

EXHIBIT 2-2

Fixed cost of an apartment rental.

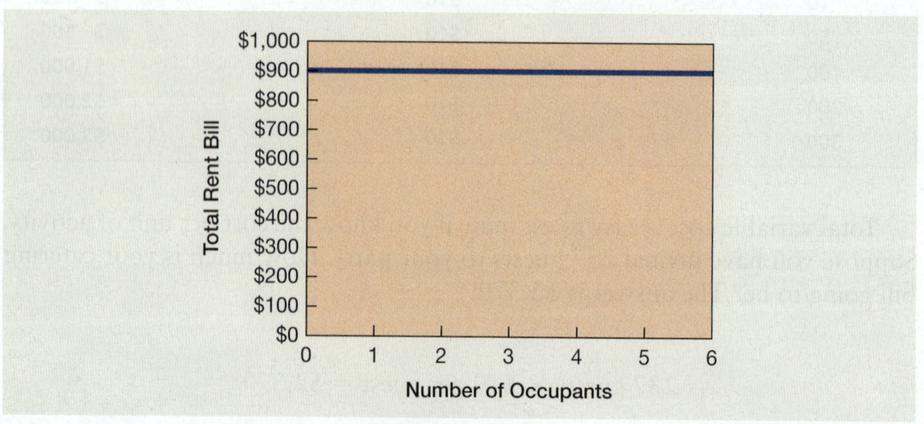

The following table illustrates the relationship between the number of occupants, the total cost, and the cost per person at various levels of activity:

Number of Occupants	Total Cost	Cost per Person
1	$900	$900
2	$900	$450
3	$900	$300
4	$900	$225
5	$900	$180

Discretionary versus Committed Fixed Costs

One important distinction between different types of fixed costs is the period over which they can be changed. **Discretionary fixed costs** are fixed costs that can be changed over the short run. For instance, the cost of an annual contract for television advertising is a fixed cost. In times of falling profits, however, a company may choose to cut such advertising costs to improve profits. **Committed fixed costs**, on the other hand, cannot be changed over the short run. For instance, a company may have signed a 10-year lease on an office building. Until the lease period ends, nothing can be done to change the amount of rent the company pays.

Companies should be careful about reducing their discretionary fixed costs during times of falling profits. Consider the cost of television advertising. Reducing advertising is likely to reduce sales further, exacerbating the problem of falling profits.

WATCH OUT!

Most students are very good at defining variable and fixed costs, but they often make mistakes in recalculating costs when the activity level changes. To avoid mistakes, keep the costs in their "constant" form. For example, if you are calculating variable costs, use the cost per unit because you know that number won't change (remember $10 per guest?). Then calculate the new total by multiplying the constant—in this case, the cost per unit—by the number of units. If you are calculating fixed costs, use the total cost (remember $900 per month for rent?), even if someone has given you the cost per unit. You know that a fixed cost per unit applies to only one activity level, so don't use it to predict fixed cost at any other level of activity.

Step Costs

Suppose your cell phone company offers a data plan under which you can buy data service in blocks of 4 gigabytes (GB). Every block of 4 GB costs $40. If you use between 0 and 4 GB, you will pay $40; if you use 4.1 GB, you will pay $80.

This data plan is an example of a **step cost**. Step costs are fixed over only a small range of activity. Once that level of activity has been exceeded, total cost increases and remains constant over another small range of activity.

With step costs, total cost remains constant over the step range, but unit cost decreases as usage within the step range increases. So while the total cost of both 1 GB and 4 GB would be $40, the cost per gigabyte of data would be $40 and $10, respectively. Exhibit 2-3 illustrates step costs.

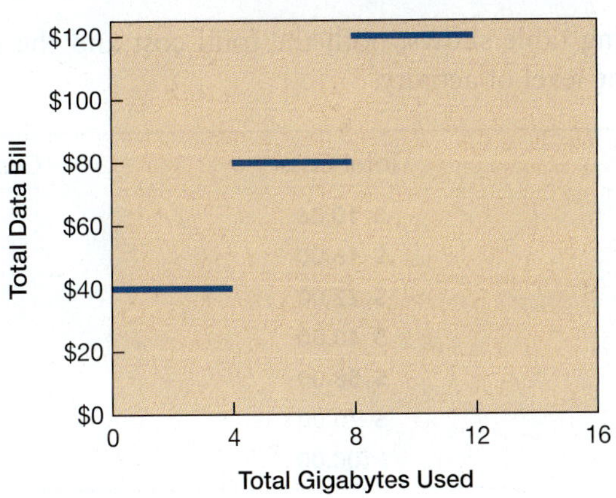

EXHIBIT 2-3

Step cost of data service.

Mixed Costs

At this point, you may be thinking that all costs are either fixed or variable. That isn't quite the case, however. Some costs have both a fixed and a variable component. These costs are referred to as **mixed costs**. Since a mixed cost has both a fixed and a variable component, both the total cost and the unit cost will vary with changes in the level of activity.

Think about the natural gas bill you might receive for heating your apartment. To receive service, you pay a base charge of $10 per month, regardless of how much gas you use. Then you pay an additional charge of $0.06 per cubic foot for the gas you use. The $10 monthly charge is the fixed component, and the $0.06 charge per cubic foot is the variable component. So the total cost can be expressed as:

Total gas cost = $10 + ($0.06 × cubic feet of gas used)

Exhibit 2-4 illustrates the concept of a mixed cost. Notice that the total cost line intersects the *y*-axis at $10, representing the fixed component of the mixed cost. The slope of the line is $0.06, representing the variable component of the mixed cost.

EXHIBIT 2-4

Mixed cost of natural gas service.

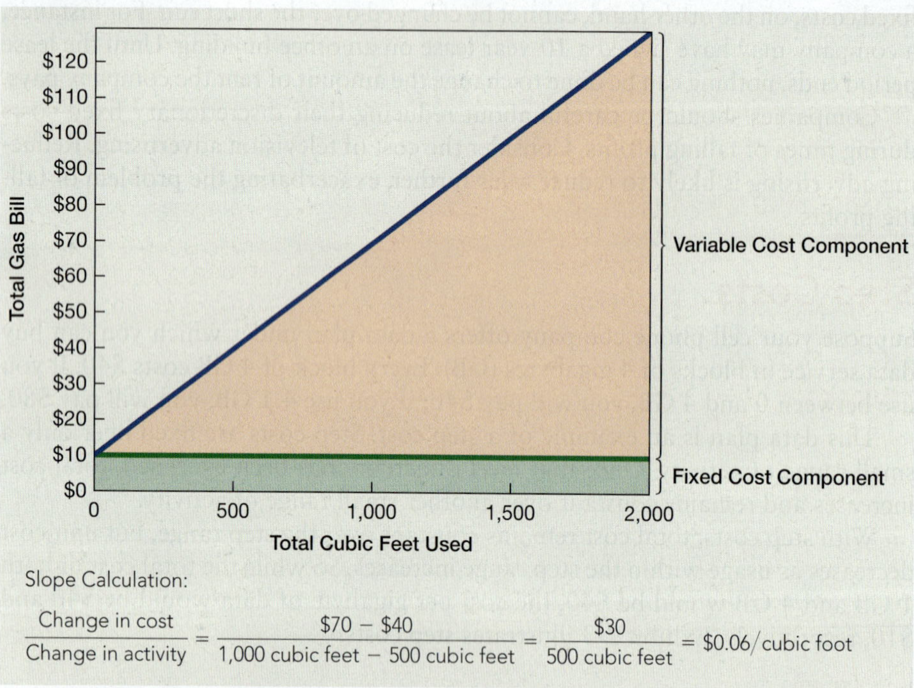

Slope Calculation:

$$\frac{\text{Change in cost}}{\text{Change in activity}} = \frac{\$70 - \$40}{1{,}000 \text{ cubic feet} - 500 \text{ cubic feet}} = \frac{\$30}{500 \text{ cubic feet}} = \$0.06/\text{cubic foot}$$

As the following table shows, both the total cost and the unit cost change with changes in the level of activity.

Cubic Feet Used	Total Cost	Cost per Cubic Foot
1	$ 10.06	$10.0600
100	$ 16.00	$ 0.1600
200	$ 22.00	$ 0.1100
500	$ 40.00	$ 0.0800
800	$ 58.00	$ 0.0725
1,000	$ 70.00	$ 0.0700
1,500	$100.00	$ 0.0667

REALITY CHECK—*If it looks like a variable cost . . .*

Monkey Business Images/Shutterstock

$596.3 billion. That's what U.S. public school systems spent during the 2012–13 academic year to educate students in grades K–12. When taken on a per-student basis, it means that it costs an average of $10,763 to educate each K–12 student. But does this mean that if one more student enters school it will cost an additional $10,763? No.

While this average cost per student may look like a variable cost, it really isn't. Think about all the different costs that are incurred to educate a student. While many of these costs, such as books, cafeteria food, and classroom supplies, are variable, there are many other costs that are not. Consider the school principal's salary. It's a fixed cost, and it will not change when one additional student enrolls in the school. Think about teachers' salaries. With maximum classroom size often legislated by state lawmakers, teachers' salaries are a step cost because a new teacher will be hired only when the maximum allowed enrollment is exceeded.

It costs an average of $10,763 to educate each K–12 student.

An analysis of Census Bureau data also reveals a wide disparity across the country in the education cost per pupil. The state of New York, for example, spends an average of $19,818 per student, while Utah spends only $6,555. Boston City Schools spent the most in the country—$20,502 per student.

So next time you see statistics reported like this, remember that the reported amount probably isn't a variable cost. Rather, it's a mixed cost that combines variable, fixed, and step cost components.

Sources: Emma Brown, "The States That Spend the Most (and the Least) on Education, in One Map," *The Washington Post*, June 2, 2015, https://www.washingtonpost.com/news/local/wp/2015/06/02/the-states-that-spend-the-most-and-the-least-on-education-in-one-map/ (accessed February 18, 2016); U.S. Department of Education, National Center for Education Statistics, *Fast Facts*, https://nces.ed.gov/fastfacts/display.asp?id=66 (accessed February 18, 2016); U.S. Census Bureau, "Per Pupil Spending Varies Heavily Across the United States," Release Number CB 15-98, June 2, 2015, https://www.census.gov/newsroom/press-releases/2015/cb15-98.html (accessed February 18, 2015).

THINK ABOUT IT 2.2

What causes a mixed cost to increase with activity? What causes the cost per unit of a mixed cost to decrease with activity?

UNIT 2.1 REVIEW

KEY TERMS

Activity p. 46
Committed fixed cost p. 49
Cost behavior p. 46
Discretionary fixed cost p. 49
Fixed cost p. 48
Mixed cost p. 50
Step cost p. 49
Variable cost p. 46

PRACTICE QUESTIONS

1. LO 1 A variable cost remains constant in total with changes in activity level. True or False?
2. LO 1 Macintosh Corporation leases a copy machine for a monthly fee of $100 plus a charge of $0.01 per copy. Macintosh's copy cost would be considered a
   - a. variable cost.
   - b. fixed cost.
   - c. step variable cost.
   - d. mixed cost.
3. LO 1 Meg Thomas maintains a membership at Woodridge Health and Fitness that costs her $120 per month. The membership fee would be considered a
   - a. variable cost.
   - b. fixed cost.
   - c. step variable cost.
   - d. mixed cost.

UNIT 2.1 PRACTICE EXERCISE

Complete the following table, identifying the following costs as fixed (F), variable (V), or mixed (M).

	ACTIVITY LEVEL			COST BEHAVIOR
	1,000 UNITS	2,000 UNITS	3,000 UNITS	F, V, or M
Cost 1	$ 12,000	$ 12,000	$ 12,000	F
Cost 2	$ 5,100	$ 5,200	$ 5,300	
Cost 3	$ 4,300	$ 8,600	$ 12,900	
Cost 4	$0.06/unit	$0.06/unit	$0.06/unit	
Cost 5	$ 600/unit	$ 300/unit	$ 200/unit	
Cost 6	$ 151/unit	$ 76/unit	$ 51/unit	

SELECTED UNIT 2.1 ANSWERS

Think About It 2.1

	VARIABLE COST	UNIT OF ACTIVITY
Starbucks	coffee, cups, cream, cup lids	cups of coffee sold
Honda Motor Co.	steel, tires, windshields	cars manufactured
UPS	jet fuel gasoline	pounds transported by air delivery miles driven
Amazon.com	shipping cartons, freight	number of shipments
Dell	computer chips, monitors	number of computers built
Hilton Hotels	laundry, mints	number of guests
Southwest Airlines	jet fuel snacks, napkins	number of miles flown number of passengers
State Farm Insurance	agent commissions	policy dollar value

Think About It 2.2

The variable component of the mixed cost increases as activity increases, so the total cost increases. The fixed component of the mixed cost causes the cost per unit to decrease with activity because those fixed costs are spread over more units.

Practice Questions

1. False
2. D
3. B

Unit 2.1 Practice Exercise

	ACTIVITY LEVEL			COST BEHAVIOR
	1,000 UNITS	2,000 UNITS	3,000 UNITS	F, V, or M
Cost 1	$ 12,000	$ 12,000	$ 12,000	F
Cost 2	$ 5,100	$ 5,200	$ 5,300	M
Cost 3	$ 4,300	$ 8,600	$ 12,900	V
Cost 4	$0.06/unit	$0.06/unit	$0.06/unit	V
Cost 5	$ 600/unit	$ 300/unit	$ 200/unit	F
Cost 6	$ 151/unit	$ 76/unit	$ 51/unit	M

Costs 1 and 4 are easy to identify because they match the "constant" definition of fixed and variable costs. Cost 1 is constant *in total* over all activity levels, so it must be a fixed cost. Cost 4 is constant *per unit* over all activity levels, so it must be a variable cost. The other costs cannot be classified just by looking at them.

Costs 2 and 3 both change with the activity level, but that doesn't make these costs variable. Variable costs vary *directly* with activity, meaning that there is a linear relationship between the cost and the activity. To determine whether such a relationship exists, compute the cost per unit (total cost ÷ activity level). For cost 2, the per unit amounts are $5.10, $2.60, and $1.77. For cost 3, the per unit amounts are $4.30, $4.30, and $4.30. Notice that cost 3 has a direct relationship to the activity level—that is, for every additional unit of activity, a cost of $4.30 is incurred. Because this unit cost is constant over all activity levels, it must be a variable cost. For cost 2, on the other hand, the per unit cost *decreases* with activity, which means it can't be variable. We know that cost 2 is not fixed because it changes with activity. If it is neither fixed nor variable, it must be mixed.

Costs 5 and 6 both decrease on a per unit basis as the activity level increases, which is a characteristic of both fixed and mixed costs. To determine whether these costs are fixed or mixed, compute the total cost (cost per unit × activity level). For cost 5, the total cost is $600,000, $600,000, and $600,000, indicating that it is a fixed cost. For cost 6, the total cost is $151,000, $152,000, and $153,000. Since cost 6 has characteristics of both fixed costs (the cost per unit decreases as the activity level increases) and variable costs (the total cost increases as the activity level increases), it is a mixed cost.

UNIT 2.2

Cost Estimation

GUIDED UNIT PREPARATION

Answering the following questions while you read this unit will guide your understanding of the key concepts found in the unit. The questions are linked to the learning objectives presented at the beginning of the chapter.

LO 2

1. Express the relationship between total cost (TC), variable cost per unit (VC), volume (x), and fixed cost (FC) in equation form.
2. Explain how a scattergraph is used to separate a mixed cost into its fixed and variable components.

3. Explain how the high-low method is used to separate a mixed cost into its fixed and variable components for cost estimation.
4. Given a choice between the high-low method, a scattergraph, or regression analysis, which method would you prefer for separating a mixed cost into its fixed and variable components? Why?
5. Explain the concept of the relevant range. How does a company's relevant range differ from the steps found in a step cost?

A large part of analyzing a business decision is predicting the level of cost that will be incurred. Once you know how a particular cost behaves, estimating the total cost is relatively simple. In this unit, we will learn how to use several techniques for making these estimates.

Total cost is a combination of fixed and variable costs.[1] It can be predicted using the standard algebraic equation

$$mx + b = y$$

where:

m = the variable cost per unit;
x = the level of activity (such as number of units);
b = total fixed cost; and
y = total cost.

Think back to the cost of natural gas, which we examined in Unit 2.1. This mixed cost included a fixed charge of \$10 per month and a variable charge of \$0.06 per cubic foot. The total cost of service at any level of usage can be estimated using the following equation:

\$0.06	(number of cubic feet used) +	\$10 =	Total gas cost
↓	↓	↓	↓
m	x	b	y

So for 100 cubic feet of gas, the estimated total cost would be

$$\$0.06(100) + \$10 = \$16$$

While using this equation to predict the total cost is a simple task, we don't always know the total fixed cost and variable cost per unit. So we need to determine those costs before we can predict future costs. Let's look at three methods of estimating costs: scattergraphs, the high-low method, and regression analysis.

Scattergraphs

Scattergraphs are the simplest method for estimating the fixed and variable components of a mixed cost. A **scattergraph** is simply a graph that shows total costs in relation to volume or activity level. The data needed to create a scattergraph can be gathered from weekly or monthly reports. Once you have plotted the individual points, draw a line through them to estimate the cost relationship.[2]

The following table shows the delivery costs that Universal Sports Exchange incurred last year with its outside delivery service. Exhibit 2-5 shows the same information in the form of a scattergraph. Notice that the level of activity—number of deliveries in this case—is plotted on the horizontal axis and the total delivery cost is plotted on the vertical axis. This is the customary format for a scattergraph. Based on a visual inspection of the scattergraph, a linear relationship appears to exist between the number of deliveries and delivery cost.

Month	Number of Deliveries	Total Delivery Cost
January	2,000	$ 3,650
February	985	1,875
March	1,500	2,600
April	2,500	4,000
May	800	1,400
June	600	1,500
July	2,800	4,800
August	1,200	2,125
September	1,350	2,200
October	725	1,600
November	1,850	3,050
December	2,200	3,400
Total	18,510	$32,200

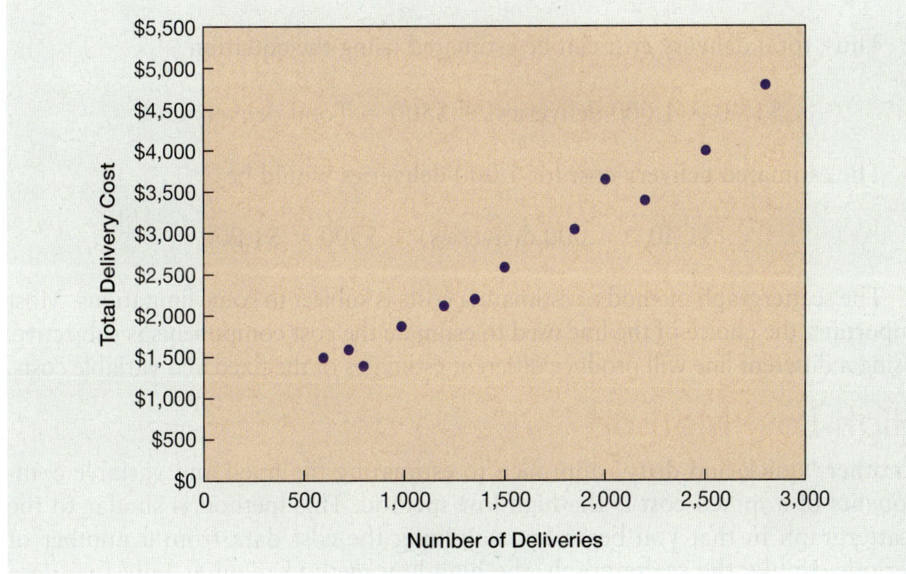

EXHIBIT 2-5

Scattergraph of delivery costs.

To estimate the fixed and variable cost components using a scattergraph, it is necessary to visually "fit" a line to the plotted points. You need to draw the line so that it appears to fit the data well, minimizing the distance between the line and the data points. Once you have drawn the line, you can calculate the fixed and variable costs using basic algebra. Exhibit 2-6 shows one possible line fitted to the plotted points. Notice that it crosses the *y*-axis (where the level of activity is 0) at $500. Thus, the estimate for fixed delivery cost is $500.

EXHIBIT 2-6

Scattergraph of delivery costs with fitted line.

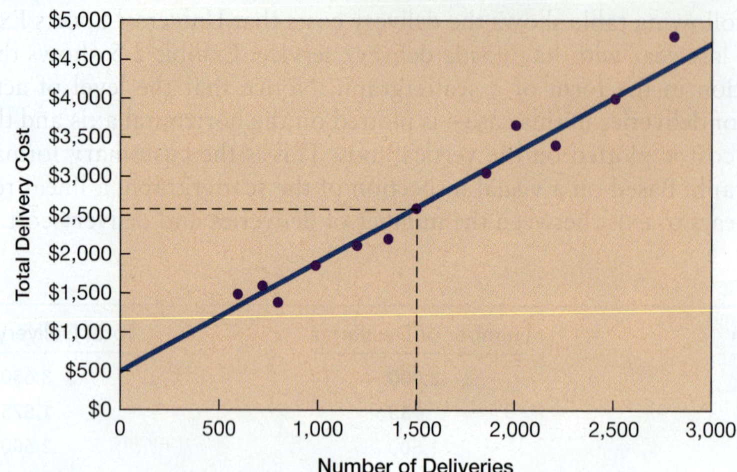

You can calculate the variable cost of a delivery as the slope of the line using any visually identified point on the line. Using the point representing 1,500 deliveries and $2,600 of total delivery cost,

$$\text{Variable cost per delivery} = \frac{\text{Change in total cost}}{\text{Change in number of deliveries}}$$

$$m = \frac{\$2{,}600 - \$500}{1{,}500 - 0}$$

$$m = \frac{\$2{,}100}{1{,}500}$$

$$m = \$1.40 \text{ per delivery}$$

Thus, total delivery cost can be estimated using the equation

$$(\$1.40 \times 1{,}000 \text{ deliveries}) + \$500 = \text{Total delivery cost}$$

The estimated delivery cost for 1,000 deliveries would be

$$(\$1.40 \times 1{,}000 \text{ deliveries}) + \$500 = \$1{,}900$$

The scattergraph method of estimating costs is subject to some limitations. Most important, the choice of the line used to estimate the cost components is subjective. Using a different line will produce different estimates of the fixed and variable costs.

High-Low Method

Another "quick and dirty" approach to estimating the fixed and variable components of a mixed cost is the **high-low method**. This method is similar to the scattergraph in that you begin by examining the cost data from a number of periods. Unlike the scattergraph, the high-low method requires only two data points—the lowest point of activity and the highest point of activity.

To estimate total cost using the high-low method:

1. Identify the highest and lowest levels of activity
2. Compute the variable cost per unit (the slope of the line):

$$\text{Variable cost per unit} = \frac{\text{Change in total cost}}{\text{Change in activity}}$$

3. Calculate the fixed cost using either the high point or the low point such that:

$$\text{Fixed costs} = \text{Total cost} - \text{Variable cost}$$

4. Complete the cost equation by showing that

$$(\text{Variable cost per unit} \times \text{Units}) + \text{Fixed cost} = \text{Total cost}$$

> **WATCH OUT!**
> Always select the high and low points based on *level of activity*, not total cost.

Let's return to the data on delivery cost that we used in the scattergraph example.

Step 1: The highest level of activity, 2,800 deliveries, occurred in July at a total cost of $4,800. The lowest level of activity, 600 deliveries, occurred in June at a total cost of $1,500.

Step 2:

$$\text{Variable cost per delivery} = \frac{\text{Change in total cost}}{\text{Change in number of deliveries}}$$

$$m = \frac{\$4{,}800 - \$1{,}500}{2{,}800 - 600}$$

$$m = \frac{\$3{,}300}{2{,}200}$$

$$m = \$1.50 \text{ per delivery}$$

Step 3: Using the high point,

$$(\text{Variable cost per unit} \times \text{Number of units}) + \text{Fixed cost} = \text{Total cost}$$
$$(\$1.50 \times 2{,}800) + \text{Fixed cost} = \$4{,}800$$
$$\$4{,}200 + \text{Fixed cost} = \$4{,}800$$
$$\text{Fixed cost} = \$4{,}800 - \$4{,}200$$
$$\text{Fixed cost} = \$600$$

Or, using the low point,

$$(\text{Variable cost per unit} \times \text{Number of units}) + \text{Fixed cost} = \text{Total cost}$$
$$(\$1.50 \times 600) + \text{Fixed cost} = \$1{,}500$$
$$\$900 + \text{Fixed cost} = \$1{,}500$$
$$\text{Fixed cost} = \$1{,}500 - \$900$$
$$\text{Fixed cost} = \$600$$

Step 4:

$$(\$1.50 \times \text{Number of deliveries}) + \$600 = \text{Total delivery cost}$$

We can now use our equation to estimate the delivery cost at any level of activity. For example, at 1,000 deliveries, estimated total delivery cost would be:

$$(\$1.50 \times 1{,}000 \text{ deliveries}) + \$600 = \$2{,}100$$

Like the scattergraph, the high-low method does have some limitations. Because it is based on only two extreme points, the high and low activity levels, the cost equation may not be truly representative of the cost relationship. Be careful not to use an obvious outlier as either the high or the low point, or it will greatly skew your cost estimate.

> **WATCH OUT!**
> In using the high-low method to separate a mixed cost into its fixed and variable components, students often stop after Step 2, forgetting half the solution. Remember to insert either the high point or the low point into the total cost equation to calculate the fixed cost component of the mixed cost (Step 3). Then, write out the total cost estimation equation (Step 4). Use *only* the high point or the low point to complete Step 3 because those were the only two points used to estimate the variable cost per unit.

Regression Analysis

A more precise approach to separating a mixed cost is **regression analysis**, a statistical technique that identifies the line of best fit for the points plotted in a scattergraph. As shown in Exhibit 2-7, spreadsheet software such as Microsoft Excel makes regression analysis easy. After entering the data points in the spreadsheet, use the INTERCEPT and SLOPE functions to determine the fixed cost and variable cost per unit, respectively.

EXHIBIT 2-7

Regression using Microsoft Excel.

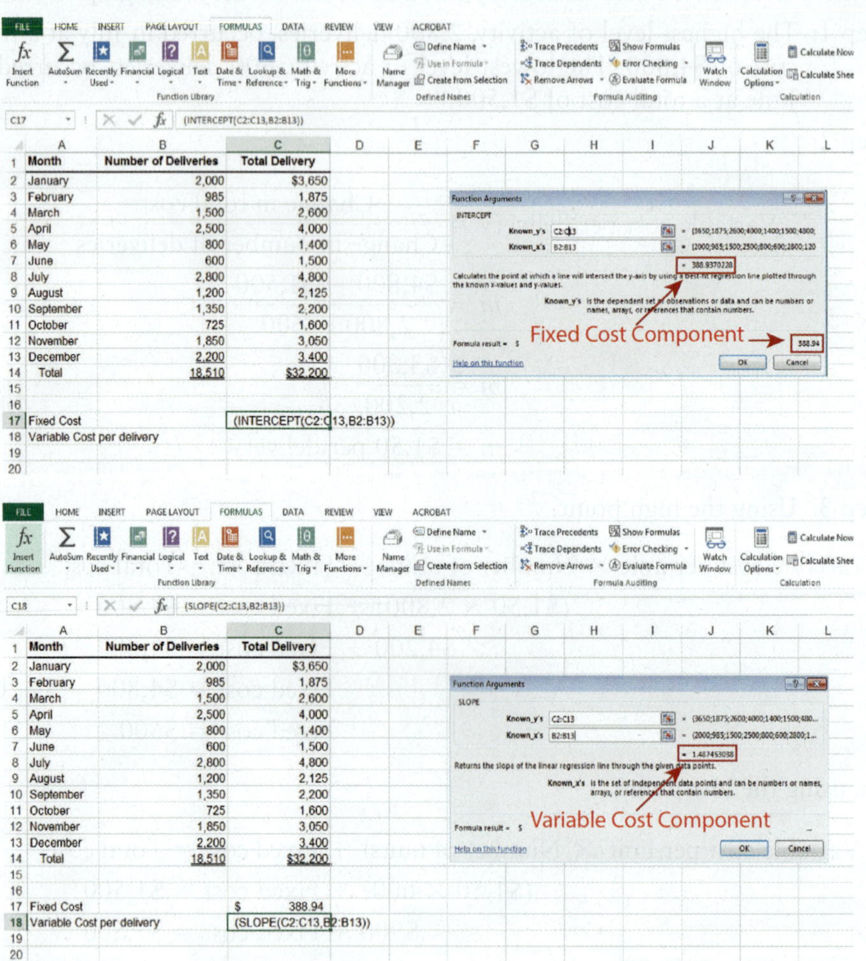

Month	Number of Deliveries	Total Delivery
January	2,000	$3,650
February	985	1,875
March	1,500	2,600
April	2,500	4,000
May	800	1,400
June	600	1,500
July	2,800	4,800
August	1,200	2,125
September	1,350	2,200
October	725	1,600
November	1,850	3,050
December	2,200	3,400
Total	18,510	$32,200

Using the same data represented in our scattergraph (Exhibit 2-5), regression analysis results in a total fixed cost of $388.94 and a variable cost of $1.49 per delivery. Thus, the equation to estimate total delivery cost would be

$$(\$1.49 \times \text{Number of deliveries}) + \$388.94 = \text{Total delivery cost}$$

Using this equation, the estimated delivery cost for 1,000 deliveries would be

$$(\$1.49 \times 1{,}000) + \$388.94 = \$1{,}878.94$$

You have now learned three ways to estimate the fixed and variable components of a mixed cost: the scattergraph, the high-low method, and regression analysis. Let's compare the results of the three methods:

REALITY CHECK—*Where does the relevant range end?*

Scott Olson/Getty Images News/Getty Images

Growth of this magnitude will definitely move BMW's production costs into a different relevant range.

How wide is the relevant range of activity? When does a company leave one relevant range and enter another one with a different cost function? The answers to these questions are company-specific and can greatly affect the cost estimates used in decision making.

Consider BMW Group's decision to expand its plant in Spartanburg, South Carolina. A March 2014 announcement of a $1 billion expansion at the plant to produce the new X4 and X7 models promised to increase production by 50%, to 450,000 cars per year, and to create 800 new jobs. And this expansion came on the heels of a $950 million expansion in 2012 and a $750 million expansion in 2008.

While it's possible that the plant will be operating in the same relevant range after the latest expansion is complete, growth of this magnitude will definitely move BMW's production costs into a different relevant range from when the plant opened in 1994 with a planned capacity of 50,000 cars and 500 employees.

Sources: BMW Group, "BMW Announces Plant Expansion," news release, March 10, 2008, https://www.bmwusfactory.com/bmw_articles/bmw-announces-plant-expansion/ (accessed June 28, 2016); Michelle Krebs, "Plant Expansion Linchpin in BMW Plan to Dominate U.S. Luxury Market," Edmunds AutoObserver, October 14, 2010, https://www.bmwusfactory.com/bmw_articles/bmw-announces-plant-expansion/ (accessed June 28, 2016); South Carolina Department of Commerce, "BMW Announces Plant Expansion in Spartanburg County," press release, January 12, 2012, http://www.fitsnews.com/2012/01/12/sc-commerce-bmw-announces-plant-expansion/ (accessed June 26, 2016); Jeffrey Collins, "BMW plans $1 billion expansion at factory in Greer, SC," *The Charlotte Observer*, March 28, 2014, http://www.charlotteobserver.com/news/business/article9108095.html (accessed February 16, 2016).

Method	Variable Cost per Delivery	Fixed Cost	Estimated Delivery Cost for 1,000 Deliveries
Scattergraph	$1.40	$500.00	$1,900.00
High-low	$1.50	$600.00	$2,100.00
Regression	$1.49	$388.94	$1,878.94

Why go through all these estimations? Remember, we started the chapter by asking what Universal's income would be if the company had achieved its original sales volume target. But we can't estimate how income will change when the activity level changes until we can estimate how costs will change with the activity level.

THINK ABOUT IT 2.3

Why do these three estimation techniques result in different predictions for delivery cost? Which one is right?

Cost Estimation and the Relevant Range

A final word of caution about cost behavior and estimation: Cost behaviors and estimates are valid only within the **relevant range**, or the normal level of operating activity. Beyond the relevant range, cost relationships are likely to change, and with them, cost estimates. (For more about relevant range, see the box at the top of this page.)

Consider the graph shown in Exhibit 2-8, which represents a cost relationship that is often encountered in business. Note that the cost relationships on

EXHIBIT 2-8

Cost relationship within the relevant range.

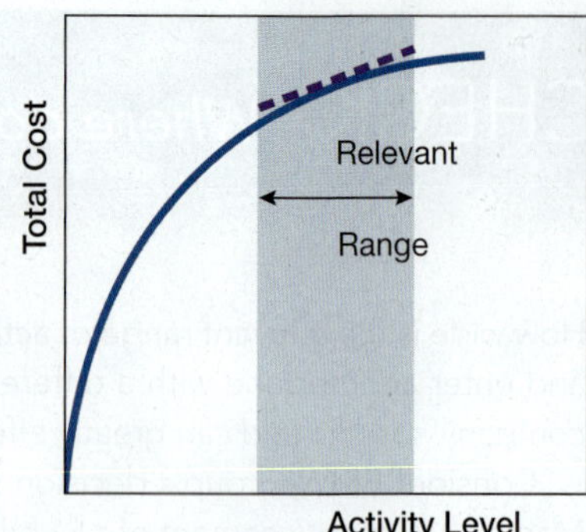

either side of the shaded relevant range differ markedly from the highlighted portion of the curves. While these graphs represent curvilinear cost relationships, within the relevant range the cost relationships approximate a linear relationship. Thus, the estimation techniques you have learned, which are based on a linear relationship, are valid, but *only over the relevant range.*

UNIT 2.2 REVIEW

KEY TERMS

High-low method p. 56 Regression analysis p. 58 Relevant range p. 59 Scattergraph p. 54

PRACTICE QUESTIONS

1. LO 2 The scattergraph method provides the most accurate cost function estimates. True or False?
2. LO 2 Bargain Booksellers sold 40,000 books in April and 65,000 books in December. Shipping costs for the two months were $150,000 and $200,000, respectively. Using these two months' data, the shipping cost function is best estimated as
   a. ($2.00 × number of books sold) + $70,000
   b. ($0.50 × number of books sold) + $167,500
   c. ($3.33 × number of books sold)
   d. ($2.00 × number of books sold) + $50,000
3. LO 2 Mike Morriss conducted a regression analysis on Morriss Medical Supplies' catalog printing costs for last year, which resulted in the following equation: $5*x* + $750. If Morriss plans to print 500 catalogs in the coming year, what are the printing costs expected to be?
   a. $755
   b. $2,500
   c. $3,250
   d. $5,000

UNIT 2.2 PRACTICE EXERCISE

This exercise extends the work you did for the Unit 2-1 exercise. This time, complete the table by estimating the cost formula. For mixed costs, use the high-low method.

	ACTIVITY LEVEL			COST FORMULA
	1,000 UNITS	2,000 UNITS	3,000 UNITS	VC + FC
Cost 1	$ 12,000	$ 12,000	$ 12,000	*$0 + $12,000*
Cost 2	$ 5,100	$ 5,200	$ 5,300	
Cost 3	$ 4,300	$ 8,600	$ 12,900	
Cost 4	$0.06/unit	$0.06/unit	$0.06/unit	
Cost 5	$ 600/unit	$ 300/unit	$ 200/unit	
Cost 6	$ 151/unit	$ 76/unit	$ 51/unit	

SELECTED UNIT 2.2 ANSWERS

Think About It 2.3

The three estimation techniques use different combinations of data points to arrive at a cost equation for deliveries. As a result, their estimated costs differ. Although none of the three techniques yields a correct answer (remember, they are estimations), most statisticians would agree that regression gives the best estimate because it calculates the line of best fit for all data points, not just one or two.

Practice Questions

1. False
2. A
3. C

Unit 2.2 Practice Exercise

	ACTIVITY LEVEL			COST FORMULA
	1,000 UNITS	2,000 UNITS	3,000 UNITS	VC + FC
Cost 1	$ 12,000	$ 12,000	$ 12,000	$ 0(units) + $ 12,000
Cost 2	$ 5,100	$ 5,200	$ 5,300	$0.10(units) + $ 5,000
Cost 3	$ 4,300	$ 8,600	$ 12,900	$4.30(units) + $ 0
Cost 4	$0.06/unit	$0.06/unit	$0.06/unit	$0.06(units) + $ 0
Cost 5	$ 600/unit	$ 300/unit	$ 200/unit	$ 0(units) + $600,000
Cost 6	$ 151/unit	$ 76/unit	$ 51/unit	$ 1(units) + $150,000

Determining the cost formulas for costs 5 and 6 might seem a little confusing at first because those costs are represented per unit instead of in total. You can easily convert them to totals, however, by multiplying the per unit amounts by the appropriate number of units. For cost 5, the total costs are $600,000, $600,000, and $600,000. For cost 6, the total costs are $151,000, $152,000, and $153,000. Applying the high-low method to these total costs is easy.

UNIT 2.3

Contribution Margin Analysis

GUIDED UNIT PREPARATION

Answering the following questions while you read this unit will guide your understanding of the key concepts found in the unit. The questions are linked to the learning objectives presented at the beginning of the chapter.

LO 3

1. Define the term *contribution margin.*
2. What is the contribution margin ratio? How is it related to the variable cost ratio?
3. If a product's variable cost per unit increases while the selling price and fixed cost decrease, what will happen to the contribution margin per unit?
4. How can a company increase a product's contribution margin?

Once you understand cost behavior, you can begin to use that knowledge in making business decisions. One of the basic tools for making such decisions is the contribution margin. In this unit you will learn how to calculate the contribution margin and how to construct a contribution format income statement to support business decision making.

Contribution Margin

If an organization wants to make a profit, it must generate more sales revenue than the expenses it incurs. This relation can be expressed using the following profit equation:

Operating income = Sales revenue − Total expenses

or

Operating income = Sales revenue − Total variable expenses − Total fixed expenses

Let's expand this profit equation based on our knowledge of cost behavior. Since variable cost per unit remains constant, we can express total variable expense as a function of the number of units sold. Likewise, we can express total sales revenue as a function of the number of units sold, resulting in the following expanded profit equation.

Operating income = (Sales price per unit × # of units sold) − (Variable cost per unit × # of units sold) − Fixed expenses

> **WATCH OUT!**
>
> You will notice that sometimes we refer to variable and fixed *costs* and at other times to variable and fixed *expenses*. A **cost** is the cash or other value given up to obtain goods or services in the expectation that they will generate future benefits. A cost can be capitalized as an asset on the balance sheet, as in the purchase of inventory for resale. Once the future benefits have been received, however, the cost becomes an expense on the income statement. So an **expense** is an expired, or used up, cost.
>
> In the inventory example, when inventory is sold, the future benefit—sales revenue—has been realized, so the original capitalized cost is expensed on the income statement as the cost of goods sold. At the same time, the inventory asset on the balance sheet is reduced. Some costs, such as salaries and wages, are expensed in the same period in which they are incurred and are never reported on the balance sheet.

Applying some basic algebra to this equation, we can express operating income in the following way:

Operating income = [(Sales price per unit − Variable cost per unit) × # of units sold] − Fixed expenses

The above equation highlights the contribution margin, an important relationship between sales and variable cost. The **contribution margin** is the difference between sales revenue and variable expenses. In other words, it is the amount that remains to cover fixed expenses and provide a profit. The contribution margin can be expressed in unit terms, as the sales price per unit minus the variable cost per unit, or as a total:

Contribution margin per unit = Sales price per unit − Variable cost per unit

or

Contribution margin = Sales revenue − Total variable expenses

Using the definition of contribution margin, we can rewrite the profit equation as

Operating income = [Contribution margin per unit × # of units sold] − Fixed expenses

This version of the profit equation should help you understand an important relation between contribution margin and profit. As the number of units sold increases, total contribution margin increases, but fixed expenses remain the same. Thus, as the number of units sold rises, profit increases by the additional contribution margin per unit.

Suppose Universal Sports Exchange pays C&C Sports $14.80 for each baseball jersey and sells the jerseys to customers for $20. Let's assume the only other

REALITY CHECK—*The contribution margin recipe*

Technological advances have made vital information more readily available to restaurant managers than it was in the past. Before restaurants had "back-office" computer systems to provide vital operating information, managers would look at a recipe, develop a best-guess estimate of the cost to prepare the item, and then increase it by 300–400% to arrive at the menu price. With today's systems, however, guessing is no longer necessary. Based on a recipe and the prices of its ingredients, these systems can calculate the contribution margin of a menu item. Armed with this information, restaurant owners can quickly perform *menu engineering* and identify dishes that aren't selling or aren't making money.

What's the bottom-line result? Using such a system, Chip Motley, the owner of four restaurants in the Washington, DC area, was able to identify a rib-eye steak special that was selling well but wasn't making much money. He decided to raise the price and increase the contribution margin. Because the increased price did little to change the sales volume, the result was a bottom-line improvement from the increased contribution margin.

An estimated 30% of all new restaurants fail within their first year of business.

An estimated 30% of all new restaurants fail within their first year of business. Perhaps if more restaurant owners understood the concept of the contribution margin, the failure rate would be lower.

Sources: "Back-Office Bonanza," *Nation's Restaurant News*, October 27, 2003, 8–12; John Nessell, "Is Your Menu Working For or Against You?" Restaurant Resource Group, http://www.rrgconsulting.com/menu_engineering.htm (accessed June 28, 2016); "Restaurant Management Tips: Sell the Big Contributors," Chef2Chef Culinary Portal, http://foodservice.chef2chef.net/restaurant-management/chapters/tip01.shtml (accessed March 12, 2008, site now discontinued); Chana R. Schoenberger, "A Burger with a Side of Losses," *Forbes*, December 9, 2002, 168, available online at http://www.forbes.com/forbes/2002/1209/168.html (accessed June 28, 2016).

variable expense Universal incurs is the 6% sales commission it pays each salesperson ($20 × 6% = $1.20 per jersey). Therefore, the jersey has a $4 contribution margin ($20 − $14.80 − $1.20). For each jersey sold, Universal earns $4 to cover its total fixed expenses and provide some profit.

In assessing business opportunities, the *contribution margin ratio* is sometimes a useful tool. The **contribution margin ratio** is the ratio of the contribution margin to sales.

$$\text{Contribution margin ratio} = \frac{\text{Contribution margin}}{\text{Sales revenue}} = \frac{\text{Contribution margin per unit}}{\text{Sales price per unit}}$$

The contribution margin ratio for Universal's baseball jersey is 20%:

$$\text{Contribution margin ratio} = \frac{\$4}{\$20} = 20\%$$

The contribution margin ratio can be used to determine the increase in profits from a given dollar increase in sales revenue. With a 20% contribution margin ratio, each dollar in baseball jersey sales generates $0.20 ($1.00 × 20%) in contribution margin for Universal. So an additional $100 in jersey sales will generate $20 in additional contribution margin.

Contribution Format Income Statement

Recall from the chapter opener that Universal missed its target sales goal by 10% and Martin Keck, vice president for sales, was trying to understand how the lower sales volume affected income. Exhibit 2-9 presents Universal Sports Exchange's income statement that raised Martin's questions.[3]

EXHIBIT 2-9
Universal Sports Exchange's functional income statement.

UNIVERSAL SPORTS EXCHANGE
Income Statement
52 Weeks Ended February 1, 2017

Sales	$1,039,500
Cost of goods sold	769,230
Gross profit	270,270
Selling and administrative expense	230,370
Operating income	39,900
Tax expense (30%)	11,970
Net income	$ 27,930

This format, which is consistent with GAAP, does not help managers predict the financial results of their decisions. This shortcoming is due to the format of GAAP statements, which is based on cost function (product, sales, administration) rather than on cost behavior.

What Martin needs to answer his questions is an income statement that classifies expenses by *behavior*. Such a statement will allow him to easily assess the impact of sales volume on operating income. This type of income statement is called a **contribution format income statement**, and it presents expenses by behavior, as follows:

Sales revenue
− Variable expenses
= Contribution margin
− Fixed expenses
= Operating income

For the purposes of illustration, let's assume that Universal sells only one product, baseball jerseys. Universal buys each jersey from C&C for $14.80 and sells it for $20. That means that both the sales revenue and cost of goods sold vary with the number of jerseys sold. Selling and administrative expenses are made up of $178,870 in selling expenses and $51,500 in administrative expenses. The selling expenses include a 6% sales commission paid to the sales staff. That is, for every dollar of sales made by a sales representative, Universal pays a $0.06 commission. Since sales revenue varies with activity, total sales commissions also vary with activity. The rest of the selling expenses are fixed, as are all the administrative expenses.

Using this information, we can prepare an income statement in the contribution format, as shown in Exhibit 2-10. Notice that we arrived at the same operating income as in the original income statement in Exhibit 2-9. Changing from a traditional functional income statement to a contribution format income statement does not change the amount of income. Rather, it just rearranges the individual components. If you notice that operating income has changed after you convert from one format of the income statement to the other, you have made an error; you should recheck your work.

EXHIBIT 2-10

Universal Sports Exchange's contribution format income statement.

UNIVERSAL SPORTS EXCHANGE Income Statement 52 Weeks Ended February 1, 2017		
Sales		$1,039,500
Less: variable expenses		
Cost of goods sold	$769,230	
Sales commissions (0.06 × $1,039,500)	62,370	
Total variable expenses		831,600
Contribution margin		207,900
Less: fixed expenses		
Selling ($178,870 − $62,370)	116,500	
Administrative	51,500	
Total fixed expenses		168,000
Operating income		$ 39,900

We are not quite ready to predict how much income Universal lost by failing to meet its sales targets because we don't have the information in "constant" form. (Recall from the *WATCH OUT!* box on page 49 that you should always put your information in constant form before you begin to estimate the results of a change in activity.) So what do we need to do? Fixed expenses are in the correct format because they are in their "constant" form—that is, in total. Variable expenses, however, need to be converted to a per unit basis, as shown in Exhibit 2-11.

EXHIBIT 2-11

Universal Sports Exchange's contribution format income statement with unit data.

UNIVERSAL SPORTS EXCHANGE Income Statement 52 Weeks Ended February 1, 2017				
			Per Unit	Ratio
Sales		$1,039,500	$20.00	100%
Less: variable expenses				
Cost of goods sold	$769,230		14.80	74%
Sales commissions	62,370		1.20	6%
Total variable expenses		831,600	16.00	80%
Contribution margin		207,900	$ 4.00	20%
Less: fixed expenses				
Selling	116,500			
Administrative	51,500			
Total fixed expenses		168,000		
Operating income		$ 39,900		

Notice that in the "Ratio" column, variable amounts are shown as a percentage of sales. The contribution margin ratio is 20%; the **variable cost ratio** is 80%, or 1 minus the contribution margin ratio.

Remember that Universal sold 10% fewer jerseys than it expected, so how many jerseys had it planned to sell? First, we need to know the current sales volume, and we can calculate that amount by dividing total sales dollars by sales price per unit:

$$\text{Shirts sold} = \frac{\$1{,}039{,}500}{\$20.00} = 51{,}975 \text{ jerseys}$$

Based on actual sales of 51,975 jerseys, Universal's original sales projection was 57,750 jerseys (51,975/0.9). Therefore, Universal would need to sell 5,775 additional jerseys to reach that goal. So how much more income would these 5,775 additional jerseys generate? Each jersey generates \$4 in contribution margin, so the total increase in operating income would be \$23,100 (\$4 × 5,775). Net income would increase by \$16,170 after taxes (\$23,100 × (1 − 0.30)). We could have obtained the same result using the contribution margin ratio:

$$\text{Additional sales revenue} \times \text{Contribution margin ratio} = \text{Additional contribution margin}$$

$$(\$20 \times 5{,}775 \text{ jerseys}) \times 0.20 = \$23{,}100$$

Exhibit 2-12 shows how the contribution format income statement would have looked had the expected level of sales been achieved. Notice that the variable items—sales, variable expenses, and contribution margin—would have varied in total, whereas the fixed expenses would have remained fixed.

EXHIBIT 2-12

Universal Sports Exchange comparison of actual and expected results.

UNIVERSAL SPORTS EXCHANGE
Comparison of Actual and Expected Results

	Actual Result	Increase 5,775 Jerseys	Expected Result
Sales	$1,039,500	$115,500	$1,155,000
Less: variable expenses			
Cost of goods sold	769,230	85,470	854,700
Sales commissions	62,370	6,930	69,300
Total variable expenses	831,600	92,400	924,000
Contribution margin	207,900	23,100	231,000
Less: fixed expenses			
Selling expenses	116,500	0	116,500
Administrative expenses	51,500	0	51,500
Total fixed expenses	168,000	0	168,000
Operating income	39,900	23,100	63,000
Income taxes (30%)	11,970	6,930	18,900
Net income	$ 27,930	$ 16,170	$ 44,100

THINK ABOUT IT 2.4

If the managers at Universal Sports Exchange had decided to lower the sales prices of jerseys to increase sales volume and total sales revenue, what would have been the effect on the following?

- Cost of goods sold per unit
- Commission per jersey sold
- Contribution margin per unit

If the strategy had worked as planned, what would have been the change in the following?

- Total sales revenue
- Total cost of goods sold
- Total commissions paid
- Total contribution margin

UNIT 2.3 REVIEW

KEY TERMS

Contribution format income statement p. 64
Contribution margin p. 62
Contribution margin ratio p. 63
Cost p. 62
Expense p. 62
Variable cost ratio p. 65

PRACTICE QUESTIONS

1. LO 3 A contribution format income statement presents all expenses by behavior rather than by function. True or False?
2. LO 3 The contribution margin is calculated as
   a. Sales revenue − Cost of goods sold.
   b. Sales revenue − Variable cost of goods sold.
   c. Sales revenue − Total variable expenses.
   d. Sales revenue − Total fixed expenses.
3. LO 3 The amount of net income presented on a functional income statement will be different from the amount of net income presented on a contribution format income statement. True or False?
4. LO 3 Jenkins Jewelers operates with a 30% contribution margin. If Jenkins's sales increase by $20,000, operating income will increase by
   a. $6,000.
   b. $10,000.
   c. $14,000.
   d. $20,000.

UNIT 2.3 PRACTICE EXERCISE

Restate the following income statement for a retailer in contribution margin format.

Sales ($50 per unit)		$5,000
Less cost of goods sold ($32 per unit)		3,200
Gross margin		1,800
Less operating expenses:		
Salaries	$800	
Advertising	400	
Shipping ($2 per unit)	200	1,400
Operating income		$ 400

SELECTED UNIT 2.3 ANSWERS

Think About It 2.4

Cost of goods sold per unit	no change
Commission per jersey sold	decrease
Contribution margin per unit	decrease
Total sales revenue	increase
Total cost of goods sold	increase
Total commissions paid	increase
Total contribution margin	increase

Practice Questions

1. True
2. C
3. False
4. A

Unit 2.3 Practice Exercise

			PER UNIT	RATIO
Sales		$5,000	$50	100%
Less variable expenses:				
Cost of goods sold	$3,200		32	64%
Shipping	200		2	4%
Total variable expenses		3,400	34	68%
Contribution margin		1,600	$16	32%
Less fixed expenses:				
Salaries	800			
Advertising	400			
Total fixed expenses		1,200		
Operating income		$ 400		

BUSINESS DECISION AND CONTEXT Wrap Up

In the chapter opener, Martin Keck wondered how much additional income Universal would have earned if the company had met its sales target. Recall that the actual sales volume was 10% lower than the original sales target of 57,750 jerseys. The answer to this question requires an understanding of Universal's cost behavior patterns.

We've seen that to achieve the original sales target, Universal would have sold 5,775 more baseball jerseys. Those additional jerseys would have generated an additional contribution margin of $23,100. After the income taxes on this additional income had been deducted, the bottom line would have increased by almost 58% to $44,100.

To be able to predict the difference in income, Martin needed to know cost behavior patterns and needed information in constant form—variable costs per unit and fixed expenses in total.

CHAPTER SUMMARY

In this chapter you learned some important terms and techniques that will be relevant throughout the rest of this book. Specifically, you should be able to meet the learning objectives set out at the beginning of the chapter:

1. ***Identify basic cost behavior patterns and explain how changes in activity level affect total cost and unit cost. (Unit 2.1)***

The two basic cost behavior patterns are variable and fixed. Costs that are a combination of these two basic patterns are referred to as mixed. The following table shows how these costs change with changes in activity:

	AS ACTIVITY INCREASES		AS ACTIVITY DECREASES	
Cost Behavior	Total Cost	Cost per Unit	Total Cost	Cost per Unit
Variable	increases	remains constant	decreases	remains constant
Fixed	remains constant	decreases	remains constant	increases
Mixed	increases	decreases	decreases	increases

2. ***Estimate a cost equation from a set of cost data and predict future total cost from that equation. (Unit 2.2)***

Total cost can be expressed in the form $y = mx + b$, where y is the total cost, m is the variable cost per unit, x is the number of units, and b is the total fixed cost. Given a set of costs and activity levels, you can estimate a cost equation using one of the following methods: scattergraph, high-low, or regression.

3. ***Prepare a contribution format income statement. (Unit 2.3)***

A contribution format income statement is an income statement that categorizes expenses by their behavior. It follows the structure:

Sales revenue
− Variable expenses
= Contribution margin
− Fixed expenses
= Operating income

Besides showing total sales revenue and expenses, the contribution format income statement should also show per unit amounts for sales revenue, variable expenses, and contribution margin.

KEY TERMS

Activity (Unit 2.1)
Committed fixed cost (Unit 2.1)
Contribution format income statement (Unit 2.3)
Contribution margin (Unit 2.3)
Contribution margin ratio (Unit 2.3)
Cost (Unit 2.3)
Cost behavior (Unit 2.1)
Discretionary fixed cost (Unit 2.1)
Expense (Unit 2.3)
Fixed cost (Unit 2.1)
High-low method (Unit 2.2)
Mixed cost (Unit 2.1)
Regression analysis (Unit 2.2)
Relevant range (Unit 2.2)
Scattergraph (Unit 2.2)
Step cost (Unit 2.1)
Variable cost (Unit 2.1)
Variable cost ratio (Unit 2.3)

EXERCISES

2-1 Identify cost behavior (LO 1) Macon Vitamins sells a variety of vitamins and herbal supplements to small health food stores. Macon purchases the vitamins and supplements from leading manufacturers. Identify each of the following costs incurred by Macon Vitamins in terms of its cost behavior—variable, fixed, mixed, or step.

a. Vitamin C tablets
b. President's salary
c. Sales commissions ($1.00 per case)
d. Straight line depreciation on office equipment
e. Shipping (billed in 100-pound increments)
f. Advertising
g. Cell phone charges (monthly fee of $35 plus data usage charges)

2-2 Identify cost behavior (LO 1) Identify each of the following costs in terms of its cost behavior—variable, fixed, mixed, or step.

a. The cost of coffee beans at a Starbucks shop
b. Depreciation of airplanes at Southwest Airlines
c. Nurses' wages at M. D. Anderson Cancer Center, assuming a ratio of one nurse to every five patients
d. Electricity cost at a Krispy Kreme Doughnuts store
e. The cost of hard drives installed in computers built by Dell
f. Store managers' salaries at Barnes and Noble bookstores
g. Actors' wages and salaries at Paramount Studios, when the star is paid a base amount plus a percentage of box office receipts
h. The cost of fabric used in making shirts at Southern Tide
i. The cost of cookies provided to guests at check-in at Doubletree Hotels
j. The cost of a national advertising campaign for Burger King

2-3 Estimate unit and total costs (LO 1) Will Jones, LLP is a small CPA firm that focuses primarily on preparing tax returns for small businesses. The company pays a $500 annual fee plus $10 per tax return for a license to use Mega Tax software.

Required

a. What is the company's total annual cost for the Mega Tax software if 300 returns are filed? If 400 returns are filed? If 500 returns are filed?
b. What is the company's cost per return for the Mega Tax software if 300 returns are filed? If 400 returns are filed? If 500 returns are filed?
c. Why does the cost per return differ at each of the three volume levels?

2-4 Cost behavior (LO 1) Identify each of the following costs, incurred monthly by Furman Flower Cart, as fixed, variable, or mixed. Explain your reasoning.

	Bouquets Sold		
	3,000	5,000	7,000
Balloons (10 per bouquet)	$ 9,000	$15,000	$21,000
Insurance	$ 7,500	$ 7,500	$ 7,500
Delivery	$ 5,300	$ 8,300	$11,300
Employee compensation	$11,000	$15,000	$19,000
Advertising	$ 2,000	$ 2,000	$ 2,000

2-5 Identify cost behavior (LO 1) Marla Mason owns and operates a home health care agency. She reported the following cost information for the first four months in 2017. Identify each of the following costs as fixed, variable, or mixed and calculate the missing values.

	Home Visit Hours			
	10,000	12,500	15,000	17,500
Medical records automation and storage	$3,000	?	$4,250	$ 4,875
Medical testing supplies	$7,500	$9,375	?	$13,125
Insurance filing services	$4,000	$5,000	$6,000	?
Communications system lease	?	$2,000	?	$ 2,000

2-6 Cost behavior (LO 1) To calculate the unit cost of the video games that he sells at his mall kiosk, Joel Lawson added up all his costs and divided by the number of units he sold during the year. He then used this unit cost to estimate total costs for the coming year.

Required

Explain to Joel why this unit cost is not useful in predicting total costs for the coming year.

2-7 Cost behavior (LO 1) The Boeing Company produces commercial aircraft. The following passage is taken from Management's Discussion and Analysis, included in Boeing's 2005 Annual Report.

> Commercial aircraft production costs include a significant amount of infrastructure costs, a portion of which do not vary with production rates.

As part of its accounting practices, Boeing spreads the fixed infrastructure costs over the "accounting quantity" for each type of airplane. The accounting quantity is the estimated number of planes that will eventually be produced. At the end of 2005, Boeing's accounting quantity for the 737 Next-Generation plane was 2,800. At the end of 2011, the accounting quantity for this plane had risen to 6,200, and to 10,105 at the end of 2015.

Required

a. What effect would this change in accounting quantity have on the total fixed infrastructure cost of the 737 Next-Generation plane?
b. What effect would this change in accounting quantity have on the unit cost of the 737 Next-Generation plane?

2-8 Scattergraphs (LO 2) Stratton, Inc., has collected the following information on its cost of electricity:

	Machine Hours	Total Electricity Costs
January	510	$240
February	540	$300
March	360	$205
April	450	$215
May	660	$290
June	690	$300
July	340	$180
August	520	$260
September	240	$120
October	750	$340
November	840	$360
December	600	$320

Required

a. Prepare a scattergraph of Stratton's electricity costs for the year. Plot the total electricity cost on the y-axis. Draw a line that you think best represents the electricity cost function. Be sure that the line runs through at least one of the data points.
b. What is the equation of the line you drew in part (a)?

c. What is the expected electricity cost when 750 machine hours are used?
d. Why does your answer to part (c) differ from the actual cost for the month of October, when 750 machine hours were used?

2-9 High-low method (LO 2) Refer to the data in Exercise 2-8.

Required

a. Using the high-low method, compute the variable cost of electricity per machine hour.
b. Compute the total fixed cost of electricity.
c. Represent the electricity cost function in equation form.
d. What is the expected electricity cost when 750 machine hours are used?
e. Why does your answer to part (d) differ from the actual cost for the month of October, when 750 machine hours were used?

2-10 High-low method (LO 2) After graduating from dental school two years ago, Dr. Lauren Farish purchased the dental practice of a long-time dentist who was retiring. In January of this year she had to replace the outdated autoclave equipment she inherited from the previous dentist. Now, as she is preparing her budget for next year, she is concerned about understanding how her cost for sterilizing her dental instruments has changed. She has gathered the following information from her records:

Month	Number of Instruments Used	Total Autoclave Cost
January	600	$ 7,400
February	500	6,500
March	700	7,000
April	900	9,000
May	800	7,600
June	1,000	8,500
July	1,200	10,000
August	1,100	9,800

Required

a. What is the variable cost of sterilizing an instrument using the new equipment?
b. What is the fixed cost of the autoclave equipment?
c. What is the cost formula that Dr. Farish should use for estimating autoclave sterilization costs for next year's budget?
d. If Dr. Farish estimates she will use 1,150 instruments next month, what cost should she include in her budget for instrument sterilization?

2-11 Estimated cost equation (LO 2) Refer to the data in Exercise 2.4. Using the form $y = mx + b$, estimate the cost formula for each cost incurred by Furman Flower Cart.

2-12 Cost estimation (LO 2) Managers of Tom Brown Distributors are evaluating the compensation system for the company's sales personnel. Currently, the two salespeople have a combined salary of $60,000 per year and earn a 3% sales commission.

The company is considering two alternatives to the current compensation system. The first alternative is to reduce total salaries to $50,000 and increase the sales commission to 5%. The second alternative is to eliminate the salaries and pay a 12% sales commission.

Sales projections under each of the compensation systems are as follows:

Current system	$1,000,000
Salary and 5% commission	$1,120,000
12% commission	$1,200,000

Required

a. Write the cost equations for the current compensation system and both alternative compensation structures.

b. Given Tom Brown's sales projections, and assuming that the cost of goods sold is equal to 30% of sales, which pay system would be the most profitable one for the company? Ignore all other costs and show your calculations.

2-13 Contribution format income statement (LO 3) Restate the following income statement for a retailer in contribution format.

Sales revenue ($100 per unit)		$50,000
Less cost of goods sold ($60 per unit)		30,000
Gross margin		20,000
Less operating costs:		
Commissions expense ($6 per unit)	$3,000	
Salaries expense	8,000	
Advertising expense	6,000	
Shipping expense ($2 per unit)	1,000	18,000
Operating income		$ 2,000

2-14 Contribution format income statement: missing values (LO 3) Complete each of the following contribution format income statements by supplying the missing numbers.

	a.	b.	c.	d.
Sales revenue	?	$425,000	?	$700,000
Variable expenses	210,000	?	86,000	?
Contribution margin	85,000	150,000	?	400,000
Fixed expenses	?	70,000	120,000	?
Operating income	27,000	?	?	?
Income taxes	?	18,000	16,000	55,000
Net income	$10,500	?	$45,000	$145,000

2-15 Contribution format income statement (LO 3) The Carpenter Company sells sports decals that can be personalized with a player's name, team name, and jersey number for $10 each. Carpenter buys the decals from a supplier for $3 each and spends an additional $0.50 in variable operating costs per decal. The results of last month's operations are as follows:

Sales revenue	$10,000
Cost of goods sold	3,000
Gross profit	7,000
Operating expenses	2,500
Operating income	$ 4,500

Required

Prepare a contribution format income statement for the Carpenter Company.

2-16 Contribution margin (LO 3) Anthony Herrera recently fulfilled his long-time dream of opening a gym that offers spinning exercise classes for $5 per person. To differentiate his gym and better serve his clients, Anthony provides a towel, a bottle of water, and an after-workout protein shake to each person participating in a class, at a cost of $1.75 per person. Anthony employs three part-time instructors and pays them each $1,000 per month. He also pays himself a monthly salary of $4,000. Anthony's other monthly costs are $1,500 for rent, $1,250 for depreciation on his 30 bikes, and $1,800 in utilities and insurance.

Required

a. What is Anthony's contribution margin per unit?
b. What is Anthony's contribution margin ratio?
c. Prepare Anthony's monthly contribution format income statement. Assume that he teaches 5,000 clients.

2-17 Contribution format income statement (LO 3) Erin Brushwood sells gourmet chocolate chip cookies. The results of her last month of operations are as follows:

Sales revenue	$50,000
Cost of goods sold (all variable)	26,250
Gross margin	23,750
Selling expenses (75% variable)	8,000
Administrative expenses (25% variable)	13,000
Operating income	$ 2,750

Required

a. Prepare a contribution format income statement for Erin.
b. If Erin sells her cookies for $2 each, how many cookies did she sell during the month?
c. What is the contribution margin per cookie?
d. What is Erin's contribution margin ratio?

2-18 Contribution format income statement (LO 3) Palmer/Davis Designs sells customized mobile phone covers. The company's controller prepared the following income statement for the upcoming monthly management meeting.

Sales revenue		$175,000
Cost of goods sold	$60,000	
Variable selling expenses	9,000	
Variable general and administrative expenses	6,250	
Total variable expenses		75,250
Contribution margin		99,750
Fixed selling expenses	17,000	
Fixed general and administrative expenses	32,000	
Total fixed expenses		49,000
Operating income		$ 50,750

Required

a. Assume that Palmer/Davis sells its phone covers for $35 each. How many covers did the company sell?
b. What is the company's contribution margin per unit?
c. What is the company's contribution margin ratio?

PROBLEMS

2-19 Calculate changes in cost; decision making (LO 1) Southwest Phone Services offers a cellular phone plan for $50 per month. Under this plan, you can make an unlimited number of phone calls and talk as long as you like.

Required

a. Prepare a table that shows the cost per minute of airtime and the total amount of the phone bill at the following usage levels: 10 minutes, 100 minutes, 250 minutes, and 500 minutes.
b. What type of cost behavior does Southwest's phone plan illustrate? Why?
c. Assume that your current cell phone plan costs you $0.02 per minute. If you use 1,000 minutes of airtime per month, which plan would you prefer, $50 per month or $0.02 per minute? What if you used 3,000 minutes per month? At what level of airtime usage would you become indifferent between the two plans?
d. How would you decide which phone plan to buy?

2-20 Scattergraph; high-low method; cost estimation (LO 2) The Aust Corporation has gathered the following data on its copy machine costs for the first eight months of the year.

Month	Number of Copies	Total Copy Cost
January	40,000	$3,500
February	35,000	$3,200
March	60,000	$4,100
April	80,000	$5,100
May	85,000	$5,600
June	75,000	$4,800
July	82,000	$5,300
August	105,000	$6,000

Required

a. Prepare a scattergraph of the cost information and then choose a line that you believe best represents the cost function. Represent your chosen line with a cost equation of the form $y = mx + b$. Show your calculations.

b. Using the high-low method, what is the variable cost per copy?

c. Using the high-low method, what is the fixed cost per month?

d. Using the high-low method, represent the cost function with a cost equation of the form $y = mx + b$.

e. Using your cost equation from part (d), provide your best estimate of the copy costs for September if 80,000 copies will be made. Why does your estimate differ from the $5,100 cost incurred in April?

2-21 High-low method; cost estimation (CMA adapted) (LO 2) Angie March owns a catering company that stages banquets and parties for both individuals and companies. The business is seasonal, with heavy demand during the summer months and year-end holidays and light demand at other times. Angie has gathered the following cost information from the past year:

Month	Labor Hours	Overhead Costs
January	3,500	$ 62,000
February	2,800	59,000
March	3,000	60,000
April	4,200	64,000
May	4,500	67,000
June	5,500	71,000
July	6,500	74,000
August	7,500	77,000
September	7,800	80,000
October	4,500	68,000
November	3,100	62,000
December	6,500	73,000
Total	59,400	$817,000

Required

a. Using the high-low method, compute the overhead cost per labor hour and the fixed overhead cost per month.

b. Angie has booked 3,200 labor hours for the coming month. How much overhead should she expect to incur?

c. If Angie books one more catering job for the month, requiring 200 labor hours, how much additional overhead should she expect to incur?

d. Angie recently attended a meeting of the local Chamber of Commerce, at which she heard an accounting professor discuss regression analysis and its business applications.

After the meeting, Angie enlisted the professor's assistance in preparing a regression analysis of the overhead data she collected. This analysis yielded an estimated fixed cost of $48,933 per month and a variable cost of $3.87 per labor hour. Why do these estimates differ from your high-low estimates, calculated in part (a)?

2-22 High-low method (LO 2) Harlan Gravity Grips produces spike sets for track shoes. CEO Brittany Harlan has gathered the following information about the company's sales volume and marketing cost for the past six months.

	Sales Volume	Total Marketing Costs
January	550,700	$82,770
February	390,500	$74,525
March	561,000	$83,050
April	543,000	$82,330
May	546,600	$82,480
June	552,900	$82,860

Required

a. Using the high-low method, compute the variable marketing cost per spike set.
b. Compute the total fixed marketing cost.
c. Represent the marketing cost function in equation form.
d. Examine the data and identify the potential outlier.
e. Recalculate the marketing cost function, removing the potential outlier.
f. Which of the two cost functions you calculated would be appropriate to use in estimating future marketing costs? Why?

2-23 Cost estimation (LO 2) Smythe, Ltd., provides nationwide passenger train service on 21,000 miles of routes. Selected operating data for the latest fiscal year are shown below.

Month	Fuel Expense (000s)	Passengers (000s)	Passenger Miles (000s)	Train Miles (000s)
October	$20,075	2,145	450,857	3,098
November	$22,037	2,154	451,448	3,091
December	$22,435	2,180	361,214	3,141
January	$19,990	2,030	377,438	3,178
February	$22,225	2,136	461,088	3,025
March	$26,204	2,174	458,762	3,175
April	$24,698	2,207	470,311	3,096
May	$24,832	2,296	492,429	3,197
June	$23,239	2,291	540,655	3,076
July	$25,480	2,480	578,133	3,191
August	$25,459	2,430	580,214	3,515
September	$25,021	2,148	448,263	3,066

Required

a. The above data provide three possible activity measures that could influence fuel expense. Use the high-low method to develop a cost formula for fuel expense for each of the three measures.
b. Do any of the cost formulas you developed in (a) appear to be a poor choice for estimating future train operations expense? Why?
c. Which formula do you think will make the most accurate predictions? Why?

2-24 Cost behavior identification; contribution format income statement (LO 1, 3) Mighty Bright Window Cleaners' monthly income statement at several levels of activity is as follows:

Windows washed	1,000	2,000	3,000
Sales revenue	$3,000	$6,000	$9,000
Cost of goods sold	1,200	2,400	3,600
Gross profit	1,800	3,600	5,400
Operating expenses			
Advertising expense	400	400	400
Salaries and wages expense	700	900	1,100
Insurance expense	200	200	200
Postage expense	400	800	1,200
Total operating expenses	1,700	2,300	2,900
Operating income	$ 100	$1,300	$2,500

Required

a. Identify each expense as fixed, variable, or mixed.
b. Prepare a contribution margin income statement based on a volume of 2,500 windows.

2-25 Cost estimation; contribution format income statement (LO 2, 3) J Bryant, Ltd. is a local coat retailer. The store's accountant prepared the following income statement for the month ended January 31:

Sales revenue		$750,000
Cost of goods sold		300,000
Gross margin		450,000
Less operating expenses		
Selling expense	$23,560	
Administrative expense	49,500	73,060
Net operating income		$376,940

Bryant sells its coats for $300 each. Selling expenses consist of fixed costs plus a commission of $6 per coat. Administrative expenses consist of fixed costs plus a variable component equal to 5% of sales.

Required

a. Prepare a contribution format income statement for January.
b. Using the format $y = mx + b$, develop a cost formula for total expenses.
c. If 2,700 coats are sold next month, what is the expected total contribution margin?

2-26 Contribution format income statement; decision making (LO 3) Harris Horticulture provides and maintains live plants in office buildings. The company's 850 customers are charged $40 per month for this service, which includes weekly watering visits. The variable cost to service a customer's location is $20 per month. The company incurs $2,000 each month to maintain its fleet of four service vans and $3,000 each month in salaries. Harris pays a bookkeeping service $3 per customer each month to handle all invoicing and accounting functions.

Required

a. Prepare Harris's contribution format income statement for the month.
b. What is the expected monthly operating income if 150 customers are added?
c. Mr. Harris is exploring options to reduce the **annual** bookkeeping costs.
   Option 1: Renegotiate the current contract with the bookkeeping service to pay a flat fee of $20,400 per year plus $1 per customer per month.
   Option 2: Hire a part-time bookkeeper for $27,000 per year to handle the invoicing and simple accounting. He would need to pay $5,000 per year to have taxes and year-end financial statements prepared.
   Compare the current bookkeeping cost with the two options at customer levels of 850, 1,000, and 1,100.
d. Besides the bookkeeping costs incurred, what should Mr. Harris consider before he makes a change in bookkeeping services?

C&C SPORTS CONTINUING CASE

2-27 Identify cost behavior (LO 1) Identify each of the following costs incurred by Universal Sports Exchange in terms of its cost behavior—variable, fixed, mixed, or step.

Required

a. Monthly sales staff payroll of $650 plus 6% sales commission on jerseys
b. $100 monthly rental for credit card processing equipment
c. Cost of goods sold of $14.80 per jersey
d. The cost of price tags attached to each jersey
e. Inventory insurance that costs $2 per $1,000 of sales
f. Website hosting cost of $25 per month

2-28 Cost Equations and Contribution Format Income Statements (LO 2, 3) Refer to Exhibit 2-11 on page 65.

Required

a. What is Universal Sports Exchange's operating profit equation?
b. If Universal Sports Exchange sells 55,000 jerseys, what total expense will be reported on the income statement?
c. The *Daily News Journal* has approached Martin Keck, Universal's vice president for sales, with a $20,000 annual ad campaign. If Martin accepts the ad campaign, what will change in Universal's operating profit equation?
d. Assume that Martin Keck accepts the *Daily News Journal*'s ad campaign and as a result Universal sells 60,000 jerseys. Prepare the contribution format income statement for the year.

CASES

2-29 Calculate expected costs (LO 1) Bohlander Botanicals develops hybrid tea roses. A relative newcomer to the field, Bohlander is looking for innovative ways to advertise its products to potential customers. Rose Mayfield, sales manager and avid online shopper, wonders about advertising the company's roses on various gardening websites. She has contacted Kimland Media, Inc., an advertising firm specializing in Internet advertising campaigns, to explore some options.

After meeting with Rose, Sami Landon, regional sales coordinator, has suggested that Bohlander use a targeted marketing strategy by placing banner ads on a few gardening websites. Bohlander would pay for the service based primarily on the number of ad impressions (the number of times the ads are shown). Using past campaigns as a guide, Sami has prepared the following quarterly estimate for Bohlander.

Banner ad development (6 banners per quarter)	$6,000
Banner ad placement	$0.80 per thousand impressions
Estimated ad impressions	3,000,000
Banner ad click-throughs	$0.04 per click-through

From past experience, Kimland Media estimates that 10% of all viewers will "click through" the banner ad to Bohlander's website. Of those viewers who click through, Kimland estimates that 5% will actually make a purchase.

Required

a. What is the expected total cost per quarter of Bohlander's Internet advertising campaign?
b. Given Sami's cost estimates, what is Bohlander's expected cost of acquiring a new customer through the campaign?
c. Using the information you just calculated, what is the estimated cost to get one more person to click through and make a purchase?

2-30 Ethics (This is a continuation of Case 2-29) On March 15, Jeff Blake, Kimland Media's sales director, stopped by Sami Landon's cubicle. "Sami, I've been reviewing your accounts, and they aren't generating as much revenue as we had hoped. If you want to achieve your quota for the quarter, you're going to have to bump it up a bit."

Sami thought for a few minutes about how she might increase her revenue pool. She could sign some new customers, but she didn't have any strong leads, and developing the ones she had would take too much time. She couldn't create new banner ads for her current customers. Then it dawned on her: She could increase her variable revenue through increased click-through counts on her existing banner ads.

Sami got on the phone and called her friends and family members. "I need a small favor. Would you go to www.tearosegarden.com and look for the Bohlander ad? Then just click through the ad as many times as you can."

Required

a. Was it ethical for Sami to enlist the help of friends and family to drive up the number of click-throughs to Bohlander's website? Why or why not?
b. Would your answer to part (a) change if Sami's friends and family members actually made a purchase from Bohlander? Why or why not?
c. What impact did Sami's actions have on Bohlander Botanicals?

ANALYTICS PROBLEM

2-31 Cost estimation using data analytics and Excel (LO 2) The city of Brownswood is trying to understand its road repair costs. As a starting point, Mark Winston, the city's finance manager, asked public works manager Rachel Morris to gather relevant data. Rachel provided Mark with a data set containing a list of completed pothole repair work orders and the related costs for a recent week. Mark has asked you to analyze this data set and provide some initial insights about the city's road repair costs.

Required

a. Prepare a visualization of the data set using the CHART function in Excel to create an XY scattergraph chart. Comment on what the visualization reveals.
b. Use the MIN, MAX, and VLOOKUP functions in Excel to estimate the road repair cost function using the high-low method.
c. Use the SLOPE and INTERCEPT functions in Excel to estimate the road repair cost function using regression.
d. Based on your work so far, do you have any concerns about the data used to calculate the cost function estimates?
e. Think about factors that might affect pothole repairs and the associated costs. What additional data would you like to have available to help you prepare a better cost estimate?

The Excel data files for answering this problem can be found in WileyPLUS.

ENDNOTES

1. You may be wondering about how mixed costs fit into this equation. Remember that a mixed cost has both a fixed and variable component. Therefore, we separate the mixed cost into its fixed and variable components and then add these amounts to the other fixed and variable costs.
2. You can use the chart function in Microsoft Excel or a similar program to easily plot points on a scattergraph.
3. Notice that the financial statements do not use the traditional December 31 date. This is because most retailers use the 4–5–4 calendar that divides the year into months using a 4 weeks/5 weeks/4 weeks pattern, with each week beginning on a Sunday. You can learn more about the 4–5–4 calendar at https://nrf.com/resources/4-5-4-calendar.

© Tischenko Irina/Shutterstock

COST–VOLUME–PROFIT ANALYSIS AND PRICING DECISIONS

UNITS	LEARNING OBJECTIVES
UNIT 3.1 Breakeven Analysis	**LO 1:** Calculate the breakeven point in units and sales dollars.
UNIT 3.2 Cost–Volume–Profit Analysis	**LO 2:** Calculate the level of activity required to meet a target income.
	LO 3: Determine the effects of changes in sales price, cost, and volume on operating income.
	LO 4: Define operating leverage and explain the risks associated with the trade-off between variable and fixed costs.
UNIT 3.3 Multiproduct CVP Analysis	**LO 5:** Calculate the multiproduct breakeven point and level of activity required to meet a target income.
UNIT 3.4 Pricing Decisions	**LO 6:** Define markup and explain cost-plus pricing.
	LO 7: Explain target costing and calculate a target cost.

© GlobalStock/iStockphoto

Business Decision and Context

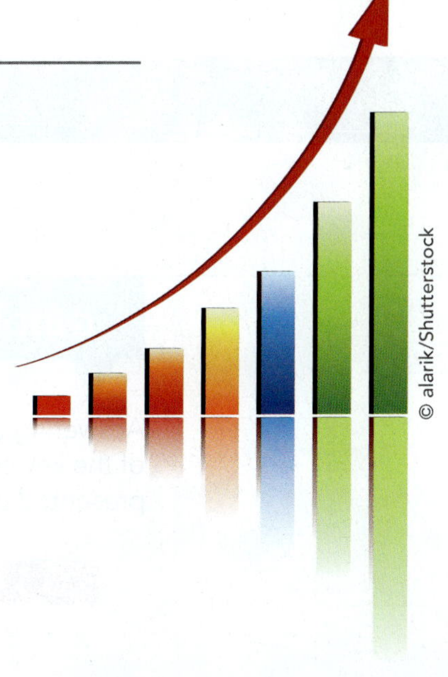

Martin Keck, vice president for sales at Universal Sports Exchange, was talking with his sales team at the monthly sales meeting. "As you know, the company missed its sales target last year. We were expecting to sell 10% more jerseys than we did. And we all saw the effect that the lower sales level had on our bottom line. When we miss our sales targets, it affects what everyone else in the company can accomplish because they count on us to generate revenue."

Sarah Yardley, one of the company's top salespeople, had been listening intently as Martin discussed the concept of cost behavior. "I think I understand all this talk about cost behavior," she said, "but I'm still not sure how it plays into my decisions."

"Sarah," Martin replied, "we have to use our knowledge of cost behaviors to *predict* what effect our decisions will have on the bottom line. We know when it is advantageous to, say, initiate a new advertising campaign instead of reducing prices, but to persuade the president and the CFO, we need to have more convincing data, and that includes the financial impact of our decisions. In fact, I'll be meeting with the president and CFO next week to discuss the relative merits of a $50,000 advertising campaign and a 10% reduction in sales price. You can be sure that I'll know the expected financial impact of each alternative before I walk into the meeting."

> "I'll be meeting with the president and CFO next week to discuss the relative merits of a $50,000 advertising campaign and a 10% reduction in sales price. You can be sure that I'll know the financial impact of each alternative before I walk into the meeting."

Decisions like this one come up frequently in business. Managers of a start-up company want to know how much they will have to sell before they generate a profit. Managers of a company that has been in business for years want to know whether they should pass their increased costs on to customers in the form of a price increase. And in a highly competitive industry, managers of another company want to know what will happen to income if they meet a competitor's lower price or offer a coupon to increase sales volume. Knowing how these changes might affect a company's income will help managers to decide which alternatives to implement.

Watch the Whole Foods video in WileyPLUS to learn more about cost-volume-profit analysis in a changing business environment.

Watch the Zappos.com video in WileyPLUS to learn more about pricing issues in the real world.

SUPPLY CHAIN KEY PLAYERS

END CUSTOMER

UNIVERSAL SPORTS EXCHANGE

Vice President of Sales, Martin Keck

Top Salesperson, Sarah Yardley

C&C SPORTS

DURABLE ZIPPER COMPANY

BRADLEY TEXTILE MILLS

CENTEX YARNS

NEFF FIBER MANUFACTURING

BRUIN POLYMERS, INC.

UNIT 3.1

Breakeven Analysis

GUIDED UNIT PREPARATION

Answering the following questions while you read this unit will guide your understanding of the key concepts found in the unit. The questions are linked to the learning objectives presented at the beginning of the chapter.

LO 1

1. What does it mean to break even?
2. If a product's variable cost per unit increases while the selling price and fixed costs remain constant, what will happen to the breakeven point?
3. How do you calculate the breakeven point in units? In dollars?
4. What actions can a company take to reduce its breakeven point?
5. What is the margin of safety? How is it calculated?

A common question for managers, particularly of start-up ventures, is, "How long will it take us to earn a profit?" Stated another way, what these managers are really asking is, "When will we break even?" Knowing the breakeven point helps managers evaluate the desirability and profitability of various business opportunities.[1]

The Breakeven Point

As managers evaluate business opportunities, they examine many factors, including profitability. But before a business can generate a profit, it must generate sufficient revenue to cover all of its expenses. In other words, the business must reach its breakeven point. At the **breakeven point**, sales revenue is exactly equal to total expenses, and there is no profit or loss. There is only one level of sales at which this relationship is true. Thus, the breakeven point can be calculated using the profit equation. To find the breakeven point, set the standard profit equation equal to zero, let x equal the number of units needed to break even, and then solve for x, as shown in the following equation:

$$\text{Sales revenue} - \text{Variable expenses} - \text{Fixed expenses} = \text{Operating income}$$
$$\text{SP}x - \text{VC}x - \text{FC} = \$0$$

As Exhibit 3-1 shows, Universal Sports Exchange, one of C&C Sports' customers, reported operating income of $39,900 for fiscal year 2017. Using the information in Universal's income statement, let's calculate Universal's breakeven point in jerseys using the profit equation above.

UNIVERSAL SPORTS EXCHANGE Contribution Format Income Statement for the 52 Weeks Ending February 1, 2017				
			Per Unit	Ratio
Sales		$1,039,500	$20.00	100%
Less Variable expenses:				
Cost of goods sold	$769,230		14.80	74%
Sales commissions	62,370		1.20	6%
Total variable expenses		831,600	16.00	80%
Contribution margin		207,900	$ 4.00	20%
Less Fixed expenses:				
Selling expenses	116,500			
Administrative expenses	51,500			
Total fixed expenses		168,000		
Operating income		$ 39,900		

EXHIBIT 3-1

Universal Sports Exchange's contribution format income statement.

$$
\begin{aligned}
&(1) \quad \$20x - \$16x - \$168,000 = \$0 \\
&(2) \quad \$4x - \$168,000 = \$0 \\
&(3) \quad \$4x = \$168,000 \\
&(4) \quad x = 42,000 \text{ jerseys}
\end{aligned}
$$

In Step (1) we put everything into "constant" form—sales price per unit, variable cost per unit, and total fixed expenses. We set the number of jerseys equal to x because that is what we want to know—the number of jerseys that must be sold to break even. Step (2) shows that we could have started the calculation with the $4 contribution margin per unit, skipping Step (1). Step (3) reveals an essential relationship: *At the breakeven point, the total contribution margin equals total fixed expenses*. In Step (4), we solved the breakeven question: 42,000 jerseys must be sold to break even.

WATCH OUT!

Break even calculations will not always yield a breakeven point that is in whole units. Since you can't sell a fractional unit of a product, always round breakeven points up to the next whole unit.

We can use our definition of the contribution margin as a shortcut to finding the breakeven point. Since the contribution margin is the amount that is available to cover fixed expenses and provide a profit ($0 in the breakeven case), we can use the following formula to calculate the breakeven point in units:

$$\frac{\text{Total fixed expenses}}{\text{Contribution margin per unit}} = \text{Breakeven point in units}$$

$$\frac{\$168,000}{\$4.00} = 42,000 \text{ jerseys}$$

Notice that this formula is just a restatement of the mathematical operations made between Steps (3) and (4).

Sometimes it is useful to know the breakeven point in terms of sales dollars rather than units. If we know the breakeven point in units, we can simply multiply it by the sales price per unit: $20 × 42,000 = $840,000. Alternatively, we

REALITY CHECK—*Who really uses breakeven analysis?*

© izusek/iStockphoto

Retail establishments and manufacturers have an obvious interest in breakeven analysis. But do service organizations such as airlines and art galleries ever use the concept? Absolutely.

Airlines calculate a "breakeven load factor," which is the average percentage of seats on an average flight that must be occupied by a customer paying an average fare before the flight generates a profit. Analysts estimated in early 2012 that "network" carriers such as **American**, **Delta**, and **United** break even when they achieve an 86.6% load factor. But at that time, these carriers filled only 86% of their seats on average. "Value" carriers such as **JetBlue** and **Southwest** should break even if they fill 79.3% of their seats, and these carriers achieved an average load factor of 83% in that period. Increasing breakeven load factors have plagued the industry since 2000, and airlines have reduced operating costs, increased fares, and implemented extra fees for checked baggage and other services to lower the breakeven load factor to acceptable levels. While these actions may have helped to some degree, US Airways reported in June 2012 that a hypothetical flight of 100 passengers paying an average domestic fare of $146 and $18 in fees had a breakeven load factor of almost 99%.

Before the Bellagio Gallery of Fine Art, housed in the **Bellagio** Casino in Las Vegas, opened a show of 21 Monets on loan from the **Museum of Fine Arts in Boston**, Marc Glimcher estimated that 400 people a day, paying between $12 and $15 each, needed to view the exhibit to achieve the breakeven point. Since shows of works by Andy Warhol and Fabergé had drawn over 150,000 visitors, this level of attendance did not appear to be out of reach. The show averaged 1,000 visitors each day, far exceeding the projected breakeven attendance. The show generated approximately $6 million in ticket sales, with more than $1 million going back to Boston's Museum of Fine Arts. Following the show's success, the gallery staged another show of Impressionist paintings from the museum, and other museums are expressing interest in showing their works at the Bellagio.

US Airways reported in June 2012 that a hypothetical flight of 100 passengers had a breakeven load factor of almost 99%.

Sources: Fred A. Bernstein, "A Loan That Keeps on Paying," *The New York Times*, March 30, 2005; Kristen Peterson, "Casino Handed Artistic Legacy," *Las Vegas Sun*, February 8, 2008, http://lasvegassun.com/news/2008/feb/08/casino-handed-artistic-legacy/(accessed March 5, 2008); Steve Friess and Peter Plagens, "Show Me the Monet," *Newsweek*, January 26, 2004, 60; Scott McCartney, "Airlines That Fill 86% of Seats and Still Lose Money on Domestic Flights," *The Wall Street Journal*, February 8, 2012; Scott McCartney, "How Airlines Spend Your Airfare," *The Wall Street Journal*, June 7, 2010; U.S. Department of Transportation, "Rising Breakeven Load Factors Threaten Airline Finances," October 2003, http://www.rita.dot.gov/bts/sites/rita.dot.gov.bts/files/publications/special_reports_and_issue_briefs/issue_briefs/number_08/html/entire.html; Ken White, "Making an Impression," *Las Vegas Review-Journal Neon*, June 10, 2005, http://www.reviewjournal.com/lvrj_home/2005/Jun-10-Fri-2005/weekly/2000819.html (accessed March 5, 2008, site now discontinued).

could use the contribution margin ratio and the profit relationships examined on the previous page, as in the following formula:

$$\frac{\text{Total fixed expenses}}{\text{Contribution margin ratio}} = \text{Breakeven point in sales dollars}$$

$$\frac{\$168{,}000}{0.20} = \$840{,}000 \text{ in sales dollars to break even}$$

Breakeven Graphs

While calculating a breakeven point is useful, managers are also interested in the profits generated at other sales levels. A **breakeven graph** illustrates this relationship between sales revenue and expenses, allowing managers to view a

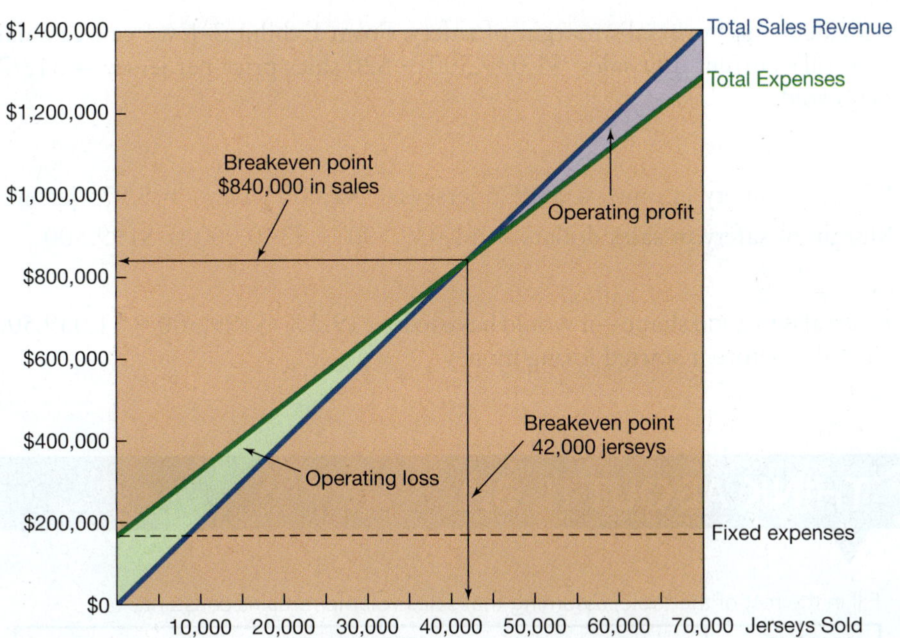

EXHIBIT 3-2

Breakeven graph for Universal Sports Exchange.

range of results at a single glance. Exhibit 3-2 shows Universal's breakeven graph based on the company's sales and expense information. Notice that the total sales revenue line intersects the *y*-axis at $0 and has a slope of $20: for every jersey sold, Universal takes in $20 of revenue. The fixed expense line intersects the *y*-axis at $168,000 and remains constant across all sales volumes. Even if no jerseys were sold, the company would incur fixed expenses of $168,000. The total cost line represents the sum of fixed and variable expenses, so it intersects the *y*-axis at $168,000 and increases at a rate (slope) of $16 per jersey. The point at which the total sales revenue line and the total expense line intersect is the breakeven point. Any level of sales to the left of the breakeven point represents an operating loss. Any level of sales to the right of the breakeven point represents operating income.

One of the activities managers like to engage in is called "what-if" analysis, or sensitivity analysis. "What if I could reduce fixed expenses—how would profits change?" Before we get into this type of analysis, let's use Universal's breakeven graph to think conceptually about these questions. What if fixed expenses decrease—how would the graph change? The fixed expense line would shift downward, as would the total expense line. The revenue line would remain unchanged, so the breakeven point would shift to the left, indicating that fewer jerseys would need to be sold to break even. And since neither sales nor variable costs changes, the contribution margin doesn't change either. The end result: when expenses go down, operating profit goes up.

Margin of Safety

A company's **margin of safety** is the difference between current sales and breakeven sales. It represents the volume of sales that can be lost before the company begins to lose money and can be **measured** in units or sales dollars.

$$\text{Margin of safety} = \text{Current sales} - \text{Breakeven sales}$$

Let's calculate Universal's margin of safety. From Exhibit 3-1 we can calculate Universal's current unit sales: \$1,039,500 ÷ \$20 sales price per jersey = 51,975 jerseys sold.

Margin of safety in units = 51,975 jerseys − 42,000 jerseys = 9,975 jerseys
Margin of safety in sales dollars = \$1,039,500 − \$840,000 = \$199,500

Universal is in good shape—it would have to lose 19.2% (\$199,500 ÷ \$1,039,500) of its sales before it started losing money.

THINK ABOUT IT 3.1

Fill in the rest of the table, assuming that sales volume remains constant.

WHAT IF . . .	EFFECT ON				
	Sales Revenue	Total Expenses	Contribution Margin per Unit	Breakeven Point	Operating Profit
fixed expenses decrease	no effect				
variable cost per unit increases					
sales price increases					

UNIT 3.1 REVIEW

KEY TERMS

Breakeven graph p. 84

Breakeven point p. 82

Margin of safety p. 85

PRACTICE QUESTIONS

1. LO 1 At the breakeven point, sales revenue and total contribution margin are equal. True or False?

2. LO 1 Reese Manufacturing has a current breakeven point of 475,642 units. To reduce the breakeven point, Reese Manufacturing should
   a. reduce the contribution margin.
   b. increase fixed expenses.
   c. reduce the sales price per unit.
   d. increase the contribution margin.

3. LO 1 Jordan Graft Images sells framed prints of various college landmarks. Jordan purchases the prints from his supplier for \$30 and sells them through his website for \$65. Jordan's fixed expenses are \$89,250. What is Jordan's breakeven point in units?
   a. 940
   b. 1,373
   c. 2,550
   d. 2,975

4. LO 1 Deaton, Inc. sells computer backpacks. The company purchases the backpacks from its supplier for $15 and sells them to office supply stores for $25. Deaton's fixed expenses are $100,000. What is Deaton's breakeven point in sales dollars?

a. $100,000

b. $166,667

c. $175,000

d. $250,000

5. LO 1 Conrad Steel sells bridge supports. Currently, the company's sales revenue is $5,000,000. If Conrad's controller has calculated the company's breakeven point to be $3,975,000, what is the company's margin of safety?

a. $1,025,000

b. $2,950,000

c. $3,975,000

d. $5,000,000

UNIT 3.1 PRACTICE EXERCISE

Use this income statement to answer the questions that follow.

Sales ($50 per unit)		$5,000
Less: Cost of goods sold ($32 per unit)		3,200
Gross margin		1,800
Less operating expenses:		
Salaries	$800	
Advertising	400	
Shipping ($2 per unit)	200	1,400
Operating Income		$ 400

Required

1. What is the variable cost per unit?
2. What is the total fixed expense?
3. What is the contribution margin per unit?
4. What is the contribution margin ratio?
5. What is the breakeven point in units? In dollars?
6. What is the margin of safety in units? In dollars?

SELECTED UNIT 3.1 ANSWERS

Think About It 3.1

WHAT IF...	EFFECT ON				
	Sales Revenue	Total Expenses	Contribution Margin per Unit	Breakeven Point	Operating Income
Fixed expenses decrease	No effect	Decrease	No effect	Decrease	Increase
Variable cost per unit increases	No effect	Increase	Decrease	Increase	Decrease
Sales price increases	Increase	No effect	Increase	Decrease	Increase

Practice Questions

1. False
2. D
3. C
4. D
5. A

Unit 3.1 Practice Exercise

1. The two variable costs are cost of goods sold ($32 per unit) and shipping ($2 per unit), for a total variable cost per unit of $34.

2. The two fixed expenses are salaries ($800) and advertising ($400), for a total fixed expense of $1,200.

3. $50 − $34 = $16

4. $\frac{\$16}{\$50}$ or $\frac{\$1,600}{\$5,000}$ = 0.32 or 32%

5. $\frac{\text{Fixed expenses}}{\text{CM per unit}} = \frac{\$1,200}{\$16} = 75 \text{ units}$

   $\frac{\text{Fixed expenses}}{\text{CM ratio}} = \frac{\$1,200}{0.32} = \$3,750$

   (Notice that this amount also equals 75 units × $50.)

6. The margin of safety equals current sales minus break-even sales. Before this calculation can be done in units, you must compute how many units the company is currently selling:

   $$\frac{\text{Sales revenue}}{\text{Sales price}} = \frac{\$5,000}{\$50} = 100 \text{ units}$$

   Margin of safety in units = 100 units − 75 units = 25 units

   Margin of safety in dollars = $5,000 − $3,750 = $1,250 (Notice that this amount also equals 25 units × $50.)

UNIT 3.2

Cost–Volume–Profit Analysis

GUIDED UNIT PREPARATION

Answering the following questions while you read this unit will guide your understanding of the key concepts found in the unit. The questions are linked to the learning objectives presented at the beginning of the chapter.

LO 2 1. How can managers use CVP analysis to determine the level of sales needed to attain a specific level of operating income?

LO 3 2. How can managers use CVP analysis to support their decision making?

3. What assumptions are made in CVP analysis? Do those assumptions invalidate the predictions managers make using CVP analysis?

LO 4 4. Explain the concept of operating leverage.

Although managers often want to know how many units they need to sell to break even, they are more interested in finding out how they can generate a profit. **Cost–volume–profit analysis**, or CVP for short, helps managers assess the impact of various business decisions on company profits.

Target Operating Income

Managers frequently have an income target in mind when they plan business activities. They might want to know what it takes to make, say, $60,000 in operating income, or income before taxes. Calculating the level of sales required to meet that goal is easy if you know some basic information. You use the same profit equation used to determine the breakeven point, but set profit equal to the target income. In Universal's case, we would solve the problem as follows:

$$
\begin{aligned}
&(1)\quad \$20x - \$16x - \$168{,}000 = \$60{,}000\\
&(2)\quad \$4x - \$168{,}000 = \$60{,}000\\
&(3)\quad \$4x = \$228{,}000\\
&(4)\quad x = 57{,}000 \text{ jerseys}
\end{aligned}
$$

Recall that Universal is already selling 51,975 jerseys. Although we can do the math to determine that the company will need to sell 5,025 additional jerseys to reach the target income of $60,000, managers must use their judgment in deciding if achieving this level of additional sales is likely.

With a simple adjustment, we can use our shortcut formulas from Unit 3.1 to answer the target income question:

$$\frac{\text{Total FC} + \text{Target OI}}{\text{CM per unit}} = \text{Units required to meet target OI}$$

$$\frac{\$168{,}000 + \$60{,}000}{\$4.00} = 57{,}000 \text{ jerseys sold to meet target OI}$$

$$\frac{\text{Total FC} + \text{Target OI}}{\text{CM ratio}} = \text{Sales dollars required to meet target OI}$$

$$\frac{\$168{,}000 + \$60{,}000}{0.20} = \$1{,}140{,}000 \text{ in sales to meet target OI}$$

Target Net Income

Suppose that instead of operating income, Universal's managers want to know how many jerseys they must sell to make $42,000 in *net* income. Remember, net income is operating income less income taxes. Since the profit equation calculates operating income, we need to convert the desired net income to operating income. Universal's income taxes are 30% of operating income. That means net income must be 70% of operating income. If we state this relationship mathematically, we can determine what operating income results in $42,000 net income:

$$\$42{,}000 = 0.70 \times \text{Operating income}$$

$$\frac{\$42{,}000}{0.70} = \text{Operating income}$$

$$\$60{,}000 = \text{Operating income}$$

Now we have the same *operating* income target—$60,000—as in the previous section. From this point, we simply follow the steps described in that section to calculate the number of units needed to reach the target operating income.

From the preceding calculations, we can develop the following general formula for converting net income to operating income:

$$\frac{\text{Net income}}{(1 - \text{Tax rate})} = \text{Operating income}$$

What-If Analysis

Managers often want to know what will happen to profit or other measures if costs or volume change. Recall that the profit equation includes sales revenue, variable expenses, and fixed expenses. If we know all but one of these variables, we can solve for the remaining unknown variable. Here are some questions that Universal's managers might ask. As we answer these questions, refer back to Exhibit 3-1, which shows Universal's contribution format income statement as of February 1, 2017. Remember that the company sold 51,975 jerseys that year and showed an operating income of $39,900.

What if C&C Sports were to raise the price of a baseball jersey by 5%?

The price Universal pays C&C Sports for each jersey is a variable cost, so we need to adjust the "constant" form of that cost, which is the $14.80 cost per jersey. A 5% increase from $14.80 would be $0.74, so the new cost of goods sold per jersey would be $14.80 + $0.74 = $15.54. The total variable cost per jersey would be $15.54 plus a $1.20 sales commission, or $16.74.

Since the variable cost per unit has gone up, the contribution margin per unit has gone down to $20 − 16.74 = $3.26. (We could just as easily reduce the original contribution margin per unit by the increase in variable costs: $4 − $0.74 = $3.26.) To calculate the new operating income, we simply substitute this revised contribution margin into the profit formula:

$$\text{Contribution margin} - \text{Fixed expenses} = \text{Operating income}$$
$$(\$3.26 \times 51{,}975 \text{ jerseys}) - \$168{,}000 = \$1{,}438.50$$

If the cost of jerseys increases 5% and Universal sells the same number of jerseys as last year, but does not raise the price it charges, the company will report a much smaller profit.

How much would Universal need to raise the price of a baseball jersey to cover the increase in cost and earn the same operating income as last year?

The solution to this problem isn't as simple as adding $0.74 to the price because Universal pays a commission based on a percentage of sales revenue—6%, to be exact. Therefore, if the sales price per unit changes, so must the commission per unit. Solving for the sales price, SP, we find that the new price per jersey would need to be $20.79:

$$\text{Sales revenue} - \text{Sales commission} - \text{Cost of goods sold} - \text{FC} = \text{OI}$$
$$(\text{SP} \times 51{,}975) - (0.06\text{SP} \times 51{,}975) - (\$15.54 \times 51{,}975) - \$168{,}000 = \$39{,}900$$
$$51{,}975\text{SP} - 3{,}118.5\text{SP} - \$807{,}691.50 - \$168{,}000 = \$39{,}900$$
$$48{,}856.5\text{SP} = \$1{,}015{,}591.50$$
$$\text{SP} = \$20.787 \text{ per jersey, rounded up to } \$20.79$$

The new sales commission would be $20.79 × 0.06 = $1.247 per jersey, rounded up to $1.25. Therefore, the contribution margin per unit would be $20.79 − 15.54 − 1.25 = $4. Notice that this amount is the same as the original contribution margin. If Universal raised the price to $20.79 *and* the number of units sold remained the same, operating income would not change.

THINK ABOUT IT 3.2

If Universal were to raise the sales price of its baseball jersey by $0.79, would the number of units sold remain the same? What if the price were to rise by $5 to $25?

Refer back to the original situation. Assume Universal is considering a new advertising campaign that would cost $10,000. By how much would sales need to increase for the company to make the same operating income as last year?

Adding a new advertising campaign would increase fixed expenses to $178,000. This is a target income problem, and the target is last year's operating income, $39,900 (see Exhibit 3-1 on page 83):

$$\frac{\$178{,}000 + \$39{,}900}{0.20} = \$1{,}089{,}500$$

So the answer to the question of how much sales would need to increase is:

$$\text{New sales revenue} - \text{Old sales revenue} = \text{Increase in sales revenue}$$
$$\$1{,}089{,}500 - \$1{,}039{,}500 = \$50{,}000$$

We could have considered this question in a different manner by asking how much *additional* contribution margin would be needed to cover the $10,000 in *additional* fixed expenses. The answer is $10,000. How much in additional sales does that amount imply? Since the contribution margin is 20% of sales, we simply divide the additional contribution margin needed by the contribution margin ratio:

$$\frac{\$10{,}000}{0.20} = \$50{,}000$$

WATCH OUT!

When volume changes, total sales revenue, total variable expenses, and total contribution margin all change. Students typically change total sales revenue but forget to change total variable expenses. The safest bet is to start with contribution margin per unit × sales volume to be sure to capture the change in total sales and variable expenses.

Limitations of CVP Analysis

CVP analysis is a powerful tool for assessing the profit implications of various business decisions. However, the predictions provided by the analysis are only as good as the data they are based on. And when using CVP as a decision tool, we have to make several assumptions about the data. The primary assumptions we have made in our use of CVP in this unit are:

- All costs can be easily and accurately separated into fixed and variable categories.
- A linear relationship exists between total variable expenses and sales activity over the relevant range of interest.
- Total fixed expenses and variable costs per unit remain constant across all sales levels.
- Inventory is sold during the same period it is purchased or produced.

Even with these assumptions, managers find CVP to be a useful tool in evaluating business opportunities.

Cost Structure and Operating Leverage

Up to this point, we have considered the levels of variable and fixed costs to be given, changeable only by increases or decreases in cost. To some degree, however, firms can, over time, control the relative size of variable and fixed costs in order to establish a particular cost structure. Why would this cost structure matter to a company? Remember that variable costs are incurred only with some type of activity. For example, variable selling expenses are incurred only when sales are made, whereas fixed selling expenses are incurred regardless of the level of sales. Companies that carry a high level of fixed costs relative to variable costs are considered to have greater risk than companies with a high level of variable costs relative to fixed costs.

One measure that is directly affected by the company's cost structure is **operating leverage,** or the change in operating income relative to a change in sales. A company with high operating leverage will experience a large percentage change in operating income as a result of a small percentage change in sales. Refer back to Exhibit 3-1, which shows Universal's contribution format income statement. If sales were to increase by 10% ($103,950), the contribution margin would increase by 10% ($20,790), increasing operating income by $20,790. Compared to the original operating income of $39,900, that is a 52.1% increase in operating income! Of course, the bad news is that if sales were to decrease by 10%, operating income would decrease by 52.1%.

Another way to compute the expected change in operating income due to a change in sales volume *at a given level of sales* is to compute the **degree of operating leverage.**

$$\text{Degree of operating leverage} = \frac{\text{Contribution margin}}{\text{Net operating income}}$$

Universal's degree of operating leverage is 5.21, computed as follows:

$$\text{Degree of operating leverage} = \frac{\$207{,}900}{\$39{,}900} = 5.21$$

That is why a 10% increase in sales due to sales volume (not due to a change in sales price) will increase operating income by 52.1%: a 10% increase in sales × 5.21 = a 52.1% increase in operating income.

Firms can manage their degree of operating leverage by converting variable costs to fixed costs, and vice versa. In a production facility, for example, welders who are paid by the hour (a variable cost) could be replaced by a welding machine (a fixed cost). In Universal's case, managers could replace the sales commission (a variable cost) with a salary (a fixed cost). Exhibit 3-3 compares Universal's contribution format income statement for last year to what it would have looked like if the sales commission had been replaced with a salary.

EXHIBIT 3-3

Universal Sports Exchange's contribution format income statement.

UNIVERSAL SPORTS EXCHANGE
Contribution Format Income Statement

	Commission		Salary	
Sales	$1,039,500	$20.00	$1,039,500	$20.00
Cost of goods sold	769,230	14.80	769,230	14.80
Sales commission	62,370	1.20	0	0.00
Variable costs	831,600	16.00	769,230	14.80
Contribution margin	207,900	$ 4.00	270,270	$ 5.20
Selling and marketing	116,500		178,870	
Administrative costs	51,500		51,500	
Fixed costs	168,000		230,370	
Operating income	$ 39,900		$ 39,900	

The $62,370 in original sales commissions has been added to the original $116,500 fixed selling and marketing expenses, yielding new fixed selling and marketing expenses of $178,870. Notice that under the salary alternative, the contribution margin per unit has risen to $5.20. For every unit sold, Universal retains $1.20 more revenue to cover fixed expenses and contribute to profit.

Under the new salary alternative, as before, a 10% increase in sales ($103,950) will increase contribution margin by 10%, or $27,027. But the $27,027 added to operating income represents a 67.7% increase ($27,027 ÷ $39,900). The degree of operating leverage, then, has increased from a factor of 5.21 to a factor of 6.77 ($270,270 ÷ $39,900). With more fixed and fewer variable costs, the new cost structure creates a higher degree of operating leverage, and thus a higher degree of risk. The payoff is bigger when sales increase, but the downside is bigger when sales decrease.

The profit–volume graph in Exhibit 3-4 compares Universal's profit over several sales levels under the two cost structures, one with a sales commission and the other with a sales salary. The point at which the profit line intersects the *y*-axis represents total fixed expenses—$168,000 under the commission scenario and $230,370 under the salary scenario. The point at which the profit line crosses the *x*-axis is the breakeven point, where profit equals zero. Under the commission scenario, only 42,000 jerseys must be sold to break even; under the salary scenario, 44,302 (rounded from 44,301.9) jerseys must be sold to break even. The difference in the breakeven points represents another type of risk related to operating leverage: As operating leverage rises, more jerseys must be sold to break even.

At 51,975 jersey sales, the point where the two profit lines cross, the two scenarios return equal profits. At lower sales levels, profit is higher under the

EXHIBIT 3-4

Profit–volume graph for Universal Sports Exchange.

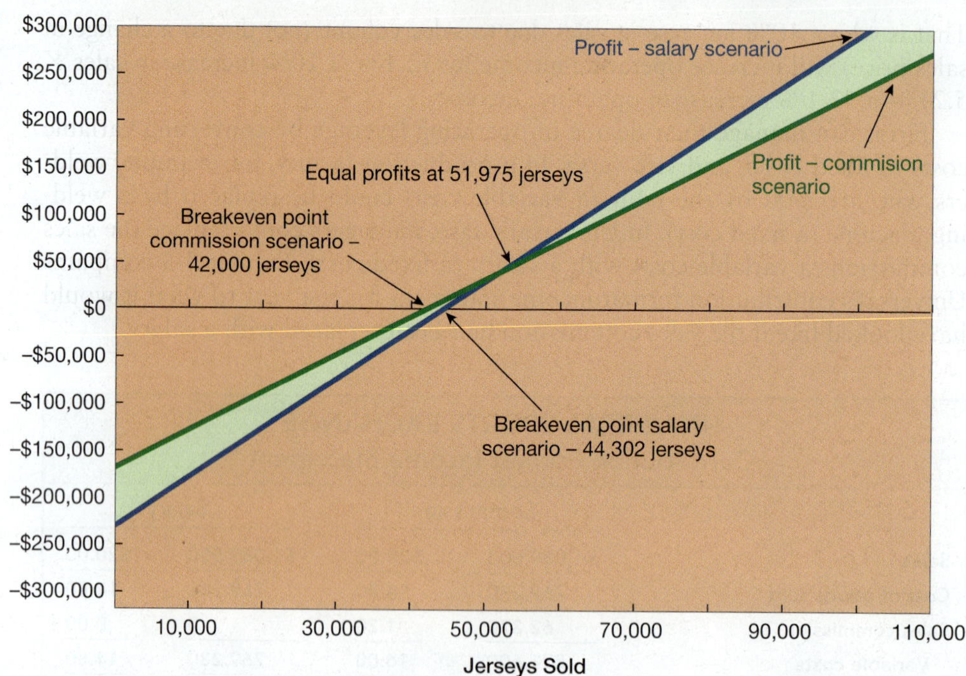

commission scenario; at higher sales levels, profit is higher under the salary scenario. The choice of cost structure, then, is critical. Depending on the company's sales volume, it can greatly affect profit.

REALITY CHECK—*Fixed versus variable costs*

© sdlgzps/iStockphoto

Fixed costs like these make it difficult for steel mills to control their costs in times of reduced production.

2,300 degrees Fahrenheit. That makes for a lot of hot air, and that's exactly what it takes to operate the preheater that blows the hot air at a giant ladle that holds melting steel at *Universal Stainless & Alloy Products Inc.* But what happens when the mill isn't producing steel and the giant ladle is empty? Nothing or everything, depending on how you look at it. Even though the ladle may be empty (the "nothing"), the preheater keeps blowing the hot air (the "everything") to prevent the refractory bricks inside the unit from disintegrating. And the mill's baghouse fans, part of the air pollution control system, run continuously, even when the mill is not operating, so the motors are not damaged.

These two pieces of equipment illustrate the high levels of fixed costs that many steel mills incur. Fixed costs like these make it difficult for steel mills to control their costs in times of reduced production. And as steel prices drop in times of weak demand, the mills become trapped in unprofitable operating cycles.

Some steel makers, such as *Nucor*, have sought to break this cycle by building smaller mills that can ramp down production, and thus costs, in times of weak demand. This increased presence of variable costs increases the mill's flexibility in responding to a varying demand and production schedule, improving the company's profitability.

Sources: Kelly Evens, "High Fixed Costs Are Makings of Steel Trap," *The Wall Street Journal*, October 25, 2011; Robert Guy Matthews, "Fixed Costs Chafe at Steel Mills," *The Wall Street Journal*, June 10, 2009.

Changing a company's cost structure affects more than its operating leverage, however. It may have behavioral implications for the employees. In Universal's case, the company paid sales commissions to encourage the sales staff to sell more units, to make more money both for themselves and for the company. When the sales commission is eliminated, so is the financial incentive for the sales staff to sell more.

THINK ABOUT IT 3.3

Assume you are running a new start-up company in which you have invested a good deal of money. What type of cost structure will you use to pay your sales staff—commission or salary? Why?

UNIT 3.2 REVIEW

KEY TERMS

Cost–volume–profit analysis (CVP) p. 88 | Degree of operating leverage p. 92 | Operating leverage p. 92

PRACTICE QUESTIONS

1. LO 2 Pete's Pretzel Stand sells jumbo pretzels for $2 each. Pete's variable cost per pretzel is $0.50, and total fixed expenses are $3,000 per month. If Pete wants to earn a monthly operating income of $9,000, how many pretzels must he sell during the month?

   a. 8,000
   b. 6,000
   c. 4,000
   d. 2,000

2. LO 2 Marisol's Parasols sells novelty umbrellas for $10 each. Marisol's variable costs are $4 per unit, and her fixed expenses are $3,000 per month. If Marisol's tax rate is 25%, how many umbrellas must Marisol sell each month if she wants to earn $9,000 in net income?

   a. 500
   b. 2,000
   c. 2,500
   d. 3,500

3. LO 3 All other things equal, a 20% increase in the number of units sold will yield a 20% increase in net income. True or False?

4. LO 3 All other things equal, an increase in the number of units sold will

   a. increase operating income.
   b. increase total variable expenses.
   c. increase total contribution margin.
   d. all of the above.

5. LO 3 Ellis McCormick and Elaine Sury are owners of MeetingKeeper, a company that sells personalized daily planners. Last month, the company sold 1,500 planners at a price of $6 per planner. Variable costs were $2.40 per unit; fixed expenses were $3,600. This month, Ellis and Elaine have decided to spend $2,000 to advertise in the local newspaper. They believe that the additional advertising will generate 25% more sales volume than last month. What will be this month's operating income?

   a. $3,150
   b. $1,150
   c. $775
   d. ($1,100)

6. LO 4 All other things equal, a company can increase its operating leverage by converting commission-based salespeople to salaries. True or False?

7. LO 4 Dawson Enterprises' current degree of operating leverage is 8. A planned promotion campaign is expected to increase sales by 15%. What is the expected increase in operating income?

a. 8%

b. 15%

c. 23%

d. 120%

8. LO 4 Festive Foods Caterers' income statement for last month follows. What is Festive Foods' degree of operating leverage?

Sales	$200,000
Variable expenses	60,000
Contribution margin	140,000
Fixed expenses	120,000
Net operating income	$ 20,000

a. 0.7 c. 7

b. 3 d. 10

UNIT 3.2 PRACTICE EXERCISE

Use this income statement and your calculations from the Unit 3.1 Practice Exercise to answer the following questions.

Sales ($50 per unit)		$5,000
Less: Cost of goods sold ($32 per unit)		3,200
Gross margin		1,800
Less operating expenses:		
Salaries	$800	
Advertising	400	
Shipping ($2 per unit)	200	1,400
Operating Income		$ 400

1. How many units would the company need to sell to earn $2,000 in operating income?
2. How many units would the company need to sell to earn $1,140 in net income if the tax rate is 25%?
3. By how much would operating income change with a 10% increase in units sold?

SELECTED UNIT 3.2 ANSWERS

Think About It 3.2

Kids who play baseball need baseball jerseys. The question is, will consumers continue to buy those jerseys from Universal, or will they go elsewhere? For an additional $0.79, Universal may not see much of a change in demand for its jerseys; the increase in price is less than 4%. At a $5 increase in price, however, consumers may look for a better deal somewhere else.

Think About It 3.3

You should offer a commission. A start-up company typically has little self-generated cash and few customers. Salaries would have to be paid no matter what, even if no sales were made. With a commission, the sales staff is paid only when the company earns revenue. Because many employees are not willing to bear the total risk of compensation tied to sales, some companies offer a combination of salary and commission (a mixed cost).

Practice Questions

1. A
2. C
3. False
4. D
5. B
6. True
7. D
8. C

Unit 3.2 Practice Exercise

1. You know from the Unit 3.1 Practice Exercise that the contribution margin is $16/unit and total fixed expenses are $1,200. Now, use the target income formula to solve for the number of units:

$$\frac{\text{Fixed expenses} + \text{Target income}}{\text{CM per unit}}$$

$$= \frac{\$1{,}200 + \$2{,}000}{\$16} = 200 \text{ units}$$

2. First, you must convert net income to operating income:

$$\frac{\text{Net Income}}{(1 - \text{Tax rate})} = \frac{\$1{,}140}{(1 - 0.25)} = \$1{,}520$$

$$\frac{\text{Fixed expenses} + \text{Target income}}{\text{CM per unit}}$$

$$= \frac{\$1{,}200 + \$1{,}520}{\$16} = 170 \text{ units}$$

3. Next, you must compute the degree of operating leverage:

$$\frac{\text{Contribution margin}}{\text{Net operating income}} = \frac{\$1{,}600}{\$400} = 4$$

Now, multiply the degree of operating leverage by the percentage change in the number of units sold to arrive at the change in operating income: 4 × 10% = 40% increase in operating income. Therefore, a 10% increase in unit sales results in a $160 (0.4 × $400) increase in operating income. This answer can also be calculated by multiplying the increase in the number of units sold (0.1 × 100 = 10) by the contribution margin per unit: 10 × $16 = $160.

UNIT 3.3

Multiproduct CVP Analysis

GUIDED UNIT PREPARATION

Answering the following questions while you read this unit will guide your understanding of the key concepts found in the unit. The questions are linked to the learning objectives presented at the beginning of the chapter.

LO 5

1. What is meant by the term *sales mix*?
2. How do you calculate the sales required to break even or achieve a target operating income in a multiproduct setting?
3. What assumption is required in multiproduct CVP analysis but is not necessary in single-product CVP analysis?

The CVP analyses you have conducted so far focus on decisions about a single product. While this type of analysis is useful in small start-up businesses and divisions with only a single product line, most companies produce or sell more than one type of product. Companies that sell multiple products need to know what results are required for the *company*, not individual products, to achieve certain targets. To solve this type of problem, managers must have a good grasp of the **sales mix**—that is, the sales of each product relative to total sales.

We will illustrate multiproduct CVP analysis with another retail sporting goods store—Landon Sports, one of Universal's competitors. Landon sells the same baseball jerseys as Universal, but it also sells athletic shoes. Unit data for the jerseys and shoes are as follows:

	Jerseys	Shoes
Sales price	$20.00	$45.00
Cost of goods sold	14.80	36.00
Sales commission	1.20	2.70
Total variable expenses	16.00	38.70
Contribution margin	$ 4.00	$ 6.30

Note that Landon prices its jerseys the same as Universal (to be competitive) and offers employees the same 6% commission on sales. The athletic shoes that Landon sells are priced higher than the jerseys, and they cost the company more to sell.

Last year, Landon sold 40,000 jerseys and 10,000 pairs of shoes, so the sales mix is four jerseys for every pair of shoes sold. Exhibit 3-5 shows Landon's income statement by product type and in total. Note that no fixed expenses are assigned to either jerseys or shoes. As long as the company keeps selling jerseys and shoes, the fixed expenses will not change, so they are deducted in total rather than allocated to the individual product lines.

LANDON SPORTS
Income Statement
for the 52 Weeks Ended February 1, 2017

	Jerseys			Shoes			Total Company	
	Total	Per Unit	Percentage	Total	Per Unit	Percentage	Total	Percentage
Sales	$800,000	$20.00	100.00%	$450,000	$45.00	100.00%	$1,250,000	100.00%
Cost of goods sold	592,000	14.80	74.00%	360,000	36.00	80.00%	952,000	76.16%
Sales commission	48,000	1.20	6.00%	27,000	2.70	6.00%	75,000	6.00%
Variable expenses	640,000	16.00	80.00%	387,000	38.70	86.00%	1,027,000	82.16%
Contribution margin	$160,000	$ 4.00	20.00%	$ 63,000	$ 6.30	14.00%	223,000	17.84%
Selling and marketing							125,000	
Administrative expenses							53,400	
Fixed expenses							178,400	
Operating income							$ 44,600	

EXHIBIT 3-5 *Landon Sports' income statement.*

The profit formula for a company with multiple products (in this case, jerseys and shoes) and a specified sales mix is:

$$(\text{Sales}_{\text{jerseys}} - \text{Variable expenses}_{\text{jerseys}}) + (\text{Sales}_{\text{shoes}} - \text{Variable expenses}_{\text{shoes}}) - \text{FC} = \text{OI}$$

or

$$\text{Contribution margin}_{\text{jerseys}} + \text{Contribution margin}_{\text{shoes}} - \text{FC} = \text{OI}$$

This equation can be expanded to accommodate as many products as the company sells.

REALITY CHECK—*Mixing it up on a high flyer*

In February 2016, Boeing delivered its 100th 787 Dreamliner produced at its facility in North Charleston, South Carolina. While it took the company three years to reach this milestone, it expects to deliver its 200th Dreamliner in about half that time.

But there's not just one Dreamliner product. There are actually three versions of the plane–small, medium, and large. The largest version, known as the 787-10 or "Dash 10," was announced at the 2013 Paris Air Show, and Boeing left the show with orders for a total of 102 airplanes from five customers. With a backlog of 164 jets at the end of 2015, the first 787-10 isn't expected to be delivered until 2018.

The 787-8 accounted for almost 80% of all Dreamliners sold through the end of 2015, but looking at the current backlog of Dreamliner orders shows a much different sales mix. The backlog mix is about 20% 787-8s, 60% 787-9s and 20% 787-10s. Since the 787-10 is the most profitable version of the three models, this changing sales mix should improve the company's profitability. In fact, one analyst estimates that the average profit on a 787-10 is as much as $15 billion greater than the profit on a 787-9. So don't be surprised if you see the company try to change the sales mix to include an even greater percentage of 787-10 Dreamliners in the future.

One analyst estimates that the average profit on a 787-10 is as much as $15 billion greater than the profit on a 787-9.

Sources: Dominic Gates, "Boeing Finishes 787-10 Design Details, *The Seattle Times*, December 2, 2015, http://www.seattletimes.com/business/boeing-aerospace/boeing-finishes-787-10-design-details/ (accessed February 26, 2016); Dominic Gates, "Boeing's S. Carolina Site Delivers 100th Dreamliner," *The Seattle Times*, http://www.seattletimes.com/business/boeing-aerospace/boeings-s-carolina-site-delivers-100th-dreamliner/ (accessed February 26, 2016); Adam Levine-Weinberg, "Why Boeing's 787-10 Is Critical for Dreamliner Profitability," The Motley Fool, http://www.fool.com/investing/general/2016/02/22/why-boeings-787-10-is-critical-for-dreamliner-prof.aspx (accessed February 26, 2016); Aerospace-Technology.com, "Boeing 787-10 Dreamliner, United States of America," http://www.aerospace-technology.com/projects/boeing-787-10-dreamliner/ (accessed February 26, 2016).

Landon Sports breaks even when:

$$(\$4.00 \times \text{\# of jerseys sold}) + (\$6.30 \times \text{\# of pairs of shoes sold}) - \$178{,}400 = \$0$$

The preceding equation has two unknowns and an infinite number of solutions. However, when we require that the sales mix is held constant, then we know the number of jerseys sold is four times the number of pairs of shoes sold. If we let x equal the number of pairs of shoes sold, we have the following equation and solution:

$$\begin{aligned}(\$4.00 \times 4x) + (\$6.30 \times x) - \$178{,}400 &= \$0\\ \$16x + \$6.30x &= \$178{,}400\\ x &= 8{,}000 \text{ pairs of shoes}\\ 4x &= 32{,}000 \text{ jerseys}\end{aligned}$$

Breakeven in sales dollars is $1,000,000: $640,000 for jerseys ($20 × 32,000) and $360,000 ($45 × 8,000) for shoes.

WATCH OUT!

Do not split fixed expenses between the multiple products and try to come up with individual product breakeven points or target income points. This will result in units sold that do not adhere to the sales mix ratio.

The formula is easily adapted to target income problems. Suppose the CFO at Landon Sports wanted to know how many jerseys and pairs of shoes needed to be sold to earn $66,900 in operating income:

$$(\$4.00 \times 4x) + (\$6.30 \times x) - \$178{,}400 = \$66{,}900$$
$$\$16x + \$6.30x = \$245{,}300$$
$$x = 11{,}000 \text{ pairs of shoes}$$
$$4x = 44{,}000 \text{ jerseys}$$

If the sales mix changes, so do the breakeven point and the other targets. Exhibit 3-6 shows what Landon's income statement would look like if Landon Sports still sold a total of 50,000 units, but the sales mix changed to 30,000 jerseys and 20,000 pairs of shoes (instead of 40,000 jerseys and 10,000 pairs of shoes). The company would make more money, even though it sold the same number of units as in the previous scenario because more of those units sold were shoes, which generate a higher contribution margin per unit.

LANDON SPORTS
Revised Income Statement
for the 52 Weeks Ended February 1, 2017

	Jerseys			Shoes			Total Company	
	Total	Per Unit	Percentage	Total	Per Unit	Percentage	Total	Percentage
Sales	$600,000	$20.00	100.00%	$900,000	$45.00	100.00%	$1,500,000	100.00%
Cost of goods sold	444,000	14.80	74.00%	720,000	36.00	80.00%	1,164,000	77.60%
Sales commission	36,000	1.20	6.00%	54,000	2.70	6.00%	90,000	6.00%
Variable expenses	480,000	16.00	80.00%	774,000	38.70	86.00%	1,254,000	83.60%
Contribution margin	$120,000	$ 4.00	20.00%	$126,000	$ 6.30	14.00%	246,000	16.40%
Selling and marketing							125,000	
Administrative expenses							53,400	
Fixed expenses							178,400	
Operating income							$ 67,600	

EXHIBIT 3-6 *Landon Sports' revised income statement.*

Let's see what the breakeven point is with this new sales mix. Since sales of jerseys are 1.5 times the number of shoe sales $\left(\frac{30{,}000}{20{,}000}\right)$, we will replace 4*x* from the original formula with 1.5*x* in the new formula:

$$(\$4.00 \times 1.5x) + (\$6.30 \times x) - \$178{,}400 = \$0$$
$$\$6x + \$6.30x = \$178{,}400$$
$$x = 14{,}504.065 \text{ pairs of shoes}$$
$$1.5x = 21{,}756.0975 \text{ jerseys}$$

Since Landon Sports cannot sell part of a shoe or part of a jersey, the breakeven points must be rounded up to the next whole unit—14,505 pairs of shoes and 21,757 jerseys. Breakeven in sales dollars is $1,087,865: $435,140 for jerseys ($20 × 21,757) and $652,725 ($45 × 14,505) for shoes. More sales dollars are needed to break even and achieve other income targets relative to the original sales mix because, although the shoes have a higher contribution margin per unit than the jerseys ($6.30

compared to $4.00), the contribution margin *ratio* for shoes is lower than the contribution margin *ratio* for jerseys. That means that with this mix, less of each sales dollar is available after covering variable expenses to cover fixed expenses and profit.

THINK ABOUT IT 3.4

Consider Landon's original sales mix of 40,000 jerseys and 10,000 shoes. In an effort to stimulate jersey sales, Landon has increased the sales commission paid on each jersey to 12.3%. The company believes that this move will generate additional sales of 10,000 jerseys, with no effect on shoe sales. How will this move alter Landon's sales mix? How will it affect the breakeven point? Do you think this change is a good move?

Limitations of Multiproduct CVP Analysis

In Unit 3.2, you learned about the assumptions of CVP analysis, and all those assumptions apply in a multiproduct environment. However, there is another assumption that we make in a multiproduct environment: *The sales mix can be determined and will remain constant.*

UNIT 3.3 REVIEW

KEY TERMS

Sales mix p. 97

PRACTICE QUESTIONS

1. LO 5 If a company sells more than one product, it cannot use CVP analysis to examine the effect of changes in costs on operating income. True or False?

2. LO 5 Which of the following is *not* a limiting assumption of multiproduct CVP analysis?

    a. Fixed cost per unit remains constant within the relevant range.

    b. All variable cost relationships are linear with respect to activity.

    c. All costs can be easily separated into variable and fixed categories.

    d. The sales mix can be determined and remains constant over time.

3. LO 5 Blalock Training sells three online training courses in database programming skills. For every 12 people who take the introductory course, 5 take the intermediate course and 3 take the advanced course. Blalock's CFO has calculated a breakeven point of 10,000 courses. How many of those 10,000 courses will be introductory?

    a. 1,200
    b. 6,000
    c. 8,000
    d. 10,000

4. LO 5 Montelone Images, a photography studio, sells two photo packages. The standard package has a contribution margin of $5, and the deluxe package has a contribution margin of $12. Montelone sells five standard packages for every one deluxe package. If fixed expenses total $74,000, how many standard and deluxe packages must be sold to break even?

    a. 14,800 standard; 6,167 deluxe

    b. 4,353 standard; 4,353 deluxe

    c. 9,280 standard; 2,300 deluxe

    d. 10,000 standard; 2,000 deluxe

5. LO 5 Assume a company sells 10,000 units—5,000 of product A and 5,000 of product B. Product A has a contribution margin of $6.00 per unit, while Product B has a contribution margin of $4.00 per unit. If the sales mix changes to 5,500 units of Product A and 4,500 units of product B, which of the following is true?

    a. The company will make more money because more of the product with the higher contribution margin per unit is being sold.

    b. It will take fewer total units to break even now that more of the product with the higher contribution margin per unit is being sold.

    c. The breakeven point depends on the current sales volume as it effects the sales mix.

    d. All of the above are true.

UNIT 3.3 PRACTICE EXERCISE

Hometown Bakery sells three types of doughnuts: glazed, jelly, and cake. The following table shows the sales price and variable costs for each type. The bakery incurs $300,000 a year in fixed expenses. Assume that it sells two glazed doughnuts for every one jelly doughnut and every one cake doughnut.

DOUGHNUT TYPE	SALES PRICE	VARIABLE COST
Glazed	$0.35	$0.20
Jelly	$0.50	$0.45
Cake	$0.40	$0.27

Required

1. How many doughnuts of each type will be sold at the breakeven point?
2. What amount of revenue would need to be generated by each type of doughnut for the company to earn $60,000 in operating income?

SELECTED UNIT 3.3 ANSWERS

Think About It 3.4

The new sales commission is expected to generate sales of an additional 10,000 jerseys. With total sales of 50,000 jerseys and 10,000 pairs of shoes, the new sales mix would be five jerseys for every one pair of shoes. The new contribution margin for jerseys would be:

Sales price	$20.00
Cost of goods sold	14.80
Sales commission ($20 × 0.123)	2.46
Variable expenses	17.26
Contribution margin	$ 2.74

Breakeven is now:

$$(\$2.74 \times 5x) + (\$6.30 \times x) - \$178{,}400 = \$0$$
$$\$13.70x + \$6.30x = \$178{,}400$$
$$x = 8{,}920 \text{ pairs of shoes}$$
$$5x = 44{,}600 \text{ jerseys}$$

By lowering the contribution margin per unit of jerseys and shifting a greater percentage of sales to those jerseys, more jerseys and more shoes will have to be sold in order to break even.

Is this change a good move? An increase in the breakeven point creates more risk for the company, but it might be considered a good move if greater income can be generated. Since the number of shoes sold is expected to remain constant at 10,000, we only need to consider the contribution margin generated by the jerseys.

Original contribution margin:	40,000 jerseys × $4.00 =	$160,000
New contribution margin:	50,000 jerseys × $2.74 =	137,000
Reduction in contribution margin		$ 23,000

If the new commission strategy only generates an additional 10,000 jersey sales, then it is not a good move, since total contribution margin, and therefore operating income, decreases by $23,000.

Practice Questions

1. False
2. A
3. B
4. D
5. D

Unit 3.3 Practice Exercise

1. $(\$0.15 \times 2x) + (\$0.05 \times x) + (\$0.13 \times x) - \$300{,}000 = \$0$

   $\$0.48x = \$300{,}000$

   $x = 625{,}000$ jelly doughnuts

   $x = 625{,}000$ cake doughnuts

   $2x = 1{,}250{,}000$ glazed doughnuts

2. $(\$0.15 \times 2x) + (\$0.05 \times x) + (\$0.13 \times x) - \$300{,}000 = \$60{,}000$

   $\$0.48x = \$360{,}000$

   $x = 750{,}000$ jelly doughnuts × $0.50 = $375,000

   $x = 750{,}000$ cake doughnuts × $0.40 = $300,000

   $2x = 1{,}500{,}000$ glazed doughnuts × $0.35 = $525,000

UNIT 3.4

Pricing Decisions

GUIDED UNIT PREPARATION

Answering the following questions while you read this unit will guide your understanding of the key concepts found in the unit. The questions are linked to the learning objectives presented at the beginning of the chapter.

LO 6

1. Define markup. How does a markup percentage differ from the gross margin percentage?
2. Explain cost-plus pricing. What are some flaws of cost-plus pricing?
3. Explain how competitors influence the price under cost-plus pricing.

LO 7

4. Explain target costing. What alternatives does a company have if it cannot make a product at the target cost?

In this chapter you have learned how to calculate several pieces of information to assist managers in their decision making. For each calculation you were provided all the necessary inputs, such as the sales price, variable and fixed expenses, and sales demand. But knowing how to plug these inputs into an equation and "do the math" is not enough. As a manager, you will need to determine the prices, costs, and demand for products and services; they will not be provided to you.

In this unit you will learn about some of the decisions managers face in setting the price to charge for a product or service. As Noel Zeller, founder of Zelco Industries, maker of the "itty bitty" Booklight, put it, "Pricing is crucial to success—knowing how to price your merchandise so that you make an adequate profit. Most people start out under-pricing their products. Why? Because they price them out on the basis of labor costs and what the components cost, and don't go by the perceived value of the product."[2]

Influences on Price

From the customer's perspective, the price paid for a product or service should reflect its value. From the company's perspective, the price charged must be high enough to cover expenses and return a reasonable profit to the company. The customer wants to pay as *little* as reasonably possible, while the company wants to charge as *much* as reasonably possible. Where do those two perspectives meet?

Economic theory suggests that price and demand are inversely related: the higher the price, the lower the demand for a product. At lower prices, customers will demand (and purchase) a higher quantity of a product than they will at higher prices. The lower the price, however, the fewer units of product a company is willing to supply. How do companies decide what price to charge in order to make an acceptable profit and deliver the goods and services customers want?

The answer depends in part on the market for their products. While customers and costs influence prices, so does the level of competition in the marketplace. If two companies are selling the same product, why would a consumer pay a higher price to one than to the other? If the products are identical, they won't. In a market in which many companies are selling the same product, each company will sell its product at the going market price, which is set by the supply of and demand for the product. These companies are "price takers": their production and sales decisions do not affect the price of their product. Producers of commodities such as corn, oil, and orange juice face this kind of market.

Since price takers can't affect product prices, they must find other ways to earn a reasonable profit. The one profit-related factor they can influence is the cost to deliver their products or services to consumers. To reduce that cost, they must focus on operational efficiency. If the cost is too high, so that net income is low or negative, they may choose to leave the market altogether.

If a company is not a price taker, how do managers decide what price to set for a product or service? This is a difficult question, one we will not answer fully in this unit. However, there are some basic guidelines these companies can follow. Most important, to justify a higher price, a company must differentiate its product or service from that of competitors, so that customers believe it is different enough to warrant the higher price.

Why pay $50 for a haircut at a fancy salon instead of $8 at the local barbershop? Why pay more for a Lexus than a Kia? The difference depends on the customer's desires and the seller's ability to convince the customer that the product is or is not worth a higher price. The luxury of the Lexus certainly adds to the cost of producing it. Since the cost of producing the Lexus is higher than the cost of producing a Kia, Lexus will need to charge a higher price. It's up to the customer to decide whether the higher price is worth it, and it's up to Lexus to convince the consumer that it is.

In a perfect world, companies would understand the relationship between the price of their products and the demand for them. If they knew that information, they could figure out exactly which price would return the greatest income. Although it is possible to calculate this information—and you may be familiar with the economic theory behind these calculations—such information may be difficult or expensive to acquire. As an alternative, some companies rely on one of two methods: cost-plus pricing or target costing.

Cost-Plus Pricing

To be profitable over the long run, a company must sell its products or services at a price that will both cover its expenses and provide a profit. **Cost-plus pricing** adds an amount to the cost of the product or service to cover the company's operating costs and contribute to its profit. The "plus" amount is often referred to as a **markup**, or the difference between the selling price and the cost of the product:

Cost
+ Markup
Sales price

Look back at Exhibit 3-1. Universal adds a $5.20 markup to the wholesale price (cost of goods sold) C&C Sports charges for baseball jerseys: $20.00 − $14.80 = $5.20. Most companies don't think of their markups as dollar amounts, however. Instead, they express markups as a percentage of the cost:

$$\frac{\text{Sales price} - \text{Cost}}{\text{Cost}} = \text{Markup\%}$$

Expressed as a percentage, Universal's jersey markup is 35% of the cost of goods sold:

$$\frac{\$20.00 - \$14.80}{\$14.80} = 35\%$$

Because cost can be defined in different ways, it is important to identify the appropriate cost basis in communicating markups. Let's look again at Exhibit 3-1. If Universal chooses to define *cost* as the total *variable* cost per unit rather than the cost of goods sold, then the markup percentage is 25% $\left(\frac{\$20 - \$16}{\$16}\right)$. If *cost* is defined as *total* cost (ignoring income taxes), then the markup percentage is 3.99% $\left(\frac{\$1{,}039{,}500 - (\$831{,}600 + \$168{,}000)}{(\$831{,}600 + \$168{,}000)}\right)$. Notice that as the cost base grows larger, the markup grows smaller. That is because, as the cost base expands, fewer costs are left to be covered by the markup.

The markup percentages we just calculated are based on existing costs and prices. How can these markup percentages be used to set the prices of new products? Suppose that to remain competitive with Landon Sports, managers of Universal Sports Exchange have decided to start selling shoes. If Universal can purchase the shoes at the same average cost ($36) as Landon (refer back to Unit 3.3), what price should the company charge to maintain a 35% markup on the cost of goods sold, as for its jerseys? The answer is $48.60 ($36 + (35% × $36)). But does it make sense to charge $48.60 for Universal's shoes when customers can buy similar shoes from Landon for only $45? Only if Universal can convince customers that they are getting better shoes or better service than they would from Landon does a price of $48.60 make sense. Otherwise, Universal will need to meet Landon's $45 price and settle for a 25% markup on cost of goods sold $\left(\frac{\$45 - \$36}{\$36}\right)$.

Although cost-plus pricing is a relatively simple approach to pricing, it has several flaws. First, the price a customer is willing to pay for a product or service should represent the value of that product or service to the customer. A markup based on cost does not represent the value to the customer. Instead, the markup represents the return to the seller. Similarly, cost-plus pricing implies that the cost of the seller's operational inefficiencies should be borne by the customer. For example, Landon may be able to charge $45 for shoes because its operating costs are lower than Universal's. If $45 provides Landon with enough return to cover operating costs and contribute to profits, should customers pay Universal more just because it has more costs to cover? No. It is not the customer's responsibility to ensure that companies stay in business. Customers should be willing to pay a fair price for a product or service. Aside from the price, they will buy from the company that delivers the product or service they want, the way they want it.

> **WATCH OUT!**
>
> All the different percentages that business people use can become confusing. In this chapter, you learned about markups as a percentage of cost. As a dollar amount, gross profit (Sales – Cost of Goods Sold) is the same as the markup on Cost of Goods Sold, but the gross margin percentage is *not* the same as the markup percentage.
>
> For example, Universal Sports Exchange buys jerseys from C&C Sports for $14.80 and sells them for $20. The gross margin, or markup on the cost of goods sold, is $5.20. The gross margin percentage is 26% ($5.20 ÷ $20.00), but the markup percentage on the cost of goods sold is 35% ($5.20 ÷ $14.80).
>
> To keep these concepts straight, remember that markups are always expressed as a percentage of *cost*. In contrast, financial ratios such as the gross margin percentage and the profit margin are based on *sales*. Finally, be sure you know what cost someone is referring to before you make a calculation. When in doubt, ask.

Target Costing

The term *target costing* may not sound like a pricing strategy, yet it is just that. Whereas cost-plus pricing starts with the cost, **target costing** starts with the price customers are willing to pay. This method computes the desired markup and the

REALITY CHECK—*Big data brings dynamic pricing strategies*

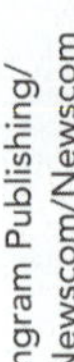

It's hard to have a business discussion today without talking about "big data," and one area where big data can offer some help is in pricing. In a dynamic pricing environment, businesses use available data to help set prices, which may be different for each customer based on what that customer values. Airlines have long used this approach to setting fares, sometimes charging frequent fliers more for a ticket than an infrequent flier on the same route, and charging more for prime departure times and arrival times.

But with big data and related data analytics tools becoming more prevalent, other businesses are jumping on the dynamic pricing bandwagon. Think about the information footprint you might leave behind every time you surf the Internet or make an online purchase—address, zip code, gender, age, browsing history, purchase history—and now think about how companies can use that information to help determine what you might be willing to pay for a product or service. Live in a well-to-do zip code? A travel site may direct you to higher priced hotels.

One consultant estimates that businesses that employ dynamic pricing practices increase profits by an average of 25%.

Grocery chain Safeway is using customer purchasing patterns to send targeted customers specific coupons and special offers. And in 2013, almost 45% of the chain's sales came from shoppers who had received a targeted digital special offer.

Looking for a tee time in Las Vegas? Two golf courses there are using dynamic pricing to fill available tee times. The greens fee depends on the time of day, current demand, and when you make the reservation. And the prices can change throughout the day as conditions change.

Is dynamic pricing worth the effort? The data indicate that it is. One consultant estimates that businesses that employ dynamic pricing practices increase profits by an average of 25%.

Sources: Lisa Gerstner, "How Online Retailers Trick Shoppers Into Paying More," *Kiplinger's Personal Finance*, June 2015, http://www.kiplinger.com/article/spending/T050-C000-S002-what-you-should-know-about-online-pricing.html (accessed February 26, 2016); Olga Kharif, "Supermarkets Offer Personalized Pricing," *Bloomberg-Business*, November 13, 2013, http://www.bloomberg.com/bw/articles/2013-11-14/2014-outlook-supermarkets-offer-personalized-pricing (accessed February 26, 2016); Greg Petro, "Dynamic Pricing: Which Customers are Worth the Most? Amazon, Delta Airlines and Staples Weigh In," *Forbes*, April 17, 2015, http://www.forbes.com/sites/gregpetro/2015/04/17/dynamic-pricing-which-customers-are-worth-the-most-amazon-delta-airlines-and-staples-weigh-in/#50ba54dcb516 (accessed February 26, 2016); PricingNews.com, "Dynamic Pricing Lets Golfers Choose Las Vegas Tee Times Rates," http://pricing-news.com/dynamic-pricing-lets-golfers-choose-las-vegas-tee-times-rates-golf-las-vegas-now/#sthash.Pr9lWejX.dpbs (accessed February 26, 2016).

maximum cost the company can incur to deliver a product or service at the market price. Management scholar Peter Drucker advocated the use of target costing in this way: "The only sound way to price is to start out with what the market is willing to pay—and thus, it must be assumed, what the competition will charge—and design to that price specification" (*The Wall Street Journal*, October 21, 1993).

Companies need to engage in target costing *before* introducing a new product. Suppose Bradley Textile Mills, one of C&C's fabric suppliers, has developed a fabric that "breathes" better than all other fabrics currently on the market. Before Bradley begins to mass produce the new fabric, managers need to know what customers like C&C are willing to pay for it. Bradley's marketing department, together with the product engineers, should conduct marketing surveys and demonstrations to assess customers' interest in its product and the price they are willing to pay.

Let's assume that Bradley's market research indicates that customers are willing to pay $4.50 per yard for the new fabric. That's $0.50 more per yard than the price of the fabric Bradley currently produces. Let's assume, too, that Bradley Textile Mills requires a 30% gross profit margin on all new products. A 30% gross margin on $4.50 would be $1.35, resulting in a target cost of goods sold of $3.15 ($4.50 − $1.35). At this point, the production engineers at Bradley Textile Mills need to figure out whether the new fabric can be made for $3.15 per yard. If it can't, the company shouldn't produce the new product because the market price will not provide the desired return.

THINK ABOUT IT 3.5

Why is it important to figure out the target cost before beginning production of a new product?

UNIT 3.4 REVIEW

KEY TERMS

Cost-plus pricing p. 104 | Markup p. 104 | Target costing p. 105

PRACTICE QUESTIONS

1. LO 6 A markup percentage can be calculated as $\frac{\text{Markup}}{\text{Cost}}$. True or False?

2. LO 6 Which of the following affects the price a company charges under cost-plus pricing?
   a. The cost of the product
   b. Competitors' prices
   c. Desired gross margin percentage
   d. b. and c. only
   e. All of the above

3. LO 6 Dunn Family Auto Repairs offers several services ranging from tire patching to complete transmission rebuilding. Since labor is the main cost of these services, the company charges customers a markup on the worker's wage rate. The most skilled workers earn $25 per hour; Dunn charges customers $40 per hour. If Dunn applies the same markup percentage to each worker, what price will the company charge for a worker who earns $15 per hour?
   a. $20
   b. $24
   c. $30
   d. $40

4. LO 7 The gross margin percentage and the markup percentage are essentially the same. True or False?

5. LO 7 Carpenter Western Wear is a retail clothing store in Lubbock, Texas. On average, the store earns a 40% gross margin on its merchandise. The owner, Carol Carpenter, wants to add jewelry to the sales mix. Carol believes that her customers won't pay more than $50 for a bracelet. If she wants to maintain the same average gross margin, what is the maximum wholesale cost she should pay for bracelets?
   a. $15
   b. $20
   c. $30
   d. $35

UNIT 3.4 PRACTICE EXERCISE

Gorrells and Sunn builds high-quality homes ranging in price from $200,000 to $1 million. John Ellis, a local physician, has asked Gorrells and Sunn to show him some house plans. Dr. Ellis has selected a plan that calls for $300,000 in building materials, $180,000 in labor, and $40,000 in add-ons, but he doesn't want to pay more than $575,000 for his home. Gorrells and Sunn typically prices its homes based on the total cost of construction plus 15%.

Required

1. What price would Gorrells and Sunn normally quote for this house plan?
2. What is the target cost Gorrells and Sunn would need to meet to sell the house for $575,000 at a 15% markup?
3. What could Gorrells and Sunn do to meet the target cost in part (2)?

SELECTED UNIT 3.4 ANSWERS

Think About It 3.5

When a company is ready to start producing a new product or offering a new service, new investments must be made. For example, new machinery might be purchased, new employees hired, or new office facilities rented. Because these costs are fixed, they will be difficult to reduce in the short run. In other words, once a company has committed to producing a new product or offering a new service, a vast majority of the costs are already incurred. If the product or service can't command the price that the company expects and costs can't be reduced, the company will end up earning less money than expected, and perhaps even losing money. If used effectively, target costing can help companies to avoid sinking money into unprofitable products or services.

Practice Questions

1. True
2. E
3. B
4. False
5. C

Unit 3.4 Practice Exercise

1.

Materials cost	$300,000
Labor cost	180,000
Add-ons	40,000
Total cost	$520,000
15% Desired markup	78,000
Quoted price	$598,000

2.

$$\frac{\$575{,}000 - x}{x} = 0.15$$

$$\$575{,}000 - x = 0.15x$$

$$\$575{,}000 = 1.15x$$

$$\frac{\$575{,}000}{1.15} = x = \$500{,}000$$

3. Gorrells and Sunn will need to reduce its cost by $20,000 to build the house. The company could use lower-quality building materials or look for cheaper subcontractors to provide labor, though such cost reductions could impact the quality of the house and the company's reputation. The builder could also work with Dr. Ellis to reduce the add-ons he has selected.

BUSINESS DECISION AND CONTEXT Wrap Up

Martin Keck now knows how to present the financial implications of the $50,000 advertising campaign and a 10% price reduction.

The advertising campaign represents a $50,000 increase in fixed expenses. Since nothing else is changing, Martin determined that Universal will need to sell at least 12,500 additional jerseys to cover the additional fixed expense ($50,000 ÷ $4 contribution margin). That's a 24% increase in sales volume just to earn the same net income that Universal earns without the extra advertising. Of course, if the campaign generates customer loyalty so that sales volume remains higher even after the advertising has been discontinued, then the company will benefit in the future.

A 10% price reduction results in a new sales price of $18 ($20 × 90%) and a new commission of $1.08 ($18 × 6%). The new contribution margin would be $2.12 ($18.00 − 14.80 − 1.08). To earn the same $207,900 contribution margin generated by the $20 price, the company would need to sell 98,067 jerseys ($207,900 ÷ $2.12), or 46,092 more jerseys than it sells now.

The worst case scenario for each of the alternatives would be no impact on current sales volume, as it is unlikely that either would reduce sales. If that were to occur, the company would lose $50,000 if it paid for the advertising campaign, but it would lose $97,713 [($4.00 − $2.12) × 51,975 jerseys] with the price reduction.

In making this decision, Martin must rely on his understanding of the industry and his company's customers. Without the numbers, however, he wouldn't know where to begin.

CHAPTER SUMMARY

In this chapter you learned some important terms and techniques that will be relevant throughout the rest of this book. Specifically, you should be able to meet the learning objectives set out at the beginning of the chapter:

1. ***Calculate the breakeven point in units and sales dollars. (Unit 3.1)***

The **breakeven point** is the level of sales at which sales revenue equals total expense and profit is $0. This point can be calculated in terms of units or sales revenue using either the profit equation or the contribution margin formula, as follows:

$$SPx - VCx - FC = 0$$

$$\frac{\text{Total fixed expenses}}{\text{Contribution margin per unit}} = \text{Breakeven point in units}$$

$$\frac{\text{Total fixed expenses}}{\text{Contribution margin ratio}} = \text{Breakeven point in sales dollars}$$

2. ***Calculate the level of activity required to meet a target income. (Unit 3.2)***

To calculate the sales level required to meet a certain level of operating income, use one of the following formulas. If you are working with a target level of *net* income, divide it by (1 minus the tax rate) to convert it to operating income before using one of the formulas.

$$SPx - VCx - FC = \text{Target OI}$$

$$\frac{\text{Total fixed expenses} + \text{Target operating income}}{\text{Contribution margin per unit}} = \text{Units required to reach target OI}$$

$$\frac{\text{Total fixed expenses} + \text{Target operating income}}{\text{Contribution margin ratio}} = \text{Sales dollars required to reach target OI}$$

3. ***Determine the effects of changes in sales price, cost, and volume on operating income. (Unit 3.2)***

Using the following equations, you should be able to solve for any unknown factors that would help in evaluating the financial impact of certain managerial decisions.

$$\text{Revenues} - \text{Expenses} = \text{Operating income}$$
$$\text{Revenues} - \text{Variable expenses} - \text{Fixed expenses} = \text{Operating income}$$
$$SPx - VCx - FC = OI$$
$$(SP - VC)x - FC = OI$$
$$CMx - FC = OI$$

Other relationships that you will find helpful in solving these problems include the contribution margin ratio (contribution margin divided by sales revenue) and the variable cost ratio (variable cost divided by sales revenue). The sum of the contribution margin ratio and the variable cost ratio is 1.

4. *Define operating leverage and explain the risks associated with the trade-off between variable and fixed costs. (Unit 3.2)*

Operating leverage indicates the change in operating income that will result from a change in sales; it is directly affected by the ratio of fixed expenses to variable expenses. The degree of operating leverage at a particular level of sales can be calculated as follows:

$$\frac{\text{Contribution margin}}{\text{Net operating income}}$$

Companies with relatively high contribution margins (meaning low variable costs) and high fixed expenses generate profits quickly once they pass the breakeven point. However, if their sales fall below the breakeven point, their losses mount quickly. To reduce the risk of covering fixed expenses, some companies prefer to carry high levels of variable costs so that expenses are incurred only as products are sold.

5. *Calculate the multiproduct breakeven point and level of activity required to meet a target income. (Unit 3.3)*

Companies that sell more than one product must consider their **sales mix** in order to solve breakeven and other problems. Holding the sales mix constant for *n* products, the breakeven point and target operating income can be calculated using the modified profit formula:

$$CM_1 + CM_2 + \ldots CM_n - \text{Fixed expenses} = \text{Operating income}$$

6. *Define markup and explain cost-plus pricing. (Unit 3.4)*

A markup is the difference between the cost of a product or service and the price a company charges for it. The markup percentage can be calculated as

$$\frac{\text{Sales price} - \text{Cost per unit}}{\text{Cost per unit}} = \text{Markup \%}$$

Cost-plus pricing begins with the cost of a product and adds a markup to determine the price to charge. The flaw in this method is that the resulting price does not reflect the value of the product to the customer. After the price has been calculated, managers must still compare it to the price of a comparable product or service. If the price is too high relative to competitors' prices, the company is unlikely to be able to sell the product.

7. *Explain target costing and calculate a target cost. (Unit 3.4)*

Target costing begins with the price a customer is willing to pay for a product or service and works backward to the maximum cost the company can incur to deliver the product or service to market. Assume, for example, that a company is considering a new product that marketing research suggests customers will pay no more than $25 for. If the company needs a 40% gross profit margin to cover its operating expenses and contribute to profit, then managers must be able to acquire or make the product for no more than $15: $25 − ($25 × 40%) = $15. If managers conclude that they can deliver the product for $15, then they should go ahead with the new venture. If they can't, then they need to halt the project before the company sinks any more funds into it.

KEY TERMS

Breakeven graph (Unit 3.1)
Breakeven point (Unit 3.1)
Cost-plus pricing (Unit 3.4)
Cost–volume–profit analysis (CVP) (Unit 3.2)
Degree of operating leverage (Unit 3.2)
Margin of safety (Unit 3.1)
Markup (Unit 3.4)
Operating leverage (Unit 3.2)
Sales mix (Unit 3.3)
Target costing (Unit 3.4)

EXERCISES

3-1 Breakeven analysis (LO 1) Lasley Cash, Ltd. operates a chain of exclusive ski hat boutiques in the western United States. The stores purchase several hat styles from a single distributor at $12 each. All other costs incurred by the company are fixed. Lasley Cash, Ltd. sells the hats for $25 each.

Required

a. If fixed costs total $130,000 per year, what is the breakeven point in units? In sales dollars?
b. What is Lasley Cash's contribution margin ratio? Its variable cost ratio?
c. Assume that Lasley Cash, Ltd. currently operates at a loss. What actions could managers take to lower the breakeven point and begin earning a profit?

3-2 Breakeven analysis (LO 1) Scott Confectionery sells its Stack-o-Choc candy bar for $0.80. The variable cost per unit for the candy bar is $0.45; total fixed costs are $175,000.

Required

a. What is the contribution margin per unit for the Stack-o-Choc candy bar?
b. What is the contribution margin ratio for the Stack-o-Choc candy bar?
c. What is the breakeven point in units? In sales dollars?
d. If an increase in chocolate prices causes the variable cost per unit to increase to $0.55, what will happen to the breakeven point?

3-3 Breakeven analysis (LO 1) Julianna Abdallah owns and operates FirstCakes, a bakery that creates personalized birthday cakes for a child's first birthday. The cakes, which sell for $40 and feature an edible picture of the child, are shipped throughout the country. A typical month's results are as follows:

Sales revenue	$840,000
Variable expenses	630,000
Contribution margin	210,000
Fixed expenses	112,000
Operating income	$ 98,000

Required

a. What is FirstCakes' contribution margin per unit?
b. What is FirstCakes' monthly breakeven point in units?
c. What is FirstCakes' contribution margin ratio?
d. What is FirstCakes' monthly breakeven point in sales dollars?

3-4 Target net income (LO 2) Delectable Dish Printery publishes the best-selling *Captain Cajun Cookbook* that sells for $8. The company incurs variable costs of $3 per cookbook and total fixed costs are $300,000.

Required

If the company's tax rate is 25%, how many cookbooks must be sold to generate $180,000 in net income?

3-5 Target operating income (LO 2) Three years ago, Marissa Moore started a business that creates and delivers holiday and birthday gift baskets to students at the local university. Marissa sells the baskets for $25 each, and her variable costs are $15 per basket. She incurs $12,000 in fixed costs each year.

Required

a. How many baskets will Marissa have to sell this year if she wants to earn $30,000 in operating income?
b. Last year, Marissa sold 4,000 baskets, and she believes that demand this year will be stable at 4,000 baskets. What actions could Marissa take if she wants to earn $30,000 in operating income by selling only 4,000 baskets? Be specific.

3-6 Target net income (LO 2) Manzoni Machine Works produces soft serve ice cream freezers. The freezers sell for $18,000, and variable costs total $12,300 per unit. Manzoni incurs $3,500,000 in fixed costs during the year. The company's tax rate is 25%.

Required

How many freezers must Manzoni sell to generate net income of $7,635,000?

3-7 Target income (LO 2) Refer to Exercise 3-3.

Required

a. How many cakes will Julianna Abdallah have to sell if she wants to earn $150,000 in operating income each month?
b. Assuming a 30% tax rate, how many cakes will Julianna Abdallah have to sell if she wants to earn $115,150 in net income each month?

3-8 Breakeven analysis; target income (LO 1, 2) Reid Recreation Products sells the Amazing Foam Frisbee for $12. The variable cost per unit is $3; fixed costs are $36,000 per month.

Required

a. What is the annual breakeven point in units? In sales dollars?
b. How many frisbees must Reid sell to earn $18,000 in operating income?
c. What operating income must Reid earn to realize net income of $16,200, assuming that the company is in the 40% tax bracket?
d. How many frisbees must Reid sell to earn $16,200 in net income?

3-9 Breakeven analysis; target income (LO 1, 2) Josh Ward is a young entrepreneur preparing to start a company that will sell floating lounge chairs for use in private pools. As part of a loan package, the bank has asked him to prepare a business plan that includes a breakeven analysis. The lounge chairs will sell for $64 each and variable costs per unit are expected to be $24. Josh anticipates incurring $600,000 in fixed costs per year.

Required

a. What is the expected contribution margin per lounge chair?
b. Based on his projections, how many lounge chairs must Josh sell to break even?
c. If Josh wants to generate annual operating income of $54,000, how many lounge chairs must he sell?
d. Assuming the company's tax rate is 25%, how many lounge chairs must the company sell to generate annual net income of $64,500?

3-10 CVP analysis (LO 3) MathTot sells a learning system that helps preschool and elementary students learn basic math facts and concepts. The company's income statement from last month is as follows:

	Total	Per Unit
Sales revenue	$600,000	$50.00
Variable expenses	210,000	17.50
Contribution margin	390,000	$32.50
Fixed expenses	292,500	
Operating income	$ 97,500	

Required

a. What is MathTot's contribution margin ratio? Its variable cost ratio?
b. What is MathTot's margin of safety?
c. If MathTot's sales were to increase by $100,000 with no change in fixed expenses, by how much would operating income increase?
d. MathTot's managers have determined that variable costs per unit will increase by 16% beginning next month. To offset this increase in costs, they are considering a 10% increase in the sales price. Market research indicates that the price increase will result in a 2% decrease in the number of learning systems MathTot sells. What will be MathTot's expected operating income if the price increase is implemented?

3-11 CVP analysis (LO 3) Carr Orthotics Company distributes a specialized ankle support that sells for $30. The company's variable costs are $18 per unit; fixed costs total $360,000 each year.

Required

a. If sales increase by $39,000 per year, by how much should operating income increase?
b. Last year, Carr sold 32,000 ankle supports. The company's marketing manager is convinced that a 10% reduction in the sales price, combined with a $50,000 increase in advertising, will result in a 25% increase in sales volume over last year. Should Carr implement the price reduction? Why or why not?

3-12 Multiple-choice questions covering various topics; consider each scenario independently (LO 1, 3)

a. James Shaw owns several shaved ice stands that operate in the summer along the Outer Banks of North Carolina. His contribution margin ratio is 60%. If James increases his sales revenue by $25,000 without any increase in fixed costs, by how much will his operating income increase? (a) $25,000; (b) $15,000; (c) $10,000; (d) $5,000.
b. Which of these events will decrease a company's breakeven point? (a) decrease in units sold; (b) increase in direct labor costs; (c) increase in sales price; (d) both (a) and (b).
c. Halloween, Inc. reported the following income statement data for February: Sales $150,000; Total costs $170,000; Loss ($ 20,000). The firm's contribution margin percentage at its current selling price of $20 is 40%. What is the company's total fixed cost? (a) $20,000; (b) $90,000; (c) $60,000; (d) $80,000.
d. Refer to the information in part (c). What would be the change in income if the company paid $6,000 for a special advertising campaign and increased sales by 1,000 units, at

$20 per unit? (a) $2,000 increase; (b) $14,000 increase; (c) $4,000 decrease; (d) $6,000 decrease.

e. A company's selling price is $50; its contribution margin ratio, 32%; its fixed costs, $200,000; and its income, $20,000. What is the company's breakeven point in units? (a) 11,250; (b) 13,750; (c) 12,500; (d) cannot be determined.

3-13 Breakeven analysis; CVP analysis (LO 1, 3) Matoaka Monograms sells stadium blankets that have been monogrammed with high school and university emblems. The blankets retail for $50 throughout the country to loyal alumni of over 1,000 schools. Matoaka's variable costs are 40% of sales; fixed costs are $120,000 per month.

Required

a. What is Matoaka's annual breakeven point in sales dollars?
b. Matoaka currently sells 100,000 blankets per year. If sales volume were to increase by 15%, by how much would operating income increase?
c. Assume that variable costs increase to 45% of the current sales price and fixed costs increase by $10,000 per month. If Matoaka were to raise its sales price by 10% to cover these new costs, what would be the new annual breakeven point in sales dollars?
d. Assume that variable costs increase to 45% of the current sales price and fixed costs increase by $10,000 per month. If Matoaka were to raise its sales price 10% to cover these new costs, but the number of blankets sold were to drop by 5%, what would be the new annual operating income?
e. If variable costs and fixed costs were to change as in part (d), would Matoaka be better off raising its selling price and losing volume or keeping the selling price at $50 and selling 100,000 blankets? Why?

3-14 Breakeven analysis; target operating income; CVP graph (LO 1, 2, 3) Wimpee's Hamburger Stand sells the Super Tuesday Burger for $4.00. The variable cost per hamburger is $2.25; total fixed cost per month is $38,500.

Required

a. How many hamburgers must Wimpee's sell per month to break even?
b. How many hamburgers must Wimpee's sell per month to make $10,500 in operating income?
c. Prepare a CVP graph for Wimpee's.
d. Assuming that the most hamburgers Wimpee's has ever sold in a month is 24,000, how likely is Wimpee's to achieve a target operating income of $10,500? What actions could Wimpee's manager take to increase the chances of reaching that target operating income?

3-15 Operating leverage (LO 4) Hogue Sports Hut provides individual instruction and coaching to children participating in the city's baseball, softball, basketball, and soccer youth leagues. Last year's results were as follows:

Sales revenue	$950,000
Variable expenses	646,000
Contribution margin	304,000
Fixed expenses	182,400
Operating income	$121,600

Required

a. What is Hogue Sports Hut's degree of operating leverage?
b. If Anna Hogue, the company's president, is successful in increasing sales revenue by 8%, by what percent will the company's operating income increase?
c. After achieving the sales increase in part (b), what will be the company's new operating income?
d. After achieving the sales increase in part (b), what will be the company's new operating leverage?

3-16 Operating leverage (LO 4) Mary Smith sells gourmet chocolate chip cookies. The results of her last month of operations are as follows:

Sales revenue	$50,000
Cost of goods sold (all variable)	26,000
Gross margin	24,000
Selling expenses (20% variable)	8,000
Administrative expenses (60% variable)	12,000
Operating income	$ 4,000

Required

a. What is Mary's degree of operating leverage?
b. If Mary can increase sales by 10%, by how much will her operating income increase?

3-17 Conceptual breakeven; margin of safety; operating leverage (LO 1, 4) On March 1, 2004, Seagram Co. CEO Edgar Bronfman, Jr., purchased Warner Music Group for $2.6 billion. The next day he fired 1,000 salaried employees and reduced top executives' salaries, slashing overhead costs by more than $250 million.

Required

a. What effect would these cuts have on Warner's breakeven point? Explain.
b. What effect would these cuts have on Warner's margin of safety? Explain.
c. What effect would these cuts have on Warner's degree of operating leverage? Explain.

3-18 Multiproduct breakeven point (LO 5) Amazon.com announced in a May 19, 2011, news release that the company was selling more Kindle books than traditional print books. From their first sales in November 2007, these ebooks have continued to grow in popularity, and by the beginning of 2011 had overtaken paperback books as the most popular book format on the site. At April 1, 2011, the company was selling 105 Kindle books for every 100 print books.

Required

a. What is Amazon.com's sales mix of Kindle ebooks to print books?
b. How do you think the contribution margin of a Kindle ebook compares to the contribution margin of a print book?
c. As Amazon.com's sales mix approaches the 2 to 1 sales mix of Kindle ebooks to print books at Amazon.co.uk, what will likely happen to the breakeven point?

3-19 Multiproduct breakeven point (LO 5) Andrew Sinclair operates a lawn care business. He offers customers a choice of two services. The first service, basic lawn care, includes mowing and trimming of all lawn areas. Andrew bills these customers $30 per hour, and his variable cost for providing this service is $22 per hour. Andrew also offers deluxe lawn care services, which includes flower bed maintenance in addition to basic lawn care. He bills his customers $60 per hour for this service, and his variable cost for providing this service is $28 per hour. Andrew currently spends 1 hour of his time providing deluxe lawn care services for every 4 hours of basic lawn care services. Andrew also incurs $140,800 in fixed costs per year running his business.

Required

a. What is Andrew's profit equation?
b. How many hours of each service type must Andrew provide in a year to break even?
c. Andrew believes that with a little persuasion, he could convert many of his basic lawn care customers to the deluxe service. If he is able to convert enough customers so that he spends an equal amount of time providing basic and deluxe services, how many hours will he need to work to break even?

3-20 Breakeven analysis; multiproduct CVP analysis (LO 1, 5) Abado Profiles provides testing services to school districts that wish to assess students' reading and mathematical abilities. Last year Abado evaluated 60,000 math tests and 20,000 reading tests. An income statement for last year follows.

	Math Testing		Reading Testing		
	Total	Per Unit	Total	Per Unit	Total Company
Sales revenue	$1,200,000	$20	$720,000	$36	$1,920,000
Variable expenses	840,000	14	360,000	18	1,200,000
Contribution margin	$ 360,000	$ 6	$360,000	$18	720,000
Fixed expenses					360,000
Operating income					$ 360,000

Required

a. What is Abado's breakeven point in sales dollars?

b. In an effort to raise the demand for reading tests, managers are planning to lower the price from $36 per test to $20 per test, the current price of the math test. They believe that doing so will increase the demand for reading tests to 60,000. Prepare a contribution format income statement reflecting Abado's new pricing and demand structure.

c. What will be Abado's breakeven point in sales dollars if this change is implemented? Do you recommend that Abado make the change?

3-21 Breakeven analysis; multiproduct CVP analysis (LO 1, 5) Kitchenware, Inc., sells two types of water pitchers, plastic and glass. Plastic pitchers cost the company $15 and are sold for $30. Glass pitchers cost $24 and are sold for $45. All other costs are fixed at $982,800 per year. Current sales plans call for 14,000 plastic pitchers and 42,000 glass pitchers to be sold in the coming year.

Required

a. How many pitchers of each type must be sold to break even in the coming year?

b. Kitchenware, Inc., has just received a sales catalog from a new supplier that is offering plastic pitchers for $13. What would be the new breakeven point if managers switched to the new supplier?

3-22 Markups; cost-plus pricing (LO 6) Payton Sanchez runs a popcorn stand in the local amusement park. Her cost to produce a bag of popcorn is $0.40, which she sells for $2.00.

Required

a. What is Payton's markup percentage on a bag of popcorn?

b. If Payton wants to earn a 500% markup on a bag of popcorn, what price must she charge?

c. If Payton lowers her price per bag to $1.50, what markup percentage will she earn on a bag of popcorn?

3-23 Markups; cost-plus pricing (LO6) On April 24, 2015, Apple entered the wearable technology market with the release of its Apple Watch. A May 1, 2015, article published in *The Wall Street Journal* estimated that the cost of materials and labor required to produce the watch totaled $83.70. The Apple Watch's retail price is $349.

Required

a. What percentage of the retail price is accounted for by the cost of materials and labor?

b. What is the markup dollar amount on the watch?

c. What is the markup percentage on the watch?

d. Estimates for the iPad mini 2 place materials and labor cost at 45% of the retail price. If Apple had wanted to maintain that same relationship between materials and labor cost and retail price for the Apple Watch, what price would Apple have set for the watch? What markup percentage would have yielded this price?

e. Why do you think Apple chose to use a higher markup percentage for the Apple Watch than for the iPad mini 2?

3-24 Markups; cost-plus pricing (LO 6) According to a March 3, 2012, EETimes.com article, Apple enjoyed a 56% gross margin on its iPad 2 when it was first released in March 2011.

Required

a. Given that the iPad 2 sold for $629, what was the cost to make it, assuming the 56% gross margin?
b. In March 2012, the second year of production, the cost of producing an iPad 2 fell to an estimated $248.07. What markup percentage would Apple need to use to maintain its $629 sales price?
c. If Apple had maintained the iPad's 56% gross margin after the cost decrease, what sales price would it have put on the iPad?
d. In March 2012, Apple announced the upcoming release of an iPad 4G that would be sold for $629. If the estimated cost to produce the new iPad 4G was $310, what markup percentage was Apple apparently willing to accept for the new iPad?

3-25 Markups; cost-plus pricing (LO 6) The following is Talley Company's income statement for the past year.

Sales revenue	$540,000
Cost of goods sold	324,000
Gross margin	216,000
Operating expenses	126,000
Operating income	$ 90,000

Required

a. What is the markup percentage on cost of goods sold?
b. What is the markup percentage on total cost?
c. What is the gross margin percentage?
d. If the company wants to sell a new product that costs $42 wholesale while keeping the same markup structure, what will be the price of the new product?

3-26 Target costing (LO 7) Justin Allen, a product engineer for L'Oso Gaming, is designing a new electronic game. Market research indicates that gamers will pay $36 for the game.

Required

a. If L'Oso desires a 60% markup on production costs, what is the target cost for the new game?
b. Justin believes it will cost $24 per unit to produce the new game. What actions should he take next?

3-27 Cost-plus pricing; target costing (LO 6, 7) Pet Designs makes various accessories for pets. Their trademark product, PetBed, is perceived to be high quality but not extravagant, and is sold in a variety of pet stores. Wanda Foster, marketing manager, has convinced her boss that they are missing an important segment of the market. "We can increase the quality of the material and design and market PetBed to a higher-end clientele," Wanda claims. "We won't compete with our existing product. It's win-win!"

PetBeds sell for $45 each. Wanda estimates the gross margin at $15. After working with production engineers and the marketing research team, Wanda has designed a bed that she believes the new market segment will pay $78 for. The production engineers and accountants believe it will cost about $58 to make.

Required

a. If Pet Designs uses cost-plus pricing and prices most products like the original PetBed, what should be the price of the high-end PetBed?
b. If Pet Designs wants to preserve the existing gross margin percentage, what is the target cost at a market price of $78?
c. Based on your answers to (a) and (b), what are Pet Designs' alternatives?

PROBLEMS

3-28 Breakeven analysis; margin of safety (LO 1) The Stafford Company sells sports decals that can be personalized with a player's name, a team name, and a jersey number for \$6 each. Stafford buys the decals from a supplier for \$2.50 each and spends an additional \$0.50 in variable operating costs per decal. The results of last month's operations are as follows:

Sales revenue	\$18,000
Cost of goods sold	7,500
Gross profit	10,500
Operating expenses	3,990
Operating income	\$ 6,510

Required

a. What is Stafford's monthly breakeven point in units? In dollars?
b. What is Stafford's margin of safety?

3-29 Breakeven analysis; target income (LO 1, 2) Briggs Herrera, president of Retro Recreation Products, Inc., is concerned about declines that he is beginning to see in the demand for the company's line of old school logo basketballs as new competitors enter the market. At a current contribution margin of \$8, the company must sell 81,250 basketballs to generate the desired \$200,000 in annual operating income. Based on a recent market research report, Briggs thinks the company can expect annual sales of only 65,000 basketballs in the future.

Required

a. What is Briggs's current level of fixed expenses?
b. What is Briggs's current breakeven point?
c. If Briggs wants to maintain the current level of operating income in the future while selling only 65,000 basketballs, what contribution margin must the basketballs generate?
d. What action(s) could Briggs take to achieve this new contribution margin?
e. If Briggs wants to earn \$175,000 in annual net income, how many basketballs must he sell? Assume a 30% tax rate.

3-30 CVP analysis (LO 3) CB Markets imports and sells small bear-shaped piñatas. In planning for the coming year, the company's owner is evaluating several scenarios. For each scenario under consideration, prepare a contribution margin income statement showing the anticipated operating income. Consider each scenario independently. Last year's income statement is as follows:

	Total	Per Unit
Sales revenue	\$600,000	\$12.00
Variable expenses	350,000	7.00
Contribution margin	250,000	\$ 5.00
Fixed expenses	175,000	
Operating income	\$ 75,000	

Required

a. The sales price increases by 10% and sales volume decreases by 5%.
b. The sales price increases by 10% and variable cost per unit increases by 5%.
c. The sales price decreases by 10% and sales volume increases by 20%.

d. Fixed expenses increase by $20,000.
e. The sales price increases by 10%, variable cost per unit increases by 10%, fixed expenses increase by $25,000, and sales volume decreases by 10%.

3-31 CVP analysis (LO 3) JenSteel, Inc., had the following results for last year:

	Total	Per Unit
Sales revenue	$2,000,000	$40.00
Variable expenses	1,250,000	25.00
Contribution margin	750,000	$15.00
Fixed expenses	400,000	
Operating income	$ 350,000	

Prepare a new income statement for each of the following scenarios. Consider each scenario independently.

Required

a. Sales volume increases by 10%.
b. The sales price decreases by 5%.
c. Variable costs per unit decrease by $1.50.
d. The sales price decreases to $38, and an additional 6,000 units are sold.
e. A new advertising campaign costing $90,000 increases sales volume by 10%.
f. Variable costs per unit increase by $3.00, the sales price per unit increases by $4.00, sales volume decreases by 2,000 units, and fixed expenses increase by $15,000.

3-32 Breakeven; CVP analysis (LO 1, 3) W Promotions sells T-shirts imprinted with high school names and logos. Last year the shirts sold for $18 each, and variable costs were $5.40 per shirt. At this cost structure, the breakeven point was 20,000 shirts. However, the company actually earned $15,120 in net income.

This year, the company is increasing its price to $21 per shirt. Variable costs per shirt will increase by one-third, and fixed expenses will increase by $30,900. The tax rate will remain at 40%.

Required

a. Prepare a contribution format income statement for last year.
b. How many T-shirts must the company sell this year to break even?
c. How many T-shirts must the company sell this year in order to earn $28,980 in net income?

3-33 Breakeven; target income; CVP analysis (LO 1, 2, 3) Adam Granger operates a kiosk in downtown Chicago, at which he sells one style of baseball hat. He buys the hats from a supplier for $14 and sells them for $20. Adam's current breakeven point is 15,000 hats per year.

Required

a. What is Adam's current level of fixed costs?
b. Assume that Adam's fixed costs, variable costs, and sales price were the same last year, when he made $21,000 in net income. How many hats did Adam sell last year, assuming a 30% income tax rate?
c. What was Adam's margin of safety last year?
d. If Adam wants to earn $37,800 in net income, how many hats must he sell?
e. How many hats must Adam sell to break even if his supplier raises the price of the hats to $15 per hat?
f. What actions should Adam consider in response to his supplier's price increase?
g. Adam has decided to increase his sales price to $21 to offset the supplier's price increase. He believes that the increase will result in a 5% reduction from last year's sales volume. What is Adam's expected net income?

3-34 Breakeven analysis; target income; CVP analysis (CMA adapted) (LO 1, 2, 3) Delphi Company has developed a new product that will be marketed for the first time next year. The product will have variable costs of $16 per unit. Although the marketing department estimates that 35,000 units could be sold at $36 per unit, Delphi's management has allocated only enough manufacturing capacity to produce a maximum of 25,000 units a year. The fixed costs associated with the new product are budgeted at $450,000 for the year. Delphi is subject to a 40% tax rate.

Required

a. How many units of the new product must Delphi sell in the next fiscal year to break even?
b. What is the maximum net income that Delphi can earn from sales of the new product in the next fiscal year?
c. Delphi's managers have stipulated that they will not authorize production beyond the next fiscal year unless the after-tax profit from the new product is at least $75,000. How many units of the new product must be sold in the next fiscal year to ensure continued production?
d. Regardless of your answer in part (c), assume that more than the allowed production of 25,000 units will be required to meet the $75,000 net income target. Given the production constraint (maximum of 25,000 units available), what price must be charged to meet the target income and continue production past the next fiscal year?
e. Assume that the marketing manager thinks the price you calculated in part (d) is too high. What actions could the project manager take to help ensure production of the new product past the current fiscal year?

3-35 Target income; CVP analysis (CMA adapted) (LO 2, 3) Kipmar Company produces a molded briefcase that is distributed to luggage stores. The following operating data for the current year has been accumulated for planning purposes.

Sales price	$ 40.00
Variable cost of goods sold	12.00
Variable selling expenses	10.60
Variable administrative expenses	3.00
Annual fixed expenses	
Overhead	$7,800,000
Selling expenses	1,550,000
Administrative expenses	3,250,000

Kipmar can produce 1.5 million cases a year. The projected net income for the coming year is expected to be $1.8 million. Kipmar is subject to a 40% income tax rate.

During the planning sessions, Kipmar's managers have been reviewing costs and expenses. They estimate that the company's variable cost of goods sold will increase 15% in the coming year and that fixed administrative expenses will increase by $150,000. All other costs and expenses are expected to remain the same.

Required

a. What amount of sales revenue will Kipmar need to achieve in the coming year to earn the projected net income of $1.8 million?
b. What price would Kipmar need to charge for the briefcase in the coming year to maintain the current year's contribution margin ratio?

3-36 Operating leverage (LO 4) Picasso's Pantry is a chain of arts and crafts stores. Results for the most recent year are as follows:

Sales revenue		$9,000,000
Variable expenses	$5,000,000	
Fixed expenses	2,000,000	
Total expenses		7,000,000
Operating income		$2,000,000

Required

a. What is Picasso's Pantry's degree of operating leverage?
b. If sales increase by 5%, what will the new operating income be?
c. Managers are considering changing Picasso's cost structure by offering employees a commission on sales rather than a fixed salary. What effect would such a change have on the firm's operating leverage?

3-37 Sales mix (LO 5) Under Armour, a company that wants to "empower athletes everywhere," started out to produce a superior T-shirt that would help regulate an athlete's body temperature during workouts. The company has expanded its product line well beyond T-shirts, now providing athletes with a wide range of workout wear, footwear, and accessories. The following chart shows the company's sales mix for 2010 and 2015.

	2010	2015
Apparel	83%	73%
Footwear	12%	18%
Accessories	4%	9%

Required

a. Discuss the effect that the change in sales mix might have had on Under Armour's breakeven point and operating income.
b. Assume that apparel has a higher contribution margin ratio than accessories. Was the decrease in the percentage of sales provided by apparel a desirable outcome in 2015?
c. Within the apparel line, do you think all products have the same contribution margin? Why or why not?

3-38 Breakeven analysis; multiproduct CVP analysis (CMA adapted) (LO 1, 5) Return to Problem 3-35. Kipmar Company's managers are considering expanding the product line by introducing a leather briefcase. The new briefcase is expected to sell for $90; variable costs would amount to $36 per briefcase. If Kipmar introduces the leather briefcase, the company will incur an additional $300,000 per year in advertising costs. Kipmar's marketing department has estimated that one new leather briefcase would be sold for every four molded briefcases.

Required

a. If managers decide to introduce the new leather briefcase, given the cost changes on the molded briefcase presented in Problem 3-35, how many units of each briefcase would be required to break even in the coming year? Cost of goods sold for the molded briefcase is expected to be $13.80 per unit.
b. After additional research, Kipmar's marketing manager believes that if the price of the new leather briefcase drops to $66, it will be more attractive to potential customers. She also believes that at that price, the additional advertising cost could be cut to $177,600. These changes would result in sales of one molded briefcase for every three leather briefcases. Based on these circumstances, how many units of each briefcase would be required to break even in the coming year?
c. What additional factors should Kipmar's managers consider before deciding to introduce the new leather briefcase?

3-39 Breakeven analysis; multiproduct CVP analysis (LO 1, 5) Herzog Industries sells two electrical components with the following characteristics. Fixed costs for the company are $200,000 per year.

	XL-709	CD-918
Sales price	$10.00	$25.00
Variable cost	6.00	17.00
Sales volume	40,000 units	60,000 units

Required

a. How many units of each product must Herzog Industries sell in order to break even?
b. Herzog's vice president of sales has determined that due to market changes, the sales price of component XL-709 can be increased to $14.00 with no impact on sales volume. What will be Herzog's new breakeven point in units?
c. Returning to the original information, Herzog's vice president of marketing believes that spending $60,000 on a new advertising campaign will increase sales of component CD-918 to 80,000 units without affecting the sales of product XL-709. How many units of each product must Herzog sell to break even under this new scenario?
d. The market changes referred to in part (b) indicate additional overall demand for component XL-709. Herzog's vice president of marketing believes that if the company spends $60,000 to advertise component XL-709 rather than CD-918, as planned in part (c), the company will be able to sell a total of 50,000 units of XL-709 at the new price of $14.00. If the company must choose to advertise only one component, which component should receive the additional $60,000 in advertising?

3-40 General pricing; markups (LO 6) Taylor Pennington produces and sells hammocks. One day during lunch he complained to his friend Steven Green, an economist, that he was having trouble setting prices. When he raised his prices, demand went down as expected, but he could never predict how much demand would change. "I understand my costs quite well," Taylor commented. "I can produce hammocks for $60 each, and I incur $350,000 in fixed costs each year. I think I could manage my business much better if I had a better idea of the demand for hammocks at different prices." Steve said he would take a look at several years' worth of sales data and try to estimate a demand curve for the hammocks. He came up with the following table:

Sales Price	Demand	Sales Price	Demand
$200	40,657	$140	69,768
$190	44,486	$130	76,338
$180	48,675	$120	83,527
$170	53,259	$110	91,393
$160	58,275	$100	100,000
$150	63,763		

Required

a. What price can be expected to result in the highest operating income?
b. What is the markup on variable cost at the price you selected in part (a)?
c. What is the markup on variable cost when the sales price is $200? $100?
d. What can you conclude about the value of cost-plus pricing compared to pricing based on a demand schedule?

3-41 Cost-plus pricing; target costing (LO 6, 7) Gail Sawyer has just started a new catering business in Dallas, Texas. Instead of establishing a fixed menu, she has decided to make whatever the customer wants until she knows how well different dishes will be received. Gail has been invited to bid on the rehearsal dinner for the wedding of the mayor's son. If she wins the bid and gets the job, some of the most prominent people in Dallas will taste her food. She can't get better advertising than that!

The mayor has decided on a menu of peanut soup, baby field greens salad with fresh mozzarella, grilled salmon, bacon-wrapped filet mignon, baby asparagus with hollandaise sauce, and white chocolate creme brulée. Gail estimates that the selected menu will require $35 of food per person. She has been quoting prices based on a 75% markup on food cost.

Required

a. What is the minimum price per person that Gail should quote for the job?
b. What price would Gail need to charge to achieve her desired 75% markup?

c. Assume the mayor has already received a bid of $56 per person and has told Gail that he will not pay more than that. If Gail agreed to a price of $56 per person for the desired menu, what markup would she realize?
d. If Gail met the lower price and took the job, what might be some potential consequences, both good and bad?

C&C SPORTS CONTINUING CASE

3-42 CVP analysis (LO 3) Universal Sports Exchange has just received notice from C&C Sports that the price of a baseball jersey will be increasing to $15.30 next year. In response to this increase, Universal is planning its sales and marketing campaign for the coming year. Managers have developed two possible plans and have asked you to evaluate them.

The first plan calls for passing on the entire $0.50 cost increase to customers through an increase in the sales price. Managers believe that $10,000 in additional advertising targeted directly to current customers will allow the sales force to reach the current year's sales volume of 51,975 jerseys.

The second plan relies on a new advertising campaign that focuses on the sales price remaining the same as last year. The campaign would include a new database that offers more potential customers than Universal has had access to in the past. The cost of the campaign is expected to be $5,000. Managers believe that the campaign will be more successful in generating new sales than the current incentive-based sales and marketing plan. As a result, they want to reduce the sales commission from 6% to 4% of sales and increase sales salaries by $22,000. The campaign is expected to generate an additional 10% in sales volume.

Using the information in Exhibit 3-1 as a starting point, answer the following questions.

Required

a. How much would operating income decrease if Universal did nothing to recover the increase in cost of goods sold, all other things equal?
b. Determine the expected operating income under each proposed sales and marketing plan.
c. Why does the first plan result in a reduction in operating income that is greater than the $10,000 advertising?
d. Which plan do you recommend to management? Why?

CASES

3-43 Operating leverage (LO 4) In 1999, Blue Nile, Inc. began selling diamonds and other fine jewelry over the Internet. Using an online retailing model, Blue Nile prices its diamonds at an average of 35% less than traditional brick-and-mortar jewelers. In fewer than five years, the company had become the eighth-largest specialty jeweler in the United States. On May 20, 2004, Blue Nile went public with an initial stock offering priced at $20.50 per share. By the end of the day, shares were trading at $28.40. Before the end of the month, the share price had doubled, before closing at month's end in the mid-$30s.

While traditional jewelers operate with gross margins of up to 50%, Blue Nile's gross margin percentage for the year ended January 4, 2015 was just 18.3%. Yet the company remains competitive despite its lower gross margin. As of January 4, 2015, Blue Nile employed 288 full-time and 13 part-time employees. It leased its 40,000-square-foot corporate headquarters in Seattle, Washington, as well as an additional 27,000-square-foot fulfillment center in the United States, a 10,000-square-foot fulfillment center in Dublin, Ireland, and 3,400 square feet of space in Shanghai, China.

Compared to Blue Nile, Tiffany & Co., one of the world's best-known in-store jewelers, is a giant. Tiffany & Co. opened its doors in New York City in 1837 and has since grown into an international operation. Regarded as one of the world's premier jewelers, the company went public in 1987 at $1.92 per share and closed that day at $1.93 per share. A month later it was trading at $1.90 per share. Seventeen years later, on the day Blue Nile went public, Tiffany & Co. closed at $33.90 per share.

As of January 31, 2015, Tiffany & Co. employed approximately 12,000 people. The company owns a 124,000-square-foot headquarters building on Fifth Avenue in New York City, 45,500 square feet of which is devoted to a retail storefront. The company has 173 other stores in the United States and 200 more abroad. The average operating profit as a percentage of sales for the retail jewelry industry is 5%.

Selected income statement information for the two companies is as follows.

	Blue Nile, Inc. Year Ended 1/4/2015		Tiffany & Co. Year Ended 1/31/15	
	$ in 000s	% of sales	$ in 000s	% of sales
Net sales revenue	$473,516	100.0%	$4,249,913	100.0%
Cost of goods sold	386,874	81.7%	1,712,738	40.3%
Gross margin	86,642	18.3%	2,537,175	59.7%
Operating expenses	72,430	15.3%	1,645,746	38.7%
Operating income	$ 14,212	3.0%	$ 891,429	21.0%

Required

a. How do Tiffany's fixed costs compare to those of Blue Nile, Inc.?

b. How can Blue Nile, Inc. remain competitive with its 18.3% gross margin percentage when Tiffany & Co. earns a 59.7% gross margin?

c. Which company do you believe has the greater operating leverage? Why?

d. In Tiffany & Co.'s 2014 Annual Report, management stated that gross margin had "increased as a result of a favorable shift in product sales mix toward the higher-margin fashion jewelry category." How would this shift have affected the company's contribution margin?

e. On April 22, 2004, Amazon.com launched its online jewelry store. Which company's cost structure do you think it resembles, Blue Nile's or Tiffany's? Why?

3-44 Comprehensive CVP analysis (LO 1, 2, 3, 5) "I'll never understand this accounting stuff," Blake Dunn yelled, waving the income statement he had just received from his accountant in the morning mail. "Last month, we sold 1,000 stuffed State University mascots and earned $6,850 in operating income. This month, when we sold 1,500, I thought we'd make $10,275. But this income statement shows an operating income of $12,100! How can I ever make plans if I can't predict my income? I'm going to give Janice one last chance to explain this to me," he declared as he picked up the phone to call Janice Miller, his accountant.

"Will you try to explain this operating income thing to me one more time?" Blake asked Janice. "After I saw last month's income statement, I thought each mascot we sold generated $6.85 in net income; now this month, each one generates $8.07! There was no change in the price we paid for each mascot, so I don't understand how this happened. If I had known I was going to have $12,100 in operating income, I would have looked more seriously at adding to our product line."

Taking a deep breath, Janice replied, "Sure, Blake. I'd be happy to explain how you made so much more operating income than you were expecting."

Required

a. Assume Janice's role. Explain to Blake why his use of operating income per mascot was in error.

b. Using the following income statements, prepare a contribution margin income statement for March.

	February	March
Sales revenue	$25,000	$37,500
Cost of goods sold	10,000	15,000
Gross profit	15,000	22,500
Rent expense	1,500	1,500
Wages expense	3,500	5,000
Shipping expense	1,250	1,875
Utilities expense	750	750
Advertising expense	750	875
Insurance expense	400	400
Operating income	$ 6,850	$12,100

c. Blake plans to sell 500 stuffed mascots next month. How much operating income can Blake expect to earn next month if he realizes his planned sales?

d. Blake wasn't happy with the projected income statement you showed him for a sales level of 500 stuffed mascots. He wants to know how many stuffed mascots he will need to sell to earn $3,700 in operating income. As a safety net, he also wants to know how many stuffed mascots he will need to sell to break even.

e. Blake is evaluating two options to increase the number of mascots sold next month. First, he believes he can increase sales by advertising in the university newspaper. Blake can purchase a package of 12 ads over the next month for a total of $1,200. He believes the ads will increase the number of stuffed mascots sold from 500 to 960. A second option would be to reduce the selling price. Blake believes a 10% decrease in the price will result in 1,000 mascots sold. Which plan should Blake implement? At what level of sales would he be indifferent between the two plans?

f. Just after Blake completed an income projection for 1,200 stuffed mascots, his supplier called to inform him of a 20% increase in cost of goods sold, effective immediately. Blake knows that he cannot pass the entire increase on to his customers, but thinks he can pass on half of the 20% increase while suffering only a 5% decrease in units sold. Should Blake respond to the increase in cost of goods sold with an increase in price?

g. Refer back to the original information. Blake has decided to add stadium blankets to his product line. He has found a supplier who will provide the blankets for $32, and he plans to sell them for $55. All other variable costs currently incurred for selling mascots will be incurred for selling blankets at the same rate. Additional fixed costs of $350 per month will be incurred. He believes he can sell one blanket for every three stuffed mascots. How many blankets and stuffed mascots will Blake need to sell each month in order to break even?

3-45 Ethics and CVP analysis (LO 3) At 3:00 P.M. on Friday afternoon, Dan Murphy, vice president of distribution, rushed into Grace Jones's office exclaiming, "This is the fourth week in a row we've filed a record number of claims against our freight carriers for products damaged in shipment. How can they all be that careless? At this rate, we'll have filed over $150,000 in claims this year to replace damaged goods. Some of the freight carriers claim we're their worst customer. Sure, we give them lots of business, but we've got the highest claims level."

"That's interesting," replied Grace, the company's CFO. "Last week Jeff and I were talking about the great cartons he just purchased for shipping our products. In fact, he had to get special permission to enter into a long-term contract with the company, so that it would provide us with the cartons at a reduced price. He prepared a great proposal outlining the increase in income we could expect based on the number of cartons we use per period and the cost savings per carton. His proposal for tying us into a long-term contract was accepted because he specifically addressed the need to maintain the quality that our customers have come to expect while at the same time improving the bottom line. If anything, I would have thought our claims would have been reduced, *and* that we would have started to save money by buying boxes in bulk. Why don't you see if Jeff has any insights into the problem?"

Dan found Jeff in the coffee room early Monday morning. "Hey Jeff, we've been having lots of trouble lately with damage claims. Grace tells me you bought some new cartons for shipping. Do you think they could be causing the problem?"

"Gee, I hope not," replied Jeff. "My evaluations have been awesome since I cut costs so dramatically. In fact, the product managers have been singing my praises since the variable costs of shipping went down and their contribution margins went up."

"Well, I've got to figure this out," said Dan, "because the freight companies are breathing down my neck, and they've threatened to quit paying our claims. The sales reps are all over me, too, because their customers are irritated at having to go through the claims process. They want their products delivered free of damage, the first time. Let me take a look at the cartons and see if I can figure out the problem."

As Dan left the room, Jeff started to worry. Jeff was aware of the crush weight standards (i.e., the strength) of the company's cartons. He decided to save the company some money by trying a carton with a slightly lower crush weight. Of course, the savings would also make Jeff look good at annual evaluation time, and this was important since he was up for a promotion. He had gotten such a great deal on the new cartons because his brother Marvin had just been named sales manager at a new carton manufacturing company. Jeff signed the long-term contract so that his brother would achieve a sizeable year-end bonus for exceeding his sales targets. Part of the bonus was a week-long trip for two to the Super Bowl, and Marvin promised Jeff he could go with him.

Wednesday morning Dan called Jeff and said, "I've been talking with our shipping department, and one of the guys figured out that the cartons on the bottom of the pallet seem to suffer the most damage. It turns out that the crush weight of the new cartons you purchased wasn't as high as that of the old boxes. We've filed all those damage claims against our carriers, and the damage hasn't been their fault at all. I guess you need to go back to purchasing the sturdier cartons."

"Can't do that for the next 15 months," Jeff moaned. "We're locked into a long-term contract."

Required

a. Identify the ethical issues in this case.
b. What steps should Dan and Jeff take next?
c. What are the costs and benefits to the company for making an ethical decision?

ANALYTICS PROBLEM

3-46 Multiproduct CVP analysis using data analytics and Excel (LO 5) Greer Golf Supplies is an online store that sells two types of golf balls: practice balls and tournament balls. The golf balls are sold in plastic sleeves containing three golf balls. Practice balls sell for $4 per sleeve; tournament balls sell for $12 per sleeve. Owner Carl Rider purchases the golf balls directly from the manufacturer and pays $1 per sleeve for the practice balls and $4 per sleeve for the tournament balls. Fixed costs total $14,000 per month and include Carl's salary, website hosting, and accounting and legal fees. When preparing the sales forecast for the year, Carl assumed he would sell twice as many sleeves of practice balls as tournament balls.

Required

a. Calculate the annual breakeven point for Greer Golf Supplies.
b. Carl has gathered the sales data for the past year. Use Excel's CHART function to prepare a 100% stacked bar chart of the monthly sales mix based on the actual sales data. You will first need to calculate the monthly sales total for each type of ball using the SUMIF function.
c. Calculate the actual sales mix for the year. Round to one decimal place as needed.

d. Calculate the sales mix for each customer's purchase. Did any customer purchase golf balls in the 2:1 assumed sales mix? In the actual mix you calculated above in part c?

e. Prepare Greer's contribution format income statement for the year using the actual sales data. Assume all prices and costs were as projected.

f. Using the actual sales mix, calculate the breakeven point for the year. Fixed costs were $14,000 per month. How does this compare to the projected breakeven point Carl used in preparing his sales forecast?

The Excel data files for answering this problem can be found in WileyPLUS.

ENDNOTES

1. The following abbreviations will be used in equations throughout the chapter:
   x = number of units
   SP = sales price per unit
   VC = variable cost per unit
   FC = fixed expenses
   OI = operating income
   CM = contribution margin
2. "Entrepreneurial Words of Wisdom," *American Way,* July 15, 2004, 58.

© jsnyderdesign/iStockphoto

PRODUCT COSTS AND JOB ORDER COSTING

© Pressmaster/Shutterstock

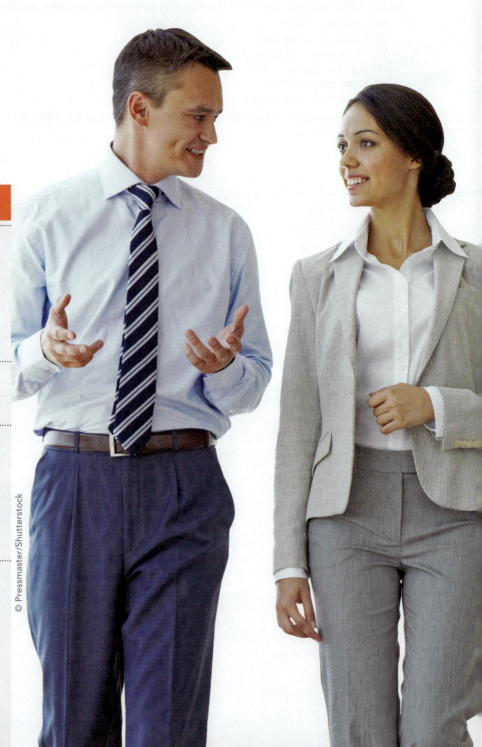

UNITS	LEARNING OBJECTIVES
UNIT 4.1 Product and Period Costs	**LO 1:** Distinguish between product and period costs. **LO 2:** Describe the three major components of product costs: direct materials, direct labor, and manufacturing overhead.
UNIT 4.2 Product Cost Flows	**LO 3:** Trace the flow of product costs through the inventory accounts.
UNIT 4.3 Job Order Costing	**LO 4:** Compute a predetermined overhead rate and apply manufacturing overhead to production. **LO 5:** Compute product costs using a job order costing system.
UNIT 4.4 Underapplied and Overapplied Manufacturing Overhead	**LO 6:** Determine and dispose of under- and overapplied manufacturing overhead.

Business Decision and Context

© iconeer/iStockphoto

Jonathan Smith, C&C Sports' vice president for marketing, was talking with **Erin Newton**, the company's **controller**. "I don't understand how you think it costs us $11.17 to make a baseball jersey. The materials cost only $6.85, and it takes only a few minutes for our sewing machine operators to put the whole thing together. I figure it costs us $9.00 at most."

"There's more to the cost of making a jersey than buying materials and paying someone to sew them into a jersey," Erin replied. "Think about all the electricity we use to run the sewing machines and heat and cool the building. And that's just the beginning of all the other costs we incur to go from a piece of fabric to a completed jersey."

"I never thought about it that way," Jonathan responded. "Even so, as long as the company is making a profit, do we really need to be so precise about what a jersey costs to make?"

"Think about it for a minute, Jonathan," Erin said. "How will you know if the $14.80 per jersey you charge a customer will generate a profit if you don't know the costs to make it?"

> "How will you know if the $14.80 per jersey you charge a customer will generate a profit if you don't know the costs to make it?"

We also need to know the cost so we can value the inventory we report on our balance sheet.

Jonathan thought for a minute before answering. "I see your point, Erin. But I still don't know how you came up with $11.17."

Watch the **Making a Hollywood Movie** *video in WileyPLUS to learn more about job order costing in the real world.*

SUPPLY CHAIN KEY PLAYERS

END CUSTOMER

UNIVERSAL SPORTS EXCHANGE

C&C SPORTS

Vice President for Marketing
Jonathan Smith

Controller
Erin Newton

DURABLE ZIPPER COMPANY

BRADLEY TEXTILE MILLS

CENTEX YARNS

NEFF FIBER MANUFACTURING

BRUIN POLYMERS, INC.

UNIT 4.1

Product and Period Costs

GUIDED UNIT PREPARATION

Answering the following questions while you read this unit will guide your understanding of the key concepts found in the unit. The questions are linked to the learning objectives presented at the beginning of the chapter.

LO 1

1. Why do managers need to understand product and period costs?
2. What is a product cost? Give three specific examples (not categories) that are not mentioned in the chapter.
3. What is a period cost? Give three specific examples (not categories) that are not mentioned in the chapter.

LO 2

4. Describe the three major categories of product costs.
5. Why are some raw materials costs and some labor costs treated as manufacturing overhead? What are those components of manufacturing overhead called?

Merchandising companies like Universal Sports Exchange purchase inventory to resell to customers. To operate effectively, they must be able to earn enough sales revenue to cover the costs of acquiring the inventory, selling it, and running (or administering) the business. Remember from financial accounting that the costs of acquiring inventory are reported on the balance sheet as an asset labeled "Inventory" and are expensed only when products are sold. The costs of selling and administration, on the other hand, are reported on the income statement as expenses when they are incurred. So you are already familiar with the concept of product and period costs. Product costs are the costs related to inventory, and period costs are the costs related to the selling and administrative functions.

Manufacturing companies like C&C Sports also have product and period costs, but their determination is more difficult. Instead of buying inventory to resell, manufacturing companies *make* inventory to sell. Thus, all the many costs incurred in the manufacture of a product become part of the inventory cost. Selling and administrative costs, however, are accounted for just as they are in merchandising companies—that is, they are expensed as they are incurred.

Product Costs

Product costs, or **manufacturing costs**, are any costs that a company incurs to acquire raw materials and convert them to finished goods ready for sale. C&C Sports incurs many costs to manufacture its baseball jerseys, baseball pants, and award jackets. Under the matching principle of financial accounting, those costs are first recorded as inventory (an asset) and then expensed as cost of goods sold on the income statement at the time they are sold. In general, product costs may be classified into three categories: direct materials, direct labor, and manufacturing overhead. Exhibit 4-1 illustrates these three major components of product costs.

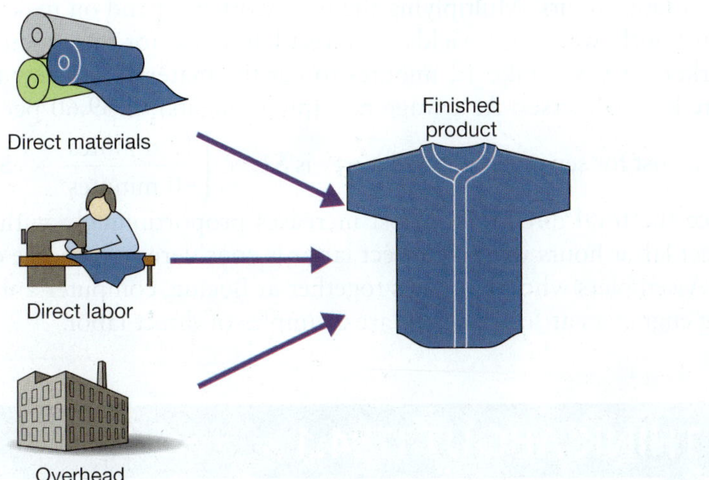

EXHIBIT 4-1

The three components of product cost.

Direct Materials

Direct materials are those materials that can be directly traced to, or easily identified with, the final product. For C&C Sports' baseball jersey, the primary direct material is the fabric. Because tracing the actual amount of fabric used in a particular jersey is easy, determining the cost of that fabric is simple. For example, each shirt takes one yard of jersey fabric and one yard of backing material. Each yard of fabric costs $4.00, and each yard of backing material costs $2.00. Therefore, the cost of the fabric for one jersey is $6.00. The baseball pants that C&C makes take 1.1 yards of fabric, and each yard of fabric costs $3.50. Therefore, the cost of the fabric for the baseball pants is $3.85 (1.1 yards × $3.50 per yard). Since the total fabric cost increases with the number of jerseys or pants produced, direct materials are a variable cost.

Let's think about some other products familiar to you. Chocolate is a direct material for Mars Incorporated's Snickers® and M&M's® candies. Coffee beans are a direct material for Starbucks. Tires and aluminum are just two of the direct materials used by Honda Motor Company in the production of Accords and Pilots. In each of these examples, it is easy to see the direct material in the final product and to measure how much of the material has been used in the production process.

Recall C&C Sports' supply chain, introduced in Topic Focus 1 (see Exhibit T1-2 on page 36). Notice that along the supply chain, one company's finished product becomes another company's direct material. For example, the fabric that C&C Sports buys from Bradley Textile Mills is a finished product for Bradley, but it becomes a direct material when it arrives at C&C Sports.

Direct materials are sometimes referred to as raw materials. While all direct materials are raw materials, not all raw materials are direct materials, as we will see when we study manufacturing overhead.

Direct Labor

To convert fabric into baseball jerseys, someone must cut the fabric and sew the pieces together. The people involved in these operations are part of C&C's **direct labor**. Direct labor costs are the wages (and possibly benefits) paid to the workers who transform direct materials into a finished product. For labor to be considered direct, the worker must actually have his or her hands on the product or on the machine as the product is being made. Direct labor workers can easily trace the time they spend working on a particular product, which is referred to as **direct labor hours**. Multiplying the time workers spend on making a product by their hourly wage rates yields the direct labor cost for the product. For example, workers at C&C take 12 minutes to cut the material and sew together a complete baseball jersey. At a wage rate (plus benefits) of $9.60 per hour, the direct labor cost for sewing a baseball jersey is $1.92 $\left[\frac{12 \text{ minutes}}{60 \text{ minutes}} \times \$9.60 \text{ per hour}\right]$. Since the total direct labor cost increases proportionately with the number of direct labor hours worked, direct labor is considered a variable cost.

Assemblers who put planes together at Boeing, computer animators at Pixar, ring engravers at Josten's—all are examples of direct labor.

THINK ABOUT IT 4.1

Is direct labor cost always a variable cost? Consider General Motors' Opel subsidiary. In August 2004, Opel announced that it would try to add five hours to its 35-hour work week, without increasing workers' pay. Would Opel consider direct labor to be a variable or fixed cost? Why?

Overhead

It takes more than direct materials and direct labor to make C&C's baseball jerseys. Electricity is needed to run the sewing machines and to light, heat, and cool the factory. Security guards and insurance are needed to protect the factory building and its contents. Supervisors are needed to oversee the production process. All these costs are examples of **overhead** costs, the indirect product costs that arise in the manufacturing process and that cannot easily be traced to a unit of product. For instance, managers can't trace the amount of electricity required to light, heat, and cool the factory building while one baseball jersey is sewn. Some companies refer to overhead as **manufacturing overhead**, **factory overhead**, **manufacturing support**, **factory support**, **manufacturing burden**, or **factory burden**. If a cost is incurred to support the factory or the manufacturing process and is not classified as direct labor or direct material, it is part of overhead.

In addition to general overhead costs, two special categories of overhead warrant further discussion: indirect materials and indirect labor. **Indirect materials** include the supplies used in supporting the production process, which may or may not be part of the final product. For instance, C&C must keep its sewing machines well lubricated. The oil and grease it uses to do so are not part of the baseball jersey. Rather, those supplies provide the production capability to produce the jersey. Similarly, the janitorial supplies that keep the factory clean are not part of the baseball jerseys. Nevertheless, the factory could not function

REALITY CHECK—*Showing cost classifications in published financial statements*

© jim kruger/iStockphoto

Does the classification of costs really matter to companies? The answer is "yes" because those costs must be reported in the company's published financial statements. Let's look at a few examples from companies' annual reports:

- Stanley Furniture Company, Inc. is a leading manufacturer of furniture headquartered in Stanleytown, Virginia. Its 2015 consolidated income statement groups all selling, general, and administrative expenses into a single category. Cost of goods sold is shown as a separate line item.
- Merck & Co., Inc. a pharmaceuticals manufacturer, reports separate line items for each of the following expenses in its 2015 income statement: materials and production, marketing and administrative, and research and development. (The materials and production amount is the company's cost of goods sold.)
- American Airlines Group, Inc., parent company of American Airlines, takes a third approach to reporting costs. As shown in its 2015 income statement, American reports ten different operating cost categories.

In *Accounting Trends and Techniques—2012,* the American Institute of Public Accountants surveyed 500 annual reports and found a variety of reporting practices. Of the 500 reports, 307 grouped selling, general, and administrative expenses as a single line item. Only 39 companies devoted a separate line item to selling expenses.

Clearly, there are several acceptable ways to report costs in published income statements. Regardless of how expenses are reported, companies know internally which costs are included in various classifications. And knowing the cost of different activities is a key to making good business decisions.

Clearly, there are several acceptable ways to report costs in published income statements.

Sources: Merck & Co., Inc., 2015 10-K; Stanley Furniture Company 2015 Annual Report; American Airlines Group, Inc, 2015 Form 10-K Annual Report; American Institute of Certified Public Accountants, *Accounting Trends and Techniques—2012.*

UNIT 4.1 REVIEW

KEY TERMS

PRACTICE QUESTIONS

1. LO 1 Which of the following is *not* a product cost?
   a. Direct materials
   b. Indirect labor
   c. Corporate controller's salary
   d. Manufacturing overhead
2. LO 1 The cost of an advertising campaign for a new product would be classified as
   a. selling, general, and administrative expense.
   b. manufacturing overhead.
   c. indirect materials.
   d. cost of goods manufactured.
3. LO 2 Which of the following would be considered direct materials?
   a. 2-liter plastic bottles used by Coca-Cola
   b. Shipping boxes used by J. Crew to fill online orders
   c. Glue used by Smuckers to attach labels to jars of Jif® peanut butter
   d. Ketchup used on a McDonald's hamburger
4. LO 2 Which of the following would *not* be a component of manufacturing overhead for an automobile manufacturer?
   a. Final assembly inspector's salary
   b. Depreciation on a robotic welder used to assemble automobile doors
   c. Lubricant used on automobile door hinges
   d. Automobile windshields

UNIT 4.1 PRACTICE EXERCISE

Classify the following costs as product or period costs. Identify whether the product costs are direct materials, direct labor, or overhead. The first item has been done for you.

	PRODUCT COST			PERIOD COST
	Direct Materials	Direct Labor	Overhead	
Cost of food in a **Stouffer's**® microwaveable dinner	X			
Cost of the plant manager's salary in a **Dell** computer production facility				
Wages of the security personnel at a **Best Buy** store				
Cost of the utilities at a **Pepsi** bottling plant				
Cost incurred by **Lands' End** to ship merchandise to customers				
Cost of upholstery leather purchased by **Toyota**				
Wages of the printing press operator at the ***New York Times***				
Cost of advertising a book published by **John Wiley & Sons**				
Wages of the assembly-line workers at a **John Deere plant**				
Cost of the commission paid to **Honda** salespeople for every Accord sold				

SELECTED UNIT 4.1 ANSWERS

Think About It 4.1

In this case, Opel appears to be treating direct labor as a fixed cost. The addition of five hours to the work week means that total labor cost will not increase with the increase in volume. An alternative treatment would be to convert the 35-hour-per-week hourly wage rate to a lower per-hour wage rate that would yield the same total pay for the new 40-hour work week.

Two conditions should exist when direct labor is considered to be variable. First, workers must be paid based on how much they produce (which is legal as long as they make more than the minimum wage). That is, the more they produce, the more they are paid, so their labor cost varies directly with production. Second, direct labor cost should vary at different levels of production, *and* management must have the flexibility to hire and fire workers based on those production levels. Direct labor should be considered fixed if the workers are guaranteed a certain number of hours of work, regardless of the level of production—even if those workers are paid by the hour.

Think About It 4.2

No, $4.00 is not Bradley's cost of goods sold. The $4.00 per yard is Bradley Textile Mills' revenue.

Practice Questions

1. C
2. A
3. A
4. D

Unit 4.1 Practice Exercise

	PRODUCT COST			PERIOD COST
	Direct Materials	Direct Labor	Overhead	
Cost of food in a Stouffer's® microwaveable dinner	X			
Cost of the plant manager's salary in a Dell computer production facility			X	
Wages of the security personnel at a Best Buy store				X
Cost of the utilities at a Pepsi bottling plant			X	
Cost incurred by Lands' End to ship merchandise to customers				X
Cost of upholstery leather purchased by Toyota	X			
Wages of the printing press operator at the *New York Times*		X		
Cost of advertising a book published by John Wiley & Sons				X
Wages of the assembly-line workers at a John Deere plant		X		
Cost of the commission paid to Honda salespeople for every Accord sold				X

UNIT 4.2

Product Cost Flows

GUIDED UNIT PREPARATION

Answering the following questions while you read this unit will guide your understanding of the key concepts found in the unit. The questions are linked to the learning objectives presented at the beginning of the chapter.

LO 3

1. Refer to the T-accounts in Exhibit 4-18. Answer the following questions in words, not numbers.
   a. What increases Raw Materials Inventory? What decreases Raw Materials Inventory?
   b. What increases Work in Process Inventory? What decreases Work in Process Inventory?
   c. What increases Finished Goods Inventory? What decreases Finished Goods Inventory?
   d. What increases Manufacturing Overhead? What decreases Manufacturing Overhead?
   e. What increases Cost of Goods Sold?
2. What is the cost of goods manufactured? How does it differ from total manufacturing cost?

Now that you know how to categorize costs by function, let's look more closely at the flow of product costs from raw materials to the finished product. At any given time, a product can be in one of three stages of completion: not started, started but not finished, or completely finished and ready for sale. Traditionally, manufacturers like C&C Sports have used three separate inventory accounts to record the costs of products in these three stages of production.

Inventory Account Definitions

When the company purchases raw materials for use in the production process, the cost of those materials is recorded in the **Raw Materials Inventory** account. At C&C Sports, this inventory account would include the cost of purchased items such as fabric, thread, elastic bands, and cleaning supplies. Alternatively, C&C Sports could choose to record only direct materials in this account and to record the cost of indirect materials like elastic bands and cleaning supplies in a separate **Supplies Inventory** account.

When C&C Sports is ready to begin making a product, employees take fabric from the warehouse shelves and move it to the cutting room to begin the first stage of the production process. Now that production has begun, the material is part of the Work in Process Inventory account and is no longer counted as part of Raw Materials Inventory. The **Work in Process Inventory** account records the costs of all products that have been started but are not yet complete. Since direct labor and

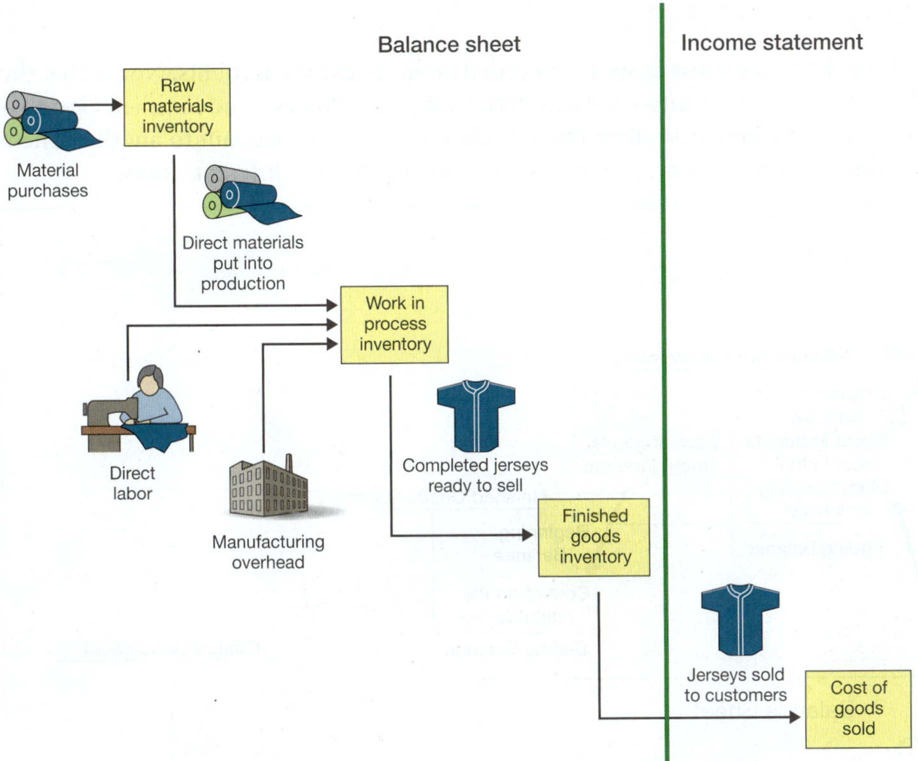

EXHIBIT 4-4

Manufacturing inventory cost flows.

manufacturing overhead are incurred during the production process, those costs are also recorded in the Work in Process Inventory account, as they are incurred.

The final inventory account is **Finished Goods Inventory**. This account records all the production costs of completed products. At C&C Sports, once a baseball jersey has been completed and is ready for sale, all the direct materials, direct labor, and manufacturing overhead costs incurred to make that jersey are transferred from the Work in Process Inventory account to the Finished Goods Inventory account, just as the jersey is moved from the factory floor to the finished goods warehouse. When the jersey is sold to a customer, its cost is removed from the Finished Goods Inventory account and transferred to Cost of Goods Sold. Exhibit 4-4 illustrates the cost flows through the three inventory accounts.

THINK ABOUT IT 4.3

Chiquita Brands International, Inc. reported the following information about its inventories in a footnote to its 2010 annual report:

Bananas	$ 44,873
Salads	7,667
Other fresh produce	4,381
Processed food products	10,629
Growing crops	74,392
Materials, supplies, and other	70,307
	$212,249

Classify each of these inventory categories as raw materials, work in process, or finished goods.

Recording of Cost Flows

Exhibit 4-5 shows how costs are recorded in the inventory accounts. Notice that the three inventory accounts—Raw Materials, Work in Process, and Finished Goods—are distinct from one another. Do not add one inventory account to another. These are three different assets, just as cash and equipment are different assets.

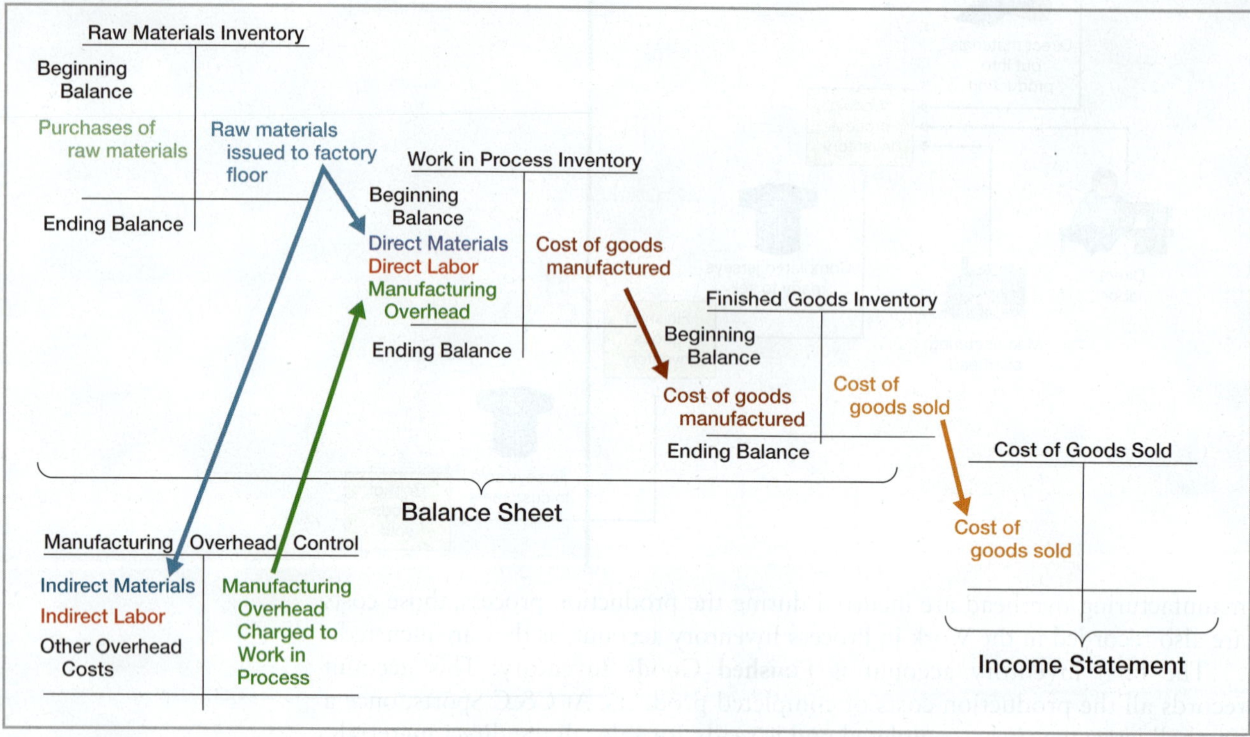

EXHIBIT 4-5 *Cost flows through the manufacturing inventory T-accounts.*

As with any balance sheet account, an inventory account may carry a beginning balance representing costs that were in the account at the end of the previous accounting period. Throughout the accounting period, costs are added to and removed from the account. At the end of the period, the following equation is used to calculate the ending balance.

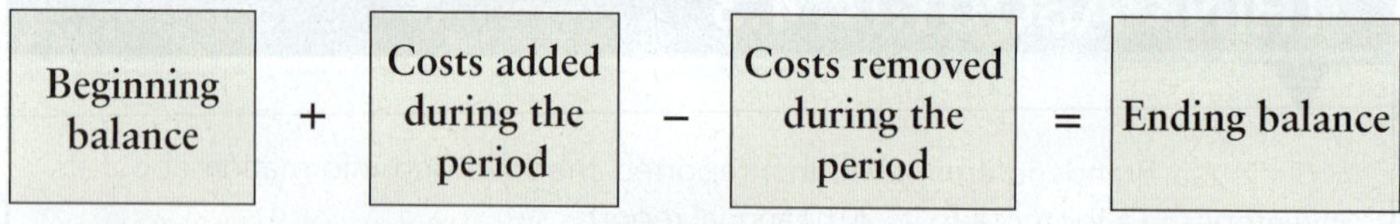

Let's look at each of the inventory accounts in detail. Raw Materials Inventory increases when materials are purchased and decreases when materials are used. The only thing you need to watch out for is whether these materials are direct or indirect materials. The use of direct materials increases Work in Process Inventory, whereas the use of indirect materials increases Manufacturing Overhead. The ending balance in the Raw Materials Inventory account represents materials that are still sitting on the storeroom shelves, waiting to be used.

Work in process, as we have seen, represents products that have been started but not completed. As direct materials are used, and direct labor and overhead costs are incurred, those costs are recorded as increases in Work in Process Inventory. When products are finished, their costs must be removed from Work in Process Inventory and added to Finished Goods Inventory. The total cost of all the good units completed during the accounting period is referred to as the **cost of goods manufactured**—the cost of everything that is finished during the period, whether or not it was started during the period. Imagine, for example, that workers began production of a unit on August 28 and finished it on September 3. For the month ended August 31, the cost of the unfinished unit would be part of Work in Process Inventory. For the month ended September 30, the total cost of the finished product would be part of the cost of goods manufactured.

The third inventory account, Finished Goods Inventory, represents finished products that are ready to be sold. This account is similar to the Inventory account of a merchandising company, which you learned about in financial accounting. Finished Goods Inventory increases by the cost of goods manufactured (good finished units) and decreases by the cost of goods sold. When products are sold, they are removed from inventory and recognized as an expense on the income statement. Remember, materials may be purchased, factory workers paid, and overhead costs incurred, but none of those costs makes it to the income statement as an expense until a product is actually sold. Has cash been paid for each of these costs? Probably, but a cash payment is not what makes a product cost an expense. Rather, the sale of the product triggers the recording of an expense.

Now that you understand how costs flow through the three inventory accounts, let's analyze the cost flows at C&C Sports. To simplify the analysis, we'll assume that C&C makes only baseball jerseys in September. At the beginning of the month, C&C Sports had a total of $132,571 in Raw Materials Inventory, $2,519 in Work in Process Inventory, and $381,620 in Finished Goods Inventory. During September, C&C Sports purchased a total of $104,810 in raw materials. Adding the September purchases to the beginning balance, C&C Sports had $237,381 of raw materials available to use in production. The journal entry to record the purchase of raw materials in September is:

Raw Materials Inventory	$104,810	
Accounts Payable (or Cash)		$104,810

During September, C&C Sports incurred the following additional costs to complete the jerseys already in process and to start 14,875 new jerseys:

Materials used ($101,894 direct; $5,912 indirect)	$107,806
Hourly wages paid ($28,723 direct; $7,532 indirect)	36,255
Production manager's salary	8,500
Factory equipment depreciation	6,698
Factory rent	9,167
Factory utilities	4,185
Factory insurance	4,200
Factory janitorial service	1,000

The journal entries to record these manufacturing costs are:

Direct Material Used in Production		
Work in Process Inventory	$101,894	
Raw Materials Inventory		$101,894
Direct Labor		
Work in Process Inventory	$ 28,723	
Wages Payable (or Cash)		$ 28,723

Manufacturing Overhead		
Manufacturing Overhead Control	$ 47,194	
Raw Materials Inventory		$ 5,912
Wages Payable (or Cash)		7,532
Salaries Payable (or Cash)		8,500
Accumulated Depreciation		6,698
Cash or Other Payables		18,552
Work in Process Inventory	$ 47,194	
Manufacturing Overhead Control		$ 47,194

The overhead entries might look strange to you. First of all, C&C is using a Manufacturing Overhead Control account to accumulate the overhead costs as they occur throughout the period. At the end of the month, one entry can be made to transfer these costs to Work in Process. Thus, at the end of the month (or other accounting period) the Manufacturing Overhead Control account will have a zero balance.

You may also remember from financial accounting that when salaries or wages are paid, you debit an expense account and credit cash. That works well for a merchandising or service company, but not for a manufacturing company. Remember, these salaries, wages, rent, insurance, and other overhead costs were incurred to support the manufacturing of *products*. That makes these costs *product costs*, which means they must become part of an inventory account until the products are sold.

By the end of September, 14,525 jerseys have been finished at a cost of $162,244. The journal entry to record the cost of goods manufactured for September is:

Finished Goods Inventory	$162,244	
Work in Process Inventory		$162,244

The final set of journal entries for September's manufacturing costs is made to cost of goods sold. In September, C&C sold 5,000 jerseys that cost $55,850 to make. Recall from Chapter 2 that C&C sells the jerseys for $14.80 each, so the sale of 5,000 jerseys generates $74,000 in revenue. Even though revenue is not a cost, you should get into the habit of recording both the expense and the revenue associated with the sale of inventory. The journal entries to record the sale of 5,000 jerseys are:

Cash (or Accounts Receivable)	$74,000	
Sales Revenue		$74,000
Cost of Goods Sold	$55,850	
Finished Goods Inventory		$55,850

The $18,150 difference between the sales revenue and the cost of goods sold ($74,000 − $55,850) represents the gross profit on the sale of 5,000 jerseys. This gross profit helps cover selling and administrative costs so that C&C can stay in business. It is *not* the same as *contribution margin*, which you learned about in Chapter 2. Gross profit includes all product costs, regardless of behavior, whereas contribution margin includes all variable costs, regardless of function.

Exhibit 4-6 summarizes C&C Sports' product cost flows for September.

REALITY CHECK—*What's satisfying your sweet tooth going to cost?*

Leading chocolatier Hershey passed on an 8% price increase to its customers.

Forrest Gump's mother might have been on to something when she said you never know what you are going to get in a box of chocolates. And if cocoa prices continue to increase, the price for that box of chocolates might be changing as much as the chocolate inside.

The West African countries of Ghana and Ivory Coast produce the majority of the world's cocoa. Due to adverse weather conditions, poor farming, and the Ebola outbreak, production in recent years has declined. As a result, the price of cocoa has doubled in the past ten years, with 40 percent of that increase coming between 2012 and 2015.

What's a chocolate manufacturer to do with such large raw material price increases? Faced with the cocoa price increase and increases in the price of both milk and nuts, leading chocolatier Hershey passed on an 8% price increase to its customers in July 2014. Other companies are reducing the size of their chocolates or replacing dark chocolate with milk chocolate in an effort to reduce costs and avoid a price increase.

Sources: Patrick Gillespie, "Chocolate lovers: prices could go up (again)!" Money.CNN.com, June 23, 2015, http://money.cnn.com/2015/06/23/investing/chocolate-cocoa-prices-go-up/ (accessed February 29, 2016); John W. Shoen, "Why Are Chocolate Prices Jumping?" CNBC.com, February 13, 2015, http://www.cnbc.com/2015/02/13/why-are-chocolate-prices-jumping.html (accessed February 29, 2016).

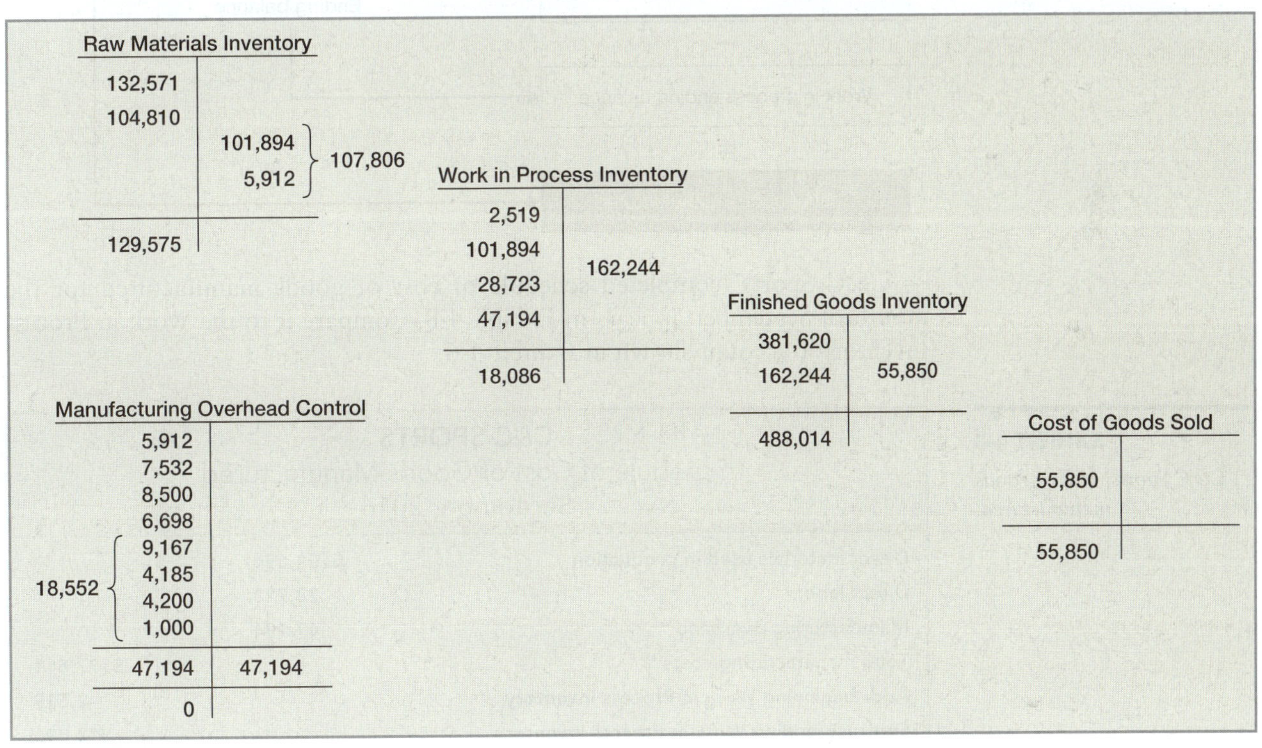

EXHIBIT 4-6 *C&C Sports' product cost flows for September.*

Schedule of Cost of Goods Manufactured

In calculating the cost of goods manufactured, it is sometimes helpful to prepare a schedule of cost of goods manufactured. The long name may make this schedule sound complex and intimidating, but it is nothing more than a restatement of the Work in Process Inventory account.

To prepare the schedule of cost of goods manufactured, begin with the **total manufacturing cost** incurred during the period—the direct materials used in production, direct labor incurred, and manufacturing overhead incurred. To that total, add the beginning balance in the Work in Process Inventory account. Finally, subtract the ending balance in the Work in Process Inventory account. The remaining amount is the cost of goods manufactured. Exhibit 4-7 shows the relationship between the schedule of cost of goods manufactured and the Work in Process Inventory T-account.

EXHIBIT 4-7

Relationship between the schedule of cost of goods manufactured and the Work in Process Inventory T-account.

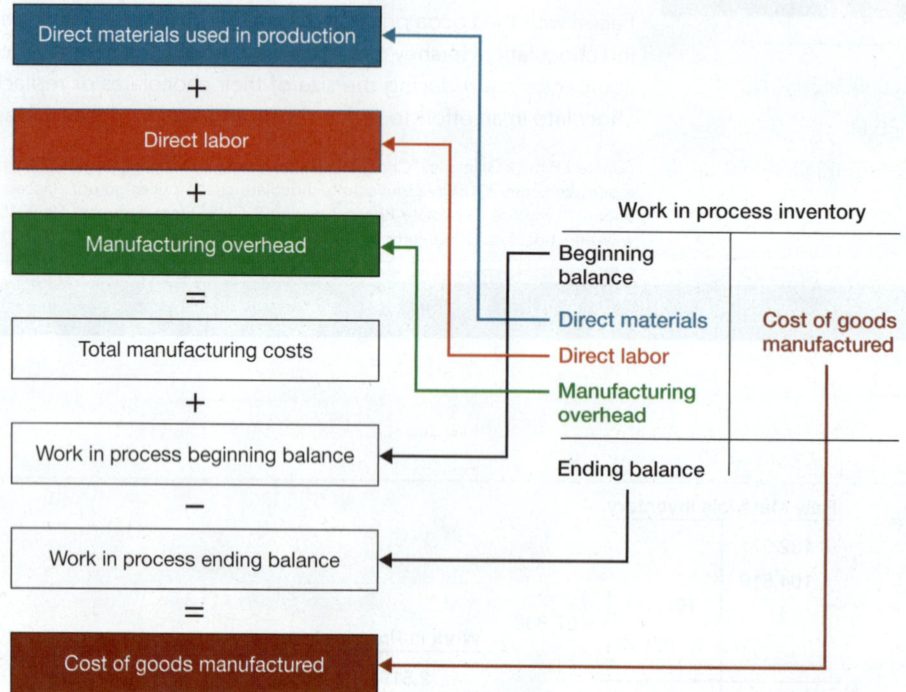

C&C Sports' completed schedule of cost of goods manufactured for the month of September appears in Exhibit 4-8. Compare it to the Work in Process Inventory T-account shown in Exhibit 4-6.

EXHIBIT 4-8

C&C Sports' cost of goods manufactured.

C&C SPORTS
Schedule of Cost of Goods Manufactured
September 2016

Direct materials used in production	$101,894	
Direct labor	28,723	
Manufacturing overhead	47,194	
Total manufacturing costs		$177,811
Add: beginning Work in Process Inventory		2,519
Subtract: ending Work in Process Inventory		(18,086)
Cost of goods manufactured		$162,244

We can also create a schedule of cost of goods sold, which is a restatement of the Finished Goods Inventory account. Exhibit 4-9 shows C&C's schedule of cost of goods sold for September. Compare it to the Finished Goods Inventory T-account shown in Exhibit 4-6.

WATCH OUT!

Total manufacturing cost and the cost of goods manufactured typically are not the same amount. The only way the two could be the same is if beginning Work in Process balance and ending Work in Process balance were exactly the same amount. That is, if there were any products in process at the beginning and end of the period, they must have been at the same level of completion *and* costs cannot have increased from one period to the next.

C&C SPORTS Schedule of Cost of Goods Sold September 2016	
Cost of goods manufactured	$ 162,244
Add: beginning Finished Goods Inventory	381,620
Goods available for sale	543,864
Subtract: ending Finished Goods Inventory	(488,014)
Cost of goods sold	$ 55,850

EXHIBIT 4-9 *C&C Sports' cost of goods sold.*

UNIT 4.2 REVIEW

KEY TERMS

Cost of goods manufactured p. 141
Finished Goods Inventory p. 139
Raw Materials Inventory p. 138
Supplies Inventory p. 138
Total manufacturing cost p. 144
Work in Process Inventory p. 138

PRACTICE QUESTIONS

1. LO 3 If the beginning balance in the Raw Materials Inventory account for May was $27,500, the ending balance in the same account for May was $28,750, and $128,900 of materials were used during the month, the materials purchased during the month cost (CMA adapted)
   a. $127,650.
   b. $130,150.
   c. $131,300.
   d. $157,650.
2. LO 3 The cost of goods manufactured is
   a. always the same as the total manufacturing cost.
   b. always the same as the cost of goods sold.
   c. recorded as a debit to the Finished Goods Inventory account.
   d. recorded as a debit to the Work in Process Inventory account.
3. LO 3 If the cost of goods sold is greater than the cost of goods manufactured, then
   a. the Work in Process Inventory has decreased during the period.
   b. the Finished Goods Inventory has increased during the period.
   c. total manufacturing cost must be greater than the cost of goods manufactured.
   d. the Finished Goods Inventory has decreased during the period.

UNIT 4.2 PRACTICE EXERCISE

Bryant Enterprises reported the following for April:

Beginning balance, Raw Materials Inventory	$30,000
Beginning balance, Work in Process Inventory	48,000
Beginning balance, Finished Goods Inventory	17,000
Purchases of raw materials	54,000
Factory electricity	10,000
Direct labor payroll	32,000
Depreciation on factory equipment	35,000
Insurance on factory building	8,000
Indirect materials used in production	7,000
Total raw materials used in production	65,000
Indirect labor payroll	24,000
Cost of goods manufactured	200,000
Cost of goods sold	210,000

Required

1. How much direct materials were used in production?
2. How much manufacturing overhead was incurred during April?
3. What was the total manufacturing cost for the month of April?
4. What were the ending balances in the Raw Materials, Work in Process, and Finished Goods inventory accounts?

SELECTED UNIT 4.2 ANSWERS

Think About It 4.3

Bananas	*Finished Goods*
Salads	*Finished Goods*
Other fresh produce	*Finished Goods*
Processed food products	*Finished Goods*
Growing crops	*Work in Process*
Materials, supplies, and other	*Raw Materials*

Practice Questions

1. B 2. C 3. D

Unit 4.2 Practice Exercise

1. $58,000 of direct materials were used in production. Raw materials of $65,000 were used, but $7,000 of that amount was for indirect materials.
2. $84,000 in manufacturing overhead was incurred during April. Included in this amount were factory electricity, depreciation on factory equipment, insurance on factory building, indirect materials used in production, and indirect labor payroll.
3. The total manufacturing cost was $174,000. Included in this amount were direct materials of $58,000, direct labor of $32,000, and manufacturing overhead of $84,000.
4. Raw materials = $19,000; work in process = $22,000; finished goods = $7,000. See the following T-accounts.

Raw Materials

	Debit	Credit
Beg. Bal.	30,000	
Purchases	54,000	
Materials Used		65,000
Ending Bal.	**19,000**	

Work in Process

	Debit	Credit
Beg. Bal.	48,000	
DM	58,000	200,000
DL	32,000	
MOH	84,000	
Ending Bal.	**22,000**	

Finished Goods

	Debit	Credit
Beg. Bal.	17,000	
COGM	200,000	
COGS		210,000
Ending Bal.	**7,000**	

UNIT 4.3

Job Order Costing

GUIDED UNIT PREPARATION

Answering the following questions while you read this unit will guide your understanding of the key concepts found in the unit. The questions are linked to the learning objectives presented at the beginning of the chapter.

LO 4

1. Why must overhead be applied instead of traced to specific jobs?
2. How is the predetermined overhead rate calculated? When is the predetermined overhead rate calculated?
3. Why do some companies prefer to use predetermined overhead rates instead of waiting for the actual rates? Give three reasons.

LO 5

4. How are job cost sheets used to determine the Work in Process account balance at any particular time?
5. How would an attorney use job order costing?
6. Refer to Exhibit 4-10. Is $390.95 the actual cost of Job 6052?

Now that you've seen how costs flow through the inventory accounts, you may be wondering how a company determines those costs. Because C&C Sports makes three different products (jerseys, pants, and jackets), each of which requires different materials, labor, and machinery, the company needs to be able to know how much a single jersey, pair of pants, or jacket costs. To determine those costs, the company uses a job order costing system.

In a **job order costing system**, products are manufactured in batches or jobs, and product costs are accumulated for each batch or job. When the job is completed, the total costs accumulated for the job are divided by the number of units produced to determine the average cost per unit. Like C&C Sports, companies that use a job order costing system produce a number of different products that require different amounts of direct materials, direct labor, and manufacturing overhead. Frequently, those products are produced to customer specifications. Because each job has a distinct beginning and end, you can watch the individual units being created during the production process.

Consider Alcoa's flexible packaging products division, a manufacturer of the plastic sleeves found on bottles of Coffee-Mate® and Nestlé® Nesquick™ chocolate milk. Although the products are similar in many ways, Alcoa produces the sleeves in batches, probably based on product flavor. Each flavor requires a different colored sleeve and thus a different combination of inks, at a different combination of costs. Therefore, Alcoa accumulates product costs separately for each batch of sleeves produced.

Job order costing systems are not used exclusively by manufacturers; many service organizations also use job order costing. For example, professional services firms such as the accounting firm PricewaterhouseCoopers and the legal firm Fulbright & Jaworski use job order costing to accumulate the costs associated with a particular client or a particular case. Hospitals such as the Mayo Clinic use job order costing to accumulate the costs incurred to treat a particular patient. Let's see how the system works.

Accumulating Direct Job Costs

When a sales order arrives or a manager reorders an inventory item, the production scheduling department creates a production order to authorize the start of a new job. For identification and tracking purposes, the production order is assigned a job number. It also initiates the creation of a **job cost sheet**, which accumulates and summarizes all the costs incurred during the job. Exhibit 4-10 shows a job cost sheet for a batch of C&C Sports' baseball jerseys. In later sections we will see how the costs on the sheet were accumulated and recorded. While the exhibit appears to illustrate a manual recording process, most companies today use computer systems to accumulate such information and produce reports.

EXHIBIT 4-10

C&C Sports' job cost sheet.

C&C Sports

Job Cost Sheet

Job Number 6052 Date Started 06/15/2016 Date Completed 06/16/2016

Item Description batch of 35 gray jerseys Units Completed 35

Direct Materials			
Date	**Req. No.**	**Description**	**Cost**
06/15/2016	50613	Jersey fabric & backing material	$210.00
06/15/2016	50614	Buttons, size label & packaging	29.75
			$239.75

Direct Labor				
Date	**Ticket No.**	**Description**	**Total Time**	**Cost**
06/15/2016	6343	Cutting	0.3hr.	$ 2.88
06/16/2016	6349	Sewing	6.7hrs.	64.32
				$67.20

Manufacturing Overhead				
Date	**Activity Base**	**Quantity**	**Rate**	**Cost**
06/15/2016	Direct labor cost	$ 2.88	125%	$ 3.60
06/16/2016	Direct labor cost	$64.32	125%	80.40
				$84.00

Cost Summary	Total Cost	Unit Cost
Direct Material	$239.75	$ 6.85
Direct Labor	$ 67.20	$ 1.92
Manufacturing Overhead Applied	$ 84.00	$ 2.40
Total Cost	$390.95	$11.17

The job cost sheets are the subsidiary ledger that supports the Work in Process Inventory account on the balance sheet. Therefore, to calculate the total in Work in Process Inventory at any point in time, you simply add up the totals on the job cost sheets for all the jobs that have not yet been completed (see Exhibit 4-11).

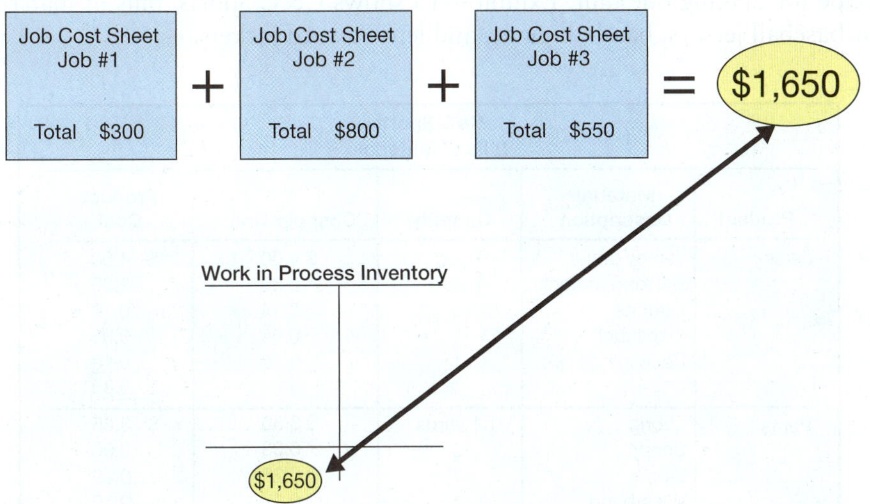

EXHIBIT 4-11

Relationship between the job cost sheets and work in process balance.

Tracing Direct Materials Costs

Once management has approved a production order, workers gather the direct materials from the storeroom and deliver them to the production area. A **materials requisition slip** releases those direct materials from the storeroom to the factory floor. Exhibit 4-12 shows a C&C Sports materials requisition slip for a batch of 35 baseball jerseys. Notice that it includes the job number, the name of the department requesting the materials, and the description, quantity, unit cost, and total cost of each direct material requested. The signature on the materials

C&C Sports
Materials Requisition Slip No. 50613

Date June 15, 2016 Job Number 6052

Department Cutting

Description	Quantity	Unit Cost	Total Cost
Gray jersey fabric	35 yds.	$4.00/yd.	$140.00
Backing material	35 yds.	$2.00/yd.	$ 70.00
			$210.00

Authorized Signature Michael Scott

EXHIBIT 4-12

C&C Sports' materials requisition slip.

requisition slip verifies that the materials have been issued to the production area. Look back at Exhibit 4-10 and find the entry for this materials requisition on the job cost sheet for Job 6052.

How do managers know how much direct material to requisition for 35 jerseys? Each product has a **bill of materials** that lists all the materials required to make a single unit of the product. You can think of the bill of materials as a recipe for making one unit. Exhibit 4-13 shows C&C Sports' bills of materials for baseball jerseys, baseball pants, and letter award jackets.

EXHIBIT 4-13

C&C Sports' bills of materials.

C&C Sports
Bills of Materials

Product	Material Description	Quantity	Cost per Unit	Product Cost
Jersey	Jersey fabric	1 yard	$ 4.00	$ 4.00
	Backing material	1 yard	2.00	2.00
	Buttons	5	0.14	0.70
	Size label	1	0.05	0.05
	Packaging	1	0.10	0.10
				$ 6.85
Pants	Fabric	1.1 yards	$ 3.50	$ 3.85
	Snaps	2	0.03	0.06
	Zipper	1	0.29	0.29
	Waistband	1	0.12	0.12
	Size label	1	0.05	0.05
	Packaging	1	0.10	0.10
				$ 4.47
Jacket	Wool	2 yards	$ 8.00	$ 16.00
	Leather	1.5 yards	15.00	22.50
	Lining material	2 yards	2.00	4.00
	Chenille lettering	1	1.86	1.86
	Snaps	7	0.03	0.21
	Size label	1	0.05	0.05
	Packaging	1	0.10	0.10
				$ 44.72

When the cutting department is ready to start a batch of 35 jerseys, the manager will order one yard of jersey fabric and one yard of backing material for each jersey.

In a company with an automated job cost system, the materials requisition can be completed simply by entering the appropriate information directly into the system. In that case, no materials requisition slip is needed. The computer system automatically posts the amount of the materials requisition to the job cost sheet.

Tracing Direct Labor Costs

The direct labor costs for a particular job are recorded in much the same way as direct materials costs. When employees begin working on a particular job, they record the starting time on a **time ticket**, as shown in Exhibit 4-14. The time ticket also records the employee's name, the date, and the job number. When a work session is completed, the employee records the ending time. (In an automated environment, employees may clock in and out on a computer or other automated time clock rather than manually completing a time ticket.) At the end of the day, the manager (or computer) calculates the total hours worked on each job that day. The total direct labor cost of the day's work can then be calculated and recorded on the job cost sheet using the employee's wage rate. Look back at Exhibit 4-10 and find the entry for this time ticket on the job cost sheet.

C&C Sports
Time Ticket

No. 6349

Employee Erin Smith

Date June 16, 2016

Department Sewing

Start Time	End Time	Total Time	Hourly Rate	Total Cost	Job Number
7:00 AM	11:00 AM	4.0 hrs	$9.60	$38.40	6052
12:00 PM	2:42 PM	2.7 hrs	$9.60	$25.92	6052
2:42 PM	2:54 PM	0.2 hrs	$9.60	$1.92	Machine Maintenance
2:54 PM	4:00 PM	1.1 hr.	$9.60	$10.56	6067

Authorized Signature Michael Scott

EXHIBIT 4-14

C&C Sports' time ticket.

Sometimes a direct labor worker may perform indirect labor activities. For example, a machine may break down, requiring the worker to stop and perform maintenance. Or a worker may sit idle while waiting for raw materials to arrive. In such cases, the worker will charge the time to a particular activity, not to a particular job. Notice in Exhibit 4-14 that Erin Smith charged 0.2 hours to machine maintenance. The labor cost associated with those hours will be charged as manufacturing overhead (indirect labor) rather than direct labor.

Allocating Manufacturing Overhead Costs

Accumulating direct materials and direct labor costs for a particular job is fairly easy. That is because those costs can be traced directly back to the job. The same is not true of manufacturing overhead. Recall from Unit 4.1 that manufacturing overhead is an indirect cost that cannot be physically or economically traced back to a specific item. Because of this lack of traceability, manufacturing overhead must be divided among the different jobs or products a company makes during the year. Dividing or allocating overhead to various jobs is called **overhead application**; the amount of manufacturing overhead allocated to each job is called **applied overhead**.

There are three additional reasons to allocate overhead. First, unlike direct materials and direct labor, the amount of manufacturing overhead actually incurred by the company may not be known at the time a job is being worked on. Consider the property tax on a factory building, which is one component of manufacturing overhead. Assume that C&C Sports' property tax is levied and billed once a year, on March 1. The company can't wait until March 1 to begin allocating this component of manufacturing overhead to the products produced in January and February. Because operating decisions must be made in January and February, the company needs to know its product costs at that time, not at the time the property tax is billed. In other words, the company can't wait until the end of the year, when the actual total amount of overhead is known, to begin developing its product costs.

REALITY CHECK—*Tracking direct labor costs*

© MousePotato/iStockphoto

You may be wondering why it is so important to track the number of hours a worker spends on a particular job. Consider the case of auto maker Fiat Chrysler. The company reached an agreement with the United Auto Workers (UAW) in 2007 on a two-tiered salary structure. Newly hired workers would be paid $14 per hour, while existing employees earned twice that wage for the same work. Knowing which group of employees worked on a particular job, then, has a great effect on the direct labor cost.

What were the results of the two-tiered pay plan? As higher-paid workers left the company and were replaced by the new lower-paid workers, the company's direct labor costs decreased dramatically. By late 2015, approximately 45% of Fiat Chrysler's workers were in the lower pay tier, and total union labor cost has dropped 45% since 2007, to $1,771 per car. Similar plans have been implemented at Ford, General Motors, and Caterpillar and in service industries, such as Safeway grocery stores in California and Mandalay Resort Group hotels in Nevada.

Total union labor cost has dropped 45% since 2007, to $1,771 per car.

As you might guess, now that the auto industry has rebounded, workers are not happy with the two-tiered wage plans. Recent negotiations have resulted in a contract proposal that reduces the wage gap between tiers, but union members rejected the proposal and sent both sides back to negotiate a new deal.

Sources: Fay Hansen, "Breaking the Grip of High Labor Costs," *Business Finance*, June, 2004, p. 51–53; Bill Vlasic, "Detroit Sets Its Future on a Foundation of Two-Tier Wages," *The New York Times*, September 12, 2011; Bernie Woodall and Nick Carey, "Proposed Fiat Chrysler UAW Pact Gradually Ends Two-tier Pay: Sources," Reuter.com, October 8, 2015, http://www.reuters.com/article/us-autos-uaw-idUSKCN0S22RX20151008 (accessed February 29, 2016); Claire Zillman, "Auto Workers Are Even Worse Off Than They Were 10 Years Ago," *Fortune*, October 7, 2015, http://fortune.com/2015/10/07/uaw-fiat-chrysler-worker-strike-pay/ (accessed February 29, 2016); Michael Hiltzik, "Are Those Detested Two-tiered UAW Contracts Finally on the Way Out?," *Los Angeles Times*, October 13, 2015, http://www.latimes.com/business/hiltzik/la-fi-mh-is-the-two-tiered-union-contract-20151013-column.html (accessed February 29, 2016).

The second reason for allocating overhead is that some overhead costs are seasonal. Consider the cost of electricity used to cool the factory building in the summer. Remember, C&C's manufacturing facility is in southern Texas. Its utilities costs will be higher in the summer, not because of any change in the manufacturing process, but because of environmental factors beyond the company's control. If C&C Sports produces the same baseball jersey in March as in August with no change in the production process, does the jersey made in August really cost more to produce than the one made in March? No. The additional cost incurred to cool the factory building in August is part of the *annual* cost of providing adequate manufacturing capacity and should be spread over production for the entire year.

The final reason for allocating overhead relates to fixed manufacturing overhead costs that are not related to the number of units produced. Consider the fixed cost of factory rent. The total cost of rent remains the same each month, regardless of the number of baseball jerseys produced. However, the fixed cost per unit decreases as more units are made. Should C&C Sports conclude that a baseball jersey produced in October, when only 5,000 jerseys are made, costs more than a jersey produced in September, when over 14,000 are produced, simply because the per unit rent cost differs? No. Much like the seasonal costs just described, these fixed costs are incurred to provide production capacity for the entire year, regardless of the number of units produced in a particular month.

THINK ABOUT IT 4.4

Assigning overhead to a job is like splitting the cost of a shared appetizer at dinner. Imagine that you and two friends shared a plate of nachos costing $6.00. What would be the easiest way to allocate the cost of the nachos? What would be the most accurate way to allocate the cost? Why is the most accurate method preferable in business applications such as the division of costs among different products or divisions?

Calculating the Predetermined Overhead Rate

Before you can apply overhead to a particular job, you must calculate a **predetermined overhead rate** based on an application base and the budgeted manufacturing overhead costs. Budgeted manufacturing overhead costs are the total overhead costs the company expects to incur during the year. An **application base** is a measure that is correlated with overhead costs. Common application bases are direct labor hours (DLH), machine hours (MH), direct labor costs (DL$), and units of production.

The predetermined overhead rate is calculated as:

$$\text{Predetermined overhead rate} = \frac{\text{Budgeted total manufacturing overhead cost}}{\text{Budgeted total level of application base}}$$

The rate is calculated at the beginning of the year so that manufacturing overhead can be allocated to all products manufactured throughout the year. As such, the predetermined overhead rate is based on estimates of both the amount of overhead to be incurred and the application base to be achieved.

Applying Manufacturing Overhead to Jobs

Once the predetermined overhead rate is known, manufacturing overhead can be applied to each job based on the actual amount of the application base used on that job. The amount of manufacturing overhead applied to a particular job is calculated as:

$$\text{Applied overhead} = \text{Predetermined overhead rate} \times \text{Actual amount of application base}$$

To illustrate the calculations, let's look at C&C Sports' manufacturing overhead application. At the beginning of 2016, C&C Sports' managers estimated that the company would incur $1,056,000 in manufacturing overhead costs. Based on historical cost trends, Claire Elliot, vice president of finance and administration, has determined that overhead costs are correlated with direct labor cost. That is, as direct labor costs increase, so do overhead costs. Therefore, the application base C&C Sports uses for manufacturing overhead is direct labor cost. The

REALITY CHECK—*Here come the robots*

© RainerPlendl/iStockphoto

At the beginning of the industrial revolution, direct laborers performed the vast majority of work in manufacturing products. But as technology has evolved, the amount of direct labor required to produce most products has declined dramatically. Automobile manufacturing is one example of an industry that has turned to robots to accomplish many jobs that were once done by hand.

When Mercedes-Benz opened its plant at Vance, Alabama, in 1997, there were only 80 robots in the body shop. That number had increased to approximately 1,300 by 2014. Nissan North America, Inc., makes engines in Decherd, Tennessee, with very little contact between the engines and human hands. And Pirelli North America changed its cost structure enough through robots that it can now produce low-volume jobs.

As direct labor cost shrinks as a proportion of the total product cost, it is no longer a relevant cost driver for manufacturing overhead for many companies.

What does this increase in the use of robotics mean for product costing? With robots now costing as little as $20,000, it's not just large manufacturers that are using robots to help with manufacturing tasks that were once performance by human workers. As direct labor cost shrinks as a portion of the total product cost, it is being replaced by manufacturing overhead. Thus, direct labor is no longer a relevant cost driver for manufacturing overhead for many companies. In job order shops, its use as the application base for manufacturing overhead is declining.

Sources: Timothy Aeppel, "Robots Work Their Way into Small Factories," *The Wall Street Journal*, September 18, 2014, B1, B7; Alisa Priddle, "The Next Chapter," *Ward's Auto World*, August 1, 2005, http://wardsauto.com/news-analysis/next-chapter (accessed October 17, 2016); "Robot Numbers Rise as Costs Tumble," *Automotive News*, February 21, 2005, 26; Patrick Rupinski, "Mercedes Plans to Hire 400–500 Workers," *TuscaloosaNews.com*, August 27, 2010, http://www.tuscaloosanews.com/article/20100827/news/100829618 (accessed October 17, 2016); Mark Venables, "MBUSI: Adding to Alabama," Automotive Manufacturing Solutions, May 7, 2014, http://www.automotivemanufacturingsolutions.com/focus/mercedes-benz-adding-to-alabama (accessed February 29, 2016).

company expects to incur $844,800 in direct labor costs during the coming year. Given this estimate, the predetermined overhead rate is

$$\frac{\$1{,}056{,}000}{\$844{,}800} = 125\% \text{ of direct labor cost}$$

Recall from Exhibit 4-14 that $64.32 of direct labor cost was incurred on job 6052 ($38.40 + $25.92). Using the above predetermined overhead rate, $80.40 of manufacturing overhead needs to be applied to the job.

$$\$64.32 \times 125\% = \$80.40$$

Look back at Exhibit 4-10 and find the entry for this application of manufacturing overhead on the job cost sheet.

Recall that the journal entry to charge overhead cost to Work in Process Inventory is

Work in Process Inventory	XXXX	
Manufacturing Overhead Control		XXXX

Instead of crediting the *actual* overhead costs to Work in Process Inventory as was done in Unit 4.2, a job order costing system charges the *applied* manufacturing overhead to Work in Process Inventory. Exhibit 4-15 shows how the Manufacturing Overhead T-account is debited and credited when overhead is allocated to jobs.

Manufacturing Overhead	
Actual overhead recorded as a debit as invoices are received	Applied overhead recorded as a credit during the period as overhead is applied to specific jobs

EXHIBIT 4-15

Manufacturing overhead T-account.

UNIT 4.3 REVIEW

KEY TERMS

Application base p. 153
Applied overhead p. 151
Bill of materials p. 150
Job cost sheet p. 148
Job order costing system p. 147
Materials requisition slip p. 149
Overhead application p. 151
Predetermined overhead rate p. 153
Time ticket p. 150

PRACTICE QUESTIONS

1. LO 4 The predetermined overhead rate is calculated as
   a. actual overhead cost divided by estimated activity level.
   b. estimated activity level divided by estimated overhead cost.
   c. estimated overhead cost divided by estimated activity level.
   d. actual activity level multiplied by estimated overhead cost.

2. LO 4 In planning for the upcoming year, managers of Manilon Industries estimated $447,000 in manufacturing overhead, 20,000 direct labor hours, and 60,000 machine hours. If overhead is applied based on direct labor hours, what is the predetermined overhead rate for the coming year?
   a. $0.04/DLH
   b. $5.5875/DLH
   c. $7.45/DLH
   d. $22.35/DLH

3. LO 4 Agee Machining had one job in Work in Process Inventory at the beginning of the month, job number 1376. The costs incurred to date on that job included $17,500 in direct materials, $22,000 in direct labor, and $33,000 in overhead. During the month, Agee added $1,000 in direct materials and $7,000 in direct labor. If Agee's predetermined overhead rate is 160% of direct labor costs, how much overhead should be applied to job 1376 for the month?
   a. $1,120
   b. $11,200
   c. $44,200
   d. $46,400

4. LO 5 Hurst Motors applies overhead based on direct labor hours. In completing the 300 motors in job 4329, the company incurred $10,500 in direct materials and 60 direct labor hours at $15 per hour. The predetermined overhead rate is $65 per direct labor hour. What is the unit cost of the motors produced in job 4329?
   a. $13
   b. $51
   c. $115
   d. $233

5. LO 5 Which of the following documents is not used to accumulate product costs in a job order costing environment?
   a. Time ticket
   b. Job cost sheet
   c. Customer invoice
   d. Materials requisition slip

6. LO 5 Weaver Mills uses a job order costing system to account for its production of specialty fabrics. On January 31 the company reported the following balances in its inventory accounts: $50,975 in Raw Materials, $24,950 in Work in Process, and $15,080 in Finished Goods. On January 31, the total of all open job order cost sheets would be

a. $15,080.
b. $24,950.
c. $50,975.
d. $91,005.

UNIT 4.3 PRACTICE EXERCISE

Foster Enterprises makes custom-order draperies. In late 2016, when managers prepared the budget for 2017, they estimated that manufacturing overhead would total $100,000. Because the production process is labor intensive, overhead is allocated to jobs based on direct labor hours. Managers expected total direct labor hours to amount to 400,000 hours.

During March and April of 2017, employees worked on only three jobs. Relevant information for each job follows:

Monthly Data Recorded	Job 76	Job 77	Job 78
March			
Direct materials cost	$12,986	—	—
Direct labor cost	$35,880	—	—
Direct labor hours	3,680	—	—
April			
Direct materials cost	$ 0	$10,855	$6,250
Direct labor cost	$ 9,750	$22,800	$2,730
Direct labor hours	1,000	2,400	280

Job 76 was started in March, finished in April, and delivered to the customer in the same month. Job 77 was started in April, finished in April, and delivered to the customer in May. Job 78 was started in April and finished in May.

1. What predetermined overhead rate will the company use for all jobs worked on during 2017?
2. Compute the cost of each job (don't forget to allocate overhead).
3. What was the Work in Process Inventory balance on March 31? On April 30?
4. What was cost of goods manufactured for April?
5. What was cost of goods sold for April?

SELECTED UNIT 4.3 ANSWERS

Think About It 4.4

The easiest way to allocate the cost would be to divide it equally among everyone at the table—$6.00 ÷ 3 = $2.00 per person. The most accurate way would be to keep track of how much each person ate and divide the cost based on the percentage of nachos each person consumed. The most accurate method is preferable in business because that is the only way to get the best information on the cost of making a product or supporting a division. Accurate cost information yields accurate profit information, which is critical to the decisions managers make about products and divisions.

Practice Questions

1. C
2. D
3. B
4. B
5. C
6. B

Unit 4.3 Practice Exercise

1. $\frac{\$100{,}000}{400{,}000 \text{ DLH}} = \$0.25/\text{DLH}$

2.

	Job 76	Job 77	Job 78
March			
Direct materials	$12,986	—	—
Direct labor	35,880	—	—
Overhead	—	—	
(3,680 DLH × $0.25/DLH)	920		
April			
Direct materials	0	$10,855	$6,250
Direct labor	9,750	22,800	2,730
Overhead			
(1,000 DLH × $0.25/DLH)	250		
(2,400 DLH × $0.25/DLH)		600	
(280 DLH × $0.25/DLH)			70
Total costs	$59,786	$34,255	$9,050

3. March 31: Job 76 = $49,786; April 30: Job 78 = $9,050
4. Jobs 76 and 77: $59,786 + $34,255 = $94,041
5. Job 76: $59,786

UNIT 4.4

Underapplied and Overapplied Manufacturing Overhead

GUIDED UNIT PREPARATION

Answering the following questions while you read this unit will guide your understanding of the key concepts found in the unit. The questions are linked to the learning objectives presented at the beginning of the chapter.

LO 6

1. Why do companies that use job order costing have under- and overapplied overhead?
2. What two methods can companies use to dispose of under- and overapplied overhead?

We have seen that during the accounting period, manufacturing overhead is applied to work in process using a predetermined overhead rate that is based on estimates of total manufacturing overhead and activity. It is unlikely, therefore, that at the end of the accounting period the actual overhead incurred during the period will equal the applied overhead for the period. That is, instead of equaling zero, the Manufacturing Overhead Control account will show a balance. This control account is just a temporary account that is used to keep track of overhead costs. Because the amount isn't reported separately in the financial statements, it needs to have a zero balance by the end of the accounting period. The way to reduce the account balance to zero is to make an adjusting entry to the Manufacturing Overhead Control account.

To determine the amount of the adjustment, look at the balance in the Manufacturing Overhead Control account. If the balance is a debit, more overhead was actually incurred than was recorded in the Work in Process Inventory account during the period. The result is **underapplied overhead**—that is, not enough overhead cost was charged to products as they were made. As a result, the inventory cost is too low and needs to be increased. If the balance in the account is a credit, on the other hand, more overhead was recorded in the Work in Process Inventory account than was actually incurred during the period. The result is **overapplied overhead**. Since the cost that was recorded in the inventory account is too high, the inventory cost needs to be decreased. Exhibit 4-16 summarizes the relationship between actual and applied manufacturing overhead.

EXHIBIT 4-16

Underapplied and overapplied overhead.

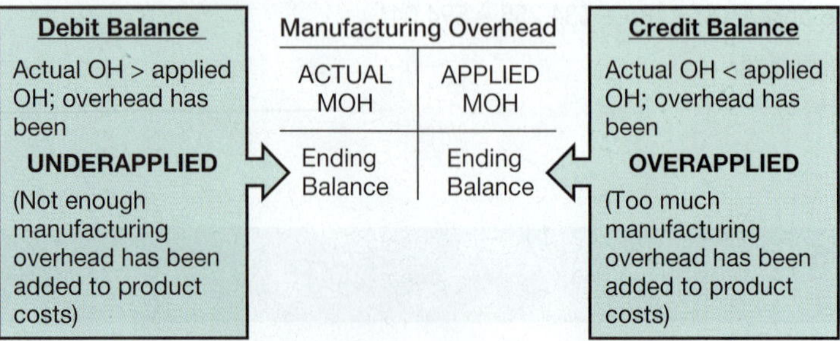

Closing Underapplied and Overapplied Overhead to Cost of Goods Sold

If the amount of underapplied or overapplied manufacturing overhead is small, most companies will make the entire adjustment to cost of goods sold. The justification is that by the end of the period most of the inventory that was incorrectly costed has been sold and the adjustment amount is small compared to the total inventory value. To make this kind of adjustment, one of the following journal entries should be recorded for the amount of underapplied or overapplied manufacturing overhead:

To Adjust for Underapplied Overhead			To Adjust for Overapplied Overhead		
Cost of Goods Sold	xxx		Manufacturing Overhead Control	xxx	
Manufacturing Overhead Control		xxx	Cost of Goods Sold		xxx

Notice that when manufacturing overhead is underapplied (left column), Cost of Goods Sold is debited. Cost of Goods Sold is an expense account that normally has a debit balance. If this account is debited, it is increased, recognizing that not enough overhead has been recorded in the financial records. Alternatively, when manufacturing overhead is overapplied (right column), Cost of Goods Sold is credited, or decreased, recognizing that too much overhead has been recorded in the financial records.

Let's look at an example. By the end of the year, C&C Sports had applied $1,043,526 of manufacturing overhead costs to work in process. The company had actually incurred $1,063,108 in manufacturing overhead costs. Since actual manufacturing overhead exceeded the amount of overhead applied during the year, overhead was underapplied by $19,582, and inventory costs recorded during the year were too low. For the inventory accounts to reflect the actual overhead costs incurred, C&C Sports should make the following journal entry:

Cost of Goods Sold	$19,582	
Manufacturing Overhead Control		$19,582

WATCH OUT!

The three different overhead terms that you have just learned cannot be used interchangeably. Make sure you can distinguish among them:

Actual overhead—the amount of overhead costs that the company really pays for. (For C&C, $1,063,108 in 2016).

Estimated overhead—the amount of overhead that the company *expects* to incur during the year. This amount is used only at the beginning of the accounting period, to determine the predetermined overhead rate. (Estimated by C&C at $1,056,000 at the beginning of 2016).

Applied overhead—the amount of overhead that is charged to Work in Process Inventory. It equals the predetermined overhead rate times the actual application base incurred by the company. (For C&C, $1,043,526 by the end of 2016).

Prorating Underapplied and Overapplied Overhead

If the amount of underapplied or overapplied manufacturing overhead is relatively large, the more appropriate treatment is to prorate the amount to all the accounts that contain applied overhead—Work in Process Inventory, Finished Goods Inventory, and Cost of Goods Sold. The proration should be based on the relative size of the ending balance in each account.

The first step in prorating underapplied or overapplied overhead is to add together the ending balances in the Work in Process Inventory, Finished Goods Inventory, and Cost of Goods Sold accounts. Next, calculate the percentage of the total represented by each of the three accounts. Finally, multiply each percentage by the underapplied or overapplied amount to determine how much overhead should be charged to each account. Exhibit 4-17 shows how the proration would be done using the same amount as in the previous example (with $19,582 in underapplied manufacturing overhead).

Account	Ending Balance	Percentage of Total	Prorated Overhead Amount
Work in process	$ 6,137	0.14%[a]	$ 27[b]
Finished goods	447,280	10.38%	2,033
Cost of goods sold	3,856,850	89.48%	17,522
	$4,310,267	100.00%	$19,582

[a]$6,137 ÷ $4,310,267 = 0.14%.
[b]$19,582 × 0.14% = $27.

EXHIBIT 4-17

C&C Sports' proration of underapplied overhead.

Notice that with either approach (closing the entire amount to Cost of Goods Sold or prorating it), the balance in the Manufacturing Overhead Control account will be zero after the adjusting entry has been posted. The zero balance indicates that actual overhead cost and applied overhead cost are equal so that all inventory is reflected at actual cost.

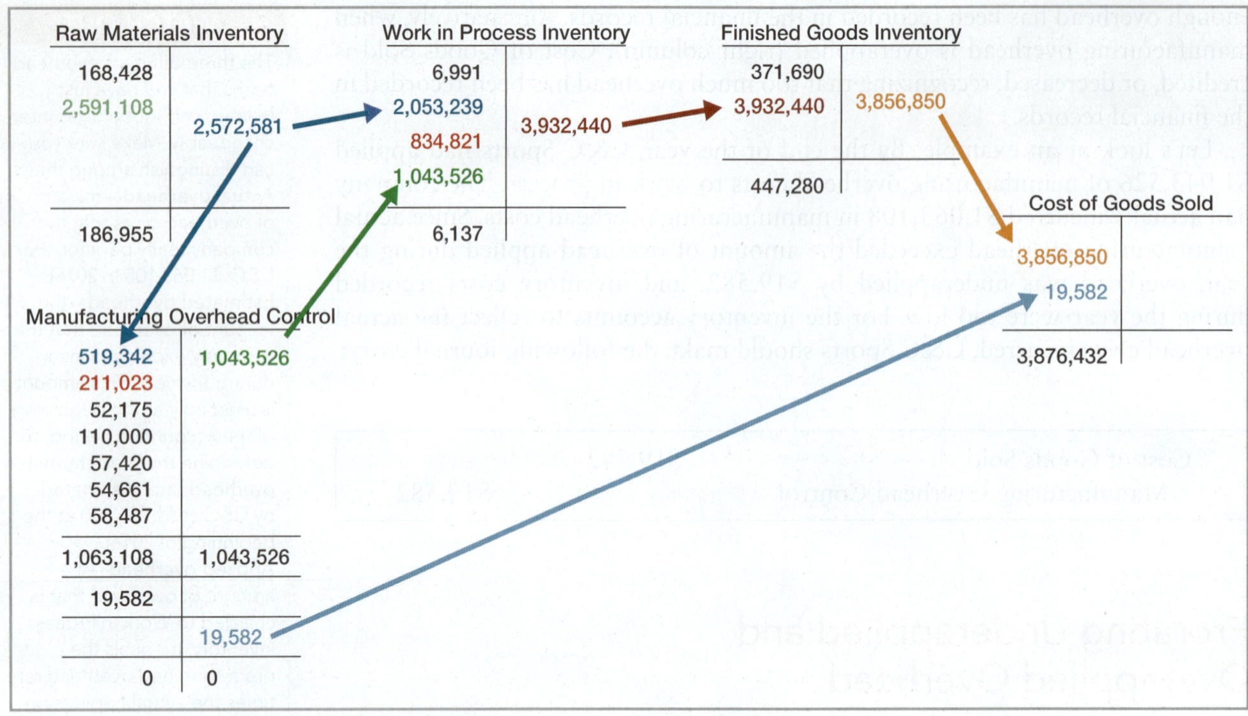

EXHIBIT 4-18 *Manufacturing cost flow summary for C&C Sports, 2016.*

Exhibit 4-18 summarizes C&C's cost flows for 2016 based on the following events. Compare the balances in the T-accounts in Exhibit 4-18 to C&C Sports' financial statements, shown in Topic Focus 1, Exhibits T1-3 on page 37 and T1-4 on page 38.

Materials purchased	$2,591,108
Materials used ($2,053,239 direct; $519,342 indirect)	2,572,581
Wages/Salaries paid ($834,821 direct; $211,023 indirect)	1,045,844
Factory equipment depreciation recorded	52,175
Factory rent paid	110,000
Utilities paid	57,420
Insurance paid	54,661
Other factory costs incurred	58,487
Overhead charged to work in process at 125% of direct labor cost ($834,821 × 125%)	1,043,526
Finished:	
202,000 pants at a total cost of $1,993,740	
70,000 jerseys at a total cost of $781,900	
15,000 jackets at a total cost of $1,156,800	$3,932,440
Sold:	
200,000 pants at a total cost of $1,974,000	
65,000 jerseys at a total cost of $726,050	
15,000 jackets at a total cost of $1,156,800	$3,856,850
Underapplied overhead charged to Cost of Goods Sold	$ 19,582

THINK ABOUT IT 4.5

Why is underapplied or overapplied overhead never charged to Raw Materials Inventory?

UNIT 4.4 REVIEW

KEY TERMS

Actual overhead p. 159 Estimated overhead p. 159 Overapplied overhead p. 158 Underapplied overhead p. 158

PRACTICE QUESTIONS

1. LO 6 Mountain Pictures, Ltd., applies overhead at a rate of $10 per direct labor hour. At the end of June, the company had accumulated 7,650 direct labor hours and incurred $81,250 in manufacturing overhead. For the month of June, manufacturing overhead was
   a. $750 overapplied.
   b. $750 underapplied.
   c. $4,750 overapplied.
   d. $4,750 underapplied.

2. LO 6 Stewart Statues had overapplied overhead totaling $50,000 during the year, which is considered to be immaterial. To dispose of this overapplied overhead, Stewart should
   a. increase Cost of Goods Sold by $50,000.
   b. decrease Cost of Goods Sold by $50,000.
   c. increase Finished Goods Inventory by $50,000.
   d. decrease Finished Goods Inventory by $50,000.

UNIT 4.4 PRACTICE EXERCISE

At the end of the year, but before an adjustment had been made to close Manufacturing Overhead Control, A-1 Frames had the following account balances:

Raw Materials Inventory	$ 126,788
Work in Process Inventory	$ 146,955
Finished Goods Inventory	$ 342,895
Cost of Goods Sold	$1,959,400

At the beginning of the year, management had estimated that total manufacturing overhead would be $630,000 and had planned to apply overhead to jobs based on an estimated use of 42,000 machine hours. The actual number of machine hours used during the year was 41,895, and actual manufacturing overhead cost for the year was $648,825.

1. What predetermined overhead rate did the company use throughout the year?
2. How much overhead was applied to jobs during the year?
3. By how much is overhead under- or overapplied? (Indicate whether under or over.)
4. What was the balance in Cost of Goods Sold if the entire amount of under- or overapplied overhead was closed to that account?
5. What were the balances in the inventory accounts and Cost of Goods Sold if the amount of under- or overapplied overhead was prorated to the appropriate accounts?

SELECTED UNIT 4.4 ANSWERS

Think About It 4.5

Under- and overapplied overhead is never allocated to Raw Materials Inventory because overhead costs are consumed only as products are made. Raw Materials Inventory represents the cost of materials that have not yet been put into production and thus have never caused any overhead to be incurred.

Practice Questions

1. D
2. B

Unit 4.4 Practice Exercise

1. $\frac{\$630{,}000}{42{,}000 \text{ machine hours}} = \$15/\text{machine hour}$
2. 41,895 machine hours × $15/machine hour = $628,425
3. $648,825 actual overhead − $628,425 applied overhead = $20,400 underapplied overhead
4. $1,959,400 + $20,400 = $1,979,800. Since overhead was underapplied, Cost of Goods Sold must be increased to reflect the actual cost.
5.

Account	Balance	Percent of Total[a]	Prorated Amount[b]	Adjusted Balance[c]
Work in Process Inventory	$ 146,955	6%	$ 1,224	$ 148,179
Finished Goods Inventory	342,895	14%	2,856	345,751
Cost of Goods Sold	1,959,400	80%	16,320	1,975,720
Total	$2,449,250	100%	$20,400	$2,469,650

[a]For Work in Process: $\frac{\$146{,}955}{\$2{,}449{,}250} = 6\%$.

[b]For Work in Process: $20,400 × 6% = $1,224.

[c]For Work in Process: $146,955 + $1,224 = $148,179.

BUSINESS DECISION AND CONTEXT Wrap Up

In the chapter opener, C&C's Vice President of Marketing Jonathan Smith was questioning how the company calculated its $11.17 cost to make a baseball jersey. Jonathan focused only on the material cost of $6.85 and was surprised to learn that there was more to the cost to produce a jersey, as follows.

Direct materials	$ 6.85
Direct labor	1.92
Overhead (125% × $1.92)	2.40
Jersey unit cost	$11.17

Now Jonathan understands how C&C uses job order costing to accumulate its product costs. He also understands that while direct materials and direct labor are directly traceable to products, manufacturing overhead must be allocated.

Jonathan knows that manufacturing overhead is allocated to products throughout the year using a predetermined overhead rate. At the end of the year when the actual amount of manufacturing overhead is known, the company adjusts the accounting records to reflect actual product costs.

Now when Jonathan looks at the unit cost of $11.17 for jerseys, $9.87 for pants, and $77.12 for jackets, he understands how those costs are calculated. More importantly, he can use that knowledge to help C&C make decisions about pricing, sales mix, and the introduction of new products.

CHAPTER SUMMARY

In this chapter you learned how to accumulate product costs using a job order costing system. You should be able to meet the learning objectives set out at the beginning of the chapter:

1. *Distinguish between product and period costs. (Unit 4.1)*

   All costs can be classified as either product or period costs. **Product costs** are the costs incurred to acquire raw materials and convert them into finished products; they are accumulated in inventory accounts and expensed when the finished units are sold. **Period costs** are the costs associated with the sale of the finished product and the administration of the business. These costs, commonly referred to as selling, general, and administrative costs, are expensed as they are incurred.

2. *Describe the three major components of product costs: direct materials, direct labor, and manufacturing overhead. (Unit 4.2)*

   Direct materials is the cost of the raw materials that can be traced directly to, or easily identified with, the final product. **Direct labor** is the cost of the wages and salaries paid to workers who have their "hands on" the product as it is made. **Manufacturing overhead** includes all manufacturing costs not classified as direct materials or direct labor.

3. *Trace the flow of product costs through the inventory accounts. (Unit 4.2)*

   The three inventory accounts are **Raw Materials, Work in Process,** and **Finished Goods.** Purchases of raw materials are debited to the Raw Materials Inventory account. When raw materials are issued to the production floor, their cost is credited to the Raw Materials Inventory account. The cost of direct materials issued to the production floor, along with the costs of direct labor and applied manufacturing overhead, are debited to the Work in Process Inventory account. The **cost of goods manufactured** is credited to the Work in Process Inventory account and debited to the Finished Goods Inventory account. Finally, the **cost of goods sold** is credited to the Finished Goods Inventory account.

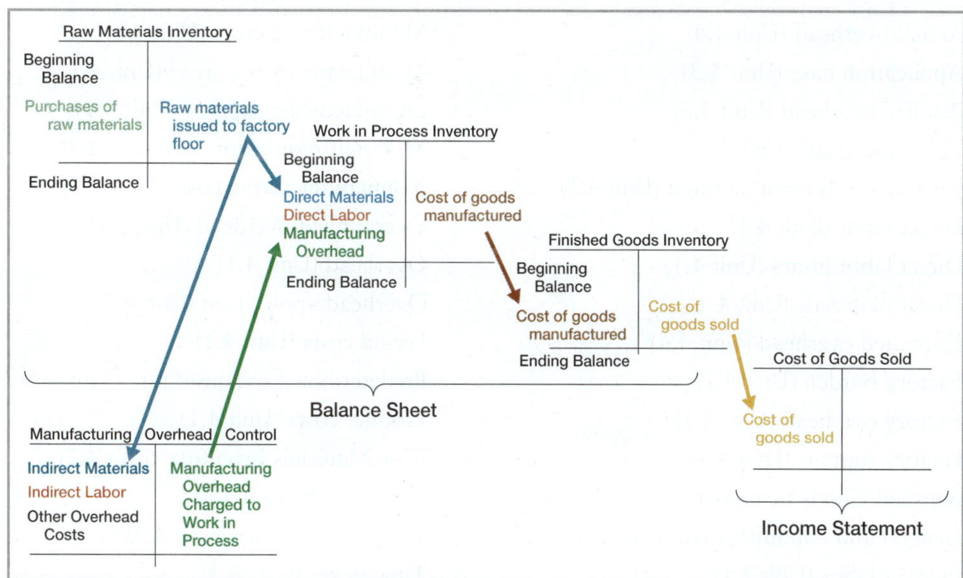

4. *Compute a predetermined overhead rate and apply manufacturing overhead to production. (Unit 4.3)*

   The **predetermined overhead rate** is calculated using the total estimated overhead cost and the total estimated **application base.** Some common application bases are machine hours, direct labor hours, and direct labor cost. The chosen application base should have a causal relationship to, or be highly correlated with, overhead costs. To apply overhead cost to production, multiply the predetermined overhead rate by the actual application base.

$$\text{Predetermined overhead rate} = \frac{\text{Budgeted total manufacturing overhead}}{\text{Budgeted level of application base}}$$

$$\text{Applied overhead} = \text{Predetermined overhead rate} \times \text{actual level of application base}$$

5. ***Compute product costs using a job order costing system. (Unit 4.3)***
   In a job order costing system, product costs are accumulated on a **job cost sheet using materials requisition slips, job time tickets,** and **applied overhead,** either on paper forms or in a computerized system. Once all the costs have been accumulated, the total cost of the job is divided by the number of good units actually produced to determine the average unit cost.

6. ***Dispose of under- and overapplied manufacturing overhead. (Unit 4.4)***
   If actual manufacturing overhead costs for the period exceed the applied manufacturing overhead, overhead has been **underapplied.** Conversely, if actual manufacturing overhead costs for the period fall short of the applied manufacturing overhead, overhead has been **overapplied.** The easiest way to dispose of under- or overapplied overhead is to adjust the Cost of Goods Sold account. The more "accurate" method is to prorate it to the three accounts that contain overhead costs: Work in Process Inventory, Finished Goods Inventory, and Cost of Goods Sold. The amount that is prorated to each account is based on the size of the account balance relative to the total balance in the three accounts.

KEY TERMS

Actual overhead (Unit 4.4)
Application base (Unit 4.3)
Applied overhead (Unit 4.3)
Bill of materials (Unit 4.3)
Cost of goods manufactured (Unit 4.2)
Direct labor (Unit 4.1)
Direct labor hours (Unit 4.1)
Direct materials (Unit 4.1)
Estimated overhead (Unit 4.4)
Factory burden (Unit 4.1)
Factory overhead (Unit 4.1)
Factory support (Unit 4.1)
Finished Goods Inventory (Unit 4.2)
General and administrative costs (Unit 4.1)
Indirect labor (Unit 4.1)
Indirect materials (Unit 4.1)
Job cost sheet (Unit 4.3)
Job order costing system (Unit 4.3)
Manufacturing burden (Unit 4.1)
Manufacturing costs (Unit 4.1)
Manufacturing overhead (Unit 4.1)
Manufacturing support (Unit 4.1)
Materials requisition slip (Unit 4.3)
Nonmanufacturing costs (Unit 4.1)
Overapplied overhead (Unit 4.4)
Overhead (Unit 4.1)
Overhead application (Unit 4.3)
Period costs (Unit 4.1)
Predetermined overhead rate (Unit 4.3)
Product costs (Unit 4.1)
Raw Materials Inventory (Unit 4.2)
Selling costs (Unit 4.1)
Supplies Inventory (Unit 4.2)
Time ticket (Unit 4.3)
Total manufacturing cost (Unit 4.2)
Underapplied overhead (Unit 4.4)
Work in Process Inventory (Unit 4.2)

EXERCISES

4-1 Product versus period costs (LO 1) Steinway Musical Instruments, Inc. is a leading manufacturer of pianos and band and orchestral instruments. The company also maintains ten retail showrooms throughout the world. Classify each of the following costs as a product or period cost.

a. Sitka spruce wood used in piano soundboards
b. Glue used to secure xylophone mallet heads to the sticks
c. Design costs for the company's sales catalog
d. Salaries of the district sales managers
e. The CEO's salary
f. Salaries of the production workers who make Vito clarinets
g. Freight charges for the delivery of a piano to a retail showroom
h. Freight charges for delivery of metal used in trumpets
i. Legal fees incurred to register the company with state sales tax agencies
j. Lease payments for a drum manufacturing facility in Monroe, North Carolina
k. Lease payments for a piano showroom in Coral Gables, Florida
l. Sandpaper used to smooth the wooden components of a piano

4-2 Product cost identification and classification (LO 1, 2) Friendly Ice Cream Corporation operates and franchises full-service restaurants from Maine to Florida. The company also manufactures the ice cream that is served in its restaurants and sold in supermarkets and other retail stores. Indicate whether each of the following costs that Friendly's might incur would be considered a product or a period cost. If the cost is a product cost, classify it as direct materials, direct labor, indirect materials, indirect labor, or other manufacturing overhead.

a. The cost of milk used in the manufacturing of ice cream
b. Salaries paid to the graphic artists responsible for the design of the corporate website
c. Salary paid to the shift supervisor in the ice cream plant
d. Wages paid to production line workers in the ice cream plant
e. Wages paid to the forklift drivers who load the filled ice cream cartons into storage freezers awaiting delivery to customers
f. The cost of empty ice cream cartons
g. The cost of hairnets worn by production line workers
h. The cost of glue used to seal the bottom of ice cream cartons
i. The cost of toner for the sales department's laser printer
j. The cost of life insurance policies for top corporate executives

4-3 Product cost classification (LO 2) Ethan Allen Interiors, Inc. is a leading manufacturer and retailer of furniture and home decorating accessories. Its company-owned operations include sawmills, manufacturing plants, and retail stores. Classify each of the following product costs as direct materials, indirect materials, direct labor, indirect labor, or other manufacturing overhead.

a. Maple logs purchased and cut in the sawmill
b. Foam used in stuffing sofa cushions
c. Silk brocade fabric used to upholster chairs
d. Wages paid to the woodworkers who assemble dresser drawers
e. Glue used to strengthen the bed frame joints
f. Staples used to secure upholstery fabric to the chair seats
g. Electricity to heat and light the factory
h. The sawmill foreman's salary
i. Wages paid to the forklift operator in the raw materials warehouse
j. Depreciation on factory equipment

4-4 Product versus period costs (LO 1, 2) Carleton Closures, Inc., manufactures clamps used in the overhead bin latches of several leading airplane models. Greg Poole, president of Carleton Closures, Inc., has gathered the following cost information from the company's accounting records for the latest month of operations.

Advertising	$25,000
Fire insurance premium for the factory building	$ 6,250
Sales office utilities	$ 2,500
Air filters for the buffing machines used to produce the clamps	$ 1,875
Aluminum used to produce the clamps	$37,500
Rent on the factory building	$10,000
Freight to ship the clamps to customers	$ 3,125
Sales department executives' salaries	$42,500
Production supervisors' salaries	$22,500
Assembly line workers' wages	$60,000

Required

a. Calculate the total period costs for the month.
b. Calculate the total product costs for the month.
c. Calculate the amount of manufacturing overhead incurred for the month.

4-5 Product cost flows (LO 3) The following T-accounts record the operations of Roddick Co.:

Direct Materials

	Debit	Credit
Beginning Balance	10,000	60,000
Purchases	?	
Ending Balance	12,000	

Work in Process

	Debit	Credit
Beginning Balance	15,000	?
Direct Material	?	
Direct Labor	48,000	
Overhead	72,000	
Ending Balance	23,000	

Finished Goods

	Debit	Credit
Beginning Balance	25,000	
COGM	?	
COGS		?
Ending Balance	16,000	

Required

a. Calculate the amount of direct materials purchased during the period.
b. Calculate the direct materials used in production during the period.
c. Calculate the total manufacturing cost for the period.
d. Calculate the cost of goods manufactured for the period.
e. Calculate the cost of goods sold for the period.

4-6 Cost of goods manufactured schedule (LO 3) Rocket Company produces small gasoline-powered engines for model airplanes. Mr. Clemens, Rocket's CFO, has presented you with the following cost information:

Direct Materials Inventory, beginning	$ 80,000
Direct Materials Inventory, ending	$122,000
Work in Process Inventory, beginning	$140,000
Work in Process Inventory, ending	$ 95,000
Direct labor	$780,000
Direct materials purchases	$940,000
Insurance, factory	$ 50,000
Depreciation, factory	$ 22,000
Depreciation, executive offices	$ 15,000
Indirect labor	$220,000
Utilities, factory	$ 17,000
Utilities, executive offices	$ 8,000
Property taxes, factory	$ 18,000
Property taxes, executive offices	$ 14,000

Required

Using this cost information, prepare a cost of goods manufactured schedule for Mr. Clemens.

4-7 Cost of goods sold schedule (LO 3) The following information relates to the operations of Favre Company:

Finished Goods Inventory, beginning	$ 80,000
Finished Goods Inventory, ending	$ 50,000
Cost of goods available for sale	$220,000

Required

a. What was Favre's cost of goods manufactured for the period?
b. What was Favre's cost of goods sold for the period?

4-8 Inventory accounts (LO 3) Brinker International, Inc. is the parent company that owns casual dining chains Chili's Grill and Bar and Maggiano's Little Italy. You can learn more about the company at http://www.brinker.com. In its 2015 annual report, Brinker reported $23,035,000 in inventories on June 24, 2015. Would you expect Brinker to use all three categories of inventory—Raw Materials, Work in Process, and Finished Goods? Why or why not?

4-9 Inventory cost flows (LO 3) The following information is taken from the accounting records of four different companies. Provide the missing amounts. Assume there are no indirect materials used in the company's finished product.

	Company 1	Company 2	Company 3	Company 4
Direct Materials Inventory, beginning	$ 15,000	?	$ 6,000	$130,500
Purchases of direct materials	?	93,200	51,600	220,800
Total direct materials available for use	394,000	101,300	?	?
Direct Materials Inventory, ending	26,000	?	?	34,600
Direct materials used in production	?	71,200	?	?
Direct labor	212,000	?	25,000	324,400
Total manufacturing overhead	254,400	97,500	64,300	?
Total manufacturing cost	?	195,000	138,300	913,200
Beginning Work in Process Inventory	?	147,500	38,000	?
Ending Work in Process Inventory	49,000	43,700	?	49,900
Cost of goods manufactured	817,400	?	103,450	920,300
Finished Goods Inventory, beginning	35,000	?	?	36,000
Cost of goods available for sale	?	393,000	140,050	?
Finished Goods Inventory, ending	?	14,600	?	42,400
Cost of Goods Sold	796,400	?	108,400	?

4-10 Appropriate manufacturing overhead application bases (LO 4) Discuss the appropriateness of the manufacturing overhead application base used in each of the following examples.

Required

a. Barlowe Manufacturing produces cell phone covers. The manufacturing process is highly automated, requiring very little human contact. The company uses direct labor hours as its manufacturing overhead application base.
b. Sky High Tumblers manufactures tumbling mats. Although part of the production process is automated, significant human effort is required to complete the mats. The company uses machine hours as its manufacturing overhead application base.
c. Hill, Hill, and Dale is a dental office that performs a variety of dental services for its patients. For most services, the dental hygienists spend much more time with the patients than the dentists do. The company uses direct labor dollars as its overhead application base.
d. Lamberti Industries is a leading manufacturer of perfumes. The entire mixing process for the perfumes is automated and controlled by highly sensitive computers. The company uses machine hours as its manufacturing overhead application base.

4-11 Predetermined overhead rates and manufacturing overhead application (LO 4) Beltran Corporation produces wooden and aluminum baseball bats. In preparing the current budget, Beltran's management estimated a total of $500,000 in manufacturing overhead costs and 10,000 machine hours for the coming year. In December, Beltran's accountants reported actual manufacturing overhead incurred of $650,000 and 10,500 machine hours used during the year. Beltran applies overhead based on machine hours.

Required

a. What was Beltran's predetermined overhead rate for the year?
b. How much manufacturing overhead did Beltran apply during the year?

4-12 Predetermined overhead rates and manufacturing overhead application (LO 4) Rector Company manufactures a line of lightweight running shoes. CEO Mark Rector estimated that the company would incur $2,500,000 in manufacturing overhead during the coming year. Additionally, he estimated the company would operate at a level requiring 250,000 direct labor hours and 400,000 machine hours.

Required

a. Assume that Rector Company uses direct labor hours as its manufacturing overhead application base. Calculate the company's predetermined overhead rate.
b. Assume that job 4375 required 300 direct labor hours to complete. How much manufacturing overhead should be applied to the job?
c. Assume that Rector Company uses machine hours as its manufacturing overhead application base. Calculate the company's predetermined overhead rate.
d. Assume that job 4375 required 140 machine hours to complete. How much manufacturing overhead should be applied to the job?

4-13 Inventory cost flows (LO 3, 4) Furr Fabricators produces protective covers for smart phones. Since the covers must be customized to each smart phone model, Furr uses a job order costing system. On September 1, the company reported the following inventory balances:

Direct Materials	$ 25,000
Work in Process	$148,000
Finished Goods	$255,000

During September, the following events occurred:

1. Furr purchased direct materials costing $415,000 on account.
2. Furr used $427,000 in direct materials in production.
3. Furr's employees clocked 18,000 direct labor hours at an average wage rate of $10.00 per direct labor hour.
4. The company incurred $169,000 in manufacturing overhead, including $18,000 in indirect labor costs.
5. Using direct labor hours as the application base, the company applied $162,000 of manufacturing overhead to jobs worked on in September.
6. The company completed production on jobs costing $850,000.
7. The company delivered jobs costing $1,075,000 to customers.

Required

a. Calculate the ending September balance of the Direct Materials, Work in Process, and Finished Goods Inventory accounts.
b. Calculate total manufacturing costs for September.

4-14 Cost flow through T-accounts (LO 3, 4) Drew Corp. designs and manufactures mascot uniforms for high school, college, and professional sports teams. Since each team's uniform is unique in color and design, Drew uses a job order costing system. On January 1, the T-accounts for some of Drew's primary balance sheet accounts were as follows:

Raw Materials Inventory	
1/1 15,000	

Work in Process Inventory	
1/1 31,000	

Finished Goods Inventory	
1/1 22,000	

Cash	
1/1 32,000	

Accounts Receivable	
1/1 56,000	

Accounts Payable	
	42,000 1/1

During the year, the following events occurred:

1. Drew purchased raw materials costing $86,000 on account.
2. Drew used $93,000 of raw materials in production. Of these, 70% were classified as direct materials and 30% as indirect materials. (Drew maintains a single Raw Materials Inventory account.)
3. Drew used 31,200 hours of direct labor. The company's average direct labor rate was $7.50 per hour (credit Wages Payable).
4. The company's only indirect labor cost was the salary of a security guard hired to watch the company's shop after hours. The guard's annual salary was $25,000 (credit Wages Payable).
5. Other manufacturing overhead costs the company incurred on account totaled $70,000.
6. Drew applied $130,000 in manufacturing overhead.
7. The company completed production of goods costing $326,000.
8. The company's Cost of Goods Sold balance was $303,750 before adjusting for over- or underapplied overhead.
9. Sales revenue was $425,000 (all sales were made on account).
10. Drew collected $450,000 from customers.
11. The company paid accounts payable of $100,000.
12. At year-end, all wages earned during the year had been paid.

Required

a. Record the transactions above in the appropriate T-accounts and calculate ending balances. Create new T-accounts if needed.
b. Calculate total manufacturing costs for the year.
c. Calculate cost of goods available for sale during the year.

4-15 Job order costing (CMA adapted) (LO 5) Lucy Sportswear manufactures a line of specialty T-shirts using a job order costing system. In March the company incurred the following costs to complete Job ICU2: direct materials, $13,700, and direct labor, $4,800. The company also incurred $1,400 of administrative costs and $5,600 of selling costs to complete this job. Job ICU2 required 800 machine hours. Factory overhead was applied to the job at a rate of $25 per machine hour.

Required

If Job ICU2 resulted in 7,000 good shirts, what was the cost of goods sold per shirt?

4-16 Job order costing (LO 4, 5) Jestus Church Furniture manufactures custom pews, altars, and pulpits for churches across the southern United States. Since each order is unique, Jestus uses a job order costing system. During the month of June, Jestus worked on orders for three churches: Faith Church, Grace Church, and Hope Church. Production on the Faith and Grace orders began in May and ended in June. Production on the Hope order began in June and was incomplete at the end of the month. Jestus applies overhead to each job based on machine hours. Prior to the year, managers had estimated manufacturing overhead at

$600,000, along with 40,000 machine hours. Additional cost information related to the three orders is as follows:

	Faith	Grace	Hope
Beginning balance, June 1	$9,000	$4,300	—
Direct materials, June	$6,000	$9,000	$3,800
Direct labor, June	$12,000	$4,500	$2,400
Manufacturing OH, June	?	?	?
Machine hours, June	2,000	4,000	1,400

Required

a. What is Jestus's predetermined overhead rate?
b. How much manufacturing overhead should Jestus apply to each job for June?
c. What is the balance in Jestus's Work in Process Inventory account at the end of June?

4-17 Job order cost flows and under- and overapplied overhead (LO 5, 6) The following events occurred over the course of a year at Bagby Corp., which uses a job order costing system:

1. Direct materials purchases totaled $460,000.
2. $230,000 of indirect materials were used in production. Bagby uses a separate Supplies Inventory account for indirect materials.
3. $415,000 of direct materials were used in production.
4. The direct labor payroll was $940,000 (credit Wages Payable).
5. Other manufacturing overhead costs incurred during the year totaled $540,000.
6. Bagby applies overhead based on a predetermined overhead rate of $15 per machine hour. The company used 50,000 machine hours during the year.
7. During the year, Bagby transferred goods costing $2,100,000 into the Finished Goods Inventory account.
8. Bagby sold products with a manufacturing cost of $2,050,000 to customers during the year.

Required

a. Prepare journal entries to record these events.
b. Prepare T-accounts for the following accounts: Direct Materials Inventory, Work in Process Inventory, Manufacturing Overhead Control, and Finished Goods Inventory. Record the transactions from part (a) in the T-accounts and calculate ending account balances. Assume the following beginning account balances:

Account	Balance
Direct Materials Inventory	$20,000
Work in Process Inventory	$12,000
Finished Goods Inventory	$35,000

c. Was overhead under- or overapplied for the year? By how much?

4-18 Under- and overapplied overhead (LO 6) Refer to the data in Exercise 4-12. At the end of the year, Rector Company had worked 245,000 direct labor hours, used 410,000 machine hours, and incurred $2,515,000 in manufacturing overhead.

Required

a. If Rector Company used direct labor hours as its manufacturing overhead application base, how much overhead was applied to jobs during the year?
b. Using direct labor hours as the application base, was manufacturing overhead under- or overapplied for the year? By how much?
c. If Rector Company used machine hours as its manufacturing overhead application base, how much overhead was applied to jobs during the year?
d. Using machine hours as the application base, was manufacturing overhead under- or overapplied for the year? By how much?

4-19 Under- and overapplied overhead (LO 6) Kim-Brooks, Inc. makes costumes for movies and television shows. Brooks Kimberly, the company's owner, prepared the following estimates for the upcoming year:

Manufacturing overhead cost	$800,000
Direct labor hours	50,000
Direct labor cost	$250,000
Machine hours	40,000

Required

a. Assume that Kim-Brooks applies manufacturing overhead on the basis of direct labor hours. During the year, 49,800 direct labor hours were worked. How much overhead was applied to work in process? If actual manufacturing overhead for the year was $792,000, was overhead under- or overapplied during the year? By how much?
b. Assume that Kim-Brooks applies manufacturing overhead on the basis of direct labor cost. During the year, $245,000 in direct labor cost was incurred. How much overhead was applied to work in process during the year? If actual manufacturing overhead for the year was $792,000, was overhead under- or overapplied during the year? By how much?
c. Assume that Kim-Brooks applies manufacturing overhead on the basis of machine hours. During the year, 40,200 machine hours were worked. How much overhead was applied to work in process during the year? If actual manufacturing overhead for the year was $792,000, was overhead under- or overapplied during the year? By how much?

4-20 Under- and overapplied overhead (LO 6) Mallet Music Company makes custom marimbas and xylophones. Since much of the work on these musical instruments is done by hand, the company uses direct labor hours as its manufacturing overhead application base. The company's annual budgeted overhead costs for 72,500 direct labor hours totaled $580,000.

Required

a. Assume that during the year, the company incurred manufacturing overhead totaling $586,000 for 72,500 direct labor hours. By how much was manufacturing overhead under- or overapplied for the year?
b. Assume that during the year, the company incurred manufacturing overhead totaling $586,000 for 73,550 direct labor hours. By how much was manufacturing overhead under- or overapplied for the year?
c. Assume that during the year, the company incurred manufacturing overhead totaling $590,000 for 73,550 direct labor hours. By how much was manufacturing overhead under- or overapplied for the year?

4-21 Disposition of under- and overapplied overhead (LO 6) Revisit Exercise 4-14 about Drew Corp. If you have not already completed that exercise, do so before answering the following questions.

Required

a. Calculate under- or overapplied overhead for the year.
b. Assuming that Drew closes under- or overapplied overhead to Cost of Goods Sold, calculate the cost of goods sold for the year.
c. Assuming that Drew prorates under- or overapplied overhead to the appropriate accounts, calculate the adjusted Work in Process Inventory, Finished Goods Inventory, and Cost of Goods Sold balances for the year.

PROBLEMS

4-22 Product and period costs (LO 1) The following passages are taken from the notes to the financial statements in Amazon.com's 2003 annual report.

> *Cost of Sales*
>
> Cost of sales consists of the purchase price of consumer products sold by us, inbound and outbound shipping charges to us, packaging supplies, and certain

costs associated with our service revenues. In instances where we incur fulfillment costs to ship products on behalf of third-party sellers or provide customer service on their behalf, such costs are classified as "Cost of sales" rather than "Fulfillment" on the consolidated statements of operations.

Fulfillment

Fulfillment costs represent those costs incurred in operating and staffing our fulfillment and customer service centers, including costs attributable to receiving, inspecting, and warehousing inventories; picking, packaging, and preparing customer orders for shipment; credit card fees and bad debts costs, including costs associated with our guarantee for certain third-party transactions; and responding to inquiries from customers. Fulfillment costs also include amounts paid to third parties that assist us in fulfillment and customer service operations. Certain of our fulfillment-related costs that are incurred on behalf of other business, such as Toysrus.com, Inc. and Target Corporation, are classified as cost of sales rather than fulfillment.

Required

a. What type of cost is Amazon.com's cost of sales, a product or a period cost?
b. What type of cost is Amazon.com's fulfillment cost, a product or a period cost?
c. Notice that in both passages, references are made to costs related to packaging orders for shipment. How can costs related to packaging be classified as both a cost of sales and a fulfillment cost?
d. In an article titled "CreativeAccounting.com" in the July 24, 2000, issue of *The Wall Street Journal*, Andy Kessler commented on a statement in an Amazon.com 10-K statement that resembled the passages reprinted here. He argued that these fulfillment costs sound more like a cost of sales than a fulfillment cost. Do you agree with his argument? Why or why not?

4-23 Product cost flows (LO 3) "Of all the times this hard drive could crash, it had to be now," Marcy cried. "How can I finish the June financial reports without all the information? I knew I should have backed up the disk last night before I left work." News of the disaster traveled quickly through the office, and people began to stop by her cubicle to offer their help.

John was the first to the rescue. "It might not be as bad as you think, Marcy. I have the financial reports from May right here. According to the balance sheet, we had a total inventory of $99,000 at the end of May. And I remember that the Finished Goods Inventory was one-third of that amount."

"I just finished the inventory counts last night," Peter chimed in from across the hall. "According to my tally sheets, we finished June with $80,000 in Direct Materials Inventory, $52,000 in Work in Process Inventory, and $25,000 in Finished Goods Inventory. This was a 100% increase from the balances in Direct Materials Inventory and Work in Process Inventory at the end of May. I bet with a little more investigative work, we can get all the numbers you need to complete the reports."

Sally called from Payroll to tell Marcy that the company had paid a total of $36,000 for direct labor during June. Juan, the billing supervisor, e-mailed Marcy that the company had sent out invoices to customers totaling $291,000.

Marcy knew that the overhead rate was 200% of direct labor costs. She also knew that the company priced its product using a 50% markup on the cost of goods sold. Armed with all this information, she sat down to reconstruct the inventory accounts for June.

Required

a. Using the information available to Marcy, prepare T-accounts to reflect the inventory cost flows for June.
b. Prepare a schedule of cost of goods manufactured in good form.

4-24 Product cost flows, journal entries, T-accounts (LO 3, 4) Oberti Guitar Company makes high-quality customized guitars. Oberti uses a job order costing system. Because the guitars are handmade, the company applies overhead based on direct labor hours. At the beginning of the year, the company estimated that total manufacturing overhead costs would be $300,000 and that 20,000 direct labor hours would be worked. At year-end, Anthony, the company's founder and CEO, gives you the following information regarding Oberti's operations:

1. The beginning balances in the inventory accounts were:

Raw Materials Inventory	$ 8,000
Work in Process Inventory	$26,000
Finished Goods Inventory	$32,000

2. During the year, the company purchased raw materials costing $97,000.
3. The production department requisitioned $100,000 of raw materials for use in production. Of those, 70% were direct materials and 30% were indirect materials.
4. The company used 21,000 direct labor hours at a cost of $14 per hour during the year (credit Wages Payable).
5. The company used 6,500 indirect labor hours at a cost of $10 per hour (credit Wages Payable).
6. The company paid $178,000 for insurance, utilities, and property taxes on the factory.
7. The company recorded factory depreciation of $40,000.
8. The company applied manufacturing overhead to inventory based on the 21,000 labor hours actually worked during the year.
9. Products costing $665,000 were completed during the year and transferred to the Finished Goods Inventory.
10. During the year, the company sold products costing a total of $672,000.
11. The company closes under- and overapplied overhead to Cost of Goods Sold.

Required

a. Prepare journal entries for each of the transactions just listed.
b. Using the information in the entries, record the transactions in T-accounts for Raw Materials Inventory, Work in Process Inventory, Finished Goods Inventory, Manufacturing Overhead, and Cost of Goods Sold. Show the ending balances for all accounts.

4-25 Departmental overhead rates and job order costing (LO 4, 5) Lassen Artworks creates hand-painted picture frames. The frames are cast from resin in an automated process. Once the casting is done, talented artisans hand-paint one of fifteen designs on each frame. In the final assembly process, a worker inserts the glass pane and attaches the backing to the frame. Lassen's budget for the current year, along with the production requirements for two of the frames it produces, are as follows:

	Department		
	Casting	Painting	Assembly
Direct labor hours	—	60,000	12,000
Machine hours	28,000	—	800
Manufacturing overhead cost	$252,000	$276,000	$48,000

Seasons of Fun Frame	Department		
	Casting	Painting	Assembly
Direct labor hours	—	1	0.25
Machine hours	1.5	—	0.5

Birth Announcement Frame	Department		
	Casting	Painting	Assembly
Direct labor hours	—	1.5	0.5
Machine hours	0.75	—	0.1

Required

a. Assume that Lassen Artworks uses a single predetermined overhead application rate based on direct labor hours. Calculate the rate for the current year.
b. Using the rate you calculated in part (a) and the production requirements given, calculate the amount of overhead applied to a *Seasons of Fun* frame and a *Birth Announcement* frame.
c. Lassen Artworks' accountant has been taking a course in managerial accounting and has just learned that overhead should be applied using a causal base. She believes that direct labor hours may not be the best application base for the company and wants to explore the use of machine hours instead. Calculate the predetermined overhead application rate for the year using machine hours as the base. Using this rate, calculate the amount of overhead applied to a *Seasons of Fun* frame and a *Birth Announcement* frame.
d. The accountant has attended a few more classes and now wants to explore the use of departmental predetermined overhead rates. She has decided that machine hours is the best overhead application base for the casting department and direct labor hours is the best base for the painting and assembly departments. Do you support her choice of an overhead application base? Why? Calculate the predetermined overhead application rate for each of the three departments using the selected base.
e. Using the departmental overhead application rates developed in part (d), calculate the amount of overhead applied to a *Seasons of Fun* frame and a *Birth Announcement* frame.
f. Compare the levels of overhead applied to a *Seasons of Fun* frame and a *Birth Announcement* frame under the three different overhead application methods. Which method is best? Why?

4-26 Job order costing (LO 5) Paladin Parabolics Company produces high-quality microscopes for education and health care uses. The company uses a job order costing system. Because the microscopes' optics require significant manual labor to ensure adherence to strict manufacturing specifications, the company applies overhead on the basis of direct labor hours. At the beginning of 2017, the company estimated its manufacturing overhead would be $1,960,000 and that employees would work a total of 98,000 direct labor hours.

During March, the company worked on the following five jobs:

Job	Beginning Balance	Direct Materials added during March	Direct Labor added during March	Direct Labor Hours added during March
134	$118,600	$ 4,000	$ 8,400	150
158	121,450	2,500	12,160	300
212	21,800	86,400	36,650	3,450
287	34,350	71,800	31,850	2,700
301		18,990	21,845	1,400
Total	$296,200	$183,690	$110,905	8,000

Jobs 134 and 158 were started in January, Jobs 212 and 287 were started in February, and Job 301 was started in March. During March, workers completed Jobs 134, 158, and 212. Jobs 134 and 212 were delivered to customers during March.

Actual overhead for the month of March was $176,300.

Required

a. Calculate the predetermined overhead rate used by Paladin Parabolics Company in 2017.
b. Calculate the total manufacturing cost for March.
c. Calculate the total cost for each of the five jobs as of March 31.
d. Calculate the cost of goods manufactured for March.
e. Calculate the balance in the Work in Process Inventory account as of March 31.
f. Calculate the Cost of Goods Sold for March.
g. Calculate the balance in the Finished Goods Inventory account as of March 31.

4-27 Job order costing (LO 5) E. Cain, Ltd. produces decorative lamps in several styles and finishes. The company uses a job order costing system to accumulate product costs. Because much of the production process is automated, E. Cain, Ltd. has selected machine hours as its overhead application base.

In April, E. Cain, Ltd. worked on four jobs. Jobs 78 and 79 were started in March and completed and delivered to customers in April. Job 80 was started and finished in April, and at the end of April, the lamps from the job were in the warehouse. Job 81 was started but not completed at the end of April.

	78	79	80	81
Costs Added in March				
Direct materials	$25,000	$10,000		
Direct labor	$36,000	$ 4,000		
Overhead	$40,000	$ 500		
Machine hours	1,600 MH	20 MH		
Costs Added in April				
Direct materials	—	$ 9,000	$ 8,000	$4,000
Direct labor	$ 8,000	$28,000	$12,000	$ 500
Machine hours	120 MH	500 MH	325 MH	45 MH

Required

a. Calculate the total manufacturing cost for April.
b. Calculate the total cost of each of the four jobs as of the end of April.
c. Calculate the balance in the Work in Process Inventory account at the end of March and the end of April.
d. Calculate the cost of goods manufactured for April.
e. Calculate the Cost of Goods Sold for April.
f. Calculate the Finished Goods Inventory balance at the end of April.

4-28 Job order costing (CMA adapted) (LO 5) ErgoFurn, Inc. manufactures ergonomically designed computer furniture. ErgoFurn uses a job order costing system. On November 30, the Work in Process Inventory consisted of the following jobs:

Job No.	Item	Units	Accumulated Cost
CC723	Computer caddy	20,000	$ 900,000
CH291	Chair	15,000	431,000
PS812	Printer stand	25,000	250,000
			$1,581,000

On November 30, ErgoFurn's Raw Materials Inventory account totaled $668,000, and its Finished Goods Inventory totaled $3,456,400. ErgoFurn applies manufacturing overhead on the basis of machine hours. The company's manufacturing overhead budget for the year totaled $4,500,000, and the company planned to use 900,000 machine hours during the year. Through the first eleven months of the year, the company used a total of 830,000 machine hours, total manufacturing overhead amounted to $4,274,500, and Cost of Goods Sold was $8,750,250.

ErgoFurn purchased $638,000 in raw materials in December and incurred the following costs for jobs in process that month:

Job No.	Materials Issued	Machine Hours	Direct Labor Hours	Direct Labor Cost
CC723	$155,000	12,000	11,600	$122,400
CH291	$ 13,800	4,400	3,600	$ 43,200
PS812	$211,000	19,500	14,300	$200,500
DS444	$252,000	14,000	12,500	$138,000

The following jobs were completed in December and transferred to the Finished Goods Inventory:

Job No.	Item	Units
CC723	Computer caddy	20,000
CH291	Chair	15,000
DS444	Desk	5,000

Required

a. Calculate the total cost of each of the four jobs worked on in December.
b. Calculate the total manufacturing cost for December.
c. Calculate the cost of goods manufactured for December.
d. Calculate the balance in the Work in Process Inventory account on December 31.
e. Assume that ErgoFurn sold 15,000 computer caddies, 12,000 chairs, and 4,500 desks in December. Calculate Cost of Goods Sold for the month of December and the ending Finished Goods Inventory balance on December 31.

4-29 Under- and overapplied overhead (LO 6) Refer to Problem 4-26. If you have *not* completed that problem, do so at this time.

Required

a. Paladin Parabolics Company incurred $176,300 manufacturing overhead in the month of March. Given that expenditure for overhead, was manufacturing overhead under- or overapplied in March? By how much?
b. Assume that Paladin Parabolics Company closes under- or overapplied overhead to the Cost of Goods Sold account. Calculate the Cost of Goods Sold amount after that adjustment.
c. Assume that Paladin Parabolics Company prorates under- or overapplied overhead to the appropriate accounts. Calculate the allocated amounts and adjust the account balances as needed.
d. Which method of under- or overapplied overhead disposition is more appropriate for Paladin Parabolics Company? Why?
e. Job 212 was for 1,000 microscopes. What was the unit cost for the microscopes produced in this job? Is this the **actual** cost of producing this job? Why or why not?

4-30 Under- and overapplied overhead (LO 6) Refer to Problem 4-28. If you have *not* completed that problem, do so at this time.

Required

a. ErgoFurn incurred $395,000 in manufacturing overhead in December. Given that expenditure, was manufacturing overhead under- or overapplied for the year? By how much?
b. Why was overhead under- or overapplied for the year?
c. Assume that ErgoFurn closes under- or overapplied overhead to the Cost of Goods Sold account. Prepare the journal entry to close the manufacturing overhead account.
d. Assume that ErgoFurn prorates under- or overapplied overhead to the appropriate accounts. Calculate the allocated amounts and adjust the account balances as needed.
e. Which method of under- or overapplied overhead disposition is more appropriate for ErgoFurn? Why?

4-31 Under- and overapplied overhead (CMA adapted) (LO 6) Northcoast Manufacturing Company, a small manufacturer of appliance parts, has just completed its first year of operations. The company's controller, Vic Trainor, has been reviewing the results for the year and is concerned about the application of factory overhead. Trainor is using the following information to assess operations.

- Northcoast uses several machines with a combined cost of $2,200,000 and no residual value. Each machine has an output of five units of product per hour and a useful life of 20,000 machine hours.
- Selected actual data on Northcoast's operations for the year just ended are as follows:

Products manufactured	650,000 units
Machine use	130,000 hours
Direct labor	35,000 hours
Labor rate	$15 per hour
Total factory overhead	$ 1,130,000
Cost of Goods Sold	$ 1,720,960
Finished Goods Inventory (year-end)	$ 430,240
Work in Process Inventory (year-end)	$ 0

- Total factory overhead is applied based on direct labor cost using a predetermined plant-wide rate.
- Budgeted activity for the year included 20 employees each working 1,800 productive hours per year to produce 540,000 units of product. Because the machines are highly automated, each employee can operate two to four machines simultaneously. Normal activity is for each employee to operate three machines. Machine operators are paid $15 per hour. Overhead was budgeted at $961,200.

Required

a. Based on Northcoast Manufacturing Company's actual operations over the past year, was manufacturing overhead underapplied or overapplied? By how much?
b. How do you suggest disposing of the underapplied or overapplied overhead? Justify your answer.
c. Vic Trainor believes that Northcoast Manufacturing Company should apply manufacturing overhead based on machine hours. Calculate the predetermined overhead rate using that activity base.
d. If Northcoast Manufacturing Company had used machine hours as its application base, would manufacturing overhead have been underapplied or overapplied? By how much?
e. Explain why machine hours would be a more appropriate application base than direct labor cost.

4-32 Comprehensive problem (LO 1, 2, 3, 4, 5, 6) Maverick Wings, Inc. manufactures airplanes for use in stunt shows. Maverick's factory is highly automated, using the latest in robotic technology. To keep costs low, the company employs as few factory workers as possible. Since each plane has different features (such as its shape, weight, and color), Maverick uses a job order costing system to accumulate product costs.

At the end of 2016, Maverick's accountants developed the following expectations for 2017 based on the marketing department's sales forecast:

Budgeted overhead cost	$1,050,000
Estimated machine hours	50,000
Estimated direct labor hours	10,000
Estimated direct materials cost	$1,500,000

Maverick's inventory count, completed on December 31, 2016, revealed the following ending inventory balances:

Raw Materials Inventory	$250,000
Work in Process Inventory	$626,000
Finished Goods Inventory	$340,000

The company's 2017 payroll data revealed the following actual payroll costs for the year:

Job Title	Number Employed	Wage Rate per Hour	Annual Salary per Employee	Total Hours Worked per Employee
President and CEO	1		$225,000	
Vice president and CFO	1		$178,000	
Factory manager	1		$ 40,000	
Assistant factory manager	1		$ 32,000	
Machine operator	5	$14.50		2,250
Security guard, factory	2		$ 20,000	
Forklift operator	2	$ 7.50		2,000
Corporate secretary	1		$ 35,000	
Janitor, factory	2	$ 6.00		2,150

The following information was taken from Maverick's Schedule of Plant Assets. All assets are depreciated using the straight-line method.

Plant Asset	Purchase Price	Salvage Value	Useful Life
Factory building	$4,000,000	$150,000	20 Years
Administrative office	$ 650,000	$125,000	30 Years
Factory equipment	$2,000,000	$ 20,000	12 Years

Other miscellaneous costs for 2017 included:

Cost	Amount
Factory insurance	$14,000
Administrative office utilities	$ 6,000
Factory utilities	$32,000
Office supplies	$ 5,000

Additional information about Maverick's operations in 2017 includes the following:

- Raw materials purchases for the year amounted to $1,945,000.
- The company used $1,870,000 in raw materials during the year. Of that amount, 85% was direct materials and 15% was indirect materials.
- Maverick applied overhead to Work in Process Inventory based on direct materials cost.
- Airplanes costing $3,450,000 to manufacture were completed and transferred out of Work in Process Inventory.
- Maverick uses a markup of 80% to price its airplanes. Sales for the year were $6,570,000. (*Note:* This transaction requires two journal entries.)

Required

Use the information just given to answer the following questions:

a. What was Maverick's predetermined overhead rate in 2017?
b. Prepare the journal entries to record Maverick's costs for 2017.
c. Prepare the appropriate T-accounts for Raw Materials Inventory, Work-in-Process Inventory, Finished Goods Inventory, Manufacturing Overhead Control, Cost of Goods Sold, and Sales, and record Maverick's transactions for 2017.
d. Was manufacturing under- or overapplied in 2017? By how much?
e. Make the adjusting entry necessary to close the under- or overapplied overhead to cost of goods sold.
f. If Maverick chooses instead to prorate under- or overapplied overhead, how much would be allocated to Work in Process Inventory, Finished Goods Inventory, and Cost of Goods Sold for 2017?
g. Job 3827 was started and completed in 2017. The job required 500 machine hours, 300 direct labor hours, and $75,000 in direct materials to complete. What was the total cost of this job? Using Maverick's 80% markup, what sales price would be charged for this airplane?

h. If Maverick had chosen to use machine hours as its overhead application base, what would the rate have been in 2017? Why would that application base have been a logical choice for Maverick?

C&C SPORTS CONTINUING CASE

4-33 Inventory cost flows (LO 3, 4, 5, 6) C&C Sports has determined the following unit costs for each of its products:

	Pants	Jerseys	Jackets
Direct materials	$ 4.47	$ 6.85	$ 44.72
Direct labor	2.40	1.92	14.40
Manufacturing overhead	3.00	2.40	18.00
Total unit cost	$ 9.87	$11.17	$ 77.12
Sales price per unit	$12.00	$14.80	$125.00

On May 31, C&C Sports' Work in Process Inventory consisted of the following items:

Job	Units	Accumulated Cost
PA-1247—Pants	100	$ 717
JE-1397—Jerseys	200	1,802
JA 426—Jackets	50	3,046
		$5,565

During June, a total of $191,591 in direct materials and $74,208 in direct labor costs were incurred. Units finished and sold during June were as follows:

Product	Units Finished	Units Sold
Pants	13,500	14,000
Jerseys	3,200	3,100
Jackets	2,500	2,500

Required

a. Given that C&C Sports uses direct labor dollars as its application base, what is the company's predetermined overhead rate?
b. Calculate the total manufacturing cost for June.
c. Calculate the Cost of Goods Manufactured for June.
d. Calculate the Ending Work in Process Inventory balance on June 30.
e. Calculate Cost of Goods Sold for June.
f. Calculate Gross Profit for June.
g. For each of the three products, state whether there are more, fewer, or the same number of finished units in Finished Goods Inventory on June 30 than there were on June 1.

CASES

4-34 Ethics and cost classification (CMA adapted) (LO 1) Healthful Foods, Inc. a manufacturer of breakfast cereals and snack bars, has experienced several years of steady growth in sales, profits, and dividends while maintaining a relatively low level of debt. The board of directors has adopted a long-term strategy of maximizing the value of the shareholders' investment. To achieve this goal, the board established the following five-year financial objectives:

- Increase sales by 12% per year.
- Increase income before taxes by 15% per year.
- Increase dividends by 12% per year.
- Maintain long-term debt at a maximum 16% of assets.

For the past three years, the company has attained these financial objectives. At the beginning of last year, the president of Healthful Foods, Andrea Donis, added a fifth financial objective: maintaining cost of goods sold at a maximum of 70% of sales. The company attained this new goal last year.

Results for the current year have been disappointing. Increased emphasis on healthful eating has driven up the cost of raw ingredients significantly. Because of a prolonged recession, the company has been unable to pass on those cost increases to customers in the form of price increases.

John Winslow, the cost accountant at Healthful Foods, has just completed a review of the year's operating results, which suggests that the cost of goods sold objective will not be met this year. Because employee bonuses are tied to performance on all five objectives, Winslow is concerned about company morale. After additional scrutiny, he decides that if he overestimates the amount of ending work in process inventory and reclassifies the fruit and grain inspection costs as administrative rather than manufacturing overhead costs, cost of goods sold for the year will fall below the 70% maximum level. Winslow makes the adjustments and presents Donis with a set of financial statements that meets the company's five financial objectives.

Required

a. Explain why the adjustments Winslow made are unethical, referring to the IMA's Statement of Ethical Professional Practice.
b. What additional costs, both monetary and nonmonetary, might Healthful Foods incur as a result of Winslow's actions?

4-35 Product and period costs (LO 3, 5) (Case and requirements c, d, and e are reprinted from *Journal of Accounting Education*, Vol. 15, Charles E. Davis, "Accounting Is Like a Box of Chocolates: A Lesson in Cost Behavior," 307–308, Copyright (1997), with permission from Elsevier.)

Forrest Gump was one of the biggest movie hits of 1994. The movie's fortunes continued to climb in 1995, as it took home Oscars in six of 13 categories in which it was nominated, including best picture, best director, and best actor. One analyst has estimated that the film could generate cash flow as much as $350 million for Viacom, Inc., Paramount Pictures' parent company. Such success has insured the film a place among the top grossing films of all time. This is quite an accomplishment for a movie that took nine years to make it to the big screen and whose script was not considered material likely to generate a runaway movie hit.

But was *Forrest Gump* a money maker for Paramount in 1994? Films are typically distributed to theaters under an agreement that splits the gross box office receipts approximately 50/50 between the theater and the movie studio. Under such an agreement, Paramount had received $191 million in gross box office receipts *from theaters* as of December 31, 1994. Paramount reports that the film cost $112 million to produce, including approximately $15.3 million each paid to star Tom Hanks and director Robert Zemeckis, and "production overhead" of $14.6 million. This production overhead is charged to the movie at a rate equal to 15% of other production costs.

Not included in the $112 million production costs were the following other expenses associated with the film. Promotion expenses incurred to advertise, premiere, screen, transport, and store the film totaled $67 million at the end of 1994. An additional $6.7 million "advertising overhead charge" (equal to 10% of the $67 million promotion expenses) was charged to the film by Paramount. These charges represent the film's allocation of the studio's cost of maintaining an in-house advertising department. Paramount also charged the film a "distribution fee" of 32% of its share of gross box office receipts. This fee is the film's allocation of the costs incurred by Paramount to maintain its studio-wide distribution services. Finally, $6 million in interest on the $112 million in production costs were charged to the film by Paramount.

Required

a. Identify each of the costs mentioned above as a product or period cost.
b. What application bases did Paramount use to apply overhead to this "job"?
c. Was *Forrest Gump* an "accounting" hit in terms of net income, as computed by Paramount?
d. In their original contracts, actor Tom Hanks and director Robert Zemeckis were to receive $7 million and $5 million, respectively, for their work on *Forrest Gump*. However, after the studio asked the producers for budget cuts, both Hanks and Zemeckis agreed to forego their standard fee for a percentage of the film's gross box office receipts. Sources estimate that the new agreement guaranteed each of the two 8% of the studio's share of gross box office receipts from the film. Using the information available about the costs of making the film, did *Forrest Gump* have a positive contribution margin? Assume that all costs not specifically identified as variable are fixed.
e. Other individuals associated with the film signed contracts based on a percentage of "net profits" rather than gross box office receipts, net profits being the films' profits after the recouping of all the studio's expenses. For example, Winston Groom, who wrote the novel on which the movie was based, received $350,000 plus 3% of the film's net profits. Eric Roth, the screenwriter, signed a similar contract with a fixed fee plus 5% of the film's net profits. Based on your calculations above, how much did these two individuals receive from their share of the film's net profits? How much in gross box office receipts will the studio have to receive from theaters before Groom and Roth receive any money under their net profit participation contract?

ANALYTICS PROBLEM

4-36 Job order costing using data analytics and Excel (LO 5) Thoni Manufacturing has gathered information from materials requisition sheets and labor time sheets for several jobs worked on during the last month and needs to calculate the job costs.

Required

a. Use the SUMIF function to calculate the direct materials cost added to each job during the month. You will find the data in the materials tab of the data worksheet.
b. Use the SUMIF function to calculate the direct labor cost added to each job during the month. You will find the data in the labor tab of the data worksheet. You will need to use the VLOOKUP function to find employee wage rates in the wage rate tab of the worksheet. Remember that time data is expressed in hours and minutes, while the wage rate is expressed on an hourly basis. You will need to convert minutes worked to their decimal equivalent before making the direct labor calculation. You may find the HOUR and MINUTE functions helpful for this calculation (HOUR(cell reference) + MINUTE(cell reference))/60.
c. Thoni Manufacturing uses direct labor hours to apply manufacturing overhead. The predetermined overhead rate is $200/DLH. Apply overhead to each job and calculate the total job costs for the month.
d. Charlie Anderson, Thoni's CFO, is concerned that some employees may not be appropriately recording the time worked on specific jobs. Sort the labor time tickets by time worked. What do you notice?
e. What other information would help Charlie evaluate the appropriateness of the time recorded?

The Excel data files for answering this problem can be found in WileyPLUS.

TOPIC FOCUS 2: PROCESS COSTING

Petek ARICI/Getty Images

FOCUS	LEARNING OBJECTIVES
TOPIC FOCUS 2	**LO 1:** Identify the kinds of companies that use process costing systems.
	LO 2: Explain how costs flow through the inventory accounts in a process costing system.
	LO 3: Calculate and explain equivalent units.
	LO 4: Assign costs to completed units and ending Work in Process Inventory.

TOPIC FOCUS 2—GUIDED UNIT PREPARATION

Answering the following questions while you read this unit will guide your understanding of the key concepts found in this unit. The questions are linked to the learning objectives presented at the beginning of the unit.

LO 1

1. What are the similarities between job order and process costing? What are the differences?

LO 2

2. What are conversion costs?

LO 3

3. What are equivalent units? Why is it necessary to calculate equivalent units?
4. Why do the equivalent units calculated for materials sometimes differ from the equivalent units calculated for conversion?

LO 4

5. How do you determine the total cost that must be assigned both to the units transferred out of the department and to the units remaining in ending Work in Process Inventory?
6. How do you determine the cost to assign to the ending Work in Process Inventory? To the units that are transferred out of the department?

Business Decision and Context

BRADLEY TEXTILE MILLS

Chief Executive Officer
Kathy Stewart

Production Manager
Jonathan Grant

Kathy Stewart was completing her first month as **CEO of Bradley Textile Mills**. Prior to joining Bradley, she served as CEO of a small custom millwork company. While Kathy knew all about job order costing, she was still developing her understanding of Bradley's process costing system, so she was having trouble interpreting the monthly production report. (See Exhibit T2-3.)

Realizing she needed some help, Kathy called **Production Manager Jonathan Grant**. "Jonathan, this production report for last month doesn't make sense to me," Kathy said. "I know that during the month we had 500,000 yards of jersey fabric working its way through the Weaving Department. Your report shows only 450,000 yards accounted for in the department. What happened to the other 50,000 yards? I hope it wasn't all defective."

> "Your report shows only 450,000 yards accounted for in the department. What happened to the other 50,000 yards? I hope it wasn't all defective."

"Everything's fine," Jonathan said, hoping to reassure Kathy. "Yes, we were working on 500,000 yards of jersey fabric in the Weaving Department. But since we hadn't finished it all yet, we can't report all 500,000 yards as completed inventory."

"I know all 500,000 yards weren't finished yet," Kathy replied. "But you still had a total of 500,000 yards of fabric sitting in the department. And why is this fabric designated as 'EU'? Is it going to customers in the European Union?"

"No, this fabric is not destined for the European Union," Jonathan responded. "That's an abbreviation for 'equivalent units.' Why don't I come down and help you interpret the report."

Kathy breathed a sigh of relief. "That would be great. Come on down."

Watch the Jones Soda video in WileyPLUS to learn more about process costing in the real world.

In Chapter 4 we saw that C&C Sports uses a job order costing system to accumulate product costs. This system allows managers to determine how much a single jersey, pair of pants, or jacket costs to make. A job order costing system is appropriate for C&C Sports because its products differ markedly in terms of the materials and labor they require. But job order costing isn't appropriate for all production systems.

Companies that mass-produce similar products or employ a continuous production process typically use a **process costing system.** In this type of costing system, all product costs for the period are accumulated and divided evenly over all units produced during the period. The Jelly Belly Candy Company is an example of the type of company that would use a process costing system. All the jelly beans are manufactured the same way using similar ingredients.[1] Other companies that use a process costing system to accumulate product costs include the oil refiner Phillips66, the soft drink bottler Dr Pepper, and the paint manufacturer Sherwin Williams.

Cost Flows

Let's consider how product costs flow through a process costing system. We'll start with a simple example that you may be quite familiar with: baking cookies. When you decide to bake cookies, you "requisition" or remove the raw materials (eggs, flour, chocolate chips) from storage (the pantry or refrigerator). Then you preheat the oven and start mixing the ingredients. At this point, what do you have? Literally, you have work in process. What costs have you incurred? Direct materials, direct labor, and overhead. The materials cost is from the ingredients used, the labor cost is due to the mixing effort you supplied, and the overhead costs are comprised of the costs to run the kitchen (the oven, electricity, counter space, and cooking utensils).

When you put a sheet of cookies in the oven, you still have work in process, though your cookies are more finished than the dough left in your mixing bowl. These different states of work in process probably don't matter to you, but they do matter in certain industries. When the sheet of cookies is fully baked and cooled, you have some finished cookies and some other cookies at various stages of work in process. When all the cookies have been baked, you add up the raw materials, direct labor, and overhead costs and divide by the number of cookies you produced. This is your cost per cookie.

So far, this process should sound a lot like the product cost flows you learned in Chapter 4. The top portion of Exhibit T2-1 shows how the cost of the raw materials flows out of Raw Materials Inventory and into Work in Process Inventory. Direct labor and overhead costs are added to Work in Process Inventory. When the cookies are finished, the cost of the finished cookies is transferred to Finished Goods Inventory.

Recall that in a job order costing system, the costs of each job are accumulated on a job cost sheet. The total of all the job cost sheets equals the total Work in Process Inventory account balance. In process costing, by contrast, the costs are accumulated by department. The bottom part of Exhibit T2-1 shows that the Work in Process Inventory account is made up of three subaccounts—one for mixing, one for baking, and one for cooling. When the cookies have been mixed, they are transferred to baking. After they have been baked, they are transferred to cooling. When the cookies are cool, they are ready to sell (or eat) and are transferred to Finished Goods Inventory.

In our cookie example, all direct materials were added in the Mixing Department at the beginning of the production process. This is not always the case, as

EXHIBIT T2-1

Cost flows in the cookie-baking process.

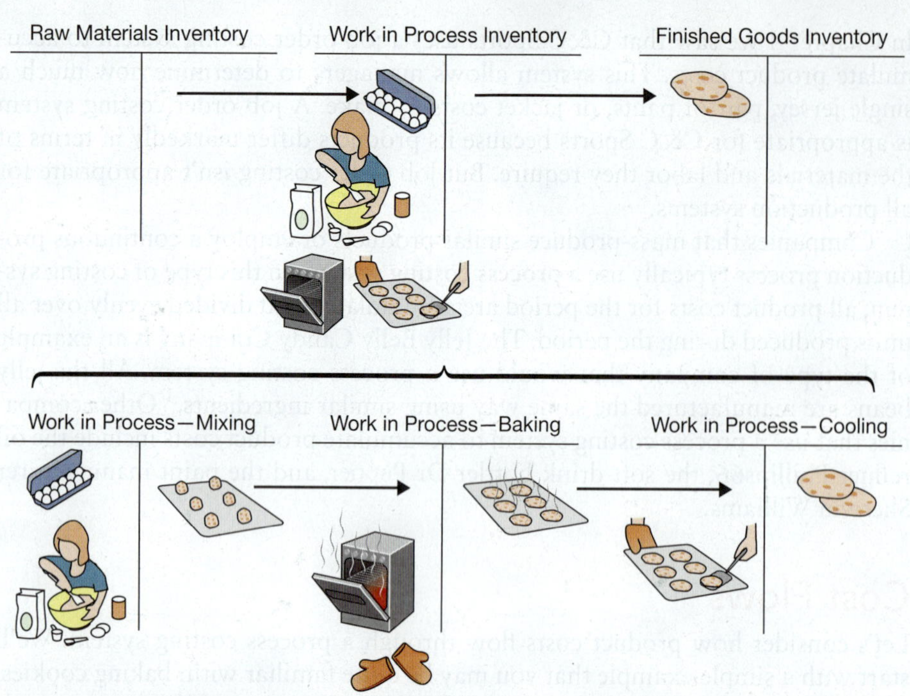

direct materials may be added at different points of the department's production process. It is also possible that direct materials are added in multiple departments throughout the production process. For example, if we choose to decorate the cookies, additional direct materials will be added in the Cooling Department.

The journal entries used to record cost flows in a process costing system are the same as those you learned in Chapter 4 for a job order costing system. While we did not look at multiple Work in Process accounts in Chapter 4, job order costing systems often use a Work in Process account for each department, just as Exhibit T2-1 shows.

THINK ABOUT IT T2.1

Give an example of a product for which materials would be added in a later phase of the production process.

Comparison of Process Costing and Job Order Costing

Now that you have been through a relatively simple example of process costing, let's compare and contrast process costing and job order costing.[2] Both systems accumulate product costs, but they differ in *how* those costs are accumulated. Exhibit T2-2 summarizes the similarities and differences between job order costing and process costing.

Similarities

1. **Objective:** Both process costing and job order costing systems accumulate product costs throughout the production process and assign those costs to individual units of production.

		Process Costing	Job Order Costing
Similarities	Objective	To accumulate and assign manufacturing costs to products	To accumulate and assign manufacturing costs to products
	Product costs	Direct material, direct labor, manufacturing overhead	Direct material, direct labor, manufacturing overhead
	Cost flows	From raw materials to work in process to finished goods to cost of goods sold	From raw materials to work in process to finished goods to cost of goods sold
Differences	Production schedule	Identical products produced over a long period, often in a continuous production process	Many different products produced, each with different materials, labor, and/or overhead requirements
	Cost accumulation	By production department	By job
	Key document	Department production report	Job cost sheet

EXHIBIT T2-2 *Process costing versus job order costing.*

2. **Product Costs:** Both process costing and job order costing systems accumulate direct materials, direct labor, and manufacturing overhead costs.
3. **Cost Flows:** Both process costing and job order costing systems track cost flows from Raw Materials Inventory to Work in Process Inventory, from Work in Process Inventory to Finished Goods Inventory, and from Finished Goods Inventory to Cost of Goods Sold.

Differences

1. **Production schedule:** Companies that use a process costing system mass-produce identical products or employ a continuous production process. Because the number of different product types is relatively small, these companies make no attempt to track an individual product's cost; all the products have similar costs. Companies that use a job order costing system produce many different types of products, often to customer specifications. Each product has different direct materials, direct labor, and/or manufacturing overhead requirements.
2. **Cost accumulation:** Companies that use a process costing system accumulate product costs in each production department throughout the period. Costs are then allocated evenly across all units produced in the department during the period. Unit product costs are calculated at the end of each period. In contrast, companies that use a job order costing system accumulate product costs by job and allocate those costs only to the units in that particular job. Unit costs are calculated only when all units in the job have been completed.
3. **Key document:** Companies that use a process costing system accumulate product costs on the departmental production report. Companies that use a job order costing system accumulate product costs on the job cost sheet.

THINK ABOUT IT T2.2

Name three companies that are likely to use a process costing system and three that are likely to use a job order costing system.

Cost Accumulation and Reporting

When there is no Work in Process Inventory at the end of a period, cost accumulation and reporting is extremely easy under process costing. The product costs are simply added up and divided evenly among the products produced. When work is in process at the end of an accounting period, however, cost accumulation and reporting become more complicated. The costs incurred to get the in-process units to their present state need to remain in the Work in Process Inventory account, while the costs incurred to produce the completed goods need to be transferred to the Finished Goods Inventory account. So we need a way to assign costs to the completed units and to the partially completed goods that remain in Work in Process Inventory.

Let's consider the case of Bradley Textile Mills, the fabric producer in C&C Sports' supply chain. Fabric production can be very complicated, but we will simplify the process by considering only three stages of production: weaving, preparation, and finishing. At Bradley, production begins in the Weaving Department, where yarns purchased from Centex Yarns are loaded onto high-speed looms. This process is largely automated, though some labor is needed to load and monitor the machines. The looms weave what are called greige (pronounced "gray") goods, which are rolled onto bolts as they come off the machines. After 100,000 yards of greige goods have been completed, the fabric is cut from the loom and the bolt is transferred to the Preparation Department.

Once the greige goods have arrived in the Preparation Department, the fabric is washed with chemicals to remove impurities and to make it more receptive to dyes and other additives. It is then dried and straightened. The last step is applying the dye and re-drying the fabric. Once this process is complete, the fabric is moved to the Finishing Department, where softeners are added along with other chemicals to make it wrinkle resistant. The fabric is then inspected, packaged in 2,000-yard rolls, and moved to the finished goods warehouse.

Bradley Textile Mills charges C&C Sports $4.00 per yard for its jersey fabric. The $4.00 is revenue for Bradley Textile Mills, but how does the company determine the cost to produce a yard of fabric? To answer this question, let's look at how the company accumulated costs during the month of June.

Reconciling Activity and Costs

At the beginning of June, 80,000 yards of fabric were in process in the Weaving Department. During the month, 420,000 additional yards were started into production, for a total of 500,000 yards worked on during the month. By the end of June, 400,000 yards of greige goods had been completed and transferred to the Preparation Department, leaving 100,000 yards in process on June 30. The T-account that follows shows that the yards in beginning inventory plus the yards started during the month equal the yards completed and transferred to the Preparation Department plus the yards in ending Work in Process Inventory.

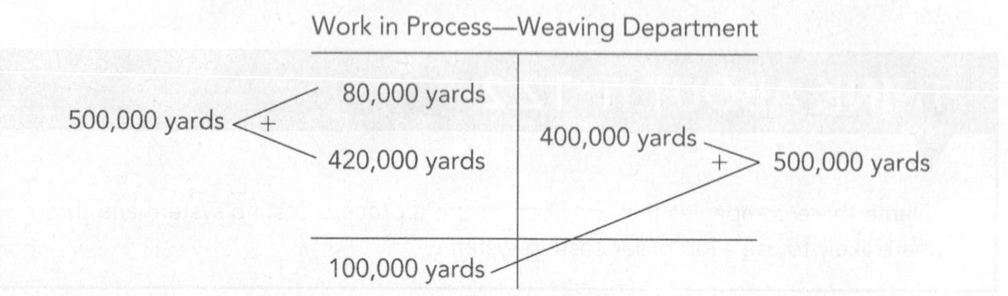

Not only must the units (yards) produced be reconciled in this manner, but their costs must be reconciled as well. The June 1 beginning balance in the Work in Process Inventory account was $66,280, and the costs added during June amounted to $565,020. The total cost of $631,300 must be assigned both to the 400,000 yards completed and transferred to the Preparation Department and to the 100,000 yards remaining in the ending Work in Process Inventory. Is the process as simple as dividing $631,300 by the 500,000 yards worked on during the month? Unfortunately not. Some of those yards are still unfinished, so they are not equivalent to finished goods yards.

Calculating Equivalent Units

Because the 100,000 yards remaining in the Weaving Department's Work in Process Inventory aren't complete, we shouldn't allocate as much cost to them as to the completed yards. Instead, we need to determine the percentage of completion for the work in process. Based on that percentage, we can calculate **equivalent units (EU)** of production. If the 100,000 yards were 60% complete, for example, we would calculate 60,000 (60% × 100,000 yards) equivalent units of production.

Think about it this way. Suppose an ice cream manufacturer has two machines that fill five-gallon cartons of ice cream. At the end of the day, each machine has filled a carton half full. So we have two cartons that are 50% complete. If we add them together, they contain a total of five gallons of ice cream, equivalent to one "complete" unit. So the two incomplete units represent one equivalent unit of production (2 cartons × 50% completion):

To complicate matters further, products can be more or less complete for materials than for direct labor and overhead. Think back to the cookie example. All the ingredients were added together at the beginning of the process, so the cookies were 100% complete in terms of materials. But at any point before the cookies cool, they are less than 100% complete in terms of direct labor and overhead. In a process costing system, labor and overhead costs are typically combined and referred to as **conversion costs**—that is, the production costs required to convert raw materials into finished goods.

According to Jonathan Grant, the production manager at Bradley Textile Mills, the 100,000 yards remaining in the Weaving Department's Work in Process Inventory are 60% complete with respect to materials and 50% complete with respect to conversion. So we can represent ending work in process as 60,000 EU in calculating materials costs and 50,000 EU in calculating conversion costs. The top portion of Exhibit T2-3 shows these amounts. If we add the 400,000 completed yards to these equivalent units, we get a total of 460,000 equivalent units for materials and 450,000 equivalent units for conversion.

WATCH OUT!

Do not add the equivalent units for materials to the equivalent units for conversion; that total is meaningless. These equivalent units should be added separately to total units completed to arrive at the total equivalent units for materials and the total equivalent units for conversion.

Allocating Product Costs to Units

Since the equivalent units for materials and conversion differ, we must separate the $631,300 total cost into materials cost and conversion cost. As you can see in the bottom of Exhibit T2-3, the $66,280 of beginning Work in Process consists of $37,120 in materials cost and $29,160 in conversion costs. Likewise, the $565,020 of costs added during the period consists of $229,680 in materials cost and $335,340 in conversion costs. Therefore, total materials cost for the month is $266,800 and total conversion cost is $364,500.[3] With these amounts, we can compute a materials cost and a conversion cost per equivalent unit:

$$\text{Material EU cost} = \frac{\$266{,}800}{460{,}000} = \$0.58 \text{ per EU}$$

$$\text{Conversion EU cost} = \frac{\$364{,}500}{450{,}000} = \$0.81 \text{ per EU}$$

The final step is to use these EU costs to assign costs to the units transferred to the Preparation Department and to the units remaining in the Weaving Department's Work in Process Inventory. The 400,000 yards transferred to the Preparation Department are assigned the total EU cost of $1.39 per yard ($0.58 materials + $0.81 conversion), resulting in a cost transferred of $556,000 ($1.39 × 400,000 EU). For the ending Work in Process, the materials cost is $34,800 ($0.58 × 60,000 EU) and the conversion cost is $40,500 ($0.81 × 50,000 EU), resulting in a total ending Work in Process in the Weaving Department of $75,300 ($34,800 + $40,500). Exhibit T2-3 summarizes these calculations

EXHIBIT T2-3

Bradley Textile Mills' weaving department production report, June.

Unit Information:

Work in Process, June 1 (materials 80% complete; conversion 45% complete)	80,000 yards		
Started into production	420,000 yards		
Total units to be accounted for	500,000 yards		
		Equivalent Units	
		Materials	Conversion
Yards transferred to Preparation Department	400,000	400,000	400,000
Work in Process, June 30 (materials 60% complete; conversion 50% complete)	100,000	60,000[a]	50,000[b]
Total units accounted for	500,000	460,000	450,000

[a]100,000 yards × 60%
[b]100,000 yards × 50%

Cost Information:

		Total Costs	Materials	Conversion
	Work in Process, June 1	$ 66,280	$ 37,120	$ 29,160
+	Costs added during June	565,020	229,680	335,340
=	Total costs to be accounted for	$631,300	$266,800	$364,500
÷	Equivalent units		460,000	450,000
=	Cost per equivalent unit		$0.58	$ 0.81
Transferred to Preparation Department [400,000 yards × ($0.58 + $0.81)]			$556,000	
Work in Process, June 30				
Materials: $0.58 × 60,000 EU		$ 34,800		
Conversion: $0.81 × 50,000 EU		40,500		
Total Work in Process, June 30			75,300	
Total Costs Accounted for			$631,300	

and shows how the total cost to be accounted for, $631,300, equals (or reconciles with) the total costs assigned to the units transferred to the Preparation Department plus the costs remaining in Work in Process Inventory. The T-account to reconcile these costs would appear as follows:

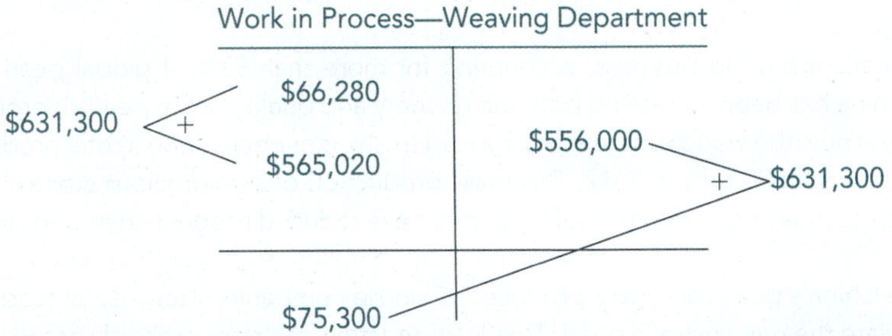

To complete the cost allocation for the month of June, similar calculations must be done for the Preparation and Finishing departments. For simplicity, we'll assume that all 400,000 yards of greige goods transferred out of the Weaving Department in June were completely prepared and finished that month, so that there was no ending Work in Process Inventory in either of those departments. Exhibit T2-4 shows the final results of these allocations in the T-accounts for the Work in Process Inventory in each of the three production departments. You can see that as products are completed in one department, the costs are transferred to the next department. (Remember from Exhibit T2-1 that costs are accumulated by department under process costing.) For example, the $556,000 cost of the 400,000 yards of completed greige goods is transferred out of the Weaving Department's Work in Process Inventory and into the Preparation Department's Work in Process Inventory.

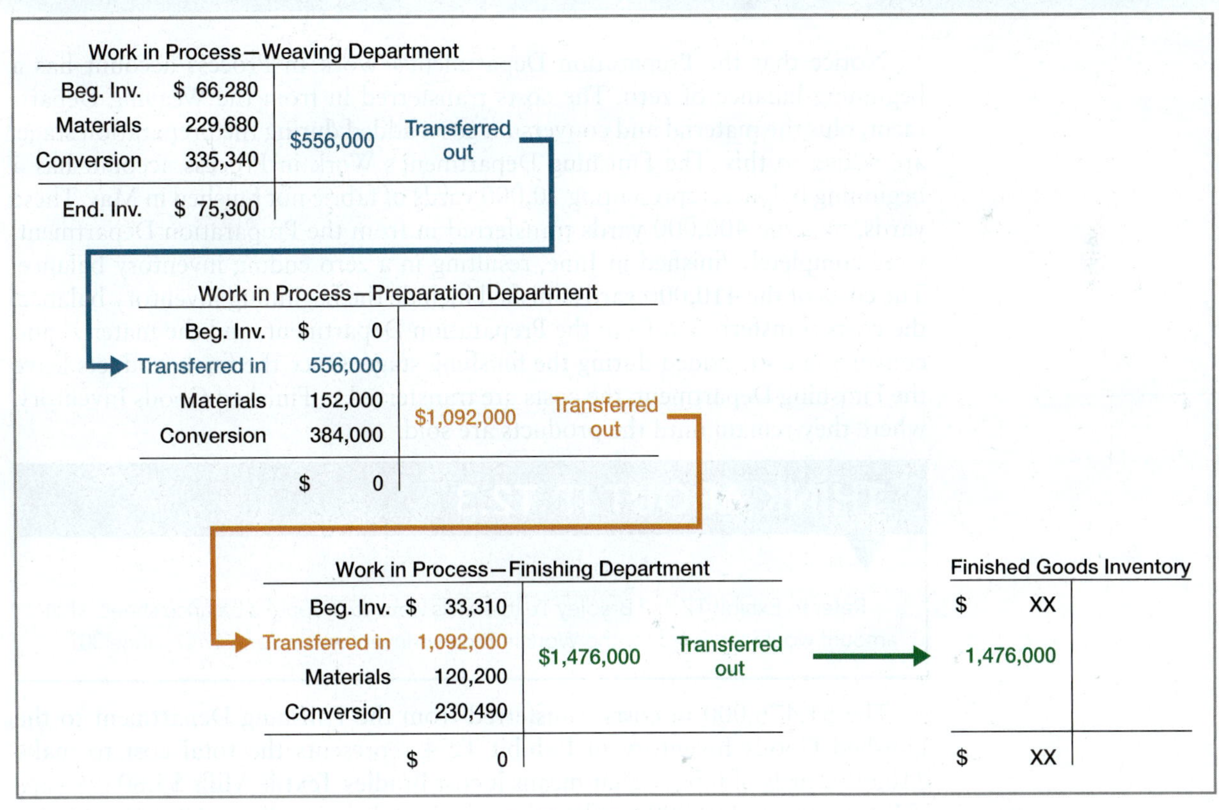

EXHIBIT T2-4 *Bradley Textile Mills' cost flows through work in process, June.*

REALITY CHECK—*Costs in the oyster bed*

© Jim Barber/Shutterstock

Because China's pearls are mass-produced, Chinese companies likely use process costing to calculate the unit cost of a pearl.

Cultured pearls are a big business, accounting for more than 95% of global pearl sales. Recently, China has been increasing both the quantity and quality of the pearls it produces. The country is now the world's largest producer of freshwater pearls, with a total production of approximately 1,500 tons in 2012. This mass production of semiprecious stones has no doubt led to cost-saving economies of scale that have reduced product costs and lowered prices.

Because China's pearls are mass-produced, Chinese companies likely use process costing to calculate the unit cost of a pearl. That is, production costs are probably accumulated during the period and then spread over the period's production to arrive at a unit cost. Not everyone in the pearl supply chain will use process costing, however. Harvested pearls are purchased by jewelry manufacturers such as Tiffany and Harry Winston, who turn them into expensive pieces of jewelry worth thousands of dollars. Given the uniqueness of design and high cost of the gems included in each piece, job order costing is a better way to account for their production than process costing.

Sources: Lorraine Yapps Cohen, "Freshwater Pearl Production in China," *Examiner.com*, August 12, 2012, http://www.examiner.com/article/freshwater-pearl-production-china (accessed December 20, 2012); Vanessa O'Connell, "Pursuits: Gem Wars," *The Wall Street Journal*, January 13, 2007; Margaret Studer, "Jewelry Sales Will Shine With Precious Stones," *The Wall Street Journal Online*, November 10, 2006.

Notice that the Preparation Department's Work in Process account has a beginning balance of zero. The costs transferred in from the Weaving Department, plus the material and conversion costs added during the preparation stage, are added to this. The Finishing Department's Work in Process account has a beginning balance, representing 10,000 yards of fabric not finished in May. These yards, plus the 400,000 yards transferred in from the Preparation Department, were completely finished in June, resulting in a zero ending inventory balance. The costs of the 410,000 yards finished include the beginning inventory balance, the costs transferred in from the Preparation Department, and the material and conversion costs added during the finishing stage. Once the final products leave the Finishing Department, the costs are transferred to Finished Goods Inventory, where they remain until the products are sold.

THINK ABOUT IT T2.3

Refer to Exhibit T2-4. If Bradley Textile Mills were to prepare a balance sheet, what amount would be listed for the Work in Process Inventory on June 1? On June 30?

The $1,476,000 in costs transferred from the Finishing Department to the Finished Goods Inventory in Exhibit T2-4 represents the total cost to make 410,000 yards of fabric. That means it cost Bradley Textile Mills $3.60 per yard ($1,476,000 ÷ 410,000 yards) to make the fabric it sells to C&C Sports for $4.00.

THINK ABOUT IT T2.4

What is the gross profit that Bradley Textile Mills earns on the fabric it sells to C&C Sports? What would you need to know to help Bradley's managers forecast the effects of changes in price or cost on the company's operating income?

Process Costing Recap

The objective of process costing is the same as job order costing: to develop a product unit cost to use in decision making and inventory valuation. At this point, process costing may seem more complicated to you than job order costing. True, there are some additional steps in calculating the unit product cost. But if you follow these steps, you will be able to work through the complexities without becoming overwhelmed.

1. **Calculate the physical unit flow:** Add the number of units started into production during the period to the number of units in beginning inventory. The total is the number of units you must account for. Then subtract the number of units that were completed and transferred out of the department. The remaining units constitute the ending work in process inventory. Reconcile the physical unit flow using the following equation:

   Beginning WIP units + Units started = Units transferred out + Ending WIP units

2. **Calculate the equivalent units of production:** The units of product in the ending Work in Process Inventory must be converted to equivalent units of production. This calculation must be done separately for the direct materials and conversion costs, since the units may not be at the same stage of completion in the two cost categories. To determine the number of equivalent units produced, multiply the percentage of completion for each cost category by the number of physical units in the ending Work in Process Inventory. Add these results to the number of units transferred out of the department during the period to obtain the total equivalent units of production for the period.
3. **Calculate the cost per equivalent unit:** Add the cost of direct materials placed into production during the period to the direct materials cost in the beginning Work in Process Inventory. Divide this total by the equivalent units of production for direct materials. This is the direct materials equivalent unit cost. Next, add the direct labor and manufacturing overhead costs incurred during the month to the direct labor and manufacturing overhead costs in beginning Work in Process Inventory. Divide this total cost by the equivalent units of production for conversion costs to obtain the conversion equivalent unit cost.
4. **Allocate the equivalent unit costs of production:** Using the amounts calculated in Steps 2 and 3, multiply the number of equivalent units in the ending Work in Process Inventory by the cost per equivalent unit to determine the ending dollar balance in the Work in Process Inventory account. Then multiply the number of units transferred out of the department during the period by the cost per equivalent unit to determine the total cost transferred out of the department during the period. Remember to do separate calculations for the direct materials and conversion costs.

5. **Reconcile the costs of production:** To be sure that you have accounted for all production costs, use the following equation:

Beginning WIP balance + Costs added = Costs transferred out + Ending WIP balance

6. **Repeat Steps 1–5 for each department:** Equivalent units and costs must be calculated separately for each department in the production process. Since these calculations include costs transferred in from other departments, they must be performed in the same order as the production process so that the required information will be available.

TOPIC FOCUS REVIEW

KEY TERMS

Conversion costs p. 189   Equivalent units (EU) p. 189   Process costing system p. 185

PRACTICE QUESTIONS

1. LO 1 Which of the following companies is *least* likely to use process costing for the majority of its products?

   a. ConocoPhillips
   b. Dupont Chemical
   c. Crocs, Inc.
   d. Boeing

2. LO 1, 2 Process costing differs from job order costing because

   a. only job order costing assigns manufacturing overhead to products.
   b. job order costing accumulates costs by the job, whereas process costing accumulates costs by department.
   c. only job order costing uses a Work in Process Inventory account.
   d. job order costing uses equivalent units.

3. LO 2 When a company produces products in multiple departments, materials are transferred from Raw Materials Inventory to the first department only. In subsequent departments, only direct labor and manufacturing overhead costs are added. True or False?

4. LO 3 By the end of March, Flanders Co. had completed 10,000 units and left 3,000 units in work in process. The 3,000 units were 40% complete with respect to materials and 15% complete with respect to conversion. How many equivalent units will be used to determine the cost per equivalent unit for materials?

   a. 1,200
   b. 3,000
   c. 11,200
   d. 13,000

5. LO 3 Refer to question 4. Conversion costs will be assigned to how many equivalent units in the ending Work in Process Inventory?

   a. 450
   b. 1,500
   c. 3,000
   d. 10,000

6. LO 4 On December 31, Talley Company recorded the following information in the Grating Department's Work in Process Inventory account:

	Units	Cost
Beginning balance (80% complete)	5,000	$ 56,000
Started into production	115,000	$1,505,800
Completed and transferred to Assembly Department	105,000	?
Ending balance (60% complete)	15,000	?

   Assume that the unfinished units in ending inventory are 60% complete for both materials and conversion. What is the cost per equivalent unit?

   a. $13.09
   b. $13.58
   c. $13.02
   d. $13.70

7. LO 4 Refer to question 6. What is the ending balance in the Work in Process Inventory account on December 31?

   a. $123,300
   b. $205,500
   c. $195,300
   d. $168,000

TOPIC FOCUS 2 PRACTICE EXERCISE

Smash-It Company mass-produces tennis balls in two departments: Shaping and Covering. In the Shaping Department, long sheets of rubber are put through a machine that cuts the required pieces and then cements them together. From the Shaping Department, the balls go to the Covering Department. During April the following information was recorded for the Shaping Department:

	Units	Costs	
		Materials	Conversion
Work in Process			
Beginning inventory, April 1	15,000	$ 2,110	$ 2,625
Added to production	250,000	34,815	52,395
Completed and transferred out	260,000	?	?
Ending inventory, April 30	5,000	?	?

Ending inventory was 75% complete with respect to materials and 40% complete with respect to conversion.

1. What is the total cost to be accounted for—that is, what total cost needs to be assigned to the units completed and transferred out of the Shaping Department and to those remaining in the ending Work in Process Inventory?
2. Compute the equivalent units for materials.
3. Compute the equivalent units for conversion.
4. Determine the cost per equivalent unit for both materials and conversion.
5. Determine the cost that should be assigned to the completed units transferred to the Covering Department.
6. Determine the cost that should be assigned to the Shaping Department's ending Work in Process Inventory.

SELECTED TOPIC FOCUS 2 ANSWERS

Think About It T2.1

A paint manufacturer will add pigment to paint at a later phase in the process. An oil refinery will introduce gasoline additives at a later phase in the process.

Think About It T2.2

Examples of companies that are likely to use process costing would include Kellogg's, ExxonMobil, and Procter & Gamble. Companies that are likely to use job order costing would include Ernst & Young, the law firm Baker & McKenzie, and Dell Computers.

Think About It T2.3

	June 1	June 30
Weaving Department	$66,280	$75,300
Preparation Department	0	0
Finishing Department	33,310	0
Total Work in Process	$99,590	$75,300

Think About It T2.4

Gross profit = $0.40/yard ($4.00 − $3.60). To forecast operating income, managers need to know which costs are variable and which costs are fixed.

Practice Questions

1. D
2. B
3. False
4. C
5. A
6. D
7. A

Topic Focus 2 Practice Exercise

1.

Beginning inventory, materials	$ 2,110
Beginning inventory, conversion	2,625
Added materials costs	34,815
Added conversion costs	52,395
Total	$91,945

2. Completed units 260,000
Ending Work in Process Inventory 3,750 — 5,000 units × 75% complete
Total equivalent units, materials 263,750

3. Completed units 260,000
Ending Work in Process Inventory 2,000 — 5,000 units × 40% complete
Total equivalent units, conversion 262,000

4.

	Materials	Conversion
Beginning inventory	$ 2,110	$ 2,625
Costs added to production	34,815	52,395
Total costs	$ 36,925	$ 55,020
÷ Equivalent units	263,750	262,000
Cost per equivalent unit	$ 0.14	$ 0.21

5. 260,000 units × ($0.14 + $0.21) = $91,000

6.

Materials (5,000 units × 75% × $0.14)	$525
Conversion (5,000 units × 40% × $0.21)	420
Total cost of ending inventory	$945

BUSINESS DECISION AND CONTEXT Wrap Up

After Jonathan Grant left her office, Kathy Stewart reflected on the conversation and her first month at Bradley Textile Mills. With her years of experience running a production operation, she didn't expect to run into an obstacle reading production reports. She was a little embarrassed that she hadn't realized different production processes are accounted for differently and, as a result, reported differently.

Now that Kathy knows what an equivalent unit is, she has a better understanding of process costing. Even though 500,000 yards of jersey fabric were in the Weaving Department during the month, the 100,000 that remain in work in process inventory at the end of the month are only partially completed. Based on the department's production report, the ending inventory is 60,000 equivalent yards for materials cost and 50,000 equivalent yards for conversion costs. Kathy also learned that valuing inventory in a process costing system requires calculation of both a materials cost and conversion cost per equivalent unit.

Now that Kathy understands process costing, she can read and interpret the company's production reports and make informed decisions.

TOPIC FOCUS SUMMARY

In this focus unit you learned about process costing, which is used by companies that mass-produce similar products. Now you should be able to meet the learning objectives set out at the beginning of the focus unit:

1. ***Identify the kinds of companies that use process costing systems.***

Companies that mass-produce their products or use a continuous production process use process costing systems. Industries that use process costing systems include chemicals, textiles, paper, and food processing.

2. ***Explain how costs flow through the inventory accounts in a process costing system.***

Costs flow through the inventory accounts in a process costing system just as they do in a job order costing system. The process begins with materials requisitioned from the Raw Materials Inventory being moved into the Work in Process Inventory. Direct labor and overhead costs are added to the Work in Process Inventory. When products are finished, they are transferred either to another Work in Process Inventory account or to the Finished Goods Inventory.

3. ***Calculate and explain equivalent units.***

Equivalent units are a way of representing partially completed units in completed form. For example, 100 units that are 80% complete are the equivalent of 80 completed units. Calculating equivalent units is necessary when costs must be assigned to both units that have been completed and transferred out of Work in Process and to units that remain in the Work in Process Inventory.

4. ***Assign costs to completed units and ending Work in Process Inventory.***

To assign costs to completed units and ending Work in Process Inventory, multiply the number of completed units and the number of equivalent units in ending Work in Process Inventory by the cost per equivalent unit. The cost per equivalent unit equals:

$$\frac{\text{Costs to be assigned}}{\text{Complete units} + \text{Equivalent units in ending inventory}}$$

EXERCISES

T2-1 Process costing and job order costing (LO 1) Identify which costing method is more likely to be used to accumulate costs for the following products or services by marking an X in the appropriate column. *Hint:* Think about the cost object and whether it is treated as distinct from other cost objects or as one of many cost objects.

PRODUCT/SERVICE	PROCESS COSTING	JOB ORDER COSTING
A completed tax return		
A box of Kellogg's Frosted Flakes®		
A gallon of gasoline		
Legal representation		
Knee surgery		
A bottle of Coca-Cola®		
A roll of newsprint paper		
A custom-built home		
A bottle of Robitussin® cough syrup		

T2-2 Processing costing: Cost flows (LO 2) Fill in the missing data (ignore indirect materials).

	Raw Materials Inventory		WIP—Department 1		WIP—Department 2		Finished Goods Inventory	
Beginning balance	$150,000		$ 60,000		$ 51,000		$250,000	
Materials purchased	805,000							
Direct materials used		$800,000	630,000		c.			
Conversion costs incurred			516,000		180,000			
Transfers of completed units				$1,100,000	d.	e.	f.	g.
Cost of goods sold								
Ending balance	a.		b.		$ 31,000		$150,000	

T2-3 Process costing: Cost flows (LO 2) Fill in the missing data (ignore indirect materials).

	Raw Materials Inventory		WIP—Department 1		WIP—Department 2		Finished Goods Inventory	
Beginning balance	a.		$ 36,000		$ 13,000		$63,000	
Materials purchased	$250,000							
Direct materials used		b.	200,000		80,000			
Conversion costs incurred			85,000		e.			
Transfers of completed units				d.	300,000	f.	g.	
Cost of goods sold								$512,000
Ending balance	$ 16,000		c.		$ 8,000		$41,000	

T2-4 Calculate equivalent units (LO 3) In February, Parsons, Inc. completed 12,000 units; 3,000 units still in process were 40% complete with respect to materials and conversion.

Required

a. How many equivalent units were in Parsons's ending Work in Process Inventory?
b. How many equivalent units will be used to calculate the cost per equivalent unit?

T2-5 Calculate equivalent units (LO 3) Sury Company reported the following information for the month of April:

	Units
Work in Process	
Beginning inventory, April 1	8,000
Added to production	45,000
Completed and transferred out	?
Ending inventory, April 30	5,000

Ending inventory was 100% complete with respect to materials and 80% complete with respect to conversion costs.

Required

a. How many units were transferred out of Work in Process Inventory?
b. What were the equivalent units of production for materials?
c. What were the equivalent units of production for conversion?

T2-6 Assign costs to completed units and ending Work in Process Inventory (LO 4) Refer to the information in T2-5. Sury also reported the following cost information in April:

	Costs	
	Materials	Conversion
Work in Process		
Beginning inventory, April 1	$11,000	$ 17,160
Added to production	66,380	104,000

Required

a. What was the cost per equivalent unit for materials?
b. What was the cost per equivalent unit for conversion?
c. What cost would be assigned to the units transferred out of Work in Process Inventory?
d. What cost would be assigned to the ending Work in Process Inventory?

T2-7 Assign costs to completed units and ending Work in Process Inventory (LO 4) Monk, Inc. reported the following results for the month of November.

	Units	Materials	Conversion
Work in process			
Beginning inventory	?	$ 5,900	$15,000
Added to production	?	47,300	65,000
Completed and transferred out	?	?	?
Ending inventory	40,000	60% complete	40% complete
Cost per equivalent unit		$0.40	$0.64

Required

a. How many units were completed and transferred out of Work in Process Inventory?
b. What cost should be assigned to the units transferred out of Work in Process Inventory?
c. What cost should be assigned to the ending Work in Process Inventory?

PROBLEMS

T2-8 Process costing: Cost flows (LO 2) Jenkins, Inc. started the period with the following account balances:

Raw Materials	$115,000
Work in Process:	
Grinding Department	$ 25,000
Mixing Department	$ 7,000
Finishing Department	$ 10,000
Finished goods	$ 41,000

The following events occurred during the year:

1. Production of a new set of products began with a transfer of $60,000 worth of raw materials to the Grinding Department.
2. Conversion costs of $82,000 were incurred in the Grinding Department.
3. Products costing $150,000 were transferred from Grinding to the Mixing Department.
4. Materials costing $8,000 were added to the Mixing Department.
5. Conversion costs of $33,000 were incurred in the Mixing Department.
6. Products costing $178,000 were transferred from Mixing to the Finishing Department.
7. Conversion costs of $41,000 were incurred in the Finishing Department.
8. Products costing $206,000 were completed and transferred to the Finished Goods Inventory.
9. Products costing $230,000 were sold.

Required

a. Record the events in the inventory T-accounts. Be sure to show ending balances for all accounts.

b. Review your T-accounts and answer the following questions:
   1. Which process does not require any materials to be added?
   2. Which process appears to be the most expensive?
   3. Assume 10,300 good units were produced during the year. What was the cost per unit? How many units were sold?

T2-9 Process costing and equivalent units (CMA adapted) (LO 3, 4) Gray Manufacturing Company makes pennants for college and university athletic teams. The company uses a process costing system to accumulate product costs as the pennants move through the two stages of production: cutting and silk-screening. All materials are added at the beginning of both cutting and silk-screening processes, while conversion costs are applied evenly throughout the process.

At the beginning of September, the Cutting Department had 1,000 pennants in process that were 50% complete. The company had incurred $1,300 in direct materials cost and $1,250 in conversion cost to make them. During the month the department added $13,195 more of direct materials and $32,875 in conversion costs. A total of 9,150 pennants were finished during September and transferred to the Silk-screening Department. At the end of the month, 2,000 pennants that were 30% complete remained in the Cutting Department.

Required

a. Calculate the number of pennants started in the Cutting Department during September.

b. Calculate the equivalent units of production for the Cutting Department for September. (*Hint:* Materials equivalent units and conversion equivalent units will not be the same.)

c. What was the ending balance in the Cutting Department's Work in Process Inventory account in dollars?

d. How much cost was transferred from the Cutting Department to the Silk-screening Department during September?

e. Reconcile both the physical units and the product costs for the Cutting Department in September.

T2-10 Process costing and equivalent units (CMA adapted) (LO 3, 4) Bricktown Bats buys wood as a direct material for its baseball bats. The Forming Department processes the baseball bats, which are then transferred to the Finishing Department, where a sealant is applied. During the month of March the Forming Department began manufacturing 10,000 "Casey Sluggers." There was no beginning inventory that month. Costs added to the Forming Department that month were as follows:

Direct materials	$33,000
Conversion costs	17,000
Total	$50,000

A total of 8,000 bats were completed and transferred to the Finishing Department in March; the remaining 2,000 bats were still in process at the end of the month. The bats in ending inventory were 100% complete with respect to materials but were only 25% complete with respect to conversion.

Required

a. What was the cost of the units transferred to the Finishing Department?

b. What was the Forming Department's Work in Process Inventory balance at the end of March?

CASES

T2-11 Process costing and equivalent units (CMA adapted) (LO 2, 3, 4) Lendrim, Ltd. is an established firm that manufactures a variety of high-quality sports clothing used by college and high school football teams. Over the last year the company's profits have declined. Lendrim's managers have been using product cost information that was developed almost two years ago. In an effort to determine the causes of weakened earnings performance, the company's controller, Al Lovelace, has asked Melanie Roberts, senior cost analyst, to investigate product costing at one of the company's largest plants, in Williamsburg, Virginia.

The Williamsburg plant manufactures high-grade insulated warm-up jackets that are produced in a two-department process. The Assembly Department completes the basic assembly of materials using Materials Packet #1 (insulated liner, outer jacket shell, hood, pocket lining, and zipper or snap attachments). After completion of the basic assembly, the jackets are transferred to the Finishing Department, where Materials Packet #2 is used to embroider school names, logos, monograms, and players' names on the jackets. When the finishing work is completed, the jackets are inspected before being transferred to the Finished Goods Inventory. In each department, all materials are added at the beginning of the manufacturing process. Direct labor and manufacturing overhead are applied continuously in both departments.

Roberts has traveled to the Williamsburg plant to develop accurate unit cost information, which will be used to determine whether the production process should be changed or the pricing structure should be altered. The unit cost that is used at the Williamsburg plant for planning, control, and pricing purposes is $75 per jacket. The jackets normally sell for $125.25 each.

When Roberts arrives at the plant, she is given a tour by plant manager B. J. Lendrim. Everything looks in order, and Lendrim claims everything has been running smoothly. His only complaint is that he is being evaluated against product costs that were set two years ago; he is sure that most of the plant's costs have increased since then. Roberts reviews the production costs for May and develops the following information:

- The beginning Work in Process Inventory for the Assembly Department held 560 units that were 25% complete as to conversion costs. There was no beginning inventory in the Finishing Department.
- The costs in beginning Work in Process Inventory were: Materials, $12,500; Conversion, $4,500.
- During May, the Assembly Department started 7,600 jackets, and completed and transferred to the Finishing Department a total of 7,260 jackets.
- At the end of May the Assembly Department had 900 jackets in process that were 40% complete as to conversion costs, and the Finishing Department had 300 jackets in process that were 50% complete as to conversion costs.
- The following costs were incurred during May:
    - Materials Packet #1 $252,700
    - Materials Packet #2 $ 76,230
    - Conversion Costs—Assembly $231,720
    - Conversion Costs—Finishing $106,650

Required

a. Calculate the equivalent units in the Assembly and Finishing departments for the month of May.

b. What was the cost per equivalent unit in the Assembly Department? In the Finishing Department? (Only consider the materials and conversion costs added to the department, not the costs of assembled units transferred in.)

c. What was the total unit product cost for the warm-up jackets?

d. Lendrim has been using the two-year-old $75-per-unit cost and a 67% markup ($75 × 167% = $125.25) as a basis for pricing the warm-up jackets. Based on the new costs you calculated for May, what markup is Lendrim *actually* achieving on the product cost? If Lendrim wants to continue using a 67% markup on the product cost, what price should the company charge for the warm-up jacket?

e. Assume you are Melanie Roberts. Write a memo to B. J. Lendrim either supporting or refuting his claim that product costs have risen over the past two years. Be sure to support your position with facts.

ENDNOTES

1. To learn more about the Jelly Belly production process, visit http://manufacturing.stanford.edu/ and click on the "How Everyday Things Are Made" hyperlink and look for "jelly beans."
2. For a review of job order costing, see Chapter 4.
3. This method of cost allocation is referred to as the weighted-average method. Another method, FIFO, is explained in more advanced cost accounting textbooks.

TOPIC FOCUS 3: VARIABLE AND ABSORPTION COSTING

Petek ARICI/Getty Images

FOCUS	LEARNING OBJECTIVES
TOPIC FOCUS 3	**LO 1:** Explain the difference between variable costing and absorption costing.
	LO 2: Calculate operating income under variable costing and absorption costing.

TOPIC FOCUS 3—GUIDED UNIT PREPARATION

Answering the following questions while you read this focus unit will guide your understanding of the key concepts found in this unit. The questions are linked to the learning objectives presented at the beginning of the unit.

LO 1

1. Under absorption costing, which costs are considered product costs? Which costs are considered period costs?
2. Under variable costing, which costs are considered product costs? Which costs are considered period costs?

LO 2

3. What income statement format is appropriate for variable costing?
4. When is income under variable costing higher than income under absorption costing?
5. What formula can be used to calculate the difference between income under variable costing and income under absorption costing?
6. What managerial behavior does variable costing render ineffective?

Business Decision and Context

BRADLEY TEXTILE MILLS

Chief Executive Officer
Kathy Stewart

Chief Financial Officer
Michael Schwaig

Kathy Stewart, CEO of Bradley Textile Mills, couldn't understand why predicting income from one period to the next was so difficult. She had been told by her accounting staff that a yard of fabric costs $3.60 to make. At a selling price of $4.00 per yard, she figured the company should make $0.40 on each yard sold.

But every month when she ran the numbers, the actual results never seemed to match her predictions.

Kathy confronted **CFO Michael Schwaig**. "Either it costs \$3.60 to make a yard of fabric or it doesn't," she said. "How can I predict sales and costs accurately from one period to the next?"

"Income depends on how much we produce *and* how much we sell," Mike responded. "We've discussed variable and fixed costs before. If we ramp up production and spread our fixed costs over more yards of fabric, we can reduce the cost to produce each yard and increase our margin. Producing more units makes better use of our facilities."

"I understand that," Kathy replied, "but if we can't sell the extra fabric, it just sits in inventory. That extra inventory increases our insurance costs. And we pay the same amount of fixed costs from one month to the next. Spreading these costs over more units doesn't reduce the amount we pay. In the meantime, we can't generate cash from inventory that is just sitting in the warehouse."

> "Spreading these costs over more units doesn't reduce the amount we pay. In the meantime, we can't generate cash from inventory that is just sitting in the warehouse."

Kathy and Mike both had valid points. Who was correct?

Accounting for inventory costs in a manufacturing company like Bradley Textile Mills or C&C Sports is much more complicated than it is for a retail operation like Universal Sports Exchange. Trying to forecast the effects of financial decisions on the income statement can also be more difficult. In the opening scenario, Kathy Stewart was confused by Bradley Textile Mills' sales and income trends. If a manager can't predict the effects of various events and decisions on income, then planning is useless. This unit will introduce the concept of variable costing, a method of accumulating product costs that provides information that is useful in decision making.

Absorption Costing versus Variable Costing

You have learned that product costs consist of all the costs incurred in the production of a product: direct materials, direct labor, and manufacturing overhead. The process of classifying all these costs as product costs is referred to as **absorption costing** (or **full costing**). Absorption costing is the cost accumulation method required by generally accepted accounting principles (GAAP) and by regulatory bodies such as the Internal Revenue Service. This is the type of costing you have done in previous chapters.

The underlying principle that absorption costing satisfies is the **matching principle**, which states that expenses should be matched with the revenues they generate. You may remember discussing this principle in your financial accounting course. Based on the matching principle, all product costs flow through Raw Materials Inventory, Work in Process Inventory, and Finished Goods Inventory until the goods are sold. Even though the company may have already paid cash for these items, the costs are not expensed on the income statement until the inventory has been sold. For example, the wages paid to direct labor workers are not treated as an expense at the time the payroll checks are written. Instead, they are charged to Work in Process Inventory so that they will become part of the product's cost.

You have learned that some costs are variable and some costs are fixed. You have also learned that to make predictions about costs and income, you must first separate costs by their behavior, whether fixed or variable. Any costs that are mixed must be divided into their fixed and variable components. If inventory unit costs combine variable costs (typically direct materials, direct labor, and overhead) with fixed costs (typically overhead), how can managers make sound decisions? One way is to use **variable costing** (or **direct costing**), in which only variable product costs are accumulated in the inventory accounts. In variable costing, fixed manufacturing overhead is treated as a period expense rather than a product cost, meaning it is expensed in the period in which it is incurred. Exhibit T3-1 shows how various product cost components are accounted for under variable versus absorption costing. As you can see, the only difference between the two methods is the treatment of fixed overhead costs.

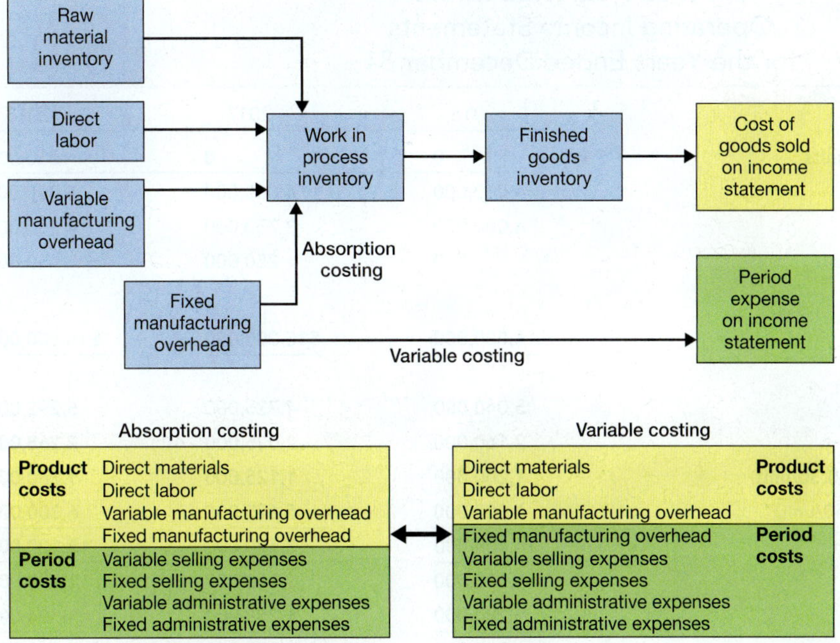

EXHIBIT T3-1

Comparison of variable and absorption costing.

Income Effects of Variable Costing

It should be clear now that the difference between absorption and variable costing is a timing difference in the expensing of fixed overhead costs. Of course, changing the timing of an expense will change reported income. Let's explore these changes using Bradley Textile Mill's cost for jersey fabric. We'll look at three scenarios: one in which production volume and sales volume are equal, one in which production volume is greater than sales volume, and one in which production volume is less than sales volume. The absorption and variable product costs for a yard of Bradley's fabric are as follows:

	Absorption Costing	Variable Costing
Direct materials	$1.26	$1.26
Direct labor	0.54	0.54
Variable overhead	0.30	0.30
Fixed overhead	1.50	
Total cost per yard	$3.60	$2.10

When Production Volume Equals Sales Volume

Let's assume that in 2016, Bradley had no beginning inventory, produced 4,000,000 yards of fabric, and sold 4,000,000 yards of fabric. So the company sold everything it produced during the year. Exhibit T3-2 shows two versions of Bradley's operating income statement for 2016. The top version, based on absorption costing, is presented in the functional format used in GAAP reporting. The bottom version, based on variable costing, is presented in the contribution margin format. Because the contribution margin format separates costs by their behaviors, it easily accommodates variable costing. This format is the more useful one for managerial decision making.

EXHIBIT T3-2

Comparison of Bradley Textile Mills' operating income.

BRADLEY TEXTILE MILLS
Operating Income Statements
for the Years Ended December 31

	2016	2017	2018
Beginning Finished Goods Inventory units	0	0	250,000
Units produced	4,000,000	4,000,000	4,000,000
Units sold	4,000,000	3,750,000	4,200,000
Ending Finished Goods Inventory units	0	250,000	50,000
Absorption Costing			
Sales ($4.00/unit)	$16,000,000	$15,000,000	$16,800,000
Cost of goods sold:			
Direct material ($1.26/unit)	5,040,000	4,725,000	5,292,000
Direct labor ($0.54/unit)	2,160,000	2,025,000	2,268,000
Variable manufacturing overhead ($0.30/unit)	1,200,000	1,125,000	1,260,000
Fixed manufacturing overhead ($1.50/unit)	6,000,000	5,625,000	6,300,000
Total cost of goods sold ($3.60/unit)	14,400,000	13,500,000	15,120,000
Gross profit ($0.40/unit)	1,600,000	1,500,000	1,680,000
Selling and administrative expenses	1,280,000	1,250,000	1,304,000
Operating income	$ 320,000	$ 250,000	$ 376,000
Variable Costing			
Sales ($4.00/unit)	$16,000,000	$15,000,000	$16,800,000
Variable expenses:			
Direct material ($1.26/unit)	5,040,000	4,725,000	5,292,000
Direct labor ($0.54/unit)	2,160,000	2,025,000	2,268,000
Variable manufacturing overhead ($0.30/unit)	1,200,000	1,125,000	1,260,000
Variable selling and administrative expenses ($0.12/unit)	480,000	450,000	504,000
Total variable expenses ($2.22/unit)	8,880,000	8,325,000	9,324,000
Contribution margin ($1.78/unit)	7,120,000	6,675,000	7,476,000
Fixed expenses:			
Fixed manufacturing overhead	6,000,000	6,000,000	6,000,000
Fixed selling and administrative expenses	800,000	800,000	800,000
Total fixed expenses	6,800,000	6,800,000	6,800,000
Operating income	$ 320,000	($ 125,000)	$ 676,000
Absorption income less variable income	$ 0	$ 375,000	($ 300,000)

Bradley's fixed manufacturing overhead cost for 2016 totaled $6,000,000, or $1.50 per yard of fabric ($6,000,000 ÷ 4,000,000 yards *produced*). In the absorption costing income statement (top of Exhibit T3-2), we expense, as cost of goods sold, $1.50 per yard sold. Since all 4,000,000 yards produced were sold, $6,000,000 (4,000,000 yards *sold* × $1.50 per yard) is subtracted from Sales to arrive at the Gross Margin. In the variable costing income statement (bottom of Exhibit T3-2), the entire $6,000,000 of fixed overhead is grouped with the other fixed expenses and is subtracted from the Contribution Margin to arrive at Operating Income. In this scenario, because production volume equals sales volume, the amount of fixed overhead expensed is the same in both statements.

When Production Volume Exceeds Sales Volume

Let's assume that in 2017 Bradley produced 4,000,000 yards of fabric but sold only 3,750,000 yards. This difference between the production and sales volumes resulted in a 250,000-yard increase in the ending finished goods inventory. Exhibit T3-2 shows the effects on the income statement (middle column). Notice that there is a $375,000 difference in reported operating income between the two versions of the statement, even though they reflect the same operating events. Both statements report the results of producing 4,000,000 yards of fabric and selling 3,750,000 yards.

What caused this $375,000 difference in operating income? It's all in the way that fixed manufacturing overhead is expensed and reported. With total fixed manufacturing overhead of $6,000,000, $1.50 is allocated to each yard ($6,000,000 ÷ 4,000,000 yards produced). Under absorption costing, only $5,625,000 of that amount is expensed ($1.50 per yard × 3,750,000 yards *sold*) in 2017; under variable costing, the entire $6,000,000 is expensed. So the difference in operating income between the two methods is the fixed overhead cost related to the 250,000-yard increase in ending inventory (from 0 yards to 250,000 yards).

If you are thinking that $375,000 can't just disappear, you are correct. If this amount is not on the income statement under absorption costing, then where is it? You have to look in the inventory account on the balance sheet. Remember that because production volume was greater than sales volume, some fabric is left in Finished Goods Inventory at the end of the year. The same unit cost that is used to calculate the cost of goods sold on the income statement is used to value that ending inventory. The following table shows the valuation of the Finished Goods Inventory (250,000 yards) in detail:

WATCH OUT!

Remember, inventory (or product) costs are based on the number of units produced. Income statement expenses are based on the number of units sold.

	Absorption Costing		Variable Costing	
	Unit Cost	Total Cost	Unit Cost	Total Cost
Direct materials	$1.26	$315,000	$1.26	$315,000
Direct labor	0.54	135,000	0.54	135,000
Variable manufacturing overhead	0.30	75,000	0.30	75,000
Fixed manufacturing overhead	1.50	375,000		
Total product cost	$3.60	$900,000	$2.10	$525,000

Notice that under absorption costing, the inventory balance is $375,000 higher than it is under variable costing. That is because the cost of the 250,000 yards of fabric in ending inventory includes $1.50 per yard in fixed manufacturing overhead cost. Under absorption costing, these inventory costs will not be expensed until the units are actually sold.

REALITY CHECK—*Variable costing, German style*

Michael Taylor/Lonely Planet Images/Getty Images

When 98% of managers in the United States don't have confidence in the cost information they use in their decision making, their companies may be ripe for a change.

Grenzplankostenrechnung—some dreaded disease? Just a random collection of letters? Neither. It's the German approach to cost accounting, which translates roughly as "flexible margin costing." In the United States it's referred to simply as GPK.

Developed after World War II by Georg Plaut and Wolfgang Kilger, GPK is similar to variable or direct costing. The main idea is that product costs should include only variable costs so that cost accounting information can better support managerial decisions, such as whether to make a component in-house or to outsource its production. Of course, this approach means that all costs must be classified as either fixed or variable.

Who uses GPK? Currently, GPK is used primarily in German-speaking countries, such as Germany, Austria, and Switzerland. Automakers Porsche, BMW, and Daimler Benz and the chainsaw manufacturer Stihl use GPK.

Will GPK be adopted in the United States? Although the Institute of Management Accountants has sponsored research to explore the system and several articles have been published about it, GPK's adoption in the United States is almost nonexistent. Chrysler doesn't use it, despite its former connection to Daimler Benz. However, Stihl's U.S. subsidiary has implemented GPK.

Why the lack of broad GPK use in the United States? A lot can be explained by cultural differences. U.S. companies don't emphasize cost management systems as much as German companies do. And U.S. and German companies differ in their cost center structures.

Only time will tell whether U.S. companies will switch to GPK. But when 98% of managers in the United States don't have confidence in the cost information they use in their decision making, their companies may be ripe for a change.

Sources: Ashish Garg, Debashis Ghosh, James Hudick, and Chuen Nowacki, "Roles and Practices in Management Accounting Today: Results from the 2003 IMA-E&Y Survey," *Strategic Finance*, July 2003, 30–35; Kip Krumwiede, "Rewards and Realities of German Cost Accounting," *Strategic Finance*, April 2005, 27–34; Kris Portz and John C. Lere, "Cost Center Practices in Germany and the United States: Impact of Country Differences on Managerial Accounting Practices," *American Journal of Business*, Spring 2010, 25(1), 45–51; Paul A. Sharman and Kurt Vikas, "Lessons from German Cost Accounting," *Strategic Finance*, December 2004, 28–35; Carl Smith, "Going for GPK," *Strategic Finance*, April 2005, 36–39; Rosanne Weaver, Robert W. Rutledge, and Khondkar E. Karin, "Is GPK Right for U.S. Companies?," *Internal Auditing*, July/August 2011, 3–9.

When Production Volume Is Less Than Sales Volume

At this point, you may think that absorption costing is preferable to variable costing because it shows a higher operating income. That isn't always the case, however. Let's look at what happens when production volume is less than sales volume. This scenario can occur only if the company has a beginning inventory, which Bradley did have at the beginning of 2018.

Let's assume that in 2018 all costs remained the same, and the company produced 4,000,000 yards of fabric and sold 4,200,000 yards. This sales volume resulted in a 200,000-yard decrease in ending inventory (from 250,000 to 50,000 yards). Exhibit T3-2 shows the resulting income statements for 2018. Notice that there is a $300,000 difference in reported net income between the two accounting methods, and that this year, variable costing, not absorption costing, has generated the higher operating income. Once again, these two versions of the income statement report the results of the same operating events. In 2018, those events were the production of 4,000,000 yards of fabric and the sale of 4,200,000 yards of fabric.

What caused this $300,000 difference in operating income? Again, it's all in the way fixed overhead is expensed and reported. Under absorption costing, fixed overhead of $6,300,000 (4,200,000 yards *sold* × $1.50 per yard) is expensed as part of the cost of goods sold. Under variable costing, only the $6,000,000 actually incurred during the year is expensed. So the difference in operating income is the fixed overhead cost related to the 200,000-yard decrease in ending inventory (from 250,000 yards to 50,000 yards) that is sold out of beginning inventory under the absorption costing method ($1.50 × 200,000 yards).

WATCH OUT!

Don't confuse the unit product cost under variable costing with the total variable cost per unit used in calculating contribution margin. Variable selling and administrative costs are ***never*** part of product costs.

Reconciling Income under Absorption Costing and Variable Costing

As Exhibit T3-3 shows, whenever there is a difference between the production volume and the sales volume, absorption costing and variable costing will result in different amounts for operating income. When costs don't change from one period to the next, you can reconcile this difference by multiplying the change in ending inventory units by the fixed overhead cost per unit used under absorption costing.

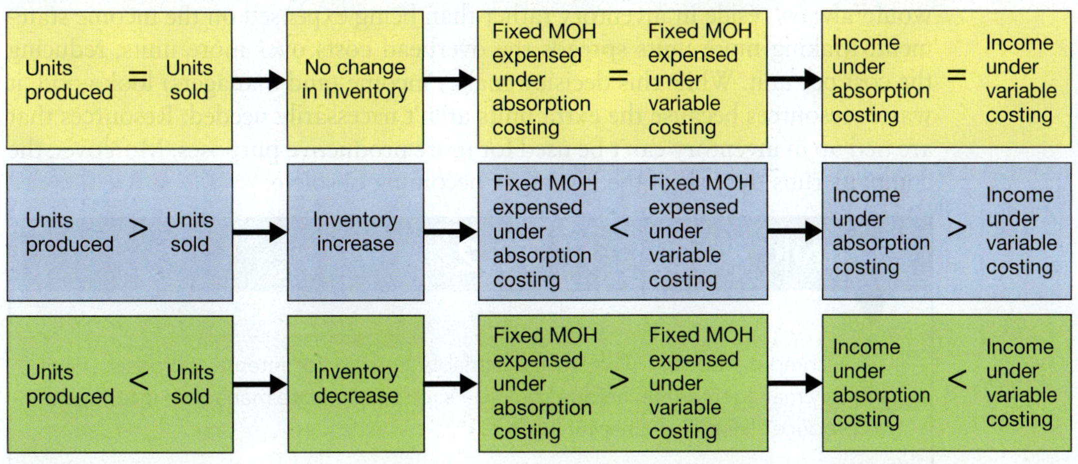

EXHIBIT T3-3 *Summary of income differences between absorption costing and variable costing.*

The table that follows reconciles the operating incomes shown in Exhibit T3-2.

		2016	2017	2018
	Absorption costing income	$320,000	$250,000	$376,000
–	Variable costing income	– 320,000	– (125,000)	– 676,000
	Difference	$0	$375,000	($300,000)
	Change in ending inventory units	0	250,000	(200,000)
×	Fixed overhead per unit	× $1.50	× $1.50	× $1.50
	Reconciliation	$0	$375,000	($300,000)

Looking across the years in Exhibit T3-2, you will notice that income varies less under absorption costing than under variable costing. Which income measure is the right one? Neither amount is necessarily right or wrong. In the long run, the same amounts will be recorded for revenues and expenses under both methods. The difference is just a matter of timing.

THINK ABOUT IT T3.1

Refer back to Exhibit T3-2. If Bradley had produced 3,750,000 units instead of 4,000,000 in 2017, what would the fixed overhead cost per unit have been? What would have been the new product cost per unit under absorption costing? If those 3,750,000 units had been sold, what operating income would Bradley have recorded for 2017?

From your answers to *Think About It T3.1*, you can conclude that when a company's production volume and sales volume vary from one year to the next, income will be harder to forecast under absorption costing because the fixed cost per unit changes with the number of units produced. So variable costing is better for purposes of forecasting and decision making. Is there any other reason to use variable costing for internal reporting purposes? The answer is yes. Absorption costing can encourage managers to engage in gaming behavior in an attempt to affect the income statement. Notice that if the production manager were to ensure that production is always greater than sales, a portion of the manufacturing overhead cost would always reside in inventory rather than being expensed on the income statement. Making more units spreads the overhead costs over more units, reducing the cost per unit. While this decision makes income (and managers) look good, it wastes resources because the extra units aren't necessarily needed. Resources that are tied up in inventory can't be used for more productive purposes. Moreover, the company runs the risk of the inventory becoming obsolete.

THINK ABOUT IT T3.2

If a company doesn't want to use variable costing for internal purposes, what inventory management technique could be used to eliminate managers' incentive to overproduce? (Hint: See Chapter 1.)

TOPIC FOCUS REVIEW

KEY TERMS

Absorption costing p. 204
Direct costing p. 205
Full costing p. 204
Matching principle p. 204
Variable costing p. 205

PRACTICE QUESTIONS

1. LO 1 Which of the following costs are *not* considered product costs under variable costing?
   a. Fixed manufacturing overhead
   b. Variable selling and administrative costs
   c. Fixed selling and administrative costs
   d. All of the above

2. LO 1 If a company uses a just-in-time inventory system, the differences between income under variable costing and income under absorption costing will be minimal. True or False?

3. LO 1 Which of the following is *not* a reason for a company to use variable costing?
   a. Variable costing is required by GAAP.
   b. Variable costing eliminates the temptation to overproduce in order to reduce the cost per unit.
   c. Variable costing highlights the fact that all of fixed overhead cost is incurred each period whether products are sold or sit in inventory.
   d. Variable costing is useful for decision making.

4. LO 2 Carlisle Gifts began its operations on January 1. The company produced 110,000 units; by the end of the year, 100,000 had been sold at an average price of $14/unit. Variable production costs were $5/unit; variable selling costs, $1/unit; fixed manufacturing overhead, $220,000; and fixed selling and administrative expenses, $80,000. Under absorption costing, what was Carlisle's operating income?

   a. $500,000
   b. $520,000
   c. $600,000
   d. $720,000

5. LO 2 Refer to question 4. Under variable costing, what was Carlisle's operating income?

   a. $500,000
   b. $520,000
   c. $600,000
   d. $720,000

TOPIC FOCUS 3 PRACTICE EXERCISE

The following table summarizes annual production and sales for Feldman Incorporated:

Units produced	100,000
Units sold	80,000
Sales price	$ 20/unit
Direct materials cost	$ 4/unit
Direct labor cost	$ 3/unit
Variable overhead cost	$ 2/unit
Fixed manufacturing overhead cost	$500,000
Variable and administrative selling cost	$ 1/unit
Fixed selling and administrative cost	$125,000

Feldman held no inventory at the beginning of the year.

Required

1. Calculate operating income using the absorption costing method.
2. Calculate operating income using the variable costing method.
3. Show that the difference in operating income is due to the fixed overhead cost in ending inventory.

SELECTED TOPIC FOCUS 3 ANSWERS

Think About It T3.1

Fixed overhead per unit = $1.60 ($6,000,000 ÷ 3,750,000). New product cost = $3.70.

Absorption Costing	
Sales ($4.00/unit)	$15,000,000
Cost of goods sold:	
Direct material ($1.26/unit)	4,725,000
Direct labor ($0.54/unit)	2,025,000
Variable manufacturing overhead ($0.30/unit)	1,125,000
Fixed manufacturing overhead ($1.60/unit)	6,000,000
Total cost of goods sold ($3.60/unit)	13,875,000
Gross profit ($0.30/unit)	1,125,000
Selling and administrative expenses	1,250,000
Operating income	$ (125,000)

Think About It T3.2

The company could use a just-in-time inventory system, making only enough units to fill customers' orders as they are received. As a result, the company would hold very little inventory.

Practice Questions

1. D
2. True
3. A
4. B
5. A

Topic Focus 3 Practice Exercise

1. Absorption Costing Unit Costs

Direct materials	$ 4	
Direct labor	3	
Variable overhead	2	
Fixed overhead	5	Fixed overhead per unit = $500,000 ÷ 100,000 units
Total	$14	

Sales	$1,600,000	$20 per unit × 80,000 units
Variable cost of goods sold	720,000	($4 + $3 + $2) × 80,000 units
Fixed overhead	400,000	$5 × 80,000 units
Gross margin	480,000	
Variable selling & administrative expenses	80,000	$1 × 80,000 units
Fixed selling & administrative expenses	125,000	
Operating Income	$ 275,000	

2. Variable Costing Unit Cost

Direct material	$4
Direct labor	3
Variable overhead	2
Total	$9

Sales	$1,600,000	$20 per unit × 80,000 units
Variable cost of goods sold	720,000	($4 + $3 + $2) × 80,000 units
Variable selling & administrative expenses	80,000	$1 × 80,000 units
Contribution margin	800,000	
Fixed overhead	500,000	
Fixed selling & administrative expenses	125,000	
Operating Income	$ 175,000	

3.

Absorption costing operating income	$ 275,000	
Variable costing operating income	$ 175,000	
Difference	$ 100,000	
Change in ending inventory units	20,000	100,000 − 80,000
Fixed overhead per unit	× $5	
Reconciliation	$ 100,000	

BUSINESS DECISION AND CONTEXT Wrap Up

In the opening scenario, Kathy Stewart, CEO of Bradley Textile Mills, couldn't predict the company's income from one period to the next. Her problem was that under absorption costing, all manufacturing costs, including fixed manufacturing overhead, must be assigned to products. Thus, if the number of units produced changes from one period to the next, unit product costs will change as fixed manufacturing overhead costs are spread over a greater or lesser number of units. Variable costing removes the variability in income due to changes in production volumes so that income changes only with changes in the number of units sold. Companies that use variable costing, or that at least separate their costs into variable and fixed components, can use CVP analysis to forecast the effects of various decisions on income or components of income. But remember that although variable costing is useful for internal decision making, it is not acceptable for external reporting.

This does not, however, completely invalidate Mike's argument in the opening scenario. Mike is correct that producing more units makes better use of Bradley's facilities. However, managers should not produce more units solely for the purpose of reducing unit product costs. Managers should produce enough units to meet demand.

TOPIC FOCUS SUMMARY

In this focus unit you learned about variable costing, a system that can be used only for internal reporting to help in managerial decision making. Now you should be able to meet the learning objectives set out at the beginning of the unit:

1. *Explain the difference between variable costing and absorption costing.*

   In absorption costing, which is required by GAAP, all manufacturing costs are considered to be product costs. Only selling and administrative costs are treated as period costs. In variable costing, only variable manufacturing costs are considered to be product costs. Fixed manufacturing overhead and all selling and administrative costs are treated as period costs.

2. *Calculate operating income under variable costing and absorption costing.*

   Under the absorption costing method you subtract the cost of goods sold from sales to arrive at the gross profit. Then you subtract the selling and administrative expenses to arrive at operating income. Under the variable costing method you subtract the variable costs from sales to arrive at the contribution margin. Then you subtract all fixed costs to arrive at the operating income.

EXERCISES

T3-1 Variable costing income statement (LO 1, 2) Following is Hartzberg's latest income statement. The company produced and sold 100,000 units during the year.

Sales (100,000 units at $50)		$ 5,000,000
Cost of goods sold:		
Direct material	$1,500,000	
Direct labor	800,000	
Variable manufacturing overhead	300,000	
Fixed manufacturing overhead	1,200,000	
Total cost of goods sold		3,800,000
Gross profit		1,200,000
Selling expenses:		
Variable	200,000	
Fixed	700,000	
Total selling expenses		900,000
Operating income		$ 300,000

Required

Restate the income statement in contribution margin format, as if Hartzburg had used a variable costing system to report income.

T3-2 Variable costing versus absorption costing (LO 1, 2) Fiendish Friends makes Halloween costumes. The company incurred the following total costs to produce 25,000 costumes.

Direct materials	$200,000
Direct labor	150,000
Variable overhead	50,000
Fixed overhead	100,000

Required

a. Under the absorption costing method, what is the average unit product cost? Using this method, how much product cost would be recorded on the income statement if 20,000 units were sold?

b. Under the variable costing method, what is the average unit product cost? Using this method, how much product cost would be recorded on the income statement if 20,000 units were sold?

T3-3 Variable versus absorption costing (LO 1, 2) The following table shows the inventory balances, in units, for years 1, 2, and 3. Total fixed manufacturing costs were $30,000 for each of the last five years. The units in Year 1 beginning inventory were based on production of 500 units.

	Year		
	1	2	3
Beginning inventory	50	0	100
Production	500	600	600
Sales	(550)	(500)	(600)
Ending inventory	0	100	100

Required

For each year, calculate the difference between absorption costing and variable costing operating income. Be sure to indicate which costing system has the higher net income.

T3-4 Variable versus absorption costing (LO 2) As Jacob walked back to his office after the weekly financial meeting, he reviewed his notes and saw that he had written down two operating income numbers: $110,000 and $50,000. He knew that the difference in the numbers was due to using different costing methods, but he had forgotten to write down which was based on variable costing and which was based on absorption costing.

Required

a. Jacob remembered that inventory has been increasing. Which of the operating income numbers results from variable costing and which results from absorption costing?
b. If all other operations remain the same but sales exceeds production next week, what will be the relation between the operating incomes calculated based on variable and absorption costing?
c. For decision-making purposes, does it make sense to report incomes generated by both costing systems at the weekly financial meeting? Explain your reasoning.

T3-5 Variable versus absorption costing (LO 1, 2) Sarah Stoner sells handmade jewelry that she designs herself. The items aren't expensive, and she has a loyal following in her town and the surrounding area. Sarah incurred the following unit costs to produce 60,000 items.

Direct materials	$3.00
Direct labor	$1.75
Variable overhead	$0.75
Fixed overhead	$4.25

Sarah began the year with no inventory. During the year she sold 45,000 items for $15 each, incurring $0.50 in selling costs per item plus $5,000 in advertising and other selling expenses.

Required

a. Under variable costing, what is Sarah's operating income?
b. Under absorption costing, what is Sarah's ending Finished Goods Inventory balance?

T3-6 Variable versus absorption costing (LO 1, 2) Regal Printing, Inc., prints and binds encyclopedias. The following information was found in the accounting records:

Sales price per unit	$ 103
Direct materials per unit	$ 50
Direct labor per unit	$ 16
Variable overhead per unit	$ 10
Fixed overhead per unit	$ 23
Fixed selling costs	$ 55,000
Variable selling costs	$180,000
Beginning inventory	0
Units produced	100,000
Units sold	90,000

Required

a. Under absorption costing, what is Regal's operating income?
b. Under variable costing, what is Regal's ending Finished Goods Inventory balance?

T3-7 Variable costing versus absorption costing (LO 1, 2) The following data were prepared by the Waco Wagon Company.

	Total	Variable	Fixed
Sales price	$20/unit		
Direct materials used	$ 90,000		
Direct labor	$ 99,000		
Manufacturing overhead	$ 90,000	$ 9,000	$81,000
Selling and administrative expense	$ 23,000	$14,000	$ 9,000
Units manufactured	18,000 units		
Beginning Finished Goods Inventory	20,000 units		
Ending Finished Goods Inventory	24,000 units		

Required

a. Under absorption costing, what is the unit product cost?
b. Under variable costing, what is the unit product cost?
c. Under absorption costing, what is the cost of goods sold?
d. Under variable costing, what is the cost of goods sold?
e. Under absorption costing, what is the operating income?
f. Under variable costing, what is the operating income?
g. Reconcile the difference in operating income under absorption costing versus variable costing.

PROBLEMS

T3-8 Absorption costing versus variable costing (LO 1, 2) Ruth Dennis, CEO of Prescott Industries, is concerned about the recent volatility in the company's operating income. She believes that since the number of units sold has been fairly stable over the past three years that operating income also should have been stable. Ruth asked Jim Randall, Prescott's inventory manager, to help her understand the issue.

Jim reviewed the company's records and compiled the following changes to Finished Goods Inventory (in units) for the years 2016, 2017, and 2018.

	Year		
	2016	2017	2018
Beginning inventory	1,000	2,000	500
Production	40,000	38,000	40,000
Sales	(39,000)	(39,500)	(39,500)
Ending inventory	2,000	500	1,000

Jim also gathered the 2016 income statements prepared using absorption costing and variable costing, which follow.

Income Statement—Absorption Costing	
Sales	$ 4,290,000
Cost of goods sold	
Units in beginning inventory	(90,000)
Units sold from current year production	(3,420,000)
Total cost of goods sold	(3,510,000)
Gross margin	780,000
Selling expense	(645,000)
Operating Income	$ 135,000

Income Statement—Variable Costing	
Sales	$ 4,290,000
Variable production expenses	(2,028,000)
Variable selling expenses	(195,000)
Contribution margin	2,067,000
Fixed manufacturing expenses	(1,520,000)
Fixed selling expenses	(450,000)
Operating income	$ 97,000

Required

a. Compute the unit product cost for 2016, 2017, and 2018 for variable and absorption costing. Assume costs do not change from one year to the next.

b. Prepare variable and absorption costing income statements for 2017 and 2018.
c. What do you notice about the trend in operating income from 2016 to 2018 under absorption costing? Compare this trend to the trend in unit sales.
d. Add the operating incomes across the three years for variable costing and absorption costing. What do you notice about the two totals? Why did this happen?

T3-9 Absorption costing versus variable costing (LO 1, 2) Barnes & Coffman Industries makes artificial Christmas trees. The unit costs for producing a tree are:

Direct materials	\$25
Direct labor	\$15
Variable overhead	\$15
Fixed overhead	\$ 5

The company also incurs \$1 per tree in variable selling and administrative costs and \$4,000 in fixed marketing costs.

At the beginning of the year the company had 900 trees in the beginning Finished Goods Inventory. The company produced 2,000 trees during the year. Sales totaled 1,500 trees at a price of \$100 per tree.

Required

a. Based on absorption costing, what was the company's operating income for the year?
b. Based on variable costing, what was the company's operating income for the year?
c. Assume that in the following year the company produced 2,000 trees and sold 2,500. Based on absorption costing, what was the operating income for that year? Based on variable costing, what was the operating income for that year?
d. For both years, explain why the operating income based on absorption costing differed from the operating income based on variable costing.

T3-10 Absorption versus variable costing (CMA Adapted) (LO 2) Bob Jones owns a catering company that prepares banquets and parties for individual and corporate functions throughout the year. Jones's business is seasonal, with a heavy schedule during the summer and on year-end holidays and a light schedule the rest of the year. Fixed operating costs are incurred evenly throughout the year.

One of Jones's most requested functions is a cocktail party. Bob has developed the following costs per person for a standard cocktail party:

Food and beverages	\$15
Direct labor	\$ 5
Variable overhead	\$ 2
Fixed overhead	\$ 5

Required

a. Based on absorption costing, what is Jones's cost per person? Based on variable costing, what is his cost per person?
b. Jones prices his cocktail parties by adding a 15% markup to his costs. What price will Jones charge per person if he uses absorption costing? If he uses variable costing?
c. Jones has been asked to bid on a 200-person cocktail party to be given next month. What is the minimum price he should bid for the party? Why?

T3-11 Absorption versus variable costing (LO 2) Joan Keathley has been trying to convince her boss, Jeff Hamilton, to use variable costing for internal reporting purposes. "If we could predict demand better, it wouldn't be an issue," argued Joan. Jeff doesn't think it is worth the extra effort or confusion of maintaining two sets of books. As a last resort, Joan has prepared income statements under five different scenarios of production volume. She believes that if this doesn't convince Jeff that their current income statements have been misleading, nothing will.

The following table shows the inventory unit data under five scenarios. Each scenario should be considered independently.

	Scenario				
	A	B	C	D	E
Beginning inventory	200	200	200	200	200
Production	500	600	700	800	900
Sales	(700)	(700)	(700)	(700)	(700)
Ending inventory	0	100	200	300	400

Joan gathered the following information from the accounting records. Fixed manufacturing costs per unit were determined based on normal production of 700 units per year. The 200 units in beginning inventory are valued at $63.20.

Sales price per unit	$ 99.00
Variable manufacturing costs per unit	$ 20.00
Fixed manufacturing costs per unit	$ 43.20
Total fixed manufacturing costs	$30,240
Total selling expense (all fixed)	$24,650

Required

a. Complete the following table. Scenario A is completed for you as a guide.

	Scenario				
	A	B	C	D	E
Product cost per unit					
Variable cost	$20.00	$20.00	$20.00	$20.00	$20.00
Fixed cost	60.48	?	?	?	?
Total unit cost	$80.48	?	?	?	?
Income Statement—Absorption Costing					
Sales	$ 69,300	?	?	?	?
Cost of goods sold					
Units in beginning inventory	(12,640)	?	?	?	?
Units sold from current year production	(40,240)	?	?	?	?
Total cost of goods sold	(52,880)	?	?	?	?
Gross margin	16,420	?	?	?	?
Selling expense	(24,650)	?	?	?	?
Operating income	($ 8,230)	?	?	?	?
Income Statement—Variable Costing					
Sales	$ 69,300	?	?	?	?
Variable expenses	(14,000)	?	?	?	?
Contribution margin	55,300	?	?	?	?
Fixed manufacturing expenses	(30,240)	?	?	?	?
Fixed selling expenses	(24,650)	?	?	?	?
Operating income	$ 410	?	?	?	?

b. How did unit sales change from one scenario to the next?

c. What causes the difference in income between variable and absorption costing?

d. The operating incomes for scenario C should be the same. Why?

e. Suppose Jeff Hamilton says he prefers the absorption costing statements because income increases from scenario to scenario. How would you respond?

CASES

T3-12 Inventory management and ethics (LO 1, 2) Venus Family Packaging is a privately owned business that has been in operation since the late 1800s. The business, which has grown at a moderate pace, has remained competitive due to its dedication to customer service and quality.

In February 2015 the company hired production manager Marcy Lambert and controller Keith Waldrop. Both Lambert and Waldrop came from publicly held companies with performance-based compensation systems. Missing the opportunity they had once had to influence a significant portion of their total compensation, these two employees made several presentations to upper management about the desirability of changing the company's compensation system.

Company president and major stockholder John Williams, who is not one to adopt the latest fads, listened patiently to Lambert and Waldrop for two years. He also attended a couple of seminars on performance-based compensation systems. After much information gathering, he decided to implement a compensation system to reward managers based on the company's performance beginning in January 2017.

The new system was based on two benchmarks: unit product cost and operating income. As the production supervisor, Lambert was rewarded on what she could control—production costs. Specifically, she was given a benchmark unit cost to achieve along with quality requirements. If she met or beat the benchmark unit cost (with a lower unit cost) while maintaining product quality, she would receive a bonus equal to 25% of her annual salary. The controller, vice president of marketing, and president would be given 25% bonuses if operating income exceeded the benchmark.

At first the plan seemed to be working well. Income was growing, customers were happy because their orders were always filled quickly, and management had gained a newfound pride in the company's financial performance. But as the end of the year approached, people's behavior began to change. In November 2017, Lambert instructed David Daughdrill, the purchasing agent, to buy additional raw materials. When the inventory manager, Larissa Denton, got wind of the new purchases, she confronted Lambert. Lambert's response was, "We need to make several thousand additional medium-sized boxes." Denton informed Lambert that the company had more than enough medium-sized boxes to make it through March of 2018, and there was no room to store the extra inventory. Lambert responded in a forceful tone, "Then you are going to have to rent some storage space because the products need to be made. I know of issues that you needn't be concerned with."

Since Lambert was her boss, Denton did as she was told. But three weeks later, over morning coffee, she mentioned the growing inventory to Keith Waldrop. "I've noticed an increase in our inventory on the balance sheet and have wondered what was happening," Waldrop replied. "But our inventory doesn't spoil, and the packaging is standard, so it won't become obsolete. I just record the events the way they occur. I don't see anything wrong with Lambert's actions."

Required

a. What might explain production manager Lambert's actions at the end of 2017?

b. If the company uses variable costing for internal reporting purposes, how do you think net income would compare to the net income reported under absorption costing in 2017?

c. How long do you think Lambert can keep building up inventory before someone calls a halt to it?

d. What responsibility does controller Keith Waldrop have to question Lambert's methods? Why does he choose to "look the other way"? By not following up on the unusual inventory increase he has noticed on the balance sheet, has Waldrop violated any ethical obligation he has to the company? Why or why not?

e. If Lambert overproduces inventory only in 2017, returning to normal production and inventory levels in 2018, do you think she has violated any ethical obligation she has to the company? Why or why not?

f. How might the compensation system be altered to mitigate Lambert's actions?

© jsnyderdesign/iStockphoto

CHAPTER 5 PLANNING AND FORECASTING

UNITS	LEARNING OBJECTIVES
UNIT 5.1 Planning and the Budgeting Process	**LO 1:** Describe the budget development process and explain how it fits into management's planning process.
UNIT 5.2 Performance Standards	**LO 2:** Calculate the standard cost of a product.
UNIT 5.3 Building the Master Budget: The Operating Budget	**LO 3:** Prepare the operating budget and describe the relationships among its components.
UNIT 5.4 Building the Master Budget: The Cash Budget	**LO 4:** Prepare the cash budget and describe the relationships among its components.
UNIT 5.5 Pro-Forma Financial Statements	**LO 5:** Prepare pro-forma financial statements and describe their relationship to the master budget components.

© dmitryzubarev/iStockphoto

Business Decision and Context

© Robyn Mackenzie/Shutterstock

During 2016, **George Douglas, president of C&C Sports,** became increasingly concerned about the company's cash difficulties. Near the end of the year, he raised this issue with his management team. "It looks like we're going to end the year with only about $7,000 in cash, and if we don't change operations in 2017, I'm worried that we could have some real problems if unexpected expenses should arise," said George. "You're absolutely right," added **Claire Elliot, vice president for finance and administration.** "For the last few years, the company has not generated enough cash to sustain operations, and we've had to acquire short-term loans while at the same time paying off long-term debt. Sales and income are increasing, but so are inventories, which tie up our cash." "Okay, then, as we plan for 2017, what can we do differently to increase cash and reduce debt?" challenged George.

Jonathan Smith, vice president for marketing, offered the first suggestion. "Well, we can increase sales, reduce inventories, or both. Sales of baseball pants and jerseys are already high, but they are low-margin items that contribute very little to profit. Sales of award jackets generate a higher gross margin and contribution margin, but make up only a small part of our business. So increasing sales of award jackets should help to increase cash. I can get my sales team to concentrate on increasing jacket sales while maintaining or increasing sales of pants and jerseys."

"Claire is right that we have too much cash tied up in inventory," said **Chad Davis, vice president for operations.** "Reducing inventories at the same time that sales are increasing will be a challenge. Customer response time must remain fast, since that is a major advantage we have over our competitors. If we hold too little inventory, customers' needs will not be met, and the company will lose its competitive edge. Nevertheless, I'm confident we can come up with a plan to tighten our management of inventory."

George was pleased with the ideas generated by his management team. "These are great ideas. Let's forecast what results we might expect if we can increase sales and manage inventory better. Claire, Jonathan, and Chad, get your groups together and start working on your pieces of the 2017 budget with these new strategies in mind."

> "Let's forecast what results we might expect if we can increase sales and manage inventory better. Claire, Jonathan, and Chad, get your groups together and start working on your pieces of the 2017 budget with these new strategies in mind."

Watch the Babycakes video in WileyPLUS to learn more about budgetary planning in the real world.

SUPPLY CHAIN KEY PLAYERS

END CUSTOMER

UNIVERSAL SPORTS EXCHANGE

C&C SPORTS

President
George Douglas

Vice President for Finance and Administration
Claire Elliot

Vice President for Marketing
Jonathan Smith

Vice President for Operations
Chad Davis

DURABLE ZIPPER COMPANY

BRADLEY TEXTILE MILLS

CENTEX YARNS

NEFF FIBER MANUFACTURING

BRUIN POLYMERS, INC.

UNIT 5.1

Planning and the Budgeting Process

GUIDED UNIT PREPARATION

Answering the following questions while you read this unit will guide your understanding of the key concepts found in the unit. The questions are linked to the learning objectives presented at the beginning of the chapter.

LO 1

1. Why do organizations prepare budgets?
2. Whose responsibility is it to set the budget?
3. "Budgeting is needed only in large organizations. As a small business owner, I don't need to waste time preparing a budget." Do you agree with this statement? Why or why not?
4. How does top-down budgeting differ from bottom-up budgeting? What are the advantages of each approach?
5. What is budgetary slack? Why is it an issue in budget preparation?
6. What is zero-based budgeting?

Most organizations have a plan for success. Those plans may be formal or informal, but leaders should be able to identify what they want their organizations to achieve. In Chapter 1, you read about the need for organizations to have strategies to achieve their goals. **Strategic planning** is very broad and helps to identify the overall focus of an organization. **Tactical planning** develops concrete actions that turn strategic plans into reality.

One type of tactical planning is the budgeting process. The budgeting process is a means of allocating organizational resources among various divisions, projects, or other subsets of an organization. Just as strategic planning is ineffective without a tactical plan that specifies how to achieve management's goals, budgeting will be ineffective unless it is tied to strategy and is used to manage an organization's overall performance. Yet a 2014 survey by Deloitte found that 37% of respondents believed that their budgeting process was not aligned with corporate strategy.[1]

What Is a Budget?

A **budget** is an operating plan that is expressed primarily in financial terms—that is, in dollars. The budget has its beginnings in the organization's strategic plan. As managers develop the steps required to implement a strategy, they begin also to develop the budget, which shows how resources will be used to operationalize those steps. In other words, you can think of a budget as "putting your money where your mouth is." The budget helps to communicate this commitment of resources throughout the organization.

But budgets do more than show how resources are to be committed. Preparing a budget allows managers to plan for the future, reducing the need for knee-jerk responses to unexpected situations. For example, if the budget indicates that the organization will experience a short-term cash shortage, plans can be made to secure a line of credit that will see the company through the shortage. That way, employees will receive their paychecks as scheduled, vendors will receive payment for the company's purchases, and customers will receive their goods and services at the requested time.

The budget also helps divisions within the organization to communicate with one another, getting them all going in the same direction toward overall corporate goals. As managers review divisional budgets, they can assess whether the division's strategic direction is in line with corporate strategy, and request corrective action if needed. For example, corporate executives who have decided to pursue new international markets might find some divisional budgets that don't commit any resources to international market growth. If so, they can then meet with the divisional heads and encourage them to prepare new budgets that commit resources to help achieve the corporation's international strategy.

As Exhibit 5-1 shows, budgets assist managers in all four aspects of management discussed in Chapter 1—planning, controlling, evaluating, and decision making. This chapter concentrates on the planning aspects of budgeting. We will explore the controlling, evaluating, and decision-making aspects of budgeting in later chapters.

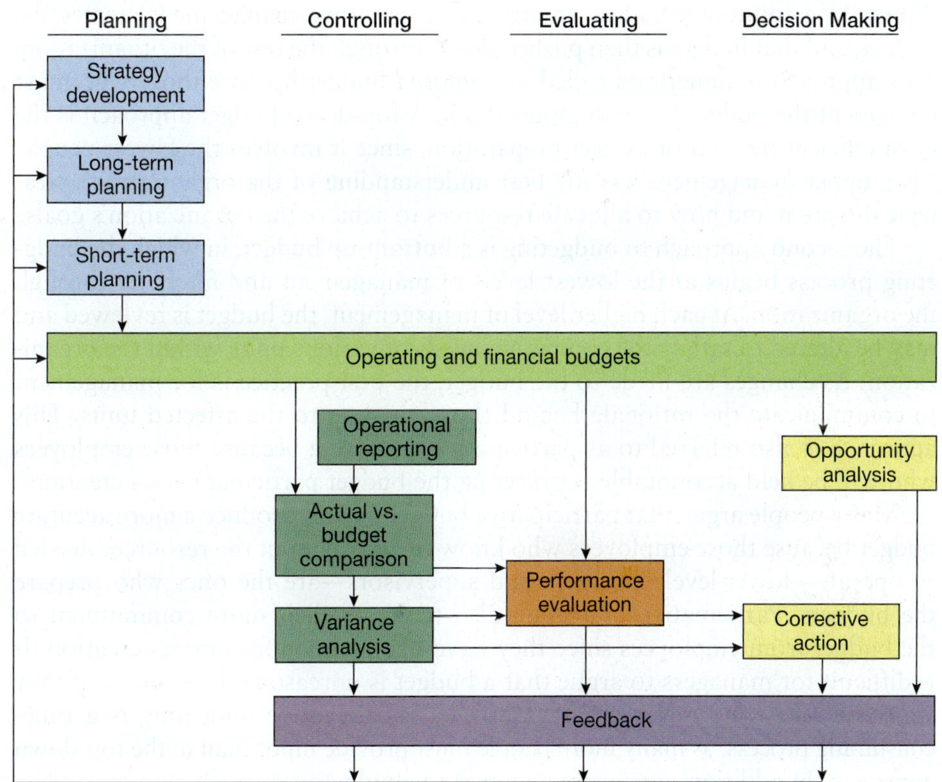

EXHIBIT 5-1

Uses of budgeting in managing an organization.

The Budgeting Process

How does an organization prepare a budget? The mechanics of the process are straightforward, as we will see in the following units. However, budgeting isn't just about the numbers. Choices related to who creates the budget or how standards are set may result in unintended consequences if managers are not aware of how employees are affected by these choices. Before we learn the mechanics, we are going to explore various choices managers have when implementing the budget process and the related behavioral issues that all managers should understand.

EXHIBIT 5-2

Information flows during budget preparation.

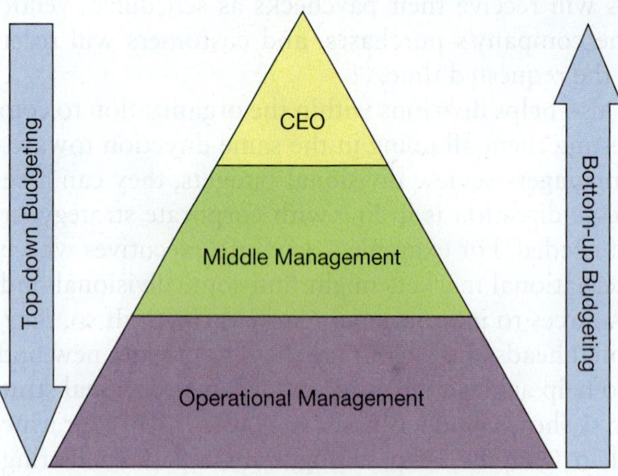

Information Flows

Information flows in two primary directions in the budgeting process, as Exhibit 5-2 shows. In a **top-down budget** environment, executive management creates the budget, and that budget is then pushed down through the rest of the organization. This approach is sometimes called an *imposed* budget because those who must implement the budget have no input into it. A top-down budget approach is the most efficient method of budget preparation, since it involves the fewest people. Also, upper management has the best understanding of the organization's strategic direction and how to allocate resources to achieve the organization's goals.

The second approach to budgeting is a **bottom-up budget**, in which the budgeting process begins at the lowest levels of management and filters up through the organization. At each higher level of management, the budget is reviewed and may be altered to satisfy the competing needs of various units within the organization. As changes are made to the budget, the best practice is for management to communicate the rationale behind those changes to the affected units. This approach is also referred to as **participative budgeting** because those employees who will be held accountable for meeting the budget participate in its creation.

Many people argue that participative budgeting will produce a more accurate budget because those employees who know the most about the resources needed to operate—lower-level managers and supervisors—are the ones who prepare the budgets. Participative budgeting also tends to elicit more commitment to the budget from employees since they have had some input into its creation. It is difficult for managers to argue that a budget is unreasonable or unfair if they were the ones who developed it. However, participative budgeting is a time-consuming process, as many more people must provide input than in the top-down approach. In addition, managers may pad the budgets.

In Exhibit 5-2, both the top-down and bottom-up approaches to budgeting appear to be linear, with budget information flowing in a single direction. That is not the case in practice. Under both approaches, budget preparation is iterative. That is, as the initial budget is developed and communicated through various levels of management, it is revised to incorporate additional factors and returned to the original preparer. So the budget process is really more circular than linear.

Behavioral Issues

Budgets should not be prepared simply as an exercise. Instead, budgets should be used to guide employee actions and decisions throughout the year as part of an overall performance management plan. Deviations from the budget can identify the need to correct a situation gone wrong. This use of the budget is part of managerial control.

As the year progresses, actual results should be compared to budgeted results. Deviations from the budget can occur because of good decisions, bad decisions, or events beyond the company's control. Some middle managers, no doubt, will be called on to explain why such deviations occurred. Those managers may be praised for favorable outcomes (such as higher revenue), whether or not they are in control of the factors that caused the outcomes. Conversely, they may be reprimanded for unfavorable outcomes (such as higher expenses), whether or not they control the factors causing the outcomes. The need to explain such outcomes and the fear of repercussions may cause some managers to behave defensively, perhaps by over- or underestimating budget items. In fact, a survey published in *CFO* reports that of 164 financial executives polled, 53% believed that the budgeting process used in their organizations encouraged managers to engage in some form of undesirable behavior.[2]

This type of problem is especially common in a bottom-up budget environment, in which managers prepare the budget that they will eventually be evaluated against. Often, managers are tempted to include **budgetary slack**, or **budgetary padding**, in the budget. For example, a manager may budget lower revenues or higher costs than are expected to occur. If the manager believes that revenues for the coming year will be $100,000, she may budget for only $85,000. At the end of the year if revenues are really $100,000 as originally expected, the manager who has "beat the budget" looks as if she did a great job managing her division. Likewise, if expenses are expected to be $50,000, a manager may budget for $60,000 to increase his chances of beating the budget.

The addition of budgetary slack may appear to be harmless, but it has real consequences for the organization. First, resources may not be allocated in the optimal way. The suboptimal allocation of resources may lead to the postponement or cancellation of projects that would be beneficial to the organization because resources do not appear to be available to fund them. In the above scenario, for example, if management expected an extra $15,000 in revenues ($100,000 − $85,000), that $15,000 could be committed to a worthwhile, income-generating project. Second, if managers receive bonuses based on their beating a padded budget, they receive additional compensation that they would not have earned had the budget been prepared realistically.

Top-down budgets are not without behavioral issues, either. Employees may feel that an imposed budget is unfair, that there is no way to operate within its parameters. If they are not committed to the budget, they will have no motivation to attempt to meet it. As employees fail to control expenses or generate revenues, the organization's resources may be wasted.

THINK ABOUT IT 5.1

How might a company reward employees for meeting or exceeding the budget, yet discourage them from creating budgetary slack? In a bottom-up budget environment, is it possible to completely eliminate budgetary slack? Why or why not?

REALITY CHECK—*What's up with the budget?*

© Dean Mitchell/iStockphoto

Budget. The mere mention of the word conjures up unpleasant ideas for many business people—hours and hours of data analysis, a seemingly never-ending process with questionable results, an unreliable yardstick used to measure performance. In his best-selling book *Winning*, former General Electric CEO Jack Welch stated that budgeting "sucks the energy, time, fun and big dreams out of an organization." Yet despite this apparent unpleasantness, a 2014 Deloitte survey found that over 90% of the responding firms prepared a budget to help guide operations.

With all the economic uncertainty facing organizations today, preparing a useful budget is a challenge. The Deloitte survey found that more than 80% of respondents spent 2 months or longer preparing the budget. While a recent Performance Architects survey found that 73% of firms prepare a budget that covers 12 months, a 2012 Quantrix survey reports that 37% of budgets are obsolete within the first three months of the year. Perhaps that's why 80% of the Deloitte global survey respondents prepare updated forecasts at least quarterly.

What can be done to make budgeting a more useful tool? For some organizations, it's changing the approach to budgeting. Rolling forecasts, bottom-up budgeting, and zero-based budgeting are all tools that more and more companies are embracing to improve their budgeting process.

While 73% of firms prepare a budget that covers 12 months, 37% of budgets are obsolete within the first three months of the year.

Sources: Jack Welch, *Winning* (New York: Harper Business, 2005, p. 189); Richard Horton, Paul Searles, and Kimberly Stone, *Integrated Performance Management: Plan. Budget. Forecast*. Deloitte LLP, 2014, https://www2.deloitte.com/content/dam/Deloitte/au/Documents/technology/deloitte-au-tech-integrated-performance-management-plan-budget-forecast-0614.pdf (accessed March 1, 2016); Kirby Lunger, Performance Architects, "Budgeting and Forecasting 2010 Survey Results," http://www.techrepublic.com/whitepapers/budgeting-and-forecasting-2010-survey-results/2502859 (accessed March 1, 2013); Quantrix, *2012 Budgeting, Forecasting, and Planning Survey*, http://www.quantrix.com/en/news-events/press-releases/2012/04/quantrix-releases-results-of-2012-budgeting,-forecasting,-and-planning-survey/ (accessed July 4, 2016).

Starting Points

How does a company begin the budgeting process? There are two main ways to begin, the more popular of which is the incremental approach. Using this type of approach, the manager begins with the current year's budget and adds or subtracts funds for any anticipated changes in operations. This approach may be as simple as increasing the entire budget by a flat percentage, say 5%, or it may be as complicated as marking each budget item for an increase or decrease.

Although the incremental method is fairly easy to implement, it perpetuates budget errors. If a manager has padded this year's budget, that padding will carry forward to the next year. Furthermore, programs will not be reviewed to ensure that they continue to meet corporate goals and objectives. Rather, they will become "perpetual" budget items that consume resources better invested elsewhere.

An alternative to incremental budgeting is **zero-based budgeting**, under which the budget begins each year at $0 and each individual budget item must be justified. Just because an item was included in last year's budget, it is not guaranteed a place in this year's budget. If an item cannot be justified, it is not added to the budget. This method of budgeting is often used in governmental entities and is much more time-consuming than incremental budgeting.

Time Frames

Different companies use different time frames to prepare their budgets. The most common time frame is one year. A typical approach to preparing an annual budget is to compile detailed monthly budgets. But the further into the future you project, the harder it is to get "good" numbers. If C&C is budgeting in November to buy fabric the following October, how accurate is the projected price 11 months in the future? A lot of unexpected price changes can occur in a short period of time. Consider what can happen to polyester prices in the wake of a hurricane. If the storms damage refineries and chemical plants along the Gulf Coast, the prices of polyester inputs can increase dramatically as they did in 2006 after Hurricanes Katrina and Rita. There is no way that C&C can know to budget for such a price increase before it occurs.

To protect against such uncertainties, some organizations will begin the budget period by breaking down only the first quarter into months. As the second quarter approaches, managers review the budget and break it down into months. Other companies prepare a **rolling budget**, which always includes 12 months of data. As one month ends, it is removed from the budget, and the entire budget rolls forward one month. Regardless of the period chosen, however, the mechanics of calculating the budget remain the same.

Once prepared, budgets don't have to be set in stone. Companies can prepare updated forecasts throughout the year to provide the best estimate of what to expect. In fast-paced, highly competitive industries, product life cycles are short, and competitors' actions can change the nature of the market quickly. Consider the cell phone industry, in which new features are advertised almost weekly. If a competitor introduces a popular new phone, a phone that sells for $250 today may sell for only $150 next quarter. Under these conditions, forecasts need to be updated frequently.

The budgeting process should also be flexible enough to allow managers to take advantage of opportunities or to discontinue unproductive programs. In allowing for revisions, however, managers need to distinguish between changes that are necessary to manage the business successfully and changes that merely relax standards. Before explaining the creation of a budget, then, we will discuss the development and need for standards in determining budget amounts.

UNIT 5.1 REVIEW

KEY TERMS

Bottom-up budget p. 224
Budget p. 222
Budgetary padding p. 225
Budgetary slack p. 225
Participative budgeting p. 224
Rolling budget p. 227
Strategic planning p. 222
Tactical planning p. 222
Top-down budget p. 224
Zero-based budgeting p. 226

PRACTICE QUESTIONS

1. LO 1 Which of the following statements about budgeting is *not* true?

   a. Budgeting is an aid to planning and control.

   b. Budgets create standards or benchmarks for performance evaluation.

   c. Budgets coordinate the activities of the whole organization.

   d. Budgets should always be prepared by top management, since executives see the "big picture."

2. LO 1 Bottom-up budget planning is more efficient than top-down planning because the operational managers have a better grasp of reality than top management, so that fewer changes need to be made after the budget has been submitted for review. True or False?

3. LO 1 Once a company has prepared a budget for the year, no changes can be made to the budget during the year. True or False?

4. LO 1 Joe Sneed requested $50,000 in his budget to cover advertising expenses he believed would cost only $35,000. This is an example of
   a. budgetary slack.
   b. zero-based budgeting.
   c. rolling budgeting.
   d. top-down budgeting.

UNIT 5.1 PRACTICE EXERCISE

On September 20, Jeff DeHay, manager of Briloff's Central Texas region, received the annual email from the budget office. It was time to prepare his annual budget. Included in the email were instructions that DeHay should estimate the revenues and expenses his region would report for the coming year. Anything greater than a 5% deviation from the current year's budget would need to be explained, though there was no indication that the budgeted numbers wouldn't be accepted.

Required

1. Describe Briloff's budget process as top-down or bottom-up.
2. What are the advantages and disadvantages of this budget approach?

SELECTED UNIT 5.1 ANSWERS

Think About It 5.1

There is no simple answer to this question. Such a reward system would need to include some type of punishment or disincentive for not telling the truth. One way might be to reward the managers with a bonus for meeting or exceeding the budgets they proposed up to a certain point, but to penalize them if they beat the budget by too much. For example, a sales manager who budgets for sales of $100,000 should receive a graduated bonus for meeting that goal or exceeding it up to, say, $110,000. For sales over $110,000, the manager loses bonus dollars. The penalty does give him an incentive to stop selling once sales hit $110,000—a problem for the company. However, the sales staff could receive bonuses for selling as much as possible, with no limit on their earnings. They would have no incentive to stop selling, and they would strive for the highest possible sales level. Because the manager knows that the sales staff will reach for the stars, he or she is more likely to budget for the maximum sales level.

It is unlikely that budgetary slack will ever be eliminated completely. It is human nature to "play it safe."

Practice Questions

1. D
2. False
3. False
4. A

Unit 5.1 Practice Exercise

1. Briloff's budget process is a bottom-up approach, since managers develop and submit their budgets rather than receiving the budgets from executive management. This process can also be described as participative budgeting.
2. Advantages: More accurate, greater employee commitment to the budget

   Disadvantages: More time-consuming, potential for budgetary slack

Performance Standards

GUIDED UNIT PREPARATION

Answering the following questions while you read this unit will guide your understanding of the key concepts found in the unit. The questions are linked to the learning objectives presented at the beginning of the chapter.

LO 2

1. What is a standard? Give three examples of standards that were not discussed in this unit.
2. Explain the difference between ideal and practical standards. Which type of standard would you want to be evaluated against? Why?
3. What is the difference between a standard price and a standard cost?
4. What are the components of a product's standard cost?

Have you ever seen a health department sanitation certificate displayed on a restaurant's wall? The certificate attests that inspectors visited the restaurant and evaluated it against a set of expectations established by the issuing body. Such expectations, often called **standards**, specify the characteristics, rules, or guidelines that define a particular level of performance or quality.

Many facets of our lives are subject to standards. Your grade in this class is based on your professor's standards for achievement. The water you drink meets standards for clean drinking water specified by the Environmental Protection Agency. (For instance, drinking water can contain no more than 4 milligrams of chlorine per liter.)[3] Editors of the *Mobil Travel Guide* set the guide's standards for its five-star hotels and restaurants.

Some standards, such as your grade in this course, are set by individuals. Other standards are set through a more rigorous process of review and comment. The International Organization for Standardization (ISO) is an international body with over 19,500 standards for a variety of products, ranging from paper sizes (letter, legal, and A4) to information security. You may have seen companies that advertise "ISO 9000" certification, an application of ISO-specified quality management standards.[4] Another standard-setting group that you may have encountered is the American National Standards Institute (ANSI).

In this unit, we will explore how companies develop the standards they use in planning their operations. In the next unit we will show how to use those standards to develop a budget. But planning activities are only one way that firms use standards. In Chapter 6 we will explore how to use the same standards in evaluating organizational performance.

REALITY CHECK—*The diamond standard*

© Simfo/iStockphoto

Many people have heard of the 4 Cs of diamond quality—color, cut, clarity, and carat. This method of referring to diamond quality was developed in the late 1930s by the Gemological Institute of America (GIA) to help the public understand what to look for when purchasing a diamond. Not long thereafter, GIA developed the grading system that has been adopted internationally as the industry standard for communicating diamond quality.

The color standard runs from "D," which is a colorless diamond, to "Z," which is light yellow, brown, or gray. Most people can't tell a difference in color unless they compare stones that are at least two or three grades apart. The online jeweler Blue Nile recommends a diamond of "J" color or better, while Diamonds.com recommends grade "K" or better.

Clarity standards are used to measure "inclusions" and "blemishes," which are imperfections in the stone. To apply these standards, the diamond grader examines a stone under 10 times magnification. The clarity standard ranges from "Flawless" (Fl), meaning no imperfections, to "Included" (I3), which contains obvious and possibly large imperfections. Blue Nile recommends stones that meet at least the "SI2" (slightly included) grade, while Diamonds.com recommends that stones be at least "I1" in clarity.

The standards for grading a diamond are subject to a bit of interpretation.

The standards for grading a diamond are subject to a bit of interpretation. In fact, the same diamond may receive different grades from different graders. But technological advances, such as Overseas Diamonds' "Isee2" machine, are making the grading process less subjective.

Sources: Ann Zimmerman and Anita Raghavan, "Diamond Grader Tries Polishing Its Image," *The Wall Street Journal*, March 24, 2006; Robert Weldon, "Sight for Sore Eyes'" *Professional Jeweler Magazine*, November 2005, http://www.professionaljeweler.com/archives/articles/2005/nov05/1105md1.html (accessed July 6, 2016); http://www.diamonds.com/Education/Education_Intro.aspx (accessed March 1, 2013); http://www.bluenile.com/diamond-and-jewelry-education?track=NavEdu (accessed March 1, 2013).

Ideal versus Practical Standards

Standard setting is not an exact science; in fact, it is often subjective. Take academic standards, for example. Some professors may set the standard for an "A" at 90%, while others may set it at 93%. Even if two professors set the standard at 90%, they may differ on what constitutes A-level work. There is no hard and fast criterion for proving one standard right and the other one wrong. Standards are a matter of choice exercised by the individual who sets the standard.

Standards generally fall along a continuum based on the likelihood that they will be achieved. An **ideal standard** signifies perfection. Think about academic performance, in which the 4.0 GPA represents the ideal standard. In a manufacturing environment, the ideal standard is a kind of "factory heaven": machines never break down; workers always operate at 110% efficiency, never needing breaks; and materials always arrive on time, in the quantity and quality ordered. Unfortunately, this scenario never occurs in manufacturing.

At the other end of the continuum are **practical standards**, which represent a level of performance that can be attained with reasonable effort. A practical standard is not set at a level so low that it is always reached or can be reached with no effort at all. In an academic context, a 3.0 GPA might be considered a practical standard. In a manufacturing setting, practical standards allow for machine breakdowns, employee fatigue, and other normal operating glitches.

The type of standard adopted can have a behavioral impact on workers. Suppose a manager sets an ideal standard, believing that employees will work hard to attain the expected level of performance. Since the standard is ideal, they will rarely, if ever, reach it. Ideal standards are very popular in Japanese manufacturing. The standard of "zero defects," for example, is a goal Japanese companies desire to achieve. That is, all products should be made or services provided with no lapses in quality. Even if the goal of no defects is impossible to achieve over the long term, companies that use these standards want their employees to know that they should always strive for that level of performance.

Critics of ideal standards believe that after a period of performing below standard, employees will likely lose motivation because no matter how hard they work, they cannot attain the standard. Their morale will likely suffer, and performance will continue to decline. Worse yet, in an effort to meet an ideal standard, employees may take shortcuts. The result could be a decline in product quality.

If the manager sets a practical standard, however, employees will be able to reach it with some effort. Once they see that they can meet the standard with a little hard work, they will be more motivated to continue working at the level necessary to meet the standard. Employees will take pride in their work and their ability to reach the standard, and their morale will remain high. Once they begin to achieve a practical standard on a regular basis, it should be raised to a higher level of performance. Striving for performance improvement may be the only way a company can maintain its competitive advantage.

THINK ABOUT IT 5.2

Reread "The Diamond Standard" Reality Check. What would be considered the ideal standard for diamond color and clarity? What would be considered a practical standard for diamond color and clarity? What trade-offs does a buyer make when choosing between ideal and practical standards?

Product Standards

Manufacturing companies like C&C Sports often set standards for the maximum cost that should be incurred to produce a unit of product. Such cost standards are useful in the planning (budgeting) process and can be helpful in evaluating how well manufacturing operations are managed. In developing product standards, managers must set a separate standard for each component of product cost—direct materials, direct labor, variable manufacturing overhead, and fixed manufacturing overhead. When the standards for all these cost components have been determined, a **standard cost**, representing the cost to produce one unit of product, can be calculated.

Direct Materials

Direct materials standards specify both the *quantity* of material needed per unit of product and the *price* to be paid for the material. Let's develop the materials standards for C&C Sports' baseball pants. The primary direct material used in the production of baseball pants is the fabric. In addition to the list price of $3.65 per yard, the standard price includes the cost of shipping the fabric from Bradley Textile Mills to C&C's plant, as well as any volume discounts Bradley grants C&C. In all, the standard price for one yard of fabric is $3.50:

Item	Price
List price	$ 3.65
Quantity discount	(0.25)
Freight	0.10
Standard price per yard	$ 3.50

You may be wondering who calculates the standard price for the material. The purchasing agent responsible for ordering the fabric knows the list prices that various suppliers charge C&C, so she likely would be the one to negotiate a volume discount. Of course, since the price of the fabric may be influenced by its grade or quality, the agent must confer with the product designer, product engineer, and production manager to verify the appropriate grade to purchase before setting the standard price. Furthermore, if the inventory manager is trying to control the volume of raw materials, the purchasing agent will need to know whether she should buy in bulk to get volume discounts. If cash must be borrowed to finance the extra inventory, saving money on materials purchases may cost the company more in storage costs, insurance, and interest.

The quantity of fabric used in each pair of baseball pants is determined by product designers and engineers when a product is designed. If practical standards are used, the standard quantity for direct materials should include allowances for waste and spoilage in the normal course of manufacturing. The calculation of the standard quantity of fabric for a pair of C&C's baseball pants is as follows:

Item	Quantity (in yards)
Required fabric	0.9
Waste	0.1
Spoilage	0.1
Standard quantity per pair, in yards	1.1

The final step in setting the direct material standard for fabric is to calculate the standard cost of fabric for a pair of baseball pants. The standard cost is the standard price of the fabric multiplied by the standard quantity of fabric needed for one pair of pants:

$$\begin{pmatrix}\text{Standard price of}\\\text{direct material input}\end{pmatrix} \times \begin{pmatrix}\text{Standard quantity of}\\\text{direct material inputs}\end{pmatrix} = \begin{matrix}\text{Standard cost of}\\\text{direct material}\end{matrix}$$

$$\$3.50\text{ per yard} \times 1.1\text{ yards} = \$3.85\text{ per unit}$$

WATCH OUT!

You may have noticed that we refer to both the standard *price* and the standard *cost*. Because these two terms have different meanings, they are not interchangeable. The standard price is the amount C&C pays to obtain one unit of direct material from the vendor. The standard cost is the total cost C&C incurs to produce one unit of product. C&C pays a standard price of $3.50 to obtain a yard of fabric, but incurs a total standard fabric cost of $3.85 to produce one pair of pants.

Fabric isn't the only direct material in baseball pants. Recall from Chapter 4 that companies prepare a bill of materials for each product, which lists all the direct materials required to produce a single unit. We can use the bill of materials, along with the standard prices and quantities, to calculate the total standard direct materials cost for a pair of baseball pants. As Exhibit 5-3 shows, the standard direct materials cost for a pair of C&C's baseball pants is $4.47.

Product	Material Description	Standard Quantity	Standard Price	Standard Product Cost
Pants	Fabric	1.1 yards	$3.50	$3.85
	Snaps	2	0.03	0.06
	Zipper	1	0.29	0.29
	Waistband	1	0.12	0.12
	Size label	1	0.05	0.05
	Packaging	1	0.10	0.10
				$4.47

EXHIBIT 5-3

Calculation of standard direct materials cost.

Direct Labor

The calculation of direct labor standards follows the same basic process as for direct materials standards. Direct labor price standards begin with the employees' wage rates. When setting direct labor standards, remember that employees with different skill levels may perform different tasks, so that they are generally paid different wage rates. The standard price will also include payroll taxes (such as FICA) and fringe benefits (such as health insurance and retirement contributions). These amounts are typically provided by the payroll and human resources departments.

Because people talk about wage rates rather than wage prices, we will refer to standard direct labor prices as direct labor *rates*, expressed per direct labor hour. The calculation of the standard direct labor rate of $9.60 for C&C's cutters and sewing machine operators is as follows:

Item	Rate
Base hourly rate	$8.00
Payroll taxes	0.60
Fringe benefits	1.00
Standard direct labor rate	$9.60

The direct labor quantity standard is the time needed to produce one unit of product. In addition to the actual production time expended by C&C's direct laborers, allowances are made for rest time and machine downtime based on the engineering department's estimates. Those estimates can be derived from published benchmarking studies, or they can be developed internally through time-and-motion studies in which researchers use a stopwatch to time workers as they perform the activities. Adding up the times required for each individual activity yields the number of standard direct labor hours for one unit. The calculation of the standard direct labor hours for C&C's baseball pants is as follows:

Activity	Direct Labor Hours
Cutting	0.02
Sewing	0.18
Machine downtime	0.02
Rest period	0.03
Standard direct labor hours	0.25

The final step in the standard-setting process for direct labor is to calculate the standard direct labor cost for a pair of baseball pants, $2.40.

$$\begin{pmatrix}\text{Standard wage rate per}\\ \text{direct labor hour}\end{pmatrix} \times \begin{pmatrix}\text{Standard quantity of}\\ \text{direct labor hours}\end{pmatrix} = \begin{matrix}\text{Standard direct}\\ \text{labor cost}\end{matrix}$$

$$\$9.60 \text{ per direct labor hour} \times 0.25 \text{ direct labor hours} = \$2.40$$

Manufacturing Overhead

Without realizing it, you have already been using manufacturing overhead standards. In Chapter 4 you learned about applying manufacturing overhead using a predetermined overhead rate. The predetermined overhead rate is the standard manufacturing overhead price or rate. Recall that the rate is calculated as:

$$\text{Predetermined overhead rate} = \frac{\text{Budgeted total manufacturing overhead}}{\text{Budgeted activity level of application base}}$$

For 2017, C&C expects to incur a total of $1,033,250 in overhead costs and $826,600 in direct labor costs. So the standard manufacturing overhead rate is 125% of direct labor cost:

$$\frac{\$1{,}033{,}250}{\$826{,}600} = 125\% \text{ of direct labor cost}$$

You may recall that overhead is typically divided into two components, variable and fixed. Historically, C&C's variable overhead has been 55% of direct labor cost, a rate that is not expected to change. With an anticipated direct labor cost of $826,600, variable overhead is expected to be $454,630 ($826,600 × 55%). That leaves $578,620 ($1,033,250 − $454,630) in fixed overhead, or 70% of direct labor cost.

Talking about a quantity standard for overhead doesn't make much sense. Instead, we multiply the overhead rate by the appropriate standard activity base—in C&C's case, direct labor cost. A company that applies overhead based on direct labor *hours* would multiply the overhead rate by the number of direct labor hours required to make one unit of product.

For C&C, the standard overhead cost for a pair of baseball pants is $3.00.

$$\begin{aligned}\text{Variable overhead} &= 55\% \times \$2.40 \text{ direct labor cost} = \$1.32\\ \text{Fixed overhead} &= 70\% \times \$2.40 \text{ direct labor cost} = \underline{1.68}\\ &\text{Total standard overhead cost} = \underline{\underline{\$3.00}}\end{aligned}$$

Now we can calculate the total standard cost of a pair of C&C's baseball pants:

Direct material	$4.47
Direct labor	2.40
Variable overhead	1.32
Fixed overhead	1.68
	$9.87

UNIT 5.2 REVIEW

KEY TERMS

Ideal standard p. 230 Practical standards p. 230 Standard cost p. 231 Standards p. 229

PRACTICE QUESTIONS

1. LO 2 Bongo Company is planning to make 1,000 drums in March. Each drum requires 2.5 feet of high-quality wood, which costs $7.00 per foot. What standard material cost per drum would the company use to plan for production?

   a. $7.00

   b. $17.50

   c. $7,000

   d. $17,500

2. LO 2 The standard cost of a product is the total budgeted manufacturing cost for all units of the product that the company expects to make in one year. True or False?

3. LO 2 The standard wage rate includes more items than just the hourly rate paid directly to the employee. True or False?

4. LO 2 Hickman & Reid manufactures hand-sewn silk ties. The company applies overhead using direct labor hours as the application base. The direct labor quantity standard for making a tie is 6 minutes. The company estimates overhead to be $2,250,000 for the coming year, based on production of 1,500,000 ties. The standard overhead cost per tie is

   a. $1.50.

   b. $6.00.

   c. $8.00.

   d. $9.00.

UNIT 5.2 PRACTICE EXERCISE

PuzzleJigs manufactures custom jigsaw puzzles by turning a customer's 8 × 10 photograph into a 300-piece puzzle. The following information has been provided by various units within the company. Each photograph is mounted onto a 9 × 12 sheet of cardboard using one ounce of adhesive. The company buys the cardboard in bundles of 500 sheets for $100. PuzzleJigs pays shipping costs of $15 per bundle on the cardboard. The mounting adhesive costs $0.25 per ounce. Each finished puzzle is packaged in a box that costs PuzzleJigs $0.50 to purchase. It takes 24 minutes for a worker to mount the picture, cut the puzzle, and pack it in a box. Workers are paid $6.60 per hour; fringe benefits amount to an additional 25% of wages. PuzzleJigs applies overhead at a rate of $10 per direct labor hour.

Required

1. Calculate the standard price and quantity for each component of direct materials.
2. Calculate the standard price and quantity for direct labor.
3. Calculate the standard price and quantity for manufacturing overhead.
4. Compute the standard cost of producing one puzzle.

SELECTED UNIT 5.2 ANSWERS

Think About It 5.2

The ideal standard for diamond color is D, and the ideal standard for clarity is F1. A practical standard for diamond color is J; for clarity, SI2. In choosing between a D and a J or an F1 and an SI2, the buyer makes a trade-off between availability, beauty, and cost. Js and SIs are more readily available in the marketplace. Ds and FIs are more beautiful, more expensive, and rarer.

Practice Questions

1. B
2. False
3. True
4. A

Unit 5.2 Practice Exercise

1.

Material	Standard Quantity	Standard Price
9 × 12 cardboard	1 sheet	Purchase price = $100 ÷ 500 = $0.20 per sheet Shipping = $15 ÷ 500 = $0.03 per sheet Total = $0.20 + $0.03 = $0.23 per sheet
Mounting adhesive	1 ounce	$0.25 per ounce
Packing box	1 box	$0.50 per box

2.

	Standard Quantity	Standard Price
Direct labor	24 minutes = 0.4 hour	Hourly rate = $6.60
		Fringe benefits per DLH = $6.60 × 25% = $1.65
		Total standard rate per DLH = $6.60 + $1.65 = $8.25

3.

	Standard Quantity	Standard Price
Overhead	24 minutes = 0.4 hour	Hourly rate = $10.00

4.

Cost Component	Standard Quantity	Standard Price	Standard Cost per Puzzle
Direct materials			
9 × 12 cardboard	1 sheet	$0.23	$0.23
Adhesive	1 ounce	$0.25	0.25
Packing box	1 box	$0.50	0.50
Total materials			0.98
Direct labor	0.4 DLH	$ 8.25/DLH	3.30
Overhead	0.4 DLH	$10.00/DLH	4.00
Total standard cost			$8.28

UNIT 5.3

Building the Master Budget: The Operating Budget

GUIDED UNIT PREPARATION

Answering the following questions while you read this unit will guide your understanding of the key concepts found in the unit. The questions are linked to the learning objectives presented at the beginning of the chapter.

LO 3

1. What is an operating budget?
2. List the components of the operating budget. How are the components of the operating budget related?
3. Why is an accurate sales forecast so important in budget preparation?
4. How does a budget that is prepared using interim periods, such as quarters or months, provide additional information that is not available in a budget that reports the year's final results?
5. What is a master budget? What are the component parts of the master budget, and how are those components related?

Whether a company uses standard costs or last year's actual costs, incremental or zero-based budgeting, top-down or bottom-up budgeting, the final product is the master budget. The **master budget** is a collection of smaller budgets that lead to pro-forma (budgeted) financial statements. Exhibit 5-4 illustrates the major components of the master budget and the relationships among them.

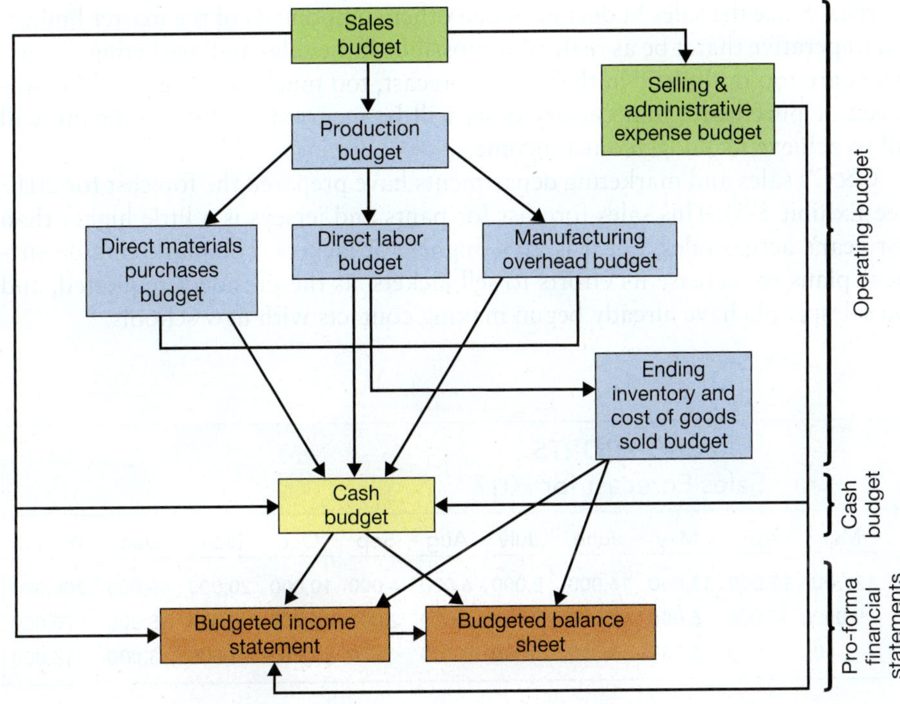

EXHIBIT 5-4

Components of the master budget.

If the master budget looks complex, it is. Exhibit 5-4 makes clear that all areas must work together to achieve the organization's goals. Not only do information and decisions in one area of the organization affect other areas, but information from each of the operating budgets flows to one or more of the pro-forma financial statements. We will cover the preparation of the pro-forma financial statements in detail in Unit 5.5. Here we will note the ways in which each budget flows into those statements. As we work through the next two units, be aware of how each of those budgets impacts the company's cash position, income statement, and balance sheet.

THINK ABOUT IT 5.3

How might the master budget diagram for a merchandising company look?

The first component of the master budget is the **operating budget**, which provides a plan for operations during the budget period. Development of the operating budget begins with the sales budget. From those sales estimates, budgeted production, direct materials, direct labor, manufacturing overhead, and selling and administrative expenses are determined. This unit illustrates the mechanics for preparing each section of the operating budget.

The Sales Budget

The sales and marketing departments prepare the **sales budget**, which forecasts the number of units expected to be sold, as well as the prices expected to be charged. Since the sales budget drives all other components of the master budget, it is imperative that it be as realistic as possible. If the sales and marketing departments are too optimistic in their sales forecast, too much inventory will be produced or purchased, unnecessary costs will be incurred, and the company will fail to achieve its budgeted net income.

C&C's sales and marketing departments have prepared the forecast for 2017 (see Exhibit 5-5). This sales forecast for pants and jerseys is a little higher than last year's actual sales, but it is 20% higher for jackets. The marketing department plans to increase its efforts to sell jackets, as the president requested, and the salespeople have already begun making contacts with new schools.

C&C SPORTS
Sales Forecast for 2017

	Jan	Feb	Mar	Apr	May	June	July	Aug	Sep	Oct	Nov	Dec	Annual
Baseball pants	38,000	20,000	12,000	12,000	12,000	16,000	8,000	6,000	6,000	10,000	20,000	40,000	200,000
Baseball jerseys	12,000	9,000	5,000	4,000	6,000	3,000	2,000	2,000	2,000	4,000	6,000	15,000	70,000
Award jackets	0	0	0	1,000	5,000	3,000	0	0	0	1,000	5,000	3,000	18,000

EXHIBIT 5-5 *C&C Sports' sales forecast.*

Notice the cyclical nature of C&C's business, indicated in the sales forecast. Baseball pants and jerseys are sold primarily in the first (January–March) and fourth (October–December) quarters, since most teams order their uniforms before the spring season. Award jackets are sold only in the second (April–June) and fourth quarters, since schools typically make their awards at the end of the fall and spring semesters. Sales of all product lines are low in the third quarter (July–September), and if managers don't plan correctly, C&C could find itself in financial trouble due to a lack of cash.

To prepare the sales budget, we need both the budgeted sales price and the unit sales forecast. C&C plans to sell its baseball pants for $12.00, its baseball jerseys for $14.80, and its award jackets for $125.00. To prepare the sales budget, we multiply the forecasted sales units by the budgeted sales price per unit. For the sake of simplicity, we will illustrate many of the concepts of master budget preparation for the fourth quarter using baseball pants.

Exhibit 5-6 shows the calculations for C&C's sales budget for baseball pants and the total sales budget for all three product lines. The actual master budget would include detailed information for all three product lines. The total budgeted sales revenue for all products flows to the budgeted income statement as budgeted revenue.

Throughout the year C&C plans to charge an average price of $12.00 for a pair of baseball pants; some pants may be sold for less and some for more.

EXHIBIT 5-6

C&C Sports' sales budget.

C&C SPORTS 4th Quarter Sales Budget—Baseball Pants				
	October	November	December	4th Quarter
Budgeted unit sales (Exhibit 5-5)	10,000	20,000	40,000	70,000
Budgeted sales price	× $ 12.00	$ 12.00	$ 12.00	$ 12.00
Budgeted sales revenue	= $120,000	$240,000	$480,000	$840,000

4th Quarter Sales Budget—All Products				
	October	November	December	4th Quarter
Baseball pants	$120,000	$240,000	$ 480,000	$ 840,000
Baseball jerseys	59,200	88,800	222,000	370,000
Award jackets	125,000	625,000	375,000	1,125,000
Total	$304,200	$953,800	$1,077,000	$2,335,000

Flows to budgeted income statement

A company may not always plan to charge the same average price throughout the year. If the company is planning a price increase or decrease, that should be reflected in the sales budget.

THINK ABOUT IT 5.4

The master budget diagram shows the sales budget affecting the income statement and the cash budget. But many times the effect on the cash budget is different from that on the income statement. Why would that be true? (Hint: Think about the journal entries that would be used to record sales.)

The Selling and Administrative Expense Budget

To support the sales that are planned in the sales budget, C&C must incur selling and administrative expenses. The **selling and administrative expense budget** estimates when and how much selling and administrative expense will be incurred. Recall from Unit 4.1 that selling and administrative expenses (period costs) may be fixed or variable in nature. To prepare the budget, then, C&C will need to understand the cost behavior of these items.

Three of C&C's selling expenses are variable. First, salespeople earn a 5% commission on all sales. Second, bad debt expense is estimated to be 5% of sales, but it applies only to baseball pants and jerseys. (Sales of award jackets are prepaid, so there is no bad debt expense on jacket sales.) Finally, shipping expenses are estimated to be $0.40 per unit. Based on this cost information, we can calculate variable selling and administrative expenses for October, as follows:

Expense	Calculation	Total
Sales commission	$304,200 October budgeted sales × 5% commission	$15,210
Bad debts	($120,000 + $59,200) October budgeted sales of pants and jerseys × 5% estimated bad debt expense	$ 8,960
Shipping	(10,000 pants + 4,000 jerseys + 1,000 jackets) × $0.40	$ 6,000

The remaining selling and administrative expenses are fixed *annual* amounts: office equipment depreciation, $15,612; advertising, $160,000; administrative salaries, $385,000; and utilities, $7,000. Since these expenses are incurred evenly throughout the year, we can calculate the monthly budgeted amounts by dividing the fixed annual amount by 12.

Exhibit 5-7 shows C&C's selling and administrative expense budget. As indicated, total budgeted selling and administrative expenses flow to the budgeted income statement. Most of these expenses also require a cash payment to a vendor, so this payment information is used to prepare the cash budget. Notice that total budgeted expenses has been reduced by the noncash items to arrive at total cash costs. For example, recall from financial accounting that bad debt expense and office equipment depreciation are not cash items. Bad debt expense represents sales that C&C does not expect to collect; therefore, no outlay of cash is required. Office equipment depreciation is the systematic expensing of the cost of office equipment as it is used and as its economic value declines. C&C has already paid for the machinery, so its depreciation is not a cash expense.

C&C SPORTS
4th Quarter Selling and Administrative Expense Budget

	October	November	December	4th Quarter	
Sales commissions	$15,210[a]	$ 47,690	$ 53,850	$116,750	
Bad debt expense	8,960[b]	16,440	35,100	60,500	
Shipping	6,000[c]	12,400	23,200	41,600	
Office equipment depreciation	1,301	1,301	1,301	3,903	
Advertising	13,333	13,333	13,334	40,000	
Administrative salaries	32,083	32,083	32,084	96,250	
Utilities	583	583	584	1,750	
Total budgeted expenses	77,470	123,830	159,453	360,753	→ Flows to budgeted income statement
Less: Noncash items					
Bad debt expense	8,960	16,440	35,100	60,500	
Office equipment depreciation	1,301	1,301	1,301	3,903	
Total cash costs	$67,209	$106,089	$123,052	$296,350	

Flows to cash budget

[a]October budgeted sales (Exhibit 5-6) × commission percentage: $304,200 × 5%.
[b]October budgeted sales of pants and jerseys (Exhibit 5-6) × estimated bad debt percentage: ($120,000 + $59,200) × 5%.
[c]October total units sold (Exhibit 5-5) × shipping cost per unit: (10,000 pants + 4,000 jerseys + 1,000 jackets) × $0.40.

EXHIBIT 5-7 *C&C Sports' selling and administrative expense budget.*

The Production Budget

If C&C is going to sell 200,000 pairs of pants during 2017, the pants must be available when customers want them. If they are not already available in beginning inventory, then they will have to be manufactured during the period. The **production budget** provides C&C with a plan for when and how many pants must be manufactured. This budget shows not only the beginning inventory for the period, but the desired ending inventory. The logic behind the production budget is as follows:

Budgeted sales	+	Budgeted ending inventory	−	Budgeted beginning inventory	=	Budgeted production

You may wonder why C&C would plan to have ending inventory. The ending inventory provides a safety net to absorb any unexpected sales that may occur. It becomes beginning inventory for the next period, providing units ready for sale in the first few days of the period, before current production is complete.

From the opening scenario we know that C&C's president thinks inventory levels are too high. After some discussion and a review of historical sales trends, the vice president of operations and the inventory manager decide to hold monthly ending inventory equal to 25% of the following month's sales.

The production budget is prepared using four simple steps:

1. Enter budgeted sales units from the sales budget (Exhibit 5-5).
2. Calculate budgeted ending inventory units for the period.
3. Add budgeted ending inventory units to budgeted sales units to determine the number of units required during the period.
4. Subtract beginning inventory units from required units to determine the budgeted production.

Exhibit 5-8 shows the fourth quarter production budget for baseball pants. For October, these four steps result in planned production of 12,500 pairs of pants:

1. 10,000 pants to be sold in October
2. 5,000 pants in ending inventory: 25% × 20,000 pants to be sold in November
3. 10,000 + 5,000 = 15,000
4. 15,000 − 2,500 = 12,500

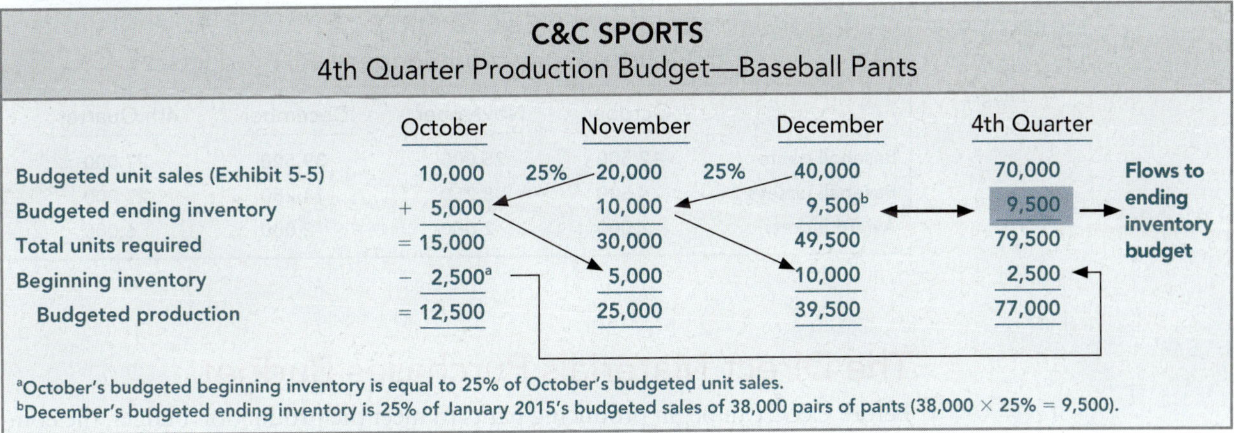

C&C SPORTS
4th Quarter Production Budget—Baseball Pants

	October	November	December	4th Quarter
Budgeted unit sales (Exhibit 5-5)	10,000	20,000	40,000	70,000
Budgeted ending inventory	+ 5,000	10,000	9,500[b]	9,500
Total units required	= 15,000	30,000	49,500	79,500
Beginning inventory	− 2,500[a]	5,000	10,000	2,500
Budgeted production	= 12,500	25,000	39,500	77,000

[a]October's budgeted beginning inventory is equal to 25% of October's budgeted unit sales.
[b]December's budgeted ending inventory is 25% of January 2015's budgeted sales of 38,000 pairs of pants (38,000 × 25% = 9,500).

EXHIBIT 5-8 *C&C Sports' production budget—baseball pants.*

WATCH OUT!

The final column in the production budget requires special attention during budget preparation. The beginning inventory amount in the final column is the beginning inventory for the entire budget period, not the total of the beginning inventories for each period. So the final column will show whatever beginning inventory is shown in the first period. Similarly, the budgeted ending inventory is the ending inventory for the entire budget period. So the final column will show whatever ending inventory is shown in the last period.

To avoid confusion, it might be helpful to include the dates covered by the budget in the heading for the total column. So if the final heading is October 1–December 31, then beginning inventory is what is on hand on October 1, and ending inventory is what is on hand on December 31.

Let's take a more detailed look at Steps 2 and 4. When a company budgets ending inventory as a percentage of the following period's sales (Step 2), special attention must be paid to the last period in the budget cycle. For a company that budgets ending inventory as a percentage of the following month's sales, the only way to calculate December 2017's ending inventory is to know the budgeted sales level for January 2018. C&C is forecasting the same level of sales in January 2018 as in January 2017—38,000 pairs of pants. Therefore, the company will budget ending inventory for December 2017 at 9,500 pairs of pants (38,000 × 25%).

Determining beginning inventory (Step 4) may be as simple as reading amounts that are already given to you, or it may require a little bit of computation. In general, beginning inventory for one period is always the ending inventory of the previous period. Since C&C is preparing the production budget for the fourth quarter, the beginning inventory for the first month of the quarter, October, will be the ending inventory for the last month of the third quarter, September. If you are not given the beginning inventory amount, you can assume that the ending inventory balance of the previous month was budgeted just like all ending inventory balances of this period—in this case, 25% of the following month's sales. September's budgeted ending inventory is 25% of October's sales, or 2,500 (10,000 units × 25%).

THINK ABOUT IT 5.5

Why does the sales budget determine the production budget instead of the other way around?

Using the method just described, C&C prepared production budgets for baseball jerseys and award jackets for the fourth quarter (see Exhibit 5-9). Once the production budget has been determined, the direct materials, direct labor, and manufacturing overhead budgets can be prepared.

EXHIBIT 5-9

C&C Sports' production budget.

C&C SPORTS
4th Quarter Production Budget—All Products

	October	November	December	4th Quarter
Baseball pants	12,500	25,000	39,500	77,000
Baseball jerseys	4,500	8,250	14,250	27,000
Award jackets	2,000	2,000	2,000	6,000

The Direct Materials Purchases Budget

Before C&C can begin producing pants to meet the production budget, the company must obtain the required direct materials. The **direct materials purchases budget** itemizes the direct materials that must be purchased to meet budgeted production. It will help C&C's managers to plan the quantity and timing of those purchases. Careful planning helps to minimize the resources invested in inventory and helps to ensure an adequate level of inventory—one that will allow the company to meet customer demand in a timely manner.

Once the production budget has been completed, preparing the direct materials purchases budget is fairly simple. The logic is similar to that of the production budget. The key inputs are the production budget and the direct materials standards for each product. A separate direct materials purchases budget must be completed for every direct material that goes into the product.

C&C has already determined the direct materials standards for one pair of pants. For baseball pants, that includes fabric, snaps, one zipper, one waistband, one size label, and packaging (see Exhibit 5-3).

The direct materials purchases budget is prepared using the following steps:

1. Enter budgeted production from the production budget (Exhibit 5-8).
2. Calculate the direct materials production needs by multiplying the number of units to be produced during the period by the direct materials standard quantity for one unit.
3. Calculate the desired budgeted ending inventory of direct materials.
4. Calculate the total direct materials required for the period by adding the budgeted ending inventory to the direct materials production needs.
5. Calculate the required purchases of direct materials by subtracting the beginning direct materials balance from the total direct materials required for the period.
6. Calculate the budgeted dollar amount of direct materials purchases by multiplying the required purchases of direct materials by the standard price per unit.

In their planning meetings for 2017, C&C's president, vice president for operations, and inventory manager settled on a budgeted ending direct materials inventory balance of 20% of the following month's production requirements. Why would these managers select a lower percentage of direct materials to have on hand (20%) than finished goods to have on hand (25%)? It could be due to the differences in predictability of production and sales. Although the higher percentage of finished goods on hand means more dollars are tied up in inventory, it will result in fewer stockouts, or lost sales. When sales patterns are not known with certainty, managers may tend to desire a greater cushion. If sales are higher than expected, meaning more units need to be produced, managers can monitor the inventory balances and know when they need to order more materials. Good relationships with suppliers that deliver quickly can minimize the amount of raw materials that need to be held.

Exhibit 5-10 shows the fourth quarter direct materials purchases budget for baseball pants fabric. For October, these six steps result in planned purchases of 16,500 yards of fabric at $3.50 per yard, for a total purchase price of $57,750:

1. 12,500 pants to be produced in October
2. 13,750 yards needed to make 12,500 pants: 12,500 pants × 1.1 yards/unit
3. 5,500 yards in ending inventory: 20% × 27,500 yards needed for November production
4. 19,250 yards required = 13,750 yards needed for production + 5,500 yards in budgeted ending inventory

EXHIBIT 5-10

C&C Sports' direct materials purchases budget—baseball pants fabric.

C&C SPORTS 4th Quarter Direct Materials Purchases Budget—Pants Fabric		October	November	December	4th Quarter
Budgeted production (Exhibit 5-8)		12,500	25,000	39,500	77,000
Standard materials per unit (yards)	×	1.1	1.1	1.1	1.1
Production needs (yards)	=	13,750	27,500	43,450	84,700
Budgeted ending inventory (yards)	+	5,500	8,690	7,480[b]	7,480
Total materials required (yards)	=	19,250	36,190	50,930	92,180
Beginning inventory (yards)	−	2,750[a]	5,500	8,690	2,750
Budgeted materials purchases (yards)	=	16,500	30,690	42,240	89,430
Standard price per yard	×	$ 3.50	$ 3.50	$ 3.50	$ 3.50
Budgeted purchases cost	=	$57,750	$107,415	$147,840	$313,005

[a]October's beginning inventory is 20% of October's production needs (2,750 = 20% × 13,750 yards).
[b]December's ending inventory is 20% of January 2015's budgeted production needs (7,480 = 20% × 34,000 pants × 1.1 yards).

5. 16,500 yards purchased = 19,250 yards required − 2,750 yards in beginning inventory
6. $57,750 = 16,500 yards × $3.50/yard

Just as with the production budget, when a company budgets the ending Direct Materials Inventory as a percentage of the following period's production requirements, special attention must be paid to the last period in the budget cycle. Since C&C budgets the ending inventory as a percentage of the following month's production needs, the only way to calculate December's ending Direct Materials Inventory is to know the direct material production needs for January 2018. To determine this amount, we will need to prepare a production budget for January. Sales in January 2018 are budgeted to be the same as for January 2017, and February 2018 sales are expected to be 22,000 pants.

	January 2018
Sales (pants)	38,000
Budgeted ending inventory (25% × 22,000 pants)	+ 5,500
Total units required	43,500
Beginning inventory	− 9,500
Budgeted production (pants)	34,000
Materials per unit	× 1.1
Production needs (yards)	37,400

The ending inventory for pants fabric in December 2017 will be 7,480 yards (37,400 yards needed in January 2018 × 20%).

As stated earlier, C&C must prepare a separate purchases budget for each type of direct material. Exhibit 5-11 shows the total direct materials purchases C&C is budgeting for the fourth quarter. Notice that all the direct materials for a pair of baseball pants are listed, just to give you an idea of the required level of detail. In practice, the same would be done for jerseys and jackets.

THINK ABOUT IT 5.6

The master budget diagram in Exhibit 5-4 shows the direct materials purchases budget affecting both the ending inventory budget and the cash budget. Yet many times the effect on the cash budget is different from the effect on the ending inventory budget. Why would that be true? (Hint: Think about the journal entries that would be used to record purchases of direct materials.)

EXHIBIT 5-11

C&C Sports' direct materials purchases budget—all products.

C&C SPORTS 4th Quarter Materials Purchases Budget					
	October	November	December	4th Quarter	
Baseball pants:					
Fabric (Exhibit 5-10)	$ 57,750	$107,415	$147,840	$313,005	
Snaps	900	1,674	2,304	4,878	
Zipper	4,350	8,091	11,136	23,577	
Waistband	1,800	3,348	4,608	9,756	
Size label	750	1,395	1,920	4,065	
Packaging	1,500	2,790	3,840	8,130	
Total for pants	67,050	124,713	171,648	363,411	
Baseball jerseys	6,480	69,870	93,502	169,852	
Award jackets	107,328	89,439	71,552	268,319	
Total purchases	$180,858	$284,022	$336,702	$801,582	→ Flows to budgeted ending inventory

The Direct Labor Budget

The **direct labor budget** calculates the number of direct labor hours required to meet the budgeted level of production, and it is prepared using the following steps:

1. Enter budgeted production from the production budget (Exhibit 5-8).
2. Calculate the number of direct labor hours needed to meet the production schedule by multiplying the number of units to be produced during the period by the standard number of direct labor hours for one unit.
3. Calculate the total budgeted direct labor payroll by multiplying the total required direct labor hours by the standard *average* wage rate for the period. If the company pays a wide range of direct labor wage rates, the direct labor budget will be more accurate if direct labor hours are calculated separately for each pay level.

Exhibit 5-12 shows C&C's direct labor budget for baseball pants for the fourth quarter. For October, these three steps result in 3,125 budgeted direct labor hours at $9.60 per hour for a total cost of $30,000:

1. 12,500 pants to be produced in October
2. 3,125 direct labor hours are needed to make 12,500 pants: 12,500 pants × 0.25 hours/pant

3. $30,000 direct labor cost: $9.60/direct labor hour × 3,125 direct labor hours needed

EXHIBIT 5-12

C&C Sports' direct labor budget—baseball pants.

C&C SPORTS
4th Quarter Direct Labor Budget—Baseball Pants

		October	November	December	4th Quarter
Budgeted production (Exhibit 5-8)		12,500	25,000	39,500	77,000
Standard direct labor hours per pair	×	0.25	0.25	0.25	0.25
Total direct labor hours required	=	3,125	6,250	9,875	19,250
Standard average wage rate	×	$ 9.60	$ 9.60	$ 9.60	$ 9.60
Budgeted direct labor cost	=	$30,000	$60,000	$94,800	$184,800

Remember that Exhibit 5-12 is the direct labor budget just for baseball pants. To complete the direct labor budget, C&C will need to do the same calculations for baseball jerseys and award jackets. Exhibit 5-13 shows C&C's total budgeted direct labor cost for the fourth quarter. Note that the direct labor budget flows through to the cash budget and the ending inventory budget.

EXHIBIT 5-13

C&C Sports' direct labor budget—all products.

C&C SPORTS
4th Quarter Direct Labor Budget—All Products

	October	November	December	4th Quarter	
Baseball pants (Exhibit 5-12)	3,125	6,250	9,875	19,250	
Baseball jerseys	900	1,650	2,850	5,400	
Award jackets	3,000	3,000	3,000	9,000	
Total direct labor hours required	7,025	10,900	15,725	33,650	
Standard average wage rate	$ 9.60	$ 9.60	$ 9.60	$ 9.60	
Total direct labor cost	$67,440	$104,640	$150,960	$323,040	→ Flows to budgeted COGS in ending inventory budget
	Flows to cash budget				

The Manufacturing Overhead Budget

The next component of the operating budget is the **manufacturing overhead budget**, which shows the expected overhead costs for the period. In Chapter 4 you learned that overhead costs include costs that are required to operate the manufacturing plant, but cannot be classified as direct materials or direct labor. Exhibit 5-14 shows the budgeted annual overhead costs. Notice that the amounts are separated into their fixed and variable components. Compare these totals to the overhead rate calculation on page 154. You will see that total fixed overhead was budgeted to be $578,620 and variable overhead is budgeted to be $0.55 per direct labor dollar.

C&C SPORTS Budgeted Annual Manufacturing Overhead Costs		
	Fixed Costs	Variable Costs
Indirect labor	$211,000	
Depreciation	46,184	
Indirect materials	98,000	$0.50 per direct labor dollar
Rent	110,000	
Utilities	17,000	$0.05 per direct labor dollar
Insurance	55,000	
Other	41,436	
Total	$578,620	$0.55 per direct labor dollar

EXHIBIT 5-14

C&C Sports' budgeted annual manufacturing overhead.

If overhead were only fixed, then the monthly overhead cost would be easy to calculate: Just take the total amount and divide by 12. However, since overhead also has a variable component, you can calculate monthly overhead costs using the following steps:

1. Enter the budgeted activity base from the appropriate budget.
2. Calculate the variable overhead cost per period using the variable rate and the budgeted activity base.
3. Calculate the fixed overhead cost per period assuming that costs are incurred evenly throughout the period.
4. Calculate the total overhead cost for the period by adding the fixed and variable overhead costs.
5. Subtract the noncash overhead items from the total overhead cost to determine the cash payments for overhead.

Exhibit 5-15 shows C&C's manufacturing overhead budget for the fourth quarter. For October, these five steps result in total budgeted overhead of $85,310 and total cash costs for overhead of $81,462:

1. $67,440 direct labor cost to be incurred in October
2. $37,092 = $67,440 direct labor cost × $0.55/direct labor dollar
3. $48,218 = $578,620 budgeted fixed cost ÷ 12 months = $48,218.33 → use $48,218 for October and November and $48,219 for December
4. $85,310 = $37,092 variable overhead + $48,218 fixed overhead
5. $81,462 = $85,310 − $3,848 depreciation expense

Total budgeted manufacturing overhead costs flow to the ending inventory and cost of goods sold budget. Just as we did on the selling and administrative expense budget (Exhibit 5-7), noncash items are subtracted from "Total budgeted manufacturing overhead" to arrive at "Total cash costs," and this amount flows to the cash budget. Upon review of Exhibit 5-14, you will see that depreciation is the only noncash item.

Depreciation of $46,184 annual ÷ 12 months = $3,848.67 per month.

Use $3,848 for October and $3,849 for November and December.

EXHIBIT 5-15

C&C Sports' budgeted manufacturing overhead—4th quarter.

C&C SPORTS
4th Quarter Manufacturing Overhead Budget

	October	November	December	4th Quarter	
Direct labor cost (Exhibit 5-13)	$67,440	$104,640	$150,960	$323,040	
Variable overhead cost (DL cost × $0.55)	37,092	57,552	83,028	177,672	
Fixed overhead cost[a]	48,218	48,218	48,219	144,655	
Total budgeted manufacturing overhead	85,310	105,770	131,247	322,327	→ Flows to budgeted COGS in ending inventory budget
Less: Noncash items					
Depreciation[b]	3,848	3,849	3,849	11,546	
Total cash costs	$81,462	$101,921	$127,398	$310,781	

Flows to cash budget

[a]Monthly fixed overhead cost equals annual fixed overhead cost (Exhibit 5-14) ÷ 12: $578,620 ÷ 12 = $48,218.33. For ease of presentation, two months are budgeted at $48,218 and one month is budgeted at $48,219.

[b]Monthly depreciation equals annual depreciation (Exhibit 5-14) ÷ 12: $46,184 ÷ 12 = $3,848.67. For ease of presentation, one month is budgeted at $3,848 and two months are budgeted at $3,849.

The Ending Inventory and Cost of Goods Sold Budget

The final component of the operating budget is the **ending inventory and cost of goods sold budget**. Preparing these budgets makes the preparation of the pro-forma income statement and balance sheet much easier. C&C's ending inventory and cost of goods sold budget for the fourth quarter is shown in Exhibit 5-16.

Notice that this budget is prepared in three sections—Raw Materials Inventory, Finished Goods Inventory, and Cost of Goods Sold. These sections are similar in format to the product cost flows presented in Chapter 4. If C&C had budgeted to end the year with Work in Process Inventory, a fourth section would have been included.

Ending Raw Materials

To prepare the ending Raw Materials Inventory budget, follow these steps, which mirror the entries in the Raw Materials Inventory T-account:[5]

1. Enter the beginning Raw Materials Inventory balance. It will be the same amount as the ending Raw Materials Inventory balance on the previous period's balance sheet.
2. Add budgeted purchases from the direct materials purchases budget.
3. Subtract the direct materials used in the production of new units started during the period.

Let's look at C&C's ending Raw Materials Inventory budget shown in the first part of Exhibit 5-16. The beginning raw materials balance of $89,281 comes from the beginning balance sheet (Exhibit 5-23). To that we add

C&C SPORTS 4th Quarter Ending Inventory and Cost of Goods Sold Budget					
Raw Materials Inventory:					
Beginning Raw Materials Inventory (Exhibit 5-23)				$ 89,281	
Purchases of direct materials (Exhibit 5-11)			+	801,582	
Direct materials used					
Pants: 77,000 units × $4.47	344,190				
Jerseys: 27,000 units × $6.85	184,950				
Award jackets: 6,000 units × $44.72	268,320		–	797,460	
Ending Raw Materials Inventory			=	$ 93,403	→ Flows to budgeted balance sheet

Finished Goods Inventory:	Pants	Jerseys	Jackets	Total	
Unit costs					
Direct materials	$ 4.47	$ 6.85	$44.72		
Direct labor	+ 2.40	1.92	14.40		
Overhead	+ 3.00	2.40	18.00		
Total standard unit cost	= $ 9.87	$ 11.17	$77.12		
Ending inventory units (see Exhibit 5-8 for pants)	× 9,500	3,000	0		
Ending Finished Goods Inventory	= $93,765	$33,510	0	$127,275	→ Flows to budgeted balance sheet

Cost of Goods Sold:			
Beginning Work in Process Inventory (Exhibit 5-23)		$ 0	
Direct materials used (see Raw Materials Inventory budget above)	$797,460		
Direct labor (Exhibit 5-13)	323,040		
Manufacturing overhead (Exhibit 5-15)	322,327		
Total manufacturing costs		1,442,827	
Less: Ending Work in Process Inventory		0	
Cost of goods manufactured		1,442,827	
Add: beginning finished goods (Exhibit 5-23)		267,205	
Less: ending finished goods (see Finished Goods Inventory budget above)		127,275	
Cost of goods sold		$1,582,757	→ Flows to budgeted income statement

EXHIBIT 5-16 *C&C Sports' ending inventory and cost of goods sold budget.*

$801,582 in purchases of direct materials from the direct materials purchases budget (Exhibit 5-11).

Now we need to subtract the budgeted materials used for the period. This takes a bit of calculation. C&C plans to use direct materials to make 77,000 pants, 27,000 jerseys, and 6,000 jackets. These numbers come straight from the production budget in Exhibit 5-9. To calculate the direct materials that will be put into production during the fourth quarter, we multiply the number of products we need materials for by the standard materials cost per unit: (77,000 pairs of pants × $4.47) + (27,000 jerseys × $6.85) + (6,000 award jackets × $44.72) = $797,460. The resulting budgeted ending Raw Materials Inventory balance is $93,403. As you will see in Unit 5.5, this amount will also be reported on the pro-forma balance sheet.

REALITY CHECK—*Is there a crystal ball for forecasting sales?*

© VallarieE/iStockphoto

What part of budget preparation could be more daunting than forecasting sales? If you get the sales forecast wrong, everything else—from production to the final cash balance—will be incorrect. The company could wind up short of cash. In fact, many new businesses fail not because they are unprofitable, but because they run out of cash.

It may be tempting to see a sales forecast as a one-time exercise to jump-start the budgeting process, but it's much more than that. Sales forecasting needs to be an ongoing process that considers both what has been planned and what has already happened. That means the forecast should be updated periodically to reflect the revised expected level of future sales.

Sales forecasts are subject to a variety of behavioral influences on those preparing the forecasts. For instance, salespeople may be overly optimistic about the likelihood of landing a large sale, or they may just "guess" in the absence of more reliable data. But data analytics are now bringing a new level of objectivity to sales forecasting. And while you may think taking more time to prepare a forecast increases its accuracy, research has shown just the opposite. Companies that took an average of 8 days to develop the forecast had a 6% forecast error, while those taking 17 days missed the forecast by 10% or more.

Companies that took an average of 8 days to develop the forecast had a 6% forecast error, while those taking 17 days missed the forecast by 10% or more.

What's the price of missing the forecast? For former Walgreen CFO Wade Miquelon, the price was his job. After revealing a fiscal 2016 forecast revision of $1.1 billion (an almost 13% correction), Miquelon suddenly left the company, in what some say was a "pressured resignation." Kermit Crawford, Walgreen's pharmacy-unit chief, also announced his upcoming retirement.

Sources: David McCann, Forecasting Error Cost Walgreen's CFO His Job," CFO.com, August 20, 2014, http://ww2.cfo.com/people/2014/08/forecasting-error-cost-walgreens-cfo-job/ (accessed March 7, 2016); Maxwell Murphy, "The Big Number," *The Wall Street Journal*, February 16, 2016, B5; K. V. Rao, "The Mind of a Salesperson: How Human Nature Can Muddle Sales Forecasting," *Huffington Post*, January 12, 2016, www.huffingtonpost.com/k-v-rao/the-mind-of-a-salesperson-how-human-nature-can-muddle-sales-forecasting_b_8942048.html (accessed March 7, 2016).

Ending Finished Goods

To prepare the ending Finished Goods Inventory budget, follow these steps:

1. Enter the standard cost of each product.
2. Calculate the ending Finished Goods Inventory balance by multiplying the total standard cost per unit by the budgeted number of units in the ending Finished Goods Inventory shown in the production budget.

C&C has budgeted 9,500 pairs of pants (Exhibit 5-8) and 3,000 jerseys for the ending Finished Goods Inventory. Since jackets are made only as orders are received, no jackets are left in Finished Goods Inventory. At a standard cost of $9.87 and $11.17, respectively, the budgeted ending Finished Goods Inventory for pants is $93,765 ($9.87 × 9,500), and for jerseys it is $33,510 ($11.17 × 3,000). Total budgeted ending Finished Goods Inventory for the fourth quarter is $127,275 ($93,765 + $33,510). This amount will also be reported on the pro-forma balance sheet, as we will see in Unit 5.5.

Budgeted Raw Materials and Finished Goods Inventory total $220,678. This is down from the 2016 ending balance of $640,327 (Exhibit T1-4 on page 38). By adopting a practice of maintaining ending inventory equal to a percentage of next month's sales, C&C managers expect to reduce the amount of cash tied up in inventory by over $400,000. This is a huge departure from past experience, though, so the inventory manager and vice president of operations are going to need to keep a close watch on inventory levels. They will also need to work closely with the vice president of marketing to ensure customer needs are met.

Cost of Goods Sold

To prepare the cost of goods sold budget, follow these steps:

1. Enter the Beginning Work in Process Inventory balance (from the beginning balance sheet).
2. Add the budgeted direct materials, budgeted direct labor, and budgeted manufacturing overhead used in production.
3. Subtract the budgeted ending Work in Process Inventory balance to determine the budgeted cost of goods manufactured.
4. Add the beginning Finished Goods Inventory balance (from the beginning balance sheet).
5. Subtract the budgeted ending Finished Goods Inventory balance.

C&C plans to have $0 in Work in Process Inventory at the beginning of October. The various components of the operating budget for the fourth quarter provide direct materials used of $797,460, direct labor of $323,040, and manufacturing overhead of $322,327. There will be no ending Work in Process Inventory balance because the fourth quarter production budget calls for all units to be completed. With the beginning Finished Goods Inventory of $267,205 and a budgeted ending Finished Goods Inventory of $127,275, the budgeted cost of goods sold for the fourth quarter is $1,582,757. This amount will appear on the budgeted income statement, as we will see in Unit 5.5.

UNIT 5.3 REVIEW

KEY TERMS

Direct labor budget p. 245

Direct materials purchases budget p. 242

Ending inventory and cost of goods sold budget p. 248

Manufacturing overhead budget p. 246

Master budget p. 237

Operating budget p. 237

Production budget p. 241

Sales budget p. 238

Selling and administrative expense budget p. 239

PRACTICE QUESTIONS

1. LO 3 The master budget process usually begins with the
   a. sales budget.
   b. production budget.
   c. operating budget.
   d. cash budget.

2. LO 3 Modesto Company produces and sells Product Alpha. In budgeting for production needs, the company requires that 20% of the next month's sales be on hand at the end of each month. Budgeted sales of Product Alpha over the next four months are:

	June	July	August	September
Budgeted unit sales	30,000	40,000	60,000	50,000

   Budgeted production for August would be
   a. 44,000
   b. 52,000
   c. 58,000
   d. 70,000

3. LO 3 Stacy Moore is preparing the materials purchases budget for the second quarter. The production manager has provided the following production budget: April—65,000 units, May—50,000 units, June—70,000 units. Each unit requires 8 pounds of direct materials, and Stacy wants to maintain an ending inventory equal to 20% of the next month's production needs. How many pounds of material will Stacy budget to purchase in May?
   a. 480,000
   b. 456,000
   c. 432,000
   d. 400,000

4. LO 3 Martin Bradstone is gathering information to complete the direct labor budget for next quarter. Which of the following will he *not* need to complete the budget?

a. Budgeted production
b. Standard hourly labor rate
c. Standard direct labor hours per unit
d. Predetermined overhead rate

UNIT 5.3 PRACTICE EXERCISE

Hurtt's Java Seeds is an independent roaster of specialty coffee beans. The company budgets two months ahead, so that in early January, it is time to plan for March. During March, the company plans to sell 10,000 pounds of beans. At the end of February, the company expects to have 2,000 pounds of raw green coffee beans (costing $4,000) and 800 pounds of roasted beans (costing $4,000) in inventory. Hurtt's would like to have 1,000 pounds of green coffee beans and 500 pounds of roasted beans in inventory at the end of March. Hurtt's purchases green coffee beans from the grower at $2.00 per pound and sells the roasted beans for $12 per pound.

Hurtt's roasters hold 25 pounds of green coffee beans. It takes 15 minutes to roast the beans to perfection. Because the roaster must be monitored by an employee at all times, each batch requires 0.25 direct labor hours. During the roasting process, the green beans lose 20% of their weight, so that 1.25 pounds of green (raw) beans must be used to produce one pound of roasted beans. The standard direct labor rate is $12 per direct labor hour. Variable overhead is applied at the rate of $80 per direct labor hour, and fixed overhead is budgeted at $13,095 per month, including $1,500 in equipment depreciation.

Required

1. Prepare Hurtt's sales budget for March.
2. Prepare Hurtt's production budget for March.
3. Prepare Hurtt's coffee bean purchases budget for March.
4. Prepare Hurtt's direct labor budget for March.
5. Prepare Hurtt's overhead budget for March.
6. Compute Hurtt's ending inventory balances and cost of goods sold for March.

SELECTED UNIT 5.3 ANSWERS

Think About It 5.3

The master budget for a merchandising company will not have any production components. Instead, the sales budget will flow into an inventory purchases budget, which will flow into the cash budget. A diagram of the master budget might look like the following:

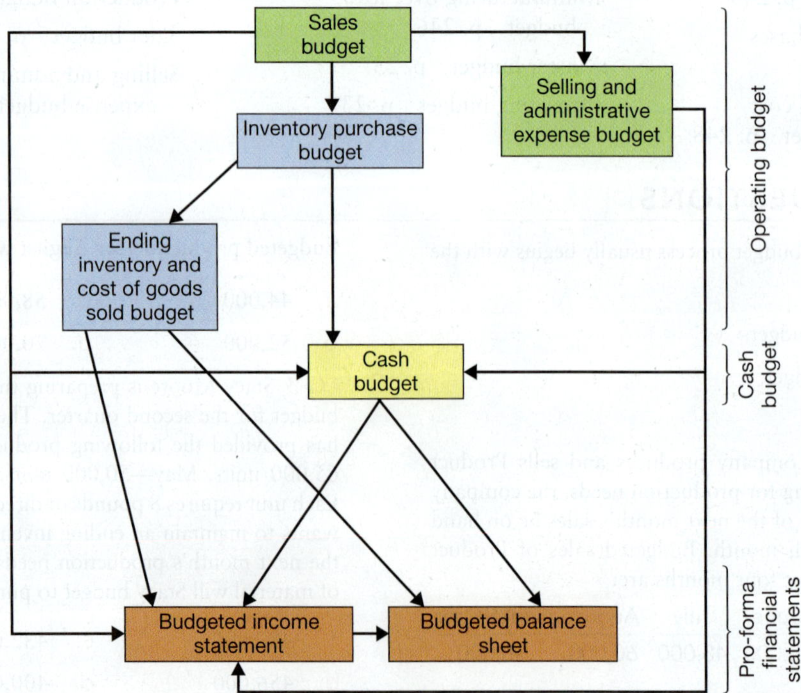

Think About It 5.4

Customers don't always pay cash at the time they make a purchase. If customers buy on credit, the company has an account receivable and collects the cash in a future period.

Think About It 5.5

By starting with the sales budget, a company first determines what customers want and then makes the products. The sales and marketing departments don't just dream up the sales numbers. Instead, they use surveys and market research to find out what customers want. If companies started with the production budget and then made products, managers couldn't be sure they were making what customers want to buy. By starting with the production budget, managers might produce too much or too little inventory relative to customer demand, resulting in excess inventory and increasing the risk of obsolescence or backorders and unhappy customers.

Think About It 5.6

Companies don't always pay cash at the time a purchase is made. If a company buys on credit, then it has an account payable for which cash must be paid in the future.

Practice Questions

1. A
2. C
3. C
4. D

Unit 5.3 Practice Exercise

1.

Budgeted pounds sold	10,000
Budgeted sales price per pound	× $12.00
Budgeted sales revenue	$120,000

2.

Budgeted roasted pounds sold	10,000
Budgeted roasted beans ending inventory (pounds)	500
Roasted pounds needed	10,500
Beginning inventory roasted beans	(800)
Budgeted roasted bean production (pounds)	9,700

3.

Budgeted production	9,700
Green beans per roasted pound	× 1.25
Green beans needed for production (pounds)	12,125
Budgeted ending inventory of green beans	1,000
Total green beans needed (pounds)	13,125
Beginning green bean inventory (pounds)	(2,000)
Budgeted green bean purchases (pounds)	11,125
Standard price per pound	× $2.00
Budgeted purchases	$22,250

4. Based on the purchases budget, 12,125 pounds of green coffee beans must be roasted during the month to yield the 9,700 pounds of required production of roasted beans. Since each batch starts with 25 pounds of green beans, 485 batches (12,125 pounds ÷ 25 pounds per batch) will be roasted during the month.

Batches roasted	485
Direct labor hours per batch	× 0.25
Budgeted direct labor hours	121.25
Standard labor rate	× $12.00
Budgeted direct labor cost	$ 1,455

5.

Budgeted direct labor hours	121.25
Variable overhead rate per direct labor hour	× $80
Budgeted variable overhead	$ 9,700
Fixed overhead	13,095
Budgeted overhead	$22,795

6. Raw Materials Ending Inventory: 1,000 pounds × $2.00/pound = $2,000

Finished Goods Ending Inventory:

Direct materials used (12,125 × $2.00)	$24,250
Direct labor	1,455
Manufacturing overhead	22,795
Cost of goods manufactured	$48,500
Units produced	÷ 9,700
Cost per pound	$ 5.00
Ending inventory units	× 500
Ending Finished Goods Inventory balance	$ 2,500

Cost of Goods Sold:

Cost of goods manufactured	$48,500
Add: Beginning Finished Goods Inventory	4,000
Less: Ending Finished Goods Inventory	(2,500)
Cost of goods sold	$50,000

UNIT 5.4

Building the Master Budget: The Cash Budget

GUIDED UNIT PREPARATION

Answering the following questions while you read this unit will guide your understanding of the key concepts found in the unit. The questions are linked to the learning objectives presented at the beginning of the chapter.

LO 4

1. Describe the components of the cash budget.
2. Why do companies set a minimum cash balance?
3. Why is it better to prepare monthly or quarterly cash budgets instead of annual cash budgets?

Managing cash is a common problem for individuals and organizations alike. In fact, inadequate cash flow is one of the major reasons that small businesses fail. What can managers do to ensure that enough cash is available to run the business? The answer lies in one of the four basic managerial functions we explored in Chapter 1: planning.

The plan that helps to manage cash flow is the **cash budget**, which summarizes all budgeted cash receipts and disbursements for the period. The cash budget is prepared after all the operating budgets have been completed. The final result is the budgeted cash balance. Exhibit 5-17 presents C&C's cash budget for the fourth quarter. Although it may appear overwhelming at first, breaking down the cash budget into its five major sections will help you to understand it:

Cash available to spend
− Cash disbursements
= Cash excess or cash needed
+ Short-term financing
= Ending cash balance

In this unit we'll look at each section in detail. As we do so, we'll comment on the entire quarter. However, the cash budget must be completed one month at a time.

Cash Available to Spend

The first section of the cash budget shows the amount of cash that will be available to spend during the period. As Exhibit 5-18 shows, this section is simply the beginning cash balance plus cash payments collected from customers during the

C&C SPORTS
4th Quarter Cash Budget

		Source	October	November	December	4th Quarter
	Beginning cash balance	Beginning balance sheet (Exhibit 5-23)	$ 48,720	$ 40,448	$ 284,478	$ 48,720
	Collections from sales	Cash receipts budget (Exhibit 5-19)	268,080	885,000	911,280	2,064,360
A	Total Cash Available to Spend		316,800	925,448	1,195,758	2,113,080
	Less disbursements:					
	Material purchases	Cash payments for material purchases budget (Exhibit 5-21)	154,241	232,440	310,362	697,043
	Direct labor	Direct labor budget (Exhibit 5-13)	67,440	104,640	150,960	323,040
	Manufacturing overhead	Manufacturing overhead budget (Exhibit 5-15)	81,462	101,921	127,398	310,781
	Selling & administrative expenses	Selling & administrative expense budget (Exhibit 5-7)	67,209	106,089	123,052	296,350
	Equipment purchases		0	0	150,000	150,000
B	Total Cash Disbursements		370,352	545,090	861,772	1,777,214
C = A − B	Cash excess (deficiency)		(53,552)	380,358	333,986	335,866
D	Minimum cash balance		40,000	40,000	40,000	40,000
E = C − D	Cash Excess (Needed)		(93,552)	340,358	293,986	295,866
	Short-term financing:					
	Borrowing		94,000	0	0	94,000
	Repayments		0	(94,000)	0	(94,000)
	Interest (annual rate = 12%)		0	(1,880)	0	(1,880) → To income statement
F	Total Short-Term Financing		94,000	(95,880)	0	(1,880)
C + F	Ending Cash Balance		$ 40,448	$284,478	$ 333,986	$ 333,986 ↓ Flows to budgeted balance sheet

EXHIBIT 5-17 *C&C sports' cash budget.*

period. The beginning cash balance is taken from the beginning balance sheet or from the prior period's ending cash balance.

Determining the amount of cash collected from sales is a bit more involved. If all customers paid for their purchases in cash at the time the sales were made, estimating how much cash would be collected during a period would be easy. The cash collected would equal the budgeted sales for the period. However, most businesses offer customers some form of credit, and many customers take advantage of that offer and pay for their purchases at some time *after* the sale is made and the goods have been delivered or the services rendered. Furthermore, credit sales are not always collected in the same month as the sale, since many companies offer payment terms of 30 days or more. Some customers never pay

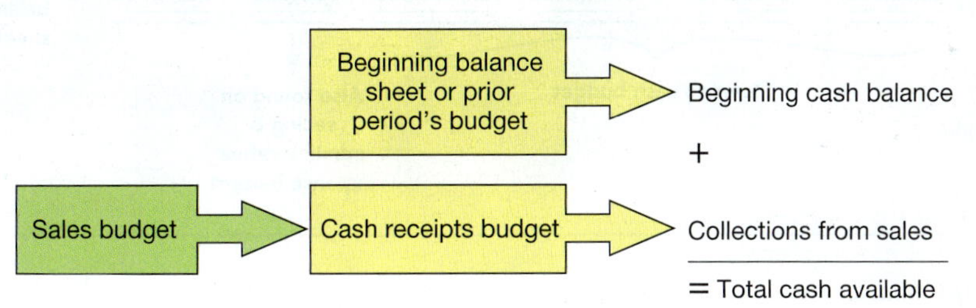

EXHIBIT 5-18
Cash available to spend section information flows.

their bills, so that cash is never collected. To determine cash collections during a period under these conditions, companies prepare a cash receipts budget.

The Cash Receipts Budget

When customers purchase goods or services from an organization, the organization expects to collect cash from those customers. The **cash receipts budget** shows when and how much cash is expected to be collected from the sale of products or services.

To prepare the cash receipts budget, a company must first review its past collections history in order to estimate its collection pattern and bad debt percentage. Once the collection pattern has been established, the company can apply it to the sales budget to determine the budgeted cash receipts from customers.

C&C's collection review has identified two cash receipts patterns. First, because all award jacket orders are prepaid, cash is collected in the same period as the sale. However, baseball pants and jerseys are always sold on credit. C&C has found that historically, 5% of credit sales become bad debts and are not collected. No cash is ever received for those sales. C&C has also found that 60% of each month's sales is collected during the month, and the remaining 35% is collected the following month.

Exhibit 5-19 shows C&C's cash receipts budget for the fourth quarter. It was prepared using the following steps:

1. Apply the established collections pattern to the existing accounts receivable.
2. Apply the established collections pattern to budgeted sales.

C&C's balance sheet (see Exhibit 5-23) shows a balance of $35,560 in accounts receivable (net of allowance for doubtful accounts) from sales made in September. Based on C&C's historical collections pattern, the entire amount is expected to be collected in October.

C&C SPORTS
4th Quarter Cash Receipts Budget

	October	November	December	Total Cash Receipts	Bad Debts	Accounts Receivable
September accounts receivable (Exhibit 5-23)	$ 35,560			$ 35,560		
Pants (sales figures from Exhibit 5-6)						
October sales, $120,000	72,000	$ 42,000		114,000	$ 6,000	
November sales, $240,000		144,000	$ 84,000	228,000	12,000	
December sales, $480,000			288,000	288,000	24,000	$168,000
Jerseys						
October sales, $59,200	35,520	20,720		56,240	2,960	
November sales, $88,800		53,280	31,080	84,360	4,440	
December sales, $222,000			133,200	133,200	11,100	77,700
Jackets						
October sales, $125,000	125,000			125,000		
November sales, $625,000		625,000		625,000		
December sales, $375,000			375,000	375,000		
Totals	$268,080	$885,000	$911,280	$2,064,360	$60,500	$245,700 → Flows to budgeted balance sheet

Flows to cash budget (October through Total Cash Receipts)

Bad Debts: Also found on selling & administrative expense budget

Collection pattern

Pants and jerseys: 60% in month sold
35% in month following sale
5% uncollectible

Award jackets 100% in month sold

EXHIBIT 5-19 *C&C Sports' cash receipts budget.*

By applying the historical collections pattern to the fourth quarter sales budget (Exhibit 5-6), managers can calculate the company's expected cash collections and bad debt expense. October's pants sales of $120,000 will generate $6,000 in bad debts ($120,000 × 5% expected bad debts). That amount will never be collected. Of the remaining $114,000 in October pants sales, $72,000 ($120,000 × 60%) will be collected in October and $42,000 ($120,000 × 35%) in November. This calculation must be repeated for jersey and jacket sales. The total of each month's cash collections flows to the cash budget; total bad debts flows to the selling and administrative expense budget.

One last item to consider is the balance (35%) of December 2017 pants and jersey sales that will not be collected until January 2018. This amount will be reported as the accounts receivable balance on the pro-forma balance sheet.

Notice how much cash collections vary from one month to the next. The cash receipts budget gives C&C's managers an early warning regarding the low level of cash receipts expected in October, so they can take corrective action in advance. Otherwise the company could find itself in financial trouble.

Now that we have seen how to calculate both components of cash available to spend, let's revisit C&C's cash budget shown in Exhibit 5-17. The beginning cash balance for October, $48,720, is the balance in the cash account on the September 30 balance sheet (see Exhibit 5-23). From that point, each period's budgeted ending cash balance rolls forward to become the next period's budgeted beginning cash balance. For example, October's ending cash balance of $40,448 becomes the beginning balance for November. As a result, the cash budget must be completed one period at a time, in order to determine what ending cash balance will roll forward.

The second line of this section of the cash budget is based on the cash receipts budget. Compare the highlighted totals in columns 1–4 of the cash receipts budget (Exhibit 5-19) to the "Collections from Sales" line in Exhibit 5-17 and you will see that they flow directly into the cash budget. Following the cash receipts entry, the total cash available to spend is calculated as the sum of the beginning cash balance and all cash collections from sales made during the period.

WATCH OUT!

Be sure you understand the cash collection pattern before preparing the cash receipts budget. Cash sales are always collected in the period in which the sale is made. Credit sales are collected based on a collection pattern that may include some receipts in the period of sale and other receipts in later periods.

WATCH OUT!

Remember that the beginning balance in the 4th quarter column of the cash budget is the beginning balance for the entire budget period—that is, the beginning balance from October. Similarly, the ending balance in the 4th quarter column is the ending balance for the entire budget period—that is, the ending balance from December.

Cash Disbursements

The cash disbursements section of the cash budget lists each type of cash disbursement that is expected to occur during the period. You will find much of this information in the operating budgets you have already prepared, as Exhibit 5-20 shows. However, some cash disbursements are not included anywhere else in the master budget and are known only as part of the organization's overall operational plans.

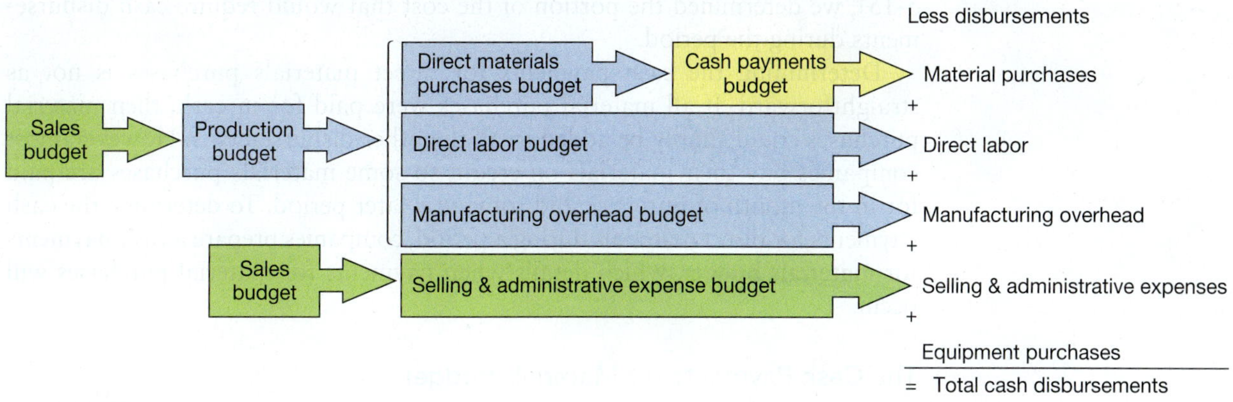

EXHIBIT 5-20 *Cash disbursements section information flows.*

REALITY CHECK—*Budgeting around the world*

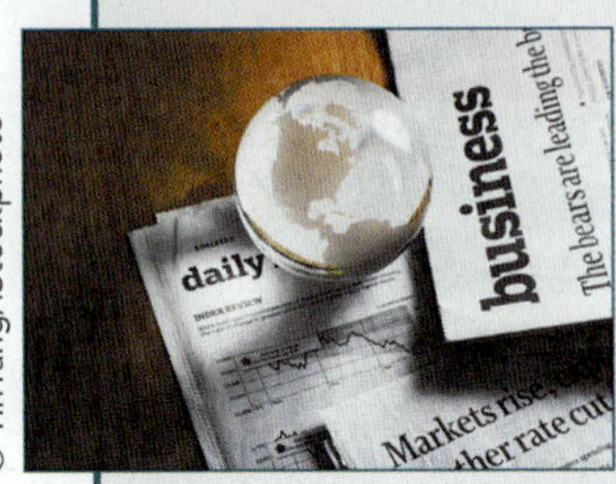

© YinYang/iStockphoto

For companies that operate in different countries, exchange rates are a budgeting issue because they cannot be predicted with any accuracy.

Budgeting is a common practice throughout the world. But do all companies around the world budget in the same way? The answer is yes and no. Surveys have found many similarities around the globe. Companies in the United States, Australia, Japan, Holland, and the United Kingdom all use master budgets. These companies also distinguish between variable and fixed costs in preparing these budgets.

But international operations raise some special budgeting concerns. For companies that operate in different countries, exchange rates are a budgeting issue because they cannot be predicted with any accuracy. Although assumptions can be made, the exchange rate simply is not under management's control. And a change in the exchange rate can dramatically alter both the budget and the company's actual results.

How might fluctuating exchange rates affect the budget? Suppose that the cash payments budget prepared on November 2, 2015, requires a 500,000 EUR payment for direct materials on February 15, 2016 (EUR stands for euro, the European Union's currency). Using the exchange rates at the time the budget was prepared, a U.S.-based company would pay $453,432 to obtain the 500,000 EUR. When the payment comes due, however, the exchange rate is different, and the 500,000 EUR cost the U.S.-based company $448,551. Because the cash payment is less than was budgeted, the original cash budget is no longer accurate. Clearly, large swings in exchange rates could have a dramatic impact on the budget.

Sources: http://www.x-rates.com/cgi-bin/hlookup.cgi; Marc Lynn and Roland Madison, "A Closer Look at Rolling Budgets," *Management Accounting Quarterly*, Fall 2004, 60; Ken Milani and Juan Rivera, "The Rigorous Business of Budgeting for International Operations," *Management Accounting Quarterly*, Winter 2004, 38–39.

The first category of cash disbursements information comes from the production-related budgets. Each of the product cost components—direct materials, direct labor, and manufacturing overhead—requires cash disbursements. In the direct labor budget (Exhibit 5-13), we determined the number and total cost of direct labor hours required to meet the production budget. While payroll periods, particularly those for hourly workers, don't always coincide with the end of an accounting period, a common assumption is that all wages are paid in the period in which they are incurred. For manufacturing overhead (Exhibit 5-15), we determined the portion of the cost that would require cash disbursements during the period.

Determining the cash payments for direct materials purchases is not as straightforward. If all material purchases were paid for in cash, then material purchases could simply be added to all the other disbursements. However, most companies buy their materials on credit, so some materials purchases are paid for in the month of purchase and some in a later period. To determine the cash payments for direct materials during a period, companies prepare a **cash payments for materials budget**, which details when payments for material purchases will occur.

The Cash Payments for Materials Budget

Like most companies, C&C purchases its raw materials on account. That means that payment for those purchases is made after receipt of the materials, based on vendors' payment terms. C&C's zipper supplier requires payment within 30 days; other suppliers require payment within 15 days, or on receipt of the invoice.

Just as companies review their cash collections history to determine which pattern of collections to use in preparing their cash receipts budget, they review their cash payments history and credit terms to develop a cash disbursements pattern. They then apply the cash disbursements pattern to budgeted materials purchases to estimate when cash payments will be made. Based on vendors' payment terms and past history, C&C managers estimate that the company pays for 50% of direct materials purchases in the period of purchase and the remaining 50% in the following period.

Exhibit 5-21 shows C&C's cash payments for materials budget. This budget was prepared using the following steps:

1. Apply the established disbursements pattern to existing accounts payable.
2. Apply the established disbursements pattern to budgeted materials purchases.

C&C SPORTS
4th Quarter Cash Payments
for Materials Purchases Budget

	October	November	December	Total Cash Disbursements	Accounts Payable
September accounts payable (Exhibit 5-23)	$ 63,812			$ 63,812	
October purchases (Exhibit 5-11), $180,858	90,429	$ 90,429		180,858	
November purchases, $284,022		142,011	142,011	284,022	
December purchases, $336,702			168,351	168,351	168,351
Totals	$154,241	$232,440	$310,362	$697,043	$168,351

Flows to cash budget

Flows to budgeted balance sheet

Payment history:
50% in month purchased
50% in month following purchase

EXHIBIT 5-21 *C&C Sports' cash payments for materials purchases budget.*

The first line of the cash payments budget is the payment of accounts payable from the previous year. C&C's balance sheet (Exhibit 5-23) shows a balance of $63,812 in accounts payable. This balance represents 50% of purchases of direct materials in September. Based on the established cash disbursements pattern, the entire amount will be paid in October (the period after the purchase).

Applying the historical cash payments pattern to budgeted direct materials purchases, C&C calculates that October's purchase of direct materials worth $180,858 will generate $90,429 in cash payments ($180,858 × 50%) in October, and the same amount in November. This calculation is repeated for the two remaining months. One-half of December 2017's purchases will not be paid until January 2018. That amount will be reported as the accounts payable balance on the pro-forma balance sheet.

Other Cash Disbursements

Disbursements for selling and administrative expenses are based on the selling and administrative expense budget (see Exhibit 5-7). Recall that not all of these expenses involved cash disbursements. Therefore, only the cash disbursements for selling and administrative expenses—not the total expenses—should appear in the cash disbursements section of the cash budget.

The remaining item in the cash disbursements section of Exhibit 5-17 has not appeared anywhere else in the budget preparation process. C&C plans to purchase new equipment costing $150,000 at the end of December. This budgeted cash disbursement will be made based on the organization's operational plans. Some firms may make other cash disbursements, such as dividend payments and income tax payments, that C&C is not planning to incur. The bottom line is that all planned cash disbursements during the period should be included in this section of the cash budget. Otherwise, the company may come up short of cash.

THINK ABOUT IT 5.7

Where should a company report cash collections other than sales receipts, such as proceeds from the sale of equipment?

Cash Excess (Cash Needed)

Once managers know the total cash available to spend and the total cash disbursements for the period, they can calculate whether the company will have enough cash on hand to make the budgeted disbursements on time. That is what the cash excess (cash needed) section of the cash budget is all about. It can be completed using the following steps:

1. Subtract the total cash disbursements from the total cash available to spend to determine whether the cash available to spend is adequate to cover the budgeted cash disbursements for the period.
2. Subtract the minimum desired cash balance from the result in Step 1 to determine the cash excess or cash needed.

If the difference between the total cash available to spend and the budgeted cash disbursements in Step 1 is positive, more cash is available than is required to make budgeted disbursements in the period. If the difference is negative, not enough cash is available to make budgeted disbursements.

Many firms establish a **minimum cash balance** that they want to have on hand at the end of every period. Sometimes this minimum balance may be required by a creditor, such as a bank, that has made a loan to the organization. In other cases, managers determine the appropriate amount to hold for contingencies. Recall from the chapter-opening story that C&C's president was concerned that the company's cash balance was too low at the end of last year. After consulting with the chief financial officer, he concluded that C&C should maintain a minimum cash balance of $40,000. The minimum cash balance is subtracted from the cash excess/deficiency to determine whether short-term borrowing is required to meet the organization's cash needs. If the difference is positive, no short-term borrowing is required. If the difference is negative, the company will need to secure short-term borrowing to meet its cash obligations.

WATCH OUT!

For these calculations to work, you must treat the amount of the cash deficiency as a negative number. That way, when you subtract the minimum cash balance, you will get a larger negative number, indicating a shortage of cash and a need for short-term borrowing.

In October, C&C has a cash deficiency of $53,552 before the minimum balance of $40,000 is subtracted. After subtracting the minimum cash balance, C&C is short $93,552 and must borrow to cover its cash needs in October. Notice, however, that the company's cash position reverses in November, when it generates excess cash.

Short-Term Financing

This section of the cash budget is prepared only if there is a need to secure a new round of short-term borrowing or to repay previous short-term borrowing.[6] If there is a need for new short-term borrowing, managers must determine how much additional cash should be borrowed to meet the company's cash disbursements and maintain the minimum desired cash balance.

In C&C's case, there is a budgeted cash shortfall of $93,552 in October. C&C has an agreement with its bank to cover this type of short-term borrowing. That agreement specifies that cash may be borrowed at the beginning of the month in increments of $1,000, at 12% annual interest. Accrued interest on the loan is paid only when the principal is repaid. Based on those terms, C&C will need to borrow $94,000 for the first quarter.

To see how to include principal repayments and interest in the cash budget, we need to look at November's budget. C&C expects to have $340,358 in excess cash at the end of November, so there will be more than enough cash to repay the $94,000 loan from October. In addition to the principal payment, C&C will pay the accrued interest on that amount. C&C plans to repay the principal at the end of November since that is when managers will be certain that enough funds are available. Since the money will be borrowed at the beginning of October and repaid at the end of November, C&C will need to pay two months' accrued interest of $1,880 ($\$94,000 \times 12\% \times \frac{2}{12}$).

Ending Cash Balance

The last line of the cash budget is the ending cash balance for each period. This balance is calculated as

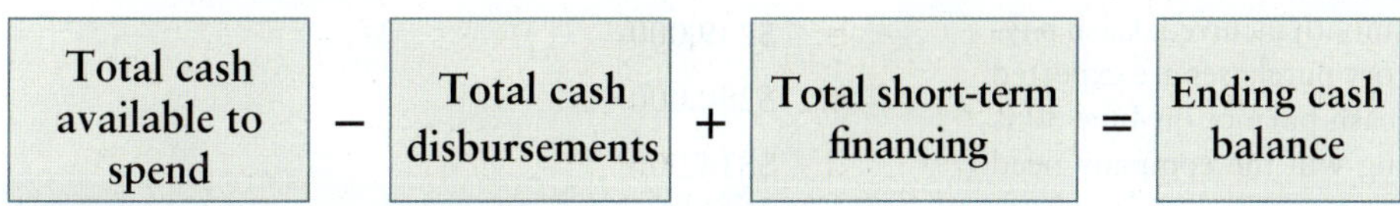

A couple of points about the ending cash balance warrant special attention. First, while the diagram shows that total short-term financing is added to total cash available to spend to find the ending cash balance, if the financing is a repayment of principal and interest, that amount will be a negative number. (Recall from algebra that adding a negative number is the same as subtracting a positive number.) Second, remember that the ending cash balance for the period becomes the beginning cash balance for the next period.

An examination of C&C's monthly cash budget reveals several interesting facts.

- If the cash budget had been prepared only on a quarterly basis, it would have shown sufficient cash to cover the fourth quarter's disbursements.

However, the monthly budget shows a different picture: short-term financing is needed in October to meet expected cash disbursements. Knowing that in advance will help C&C's managers make the necessary arrangements before a cash emergency arises.

- Notice how much C&C's ending cash balance varies from month to month. This variation is due to the seasonality of its business. C&C generates large ending cash balances in November and December. Upon review of the sales forecast in Exhibit 5-5, you would expect cash deficits in the third quarter when demand is particularly low.
- Based on the fourth quarter cash budget, C&C's managers may want to explore options for investing the excess cash generated during November and December to earn a return on excess cash. However, the investments they select must be short-term instruments that allow C&C to access the money as needed during other months of the year.

UNIT 5.4 REVIEW

KEY TERMS

Cash budget p. 254

Cash payments for materials budget p. 258

Cash receipts budget p. 256

Minimum cash balance p. 260

PRACTICE QUESTIONS

1. LO 4 A company is preparing its cash budget for the second quarter of the year. It has $10,000 in cash on March 31. Sales for the quarter are expected to be $300,000, all in cash. Operating expenses are expected to be $65,000, which includes $15,000 of depreciation. Cash expenses are paid in the month incurred. Cash payments for merchandise inventory purchases are expected to be $270,000. The desired cash balance on June 30 is $20,000. How much financing will the company need during the quarter?

   a. $30,000
   b. $25,000
   c. $45,000
   d. $10,000

2. LO 4 Joshua Studios expects the following sales in March, April, and May:

	Cash Sales	Credit Sales
March	$55,000	$240,000
April	50,000	250,000
May	75,000	300,000

   The controller has determined that the company collects credit sales in the following pattern: 30% in the month of sale, 50% in the first month after sale, 10% in the second month after sale, and 10% uncollectible. How much cash will be collected from customers in May?

   a. $ 75,000
   b. $239,000
   c. $290,000
   d. $314,000

3. LO 4 Sleep Systems, Inc. budgeted the following selling and administrative expenses for July:

Utilities	$8,500
Advertising	675
Office equipment depreciation	1,230
Supplies	530
Bad debts	1,920

   How much will Sleep Systems, Inc. show on its July cash budget for selling and administrative expenses?

   a. $12,855
   b. $11,625
   c. $ 9,705
   d. $ 3,150

4. LO 4 Marvin's Garden Supply is preparing its cash budget for the fourth quarter. The inventory manager has provided the following budgeted materials purchases amounts: October—$58,000, November—$80,000, December—$74,000. Historically, Marvin's has paid for 20% of its purchases in the month of purchase, 70% in the month following the purchase, and 10% in the second month after the purchase. What is Marvin's budgeted cash payments for purchases in December?

a. $80,000
b. $76,600
c. $74,000
d. $56,000

UNIT 5.4 PRACTICE EXERCISE

(This problem is a continuation of the Unit 5.3 Practice Exercise.)

Hurtt's Java Seeds is an independent roaster of specialty coffee beans. During March, the company plans to sell 10,000 pounds of beans at $12.00 per pound. Internet sales account for 50% of total sales and are paid for by customers when they place their orders. Of the remaining 50%, three-fifths are paid for in the month of sale and two-fifths in the month following the sale. In February, roasted coffee bean sales are expected to total $99,600.

Hurtt's pays for 40% of its green coffee beans in the month of purchase and the remaining 60% in the month following the purchase. (Refer to your answer for Unit 5.3 Exercise for March purchases.) February's purchases of green coffee beans are expected to total $25,000.

Variable selling and administrative expenses are 20% of sales, and fixed administrative expenses are $30,000 per month. Both are paid in the month incurred, as are direct labor costs and manufacturing overhead. In March, Hurtt's must make a $30,000 payment on its long-term loan, of which $5,000 is interest.

At the end of February, Hurtt's cash balance is expected to be $14,000. The company must maintain a minimum cash balance of $12,000 as a condition of a long-term loan. Any cash required to maintain the minimum balance can be borrowed in $1,000 increments at a 12% annual interest rate. Interest is paid only when principal is repaid. However, it is accrued at the end of every month.

Required

1. Prepare Hurtt's cash receipts budget for March.
2. Prepare Hurtt's cash payments for purchases budget for March.
3. Prepare Hurtt's cash budget for March.

SELECTED UNIT 5.4 ANSWERS

Think About It 5.7

Other cash collections can be posted either as an addition to cash available or as an offset to cash disbursements. The budget is prepared for the managers' benefit, so the format needs to be whatever provides the best information for the managers.

Practice Questions

1. A
2. D
3. C
4. B

Unit 5.4 Practice Exercise

1.

Cash sales—March ($120,000 × 50%)	$ 60,000
Credit sales collections—March ($120,000 × 50% × 60%)	36,000
Credit sales collections—February ($99,600 × 50% × 40%)	19,920
Total cash collections	$115,920

2. Payment on March purchases ($22,250* × 40%) $ 8,900
Payment on February purchases ($25,000 × 60%) 15,000
Total cash payments for purchases $ 23,900

*Answer to Unit 5.3 Practice Exercise, part 3

3.

Beginning cash balance	$ 14,000
Collections from sales	115,920
Total cash available	129,920
Less disbursements:	
Direct material purchases	23,900
Direct labor (Unit 5.3 Practice Exercise, part 4)	1,455
Manufacturing overhead ($22,795 − $1,500 depreciation) (Unit 5.3 Practice Exercise, part 5)	21,295
Variable selling & administrative expenses ($12 × 10,000 × 2)	24,000
Fixed selling & administrative expenses	30,000
Long-term debt payment	30,000
Total cash disbursements	130,650
Excess (inadequacy of cash)	(730)
Minimum cash balance	(12,000)
Cash available (needed)	(12,730)
Short-term financing	
Borrowing	13,000
Repayments	
Interest	
Total financing	13,000
Ending cash balance	$ 12,270

UNIT 5.5

Pro-Forma Financial Statements

GUIDED UNIT PREPARATION

Answering the following questions while you read this unit will guide your understanding of the key concepts found in the unit. The questions are linked to the learning objectives presented at the beginning of the chapter.

LO 5

1. Explain the relationship between the master budget and the pro-forma financial statements.
2. Which financial statement is prepared last? Why is that the case?

Given our focus on the importance of cash flows in Unit 5.4, you may think that once the cash budget has been prepared, the budgeting process is complete. That is not the case. Although cash flow is important, the financial statements also provide a wealth of information about a company. To get a complete picture of the expected results of budgeted operations, we need to prepare pro-forma financial statements.

Pro-forma financial statements are prepared based on assumed rather than actual results. Like a budget, they are predictions of what will happen in the future. As part of the budgeting process, the pro-forma statements predict the organization's financial position if all the components of the master budget are achieved as planned. The income statement is prepared first, since net income needs to flow through to retained earnings on the balance sheet.

The Pro-Forma Income Statement

Recall from your financial accounting course that the income statement shows the results of operations for the entire period. The various components of the master budget provide the information to prepare the pro-forma income statement. Exhibit 5-22 shows C&C's pro-forma income statement based on the master budget components for the fourth quarter, as prepared in Units 5.3 and 5.4. Let's look at each line item on the pro-forma income statement and trace it back to the master budget.

EXHIBIT 5-22

C&C Sports' pro-forma income statement.

C&C SPORTS
Pro-Forma Income Statement
for the Quarter Ended December 31, 2017

	Source	
Sales	Sales budget (Exhibit 5-6)	$2,335,000
Cost of goods sold	Ending inventory and COGS budget (Exhibit 5-16)	1,582,757
Gross profit		752,243
Selling and administrative expense	Selling and administrative expense budget (Exhibit 5-7)	360,753
Operating income		391,490
Interest expense	Cash budget (Exhibit 5-17)	1,880
Income before taxes		389,610
Income tax expense (30%)		116,883
Net income		$ 272,727

- Sales revenue: Sales revenue for the year comes directly from the sales budget in Exhibit 5-6.
- Cost of goods sold: Cost of goods sold for the year comes directly from the cost of goods sold budget in Exhibit 5-16.
- Gross profit: Budgeted sales revenue minus budgeted cost of goods sold.
- Selling and administrative expense: Selling and administrative expense comes directly from the selling and administrative expense budget in Exhibit 5-7. (Remember to use the expense amount, not the cash payments amount.)
- Operating income: Budgeted gross profit minus budgeted selling and administrative expense.

- Interest expense: For C&C, budgeted interest expense comes from the short-term borrowing in October. Recall from the cash budget (Exhibit 5-17) that $1,880 of interest was paid when the short-term loan was repaid. Even if the loan had not been repaid, interest expense would have been accrued for the quarter. Not all companies will have the same interest expense items. To know what a company's interest expense will be, you will need to be aware of the types of loans the company has.
- Income before taxes: Budgeted operating income minus budgeted interest expense.
- Income tax expense: Multiply the budgeted income before taxes by the budgeted 30% tax rate.
- Net income: Income before taxes minus income tax expense.

The Pro-Forma Balance Sheet

The pro-forma balance sheet in Exhibit 5-23 shows C&C's budgeted financial position at the end of the fourth quarter. To prepare the pro-forma balance sheet for the quarter, we begin with the previous quarter's balance sheet (left-hand column) and adjust the balances to reflect budgeted operations for the next quarter (right-hand column). Let's look at each account and trace the balances back to the master budget.

C&C SPORTS
Pro-Forma Balance Sheets
As of

	September 30, 2017		Changes/Source	December 31, 2017	
Cash		$ 48,720	Cash budget (Exhibit 5-17)		$ 333,986
Accounts receivable, net		35,560	Cash receipts budget (Exhibit 5-19)		245,700
Raw materials	$ 89,281		Ending inventory budget (Exhibit 5-16)	$ 93,403	
Finished goods inventory	267,205		Ending inventory budget (Exhibit 5-16)	127,275	
Total inventories		356,486			220,678
Total current assets		440,766			800,364
Machinery and equipment, net		486,511	+ 150,000 – 11,546 – 3,903[a]		621,062
Other assets		41,704	*No change*		41,704
Total assets		$968,981			$1,463,130
Accounts payable		$ 63,812	Cash payments for materials budget (Exhibit 5-21)		$ 168,351
Income taxes payable		0	+ $116,883 Income tax expense (Exhibit 5-22)		116,883
Total current liabilities		63,812			285,234
Long-term debt		0			0
Total liabilities		63,812			285,234
Common stock		$210,000	*No change*		210,000
Retained earnings		695,169	+ $272,727 Net income (Exhibit 5-22)		967,896
Total stockholders' equity		905,169			1,177,896
Total liabilities and stockholders' equity		$968,981			$1,463,130

[a]$150,000 equipment purchase (Exhibit 5-17) – $11,546 manufacturing overhead depreciation (Exhibit 5-15) – $3,903 selling and administrative depreciation (Exhibit 5-7).

EXHIBIT 5-23 *C&C Sports' pro-forma balance sheets.*

REALITY CHECK—*How the pros use pro-formas*

Pro-forma financial statements give users a what-if picture of an organization. These statements do not report real results; rather, they project future results based on a set of assumptions about the future.

Consider the case of an entrepreneur searching for funding for her latest venture. A key component in her pitch to investors will be a thoughtfully prepared business plan—and a key component of that business plan will be a set of pro-forma financial statements, projecting the financial health and performance of the venture. In a survey of *INC.* 500 companies (the 500 fastest-growing, privately held companies in the United States), CEOs reported that their pro-forma statements were a critical success factor in obtaining outside funding for their businesses. They also believed that the pro-forma statements were the most important part of the business plan in the day-to-day management of the company.

Reported earnings under GAAP were 25% lower than what was reported using the pro-forma measures.

Analysts and investors also make frequent use of pro-forma financial statements. Many companies release pro-forma earnings along with generally accepted accounting principles (GAAP) earnings. For instance, Del Taco Restaurants (2015) and Kraft Heinz (2016) both reported pro-forma information to illustrate the possible effects of an acquisition.

Many companies are now choosing to report pro-forma results of a different type. Companies argue that this new type of pro-forma reporting, which reports numbers that do not comply with GAAP, provides financial statement users with "better" measures of operations and financial results. For example, Valeant Pharmaceuticals International reported pro-forma earnings of $2.74 for the quarter ended September 30, 2015, while the GAAP earnings were only $0.14. A recent study by *The Wall Street Journal* found that 25% of public companies used these non-GAAP pro-forma measures in securities filings, and reported earnings under GAAP were 25% lower than what was reported using the pro-forma measures.

Some people, including investor Warren Buffett, are sounding alarms about this type of pro-forma reporting. So when reading pro-forma financial results, be sure and do your homework to understand exactly what the pro-forma numbers are reporting.

Sources: "Del Taco Restaurants, Inc. Announces Fiscal Fourth Quarter and Fiscal Year 2015 Financial Results," March 7, 2016, http://www.businesswire.com/news/home/20160307005383/en/Del-Taco-Restaurants-Announces-Fiscal-Fourth-Quarter (accessed March 7, 2016); Stephen Gandel, "Warren Buffet Attacks Wall Street Over 'Phoney' Earnings," *Fortune*, February 27, 2016, http://fortune.com/2016/02/27/warren-buffett-wall-street-earnings/(accessed March 7, 2016); Jeff Gelski, "Kraft Heinz Placing 'Big Bets' on Specific items," *Food Business News*, February 29, 2016, http://www.foodbusinessnews.net/articles/news_home/Financial-Performance/2016/02/Kraft_Heinz_placing_big_bets_o.aspx?ID=%7BC1A8A8DA-0AA8-43FA-ABF5-44BC8AC2B781%7D&cck=1 (accessed March 7, 2016); Charley Grant, "Should You Trust These Financial Reports?," *The Wall Street Journal*, February 15, 2016, http://blogs.wsj.com/moneybeat/2016/02/15/should-you-trust-these-financial-reports/(accessed March 7, 2016); Gretchen Morgenson, "A Troubling Timeline at Valeant," *The New York Times*, March 4, 2016, http://www.nytimes.com/2016/03/06/business/a-troubling-timeline-at-valeant.html?_r=0 (accessed March 7, 2016); David Reilly, "Herbalife's Made-Up Measure Goes Kerflooey," *The Wall Street Journal*, March 3, 2016, http://blogs.wsj.com/moneybeat/2016/03/03/herbalifes-made-up-measure-goes-kerflooey/ (accessed March 7, 2016).

Assets

- Cash: The cash balance at December 31, 2017 (right-hand column) comes directly from the ending balance shown on the cash budget (Exhibit 5-17).
- Accounts Receivable, net: The Accounts Receivable balance for the fourth quarter is the amount of uncollected credit sales shown on the cash receipts budget in Exhibit 5-19.

- Raw Materials Inventory: The Raw Materials Inventory balance for the fourth quarter comes directly from part one of the ending inventory budget in Exhibit 5-16.
- Work in Process Inventory: The Work in Process Inventory balance is zero because the production budget calls for all units started in the fourth quarter to be finished. If units remained in process at the end of the period, the cost of these units would be reflected on the Ending Inventory and Cost of Goods Sold Budget.
- Finished Goods Inventory: The Finished Goods Inventory balance for the fourth quarter comes directly from part two of the ending inventory budget in Exhibit 5-16.
- Machinery and Equipment, net: This line item is affected by three other items. First, new equipment totaling $150,000 is to be purchased, as shown on the cash budget in Exhibit 5-17. Second, production equipment is to be depreciated by $11,546, as shown on the manufacturing overhead budget in Exhibit 5-15. Third, office equipment is to be depreciated by $3,903, as shown on the selling and administrative expense budget in Exhibit 5-7. Thus, the balance is $486,511 + 150,000 − 11,546 − 3,903 = $621,062.
- Other Assets: No activity is planned in the Other Assets account, so the balance remains the same from the third to the fourth quarter.

Liabilities and Stockholders' Equity

- Accounts Payable: The Accounts Payable balance is the amount of unpaid purchases of direct materials shown on the December accounts payable line in the cash payments for materials budget (Exhibit 5-21).
- Income Taxes Payable: The beginning balance of Income Taxes Payable is $0, indicating that no tax liability exists at the end of the third quarter. Taxes totaling $116,883 are expected to be owed for the fourth quarter, as shown on the income statement in Exhibit 5-22. The resulting balance is $0 + 116,883 = $116,883.
- Long-Term Debt: C&C did not have any long-term debt at the end of the third quarter, and it did not issue any new long-term debt during the fourth quarter. Recall that the company had to borrow $94,000 in October but paid it back in November. If any of that debt was still outstanding, it would have been reported as "Short-term debt" in the current liabilities section.
- Common Stock: Common stock is not expected to change, since no new stock will be issued during the year.
- Retained Earnings: Retained Earnings increases by the amount of budgeted net income shown on the pro-forma income statement in Exhibit 5-22: $695,169 + 272,727 = $967,896. If C&C were planning to declare dividends, the amount of the dividends would reduce Retained Earnings.

We already noted at the end of Unit 5.3 that C&C was able to reduce inventory by more than $400,000. Comparing the cash balance and the liability section of this fourth quarter balance sheet to the 2016 balance sheet (Exhibit T1-4 on page 38), you can see that the cash balance is predicted to increase, and an unexpected, but positive, result is that the short-term and long-term debt is expected to be paid off. Now that the company has finalized this plan, it will be important for managers to track the company's operating performance through 2017, comparing actual results to the budget to ensure that they stay on track. The next chapter will focus on how to compare budgeted and actual performance.

THINK ABOUT IT 5.8

After reviewing the pro-forma financial statements, the president regards his plan of increasing jacket sales and reducing inventory balances as potentially successful. However, total assets are expected to decrease from $1,870,787 at the end of 2016 to $1,463,130 at the end of 2017. Why would he consider a reduction in total assets to be a good thing?

UNIT 5.5 REVIEW

KEY TERM

Pro-forma financial statements p. 265

PRACTICE QUESTIONS

1. LO 5 The pro-forma balance sheet is the final financial statement to be prepared because information from both the statement of cash flows (or cash budget) and the income statement flows into the balance sheet. True or False?

2. LO 5 The budgeted year-end Accounts Payable balance, which must be entered on the pro-forma balance sheet, can be found on which budget?
   a. Cash Budget
   b. Purchases of Direct Materials Budget
   c. Cash Payments for Materials Budget
   d. Cash Receipts Budget

3. LO 5 Sleep Systems, Inc. budgeted the following selling and administrative expenses for July:

Utilities	$8,500
Advertising	675
Office equipment depreciation	1,230
Supplies	530
Bad debts	1,920

How much will Sleep Systems, Inc., show on its July pro-forma income statement for selling and administrative expenses?

a. $12,855 c. $ 9,705
b. $11,625 d. $ 3,150

UNIT 5.5 PRACTICE EXERCISE

(This problem is a continuation of the Unit 5.4 Practice Exercise.)

Prepare the March pro-forma income statement and balance sheet for Hurtt's Java Seeds (ignore income taxes). The expected February 28 balance sheet is:

Cash	$ 14,000	Accounts payable	$ 15,000
Accounts receivable	19,920	Short-term notes payable	0
Raw materials (green beans)	4,000	Long-term debt	50,000
Finished goods (roasted beans)	4,000	Total liabilities	65,000
Equipment	125,000	Common stock	40,000
Accumulated depreciation	(54,000)	Retained earnings	7,920
Total assets	$112,920	Total liabilities and equity	$112,920

SELECTED UNIT 5.5 ANSWERS

Think About It 5.8

Total assets are expected to decrease primarily due to the decrease in inventory. Along with the decrease in assets is a decrease in short-term and long-term debt. A company needs assets only if they are generating a return. Excess inventory, as it sits in the warehouse, is not generating a return and in fact costs the company interest expense on the debt incurred to purchase the inventory. If the president's plan works, he and the other managers should explore ways to use excess cash and debt to invest in assets that generate a return for the company.

Practice Questions

1. True
2. C
3. A

Unit 5.5 Practice Exercise

Income Statement:

Sales revenue (Unit 5.3 Practice Exercise, part 1)	$120,000
Cost of goods sold (Unit 5.3 Practice Exercise, part 6)	50,000
Gross profit	70,000
Selling and administrative expenses (Unit 5.4 Practice Exercise, part 3)	54,000
Interest expense*	5,130
Operating income	$ 10,870

*From Unit 5.4 Practice Exercise, part 3: $5,000 on long-term debt plus $130 accrued on short-term financing ($13,000 × 12% ÷ 12 months).

Balance Sheet:

Cash	$ 12,270	Accounts payable	$ 13,350
Accounts receivable	24,000	Interest payable	130
Raw materials (green beans)	2,000	Short-term notes payable	13,000
Finished goods (roasted beans)	2,500	Long-term debt	25,000
Equipment	125,000	Total liabilities	51,480
Accumulated depreciation	(55,500)	Common stock	40,000
		Retained earnings	18,790
Total assets	$110,270	Total liabilities and equity	$110,270

Balance Sheet Calculations

Cash: from Unit 5.4 Practice Exercise, part 3
Accounts receivable: March sales $120,000 × 20% = $24,000 (from Unit 5.4 Practice Exercise, part 1)
Raw materials: from Unit 5.3 Practice Exercise, part 6
Finished goods: from Unit 5.3 Practice Exercise, part 6
Equipment: no change from February balance sheet
Accumulated depreciation: $54,000 + 1,500 (February balance + March depreciation given in Unit 5.3 Practice Exercise)
Accounts payable: March purchases $22,250 × 60% = $13,350 (from Unit 5.4 Practice Exercise, part 2)
Interest payable: unpaid interest on short-term loan: $13,000 × 12% ÷ 12 months (from Unit 5.4 Practice Exercise, part 3)
Short-term notes payable: from Unit 5.4 Practice Exercise, part 3
Long-term notes payable: $50,000 − 25,000 = $25,000 (February balance less March payment from Unit 5.4 Practice Exercise, part 3)
Common stock: no change from February balance sheet
Retained earnings: $7,920 + $10,870 = $18,790 (February balance + Net income)

BUSINESS DECISION AND CONTEXT Wrap Up

In the story that opened the chapter, George Douglas expressed concern about C&C's cash balance. Recent cash shortages have led to short-term borrowings to provide the company with the cash needed to stay in business. Inventory balances have also been increasing, requiring additional investment and resources. Douglas wants to find a way to reduce inventory and increase cash flow. He has suggested increasing the sales of award jackets.

C&C's managers met to discuss the inventory balances and determined that the direct materials inventory could be reduced to 20% of the following period's production needs. They also determined that the Finished Goods Inventory could be reduced to 25% of the following period's sales. Based on C&C's budget for 2017, implementation of those inventory levels will reduce inventory by over $400,000, freeing up resources for use in more profitable areas of the business.

The 2017 budget provides a roadmap for cash management. Based on the budgeted operating plan, C&C should finish the year with a Cash balance more than $300,000 greater than that at the end of 2016. The cash budget also shows that existing debt can be repaid on an accelerated schedule, reducing the firm's level of indebtedness. Another contribution of the cash budget is the identification of cash shortages in the first and third quarters. According to the budget, short-term financing will be paid off by the end of the year.

Based on the new budget, C&C now has a plan for operating under George Douglas's mandate of reduced inventory, increased sales of award jackets, and higher cash balances. It appears that Douglas's strategy can work.

CHAPTER SUMMARY

In this chapter you learned how to calculate product standards and prepare the master budget. Specifically, you should be able to meet the objectives set out at the beginning of the chapter:

1. ***Describe the budget development process and explain how it fits into management's planning process. (Unit 5.1)***

   Budgets can be completed in either a top-down, imposed process or a bottom-up, participative process. Either way, the process is iterative, as information is passed throughout the organization and updated for changes in planned activity. Budgets can be prepared using the prior year's budget as a starting point, or they can be prepared using zero-based budgeting, in which each item must be justified anew each year. A budget may be prepared to cover a monthly, quarterly, or annual time frame.

   Executive management sets out a strategy to guide a company's actions. The budgeting process translates that strategy into action by allocating financial resources across the organization to ensure that the necessary steps can be taken. The budget also communicates decisions about resource allocation throughout the organization, allowing managers to plan for the future in order to mitigate potential operational risks, such as cash shortages.

2. ***Calculate the standard cost of a product. (Unit 5.2)***

   To calculate the standard cost of a product, multiply the standard price of each input (direct materials, direct labor, and manufacturing overhead) by the standard quantity of the input and sum. The standard cost is the expected cost to manufacture one unit of output.

   Price standards are the expected cost of obtaining each input used in producing a product.

   - The *direct materials* price standard includes the cost of getting the materials to the factory (purchase price, freight, and discounts).
   - The *direct labor* price standard includes wages, fringe benefits, and payroll taxes.
   - The *manufacturing overhead* price standard is the predetermined overhead rate.

   Quantity standards are the expected amount of inputs required to produce one good unit of output.

   - The *direct materials* quantity standard is the quantity of direct materials needed to produce one unit of good output, including allowances for waste and spoilage.
   - The *direct labor* quantity standard is the amount of direct labor time required to produce one good unit of output.
   - The *manufacturing overhead* quantity standard is based on usage of the overhead application base.

3. ***Prepare the operating budget and describe the relationships among its components. (Unit 5.3)***

   The operating budget begins with the creation of the sales budget. Once budgeted sales have been forecast, a selling and administrative expense budget to support that level of sales is calculated. The sales budget also provides input for the production budget, which details when and how much of a product must be produced. Once budgeted production is known, the direct materials purchases, direct labor, and manufacturing overhead budgets can be prepared to support the acquisition of the required inputs.

- The sales budget is a forecast of expected sales, expressed in both units and dollars. This budget is the key to the entire master budgeting process, since most other master budget components depend on the level of sales.
- The selling and administrative expense budget details all the expenditures for selling and administrative expenses.
- The production budget determines the level of production required to meet budgeted sales and maintain desired levels of ending Finished Goods Inventory.
- The direct materials purchases budget shows the quantity of direct materials that will be needed to meet the production requirements shown in the production budget and maintain the desired ending inventory of direct materials. This budget also shows the quantity of direct materials that must be purchased.
- The direct labor budget shows how many direct labor hours must be incurred to meet the budgeted level of production.
- The manufacturing overhead budget details the fixed and variable overhead costs to be incurred.

4. ***Prepare the cash budget and describe the relationships among its components. (Unit 5.4)***

The cash budget is comprised of the following sections:

- The cash available to spend section of the cash budget shows how much cash is available to spend in each period. It includes the beginning Cash balance and cash collections from sales shown in the cash receipts budget.
- The cash disbursements section of the cash budget lists all budgeted cash disbursements. In addition to various planned operational disbursements, such as equipment purchases and debt service payments, the cash disbursements section includes information from the cash payments for materials, direct labor, manufacturing overhead, and selling and administrative expense budgets.
- The cash excess (cash needed) section of the cash budget subtracts the budgeted cash disbursements from the budgeted cash available to spend to determine the cash excess or shortage. It includes any minimum Cash balance required.
- The short-term financing section of the cash budget details the short-term financing activities needed to maintain an adequate Cash balance. It is completed only if additional short-term borrowings or repayments of existing short-term borrowings or interest are required.
- The ending Cash balance is determined by the following formula:

	Cash available to spend
−	Cash disbursements
=	Cash excess or cash needed
+	Short-term financing
=	Ending cash balance

The ending Cash balance should always be at least as much as the minimum Cash balance required. The ending Cash balance for one period is the beginning Cash balance for the next period.

5. ***Prepare pro-forma financial statements and describe their relationship to the master budget components. (Unit 5.5)***

Pro-forma income statements and balance sheets are prepared using the information developed in the budget process. These statements reflect the results of operations and the financial position of the organization *as if* all actions planned in the budget had occurred.

Many of the master budget components provide direct input to the pro-forma financial statements, as follows:

Budget Component	Income Statement Accounts	Balance Sheet Accounts
Sales budget	Revenue	
Selling and administrative expense budget	Selling and Administrative Expense	Accumulated Depreciation
Manufacturing overhead budget		Accumulated Depreciation
Ending inventory and cost of goods sold budget	Cost of Goods Sold	Raw Materials Inventory, Work in Process Inventory, Finished Goods Inventory
Cash receipts budget	Bad Debt Expense	Accounts Receivable
Cash payments for materials budget		Accounts Payable
Cash budget	Interest Expense	Cash, Accrued Expenses, Equipment, Short- and/or Long-Term Debt

KEY TERMS

- Bottom-up budget (Unit 5.1)
- Budget (Unit 5.1)
- Budgetary padding (Unit 5.1)
- Budgetary slack (Unit 5.1)
- Cash budget (Unit 5.4)
- Cash payments for materials budget (Unit 5.4)
- Cash receipts budget (Unit 5.4)
- Direct labor budget (Unit 5.3)
- Direct materials purchases budget (Unit 5.3)
- Ending inventory and cost of goods sold budget (Unit 5.3)
- Ideal standard (Unit 5.2)
- Manufacturing overhead budget (Unit 5.3)
- Master budget (Unit 5.3)
- Minimum cash balance (Unit 5.4)
- Operating budget (Unit 5.3)
- Participative budgeting (Unit 5.1)
- Practical standards (Unit 5.2)
- Production budget (Unit 5.3)
- Pro-forma financial statements (Unit 5.5)
- Rolling budget (Unit 5.1)
- Sales budget (Unit 5.3)
- Selling and administrative expense budget (Unit 5.3)
- Standard cost (Unit 5.2)
- Standards (Unit 5.2)
- Strategic planning (Unit 5.1)
- Tactical planning (Unit 5.1)
- Top-down budget (Unit 5.1)
- Zero-based budgeting (Unit 5.1)

EXERCISES

5-1 Developing a budget (LO 1) Mark Newton has just opened a gourmet coffee bar, the first of its kind in Fountain, North Carolina. You are Mark's accountant. On a recent visit to the store, you asked how the budget was coming along. Mark replied that since there was no history of gourmet coffee sales in Fountain, he didn't know how to prepare a budget, and he didn't really see the need for one.

Required

Explain to Mark the importance of budgeting and provide some guidance on how he should go about the process.

5-2 Calculating direct material price standards (LO 2) Graymont Industries purchases Solvate, a chemical compound used in several of its products, from ChemMaster. ChemMaster has just increased the list price of Solvate to $6.50 per gallon. However, because Graymont purchases a high volume of Solvate, ChemMaster grants the company a 10% discount off the list price. Charges for shipping Solvate from ChemMaster to Graymont's factory are $100 for a shipment of twenty-five 50-gallon drums. Special storage requirements cost $0.55 per gallon.

Required

Calculate Graymont's standard price for a gallon of Solvate.

5-3 Calculating direct labor rate standards (LO 2) Interpretive Dimensions provides sign language interpreters for major business conferences. Interpreters are paid an hourly rate of $20. Fringe benefits are estimated to be 30% of wages, and employment taxes amount to 10% of wages.

Required

Calculate the standard hourly rate for an interpreter.

5-4 Calculating direct materials quantity standards (LO 2) Mathis Music Stands manufactures decorative wooden music stands for discriminating musicians. Each completed music stand contains 2.5 board feet of American cherry wood. In the process of matching the wood grain and cutting decorative scrollwork, 1.5 board feet of wood are scrapped.

Required

Calculate the standard quantity of American cherry in Mathis's music stand.

5-5 Calculating direct labor quantity standards (LO 2) Caro-Lind Inc. manufactures personalized baby quilts. An experienced embroiderer can personalize 8 quilts per hour. Because the repetitive nature of the sewing can lead to carpal tunnel syndrome, workers take a 20-minute break after every 8 quilts. Before beginning each batch of 8 quilts, workers spend 10 minutes cleaning and setting up their sewing machines.

Required

Calculate the standard quantity of direct labor for one quilt.

5-6 Calculating standard product cost (CMA adapted) (LO 2) Mama Fran's Bakery makes a variety of home-style cookies for upscale restaurants in the Atlanta metropolitan area. The company's best-selling cookie is the double chocolate almond supreme. Mama Fran's recipe requires 10 ounces of a commercial cookie mix, 5 ounces of milk chocolate, and 1 ounce of almonds per pound of cookies. The standard direct materials costs are $0.80 per pound of cookie mix, $4.00 per pound of milk chocolate, and $12.00 per pound of almonds. Each pound of cookies requires 1 minute of direct labor in the mixing department and 2 minutes of direct labor in the baking department. The standard labor rates in those departments are $14.40 per direct labor hour (DLH) and $18.00 per DLH, respectively. Variable overhead is applied at a rate of $32.40 per DLH; fixed overhead is applied at a rate of $60.00 per DLH.

Required

Calculate the standard cost for a pound of Mama Fran's double chocolate almond supreme cookies.

5-7 Preparing a sales budget (CMA adapted) (LO 3) Hammarstrom and Company makes and sells high-quality glare filters for computer monitors. John Stanford, controller, is responsible for preparing Hammarstrom's master budget. He has received the following sales forecast for the coming year from the sales manager.

	January	February	March	April
Forecasted unit sales	15,000	12,500	14,000	18,000
Sales price per unit	$80	$80	$80	$75

Required

Prepare Hammarstrom's sales budget for the first quarter.

5-8 Preparing a sales budget (LO 3) Bates & Hill Fabricators produces commemorative bricks that organizations use for fundraising projects. Aaron Bates, the company's vice president of marketing, has prepared the following sales forecast for the first six months of the coming year. The company plans to sell the bricks for $15 each.

January	February	March	April	May	June
20,000	39,000	35,000	29,000	23,000	20,000

Required

Prepare Bates & Hill's sales budget for the first quarter of the coming year.

5-9 Preparing a selling and administrative expense budget (LO 3) Bates & Hill Fabricators' marketing department has identified the following monthly expenses that will be needed to support the company's sales and administrative functions (see Exercise 5-8). In addition to these monthly expenses, the company will pay a commission to its salespeople equal to 5% of the sales revenue from each brick sold. The company expects bad debt expense to be 4% of sales revenue.

Depreciation	$10,000
Sales staff salaries	$25,000
Advertising	$1,000
Executive salaries	$10,000
Miscellaneous	$500

Required

Prepare Bates & Hill's selling and administrative expense budget for the first quarter of the coming year.

5-10 Preparing a production budget (CMA adapted) (LO 3) Rossano, Inc., makes and sells drum sets. Nick Ross, controller, is responsible for preparing the master budget. The sales manager has given Nick the following sales forecast for the coming months.

	April	May	June	July
Forecasted unit sales	12,000	15,000	10,000	11,000

Rossano expects to have 6,000 drum sets in ending inventory on March 31. The company's policy is to carry 30% of the following month's projected sales in ending inventory.

Required

Prepare Rossano's production budget for the second quarter.

5-11 Preparing a production budget (LO 3) Joshua Hill, Bates & Hill Fabricators' production manager, has just received the company's sales budget for the first quarter (see Exercise 5-8). Company policy requires an ending finished goods inventory each month that will meet 20% of the following month's sales volume. Joshua plans to have 5,600 finished bricks at a cost of $49,000 in inventory at the beginning of the year.

Required

Prepare Bates & Hill's production budget for the first quarter.

5-12 Preparing a production budget (LO 3) High Flyers manufactures competition stunt kites. In November, Jerry Box prepared the following production budget for the first quarter of the coming year. Desired ending inventory is based on the following month's budgeted sales.

	January	February	March	Quarter
Budgeted sales	20,000	35,000	30,000	85,000
Desired ending inventory	7,000	6,000	2,400	2,400
Kites needed	27,000	41,000	32,400	87,400
Less beginning inventory	4,000	7,000	6,000	4,000
Budgeted production	23,000	34,000	26,400	83,400

Following higher-than-expected sales in December, Jerry conducted an inventory count on January 2 and discovered that the company had only 2,000 completed kites on hand. He decided that given the brisk sales in December, the company should increase its desired ending inventory level from 20 to 25% of the next month's sales volume.

Required

a. Prepare a new production budget for the first quarter.
b. What other components of the master budget will be affected by this change?

5-13 Preparing a direct materials purchases budget (CMA adapted) (LO 3) Rider Auto has developed the following production plan for its new auto part.

	January	February	March	April
Budgeted production (units)	12,000	8,000	13,000	15,000

Each unit contains four pounds of raw material. The desired raw materials ending inventory is 40% of the next month's production needs, plus an additional 100 pounds. January's beginning inventory meets this requirement.

Required

Prepare the direct materials purchases budget for the first three months of the coming year.

5-14 Preparing a direct materials purchases budget (LO 3) Mackenzie Chemicals has developed a new window cleaner that requires two ingredients, AM972 and CA38. Based on forecasted sales, Mackenzie has developed the following budgeted production for the coming year.

	1st Quarter	2nd Quarter	3rd Quarter	4th Quarter	1st Quarter Next Year
Forecasted production (gallons)	5,000	7,500	9,000	12,000	6,000

Each gallon of window cleaner requires 100 ounces of AM972 and 28 ounces of CA38. An ounce of AM972 costs Mackenzie $0.15. An ounce of CA38 costs the company $0.25. Mackenzie's inventory policy requires ending inventory equal to 20% of the next quarter's production needs. At the beginning of the year, Mackenzie expects to have 80,000 ounces of AM972 and 30,000 ounces of CA38 on hand.

Required

Prepare Mackenzie's AM972 purchases budget for the coming year.

5-15 Preparing a direct materials purchases budget (LO 3) Marcy Jones, Bates & Hill Fabricators' purchasing manager, has just received the company's production budget for the first quarter (see Exercise 5-11). Each brick requires 5 pounds of clay, and Marcy expects to pay $0.40 per pound of clay in the coming year. Company policy requires an ending direct materials inventory each month that will meet 10% of the following month's production needs. Marcy expects to have 18,900 pounds of clay at a cost of $7,560 in inventory at the beginning of the year.

Required

Prepare Bates & Hill's direct materials purchases budget for the first quarter.

5-16 Preparing a direct labor budget (CMA adapted) (LO 3) Rider Auto has developed the following production plan for its new auto part.

	July	August	September	October
Budgeted production (units)	18,000	15,000	20,000	24,000

Each unit passes through two departments before completion. The company has developed the following direct labor standards:

	Machining	Assembly
DLH per unit	3.0	0.75
Hourly rate	$12.00	$8.00

Required

Prepare the direct labor budget for the third quarter of the coming year.

5-17 Preparing a direct labor budget (LO 3) Joshua Hill, Bates & Hill Fabricators' production manager, has just completed the company's production budget for the first quarter (see Exercise 5-11). Each brick requires 15 minutes to produce, and Joshua expects to pay workers $20 per direct labor hour in the coming year.

Required

Prepare Bates & Hill's direct labor budget for the first quarter.

5-18 Preparing a manufacturing overhead budget (LO 3) Sanchez Sleep Systems manufactures nylon mesh hammocks for a chain of retail outlets located throughout the Southeast. The company plans to manufacture and sell 30,000 hammocks during the fourth quarter. Overhead costs are expected to include:

Variable indirect materials	$ 4.25 per hammock
Variable indirect labor	$11.50 per hammock
Other variable overhead	$ 3.25 per hammock
Salaries	$ 60,000 per quarter
Insurance	$ 5,000 per quarter
Depreciation	$ 26,000 per quarter

Required

Prepare Sanchez's manufacturing overhead budget for the fourth quarter.

5-19 Preparing a manufacturing overhead budget (LO 3) Joshua Hill, Bates & Hill Fabricators' production manager, has just completed the company's production budget for the first quarter (see Exercise 5-11). He has identified the following monthly expenses that will be needed to support the company's manufacturing process.

	Fixed Overhead per month	Variable Overhead per DLH
Depreciation	$30,000	
Indirect materials	21,500	$0.25
Indirect labor	15,000	0.20
Utilities	30,000	0.10
Property taxes	7,000	
Maintenance	9,000	0.15

The company applies manufacturing overhead based on direct labor hours, and the current predetermined rates are $12 per direct labor hour for fixed manufacturing overhead and $0.70 per direct labor hour for variable manufacturing overhead.

Required

Prepare Bates & Hill's manufacturing overhead budget for the first quarter.

5-20 Preparing an ending inventory budget (LO 3) Joshua Hill, Bates & Hill Fabricators' production manager, has just completed the company's production budget (see Exercise 5-11) and manufacturing overhead budget (see Exercise 5-19) for the first quarter. He also has received the direct materials purchases budget (see Exercise 5-15) and direct labor budget (see Exercise 5-17).

Required

Prepare Bates & Hill's ending inventory and cost of goods sold budget for the first quarter.

5-21 Preparing a cash receipts budget (LO 4) In the coming year, Urayse, Inc. will be introducing its first product, a wrist brace that protects serious video gamers from repetitive-motion injuries. The brace will be sold for $11.25 to retailers throughout the country. All sales will be made on account. An expected 65% of sales will be collected within the quarter of the sale, and another 30% in the quarter following the sale. The remaining 5% of credit sales are expected to be uncollectible. The sales budget for the coming year is as follows:

	1st Quarter	2nd Quarter	3rd Quarter	4th Quarter
Budgeted sales units	25,000	40,000	50,000	80,000

Required

Prepare Urayse, Inc.'s cash receipts budget for the coming year.

5-22 Preparing a cash receipts budget (LO 4) Brooks/Neff, Ltd. personalizes scrapbooks for customers, using their digital photographs. Each scrapbook sells for $50. Brooks/Neff collects cash at the time of sale from 30% of customers. Of the remaining sales, 75% are collected in the month of sale and 25% are collected in the month following the sale. The sales budget for the first seven months of the year is as follows:

	January	February	March	April	May	June
Budgeted sales	$120,000	$110,000	$110,000	$112,000	$115,000	$125,000

Required

Prepare Brooks/Neff's cash receipts budget for the second quarter.

5-23 Preparing a cash receipts budget (LO 4) Laura Falk, Bates & Hill Fabricators' accounts receivable manager, has just received the company's sales budget for the first quarter (see Exercise 5-8). The company makes all sales on credit. Laura recently reviewed the company's collection history and found that 70% of the sales are collected in the month of the sale, 26% of sales are collected in the month following the sale, and 4% of sales are uncollectible. The company expects to have an accounts receivable balance of $58,500 on January 1, and this amount represents the remaining receivables from December's sales.

Required

Prepare Bates & Hill's cash receipts budget for the first quarter.

5-24 Preparing a cash payments budget (LO 4) Dakota Williams is one of Texas's premiere party planners. She purchases a variety of supplies, such as plastic tableware, stemware, and decorations, throughout the year. Dakota has prepared the following purchases budget for the coming year.

	1st Quarter	2nd Quarter	3rd Quarter	4th Quarter
Budgeted purchases	$300,000	$420,000	$435,000	$515,000

Historically, Dakota has paid for 40% of her purchases in the quarter of purchase and 60% in the quarter following purchase. On December 31 of this year Dakota had a $250,000 accounts payable balance.

Required

Prepare Dakota's cash payments budget for the coming year.

5-25 Preparing a cash payments budget (LO 4) Maria Bockman, Bates & Hill Fabricators' accounts payable manager, has just received the company's direct materials purchases budget for the first quarter (see Exercise 5-15). The company makes all of its direct materials purchases on account. Maria's recent review of the company's payment history revealed that the company pays for 50% of its direct materials purchases in the month of purchase and 50% in the month following purchase. The company expects to have an accounts payable balance of $18,000 on January 1, and this amount represents the remaining payables from December's direct materials purchases.

Required

Prepare Bates & Hill's cash payments budget for the first quarter.

5-26 Determining required financing (LO 4) Will Benjamin has been working on Heston Paints' cash budget for the coming year. Based on his projections for March, the beginning cash balance will be $45,700, cash collections will be $650,000, and cash disbursements will be $684,000. Heston Paints desires to maintain a $45,000 minimum cash balance. The company has a 12% open line of credit with its bank, which provides short-term borrowings in $500 increments. All borrowings are made at the beginning of the month, and all repayments are made at the end of the month (in $500 increments). Accrued interest is paid at the time of repayment.

Required

a. How much will Heston Paints need to borrow from the bank at the beginning of March?
b. Assuming that Heston Paints has $20,000 in excess cash budgeted for April, how much principal will the company plan to repay? How much interest will be repaid in April?

5-27 Preparing a cash budget (LO 4) Topper, Inc. prepared the following cash budget for the fourth quarter.

	October	November	December	Quarter
Beginning Cash balance	?	$ 15,500	?	$ 16,500
Collections from sales	55,000	?	?	238,600
Total cash available	71,500	96,000	120,000	?
Less disbursements				
Materials purchases	?	10,000	14,000	36,000
Direct labor	5,000	6,000	8,000	19,000
Manufacturing overhead	20,000	23,000	22,000	?
Selling & administrative expenses	29,000	30,000	?	?
Equipment purchase			?	15,000
Dividends			5,000	5,000
Total disbursements	66,000	?	?	?
Excess (deficiency) of cash	?	27,000	?	?
Minimum cash balance	15,000	15,000	15,000	?
Cash available (needed)	(9,500)	?	9,000	?
Financing:				
Borrowings	?			10,000
Repayments		?		(10,000)
Interest		(100)		(100)
Total financing	?	(10,100)		(100)
Ending Cash balance	$ 15,500	$ 16,900	?	?

Required

Fill in the missing amounts, assuming that Topper desires to maintain a $15,000 minimum monthly cash balance. Any required borrowings and repayments must be made in even increments of $1,000.

5-28 Preparing a cash budget (LO 4) John Wills, Bates & Hill Fabricators' budget director, has received budget information from several managers (see Exercises 5-8, 9, 11, 15, 17, 19, 20, 23, and 25) and is preparing the company's cash budget. In addition to the information he received from these managers, John knows the following:

- Bates & Hill plans to have $60,000 in its cash account on January 1.
- Bates & Hill plans to declare and pay dividends totaling $49,000 in January.
- Bates & Hill plans to purchase and pay cash for a piece of land in February at a cost of $72,000.
- Bates & Hill plans to make a cash purchase of equipment in March at a cost of $60,000.
- Bates & Hill's income taxes from last quarter totaling $75,260 will be paid in January.
- Bates & Hill is required to maintain a minimum cash balance of $30,000 in its account at First National Bank.

Bates & Hill has negotiated with the First National Bank to provide a $175,000 line of credit that can be borrowed against in $1,000 increments on the first day of the month. Any repayments on the line of credit must also be made in $1,000 increments and are made on the last day of the month when cash is available. The annual interest rate on this line of credit is 12%. Any time a principal payment is made, all accrued interest to date is repaid.

Required

Prepare Bates & Hill's cash budget for the first quarter.

5-29 Pro-forma financial statements (LO 5) In its latest Annual Report, Monterey Holdings reported revenues of $849,414,000 and net income of $22,682,000 for the year. Part of the revenues and income for the year was generated by Montego Motors, which Monterey Holdings acquired on February 26 for $83.4 million. Since this acquisition was made after the start of the year, the reported amounts do not reflect an entire year's worth of revenue and income from this segment of the company.

In a footnote to the financial statements, Monterey Holdings disclosed total revenues of $868,237,000 and net income of $21,921,000, which are the amounts the company would have reported if the acquisition had occurred before the beginning of the year.

Required

a. Are the revenue and income amounts disclosed in the footnote pro-forma amounts? Why?
b. Why would Monterey Holdings disclose the additional revenue and income amounts?

5-30 Preparing pro-forma financial statements (LO 5) Bill Thomas, Bates & Hill's controller, has received all the budgets prepared by the various operating units (see Exercises 5-8, 9, 11, 15, 17, 19, 20, 23, 25, and 29) and is ready to compile the pro-forma financial statements for the first quarter. The company's balance sheet as of December 31 is as follows:

Cash	$ 60,000
Accounts Receivable (net)	58,500
Finished Goods Inventory	49,000
Raw Materials Inventory	7,560
Property, Plant, & Equipment	300,000
Accumulated Depreciation	(75,000)
Total Assets	$400,060
Accounts Payable	$ 18,000
Income Tax Payable	75,260
Common Stock	100,000
Retained Earnings	206,800
Total Liabilities & Owners Equity	$400,060

The company expects a 30% income tax rate, and all quarterly taxes are paid in the first month of the following quarter.

Required

a. Prepare Bates & Hill's pro-forma income statement for the first quarter.
b. Prepare Bates & Hill's pro-forma balance sheet as of March 31.

PROBLEMS

5-31 Integrated sales budget, production budget, and purchases budget (LO 3) Simmons Enterprises is a boutique guitar manufacturer. The company produces both acoustic and electric guitars for rising and established professional musicians. Vanessa Aaron, the company's sales manager, prepared the following sales forecast for 2018. The forecasted sales prices include a 5% increase in the acoustic guitar price and a 10% increase in the electric guitar price, to cover anticipated increases in raw materials prices.

	Sales Price	1st Quarter	2nd Quarter	3rd Quarter	4th Quarter
Acoustic guitar sales	$1,250	200	280	300	325
Electric guitar sales	$2,400	400	350	320	360

Required

a. Prepare Simmons's sales budget for 2018.
b. On December 31, 2017, Simmons had 30 acoustic guitars in stock—fewer than the desired inventory level of 80 guitars, based on the following quarter's sales. The company has budgeted for sales of 240 acoustic guitars in the first quarter of 2019. Prepare the 2018 production budget for acoustic guitars.

c. Each acoustic guitar requires a maple neck blank, which Simmons purchases for $45. On December 31, 2017, Simmons had 400 neck blanks in inventory. Spoilage during the production process results in a standard quantity of 1.5 necks per acoustic guitar. Because of recent delivery problems, Simmons wants to maintain an ending inventory equal to 50% of the following quarter's production needs. Since the supplier has assured Simmons that the delivery issues will be resolved by the end of December, Simmons wants only 150 neck blanks in inventory on December 31, 2018. Prepare the purchases budget for neck blanks for 2018.

XLS **5-32 Integrated production budget, purchases budget, and direct labor budget (LO 3)** Aaron Furniture builds high-end hand-made dining tables. Attacus Simmons, the company's owner, has developed the following sales forecast for 2018.

	1st Quarter	2nd Quarter	3rd Quarter	4th Quarter
Forecasted sales (tables)	2,500	2,700	2,900	2,200

Because of the time needed to create each table, Aaron maintains an ending Finished Goods Inventory of 20% of the following quarter's budgeted sales. Aaron has been following this inventory policy for several years. The company ended 2017 with 500 tables on hand.

The standard cost card for a table is as follows:

	Standard Quantity	Standard Price	Total Standard Cost
American cherry wood	25 board feet	$5/board foot	$ 125
American cherry turning square (legs)	4 squares	$ 10/square	40
Direct labor	12 DLH	$ 18/DLH	216
Variable overhead	12 DLH	$ 60/DLH	720
Fixed overhead	12 DLH	$ 10/DLH	120
			$1,221

Required

a. Prepare Aaron's production budget for 2018. Assume that the desired ending inventory for 2018 is 600 tables.

b. Aaron maintains inventory of American cherry wood equal to 10% of the following quarter's production needs. On December 31, 2017, Aaron's physical inventory count showed 5,500 board feet of American cherry. Due to an anticipated price increase in 2019, managers want to have 10,000 board feet of American cherry wood in inventory on December 31, 2018. Prepare Aaron's 2018 direct materials purchases budget for American cherry wood.

c. Prepare Aaron's direct labor budget for 2018.

d. Assume that because of the skill level required to make the tables, Aaron cannot easily hire additional workers to handle peaks in demand. Consequently, the company maintains a steady workforce of 60 employees and guarantees each worker 500 hours per quarter. For any additional time required to complete the scheduled production, these same workers earn 1.5 times their normal hourly rate. Prepare Aaron's direct labor budget for 2018.

5-33 Integrated purchases and cash payments budget (LO 3, 4) R. Wilson Ascots, a retailer of collegiate neckwear, has completed the sales forecast for the coming year.

January	$37,000	July	$38,000
February	$28,000	August	$47,000
March	$32,000	September	$45,000
April	$40,000	October	$80,000
May	$56,000	November	$50,000
June	$31,000	December	$62,000

R. Wilson Ascots maintains an ending inventory level of 60% of the following month's cost of goods sold. The company's cost of goods sold is 40% of sales.

Required

a. Prepare R. Wilson Ascots' purchases budget for October. Use the following format:

	Budgeted sales dollars
×	Cost of goods sold percentage
=	Cost of goods sold
+	Ending inventory
=	Total inventory required
−	Beginning inventory
=	Budgeted purchases

b. Assuming that R. Wilson Ascots pays for 30% of its purchases in the month of purchase and the remaining 70% in the month following the purchase, prepare the company's cash payments budget for October.

5-34 Cash receipts budget with discounts (LO 4) Conradt Connectivity Company manufactures various electrical connectors. The company's sales budget for the first six months of the coming year is as follows. All sales are made on credit.

	January	February	March	April	May	June
Budgeted sales	$540,000	$475,000	$580,000	$625,000	$560,000	$600,000

Conradt is planning to change its credit policies in the coming year. For the first time in its history, the company is offering a 2% discount to customers who pay within 15 days of the invoice date. Based on industry trends, Conradt estimates that this change will result in 50% of credit sales being paid within the discount period; another 15% of sales, within the month of sale (but outside the discount period); and another 32% of sales, during the month after the sale. An estimated 3% of sales will be uncollectible.

Required

a. Prepare Conradt's cash receipts budget for the second quarter of the coming year.

b. How much cash will Conradt sacrifice in the second quarter by offering the new discount?

c. What do you think led Conradt to offer the new discount to customers?

5-35 Comprehensive Cash Budget (CMA adapted) (LO 4) GrowMaster Products, a rapidly growing distributor of home gardening equipment, is formulating its plans for the coming year. Carol Jones, the firm's marketing director, has completed the following sales forecast.

Month	Sales	Month	Sales
January	$ 900,000	July	$1,500,000
February	$1,000,000	August	$1,500,000
March	$ 900,000	September	$1,600,000
April	$1,150,000	October	$1,600,000
May	$1,250,000	November	$1,500,000
June	$1,400,000	December	$1,700,000

Phillip Smith, an accountant in the Planning and Budgeting Department, is responsible for preparing the cash flow projection. He has gathered the following information.

- All sales are made on credit.
- GrowMaster's excellent record in accounts receivable collection is expected to continue, with 60% of billings collected in the month after sale and the remaining 40% collected two months after the sale.

- Cost of goods sold, GrowMaster's largest expense, is estimated to equal 40% of sales dollars. Seventy percent of inventory is purchased one month prior to sale and 30% during the month of sale. For example, in April, 30% of April cost of goods sold is purchased and 70% of May cost of goods sold is purchased.
- All purchases are made on account. Historically, 75% of accounts payable have been paid during the month of purchase, and the remaining 25% in the month following purchase.
- Hourly wages and fringe benefits, estimated at 30% of the current month's sales, are paid in the month incurred.
- General and administrative expenses are projected to be $1,550,000 for the year. A breakdown of the expenses follows. All expenditures are paid monthly throughout the year, with the exception of property taxes, which are paid in four equal installments at the end of each quarter.

Salaries and fringe benefits	$ 324,000
Advertising	372,000
Property taxes	136,000
Insurance	192,000
Utilities	180,000
Depreciation	346,000
Total	$1,550,000

- Operating income for the first quarter of the coming year is projected to be $320,000. GrowMaster is subject to a 40% tax rate. The company pays 100% of its estimated taxes in the month following the end of each quarter.
- GrowMaster maintains a minimum cash balance of $50,000. If the cash balance is less than $50,000 at the end of the month, the company borrows against its 12% line of credit in order to maintain the balance. All borrowings are made at the beginning of the month, and all repayments are made at the end of the month (in increments of $1,000). Accrued interest is paid in full with each principal repayment. The projected cash balance on April 1 is $50,000.

Required

a. Prepare the cash receipts budget for the second quarter.
b. Prepare the purchases budget for the second quarter.
c. Prepare the cash payments budget for the second quarter.
d. Prepare the cash budget for the second quarter.

C&C SPORTS CONTINUING CASE

5-36 Preparing a sales budget and a production budget (LO 3) Throughout the chapter the budget preparation process was illustrated with detailed budgets for baseball pants. Using information in the text and Exhibits 5-5, 5-6 and 5-8, prepare a detailed sales budget and production budget for baseball jerseys for the fourth quarter. Budgeted sales of baseball jerseys in January 2018 is 12,000 jerseys.

CASES

5-37 Standards and behavior (CMA adapted) (LO 2) Miller Manufacturing makes several different products for the mountain biking enthusiast. In an extremely competitive market, Miller has assumed a strong position by stressing cost control. Several years ago, the company implemented a standard cost system based on practical standards that were considered fair and reasonable by both managers and line workers.

Last month, Miller hired Kate Daniel as its new controller. After a brief review of operations, Kate has decided to make some changes. She reviewed materials and labor standards, and believes they need to be revised. She has indicated to other managers that workers need to be better motivated and that tighter labor standards will provide that motivation.

Yesterday, Kate presented each departmental manager with a new annual budget based on the new standards. There was little discussion; however, one cost accountant mentioned that the new standards appeared to be quite a bit tighter than the old ones.

Required

a. Describe any negative behaviors that managers and line workers may exhibit as a result of the tightening of the standards.
b. Can Kate take any actions to mitigate the negative behaviors you have identified?
c. How can tight standards have a positive effect on employees' behavior?
d. Who should have participated in the setting of the new standards? How would their participation have improved the process?

5-38 Comprehensive master budget in a manufacturing setting (LO 3, 4, 5)

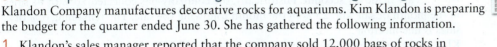

Klandon Company manufactures decorative rocks for aquariums. Kim Klandon is preparing the budget for the quarter ended June 30. She has gathered the following information.

1. Klandon's sales manager reported that the company sold 12,000 bags of rocks in March. He has developed the following sales forecast. The expected sales price is $10 per bag.

April	20,000 bags
May	50,000 bags
June	30,000 bags
July	25,000 bags
August	15,000 bags

2. Sales personnel receive a 5% commission on every bag of rocks sold. The following monthly fixed selling and administrative expenses are planned for the quarter. However, these amounts do not include the depreciation increase resulting from the budgeted equipment purchase in June (see part 7).

	Monthly Fixed Selling and Administrative Costs	Variable Cost/Unit
Depreciation	$10,000	
Salaries of sales personnel	25,000	$ .50
Advertising	1,000	
Management salaries	10,000	
Miscellaneous	500	
Bad debts		.50
Total costs	$46,500	$1.00

3. After experiencing difficulty in supplying customers in a timely fashion due to inventory shortages, the company established a policy requiring the ending Finished Goods Inventory to equal 20% of the following month's budgeted sales, in units. On March 31, 4,000 bags were on hand.
4. Five pounds of raw materials are required to fill each bag of finished rocks. The company wants to have raw materials on hand at the end of each month equal to 10% of the following month's production needs. On March 31, 13,000 pounds of materials were on hand.
5. The raw materials used in production cost $0.40 per pound. Half of the month's purchases is paid for in the month of purchase; the other half, in the following month. No discount is available.

6. The standard labor allowed for one bag of rocks is 15 minutes. The current direct labor rate is $10 per hour.
7. On June 1, the company plans to spend $48,000 to upgrade its office equipment that is fully depreciated. The new equipment is expected to have a five-year life, with no residual value.
8. The budgeted monthly variable and fixed overhead amounts are as follows. Variable overhead is based on the number of units produced. The fixed overhead budget is based on an annual production of 400,000 bags.

	Monthly Fixed Overhead	Variable Cost/Unit
Depreciation	$ 8,000	
Indirect materials	1,000	$0.05
Indirect labor	10,000	0.20
Utilities	20,000	0.10
Property taxes	5,000	
Maintenance	6,000	0.15
Total costs	$50,000	$0.50

9. All sales are made on account. Historically, the company has collected 70% of its sales in the month of sale and 25% in the month following the sale. The remaining 5% of sales is uncollectible.
10. Klandon must maintain a minimum cash balance of $30,000. An open line of credit at a local bank allows the company to borrow up to $175,000 per quarter in $1,000 increments.
11. All borrowing is done at the beginning of the month, and all repayments are made at the end of a month in $1,000 increments. Accrued interest is paid any time a principal payment is made. The interest rate is 12% per year.
12. A quarterly dividend of $49,000 will be declared and paid in April.
13. Income taxes payable for the first quarter will be paid on April 15. Klandon's tax rate is 30%.
14. The March 31 balance sheet is as follows:

	March 31
Cash	$ 40,000
Accounts receivable	30,000
Finished goods inventory	26,000
Raw materials inventory	5,200
Plant & equipment	200,000
Accumulated depreciation	(50,000)
Total assets	$ 251,200
Accounts payable	$ 12,000
Income taxes payable	50,000
Common stock	52,000
Retained earnings	137,200
Total liabilities and equities	$ 251,200

Required

a. Prepare all components of Klandon's master budget for the second quarter.
b. Prepare a pro-forma income statement for the second quarter.
c. Prepare a pro-forma balance sheet as of June 30.

5-39 Analyzing budget changes (LO 3, 4, 5) After preparing the budget for the second quarter based on the parameters in Case 5-38, Kim Klandon was not satisfied with the projected results and began to investigate the following alternatives. Each of the alternatives is independent of all others.

a. Reducing the price of a bag of rocks to $9.70 and spending an additional $1,000 per month on advertising are expected to increase sales volume by 10% each month. (March sales price and unit sales will not change. Continue using a $2.00 per unit applied overhead rate.)
b. Klandon can switch to a new supplier that has promised to provide raw materials at a price of $0.32 per pound. These rocks are a lesser quality than those provided by the current supplier. As a result, it will take 6 pounds of raw materials for each bag of finished rocks. Klandon will also need to maintain ending Raw Materials Inventory equal to 15% of the following month's production needs.
c. Klandon's current supplier has offered to provide a higher quality rock for $0.50 per pound. If the higher quality rock is used, only 4 pounds will be needed for each bag of finished rocks. As a result, Klandon will only need to maintain ending Raw Materials Inventory of 8% of the following month's production needs.
d. Klandon would like to reduce the age of accounts receivable to better manage the cash cycle. Instead of charging a fee for accounts that are paid in the second month after sale, she wants to offer a 2% cash discount. Since the company cannot afford to have total revenue decrease, Klandon plans to increase the sales price to $10.20 per bag. Customers who pay with cash at the time of purchase won't see any increase in their costs, but customers who purchase on account and pay later will. Klandon anticipates the following collection pattern if such a change is made:

Cash sales	75%
Credit:	
Month of sale	10%
Month after sale	10%
Uncollectible	5%
	100%

Required

Use your solution to 5-38 to answer the following questions for each of the alternatives:

- What budgets were impacted by the new information in the alternative?
- By how much did income change from the amount in the original budget of 5-38?
- What balance sheet accounts changed from the amounts in the original budget of 5-38? What caused the changes?
- What is your recommendation about pursuing the alternative? Why?

5-40 Comprehensive master budget in a retail setting (LO 3, 4, 5) Joseph A. Knab distributes men's suits in the Southwest. The following information was gathered to prepare the budget for the third quarter.

- Suits are budgeted to sell for an average price of $225. Unit sales are expected to be as follows:

June	4,000 suits
July	4,500 suits
August	4,700 suits
September	4,600 suits
October	4,600 suits

- Sales are made for cash and on credit. The following collection pattern is used to estimate monthly cash collections:

Cash sales	41%
Credit sales—month of sale	35
Credit sales—month after sale	20
Uncollectible	4
Total	100%

- The company tries to maintain an inventory of 25% of the following month's sales. The company expects to have 1,125 suits on hand on June 30. Knab pays an average of $146 per suit.
- The company pays for 70% of its purchases in the month of purchase and the remaining 30% in the month after purchase.
- The following monthly selling and administrative expenses are planned for the quarter, though advertising will have a one-time $30,000 increase in August.

	Fixed Overhead	Variable Cost/Unit
Depreciation	$ 9,000	
Rent	40,000	
Advertising	84,000	
Salaries	150,000	
Bad debts		$9.00

- On September 30, the company plans to purchase $45,000 of new office equipment. However, no additional depreciation will be recorded in the third quarter.
- Knab wants to maintain a minimum cash balance of $20,000. An open line of credit at a local bank allows the company to borrow up to $100,000 per quarter in $1,000 increments.
- All borrowing is done at the beginning of the month, and all repayments are made at the end of a month in $1,000 increments. Accrued interest is paid only when principal is repaid. The interest rate is 12% per year.
- Accrued expenses from the second quarter will be paid in July.
- Knab's tax rate is 30%.
- The June 30 balance sheet is budgeted as follows:

	June 30
Cash	$ 21,000
Accounts receivable	180,000
Inventory	164,250
Plant & equipment	540,000
Accumulated depreciation	(135,000)
Total assets	$ 770,250
Accounts payable	$ 175,000
Accrued expenses	75,000
Common stock	300,000
Retained earnings	220,250
Total liabilities and equities	$ 770,250

Required

a. Prepare all components of Knab's master budget for the third quarter.
b. Prepare a pro-forma income statement for the third quarter.
c. Prepare a pro-forma balance sheet as of September 30.

5-41 Ethics and budgeting (LO 1, 3, 4, 5) Faced with three young children who were always complaining "I'm bored," Ann Newton looked for an interesting after-school activity. Finding nothing available in the community, she decided to solve her problem by renting an old bakery and turning it into Kiddie Kitchen. Three afternoons a week, Ann, her children, and several other children gathered to learn the art of cooking. In less than five years, Ann's business grew to over 30 franchised kitchens located throughout the state. In 2005, she retired from active management of the company and sold the majority of her stock to Bernice Mayfield, who now runs the firm.

Today, Kiddie Kitchen has 100 franchised locations and 50 corporate locations up and down the East Coast. The company is organized into five regional territories, each run by a director who reports to the vice president of operations. In addition to the vice president of operations, executive management includes the CFO, the vice president of marketing, and the vice president of human resources. All executive personnel work at the corporate headquarters, now located in Raleigh, North Carolina. Each director maintains a regional office, complete with an administrative staff.

Shortly after taking over the company, Mayfield revamped the budgeting process, replacing a bottom-up process that had been in place since the early 1990s with a top-down process. Since the new budget process influences the bonus compensation a director can earn, directors have a great deal of interest in developing the budget. At the beginning of the budget cycle, regional directors receive corporate directives concerning the coming year's budget. These directives include projected growth in locations and revenue, salary increases, and allocated corporate expenses. Directors prepare three budgets—one for franchised locations, one for corporate locations, and one for administrative costs associated with the regional offices. These budgets are passed up to the corporate office for consolidation into the corporate budget.

Max Green is director of the southeast region. His approach to preparing the budget for the coming year budget is a typical example of budget preparation. He passed the corporate budget directives to his accountant, Henri Duvall, who prepared the first draft of the budget. When Green reviewed the draft, he did not like what he saw. Budgeted net income was too high—so high that his region would never meet the target. He asked Duvall to make some adjustments.

The corporate directive had projected a general price level increase of 2–4%. The range was intended to allow higher cost-of-living areas, such as Boston and New York, to budget higher levels of cost increases than lower cost-of-living areas. But even though Green's office was located in the lowest cost-of-living area in the country, he told Duvall to budget an across-the-board increase of 4%. Green knew that as long as he was within the directive's guidelines, the corporate office wouldn't question the increase.

Green also told Duvall that the region would open ten new stores during the coming year and that the budget should reflect enough start-up expenses to cover the new locations. Green knew that no region had ever opened more than seven stores in a single year. In fact, he thought he would be lucky to open five new stores in the coming year.

Since Green had a reputation for retaliating against employees who chose to ignore his requests, Duvall made the changes without questioning them. The result was a $250,000 reduction in budgeted net income.

Duvall, a certified management accountant, had a wife and three children, and could not afford to lose his job and his generous benefit package. Besides, his wife was in line to become owner of one of the new franchised stores in the coming year.

Required

a. Why would Green care about the level of budgeted net income?
b. What do you think Mayfield's reaction would be if she learned of Green's actions?
c. What does Duvall have to gain from his actions? Does he have anything to lose?
d. Refer to the IMA's Statement of Ethical Professional Practice in Exhibit 1-8 (pages 24–25). What responsibilities does Duvall have in this situation? Did he violate the Statement? If so, how?

ANALYTICS PROBLEM

5-42 Preparing a Sales Budget (LO 3) (Data set from "Café Data," Concetta A. DePaolo and David F. Robinson, *Journal of Statistics Education* Volume 19, Number 1 (2011) used by permission of the authors.)

The Peppy Paladin Café is an experiential learning lab at a state university in the Midwest. After the food service operator closed a dining location in the business building, students developed the concept to provide limited food and beverage options for students, faculty, and staff. Having just completed its first semester of operations, the café is operated by student volunteers who receive internship credit for running the café.

The café staff collected sales statistics from the most recent semester of operations (January–April), and it is now time to prepare the sales budget for next semester.

Required

a. Use the AVERAGE formula in Excel to determine the average number of sodas and the average number of cups of coffee sold in a day.

b. Use the STDEV.P formula in Excel to determine the variation in daily sales of sodas and cups of coffee. Which product has the highest standard deviation? What does that imply?

c. Plot the daily sales of each beverage. What trends do you identify? How does this information help you estimate daily sales better than average sales for the entire period?

d. Calculate the average number of sodas and cups of coffee sold each weekday. Does there appear to be a pattern of sales depending on the day of the week? Knowing what you know about class schedules, how might you explain your findings? (Hint: Use the AVERAGEIF or the COUNTIF and AVERAGE formulas to determine the total sales by day of the week.)

e. Develop a sales estimation function for sodas and coffee, based on the day of the week, using the SLOPE and INTERCEPT formulas. Use the RSQ formula to determine how much of the sales variation is explained by the day of the week.

f. Develop a sales estimation function for sodas and coffee, based on the daily high temperature, using the SLOPE and INTERCEPT formulas. Use the RSQ formula to determine how much of the sales variation is explained by the maximum daily temperature.

g. Which of the two sales estimation functions do you think would be the better one to use in preparing the sales budget? Why?

h. Sodas and coffee aren't as perishable as are certain food items like sandwiches. Discuss how incorrect estimates of sales of perishable items can affect a business.

The Excel data files for answering this problem can be found in WileyPLUS.

ENDNOTES

1. Richard Horton, Paul Searles, and Kimberly Stone, *Integrated Performance Management: Plan. Budget. Forecast.* Deloitte LLP, 2014, https://www2.deloitte.com/content/dam/Deloitte/au/Documents/technology/deloitte-au-tech-integrated-performance-management-plan-budget-forecast-0614.pdf (accessed March 1, 2016).
2. Don Durfee, "Alternative Budgeting," *CFO*, June 2006, 28.
3. You can learn more about the EPA's drinking water standards at http://www.epa.gov/your-drinking-water/table-regulated-drinking-water-contaminants.
4. While many companies refer to themselves as "ISO 9000 certified," the actual standard used for certification is ISO9001:2000. Furthermore, ISO certification is issued by a national certification board rather than the ISO. In the United States, that board is the ANSI-ASQ National Accreditation Board (http://www.anab.org/).
5. For simplicity, we will assume that purchases and usage of indirect materials are equal, so all changes in the Raw Materials Inventory balance are due to purchases and usage of direct materials.
6. Such short-term financing arrangements are frequently referred to as a "line of credit."

© jsnyderdesign/iStockphoto

PERFORMANCE EVALUATION: VARIANCE ANALYSIS

UNITS	LEARNING OBJECTIVES
UNIT 6.1 Flexible Budgets: A Performance Evaluation Tool	**LO 1:** Prepare a flexible budget and explain its use in evaluating performance.
UNIT 6.2 Variance Analysis: Direct Materials	**LO 2:** Calculate the direct materials price and quantity variances. **LO 3:** Identify potential causes of the direct materials price and quantity variances.
UNIT 6.3 Variance Analysis: Direct Labor	**LO 4:** Calculate the direct labor rate and efficiency variances. **LO 5:** Identify potential causes of the direct labor rate and efficiency variances.
UNIT 6.4 Variance Analysis: Overhead	**LO 6:** Calculate the variable overhead spending and efficiency variances. **LO 7:** Calculate the fixed overhead spending variance. **LO 8:** Identify potential causes of the variable overhead spending and efficiency variances and the fixed overhead spending variance.

© DNY59/iStockphoto

Business Decision and Context

Throughout 2017, George Douglas, president of C&C Sports, wondered how the year's operations would unfold. Now the picture was becoming clearer. Based on C&C's budget, the sales staff had worked hard, through increased advertising and personal contacts, to increase the sales of award jackets. They were ecstatic to learn they had beaten their sales goal of 18,000 jackets.

At a management meeting near the end of the year, George congratulated **Jonathan Smith, vice president for marketing**. "Jonathan, your team really stepped up to the plate and delivered those extra sales that we needed. Unfortunately, we didn't realize the increase in income that we had expected. In fact, net income looks like it will be $144,800 lower than budgeted, and the fourth quarter will account for more than $30,000 of the shortfall. Chad, what do you think happened?" "You know I've been less than enthusiastic about increased production throughout the year," replied **Chad Davis, vice president for operations**. "It's not that I thought it was a bad strategy. We definitely need to increase sales. However, to meet the increased production I had to hire new workers to make jackets, and those workers took much longer than the standard 1.5 hours per jacket. Then we've had to work overtime recently to meet customers' delivery dates. The extra hours, for which workers were paid a 50% premium over their regular hourly rate, caused us to exceed our direct labor budget."

"Even with the additional costs, I expected that increased sales of the 'high dollar' award jackets would have boosted net income," George added. "Before we start trying to make adjustments to operations or sales, let me provide each of you with some performance reports that will highlight where we missed our projections,"

> "Before we start trying to make adjustments to operations or sales, let me provide each of you with some performance reports that will highlight where we missed our projections."

offered **Claire Elliot, vice president for finance and administration**. "Then you can gather data from your teams to explain the differences. I'm sure that will offer us some insight for how we want to move forward in 2018."

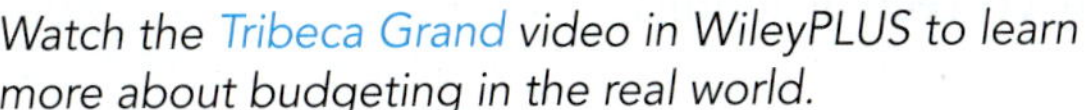

Watch the Tribeca Grand video in WileyPLUS to learn more about budgeting in the real world.

SUPPLY CHAIN KEY PLAYERS

- END CUSTOMER
- UNIVERSAL SPORTS EXCHANGE
- **C&C SPORTS**
  - **President** George Douglas
  - **Vice President for Finance and Administration** Claire Elliot
  - **Vice President for Marketing** Jonathan Smith
  - **Vice President for Operations** Chad Davis
- DURABLE ZIPPER COMPANY
- BRADLEY TEXTILE MILLS
- CENTEX YARNS
- NEFF FIBER MANUFACTURING
- BRUIN POLYMERS, INC.

UNIT 6.1

Flexible Budgets: A Performance Evaluation Tool

GUIDED UNIT PREPARATION

Answering the following questions while you read this unit will guide your understanding of the key concepts found in this unit. The questions are linked to the learning objectives presented at the beginning of the chapter.

LO 1

1. What is a static budget? When is it prepared?
2. What is a favorable variance? An unfavorable variance?
3. What is management by exception?
4. What is a flexible budget? How does it differ from a static budget?
5. Describe the two components of the static budget variance.

In Unit 1.1 we discussed the four functions of managers—planning, controlling, evaluating, and decision making. In Chapter 5 we saw how managers use managerial accounting information to plan and develop a master budget. In this unit, we will see how managers use the budgeting concepts presented in Chapter 5 to control and evaluate a company's operations.

Static Budgets

C&C Sports' managers spent hours developing the master budget you studied in Chapter 5. The master budget is an example of a **static budget**, one developed for a single level of expected output. In C&C Sports' case, that output level was 70,000 pairs of baseball pants, 25,000 baseball jerseys, and 9,000 award jackets for the fourth quarter of 2017. Throughout the quarter, these managers used the budget to plan and run the company's operations. Claire Elliot, vice president for finance and administration, evaluated the company's performance against the budget using information provided in a performance report such as the one shown in Exhibit 6-1, which compares the company's actual results for the quarter with its budgeted results.

While this performance report and the remaining examples in this chapter focus on the fourth quarter of 2017, you should not conclude that managers only concern themselves with controlling and evaluating performance every three months. Most companies monitor their performance more frequently, whether on a monthly, weekly, daily, or even hourly basis. Waiting until the end of the quarter to evaluate performance is waiting too long to take appropriate and timely corrective actions.

	Actual Results	Static Budget	Variance
Sales	$2,457,525	$2,335,000	$122,525 F
Cost of goods sold	1,724,150	1,582,757	141,393 U
Gross margin	733,375	752,243	(18,868) U
Selling and administrative expenses	385,139	360,753	24,386 U
Operating income	348,236	391,490	(43,254) U
Interest expense	2,256	1,880	376 U
Income before taxes	345,980	389,610	(43,630) U
Income taxes	103,794	116,883	(13,089) F
Net income	$ 242,186	$ 272,727	($ 30,541) U

EXHIBIT 6-1

C&C Sports' performance report for the quarter ended December 31, 2017.

Variances

Notice that the performance report in Exhibit 6-1 shows a "variance" column. A **variance** is the difference between actual results and budgeted results, and is calculated by subtracting the budgeted amount from the actual amount. When the budget being used is a static budget, the difference between actual results and budgeted results is referred to as a **static budget variance**. Note that the variances in Exhibit 6-1 are labeled as "favorable" (F) or "unfavorable" (U). A label of "favorable" or "unfavorable" doesn't depend on whether the variance is negative or positive. Rather, the labels indicate the effect on operating income. A **favorable variance** is a variance that increases operating income relative to the budgeted amount. An **unfavorable variance** is a variance that decreases operating income relative to the budgeted amount. These labels are not meant to suggest that a variance is "good" or "bad." Instead, variances direct managers' attention to items they need to investigate.

WATCH OUT!

Don't forget to identify a variance as favorable (F) or unfavorable (U). Just reporting an amount doesn't indicate the impact of the variance on operating income.

Management by Exception

What do managers do when a variance is reported? As part of their control function, they investigate the cause of the variance so that corrective action can be taken. Not all variances warrant investigation, however. Rather, managers use a method called **management by exception** that focuses only on those variances they consider important. In deciding which variances to investigate, managers consider their **materiality**, a measure of how large a variance is. A material variance is one that is large enough to make a difference in the outcome of a decision.[1] Materiality can be measured in terms of absolute dollars or relative percentages. A company will set a threshold, in either dollars or percentages, above which all variances will be investigated. For instance, C&C Sports only investigates variances that are more than $1,500 above or below the expected amount.

Does that mean managers should ignore a relatively small variance, say 1.4% higher than the budgeted amount? Don't be too quick to say yes because of its apparently small size. In a performance report like the one shown in Exhibit 6-1, small variances could be the result of combining several accounts with large offsetting variances. Managers need to wait until more detail is available before deciding which variances to investigate.

What about the favorable variances? You might be tempted to think that managers should worry only about unfavorable variances, since those have a negative impact on income. However, a favorable variance, just like an unfavorable variance, represents a difference between expectations and reality. Investigating the favorable variances may help managers plan better for the future.

Another factor managers use in deciding whether to investigate a variance is the existence of a trend. If a particular account has been running a variance for several periods, a manager might decide to investigate the variance even if it does not appear to be a material one. Another trend to consider is the size of the variance over time. If a variance has been increasing over several periods, a manager may decide to investigate it, even if it does not exceed the established threshold. This approach to investigating variances should help managers identify and correct problems before they become too large.

A final factor that influences managers' decisions to investigate a variance is the level of control they have over the expense. If a manager cannot control how the company incurs the expense, variance analysis will identify little that can be done to reduce the expense. For example, managers do not set property tax rates, so they would not be likely to investigate a variance in property tax expense.

THINK ABOUT IT 6.1

Recall from Unit 5.3 that managers use standards to develop their budgets. Which type of standard will likely result in larger variances—ideal or practical? Why?

Flexible Budgets

What does the performance report in Exhibit 6-1 tell about C&C Sports' performance in the fourth quarter? At the most basic level, sales revenue and expenses were both greater than budgeted, but operating income was less than budgeted. However, if C&C's managers are going to effectively control and evaluate operations, they need to know *why* these variances occurred. Was revenue higher than planned because more units were sold or because the company raised its prices? Was the cost of goods sold higher than planned because more units were sold or because more material than expected had to be scrapped—or perhaps because the cost of raw materials increased unexpectedly? The performance report in Exhibit 6-1 does not answer these questions. The only thing C&C's managers can be sure about is that tax expense was lower than expected because taxable income was lower than expected. To get a better handle on operations, the managers decide to focus on those items that affect operating income only.

Let's consider what C&C actually sold to achieve the reported operating results: 69,500 baseball pants, 26,000 baseball jerseys, and 10,000 award jackets. How does that compare to the budgeted sales level for each product? The company sold fewer pants, more jerseys, and more award jackets than budgeted (see Exhibit 5-5). Would you expect the direct materials cost for 10,000 jackets to be the same as for 9,000 jackets? Of course not. Does it make sense, then, to compare actual results based on one sales volume to a budget based on a different sales volume? The answer is no. Remember the old adage about comparing apples to oranges.

To generate a comparison that is useful for control and evaluation, we need to create a **flexible budget**—a budget based on the actual sales volume achieved during the period. A flexible budget shows the revenues and expenses the company should have incurred based on the actual sales level during the period. In other words, it is the static budget that managers would have prepared at the beginning of the period *if they had known the actual sales level the company*

REALITY CHECK—*Who's being flexible?*

© Graffizone/iStockphoto

In today's ever-changing business environment, organizations must be able to change plans in response to unexpected events and circumstances. Those unexpected events can quickly make a static budget irrelevant. To provide a better budgeting tool for planning purposes, and to facilitate their response to the unexpected, both for-profit and not-for-profit organizations are turning to flexible budgets. In fact, certain flexible budgeting approaches, such as frequent re-forecasting and rolling forecasts, are now considered best practices in many industries.

To provide a better budgeting tool for planning purposes, and to facilitate their response to the unexpected, both for-profit and not-for-profit organizations are turning to flexible budgets.

The **Zoological Society of San Diego**, operator of the world-famous San Diego Zoo, is one organization that relies on flexible budgeting. Every month, the Society revises its budget in light of the past month's events. What kind of events warrant this effort? Wildfires, for one. An annual occurrence in California, fires reduce zoo attendance, and thus zoo revenues. To compensate for the decreased revenue, the Society reduces future expenses and seeks to develop new revenue sources. Without a flexible approach to budgeting, the Society would not have taken these corrective actions in time.

Bacardi Limited, a privately-held producer of distilled spirits, has moved flexible budgeting into the nonfinancial realm. The company has created several sustainability key performance indicators, which it analyzes using a flexible budget approach.

Sources: Adaptive Planning, "Best Practices for Budgeting, Forecasting and Reporting," http://www.tawfikcpa.com/assets/documents/ap_best_practices_budgeting.pdf (accessed July 7, 2016); Paul Barr, "Flexing Your Budget," *Modern Healthcare*, September 12, 2005, 24; Jon Bartley, Frank Buckless, Y. S. Al Chen, Stephen Harvey, Scott Showalter, and Gilroy Zuckerman, "Flexible Budgeting Meets Sustainability at Bacardi Limited," *Strategic Finance*, December 2012, 29–34; Paula Brock, "Come Together: How to Marry Strategic and Financial Plans for a More Flexible, Accurate Budget," *California CPA*, November 2005, 14.

would achieve. Because the flexible budget is based on actual sales volume, all differences between the flexible budget and actual performance must result from operations rather than from differences in sales volume. Of course, since the flexible budget is based on actual sales volume, it cannot be prepared until *after* the end of the period—unlike the static budget, which is prepared *before* the period begins.

Although flexible budgets are used mostly as a tool for control and evaluation, they also can be used in planning. In that case, managers prepare a flexible budget for several levels of output within the relevant range. After evaluating the expected results, they choose one level on which to base the static budget for the coming period.

For the fourth quarter, managers will prepare the flexible budget using the actual sales volume of 69,500 baseball pants, 26,000 baseball jerseys, and 10,000 award jackets. The flexible budget amount is calculated by multiplying the actual number of units sold by the standard cost per unit. For instance, the flexible budget for direct materials is calculated as

$$(69{,}500 \text{ pants} \times \$4.47) + (26{,}000 \text{ jerseys} \times \$6.85) + (10{,}000 \text{ jackets} \times \$44.72) = \$935{,}965$$

EXHIBIT 6-2

C&C Sports' flexible budget for the quarter ended December 31, 2017.

Sales revenue		$2,468,800
Direct materials	$935,965	
Direct labor	360,720	
Variable manufacturing overhead	198,396	
Fixed manufacturing overhead	160,447	
Cost of goods sold		1,655,528
Gross margin		813,272
Commissions	123,440	
Bad debt expense	60,940	
Shipping costs	42,200	
Office depreciation	3,903	
Advertising	40,000	
Administrative salaries	96,250	
Utilities	1,750	
Total selling and administrative expenses		368,483
Operating income		$ 444,789

This process is repeated for each variable cost. The sales revenue for the flexible budget is calculated in a similar manner using the actual sales volume and the budgeted sales price per unit. Notice that the flexible budget amounts for fixed costs are the same as the static budget, since fixed costs do not vary with volume. Exhibit 6-2 shows C&C's flexible budget for the fourth quarter.

Using Flexible Budgets to Analyze Static Budget Variances

We've discussed how the static budget variance is not very helpful in controlling and evaluating operational performance. However, if we divide the static budget variance into its components, managers will have information that will be useful in their assessment of operations. Exhibit 6-3 shows how to separate the static budget variance into its two components: the flexible budget variance and the sales volume variance. The **flexible budget variance** is the difference between the actual results and the flexible budget. The **sales volume variance** is the difference between the flexible budget and the static budget.

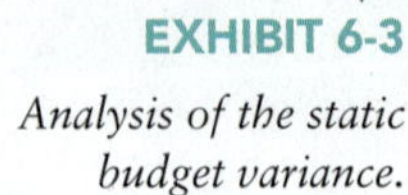

EXHIBIT 6-3

Analysis of the static budget variance.

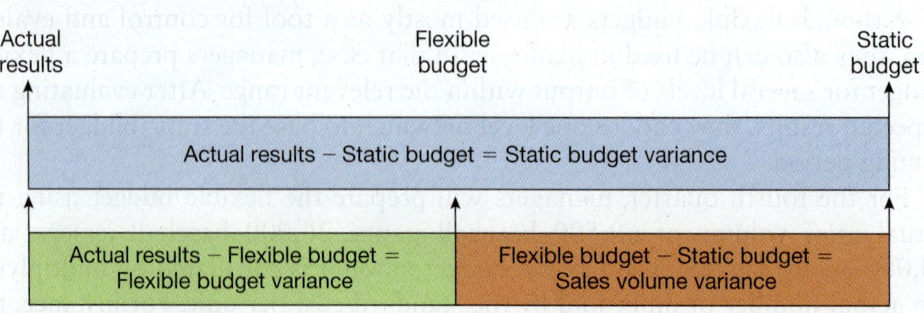

Why is it important to separate the flexible budget variance from the sales volume variance? Remember that we are using the flexible budget as a tool for controlling and evaluating performance. So we need to be able to assign responsibility for actions and results to those employees who have the ability to influence the outcome. Assigning responsibility is not the same as assigning blame. Instead, it means consulting those employees who can explain certain outcomes. The flexible budget variance reflects how efficiently the company operated in producing a given level of sales. It is influenced most heavily by the actions of operations personnel. The sales volume variance, on the other hand, reflects a different volume and/or mix of products than that specified in the static budget. This variance is influenced by the actions of sales and marketing personnel. Unless we separate the two variances, we have no way of evaluating those two areas of the organization.

A Revised Performance Report

The performance report shown in Exhibit 6-1 shows only the static budget variance, which we now know is not the information C&C's managers need. Exhibit 6-4 shows a revised performance report that includes C&C's flexible budget based on the fourth quarter's actual sales volume. Notice that the level of detail has increased to include individual components of cost of goods sold and selling and administrative expenses reported in the original performance report. The report now compares both the actual results to the flexible budget and the flexible budget to the static budget. In doing so, it allows managers to separate the static budget variance into a flexible budget variance and a sales volume variance.

	Actual Results	Flexible Budget Variance	Flexible Budget	Sales Volume Variance	Static Budget
Sales revenue	$2,457,525	($11,275) U	$2,468,800	$133,800 F	$2,335,000
Direct materials	952,117	16,152 U	935,965	49,335 U	886,630
Direct labor	367,910	7,190 U	360,720	15,120 U	345,600
Variable manufacturing overhead	228,546	30,150 U	198,396	8,316 U	190,080
Fixed manufacturing overhead	175,577	15,130 U	160,447	0	160,447
Cost of goods sold	1,724,150	68,622 U	1,655,528	72,771 U	1,582,757
Gross margin	733,375	(79,897) U	813,272	61,029 F	752,243
Commissions	123,440	0	123,440	6,690 U	116,750
Bad debt expense	60,380	(560) F	60,940	440 U	60,500
Shipping costs	44,310	2,110 U	42,200	600 U	41,600
Office depreciation	3,903	0	3,903	0	3,903
Advertising	55,000	15,000 U	40,000	0	40,000
Administrative salaries	96,250	0	96,250	0	96,250
Utilities	1,856	106 U	1,750	0	1,750
Total selling and administrative expenses	385,139	16,656 U	368,483	7,730 U	360,753
Operating income	$ 348,236	($96,553) U	$ 444,789	$ 53,299 F	$ 391,490

EXHIBIT 6-4 *C&C Sports' flexible budget performance report for the quarter ended December 31, 2017.*

Computing Sales Volume Variances

Let's look at the information in the new performance report, starting with the sales volume variances. Recall that a sales volume variance results only when actual sales volume differs from budgeted sales volume. Notice that on the sales revenue line, the sales volume variance is $133,800 favorable. Apparently, C&C sales staff sold more of at least one product, but we can't tell which one it was from the current report.

Exhibit 6-5 shows the details of C&C's sales volume variances. The report reveals an unfavorable sales volume variance for pants and favorable sales volume variances for jerseys and jackets. That means that fewer pants were sold than budgeted and more jerseys and jackets were sold than budgeted. Let's look at how the sales budget variance for pants was calculated. The easy way to calculate the variance is to subtract the static budget sales revenue from the flexible budget sales revenue: $834,000 − $840,000 = $6,000 U. Another way to calculate the variance is to multiply the difference between the actual sales volume and budgeted sales volume by the budgeted sales price: (69,500 pants actually sold − 70,000 pants budgeted to be sold) × $12 = $6,000 U. Notice that the difference in units sold is multiplied by the budgeted price. That's because we are comparing two *budgets*—one at the actual sales volume and one at the budgeted sales volume.

	Flexible Budget			Static Budget			Sales Volume Variance
	Budgeted Price (A)	Actual Sales Volume (B)	Flexible Budget (A × B)	Budgeted Price (C)	Budgeted Sales Volume (D)	Static Budget (C × D)	(Flexible Budget − Static Budget)
Pants	$ 12.00	69,500	$ 834,000	$ 12.00	70,000	$ 840,000	($ 6,000) U
Jerseys	14.80	26,000	384,800	14.80	25,000	370,000	14,800 F
Award jackets	125.00	10,000	1,250,000	125.00	9,000	1,125,000	125,000 F
Total sales revenue			$2,468,800			$2,335,000	$133,800 F

EXHIBIT 6-5 *C&C Sports' sales volume variances by product line.*

What about the sales volume variances for expenses? Exhibit 6-6 breaks down the sales volume variance by the variable production costs of each of C&C's three products. Notice that in each variance calculation, the sales volumes are multiplied by the same budgeted unit cost. Again, that's because we are comparing two *budgets*—one at the actual sales volume and one at the budgeted sales volume. You should notice a pattern: All the variances for pants are favorable, but all the variances for jerseys and award jackets are unfavorable. C&C sold fewer pants than budgeted, so those costs are lower than expected. The company sold more jerseys and award jackets than budgeted, so those costs are higher than expected. Should managers be disappointed that more jerseys were sold than budgeted? Of course not. Remember, an unfavorable sales volume variance simply indicates the effect of a higher than expected sales volume on operating income. Before managers decide if a variance is good or bad, they must consider the cause of the variance.

Return to Exhibit 6-4 and you will see that the other variable costs on the income statement follow the same pattern as the variable production costs.

	Flexible Budget			Static Budget			Sales Volume Variance
	Budgeted Cost[a] (A)	Actual Sales Volume (B)	Flexible Budget (A × B)	Budgeted Cost[a] (C)	Budgeted Sales Volume (D)	Static Budget (C × D)	(Flexible Budget – Static Budget)
Direct Materials							
Pants	$ 4.470	69,500	$310,665	$ 4.470	70,000	$312,900	($ 2,235) F
Jerseys	6.850	26,000	178,100	6.850	25,000	171,250	6,850 U
Award jackets	44.720	10,000	447,200	44.720	9,000	402,480	44,720 U
Total direct materials cost			$935,965			$886,630	$49,335 U
Direct Labor							
Pants	$ 2.400	69,500	$166,800	$ 2.400	70,000	$168,000	($ 1,200) F
Jerseys	1.920	26,000	49,920	1.920	25,000	48,000	1,920 U
Award jackets	14.400	10,000	144,000	14.400	9,000	129,600	14,400 U
Total direct labor cost			$360,720			$345,600	$15,120 U
Variable Overhead (55% × direct labor cost)							
Pants	$ 1.320	69,500	$ 91,740	$ 1.320	70,000	$ 92,400	($ 660) F
Jerseys	1.056	26,000	27,456	1.056	25,000	26,400	1,056 U
Award jackets	7.920	10,000	79,200	7.920	9,000	71,280	7,920 U
Total variable overhead cost			$198,396			$190,080	$ 8,316 U

[a]See Exhibit 5-16b.

EXHIBIT 6-6 *C&C Sports' variable cost of goods sold—sales volume variances.*

The sales volume variances for bad debt expense, shipping, and commissions are all unfavorable because total sales volume and sales dollars—the cost drivers of those expenses—are higher in the flexible budget than in the static budget.

The last thing to notice about the sales volume variances is the variances for fixed costs. Recall that fixed costs do not vary in total with activity levels. Therefore, the static budget and the flexible budget amounts should be the same; the sales volume variance for a fixed cost is always $0.

Computing Flexible Budget Variances

While the sales volume variance helps managers understand the effect of changes in sales volume on expected revenues and expenses, the variance doesn't help them understand the effects of price changes or operational efficiency on actual results. To gather this information, we need to look at the flexible budget variance. Recall that the flexible budget variance is the difference between actual results and the flexible budget. Exhibit 6-7 on the next page shows the sales revenue flexible budget variance for each product line. Since the actual sales revenue and flexible budget sales revenue are both based on the same actual sales volume, the variance must be a result of the difference between the actual sales price and the budgeted sales price. Therefore, we call this flexible budget variance the **sales price variance**.

	Actual Results			Flexible Budget			Sales Price Variance
	Actual Price (A)	Actual Sales Volume (B)	Actual Results (A × B)	Budgeted Price (A)	Actual Sales Volume (B)	Flexible Budget (A × B)	(Actual Results − Flexible Budget)
Pants	$ 11.95	69,500	$ 830,525	$ 12.00	69,500	$ 834,000	($ 3,475) U
Jerseys	$ 14.50	26,000	377,000	$ 14.80	26,000	384,800	(7,800) U
Award jackets	$125.00	10,000	1,250,000	$125.00	10,000	1,250,000	0
Total sales revenue			$2,457,525			$2,468,800	($11,275) U

EXHIBIT 6-7 *C&C Sports' sales price variances by product line.*

C&C Sports had implemented a strategy that reduced the sales price for pants and jerseys with the expectation of generating a higher sales volume. Since the actual sales price for both products was lower than budgeted, the sales price variance for both products is unfavorable. There is no sales price variance for award jackets because the actual sales price was the same as the budgeted sales price.

What about the flexible budget variances for the expenses reported in Exhibit 6-4? Let's look first at the selling and administrative expenses. All of these amounts represent a departure from the standard or budgeted cost. For example, the company had to incur $15,000 more advertising than budgeted to achieve the actual level of sales. The vice president for marketing will be responsible for explaining why such a large increase was necessary. All the other selling and administrative items can be explained in a similar fashion.

Explaining the flexible budget variances for the production costs isn't as easy. That is because production costs have two components—the quantity of inputs used to make a product and the price paid to acquire those inputs (you should recall setting standards for both price and quantity of inputs in Chapter 5). Let's consider the $16,152 unfavorable flexible budget variance for materials, shown on Exhibit 6-4. Is this variance a result of higher materials prices for rush purchases in small quantities, or is it a result of unusual waste? Similarly, is the direct labor flexible budget variance a result of poor worker productivity, or is it a result of overtime required to finish a rush order? We can't tell. To find out, managers must break down the flexible budget variance into several additional variances. In the remaining units of this chapter we will explore those additional variances in greater detail.

Using Variances to Evaluate the Sales Strategy

C&C Sports implemented a strategy that reduced the sales price for pants and jerseys with the expectation of generating a higher sales volume. To see if the company's sales strategy was beneficial overall, we need to look at the sales price variance as well as the sales volume variance (see Exhibits 6-5 and 6-7). In the case of pants, the $0.05 price reduction between the actual sales price and the budgeted sales price multiplied by the 69,500 actual pants sales volume yields a $3,475 unfavorable sales price variance. Combining that with the $6,000 unfavorable pants sales volume variance yields a $9,475 unfavorable static budget variance. The strategy appears to have backfired. One thing we can't tell from this performance report, however, is how many more pants sales might have been lost had the price *not* been lowered.

The jerseys section of the report tells a different story. The $14,800 favorable sales volume variance more than made up for the $7,800 unfavorable sales price variance, yielding a $7,000 favorable static budget variance. The $0.30 per unit price reduction appears to have generated a desired increase in sales volume.

Through the sales force's efforts, C&C was able to maintain the budgeted sales price for award jackets while selling more jackets than planned. The jackets' $125,000 favorable sales volume variance accounts for the majority of the overall $122,525 favorable static budget variance for sales revenue (see Exhibit 6-1).

It's not enough to look only at the sales-related variances to evaluate the sales strategy. Other variances that the sales strategy influenced need to be included as well. For example, the additional $15,000 in advertising was needed to boost sales, and that unfavorable variance should be included when evaluating the sales strategy. Likewise, commissions and bad debt expense variances need to be included. Therefore, the overall impact of the sales strategy on operating income is $100,395 favorable, calculated as follows:

Pants variances		
Sales volume variance	$ 6,000 U	
Sales price variance	3,475 U	
Total pants variances		$ 9,475 U
Jersey variances		
Sales volume variance	$ 14,800 F	
Sales price variance	7,800 U	
Total jersey variances		7,000 F
Jacket variances		
Sales volume variance	$125,000 F	
Sales price variance	0	
Total jacket variances		125,000 F
Commissions variance		6,690 U
Bad debt expense sales volume variance[2]		440 U
Advertising variance		15,000 U
Total variance		$100,395 F

By understanding the use of a flexible budget to help evaluate performance, managers can begin to investigate operating results using the sales volume variance and the flexible budget variance. Using a performance report such as the one shown in Exhibit 6-4, managers can see how much of the difference between actual results and budgeted expectations is due to changes in sales volume and how much is due to the operation of the manufacturing facility. In the coming units, we will examine the flexible budget variance in greater detail to determine how changes in input prices and operational efficiency affect production results.

UNIT 6.1 REVIEW

KEY TERMS

Favorable variance p. 295
Flexible budget p. 296
Flexible budget variance p. 298
Management by exception p. 295
Materiality p. 295
Sales price variance p. 301
Sales volume variance p. 298
Static budget p. 294
Static budget variance p. 295
Unfavorable variance p. 295
Variance p. 295

PRACTICE QUESTIONS

1. LO 1 When actual unit sales differ from budgeted unit sales, the static budget variance is adequate information for managers to understand the variance in sales revenue. True or False?

2. LO 1 Which of the following variances is *least* likely to be investigated by a manager following the management by exception principle?

   a. A $2,000 unfavorable variance in postage, when postage for the period was budgeted to be $5,000

   b. An unfavorable variance that has increased by 25% in each of the last five months

   c. A favorable variance in property taxes levied by the city

   d. A 20% favorable variance in sales salaries

3. LO 1 A flexible budget reports budgeted revenues and costs that should have resulted from the actual level of sales achieved during the period. True or False?

4. LO 1 The difference between the flexible budget and the static budget is known as the

   a. flexible budget variance.

   b. sales volume variance

   c. static budget variance.

   d. direct materials price variance.

UNIT 6.1 PRACTICE EXERCISE

When Carol Lindquist was planning Janovi's operations for this year, she prepared the following budgeted income statement at various levels of sales. The CEO decided that the company's best alternative was a budget based on a sales volume of 120,000 units.

	100,000	120,000	140,000
Sales	$1,500,000	$1,800,000	$2,100,000
Variable expenses			
Direct material	275,000	330,000	385,000
Direct labor	160,000	192,000	224,000
Overhead	360,000	432,000	504,000
Shipping	80,000	96,000	112,000
Total variable expenses	875,000	1,050,000	1,225,000
Contribution margin	625,000	750,000	875,000
Fixed expenses			
Overhead	26,000	26,000	26,000
Rent	15,000	15,000	15,000
Insurance	10,000	10,000	10,000
Advertising	7,000	7,000	7,000
Total fixed expenses	58,000	58,000	58,000
Operating income	$ 567,000	$ 692,000	$ 817,000

The company's income statement, reflecting actual sales of 129,000 units, follows.

Sales	$1,935,000
Variable expenses	
Direct material	352,600
Direct labor	216,400
Overhead	465,800
Shipping	110,500
Total variable expenses	1,145,300
Contribution margin	789,700
Fixed expenses	
Overhead	24,000
Rent	15,000
Insurance	10,100
Advertising	9,000
Total fixed expenses	58,100
Operating income	$ 731,600

Required

Prepare a performance report for Janovi showing both the flexible budget and sales volume variances.

SELECTED UNIT 6.1 ANSWERS

Think About It 6.1

Ideal standards will result in the largest variances. By definition, these standards will be almost impossible to meet. Practical standards, on the other hand, are achievable with moderate effort. Therefore, actual results should be closer to the practical standard than to the ideal standard.

Practice Questions

1. False
2. C
3. True
4. B

Unit 6.1 Practice Exercise

Since the CEO decided the company's best alternative was a budget based on 120,000 units, the static budget is based on 120,000 units. Actual results were 129,000 units, so the flexible budget is to be calculated at the 129,000 unit level. To prepare the flexible budget, calculate the budgeted sales price per unit and the budgeted variable costs per unit using the static budget and then multiply each of the unit amounts by 129,000 units. Fixed costs will be the same amount for both the static budget and flexible budget.

	Actual Results	Flexible Budget Variance	Flexible Budget	Sales Volume Variance	Static Budget
Units	129,000	0	129,000	9,000 F	120,000
Sales[a]	$1,935,000	$ 0	$1,935,000	$135,000 F	$1,800,000
Variable Costs					
Direct material[b]	352,600	($ 2,150 F)	354,750	$ 24,750 U	330,000
Direct labor[c]	216,400	10,000 U	206,400	14,400 U	192,000
Overhead[d]	465,800	1,400 U	464,400	32,400 U	432,000
Shipping[e]	110,500	7,300 U	103,200	7,200 U	96,000
Total variable costs	1,145,300	16,550 U	1,128,750	78,750 U	1,050,000
Contribution margin	789,700	(16,550 U)	806,250	56,250 F	750,000
Fixed Costs					
Overhead	24,000	(2,000 F)	26,000		26,000
Rent	15,000		15,000		15,000
Insurance	10,100	100 U	10,000		10,000
Advertising	9,000	2,000 U	7,000		7,000
Total fixed costs	58,100	100 U	58,000		58,000
Operating income	$ 731,600	($16,650 U)	$ 748,250	$ 56,250 F	$ 692,000

[a]Sales price = $\frac{\$1,800,000}{120,000 \text{ units}}$ = $15/unit; Flexible budget = $15 × 129,000 units = $1,935,000.

[b]Direct material = $\frac{\$330,000}{120,000 \text{ units}}$ = $2.75/unit; Flexible budget = $2.75 × 129,000 units = $354,750.

[c]Direct labor = $\frac{\$192,000}{120,000 \text{ units}}$ = $1.60/unit; Flexible budget sales revenue = $1.60 × 129,000 units = $206,400.

[d]Variable overhead = $\frac{\$432,000}{120,000 \text{ units}}$ = $3.60/unit; Flexible budget sales revenue = $3.60 × 129,000 units = $464,400.

[e]Shipping = $\frac{\$96,000}{120,000 \text{ units}}$ = $0.80/unit; Flexible budget sales revenue = $0.80 × 129,000 units = $103,200.

UNIT 6.2

Variance Analysis: Direct Materials

GUIDED UNIT PREPARATION

Answering the following questions while you read this unit will guide your understanding of the key concepts found in this unit. The questions are linked to the learning objectives presented at the beginning of the chapter.

LO 2

1. What is a direct materials price variance?
2. What is a direct materials quantity variance?
3. Define the standard quantity allowed.
4. In your own words, explain the standard quantity of tires allowed for eight bicycles. Why does your answer not depend on the number of bicycles expected to be produced?

LO 3

5. Give two reasons why actual prices might differ from standard prices, resulting in a direct materials price variance.
6. Give two reasons why actual materials usage might differ from standard materials usage, resulting in a direct materials quantity variance.

Managers have a variety of tools to use in controlling and evaluating operations. As we saw in Unit 6.1, one of those tools is variance analysis—comparing actual results against budgeted results. Unit 6.1 showed how to separate the static budget variance into its two components: the flexible budget variance and the sales volume variance. But managers of manufacturing companies need more information than what these variances provide.

In a manufacturing environment, actual product costs can differ from the flexible budget because of the price paid for inputs (direct materials, direct labor, and overhead), the quantity of inputs used for production, or a combination of both. Therefore, to evaluate the individual effects of price and quantity on product costs, we need to separate the flexible budget variance into its two components, the price variance and the quantity variance, as Exhibit 6-8 shows. Notice how the static budget breaks down into the flexible budget and sales volume variances, and how the flexible budget variance breaks down into the price and quantity variances. It is also important for you to notice that the difference between actual sales volume and budgeted sales volume has nothing to do with the price and quantity variances. Why? Because that difference is captured in the sales volume variance. The price and quantity variances explain the flexible budget variance, and the flexible budget is prepared at the actual level of production. So never explain a price or quantity variance by referring to actual sales volume being different from what was budgeted.

The price and quantity variances for the variable cost inputs (direct materials, direct labor, and variable overhead) are computed in a similar manner, although

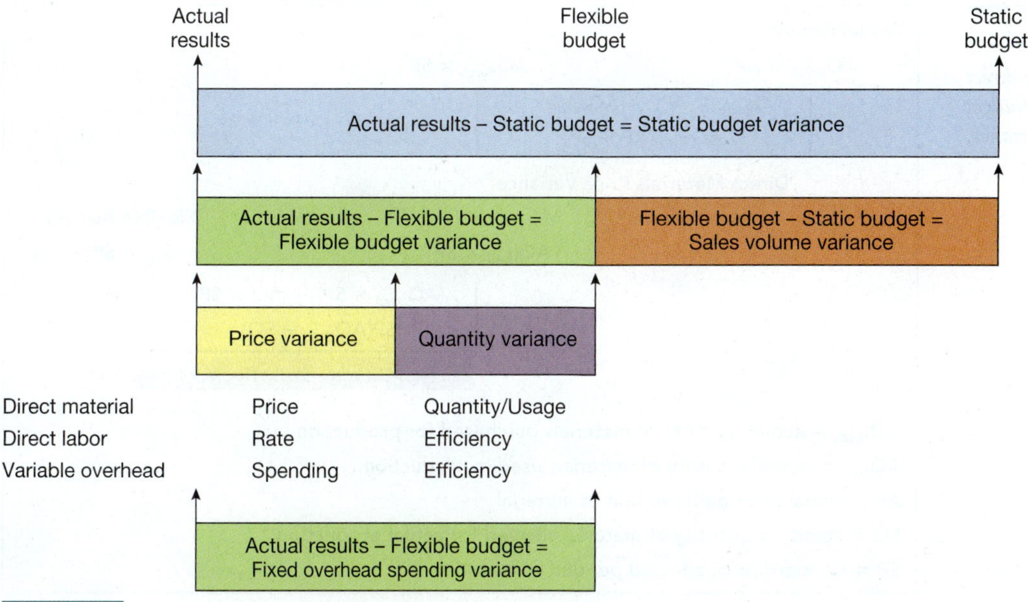

EXHIBIT 6-8 *Analyzing the flexible budget variance.*

as you will learn in this and following units, the names for each are different. Recall that fixed overhead does not vary with volume; therefore, the only reason for a fixed overhead flexible budget variance is due to the price paid for the fixed overhead item. This means that the fixed overhead flexible budget variance is not broken down into a price and quantity variance.

Since the causes for the variances differ from one input to the next, we will discuss these variances separately in the next three units. In this unit, we will explore the variances related to direct materials.

Analyzing the Direct Materials Variances

Let's think for a minute about why actual direct materials costs might differ from flexible budget costs. First, the prices the company actually paid for materials may have differed from the standard prices the company expected to pay. Second, the company may have used quantities of materials that differed from the standard amounts allowed for one unit of product. To investigate these two possibilities, we need to separate the flexible budget variance for direct materials into two components: a direct materials price variance and a direct materials quantity variance (see Exhibit 6-9).

Direct Materials Price Variance

The **direct materials price variance** is that part of the direct materials flexible budget variance that results when actual prices differ from standard prices. This variance is calculated using only three amounts: the actual quantity of direct materials purchased, the actual price paid for the direct materials, and the standard price for the direct materials. As Exhibit 6-9 on the next page shows, the calculation of the direct materials price variance can be reduced to an algebraic equation in which AQ_{Purch} represents the actual quantity of materials purchased, AP represents the actual price paid per unit of material, and SP represents the standard price allowed per unit of material:

$$\text{Direct materials price variance} = AQ_{Purch} \times (AP - SP)$$

EXHIBIT 6-9

Analyzing the direct materials flexible budget variance.

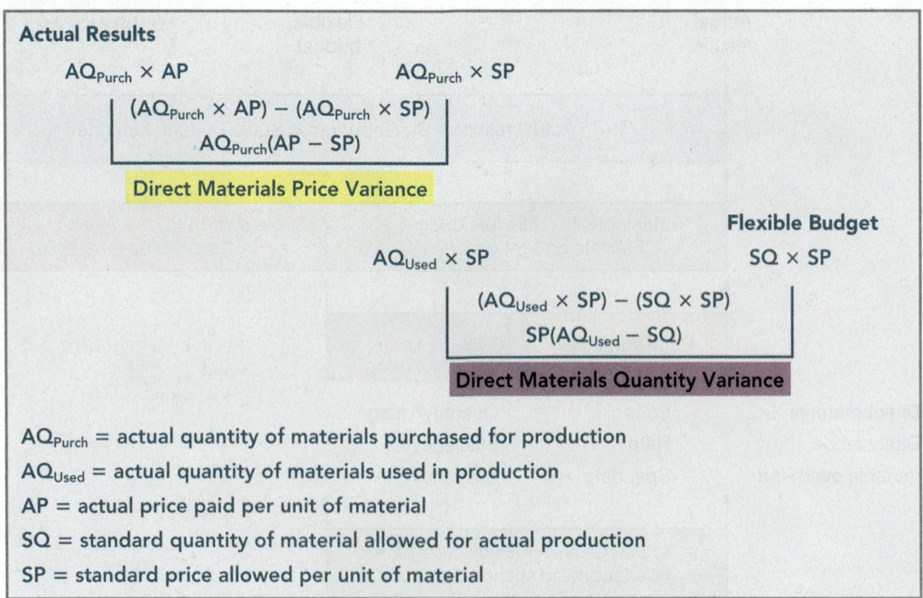

Let's look at the direct materials price variance for the lining C&C Sports uses in award jackets. The standard price for the lining is $2 per yard. However, during the fourth quarter the inventory manager purchased it at a price of $1.75 per yard. Just by comparing the standard and actual prices, we can tell there will be a direct materials price variance, since the two prices differ by $0.25. We can also tell from the prices that the variance will be favorable, since the actual price paid was lower than the standard price and operating income will be higher than budgeted. The only other amount needed to calculate the variance is the quantity of material purchased.

WATCH OUT!

Sometimes you may know only the total dollar amount of direct materials purchased rather than the actual unit price. That isn't a problem; you can still calculate the price variance using just the total purchases amount. You can also calculate the average actual price by dividing the total purchases amount by the actual number of units purchased.

During the fourth quarter, C&C purchased 25,000 yards of lining, so the direct materials price variance is $6,250 F. Exhibit 6-10 shows the calculation of the variance using the tabular format. The variance can also be calculated as 25,000 yards purchased × ($1.75 − $2.00) = $6,250 F. While we have calculated the direct materials price variance for only one type of direct material, C&C would do similar calculations for each type of direct material.

Theoretically, the company could also calculate a total direct materials price variance by adding the individual variances together. But that total would not give managers much help in controlling materials prices, since they wouldn't know which specific materials to focus on.

EXHIBIT 6-10

C&C Sports' direct materials variances for lining.

Actual Results

$AQ_{Purch} \times AP$
25,000 yards × $1.75 per yard
$43,750

$AQ_{Purch} \times SP$
25,000 yards × $2 per yard
$50,000

$43,750 − $50,000

Direct Materials Price Variance $6,250 F

Flexible Budget

$AQ_{Used} \times SP$
24,000 yards × $2 per yard
$48,000

$SQ \times SP$
(10,000 jackets × 2 yards per jacket) × $2 per yard
20,000 yards × $2 per yard
$40,000

$48,000 − $40,000

Direct Materials Quantity Variance $8,000 U

REALITY CHECK—*Going nuts over almonds*

Justin Gold had a need—healthy, vegetarian, protein-filled snacks. When he couldn't find what he wanted, he started making his own nut butter in his kitchen. And it wasn't just plain nut butter; he experimented and created tasty flavor combinations such as chocolate hazelnut, honey almond, and maple almond. Justin's has come a long way from the founder's kitchen. In addition to the original nut butters, the company's product line now includes peanut butter cups and other snacks.

Recently, Justin's faced some challenges in its almond supply. Drought conditions in California, home to 80% of the world's almond market, reduced the size of the almond harvest. As a result, the price for almonds doubled in a two-year period to a high of $4 per pound in 2014. Justin's responded by increasing its wholesale prices by 15%.

> The price for almonds doubled in a two-year period to a high of $4 per pound in 2014.

What did this increase in almond prices mean for Justin's direct material standards? It's likely that early price increases created an unfavorable direct materials price variance. But as almond prices continued to increase and the increases appeared to be more than a temporary spike, Justin's probably adjusted its price standards to reflect market conditions.

By January 2016, almond prices had begun to fall and were down about 25%. This means that Justin's will need to re-evaluate its almond price standards again.

Sources: Justins.com; Claire Groden, "Here's Some Good News for Almond Fans," *Fortune*, January 29, 2016, http://fortune.com/2016/01/29/heres-some-good-news-for-almond-fans/, (accessed March 8, 2016); Leslie Josephs, "Nut-Butter Firm's Founder Adjusts to Growth," *The Wall Street Journal*, June 25, 2015.

Direct Materials Quantity Variance

The **direct materials quantity variance** is the part of the direct materials flexible budget variance that is caused by using more or less material than the standard quantity allowed for actual production. Notice from Exhibit 6-9 that the direct materials quantity variance is calculated using only three amounts: the actual quantity of direct materials used, the standard quantity of direct materials allowed for actual production, and the standard price. As Exhibit 6-9 shows, the calculation of the direct materials quantity variance can be reduced to an algebraic equation in which SP represents the standard price allowed per unit of material, AQ_{Used} represents the actual quantity of direct materials used, and SQ represents the standard quantity of material allowed for actual production:

$$\text{Direct materials quantity variance} = SP \times (AQ_{Used} - SQ)$$

Let's look at C&C Sports' use of lining in award jackets. The standard quantity for lining is 2 yards per jacket, which means that a flexible budget for 10,000 jackets actually produced would allow for 20,000 yards of lining (10,000 jackets × 2 yards per jacket). During the fourth quarter, however, C&C used 24,000 yards of lining to make those 10,000 award jackets. Since

WATCH OUT!

Don't forget that the direct materials price variance is based on the actual quantity of direct materials *purchased*, while the direct materials quantity variance is based on the actual quantity of direct materials *used*. Only when the quantity purchased equals the quantity used will the two variances be based on the same quantity.

C&C used more lining than the standard allowed, which will increase costs and reduce operating income, the variance is unfavorable. Exhibit 6-10 shows the variance calculation using the tabular format. The variance can also be calculated as $2 per yard × (24,000 yards − 20,000 yards) = $8,000 U.

Notice that Exhibit 6-10 does not show a total direct materials variance. Because the quantity of lining purchased differs from the quantity of lining used, there is no common quantity on which to base the total variance. However, if the quantity purchased equals the quantity used, a total direct materials variance can be calculated.

THINK ABOUT IT 6.2

Determining the standard quantity to use in direct materials variance calculations sometimes causes students difficulty. Why is the standard quantity based on actual rather than budgeted production?

Interpreting Direct Materials Variances

You now know how to calculate the direct materials price and quantity variances. But that is not where the manager's work ends. The manager's job is to investigate the cause of the variances, so that corrective action can be taken. Let's explore some possible reasons for these variances, as listed in Exhibit 6-11.

EXHIBIT 6-11

Possible explanations for direct materials variances.

Favorable Price Variance	• purchased in bulk and received quantity discounts • purchased lower-quality goods than specified in standard at a cheaper price • received discount from new supplier to get our business
Unfavorable Price Variance	• purchased smaller-than-normal quantity and lost bulk purchase discount • purchased higher-quality goods than specified in standard at a higher price • price increases from suppliers • rush order with overnight delivery
Favorable Quantity Variance	• use of higher-quality goods than specified in standard reduced waste • highly trained workers generated a scrap rate that is lower than standard
Unfavorable Quantity Variance	• use of lower-quality goods than specified in standard caused higher scrap rate • machine problems ruined some output • new workers unfamiliar with process generated extra scrap • poor supervision resulted in additional scrap • employee theft

Explaining Direct Materials Price Variances

In most organizations, managers must work with the purchasing department to develop an explanation for the direct materials price variance, since the purchasing department is responsible for procuring direct materials that meet product specifications. Because the purchasing agents are the ones to negotiate the purchase price, they are typically held accountable for the direct materials price variance.

Recall that direct materials standards specify a particular quality of material. Therefore, the purchasing agent must buy materials that are of the same quality as those the product designers specified. The quality and price of materials are generally related: lower-quality materials carry a lower price. Purchasing a different quality of material from that specified in the standard will likely result in a price variance.

The size of the purchase also affects the purchase price. Many vendors give additional discounts for materials that are purchased in large quantities. The vendor may also charge a premium for small purchases and rush orders. A new vendor may offer a reduced price to generate business. Finally, vendors change their prices as a result of changes in the market. None of these occurrences would likely impact the quality of purchased materials; however, they would affect the price.

In purchasing the jacket lining, C&C's inventory manager, Bradley Austin, dealt with a new vendor that offered a lower price. The sales representative assured him that the materials were of the same quality as those he had purchased from other vendors. However, the production manager, Mary Townsley, isn't convinced that is the case.

Explaining Direct Materials Quantity Variances

While the purchasing manager is accountable for the direct materials price variance, the production manager is responsible for the direct materials quantity variance. Through adequate supervision and training of workers, the production manager can influence how much material is used during production.

A major factor in the amount of material used in production is the quality of the material. If material of a lower quality than specified in the standard is used in production, there is a good chance that it will not run through the production process as smoothly as planned. The result is usually higher levels of scrap and defective products than allowed by the standard. Alternatively, using a higher-grade material than specified in the standard may result in lower levels of scrap and defects. Thus, the direct materials price and quantity variances may be related. Global food manufacturer General Mills experienced this interaction when a purchasing manager bought cartons that were thinner than the standard called for in an effort to reduce costs. The thinner cartons caused major production problems, increasing overall production costs.[3]

The skills level of the production workers can also affect the quantity of materials used. New, untrained workers are likely to make more mistakes than workers who have been adequately trained, resulting in more scrap and product defects. Conversely, highly skilled workers may generate lower defect rates than the "average" person who was used as the basis for creating the standard allowances for scrap and defects.

You may be wondering why we base the direct materials price variance on the quantity of materials *purchased*, but the direct materials quantity variance on the quantity of materials *used*. The reason is that managers need to isolate

WATCH OUT!

Don't explain a price variance by saying "It cost more/less," or a quantity variance by saying "Workers used less/more materials than they should have." The identification of a variance as "favorable" or "unfavorable" provides that information. Instead, identify the possible *cause* for the difference in price paid or in quantity used.

REALITY CHECK—*A variance to remember*

© DNY59/iStockphoto

The whole vat of chocolate had to be thrown out, generating a likely unfavorable direct materials quantity variance.

Just when you think you've heard it all, someone comes up with an even more incredible story. Anyone who investigated the direct materials quantity variances at **Debelis Corp.** in Kenosha, Wisconsin, in August 2006 will never forget this one. On August 18, 2006, a worker at Debelis fell chest-deep into a vat of melted chocolate as he was trying to move some stuck chocolate. It took employees more than two hours and some extra cocoa butter to extract him from the thick mixture.

What does this story have to do with variances? First, the whole vat of chocolate had to be thrown out, generating a likely unfavorable direct materials quantity variance. And the cocoa butter that workers used to thin the chocolate so they could rescue the trapped worker certainly was never considered in setting the quantity standards.

The company's direct labor efficiency variances may also have been affected. The rescue, which took more than two hours, likely distracted workers, leading to an unfavorable direct labor efficiency variance.

Sources: Marie Rohde, "A Heap of Truffles: Chocolate Traps Worker," *Milwaukee Journal Sentinel*, August 12, 2006; "Worker Trapped in Vat of Chocolate for 2 Hours," MSNBC.com, August 18, 2006, available online at http://www.msnbc.msn.com/id/14412952 (accessed August 11, 2007).

variances and take corrective action as soon as possible. Suppose a purchasing manager purchased direct materials in January, but those materials weren't used until March. If she waited until March to calculate the price variance, she might lose the chance to take corrective action.

It turns out that the jacket lining purchased from the new vendor was of lower quality than material purchased in the past. It shredded more frequently during cutting, so larger seams had to be allowed. In addition, workers who had never made jackets before were employed to meet the high demand, as we will see in the next section. Those inexperienced workers made more mistakes, causing more material to be scrapped.

THINK ABOUT IT 6.3

Suppose you are investigating direct materials variances. You find that the direct materials price variance is unfavorable but the direct materials quantity variance is favorable. Assuming that the quantity purchased and used were equal, what circumstance could explain both variances?

UNIT 6.2 REVIEW

KEY TERMS

Direct materials price variance p. 307

Direct materials quantity variance p. 309

PRACTICE QUESTIONS

1. LO 2 If the actual cost of direct materials is $5.00 per unit while the standard cost of direct materials is $4.50 per unit,
   a. the direct materials quantity variance will be favorable.
   b. the direct materials quantity variance will be unfavorable.
   c. the direct materials price variance will be favorable.
   d. the direct materials price variance will be unfavorable.
2. LO 2 Stoner Concrete Creations purchased 5,000 pounds of ready-mix concrete during March at a price of $0.75 per pound. The company used 4,500 pounds of the mix during the month. The standard price for the concrete mix was $0.80 per pound. Stoner's direct materials price variance for March is
   a. $250 F.
   b. $250 U.
   c. $225 F.
   d. $225 U.
3. LO 2 Johnson Corporation used 20,000 pounds of material to make 18,000 bottles of Glime. The standard allows 1.2 pounds of material at a cost of $3.00 per pound for each bottle of Glime. Johnson's direct materials quantity variance is
   a. $4,800 F.
   b. $4,800 U.
   c. $6,000 F.
   d. $6,000 U.
4. LO 3 Direct materials price variances are usually the responsibility of the
   a. production manager.
   b. sales manager.
   c. purchasing manager.
   d. cost accounting manager.
5. LO 3 Max Deane purchased a lower grade of material than specified by the standard. A likely result of this purchase will be
   a. an unfavorable direct materials price variance.
   b. a favorable direct materials price variance.
   c. an unfavorable direct materials quantity variance.
   d. both b and c.
6. LO 3 Which of the following would be a feasible explanation for a favorable direct materials quantity variance?
   a. Purchased materials in bulk and received a quantity discount
   b. Purchased higher quality materials than specified in the standard
   c. A machine that was out of alignment caused several units of product to be scrapped
   d. New workers were hired without adequate training

UNIT 6.2 PRACTICE EXERCISE

The Beakins Company manufactures advertising banners using weather-resistant nylon whose standard price is $5 per yard. Each banner includes a standard quantity of 4 yards of nylon. During the month of March, Beakins used 5,000 yards of nylon to produce 1,200 banners. That month, the company purchased 6,000 yards of nylon at a total cost of $28,500.

Required

1. Based on the standard quantity, how many yards of nylon should Beakins have used in March?
2. Calculate the direct materials price variance for March.
3. Calculate the direct materials quantity variance for March.
4. What might have contributed to the two variances for March?

SELECTED UNIT 6.2 ANSWERS

Think About It 6.2

Direct materials variances are components of the flexible budget variance. The flexible budget is based on actual production/sales, not on static budget production/sales. Remembering that you are trying to explain a flexible budget number should make it easier to understand that the standard quantity must be based on the actual units produced/sold.

Think About It 6.3

Purchasing a higher quality of material than allowed in the standard would result in an unfavorable price variance. However, those higher quality materials may have run through the production process more efficiently, resulting in a lower rate of waste than allowed in the standard and a favorable quantity variance.

Practice Questions

1. D
2. A
3. A
4. C
5. D
6. B

Unit 6.2 Practice Exercise

1. 1,200 banners × 4 yards per banner = 4,800 yards
2. $1,500 F

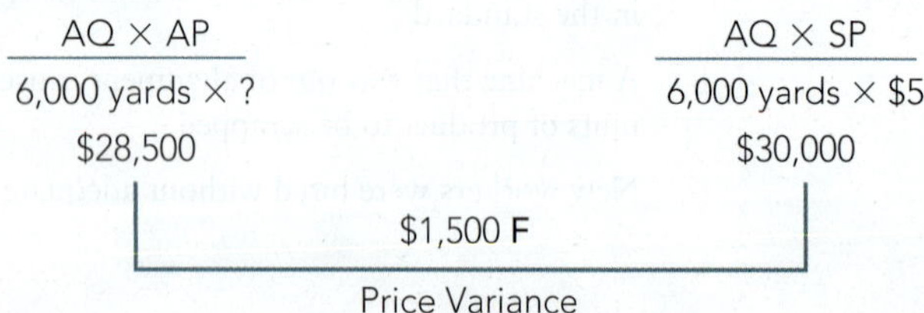

Notice that you do not need the actual price per yard to calculate the variance in this case.

3. $1,000 U

AQ × SP
5,000 yards × $5
$25,000

SQ × SP
(1,200 banners × 4 yards) × $5
$24,000

$1,000 U
Quantity Variance

4. The purchasing manager may have purchased a cheaper, lower quality nylon that led to production problems and a higher scrap rate.

UNIT 6.3

Variance Analysis: Direct Labor

GUIDED UNIT PREPARATION

Answering the following questions while you read this unit will guide your understanding of the key concepts found in this unit. The questions are linked to the learning objectives presented at the beginning of the chapter.

LO 4

1. What is a direct labor rate variance?
2. What is a direct labor efficiency variance?

LO 5

3. Give two reasons why actual labor rates might differ from standard labor rates, resulting in a direct labor rate variance.
4. Give two reasons why actual labor hours might differ from standard labor hours, resulting in a direct labor efficiency variance.

Direct labor has been decreasing as a percentage of total product costs as automation has taken over more of the factory floor. That doesn't mean that labor isn't an important component of total cost, however. Many factors can cause labor costs to deviate from the budgeted amounts. In this unit, you will learn how to calculate and interpret direct labor variances.

Analyzing the Direct Labor Variances

The direct labor flexible budget variance, much like the direct materials flexible budget variance, can be divided into two components. Why do we need to examine those two components separately? As with direct materials, part of the variance is due to what the company pays for labor and part of it is due to how efficiently employees work. To control labor costs, we need to understand which factor causes the variance.

Let's think for a minute about why actual direct labor costs might differ from the flexible budget amounts. First, although a company may set a standard wage rate, market forces sometimes require a change in that rate. Second, employees do not always operate at the desired efficiency level; sometimes they work slower, sometimes faster. These two possibilities require us to separate the flexible budget variance for direct labor into two components: a direct labor rate variance and a direct labor efficiency variance (see Exhibit 6-12 on the next page).

WATCH OUT!

Don't let the new names of these variances confuse you. The mechanics of their calculation are the same as with the direct materials price and quantity variances.

Direct Labor Rate Variance

The **direct labor rate variance** is the part of the direct labor flexible budget variance that arises when the actual wage rate differs from the standard wage rate. The direct labor rate variance is calculated using only three amounts: the actual

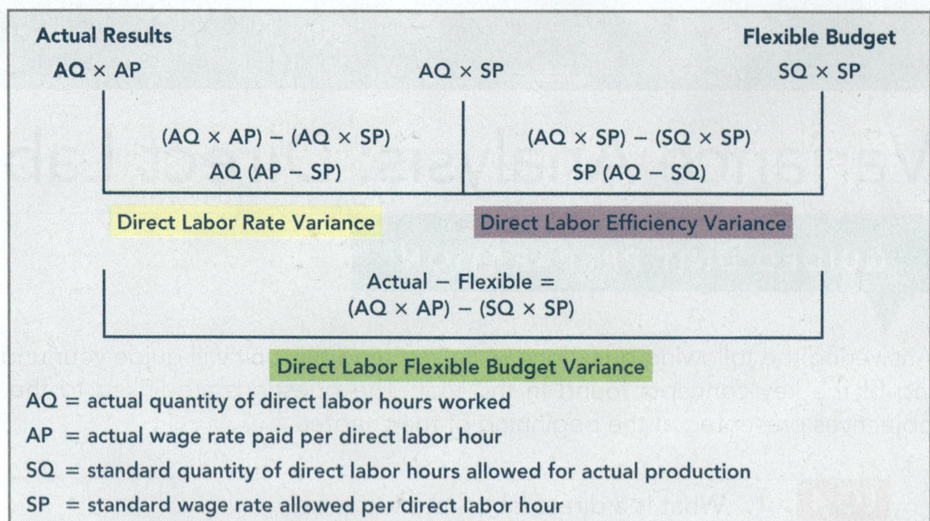

EXHIBIT 6-12 *Analyzing the direct labor flexible budget variance.*

quantity of direct labor hours worked, the actual wage rate paid, and the standard wage rate. As Exhibit 6-12 shows, the calculation of the direct labor rate variance can be reduced to an algebraic equation, in which AQ represents the actual quantity of direct labor hours worked to generate total production, AP represents the actual wage rate paid per direct labor hour, and SP represents the standard wage rate allowed per direct labor hour:

$$\text{Direct labor rate variance} = \text{AQ} \times (\text{AP} - \text{SP})$$

Consider C&C Sports' direct labor rate variance for award jackets. C&C's standard wage rate is $9.60 per direct labor hour. However, the company had to incur overtime in the fourth quarter because of the high levels of jackets and pants that had to be produced. As a result, the actual direct labor cost was $160,050. During the quarter, C&C used 16,500 direct labor hours to produce award jackets, so the average direct labor wage rate was $9.70 [$160,050 ÷ 16,500 direct labor hours], and the direct labor rate variance was $1,650 U [$160,050 − (16,500 DLH × $9.60/DLH)]. Exhibit 6-13 shows the calculation of this variance using the tabular format. The variance can also be calculated as 16,500 hours worked × ($9.70 − $9.60) = $1,650 U.

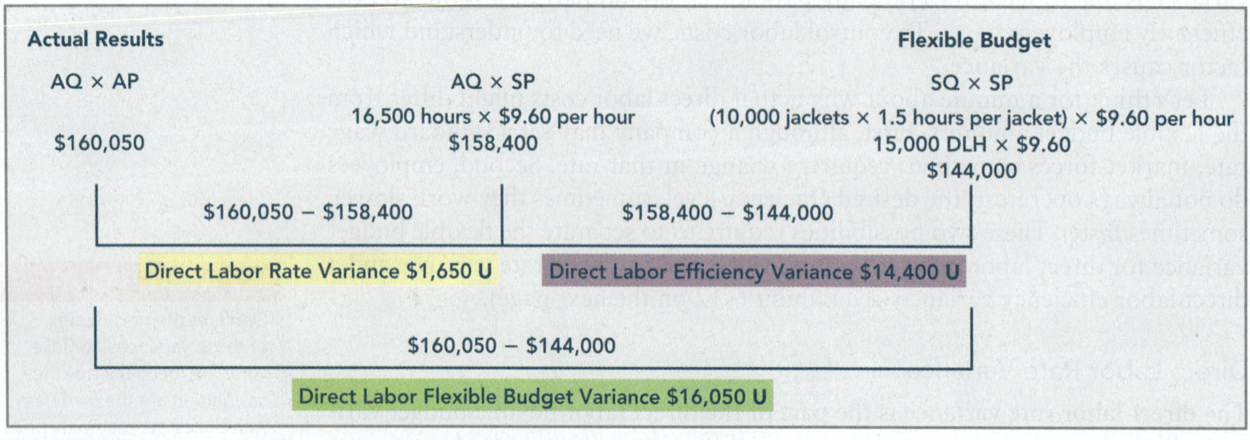

EXHIBIT 6-13 *C&C Sports' direct labor variances for jackets.*

We have illustrated the calculation of the direct labor rate variance only for award jackets. C&C would do similar calculations for the direct labor used in each of its products. By adding the individual products' variances together, the managers could also calculate a total direct labor rate variance.

All of C&C Sports' direct laborers earn the same standard wage rate. That is not true of all organizations. In many companies, different classes of workers earn different standard wage rates based on their skills. Furthermore, workers in the same skills class may earn different wage rates based on seniority or shift differentials. In those cases, managers may calculate separate labor rate variances for each class of employee. However, for the sake of simplicity, some companies calculate an average standard wage rate across worker classes for use in variance analysis.

WATCH OUT!

Sometimes you may know only the total payroll rather than the actual wage rates. That isn't a problem; you can still calculate the direct labor rate variance using the total payroll amount. You can also calculate the average actual rate by dividing the total payroll amount by the actual number of direct labor hours worked.

Direct Labor Efficiency Variance

The **direct labor efficiency variance** is that part of the direct labor flexible budget variance that is caused by using more or less direct labor than the standard allows. Notice in Exhibit 6-12 that the direct labor efficiency variance is calculated using only three amounts: the actual quantity of direct labor hours used, the standard quantity of direct labor hours allowed for actual production, and the standard wage rate. As Exhibit 6-12 shows, the calculation of the direct labor efficiency variance can be reduced to an algebraic equation in which SP represents the standard price allowed per direct labor hour, AQ represents the actual quantity of direct labor hours used in actual production, and SQ represents the standard quantity of direct labor hours allowed for actual production.

$$\text{Direct labor efficiency variance} = SP \times (AQ - SQ)$$

Let's look at C&C Sports' use of direct labor in making award jackets. The direct labor quantity standard for jackets allows 1.5 direct labor hours per jacket. Thus, a flexible budget for the 10,000 jackets actually produced would allow for 15,000 direct labor hours (10,000 jackets × 1.5 DLH per jacket). However, during the fourth quarter C&C used 16,500 direct labor hours to make the 10,000 award jackets. That is, C&C used 1,500 more direct labor hours than the standard allowed. At a standard price of $9.60 per direct labor hour, that means the direct labor efficiency variance is $14,400 (1,500 direct labor hours × $9.60 per direct labor hour). Since C&C used more direct labor hours than the standard allowed, which will reduce operating income, the variance is unfavorable. Exhibit 6-13 shows the calculation of this variance in tabular format. It can also be determined using the equation $9.60 per DLH × (16,500 DLH − 15,000 DLH) = $14,400 U.

WATCH OUT!

Remember that the standard number of direct labor hours allowed is always based on the actual number of finished units produced—that is, actual units produced × standard direct labor hours per unit.

Interpreting Direct Labor Variances

You now know how to calculate the direct labor rate and efficiency variances. But as you learned with direct materials variances, calculating the variance is only part of the process. Variances have little meaning until their causes are identified, so that corrective action can be taken. Let's explore some possible reasons for these variances (see Exhibit 6-14 on the next page).

Explaining Direct Labor Rate Variances

You may be thinking that companies should know what they will need to pay workers so that the actual labor rate should never vary from the standard. While managers do have a good idea of the wage rates they will need to pay and can set their standards accordingly, unforeseen events can cause the actual wage rate to fluctuate. The human resources manager typically makes wage rate decisions and is therefore held responsible for direct labor rate variances.

EXHIBIT 6-14

Possible explanations for direct labor variances.

Favorable Rate Variance	• used less skilled (lower paid) employees than allowed in standard
Unfavorable Rate Variance	• used more highly skilled workers than allowed in standard • employees worked overtime to complete a job
Favorable Efficiency Variance	• used more highly skilled (higher paid) workers than allowed in standard • used higher quality materials that needed less handling
Unfavorable Efficiency Variance	• new employees were still learning their job • overtime caused fatigue and reduced workers' efficiency • low quality materials required a longer production time • poor supervision resulted in employees "goofing off" • excessive machine downtime

Sometimes responsibility for direct labor variances lies with production managers. Production managers have some flexibility in assigning workers to complete a particular job, and this can affect the average actual wage rate for the period. Sometimes, to get a job done on time, the manager may need to use more highly skilled, higher paid workers than prescribed by the standard. This kind of substitution would result in an unfavorable labor rate variance. Conversely, a manager may choose to use less skilled, lower paid workers than called for in the standard, resulting in a favorable direct labor rate variance.

If a manager chooses to pay overtime to meet production requirements, a direct labor rate variance will likely result. Overtime is typically paid at time-and-a-half (1.5 times the base rate), so the actual wage rate will be higher than the standard wage rate. Because the higher wage rate will reduce operating income, the direct labor rate variance will be unfavorable. In fact, overtime is what caused C&C's unfavorable direct labor rate variance. Capacity was stretched in the fourth quarter because at the same time that the jackets needed to be made, the pants inventory had to be built up to fill the sales anticipated in the first quarter of 2018.[4]

In today's environment, many companies are seeking ways to reduce their labor costs through contract negotiations and outsourcing or offshoring. Because wage rate reductions that are achieved through these means tend to be permanent in nature, companies should revise their standard wage rates to reflect the reduced cost rather than run perpetual direct labor rate variances.

Explaining Direct Labor Efficiency Variances

When managers investigate a direct labor efficiency variance, they are trying to understand why workers took a longer or shorter amount of time than expected to produce a product. In other words, they are investigating worker productivity. Let's examine some of the factors that could influence worker productivity.

First, the level of skill and training workers possess will affect their productivity. If the work force consists of workers with a higher level of training and skill than that assumed in the standard, the result could be a favorable direct labor efficiency variance. Conversely, newly hired workers will not be as efficient as workers who have a significant amount of experience and training. If the work force consists of a number of new hires, then their lack of training could lead to an unfavorable direct labor efficiency variance. This is what happened to C&C in December. Even though some of the workers weren't new to C&C, they were new to jacket production, so they weren't as quick as the experienced jacket workers.

Workers' level of fatigue will also affect the direct labor efficiency variance. Just as you are less efficient when studying later in the day (or night!), workers

REALITY CHECK—*Labor efficiency strike out*

© RobHowarth/iStockphoto

Over 3,000 employees at Lockheed Martin's Fort Worth, Texas, plant walked off the job.

On April 23, 2012, over 3,000 employees at **Lockheed Martin's** Fort Worth, Texas, plant walked off the job in a dispute over a new union contract that would change the employees' pension benefits. While prior strikes at the plant had lasted two to three weeks, local union president Paul Black thought this one might last longer. He was right—workers didn't return to the production line until July 2, 2012. But Lockheed managed to keep the plant, which produces the U.S. Department of Defense's new F-35 Joint Strike Fighter and the F-16 jet, up and running.

How did production keep rolling if workers were on strike? The company tapped 2,200 salaried employees for possible deployment on 30-day production line rotations. While some of these contingency employees were ready for assignment, others would need to complete some training before being assigned to the production line. Over the course of the strike, the salaried workers were joined by an additional 500 temporary contract workers and some union members who decided to cross the picket line.

So how did these temporary workers fare? The company had planned to complete 29 F-35 fighters in 2012. But by May 25, 2012, the company acknowledged that production rates had decreased from prestrike levels. And on June 30, 2012, Lockheed's CEO Robert Stevens commented that the company might have to adjust its plan to produce that many fighters. Both of these acknowledgments indicate that the company was probably experiencing unfavorable direct labor efficiency variances. But given the inexperience of the salaried and temporary contract workers, these unfavorable variances would have been an expected result of the strike.

Sources: Associated Press, "Machinists End 10-week Strike vs. Lockheed," *The Daily Record*, June 28, 2012, http://thedailyrecord.com/2012/06/28/machinists-end-10-week-strike-vs-lockheed/ (accessed October 31, 2012); Doug Cameron, "Lockheed Hires Temp Workers at Fighter-Jet Plant," *The Wall Street Journal*, May 24, 2012; Andrea Sahlai-Esa, "Lockheed F-35 Workers Ready for Long Strike, Union Says," Reuters.com, April 24, 2012, http://www.reuters.com/article/2012/04/25/us-lockheed-strike-idUSBRE83O04520120425 (accessed October 31, 2012); Andrea Sahlai-Esa, "Lockheed Hires Temps at Strike-Hit Fort Worth Plant," Reuters.com, June 1, 2012, http://www.reuters.com/article/2012/06/01/us-lockheed-strike-idUSBRE8501HU20120601 (accessed October 31, 2012); Susy Solis, "Machinists Union Strike at Lockheed Threatens Company Quota," CBS DFW 11 News, June 12, 2012, http://dfw.cbslocal.com/2012/06/12/machinists-union-strike-at-lockheed-threatens-company-quota/ (accessed October 31, 2012).

who are working overtime are likely to be less efficient than expected, resulting in an unfavorable direct labor efficiency variance. Shift differentials may affect worker efficiency as well.[5] A recent study by **Circadian Technologies** found that workers on the night shift make five times as many errors and have 20% more accidents than workers on the day shift. Labor efficiency can also be affected by machine breakdowns (because idle workers remain on the clock even though they aren't producing any output) and a lack of adequate supervision (which may encourage workers to "slack off").

Finally, direct labor efficiency variances can be affected by the quality of direct materials used. When lower quality materials are used, workers must often work longer to get the job done. On the other hand, using higher quality materials can allow workers to complete a job faster. Recall from the last unit that C&C chose a new vendor to supply the lining fabric for its jackets. Because that fabric was of lower quality than specified in the standard, it required additional handling by workers.

THINK ABOUT IT 6.4

Given recent advances in information systems and automation, manufacturers can easily track an individual's actual wage rate, actual hours worked, standard wage rate, and standard hours worked. Thus, could an organization calculate direct labor wage and efficiency variances for each individual worker? What would be the benefit of such a calculation?

UNIT 6.3 REVIEW

KEY TERMS

Direct labor efficiency variance p. 317

Direct labor rate variance p. 315

PRACTICE QUESTIONS

1. LO 4 If the actual average wage rate is $4.80 per direct labor hour, but the standard wage rate is $5.00 per direct labor hour,
   a. the direct labor efficiency variance will be favorable.
   b. the direct labor efficiency variance will be unfavorable.
   c. the direct labor rate variance will be favorable.
   d. the direct labor rate variance will be unfavorable.
2. LO 4 Production line workers at Clarkson Enterprises worked a total of 5,000 direct labor hours to produce 10,000 mirrors in April. The standard for producing the mirrors allows 24 minutes per mirror at a wage rate of $10 per hour. If the actual wage rate was $11 per direct labor hour, Clarkson's direct labor rate variance for April was
   a. $5,000 U.
   b. $5,000 F.
   c. $10,000 U.
   d. $10,000 F.
3. LO 4 Production line workers at Clarkson Enterprises worked a total of 5,000 direct labor hours to produce 10,000 mirrors in April. The standard for producing the mirrors allows 24 minutes per mirror at a wage rate of $10 per hour. If the actual wage rate was $11 per direct labor hour, Clarkson's direct labor efficiency variance for April was
   a. $5,000 U.
   b. $5,000 F.
   c. $10,000 U.
   d. $10,000 F.
4. LO 5 Direct labor rate variances usually are *not* a result of
   a. the use of an average standard wage rate.
   b. the use of different skilled workers than planned.
   c. union contracts approved before the budgeting cycle.
   d. the use of overtime.
5. LO 5 Which of the following circumstances is most likely to result in an unfavorable direct labor efficiency variance?
   a. Paying workers a higher wage than expected
   b. Using higher quality direct materials than normal
   c. Using more highly skilled workers than normal
   d. Using significant overtime
6. LO 5 An unfavorable direct materials price variance combined with a favorable direct labor efficiency variance would *most* likely result from
   a. the use of unskilled workers.
   b. the use of highly skilled workers.
   c. the purchase and use of a higher-than-standard quality of material.
   d. the purchase and use of a lower-than-standard quality of material.

UNIT 6.3 PRACTICE EXERCISE

The Beakins Company manufactures advertising banners made of weather-resistant nylon. The direct labor standard for a banner allows 1.5 direct labor hours at a standard rate of $10 per direct labor hour. During the month of March, Beakins used 2,100 direct labor hours to produce 1,200 banners. The company's direct labor payroll totaled $17,850 for the month.

Required

1. Based on the direct labor standard, how many direct labor hours should Beakins have used in March?
2. Calculate the direct labor rate variance for March.
3. Calculate the direct labor efficiency variance for March.
4. What might have contributed to the two variances for March?

SELECTED UNIT 6.3 ANSWERS

Think About It 6.4

Individual direct labor rate variances would not be particularly useful in evaluating employee performance. The variance could be used to identify those employees who may have worked overtime, however. This type of information might assist a manager who wants to distribute overtime evenly across all employees.

Individual direct labor efficiency variances could be useful in assessing individual workers' performance. These variances could help to identify workers who might benefit from additional training to improve their efficiency. They might also help to identify the more efficient workers, who might be able to train new workers.

Practice Questions

1. C
2. A
3. C
4. C
5. D
6. C

Unit 6.3 Practice Exercise

1. 1,200 banners × 1.5 DLH = 1,800 DLH
2. $3,150 F
3. $3,000 U

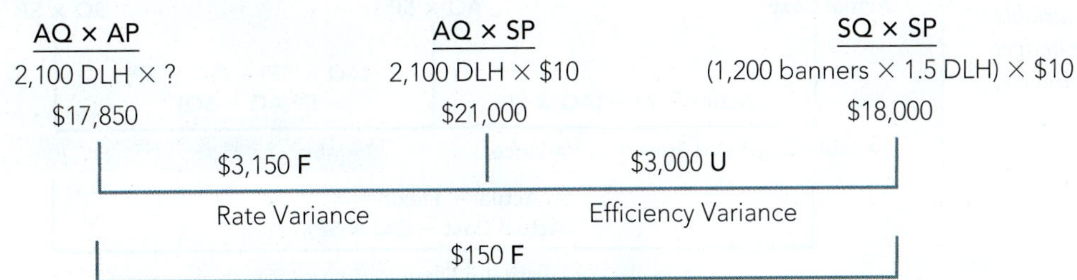

Notice that you do not need the actual direct labor rate to calculate the variance in this case.

4. Less skilled workers may have been hired at a lower wage rate, and their inexperience may have resulted in higher-than-normal scrap and defect rates.

UNIT 6.4

Variance Analysis: Overhead

GUIDED UNIT PREPARATION

Answering the following questions while you read this unit will guide your understanding of the key concepts found in this unit. The questions are linked to the learning objectives presented at the beginning of the chapter.

LO 6
1. What is a variable overhead spending variance?
2. What is a variable overhead efficiency variance?

LO 7
3. What is a fixed overhead spending variance?

LO 8
4. What are some possible explanations for the variable and fixed overhead spending variances?
5. Why would a company show a variable overhead efficiency variance?

As the level of automation in a manufacturing facility increases, manufacturing overhead becomes a more significant part of production cost. Therefore, understanding how overhead costs are incurred and how they are controlled is important. In this unit we will analyze variable and fixed overhead variances separately, since those costs are handled in very different ways.

Variable Overhead

Variable overhead cost consists of indirect production costs that are expected to vary with production activity—for example, indirect materials and utilities costs. Exhibit 6-15 shows the analysis of variable overhead variances. Notice

EXHIBIT 6-15

Analyzing the variable overhead flexible budget variance.

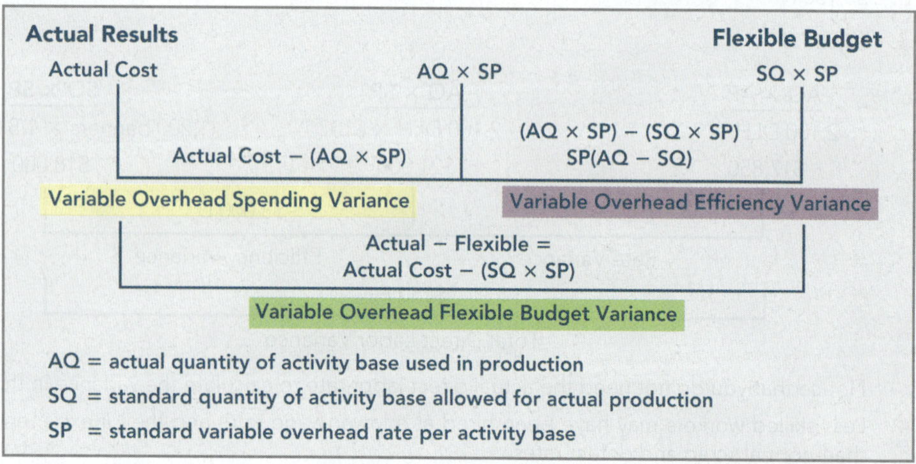

that this exhibit is almost identical to the direct materials and direct labor variance analyses. The difference is that no multiplication is required to calculate the actual cost. Although for accounting purposes these costs are charged to products based on a predetermined variable overhead rate, they are not actually incurred that way. Instead, the actual cost is determined by adding up the bills for variable overhead items. That is why the left-most column in Exhibit 6-15 reads "Actual Cost" instead of "AQ × AP." The middle and right columns are the same as for direct materials and direct labor.

Let's think about why actual variable overhead costs might differ from the flexible budget costs. First, the prices paid to acquire variable overhead items can increase or decrease. For example, utility rates might increase, causing variable overhead cost to rise. Second, variable overhead items can be used more or less efficiently than planned. For example, if a C&C worker spills a box of straight pins and doesn't recover all of them, supplies cost will be higher than budgeted. Finally, since variable overhead varies with production activity, if a company is more or less efficient with respect to that production activity, then variable overhead will be used more or less efficiently. If the variable overhead rate is based on direct labor hours, for example, then variable overhead will be used as efficiently as the direct laborers work. For these reasons we need to separate the variable overhead variance into two components: a variable overhead spending variance and a variable overhead efficiency variance.

Variable Overhead Spending Variance

The **variable overhead spending variance** is the difference between the actual cost of variable overhead items and the amount of variable overhead cost that is expected to be incurred at the actual level of activity base experienced. Exhibit 6-15 shows this calculation in tabular format. In the exhibit, this variance appears to be similar to the direct materials price and direct labor rate variances. It is, to a point. Just like the other variances, the variable overhead spending variance does capture whether the company has paid more or less for variable overhead items. However, it also captures the relative efficiency with which variable overhead items are used. You might be thinking, "Exhibit 6-15 shows an efficiency variance, so how could the spending variance have anything to do with efficiency?" That is a good question. As we will see in a minute, the variable overhead efficiency variance has to do with the efficient use of the *activity base* rather than the efficient use of the variable overhead items.

How can the variable overhead spending variance help managers to evaluate a company's performance? As long as the activity base actually *causes* the consumption of variable overhead, the spending variance really does express the difference between actual cost and the variable overhead cost that should have been incurred based on the actual activity level consumed. For example, if variable overhead cost consisted only of utilities costs and machine hours was the activity base, utility cost should go up or down as more or fewer machine hours are used. In that case, a significant unfavorable spending variance must be due either to increased utility rates or to the inefficient use of utilities, such as leaving the machines running when they are not producing anything. However, if a company incurs a lot of different variable overhead costs and the activity base is only slightly related to their consumption, then the spending variance will be virtually meaningless.

Let's consider C&C Sports' variable overhead spending variance, shown in Exhibit 6-16 on the next page. Actual variable overhead costs for the quarter were $228,546. Actual direct labor cost (the activity base for overhead) was $367,910, and the predetermined variable overhead rate was 55% of direct labor cost. Therefore, C&C's managers would expect that when direct labor cost is $367,910,

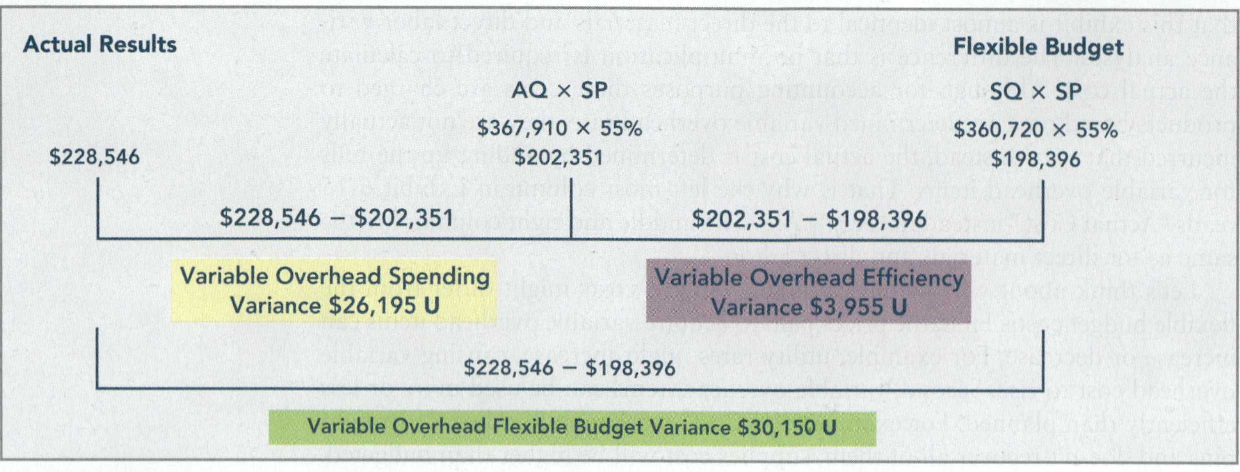

EXHIBIT 6-16 *C&C Sports' variable overhead variances.*

variable overhead cost should be $202,351 ($367,910 × 55%). The variable overhead spending variance is $26,195 U ($228,546 − $202,351). Only utilities and indirect materials are included in C&C's variable overhead. With just two types of variable overhead to track, it shouldn't be hard for the production manager to figure out why these costs are so different from expected costs.

THINK ABOUT IT 6.5

How might indirect materials generate an unfavorable usage variance that is not related to the efficient use of the variable overhead activity driver?

Variable Overhead Efficiency Variance

The **variable overhead efficiency variance** captures the effect of efficient use of the activity base on the cost of variable overhead. If variable overhead truly is caused by the activity base, efficient or inefficient use of the activity base will decrease or increase variable overhead cost. Returning to the example of a machine left running too long, if more machine hours than allowed by the standard were used, we would expect utility cost to be higher than expected. This efficiency variance is similar to the direct labor efficiency variance.

Notice in Exhibit 6-15 that the variable overhead efficiency variance is calculated using only three amounts: the actual quantity of the activity base used in production, the standard quantity of the activity base allowed for actual production, and the standard variable overhead rate. As the exhibit shows, the calculation of the variable overhead efficiency variance can be reduced to an algebraic equation in which SP represents the standard variable overhead rate, AQ represents the actual quantity of the activity base used in actual production, and SQ represents the standard quantity of the activity base allowed for actual production.

$$\text{Variable overhead efficiency variance} = SP \times (AQ - SQ)$$

Let's calculate the variable overhead efficiency variance for C&C Sports. Recall that the activity base is direct labor cost and the standard rate is 55%

of direct labor cost (see Exhibit 5-14). From Exhibit 6-16 we can see that the standard direct labor cost for all products made by C&C is $360,720. C&C actually spent $367,910, or $7,190 more than the standard allows. At a predetermined variable overhead rate of 55% of direct labor cost, the variable overhead efficiency variance is $3,955. Since actual direct labor costs were higher than the standard cost, the variance is unfavorable. Exhibit 6-16 shows this calculation in tabular format. The variance can also be determined using the equation $0.55 per direct labor dollar × ($367,910 − $360,720) = $3,955 U.

Interpreting Variable Overhead Variances

You now know how to calculate the variable overhead spending and efficiency variances. Once again, the important part of the manager's job is investigating and understanding the causes of these variances. Because variable overhead includes several items that differ from one company to another, providing a comprehensive list of explanations for these variances is difficult, but Exhibit 6-17 presents some general explanations for overhead variances.

EXHIBIT 6-17

General explanations for variable overhead variances.

Favorable Spending Variance	• paid less than expected for variable overhead items • used variable overhead items efficiently
Unfavorable Spending Variance	• paid more than expected for variable overhead items • used variable overhead items inefficiently
Favorable Efficiency Variance	• efficient use of the activity base
Unfavorable Efficiency Variance	• inefficient use of the activity base

When a variable overhead spending variance is identified, managers will want to talk with the production manager about the purchase and/or use of variable overhead items. To inquire about indirect materials, the production manager will speak with the inventory manager or the purchasing agent, to see whether the prices they paid for materials have changed. If prices haven't changed dramatically, the next place to go would be to the materials requisition log to determine who has been removing materials from inventory and whether more or less than anticipated has been used. To check on utilities, the production manager will talk with the production accountant to determine whether utility rates have increased and might also talk with a production supervisor to evaluate the use of electricity. When a variable overhead *efficiency* variance is identified, managers will again see the production manager to evaluate the use of the activity base. These are just two examples of how to investigate variable overhead variances. Similar investigative processes are used to examine other categories of variable overhead costs.

When Claire Elliot inquired about C&C's variable overhead spending variance, she learned that most of the variance was due to the inefficient use of indirect materials, specifically during the period of high award jacket production. Claire knew that the variable overhead efficiency variance was directly related to the increase in direct labor cost, since direct labor cost is the activity base. She was beginning to realize that while increasing the production of award jackets had been good for sales revenue, it might have had a bigger impact on operations than originally expected.

Fixed Overhead

Analysis of the fixed overhead variance differs from that of the other variances because of the nature of fixed overhead costs. Since fixed overhead does not vary with volume within the relevant range, the flexible budget and the static budget will report the same amount. Therefore, the flexible budget variance is the same as the static budget variance. The flexible budget variance for fixed overhead,

WATCH OUT!

Calculating the fixed overhead spending variance can be as easy as subtracting the budgeted fixed overhead from the actual fixed overhead. Sometimes, however, you may not know the budgeted fixed overhead amount. If that is the case and you know the budgeted activity base, you can use the following equation to calculate the budgeted fixed overhead amount.

$$\text{Fixed overhead rate} = \frac{\text{Budgeted fixed overhead}}{\text{Budgeted fixed base}}$$

known as the **fixed overhead spending variance**, is the difference between actual fixed overhead cost and budgeted fixed overhead cost. Normally, managers will not see many variances in these costs. Items like rent, depreciation, insurance, and maintenance are all either contracted for or known ahead of time. Sometimes unexpected costs will arise, but not often.

Let's calculate the fixed overhead spending variance for C&C Sports. As you can see from Exhibit 6-4, the calculation is simple. Actual costs were $175,577, and budgeted costs were $160,447. Quite simply, that results in a fixed overhead spending variance of $15,130 U.[6]

UNIT 6.4 REVIEW

KEY TERMS

Fixed overhead spending variance p. 326

Variable overhead efficiency variance p. 324

Variable overhead spending variance p. 323

PRACTICE QUESTIONS

1. LO 6 The variable overhead efficiency variance is a measure of how efficiently variable overhead has been used. True or False?
2. LO 6 If a company that applies variable overhead on the basis of direct labor hours records a favorable direct labor efficiency variance, the variable overhead efficiency variance will be
   a. unfavorable.
   b. favorable.
   c. zero.
   d. undeterminable.
3. LO 6 Claire's Caloric Capers produces gourmet cakes. Claire's budget for the year was based on the production of 3,200 cakes using a standard of 3 direct labor hours per cake and $3 variable overhead per direct labor hour. During the year, Claire used 8,960 direct labor hours to produce 2,800 cakes. If actual variable overhead for the year was $25,000, what was Claire's variable overhead spending variance?
   a. $1,880 unfavorable
   b. $1,880 favorable
   c. $1,680 unfavorable
   d. $1,680 favorable
4. LO 7 Super Jolt Company produces coffeemakers. The fixed overhead rate is $5 per direct labor hour, and the company budgeted for 4,608 direct labor hours for the year. During the year, Super Jolt produced 2,400 coffeemakers using 4,700 direct labor hours. Actual fixed overhead for the year was $21,000. What was the company's fixed overhead spending variance?
   a. $2,500 favorable
   b. $2,500 unfavorable
   c. $2,040 favorable
   d. $2,040 unfavorable
5. LO 8 While investigating an unfavorable variable overhead spending variance, an operations manager was told that the hourly janitorial staff had received an unexpected raise during contract negotiations. The manager could consider the raise a plausible explanation for the variance. True or False?
6. LO 8 A worker spilled a bottle of solvent used to clean ink from a printing press. This excess usage will show up in the variable overhead efficiency variance. True or False?

UNIT 6.4 PRACTICE EXERCISE

The Beakins Company manufactures advertising banners made of weather-resistant nylon. The direct labor standard for a banner allows 1.5 direct labor hours at a standard rate of $10 per direct labor hour. The predetermined variable overhead rate is $4 per direct labor hour; the predetermined fixed overhead rate is $6 per direct labor hour. These rates were based on an expected capacity of 24,000 direct labor hours, evenly distributed throughout the year.

During the month of March, Beakins used 2,100 direct labor hours to produce 1,200 banners. The company's direct labor payroll totaled $17,850 for the month. Actual variable overhead for the month was $10,800, while actual fixed overhead was $11,000.

Required

1. Calculate the variable overhead spending variance for March.
2. Calculate the variable overhead efficiency variance for March.
3. Calculate the fixed overhead spending variance for March.

SELECTED UNIT 6.4 ANSWERS

Think About It 6.5

Almost all variable overhead items may cost more or less than expected due to changes in the prices of those items or their inefficient use. But other actions may cause indirect materials variances. Materials can be stolen; over time they can spoil, shrink, or become obsolete. Because maintaining control over materials isn't easy, inventory levels are best kept as low as possible.

Practice Questions

1. False
2. B
3. B
4. C
5. True
6. False

Unit 6.4 Practice Exercise

1. $2,400 U
2. $1,200 U

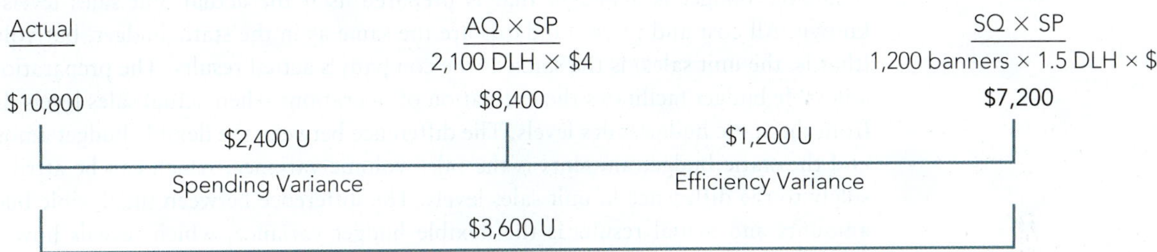

3. Actual fixed overhead – Budgeted fixed overhead = $11,000 – $12,000 = $1,000 F.

   The $6 per hour predetermined overhead rate was determined by dividing budgeted fixed overhead cost by the number of budgeted direct labor hours. So $6 = x ÷ 24,000; x = $144,000. For one month, the budgeted fixed overhead is $12,000 ($144,000 ÷ 12 months).

BUSINESS DECISION AND CONTEXT Wrap Up

In the chapter-opening story, George Douglas was searching for an explanation of why C&C's net income for the fourth quarter was lower than budgeted, even though the sales staff's extra efforts had generated higher-than-expected sales of award jackets. Through variance analysis, George was able to piece together some of the reasons for the lower net income.

Bradley Austin, C&C's inventory manager, had purchased 25,000 yards of lining at a price lower than the standard price. But because the lining was of inferior quality, it caused production problems, resulting in the use of 4,000 more yards of lining than planned in the flexible budget. So while the lining purchases saved the company $6,250, the extra fabric used due to production problems cost the company $8,000.

The additional jacket sales also caused production problems. To meet the increased customer demand, production manager Mary Townsley had scheduled overtime shifts, which increased the average wage rate paid to workers, adding an extra cost of $1,650 to the payroll.

Furthermore, some of the workers had never sewn jackets before, so they weren't as fast as the other workers. And the use of overtime meant that employees were more fatigued and worked more slowly than usual. As a result, C&C used 1,500 more direct labor hours at a cost of $14,400 to produce the extra award jackets.

In addition to these problems with materials and labor, C&C experienced increased spending on variable and fixed overhead. George concluded that his strategy of increasing the sales and production of award jackets had not played out as planned.

CHAPTER SUMMARY

In this chapter you learned how to evaluate how well a company has performed relative to the plan or budget for the period. Specifically, you should be able to meet the objectives set out at the beginning of this chapter:

1. ***Prepare a flexible budget and explain its use in evaluating performance. (Unit 6.1)***

A flexible budget is a budget that is prepared as if the actual unit sales levels are known. All cost and price standards are the same as in the static budget, but volume (that is, the unit sales) is the same as the company's actual results. The preparation of a flexible budget facilitates the evaluation of operations when actual sales levels differ from the static budget sales levels. The difference between the flexible budget amounts and the static budget amounts is the sales volume variance, which can be attributed solely to the difference in unit sales levels. The difference between the flexible budget amounts and actual results is the flexible budget variance, which reveals how well operations personnel controlled prices and costs.

2. ***Calculate the direct materials price and direct materials quantity variances. (Unit 6.2)***

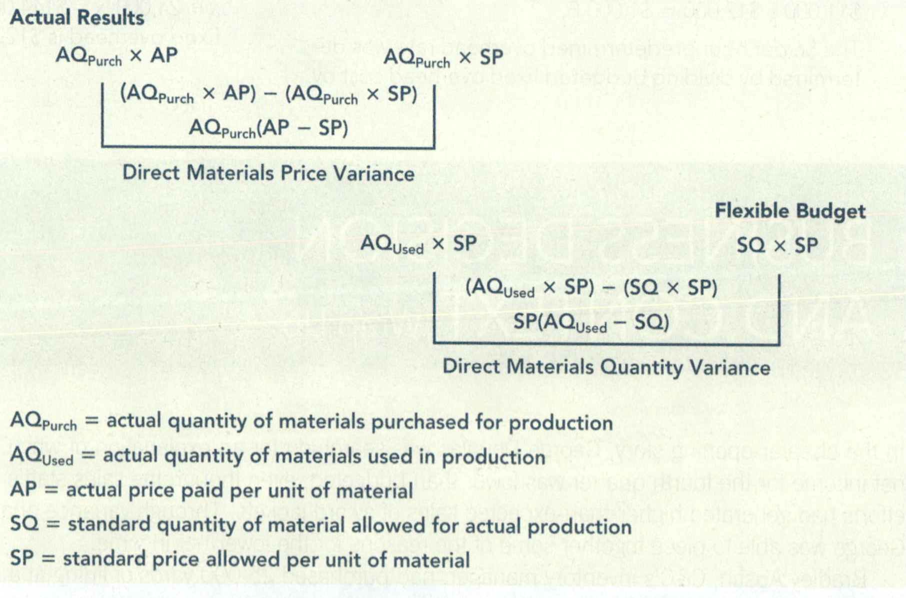

3. ***Identify potential causes of the direct materials price and quantity variances. (Unit 6.2)***

Direct materials price variances can be caused by an unexpected change in the supplier's price, by the purchase of large volumes (in bulk), or by the purchase of a different quality of material than called for by the material standard. Direct materials quantity variances can be caused by workers' experience level, the quality of materials used in production, a machine malfunction, or employee theft.

4. ***Calculate the direct labor rate and efficiency variances. (Unit 6.3)***

Actual Results | **Flexible Budget**

AQ × AP | AQ × SP | SQ × SP

(AQ × AP) − (AQ × SP) | (AQ × SP) − (SQ × SP)

AQ(AP − SP) | SP(AQ − SQ)

Direct Labor Rate Variance | Direct Labor Efficiency Variance

Actual − Flexible =

(AQ × SP) − (SQ × SP)

Direct Labor Flexible Budget Variance

AQ = actual quantity of direct labor hours worked
AP = actual wage rate paid per direct labor hour
SQ = standard quantity of direct labor hours allowed for actual production
SP = standard wage rate allowed per direct labor hour

5. ***Identify potential causes of the direct labor rate and efficiency variances. (Unit 6.3)***

Direct labor rate variances can be caused by using workers of a different skill level than called for by the standard or by paying overtime. Direct labor efficiency variances can be caused by workers' experience level, the quality of the materials used in production, a machine malfunction, or the level of supervision.

6. ***Calculate the variable overhead spending and efficiency variances. (Unit 6.4)***

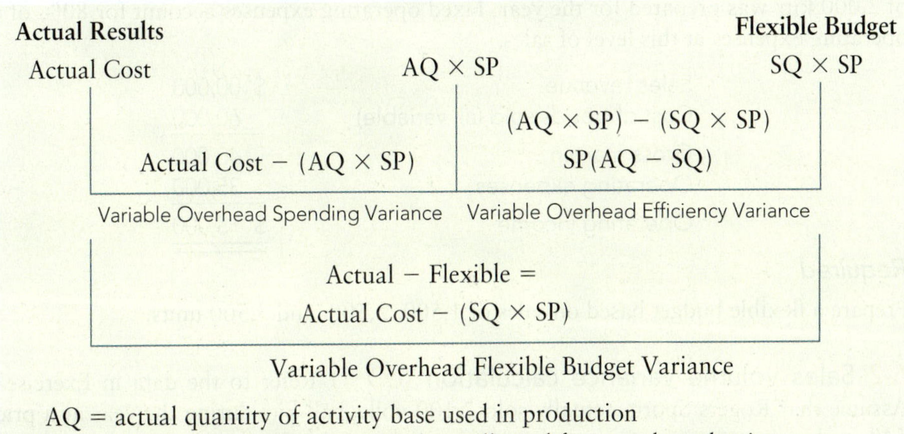

7. ***Calculate the fixed overhead spending variance. (Unit 6.4)***

Actual fixed overhead cost − Budgeted fixed overhead cost

8. ***Identify potential causes of the variable overhead spending and efficiency variances and the fixed overhead spending variance. (Unit 6.4)***

The variable overhead spending variance can be caused by paying more or less for variable overhead items than budgeted or by using variable overhead items more or less efficiently than allowed by the standard, or both. The variable overhead efficiency variance results from using the variable overhead activity base more or less efficiently than allowed by the standard. If variable overhead truly varies with this activity base, then as use of the activity base goes up or down, variable overhead costs will go up or down with it. The fixed overhead spending variance results simply from spending more or less than budgeted on fixed overhead items.

KEY TERMS

Direct labor efficiency variance (Unit 6.3)
Direct labor rate variance (Unit 6.3)
Direct materials price variance (Unit 6.2)
Direct materials quantity variance (Unit 6.2)
Favorable variance (Unit 6.1)
Fixed overhead spending variance (Unit 6.4)
Flexible budget (Unit 6.1)
Flexible budget variance (Unit 6.1)
Management by exception (Unit 6.1)
Materiality (Unit 6.1)
Sales price variance (Unit 6.1)
Sales volume variance (Unit 6.1)
Static budget (Unit 6.1)
Static budget variance (Unit 6.1)
Unfavorable variance (Unit 6.1)
Variable overhead efficiency variance (Unit 6.4)
Variable overhead spending variance (Unit 6.4)
Variance (Unit 6.1)

EXERCISES

6-1 Preparing a flexible budget (LO 1) Rogers Sports sells volleyball kits that it purchases from a sports equipment distributor. The following static budget based on sales of 2,000 kits was prepared for the year. Fixed operating expenses account for 80% of total operating expenses at this level of sales.

Sales revenue	$100,000
Cost of goods sold (all variable)	60,000
Gross margin	40,000
Operating expenses	35,000
Operating income	$ 5,000

Required

Prepare a flexible budget based on sales of 1,500, 2,500, and 3,500 units.

6-2 Sales volume variance calculation (LO 1) Refer to the data in Exercise 6-1. Assume that Rogers Sports actually sold 2,100 volleyball kits during the year at a price of $48 per kit.

Required

Calculate the sales volume variance for sales revenue and cost of goods sold.

6-3 Sales price variance calculation (LO 1) Refer to the data in Exercise 6-1. Assume that during the year Rogers Sports actually sold 2,100 volleyball kits during the year at a price of $48 per kit.

Required

Calculate the sales price variance.

6-4 Preparing a flexible budget (LO 1) Adarmes Adventures manufactures aluminum canoes. In planning for the coming year, CFO Alexis King is considering three different sales targets: 2,500 canoes, 3,000 canoes, and 3,500 canoes. Canoes sell for $800 each. The standard variable cost information for a canoe is as follows.

Direct materials	$300
Direct labor	150
Variable overhead	
Utilities	35
Indirect material	30
Indirect labor	60
Total	$575

Annual fixed overhead cost is expected to be:

Maintenance	$ 20,000
Depreciation	40,000
Insurance	27,000
Rent	30,000
Total	$117,000

Required

Prepare a flexible budget for the three sales levels under consideration.

6-5 Preparing a performance report (LO 1) Refer to the information about Adarmes Adventures given in Exercise 6-4. Alexis King chose to prepare a static budget based on sales of 3,000 canoes. Actual sales were 3,100 canoes at a price of $850 each. The company incurred the following costs for the year:

Direct material	$ 910,000
Direct labor	435,000
Variable overhead	398,000
Fixed overhead	125,000
Total	$1,868,000

Required

Prepare a performance report for the year that shows the flexible budget and sales volume variances.

6-6 Direct materials price variance calculation (LO 2) Washington WaterWorks manufactures snorkel gear. During the past month, Washington purchased 4,000 pounds of plastic to use in its dive masks, at a cost of $6,800. The standard price for the plastic is $1.60 per pound. The company actually used 3,800 pounds of the plastic to produce 15,000 dive masks.

Required

Calculate Washington's direct materials price variance for the month.

6-7 Direct materials price variance calculation (LO 2) Phelps Gold manufactures award medals. In August, Phelps produced 5,000 medals, 100 more than expected. During the month, the company purchased 1,100 ounces of gold for $875,000. The standard price for the gold is $800 per ounce. The company actually used 1,000 ounces of gold for production.

Required

Calculate Phelps's direct materials price variance for the month.

6-8 Direct materials price variance calculation (LO 2) Shevlin Enterprises purchased 60,000 gallons of direct materials during the year at a price of $2.75 per gallon. Bennett's direct materials price variance was $6,000 U.

Required

Calculate the standard price per gallon of direct materials.

6-9 Direct materials quantity variance calculation (LO 2) TechSolvers produces 8-foot USB cables. During the past year, the company purchased 500,000 feet of plastic-coated wire at a price of $0.25 per foot. The direct materials standard for the cables allows 8.5 feet of wire at a standard price of $0.23. During the year, the company used a total of 535,000 feet of wire to produce 63,000 8-foot cables.

Required

Calculate TechSolvers' direct materials quantity variance for the year.

6-10 Direct materials quantity variance calculation (LO 2) Pelligrini, Inc. makes high-quality swimsuits. During the year, the company produced 800 suits, using 1,025 yards of material, and the company purchased 900 yards of material for $4,482. The direct materials standard for the swimsuits allows 1.2 yards of material at a standard price of $5 per yard.

Required

Calculate Pelligrini's direct materials quantity variance for the year.

6-11 Direct materials quantity variance calculation (LO 2) Levine Labs used 50,000 ounces of specimen adhesive during the year. The direct materials standard allows 1.5 ounces of adhesive at a price of $0.40 per ounce for each pathology test. The direct materials quantity variance was $880 F.

Required

How many pathology tests did Levine Labs complete during the year?

6-12 Interpretation of direct materials variances (LO 3) The sole supplier of Montrose, Inc.'s critical direct material declared bankruptcy last year. As a result, Montrose had to quickly find alternative sources for the material. Since no one supplier had enough material to meet the company's needs, Montrose had to use twelve different vendors that were located throughout the country. Shipments frequently had to be sent overnight in small quantities. On three occasions, Montrose had to accept materials that were of higher quality than desired in order to meet promised delivery dates.

Required

What will be the likely impact of these circumstances on Montrose's direct materials price and quantity variances for the year?

6-13 Direct materials variance calculation and interpretation (LO 2, 3) The following information is available for Coady's Chocolates:

Actual production	3,000 boxes
Budgeted production	3,200 boxes
Direct Materials	
Standard	2 pounds of chocolate per box @ $8.00 per pound
Actual	7,000 pounds purchased @ $7.80 per pound
	6,500 pounds used @ $7.80 per pound

Required

a. Calculate the direct materials price and quantity variances.
b. What might have caused the variances you calculated?

6-14 Direct labor rate variance calculation (LO 4) ImpressMe Products embosses notebooks with school and corporate logos. Last year, the company's direct labor payroll totaled $352,100 for 50,300 direct labor hours. The standard wage rate is $6.75 per direct labor hour.

Required

Calculate ImpressMe's direct labor rate variance.

6-15 Direct labor rate variance calculation (LO 4) Pochard Paints manufactures artist's oil paints. Each 40 ml tube of paint requires 5 minutes of direct labor, and the standard labor rate is $9.00 per direct labor hour. In September, Pochard incurred 10,800 direct labor hours at a cost of $95,000 to produce 120,000 tubes of paint.

Required

Calculate Pochard's direct labor rate variance for September.

6-16 Direct labor rate variance calculation (LO 4) Workers at Banner News were paid a total of $33,400 during the month of July. The company's standard wage rate was $8 per hour, and the direct labor rate variance for the month was $1,400 U.

Required

How many direct labor hours were worked during July?

6-17 Direct labor efficiency variance calculation (LO 4) POD Incasements manufactures protective cases for MP3 players. During November, the company's workers clocked 800 more direct labor hours than the flexible budget amount of 25,000 hours to complete 100,000 cases for the Christmas season. All workers were paid $9.25 per hour, which was $0.50 more than the standard wage rate.

Required

Calculate POD's direct labor efficiency variance.

6-18 Direct labor efficiency variance calculation (LO 4) Holleyman Industries is a leading manufacturer of golf balls. Each golf ball requires 1 minute of direct labor time to complete. Holleyman used 7,200 direct labor hours in July to produce 420,000 golf balls. Holleyman's standard labor rate is $9 per direct labor hour, and the actual labor rate in July was $8.75.

Required

Calculate Holleyman's direct labor efficiency variance for July.

6-19 Direct labor efficiency variance calculation (LO 4) Buddie Paper Company produces specialty papers. During August, the company produced 50,000 reams of paper. The standard wage rate is $7.50 per hour, and each ream of paper requires 12 minutes of direct labor. The direct labor efficiency variance for August was $1,500 F.

Required

How many direct labor hours were actually worked during August?

6-20 Direct labor variance calculation and explanation (LO 4, 5) Hunter Family Instruments makes cellos. During the past year, the company made 6,400 cellos even though the budget planned for only 5,600. The company paid its workers an average of $15 per hour, which was $1 higher than the standard labor rate. The production manager budgets four direct labor hours per cello. During the year, a total of 24,320 direct labor hours were worked.

Required

a. Calculate the direct labor rate and efficiency variances.
b. What might have caused the variances you calculated?

6-21 Variable overhead variance calculation (LO 6) The following information is available for Harrison's Hot Dogs:

Actual production	12,320 packages
Budgeted production	12,500 packages
Standard direct labor hours	1.5 direct labor hours per package
Actual direct labor hours	19,500
Standard variable overhead rate	$3 per direct labor hour
Actual variable overhead costs	$50,000

Required

Calculate the variable overhead spending and efficiency variances.

6-22 Fixed overhead spending variance calculation (LO 7) Merkt Merchandise planned to produce 40,000 fleece jackets in its Metairie, Louisiana, factory. Fixed overhead costs for the factory were budgeted to be $520,000. The company actually spent $534,000 on fixed overhead and produced 38,000 jackets.

Required

Calculate the fixed overhead spending variance.

6-23 Fixed overhead spending variance calculation (LO 7) Scott Sykes publishes a pilot training course curriculum kit that he sells to flight schools across the country. He prepared the following static budget for the year based on expected sales of 30,000 curriculum kits.

Sales revenue	$3,750,000
Variable cost of goods sold	1,500,000
Variable selling and administrative expenses	450,000
Contribution margin	1,800,000
Fixed manufacturing overhead	840,000
Fixed selling and administrative expenses	370,000
Operating income	$ 590,000

At the end of the year, Scott had sold 31,000 curriculum kits at an average price of $128 per kit. During the year, he incurred fixed overhead totaling $834,000.

Required

Calculate the fixed overhead spending variance.

6-24 Fixed overhead spending variance calculation (LO 7) Devaney Foods Company manufactures single-serve mustard packets used in fast-food restaurants. Al Devaney, the company's CFO, prepared the following standard cost card for a box of mustard packets (100 packets in a box), based on expected production of 50,000 boxes.

Direct materials	$1.37
Direct labor	0.50
Variable overhead	0.34
Fixed overhead	1.75
Total standard cost per box	$3.96

During the year, Devaney Foods actually produced 51,075 boxes and incurred $85,000 in fixed manufacturing overhead.

Required

Calculate the fixed overhead spending variance.

6-25 Comprehensive variance calculations (LO 2, 4, 6, 7) Carson Construction Consultants performs cement core tests in its Greenville laboratory. The following standard costs for the tests have been developed by the company's controller, Landon Carson, based on performing 2,100 core tests per month.

	Standard Price	Standard Quantity	Standard Cost
Direct materials	$0.50 per pound	4 pounds	$ 2.00
Direct labor	$10 per DLH	.5 DLH	5.00
Variable overhead	$9 per DLH	.5 DLH	4.50
Fixed overhead	$16 per DLH	.5 DLH	8.00
Total standard cost per test			$19.50

At the end of March, London reported the following operational results:

- The company actually performed 2,250 core tests during the month.
- 8,500 pounds of direct materials were purchased during the month at a total cost of $5,600.
- 6,300 pounds of direct materials were used to conduct the core tests.

- 850 direct labor hours were worked at a total cost of $9,775.
- Actual variable overhead was $7,800.
- Actual fixed overhead was $15,750.

Required

a. Calculate the direct materials price variance for March.
b. Calculate the direct materials quantity variance for March.
c. Calculate the direct labor rate variance for March.
d. Calculate the direct labor efficiency variance for March.
e. Calculate the variable overhead spending variance for March.
f. Calculate the variable overhead efficiency variance for March.
g. Calculate the fixed overhead spending variance for March.
h. Prepare a memo to Landon Carson providing possible explanations for the direct materials and direct labor variances.

6-26 Comprehensive variance calculations (CMA adapted) (LO 2, 4, 6, 7)

Sommers Irrigation, Inc. is known throughout the world for its H2O-X high-capacity water pump, used in irrigation systems. The pump's standard cost is as follows. The company's predetermined fixed overhead rate is based on an expected capacity of 100,000 direct labor hours per month.

	Standard Price	Standard Quantity	Standard Cost
Direct materials	$7 per pound	15 pounds	$105
Direct labor	$12 per DLH	4 DLH	48
Variable overhead	$8 per DLH	4 DLH	32
Fixed overhead	$6 per DLH	4 DLH	24
			$209

During the month of September, the company produced 22,000 of the 25,000 pumps that had been scheduled for production in the budget. The company used 382,000 pounds of material during September. The direct labor payroll for the month was $980,000 for 95,000 direct labor hours. Variable overhead costs were $725,000; fixed overhead costs were $575,000. The company's purchasing agent signed a new supply contract that resulted in purchases of 500,000 pounds of direct materials at a total price of $3,300,000.

Required

Calculate Sommers' direct materials, direct labor, and overhead variances for September.

PROBLEMS

6-27 Preparing flexible budgets (CMA adapted) (LO 1)

Barnes Entertainment Corporation prepared a master budget for the month of November that was based on sales of 150,000 board games. The budgeted income statement for the period is as follows.

Sales Revenue		$2,400,000
Variable expenses		
Direct materials	$ 675,000	
Direct labor	300,000	
Variable overhead	450,000	
Total variable expenses		1,425,000
Contribution margin		975,000
Fixed Expenses		
Fixed overhead	250,000	
Fixed selling and administrative expenses	500,000	
Total fixed expenses		750,000
Operating income		$ 225,000

During November, Barnes produced and sold 180,000 board games. Actual results for the month are as follows.

Sales Revenue		$2,870,000
Variable expenses		
Direct materials	$798,000	
Direct labor	375,000	
Variable overhead	550,000	
Total variable expenses		1,723,000
Contribution margin		1,147,000
Fixed Expenses		
Fixed overhead	270,000	
Fixed selling and administrative expenses	500,000	
Total fixed expenses		770,000
Operating income		$ 377,000

Required

a. Prepare a flexible budget for November.
b. Calculate Barnes's static budget variance for November.
c. Will the static budget variance that you calculated in part (b) be useful to management? Why or why not?
d. Based on the available information, prepare a performance report for management.
e. Comment on the results of your report.

6-28 Interpreting direct materials variances and direct labor variances (LO 3, 5) Russell Marks shook his head in disbelief as he and operations manager Tom Hanover reviewed the month's flexible budget performance report. "How did you manage to make such a poor showing last month?" he asked Hanover. "You didn't meet your production schedule, and we have three customers who are unhappy about their missed delivery dates. Now we have this $375,000 unfavorable direct materials quantity variance, plus a $250,000 unfavorable direct labor efficiency variance. Tom, are you the right person for this job?"

Tom reflected for a moment on how the month had gone. He recalled that workers had complained all month about machine breakdowns and slow response from the maintenance department. One batch of products had to be thrown away because of materials defects that had been discovered after all the assembly was complete. Tom had been working hard to keep the plant running smoothly, but lately everything had gone wrong. And he couldn't seem to find the cause.

Russell interrupted Tom's thoughts. "Thank goodness for the $400,000 favorable direct materials price variance Brian generated by purchasing materials from that new supplier he found. Without that, we would have been in even worse shape. You know, he's been saving us a lot of money over the last several months by seeking out new suppliers. Maybe I should give him a bonus."

Required

a. How might Tom respond to Russell?
b. Should Russell investigate further before he awards Brian a bonus? Why or why not?

6-29 Calculating overhead variances (CMA Adapted) (LO 6, 7) Attacus Company manufactures deep-sea fishing rods, which it distributes internationally through a chain of wholesalers. The following data are taken from the budget prepared at the beginning of the year by Attacus's controller. The company applies overhead on the basis of machine hours.

	Annual Budget	May Budget
Variable manufacturing overhead	$2,000,000	$220,000
Fixed manufacturing overhead	$1,200,000	$100,000
Direct labor hours	48,000	4,000
Machine hours	250,000	22,000

During the month of May, Attacus used 4,200 direct labor hours and 21,800 machine hours. The flexible budget for the month allowed 4,000 direct labor hours and 21,000 machine hours. Actual fixed manufacturing overhead incurred was $102,000; variable manufacturing overhead incurred was $173,000.

Required

a. Calculate the variable overhead spending and efficiency variances for May.
b. Calculate the fixed overhead spending variance for May.

6-30 Comprehensive flexible budgets and variance analysis (LO 1, 2, 3, 4, 5, 6, 7, 8) Lexi Belcher picked up the monthly report that Irvin Santamaria left on her desk. She smiled as her eyes went straight to the bottom line of the report and saw the favorable variance for operating income, confirming her decision to push the workers to get those last 250 cases off the production line before the end of the month.

But as she glanced over the rest of numbers, Lexi couldn't help but wonder if there were errors in some of the line items. She was puzzled at how most of the operating expenses could be higher than the budget since she had worked hard to manage the production line to improve efficiency and reduce costs. Yet the report, shown below, showed a different story.

	Actual	Budget	Variance
Cases produced and sold	10,250	10,000	250 F
Sales revenue	$1,947,500	$1,870,000	$77,500 F
Less variable expenses			
Direct material	561,000	550,000	11,000 U
Direct labor	267,650	260,000	7,650 U
Variable manufacturing overhead	285,012	280,000	5,012 U
Variable selling expenses	93,130	90,000	3,130 U
Variable administrative expenses	41,740	40,000	1,740 U
Total variable expenses	1,248,532	1,220,000	28,532 U
Contribution margin	698,968	650,000	48,968 F
Less fixed expenses			
Fixed manufacturing overhead	111,000	110,000	1,000 U
Fixed selling expenses	69,500	70,000	(500 F)
Fixed administrative expenses	129,800	130,000	(200 F)
Total fixed expenses	310,300	310,000	300 U
Operating income	$ 388,668	$ 340,000	$48,668 F

Lexi picked up the phone and called Irvin. "Irvin, I don't get it. We beat the budgeted operating income for the month, but look at all the unfavorable variances on the operating costs. Can you help me understand what's going on?" "Let me look into it and I'll get back to you," Irvin replied.

Irvin gathered the following additional information about the month's performance.

- Direct materials purchased: 102,000 pounds at a total of $561,000
- Direct materials used: 102,000 pounds
- Direct labor hours worked: 26,500 at a total cost of $267,650
- Machine hours used: 40,950

Irvin also found the standard cost card for a case of product.

	Standard Price	Standard Quantity	Standard Cost
Direct materials	$5.50 per pound	10 pounds	$ 55
Direct labor	$10.00 per DLH	2.6 DLH	26
Variable overhead	$7.00 per MH	4 MH	28
Fixed overhead	$2.75 per MH	4 MH	11
Total standard cost per case			$120

Required

a. Calculate the direct materials price variance for the month.
b. Calculate the direct materials quantity variance for the month.
c. Calculate the direct labor rate variance for the month.
d. Calculate the direct labor efficiency variance for the month.

e. Calculate the variable overhead spending variance for the month.
f. Calculate the variable overhead efficiency variance for the month.
g. Calculate the fixed overhead spending variance for the month.
h. Prepare a performance report that will assist Lexi in evaluating her efforts to control production costs.
i. Based on your review of the performance report you prepared, do you think Lexi did a good job of controlling production expenses during the month? Why or why not?

6-31 Comprehensive flexible budgets and variance analysis (LO 1, 2, 3, 4, 5, 6, 7, 8) Pressure Reducers, Inc. produces and sells lumbar support cushions for office chairs using a special foam that molds to a person's back. Since all products are made to order, the only inventory the company maintains is raw materials. Thus, all costs of production are recognized in the period in which they are incurred. The following annual performance report was prepared from the company's accounting records:

	Actual	Budget	Variance
Units sold	14,500	15,000	(500 U)
Sales revenue	$2,972,500	$3,000,000	($27,500 U)
Cost of goods sold	2,051,000	2,075,000	(24,000 F)
Gross margin	921,500	925,000	(3,500 U)
Selling and administrative expenses	288,625	290,000	(1,375 F)
Operating income	$ 632,875	$ 635,000	($ 2,125 U)

The following fixed costs are included in these amounts.

	Actual	Budget
Cost of goods sold	$195,000	$200,000
Selling and administrative expenses	140,000	140,000

Hank Martinez, Pressure Reducers' CFO, used the following standard cost card in preparing the budget and thought he had done a good job estimating production and sales. He wonders why the variable cost of goods sold deviated from that budget.

	Standard Quantity per Unit	Standard Price	Total Cost per Unit
Direct material	10 yards	$5 per yard	$ 50
Direct labor	5 hours	$8 per DLH	40
Variable overhead	5 hours	$7 per DLH	35
			$125

Actual variable costs incurred during the year were as follows.

Direct materials purchased and used (133,400 yards @ $5.25)	$ 700,350
Direct labor cost incurred (79,750 DLH @ $7.80)	622,050
Variable overhead costs incurred	533,600
	$1,856,000

Required

a. Prepare a performance report that isolates Pressure Reducers' flexible budget and sales volume variances.
b. Calculate the direct materials price and quantity variances.
c. Calculate the direct labor rate and efficiency variances.
d. Calculate the variable overhead spending and efficiency variances.
e. Show that the sum of direct materials, direct labor, and variable overhead variances equals the flexible budget variance for variable cost of goods sold in part (a).
f. Prepare a memo to Hank Martinez explaining why the actual variable cost of goods sold differed from the budgeted amount.

6-32 Comprehensive variance calculations (CMA Adapted) (LO 2, 3, 4, 5, 6, 7, 8) Stratton, Ltd. manufactures shirts, which it sells to customers for embroidering with various slogans and emblems. The standard cost card for the shirts is as follows.

	Standard Price	Standard Quantity	Standard Cost
Direct materials	$ 4 per yard	1.5 yards	$ 6.00
Direct labor	$12 per DLH	0.5 DLH	6.00
Variable overhead	$ 4 per DLH	0.5 DLH	2.00
Fixed overhead	$ 6 per DLH	0.5 DLH	3.00
			$17.00

Sandy Robison, operations manager, was reviewing the results for November when he became upset by the unfavorable variances he was seeing. In an attempt to understand what had happened, Sandy asked CFO Suzy Summers for more information. She provided the following overhead budgets, along with the actual results for November.

The company purchased and used 80,200 yards of fabric during the month. Fabric purchases during the month were made at $3.90 per yard. The direct labor payroll ran $319,725, with an actual hourly rate of $12.25 per direct labor hour. The annual budgets were based on the production of 50,000 shirts, using 250,000 direct labor hours. Though the budget for November was based on 50,000 shirts, the company actually produced 52,000 shirts during the month.

Variable Overhead Budget

	Annual Budget	Per Shirt	November—Actual
Indirect material	$ 450,000	$0.90	$ 49,200
Indirect labor	300,000	0.60	31,400
Equipment repair	200,000	0.40	20,500
Equipment power	50,000	0.10	6,900
Total	$1,000,000	$2.00	$108,000

Fixed Overhead Budget

	Annual Budget	November—Actual
Supervisory salaries	$ 260,000	$ 22,000
Insurance	350,000	27,500
Property taxes	80,000	6,500
Depreciation	320,000	26,000
Utilities	210,000	20,300
Quality inspection	280,000	25,000
Total	$1,500,000	$127,300

Required

a. Calculate the direct materials price and quantity variances for November.
b. Calculate the direct labor rate and efficiency variances for November.
c. Calculate the variable overhead spending and efficiency variances for November.
d. Calculate the fixed overhead spending variance for November.
e. Provide an explanation for each variance you calculated.
f. Which of these variances should Sandy be held responsible for? Why?

C&C SPORTS CONTINUING CASE

6-33 Interpreting variances (LO 3, 5) As discussed in Units 6.2 and 6.3, C&C Sports experienced direct materials and direct labor variances as a result of purchasing lower-quality jacket lining from a new vendor. Review Exhibits 6-10 and 6-13 to refresh your understanding of these variances.

Required

Consider each scenario independently.

a. Assume that after experiencing the variances associated with the lower-quality lining, C&C Sports decides to purchase lining from its previous vendor. Based on past experience, C&C's inventory manager, Bradley Austin, does not anticipate any problems with the previous vendor providing an adequate supply of lining at the appropriate quality level. Provided that C&C's standards are current, what effect would you anticipate this move to have on the direct materials price variance? On the direct materials quantity variance? On the direct labor rate variance? On the direct labor efficiency variance?

b. Assume that after investigating the recent variances arising from the lower-quality lining purchase, C&C Sports decides to continue purchasing this lining and to focus on training its workers to improve their ability to cut and sew the lining. Those workers who had never worked on jackets and were pulled into service to meet the production schedule are also included in this training effort. What effect would you anticipate this move to have on the direct materials price variance? On the direct materials quantity variance? On the direct labor rate variance? On the direct labor efficiency variance?

c. After completing the December production rush, C&C Sports' sales budget does not require any award jacket production in the first quarter. When production resumes at a low level in April, what effect would you anticipate the lack of recent production experience to have on the direct materials price variance? On the direct materials quantity variance? On the direct labor rate variance? On the direct labor efficiency variance?

CASES

6-34 Flexible budgeting (CMA Adapted) (LO 1) Spitzer Specialty Furniture manufactures furniture for specialty shops throughout the Southwest. With annual sales of $12 million, the company has four major product lines—bookcases, magazine racks, end tables, and bar stools—each of which is managed by a different production manager. Since production is spread fairly evenly over the year, controller Sara Massey has prepared an annual budget that is divided into 12 monthly reporting periods.

Spitzer uses a standard cost system and applies variable overhead on the basis of machine hours. Fixed manufacturing overhead is allocated to the product lines based on the square footage they occupy using a predetermined plantwide rate. The size of the occupied space varies considerably across product lines. At the monthly meeting to review June's results, Ken Ashley, manager of the bookcase line, received the following performance report.

Spitzer Specialty Furniture
Bookcase Production Performance Report
For the Month Ended June 30

	Actual	Budget	Variance
Units	3,000	2,500	500 F
Sales Revenue	$161,000	$137,500	$23,500 F
Variable production expenses:			
Direct material	23,100	20,000	3,100 U
Direct labor	18,300	15,000	3,300 U
Overhead	60,200	51,250	8,950 U
Fixed production expenses:			
Indirect labor	9,400	6,000	3,400 U
Depreciation	5,500	5,500	
Taxes	2,400	2,300	100 U
Insurance	4,500	4,500	
Administrative expense	12,000	9,000	3,000 U
Marketing expense	8,300	7,000	1,300 U
Research & development	6,000	4,500	1,500 U
Operating profit	$ 11,300	$ 12,450	($ 1,150 U)

While distributing the performance report at the meeting, Sara remarked to Ken, "We need to talk about getting your division back on track. See me after the meeting."

Ken had been so convinced that his division did well in June that Sara's remark surprised him. He spent the balance of the meeting avoiding eye contact with his fellow managers and trying to figure out what could have gone wrong. The monthly performance report was no help to him.

Required

a. Identify at least three weaknesses in the June production performance report.
b. Discuss the behavioral implications of Sara's remark to Ken.
c. Prepare a more informative production performance report for June to assist in the evaluation of Ken's division.
d. Discuss how your recommended changes in reporting are likely to affect Ken's behavior.

6-35 Ethics; responsibility for direct materials and direct labor variances (CMA Adapted) (LO 2, 3, 4, 5) Taylor Jenkins jumped out of his chair. Harrington Chemicals, a sales lead that Taylor had been working on for six months, had just placed its first order for 8,000 bottles of Omnigar. To get the order, Taylor had had to promise a delivery date of May 20. Though he didn't take the time to check with the production scheduler, he was sure the company wouldn't have any problems filling an order for this important new customer. Harrington's order was more than enough to push Taylor over the April bonus threshold. Since Taylor was retiring at the end of April, it would be a satisfying way to end his 30-year career. If the company missed the delivery date, he would be long gone by the time it happened.

Harrington's order was not met with much enthusiasm when it reached the desk of production scheduler Missy Price. "What was Jenkins thinking when he promised a May 20 delivery date?" she complained. "He knows I have to approve all the delivery dates. We've already scheduled all our available labor for May on the Omnigar line." Purchasing agent Pat Melton's reaction was similar. "I don't know where I'll get the raw materials for those extra 8,000 bottles. Our supplier is running low and only has enough material for the 12,000 bottles already scheduled for May."

In response to these concerns, Omnigar's production manager, Charles Elliot, called a meeting to decide how to handle the Harrington order without disrupting the schedule. Pat Melton reported, "Another supplier of raw materials is willing to ship to us, but we have to commit to buy 18,000 pounds at a total cost of $142,200. He promises that the materials are the same quality as those we normally use." Missy Price reported that she could move Class II labor from another product to help with the extra 8,000 bottles. The standard wage for Class II labor is $16 per direct labor hour.

The standard direct materials and labor costs for one bottle of Omnigar are as follows:

Direct materials:	1.5 pounds at $8 per pound
Direct labor:	1.2 Class III direct labor hours at $14 per direct labor hour

At the end of May, Controller Aiden Brown called Charles to discuss the month's results.

Aiden: Charles, what's up with Omnigar this month? You're usually right on target with standard costs. Just glancing at this performance report makes me think there must be a huge labor variance. Can you give me some insight before I start crunching the numbers?

Charles: I'm not surprised. Everything seemed to go wrong in May, but none of it was under my control. We were all set to produce 12,000 bottles of Omnigar based on the orders we had in house. Then Taylor Jenkins decided to do the company one last favor before he retired by accepting a rush order from Harrington Chemical for 8,000 more bottles. He promised a firm delivery date of May 20 without checking with anyone to see if we could meet it. I was able to work with Missy to move some Class II workers over to Omnigar. And as you know, they earn $2 more per hour than the Class III workers who normally work the Omnigar line. If I could have done all the production with Class III workers, I think the labor rate variance would have been negligible.

Aiden: I didn't know that Class II workers knew how to make Omnigar. I bet their inexperience affected their productivity as well.

Charles: Luckily, the Class II workers got up to speed quickly. The real problem was with the raw materials Pat purchased to do the Harrington order. I know she did the best she could under the circumstances. Our regular supplier couldn't provide any more materials, so Pat found a new supplier with a great price. He promised that the materials were the same quality as those we usually buy, but they were nowhere near the same quality as those of our regular supplier. Spoilage went through the roof! The problem was, we couldn't tell whether the material was good or bad until we had almost finished production. And the error rate didn't seem to be affected by the class of workers we used.

Aiden: Well, it certainly sounds as if this was an atypical month for your group. Do you have any information that will help me to analyze the problem?

Charles: Yes, I do. And I think all the variances need to be charged to the sales department, not to me. They are the ones who caused all the problems, by accepting the Harrington order and promising delivery on May 20.

To get a better picture of the problem, Aiden drew up the following breakdown of the production costs associated with the two different materials:

	Regular Materials	Alternative Materials
Direct materials used (in pounds)	18,200	15,800
Production (in bottles)		
Class III workers	7,200	4,800
Class II workers	4,800	3,200
Total production	12,000	8,000
Actual direct labor hours		
Class III workers	8,600	6,600
Class II workers	5,900	4,400
Total direct labor hours	14,500	11,000

	Class II	Class III
Actual direct labor payroll	$163,770	$216,600

Required

a. Was Charles correct in asserting that the alternative material from the new supplier was inferior in quality? Calculate a direct materials quantity variance for both the regular and the alternative materials.

b. Prepare a labor rate variance analysis by worker class for Aiden.

c. Was Charles correct in asserting that both classes of labor experienced similar efficiency problems in working with the materials? Compare the direct labor efficiency variances for both classes of workers using (a) regular materials and (b) alternative materials. (Perform four separate variance calculations.)

d. Which of the variances do you believe should be the sales department's responsibility? Why?

e. Did Taylor Jenkins act ethically in accepting Harrington's order? Why or why not? Did Pat Melton act ethically in acquiring the alternative materials from the new vendor? Why or why not?

6-36 Comprehensive flexible budgets and variance analysis (CMA Adapted) (LO 1, 2, 3, 4, 5, 6, 8) At the monthly management meeting, Leslie Smith, president of Mama Fran's Fantastic Foods, was reviewing the April budget report with some satisfaction. "Our actual results are never exactly what we budget, but I guess if we're off by only 2% to 3%, we've done a good job forecasting." The report she referred to follows.

April Budget Report	Actual	Budget	Variance
Sales (in pounds)	450,000	400,000	50,000 F
Revenue	$3,555,000	$3,200,000	$355,000 F
Less variable expenses			
Direct material	865,000	580,000	285,000 U
Direct labor	348,000	336,000	12,000 U
Variable overhead	750,000	648,000	102,000 U
Total variable expenses	1,963,000	1,564,000	399,000 U
Contribution margin	$1,592,000	$1,636,000	($ 44,000 U)

Nathan Porter, the company's purchasing manager, chimed in. "It surprises me that we did as well as we did. I know that chocolate prices went up dramatically last month, so I expected a much larger variance. And we had that little mix-up when we ordered a batch of whole almonds instead of sliced almonds."

But controller Ashley Corley looked concerned. "Hang on a minute, guys. I don't think this budget report gives us the true picture. Let me work on it some more and get back to you."

Ashley's first step was to track down the following standard cost card for the cookies.

Chocolate Nut Supreme Cookies

Item	Quantity	Standard Unit Cost	Total Cost	
Direct materials				
Cookie mix	10 ounces	$0.02 per ounce	$0.20	
Milk chocolate	5 ounces	$0.15 per ounce	0.75	
Almonds	1 ounce	$0.50 per ounce	0.50	
Total direct materials				$1.45
Direct labor				
Mixing	1 minute	$14.40 per hour	0.24	
Baking	2 minutes	$18.00 per hour	0.60	
Total direct labor				0.84
Variable overhead	3 minutes	$32.40 per hour		1.62
Total standard cost per pound				$3.91

Ashley also tracked down this additional information about the month's operations.

Item	Actual Quantity Used	Actual Cost
Direct materials		
Cookie mix	4,650,000 ounces	$ 93,000
Milk chocolate	2,660,000 ounces	532,000
Almonds	480,000 ounces	240,000
Direct labor		
Mixing	540,000 minutes	108,000
Baking	800,000 minutes	240,000
Variable overhead		750,000
Total actual variable costs		$1,963,000

Required

a. Prepare a more informative performance report for the month of April.
b. Are the results better or worse than Leslie had first thought? Explain your answer.
c. Did Mama Fran's sell its cookies at the budgeted selling price? If not, was the trade-off between the price and the sales quantity a good choice? Why or why not?
d. Calculate the direct materials variances for each input, assuming that all materials purchased were used during the month.
e. Calculate the direct labor variances for April.
f. Calculate the variable overhead variances for April.
g. What do you think might have caused the April variances?
h. Prepare a memo that Ashley Corley can send to Leslie Smith explaining the month's results.

ANALYTICS PROBLEM

Direct materials variance calculation and interpretation (LO 2) (Data set from "The Weight of Euro Coins: Its Distribution Might Not Be As Normal As You Would Expect," Ziv Shkedy, Marc Aerts, and Herman Callaert, *Journal of Statistics Education*, Volume 14, Number 2 [2006], used by permission of the authors.)

The 1 Euro coin has a silver-colored inner core and a yellow outer ring. The center core is made from a copper-nickel alloy, while the outer ring is made of nickel brass. The coins are minted through a series of steps that combine two separate metal disks into the final coin that should weigh 7.5 grams. (You can watch a video of the process to make a 2 Euro coin at https://www.youtube.com/watch?v=rFDsSMDeV3w.) You are a quality control technician in the mint and are responsible for ensuring that the coins meet the official weight and size specifications. As part of this work, you have weighed 2,000 coins from eight different production runs to determine whether the machines producing the metal disks are operating to specifications.

Required

a. Assume that the standard cost of metal in the coin is €.09. Calculate the direct materials quantity variance for each batch of the coin sample. Do the coins appear to be too heavy or too light? (You may find the COUNTIF and SUMIF functions helpful.)
b. Prepare an XY scatterplot of the data using Excel's charting tool. The horizontal axis should be coin weight and the vertical axis should be batch number. What do you notice about the coin weights?
c. Calculate the average weight of the coins.
d. Calculate the average coin weight for each batch. (You may find the AVERAGEIF function helpful.)
e. Recognizing that there may be some variation in the weight of the disks, assume that specifications allow the coins to be within +/–.01 gram of the target 7.5 gram weight. Based on the information you have gathered, do you believe there is a problem with the weights of the disks being used to make the Euro coins? What if the tolerance is +/–.03 gram?
f. Given that the coins are a combination of two separate disks of different metals, how would you determine which of the two disks is outside of specification?

The Excel data files for answering this problem can be found in WileyPLUS.

ENDNOTES

1. In this usage, "material" is not to be confused with direct material or indirect material.
2. The bad debt expense flexible budget variance is not included here because it is unlikely that the sales strategy had anything to do with customers' payment practices.
3. "Thinking Outside the Cereal Box," Pallavi Gogoi, *BusinessWeek*, July 28, 2003, 74–75.
4. Not all companies agree on where to classify overtime charges. Some companies, like C&C, choose to classify overtime premiums as direct labor. Other companies choose to treat overtime premiums as a cost of providing production capacity and therefore consider the premiums to be part of manufacturing overhead. Of course, if overtime premiums are classified as manufacturing overhead, the premium cannot be an explanation for the direct labor rate variance.
5. "Is the Third Shift Pulling Its Weight?" Kate Hazelwood, *BusinessWeek*, July 28, 2003, 14.
6. You might recall from Chapter 5 that C&C's budgeted fixed overhead cost for the quarter was $144,655. How can that number be different here? When the number of units produced and the number of units sold are the same, all of fixed overhead is recognized in the period it was incurred. Remember, though, that C&C budgeted to produce fewer units than needed to meet sales, causing the Finished Goods Inventory balance to go down. When sales is greater than production, some fixed overhead cost from prior periods is recorded on the income statement (see also Chapter 4).

TOPIC FOCUS 4: STANDARD COSTING SYSTEMS

TOPIC FOCUS

4

FOCUS	LEARNING OBJECTIVES
TOPIC FOCUS 4	**LO 1:** Understand how a standard costing system is used to value inventory and control costs.
	LO 2: Calculate the fixed overhead volume variance.

TOPIC FOCUS 4—GUIDED UNIT PREPARATION

Answering the following questions while you read this focus unit will guide your understanding of the key concepts found in the unit. The questions are linked to the learning objectives presented at the beginning of the focus unit.

LO 1

1. What is the difference between a normal costing system and a standard costing system?
2. In recording variances, is an unfavorable variance recorded as a debit or a credit? Why?
3. How are variances typically disposed of?

LO 2

4. What is the only reason for a fixed overhead volume variance?

Business Decision and Context

Kelly MacGregor, Durable Zipper Company's inventory accountant, was ready to pull her hair out. Keeping up with inventory costs was a real challenge, since actual costs could fluctuate on a daily basis. She always had to try to figure out which zippers were made with which batch of inputs so that costs would be properly recorded. Once the zippers were finished and sold, it was an even greater challenge to get the correct costs recorded in cost of goods sold.

DURABLE ZIPPER COMPANY

Inventory Accountant
Kelly MacGregor

"There has to be a better way of recording these costs in our accounting records,"

"There has to be a better way of recording these costs in our accounting records."

Kelly lamented. "How do companies that are larger than us, with more inputs and products, do it?"

Watch the Starbucks video in WileyPLUS to learn more about standard costing systems in the real world.

In Chapter 6, we learned how to calculate variances as a way of evaluating a company's performance. Some companies will calculate variances at the end of a period (monthly, quarterly, and so on) by comparing their recorded costs to the standard costs they should have incurred. That is what C&C Sports does. Specifically, C&C uses a **normal costing system** in which direct materials and direct labor are recorded at actual cost, and overhead is applied to products using a predetermined overhead rate. At the end of the period, only over- or underapplied overhead cost needs to be adjusted to the actual overhead cost.

Other companies use a **standard costing system**, in which all product costs are recorded at standard cost while the products are being made. A unit recorded in inventory last week and one recorded in inventory today both will have been recorded at the same standard cost, regardless of the *actual* cost of the unit. This way, there is never any question about the recorded cost of a unit in inventory; it's always at the standard cost.

At the end of an accounting period, the balances in all inventory and cost of goods sold accounts will be at standard amounts. Because the inventory and cost of goods sold amounts must be reported on financial statements at actual cost rather than standard cost, companies make adjustments to the recorded balances through a series of journal entries using the variances we learned to calculate in Chapter 6 to change from standard cost to actual cost. This Topic Focus Unit will take you through the standard costing process using one of the companies in C&C's supply chain—Durable Zipper Company—as an example.

Durable Zipper Company makes the brass zippers that C&C uses in the production of its baseball pants. Recall from the bill of materials in Chapter 4 (see Exhibit 4-13) that C&C pays $0.29 per zipper. C&C purchases the zippers in batches of 1,000, and Durable's standard cost for a batch of 1,000 zippers is $220. Exhibit T4-1 shows Durable's standard cost card for one batch of 1,000 zippers. Machine hours is the activity base used to apply overhead.

The company expects to use its five machines a total of 10,000 hours each year (2,000 hours per machine). Because all five machines do exactly the same thing, five batches of zippers are always in process. Each batch of zippers takes one machine hour to make, so the company expects to make 10,000 batches of

EXHIBIT T4-1

Standard cost card for one batch of brass zippers.

Direct materials	27.5 pounds of brass @ $3.60/pound	$ 99
Direct labor	4 direct labor hours @ $11/DLH	44
Variable overhead	1 machine hour @ $27/machine hour	27
Fixed overhead	1 machine hour @ $50/machine hour	50
Total standard cost per 1,000 zippers		$220

zippers each year. Variable overhead costs are expected to be $270,000, resulting in a variable overhead rate of $27 per machine hour ($270,000 ÷ 10,000 MH). Fixed overhead costs are expected to be $500,000, resulting in a fixed overhead rate of $50 per machine hour ($500,000 ÷ 10,000 MH).

The following production events occurred at Durable Zipper Company during the year.

- 9,858 batches of zippers were produced and sold.
- 280,000 pounds of brass were purchased at $3.65 per pound.
- 273,395 pounds of brass were used during the year.
- 40,000 direct labor hours were worked at a cost of $10.50 per hour.
- Machines ran for 9,990 hours.
- Variable overhead costs totaled $263,000.
- Fixed overhead costs totaled $510,000.

The next sections will show how to record these events using a standard costing system.

Recording Direct Materials

When materials are purchased, the transaction is recorded in the Direct Materials Inventory account at the standard price, and Accounts Payable is charged for the full amount owed to the supplier. For Durable Zipper Company, Raw Materials Inventory is credited for $1,008,000 (280,000 pounds of brass purchased × $3.60 standard price per pound), and Accounts Payable is credited for $1,022,000 (280,000 pounds of brass purchased × $3.65 actual price per pound). The difference between those two amounts is charged to the direct materials price variance to balance the journal entry. The variance is calculated using the equation in Exhibit 6-9:

Direct materials price variance = AQ × (AP − SP) = 280,000 × ($3.65 − $3.60) = $14,000 U

The following journal entry would be used to record Durable Zipper's materials price variance at the time the brass is purchased.

Account	Debit	Credit
Raw Materials Inventory	1,008,000	
Direct Materials Price Variance	14,000	
Accounts Payable		1,022,000
To record the purchase of direct materials		

While this entry suggests that all the brass was purchased at one time, it is actually a summary of the individual entries that would have been made with each purchase. If the actual price had been less than the standard price, Direct Materials Price Variance would have been credited, rather than debited.

When direct materials are transferred to the production floor, Work in Process Inventory is debited for the standard cost of materials. For the production of 9,858 batches of zippers, 271,095 pounds of brass (27.5 standard pounds per batch × 9,858 batches = 271,095 pounds) would be transferred at a standard cost of $975,942 (271,095 pounds × $3.60 standard price per pound). The credit to Raw Materials Inventory is recorded using the *actual* amount of material transferred at the standard price. Since 273,395 pounds of brass were actually used, the credit to Raw Materials Inventory is $984,222 (273,395 pounds × $3.60 per pound). The direct materials quantity variance is the difference between these two entries and is calculated using the equation in Exhibit 6-9:

Direct materials quantity variance = SP × (AQ − SQ) = $3.60 × (273,395 − 271,095) = $8,280 U

The following journal entry would be used to record Durable Zipper's materials quantity variance at the time the brass is used in production.

Work in Process Inventory	975,942	
Direct Materials Quantity Variance	8,280	
Raw Materials Inventory		984,222
To record the use of direct material		

Again, this entry suggests that all the brass was requisitioned at one time. Actually, it is a summary of the individual entries that would have been made with each direct materials requisition. If the actual usage had been less than the standard quantity allowed, Direct Materials Quantity Variance would have been credited rather than debited.

THINK ABOUT IT T4.1

When direct materials are issued to the production line, why is Raw Materials Inventory credited for the actual quantity at standard price instead of the actual quantity at actual price?

Recording Direct Labor

As products are being made, Work in Process Inventory is debited for the standard cost of labor. The standard cost of labor consists of two components: standard quantity of direct labor hours allowed for actual production and standard direct labor rate per hour. For Durable Zippers, the standard quantity of direct labor allowed is 39,432 hours (9,858 batches × 4 hours per batch), and the standard direct labor rate is $11 per hour. Therefore, the amount debited to Work in Process Inventory is $433,752 (39,432 direct labor hours × $11 per hour). The credit to Wages Payable is the actual amount of the payroll, $420,000 (40,000 direct labor hours × $10.50 per hour).

The direct labor rate and efficiency variances are recorded at the same time as the payroll. The direct labor rate variance is calculated using the equation in Exhibit 6-12:

Direct labor rate variance = AQ × (AP − SP) = 40,000 × ($10.50 − $11.00) = $20,000 F

The direct labor efficiency variance can also be calculated using the equation in Exhibit 6-12:

Direct labor efficiency variance = SP × (AQ − SQ) = $11 × (40,000 − 39,432) = $6,248 U

The following journal entry summarizes the journal entries that Durable Zipper made each pay period.

Work in Process Inventory	433,752	
Direct Labor Efficiency Variance	6,248	
Direct Labor Rate Variance		20,000
Wages Payable		420,000
To record direct labor costs incurred		

Recording Variable Overhead

Recording events related to variable overhead requires three separate journal entries. First, as products are made during the period, variable overhead is applied to Work in Process Inventory using the predetermined variable overhead rate and the standard quantity of the application base allowed. Durable Zipper's applied variable overhead for the period is $266,166 (9,858 batches × 1 machine hour per batch × $27 per machine hour), recorded through the following journal entry. (See Unit 4.3 for a review of how to apply overhead.)

Work in Process Inventory	266,166	
Manufacturing Overhead		266,166
To apply variable overhead costs to production		

The second journal entry to record variable overhead in a standard costing system is for the actual overhead incurred. When invoices are received for the variable overhead components, the following journal entry is made. Again, this journal entry suggests that all variable overhead is recorded at one time. In actuality, a separate entry would be made for each individual invoice received.

Manufacturing Overhead	263,000	
Accounts Payable or Cash		263,000
To record actual variable overhead costs incurred		

The final journal entry is made at the end of the period, to record the variable overhead spending and efficiency variances and close over- or underapplied overhead. Recall from Chapter 4 that Manufacturing Overhead is a temporary

REALITY CHECK—*Are standard costing systems headed for extinction?*

© Brasil2/iStockphoto

Standard costing systems were first developed in the early 1900s as a means of controlling operations and valuing inventory, among other business decisions. In fact, they appear to have been a popular thesis topic, as students explored standard costing systems in the lumber, ice cream, and rubber footwear industries.

Within the last 20 years, standard costing systems have come under fire as new tools and techniques, such as activity-based costing and just-in-time inventory, have developed. While many people have warned of the decline of standard costing systems, studies show that this talk may be premature. Standard costing systems are still prevalent throughout the world.

Proponents of lean accounting believe standard costing systems encourage wasteful practices and, therefore, should be eliminated.

The latest threat to standard cost systems relevance is lean accounting, which seeks to eliminate all forms of waste throughout the organization. Proponents of lean accounting believe standard costing systems encourage wasteful practices and, therefore, should be eliminated. As this latest movement gathers steam, we may well see standard costing systems move down the path of extinction.

Sources: D. M. Colton, *The National Retail Lumber Dealers Association Standard Cost System*, Columbia University, 1930; R. C. Cox, *A Standard Cost System for an Ice Cream Company*, University of North Carolina at Chapel Hill, 1937; Mark C. DeLuzio, "Accounting for Lean," *Manufacturing Engineering*, 137, no. 6 (December 2006): 83–89; Frances A. Kennedy and Peter C. Brewer, "Lean Accounting: What's It All About," *Strategic Finance*, 87, no. 5 (November 2005): 27–34; H. A. Raymond, *Operation of a Standard Cost System in a Rubber Footwear Factory*, Boston University, 1934; F. E. Smetheram, *A Standard Cost System for a Manufacturer*, University of Washington, 1930; Anura De Zoysa and Siriyama Kanthi Herath, "Standard Costing in Japanese Firms: Reexamination of Its Significance in the New Manufacturing Environment, *Industrial Management & Data Systems*, 107, no. 2 (2007): 271–283.

account that must have a zero balance at the end of the accounting period. After recording the previous two journal entries, Manufacturing Overhead has a credit balance of $3,166 [$263,000 actual − $266,166 applied]. A credit balance means that overhead was overapplied, so the account is closed by debiting Manufacturing Overhead for the $3,166 difference. (If Manufacturing Overhead is *underapplied*, this entry would be a credit.)

The overapplied balance can be separated into the variable overhead spending and variable overhead efficiency variances. The variable overhead spending variance is calculated using the equation in Exhibit 6-15:

Variable overhead spending variance = Actual cost − (AQ × SP) = $263,000 − (9,990 machine hours × $27) = $6,730 F

The variable overhead efficiency variance is calculated using the equation in Exhibit 6-15:

Variable overhead efficiency variance = SP × (AQ − SQ) = $27 × (9,990 machine hours − 9,858 machine hours) = $3,564 U

Unfavorable variances require a debit entry; favorable variances, a credit entry. The following journal entry records Durable Zipper's variable overhead variances and disposes of the overapplied variable overhead for the period.

Manufacturing Overhead	3,166	
Variable Overhead Efficiency Variance	3,564	
Variable Overhead Spending Variance		6,730
To record the variable overhead efficiency and spending variances		

Recording Fixed Overhead

As with variable overhead, three separate journal entries are required to record fixed overhead in a standard costing system. As products are made, fixed overhead cost is applied to Work in Process Inventory using the predetermined fixed overhead rate and the standard quantity of the application base allowed. Thus Durable Zipper's applied fixed overhead for the period is $492,900 (9,858 batches × 1 machine hour per batch × $50 per machine hour), recorded through the following journal entry. (See Unit 4.3 for a review of how to apply overhead.)

Work in Process Inventory	492,900	
Manufacturing Overhead		492,900
To apply fixed overhead costs to production		

The second journal entry to record fixed overhead in a standard costing system is for the actual overhead incurred. When invoices are received for the various fixed overhead costs, the following journal entry is made. This journal entry suggests that all fixed overhead is recorded at one time. In actuality, a separate entry would be made for each individual invoice received.

Manufacturing Overhead	510,000	
Accounts Payable or Cash		510,000
To record actual fixed overhead costs incurred		

After recording the previous two journal entries, Manufacturing Overhead has a debit balance of $17,100 [$510,000 actual − $492,900 applied]. A debit balance means that overhead was underapplied, so the account is closed by crediting Manufacturing Overhead for the $17,100 difference. (If Manufacturing Overhead is *overapplied*, this entry would be a debit.)

The underapplied balance can be separated into the fixed overhead spending and fixed overhead volume variances. You learned in Unit 6.4 that the fixed overhead spending variance is quite easy to calculate: it is simply the difference between budgeted and actual fixed overhead cost: $510,000 actual fixed overhead − $500,000 budgeted fixed overhead = $10,000 U. The **fixed overhead volume variance** is the difference between budgeted fixed overhead and applied fixed overhead: $500,000 budgeted fixed overhead − $492,900 applied fixed overhead = $7,100 U. Exhibit T4-2 shows how these variances are calculated in tabular format.

When actual activity differs from the expected level of activity, a fixed overhead volume variance occurs. If production is greater than expected, the volume variance is favorable, because the fixed overhead is spread over more units than expected, reducing the per unit cost. If production is less than expected, the volume variance is unfavorable because fixed overhead must be spread over fewer

EXHIBIT T4-2

Analyzing fixed overhead variances under a standard costing system.

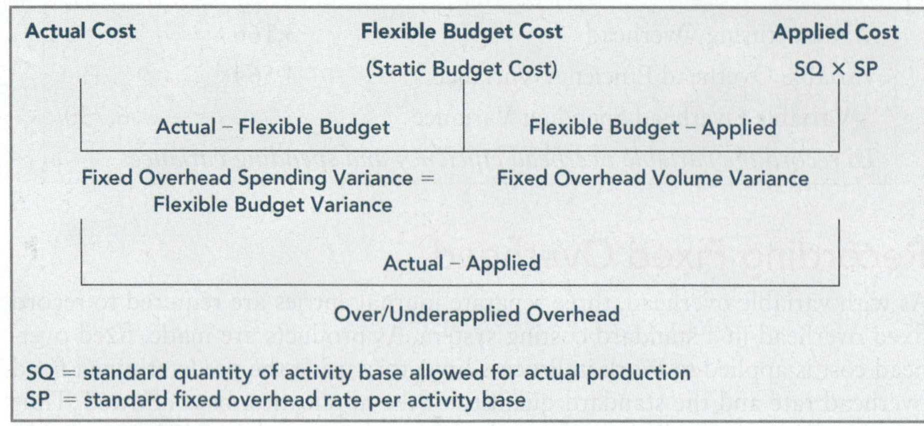

units than expected, raising the per unit cost. If Durable Zipper Company's managers had known that only 9,858 batches would be made requiring a standard of 9,858 machine hours, they would have set the predetermined fixed overhead rate at $50.72 per machine hour, or ($500,000 ÷ 9,858 machine hours), instead of $50, and there would have been no volume variance. The following journal entry records Durable Zipper's fixed overhead variances and disposes of the underapplied fixed overhead for the period.

Fixed Overhead Spending Variance	10,000	
Fixed Overhead Volume Variance	7,100	
Manufacturing Overhead		17,100
To record the fixed overhead spending and volume variances		

The $17,100 adjustment to Manufacturing Overhead closes out the fixed overhead from this account. Combining this adjustment with those from variable overhead results in a zero balance in the Manufacturing Overhead account, as required.

THINK ABOUT IT T4.2

The fixed overhead volume variance can easily be explained as being caused by the production level—that is, by making more or fewer units than budgeted. Why is the same not true of the direct materials quantity variance, the direct labor efficiency variance, and the variable overhead efficiency variance?

Transferring Completed Units to Finished Goods Inventory

Once units are complete, their cost must be transferred from Work in Process Inventory to Finished Goods Inventory. Since all inventory accounts in a standard costing system are recorded at the standard cost, this transfer is recorded at the standard cost of the completed units.

Durable Zipper Company completed 9,858 batches of zippers that must be transferred from Work in Process Inventory to Finished Goods Inventory. The standard cost for one batch of zippers is $220 (see Exhibit T4-1), so $2,168,760 (9,858 batches × $220 standard cost per batch) must be transferred to Finished Goods Inventory through the following journal entry.

Finished Goods Inventory	2,168,760	
Work in Process Inventory		2,168,760
To transfer completed units to finished goods inventory		

This journal entry suggests that all transfers are recorded at one time. In actuality, a separate entry would be made for each individual batch transfer.

Recording Cost of Goods Sold

When units are sold, their cost must be transferred from Finished Goods Inventory to Cost of Goods Sold. Since all inventory accounts in a standard costing system are recorded at the standard cost, this transfer is recorded at the standard cost of the sold units.

Durable sold 9,858 batches of zippers that must be transferred from finished goods to cost of goods sold. The standard cost for one batch of zippers is $220 (see Exhibit T4-1), so $2,168,760 (9,858 batches × $220 standard cost per batch) must be transferred to Cost of Goods Sold through the following journal entry.

Cost of Goods Sold	2,168,760	
Finished Goods Inventory		2,168,760
To transfer sold units to Cost of Goods Sold		

This journal entry suggests that all sales are recorded at one time. In actuality, a separate entry would be made for each sale. Additionally, a journal entry is required to record the sales revenue and related accounts receivable or cash payment.

Disposing of Variances

The variances are recorded in actual general ledger accounts, though the accounts are temporary ones. This means they need to be closed to a permanent general ledger account at the end of the accounting period. The easiest approach is to close the variance accounts to the Cost of Goods Sold account. However, if the variances are considered material (significant in dollar amount), they should be closed to the appropriate inventory accounts, similar to the way overhead was disposed of in Unit 4.4. This final adjustment brings the inventory and Cost of Goods Sold accounts back to actual cost.

Let's look at one variance as an example. The Direct Labor Rate Variance account has a $20,000 credit balance from the journal entry that recorded the variance. To bring this account to a zero balance, we must debit the account for $20,000. This process is followed for each of the variances, and the amount needed to balance the debits and credits is made to Cost of Goods Sold. The following journal entry shows how Durable Zipper's variances would be closed to the Cost of Goods Sold account:

Cost of Goods Sold	22,462	
Direct Labor Rate Variance	20,000	
Variable Overhead Spending Variance	6,730	
Direct Materials Price Variance		14,000
Direct Materials Quantity Variance		8,280
Direct Labor Efficiency Variance		6,248
Variable Overhead Efficiency Variance		3,564
Fixed Overhead Spending Variance		10,000
Fixed Overhead Volume Variance		7,100
To close variances to Cost of Goods Sold		

Advantages of Standard Costing

After all of these journal entries, you might wonder why a company would want to implement a standard costing system. A standard costing system gives visibility to the variances that arise in the production process. Because the variances must be recorded and closed to Cost of Goods Sold, the impact of missing standards becomes unavoidably clear to managers. Alternatively, if the variances are small, then managers don't need to spend their time evaluating processes that are in control. Essentially, standard costing systems provide managers with information to keep production processes operating as planned.

TOPIC FOCUS REVIEW

KEY TERMS

Fixed overhead volume variance p. 351

Normal costing system p. 346

Standard costing system p. 346

PRACTICE QUESTIONS

1. LO 1 Which of the following journal entries would be used to record a variance that arose when materials with a standard price of $5.00 per unit were purchased at a price of $4.00 per unit?

a.

Direct Materials Inventory	XXXX	
Direct Materials Price Variance		XXXX
Accounts Payable		XXXX

b.

Direct Materials Inventory	XXXX	
Direct Materials Price Variance	XXXX	
Accounts Payable		XXXX

c.

Direct Materials Inventory	XXXX	
Direct Materials Quantity Variance		XXXX
Accounts Payable		XXXX

d.

Direct Materials Inventory	XXXX	
Direct Materials Quantity Variance	XXXX	
Accounts Payable		XXXX

2. LO 2 Which of the following statements is true?

a. Any company that calculates variances will need to close those variances at the end of the accounting period.

b. Companies that use standard costing systems record variances in temporary accounts that must be closed at the end of an accounting period.

c. Companies that use a normal costing system will record direct materials and direct labor variances.

d. All of the statements are true.

3. LO 2 Marston Co. applies fixed overhead on the basis of machine hours. At the end of the year the company had a fixed overhead volume variance of $5,000 U. Based on this information,

a. Marston spent more on fixed overhead than budgeted.

b. Marston spent less on fixed overhead than budgeted.

c. Marston made fewer units than budgeted.

d. Marston made more units than budgeted.

TOPIC FOCUS 4 PRACTICE EXERCISE

Pressure Reducers, Inc., produces and sells ergonomic computer keyboard trays that telescope and adjust to accommodate any user's needs. At the beginning of the year, the company planned to produce and sell 15,000 trays. However, only 14,500 trays were actually produced and sold during the year. Beginning Work in Process and Finished Goods Inventories had zero balances.

The company uses the following standard cost card in its standard costing system.

	Standard Quantity/Unit	Standard Price	Total Cost/Unit
Direct material	10 pounds	$ 5 per pound	$ 50
Direct labor	5 direct labor hours	$ 8 per DLH	40
Variable overhead	5 direct labor hours	$ 7 per DLH	35
Fixed overhead	5 direct labor hours	$12 per DLH	60
			$185

Actual costs incurred during the year were as follows.

Direct materials purchased and used (133,400 pounds @ $5.25 per pound)	$ 700,350
Direct labor cost incurred (79,750 direct labor hours @ $7.80 per hour)	622,050
Variable overhead costs incurred	533,600
Fixed overhead incurred	915,000
	$2,771,000

Required

a. Prepare the journal entries to record the purchase and use of direct materials.
b. Prepare the journal entry to record the use of direct labor.
c. Prepare the journal entry to record the application of variable overhead to production.
d. Prepare the journal entry to record actual variable overhead costs incurred.
e. Prepare the journal entries to record the variable overhead variances.
f. Prepare the journal entry to record the application of fixed overhead to production.
g. Prepare the journal entry to record actual fixed overhead costs incurred.
h. Prepare the journal entries to record the fixed overhead variances.
i. Prepare the journal entry to transfer the completed units from Work in Process Inventory to Finished Goods Inventory.
j. Prepare the journal entry to transfer sold units from Finished Goods Inventory to Cost of Goods Sold.
k. Prepare the journal entry to close all variances to Cost of Goods Sold.

SELECTED TOPIC FOCUS 4 ANSWERS

Think About It T4.1

When raw materials are purchased, Raw Materials Inventory is debited for the actual amount of materials purchased at standard price. Therefore, when the materials are removed from inventory, they need to be removed at the price at which they were initially recorded, that is, the standard price.

Think About It T4.2

The fixed overhead volume variance is caused by the misestimation of expected production activity at the beginning of the period. If more units are produced than expected, the predetermined fixed overhead rate is higher than necessary, causing a favorable volume variance. If fewer units are produced than expected, the predetermined fixed overhead rate is lower than necessary, causing an unfavorable volume variance. The direct materials quantity, direct labor efficiency, and variable overhead efficiency variances are used to help explain the difference between actual costs and flexible budget costs. Flexible budget costs are calculated at the actual level of activity, not the expected level of activity.

Practice Questions

1. A 2. B 3. C

Topic Focus 4 Practice Exercise

a.

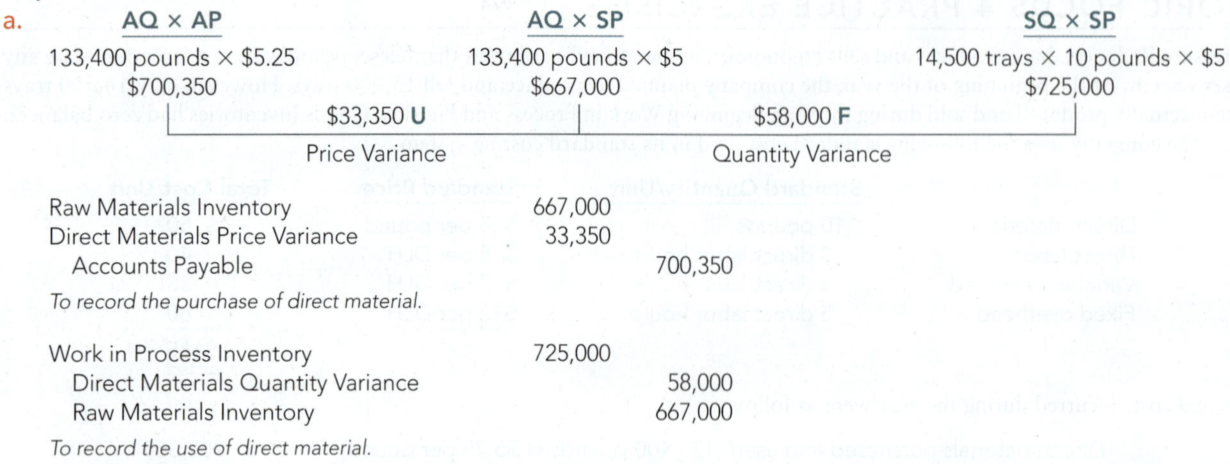

AQ × AP	AQ × SP	SQ × SP
133,400 pounds × $5.25	133,400 pounds × $5	14,500 trays × 10 pounds × $5
$700,350	$667,000	$725,000
$33,350 **U** Price Variance	$58,000 **F** Quantity Variance	

Raw Materials Inventory	667,000	
Direct Materials Price Variance	33,350	
Accounts Payable		700,350

To record the purchase of direct material.

Work in Process Inventory	725,000	
Direct Materials Quantity Variance		58,000
Raw Materials Inventory		667,000

To record the use of direct material.

b.

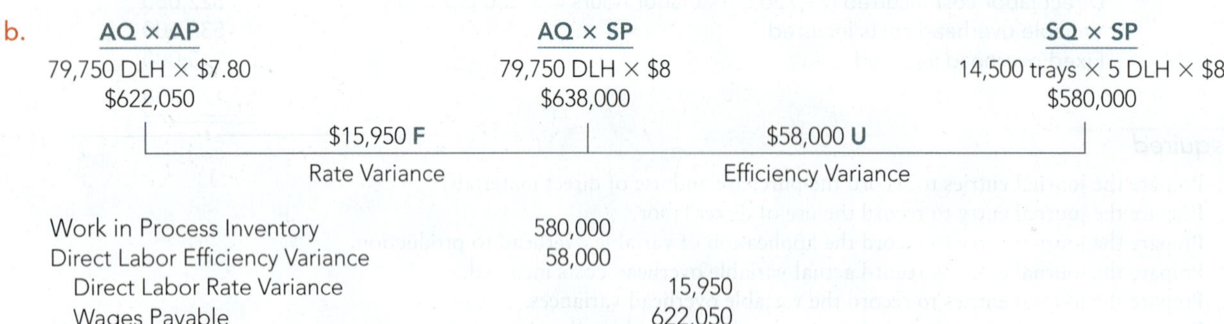

AQ × AP	AQ × SP	SQ × SP
79,750 DLH × $7.80	79,750 DLH × $8	14,500 trays × 5 DLH × $8
$622,050	$638,000	$580,000
$15,950 **F** Rate Variance	$58,000 **U** Efficiency Variance	

Work in Process Inventory	580,000	
Direct Labor Efficiency Variance	58,000	
Direct Labor Rate Variance		15,950
Wages Payable		622,050

To record direct labor cost.

c.

Actual	AQ × SP	SQ × SP
	79,750 DLH × $7	14,500 trays × 5 DLH × $7
$533,600	$558,250	$507,500
$24,650 **F** Spending Variance	$50,750 **U** Efficiency Variance	

Work in Process Inventory	507,500	
Manufacturing Overhead		507,500

To apply variable overhead cost to production.

d.

Manufacturing Overhead	533,600	
Accounts Payable or Cash		533,600

To record actual variable overhead cost incurred.

e.

Variable Overhead Efficiency Variance	50,750	
Variable Overhead Spending Variance		24,650
Manufacturing Overhead		26,100

To record the variable overhead efficiency and spending variances.

f.

Actual	Static Budget	SQ × SP
	15,000 trays × 5 DLH × $12	14,500 trays × 5 DLH × $12
$915,000	$900,000	$870,000
$15,000 **U**		$30,000 **U**
Spending Variance		Volume Variance

Work in Process Inventory	870,000	
Manufacturing Overhead		870,000

To apply fixed overhead cost to production.

g.

Manufacturing Overhead	915,000	
Accounts Payable or Cash		915,000

To record actual fixed overhead costs incurred.

h.

Fixed Overhead Spending Variance	15,000	
Fixed Overhead Volume Variance	30,000	
Manufacturing Overhead		45,000

To record the fixed overhead spending and volume variances.

i. 14,500 trays produced × $185 standard cost per tray = $2,682,500

Finished Goods Inventory	2,682,500	
Work in Process Inventory		2,682,500

To transfer completed units to Finished Goods Inventory.

j. 14,500 trays sold × $185 standard cost per tray = $2,682,500

Cost of Goods Sold	2,682,500	
Finished Goods Inventory		2,682,500

To transfer sold units to Cost of Goods Sold.

k.

Cost of Goods Sold	88,500	
Direct Materials Quantity Variance	58,000	
Direct Labor Rate Variance	15,950	
Variable Overhead Spending Variance	24,650	
Direct Materials Price Variance		33,350
Direct Labor Efficiency Variance		58,000
Variable Overhead Efficiency Variance		50,750
Fixed Overhead Spending Variance		15,000
Fixed Overhead Volume Variance		30,000

To close variances to Cost of Goods Sold.

BUSINESS DECISION AND CONTEXT Wrap Up

Kelly MacGregor's job is easier now. With the implementation of a standard costing system, she records all inventory amounts using standard costs. Differences between actual costs and standards are recorded in variance accounts. At the end of the month, Kelly closes the variance and manufacturing overhead accounts to Cost of Goods Sold to convert the standard costs back to actual costs for financial reporting.

More important than the accounting for inventory, Kelly has better information to use in making decisions. As she calculates variances, she is able to notify the appropriate manager to take action if the variances are significant.

TOPIC FOCUS SUMMARY

In this focus unit you learned how a standard costing system is used to value inventory. Specifically, you should be able to meet the objectives set out at the beginning of this focus unit:

1. ***Understand how a standard costing system is used to value inventory and control costs.***

Standard costing systems record all inventory accounts at standard cost. Differences between standard and actual costs are recorded in variance accounts. At the end of an accounting period, the variance accounts are closed to Cost of Goods Sold.

The journal entries used in a standard costing system are as follows. For ease of presentation, all the variances are recorded as debits, representing unfavorable variances. If a variance is favorable, you should record it as a credit.

Raw Materials Inventory	$AQ_{purchased} \times SP$	
Direct Materials Price Variance	$AQ_{purchased} \times (AP - SP)$	
Accounts Payable		$AQ_{purchased} \times AP$
To record the purchase of direct material.		
Work in Process Inventory	$SQ \times SP$	
Direct Materials Quantity Variance	$SP \times (AQ_{used} - SQ)$	
Raw Materials Inventory		$AQ_{used} \times SP$
To record the use of direct material.		
Work in Process Inventory	$SQ \times SP$	
Direct Labor Rate Variance	$AQ \times (AP - SP)$	
Direct Labor Efficiency Variance	$SP \times (AQ - SQ)$	
Wages Payable		$AQ \times AP$
To record direct labor cost.		
Work in Process Inventory	$SQ \times SP$	
Manufacturing Overhead		$SQ \times SP$
To apply variable overhead cost to production.		
Manufacturing Overhead	Actual	
Accounts Payable or Cash		Actual
To record actual variable overhead costs incurred.		
Variable Overhead Spending Variance	Actual − $(AQ \times SP)$	
Variable Overhead Efficiency Variance	$SP \times (AQ - SQ)$	
Manufacturing Overhead		Sum
To record the variable overhead efficiency and spending variances.		
Work in Process Inventory	$SQ \times SP$	
Manufacturing Overhead		$SQ \times SP$
To apply fixed overhead cost to production.		
Manufacturing Overhead	Actual	
Accounts Payable or Cash		Actual
To record actual fixed overhead costs incurred.		

Account	Debit	Credit
Fixed Overhead Spending Variance	Actual − Budget	
Fixed Overhead Volume Variance	Budget − (SQ × SP)	
Manufacturing Overhead		Sum
To record the fixed overhead spending and volume variances.		
Finished Goods Inventory	Actual units produced × Standard cost	
Work in Process Inventory		Actual units produced × Standard cost
To transfer completed units to Finished Goods Inventory.		
Cost of Goods Sold	Actual units sold × Standard cost	
Finished Goods Inventory		Actual units sold × Standard cost
To transfer sold units to Cost of Goods Sold.		
Cost of Goods Sold	Sum	
Direct Materials Price Variance		$AQ_{purchased}$ × (AP − SP)
Direct Materials Quantity Variance		SP × (AQ_{used} − SQ)
Direct Labor Rate Variance		AQ × (AP − SP)
Direct Labor Efficiency Variance		SP × (AQ − SQ)
Variable Overhead Spending Variance		Actual − (AQ × SP)
Variable Overhead Efficiency Variance		SP × (AQ − SQ)
Fixed Overhead Spending Variance		Actual − Budget
Fixed Overhead Volume Variance		Budget − (SQ × SP)
To close variances to Cost of Goods Sold.		

2. ***Calculate the fixed overhead volume variance.***
Budgeted fixed overhead cost − (SQ × SP)

EXERCISES

T4-1 Recording direct materials in a standard costing system (LO 1) Washington WaterWorks manufactures snorkel gear. During the past month, Washington purchased 4,000 pounds of plastic to use in its dive masks, at a cost of $6,800. The standard price for the plastic is $1.60 per pound, and each mask requires 1/4 pound of plastic. The company actually used 3,800 pounds of the plastic to produce 15,000 dive masks.

Required

a. Prepare the journal entry to record the purchase of plastic during the month.
b. Prepare the journal entry to record the use of plastic during the month.

T4-2 Recording direct materials in a standard costing system (LO 1) TechSolvers produces 8-foot USB cables. During the past year, the company purchased 500,000 feet of plastic-coated wire at a price of $0.25 per foot. The direct materials standard for the cables allows 8.5 feet of wire at a standard price of $0.23. During the year, the company used a total of 535,000 feet of wire to produce 63,000 8-foot cables.

Required

a. Prepare the journal entry to record the purchase of wire during the month.
b. Prepare the journal entry to record the use of wire during the month.

T4-3 Recording direct labor transactions in a standard costing system (LO 1) The following information is available for Claire's Delights:

Actual production	16,000 units
Budgeted production	16,200 units
Direct Labor:	
Standard	4 hours per unit @ $10 per hour
Actual	65,600 hours @ $9.85 per hour

Required

Prepare the journal entry to record the direct labor payroll.

T4-4 Recording direct labor in a standard costing system (LO 1) POD Incasements manufactures protective cases for cell phones. During November, the company's workers clocked 800 more direct labor hours than the flexible budget amount of 25,000 hours to complete 100,000 cases for the Christmas season. All workers were paid $9.25 per hour, which was $0.50 more than the standard wage rate.

Required

Prepare the journal entry to record the direct labor payroll for November.

T4-5 Recording variable overhead in a standard costing system (LO 1) Waterworks, Inc. makes plastic water bottles that are used by various beverage makers. Demand for bottles was so high during the year that the company made 255,000 bottles, 15,000 more than budgeted. Bottles are made in batches of 100, and the standard amount of machine time to make one batch of bottles is 1 hour. During the year, $38,250 of variable overhead cost was applied to Work in Process Inventory. Actual variable overhead cost incurred was $40,000, and 2,600 machine hours were used.

Required

a. Prepare the journal entry to record actual variable overhead costs incurred.
b. Prepare the journal entry to record the application of variable overhead to production.
c. Prepare the journal entry to record the variable overhead spending and efficiency variances.

T4-6 Recording variable overhead in a standard costing system (LO 1) Dunlap Company produces 3-inch binders at its Killeen plant. The following information is available for the year:

Production:	
Budgeted	100,000 binders
Actual	98,000 binders
Standard costs:	
Direct labor	.5 DLH per binder @ $12 per hour
Variable overhead	.5 DLH per binder @ $6 per hour
Actual costs:	
Direct labor	47,040 DLH @ $11.90 per hour
Variable overhead	$282,000

Required

a. Prepare the journal entry to record actual variable overhead costs incurred.
b. Prepare the journal entry to record the application of variable overhead to production.
c. Prepare the journal entry to record the variable overhead spending and efficiency variances.

T4-7 Calculating variable and fixed overhead variances (LO 1, 2) The following information is available for Talley Company:

Production:	
Budgeted	75,000 units
Actual	76,000 units
Standard costs:	
Direct labor	10 DLH per unit @ $15 per hour
Variable overhead	10 DLH per unit @ $8 per hour
Fixed overhead	10 DLH per unit @ $9 per hour
Actual costs:	
Direct labor	756,000 DLH @ $15.50 per hour
Variable overhead	$6,040,000
Fixed overhead	$6,758,000

Required

a. Calculate the variable overhead spending and efficiency variances.
b. Calculate total budgeted fixed overhead cost.
c. Calculate the fixed overhead variances.

T4-8 Recording fixed overhead in a standard costing system (LO 2) The following information is available for Chad's Chocolates:

Actual production	2,800 boxes
Budgeted production	3,200 boxes
Standard direct labor hours	3 DLH per box
Actual direct labor hours	8,960
Fixed Overhead	
Standard	$5 per direct labor hour
Actual	$52,000

Required

a. Prepare the journal entry to record actual fixed overhead costs incurred.
b. Prepare the journal entry to record the application of fixed overhead to production.
c. Prepare the journal entry to record the fixed overhead spending and volume variances.

PROBLEMS

T4-9 Calculating and recording fixed overhead variances (CMA Adapted) (LO 1, 2) Jonah Company manufactures deep-sea fishing rods, which it distributes internationally through a chain of wholesalers. The following data is taken from the budget prepared by Jonah's controller at the beginning of the year. The company uses a predetermined overhead rate based on annual budgeted amounts and applies overhead on the basis of machine hours.

	Annual Budget
Variable manufacturing overhead	$2,400,000
Fixed manufacturing overhead	$1,200,000
Direct labor hours	48,000
Machine hours	240,000

During the year, Jonah used 51,500 direct labor hours and 250,010 machine hours. The standard quantity for actual production was 50,000 direct labor hours and 250,000 machine hours. Actual fixed manufacturing overhead incurred was $1,198,500; variable manufacturing overhead incurred was $2,455,000.

Required

a. Prepare the journal entries to record actual and applied fixed overhead for the year.
b. Calculate the fixed overhead spending and volume variances for the year.
c. Why did Jonah have a fixed overhead volume variance?
d. Was fixed overhead under- or overapplied? By how much?
e. Prepare the journal entry to record the fixed overhead spending and volume variances.
f. Prepare the journal entry to close the fixed overhead variances to Cost of Goods Sold.

T4-10 Calculating fixed overhead volume variance (CMA Adapted) (LO 2)

Gerald/Brooke, Ltd., manufactures shirts, which it sells to customers for embossing with various slogans and emblems. The standard cost card for the shirts is as follows.

	Standard Price	Standard Quantity	Standard Cost
Direct materials	$1.60 per yard	1.25 yards	$2.00
Direct labor	$12 per DLH	0.25 DLH	3.00
Variable overhead	$4 per DLH	0.25 DLH	1.00
Fixed overhead	$6 per DLH	0.25 DLH	1.50
			$7.50

The annual budgets were based on the production of 1,000,000 shirts, using 250,000 direct labor hours. Due to slight seasonal demands, the company plans to produce 80,000 shirts per month, January through August, and 90,000 shirts per month, September through December.

Required

a. Calculate total budgeted fixed overhead cost.
b. What is the monthly fixed overhead budget amount? Does it depend on the number of shirts that are produced each month?
c. What monthly fixed overhead volume variance does management expect between January and August? Between September and December? At the end of the year? Why does this happen?
d. What overhead rates would eliminate the expected monthly fixed overhead volume variances and still result in no volume variance at year-end? What do you think of this alternative to one annual overhead rate?

T4-11 Recording transactions in standard costing systems (CMA Adapted) (LO 1, 2)

Water Movers, Inc. is known throughout the world for its H2O-X high-capacity water pump, used in irrigation systems. The company uses a standard costing system, and the pump's standard cost is as follows. The company's predetermined fixed overhead rate is based on an expected capacity of 100,000 direct labor hours per month.

	Standard Price	Standard Quantity	Standard Cost
Direct materials	$6 per pound	15 pounds	$ 90
Direct labor	$9 per DLH	4 DLH	36
Variable overhead	$8 per DLH	4 DLH	32
Fixed overhead	$5 per DLH	4 DLH	20
			$178

During the month of September, the company produced 22,000 of the 25,000 pumps that had been scheduled for production in the budget. The company used 382,000 pounds of material during September. The direct labor payroll for the month was $940,000 for 94,000 direct labor hours. Variable overhead costs were $740,000; fixed overhead costs were $540,000.

The company's purchasing agent signed a new supply contract that resulted in purchases of 500,000 pounds of direct materials at a price of $2,750,000.

Required

a. Prepare the journal entries to record the purchase and use of direct materials during September.
b. Prepare the journal entry to record the use of direct labor during September.
c. Prepare the journal entry to record actual variable overhead costs incurred.
d. Prepare the journal entry to record the application of variable overhead to production.
e. Prepare the journal entry to record actual fixed overhead costs incurred.
f. Prepare the journal entry to record the application of fixed overhead to production.
g. Prepare the journal entries to record the variable and fixed overhead variances.
h. Prepare the journal entry to close all variances to Cost of Goods Sold.

© jsnyderdesign/iStockphoto

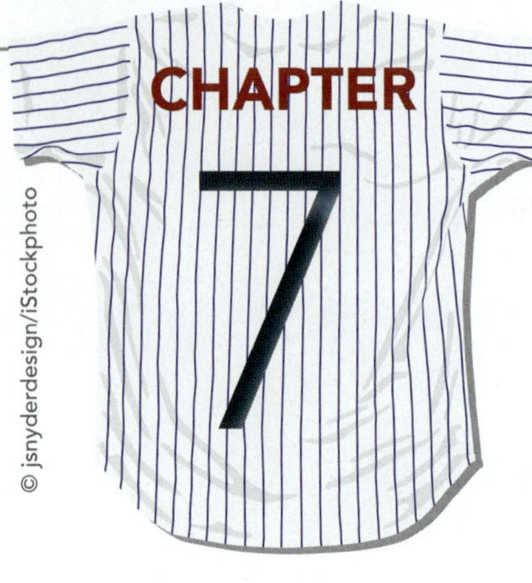

ACTIVITY-BASED COSTING AND ACTIVITY-BASED MANAGEMENT

UNITS	LEARNING OBJECTIVES
UNIT 7.1 Activity-Based Costing	**LO 1:** Classify activities as unit-level, batch-level, product-level, customer-level, or organization-level.
UNIT 7.2 Developing Activity-Based Product Costs	**LO 2:** Calculate activity-based product costs. **LO 3:** Explain the difference between traditional product costs and activity-based product costs.
UNIT 7.3 Activity-Based Management	**LO 4:** Distinguish between value-added and non-value-added activities. **LO 5:** Explain how information about activities can be used to make decisions.

© Rehan Qureshi/Shutterstock

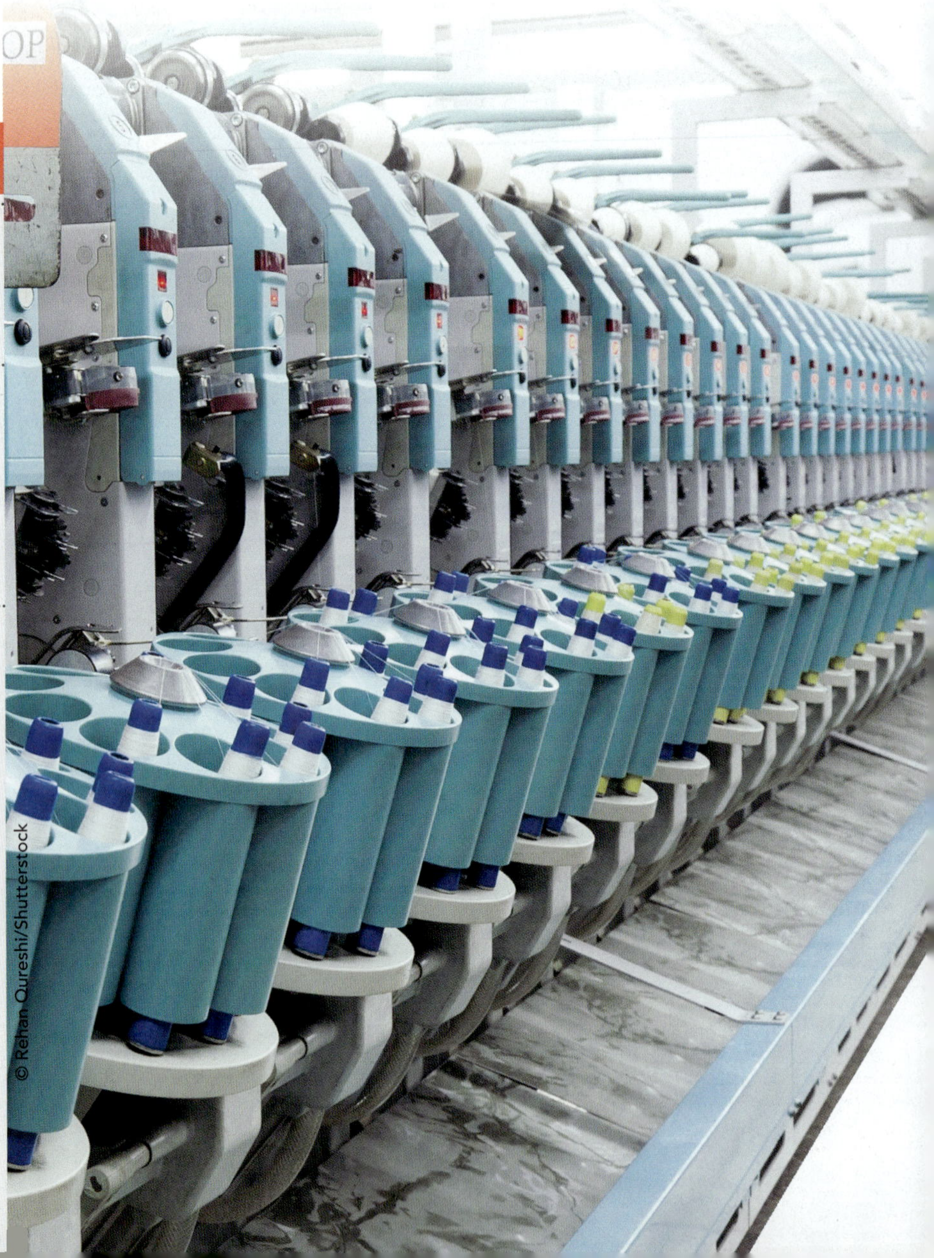

Business Decision and Context

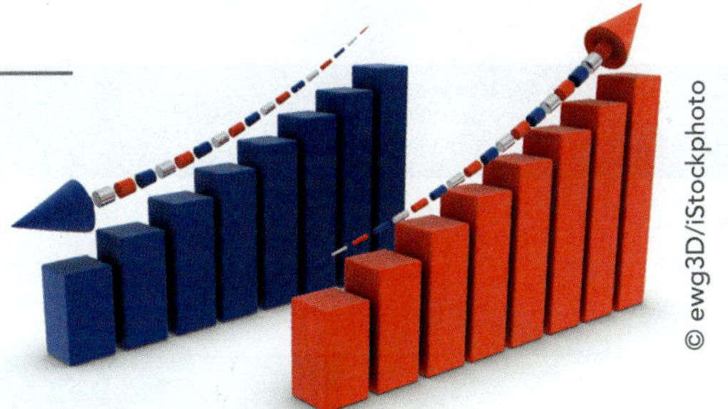

© ewg3D/iStockphoto

It was early in 2018, and C&C Sports' managers were reeling from the recently released operating results for 2017. Selling more award jackets than budgeted should have increased C&C's operating income, but that hadn't happened. Instead, costs had skyrocketed (see Chapter 6). Direct material and direct labor costs were part of the problem, but other production costs had come in much higher than expected.

George Douglas, C&C Sports' president, called a meeting of upper management to discuss the unexpected results. "We've never missed budgeted income by this much," said Douglas. "I am more convinced than ever that we don't understand what it costs to make our products," **vice president for finance and administration**, **Claire Elliot** replied. "You're right," **Chad Davis**, **vice president for operations**, chimed in, "but our production has been fairly stable for the last several years. As we've added more award jackets to the mix, operations have become more complex. I've been telling you all that making jackets isn't the same as making pants and jerseys. I'm not saying that they're a bad product line, but we have to do a lot more to make a jacket than we do for the other two products."

> "Our production has been fairly stable for the last several years. As we've added more award jackets to the mix, operations have become more complex."

"Selling the jackets is no easy job, either," commented **Jonathan Smith**, **vice president for marketing**. "It takes a lot more time and advertising to complete a sale. Thank goodness the jackets are priced high enough to make it worthwhile. Apparently our competitors don't want to go to as much trouble as we do. We've been hearing that our jackets are higher quality and less expensive than our competitors'. I'm convinced that we could sell even more jackets next year."

"Well, we can't just stop operations until we figure out this problem," said George. "Let's keep to our plan of improving cash flow and meeting sales targets, but let's not sell any more jackets than we did last year until we know what's going on. In the meantime, we need to find out why our costs have increased so dramatically." The meeting adjourned with everyone still scratching their heads.

Watch the Precor video in WileyPLUS to learn more about activity-based costing in the real world.

SUPPLY CHAIN KEY PLAYERS

END CUSTOMER

UNIVERSAL SPORTS EXCHANGE

C&C SPORTS

President
George Douglas

Vice President for Finance and Administration
Claire Elliot

Vice President for Operations
Chad Davis

Vice President for Marketing
Jonathan Smith

DURABLE ZIPPER COMPANY

BRADLEY TEXTILE MILLS

CENTEX YARNS

NEFF FIBER MANUFACTURING

BRUIN POLYMERS, INC.

UNIT 7.1

Activity-Based Costing

GUIDED UNIT PREPARATION

Answering the following questions while you read this unit will guide your understanding of the key concepts found in this unit. The questions are linked to the learning objectives presented at the beginning of the chapter.

LO 1

1. What is an activity? Provide some examples.
2. Define the following activity types and provide one example of each:
   a. Unit-level activity
   b. Batch-level activity
   c. Product-level activity
   d. Customer-level activity
   e. Organization-level activity
3. What characteristics of an organization make it a good candidate to implement activity-based costing? When is activity-based costing not likely to benefit an organization?

In preceding chapters, you have learned how managers use product cost information to make a variety of decisions. But what happens if that product cost information is distorted? Managers may make poor decisions, and results may not occur as expected. That is what C&C Sports' managers experienced when the company produced and sold more award jackets than budgeted. Revenue increased, but costs increased more than they expected, decreasing the company's income. Apparently, award jackets cost more to produce than the managers realized.

Managers at Starn Tool & Manufacturing in Meadville, Pennsylvania, had a similar experience. The company's product costing system did not reflect the way costs were actually incurred on the shop floor. As president and owner Bill Starn realized, some jobs that looked profitable were actually losing money, while others that looked unprofitable were making money. The company turned to activity-based costing. Now that managers better understand the costs the company incurs, job bidding is more accurate.[1]

In this unit we will explore the differences between traditional, GAAP-based product costing (see Chapter 4) and activity-based costing.

Why Activity-Based Costing?

What leads a manager to question the accuracy of the reported costs of products or services? Typically, doubt arises when a company's operating or financial results haven't materialized as expected. At C&C Sports, higher revenue coupled with lower operating income suggested that award jackets might be more costly to produce than profitability reports showed. At other companies, the continual loss of business to a lower bidder, even when managers believe that their bid barely covers costs, might be the source of suspicion.

Recall from Chapter 4 that direct materials and direct labor costs are directly traceable to products and services. Calculating the direct materials and direct labor costs that have been incurred to produce a product or deliver a service is relatively simple. If *all* costs could be traced directly to cost objects in this way, there would be no problem. Managers would know exactly how much it cost to produce a product or deliver a service. So if product costs have become a problem, nontraceable costs, such as manufacturing overhead, must be the source. The problem is the way that these manufacturing overhead costs are allocated to a product or service.

When direct materials and direct labor comprise the majority of product costs, manufacturing overhead allocation is not a major issue. But in recent decades, manufacturing overhead has increased in size relative to direct materials and direct labor. Armstrong Laing Group estimates that in the last 35 years, manufacturing overhead cost has more than doubled, climbing to approximately 40% of total product cost.[2] In that same period, direct labor cost has fallen by more than half, to approximately 10% of total product cost. With such a dramatic increase in manufacturing overhead cost, the choice of a method for allocating the cost has become an important managerial decision.

Activity-based costing (ABC) is a costing technique that assigns costs to cost objects such as products or customers, based on the activities those cost objects require. An **activity** is an event that consumes resources. Activities include tasks such as ordering materials, processing purchase orders, and setting up machines. When Oxford University Library Services implemented an ABC system, it identified activities such as ordering books from publishers, shelving and reshelving books, answering customer inquiries, and processing interlibrary loan requests.[3] A simple ABC model can have fewer than 20 activities; a complex model may include over 500 activities.[4]

Frederick Taylor was the first to understand the importance of a business's activities. In the early 1900s, Taylor examined workers' jobs as a set of tasks, each of which had a standard completion time.[5] But his idea was slow to catch on. In *The Practice of Management* (1954), Peter Drucker lamented, "To find out what activities are needed to attain the objectives of the business is such an obvious thing to do that it would hardly seem to deserve special mention. But analyzing the activities is as good as unknown to traditional theory."[6] Activity-based costing did not gain widespread popularity until 1987, when Robin Cooper and Robert Kaplan discussed it in their article "How Cost Accounting Systematically Distorts Product Costs."[7] By 2005, 55% of companies surveyed were actively using activity-based costing; another 32% were considering its adoption.[8]

Exhibit 7-1 illustrates the basic concept of overhead usage in activity-based costing. A company incurs costs to obtain resources such as factories, machinery,

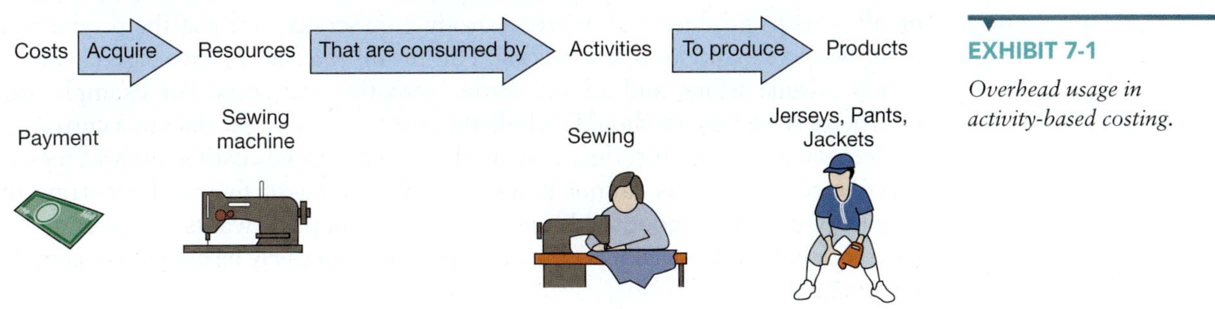

EXHIBIT 7-1

Overhead usage in activity-based costing.

and workers. Those resources are consumed by the activities performed that produce the product or deliver the service to the customer. With activity-based costing, the goal is to allocate a *cost* in a manner that reflects the amount of each *resource* consumed by *the activities* performed to produce a specific *product*. For example, C&C makes cash payments (a cost) to obtain a sewing machine (a resource) for use in sewing (an activity) the company's pants, jerseys, and jackets (products).

Let's look at a simple example to illustrate the problem of manufacturing overhead cost allocation. C&C incurs costs to purchase and operate a forklift that moves bolts of fabric from the warehouse to the cutting department. In Chapter 4 you learned that C&C applies manufacturing overhead to its products based on direct labor cost. Of a total $826,600 in direct labor costs, $440,000 is incurred to produce 183,500 pairs of pants, $127,400 to produce 66,500 jerseys, and $259,200 to produce 18,000 award jackets. Since pants have the highest direct labor cost, they are assigned the largest share of the manufacturing overhead costs related to the forklift. But does the cost of labor affect how often the forklift is used to move a pair of pants or a jacket? It takes one trip from the warehouse to deliver the fabric for a batch of pants and one trip to deliver the fabric for a batch of jackets. Use of the forklift, then, is related to the number of batches moved, not to the direct labor cost incurred.

Are manufacturing overhead costs a problem for all companies? Not necessarily. If a company produces products or delivers services that are very similar, or that consume resources in the same way, then analyzing the details associated with overhead is unlikely to offer greater precision in product costing. Likewise, if a company makes different products, but does so in a separate production facility for each product, there would be no confusion about which overhead costs are incurred for specific products. However, if a company produces products or delivers services that differ in complexity or in their consumption of common (overhead) resources, then greater attention to overhead and the activities that generate overhead costs could provide better cost information for decision making. Indicators that an activity-based costing analysis may be appropriate include the following:[9]

- Bids for complex products are accepted, while bids for simple products are rejected.
- High-volume jobs show losses or minimal profits, while low-volume jobs show healthy profits.
- Bids for jobs that require "special" processing are always accepted.
- Some manufacturing departments run at capacity, whereas others have minimal operations.

Would an activity-based analysis that focused only on manufacturing overhead improve GAAP-based financial statements? No. Because the balances in inventory and cost of goods sold, the two accounts that contain product costs, are aggregate numbers, not much will be gained from shifting costs from one product to another (only to add them together again). But an activity-based analysis that focused on all costs to produce and deliver a product or service, not just the production costs, would enhance decision making. This means that the activity-based analysis would include selling and administrative activities and costs. For example, the total activity-based cost should include the cost to deliver a product to a customer.

Including these nonproduct costs in the activity-based costing analysis means that the resulting costs cannot be used for GAAP-based financial reporting of inventory or cost of goods sold. However, if a company wants to use activity-based costing for financial reporting, the approach can easily be adapted to comply with GAAP.

Analyzing the activities that consume manufacturing overhead, selling, and administrative resources is a time-consuming process. Therefore, managers need to decide what the information will be used for and whether the expected benefit from the new information will be worth the cost to gather it. Because the main reason for generating new information is to help managers make better decisions, we will focus our discussion on providing better product costing information for internal decision making.

Classification of Activities

All activities are not created equal. In an activity-based costing system, activities are classified into five categories: (1) unit-level, (2) batch-level, (3) product-level, (4) customer-level, and (5) organization-level. This classification recognizes that different activities consume resources differently and that different cost objects use activities differently.

Unit-level activities are performed for each individual unit of product. Since each unit of a particular product requires the same level of activity, each unit consumes the same amount of resources that provide that activity. The total level of activity performed varies proportionately with the number of units produced. At C&C Sports, providing electricity to run the sewing machines is a unit-level activity, since the amount of electricity used is a function of the number of units sewn.

Batch-level activities are performed all at once on groups, or batches, of products. Since the activity is based on the existence of the batch rather than on the number of units in the batch, a batch consumes the same amount of resources whether it contains 20 units or 2,000 units. At C&C Sports, pants are produced in batches of 50, jerseys in batches of 35, and jackets in batches of 5. When production begins on pants, the forklift operator gathers enough fabric to make 50 pairs of pants and moves it from the raw materials warehouse to the cutting tables, all at once. The same is true for jerseys and jackets, except that the amount of fabric moved is enough to make 35 jerseys or 5 jackets, respectively. So even though the batches include fabric for ten times more pants than jackets, the cost of moving each batch is the same.

THINK ABOUT IT 7.1

If a batch of 5 jackets and a batch of 50 pants cost the same amount to move, what is the relative moving cost of one jacket compared to one pair of pants?

Product-level activities, also referred to as product-sustaining activities, are those that support the products or services a company provides. These activities are performed for the entire product line, regardless of how many units or batches are produced. At C&C Sports, creating a pattern for a new style of jersey is a product-level activity. When a product is eliminated, these activities are no longer performed.

Customer-level activities are performed for specific customers. For example, making a sales call and processing a sales order are customer-level activities. These activities, and the resources consumed to perform them, do not affect product costs. Rather, the resources are consumed to deliver customer support services, so the associated costs should be used to determine the cost to serve a particular customer. These activities are explored further in Topic Focus 5: *Customer Profitability*.

REALITY CHECK—*At the center of activity*

AFP/Getty Images

Understanding business activities is critical to understanding costs. Without such an understanding, a manager can unwittingly drive an organization into a financial tailspin.

One company that appears to understand how activities work is Plexus Corp., an assembler of electronic goods. Plexus has built a profitable niche by producing a relatively high number of different products in numerous small batches. This company takes on jobs that many larger companies find too small.

Understanding how resources are consumed by batch activities is essential to Plexus's success. Each time the company changes from one small batch to the next, the production line must be retooled for the next product. Through careful facility arrangement and cross-training, Plexus has reduced the time required for such changeovers to as little as 30 minutes.

But just because an organization understands activities doesn't mean that its customers do. Following a U.S. Postal Service rate increase for magazines in July 2007, some publishers showed a clear misunderstanding of the relationship between activities and resource consumption. In a *Los Angeles Times* editorial, they commented that "Rather than base rates on total weight and total number of pieces mailed, the new, complex formula is full of incentives that take into account packaging, shape, distance traveled and more."

Plexus has built a profitable niche by producing a relatively high number of different products in numerous small batches.

The incentives referred to in this quotation include a discounted rate for magazines that bear computer-readable mailing labels, which eliminate the need for human sorting, and a discount for dropping off magazines at a location closer to their final destination, which minimizes final delivery transportation cost. Basically, the new pricing structure is designed to charge for the resources consumed based on the activities performed. But apparently, some people don't want to pay for what they get.

Sources: William M. Bulkeley, "Plexus Strategy: Smaller Runs of More Things," *The Wall Street Journal*, October 8, 2003; Nate Guidry, "Magazines Brace for Higher Postage," *Pittsburgh Post-Gazette*, July 10, 2007; Teresa Stack and Jack Fowler, "Magazines Feeling Postal Pinch," *Los Angeles Times*, May 28, 2007.

Organization-level activities are required to provide productive capacity and to keep the business in operation. These activities do not provide identifiable benefits to specific products or services, but without them there would be no business. At C&C Sports, renting factory space and managing the organization (by the CEO or CFO, for example) are examples of organization-level activities that support the entire business. Regardless of how many units, batches, or products are produced or how many customers are served, these activities must continue. Therefore, the cost of the resources consumed by these activities should not be allocated to products or customers. Notice that this approach differs from GAAP-based product costing, in which costs such as factory rent are included as part of overhead and in the product costs that are used to prepare the financial statements.

Of the five categories of activities, only the first three are product- or service-related. Therefore, we will focus only on those activities in determining the resources that a product or service consumes. Exhibit 7-2 compares the components of product cost used in traditional costing under GAAP-based financial reporting to the components used in internal decision making under activity-based costing.

Although costs of the resources consumed by customer-level and organization-level activities can be allocated to products or services, determining a reasonable

Cost Category	GAAP-Based Product Cost	Activity-Based Product Cost
Direct materials	✓	✓
Direct labor	✓	✓
Manufacturing Overhead		
Unit level	✓	✓
Batch level	✓	✓
Product level	✓	✓
Organization level	✓	
Selling and Administrative Expense		
Unit level		✓
Batch level		✓
Product level		✓
Organization level		

EXHIBIT 7-2

Comparison of GAAP-based and activity-based product costs.

activity measure for use in allocating the costs would be difficult, and the information would not be helpful in decision making. Does that mean managers should ignore these costs? Absolutely not. Instead, managers need to find other ways of determining whether the benefits received from these resources are worth their cost.

Once a company has classified its activities and identified the related resources, managers may discover that some manufacturing overhead costs can be traced directly to products. A "traceable overhead cost" may sound like an oxymoron, because if a cost is traceable, it doesn't need to be allocated. The problem is that companies will often aggregate any manufacturing costs that are not for direct materials or direct labor in manufacturing overhead without considering whether they are traceable. An example of a traceable manufacturing overhead cost at C&C Sports is the cost of operating the chenille machine. This cost, which totals $132,600 and includes depreciation and indirect materials, is directly traceable to the award jackets because the chenille machine is used only to produce award jackets, and should not be allocated to pants and jerseys.

Under GAAP-based product costing, selling and administrative costs are not allocated to products. However, under activity-based costing, these costs should be allocated to products if they are incurred to provide resources that are consumed by unit-level, batch-level, or product-level activities. As with manufacturing overhead costs, some selling and administrative costs may be directly traceable to products. At C&C Sports, three selling costs are traceable to products: shipping, commissions, and a portion of advertising costs. Shipping of $0.40 per unit and commissions of 5% of the sales price are unit-level costs that are easily assigned to products. Direct advertising costs include $85,000 to advertise award jackets and $20,000 each to produce a pants catalog and a jerseys catalog.

As we develop C&C Sports' activity-based product costs, we will use budgeted information to establish performance standards. Exhibits 7-3 and 7-4 show C&C Sports' budgeted production and selling and administrative costs for 2017. This is the same information used to calculate the master budget in Chapter 5. The 2017 budget is based on the following estimated production and sales levels:

	Budgeted Production	Budgeted Sales
Pants	183,500	200,000
Jerseys	66,500	70,000
Award jackets	18,000	18,000

Since the number of units produced differs from the number of units sold, we will analyze production activities separately from selling and administrative activities.

EXHIBIT 7-2

2017 budgeted annual manufacturing overhead costs.

	Fixed Costs	Variable Costs	Total Costs
Indirect labor	$211,000		$ 211,000
Depreciation	46,184		46,184
Indirect materials	98,000	$413,300	511,300
Rent	110,000		110,000
Utilities	17,000	41,330	58,330
Insurance	55,000		55,000
Other	41,436		41,436
Total	$578,620	$454,630	$1,033,250

Based on production of 183,500 pants, 66,500 jerseys, and 18,000 award jackets.

EXHIBIT 7-4

2017 budgeted annual selling and administrative costs.

	Annual
Commissions	$ 284,300
Bad debt expense	171,800
Shipping	115,200
Office equipment depreciation	15,612
Advertising	160,000
Administrative salaries	385,000
Utilities	7,000
Total budgeted expenses	$1,138,912

Based on sales of 200,000 pants, 70,000 jerseys, and 18,000 award jackets.

UNIT 7.1 REVIEW

KEY TERMS

Activity p. 367

Activity-based costing (ABC) p. 367

Batch-level activity p. 369

Customer-level activity p. 369

Organization-level activity p. 370

Product-level activity p. 369

Unit-level activity p. 369

PRACTICE QUESTIONS

1. LO 1 Which of the following would be considered a unit-level activity?
   a. Ordering direct materials
   b. Making a sales call
   c. Preparing the annual budget
   d. Placing a UPC label on each package

2. LO 1 Mary's Mix-ins makes custom ice cream by mixing various candies into vanilla and chocolate ice cream. Orders range in size from 1 to 5 quarts. After each order has been mixed and packed into one-quart containers, the mixing equipment must be cleaned. Cleaning the mixing equipment is an example of a(n)
   a. unit-level activity.
   b. batch-level activity.
   c. product-level activity.
   d. organization-level activity.

3. LO 1 Increasing the number of units in a batch will increase the batch-level costs associated with the product. True or False?

4. LO 1 Which of the following would be considered a product-level activity?

   a. Building a prototype of a product
   b. Creating the company's advertising campaign
   c. Training warehouse employees
   d. Organizing the annual sales meeting

5. LO 1 Which of the following would be considered a customer-level activity?

   a. Ordering the direct materials used in all products
   b. Cleaning the machines before beginning a production run
   c. Making a sales call
   d. Supervising production workers

UNIT 7.1 PRACTICE EXERCISE

Place an X in the column that corresponds to the type of activity level referred to in each scenario.

	UNIT	BATCH	PRODUCT	CUSTOMER	ORGANIZATIONAL
a. Managing the corporate office					
b. Preparing a press release for a new product					
c. Cleaning hotel rooms					
d. Making on-site visits to clients' offices					
e. Making daily deposits of cash receipts					

SELECTED UNIT 7.1 ANSWERS

Think About It 7.1

One jacket costs ten times more to move than one pair of pants. To illustrate, let's say that the cost to move a batch is $100. For a batch of 50 pants, the cost would be $2 per pair ($100 ÷ 50 pairs). For a batch of 5 jackets, the cost would be $20 per jacket ($100 ÷ 5 jackets).

Practice Questions

1. D
2. B
3. False
4. A
5. C

Unit 7.1 Practice Exercise

	UNIT	BATCH	PRODUCT	CUSTOMER	ORGANIZATIONAL
a. Managing the corporate office					X
b. Preparing a press release for a new product			X		
c. Cleaning hotel rooms	X				
d. On-site visits to clients' offices				X	
e. Making daily deposits of cash receipts		X			

UNIT 7.2

Developing Activity-Based Product Costs

GUIDED UNIT PREPARATION

Answering the following questions while you read this unit will guide your understanding of the key concepts found in this unit. The questions are linked to the learning objectives presented at the beginning of the chapter.

LO 2 1. What is an activity cost pool?

LO 2 2. How are activity cost pool rates calculated?

LO 2 3. How many overhead charges will a cost object have under an activity-based costing system?

LO 2 4. How are product costs determined in an activity-based costing system?

LO 2 5. Why are organization-level costs not allocated to products under activity-based costing?

LO 3 6. What does using a "traditional" costing system mean in terms of overhead costs?

LO 3 7. When a company switches from a traditional costing system to activity-based costing, overhead costs typically shift from the high-volume/low-complexity product to the low-volume/high-complexity product. Why is this the case?

Once a company has decided to implement an activity-based costing system, work begins to identify activities and the resources consumed by those activities. By completing the following five steps, a company can implement an activity-based costing system. To be successful, these efforts must have the full support of top management. Although the following discussion may make the process appear to be relatively easy, in reality it is a complex, time-consuming effort. Once the system is in place, however, decision makers will benefit from improved information.

Step 1: Identify Activities

The first step in developing activity-based product costs is to identify the activities performed in the organization. Think of activities as "verbs" that answer the question "What do you do?" If you had to answer the question, what might be some of your responses? "I study, I sleep, I eat." Asking this question of employees is one way to determine the activities they perform; another is to observe what they do. Either way, this step is the most time-consuming part of implementing an activity-based costing system and the one that can generate the greatest error.

In addition to identifying the activities, you need to determine how much time employees spend performing each activity. Let's go back to your answer to the question "What do I do?" While you might find it easy to list what you do, saying how much time you spend on each activity might be harder. For instance, the amount of time you spend studying probably varies each week, depending on what tests you have. The same is true for many employees; the time they spend on certain tasks varies from one month to the next. Nevertheless, employees must make such an estimate so that the resources consumed by the activities (that is, their salaries and other costs) can be calculated.

A critical question to ask during activity identification is "What level of detail does the company want to collect?" The greater the level of detail, the greater the chance of misclassifying some costs and activities. For example, instead of identifying "studying" as an activity, let's say you provide greater detail, such as "studying accounting" or "studying economics." You will likely misestimate the time you spend on each, although you may be fairly confident of the total time you spend studying. Of course, if you could make a detailed estimate without error, breaking "studying" down by your courses would provide better information. The same would be true of any activity costing system: the greater the error-free distinction between activities, the better the information.

As you identify activities, remember that once an activity has been defined, the time spent on that activity and the resources consumed by that activity must be tracked. Thus, defining activities in greater detail will require more monitoring. Will the benefits of defining more detailed activities outweigh the effort needed to monitor activity performance, and the resulting potential for error? To minimize both the cost of collecting the information and the potential for error, most companies that use activity-based costing systems combine related activities into one larger activity. For example, the activities in C&C Sports' cutting department include layering fabric, laying out the pattern, cutting the fabric, collecting the cut pieces, and disposing of waste fabric. While C&C's managers could have chosen to monitor the time spent on each of those activities, they chose instead to group them as a single cutting activity. Since all these activities are batch-level activities, combining them is not an issue. One caution, however: Activities from different categories (say, unit-level versus batch-level) should not be combined.

Step 2: Develop Activity Cost Pools

After all the activities have been identified and the appropriate level of detail has been selected, the activities are combined into **activity cost pools** based on their cost drivers. For example, C&C Sports' managers determined that "moving materials from the storeroom to the cutting room" and "packing finished products" were both batch activities. Because pants, jerseys, and jackets are produced in batches, the number of batches produced determines the frequency of these warehousing and packaging activities and the resources consumed. Therefore, managers combined those two activities into one pool. After gathering all the relevant information about activities and their drivers, C&C Sports' managers determined that the company had the following five activity pools:[10]

Activity Pool	Activity Driver
Product design	Number of product lines
Warehousing/packaging	Number of batches
Cutting	Number of cuts
Sewing	Direct labor hours
General	Not assigned to products

Once the activity pools have been determined, manufacturing overhead costs can be assigned to them. This is referred to as a **first-stage allocation** because costs are assigned first to the activity pools before being assigned to cost objects. Exhibit 7-5 shows the first-stage allocation of manufacturing overhead resources for C&C Sports. These allocations were based on employee estimates of time spent and the resources used to complete the activities. Notice that the $132,600 that relates to the chenille machine is not included in the costs allocated to the activity pools, since those costs are traceable directly to the jackets. All the remaining manufacturing overhead costs are allocated to the activity pools. Compare Exhibit 7-5 to Exhibit 7-3 to see that all the manufacturing overhead costs have been accounted for.

	Chenille Machine Costs Traceable to Jackets	Product Design	Warehousing/ Packaging	Cutting	Sewing	General	Total
Indirect labor	$ 2,514	$40,000	$ 40,000	$ 7,500	$ 15,000	$105,986	$ 211,000
Depreciation	4,092		7,396			34,696	46,184
Indirect materials	125,994	37,512	110,869	135,861	101,064		511,300
Rent						110,000	110,000
Utilities					41,330	17,000	58,330
Insurance						55,000	55,000
Other		6,377	12,297	3,747	14,730	4,285	41,436
Total	$132,600	$83,889	$170,562	$147,108	$206,820	$292,271	$1,033,250

EXHIBIT 7-5 *Step 2: Allocation of manufacturing overhead costs to activity pools.*

Step 3: Calculate Activity Cost Pool Rates

After the manufacturing overhead costs have been assigned to activity cost pools, the next step in developing activity-based product costs is to calculate an **activity rate** for each cost pool. This calculation is similar to the predetermined overhead rate calculation under traditional job order costing (see Chapter 4):

$$\text{Activity Rate} = \frac{\text{Total activity cost pool resources}}{\text{Total activity driver volume}}$$

Exhibit 7-6 shows the calculation of the four activity rates for C&C Sports. Let's review the calculations. For product design, the activity cost totals $83,889 (see Exhibit 7-5). Since the number of product lines is the cost driver and C&C has three product lines (pants, jerseys, and jackets), the denominator is 3 product lines. The calculation of the activity rate is:

$$\frac{\$83,889}{3 \text{ product lines}} = \$27,963 \text{ per product line}$$

	Total Cost (A)	Total Activity (B)	Activity Rate (A) ÷ (B)
Product design	$ 83,889	3 product lines	$27,963 per product line
Warehousing/ packaging	$170,562	9,170 batches	$18.60 per batch
Cutting	$147,108	56,580 cuts	$2.60 per cut
Sewing	$206,820	86,175 direct labor hours	$2.40 per direct labor hour

EXHIBIT 7-6

Step 3: Calculation of activity rates.

For warehousing/packaging, the activity cost totals $170,562. The number of batches produced is the cost driver for this activity pool. It is calculated as follows:

	Budgeted Production		Units per Batch		Number of Batches
Pants	183,500	÷	50	=	3,670
Jerseys	66,500	÷	35	=	1,900
Jackets	18,000	÷	5	=	3,600
Total					9,170

Given this number of batches, the activity rate for this pool is calculated as:

$$\frac{\$170{,}562}{9{,}170 \text{ batches}} = \$18.60 \text{ per batch}$$

THINK ABOUT IT 7.2

Why would the batch size differ for the three product lines?

For cutting, the activity cost totals $147,108. The number of cuts is the cost driver for this activity pool; it is calculated as follows:

	Batches		Cuts per Batch		Total Cuts
Pants	3,670	×	4	=	14,680
Jerseys	1,900	×	5	=	9,500
Jackets	3,600	×	9	=	32,400
Total					56,580

Given this number of cuts, the activity rate is calculated as:

$$\frac{\$147{,}108}{56{,}580 \text{ cuts}} = \$2.60 \text{ per cut}$$

THINK ABOUT IT 7.3

Refer to Exhibit 7-5 to see what costs were allocated to the cutting pool. What specific costs might be included in the cutting pool?

WATCH OUT!

Always label the activity rate with the activity driver. Saying, for example, that the sewing activity rate is $2.40 is not sufficient; it is $2.40 **per direct labor hour**. With the activity driver included, you will know what to multiply the rate by to calculate the allocated cost. To calculate the allocated cost for sewing, for example, you will know that you should multiply the $2.40 by the number of direct labor hours—not, say, the number of units produced.

Finally, for sewing, the activity cost totals $206,820. Direct labor hours is the cost driver for this activity pool, and it is calculated as follows:

	Budgeted Production		Direct Labor Hours per Unit		Total Direct Labor Hours
Pants	183,500	×	0.25 hours	=	45,875
Jerseys	66,500	×	0.20 hours	=	13,300
Jackets	18,000	×	1.50 hours	=	27,000
Total					86,175

Given this number of direct labor hours, the activity rate is calculated as:

$$\frac{\$206{,}820}{86{,}175 \text{ direct labor hours}} = \$2.40 \text{ per direct labor hour}$$

Step 4: Allocate Costs to Products or Services

With the activity rates calculated, you are ready to allocate the costs to products or services.[11] This calculation is similar to the calculation for applying overhead costs to products or services under traditional job order costing (see Chapter 4):

$$\text{Allocated cost} = \text{Activity rate} \times \text{Activity driver consumption}$$

Exhibit 7-7 shows the cost allocations to the three products. Notice that each product has four allocations, one for each of the activity pools. Notice, too, that the activity rate column for each product is the same, since the activity rates are constant, regardless of the product that is consuming the resource. However, each product uses the activities to different degrees, and those differences in usage drive the differences in allocated costs. For example, the cutting cost allocated to pants is $2.60 × 14,680 cuts = $38,168; to award jackets, it is $84,240—why? The answer is that jackets require many more cuts than pants, even though the company makes fewer jackets than pants.

Let's reconcile how the overhead costs from the first-stage allocation (see Exhibit 7-5) were allocated to the three products:

		Overhead Costs
Pants		$ 244,493
Jerseys		119,923
Award jackets		
ABC allocation	$243,963	
Chenille machine costs	132,600	376,563
Total costs allocated		$ 740,979
General costs not allocated		292,271
Total overhead costs		$1,033,250

All the overhead costs have been accounted for. When the overhead cost allocated to the award jackets is added to the chenille costs traced to the award

Pants	Activity Rate		Activity		ABC Cost
Product design	$27,963 per product line	×	1 line	=	$ 27,963
Warehousing/packaging	$18.60 per batch	×	3,670 batches	=	68,262
Cutting	$2.60 per cut	×	14,680 cuts	=	38,168
Sewing	$2.40 per direct labor hour	×	45,875 direct labor hours	=	110,100
					$244,493

Jerseys	Activity Rate		Activity		ABC Cost
Product design	$27,963 per product line	×	1 line	=	$ 27,963
Warehousing/packaging	$18.60 per batch	×	1,900 batches	=	35,340
Cutting	$2.60 per cut	×	9,500 cuts	=	24,700
Sewing	$2.40 per direct labor hour	×	13,300 direct labor hours	=	31,920
					$119,923

Award Jackets	Activity Rate		Activity		ABC Cost
Product design	$27,963 per product line	×	1 line	=	$ 27,963
Warehousing/packaging	$18.60 per batch	×	3,600 batches	=	66,960
Cutting	$2.60 per cut	×	32,400 cuts	=	84,240
Sewing	$2.40 per direct labor hour	×	27,000 direct labor hours	=	64,800
					$243,963

EXHIBIT 7-7 *Step 4: Allocating activity costs to products.*

jackets, the total overhead cost of the award jackets becomes $376,563. Notice that this amount is more than the overhead cost allocated to pants. Even though budgeted production called for only 18,000 jackets as compared to 183,500 pants, jacket production requires many more activities than pants production.

Step 5: Calculate Unit Product Costs

The last step in the preparation of activity-based costing data is to calculate the unit product cost. In Step 4 we calculated the *total* overhead allocated to each product. For decision-making purposes, we need to convert that amount to a *unit* cost by dividing the total overhead cost by the total number of units produced. For example, the overhead cost for a pair of pants would be $1.33 (rounded), calculated as

$$\frac{\$244{,}493}{183{,}500 \text{ pants}} = \$1.33 \text{ per pair of pants}$$

To calculate the total product cost per unit, we need to add the direct materials and direct labor costs to this overhead cost. The total activity-based cost for a pair of pants would be

Direct materials	$4.47
Direct labor	2.40
Overhead	1.33
Total product cost per unit	$8.20

WATCH OUT!

With all the work they put into calculating overhead allocations, students sometimes forget the easiest part of calculating the total product cost—adding the direct materials and direct labor costs to overhead.

REALITY CHECK—*Putting ABC in the recipe for profitability*

Image Source/Getty Images

Managers discovered that the restaurant's main dishes were among the most unprofitable items on the menu.

The restaurant business is a highly competitive industry, known for small profit margins. With over 50% of new restaurants failing within three years of opening the doors, restaurant managers should be on the lookout for ways to increase the chances of survival. Perhaps one solution to increasing restaurant success rates is as easy as ABC—activity-based costing.

It is common practice for a restaurant to set menu prices based on a simple markup over food costs. But this practice fails to explicitly recognize all the activity that is needed to prepare the food and run the restaurant. In several studies, researchers have found that an activity-based costing approach in a restaurant setting provides important information for setting menu prices at a level that can increase the restaurant's profitability and therefore its chances of long-term survival.

From the Bellagio casino bakery in Las Vegas to a buffet restaurant in Hong Kong to an "à la carte" restaurant in Tunisia, activity-based costing has been shown to provide improved meal cost information. The results of the ABC analysis can be startling, as when the Tunisian restaurant managers discovered that the restaurant's main dishes were among the most unprofitable items on the menu. Armed with the new ABC information, managers can improve a menu item's profitability through activity reductions or price increases.

Sources: A. B. H. Salem-Mhamdia and B. B. Ghadhab, "Value Management and Activity Based Costing Model in the Tunisian Restaurant," *International Journal of Contemporary Hospitality Management*, 2012, 24(2), 269–288; H. G. Parsa, John T. Self, David Njite, and Tiffany King, "Why Restaurants Fail," *Cornell Hotel and Restaurant Administration Quarterly*, August 2005, 46(3), 204–322; Paige Vaughn, Carola Raab, and Kathleen B. Nelson, "The Application of Activity-Based Costing to a Support Kitchen in a Las Vegas Casino," *International Journal of Contemporary Hospitality Management*, 2010, 22(7), 1033–1047.

Exhibit 7-8 shows the calculation of the total product costs and unit costs for all three products based on the budgeted production for 2017.

EXHIBIT 7-8

Step 5: Calculating unit product costs.

	Pants	Jerseys	Jackets	Total Costs
Traceable overhead			$132,600	$132,600
Allocated overhead	$244,493	$119,923	243,963	608,379
Total overhead cost	244,493	119,923	376,563	$740,979
Units produced	÷ 183,500	÷ 66,500	÷ 18,000	
Overhead unit	$ 1.33	$ 1.80	$ 20.92	
Direct materials	4.47	6.85	44.72	
Direct labor	2.40	1.92	14.40	
	$ 8.20	$ 10.57	$ 80.04	

Let's compare the activity-based overhead allocation to C&C's original allocation, based on direct labor dollars. Exhibit 7-9 shows the manufacturing overhead costs allocated to each of the products under the two methods. Notice that the total amount of manufacturing overhead allocated to the products differs between the two methods—$1,033,250 under the traditional approach and $740,979 under the activity-based approach. The difference between the

	Pants	Jerseys	Jackets	Total
Traditional				
Direct labor $	$440,000	$127,400	$259,200	$ 826,600
× Overhead rate	125%	125%	125%	125%
= Allocated overhead	$550,000	$159,250	$324,000	$1,033,250
% of total overhead	53.23%	15.41%	31.36%	
ABC				
Traceable			$132,600	$ 132,600
+ Product design	$ 27,963	$ 27,963	27,963	83,889
+ Warehousing/packaging	68,262	35,340	66,960	170,562
+ Cutting	38,168	24,700	84,240	147,108
+ Sewing	110,100	31,920	64,800	206,820
= Allocated overhead	$244,493	$119,923	$376,563	740,979
% of allocated overhead	33.00%	16.18%	50.82%	
+ Organizational-level overhead (not allocated)				292,271
= Total overhead				$1,033,250

EXHIBIT 7-9

Comparison of traditional and activity-based costing.

amount of manufacturing overhead allocated under the two methods is the $292,271 general overhead cost pool that was not allocated to products under activity-based costing.

Although the total amount of allocated overhead differs between the two methods, we can still compare the percentage of overhead allocated to each product. Notice where the big differences occur in Exhibit 7-9. Under the traditional costing method, pants were allocated 53.23% of manufacturing overhead, yet under activity-based costing, pants received just 33% of manufacturing overhead. The other major difference between the two methods was for award jackets, which were allocated 31.36% of total overhead under the traditional method and 50.82% under activity-based costing.

What caused the differences in the relative amount of manufacturing overhead allocated under the two methods to pants, a high-volume product, and jackets, a low-volume product? One obvious cause is the costs associated with the chenille machine. Under traditional costing, these costs were shared by all three products. However, under activity-based costing, these costs are traced directly to jackets, reducing the amount of overhead allocated to pants and increasing the amount of overhead allocated to jackets.

A second cause of the difference in costs results from the cutting operation. Jacket production required more cutting than pant production, even though C&C produced only one-tenth the number of jackets as pants. This shift in cost from a high-volume to a low-volume product is quite common in newly implemented activity-based costing systems. That is because low-volume products, like jackets, tend to use as many product-level activities as other products, while generating as many or more batch-level activities.

You have now learned the five steps of calculating product costs under activity-based costing. Exhibit 7-10 summarizes the results of these steps for C&C Sports. Remember, however, that the product costs shown there include just direct materials, direct labor, and manufacturing overhead. To get a more accurate picture of total product costs, C&C will need to complete an activity-based analysis of selling and administrative costs.

EXHIBIT 7-10

Activity-based costing at C&C Sports: An overview.

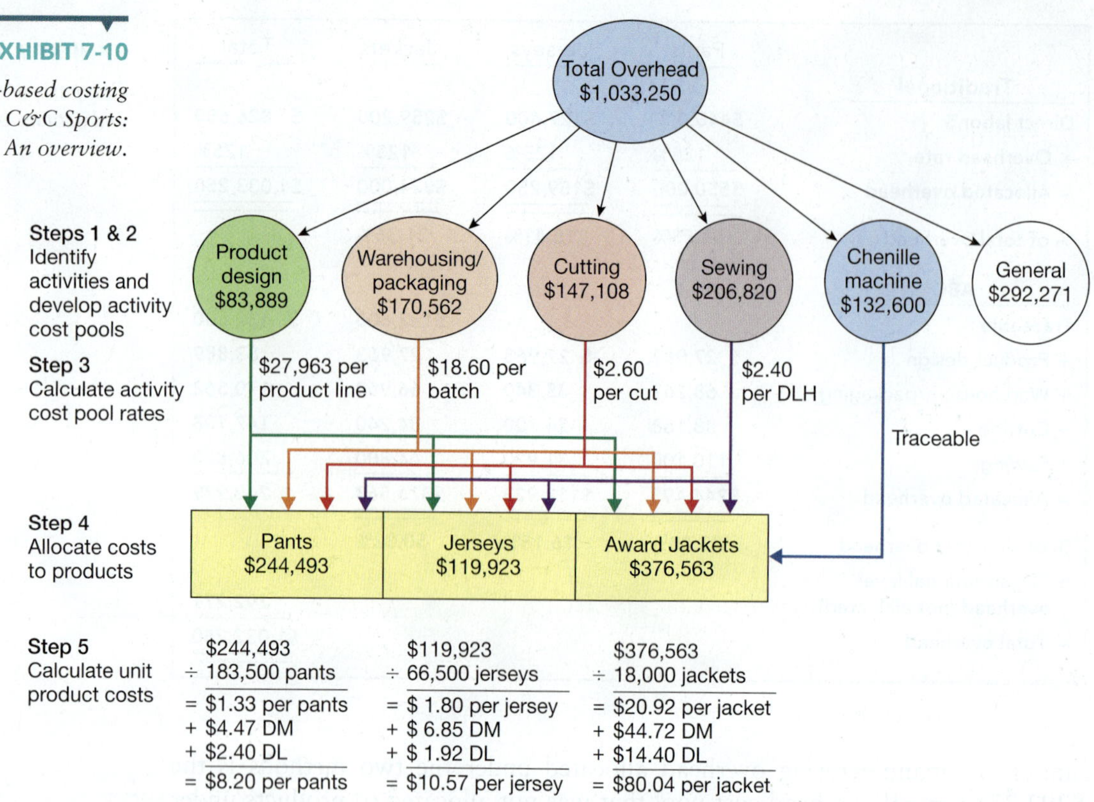

UNIT 7.2 REVIEW

KEY TERMS

Activity cost pool p. 375 | Activity rate p. 376 | First-stage allocation p. 376

PRACTICE QUESTIONS

1. LO 2 In an activity-based costing system, which of the following costs would most likely **not** be included in the allocation of overhead cost to products, but would instead be left in the "General" category?

   a. Indirect materials
   b. Factory rent
   c. Equipment depreciation
   d. Machine maintenance

2. LO 2 Managers of the Chadwick Company want to identify an appropriate cost driver for the quality control overhead cost pool. Which of the following would be the most appropriate choice?

   a. Number of units produced
   b. Number of quality engineers employed
   c. Number of quality inspections performed
   d. Number of returned units

3. LO 2 A firm produces and sells two products, SG8 and DY9. The following information relates to setup costs (a part of factory overhead) of $120,000.

	SG8	DY9
Units produced	1,500	1,500
Number of setups	75	25
Direct labor hours per unit	2	2
Total direct labor hours	3,000	3,000

Activity-based costing would allocate which of the following amounts of setup cost to each unit (rounded to the nearest dollar)?

	SG8	DY9
a.	$40	$40
b.	$60	$20
c.	$30	$10
d.	$20	$60

4. LO 2 Walker Texas produces two kinds of recliners, Standard and Deluxe. Information about the two products follows.

	Deluxe	Standard
Units produced	15,000	30,000
Direct materials cost per unit	$ 125	$ 80
Direct labor cost per unit	$ 30	$ 10
Direct labor hours required for production	45,000	30,000
Machine hours required for production	60,000	45,000
Batches	1,000	1,000

Production costs are as follows:

Activity	Cost	Activity Driver
Machining	$ 840,000	Machine hours
Moving/warehousing	$ 510,000	Batches
Total overhead cost	$1,350,000	

The activity rate for the cost of moving and warehousing is

a. $255 per batch.

b. $11.33 per unit.

c. $675 per batch.

d. $30 per unit.

5. LO 2 Refer to the information in question 4. Under activity-based costing, the total product cost per unit for the Deluxe recliner is

a. $49.

b. $155.

c. $174.

d. $204.

6. LO 2 Refer to the information in question 4. Under activity-based costing, the total product cost per unit for the Standard recliner is

a. $615,000.

b. $735,000.

c. $20.50.

d. $110.50.

7. LO 3 Under traditional costing systems, machine costs incurred specifically for one product might be allocated to all products. True or False?

8. LO 3 Activity-based costs can be higher than traditional product costs because of the inclusion of selling and administrative costs. True or False?

9. LO 3 In changing from a traditional costing system to an activity-based costing system, overhead costs tend to shift from high-volume standard products to low-volume premium products because

a. companies usually make more premium products than standard products.

b. standard products use more total activities than premium products.

c. premium products use more total direct materials and direct labor than standard products.

d. premium products usually consume more activities per unit than standard products.

UNIT 7.2 PRACTICE EXERCISE

Babytime, Inc. manufactures two products, Piglets and Rattles. Piglets are the more complex of the two products, requiring more direct labor time and more machine time per unit than Rattles.

Manufacturing overhead is currently assigned to the products on the basis of direct labor hours. The company has gathered some activity information and is interested in the differences between its present costing method and activity-based costing. All overhead costs should be allocated to the products. The overhead cost pools and activity drivers are as follows:

Activity Pool	Overhead Costs	Total Driver Usage
Setup	$256,000	3,200 setups
Materials purchasing	110,000	2,750 purchase orders
Machining/fabricating	136,000	27,200 machine hours
Total overhead costs	$502,000	

Other product information is as follows:

	Rattles	Piglets
Number of units produced	40,000	10,000
Direct materials cost	$ 15.00 per unit	$ 30.00 per unit
Direct labor cost	$ 5.25 per unit	$ 14.00 per unit
Direct labor hours	30,000	20,000
Setups	400	2,800
Purchase orders	2,070	680
Machine hours	8,000	19,200

Required

a. Using the traditional method of allocating overhead based on direct labor hours, compute the unit product cost of Rattles and Piglets:
   i. Determine the overhead rate per direct labor hour.
   ii. Allocate overhead to each product based on the direct labor hours used by each.
   iii. Divide the total overhead allocated to each product by the number of products produced to obtain the overhead cost per unit.
   iv. Add the overhead cost per unit to the direct materials and direct labor costs per unit to obain the unit product cost.

b. Using an activity-based costing approach, compute the unit product cost of Rattles and Piglets:
   i. Determine the three activity rates.
   ii. Allocate overhead to each product based on the activity drivers used by each. Total the three activity allocations to arrive at the total overhead allocated to each product.
   iii. Divide the total overhead allocated to each product by the number of products produced to obtain the overhead cost per unit.
   iv. Add the overhead cost per unit to the direct materials and direct labor costs per unit to obtain the unit product cost.

c. Why do your answers to a(iv) and b(iv) differ? Be specific.

SELECTED UNIT 7.2 ANSWERS

Think About It 7.2

Something in the processing of the different products must require different batch sizes. In a clothing factory, fabric characteristics (for example, its thickness) determine how many units can be cut at one time. Cutting several units at once is more efficient and uses less labor than cutting units individually. However, the quality of the cut must be taken into consideration. C&C Sports' production manager has likely determined the maximum number of units per batch required to balance efficiency and quality.

Think About It 7.3

The three categories of costs allocated to the cutting pool were indirect labor, indirect materials, and other. Indirect labor is likely to include the costs of cleaning around the cutting tables and setting up various machines and tables for cutting. It would not include the labor cost of cutting the fabric—that is included in the direct labor cost of making various products (refer back to Chapter 4 to see that cutting and sewing are direct labor costs). Indirect materials would include the knives and any other materials necessary to cut the fabric. It is difficult to say what "other" might include, since companies use that category for a variety of items.

Practice Questions

1. B
2. C
3. B
4. A
5. D
6. D
7. True
8. True
9. D

Unit 7.2 Practice Exercise

a. i. $\dfrac{\$502{,}000}{(30{,}000 + 20{,}000)\text{ direct labor hours}} = \$10.04$ per direct labor hour

ii. Rattles: $10.04 × 30,000 direct labor hours = $301,200
Piglets: $10.04 × 20,000 direct labor hours = $200,800

iii. Rattles: $301,200 ÷ 40,000 units = $7.53 per unit
Piglets: $200,800 ÷ 10,000 units = $20.08 per unit

iv.

	Rattles	Piglets
Direct materials	$15.00	$30.00
Direct labor	5.25	14.00
Overhead	7.53	20.08
Unit product cost	$27.78	$64.08

b. i. Setup activity rate $= \dfrac{\$256{,}000}{3{,}200\text{ setups}} = \$80$ per setup

Materials purchasing activity rate $= \dfrac{\$110{,}000}{2{,}750\text{ purchase orders}} = \$40$ per purchase order

Machining/fabricating activity rate $= \dfrac{\$136{,}000}{27{,}200\text{ machine hours}} = \$5$ per machine hour

ii.

	Rattles		Piglets	
Setup	$80 × 400 setups =	$ 32,000	$80 × 2,800 setups =	$224,000
Machining/fabricating	$40 × 2,070 purchase orders =	82,800	$40 × 680 purchase orders =	27,200
Machine operating cost	$5 × 8,000 machine hours =	40,000	$5 × 19,200 machine hours =	96,000
Total overhead allocation		$154,800		$347,200
iii. Units produced		÷ 40,000		÷ 10,000
Unit product cost		$ 3.87		$ 34.72

iv.

	Rattles	Piglets
Direct materials	$15.00	$30.00
Direct labor	5.25	14.00
Overhead	3.87	34.72
Unit product cost	$24.12	$78.72

c. The unit product costs in a(iv) and b(iv) differ because of the activities consumed by each product. In the traditional system, with overhead cost allocated by direct labor hours, each Rattle uses only 0.75 hours (30,000 hours ÷ 40,000 units), whereas each Piglet requires 2 hours (20,000 hours ÷ 10,000 units). Because Piglets use 2.667 times more direct labor hours than Rattles, they are allocated 2.667 times the overhead cost ($20.08 = 2.667 × $7.53).

Under activity-based costing, resources are used by each product as shown in the following table:

	Rattles	Piglets
Setups	$\dfrac{400\text{ setups}}{40{,}000\text{ units}} = 0.01$ setups per unit	$\dfrac{2{,}800\text{ setups}}{10{,}000\text{ units}} = 0.28$ setups per unit
Materials Purchasing	$\dfrac{2{,}070\text{ purchase orders}}{40{,}000\text{ units}} = 0.052$ purchase orders per unit	$\dfrac{680\text{ purchase orders}}{10{,}000\text{ units}} = 0.068$ purchase orders per unit
Machining/fabricating	$\dfrac{8{,}000\text{ machine hours}}{40{,}000\text{ units}} = 0.2$ machine hours per unit	$\dfrac{19{,}200\text{ machine hours}}{10{,}000\text{ units}} = 1.92$ machine hours per unit

In terms of setups, one Piglet consumes 28 times the resources that one Rattle does. Another way to think about this problem is that Rattles are produced in batches of 100 (40,000 units ÷ 400 setups = 100 units per setup); Piglets, on the other hand, are produced in batches of three or four. Therefore, each Piglet consumes a much larger share of the setup cost than each Rattle—more than its relative share of overhead based on direct labor hours. In terms of machine hours, each Piglet consumes 9.6 times the resources that one Rattle does. Again, each Piglet consumes a much larger share of the machine operating cost than each Rattle. Consumption of purchasing resources is almost the same for the two products.

UNIT 7.3

Activity-Based Management

GUIDED UNIT PREPARATION

Answering the following questions while you read this unit will guide your understanding of the key concepts found in this unit. The questions are linked to the learning objectives presented at the beginning of the chapter.

LO 4

1. What is a value-added activity? Give an example.
2. What is a non-value-added activity? Give an example.
3. How do non-value-added activities affect product costs?

LO 5

4. How does activity-based management allow managers to use information about activities to improve operations?
5. Raising the selling price of a product that is unprofitable based on activity-based costs is not always a good idea. What do managers need to evaluate before taking such an action?

What happens once product costs have been determined using activity-based costing? It's up to managers to use the new information to make better-informed decisions. The process of using activity-based costing information to manage a business's activities, and thus its costs, is called **activity-based management**. Exhibit 7-11 shows the results of one survey concerning how companies use activity-based costing information. By far its greatest use is for product costing and cost control, but activity-based costing is also used to make decisions regarding pricing, customer profitability, distribution channel profitability, and process improvement. In this unit, we will explore how companies can use activity-based costing to manage their activities.

Activity Management

Why is managing an organization's activities so important? Let's consider the case of a company that reduces costs by reducing the number of workers. If managers

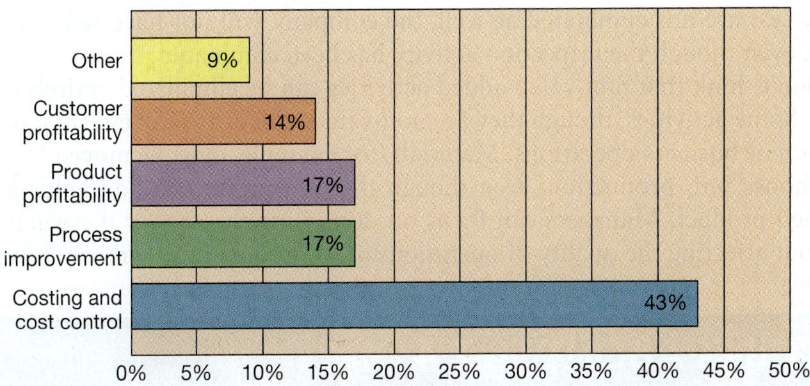

Source: *Activity Based Costing: How ABC Is Used in the Organization*, Copyright 2005, SAS Institute Inc., Cary, NC, USA. All Rights Reserved. Reproduced with permission of SAS Institute Inc., Cary, NC.

EXHIBIT 7-11

Primary use of activity-based costing.

reduce the workforce without considering the activities that employees perform, they will have done nothing to reduce the amount of work (the activities) that must be done. The remaining workers will face heavier workloads, which may decrease their job satisfaction and increase employee turnover. The company may end up having to pay overtime to meet its deadlines. In addition, customer satisfaction may fall as overworked employees miss deadlines and make more mistakes, causing product and service quality to decline. In reality, the company may see an *increase* in costs after the workforce reduction. Cost reduction, then, will be more effective when it is implemented by managing the level of activity, and hence the required resources.

Furthermore, as a result of implementing activity-based costing, managers know the cost of performing the activities required to produce and sell products. Activity-based management focuses on using that information to identify activities that are non-value-added and that can therefore be eliminated without affecting the quality of products. **Non-value-added activities** are those activities that consume resources but do not contribute to the value of the product. **Value-added activities** are those activities that create the product the customer wants to buy. These categories—value-added or non-value-added—are defined from the customer's perspective.

The customers who buy C&C Sports' award jackets value the cutting, sewing, and chenille lettering that are built into the high-quality jackets. They don't value activities such as moving materials, inspecting products, storing products, and setting up machines, which don't contribute to the quality of the jackets. C&C's customers deem these activities to be non-value-added. Consider inspection activities, for instance. Obviously, a company doesn't want defective products to be shipped to the customer; the result would be an unhappy customer and the extra cost of replacing the defective merchandise. So why isn't inspection a value-added activity? If the manufacturing process had occurred as it should have, there would be no defective products. Inspections would not be needed, and the cost incurred to conduct the inspections would be eliminated. So managers should focus on the manufacturing steps or material inputs that appear to be causing defects.

As non-value-added activities and their associated resources are eliminated, a company's costs will decrease. The key to reducing costs through activity management is *eliminating the resources* associated with the reduced activities. Let's assume that in the case of inspection costs, the company corrects the manufacturing process and eliminates the inspection process. If the inspectors (the

WATCH OUT!

Some activities may be non-value-added in one scenario but not in another. For example, inspecting a bicycle after it has gone through the production process is non-value-added. Inspection doesn't improve the bicycle production process; it just catches mistakes. On the other hand, inspecting meat for compliance with FDA regulations is value-added. People are willing to pay for that extra assurance that the meat is safe to eat.

resources) are not eliminated as well, the company will not have reduced total costs, even though the inspection activity has been eliminated.

Don't think that non-value-added activities can be eliminated entirely—they can't. Some activities, though they are non-value-added, are still essential to production or business operations. Materials, for example, must be moved from the warehouse into production, even though the moving doesn't add value to the finished product. Managers can focus on decreasing the cost of these activities without affecting the quality of operations or of products and services, however.

THINK ABOUT IT 7.4

Identify the following activities in a bicycle production plant as value-added or non-value-added.

ACTIVITY	VALUE-ADDED	NON-VALUE-ADDED
Inspecting a finished bicycle		X
Assembling the bicycle frame		
Ordering materials		
Cleaning the machines		
Calibrating the bicycle gears		
Moving tires from the warehouse to the assembly line		

Process Improvement

One way to implement activity-based management is to take a fresh look at the activities performed in the organization to see if a business process can be changed to reduce costs. **Process improvement** is the examination of business processes to identify incremental changes that may reduce operating costs. **Business process reengineering (BPR)** is a managerial tool that focuses on improving the efficiency and effectiveness of an organization's business processes through radical change.

C&C Sports' managers took a look at the activities that emerged from the implementation of activity-based costing. They decided to focus first on warehousing and packaging activities because, for the most part, those activities are non-value-added. It seemed particularly strange to them that the cost driver for the activities was the number of batches produced, since there was no relationship between the size of the batch and the activities.

C&C's products are produced in batches of different sizes based on how many items can be cut error-free at one time. For example, pants are cut in batches of 50 because their fabric is thin and few cuts are required. The pants fabric can be stacked fairly high and cut with very sharp knives. Jackets are cut in batches of five because their fabric is thick and slick, and cutting a taller stack of fabric results in uneven edges. Over the years, moving and packaging fabric and other raw materials in these same batch sizes became easier. When Chad Davis, vice president of operations, realized that the batch sizes were driving the costs of warehousing and packaging, he asked production manager Mary Townsley to devise a more efficient, less expensive way to move raw materials into the factory.

Reassessment of Product Profitability

A company that is interested in maximizing profits will instruct its sales force to emphasize its most profitable products. It is probable that after completing an activity-based costing study, the company's perception of its most profitable products will change.

Using activity-based costing, C&C Sports' managers discovered that, based solely on manufacturing costs, jackets were much more expensive to produce and pants were much less expensive to produce than they had thought. By expanding their activity-based costing exercise to include selling and administrative activities, they got an even better idea of the costs incurred to make and sell each product. Exhibit 7-12 shows the calculation of C&C's product margins using both the traditional costing method and activity-based costing.

Panel A: Traditional Costing

	Pants		Jerseys		Award Jackets	
Sales price	$ 12.00	100.00%	$ 14.80	100.00%	$ 125.00	100.00%
− Production costs	9.87	82.25%	11.17	75.47%	77.12	61.70%
= Product margin/unit	2.13	17.75%	3.63	24.53%	47.88	38.30%
× Budgeted unit sales	200,000		70,000		18,000	
= Total margin	$426,000		$254,100		$861,840	
% of total margin generated	27.63%		16.48%		55.89%	

Panel B: Activity-Based Costing

	Pants		Jerseys		Award Jackets	
Sales price	$ 12.00	100.00%	$ 14.80	100.00%	$ 125.00	100.00%
− Production costs	8.20	68.33%	10.57	71.42%	80.04	64.03%
− Selling and administrative costs	1.65	13.75%	2.02	13.65%	20.82	16.66%
= Product margin/unit	2.15	17.92%	2.21	14.93%	24.14	19.31%
× Budgeted unit sales	200,000		70,000		18,000	
= Total margin	$430,000		$154,700		$434,520	
% of total margin generated	42.19%		15.18%		42.63%	

EXHIBIT 7-12 *C&C Sports' product margins.*

The top half of Exhibit 7-12 shows the product margin calculation using traditional costing, based on the sales price per unit and the product cost per unit (see Chapter 4). These are the same numbers C&C Sports' managers used to prepare the 2017 budget. Notice that award jackets were expected to generate the highest product margin at 38.30%. Based on this product margin, award jackets would account for over half of C&C's total product margin, even though only 18,000 jackets were expected to be sold. Pants, on the other hand, have the lowest product margin, 17.75%. Even at the budgeted sales volume of 200,000 pairs, pants would account for only about 27% of C&C's total product margin. With this information, it is not surprising that C&C's president wanted to focus on increasing jacket sales. The bottom half of Exhibit 7-12 tells a different story: Pants and jackets have similar product margins—17.92% for pants and 19.31% for jackets. And based on expected sales volumes, each generates about 42% of C&C's total product margin.

What caused the change? Production costs differ between the two methods as activity-based costing matched resources consumed with the products that consume them. But the greatest difference between the two methods is including the

REALITY CHECK—*Even doctors need to know their ABCs*

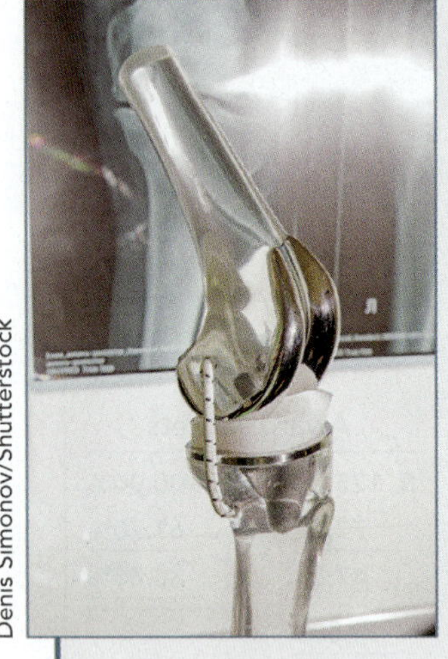

Denis Simonov/Shutterstock

Healthcare is one of today's big issues. Many people have expressed concerns over the continued rising cost of care. Among healthcare providers, there's new discussion about the *value* of healthcare delivery. Value, in this context, is measure by the health outcome achieved per dollar spent. While this may sound like a simple measure, the reality is far from simple.

There isn't a standard approach to cost accounting among healthcare providers. But one new tool that is being used to improve the value of healthcare delivery is "time-driven activity based costing," a simpler version of ABC. In this costing method, activities are measured in terms of the time it takes to complete one activity, and overhead costs are calculated per time unit of capacity (say, per minute of operating room use). Cost driver rates are then measured as the cost per minute × minutes per a single activity.

The Mayo Clinic is one of the early adopters of this costing method to help increase value. Working with a team from Harvard Business School, the clinic first focused on examining the costs for total knee and hip replacements. Through this initial effort, improvements in value have been realized in a number of ways, from reduced patient pain scores to reduced number of in-patient hospital days and reduced need for postoperative skilled nursing care. As a result of the project, the clinic's Florida site reduced its costs by 15%.

As a result of the project, the clinic's Florida site reduced its costs by 15%.

Sources: Marquis Cabrera, "Harvard Grad Develops Analytics Tool for Providers to Deliver High Quality and Cost Effective Health Care," *Huffington Post*, March 1, 2016, http://www.huffingtonpost.com/marquis-cabrera/avantgarde-health_b_9332036.html (accessed March 9, 2016); Derek A. Haas, Richard A. Helmers, March Rucci, Meredith Brady, and Robert S. Kaplan, "The Mayo Clinic Model for Running a Value-Improvement Program," *Harvard Business Review*, October 22, 2015, https://hbr.org/2015/10/the-mayo-clinic-model-for-running-a-value-improvement-program (accessed March 9, 2016); Robert S. Kaplan and Steven R. Anderson, "Time-Driver Activity-Based Costing," *Harvard Business Review*, November 2004, https://hbr.org/2004/11/time-driven-activity-based-costing (accessed March 9, 2016); Michael E. Porter, "What Is Value in Health Care?," *The New England Journal of Medicine*, December 23, 2010, http://www.nejm.org/doi/full/10.1056/NEJMp1011024 (accessed March 9, 2016).

selling and administrative costs under activity-based costing. We have omitted the specific calculation of selling and administrative costs in the interest of brevity, but the procedure is the same as that used to determine production costs. Note that selling and administrative expenses are exceptionally high for the award jackets because of the special advertising and extra administrative time needed to generate and process orders.

THINK ABOUT IT 7.5

If you calculate C&C's total margin in panels A and B of Exhibit 7-12, you will get different numbers. Why? Using Exhibit 7-4, determine how much of C&C's selling and administrative expense was *not* allocated to its products.

Implementing activity-based costing and obtaining the results reported in Exhibit 7-12 didn't make the award jackets more expensive to produce and sell. After all, nothing was done to change C&C's operations. The only difference is that C&C Sports' managers now have better information about what their products are contributing to the company's bottom line. Clearly, these products are all "keepers." Given that the only remaining costs not allocated to the products are general support costs, all three are covering their variable costs as well as some fixed costs and are therefore contributing to the bottom line.

C&C's managers now need to decide what to do with this information. If they want to increase their bottom line, they can either increase sales revenue or decrease costs. To increase sales revenue, they could either sell more units or increase their selling prices. Recall from Chapter 6 that C&C has already increased its sales revenue by selling more jackets and jerseys. However, the increase in revenue didn't translate into increased operating income because costs increased by a much higher amount. Raising the prices of pants and jerseys could be problematic. While the company touts the products' exceptional quality, they functionally are not much different from those available from competitors. C&C's award jackets, on the other hand, are perceived to be of higher quality and lower cost than other jackets. Therefore, pursuing a price increase for the jackets may be a reasonable strategy for increasing sales revenue.

Activity-Based Budgeting

Activity-based costing and management aren't the only ways a company can use information about activities to manage their operations. **Activity-based budgeting** is the practice of using activity-based costing information and knowledge about activities and resource consumption to prepare an organization's budget.

Traditional budgeting often means applying a fixed percentage increase to last year's budget. Any inefficiencies in the budget are simply carried forward from year to year. Under activity-based budgeting, the budget is based on the activities that will be performed to support the planned level of production. Knowing the activity-based cost of those activities, managers can include the appropriate level of resources in the budget. As the level of activities changes, the resources can be adjusted accordingly.

UNIT 7.3 REVIEW

KEY TERMS

Activity-based budgeting p. 391

Activity-based management p. 386

Business process reengineering (BPR) p. 388

Non-value-added activity p. 387

Process improvement p. 388

Value-added activity p. 387

PRACTICE QUESTIONS

1. LO 4 In a company that manufactures potato chips, which of the following is *not* a value-added activity?

   a. Washing the potatoes
   b. Peeling the potatoes
   c. Frying the potatoes
   d. Moving packages of chips to the warehouse

2. LO 4 Which of the following statements is *not* true of non-value-added activities?

   a. If a manager is creative enough, all non-value-added activities can be eliminated completely.
   b. An activity is defined as non-value-added from the customer's perspective.
   c. Activities can be considered non-value-added in some scenarios and value-added in others.
   d. Eliminating non-value-added activities will not result in significant cost savings if the resources consumed by those activities are not eliminated.

3. LO 5 Activity-based management

a. is a by-product of activity-based costing.
b. typically results in the elimination of resources prior to the elimination of activities.
c. can be used to evaluate the profitability of distribution channels.
d. results in the identification of value-added activities that can be eliminated.

4. LO 5 If under activity-based costing a manager realizes that the price of a product does not cover its activity-based cost, the best solution is to raise the price of the product. True or False?

5. LO 5 Which of the following is likely to generate the largest reduction in batch costs?

a. Increasing the size of a batch, which results in fewer batches
b. Eliminating specific batch costs, such as indirect materials used for machine setup
c. Both a and b are equally effective
d. Neither a nor b

UNIT 7.3 PRACTICE EXERCISE

Refer to your work on the Unit 7.2 Exercise. The managers at Babytime, Inc. were surprised that the activities associated with the production of Piglets were more extensive than they had imagined. They wondered if anything could be done to reduce the cost of producing Piglets.

Required

a. Compare the number of activities (setups, purchase orders, and machine hours) consumed per unit by Rattles and Piglets.
b. Identify whether each of the following activities is value-added or non-value-added. Explain your reasoning.
   i. Setting up production machines
   ii. Preparing purchase orders
   iii. Operating production machines
c. For each of the activities you identified as non-value-added in part (b), indicate how managers might go about reducing the activity and the associated resources without affecting the quality of the product.

SELECTED UNIT 7.3 ANSWERS

Think About It 7.4

ACTIVITY	VALUE-ADDED	NON-VALUE-ADDED
Inspecting a finished bicycle		X
Assembling the bicycle frame	X	
Ordering materials		X
Cleaning the machines		X
Calibrating the bicycle gears	X	
Moving tires from the warehouse to the assembly line		X

Think About It 7.5

The total margin is lower in panel B because a portion of the selling and administrative costs has been allocated to the products. Under the traditional costing method, selling and administrative costs are subtracted from the total gross margin, with no attempt to determine which products consume selling and administrative activities.

	Pants	Jerseys	Award Jackets
Selling and administrative cost per unit	$ 1.65	$ 2.02	$ 20.82
× Budgeted unit sales	200,000	70,000	18,000
= Total selling and administrative cost	$330,000	$141,400	$374,760

We can figure out how much selling and administrative cost was allocated to the products by multiplying the selling and administrative cost per unit by the number of units.

The total selling and administrative cost allocated to the three products was $846,160. Since the total selling and administrative cost (from Exhibit 7-4) was $1,138,912, we can conclude that $292,752 was not allocated to the products.

Practice Questions

1. D
2. A
3. C
4. False
5. B

Unit 7.3 Practice Exercise

a. See the answer to Exercise 7-2, part (c).

b. i. Setups are non-value-added. The activity consists of preparing machines to complete a production run, not of actually producing a product.

   ii. Preparing purchase orders is non-value-added. The activity consists of preparing paperwork (or electronic orders) with which to acquire materials and other production items.

   iii. Operating production machines is value-added. Running the machines produces the product.

c. *Setups*: Piglets are made in batches of three or four units at a time. A lot of time is likely to be wasted setting up the machines so frequently for so few items. Increasing the batch size would reduce the number of setups needed. Without additional information on the production process, it is difficult to say what the effect on quality might be. If the number of setups was decreased, some indirect materials (for example, cleaning materials) would likely be saved automatically. However, if the labor related to the setups was not either eliminated or redirected to a value-added activity, the company would not be able to reduce costs significantly.

   Purchase orders: For both Piglets and Rattles, purchase orders have more to do with the company's inventory management practices than with the products themselves. Given that 2,750 purchase orders are required to make 50,000 products, an average of only about 18 products' worth of materials are ordered at one time. Still, decreasing the number of purchase orders by increasing the quantity of materials purchased at one time might increase the costs associated with storing and insuring inventory. Before changing the purchase order activity, the production manager should work with the purchasing manager to ensure that the best overall inventory management policy is implemented.

BUSINESS DECISION AND CONTEXT Wrap Up

In the chapter opener, C&C Sports' managers were confused by the 2017 operating results: Revenues had increased, but income had gone down. They concluded that they must not understand what their products cost to produce. In fact, they were correct. After implementing an activity-based costing system, they learned that award jackets were much more expensive to produce and sell than they had thought. Award jackets are more complicated to make, and they consume almost as many activities as pants, even though the company sells ten times more pants than jackets. C&C can probably raise the price of jackets because they are higher quality and less expensive than competitors' jackets. Managers will also need to evaluate production and sales activities to identify and reduce non-value-added activities, which will reduce costs without compromising quality.

CHAPTER SUMMARY

In this chapter you learned that providing products and services to customers requires activities, and those activities consume organizational resources. Managers who understand the activities that are required to deliver products or services to the customer can make better decisions and obtain better operational and financial results for the organization. You should now be able to meet the objectives set out at the beginning of the chapter:

1. *Classify activities as unit-level, batch-level, product-level, customer-level, or organization-level. (Unit 7.1)*

   Unit-level activities are performed for each individual unit. Since each unit of a particular product requires the same level of activity, each unit consumes the same amount of resources that provide for that activity. The total level of activity performed varies proportionately with the number of units produced.

   Batch-level activities are performed on groups, or batches, of products at one time. Since the activity is based on the existence of the batch rather than on the number of units in the batch, a batch consumes the same quantity of resources whether it includes 20 units or 2,000 units.

   Product-level activities, also referred to as product-sustaining activities, support the products or services provided by the company. These activities are performed for the entire product line, regardless of how many units or batches are produced.

   Customer-level activities are performed for specific customers. These activities, and the resources consumed to perform them, do not affect product costs. Rather, the resources are consumed in the delivery of customer support services, and the associated costs are then used to determine the cost to serve a particular customer.

   Organization-level activities are required to provide productive capacity and to keep the business in operation. Although these activities do not provide identifiable benefits to specific products or services, without them there would be no business.

2. *Calculate activity-based product costs. (Unit 7.2)*

   Step 1: Identify activities.

   Step 2: Develop activity cost pools.

   Step 3: Calculate activity cost pool rates.

$$\text{Activity rate} = \frac{\text{Total activity cost pool resources}}{\text{Total activity driver volume}}$$

   Step 4: Allocate costs to products or services.

$$\text{Allocated cost} = \text{Activity rate} \times \text{Activity driver consumption}$$

   Step 5: Calculate unit product costs.

	Total direct materials cost
+	Total direct labor cost
+	Allocated activity cost 1
+	Allocated activity cost 2*
=	Total product cost
÷	Number of units produced
=	Unit product cost

*This calculation will have as many allocated costs as there are activity cost pools.

3. ***Explain the difference between traditional product costs and activity-based product costs. (Unit 7.3)***

The difference between traditional product costs and activity-based product costs lies in the way manufacturing overhead is allocated and in the inclusion of selling and administrative costs as a component of product cost. (Direct materials and direct labor costs do not differ between the two methods.) Activity-based product costs are based on the consumption of activities by each product rather than on consumption of the overhead base as in the traditional method.

4. ***Distinguish between value-added and non-value-added activities. (Unit 7.4)***

Value-added activities are those activities that create the product or service the customer wants to buy. Non-value-added activities are those activities that consume resources but do not contribute to the product's value.

5. ***Explain how information about activities can be used to make decisions. (Unit 7.5)***

Activity-based management uses activity-based costing information to manage business activities. Decisions regarding pricing, customer profitability, distribution channel profitability, and process improvement can all benefit from the use of activity-based costing information.

KEY TERMS

Activity (Unit 7.1)
Activity-based budgeting (Unit 7.3)
Activity-based costing (ABC) (Unit 7.1)
Activity-based management (Unit 7.3)
Activity cost pool (Unit 7.2)
Activity rate (Unit 7.2)
Batch-level activity (Unit 7.1)
Business process reengineering (BPR) (Unit 7.3)
Customer-level activity (Unit 7.1)
First-stage allocation (Unit 7.2)
Non-value-added activity (Unit 7.3)
Organization-level activity (Unit 7.1)
Process improvement (Unit 7.3)
Product-level activity (Unit 7.1)
Unit-level activity (Unit 7.1)
Value-added activity (Unit 7.3)

EXERCISES

7-1 Classifying activities (LO 1) Mitchell Manufacturing's single finished goods warehouse is located across the street from its manufacturing facility. A recent study of product sales showed that most product lines are sold primarily in a single geographical region. For instance, the Willamette line is sold primarily in the Northwest, while the Neuse line is sold primarily in the Southeast. To reduce delivery time to customers, the company has decided to close the existing warehouse and lease five smaller regional warehouses that will each serve a single product line.

Required

a. Classify the warehouse costs under the current single-warehouse scenario as unit-level, batch-level, product-level, customer-level, or organization-level.
b. Classify the warehouse costs under the proposed multiple-warehouse scenario as unit-level, batch-level, product-level, customer-level, or organization-level.
c. Under an activity-based accounting system, what effect will the change in warehouse strategy have on product costs?

7-2 Classifying activities (LO 1) Using the table below, place an X in the column that corresponds to the type of activity level referred to in each scenario.

		UNIT	BATCH	PRODUCT	CUSTOMER	ORGANIZATIONAL
a.	Setting up a machine for a production run of 500 units					
b.	Conducting a seminar for local doctors on the benefits of a new drug					
c.	Embossing a company logo on every product made					
d.	Seating a party of 11 at a restaurant					
e.	Providing technical support for two years following a sale					
f.	Managing a corporation's accounting department					
g.	Attaching a price tag to each product					
h.	Issuing an invoice					
i.	Developing a corporate advertising campaign					
j.	Recalling a defective product					

7-3 Determining cost drivers (LO 2) Grimes Grocery operates a chain of convenience stores in the Northwest. As a result of a recent consultant's visit, the company is in the beginning stages of implementing an activity-based costing system. The following activity cost pools have been identified:

- Stocking shelves
- Managing stockroom inventory
- Maintaining refrigeration units
- Processing lottery tickets
- Maintaining employee records

Required

Identify at least one possible cost driver for each activity cost pool.

7-4 Selecting a cost driver (LO 2) Brett Graham has been working on Hiltech's activity-based cost implementation team. One of his assignments is to study the information services department. One activity cost pool in the department is providing support for computer users by providing a help desk that users can call and ask questions. Brett has identified two possible cost drivers for this activity cost pool: number of calls and length of call in minutes.

Required

a. Identify some of the costs that will be included in this activity cost pool.
b. Which of the proposed cost drivers would be best for this activity cost pool? Why?

7-5 Establishing activity cost pools (LO 2) Pletzke Company manufactures dental instruments. The company's product line includes products as simple as dental picks and products as complex as panoramic x-ray machines. Carol Lindquist, a senior product manager responsible for implementing an activity-based costing system at Pletzke, identified the following three activity cost pools: assembling, packaging, and designing. Carol also investigated the components of overhead cost and determined that each cost is split among the three cost pools based on the following percentages.

Cost Category	Total Cost	Assembling	Packaging	Designing
Salaries	$4,000,000	45%	20%	35%
Supplies	1,250,000	50%	30%	20%
Utilities	800,000	70%	20%	10%

Required

a. Using the percentages above, calculate the costs included in each of the three activity cost pools.

b. Why might Carol have felt the need to implement an activity-based costing system? Be sure to consider how costs are incurred within the three categories.

7-6 Calculating traditional and ABC overhead rates (LO 2) Smith Machining makes three products. The company's annual budget includes $1,000,000 of overhead. In the past, the company allocated overhead based on expected capacity of 40,000 direct labor hours. The company recently implemented an activity-based costing system and has determined that overhead costs can be broken into four overhead pools: order processing, setups, milling, and shipping. The following is a summary of company information:

	Expected Cost	Expected Activities
Order processing	$ 175,000	10,000 orders
Setups	160,000	4,000 setups
Milling	410,000	20,500 machine hours
Shipping	255,000	25,000 shipments
	$1,000,000	

Required

a. Calculate the company's overhead rate based on direct labor hours.

b. Calculate the company's overhead rates using the activity-based costing pools.

7-7 Calculating traditional and ABC overhead rates (LO 2) Eric Parker has been studying his department's profitability reports for the past six months. He has just completed a managerial accounting course and is beginning to question the company's approach to allocating overhead to products based on machine hours. The current department overhead budget of $1,140,000 is based on 40,000 machine hours. In an initial analysis of overhead costs, Eric has identified the following activity cost pools.

Cost Pool	Expected Cost	Expected Activities
Product assembly	$ 600,000	40,000 machine hours
Machine setup and calibration	320,000	2,000 setups
Product inspection	90,000	1,500 batches
Raw materials storage	130,000	500,000 pounds
	$ 1,140,000	

Required

a. Calculate the company's overhead rate based on machine hours.

b. Calculate the company's overhead rates using the proposed activity-based costing pools.

7-8 Calculating product costs using activity-based costing (CIMA adapted) (LO 2) Wieters Industries manufactures several products including a basic case for a popular smartphone. The company is considering adopting an activity-based costing approach for setting its budget. The company's production activities, budgeted activity costs, and cost drivers for the coming year are as follows.

Activity	Activity Overhead $	Cost Driver	Cost Driver Quantity
Machine setup	$ 200,000	# of setups	800
Inspection	120,000	# of quality tests	400
Materials receiving	252,000	# of purchase orders	1,800

The budgeted data for smartphone case production are as follows.

Direct materials	$2.50 per unit
Direct labor	$0.54 per unit
Number of setups	92
Number of quality tests	400
Number of purchase orders	50
Production	15,000 units

Required

a. Calculate the activity rate for each cost pool.
b. Calculate the activity-based unit cost of the smartphone case.

7-9 Allocating overhead to products using activity-based costing (LO 2) Refer to the data in exercise 7-7. Eric Parker is taking the next step in his exploration of activity-based costing and wants to examine the overhead costs that would be allocated to two of the department's four products. He has gathered the following budget information about each product.

Driver Usage	Component 3F5	Component T76
Machine hours	1,000	10,000
Setups	40	20
Batches	20	10
Pounds of raw materials	10,000	10,000

Required

a. Calculate the total overhead allocated to each component under the traditional method using machine hours as the overhead application base.
b. Calculate the total overhead allocated to each component under activity-based costing.
c. What can you conclude about the costs of the other two products?

7-10 Calculating product costs using traditional and activity-based costing (LO 2) Refer to the data in exercises 7-7 and 7-9. Eric Parker found that the budget included production of 500 units of Component 3F5 and 5,000 units of Component T76.

Required

a. Calculate the overhead cost per unit of Component 3F5 and Component T76 under traditional costing using machine hours as the overhead application base.
b. Calculate the overhead cost per unit of Component 3F5 and Component T76 under activity-based costing.

7-11 Allocating overhead to products using activity-based costing (LO 2) Clifton Informatics provides data processing services to small businesses in the Northeast. For years, the company has allocated the cost of the data storage department using the number of tape mounts (how many times a data tape is loaded onto the computer's tape drive). This rate was tied closely to direct labor usage, since the more tapes that were mounted, the more operators that were needed to mount them. Under the current system, a customer is charged $1.50 each time a tape is mounted.

Three months ago the company implemented a new data storage system that uses an automated tape library. As a result, operators are no longer needed to mount the tapes. Some data that is used only temporarily is stored on a computer disk and never transferred to tape. With the new system, the department's payroll has dropped from 20 operators to 3.

Emma Davis, manager of the data center, believes that the new system's costs are more the result of data storage than of number of tape mounts. She has gathered the following information on the operation of the storage system, which is expected to cost $340,818 per year to operate.

Customer	Gigabytes of Storage	Number of Tape Mounts
Dale	36,254	69,388
Matthews	75,236	142,392
Johnson	830	5,072
Flowers	18	1,972
Daniel	19,762	8,388
Total	132,100	227,212

Required

a. Calculate the activity cost rate for the data storage department using the number of tape mounts as the activity driver. Using this rate, determine the data storage costs that should be allocated to each customer.

b. Calculate the activity cost rate for the data storage department using gigabytes of data storage as the activity driver. Using this rate, determine the data storage costs that should be allocated to each customer.

c. Which activity measure will customers prefer? Why?

d. Is the number of tape mounts still a good cost driver for the data storage department? Why or why not?

7-12 Comparing product costs under traditional and activity-based costing (LO 3)

Harrison-Brown is a book publisher that reissues old titles. The company offers these books with either a standard machine-glued hard cover or a deluxe, hand-embossed, hand-stitched, leather cover. Harrison-Brown currently allocates overhead to the books based on direct labor hours.

A recent activity analysis conducted by the controller revealed the following information.

	Standard Edition	Deluxe Edition
Units produced	500,000	8,000
Direct labor hours	550,000	30,000
Printing press hours	90,000	1,600
Sales orders	10,000	10,000

Required

a. Calculate the following for each product:
   i. Direct labor hours per unit
   ii. Printing press hours per unit
   iii. Sales orders per unit

b. What do your calculations above reveal about how standard edition books and deluxe edition books consume activities?

c. If Harrison-Brown implements an activity-based costing system, what will likely happen to the cost of a standard edition book and a deluxe edition book?

7-13 Explaining the differences between traditional and activity-based product costs (LO 3) "You're killing me!" exclaimed Myles Werntz, product manager for Premium products. "All along I've been told that the Premium line costs the company $125; we charge $225 and make a $100 profit. Now you're saying that costs have increased to $200. That's crazy."

Required

As the company controller you were part of the team that implemented an activity-based costing (ABC) system. Explain to Myles what typically happens to the cost of premium products under ABC. Consider what kinds of cost were included in the $125 amount and what kinds of cost are likely to be included in the $200 amount.

7-14 Calculating product costs using traditional and activity-based costing (LO 2, 3) Jay Krue makes two products, Simple and Complex. As their names suggest, Simple is the more basic product, and Complex comes with all the bells and whistles. The company has always allocated overhead costs to products based on machine hours. Last year, the company implemented an activity-based costing system, and managers determined the following activity pools and rates based on total overhead of $1,599,000:

	Rate
Assembly	$1.25 per direct labor hour
Fabrication	$9.75 per machine hour
Setups	$18.00 per batch
Bonding	$170,000 direct to Complex

Only the Complex product requires bonding, so all the costs of bonding should be allocated to Complex. The following data relate to both products.

	Simple	Complex
Units produced	125,000	40,000
Direct labor hours	250,000	160,000
Machine hours	50,000	32,000
Batches	2,500	4,000

Required

a. Using the traditional method of allocating overhead costs,
- allocate overhead cost to the products.
- show that the overhead assigned to each product sums to the total company overhead.
- determine the overhead cost per unit for each product.

b. Using the activity-based costing rates,
- allocate overhead cost to the products.
- show that the overhead assigned to each product sums to the total company overhead.
- determine the overhead cost per unit for each product.

c. Explain why overhead costs differ under the two costing methods. Refer specifically to the characteristics of the two products.

7-15 Value-added and non-value-added activities (LO 4) The following list includes activities that are performed in a physician's office. Classify each activity as value-added or non-value-added. For each non-value-added activity, state whether it can be eliminated without jeopardizing the office's operations.

a. Patient checks in.
b. Medical records clerk pulls patient's medical records.
c. Patient waits in reception area to be called to exam room.
d. Nurse takes vital signs (temperature, blood pressure, height, weight).

e. Patient waits in exam room.
f. Doctor completes examination.
g. Billing clerk files insurance claim.
h. Accounting clerk processes patient payments.
i. Accounting clerk resolves billing errors.

7-16 Value-added and non-value-added activities (LO 4) The following list includes activities that are performed in a clothing store. Classify each activity as value-added or non-value-added. For each non-value-added activity, state whether it can be eliminated without jeopardizing the store's operations.

a. Unpacking shipments.
b. Stocking shelves.
c. Changing clothing on mannequins.
d. Taking items to the dressing room for the customer.
e. Ringing up sales.
f. Cleaning dressing rooms.
g. Restocking shelves after customers try on items.
h. Closing the register at the end of the day (balancing sales totals with cash, checks, and credit card slips).
i. Cleaning the store.
j. Depositing daily receipts at the bank.

7-17 Managing activities (LO 5) Clive Franks was reviewing the product costs for his line of artist's oil paints. The current production schedule calls for the paints to be produced in batches of 1,000 tubes. Between each batch, the mixing and packaging lines must be completely cleaned to remove all remnants of color before changing to the next batch.

Currently, Clive makes 50 colors in 50,000 batches. Under the company's activity-based costing system, each batch incurs setup and cleaning charges of $50, for a total charge of $2,500,000 in setup costs. To reduce his costs in the coming year, Clive plans to increase the batch size to 2,000 tubes, which will reduce the number of required setups to 25,000.

Required

a. What effect will Clive's decision to increase the batch size have on his total setup costs?
b. What effect will Clive's decision to increase the batch size have on the cost of a tube of paint?
c. What effect will Clive's decision to increase the batch size have on other costs incurred by the company?
d. What negative effects should Clive consider before increasing the batch size?

7-18 Managing activities (LO 5) In the Reality Check on page 370, you read that the U.S. Postal Service altered its pricing strategy based on the results of an activity-based costing analysis. Specifically, the new rates were designed to encourage customers to use computer-readable mailing labels, which eliminate the need for human sorting, and to drop off magazines at a location closer to their final destination, which consumes fewer delivery resources. Customers who don't alter their behavior when bringing items to the post office pay higher rates.

Required

a. What risk does the U.S. Postal Service assume when changing its pricing strategy based on activity-based costing? In general, what kinds of organizations are likely to benefit from such a strategy and what kinds are not?
b. If all customers changed their behavior, would the U.S. Postal Service experience immediate savings? What kinds of costs do you think are incurred for "human sorting" and "magazine delivery"? What actions would the U.S. Postal Service need to take to save money?

PROBLEMS

7-19 Allocating overhead cost to products in a service industry (LO 2) The Trust Department of First National Bank offers two types of service, Basic and Premier. Trust customers with basic service do not grant trust officers any discretion in managing their accounts. The trust officers or their assistants merely execute the actions prescribed by the customer and send monthly statements. Premier customers grant the trust officers broad discretion in managing their accounts, including the buying, selling, and distribution of trust assets.

For years, the Trust Department's vice president assumed that the cost of these services was based on the amount of time the trust officers spent working on the accounts. But after some ebbs and flows in the market and the advent of various software packages for executing transactions, the vice president has begun to suspect that the costs of the services may have shifted. He has gathered the following information about the activities required by each service:

Activity Pool	Department Costs	Cost Driver
Basic account maintenance	$ 576,000	Number of accounts
Transaction processing	1,296,000	Number of transactions
Account analysis	1,008,000	Trust officer labor hours
Total Trust Department costs	$2,880,000	

Other information is as follows:

	Basic	Premier
Number of accounts	2,000	1,000
Number of transactions	6,000	14,000
Total trust officer labor hours	15,000	15,000

Required

a. How many trust officer hours does each type of account consume, on average?

b. How many transactions does each type of service generate, on average?

c. Using the traditional method of allocating Trust Department costs, which is based on trust officer labor hours, compute the cost per account to provide services to Basic and Premier customers.

d. Using activity-based costing, compute the cost per account to provide services to Basic and Premier customers.

7-20 Determining product costs using traditional and activity-based costing (LO 2) Voss Visuals produces tablets and books. Total overhead costs traditionally have been allocated on the basis of direct labor hours. After implementing activity-based costing, managers determined the following cost pools and cost drivers. They also decided that general costs should no longer be allocated to products.

Activity Pool	Department Costs	Cost Driver
Binding	$ 297,000	Number of units
Printing	955,500	Machine hours
Product design	234,000	Change orders
General	727,500	None
Total overhead costs	$2,214,000	

Other information is as follows:

	Tablets	Books
Units	62,500	20,000
Direct materials cost per unit	$3.00	$10.00
Direct labor cost per unit	$4.00	$ 8.00
Direct labor hours	30,000	19,200
Machine hours	150,000	144,000
Change orders	1,500	2,400

Required

a. Determine the unit product cost for tablets and books using the traditional costing system.

b. Determine the unit product cost for tablets and books using the activity-based costing system.

c. Show that General cost is the difference between the total overhead costs allocated to products under the traditional system and the total cost allocated to products under the activity-based costing system.

7-21 Comparing traditional and ABC costs (LO 2, 3) Ellis Perry is an electronics components manufacturer. Information about the company's two products follows:

	AM-2	FM-9
Units produced	15,000	2,000
Direct labor hours required for production	15,000	14,000
Units per batch	3,000	50
Shipping weight per unit	0.5 lbs.	4 lbs.

The company incurs $899,000 in overhead per year and has traditionally applied overhead on the basis of direct labor hours.

Required

a. How much overhead will be allocated to each product using the traditional direct labor hours allocation base? What overhead cost per unit will be allocated to each product?

b. Assume that Ellis Perry has identified three activity cost pools.

Pool	Cost	Cost Driver
Assembly	$638,000	Direct labor hours
Setup	121,500	Number of setups (1 per batch)
Packaging	139,500	Weight

Given these activity pools and cost drivers, how much overhead should be allocated to each product? What overhead cost per unit will be allocated to each product?

c. Explain the change in overhead costs per unit.

7-22 Allocating selling expenses to products using activity-based costing, activity management (LO 2, 5) Refer to the information about Voss Visuals in Problem 7-20. Voss's managers have gathered the following information about selling and administrative costs.

Activity Pool	Total Cost	Cost Driver
Shipping	$240,000	Pounds shipped
Advertising	157,500	Number of mailings
Commissions	168,125	5% of sales price
Total selling and administrative costs	$565,625	

	Tablets	Books
Weight	20,000 pounds	40,000 pounds
Advertising mailings	125,000	100,000
Sales commission	5% of sales price	5% of sales price
Selling price per unit	$35	$75

Required

a. Using the information given here and in Problem 7-20, calculate the product margin per unit for tablets and books using the traditional costing system.

b. Prepare a report like the one in Exhibit 7-12, Panel A.

c. Using the information given here and in Problem 7-20, calculate the product margin per unit for tablets and books using the activity-based costing system. Be sure to include selling and administrative costs.

d. Prepare a report like the one in Exhibit 7-12, Panel B.

e. Based on your analysis, what actions might the managers consider taking to improve the profitability of books and of the company overall?

7-23 Activity-based costing in a service setting (LO 2, 5) Chevis Consulting provides weekly payroll processing for a number of small businesses. Gia Chevis, the company's owner, has been using an activity-based costing system for several years. She used the following information in preparing this year's budget.

Activity Cost Pool	Total Cost	Cost Driver	Expected Driver Volume
Setting up new employees	$ 93,750	Number of new employees	500
Processing weekly payroll	$975,000	Number of paychecks printed	2,500,000
Weekly reporting	$375,000	Number of clients	200
Annual tax reporting	$300,000	Number of W-2s printed	80,000

Required

a. Calculate the cost rates for each activity cost pool.

b. Gia is preparing a proposal for a prospective client, Jason's Juice Bar. The client has 20 employees. What is the estimated cost of providing weekly payroll services to this client for the first year?

c. How can Gia use the estimated cost information you have calculated to price the service it will provide to Jason's Juice Bar?

7-24 Calculating product profitability using traditional and activity-based costing in a service setting (CIMA adapted) (LO 2, 3, 5) Lancaster Orthopedics specializes in hip, knee, and shoulder replacement surgery. In addition to the actual surgery, the company provides its patients with preoperative and postoperative inpatient care in a fully equipped hospital. Lancaster pays its surgeons a fixed fee for each surgical procedure they perform.

The company provides doctors and patients a variety of support services during treatment and allocates the cost of these activities through the company's costing system, which uses a single overhead rate. Currently, the company uses an allocation rate of 65% of the surgical fee charged to the patient.

Managers have expressed concern that the current system is producing inaccurate costs and profitability for the joint replacement procedures. As a result, Bree Lancaster, the company's controller, initiated a study to explore the potential for implementing an activity-based costing system. She has collected the following data on each of the procedures.

	Hip	Knee	Shoulder
Fee charged to patient	$8,000	$10,000	$6,000
Number of procedures per year	600	800	400
Average time per procedure	2.0 hours	1.2 hours	1.5 hours
Number of procedures per operating room session	2	1	4
Inpatient days per procedure	3	2	1
Surgeon's fee per procedure	$1,200	$1,800	$1,500
Medical supplies per procedure	$400	$200	$300

After analyzing the company's support activities, Bree determined that five activity cost pools would be sufficient for the company. The proposed activity cost pools, along with the proposed cost drivers, are presented below.

Activity	Cost Driver	Total Cost
Operating room preparation	Number of sessions	$864,000
Operating room use	Procedure time	1,449,000
Nursing and ancillary services	Inpatient days	5,415,000
Administration	Sales revenue	1,216,000
Miscellaneous	Number of procedures	936,000
		$9,880,000

Required

a. Calculate the profit per procedure for each of the three procedures using the current basis for allocating overhead.

b. Calculate the profit per procedure for each of the three procedures using the proposed activity-based costing system.

c. Discuss the causes of the difference in profitability between the two costing systems.

d. Based on the profit calculations, what action do you recommend?

7-25 Allocating overhead to products using activity-based costing (CMA adapted) (LO 2, 5) Nancy's Nut House is a processor and distributor of a variety of different nuts. The company buys nuts from around the world and roasts, seasons, and packages them for resale. Nancy's Nut House currently offers 15 different types of nuts in one-pound bags through catalogs and gourmet shops. The company's major cost is that of the raw nuts; however, the predominantly automated roasting and packing processes consume a substantial amount of manufacturing overhead cost. The company uses relatively little direct labor.

Some of Nancy's nuts are very popular and sell in large volumes, but a few of the newer types sell in very low sales volumes. Nancy's prices its nuts at cost (including overhead) plus a markup of 40%. If the resulting prices of certain nuts are significantly higher than the market price, adjustments are made. Although the company competes primarily on the quality of its products, customers are price conscious.

Data for the annual budget include manufacturing overhead of $6,000,000, allocated on the basis of each product's direct labor cost. The annual budgeted direct labor cost totals $1,200,000. Based on the sales budget and raw materials standards, purchases and use of raw materials are expected to total $9,000,000 for the year.

The unit costs of a one-pound bag of two of the company's products follows.

	Cashews	Chestnuts
Raw materials	$4.20	$3.20
Direct labor	0.30	0.30

Nancy's controller believes that the traditional costing system may be providing misleading cost information, so she has developed the following analysis of the annual budgeted manufacturing costs.

Activity	Cost Driver	Budgeted Activity	Budgeted Cost
Purchasing	Purchase orders	11,460	$1,146,000
Material handling	Number of setups	1,800	1,440,000
Quality control	Number of batches	600	300,000
Roasting	Roasting hours	96,100	1,922,000
Seasoning	Seasoning hours	33,600	672,000
Packaging	Packaging hours	26,000	520,000
Total manufacturing overhead cost			$6,000,000

Data regarding the annual production of cashews and chestnuts follow. There will be no Raw Materials Inventory for either type of nuts at the beginning of the year.

	Cashews	Chestnuts
Expected sales	100,000 lbs.	2,000 lbs.
Batch size	10,000 lbs.	500 lbs.
Setups	3 per batch	3 per batch
Purchase order size	2,500 lbs.	50 lbs.
Roasting time	1 hour/100 lbs.	1 hour/100 lbs.
Seasoning time	0.5 hour/100 lbs.	0.5 hour/100 lbs.
Packaging time	0.1 hour/100 lbs.	0.1 hour/100 lbs.

Required

a. Using the current costing system, calculate the cost and selling price of one pound of cashews and one pound of chestnuts.

b. Using an activity-based costing approach and the information provided, calculate the cost and selling price of one pound of cashews and one pound of chestnuts.

c. Given the activity-based costing information you have just calculated, what action do you suggest Nancy's Nut House should take regarding cashews and chestnuts?

7-26 Activity-based costing and activity-based management in a service industry (CMA adapted) (LO 2, 5) Best Test Laboratories was founded 25 years ago to evaluate the reaction of materials to extreme increases in temperature. Much of the company's early growth was attributable to government contracts to test the suitability of weapons, transportation equipment, and clothing for use in arid desert regions. Recent growth has come from diversification and expansion into commercial markets. Environmental testing at Best Test now includes the following:

- heat testing (HTT)
- air turbulence testing (ATT)
- stress testing (SST)
- arctic condition testing (ACT)
- aquatic testing (AQT)

Currently, all the company's budgeted operating costs are collected in a common overhead pool. All of the estimated testing hours are collected in another common pool. One rate per test hour is used to estimate the cost of all five types of testing. In determining the sales price, this hourly rate is marked up by 45% to cover administrative expenses, taxes, and profit.

Rick Shaw, Best Test's operations engineer, believes that there is enough variation in the test procedures and cost structure to establish separate costing and billing rates. After analyzing the following data, he has recommended that new rates be put into effect at the beginning of Best Test's fiscal year.

The budgeted total costs for the coming year are as follows:

Test pool labor (10 employees)*	$ 420,000
Supervision	72,000
Equipment depreciation	178,000
Heat	170,000
Electricity	124,000
Water	74,000
Setup	58,000
Indirect materials	104,000
Operating supplies	60,000
Total costs	$1,260,000
Total estimated test hours	105,000

*All employees are paid the same salary.

The following chart reports Shaw's analysis of resource usage by test type.

	HTT	ATT	SST	ACT	AQT
Test pool labor employees	3	2	2	1	2
Supervision	40%	15%	15%	15%	15%
Equipment depreciation	$48,000	$22,000	$39,000	$32,000	$37,000
Heat	50%	5%	5%	30%	10%
Electricity	30%	10%	10%	40%	10%
Water	—	—	20%	20%	60%
Setup	20%	15%	30%	15%	20%
Indirect materials	16,500	15,600	31,200	20,600	20,100
Operating supplies	10%	10%	25%	20%	35%
Test hours	31,500	10,500	26,250	21,000	15,750
Competitors' hourly billing rates	$ 17.50	$ 19.00	$ 15.50	$ 16.00	$ 20.00

Required

a. Compute the common pool hourly cost and hourly billing rate for Best Test Laboratories.

b. Compute the activity-based hourly cost for each of the five tests performed by Best Test Laboratories.

c. Calculate the activity-based hourly billing rate for each of the five tests performed by Best Test Laboratories.

d. Based on the new hourly cost data, what recommendations would you make to Rick Shaw on the pricing of the company's five tests?

7-27 Calculating activity-based product costs; activity-based management (CIMA adapted) (LO 2, 3, 5) Santamaria Skiffs manufactures three models of speedboats—Superior, Deluxe, and Ultra—which are sold through marine retail stores. Budgeted information for the coming year is as follows.

	Superior	Deluxe	Ultra	Total
Sales revenue	$54,000,000	$86,400,000	$102,000,000	$242,400,000
Direct material	17,600,000	27,360,000	40,200,000	85,160,000
Direct labor	10,700,000	13,320,000	16,600,000	40,620,000
Overhead				69,600,000
Gross profit				$ 47,020,000

	Superior	Deluxe	Ultra
Boats produced and sold	1,000	1,200	800
Machine hours per boat	100	200	300

Currently, the company allocates overhead using a single predetermined rate based on machine hours.

Irvin Santamaria is considering implementing an activity-based costing system. After studying the company's operations, he developed the following five activity cost pools.

Activity	Cost Driver	Overhead Cost
Machining	Machine hours	$ 13,920,000
Machine setup and calibration	Number of setups	24,000,000
Quality inspections	Number of inspections	14,140,000
Materials receiving	Number of deliveries	6,760,000
Materials requisitions	Number of requisitions	10,780,000
		$ 69,600,000

Irvin also developed the following operating data for the coming year.

	Superior	Deluxe	Ultra
Boats per batch	5	3	2
Quality inspections per batch	10	15	30
Number of deliveries	600	600	800
Number of requisitions	3,275	4,200	6,000

To ensure the highest level of production quality, all machines are set up and calibrated at the beginning of every batch.

Required

a. Calculate the unit cost of each of the three speedboat models using the current system of allocating overhead.
b. Calculate the unit cost of each of the three speedboat models using the proposed activity-based costing system of allocating overhead.
c. Discuss how the change in costing systems will affect the reported profitability of the three speedboat models. How will this change affect the overall profitability of the company?
d. Suppose Santamaria doubles the batch size of each production run. What effect will this change have on the profitability of each model?
e. Based on your findings, what recommendations do you have for improving the company's profitability?

7-28 Calculating activity-based product costs; activity-based management (CMA adapted) (LO 2, 3, 5) Elliot-Jones manufactures two large-screen television models. The 65-inch flat-panel LED model has been in production since 2012 and sells for $900. The company introduced a 55-inch 4K ultra HD in 2016; it sells for $1,140.

The company's income statement for the current year follows. Based on these results, management has decided to concentrate the company's marketing efforts on the 4K ultra HD model and begin to phase out the LED model.

Elliot-Jones
Income Statement
For the Year Ended December 31

	65" LED	55" 4K Ultra HD	Total
Sales revenue	$18,000,000	$4,560,000	$22,560,000
Cost of goods sold	11,800,000	3,212,400	15,012,400
Gross margin	6,200,000	1,347,600	7,547,600
Selling and administrative expenses	5,300,000	978,000	6,278,000
Operating income	$ 900,000	$ 369,600	$ 1,269,600
Units produced and sold	20,000	4,000	
Operating income per unit sold	$ 45.00	$ 92.40	

The unit costs for the two television models are as follows:

	65" LED	55" 4K Ultra HD
Direct materials	$352.00	$656.00
Direct labor	18.00	42.00
Manufacturing overhead	220.00	105.10
Total unit cost	590.00	803.10

Mark Renn, Elliot-Jones' controller, just attended a seminar on activity-based costing and believes the company should implement such a system. He has gathered the following annual information to explore the possibility.

Activity Cost Pool	Cost Driver	Traceable Costs	Number of Events 65″ LED	55″ 4K Ultra HD	Total
Soldering	number of solder joints	$ 942,000	1,185,000	385,000	1,570,000
Shipping	number of shipments	860,000	16,000	4,000	20,000
Quality control inspecting	number of inspections	1,248,000	56,250	21,750	78,000
Purchasing	number of orders	950,000	80,000	110,000	190,000
Machining	number of machine hours	70,400	160,000	16,000	176,000
Machine setups	number of setups	750,000	16,000	14,000	30,000
Total traceable costs		$4,820,400			

Required

a. Calculate the activity rate for each activity cost pool.
b. Allocate overhead costs to each of the products using activity-based costing.
c. Calculate the total product cost of each product using activity-based costing.
d. Are the product costs you calculated in part (c) the total costs of the two products? Why or why not?
e. Evaluate Elliot-Jones' decision to focus on the 55″ 4K Ultra HD television and phase out the 65-inch LED television.
f. In what other ways could Elliot-Jones' use the activity-based cost information calculated in part (c)?

7-29 Calculating activity-based product costs; activity-based management (CMA adapted) (LO 2, 3, 5)

Highland Manufacturing produces two products in its Saratoga plant, balzene and galvene. Since it opened its doors in 1965, Highland has been using a single manufacturing overhead pool to accumulate overhead costs. Overhead has been allocated to products based on direct labor hours.

Until recently, Highland was the sole producer of galvene in the country and was therefore able to dictate the selling price. However, last year Marcella Products began marketing a comparable product at $37 per unit—a price that is below Highland's product cost. Highland's market share of galvene has declined rapidly as a result. The company's managers must now decide whether to meet the competitive price or discontinue the product. Highland's cost accountant has suggested that the company do an activity-based cost analysis before managers make the decision.

The two main indirect costs of manufacturing balzene and galvene are power usage and setup costs. Most of the power usage occurs in the fabricating department; most of the setup costs are incurred in the assembly department. Setup costs are incurred predominantly in the production of balzene. The fabricating department has identified machine hours as the appropriate cost driver; the assembly department has identified setups as the appropriate cost driver. Direct labor rates are the same in both departments.

The combined budget for manufacturing is as follows.

	Total	Balzene	Galvene
Number of units		20,000	20,000
Direct labor	$800,000	2 hours per unit	3 hours per unit
Direct material		$5 per unit	$3 per unit
Overhead			
Indirect labor	$ 24,000		
Fringe benefits	5,000		
Indirect materials	31,000		
Power	180,000		
Setup	75,000		
Quality assurance	10,000		
Other utilities	10,000		
Depreciation	15,000		

The cost accountant has prepared the following estimates of overhead usage by the two departments:

	Fabricating	Assembly
Indirect labor	75%	25%
Fringe benefits	60%	40%
Indirect materials	$ 20,000	$11,000
Power	$160,000	$20,000
Setup	$ 5,000	$70,000
Quality assurance	70%	30%
Other utilities	50%	50%
Depreciation	80%	20%

Activity Base Usage	Machine Hours	Setups
Balzene	4 MH/unit	1,000
Galvene	6 MH/unit	250

Required

a. Calculate the unit costs of balzene and galvene using the current overhead allocation basis of direct labor hours.

b. Calculate the amount of overhead cost assigned to the Fabricating and Assembly activity cost pools using the cost accountant's estimates. Determine the overhead rate for each cost pool.

c. Calculate the unit costs of balzene and galvene using activity-based costing. Round your answer to two decimal places.

d. Did the switch to activity-based costing change the actual cost to produce galvene? Why or why not?

e. What action should Highland's managers take regarding the production of galvene? Why?

C&C SPORTS CONTINUING CASE

7-30 Calculating activity-based product costs; activity-based management

(LO 2, 5) Chad Davis, C&C Sports' vice president for operations, recently received a sales brochure for a new electric cutting tool. Based on the tool's specifications, Chad believes that C&C Sports could increase the batch size on jersey production to 50 jerseys, up from the current 35 jerseys. While the cutting tool would be used on pants and award jackets as well, other production factors prevent increasing the batch sizes for these products.

The new tool would increase annual operating costs by $14,082. Before deciding whether to purchase the cutting tool, Chad wants to know how the new tool will affect the cost of producing the company's three products.

Required

a. Review the information in Exhibit 7-5. Calculate the total annual cost included in the cutting activity cost pool assuming the cutting tool is purchased.

b. Review the information in Exhibit 7-6 and on page 377. Calculate the cost per cut assuming the cutting tool is purchased.

c. Review the information in Exhibit 7-6. Identify any other activity rates that will be affected by the purchase of the new cutting tool.

d. Explain to Chad why unit costs for all three products will change after the purchase of the new cutting tool.

e. Do you recommend that Chad purchase the new cutting tool? Why or why not?

CASE

7-31 Activity-based costing and ethics (CMA adapted) (LO 2) Thomas-Britt Industries was founded by Matt Thomas in 1950 as a small machine shop that produced parts for the aircraft industry. The Korean War brought rapid growth to Thomas-Britt. By the end of the war, the company's annual sales had reached $15 million, almost exclusively from government contracts. The next 40 years brought slow but steady growth. Cost-reimbursement contracts from the government continued to be the main source of revenue.

In the early 1990s, president Will Thomas, son of the founder, realized that Thomas-Britt could not depend on government contracts for long-term growth and stability. Consequently, he began planning for diversified commercial growth. By the end of 2003, Thomas-Britt had succeeded in reducing government contract sales to 50% of total sales.

Traditionally, the costs of the Materials Handling Department have been allocated to other departments as a percentage of the dollar value of direct materials. Peter Anderson, manager of the government contracts unit, has been complaining about this allocation for several months. He believes that since his unit's materials costs are high and materials handling activities are low relative to the commercial unit, he is absorbing more than his fair share of this overhead. He wants to find a way to transfer some of these charges to another unit, thereby increasing the government contracts unit's profitability and his year-end performance bonus.

Peter shared his views in a recent meeting with Sarah Lindley, the newly hired cost accounting manager, and Reese Mason, manager of the commercial unit. After a heated discussion, Sarah agreed to investigate the current allocation method and, if appropriate, recommend an alternative method.

After doing some research, Sarah learned the following:

- The majority of the direct materials purchases for government contracts are high-dollar, low-volume purchases. Direct materials purchases for commercial contracts are mostly low-dollar, high-volume purchases.
- There are other departments that use the services of the Materials Handling Department on a limited basis, but they have never been charged for materials handling costs.
- One purchasing agent with a direct phone line is assigned exclusively to purchasing high-dollar, low-volume materials for government contracts, at an annual salary of $36,000. His employee benefits are estimated to amount to 20% of his annual salary. The dedicated phone line costs $2,800 a year.

The Materials Handling Department's budget for 2017, as proposed by Sarah Lindley's predecessor, follows.

Payroll	$ 180,000
Employee benefits	36,000
Telephones	38,000
Other utilities	22,000
Materials and supplies	6,000
Depreciation	6,000
Total materials handling costs	$ 288,000
Direct materials budget	
Government contracts	$1,958,400
Commercial products	921,600
Total direct materials budget	$2,880,000

After reviewing the situation, Lindley has recommended that allocating materials handling costs based on the number of purchase orders issued is preferable to the current allocation based on direct materials cost. She estimated the number of purchase orders to be processed in 2017 as follows:

Government contracts	79,860
Commercial products	154,880
Other	7,260
Total	242,000

Using the 2017 estimates, she provided the following analysis to Anderson and Mason.

	Government Contracts Unit	Commercial Unit
Materials handling cost based on purchase orders issued	$ 95,040	$184,320
Materials handling cost based on direct materials cost	195,840	92,160
Difference in cost allocated to unit	($100,800)	$ 92,160

When Mason saw the projected increase in the commercial unit's costs, he exploded. He was not going to lose any of his year-end performance bonus just because Lindley wanted to change the way she calculated the numbers. He marched into Lindley's office and reminded her that he had been with the company for 25 years and had "plenty of pull" with Thomas as a member of the senior management team. He then told her to "adjust" her numbers and modify her recommendation so that the results would be more favorable to the commercial unit. He added that since materials handling costs were only allocated to the government contract and commercial units, she could just hide some of the commercial unit's purchase order volume in those other units.

Given her new position, Lindley is not sure how to proceed. She questions Mason's motivation. To complicate matters, Thomas has asked her to prepare a three-year forecast of the two units' results, for which she believes the new allocation method would provide the most accurate data. Using the new method would put her in direct opposition to Mason's directives, however.

Lindley has assembled the following forecasted data to project the units' direct materials handling costs.

	2017	2018	2019
Total materials handling costs	$ 288,000	$ 326,785	$ 374,420
Direct materials cost			
Government contracts unit	$1,958,400	$2,275,000	$2,576,000
Commercial unit	921,600	975,000	1,104,000
Total direct materials cost	$2,880,000	$3,250,000	$3,680,000

	2017	2018	2019
Purchase orders			
Government contracts unit	79,860	85,024	89,400
Commercial unit	154,880	164,734	172,840
Other units	7,260	15,942	35,760
Total purchase orders	242,000	265,700	298,000

Required

a. Using the forecasted information, calculate the materials handling costs that would be allocated to each unit under both allocation methods. Show the cumulative dollar impact over the three-year period 2017–2019.

b. Why might the number of purchase orders be a better cost driver for materials handling costs than direct materials cost?

c. Are there other factors in the allocation that Lindley should consider?
d. In a recent meeting between Sarah Lindley and Reese Mason, Mason said that there is nothing in any accounting pronouncement that requires the use of activity-based costing. Therefore, there is no reason to make Lindley's recommended change in allocation methods. Do you agree with Mason? Why or why not?
e. What ethical conflict does Sarah Lindley face? What specific steps should she take to resolve it? Refer to the *IMA Statement of Ethical Professional Practice* (Exhibit 1-8) in developing your answer.

ANALYTICS PROBLEM

7-32 Determining appropriate activity cost drivers (LO2) Plyler Plastics Company produces a variety of custom plastics products for a worldwide clientele. The company's cost accounting manager, Martha Johns, is beginning to implement an activity-based costing system and has gathered data on the quality inspections activity. She is unsure what the most appropriate driver is for this activity cost pool, but she is considering number of units produced, number of batches produced, machine hours, and direct labor hours. She has gathered weekly information for the past two years and has asked you to help her determine which activity driver to select.

Required

a. Using the activity cost pool and activity driver data, prepare a scatterplot for each potential activity driver. What do you notice about the appropriateness of each as the selected driver for assigning inspections costs to products under the new activity-based costing system?
b. Using Excel's CORREL formula, determine the correlation between each activity driver level and the inspections cost.
c. Using Excel's RSQ formula, determine how much of the variation in activity costs each activity driver explains.
d. Based on your analysis, which activity driver do you recommend? Why?
e. Assuming the past two years represent the expected level of costs and activity for the coming year, what activity cost rate for quality inspections should be used to assign costs to products in the coming year?

The Excel data files for answering this problem can be found in WileyPLUS.

ENDNOTES

1. Mark Albert, "The ABCs of Activities Based Costing," *Modern Machine Shop*, www.mmsonline.com, http://www.mmsonline.com/articles/the-abcs-of-activities-based-costing (accessed February 16, 2016).
2. *Introduction to Activity-Based Cost Management*, Armstrong Laing Group, 2004, http://www.fds.hu/pdf/introduction%20to%20activity%20based%20cost%20management.pdf (accessed May 28, 2007; site now discontinued).
3. Michael Heaney, "Easy as ABC? Activity-Based Costing in Oxford University Library Services," *The Bottom Line: Managing Library Finances*, 17, no. 3 (2004): 93–97.
4. Tad Leahy, "Where Are You on the ABC Learning Curve?" *BusinessFinance*, December 2004, http://businessfinancemag.com/bpm/where-are-you-abc-learning-curve (accessed February 16, 2016).

5. For a more complete history of the development of activity-based costing, see Steve Player and Carol Cobble, *Cornerstones of Decision Making: Profiles of Enterprise ABM* (Greensboro, NC: Oakhill Press 1999), from which this information is taken.
6. Peter F. Drucker, *The Practice of Management* (New York: Harper, 1954), 195.
7. Robin Cooper and Robert S. Kaplan, "How Cost Accounting Systematically Distorts Product Costs," in William J. Bruns, Jr. and Robert S. Kaplan (eds.), *Accounting and Management: Field Study Perspectives* (Boston: Harvard Business Publishing, 1987).
8. *Activity Based Costing: How ABC Is Used in the Organization*, BetterManagement, http://www.bettermanagement.com/images/Library/pdf/Activity_Based_Costing_Survey_Result.pdf (accessed June 2, 2007; site now discontinued).
9. Miles Free, "Is Your Order Book Telling You to Consider Activity-Based Costing?" *Production Machining*, April 17, 2007, http://www.productionmachining.com/articles/is-your-order-book-telling-you-to-consider-activity-based-costing (accessed December 20, 2012).
10. In this chapter, we will illustrate the development of activity-based costs using only manufacturing overhead. A similar analysis may be completed for selling and administrative costs to develop a truer ABC product cost.
11. This step is sometimes referred to as "second-stage allocation."

TOPIC FOCUS 5: CUSTOMER PROFITABILITY

Petek ARICI/Getty Images

FOCUS	LEARNING OBJECTIVES
TOPIC FOCUS 5	**LO 1:** Use activity-based costing techniques to measure customer profitability.
	LO 2: Identify alternatives for managing unprofitable customer accounts.

TOPIC FOCUS 5—GUIDED UNIT PREPARATION

Answering the following questions while you read this unit will guide your understanding of the key concepts found in the unit. The questions are linked to the learning objectives presented at the beginning of the topic focus unit.

LO 1

1. What kinds of costs do companies incur in making sales to customers?
2. Why are selling costs pooled and allocated to customers rather than directly traced to customers?
3. How do you calculate customer net profit? Customer profit margin?
4. Give an example of customers who tend to drive up a company's costs. Explain.

LO 2

5. What can a company do if it has identified customers who are unprofitable?
6. Why might a company decide to keep a customer who is unprofitable?

Business Decision and Context

BRADLEY TEXTILE MILLS

Vice President for Marketing and Sales
Lindsay Stang

Sales managers, Terrence Gleason and **Beth Wommack** sat in the main conference room at Bradley Textile Mills, chatting as they waited for the monthly sales staff meeting to begin. "I thought I was going to be late," Beth said. "Taylor Byrd from Sparrow Designs just called with another rush order; I don't know why they can't plan any better. All their orders seem to be rush jobs."

"Well, they generate almost $2 million in revenue for us, so we need to keep them happy," Terrence responded.

"I know, I know, but they take up so much of my time. I think I spend more time with them than with all my other customers combined," said Beth. "At least they're really nice to work with," she added.

As the meeting began, **Lindsay Stang, vice president for marketing and sales**, announced that the top brass at Bradley Textile Mills wanted a complete review of all sales accounts. "Selling expenses have been growing rapidly—faster than sales—and management wants to know where all those dollars are going. I told them it's a cost of doing business and keeping our customers happy," Lindsay said. "Apparently, the chief financial officer just returned from a conference on customer profitability. He claims we don't really know which customers are making money for us and which are costing us more than they generate in revenues. There's no point arguing with him. If we want to continue to get the financial resources we need, we're going to have to demonstrate that our customers are profitable."

> "If we want to continue to get the financial resources we need, we're going to have to demonstrate that our customers are profitable."

Many organizations believe that as long as the sales revenue a customer generates exceeds the cost of goods sold, that customer is profitable. That isn't the case, however. Measuring customer profitability in this way ignores all the selling and administrative costs incurred to provide customer service and support, such as warehousing, billing, and order processing. In this topic focus unit, you will learn how to measure customer profitability more accurately.

In their book *Killer Customers*, Larry Selden and Geoffrey Colvin estimate that the top 20% of a company's customers generates approximately 120% of the company's profits, while the bottom 20% loses as much as 100%.[1] A customer profitability analysis at some fine paper distributors produced similar results—the top 20% of customers were very profitable, while the bottom 20% were very unprofitable. The middle 60% contributed little in the way of profit.[2] This finding highlights the importance of identifying the unprofitable customers and finding ways to make them profitable. If unprofitable customers cannot be turned into profitable ones, the company should consider dropping them.

Identifying Unprofitable Customers

When asked if their companies have unprofitable customers, many managers claim they do not. When Bradley Textile Mills' sales manager, Terrence Gleason, was asked this question, he quickly pulled out the customer profitability report shown in Exhibit T5-1. "Granted, some of our customers are more profitable than others," he replied, "but all 375 of our customers are profitable at some level."

BRADLEY TEXTILE MILLS Customer Profitability (Based on Cost of Goods Sold)					
Profitability Rank	Customer	Revenues	Cost of Sales	Gross Profit[a]	Profit Margin[b]
1	Morris & Morris	$ 4,819,150	$ 3,585,455	$ 1,233,695	25.6%
2	Sparrow Designs	1,978,812	1,484,109	494,703	25.0%
3	Harps of London	168,600	126,450	42,150	25.0%
4	Gold's Upholstery	482,000	361,982	120,018	24.9%
5	Unique Uniforms	2,098,915	1,580,483	518,432	24.7%
6	C&C Sports	1,540,951	1,163,418	377,533	24.5%
7	MedTogs	4,154,500	3,157,420	997,080	24.0%
8	Florstan	67,200	51,408	15,792	23.5%
.					
.					
.					
368	House of Drew	879,520	835,544	43,976	5.0%
369	Mullins and Jones	164,826	157,244	7,582	4.6%
370	Potter Drapery	94,608	90,256	4,352	4.6%
371	Huffmeyer Mills	648,425	622,488	25,937	4.0%
372	Mooney Productions	540,895	520,340	20,555	3.8%
373	Dawson Shade	64,572	62,183	2,389	3.7%
374	Shadowbox Supply	267,400	262,052	5,348	2.0%
375	Ralston Fabrics	349,800	342,804	6,996	2.0%
Total		$200,000,000	$172,000,000	$28,000,000	14.0%

[a]Revenue − Cost of sales
[b]Gross profit / Revenues

EXHIBIT T5-1 *Bradley Textile Mills' customer profitability.*

The problem with Gleason's analysis was that the only expense it considered was the cost of goods sold. A business also incurs selling and administrative expenses. Recall from Chapter 4 that selling expenses are associated with the storage, sale, and delivery of products to the customer. Administrative expenses are associated with the general management of the business. When we examined activity-based costing in Chapter 7, these costs were not included in our analysis, since they are not considered product costs. However, in addition to covering the cost of the product, the revenue a customer generates should also cover the selling costs associated with the purchase and provide enough margin to pay for administrative expenses and contribute to profit.

What can managers do to get a better estimate of customer profitability? One way is to allocate selling expenses to customers through activity-based costing (see Chapter 7) using the following steps:

1. Identify selling activities.
2. Develop activity cost pools.
3. Calculate activity cost pool rates.
4. Allocate selling costs to customers.
5. Calculate customer profitability.

Let's look at the selling costs incurred by Bradley Textile Mills. As Exhibit T5-2 shows, the company incurred $16,815,000 in selling costs last year. After identifying all selling activities, Terrence Gleason's group narrowed the list down to seven main activities. Then they developed seven cost pools and selected an activity driver for each. By dividing each cost pool by its annual driver activity, the company can determine the cost pool rates. For example, the company incurs an annual cost of $3,200,000 to make 3,200 sales calls to current and potential customers. That is $1,000 per sales call ($3,200,000 ÷ 3,200). Once all the activity rates have been calculated, Gleason can use the information shown in Exhibit T5-2 to allocate selling costs to customers and calculate customer profitability.

EXHIBIT T5-2

Calculation of cost pool rates for selling activity.

Activities	Annual Cost	Annual Driver Activity	Activity Cost Pool Rate
Sales calls	$ 3,200,000	3,200 sales calls	$1,000 per call
Internet orders	2,600,000	130,000 orders	$20 per order
Catalog orders	2,925,000	45,000 orders	$65 per order
Standard packing and shipping	5,000,000	50,000,000 yards	$0.10 per yard
Support call center	480,000	960,000 minutes	$0.50 per minute
Product returns	210,000	600 returns	$350 per return
Express packing and shipping	2,400,000	800,000 yards	$3.00 per yard
	$16,815,000		

THINK ABOUT IT T5.1

Why aren't administrative costs included in these selling cost activity pools?

Two different calculations can be made to measure customer profitability: *customer net profit* and *customer profit margin*. **Customer net profit** starts with the revenues the customer generates and subtracts both the cost of goods sold associated with those revenues and the selling expenses allocated based on the customer-specific selling activities. This measure shows managers how many dollars a customer contributes to the company's bottom line. **Customer profit margin** divides customer net profit by customer revenues to obtain the profit percentage the customer generates for the company. The customer profit margin allows managers to compare customers based on how much each dollar of revenue they generate goes to the bottom line, regardless of the customers' absolute sales volume.

$$\text{Customer net profit} = \text{Customer revenues} - \text{Cost of goods sold} - \text{Allocated selling expenses}$$

$$\text{Customer profit margin} = \frac{\text{Customer net profit}}{\text{Customer revenues}}$$

Let's use Morris & Morris, Bradley's most profitable customer according to Gleason's analysis, to show how to measure customer profitability. As Exhibit T5-1 shows, based solely on cost of goods sold, last year Morris & Morris provided a 25.6% profit margin. Exhibit T5-3 shows an activity-based profitability analysis for this customer. Notice that Morris & Morris generates a customer net profit of $1,045,895 on sales of $4,819,150, which translates to a 21.7% profit margin.

Sales		$4,819,150
Cost of goods sold		3,585,455
Gross profit		1,233,695
Selling costs		
Sales calls	12 calls × $1,000 per call	12,000
Internet orders	1,000 orders × $20 per order	20,000
Catalog orders	10 orders × $65 per order	650
Packing and shipping	1,230,000 yards × $0.10 per yard	123,000
Call center support	100 minutes × $0.50 per minute	50
Product returns	6 returns × $350 per return	2,100
Express shipping	10,000 yards × $3.00 per yard	30,000
Customer net profit		$1,045,895
Customer profit margin	$1,045,895 ÷ $4,819,150	21.7%

EXHIBIT T5-3

Activity-based profitability analysis for Morris & Morris.

Even though the customer profit margin is lower than Gleason first thought, Morris & Morris is still a very profitable customer for Bradley Textile Mills.

How does that customer profit margin compare to Bradley's average customer profit margin? We can calculate the average customer profit margin using the numbers for the company as a whole (see Exhibit T5-1):

Revenues	$200,000,000
Cost of goods sold	172,000,000
Gross margin	28,000,000
Selling expenses (Exhibit T5-2)	16,815,000
Customer net profit	$ 11,185,000
Customer profit margin	5.6%

No wonder the chief financial officer wants to review the accounts (see Business Decision and Context). Administrative costs still need to be paid from the $11,185,000 net profit, so Bradley's net income is likely to be very low. With a customer profit margin of 21.7%—well above the average customer margin—Morris & Morris is a real winner for Bradley.

A different picture emerges from an analysis of Bradley's number two customer, Sparrow Designs. Gleason believes that Sparrow generates a 25% profit margin, but an activity analysis of the resources Sparrow Designs consumes, presented in Exhibit T5-4, shows otherwise. Gleason may need to reconsider his plans for this customer. What he thought was a 25.0% profit margin is really a 0.2% loss (($3,547) ÷ $1,978,812). For every dollar in sales, Sparrow costs the company $1.02.

Sales		$1,978,812
Cost of goods sold		1,484,109
Gross profit		494,703
Selling costs		
Sales calls	6 calls × $1,000 per call	6,000
Internet orders	0 orders × $20 per order	0
Catalog orders	230 orders × $65 per order	14,950
Packing and shipping	400,000 yards × $0.10 per yard	40,000
Call center support	3,000 minutes × $0.50 per minute	1,500
Product returns	28 returns × $350 per return	9,800
Express shipping	142,000 yards × $3.00 per yard	426,000
Customer net profit		($3,547)
Customer profit margin	($3,547) ÷ $1,978,812	(0.2%)

EXHIBIT T5-4

Activity-based profitability analysis for Sparrow Designs.

After following these same steps for each customer, Gleason obtained the customer profitability analysis shown in Exhibit T5-5. Now he cannot claim that all Bradley's customers are profitable.

EXHIBIT T5-5

Activity-based customer profitability analysis for Bradley Textile Mills.

Customer	Revenues	Cost of Sales	Selling Costs	Customer Net Profit	Customer Profit Margin
Morris & Morris	$4,819,150	$3,585,455	187,800	$1,045,895	21.7%
Sparrow Designs	1,978,812	1,484,109	498,250	($3,547)	−0.2%
Harps of London	168,600	126,450	8,100	34,050	20.2%
Gold's Upholstery	482,000	361,982	44,835	75,183	15.6%
Unique Uniforms	2,098,915	1,580,483	65,015	453,417	21.6%
C&C Sports	1,540,951	1,163,418	57,030	320,503	20.8%
MedTogs	4,154,500	3,157,420	204,400	792,680	19.1%
Florstan	67,200	51,408	20,495	(4,703)	−7.0%
.					
.					
.					
House of Drew	879,520	835,544	32,625	11,351	1.3%
Mullins and Jones	164,826	157,244	1,560	6,022	3.7%
Potter Drapery	94,608	90,256	5,234	(882)	−0.9%
Huffmeyer Mills	648,425	622,488	31,087	(5,150)	−0.8%
Mooney Productions	540,895	520,340	207,800	(187,245)	−34.6%
Dawson Shade	64,572	62,183	1,578	811	1.3%
Shadowbox Supply	267,400	262,052	37,337	(31,989)	−12.0%
Ralston Fabrics	349,800	342,804	70,100	(63,104)	−18.0%

THINK ABOUT IT T5.2

The customer profitability analyses in Exhibits T5-3 and T5-4 assume that cost of goods sold is the only direct cost, and all selling expenses are indirect (that is, they need to be allocated). What selling expenses might be traced directly to the customer?

Addressing Unprofitable Customers

Now that the managers of Bradley Textile Mills have a better understanding of each customer's profitability, they must decide what to do with the information. Recall from your study of activity-based management (Unit 7.3) that, to the extent possible, non-value-added activities should be eliminated. Because most of these activities are generated by the customer, we can assume that they have some value to the customer, but managers need to investigate other, less costly ways to deliver the service. Drastically reducing the activities would not be a viable option. Customers generally want good service, and developing a reputation for good customer service is one way for a company to differentiate itself from its competitors. Therefore, we cannot expect selling costs to be reduced to some nominal level. For purposes of this discussion, we will assume that Bradley Textile Mills is delivering customer service as efficiently and effectively as possible.

At first glance, it may appear that all unprofitable customers should be dropped, and that is exactly what some companies do. However, that is not the

REALITY CHECK—*Banking on customer profitability*

© YinYang/iStockphoto

The last few years have not been kind to the banking industry. In the wake of the U.S. banking crisis of the late 2000s, banks now face a host of new regulations that increase compliance costs. If the banks are to maintain an acceptable level of profitability, they will need to understand profitability at the customer level now more than ever before.

And bank customer profitability is not just an issue in the United States. At a recent meeting of Asia Pacific retail banking risk officers, understanding customer profitability was a big topic of conversation. Industry experts told the risk officers that knowing just 20–30 aspects of a customer could provide 80–90% of the increased customer profitability.

So how should a bank start looking at customer profitability? First, determine the products and services that each customer uses. Then, based on the cost of those products and services and the income from the customer, a bank can calculate the profit generated by each customer. Given that some industry estimates place as many as 60% of a bank's customers in the unprofitable category, imagine how a bank's profits would increase if all these unprofitable customers could be turned into profitable ones!

Some industry estimates place as many as 60% of a bank's customers in the unprofitable category.

Sources: Frank Brienzi, "It's Time to Embrace Core Systems Transformation," *Bank Systems & Technology*, November 29, 2012, http://www.banktech.com/core-systems/its-time-to-embrace-core-systems-transfo/240142937 (accessed December 20, 2012); "FICO Says Asian Banks Can Gain Double-Digit Growth in Customer Profitability with More Focus on Existing Customers," December 19, 2012, http://www.fico.com/en/newsroom/fico-says-asian-banks-can-gain-double-digit-growth-in-customer-profitability-with-more-focus-on-existing-customers-12-19-2012 (accessed July 7, 2016); Gary Shaivitz, "Customer-Profitability Analysis for Community Banks," *Banknews*, September 2011, 26–27.

first action a manager should take after identifying an unprofitable customer. Before any action is taken, managers should evaluate all the implications of the action for the affected customer, for other customers, and for the company.

Rather than drop an unprofitable customer, managers should first identify the reason the customer is unprofitable and then work with the customer to return to profitability. Let's look at Sparrow Designs again. Exhibit T5-4 shows the activities performed to support this customer. Does anything look out of the ordinary to you? Do you see any opportunities for cost reduction? One that should jump out at you is express shipping, which consumes over 86% of Sparrow's gross profit. Perhaps Beth Wommack, Bradley's customer service representative, can work with Sparrow's managers to encourage them to order earlier or in larger quantities, to avoid the need for express shipping.

Another opportunity for improvement is order placement. Notice that Sparrow places all its orders through the catalog sales channel rather than the cheaper Internet sales channel. Again, Beth could educate Sparrow's purchasing agents on the benefits of Internet ordering, which would reduce the cost to serve Sparrow while still meeting the company's needs. That is what managers at Fidelity Investments did when they discovered how frequently some unprofitable customers called Fidelity's customer service representatives. Representatives instructed the customers in how to use the company's website—a much cheaper delivery method for Fidelity. As customers became more comfortable with the technology, their satisfaction increased, and unprofitable customers turned into profitable ones.

Customer profitability can also be improved by raising the prices unprofitable customers pay. If customers are using a service, they should value it enough to pay for it. For example, Terrence Gleason might consider charging Sparrow for express shipping. The same could be required of customers who order in small quantities that require warehouse workers to select and pack individual items rather than ship a full case. Prices for such customers may be higher than for customers whose orders require less handling.

Raising prices for these customers is not a punishment for their unprofitability; it is merely a reflection of the cost of doing business with them. If the customer accepts the price increase or stops requiring costly activities, the company has turned an unprofitable customer into a profitable one. If the customer rejects the price increase and buys from a competitor, the company will be better off financially. All other things held equal, either result will improve the company's profitability.

Perhaps not all customers can be returned to profitability. If a customer remains unprofitable after efforts have been made to increase profitability, managers may reluctantly decide to drop the customer. Doing so will increase the company's overall profitability, even though total sales revenue will decrease. Managers then will have more resources with which to serve profitable customers, and overall sales may eventually increase.

Just as we saw in Chapter 7, however, the company cannot increase its profitability simply by dropping a customer. To increase the company's overall profitability, the resources used to serve the unprofitable customer must be divested. If Bradley Textile Mills decides to eliminate some of its unprofitable customers but does not eliminate the resources (people and supplies) used to serve those customers, the remaining costs will be redistributed to other customers, reducing their profitability, even though there has been no change to Bradley's overall profitability.

THINK ABOUT IT T5.3

What kind of impact might product demand have on your strategy for improving customer profitability?

TOPIC FOCUS REVIEW

KEY TERMS

Customer net profit p. 418   Customer profit margin p. 418

PRACTICE QUESTIONS

1. LO 1 If you add up all a company's customer profit margins, the total will equal net income. True or False?
2. LO 1 Which of the following selling expenses would be traceable directly to a customer?
   a. Commissions based on the sales amount
   b. Invoice processing
   c. Technical support
   d. Returns processing
3. LO 2 The only way to recover the losses from an unprofitable customer is to stop selling to that customer. True or False?
4. LO 2 Which of the following will *not* increase a company's net income, all other things held equal?
   a. Reducing the resources dedicated to serving a customer
   b. Dropping a customer with a 2.5% customer profit margin when the average customer profit margin is 6%
   c. Persuading a customer to accept an inexpensive activity rather than an expensive activity
   d. All these actions will increase the company's net income

TOPIC FOCUS 5 PRACTICE EXERCISE

Compass Directives prints road maps of major cities and distributes them to bookstores, convenience stores, and gas stations. Each map costs $1.30 to produce and is sold to retail outlets for $2.00. Sales to three of Compass's best customers last month were as follows:

BookMasters	20,000 maps
Price's QuikStop	15,000 maps
FastLanes	12,000 maps

Jason Paul, Compass's sales manager, has gathered the following information concerning the company's sales support activities:

	Total Annual Costs	Annual Activity Level
Small-quantity bundling	$400,000	50,000 bundles
Order processing	840,000	200,000 orders
Display setup	238,000	1,000 setups
Display replenishment	110,000	20,000 replenishments

As part of the study, Paul also calculated the following data on monthly usage of sales support services by the top three customers:

	Small Bundles	Orders	Display Setups	Display Replenishments
BookMasters	400	400	25	100
Price's QuikStop	20	100	5	10
FastLanes		10		

Required

1. Calculate an activity rate for each of the four sales support services.
2. Calculate the customer net profit and customer profit margin for each of the top three customers.
3. What actions could Paul suggest that BookMasters take to increase its profitability?

SELECTED TOPIC FOCUS 5 ANSWERS

Think About It T5.1

Administrative costs, which are related to running the entire business, include rent (or depreciation) on the corporate office building, the president's salary, and filing expenses for tax returns and other corporate documents. Though customers benefit from these organizational expenditures, allocating such costs to customers is not practical. You may recall that general overhead costs were treated the same way in Chapter 7.

Think About It T5.2

Commissions on sales and shipping cost per unit are examples of direct selling expenses.

Think About It T5.3

When demand for a company's products and services is greater than the supply, managers are not likely to be concerned about dropping customers. In a highly competitive environment, however, managers must carefully weigh the implications of charging for services that were once considered free. If customers can get the services they want from another company, they may be quick to leave, and other customers may not replace them. Losing those customers could require more than simply cutting back on selling and administrative resources. If total sales decline as a result, it may require cutting back on production.

Practice Questions

1. False
2. A
3. False
4. B

Topic Focus 5 Practice Exercise

1.

	Total Annual Costs	Annual Activity Level	Activity Rate
	A	B	A ÷ B
Small-quantity bundling	$400,000	50,000 bundles	$8.00 per bundle
Order processing	840,000	200,000 orders	$4.20 per order
Display setup	238,000	1,000 setups	$ 238 per setup
Display replenishment	110,000	20,000 replenishments	$5.50 per replenishment

2.

		BookMasters		Price's QuikStop		FastLanes	
	Unit Price/ Cost	Units	Revenue/ (Cost)	Units	Revenue/ (Cost)	Units	Revenue/ (Cost)
Revenues	$ 2.00	20,000 maps	$ 40,000	15,000 maps	$ 30,000	12,000 maps	$ 24,000
Cost of goods sold	$ 1.30	20,000 maps	(26,000)	15,000 maps	(19,500)	12,000 maps	(15,600)
Small-quantity bundling	$ 8.00	400 bundles	(3,200)	20 bundles	(160)	0 bundles	0
Order processing	$ 4.20	400 orders	(1,680)	100 orders	(420)	10 orders	(42)
Display setup	$238.00	25 setups	(5,950)	5 setups	(1,190)	0 setups	0
Display replenishment	$ 5.50	100 replenishments	(550)	10 replenishments	(55)	0 replenishments	0
Customer net profit			$ 2,620		$ 8,675		$ 8,358
Customer profit margin			6.55%		28.92%		34.83%

3. BookMasters consumes many more activities than the other two customers, even allowing for the number of units the company purchases throughout the year. Display setups, replenishment, and small-quantity bundling seem to be special services that BookMasters values more than other customers. Paul needs to find out whether BookMasters values these services enough to pay a premium for them, or whether the level of service can be reduced without losing BookMasters' business. To bring BookMasters' requirements in line with those of other customers, Paul may want to establish a standard order size. If BookMasters values small orders (probably because they eliminate excess inventory), Paul might consider adding a surcharge for this service. However, before Paul changes the pricing or order size, he should determine what services competitors offer and the impact that such changes would have on existing customers.

BUSINESS DECISION AND CONTEXT Wrap Up

After performing a profitability analysis of all 375 customers, Terrence Gleason understood that there was more to understanding a customer's profitability than gross margin. He realized that some customers, such as Morris & Morris, remained profitable after considering customer service costs. Others, such as Sparrow Designs, were unprofitable.

Gleason examined the activities required to service the unprofitable customers to identify ways to move them to profitability. He encouraged Sparrow's Taylor Byrd to begin using Internet orders instead of catalog orders and to order with enough lead time to avoid express shipping services. He also informed Byrd that should Sparrow continue to require express shipping services, there would be an additional charge to cover the higher shipping cost. Byrd's initial reaction to these changes was favorable.

At this point, Gleason wasn't ready to make drastic changes for all customers. He knew that alienating customers or changing the way the company provides service could well have a detrimental effect on the company's reputation for high-quality products and excellent customer service. Gleason wanted to study the services Bradley provides to customers and compare them to competitors' services. He also wanted to monitor Sparrow's activities closely for a couple of months to see how the changes affected customer profitability. Only after he feels reasonably confident that he can anticipate customers' reactions will he make sweeping changes to Bradley's selling activities.

TOPIC FOCUS SUMMARY

In this focus unit you learned how to evaluate customer profitability. Specifically, you should be able to meet the objectives set out at the beginning of this chapter:

1. *Use activity-based costing techniques to measure customer profitability.*

   To use activity-based costing techniques for measuring customer profitability, a company should follow these five steps for allocating selling expenses to customers:

   Step 1. Identify selling activities.

   Step 2. Develop activity cost pools.

   Step 3. Calculate activity cost pool rates.

   Step 4. Allocate selling costs to customers.

   Step 5. Calculate customer profitability.

2. *Identify alternatives for managing unprofitable customer accounts.*

   Companies that find they have unprofitable customers might try to manage those accounts in the following ways:

   - Reduce the customer's use of selling activities.
   - Add a service charge for certain selling activities or the excessive use of selling activities.
   - Stop providing the service to the customer.

EXERCISES

T5-1 Identify activities (LO 1) Place an X in the columns to indicate whether each of the following activities would be included in a bank's customer profitability analysis.

	INCLUDED	NOT INCLUDED
a. Opening a bank account		
b. Supporting an online banking system		
c. Developing a corporate logo		
d. Preparing bank statements for mailing		
e. Renting off-site document storage facilities (to preserve company data)		
f. Hosting the board of directors' annual meeting		
g. Gathering information for federal bank auditors		
h. Balancing transactions at the end of the day		
i. Taking deposits at the drive-in window		
j. Providing access to safety deposit boxes		

T5-2 Identify activity drivers (LO 1) Williams Enterprises is a small, locally owned provider of network services. Brian Williams, CEO, has considerable experience in the industry and knows that certain customers can run a company out of business. He has determined that the following customer activities are the major ones in which the company engages:

a. Establishing new customers and new orders
b. Installing new systems
c. Processing customer invoices
d. Making service calls
e. Customer training

Required

Identify an activity driver for each of the major activities.

T5-3 Identify high-cost activities (Adapted from Robert S. Kaplan and V. G. Narayanan, "Measuring and Managing Customer Profitability," *Journal of Cost Management*, 15, no. 5 (September/October 2001): 5–15.) **(LO 1)** Customer profitability is influenced by the activities that customers consume. Indicate whether each activity listed in the following table would be associated with a high cost-to-serve customer or a low cost-to-serve customer.

	HIGH COST-TO-SERVE	LOW COST-TO-SERVE
Orders custom products in small quantities		
Uses standard delivery services		
Frequently changes delivery requirements		
Places orders using the Internet		
Requires little to no presales support		
Requires installation and training		
Requires frequent deliveries to accommodate just-in-time inventory system		
Pays slowly (high accounts receivable)		

T5-4 Calculate customer net profit and customer profit margin (LO 1) Wingo Widgets makes and sells widgets to individual and corporate customers. Widgets cost $3.65 to make and are sold for $5.00 each. Individual customers typically require little service beyond order processing. Because widgets don't differ much from one producer to the next, corporate customers demand additional services before they will commit to a purchase. Wingo's selling activities and cost pools are as follows:

Cost Pool	Annual Cost	Annual Driver Activity
Order processing	$250,000	2,500 orders
Telephone technical support	70,000	3,500 hours
Product demonstrations	46,000	100 demonstrations
Express deliveries	42,000	400 deliveries
	$408,000	

The following table compares the activity levels for the average individual customer and the average corporate customer:

	Individual	Corporate
Widgets purchased	1,200	10,000
Orders	10	45
Technical support hours	2	80
Product demonstrations	0	10
Express deliveries	1	13

Required

a. Calculate the activity rate for each cost pool.

b. Calculate the customer net profit and customer profit margin for the average individual customer and the average corporate customer.

c. If Wingo wanted to drop one average corporate customer, how many average individual customers would need to be added to make up the lost net income?

T5-5 Calculate customer net profit and customer profit margin (LO 1) Stoner Excursions offers several services to customers. Susan Stoner realizes that some customers use more services than others, so the company has conducted a customer profitability analysis that identified the following cost pools and activity drivers:

Cost Pool	Annual Cost	Annual Driver Activity
Online reservations	$ 240,000	40,000 online reservations
Phone reservations	980,000	98,000 phone reservations
Ticket mailings	500,000	125,000 mailings
Courier deliveries	160,000	10,000 deliveries
	$1,880,000	

Required

a. Calculate the activity rate for each cost pool.

b. Two of Stoner's customers have the following activity levels. Calculate the customer net profit and customer profit margin for each customer:

	Customer A	Customer B
Ticket purchases	$172,500	$180,000
Ticket cost	$129,375	$135,000
Online reservations	500	0
Phone reservations	0	600
Ticket mailings	500	120
Courier deliveries	0	480

T5-6 Calculate the customer profit margin; calculate the income effect of dropping customers (LO 1) Corley Communications performed a customer profitability analysis and obtained the following results for its bottom five customers:

Customer	Sales	Customer Net Profit	Customer Profit Margin
Albert	$ 525,000	$ 9,450	1.80%
Brown	$1,200,000	$16,800	1.40%
Carter	$1,400,000	$ 5,600	0.40%
Dyson	$ 600,000	($ 1,500)	(0.25%)
English	$ 460,000	($ 4,140)	(0.90%)

Chris Corley, vice president for marketing, believes that if these five customers are dropped, the selling expenses required to serve them will be eliminated. Company revenues total $18,000,000; the current average customer profit margin is 7.2%, and net income is $400,000.

Required

a. Calculate the total customer net profit.
b. What effect would dropping all five customers have on the average customer profit margin?
c. What effect would dropping all five customers have on net income?
d. What action would you recommend? Why?

T5-7 Identifying Unprofitable Customers (LO 1, 2) Dan Brown, Griffin Industries' sales manager, recently read an article that described ways to evaluate customer profitability. After learning that 80% of a company's profits may be generated by less than 20% of its customers, Dan was ready to take steps to identify unprofitable customers and figure out how to turn them into profitable ones. Descriptions of two of Griffin's customers follow.

> Morgan Light and Sound has been a customer since 2008. The company orders standard products in case quantities. Morgan places 90% of its orders through Griffin's website. During the last year, Morgan placed 20 orders and made one merchandise return. Morgan called Griffin's customer service department twice during the year to resolve shipping problems; these calls lasted a total of 20 minutes. Brown makes an annual sales visit to Morgan to explain new product updates and maintain the customer relationship. Morgan's purchases for the year totaled $400,000 and generated a gross profit of $90,000.
>
> Holmes Holographics, one of Griffin's first customers, has been a customer since 1998. The company orders a wide variety of products, half of which are specialty products that Griffin must special order. Holmes places 20% of its orders through Griffin's website and 80% through the customer call center. During the last year, Holmes placed 100 orders and made 25 merchandise returns. In addition to placing orders, Holmes called the customer service department 32 times to resolve a variety of issues; these calls lasted a total of four hours. Brown visits Holmes' office twice a month to maintain the relationship. Holmes' purchases for the year totaled $500,000 and generated a gross profit of $98,000.

Required

a. Which of the customers is most likely unprofitable for Griffin? Why?
b. What suggestions do you have for Brown that may improve the unprofitable customer's profitability?

PROBLEMS

T5-8 Customer profitability (Adapted from D. L. Searcy, "Using activity-based costing to assess channel/customer profitability," *Management Accounting Quarterly*, 5, no. 2 (Winter 2004): 51–60.) **(LO 1, 2)** Time Solutions, Inc. is an employment services firm that places both temporary and permanent workers with a variety of clients. Temporary placements account for 70% of Time Solutions' revenue; permanent placements provide the remaining 30%. President Gia Johnson recently read an article that discussed the need to consider selling and administrative costs in determining customer profitability—a practice that Time Solutions does not follow. Johnson is concerned that the company may be making poor choices in the selection of customers.

In the temporary market, Time Solutions advertises and searches for workers, hires them, and pays them for the hours they work. The company then bills customers for an amount that is higher than the workers' pay plus taxes. Because the temporary market is very competitive, Time Solutions has had to reduce the rates charged to customers to keep their business.

After reviewing the year's operations, Johnson has determined that the company's customer service activities for the temporary business could be divided into three cost pools: filling work orders, hiring temporary employees, and processing payroll/billing customers. The following table shows the three cost pools and their annual capacity:

Cost Pool	Total Cost	Annual Capacity
Filling work orders	$175,875	3,500 orders
Hiring temporary employees	$ 81,125	2,950 applicants
Processing payroll/billing customers	$ 43,000	215,000 hours worked

Time Solutions' largest four customers account for about 42% of total sales, so Johnson has decided to analyze those customers' accounts first to determine how much they are contributing to the bottom line. The gross margin the companies generate and the activities they use are as follows:

	Chemical Company	Trailer Manufacturer	Newspaper Publisher	Food Processor
Sales	$466,733	$145,764	$122,604	$167,327
Cost of sales				
Wages	341,620	110,473	92,205	120,451
Taxes and fees	65,366	24,350	18,621	23,411
Total cost of sales	406,986	134,823	110,826	143,862
Gross margin	$ 59,747	$ 10,941	$ 11,778	$ 23,465
Temps ordered	88	56	928	332
Applicants	74	48	794	284
Hours worked	47,370	15,115	13,000	22,765

Required

a. Calculate the gross margin percentage for each customer.
b. Determine the activity rates for each of the three cost pools.
c. Determine the customer net profit and customer profit margin for each customer.
d. What suggestions would you make for managing each customer's profitability?

T5-9 Customer profitability (LO 1, 2) After attending a seminar on measuring customer profitability, Mason Ford decided to examine Olson Optics' customers to determine if the company truly knew how profitable its customers were.

Olson Optics already uses an activity-based costing system to determine the product cost of its two products: RF30 and LF45. Each RF30 sells for $15.00 and requires $7.05 in direct materials and $4.00 in direct labor. Each LF45 sells for $50.00 and requires $15.45 in direct materials and $14.00 in direct labor. The following table provides cost and activity information for manufacturing overhead for the two products.

			Number of Activities		
Activity Cost Pool	Cost Driver	Manufacturing Overhead Costs	RF30	LF45	Total
Packing	Cartons	$ 200,000	500,000	300,000	800,000
Setup	Setup hours	450,000	10,000	27,500	37,500
Assembly	Spot welds	730,000	125,000	240,000	365,000
Finishing	Machine hours	300,000	25,000	75,000	100,000
Total manufacturing overhead costs		$1,680,000			
Units produced			600,000	200,000	

Based on what Ford learned at the seminar, he has gathered the following information about customer support activities.

Activity Cost Pool	Cost Driver	Selling Costs	Driver Volume
Order entry	Orders	$200,000	40,000
Customer support	Support hours	150,000	5,000
Sales calls	Sales calls	250,000	2,000
Express shipping	Shipments	140,000	7,000
Total selling costs		$740,000	

Ford wants to apply his new profitability analysis techniques to Infrared Technologies, a company he believes is representative of Olson's average customer. Information about Infrared's account activity is as follows.

RF30 purchases	10,000 units
LF45 purchases	3,000 units
Orders placed	300
Customer support	500 hours
Sales calls	24
Express shipments	250

Required

a. Calculate the activity-based product cost for RF30 and LF45.
b. Calculate the cost pool rates for Olson's customer service activities.
c. Calculate the gross profit, customer net profit, and customer profit margin for Infrared Technologies.
d. Is Infrared Technologies a profitable customer? Why or why not?
e. What actions could Ford take to increase Infrared Technologies' profitability? Should these actions be applied to all of Olson's customers?

T5-10 Customer profitability (LO 2) Ray Panneton, president of Okus Designs, met with his CFO and vice president of marketing to discuss the profitability of the company's top 10 customers. These customers account for 80% of the company's revenues. The following table was prepared by the accounting department to assist Ray in his decision making.

Customer	Revenues	Cost of Sales	Selling Costs	Customer Net Profit	Customer Profit Margin
Meredith's Boutique	$ 5,000,000	$ 3,750,000	$ 750,000	500,000	10.00%
Stewart Industries	4,890,000	3,618,600	978,000	293,400	6.00%
T&P Incorporated	4,500,000	3,375,000	1,129,500	(4,500)	(0.10%)
Talley Design Studios	4,200,000	3,192,000	378,000	630,000	15.00%
UPPtown Productions	4,100,000	2,870,000	902,000	328,000	8.00%
O'Brien's Tavern	3,900,000	2,730,000	1,365,000	(195,000)	(5.00%)
House of Claire	3,850,000	2,887,500	885,500	77,000	2.00%
Copper Metalworks	3,700,000	2,664,000	888,000	148,000	4.00%
J Floral Designs	3,625,000	2,501,250	1,486,250	(362,500)	(10.00%)
Old Main Masonry	3,500,000	2,485,000	770,000	245,000	7.00%
Total/Average	$41,265,000	$30,073,350	$9,532,250	1,659,400	4.02%

Required

a. Ray is concerned about the customers with negative customer profit margins. If these customers are dropped, what will be the new total customer net profit and customer profit margin (assume the cost of sales and selling costs can be eliminated)?

b. Ray is also concerned about customers with customer profit margins below the current company average. If all customers with below-average profit margins are dropped, what will be the new total customer net profit and customer profit margin (assume the cost of sales and selling costs can be eliminated)?
c. Compare your answers to parts (a) and (b). What do you notice?
d. If Ray were to drop all customers with profit margins below average, how much in new customer revenues would need to be added to make the company as well off as it would be if it only dropped the customers with negative profit margins? Use an average profit margin for the new customers equal to the one you calculated in part (a).
e. What action do you recommend Ray take?

T5-11 Customer Profitability (LO 2) Customer centricity is a business philosophy that puts a company's customer at the heart of operations. Rather than adopting a "build it and they will buy it" mentality, a customer-centric organization seeks to understand its customers' needs and then designs and delivers products and services to meet those needs. As part of this process, companies may group their customers into various segments so that customers receive products and services that are best aligned with their needs.

One result of adopting a customer-centric operating focus is creating value for the customer through product and service offerings. However, the customer must also generate value back to the company, and this value is commonly measured through customer profitability. According to consulting firm Booz Allen Hamilton, a customer-centric company focuses on "delivering the greatest value to the best customers for the least cost" (*The Customer-Centric Organization,* http://www.boozallen.com/content/dam/boozallen/media/file/141263.pdf).

Required

a. Explain how activity-based customer profitability analysis can assist in implementing customer centricity.
b. Assume that as part of Bergquist Electronics' customer profitability analysis, marketing manager Brittany Mathis identified customers who shopped primarily during sales events. Those customers, who purchased a large volume of merchandise, had been considered desirable customers. After the analysis, however, the company ceased to mail sales notices to them. Why would Bergquist decide to ignore those customers?
c. After implementing its customer-centric approach, Bergquist's sales revenue increased. As a result, would you conclude that the move to customer centricity was a profitable one for Bergquist? How should the company determine the profitability of the change?

ENDNOTES

1. Larry Selden and Geoffrey Colvin, *Killer Customers: Tell the Good from the Bad—And Dominate Your Competitors* (New York: The Penguin Group, 2003). This book was originally published as *Angel Customers & Demon Customers.*
2. Vincent J. Shea, Steven Williamson, and Bobby E. Waldrup, "The ABCs of Customer Profitability: Insights from the PAPER Industry in Florida," *Research in Business and Economics Journal*, Special Edition–Florida Economic Symposium, May 2012, http://www.aabri.com/manuscripts/FSC-12-3.pdf.

CHAPTER 8 USING ACCOUNTING INFORMATION TO MAKE MANAGERIAL DECISIONS

UNITS	LEARNING OBJECTIVES
UNIT 8.1 Identifying Relevant Information	**LO 1:** Identify relevant information for decision making.
UNIT 8.2 Special Order Pricing	**LO 2:** Determine the qualitative and quantitative impacts of special order pricing.
UNIT 8.3 Outsourcing	**LO 3:** Determine the qualitative and quantitative impacts of outsourcing decisions.
UNIT 8.4 Allocating Constrained Resources	**LO 4:** Determine how to allocate constrained resources to maximize income.
UNIT 8.5 Keeping or Eliminating Operations	**LO 5:** Calculate the effects on operating income of keeping or eliminating operations.

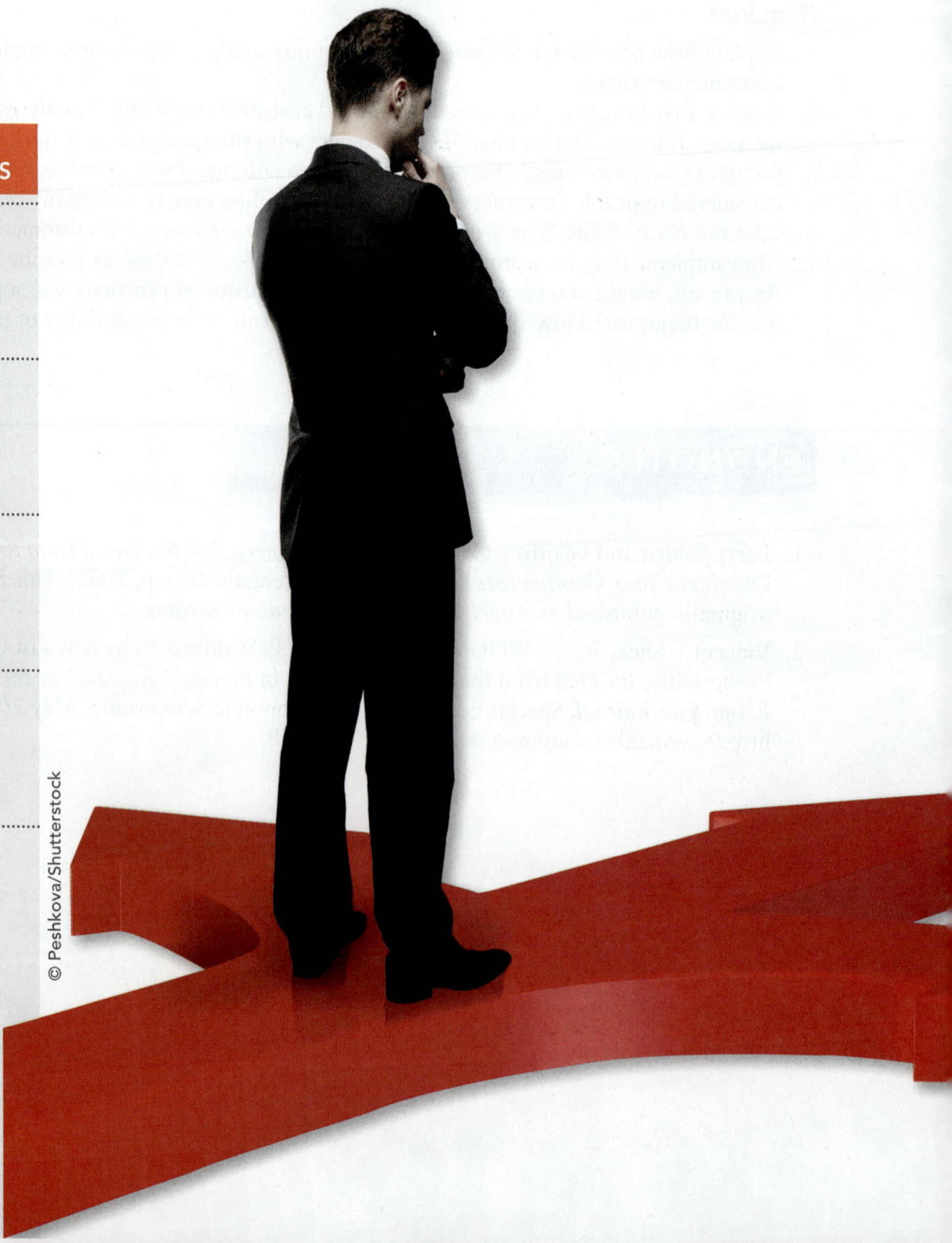

Business Decision and Context

© Natykach Nataliia/Shutterstock

At the weekly meeting of C&C Sports' management team, **President George Douglas** began his usual polling of the vice presidents to learn the issues they were facing in the coming week. **Jonathan Smith, vice president for marketing**, spoke first. "I'll start with some good news. I just got a text message from Jim Shaw, one of our sales reps. He thinks Central Independent School District is ready to sign a five-year contract to purchase 1,000 practice jerseys a year. That really would give us a head start on our move to supply school districts. The district's athletic director wants a couple of changes to our standard jersey, but I'm sure it's something we can accommodate."

Chad Davis, vice president for operations, chimed in, "I have good news, too. Bonadeo Embroidery wants to supply us with the chenille letters we use on the award jackets. You know, we make them ourselves, but the price Bonadeo is offering is less than our cost to make them. Looks like a money-saving move." "Unfortunately, I also have some bad news," Chad continued. "Austin told me yesterday that our rep at Bradley Textile Mills said that they were having some problems scheduling our jersey fabric. It seems they've had an increase in demand for their wool fabric, and they may not have enough capacity to produce all the fabric customers want to buy."

> "Our rep at Bradley Textile Mills said that they were having some problems scheduling our jersey fabric. It seems they've had an increase in demand for their wool fabric, and they may not have enough capacity to produce all the fabric customers want to buy."

George thought for a minute and replied, "Well, surely we're one of Bradley's top customers. I can't imagine that they wouldn't produce our fabric to meet our schedule. Any other issues?"

"I've been hearing some rumblings among our sales representatives," Jonathan replied. "Not everyone in the field is convinced that all the reps are pulling their weight in terms of generating profits. I want to look into it this week and develop a recommendation for our next meeting." Glancing at **Claire Elliot, vice president for finance and administration**, he said, "I'm going to need your group to prepare statements that show the profitability of each of our sales territories."

"Do you think we have a territory that is losing money?" George asked. "We really can't afford to have an unprofitable territory, so if we find we're losing money somewhere, I want to shut it down immediately."

"Not so fast," Claire interjected. "We need to make sure we don't get ourselves into even worse financial shape by making hasty decisions. I suggest we take the time to gather all the pertinent information about each of these matters before we jump to an incorrect conclusion that could cost us a lot of money."

"So, how do we avoid a potential disaster?" George asked.

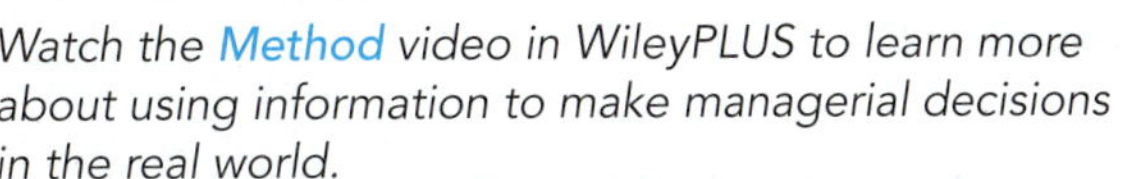

Watch the Method video in WileyPLUS to learn more about using information to make managerial decisions in the real world.

SUPPLY CHAIN KEY PLAYERS

END CUSTOMER

UNIVERSAL SPORTS EXCHANGE

C&C SPORTS

President
George Douglas

Vice President for Finance and Administration
Claire Elliot

Vice President for Marketing
Jonathan Smith

Vice President for Operations
Chad Davis

DURABLE ZIPPER COMPANY

BRADLEY TEXTILE MILLS

CENTEX YARNS

NEFF FIBER MANUFACTURING

BRUIN POLYMERS, INC.

UNIT 8.1

Identifying Relevant Information

GUIDED UNIT PREPARATION

Answering the following questions while you read this unit will guide your understanding of the key concepts found in the unit. The questions are linked to the learning objectives presented at the beginning of the chapter.

LO 1

1. What two criteria must information meet to be considered relevant for decision making?
2. Define the terms *avoidable* and *unavoidable* in the context of decision making. Provide a decision scenario and identify the avoidable and unavoidable costs.
3. What is a sunk cost? Could sunk costs ever be informative?

Think about the last time you had an important decision to make. How did you make it? Chances are, you spent some time gathering information that would help you to choose between the alternatives. When managers in an organization need to make a decision, they do the same. They sort through mounds of information, searching for the pieces that will make a difference in their deliberations.

Some of the decisions managers face are complex, requiring them to evaluate a lot of information. To focus on the facts that make a difference in the decision, managers need to know how to eliminate irrelevant information. In this unit, you will learn how managers sift through information to identify only the pieces they need to consider. By identifying the relevant pieces of information, managers can avoid becoming overwhelmed by the huge amount of information available to them, a phenomenon called **information overload.**

What Is Relevant Information?

Let's imagine that you are shopping for a new car and have narrowed your search down to the Honda Accord and Nissan Altima. These two models are your decision alternatives, only one of which can be implemented. Exhibit 8-1

EXHIBIT 8-1

Honda Accord versus Nissan Altima[a]

	Honda Accord	Nissan Altima
Base manufacturer's suggested retail price (MSRP)	$23,005	$22,500
Miles per gallon, city (MPG)	27	27
Miles per gallon, highway (MPG)	37	39
Base warranty period	36,000 miles, 36 months	36,000 miles, 36 months
Leg room, front (inches)	42.5	45
Wheelbase (inches)	109.3	109.3

[a]Specifications are for 2016 models.

REALITY CHECK—*Watch out for big data*

© moodboard/Corbis

Walmart captures information on more than 1,000,000 customer transactions each hour.

Five exabytes—the equivalent of 500,000 libraries the size of the Library of Congress. That's how much new information was generated in 2002. In 2007, 281 exabytes of new digital data was created. And in 2013, 5 exabytes of new data were created *each day*. There is so much data available today that a new term—big data—has been coined to describe the huge datasets that organizations now have at their disposal.

Where is all this data coming from? Much of it comes from organizations such as Walmart, which captures information on more than 1,000,000 customer transactions each hour. Searching through all this data to find the relevant information for decision making can be an overwhelming task, and employees' productivity falls as they wade through information that has little or no value. In fact, a recent survey conducted by the AICPA and CIMA found that information overload was slowing down decision making at 37% of the respondents' companies. Some researchers warn that information overload can even lead to Information Fatigue Syndrome and other physical ills.

One way companies have tried to combat information overload is through the creation of information dashboards, which look a lot like the cockpit instrument panel in an airplane. These displays allow executive decision makers to focus on critical information. But sometimes even the dashboards become cluttered with too much information. One company was monitoring over 100 supply-and-demand indicators, but paying attention to only five of them.

And then there's the Internet, a prime source of information overload, where Google processes over 4,000,000 searches each minute!

Sources: "Bringing Big Data to the Enterprise," IBM, http://www-01.ibm.com/software/data/bigdata/ (accessed January4,2013); RogerE.BohnandJamesE.Short, "HowMuchinformation?2009:ReportonAmericanConsumers," https://www.researchgate.net/publication/242562463_How_Much_Information_2009_Report_on_American_Consumers (accessed July 8, 2016); "Data, Data Everywhere," *The Economist*, February 25, 2010, http://www.economist.com/node/15557443/ (accessed January 4, 2013); F. Heylighen, "Change and Information Overload: Negative Effects," in F. Heylighen, C. Joslyn, and V. Turchin (eds.), *Principia Cybernetica Web* (Brussels: Principia Cybernetica), http://clearmc11.vub.ac.be/REFERPCP.html (accessed February 20, 2007); Erik Keller, "A Backlash to 'Too Much Information' Is a Real Possibility," *Manufacturing Business Technology*, November 2005, 18; Peter Lyman and Hal R. Varian, "How Much Information? 2003," http://www2.sims.berkeley.edu/research/projects/how-much-info-2003 (accessed July 8, 2016); Susan Gunelius, "The Data Explosion in 2014 Minute by Minute - Infographic," July 12, 2014, http://aci.info/2014/07/12/the-data-explosion-in-2014-minute-by-minute-infographic/ (accessed April 5, 2016).

shows the information you have gathered for each model. Is it relevant to your decision? It depends.

Relevant information meets two criteria: (1) it differs between the alternatives (that is, it is **differential**); and (2) the differences will occur in the future. Looking at the information you have gathered, we can see that the two models' MSRP, city MPG, highway MPG, and front leg room differ, and, of course, the costs related to these differences will arise in the future since you haven't yet purchased a car. Therefore, these four pieces of information are relevant to your decision. The remaining two pieces of information, wheelbase and warranty period, are the same for both models. Therefore, that information is irrelevant and should be ignored.

Based on what you have learned about the Accord and Altima, can we assume that wheelbase and warranty period will always be irrelevant to a car purchase? The answer is no. Relevance depends on context, so the same piece of information could be relevant to one decision but not to another. If you were considering the Accord and the Kia Optima, for example, both wheelbase and warranty period would become relevant. (The Optima has a 110.4 inch wheelbase and carries a 60-month/60,000 mile warranty.) So in evaluating the relevance of specific information, be sure you know the context of the decision.

Finally, in comparing the Accord to the Altima and then to the Optima, the implication was that you would purchase one of the cars. But there is another alternative that we haven't explored: maintaining the status quo. Many times, doing nothing is a viable alternative that must be considered.

In sum, information is relevant to a decision when it differs between alternatives *and* those differences occur in the future, as shown in the following decision matrix.

When does the information occur?	Does the information differ between alternatives? Yes	No
Future	Relevant (avoidable)	Not relevant (unavoidable)
Past	Not relevant (sunk)	Not relevant (sunk)

Other terms that are sometimes used to describe whether costs are relevant are *avoidable* and *unavoidable*. **Avoidable costs** occur only with the implementation of a particular alternative. They are relevant to a decision because they differ between alternatives. **Unavoidable costs** are incurred under all alternatives; thus they are irrelevant.

Another term, **sunk cost**, represents a cost that has been incurred in the past. Sunk costs are irrelevant in deciding between two alternatives because they were incurred in the past, not the future. There is no action you can take to change a sunk cost, since it has already been incurred. Assume, for example, that two months ago your current car was in the shop, and the repairs cost you $500. In your decision to purchase either an Accord or an Altima, that $500 is a sunk cost and should have no effect on your decision.

THINK ABOUT IT 8.1

Suppose you are trying to decide whether to take a job or go to graduate school after graduation. Indicate whether each of the following pieces of information is relevant or irrelevant to your decision:

	Relevant	Irrelevant
Cost of your undergraduate education		
Salary achievable with an undergraduate degree		
Salary achievable with a graduate degree		
Cost of toiletries		
Car insurance		
Graduate school tuition, fees, etc.		
Cost of breakfast food (assuming your eating habits don't change after you graduate)		

Relevant Cost Identification: An Example

Let's look at a decision Mathis Mills' managers are considering: expansion of the company's product line into a new sales territory. Mathis Mills is a competitor of Bradley Textile Mills and an infrequent supplier of C&C Sports' fabric. Right now, Mathis sells 4,250,000 yards of jersey fabric per year. Managers predict that a new territory could increase sales by 200,000 yards. The company already has adequate production capacity (machines and other overhead) to meet the increased demand, but would have to add a new sales representative to cover the territory. Thus, the decision alternatives are "add a new territory" or "maintain the status quo."

Exhibit 8-2 categorizes the available information regarding this decision, highlighting the relevant facts. The sales revenues and variable costs of the fabric sold in the new territory, as well as the salary and benefits of the new sales representative, are differential and will occur in the future. This information is relevant to the decision to expand into the new territory.

EXHIBIT 8-2

Information for Mathis Textile Mills' decision to enter a new sales territory.

When does the information occur?	Does the information differ between alternatives? Yes	No
Future	• Revenue on sale of 200,000 new yards • Variable cost of producing and selling 200,000 new yards • Salary of new sales representative	• Revenue on continuing sales of 4,250,000 yards • Variable cost of continuing to produce and sell 4,250,000 yards • Fixed cost of production—salaries, insurance, etc.
Past	• none	• Purchase of production equipment

The exhibit also shows the information that doesn't differ between the two alternatives: the revenues and costs generated by the current sales of 4,250,000 yards of fabric. That information is irrelevant to the decision to expand. Does that mean the sale of 4,250,000 yards of fabric won't occur or isn't meaningful to the company? Absolutely not. The sale of 4,250,000 yards is irrelevant to the present decision because it will occur regardless of the expansion decision. Notice that the production manager's salary isn't relevant either. Why not? Because Mathis will pay the production manager under either alternative. So how does Mathis decide whether to expand? All other things held equal, if the additional contribution margin from the sale of an extra 200,000 yards of fabric, minus the salary of the new sales representative, is positive, then the company should expand; otherwise, it should not.

Exhibit 8-3 on the following page shows a detailed analysis of the available alternatives. The first column represents the company's current operations, or the "status quo." The second column reflects expected operating income if the new territory is added. The third column, labeled "Incremental Revenues and Costs,"

	Alternative 1: Maintain Current Sales Territories	Alternative 2: Expand Sales Territories	Incremental Revenues and Costs
	4,250,000 yards	4,450,000 yards	200,000 yards
Sales ($4.00/unit)	$17,000,000	$17,800,000	$800,000
Variable expenses:			
Direct material ($1.26/unit)	5,355,000	5,607,000	252,000
Direct labor ($0.54/unit)	2,295,000	2,403,000	108,000
Variable manufacturing overhead ($0.30/unit)	1,275,000	1,335,000	60,000
Variable selling and administrative expenses ($0.12/unit)	510,000	534,000	24,000
Total variable costs ($2.22/unit)	9,435,000	9,879,000	444,000
Contribution margin ($1.78/unit)	7,565,000	7,921,000	356,000
Fixed expenses:			
Fixed manufacturing overhead	6,000,000	6,000,000	0
Fixed selling and administrative expenses	800,000	900,000	100,000
Total fixed expenses	6,800,000	6,900,000	100,000
Operating income	$ 765,000	$ 1,021,000	$256,000

EXHIBIT 8-3 *Mathis Mills' comparison of alternatives.*

reflects the difference between the two alternatives. These are the incremental (additional) revenues and costs expected to result from the expansion. Notice that the operating income in the third column is simply the contribution margin from the additional 200,000 yards less the additional salary and benefits of the new sales representative.

Calculations such as those in the third column, which show the additional impact of one alternative over another, are referred to as **incremental analysis**. This kind of analysis helps decision makers to understand the impact of their choices. "We should expand because we can make an additional $256,000 in operating income" more accurately communicates the result of the decision than "We should expand because we can make $1,021,000."

WATCH OUT!

Don't assume that all variable costs are relevant and all fixed costs are irrelevant. Cost behavior doesn't determine whether a cost is relevant. Costs that are relevant are those that differ between the alternatives, whether they are variable or fixed.

Should Mathis Mills consider anything other than the financial impact of the expansion? Of course. First, the 200,000 yards of additional sales is an estimate, not a guarantee. Management will have to decide whether to risk hiring a new sales representative and producing additional yards of material. Managers should also talk with support personnel, to ensure that an increase in production and sales will not strain the system to the point of reducing existing customer service levels.

A Relevant Cost Decision Model

With this expansion example, you have worked through a basic decision faced by many managers. While managers make many different types of decisions, most of them can be approached using the following decision model.

1. What is the decision to be made?
2. What are the available alternatives?

3. What are the relevant revenues and costs?
4. What are the qualitative issues that must be considered?
5. Which alternative offers the greatest benefit or least cost?

The first step in making any decision is to understand exactly what decision is being made. While that may sound simple, decision contexts can be very complex. In the car-buying decision, for example, was the decision "Which car should I buy?" or was it "How can I obtain reliable transportation to and from work?" Without understanding the decision context, you can't satisfactorily complete the remaining steps in the process. Worse, you may end up with an answer to a completely different decision.

Once you understand the decision context, you can develop a list of available alternatives. In our car-buying decision, we began with two alternatives, an Accord and an Altima, and hinted at a third, the Optima. But if the decision was really "How can I obtain reliable transportation to and from work?" we may have left out some viable alternatives, such as using a mass transit system. Again, understanding the decision is imperative if you are going to identify and evaluate all the viable alternatives.

In enumerating the alternatives, you may come up with an alternative that isn't really viable. For instance, mass transit will not be a viable transportation option if no such system exists in your city. So considering that alternative isn't warranted.

Once all the viable alternatives have been identified, you must develop a list of all the relevant revenues and costs. Remember that those revenues and costs must be differential, and they must occur in the future. You should also identify any qualitative factors that may affect your decision. In the car-buying example, those factors might include the car's repair history, its exterior and interior colors, and the dealer's reputation. With this information in hand, you are ready to reach a decision—choose the alternative that produces the greatest benefit or the lowest cost.

The remainder of this chapter will introduce you to four common decisions that most organizations face. Though the contexts and alternatives for each are different, you will see that they all require managers to identify and analyze the relevant information. All four decisions are short run in that they focus on the incremental contribution margin they generate. While implementing a decision that generates a small contribution margin will benefit an organization in the short run, that is not a good way to approach a long-term decision. In the long run, a viable alternative must generate enough contribution margin to cover fixed costs and provide an acceptable level of profit. We will examine long-term decisions in Chapter 9.

UNIT 8.1 REVIEW

KEY TERMS

Avoidable cost p. 436
Differential p. 435
Incremental analysis p. 438
Information overload p. 434
Relevant information p. 435
Sunk cost p. 436
Unavoidable cost p. 436

PRACTICE QUESTIONS

1. LO 1 Which of the following is *not* required for an item to be considered relevant to a decision?
   a. It arises in the future.
   b. It is variable.
   c. It differs between choices.
   d. It is avoidable.

2. LO 1 Costs that are always irrelevant in decision making are
   a. fixed costs.
   b. sunk costs.
   c. future costs that do not differ between the alternatives.
   d. both b and c.

3. LO 1 Which of the following is unavoidable, and thus irrelevant, when deciding between two job offers in different cities?
   a. The proposed salaries
   b. Relocation costs
   c. Monthly student loan payment
   d. Advancement potential

UNIT 8.1 PRACTICE EXERCISE

Jennifer Grant is the southwest regional recruiting manager for James & Smith, LLC, a large advertising firm in Houston, Texas. Jennifer needs to go to Baylor University in Waco, Texas, for a one-day recruiting event that begins at 9 A.M. on Monday morning. Waco is 183 miles from Jennifer's office. If she drives her personal car, the company will reimburse her at the rate of $0.50 per mile. Company policy allows her to spend the night if she would need to leave town before 6 A.M. to arrive at her destination. The Harrington House, a hotel close to the campus, charges $67 per night. Instead of driving, Jennifer could catch a 7:30 A.M. flight at a round-trip price of $260. Flying to Waco would require her to rent a car for $29 per day. To cover incidental costs, the company will pay her $35 per day (called a per diem) if she spends at least 6 working hours a day out of town. As a manager, Jennifer is responsible for keeping recruiting costs within budget, so she wants to determine which is more economical, driving or flying.

1. What is the total amount of expenses Jennifer will include on her expense report if she drives? If she flies?
2. What is the relevant cost of driving? What is the relevant cost of flying?
3. What is the incremental cost of flying over driving?
4. What other factors might Jennifer need to consider in her decision between driving and flying?

SELECTED UNIT 8.1 ANSWERS

Think About It 8.1

	Relevant	Irrelevant
Cost of your undergraduate education		X
Salary achievable with an undergraduate degree	X	
Salary achievable with a graduate degree	X	
Cost of toiletries		X
Car insurance		X
Graduate school tuition, fees, etc.	X	
Cost of breakfast food (assuming your eating habits don't change after you graduate)		X

Practice Questions

1. B
2. D
3. C

Unit 8.1 Practice Exercise

1.

	Costs to Drive	Costs to Fly
Mileage (183 miles × 2 × $0.50 per mile)	$183	
Hotel	67	
Airfare		$260
Car rental		29
Per diem	35	35
Total cost	$285	$324

2. Driving: $183 + 67 = $250
   Flying: $260 + 29 = $289
3. $289 − $250 = $39
4. Other items to consider:
   - Driving would give Jennifer more flexibility to change her schedule at the last minute.
   - Six hours of round-trip driving could be put to better use, perhaps by doing some other work-related activity.

UNIT 8.2

Special Order Pricing

GUIDED UNIT PREPARATION

Answering the following questions while you read this unit will guide your understanding of the key concepts found in the unit. The questions are linked to the learning objectives presented at the beginning of the chapter.

LO 2

1. Why might a business be willing to sell a product or service for an amount that is lower than the normal price?
2. If a business continually has the capacity to accept special orders, what should managers consider?
3. How should a company that is operating at capacity decide whether to accept a special order?
4. What is the minimum price that a business could charge for a special order and not lose money on the order?

Companies are like consumers—they are looking for a good deal, particularly when they buy large quantities or promise a supplier new business. So it isn't unusual for them to request special pricing from a supplier. But beware of the Robinson–Patman Act of 1936, which prohibits companies from engaging in price discrimination—that is, from offering the same item to different customers at different prices. Given that restriction, let's see how an informed supplier can respond to requests for special order pricing.

Characteristics of a Special Order

Jim Shaw has been trying to expand C&C Sports' jersey and pants sales by selling directly to large independent school districts and colleges. During his recent sales call at Central Independent School District, athletic director Carlisle Reid said he would be willing to buy C&C's jerseys for Central's junior high and high school baseball programs if Jim would strike a deal with him on the price. Specifically, Reid said he would commit to purchasing 1,000 practice jerseys a year for the next five years at a price of $10 each. The jerseys wouldn't need to be of the same quality fabric as the ones C&C normally sells, but otherwise, they would be identical to the standard C&C jersey.

Jim returned to the office and presented Reid's offer to C&C's purchasing agent, Mark Newton. Mark talked with his contacts at Bradley Textile Mills and found a lower-quality jersey fabric that would cost $2 less per jersey than C&C's standard jersey fabric. The unit cost of a regular jersey is $11.17, so Mark and Jim concluded that the new, lower-quality jerseys would cost $9.17 to make. With sales commissions and delivery costs added, Jim thinks it would be a bad deal and is reluctant to propose it to Jonathan Smith, vice president of marketing.

Why would Jim even consider Reid's offer? Sometimes companies will accept new business at a loss, with the expectation that they will make up for it in later years. Also, certain customers can influence other potential customers. Reid is past president of the Texas High School Athletic Directors Association, whose members represent over 1,000 public school districts. His endorsement could direct a great deal of business to C&C.

Relevant Costs of a Special Order

Is Reid's offer a bad deal for C&C? To find out, we need to identify the relevant costs of manufacturing and selling the special jerseys. Demonstrating a cost differential between products is one way a company can offer different customers a different price without violating the Robinson–Patman Act. The standard unit cost for producing a regular jersey is as follows:

Direct materials	$ 6.85
Direct labor	1.92
Variable overhead	1.05
Fixed overhead	1.35
Total jersey cost	$11.17

How would this cost compare to the cost of the special jersey? The direct materials for the new jersey are expected to cost $4.85, based on estimates Mark received from Bradley Textile Mills. The new jersey would require the same amount of time in cutting and sewing as the regular jersey. Although current production already takes up all C&C's time, Jim is convinced that he can hire a few more workers temporarily to make the jerseys on idle sewing machines. So labor and variable overhead costs should be the same. And because no new fixed costs will be added, fixed costs aren't relevant to this decision.

Relevant costs to sell the jersey must be added to the relevant cost to produce the jersey to arrive at the total relevant cost for the special order. On a $10 sale, the commission will be $0.50, and shipping is expected to stay at $0.40 per jersey. The relevant unit cost of this special order is $8.72:

Direct materials	$4.85
Direct labor	1.92
Variable overhead	1.05
Commission	0.50
Shipping	0.40
Total relevant cost	$8.72

REALITY CHECK—*If the price is right*

© John Peter Photography/Alamy

Have you ever used priceline.com or Hotwire.com to reserve a hotel room or a seat on a plane? Those are the two major players in the opaque travel market, where consumers place bids for hotel rooms, rental cars, and airline tickets without knowing the supplier, in hopes of reaping large savings. Studies have found that these websites are the ones that most frequently deliver the lowest prices.

How do these websites operate? They join with various travel partners to sell an "inventory" of rooms, seats, and cars. Priceline.com customers use the site's Name Your Own Price® system to register their bids for a room, car, or plane ticket. The suppliers consider the bids and either accept or reject them. Priceline.com also offers Tonight-Only Deals®, which posts last-minute hotel deals at 11:00 A.M. each day. These deals can be booked until 11:00 P.M. for the current night only and can save customers 35% off the published room rate. So from the partners' standpoint, this is a special order pricing decision in which a potential customer asks for a product or service at less than the normal price.

These deals can save customers more than 35% off the retail room rate.

And now special order pricing is seen in "reverse" when companies such as Uber, Disneyland, and the Toronto Blue Jays use dynamic pricing to match prices with consumer demand.

Sources: Priceline.com 2010 10-K; "Priceline.com Launches Tonight-Only Deals Service for iPhone & iPod Touch Users for Same-Day Hotel Bookings," PRNewswire, September 29, 2011, http://ir.priceline.com/releasedetail.cfm?ReleaseID=609581 (accessed January 23, 2013); James F. Peltz, "Why 'Dynamic' Pricing Based on Real-Time Supply and Demand Is Rapidly Spreading," *Los Angeles Times*, March 14, 2016, http://www.latimes.com/business/la-fi-agenda-dynamic-pricing-20160314-story.html (accessed April 5, 2016).

Each special jersey will generate a contribution margin of $1.28 ($10.00 sales price − $8.72 variable cost). At 1,000 special jerseys a year, this special order will generate a total annual contribution margin of $1,280. Since no additional fixed costs will be incurred on the special order, this amount will flow straight into operating income. In the grand scheme of C&C's current production, $1,280 in additional operating income is an inconsequential amount. However, if C&C could make a similar sale at even 10% of the school districts in Texas (that is, at over 100 districts), the result could be a significant increase in the company's bottom line.

Qualitative Issues in Special Order Pricing

Should C&C pursue the special order? The numbers indicate that it will generate a positive contribution margin, but there are some additional factors to consider. After Central ISD's five-year contract expires, there is no guarantee that the contract will be renewed. Furthermore, if it is renewed, there is no guarantee that the district will agree to a higher price.

Then there is the fact that the special jersey is made of lower quality fabric. Will its lower quality negatively affect C&C's reputation and possibly harm existing retail sales? And if Jim can't find the temporary workers he needs to make the special order, the regular staff will have to work overtime. That means they will be paid time and a half, which will add another $1.50 in direct labor and variable overhead to the cost of each shirt, wiping out any profit on the special order.

Let's say that instead of working overtime, C&C's staff makes the practice jerseys rather than the regular jerseys. What effect would that have on C&C's operating income? The contribution margin for a regular jersey is $3.84:

Sales price	$14.80
Direct materials	$ 6.85
Direct labor	1.92
Variable overhead	1.05
Commission	0.74
Shipping	0.40
Total variable cost	$10.96
Contribution margin	$ 3.84

WATCH OUT!

When a customer requests a special order and the supplier has capacity constraints, the options are: (1) reject the special order; or (2) accept the special order and cut back on normal production. Reducing the special order is not normally an option; if the customer needed fewer units, presumably he or she would have asked for that quantity. To be safe, determine the total effect of option 2 by calculating the total amount to be received from the special order and subtracting the total amount to be lost from regular sales.

If regular sales are given up to take a special order, the lost contribution margin on the regular sales must be subtracted from the contribution margin of the special order to arrive at the total impact on operating income. In this case, C&C would lose $2,560 per year for the next five years if it took the special order:

Contribution earned on special order ($1.28 per jersey × 1,000 jerseys)	$1,280
Contribution margin lost on regular jerseys ($3.84 per jersey × 1,000 jerseys)	($3,840)
Net effect of special order	($2,560)

Finally, if the special order jersey becomes popular with Texas schools and demand increases, additional shifts, workers, and perhaps production supervisors will be needed. With C&C's current cost structure, the company can't make money on a $10 practice jersey. So while the deal with Central ISD isn't a bad deal in the short run, it may not be worth pursuing in the long run.

THINK ABOUT IT 8.2

Why do airlines fly with empty seats rather than allow last-minute passengers with only carry-on baggage to pay, say, $50 for that seat?

Special orders aren't always problematic like the one for C&C Sports. Sometimes seasonality will affect a company's ability to profit from a special order. For example, Patillo, Therrell and Oatman, LLP (PTO), which provides C&C's tax services, is extremely busy between November and May. But the rest of the year the firm is only moderately busy with quarterly reports and various other returns. As you might expect, most CPAs aren't willing to work for only seven months a year. Therefore, PTO needs to find work to occupy employees in the months from June through October.

To keep employees working and generate revenue in the slow season, the company has come up with a special plan. PTO normally charges $80 per hour for its staff accountants to work on a client's returns. (The hourly rate is higher for more experienced workers, but we'll focus on the staff accountants.) Between June and October, however, PTO charges $60 per hour for its staff accountants' time. Is this a good idea? PTO's only variable costs are its supplies, the cost of which is very small. If all other costs are fixed, then the lower rate of $60 per hour contributes quite a bit to cover the firm's costs.

Recap of the Decision Process

Decision to be made:	Accept or reject a special order
Relevant cost information:	Avoidable costs (costs to produce and sell the special order that would not be incurred without the special order), contribution margin lost on forfeited normal sales
Qualitative issues to consider:	Effect on regular sales; possibility that the special price will become the customer's expected normal price
Watch out for:	Unavoidable fixed costs
Decision rule:	If a special order returns a positive increase in income, take the order; if the company continually has the capacity available to fill special orders, reevaluate capacity

EXHIBIT 8-4

Recap of the special order decision.

UNIT 8.2 REVIEW

PRACTICE QUESTIONS

1. LO 2 Accepting a special order is always a good idea if the price exceeds the relevant costs to produce and deliver the order. True or False?
2. LO 2 A private university is considering a plan to offer summer school courses at a special rate because summer enrollments have been dropping. Which of the following is not a relevant consideration in this decision?
   a. If summer enrollments don't increase enough, total revenues will be lower under the new pricing system.
   b. Professors who aren't normally paid during the summer will be needed to teach the courses.
   c. Higher enrollments will increase copying charges for course materials.
   d. Depreciation will be recorded on the academic buildings.
3. LO 2 The manufacturing capacity of Jordan Company's facilities is 30,000 units per year. Last year's operating results are as follows:

Sales (18,000 units @ $100)	$1,800,000
Variable costs	990,000
Contribution margin	810,000
Fixed costs	495,000
Net operating income	$ 315,000

A foreign distributor has offered to buy 15,000 units next year at a price of $90 per unit. If Jordan accepts the offer it can sell only 15,000 units at the regular price in order not to exceed capacity. What will be the company's total net operating income next year?

   a. $1,335,000
   b. $ 840,000
   c. $ 855,000
   d. $ 705,000

UNIT 8.2 PRACTICE EXERCISE

Schwaig Corporation has excess manufacturing capacity. The company has received a special order from Stewart, Inc. requesting 500 of Schwaig's computer keyboards at a price of $65. The keyboards will require special engraving of Stewart's corporate logo. Stewart needs the keyboards because its normal vendor has shut down production due to a labor strike.

Schwaig's normal selling price for the keyboards is $85. Managers estimate the variable cost of the keyboards at $35 per unit; fixed manufacturing overhead is $40 per unit. Of the fixed costs assigned to this order, $8,000 is the rent on a special machine needed to etch Stewart's corporate logo; the remainder is attributable to costs that will be incurred regardless of whether the keyboards are produced.

Required

Should Schwaig accept Stewart, Inc.'s special order? Why or why not?

SELECTED UNIT 8.2 ANSWERS

Think About It 8.2

We could ask a similar question about movie theaters, concerts, or any other service that has high fixed costs and serves different customers at each event. It does seem strange that an airline, faced with a choice between $50 or $0, would opt for $0. What are the marginal costs of a flight—beverage service and perhaps the use of the restroom? All other things held equal, $50 is better than $0, so all other things must *not* be equal. If passengers knew they could walk onto a flight at the last minute for $50, why would they pay in advance? The only reason would be to guarantee a seat. If customers don't need to fly somewhere or see a movie right away, they might as well wait to see what's available. This practice would begin to shape consumer beliefs about the value of these services, and the companies wouldn't be able to stay in business at the special lower prices.

Practice Questions

1. False
2. D
3. D

Unit 8.2 Practice Exercise

Sales price/unit ($65 × 500)	$32,500
Less: Variable costs ($35 × 500)	17,500
Contribution margin ($30 × 500)	15,000
Less: Direct fixed costs	8,000
Operating income generated by special order	$ 7,000

The special order will generate additional operating income, so Schwaig should consider accepting it. The only concern might be that the product is not substantially different from Schwaig's regular product. Current customers might become angry and take their business elsewhere if they feel they have been treated unfairly. Thus, Schwaig cannot continue to take this kind of special order indefinitely. If the company can't find a use for its excess capacity, managers should try to reduce it to the level needed to meet current operations.

UNIT 8.3

Outsourcing

GUIDED UNIT PREPARATION

Answering the following questions while you read this unit will guide your understanding of the key concepts found in the unit. The questions are linked to the learning objectives presented at the beginning of the chapter.

LO 3

1. What kinds of processes or inputs can be outsourced?
2. What information needs to be evaluated in an outsourcing arrangement?
3. What is an opportunity cost? How does it relate to an outsourcing decision?

Although many people think of outsourcing as a relatively new approach to doing business, it has existed for years. ADP, LLC, a payroll outsourcing company, began providing payroll services for others in 1949. Today, the company has approximately 620,000 clients throughout the world.[1] As with all decisions, the choice to outsource requires careful analysis of the relevant information. In this unit you will learn how to evaluate that information.

Outsourcing Defined

Today, people use the term *outsourcing* to describe a number of business arrangements. Technically, however, **outsourcing** is moving the production of goods or the delivery of services from within the organization to a provider outside the organization. For instance, all major U.S. airlines contract with external maintenance companies for the repair and maintenance of their aircraft rather than maintain a staff of mechanics on the company payroll. Recently, these same companies started outsourcing airport jobs such as customer service and baggage handling.[2]

In contrast, the term **offshoring** means moving a company's business processes to a foreign country. A company may choose to offshore its operations to a foreign subsidiary or to a completely unrelated foreign company. While many U.S. companies have offshored services and production in the past, there is a current trend by companies such as Whirlpool and K'Nex to bring some of this activity back to the United States.[3]

While these two terms are often used interchangeably, outsourcing and offshoring are not synonymous. Only when products are made or services performed by an unrelated company is offshoring considered outsourcing. An example will help to clarify the difference. Michelin, a French company, makes automobile tires in Greenville, South Carolina. Because Michelin owns the production facility in Greenville, this is an offshoring arrangement. However, if Michelin were to contract with Goodyear to manufacture its tires at the Goodyear plant in Gadsden, Alabama, that arrangement would constitute offshore outsourcing, since Goodyear is unrelated to Michelin.

When the outsourcing decision refers to the components of a manufactured product, it is more commonly called a **make-or-buy decision**, indicating that the company is choosing whether to make the part internally or buy it externally. Dell chooses to buy computer chips from Intel and AMD rather than manufacture them internally—why? When choosing the products and services to outsource, companies look primarily at areas where they do not have a core competency or strategic advantage. Rather than make a long-term investment to develop those competencies, they generally turn to other companies that have acquired the competencies through specialization. Dell's core competencies are computer assembly, sales and distribution, and customer service, not the manufacturing of computer chips. Exhibit 8-5 lists ten reasons companies choose to outsource their operations.

EXHIBIT 8-5

Ten reasons companies outsource their operations.

Short-term, Tactical Benefits

- **Releases capital funds for use in other projects**
- **Provides a cash infusion as freed-up assets are sold**
- **Reduces and controls operating costs**
- **Provides a solution when expertise is not available internally**
- **Provides external expertise to improve difficult-to-manage business processes**

Long-term, Strategic Benefits

- **Frees managers' time to focus on more important issues**
- **Provides world-class capabilities at lower cost**
- **Accelerates the benefits of process reengineering**
- **Transfers a portion of business risk to an outsource provider**
- **Redirects resources to core activities**

Source: Charles E. Davis, Elizabeth B. Davis, and Lee Ann Moore, "Outsourcing the Procurement-through-Payables Process," *Management Accounting*, July 1998, 38–44.

REALITY CHECK—*It's time to shore up production*

Kent International, Inc.

After years of offshoring work to low-cost locations, many companies are beginning to rethink their decisions and to bring manufacturing back home. Among those companies that are "reshoring" is Kent International, Inc., a bicycle manufacturer located in Parsippany, New Jersey. Kent has been manufacturing its bikes in China but is now bringing some of the production back to the United States.

Why are companies such as Kent reshoring after years of producing in offshore locations? In Kent's case, at least part of the motivation is participation in Walmart's "Made in USA" program. For other companies, it may be related to lead times required for getting products from the offshore plant back to domestic markets. Harry Moser, founder of the Reshoring Initiative, estimates that it can require as long as six months for offshore locations to respond to customization requests and seasonal demand variations. As a result, companies face significant losses from stockouts and overstocks.

It can require as long as six months for offshore locations to respond to customization requests.

What is clear is that companies are now reevaluating offshore decisions and finding that moving home sometimes makes sense.

Sources: Reshoring Initiative, *Reshoring Initiative Data Report: Reshoring and FDI Boost US Manufacturing in 2015*, http://reshorenow.org/blog/reshoring-initiative-data-report-reshoring-and-fdi-boost-us-manufacturing-in-2015/ (accessed April 5, 2016); Karen Thuermer, "WalMart's Made in USA Program Encourages Reshoring," Q4 2015, http://www.areadevelopment.com/BusinessGlobalization/Q4-2015/Walmart-Made-in-USA-Program-Encourages-Reshoring-234556.shtml (accessed April 5, 2016); Jeff Yoders, "Long Supply Chains Created Consumer Disappointment This Holiday Season," Reshoring Initiative, December 28, 2105, http://reshorenow.org/news/long-supply-chains-created-consumer-disappointment-this-holiday-season/ (accessed April 5, 2015).

A Basic Outsourcing Decision Model

You may recall from Chapter 4 that C&C Sports' award jacket includes a chenille letter that identifies the school (see Exhibit 4-13). Currently, C&C produces this letter internally, at a total unit cost of $1.86:

Direct materials	$0.78
Direct labor	0.48
Variable overhead	0.26
Fixed overhead	0.34
Total unit cost	$1.86

Yesterday, John Wiles, Bonadeo Embroidery's sales manager, approached C&C's vice president of operations, Chad Davis, with a proposal to provide all the chenille letters C&C needs at a unit price of $1.65. At first glance, it appears that Chad should accept Bonadeo's offer, since $1.65 is $0.21 less than the $1.86 C&C currently spends to make a letter. Based on the normal production quantity of 18,000 jackets, Bonadeo's offer should result in an annual savings of $3,780 (18,000 letters × $0.21 per letter). Before jumping to a conclusion about Bonadeo's proposal, however, Chad needs to determine whether the entire unit cost of $1.86 is relevant. He needs to determine which costs C&C will not incur if Bonadeo provides the chenille letters—in other words, which costs are *avoidable*.

Obviously, if Chad accepts Bonadeo's proposal, C&C will not incur the cost of direct materials for the chenille letters. The chenille machine operator will be let go, so the direct labor cost will be saved. The variable overhead associated with the letter production is based on the direct labor cost of the product (remember from Chapter 4 that C&C allocates variable overhead based on direct labor incurred). If labor isn't used, those variable overhead costs will be saved, too. Since none of these costs will be incurred if C&C chooses to accept Bonadeo's proposal, they are avoidable and relevant to Chad's decision.

THINK ABOUT IT 8.3

When a company like C&C Sports accepts an outsourcing offer, managers must take specific action to eliminate the internal costs. For example, the chenille machine operator will have to be laid off. Imagine what would happen if a company were to outsource accounts payable—all the workers in that department would have to be let go. Discuss the qualitative and perhaps the quantitative impacts of such a decision on the business.

Let's consider the remaining unit cost assigned to the production of chenille letters, fixed overhead. This cost includes depreciation of the chenille machine, as well as general factory operating costs, such as supervisory salaries and electric heating and cooling of the factory building. Depreciation on the machine is a sunk cost. The other fixed overhead costs will be incurred regardless of Chad's decision whether to outsource the chenille letters. Because these fixed overhead costs are *not* avoidable, they are irrelevant to Chad's decision.

Based on Chad's analysis of relevant costs, C&C should *not* accept Bonadeo's proposal to supply the chenille letters for the award jackets. As Exhibit 8-6 shows, the relevant unit cost of producing a letter internally is only $1.52. Accepting Bonadeo's proposal would cost C&C an additional $2,340 (18,000 letters × $0.13 per letter) beyond what it pays to produce the letters internally.

You may be thinking that variable costs are always avoidable and fixed costs are always unavoidable in outsourcing decisions. That is not the case. Suppose C&C outsources production of the letters but does not lay off the

	Relevant Cost to ...	
	Produce Internally	Outsource to Bonadeo
Direct materials	$ 0.78	
Direct labor	0.48	
Variable overhead	0.26	
Total unit cost	$ 1.52	$ 1.65
× letters required	× 18,000	× 18,000
Total relevant cost	$27,360	$29,700

$2,340 advantage to produce internally

EXHIBIT 8-6

Relevant costs of outsourcing chenille letter production.

chenille machine operator. Instead, managers transfer her to the sewing department, to work on baseball pants and jerseys. In this situation, the direct labor cost would *not* be avoidable, since it would be incurred regardless of the decision.

To give another example, assume that a portion of the fixed cost includes an annual preventive maintenance contract for the chenille machine. If the machine is no longer used as a result of the outsourcing decision, the contract will be canceled. Because this fixed cost will not be incurred if production of the letters is outsourced, it is avoidable and relevant to the decision.

Alternative Uses for Facilities

Sometimes, when the production of an item is outsourced, the resources that are freed up can be put to another use. If so, the alternative use is considered an *opportunity cost* of using the resources. An **opportunity cost** is the contribution margin of the next-best alternative use of the facilities. Assume that instead of making chenille letters for award jackets, C&C can use the chenille machine to produce a new product that is expected to generate a total annual contribution margin of $15,000. Essentially, C&C is incurring an opportunity cost of $15,000 by using its facilities to make chenille letters. Without the alternative provided by Bonadeo, making chenille letters for award jackets is presumably the best use of the machine. Given Bonadeo's alternative, however, the net out-of-pocket cost of outsourcing the chenille letters will be $14,700 (see Exhibit 8-7). So even though buying the chenille letters from Bonadeo is more expensive, the opportunity to use the freed-up resources to produce another product makes the outsourcing alternative attractive.

WATCH OUT!

The contribution margin from an alternative use of facilities increases operating income, whereas paying for an outsourcing arrangement decreases operating income. Therefore, to determine the combined effect on operating income, you need to net the contribution margin and the cost of the outsourcing.

EXHIBIT 8-7

Opportunity cost of an alternative use of facilities.

	Relevant Cost to ...	
	Produce Internally	Outsource to Bonadeo
Direct materials	$ 0.78	
Direct labor	0.48	
Variable overhead	0.26	
Total unit cost	$ 1.52	$ 1.65
× letters required	× 18,000	× 18,000
Total relevant cost	$27,360	$29,700
Additional contribution margin from alternative use of resources		(15,000)
Net cost of production	$27,360	$14,700
	$12,660 advantage to outsource	

Qualitative Issues in Outsourcing

While the "numbers" are important in making an outsourcing decision, they cannot be the sole driver. Several qualitative issues must also be considered before reaching a decision to outsource.

One important consideration in outsourcing is the quality of the outsourced product. When a company produces a product internally, it is easier to control product quality than it is if the product is made by another firm. Toy giant Mattel, Inc., learned this the hard way when it had to recall millions of toys because of lead paint used by the toys' manufacturer in China. When companies outsource a product, they should specify minimum acceptable quality levels. A related issue is the reliability of the outsource provider. The company must meet production schedules if customers are to receive their products on time. A supplier that cannot be counted on to meet required delivery schedules will not be a good choice, regardless of the price of the outsourced product.

A company also will want to consider the stability of the price offered by an outside supplier. Beware of an outsource provider that makes a price offer that is too good to be true. It is possible that the company is planning to increase the price at a later date. Once a company has outsourced a production process, bringing it back in house can be difficult and expensive. The equipment and employees needed to produce the product may have been divested.

A final concern raised by outsourcing is the potential theft of intellectual property. A company may be required to divulge trade secrets to an outside supplier to ensure that the outsourced products conform to requirements. Once a trade secret is known outside the organization, there is some risk that it will be communicated to competitors.

On the other hand, outsourcing offers a way for companies to transfer some of their technological risk to an outside supplier. For instance, a computer manufacturer like Hewlett-Packard (HP) will outsource chip production, partly because the rapid technological advancement in this area carries a great deal of risk of product obsolescence. By outsourcing chip production, HP transfers that risk to companies such as AMD, which specialize in the production of computer chips.

Recap of the Decision Process

Decision to be made:	Outsource certain operations or produce internally
Relevant cost information:	Avoidable costs (costs that would not be incurred if process is outsourced), purchase price from outside supplier, alternative use of resources
Qualitative issues to consider:	Supplier reliability and quality, theft of intellectual property, transfer of technological risk
Watch out for:	Allocated fixed costs
Decision rule:	All other things held equal, if the purchase price is less than the avoidable costs to produce plus any opportunity costs, outsource the operation

EXHIBIT 8-8

Recap of the outsourcing decision.

UNIT 8.3 REVIEW

KEY TERMS

Make-or-buy decision p. 447
Opportunity cost p. 450
Outsourcing p. 447
Offshoring p. 447

PRACTICE QUESTIONS

1. LO 3 The costs that should be included in an outsourcing decision are the

   a. variable costs.

   b. relevant costs.

   c. nonrecurring costs.

   d. sunk costs.

2. LO 3 Given the following data, what is the total relevant cost of internal production of 300,000 parts?

Cost per part from supplier	$ 12.00
Internal costs per part:	
Direct materials	$ 5.50
Direct labor	$ 4.00
Variable overhead	$ 0.50
Total fixed overhead	$90,000
Avoidable fixed overhead	$65,000

   a. $3,000,000

   b. $3,090,000

   c. $3,065,000

   d. $3,025,000

3. LO 3 Williams Company makes a key component for one of its products but is considering purchasing the part from an outside supplier. If the company purchases the component, it can rent the unused factory space to another business for $5,000 per month. The rent represents

   a. a variable production cost.

   b. a fixed production cost.

   c. an opportunity cost of making the component.

   d. a cost that is irrelevant to the make-or-buy decision.

4. LO 3 The only difference between outsourcing and offshoring is that the outsource provider is located in the home country and the offshore provider is located in a foreign country. True or False?

UNIT 8.3 PRACTICE EXERCISE

Bruin Manufacturing currently makes the 15,000 ball bearings it uses each year in its railroad car wheels. There is no other use for these production facilities, nor is there a market for the depreciable items. Raider, Inc., has just submitted a bid to manufacture the ball bearings for Bruin at a price of $20 per bearing. If Bruin no longer makes the ball bearings, the product manager will lose his job. The standard cost card lists the following costs of making one ball bearing:

Direct materials	$ 6	
Direct labor	8	
Variable overhead	1	
Direct fixed overhead	5	(40% salary of product manager, 60% depreciation)
Nondifferential fixed overhead	10	
Total cost	$ 30	

Required

a. Does it make sense for Bruin to purchase the ball bearings from Raider? Show your calculations.

b. Assume the same information just presented, except that Bruin has the opportunity to use the freed-up manufacturing facilities to increase production of its existing line of bicycle tires. This additional production would generate $65,000 a year in contribution margin. Does it make financial sense for Bruin to purchase the ball bearings from Raider? What nonfinancial considerations should have an impact on the decision?

SELECTED UNIT 8.3 ANSWERS

Think About It 8.3

Outsourcing operations can result in poor employee morale: No one is happy when employees who by all accounts are doing a good job are let go. In these situations, managers need to be honest, explain the reason for the change, and let the remaining employees know whether their jobs are at risk. Furthermore, the bad feelings aren't limited to those within the company. When large outsourcing arrangements receive local or national press, some companies may find themselves the target of outside criticism. Though the responsibility that comes with dismissing one or more employees is difficult for managers, delaying the change or trying to find other roles for the employees will only cost the company money.

Practice Questions

1. B
2. C
3. C
4. False

Unit 8.3 Practice Exercise

a.

	Make	Buy
Purchase price		$ 20
Direct materials	$ 6	
Direct labor	8	
Variable overhead	1	
Fixed overhead ($5 × 40%)	2	
Relevant cost per unit	$ 17	$ 20
Number of units	× 15,000	× 15,000
Total cost	$255,000	$300,000

No, it does not make sense to purchase the ball bearings; it is less expensive to keep making them.

b.

	Make	Buy
Total cost	$255,000	$300,000
Contribution margin from freed-up space		($ 65,000)
Net cost	$255,000	$235,000

Now it makes financial sense for Bruin to purchase the ball bearings. Bruin will want to make sure that Raider can deliver high-quality ball bearings when they are needed and that their price won't rise at a rate that is faster than the cost of production.

UNIT 8.4

Allocating Constrained Resources

GUIDED UNIT PREPARATION

Answering the following questions while you read this unit will guide your understanding of the key concepts found in the unit. The questions are linked to the learning objectives presented at the beginning of the chapter.

LO 4

1. What are some limited resources that can constrain business operations?
2. How should managers determine the best way to allocate constrained resources among products or operations?
3. How does customer demand affect the allocation of constrained resources?
4. What is a bottleneck?
5. What are some ways a bottleneck can be alleviated?

Machinery, space, materials, and labor provide the capacity businesses need to deliver their products and services to customers. When entrepreneurs visualize a new company, they will make long-term decisions about what machines, buildings, and labor will be needed to get the business off the ground. Such decisions require high-dollar investments and are made with the utmost care and planning.

As products are made or services provided, capacity is used up. Many times, companies will have enough capacity to make all the products or deliver all the services that customers demand. At other times, however, they will face constraints due to a shortage of some required resource. When that time arrives, managers once again must engage in long-term planning to evaluate the profitablity of investing in additional assets. Until such decisions are made, it is important for managers to allocate the constrained resource to products and services in a way that will maximize the company's contribution margin.

Let's consider the situation at Bradley Textile Mills, the fabric producer in C&C Sports' supply chain. Bradley sells jersey fabric to C&C Sports for $4 per yard. However, jersey fabric isn't the only fabric Bradley makes; the company also makes a heavy wool fabric that sells for $15 per yard. How should Bradley decide how much of each product to make?

This decision requires managers to consider more than just the sales price, because every time a yard of fabric is made, variable costs are incurred. Exhibit 8-9 shows that jersey fabric has a contribution margin of $1.98 per yard, while the wool fabric has a contribution margin of $5.25 per yard. Based on this information, managers might conclude that to maximize income, Bradley should make as much wool as it can sell. And that will be true as long as Bradley's resources are unlimited.

EXHIBIT 8-9

Bradley Textile Mills' product costs.

	Jersey Fabric	Wool Fabric
Sales price per yard	$4.00	$15.00
Variable costs:		
Direct materials	$1.24	$ 6.85
Direct labor	0.50	1.60
Variable overhead	0.20	0.90
Variable selling and administrative costs	0.08	0.40
Total variable costs	$2.02	$ 9.75
Contribution margin per yard	$1.98	$ 5.25

Contribution Margin per Constrained Resource

Bradley, however, faces a production constraint: The company has only ten weaving machines. These machines operate 24 hours a day (three eight-hour shifts), except for one full day a year when they are shut down for maintenance. Thus, Bradley has a total of 62,160 machine hours available for weaving: ([24 hours per day × 5 days per week × 52 weeks per year] − 24 hours down) × 10 machines. Bradley's managers need to know how to put those 62,160 machine hours to best use.

Managers first need to determine how long it takes to make each product. The weaving machines are high-speed; each can produce 150 yards of jersey fabric per hour, or 1 yard every 0.4 minutes. Alternatively, each machine can make 48 yards of wool fabric per hour, or 1 yard every 1.25 minutes.

Let's consider the wool first, since that product has the higher contribution margin per yard. If Bradley were to use all 62,160 machine hours to make wool, it could make 2,983,680 yards per year ([62,160 hours × 60 minutes] ÷ 1.25 minutes per yard). At a contribution margin of $5.25 per yard, Bradley would earn a total contribution margin of $15,664,320 (2,983,680 yards × $5.25 per yard).

What if Bradley decided to make only jersey fabric? Since each yard of jersey fabric takes just 0.4 minutes to weave, the company could make 9,324,000 yards of jersey fabric per year ([62,160 hours × 60 minutes] ÷ 0.4 minutes per yard). At a contribution margin of $1.98 per yard, Bradley would earn a total contribution margin of $18,461,520 (9,324,000 yards × $1.98 per yard).

Why does jersey fabric generate a higher total contribution margin than wool? The answer is that jersey fabric generates a higher contribution margin *per machine minute*. Exhibit 8-10 illustrates how to calculate the contribution margin per machine minute. Notice that jersey fabric generates a $4.95 contribution margin per machine minute, compared to only $4.20 per machine minute for wool.

EXHIBIT 8-10

Calculation of the contribution margin per minute.

	Jersey Fabric	Wool Fabric
Contribution margin per yard	$1.98	$5.25
÷ Machine minutes per yard	0.40	1.25
= Contribution margin per machine minute	$4.95	$4.20

This example shows that when multiple products share a constrained resource, the way to determine how to allocate the resource is to compute the contribution margin per constrained resource for each product:

$$\text{Contribution margin per constrained resource} = \frac{\text{Contribution margin per unit}}{\text{Constrained resource per unit}}$$

The constrained resource should be allocated first to the product with the highest contribution margin per constrained resource, followed by the product with the second-highest contribution margin per constrained resource, and so on. Each product should receive only as much of the constrained resource as needed to meet customer demand. If the company can sell all the product with the highest contribution margin per constrained resource that it can produce, then the best decision is to make only that product. However, qualitative factors such as customer service and customer preferences may well dictate that a mix of products should be available for sale.

THINK ABOUT IT 8.4

Qualitative issues aside, why would Bradley not simply produce as much jersey fabric as it can?

Allocation of Constrained Resources

Bradley estimates that it can sell 4,200,000 yards of jersey fabric per year. A total of 28,000 machine hours is required to make that many yards of fabric ([4,200,000 yards × 0.4 machine minutes per yard] ÷ 60 minutes), leaving 34,160 machine hours to make wool. If each yard of wool takes 1.25 minutes, then 1,639,680 yards of wool can be made ([34,160 machine hours × 60 minutes] ÷ 1.25 machine minutes per yard). Of course, Bradley would want to make that many yards of wool only if they can be sold.

How will the total contribution margin from 4,200,000 yards of jersey fabric and 1,639,680 yards of wool compare to the contribution margin from just one product? It will be more than the contribution margin from making only wool ($15,664,320), but less than the contribution margin from making only jersey fabric ($18,461,520):

(4,200,000 yards × $1.98 per yard) + (1,639,680 × $5.25 per yard) = $16,924,320

THINK ABOUT IT 8.5

What should Bradley or any other company do if more than one of its resources is constrained?

Theory of Constraints

So far, we have considered only constraints on capacity and resources. Other kinds of constraints exist, especially for companies that use multiple processes to make their products or deliver their services. Companies that experience frequent work-in-process buildups or that can't meet customer demand may have one or more processes that constrain their output. The **Theory of Constraints** was developed by Eli Goldratt to maximize the performance of a value chain by focusing on constraints that limit an organization's output.[4] While a detailed exposition of the theory is beyond the scope of this course, you should understand its basic tenets. According to the theory, five steps are required to maximize and improve the performance of a value chain:

1. *Identify* the constraint.
2. Decide how to *exploit* the constraint.
3. *Subordinate* and *synchronize* everything else to the first two decisions.
4. *Elevate* the performance of the constraint.
5. If during any of these steps the constraint has shifted, *go back to Step 1.*

REALITY CHECK—*Money doesn't grow on trees*

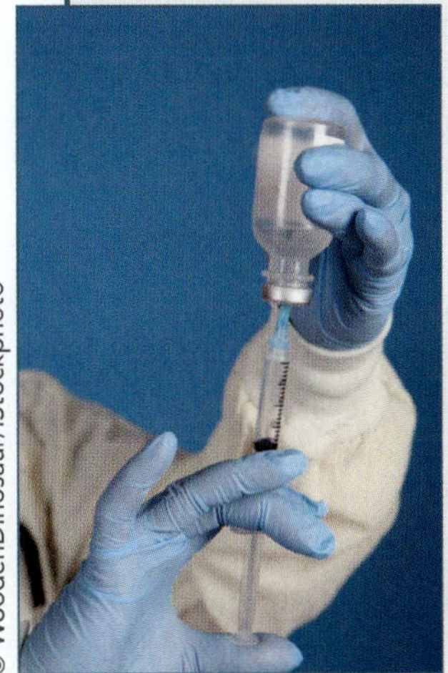
© WoodenDinosaur/iStockphoto

Homeland security, health care, hunger relief, flood relief—where should the funding go? How should legislators and government officials measure the benefits of various programs? While most people think about constrained resources in a corporate setting, government agencies also face constraints. Officials must decide how best to allocate a fixed amount of funding among competing programs.

But money isn't the only scarce resource facing these agencies. Organ transplant candidates far exceed the availability of transplantable organs. Public health emergencies resulting from natural disasters such as hurricanes Katrina and Sandy require medical personnel to ration medical services ranging from ventilators to vaccines.

Instead of contribution margin per constrained resource, government officials use a variety of other measures. While several criteria may be used in making the allocation decision, one common measure called quality-adjusted life years (QALYs) combines both the quality and quantity of life resulting from a medical treatment (see http://en.wikipedia.org/wiki/Quality-adjusted_life_years to learn more). The number of QALYs a program saves, combined with the program's cost estimates, can be used to determine which programs produce the greatest health benefits per dollar.

Who gets the next transplantable heart? Who gets the remaining flu vaccine? Who receives emergency government funding to rebuild hospitals and schools? These are tough decisions with real consequences.

Who should receive emergency funding from the government first?

Sources: Agency for Healthcare Research and Quality, "Allocation of Scarce Resources During Mass Casualty Events," Evidence Report/Technology Assessment #207, http://effectivehealthcare.ahrq.gov/ehc/products/400/1152/ER207_AllocationofScarceResources_ExecutiveSummary_20120626.pdf (accessed January 24, 2013); Fred Kuchler and Elise Golan, "Where Should the Money Go? Aligning Policies with Preferences," *Amber Waves*, June 2006, 30–38; National Institutes of Health, "Exploring Bioethics," https://science.education.nih.gov/supplements/nih9/bioethics/guide/pdf/teachers_guide.pdf (accessed July 8, 2016); Leslie Wolf and Wendy Hensel, "Valuing Lives: Allocating Scarce Medical Resources During a Public Health Emergency and the Americans with Disabilities Act (perspective)," *PLOS Currents Disasters* (September 21, 2011 [last modified: August 29, 2012]), Edition 1. doi:10.1371/currents.RRN1271.

Let's consider the situation faced by C&C's button manufacturer, Jackson & Chesser, Inc. Button making involves two processes, pressing and sealing. The demand for buttons is 1,000,000 per year. Exhibit 8-11 shows the annual capacity and production of the two processes. Notice that although the sealing department is capable of producing 900,000 buttons, it is limited by the fact that only 700,000 buttons can be pressed. According to the Theory of Constraints, the pressing operation is the process that limits total output. That is, it is the **bottleneck process**.

EXHIBIT 8-11

Jackson & Chesser, Inc.'s button production by operation.

	Pressing	Sealing
Annual capacity	700,000 units	900,000 units
Annual production	630,000 units	630,000 units

If the pressing department has the capacity to produce 700,000 buttons a year, why then does it produce only 630,000 buttons? The answer is that 10% of the buttons that are pressed turn out to be defective. What can be done to elevate the performance of this constraint? Jackson & Chesser could improve the quality of the pressing operation, which should reduce defects. The company could also

WATCH OUT!

Improving a production process that does not suffer from a bottleneck will not necessarily improve the organization's output. If a bottleneck exists in the second of three processes, improving the quality of the first process will not get more units through the bottleneck.

outsource part of the pressing operation (that is, buy pressed buttons from another source) to obtain the additional 270,000 units needed. Finally, Jackson & Chesser could purchase additional pressing machines to provide the required production capacity.

Instead of maximizing income, as measured by traditional accounting methods, the Theory of Constraints seeks to maximize **throughput contribution**, which equals sales revenue less direct materials cost. All other expenses are considered period costs. Fixed overhead costs are not allocated to products; rather, they are expensed in the period incurred. How does a company increase its throughput, then? Increase sales, decrease costs, or both.

Recap of the Decision Process

EXHIBIT 8-12

Recap of the allocation of constrained resources decision.

Decision to be made:	How to allocate constrained resources among a company's products
Relevant cost information:	Contribution margin per unit of constrained resource; demand for products
Qualitative issues to consider:	Customer preferences for a mix of products; customer service issues that arise when customer demand can't be met because of a constraint
Watch out for:	Contribution margin per unit of product
Decision rule:	Produce the product with the highest contribution margin per unit of constrained resource, up to the quantity demanded by customers

UNIT 8.4 REVIEW

KEY TERMS

Bottleneck process p. 457 Theory of Constraints p. 456 Throughput contribution p. 458

PRACTICE QUESTIONS

1. LO 4 Which of the following is *not* relevant to a decision involving the allocation of a single constrained resource among multiple products?
   a. Sales price of each product
   b. Sales demand for each product
   c. Fixed production costs
   d. Variable production costs for each product

2. LO 4 Which of the following is *not* likely to be a constrained resource?
   a. Oranges used to make orange juice
   b. Specialized labor
   c. Machine hours
   d. All of the above could be constrained resources

3. LO 4 Manico Company produces three products, X, Y, and Z, with the following characteristics:

	X	Y	Z
Selling price per unit	$20	$16	$15
Variable cost per unit	12	12	6
Contribution margin per unit	$ 8	$ 4	$ 9
Machine hours per unit	5	3	6

The company has only 2,000 machine hours available each month. If demand exceeds the company's capacity, in what sequence should orders for the three products be filled to maximize the company's total contribution margin?

   a. Y first, X second, and Z third
   b. Z first and no orders for X or Y
   c. X first, Z second, and Y third
   d. Z first, X second, and Y third

4. LO 4 According to the Theory of Constraints, all production should be subordinated to the bottleneck operation. True or False?

5. LO 4 Which of the following actions is *least* likely to relieve a bottleneck?

a. Increase the capacity of the bottleneck operation.

b. Improve the quality of the operation immediately preceding the bottleneck.

c. Decrease the production time per unit in the bottleneck operation.

d. Reduce defects in the bottleneck operation.

UNIT 8.4 PRACTICE EXERCISE

The Good Health Baking Company produces a salt-free whole-grain bread and a carob-chip cookie. The demand for these products is exceeding Good Health's production capacity. The company has only 80,000 direct labor hours available. A case of bread requires one direct labor hour, while a case of cookies requires half a direct labor hour. The company estimates that it can sell 100,000 cases of bread and 50,000 cases of cookies in the next year. The following financial information is available:

	Bread	Cookies
Selling price per case	$60	$30
Variable costs per case:		
Direct materials	13	4
Direct labor	8	4
Variable overhead	2	1
Variable marketing costs	2	1

Required

How should Good Health allocate its production capacity between bread and cookies?

SELECTED UNIT 8.4 ANSWERS

Think About It 8.4

Demand for the jersey fabric should determine the maximum amount that Bradley produces. Producing more fabric than demanded would increase the resources tied up in inventory without generating income.

Think About It 8.5

Instead of maximizing its contribution margin subject to one constraint, the company would need to maximize its contribution margin subject to all constraints. The maximization of two constraints can be calculated by hand, but for three or more constraints, linear programming is more efficient. By considering the constraints together instead of apart, a company can determine the appropriate combination of products that uses its resources most fully, to maximize the contribution margin.

Practice Questions

1. C
2. D
3. C
4. True
5. B

Unit 8.4 Practice Exercise

	Bread	Cookies
Sales price per unit	$60	$30
Variable costs:		
Direct materials	$13	$ 4
Direct labor	8	4
Variable overhead	2	1
Variable marketing costs	2	1
Total variable costs	$25	$10
Contribution margin per unit	$35	$20
÷ Direct labor hours per unit	1	0.5
Contribution margin per direct labor hour	$35	$40

Make cookies first up to the quantity demanded, then make bread:

Direct Labor Hours Needed	Direct Labor Hours Remaining
50,000 cases of cookies × 0.5 DLH = 25,000 DLH	80,000 − 25,000 = 55,000
55,000 cases of bread × 1 DLH = 55,000 DLH	55,000 − 55,000 = 0

UNIT 8.5

Keeping or Eliminating Operations

GUIDED UNIT PREPARATION

Answering the following questions while you read this unit will guide your understanding of the key concepts found in the unit. The questions are linked to the learning objectives presented at the beginning of the chapter.

LO 5

1. What event or series of events often motivates managers to consider eliminating an operation or product line?
2. Define the term *segment margin.*
3. What is an allocated cost? What happens to allocated costs if one of the cost objects (operations, products) is eliminated?
4. If a product has a positive segment margin but isn't as profitable as other products, what should managers do?

Macy's, Lord & Taylor, Bloomingdale's, Filene's—these are some of the most recognizable names in retailing. At one time, they were all part of Federated Department Stores. But Federated sold Lord & Taylor and closed its Strawbridge's store in downtown Philadelphia and its Robinsons-May store in Scottsdale, Arizona. Retail closings aren't infrequent events. Cerberus Capital, a private equity investment firm, engaged in similar transactions when it purchased 655 Albertson's grocery stores after the Albertson's chain decided to let go of many of its store locations. In less than six months, Cerberus closed 96 of the stores it had just purchased. And General Motors closed its Pontiac and Oldsmobile divisions.

Why all the closings? Usually operations close because they aren't performing at an acceptable level. Since resources are limited in almost every organization, managers need to use them wisely to generate the best possible returns. If a product, service, or location is not making money, perhaps it should be eliminated and the resources deployed elsewhere. But before managers make such a major operating decision, they must be certain they are evaluating the information correctly. In this unit, you will learn how to evaluate information regarding the decision to enter into or exit a particular operation.

Identification of Common Costs

Jonathan Smith, C&C Sports' vice president for marketing, has divided the state of Texas into four sales territories: North, South, East, and West. Each territory has one dedicated sales representative, who is paid an annual salary of $20,000 plus commission; other sales staff are paid on commission only.

Recently, the sales rep in West Texas has complained that he can't make as much commission as the other three sales reps. Jonathan has noticed that he doesn't seem as busy as the other reps, particularly those in the North and East, who seem to have more business than they can handle. On hearing this complaint, some managers might be tempted to conclude that the sales rep is just lazy. But in fact, the West Texas territory has experienced excessive employee turnover because the demand for C&C's sports apparel isn't high there.

Jonathan thinks it may be time to consider a change in the distribution of C&C's products. To assess how the West compares to the other territories, he has asked the accounting group to prepare an income statement that breaks down 2014 income by territory. One week later, his suspicions are confirmed when he receives the income statement shown in Exhibit 8-13. West Texas lost

	North	South	East	West	Total
Sales	$2,095,685	$1,331,150	$1,858,630	$514,135	$5,799,600
Cost of goods sold					
Direct materials	814,458	524,240	726,105	208,552	2,273,355
Direct labor	325,324	211,489	287,183	82,681	906,677
Variable overhead	202,241	131,241	178,534	51,212	563,228
Fixed overhead	247,044	160,407	218,086	62,630	688,167
Total cost of goods sold	1,589,067	1,027,377	1,409,908	405,075	4,431,427
Gross margin	506,618	303,773	448,722	109,060	1,368,173
Selling & administrative expenses					
Commissions	104,784	66,558	92,931	25,707	289,980
Shipping	41,496	30,051	36,939	13,314	121,800
Dedicated sales representative	20,000	20,000	20,000	20,000	80,000
Other allocated expenses	243,630	154,750	216,072	59,770	674,222
Total selling & administrative expenses	409,910	271,359	365,942	118,791	1,166,002
Operating income	$ 96,708	$ 32,414	$ 82,780	$ (9,731)	$ 202,171

EXHIBIT 8-13 *C&C Sports' sales territory income detail.*

$9,731 in 2014—results that are consistent with the previous year. Jonathan decides to meet with president George Douglas and vice president for finance and administration Claire Elliot, to let them know he is going to close the West Texas territory. If nothing else, the company will save $9,731.

Jonathan has committed a common mistake in deciding to close the West Texas territory: He has allowed allocated fixed costs, which are not relevant, to influence his decision. Those allocated fixed costs are incurred at the corporate level for the benefit of the entire organization. Jonathan's salary, for instance, is a fixed component of corporate selling and administrative expenses, which has been allocated back to each territory. If the West Texas territory is closed, Jonathan's salary won't be reduced by the amount that was allocated to that territory; it will simply be reallocated among the three remaining territories. Therefore, Jonathan's salary is nondifferential and is not relevant to his decision.

Let's look at the statement more closely, to see how the accountants put it together. Managers can split operations into a variety of **segments**, or business units, that provide detailed information about certain portions of the business. Unfortunately, the statement is presented in a functional format that is not helpful for decision making. For example, cost of goods sold includes fixed overhead costs. Those costs, such as rent and the production manager's salary, won't go away if C&C closes the West Texas territory. They are nondifferential and therefore not relevant to the decision to close the territory. Commissions, shipping, and the dedicated sales representative's salary, on the other hand, are all direct costs of each territory. That is, they occur because of sales made in the territory, so that if the territory is closed, they will not be incurred. Because these costs are differential and future oriented, they are relevant to the decision to close the territory.

"Other allocated expenses" were assigned to the territories based on the percentage of total sales dollars generated in each. For example, the North Texas territory was charged $36\%\left(\frac{\$2{,}095{,}685}{\$5{,}799{,}600}\right)$ of the $674,222 total, or $243,630. The terms **allocated cost**, **assigned cost**, and **common cost**, indicate that costs are not directly caused by the cost object (e.g., the territory), but instead are general corporate costs incurred to support operations as a whole. These costs are nondifferential and therefore are not relevant to the decision.

THINK ABOUT IT 8.6

What other ways might C&C managers want to segment the business to evaluate profitability?

Segment Margin Analysis

Because the statement shown in Exhibit 8-13 shows the *full* cost allocation to the sales territories, not all of the reported costs it lists will go away if the West Texas territory is dropped. True, the territory doesn't contribute to the company's bottom line the way the other areas do. But before a decision is made to eliminate it, the income statement should be recast to highlight only those costs directly associated with the West Texas territory.

Since we know what kinds of costs were included in the operating income statement, we can recast it easily enough. Exhibit 8-14 shows a segment margin

	North	South	East	West	Total
Sales	$2,095,685	$1,331,150	$1,858,630	$514,135	$5,799,600
Variable expenses					
Direct materials	814,458	524,240	726,105	208,552	2,273,355
Direct labor	325,324	211,489	287,183	82,681	906,677
Variable overhead	202,241	131,241	178,534	51,212	563,228
Commissions	104,784	66,558	92,931	25,707	289,980
Shipping	41,496	30,051	36,939	13,314	121,800
Total variable expenses	1,488,303	963,579	1,321,692	381,466	4,155,040
Contribution margin	607,382	367,571	536,938	132,669	1,644,560
Direct fixed expenses					
Dedicated sales representative	20,000	20,000	20,000	20,000	80,000
Segment margin	$ 587,382	$ 347,571	$ 516,938	$112,669	1,564,560
Allocated fixed expenses					
Fixed overhead					688,167
Other allocated expenses					674,222
Total allocated fixed expenses					1,362,389
Operating income					$ 202,171

EXHIBIT 8-14 *C&C Sports' sales territory segment margin income statement.*

income statement for the sales territories. Notice that this statement looks a lot like the contribution format income statement presented in Chapter 2. The key to this statement is the calculation of the **segment margin**, or the contribution margin of a particular segment less any direct fixed costs. In this case, the segments are the sales territories, and the direct fixed costs are those that will not be incurred if a segment is eliminated. Since these costs are differential, they are relevant to any decision about the segment's future.

When the income statement has been reformatted to highlight the segment margins, we can see that sales in West Texas generate a $132,669 contribution margin and a $112,669 segment margin. In other words, the West Texas territory contributes $112,669 to cover corporate fixed costs and add to operating income. If Jonathan were to drop the territory without replacing its sales somewhere else, the company would lose $112,669—not gain $9,731—in operating income. Notice that previously allocated common fixed costs are shown after the segment margin, and then only in the total column. There is no allocation of common fixed costs to misdirect Jonathan's decision. Based on this analysis, Jonathan should continue to sell to customers in West Texas until he develops a better plan to increase C&C's overall income.

THINK ABOUT IT 8.7

Given our segment analysis, we have concluded that the West Texas territory should be kept, not eliminated. But does C&C want all its territories to operate like West Texas? Even though Exhibit 8-13 isn't the appropriate analysis to use in making the keep-or-eliminate decision, what might its full-cost analysis suggest to Jonathan?

REALITY CHECK—*Sometimes less is more*

Bloomberg/Contributor/ Getty Images, Inc.

Sometimes less is more, and that's exactly what General Electric (GE) and Procter and Gamble (P&G) are counting on. Each company has recently divested itself of non-core businesses, in the belief that the remaining smaller company will offer greater returns when focused on fewer core brands and businesses.

P&G began a product simplification strategy in December 2010 after identifying 150 non-industry-leading brands that, in total, accounted for only about 10% of revenues and profits. So the company said goodbye to many of its lesser products. Gone are the pet foods brands; gone are the Duracell batteries; and gone are 43 beauty brands, including Clairol and Cover Girl. Left are just 65 brands, and most of those brands hold the number one or number two spot in their market.

P&G identified 150 non-industry-leading brands that, in total, accounted for only about 10% of revenues and profits.

GE is remaking itself into a "digital industrial company." To accomplish this makeover, GE is exiting some long-time business lines. It has dismantled most of its GE Capital subsidiary, keeping only the financing arms associated with its remaining core businesses. And after more than 100 years, GE will no longer be making electrical appliances.

What's next for these two companies? Will less become more? Only time will tell.

Sources: Procter and Gamble, "The Strategy is Simple," December 24, 2010, http://news.pg.com/blog/company-strategy/strategy-simple%E2%80%A6 (accessed April 7, 2016); Serena Ng, "P&G to Shed More Than Half Its Brands," *The Wall Street Journal*, August 1, 2014, http://www.wsj.com/articles/procter-gamble-posts-higher-profit-on-cost-cutting-1406892304 (accessed April 7, 2016); Trefis, "P&G Expects Brand Consolidation to be Over by Summer," February 20, 2015, http://www.trefis.com/stock/pg/articles/281612/pg-expects-brand-consolidation-to-be-over-by-summer/2015-02-20 (accessed April 7, 2016); General Electric 2015 Annual Report.

Additional Factors to Consider

While the segment margin income statement provides a useful analysis in the decision to eliminate a segment, it doesn't provide *all* the information needed to make the decision. Consider Universal Sports Exchange's recent analysis of its retail departments. The uniform department has a negative segment margin of ($65,000), which on the surface might lead you to recommend closing the uniform department. But Universal's managers know there is a relationship between uniform sales and equipment sales. In fact, if Universal closes its uniform department, customers who need both uniforms and equipment will shop at a store that carries both product lines. Furthermore, if the lost equipment sales generated a contribution margin of $125,000, then closing the uniform department would *reduce* operating income by $60,000:

Equipment contribution margin lost	($125,000)
Uniform segment margin saved	65,000
Net decrease in operating income	($ 60,000)

WATCH OUT!

In evaluating which costs (product, division, territory) are direct to a segment, you need to decide whether costs are avoidable. The variable costs associated with the segment's sales are always avoidable—if the sales go away, so do the variable costs. In the example of the West Texas territory, the dedicated sales representative's salary is avoidable (relevant) **only** if the representative is fired when the territory is eliminated. If the representative is reassigned to another part of the company, then the salary cost will not be saved by eliminating the territory.

Sometimes, resources that are freed up as a result of eliminating a segment can be redeployed in a more profitable way. For example, although the West Texas territory will be kept for the time being, Jonathan believes there might be more profitable ways to use the territory's sales representative. One of those options could be to generate more sales in the North Texas territory since the population of Texas is growing fastest in that area. The direct fixed cost of $20,000 would remain the same with either alternative, so to make this a profitable move, the additional sales in the North would need to generate a total contribution margin of at least $132,669, almost a 22% increase over the current contribution margin.

Now, Jonathan has a couple of things to consider. Can the company generate $132,669 more in contribution margin in the North without incurring additional advertising costs? What are the qualitative implications of eliminating the West Texas territory? Once the territory is eliminated, it will be difficult to reestablish it in the future. Can customer relationships in the West be developed to achieve a higher payoff in the future than the company would gain from the additional sales in the North? The numbers tell part of the story, but Jonathan's expertise in managing customer relationships may give him the final word in this decision.

Recap of the Decision Process

Decision to be made:	Keep or eliminate a "losing" operation
Relevant cost information:	Contribution margin, segment margin, direct fixed costs, contribution margin of complementary products
Qualitative issues to consider:	Customer relations, customer preferences for product mix
Watch out for:	Allocated common fixed costs
Decision rule:	If segment margin is positive, keep the segment until a better use of resources is found

EXHIBIT 8-15

Recap of the keeping or eliminating business segments decision.

UNIT 8.5 REVIEW

KEY TERMS

Allocated cost p. 462

Assigned cost p. 462

Common cost p. 462

Segment p. 462

Segment margin p. 463

PRACTICE QUESTIONS

1. LO 5 In a decision to add or eliminate a product or service, which one of the following is an avoidable expense?

   a. Allocated overhead

   b. Depreciation

   c. Insurance on the building

   d. Variable overhead

2. LO 5 The segment margin will always be greater than or equal to the contribution margin. True or False?

3. LO 5 A study has been conducted to determine whether one of Parry Company's departments should be eliminated. The department's contribution margin is $50,000 per year. The fixed expenses charged to the department total $65,000 per year; an estimated $40,000 of those expenses would be eliminated if the department were discontinued. These data indicate that if the department were eliminated, the company's overall net operating income would

   a. decrease by $10,000 per year.

   b. increase by $10,000 per year.

   c. decrease by $25,000 per year.

   d. increase by $25,000 per year.

4. LO 5 Kuskela Company makes hats in three sizes: small, medium and large. Medium hats have shown a loss for several years, similar to the operating loss shown in the following table:

	Small	Medium	Large	Total
Sales	$125,000	$175,000	$250,000	$550,000
Variable costs	50,000	100,000	150,000	300,000
Contribution margin	75,000	75,000	100,000	250,000
Fixed costs	70,000	80,000	85,000	235,000
Operating income	$ 5,000	$ (5,000)	$ 15,000	$ 15,000

Of the total $235,000 in fixed costs, $180,000 is common costs that have been allocated equally to each product line. What will total operating income be if medium hats are dropped?

a. $(75,000)
b. $(55,000)
c. $(40,000)
d. $20,000

UNIT 8.5 PRACTICE EXERCISE

The most recent income statement for Department C of Merrill's Department Store is as follows:

Sales		$500,000
Less variable expenses		200,000
Contribution margin		300,000
Less fixed expenses:		
Salaries and wages	$150,000	
Insurance on inventories	10,000	
Depreciation of equipment	65,000	
Advertising	100,000	325,000
Operating income (loss)		$ (25,000)

The department's equipment has a remaining useful life of six years, with little or no current resale value. Management is thinking about closing the department due to its poor showing. If the department is closed, one employee with a salary of $30,000 will be retained. The equipment has no resale value. Should the department be closed?

SELECTED UNIT 8.5 ANSWERS

Think About It 8.6

C&C Sports' managers already segment the business by product line. They may also want to segment the business by customer or customer type (e.g., wholesale or retail) or distribution channel (e.g., online or catalog orders). Managers need to evaluate the business from various angles to ensure that they are making good decisions about how resources are invested.

Think About It 8.7

C&C Sports wants all its operations to provide an acceptable return. The West Texas territory receives the same level of resources as the other territories (a sales representative), yet it is not providing the same level of returns. If all the territories earned the same segment margin as West Texas, the company would lose money. The full-cost analysis might suggest that the company could use its time and resources better than operating in the West Texas territory *if* it can find an alternative that will generate as much or more contribution margin.

Practice Questions

1. D
2. False
3. A
4. C

Unit 8.5 Practice Exercise

Avoidable items if Department C is dropped:

Sales		$500,000
Less variable expenses		200,000
Contribution margin		300,000
Less direct fixed expenses:		
Salaries and wages	$120,000	
Insurance on inventories	10,000	
Advertising	100,000	230,000
Segment margin		$ 70,000

The $30,000 salary of the employee who will remain if the department is closed is nondifferential and therefore irrelevant. Depreciation is unavoidable because the equipment will either continue to be depreciated or will be written off.

When the relevant costs are identified and used in the analysis, we can see that Department C is contributing a $70,000 segment margin. The department should be kept until a better alternative is identified.

BUSINESS DECISION AND CONTEXT Wrap Up

While the decisions C&C's vice presidents faced at the beginning of the chapter may have seemed different, they all shared something in common: the need to identify and evaluate relevant information. Jonathan Smith avoided the costly mistake of closing the West Texas sales territory when he received the appropriate information. Although the territory appeared to be losing money, when its segment margin was calculated, Jonathan realized that it contributed over $100,000 to the bottom line! Another deal Jonathan was ready to jump into was the special order from Central Independent School District. Though special orders can take advantage of excess capacity or generate new business, the long-term implications of the order didn't make much sense for C&C.

Bradley Textile Mills discovered that its jersey fabric was more profitable than its wool fabric, so Chad Davis was pleased to learn that C&C's fabric orders will be delivered on time. Even though Bradley Textile Mills realizes a much higher contribution margin per yard on wool than on jersey fabric, wool takes up more time on the weaving machine, consuming a constrained resource and generating less profit than first thought. This close call on the availability of jersey fabric reminded Chad that he needs to maintain good relationships with C&C's major suppliers. The quality of the jerseys can't be better than the quality of the fabric with which they are made.

Finally, Chad was able to evaluate how to best use the chenille machine as a result of Bonadeo Embroidery's offer to provide chenille letters for C&C's award jackets. Bonadeo's price looked like a cheaper alternative until Chad found out that the relevant cost of making the letters internally was actually lower than Bonadeo's price. However, the analysis encouraged Chad to consider other options for the chenille machine, and in the long run, C&C will be better off financially with the outsourcing arrangement he settled on.

By approaching the various decisions in the correct manner, C&C's vice presidents now have a better understanding of the company's relevant costs. As future short-term operating opportunities arise, they will be able to analyze the relevant costs accurately.

CHAPTER SUMMARY

In this chapter you learned how to identify the relevant information in various short-run business decisions. Specifically, you should be able to meet the objectives set out at the beginning of the chapter:

1. *Identify relevant information for decision making. (Unit 8.1)*

Relevant information satisfies two criteria: (1) it differs between the alternatives, and (2) the differences will occur in the future.

2. *Determine the qualitative and quantitative impacts of special order pricing. (Unit 8.2)*

Special orders arise because a customer wants a pricing arrangement that differs from the normal price. The justification for the price difference could be that the requested product differs from the normal product, that the customer is buying in large quantities for which no regular volume discount is available, or that the customer is new and willing to try the product or service only at a special rate. Special orders can be advantageous to the company if excess capacity is available or if the new business they generate is expected to have a long-term payoff.

To calculate the effect of a special order on operating income, first identify the avoidable costs associated with the special order. If capacity is available, then fixed overhead is an unavoidable cost. Watch out for the loss of normal sales if the entire special order can't be filled with available capacity. In that case, lost contribution margin from normal sales is one cost of the special order.

If a company continually accepts special orders to fill capacity, then the larger issue to evaluate is whether a permanent use can be found for the capacity, or if not, whether some assets can be eliminated to reduce capacity costs.

3. *Determine the qualitative and quantitative impacts of outsourcing decisions. (Unit 8.3)*

Outsourcing means moving the production of goods or the delivery of services from within the organization to a provider outside the organization. Quantitatively, outsourcing an operation will free up the resources it uses. However, it is critical that unavoidable costs be identified. Because those costs will continue with or without the outsourcing arrangement, they should not be included in the costs projected to be saved by outsourcing. Qualitatively, outsourcing can provide expertise the company doesn't have, transfer risk to an outside supplier, and allow the company to focus on its core competencies. Potential dangers of outsourcing include poor quality, poor delivery time, and intellectual theft.

4. *Determine how to allocate constrained resources to maximize income. (Unit 8.4)*

When company resources are limited in the amount of output they can generate, the best use of these resources is to make the product that generates the highest contribution per constrained resource. Do not, however, produce more product than the quantity customers demand.

5. *Calculate the effects on operating income of keeping or eliminating operations. (Unit 8.5)*

The decision of whether to keep or eliminate an operation should be based on the operation's segment margin. Common fixed costs should not be included in the operation's income. If the segment margin is positive, the operation should be kept until a better use can be found for its resources. If the segment margin is negative, the operation should be dropped. Watch out for related sales or operations that might be affected by the operation under evaluation.

KEY TERMS

Allocated cost (Unit 8.5)
Assigned cost (Unit 8.5)
Avoidable cost (Unit 8.1)
Bottleneck process (Unit 8.4)
Common cost (Unit 8.5)
Differential (Unit 8.1)
Incremental analysis (Unit 8.1)
Information overload (Unit 8.1)
Make-or-buy decision (Unit 8.3)
Offshoring (Unit 8.3)
Opportunity cost (Unit 8.3)
Outsourcing (Unit 8.3)
Relevant information (Unit 8.1)
Segment (Unit 8.5)
Segment margin (Unit 8.5)
Sunk cost (Unit 8.1)
Theory of Constraints (Unit 8.4)
Throughput contribution (Unit 8.4)
Unavoidable cost (Unit 8.1)

EXERCISES

8-1 Identifying relevant information (LO 1) Cherry, Inc., currently has a machine that costs $10,000 per year to operate. The machine can produce 50,000 units per year. Three years ago the company borrowed $200,000 to purchase the machine; it still owes $125,000 of that amount. Cherry could sell the machine for $70,000 and purchase a new, more efficient machine at a cost of $220,000. The new machine can produce 85,000 units per year; its annual operating costs would be $12,000.

Required

Identify each piece of information in this scenario and indicate whether it is relevant or irrelevant to the decision to purchase the new machine.

8-2 Identifying alternatives and relevant information (LO 1) Madison Ironworks made 500 defective units last month. Fortunately, the units were identified as defective before they were sold to customers. They are currently included in Madison's ending inventory balance at $200 each. At the end of the quarter, the company will have to write off their $100,000 cost, since the units have no value in their present condition. The production manager has determined that the units could be reworked for $10 each and then sold for $100. He has also received a bid from a liquidation company to purchase the defective units for $80 each.

Required

a. What alternatives are available to Madison?
b. What information is irrelevant to the decision?
c. Which alternative would generate the best financial result?

8-3 Identifying relevant information (LO 1) Jason McGregor manages an IT department for a large corporation. Kelly Preston, vice president for marketing, has asked him to help her evaluate two statistical packages for monitoring customer purchases. StatMax costs $912,000, requires 2 gigabytes of disk storage space and 80 programmer hours for customization, and has no annual license fee. The software vendor provides 150 hours of user training and offers 24-hour technical support. Buy Tracker costs $500,000, requires 2 gigabytes of disk storage space and 125 programmer hours for customization, and carries a $10,000 annual license fee. The software vendor provides 150 hours of user training and offers technical support from 8:00 A.M. to 5:00 P.M. Central Standard Time.

Required

a. What information is relevant to the decision to purchase one of these statistical packages?
b. What other information would you want to know?
c. Will the out-of-pocket cost of the software be more or less than the relevant cost? What causes the difference?

8-4 Special order pricing (LO 2) Graham Corporation has the excess manufacturing capacity to fill a special order from Nash, Inc. Using Graham's normal costing process, variable costs of the special order would be $15,000 and fixed costs would be $25,000. Of the fixed costs, $4,000 would be for unavoidable overhead costs, and the remainder for rent on a special machine needed to complete the order.

Required

What is the minimum price Graham should quote to Nash?

8-5 Special order pricing (LO 2) Marston Manufacturing has an annual capacity of 85,000 units per year. Currently, the company is making and selling 78,000 units a year. The normal sales price is $120 per unit, variable costs are $90 per unit, and total fixed expenses are $2,000,000. An out-of-state distributor has offered to buy 12,000 units at $105 per unit. Marston's cost structure should not change as a result of this special order.

Required

By how much will Marston's income change if the company accepts this order?

8-6 Special order pricing (LO 2) Lybrand Company is a leading manufacturer of sunglasses. One of Lybrand's products protects the eyes from ultraviolet rays. An upscale sporting goods store has contacted Lybrand about purchasing 15,000 pairs of these sunglasses. Lybrand's unit manufacturing cost, based on a full capacity of 100,000 units, is as follows:

Direct materials	$ 6
Direct labor	4
Manufacturing overhead (60% fixed)	15
Total manufacturing costs	$ 25

Lybrand also incurs selling and administrative expenses of $75,000 plus $2 per pair for sales commissions. The company has plenty of excess manufacturing capacity to use in manufacturing the sunglasses. Lybrand's normal price for these sunglasses is $40 per pair. The sporting goods store has offered to pay $35 per pair. Since the special order was initiated by the sporting goods store, no sales commission will be paid.

Required

What would be the effect on Lybrand's income if the special order were accepted?

8-7 Special order pricing (LO 2) The following operating information reports the results of Chappell Company's production and sale of 12,500 air-conditioned motorcycle helmets last year. Based on early market forecasts, Chappell expects the same results this year.

Sales	$1,920,000
Variable manufacturing expenses	880,000
Fixed manufacturing expenses	272,000
Variable selling and administrative expenses	128,000
Fixed selling and administrative expenses	224,000

The American Motorcycle Club has offered to purchase 1,500 helmets at a price of $100 each. Chappell has sufficient idle capacity to fill the order, which would not affect the company's cost structure or regular sales.

Required

If Chappell accepts this order, by how much will its income increase or decrease?

8-8 Outsourcing (LO 3) The Outland Company manufactures 1,000 units of a part that could be purchased from an outside supplier for $12 each. Outland's costs to manufacture each part are as follows:

Direct materials	$ 2
Direct labor	3
Variable manufacturing overhead	4
Fixed manufacturing overhead	8
Total	$17

All fixed overhead is unavoidable and is allocated based on direct labor. The facilities that are used to manufacture the part have no alternative uses.

Required

a. Should Outland continue to manufacture the part? Show your calculations.
b. Would your answer change if Outland could lease the manufacturing facilities to another company for $5,000 per year? Show your calculations.

8-9 Outsourcing (LO 3) Steeple Rides makes bicycles. It has always purchased its bicycle tires from the Balyo Tires at $15 each but is currently considering making the tires in its own factory. The estimated costs per unit of making the tires are as follows:

Direct materials	$4
Direct labor	$5
Variable manufacturing overhead	$2

The company's fixed expenses would increase by $38,000 per year if managers decided to make the tire.

Required

a. Ignoring qualitative factors, if the company needs 8,000 tires a year, should it continue to purchase them from Balyo or begin to produce them internally?
b. What qualitative factors should Steeple Rides consider in making this decision?

8-10 Outsourcing (LO 3) Every year Underwood Industries manufactures 15,000 units of part 231 for use in its production cycle. The per unit costs of part 231 are as follows:

Direct materials	$ 6
Direct labor	12
Variable manufacturing overhead	10
Fixed manufacturing overhead	15
Total	$ 43

Flintrock, Inc., has offered to sell 5,000 units of part 231 to Underwood for $40 per unit. If Underwood accepts Flintrock's offer, its freed-up facilities could be used to earn $10,000 in contribution margin by manufacturing part 240. In addition, Underwood would eliminate 75% of the fixed overhead applied to part 231.

Required

Should Underwood accept Flintrock's offer? Why or why not?

8-11 Outsourcing (LO 3) Merit Bay Communications operates a customer call center that handles billing inquiries for several large insurance firms. Since the center is located on the outskirts of town, where there are no restaurants within a 20-minute drive, the company has always operated an on-site cafeteria for employees. The cafeteria uses $180,000 in food products each year and serves 5,000 meals per month, at a price of $5 each. It employs five workers whose salaries and benefits total $90,000 per year. Depreciation on the cafeteria equipment is $35,000 per year. Other fixed overhead that is directly related to operating the cafeteria totals $12,000 per year.

Best Ever Foods has offered to take over Merit Bay's cafeteria operations. As part of the transition, current cafeteria employees would become Best Ever employees, and Best Ever would assume all out-of-pocket costs to operate the cafeteria. Best Ever would continue to offer meals at $5 each and would pay Merit Bay $0.50 per meal for the use of its cafeteria facilities.

Required

a. Should Merit Bay continue to operate the employee cafeteria, or should the company accept Best Ever's offer? Why?

b. Assume that Merit Bay accepted Best Ever's offer two years ago and that all costs have remained constant. Since then, a new shopping mall has opened close to the company's location, bringing in several fast-food and quick-service restaurants. Employee demand for cafeteria service has dropped to 1,000 meals per month, and Best Ever has laid off two of the five cafeteria workers. Does it make financial sense for Merit Bay to renew Best Ever's contract for another year, or should it resume operation of the cafeteria operation?

8-12 Allocating constrained resources (LO 4) Balloon, Inc. produces three types of balloons—small, medium, and large—with the following characteristics:

	Small	Medium	Large
Selling price per unit	$ 5	$ 8	$ 10
Variable cost per unit	3	5	6
Contribution margin per unit	$ 2	$ 3	$ 4
Machine hours per unit	1	2.4	3
Demand in units	500	1,000	800

The company has only 2,000 machine hours available each month.

Required

How many units of each type of balloon should the company make to maximize its total contribution margin?

8-13 Allocating constrained resources (LO 4) Umbrella Co. is considering the introduction of three new products. Per unit sales and cost information are as follows:

	A	B	C
Sales price	$3.00	$5.00	$16.00
Variable costs	$1.20	$3.40	$10.00
Fixed costs	$0.50	$1.00	$ 3.50
Labor hours per unit	1.2 hours	0.5 hours	5 hours
Monthly demand in units	500	600	240

The company has only 1,800 direct labor hours available to commit to production of any new products.

Required

How many of each product should Umbrella Co. produce and sell to maximize its profit?

8-14 Allocating constrained resources (LO 4) Wendy's Wind Toys manufactures decorative kites, banners, and windsocks. During the month of January, Wendy received orders for 3,000 Valentine's Day banners and 1,200 Easter kites. Because several sewing machines are in the shop for repairs, Wendy's has only 1,000 sewing machine hours available for production of these orders. Each Valentine's Day banner sells for $12. The banners take one hour to sew and have a total variable cost of $9 per banner. The Easter kites sell for $15. They take 15 minutes to sew and have a total variable cost of $14.

Required

a. With only 1,000 sewing machine hours available, how many of each product should Wendy schedule for production in January?

b. If Wendy's has promised all customers that their orders will be completed in January, what steps should managers take to meet those production demands?

8-15 Allocating constrained resources (LO 4) In response to a growing awareness of gluten allergies, Outland Bakery tried using gluten-free flour in its three most popular cookies. After several attempts and a lot of inedible cookies, the company perfected new recipes that yield delicious gluten-free cookies. The costs of producing a batch of 100 cookies are as follows:

	Chocolate Chip	Sugar	Oatmeal Raisin
Sales price	$130	$125	$120
Variable cost	$81	$86	$78
Fixed cost	18	15	20
Total cost	99	101	98
Gross profit	$31	$24	$22
Pounds of flour	2.5	2.5	2

Required

a. Assuming no raw material constraints and unlimited demand for cookies, what type of cookie would maximize the company's contribution margin? Why?

b. Assume that, based on typical customer demand, Outland will sell 12,000 batches of chocolate chip cookies, 8,000 batches of sugar cookies, and 10,000 batches of oatmeal raisin cookies. What will the company's contribution margin be?

c. Outland's flour supplier has announced a shortage of gluten-free flour. As a result, Outland will only be able to purchase 50,000 pounds of flour. How many batches of each type of cookie should the company bake? What will the company's contribution margin be?

d. If Outland uses gluten-free flour in other products, will the allocation you recommend in part (c) change? Why or why not?

8-16 Keeping or eliminating operations (LO 5) In 2015, Yum! Brands, Inc., the world's largest quick-service restaurant company (Pizza Hut, Kentucky Fried Chicken, and Taco Bell), opened 577 new Pizza Hut restaurants and closed 456 others.

Required

If you were in charge of these decisions, what information would you want to collect?

8-17 Keeping or eliminating operations (LO 5) Twinkie Trivia Co. manufactures and sells two trivia products, the Square Trivia Game and the Round Trivia Game. Last quarter's operating profits, by product, and for the company as a whole, were as follows:

	Square	Round	Total
Sales revenue	$11,000	$6,600	$17,600
Variable expenses	4,400	3,000	7,400
Contribution margin	6,600	3,600	10,200
Fixed expenses	2,750	4,200	6,950
Operating income	$ 3,850	$ (600)	$ 3,250

Forty percent of the Round Game's fixed costs could have been avoided if the game had not been produced or sold.

Required

If the Round Game had been discontinued before the last quarter, what would operating income have been for the company as a whole?

8-18 Keeping or eliminating operations (LO 5) Physical Phitness, Inc. operates three divisions, Weak, Average, and Strong. As it turns out, the Weak division has the lowest operating income, and the president wants to close it. "Survival of the fittest, I say!" was his response when the Weak division's manager insisted that his division earned money for the company. Following is the most recent financial analysis for each division:

	Weak	Average	Strong
Sales revenue	$125,000	$350,000	$500,000
Variable expenses	50,000	200,000	300,000
Contribution margin	75,000	150,000	200,000
Direct expenses	30,000	80,000	110,000
Allocated expenses	50,000	50,000	50,000
Operating income	$ (5,000)	$ 20,000	$ 40,000

Required

a. Prepare a revised income statement showing the segment margin for each division; add a column for the company as a whole.
b. By how much would total income change if the Weak division were dropped?
c. Based on the way allocated expenses are divided among the divisions, what do you think will happen to the Average division if the company continues to prepare financial statements in this way?

8-19 Adding a product line (LO 5) Luis Herrera, an up-and-coming fashion designer, created a new line of men's fashion socks in response to the growing number of celebrities who are expressing their individuality by replacing traditional navy and black socks with brighter colors and bold patterns. At a sales price of $10 per pair, Luis estimates monthly sales volume will be 20,000 pairs. Variable product costs will be $6.50 per pair and fixed overhead will be $1.60 per pair. Half of the fixed overhead is directly traceable to the new sock line. To promote the socks, Herrera proposes a $0.50 per pair commission to the company's salespeople and a $10,000 per month advertising campaign. In compliance with corporate policy, the socks will also be allocated $25,000 in fixed corporate support costs.

Required

a. Prepare a traditional monthly income statement for the proposed sock line.
b. Prepare a monthly income statement that highlights the proposed sock line's segment margin.
c. Which income statement would you recommend that Luis use when pitching the proposed sock line to company managers? Why would you recommend that he use this statement?

PROBLEMS

8-20 Special order pricing (LO 2) Guilford Packaging Company is a leading manufacturer of cardboard boxes and other product packaging solutions. One of the company's major product lines is custom-printed cake boxes that are sold to some of the country's best-known bakeries at a price of $0.50 per box. To maintain its high-quality image, Guilford uses a thick premium coated paper for all of its cake boxes. Based on annual production of 1,000,000 boxes, Guilford's cost for producing a box is as follows:

Paper	$0.15
Ink	0.04
Direct labor	0.05
Variable overhead	0.08
Fixed overhead	0.10
Total cost per box	$0.42

Andrea Borden, a recent graduate of the Culinary Institute of America, is opening a new bakery in her hometown. She recently contacted Brad Lail, Guilford's top salesperson, about purchasing cake boxes for her new store. Brad described Guilford's boxes, emphasizing the high-quality paper and the unique printing process the company uses. Andrea is looking for ways to lower her operating costs, so after hearing Brad describe Guilford's boxes, she told him that all she needed was a simple, unprinted box. Andrea also told Brad that she needs 10,000 boxes and is willing to pay $0.25 per box.

Required

a. Based on Andrea's offer of $0.25 per box for an unprinted box, should Guilford accept Andrea's order? Guildford currently has excess production capacity and can easily accommodate Andrea's order in the production schedule.
b. Since Andrea wants a simple box, Brad is exploring using a lighter-weight paper for her boxes. He has found a suitable paper that will cost $0.10 per box. If Guilford uses this lighter-weight paper for Andrea's boxes, should the company accept Andrea's order at a price of $0.25 per box? Guildford currently has excess production capacity and can easily accommodate Andrea's order in the production schedule.
c. After visiting with Andrea, Brad received a fax from one of London's top bakeries. The bakery's normal box supplier suffered some fire damage and is unable to ship the bakery's order of 10,000 boxes this month. The bakery's owner is asking if Guilford can fill a one-time rush order of 10,000 boxes printed with the bakery's logo. The bakery is willing to pay a 10% price premium to expedite the order. If Guilford accepts the order, it will incur $800 in export taxes and shipping. Should Guilford accept the London bakery's offer?
d. What qualitative issues should Guilford consider as it evaluates both Andrea's order and the London bakery's order? Are these issues different for the two orders?

8-21 Special order pricing (LO 2) Wilson Vistas is a leading producer of vinyl replacement windows. The company's growth strategy focuses on developing domestic markets in large metropolitan areas. The company operates a single manufacturing plant in Kansas City with an annual capacity of 500,000 windows. Current production is budgeted at 450,000 windows per year, a quantity that has been constant over the past three years. Based on the budget, the accounting department has calculated the following unit costs for the windows:

Direct materials	$40
Direct labor	18
Manufacturing overhead	20
Selling and administrative	14
Total unit cost	$92

The company's budget includes $5,400,000 in fixed overhead and $3,150,000 in fixed selling and administrative expenses. The windows sell for $150 each. A 2% distributor's commission is included in the selling and administrative expenses.

Required

a. ScandiHomes, Finland's second largest homebuilder, has approached Wilson with an offer to buy 75,000 windows during the coming year. Given the size of the order, ScandiHomes has requested a 40% volume discount on Wilson's normal selling price. Should Wilson grant ScandiHomes' request?
b. List the qualitative issues Wilson should consider in deciding whether to grant ScandiHomes' request for a discount. For each issue you list, identify whether or not it supports a decision to grant ScandiHomes' request.
c. Return to the original data. Monk Builders has just signed a contract with the state government to replace the windows in low-income housing units throughout the state. Monk needs 80,000 windows to complete the job and has offered to buy them from Wilson at a price of $100 per window. Monk will pick up the windows at Wilson's plant, so Wilson will not incur the $2 per window shipping charge. In addition, Wilson will not need to pay a distributor's commission, since the windows will not be sold through a distributor. Should Wilson accept Monk's offer?

d. If Wilson decides to accept Monk's offer, it will need to find an additional 30,000 windows to meet both the special order and normal sales. Panorama Panes has offered to provide them to Wilson at a price of $120 per window. Panorama Panes will deliver the windows to Wilson, and Wilson would then distribute them to its customers. Should Wilson outsource the production of the extra windows to Panorama Panes?

8-22 Relevant costs and outsourcing (CMA adapted) (LO 1, 3) Klump Trekkers, Inc., manufactures engines that are used in recreational equipment, such as motorcycles and personal watercraft. The company currently assembles the camshafts for these motors in its assembly department, which employs 40 skilled technicians. Due to crowded plant conditions and a shortage of skilled technicians, Klump is considering outsourcing the camshaft assembly to Mercury Motors, a specialist in the field. Mercury would supply 125,000 camshafts at a price of $88 each.

Mark Tobian is studying the proposed outsourcing deal and has prepared the following analysis.

Savings:	
1. Reduction in assembly technicians ($32,500 × 36)	$1,170,000
2. Supervisor transferred	43,000
3. Purchasing clerk transferred	19,000
4. Floor space savings [(1,500 × $12) + (6,000 × $10.50)]	81,000
5. Reduced purchase orders (1,200 × $1.40)	1,680
Total savings	$1,314,680
Costs:	
6. Increased component cost [125,000 × ($88.00 − $79.50)]	1,062,500
7. Hire junior engineer	28,000
8. Hire quality control inspector	26,000
9. Increased storage cost for safety stock (12% × 125,000 × $3.25)	48,750
Total costs	1,165,250
Net annual savings	$ 149,430

Additional information Tobian has gathered includes the following:

- Of the 40 technicians employed in the assembly department, 36 will be let go. Four technicians will be retained and transferred to the field service department to perform repair work. The supervisor of the assembly department will be transferred and promoted to assistant floor supervisor. No such position currently exists in the plant.
- A junior engineer will be hired to act as a liaison between Klump and Mercury, to ensure technical conformity. A quality control inspector will be hired to monitor Mercury's adherence to quality standards. The clerk in the purchasing department who handled all the camshaft purchasing will be transferred to an open clerical position in the sales department. Funds are available in the sales department to cover this position.
- The standard cost of producing a camshaft is as follows:

Direct materials	$36.00
Direct labor	14.50
Variable manufacturing overhead	11.60
Fixed manufacturing overhead	17.40
Total cost	$79.50

- The 6,000 square feet of space used by the assembly department will be converted to storage space. Currently, the space is valued at $10.50 per square foot. For the past year, Klump has been renting 1,500 square feet of storage space in a nearby building for $12.00 per square foot. This space will not be needed after the assembly department space is freed up.

- Management wants to increase safety stock levels from the current 8% of projected volume to 12% of projected volume. The variable cost to store the camshafts is $3.25 per camshaft.
- Klump will no longer need to issue the 1,200 purchase orders for camshaft materials. The variable cost of issuing a purchase order is $1.40.

Required

a. For each of the nine items listed in Tobian's analysis, indicate whether the item should have been included in the analysis. If the item is not appropriate to the analysis, explain why it should not have been included. For those items that are appropriate to the analysis, indicate whether the amount Tobian included is correct or incorrect. Use the following format for your answer:

Item Number	Appropriate/Inappropriate	Correct/Incorrect
1.		
2.		
3.		

b. What would be the financial impact on Klump of outsourcing the camshaft assembly to Mercury?

c. What other factors should Klump consider before making the decision to outsource the camshaft assembly?

8-23 Outsourcing (LO 3) Benson ProSystems needs a new signal conditioner module for a large process control system it is designing. Current market conditions will support annual sales of 1,000 systems. Engineers estimate the following unit manufacturing costs for the module:

Direct materials	$25
Direct labor	18
Variable manufacturing overhead	7
	$50

Engineers estimate that 25 weeks of development work will be needed to develop, test, and verify the new design. Engineering resources (personnel and lab) to complete the development will cost $3,000 per week. If the engineers don't work on this project, they will be assigned to another.

Longan Devices has a module that is quite similar to the one Benson needs. Longan can modify the device to suit Benson in just four weeks and has offered to supply it to Benson at a price of $60 per unit.

Required

a. Should Benson go forward with its design of the new module, or should it accept Longan's offer?

b. If Benson decided to outsource the new module to Longan, how much would the other projects Benson's engineers work on have to return (or save) to make outsourcing financially beneficial?

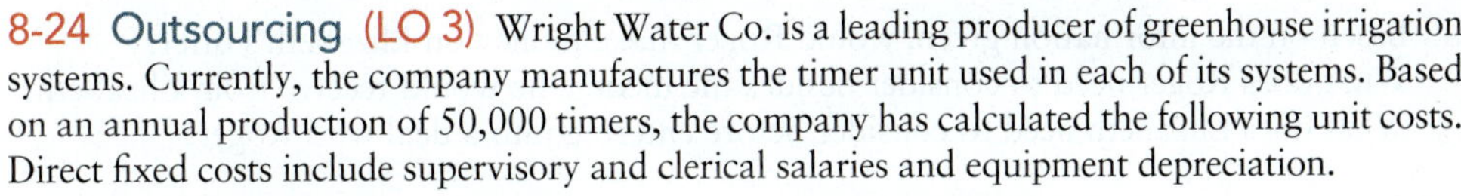

8-24 Outsourcing (LO 3) Wright Water Co. is a leading producer of greenhouse irrigation systems. Currently, the company manufactures the timer unit used in each of its systems. Based on an annual production of 50,000 timers, the company has calculated the following unit costs. Direct fixed costs include supervisory and clerical salaries and equipment depreciation.

Direct materials	$13	
Direct labor	5	
Variable manufacturing overhead	4	
Direct fixed manufacturing overhead	7	(40% salaries, 60% depreciation)
Allocated fixed manufacturing overhead	8	
Total unit cost	$37	

Clifton Clocks has offered to provide the timer units to Wright at a price of $34 per unit. If Wright accepts the offer, the current timer unit supervisory and clerical staff will be laid off.

Required

a. Assuming that Wright Water has no other use for either the facilities or the equipment currently used to manufacture the timer units, should the company accept Clifton's offer? Why or why not?

b. Assume that if Wright Water accepts Clifton's offer, the company can use the freed-up manufacturing facilities to manufacture a new line of growing lights. The company estimates it can sell 120,000 of the new lights each year at a price of $12. Variable costs of the lights are expected to be $7 per unit. The timer unit supervisory and clerical staff would be transferred to this new product line. Should Wright Water accept Clifton's offer? Why or why not?

8-25 Special order pricing, outsourcing (LO 2, 3) Elizabeth Lee is a top seller on eBay®. In fact, her business has grown so large that she can no longer manage her items on eBay's website and ship her products to the auction winners in a timely manner. When she first started, she had to ship only a few items each week. To save on the shipping charges, she would purchase the shipping materials (boxes, tape, cushioning, and labels), pack the items, and take them to the post office herself. Now she has several items to ship every day, and she doesn't have time to do it all.

Once or twice, Elizabeth has used the local Mail Plus store. Sometimes she will ask them to prepare and ship a package; other times, she will purchase the materials, wrap the package herself, and send it from Mail Plus. The store's prices are high, but the employees aren't incredibly busy, and they do a great job. Elizabeth has approached the owner, Roger Lippert, to see if he is interested in working out an arrangement in which she would receive a 20% discount on custom packaging. She knows she can't get a discount on the actual shipping charge—Mail Plus uses the U.S. Postal Service.

Roger has expressed interest in the idea but is having difficulty determining whether he will make any money on the deal without knowing the specific items Elizabeth would want to ship. Following is an income statement for the custom packaging portion of his business:

Revenues (1,200 custom packages)	$18,000
Cartons	(6,000)
Cushioning	(600)
Tape, labels	(1,500)
Salaried labor	(4,000)
Overhead	(4,100)
Income	$ 1,800

Roger's pricing system is simple: He multiplies the cost of the carton required for the job by three. The larger the carton, he reasons, the longer it takes to pack, and the more materials it requires. He feels he has done quite well with this pricing system. If he gives Elizabeth a 20% discount, he thinks he will lose money.

Required

a. Based on the information given, would Roger make money on Elizabeth's offer?

b. What does Roger need to consider besides the income he would receive from Elizabeth?

c. What does Elizabeth need to consider before entering into a deal with Roger?

8-26 Allocating constrained resources (LO 4) Marwick Innovations, Inc. produces exercise and fitness gear. Two of its newer products require a finishing process that can only be completed on machines that were recently purchased for this purpose. The machines have a maximum capacity of 6,000 machine hours, and no other products that the company makes use these machines.

Sarah Jacob, the company's operations manager, is preparing the production schedule for the coming month and can't seem to find enough machine time to produce enough units to meet the customer demand that the marketing department has included in the sales budget.

Michael Stoner, the company's controller, has gathered the following information about the two products:

	Dumbbell Rack	Weight Bench
Selling price per unit	$50	$61
Direct materials	20	15
Direct labor	4	8
Variable overhead	3	6
Fixed overhead	5	10
Profit per unit	$18	$22
Unit sales demand	4,000	7,000
Machine hours per unit	0.5	0.8

Required

a. Calculate the total number of machine hours needed to produce enough units to meet the sales demand for the two products.
b. How should Sarah allocate the 6,000 available machine hours between the two products so that Marwick maximizes its profits?
c. What total contribution margin will Marwick realize based on your answer to part (b)?
d. Sarah has talked with the marketing department about the situation and suggested that the company raise the sales price on the weight bench to $69 to reduce customer demand. The marketing department believes that at the higher price, demand for the weight bench will drop to 5,800 units. How should Sarah allocate the 6,000 machine hours based on this new information? What total contribution margin will Marwick earn?
e. After hearing about Sarah's recommendation to increase the weight bench price to $69, Scott Wilson, the sales manager, suggested that the company raise the price of the dumbbell rack instead. He believes that if the price is increased to $56, demand will fall to 2,000 units. How should Sarah allocate the 6,000 machine hours under Scott's proposal? What total contribution margin will Marwick earn?
f. Based on your answers to parts (c), (d), and (e), which action do you suggest that Marwick take? Why?

8-27 Allocating constrained resources—service setting (LO 4) Betsy Willis owns TestTutor, an educational tutoring center in Baytown, Florida. The center offers private tutoring in math, writing, and science. Information about the tutoring sessions is as follows:

	Math	Writing	Science
Session price	$34	$50	$25
Variable labor costs	20	30	10
Variable supplies cost	2	2	1
Session length	45 minutes	90 minutes	30 minutes
Number of sessions demanded per week	180	260	130

Since the company opened five years ago, demand has grown faster than the supply of qualified tutors. Betsy currently has enough tutors to provide only 420 hours of tutoring each week.

Required

a. Can Betsy satisfy customer demand with her current supply of tutors? Why or why not?
b. How should Betsy allocate the currently available tutor hours?
c. What total contribution margin will Betsy earn based on your answer to (b)?
d. Betsy has decided that instead of offering individualized instruction in math and science, she will switch to group sessions. Each math session will accommodate two students, and each science session will accommodate four students. Each student in the group will continue to pay the original session price. All sessions will have a single tutor, but each student will need supplies. How will this change in service delivery affect Betsy's ability to meet demand? How will it change her allocation of tutor hours?

e. Suppose Betsy has enough tutors lined up to provide 600 hours of tutoring each week. However, the building she currently leases has no room for expansion; when fully scheduled, it can accommodate only 420 tutoring hours each week. What is the constrained resource? How can Betsy overcome the constraint to meet the current demand for her services and provide room for future growth?

8-28 Outsourcing and capacity utilization (LO 3, 4) PlayTime, Inc., is a leading manufacturer of sporting equipment. The company is in the process of evaluating the best use of its Plastics Division, which is currently manufacturing molded fishing tackle boxes. The company manufactures and sells 8,000 tackle boxes annually, making full use of its available capacity. The selling prices and costs of the tackle boxes are as follows:

Selling price per box		$86.00
Costs per box		
Direct materials	$17.00	
Direct labor	18.75	
Variable manufacturing overhead	7.00	
Fixed manufacturing overhead[a]	6.25	
Variable selling & administrative[b]	10.00	
Fixed selling & administrative[a]	7.00	
Total cost per box		66.00
Profit per box		$20.00

[a]Allocated to products based on expected production volume.
[b]Per unit variable selling and administrative costs are the same for all products.

Managers believe they could sell 12,000 tackle boxes if the company had sufficient manufacturing capacity. Rod-N-Reel has offered to supply 9,000 tackle boxes per year at a price of $68 per box, including delivery to PlayTime's facility. Cedric Smith, Playtime's product manager, believes the company could make better use of its plastics department by manufacturing skateboards. A marketing report indicates that 17,500 skateboards could be sold at a price of $45 each. Variable costs to make the boards would be $22.50 per board.

Playtime has three options:

1. Make and sell 8,000 tackle boxes.
2. Make 8,000 tackle boxes, buy 4,000 additional tackle boxes, and sell 12,000 tackle boxes.
3. Make and sell 17,500 skateboards, and buy and sell 9,000 tackle boxes.

Required

Compare the company's operating income under the three options.

8-29 Eliminating operations (LO 5) Capital Toys' management is considering eliminating product A, which has been showing a loss for several years. The company's annual income statement, in $000s, is as follows:

	A	B	C	Total
Sales revenue	$2,200	$1,400	$1,800	$5,400
Variable expenses	1,650	600	1,080	3,330
Contribution margin	$ 550	$ 800	$ 720	$2,070
Advertising[a] expense	$ 500	$ 475	$ 520	$1,495
Depreciation[b] expense	15	10	20	45
Corporate expenses[c]	90	80	105	275
Total fixed expenses	$ 605	$ 565	$ 645	$1,815
Operating income	$ (55)	$ 235	$ 75	$ 255

[a]Specific to each product.
[b]Specific to each product; no other use available, no resale value.
[c]Allocated based on number of employees.

Required

a. Restate the income statement in segment margin format.

b. What would be the effect on income if product A were dropped?

c. Management is considering making a new product using product A's equipment. If the new product's selling price per unit were $12, its variable costs were $8, and its advertising costs were the same as for product A, how many units of the new product would the company have to sell to make the switch from product A to the new product worthwhile?

8-30 Dropping a product line (CMA adapted) (LO 5) Ridley and Scott Mercantile operates two stores, one on Maple Avenue and the other on Fenner Road. Results for the month of May, which is representative of all months, are as follows:

	Maple Avenue Store	Fenner Road Store	Total
Sales revenue	$80,000	$120,000	$200,000
Variable expenses	32,000	84,000	116,000
Contribution margin	48,000	36,000	84,000
Direct fixed expenses	20,000	40,000	60,000
Common fixed expenses	4,000	6,000	10,000
Total fixed expenses	24,000	46,000	70,000
Operating income	$24,000	$ (10,000)	$ 14,000

The following information pertains to Ridley and Scott's operations.

- One-fourth of each store's direct fixed expenses would continue if either store were closed.
- Ridley and Scott allocates common fixed expenses to each store on the basis of sales dollars.
- Management estimates that closing the Fenner Road store would result in a 10% decrease in the Maple Avenue store's sales, while closing the Maple Avenue store would have no effect on the Fenner Road store's sales.

Required

a. Management believes that the Fenner Road store should be closed, since it is operating at a loss. Do you support management's belief? Why or why not?

b. Should management consider closing the Maple Avenue store rather than the Fenner Road store? Why or why not?

c. Ridley and Scott are considering a special promotional campaign at the Fenner Road store. They expect a $6,000 monthly increase in advertising expenses to generate a 10% increase in the store's sales volume. The campaign would not affect sales at the Maple Avenue store. What effect would the promotion have on Ridley and Scott's monthly income? Should the campaign be implemented? Why or why not? Ignore your answers to parts (a) and (b).

d. Half of the Fenner Road store's dollar sales come from items that are sold at variable cost to attract customers to the store. Managers are considering deleting those items from the product mix. Doing so would reduce the Fenner Road store's direct fixed expenses by 15% but would also reduce the remaining sales volume result by an additional 20%. There would be no effect on the Maple Avenue store. Should management implement this change in the product mix? Why or why not?

C&C SPORTS CONTINUING CASE

8-31 Allocating constrained resources (LO 4) Chad Davis, vice president for operations at C&C Sports, is considering different strategies for managing the company's inventory. Earlier in the year, the company implemented a more systematic production schedule so that at the end of each month Finished Goods Inventory is 25% of the next month's anticipated sales. That strategy freed a lot of inventory space and improved the company's cash flow. However, Chad noticed that because of the seasonal nature of the purchases of all of the products, especially award jackets (see Exhibit 5-5), the need for direct labor hours fluctuated widely from one month to the next (see Exhibit 5-13). Even though Chad is able to hire workers as needed, he is concerned that eventually he won't be able to find skilled workers unless they are promised a more consistent schedule. For C&C Sports, labor and sewing machines are constrained resources. The company can produce as many of their products as they have people to make them.

Chad gathered the following unit sales and cost information about each product.

	Pants	Jerseys	Jackets
Sales price	$12.00	$14.80	$125.00
Direct materials	$4.47	$6.85	$44.72
Direct labor	2.40	1.92	14.40
Variable overhead	1.32	1.05	7.92
Fixed overhead	1.68	1.35	10.08
Total cost	$9.87	$11.17	$77.12
Gross profit	$2.13	$3.63	$47.88
Direct labor hours	.25	.20	1.50

Claire Elliot, vice president for finance and administration, reminded him that a commission of 5% of the sales price and shipping costs of $0.40 per item should also be considered when analyzing different strategies.

Required

a. Calculate the contribution margin per unit for each product.
b. Calculate the contribution margin per direct labor hour for each product.
c. If demand wasn't an issue, what preference order should be given to producing each of the products? Be sure to consider what you learned in Chapter 7 about how jackets consume activities.
d. If the sales mix continues as budgeted in 2014—200,000 pants, 70,000 jerseys, and 18,000 jackets—how many direct labor hours will be needed to produce these units? If C&C Sports chose to spread out production evenly throughout the year, how many direct labor hours would be required each week, assuming the company operates all 52 weeks per year?
e. How many employees would be needed if operations ran two 8-hour shifts per day, 5 days per week (round up to the nearest whole number)? How many sewing machines would be needed?
f. Assume that the sales team is able to increase jersey sales to 73,500 per year. What is the impact on total contribution margin if jerseys are made instead of pants? Instead of jackets? Would it be worthwhile to try to hire additional workers?

CASES

8-32 Identifying relevant costs and decision making (LO 1) It had been a quiet Monday morning for Anna Hogue, senior project manager at Flagstone Consulting. Everything seemed to be falling into place for the company's first conference, "Healthcare Management in the New Millenium," scheduled for October 11 and 12 in Boston. Then Ethan Tang, the staff consultant in charge of registration, stuck his head in the door.

"Anna," said Ethan, "I think we may have a problem with the conference. Only 15 people have registered. Our marketing consultants told us to expect at least a 3% registration rate from our direct mail campaign. Based on the 5,000 conference fliers we mailed, do you think another 135 people will register in the next three weeks?" Anna and Ethan had worked together to develop a budget for the conference, as follows. They had budgeted for registration response rates of 2%, 3%, and 4%, but a response rate of 0.3% was far outside their expectations.

	2% Response Rate		3% Response Rate		4% Response Rate	
	Total	Per Attendee	Total	Per Attendee	Total	Per Attendee
Registration fee income	$ 59,500	$595	$ 89,250	$595	$ 119,000	$595
Expenses						
Meals	12,500	$125	18,750	$125	25,000	$125
Conference materials	4,500	45	6,750	45	9,000	45
Direct mail advertising	4,500		4,500		4,500	
Meeting room rental	3,500		3,500		3,500	
Equipment rental	500		500		500	
Speaker fees:						
Newton	600		600		600	
Smith	2,000		2,000		2,000	
Townsley[a]	4,000		4,000		4,000	
Speaker travel:						
Newton	200		200		200	
Smith	1,200		1,200		1,200	
Townsley	1,000		1,000		1,000	
Compton[b]	200		200		200	
Total expenses	34,700		43,200		51,700	
Net income	$ 24,800		$ 46,050		$ 67,300	

[a]Townsley required a $1,000 deposit upon confirmation of the original conference date. The remaining $3,000 was due upon her arrival at the conference. In the event of cancellation, the $1,000 deposit was nonrefundable.

[b]Compton has agreed to speak for free.

Anna thought for a second, and then replied, "Ethan, based on what the marketing firm told us, at least 75% of all registrations are received a month before the conference. This response has me a bit worried. If we need to cancel the conference, we must do it before Thursday. Otherwise, it will be too late." Anna and Ethan called a couple of contacts at other organizations, who related similar experiences with low preconference registration. They indicated that medical professionals often wait until the last minute to register and that in some instances, conferences had been rescheduled and re-advertised to increase registration.

Anna and Ethan decided they needed more information before they could make a final decision on the fate of the conference. Rescheduling it would require them to confirm the new dates with the speakers. Conference facilities would also need to be secured for the new dates. Fortunately, the conference materials had not been sent to the printer yet, so the printed materials would not become obsolete. Anna and Ethan decided that if the conference were rescheduled, Flagstone would offer a reduced registration fee of $525 to companies that sent more than one person.

Anna called some of the Boston-area professionals who had expressed interest in the conference but had not registered yet. Some of them indicated that they had never received the registration mailing. After contacting the marketing firm about the matter, Anna learned that there had indeed been problems with the mailing. The marketing firm had subcontracted the mailing to a second firm, which could not verify that all the materials had been mailed. Anna wondered how many other prospects had not received the mailing.

Next, Anna arranged a conference call with all the speakers, to explain what was going on. They agreed that the mailing problem could have contributed to the low registration. All the speakers were available on December 8 and 9, and were willing to change their schedules to accommodate Flagstone if the firm chose to reschedule the conference. Steve Smith indicated that he had already purchased a nonrefundable airline ticket for $800. If the conference were rescheduled, he would incur an additional $100 charge to change the flight. William Townsley indicated that he was already scheduled to be in Boston on December 7, so Flagstone would not have to cover his travel expenses if the conference were rescheduled.

Ethan called the University Parks Inn to discuss the facilities contract. Although Flagstone had made no payments to the hotel yet, the special events coordinator reminded Ethan of two points in the contract:

1. A cancellation fee of $10,000 would need to be paid if the conference were canceled at this late date. However, the inn would agree to waive the cancellation fee if the conference were rescheduled within four months of the original date.
2. Flagstone had guaranteed a minimum of 40 guest rooms. If conference attendees booked fewer rooms, Flagstone would have to pay an additional $5,000 for the meeting room rental.

Ethan also contacted the marketing firm about doing additional mailings. In light of the problems with the earlier mailing, the marketing firm offered to do two additional mailings for a total of $1,500. They also agreed to expand the mailing list to include several other professional organizations, as well as students at medical and nursing schools in the area. The firm estimated the new mailings would reach 6,500 people and should result in a 2% registration rate. Of that 2%, 10% were expected to qualify for the reduced registration fee.

Required

a. What alternatives are available to Anna and Ethan with regard to holding the conference?
b. Prepare pro-forma income statements for each of the alternatives you identified in question (a).
c. Adjust the statements in part (b) by eliminating the unavoidable costs from the calculation to show only the relevant income/loss from each option.
d. What are the pros and cons of holding the conference as scheduled?
e. What are the pros and cons of canceling the conference?
f. What are the pros and cons of rescheduling the conference?
g. How should Flagstone view this conference—in the short term or in the long term?

8-33 Special order pricing, outsourcing, eliminating operations (LO 2, 3, 5)

Whirlwind Industries is a multiproduct company with several manufacturing plants. The Brownwood Plant manufactures and distributes two carpet cleaning products, Household and Commercial, under the Karpet Kleen label. The forecasted operating results for the first six months of the year are presented in the following statement.

Karpet Kleen—Brownwood Plant
Forecasted Result of Operations
For the six months ended June 30
(in thousands)

	Household	Commercial	Total
Units	100	100	200
Sales revenue	$2,000	$3,000	$5,000
Cost of goods sold	1,600	1,900	3,500
Gross profit	$ 400	$1,100	$1,500
Selling & administrative expenses			
Variable	$ 400	$ 700	$1,100
Fixed[a]	240	360	600
Total selling & administrative expenses	$ 640	$1,060	$1,700
Income (loss) before taxes	$ (240)	$ 40	$ (200)

[a]Fixed selling & administrative expenses are allocated between the two products on the basis of relative sales dollars. These expenses are avoidable only if the entire plant is closed.

The product costs per unit are as follows:

	Household	Commercial
Direct materials	$ 7	$ 8
Direct labor	4	4
Variable manufacturing overhead	1	2
Fixed manufacturing overhead	4	5
Total product cost	$16	$19

Each product is manufactured on a separate production line. Normal manufacturing capacity is 200,000 cases of each product per year. However, the plant is capable of producing 250,000 cases of the Household product and 350,000 cases of the Commercial product per year. Capacity levels assume an even flow of production throughout the year, so that the maximum capacity for the second half of the year is 125,000 cases of Household and 175,000 of Commercial cases.

The following schedule reflects the top management's consensus regarding the price/volume alternatives for Karpet Kleen products in the second six months of the year. These are essentially the same alternatives management faced during the first six months of the year.

Household		Commercial	
Alternative Prices (per Unit)	Unit Sales Volume	Alternative Prices (per Unit)	Unit Sales Volume
$18	120,000	$25	175,000
20	100,000	27	140,000
21	90,000	30	100,000
22	80,000	32	55,000
23	50,000	35	35,000

Top management believes the company's loss for the first six months of the year reflects a tight profit margin caused by intense competition. Management also believes that many companies will be forced out of this market by the next year and that long-term profits should improve.

Other Information

- Fixed manufacturing overhead per unit is based on normal manufacturing capacity.
- Depreciation constitutes 50% of the fixed manufacturing overhead cost of each product and is unavoidable.
- The remaining fixed manufacturing overhead expenses arise from factory personnel assigned to particular products.
- Variable selling and administrative expenses are $4 and $7 per unit, respectively, for the Household and Commercial products.

Required

a. What unit selling price should Whirlwind Industries assign to each of the Karpet Kleen products to maximize net income for the second six months of the year? Support your answers with calculations.

b. Based on the unit prices you have chosen in part (a), what is the company's expected income before taxes for the second six months of the year? Support your answer with an income statement prepared in the contribution margin format. Show the contribution margin and the segment margin for each product.

c. Based on the unit prices you have chosen in part (a), should the Household product be dropped for the second six months of the year? Support your answer.

d. Management has received a special order from CleanMe Corporation for 80,000 cases of the Commercial product at a price of $20 per case. No sales commission would need to be paid (sales commissions are normally $3.20 per case). Should they accept this order? Support your answer with calculations and comment on the qualitative considerations.

e. MakeIt Corporation has offered to make Karpet Kleen's Household product for $13 per case. Karpet Kleen would still sell the product to its customers. The company could use its idle resources to make a new Extra Strength product. Management believes the company could sell 45,000 cases of this new product for $40 per case; variable selling and administrative expenses would be $7 per case. They expect that introducing this product will reduce current unit sales of the Commercial product by 10%. What is the maximum variable cost per unit of the Extra Strength product that would make this proposition worthwhile? Support your answer with calculations and comment on the qualitative considerations.

f. Without considering your answers to previous questions, assume that the optimum price/volume alternatives for the second six months of the year were a selling price of $23 and a volume of 50,000 cases for the Household product, and a selling price of $35 and volume of 35,000 cases for the Commercial product. What was the company's expected income before taxes? Prepare an income statement in contribution margin format.

g. Without considering your answers to previous questions, assume that the optimum price/volume alternatives for the second six months of the year were a selling price of $23 and a volume of 50,000 cases for the Household product, and a selling price of $35 and volume of 35,000 cases for the Commercial product. Should Whirlwind Industries consider closing down its operations to minimize its losses? Support your answer with appropriate calculations and discuss the qualitative factors that should be considered.

8-34 Ethics and Outsourcing (LO 3) Wilson Owen manages administrative operations for a major medical center in Houston, Texas. In response to the rising cost of health care, he is always looking for ways to save money. In fact, part of his annual compensation is a 5% bonus for all the documented continuing cost savings he generates during the year.

Wilson recently began discussions with a firm in India to provide transcription services for the medical center. Doctors would dictate their notes from patient exams, and their recordings would be transferred to the Indian company via the Internet. There, clerks would transcribe the notes into the medical records system. The system is expected to save the medical center $500,000 each year.

When Wilson presented the idea to the practice advisory committee, questions arose regarding privacy issues. Many of the committee members did not believe that transferring patients' medical records over the Internet was a prudent business practice, much less sending them all the way to India and back. They were also concerned that the transcriptionists might not capture some of the subtleties of the English language. After heated discussion, one committee member suggested that Wilson was pursuing the arrangement solely for the $25,000 bonus. The meeting ended with the committee voting against outsourcing the records.

Wilson is torn about what to do. He believes he is obligated to provide the most cost-efficient operations possible, control operating costs, and generate higher returns for investors. But he also needs to respect the advisory committee's point of view, even though its role is only an advisory one—its actions are not binding.

Required

How should Wilson proceed? Should he act in the best interest of the shareholders or follow the advisory committee's direction? Why? As a member of the IMA, can Wilson find any direction in the organization's Statement of Ethical Professional Practice? (See Exhibit 1-8.)

ANALYTICS PROBLEM

8-35 Evaluating an Outsourcing Decision (LO3) Several years ago, Roberson Robotics outsourced component BF-365, a key component of many of its products. At the time, CFO Sam Summers concluded that outsourcing was the correct decision, but she decided to revisit that decision after overhearing some conversations on the factory floor and in the cafeteria. Based on these conversations, she has gathered information about the materials quantity variance for the part, as well as on-time delivery information of the part from the supplier and on-time delivery of the finished products to customers. Roberson Robotics uses a just-in-time inventory system, so it receives multiple shipments of BF-365 each day.

Summers has asked you to examine the data and provide insights about the continued desirability of outsourcing component BF-365.

Required

a. Prepare a scatterplot of late deliveries from the supplier and a scatterplot of missed customer delivery dates. What do you learn from these graphs?
b. Calculate the percentage of late deliveries from the supplier and the percentage of missed customer delivery dates.
c. Calculate the proportion of unfavorable materials quantity variances. How has the proportion of favorable to unfavorable variances changed over time? What do you infer about the quality of the outsourced component BF-365?
d. What other information would you like to examine before providing your insights about the outsourcing decision to Summers?

The Excel data files for answering this problem can be found in WileyPLUS.

ENDNOTES

1. For more information about ADP, Inc. visit the company's website at http://www.adp.com/.
2. Susan Carey, "United to Outsource Jobs at 12 Airports," *The Wall Street Journal*, July 8, 2014.
3. James R. Hagerty, "Once Made in China: Jobs Trickle Back to U.S. Plants," *The Wall Street Journal*, May 22, 2012; James R. Hagerty, "A Toy Maker Comes Home to the U.S.A.," *The Wall Street Journal*, March 11, 2013.
4. For more information on Goldratt's Theory of Constraints, see his book *Theory of Constraints* (North River Press, 1999) or Goldratt and Cox's *The Goal*, 3rd ed. (North River Press, 2004).

© jsnyderdesign/iStockphoto

CAPITAL BUDGETING

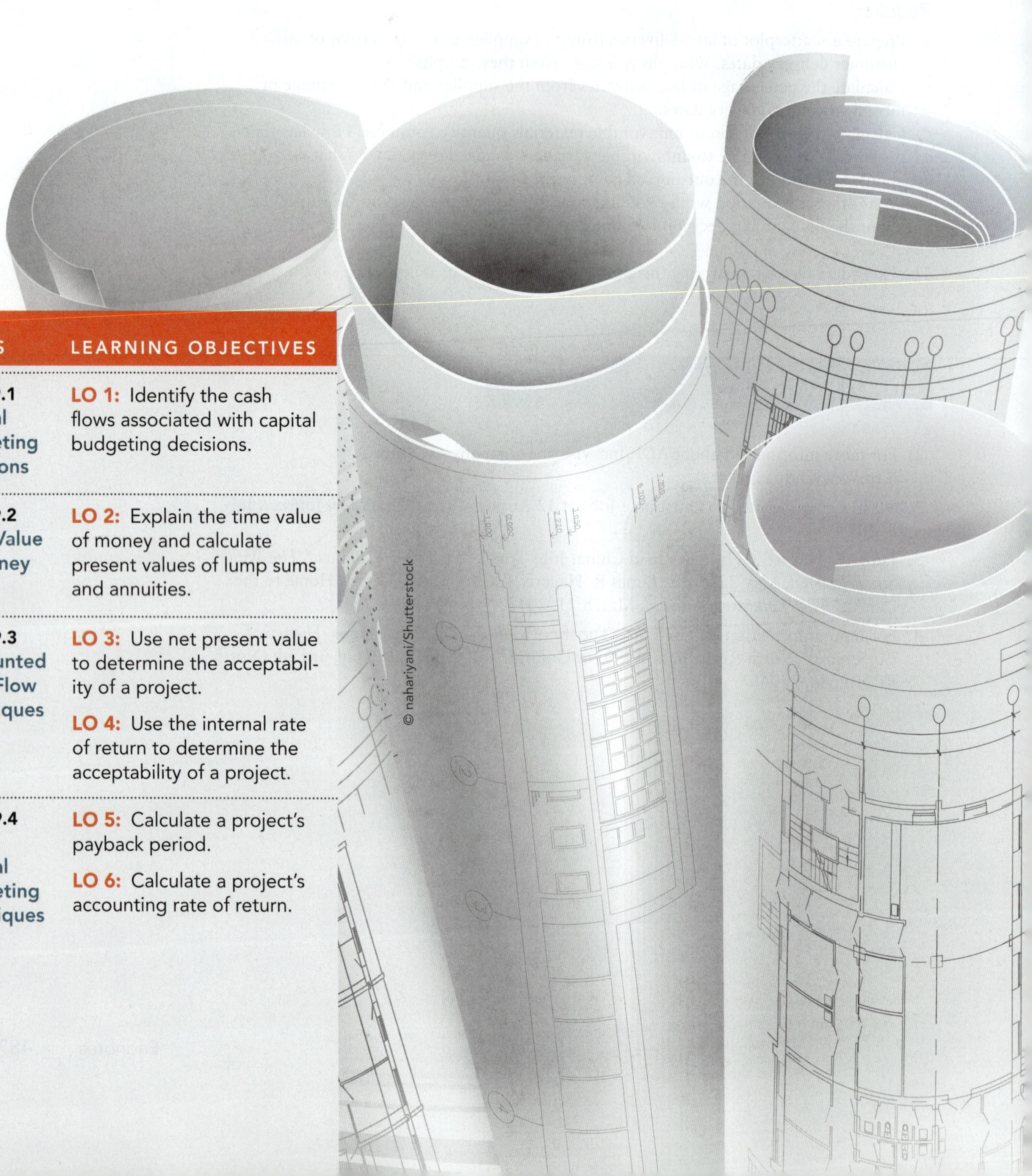

© nahariyani/Shutterstock

UNITS	LEARNING OBJECTIVES
UNIT 9.1 Capital Budgeting Decisions	**LO 1:** Identify the cash flows associated with capital budgeting decisions.
UNIT 9.2 Time Value of Money	**LO 2:** Explain the time value of money and calculate present values of lump sums and annuities.
UNIT 9.3 Discounted Cash Flow Techniques	**LO 3:** Use net present value to determine the acceptability of a project. **LO 4:** Use the internal rate of return to determine the acceptability of a project.
UNIT 9.4 Other Capital Budgeting Techniques	**LO 5:** Calculate a project's payback period. **LO 6:** Calculate a project's accounting rate of return.

Business Decision and Context

© ConnieTBallash/iStockphoto

Chad Davis, C&C's vice president for operations, and **Jonathan Smith, C&C's vice president for marketing**, were looking over the company's results from 2017. "We've got to find a way to increase our net income," Chad stated. "I don't see cost reductions alone generating the level of growth we want. The only way we can achieve a sizeable increase is from new sales. What ideas do you have, Jonathan?"

> "I don't see cost reductions alone generating the level of growth we want. The only way we can achieve a sizeable increase is from new sales. What ideas do you have?"

"I've looked at our sales estimates for baseball jerseys and pants, as well as for award jackets," Jonathan replied, "and the market doesn't appear to be able to support significant growth prospects in those product lines. I've been trying to come up with something new and different, but I don't have any ideas."

Chad pulled off his baseball cap and scratched his head. As he looked at the cap, it suddenly hit him. "I can't believe we have been so blind, Jonathan. The answer is right here on my head—every player in a C&C baseball uniform needs a cap, so why not make caps?"

Jonathan was floored. "Why didn't I think of that before? It's such a natural extension of the company's production and distribution expertise."

"We'll need to buy some new equipment," Chad said. "And since we are a bit tight on space, we may need a larger facility to house the equipment and inventory. I'll start gathering information about the cost of acquiring these assets." But Chad wondered if he needed any other information before deciding to plunge into a new product line. And once he had all the information, how would he go about making an informed decision?

SUPPLY CHAIN KEY PLAYERS

- END CUSTOMER
- UNIVERSAL SPORTS EXCHANGE
- **C&C SPORTS**
  - Vice President for Operations: Chad Davis
  - Vice President for Marketing: Jonathan Smith
- DURABLE ZIPPER COMPANY
- BRADLEY TEXTILE MILLS
- CENTEX YARNS
- NEFF FIBER MANUFACTURING
- BRUIN POLYMERS, INC.

Watch the Holland America Line video in WileyPLUS to learn more about capital budgeting in the real world.

UNIT 9.1

Capital Budgeting Decisions

GUIDED UNIT PREPARATION

Answering the following questions while you read this unit will guide your understanding of the key concepts found in the unit. The questions are linked to the learning objectives presented at the beginning of the chapter.

LO 1

1. What are capital assets?
2. What is the difference between a screening decision and a preference decision? Give an example of each.
3. What is the difference between return of investment and return on investment?

"Verizon, Partners to Build Trans-Pacific Cable to China; Catering to Multinationals"; "Hong Kong Airport to Build Ferry Terminal"; "Continental Orders Boeing Planes"; "Toyota Has Multi-Year Plan to Elevate Capital Spending"; "Refiners Rush to Build Plants Abroad"; "Hospital Building Boom Sparks Worry Cities Will Be Left Behind"—these headlines are all drawn from *The Wall Street Journal*. What do they have in common? In each case, an organization is investing in assets that are expected to generate financial returns for several years.

Capital budgeting is the process of evaluating an organization's investment in long-term assets. It differs from operational budgeting in terms of its time horizon. When completing an operating budget (see Chapter 5), managers rarely look more than a year into the future. In capital budgeting, however, managers regularly assess projects that run 5, 10, or even 20 or more years into the future.

Investing in Capital Assets

Recall from your earlier accounting studies that an asset is an economic resource that will generate future economic benefits. Cash, accounts receivable, and inventory are common examples. In this chapter we'll focus on **capital assets**, those assets that are expected to provide economic benefits for several years. On a company's balance sheet, these assets are typically shown under property, plant, and equipment. With the exception of land, they are **depreciable assets**; you may also hear people refer to them as **long-lived assets**. Regardless of what you call them, these assets are used by the organization to build products or deliver services.

Look back at C&C's 2016 balance sheet (Exhibit T1-4 on page 38), on which the company reported $532,858 in machinery and equipment. These are the company's capital assets. What future economic benefit do these capital assets provide? They provide the production capacity to make the baseball jerseys, baseball pants, and award jackets that the company will sell to generate revenue, and ultimately income.

THINK ABOUT IT 9.1

What specific capital assets might each of the following companies acquire?

Crate & Barrel (retailer of home products)

Beaver Creek ski resort

Amazon.com

Nike

Mayo Clinic (medical group)

As with any investment, organizations invest in capital assets with the expectation that they will generate a future return. According to its annual report, Hormel Foods spent over $144,000,000 acquiring capital assets in 2015. A portion of that expenditure was for building a new production facility in Jiaxing, China. Why did Hormel Foods spend so much money to acquire these assets? Managers were investing for the return the assets were expected to generate in the form of increased sales and income.

Two types of return can be expected from investment in a long-term asset: return *of* investment and return *on* investment. **Return of investment** means recouping the original investment—that is, getting your money back. **Return on investment** is any return you receive over and above the original investment. Let's look at an example that illustrates these concepts.

Suppose that on June 4, 2010, you purchased one share of ExxonMobil Corporation stock for $60.[1] Your investment would be the $60 you paid for the stock. Now assume that you sold the stock for $84 on April 12, 2016. The first $60 of the $84 you received for the sale on April 12 would be a return *of* your investment; that is, you were getting back what you originally invested. The remaining $24 ($84 − $60 return of investment) would be your return *on* investment, the amount you earned above and beyond your initial investment.

THINK ABOUT IT 9.2

You may have heard someone talk about "losing money" on an investment. Explain this phrase using the concepts of return on investment and return of investment.

Making Capital Budgeting Decisions

Capital budgeting decisions range from a few thousand dollars to the $4 billion overhaul of New York City's La Guardia airport announced in 2015.[2] Because even a project of only a few thousand dollars can be a significant investment for a small company, capital budgeting decisions are generally subject to a thorough review process. Many large companies have capital budgeting committees that review all capital project requests; large projects may require approval by executive management. Why the extensive review and approval process? These investments are made for the long term and will likely have a significant impact on the company's future financial health.

Screening Decisions versus Preference Decisions

Managers throughout an organization may submit capital projects for review and approval. Since organizations do not have an unlimited pool of money with which to fund capital requests, decisions must be made about which projects to fund and which to postpone or reject. Managers use the capital budgeting techniques explained in later units of this chapter to make two types of capital budgeting decisions, screening decisions and preference decisions. Exhibit 9-1 illustrates these two decision types.

EXHIBIT 9-1

Screening decisions versus preference decisions.

Screening Decision

Projects must exceed the required minimum rate of return, or "hurdle rate"

Preference Decision

Projects are ranked and accepted based on their expected return, with the highest ranked projects receiving preference

In a **screening decision**, a proposed project is compared to a performance benchmark to determine whether the project should be considered further. Organizations may set a minimum required return on investment, a minimum number of years in which the project must return the original investment, or both. As projects are proposed, they are compared to the benchmark. If a project's expected outcome is greater than or equal to the benchmark, it becomes a candidate for funding; otherwise, it is dismissed from further consideration. The goal of the screening decision is to narrow the list of capital proposals to include only those that are expected to bring the desired level of return. You can think of the screening decision in terms of a proposed project jumping over a hurdle. In fact, the minimum required rate of return is often referred to as the **hurdle rate**.

Once all the projects have been subjected to a screening decision, the acceptable projects must compete against one another for the available capital funds. In a **preference decision**, managers determine which projects will actually receive funds by rank-ordering them based on selected criteria, both financial and nonfinancial. Then they fund the projects in order, beginning with the most desirable one and moving down the list until all available funds have been committed. This decision is a lot like the end of a race in which participants place based on their final time. While this task may sound easy, we will see later that the more desirable projects aren't always obvious.

While much of the analysis of capital spending projects focuses on quantitative factors, qualitative issues are also important. Some projects that look like bad decisions based solely on the numbers are accepted because they are critical to the organization's strategic goals. A recent report found that small and

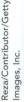

REALITY CHECK—*How much capital are we talking about?*

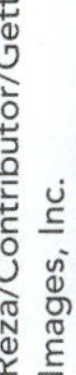

Companies invest a lot of capital in their property, plant, and equipment. But how much is a lot? ConocoPhillips, one of the world's largest oil and gas exploration and production companies, spent $10.1 billion on capital projects in 2015. Retail giant Walmart spent $11.5 billion on its capital projects in fiscal 2016. And Apple spent $11.2 billion in 2015, with a plan to increase that amount to $15 billion in 2016.

If these three companies are spending this much, how much are other companies spending? The *2014 Annual Capital Expenditures Survey* published by the U.S. Census Bureau reports total capital spending in the United States as $1,602 billion in 2014.

ConocoPhillips, spent $10.1 billion on capital projects in 2015.

Why are companies spending so much money on these projects? Automotive design and production companies and modern machine shop plants might provide insight. According to Gardner Research's *2012 Capital Spending Survey & Forecast*, 52.7% of the companies in these two fields are spending to increase capacity, while 47.7% are spending to reduce costs. Proof that the old saying "you have to spend money to make money" is true.

Sources: Apple 2015 Form 10-K; ConocoPhillips 2015 Annual Report; Gardner Research, "2012 Capital Spending Survey & Forecast," http://www.gardnerweb.com/cdn/cms/uploadedFiles/2011%20CAP%20SPENDING%20SINGLE%20PAGES%20%281%29%281%29.pdf (accessed January 28, 2013); U.S. Census Bureau, "Annual Capital Expenditures 2014" https://www.census.gov/programs-surveys/aces/news-updates/updates/2016-release.html (accessed April 29, 2016); Walmart 2016 Annual Report.

medium-sized manufacturers tend to focus on qualitative rather than quantitative factors in making their capital budgeting decisions. As CEO Karla Aaron of Hialeah Metal Spinning explains, "We buy a new machine when we see a new process capability we need. We think if we buy the machine it will open the door to new possibilities, allow us to buy into a new market niche."[3] While we don't advocate ignoring the financial impact of these decisions, neither do we believe qualitative factors should be ignored.

Cash Flow Identification

To prepare for the first step in project approval, managers need to identify the expected financial payoff from the project. Unlike most accounting decisions, which focus on income, most capital budgeting decisions focus on cash flow. For example, in evaluating the purchase of a machine, the financial impact of the purchase is the price paid for the machine, not the depreciation expense of the machine over time. In the long run, the two amounts are essentially the same, but the timing is different. Identifying the amount and timing of the cash flows associated with a project is a critical step in the capital budgeting process.

Let's look at the information Chad Davis has gathered to identify the cash flows associated with the project introduced in the chapter-opening scenario. While investigating baseball cap manufacturing, Chad discovered the TopCap system, a modular machining system that would allow C&C Sports to manufacture up to 1,000 baseball caps per day per shift. The system costs $45,265 and has a useful life of 10 years. In addition to the purchase price, Chad estimates that C&C would incur an additional $5,000 in shipping and installation costs, for

WATCH OUT!

Don't make the mistake of including depreciation as a cash flow. Depreciation is a non-cash expense.

a total acquisition cost of $50,265. The TopCap system would also require three employees per eight-hour shift to produce caps at the rate of 1,000 caps per day. Direct materials for the hats (crowns, closure fasteners, sweatbands, and visors) would run $2.00 per hat, and an additional $0.15 per hat would be incurred in variable overhead (indirect materials). C&C would incur fixed expenses of $7,000 per year for utilities, insurance, and inventory storage. These fixed expenses **do not** include depreciation, since depreciation is not a cash flow. Finally, variable selling expenses of $0.05 per hat would be required to ship the hats to customers.[4]

Based on an estimated sales volume of 250,000 hats per year at a sales price of $2.50 per hat, Chad has calculated the cash flows related to the purchase and annual operation of the TopCap system; see Exhibit 9-2. In addition to estimating the amount of the cash flows, Chad has also estimated their timing by identifying the year in which each cash flow would occur (year 0 is the time of purchase).

EXHIBIT 9-2

Cash flows from purchase of the TopCap system.

Cash Flow	Amount	Timing
Cash Inflows		
Sales revenue (250,000 caps × $2.50 per cap)	$625,000	Years 1–10
Cash Outflows		
Purchase and installation of TopCap system	$ 50,265	Year 0
Purchase of direct materials (250,000 caps × $2.00 per cap)	$500,000	Years 1–10
Direct labor (3 employees × 8 hours/day × $9.60/hour × 5 days/week × 50 weeks/year)	$ 57,600	Years 1–10
Variable overhead (250,000 caps × $0.15 per cap)	$ 37,500	Years 1–10
Variable selling expense (250,000 caps × $0.05 per cap)	$ 12,500	Years 1–10
Fixed expenses	$ 7,000	Years 1–10

WATCH OUT!

The original purchase price of an old machine (or other asset) that is being replaced is never included in capital budgeting decisions. Because the asset was purchased and paid for in a prior period, no future cash flows are associated with its purchase.

While the system C&C is considering would provide new production capacity, many of the capital projects companies consider are meant to replace or upgrade their existing capacity. At some point, for instance, C&C Sports will need to replace its sewing machines. If the old sewing machines can be sold after they are replaced, then the cash received from their sale will become a cash inflow for the replacement project. The sales price is referred to as the salvage value of the old equipment, and the related cash flow generally occurs in year 0.

Another type of cash flow occurs when new equipment generates cost savings. These cost savings are considered cash inflows in the period in which they occur. Let's think again about the possible replacement of C&C's sewing machines. Assume that the existing machines are scheduled for a $25,000 maintenance overhaul two years from now. If C&C decided to replace them today, the company would avoid the overhaul, saving $25,000. So managers should include a $25,000 cash inflow in year 2 in deciding whether to replace the machines. Other examples of potential cost savings are reduced direct labor costs and reduced direct materials costs. Any cost savings generated by a capital project should be included in the analysis as a cash inflow.

Another potential cash inflow comes from the estimated salvage value of the new equipment. This cash inflow would occur at the end of the new equipment's useful life. Suppose the new sewing machines just discussed could be sold for a total of $1,000 at the end of their eight-year life. Managers should include a $1,000 cash inflow in year 8 for the salvage value of the new equipment.

Post-Implementation Audit

After a project has successfully passed through the screening, preference, and funding decisions, the analysis isn't over. Once a project has begun, a post-implementation audit should be done to compare the actual cash flows to the original estimates. Significant variances should be investigated and, if necessary, corrective action should be taken to get the project back on track. In the worst cases, the project should be aborted to prevent future losses. Information that is gathered during the post-implementation audit should also be used to improve the cash flow estimates in future capital budgeting requests.

UNIT 9.1 REVIEW

KEY TERMS

Capital asset p. 490	Hurdle rate p. 492	Return of investment p. 491
Capital budgeting p. 490	Long-lived asset p. 490	Return on investment p. 491
Depreciable asset p. 490	Preference decision p. 492	Screening decision p. 492

PRACTICE QUESTIONS

1. LO 1 Finch, Taylor and Associates, a prominent advertising firm, has identified three color printers that can print layout drafts for clients. When the firm selects the best printer to purchase, it will be making a preference decision. True or False?

2. LO 1 Lane Lighting is considering replacing its aging telephone system with a state-of-the-art voice-activated system. The new system is expected to save the company $2,000 per month by eliminating the current operator's salary. With a cost of $100,000 and a ten-year life, the system will be depreciated at a rate of $10,000 per year. The $10,000 in depreciation will be included in the project's cash flow analysis. True or False?

3. LO 1 Martin Map Manufacturing is exploring the purchase of a new piece of equipment. If the equipment is purchased, the company will avoid a $10,000 overhaul of an existing piece of equipment that will be retired when the new equipment is installed. In determining the cash flows associated with the new equipment, the $10,000 will be

   a. considered a cash outflow in the year it would have occurred.

   b. considered a cash inflow in the year it would have occurred.

   c. considered a cash inflow at the time the new equipment is purchased.

   d. ignored in the cash flow analysis.

4. LO 1 Martin Map Manufacturing is exploring the purchase of a new piece of equipment. If the equipment is purchased, the company will incur an additional $12,000 in annual depreciation expense for the next ten years. In determining the cash flows associated with the new equipment, the additional depreciation will be

   a. considered a cash outflow in the year of occurrence.

   b. considered a cash inflow in the year of occurrence.

   c. considered a cash inflow at the time the new equipment is purchased.

   d. ignored in the cash flow analysis.

5. LO 1 Martin Map Manufacturing is exploring the purchase of a new piece of equipment. If the equipment is purchased, the company will pay $5,000 to upgrade the production line's electrical wiring. In determining the cash flows associated with the new equipment, the $5,000 payment will be

   a. considered a cash inflow in the year of occurrence.

   b. considered a cash inflow at the time the new equipment is purchased.

   c. considered a cash outflow at the time the new equipment is purchased.

   d. ignored in the cash flow analysis.

UNIT 9.1 PRACTICE EXERCISE

Forbes Festivities, a special events planner, uses a ten-year-old van to deliver decorations and supplies to customers. The company paid $18,000 for the van, which costs $2,000 per month to operate. In two years the van will need an extensive overhaul costing $5,000. Colin Forbes, the company's owner, is considering the purchase of a new delivery truck to replace the van. The truck he is looking at will cost $25,000 and has a useful life of ten years. Based on estimated gas mileage and insurance, Colin calculates that the truck will cost $1,200 per month to operate. It will require a $2,000 overhaul in year 8. Based on current blue-book values, Colin could sell the old van today for $4,000. He estimates that he will be able to sell the new truck for $7,000 at the end of its ten-year life.

Required

Identify the amount and timing of the cash flows relevant to Colin's decision to replace the delivery van.

SELECTED UNIT 9.1 ANSWERS

Think About It 9.1

Note: These are only some of the possible capital assets; you may have identified others.

- Crate & Barrel—store fixtures, warehouse, delivery vehicles
- Beaver Creek ski resort—ski lifts, snow-making machines, snow plows, shuttle buses
- Amazon.com—warehouse, computers, forklifts
- Nike—manufacturing equipment, research and development labs and equipment, warehouse
- Mayo Clinic—hospital buildings, hospital beds, X-ray machines, lab equipment

Think About It 9.2

A stock that was purchased for $25 per share but has fallen to a price of $20 per share has lost value. If the shareholder sells the stock at the lower value, then the holder will recognize a loss on the investment (the opposite of a return of investment). Even if the holder doesn't sell the stock, he will consider it to be in a loss position until its price returns to the $25 mark.

Similarly, if an investor purchases a five-year certificate of deposit (CD) at a 5% interest rate and CD rates rise to 5.25%, the investor may speak of a loss—"I'm losing money *on* my investment." The investor isn't really losing money, however; he just isn't earning the rate he could have if he had waited to purchase the CD. One of the risks of investing in long-term assets is that a better opportunity may arise later. But if you keep waiting for that better opportunity, you will never invest your money.

Practice Questions

1. True
2. False
3. B
4. D
5. C

Unit 9.1 Practice Exercise

	Cash Flow	Time Period
Purchase price	$(25,000)	0
Operating cost savings		
($2,000 old − $1,200 new) × 12 months	$ 9,600	1–10
Overhaul avoided on old van	$ 5,000	2
Overhaul on new van	$ (2,000)	8
Salvage of old van	$ 4,000	0
Salvage of new truck	$ 7,000	10

Time Value of Money

GUIDED UNIT PREPARATION

Answering the following questions while you read this unit will guide your understanding of the key concepts found in the unit. The questions are linked to the learning objectives presented at the beginning of the chapter.

LO 2

1. What is present value?
2. What three factors does present value depend on?
3. What is an annuity?

Long-term investment decisions, including capital budgeting decisions, involve outflows of cash in some periods and inflows of cash in others. How do managers decide whether the inflows justify the outflows? Answering this question isn't as straightforward as adding up the inflows and subtracting the outflows because of the time value of money—one dollar today is worth more than one dollar in the future. Why? Because a dollar today can be invested to earn interest, which will make it worth more than a dollar in the future. We need to compare the cash flows not just in terms of their amounts, but in terms of when they occur. One way to do so is to determine the present value—that is, the value today—of the dollars to be paid or received in the future.

Present Value of $1

Assume you have just been offered a business opportunity that will pay you either $20,000 today or $20,000 in one year. Your investment, whether of time or money, will be the same with either option; you just need to decide which return is better for you. Which one would you choose? If you are like most people, you would choose to receive $20,000 today. But what if the offer were for $20,000 today or $22,000 in one year? The choice between those two options may not be quite as obvious.

Let's look at the first scenario, which illustrates the concept of present value. Why would you choose $20,000 today over $20,000 a year from now? An obvious reason is that you could take the $20,000 you receive today and invest it to earn more money. At a minimum, you could deposit the money in an interest-bearing bank account; if you left it in the account for the entire year, you would have more than $20,000 at the end of the year. In a money market savings account that pays 8% simple interest, for example, you would have $21,600 ($20,000 + [0.08 × $20,000]) at the end of the year. If you could find an investment option that offers a higher rate of return, you would have even more than $21,600. Thus, a dollar received today is worth more than a dollar received at any time in the future because today's investment is expected to earn additional money.

What about the choice between $20,000 today and $22,000 a year from now? To make an appropriate comparison, you need to evaluate how much money each option is worth at the same point in time. Let's assume that you choose the $20,000 and invest it today. The following table summarizes how much money you would have at the end of the year if you invested the $20,000 at an 8%, 10%, or 12% rate of return. If you can only earn an 8% return (or lower), you should take the $22,000 in one year, since $22,000 is greater than the $21,600 you would have after earning 8% interest (all other things held equal). At a 10% rate of return, you would have $22,000 at the end of the year, so you would be indifferent between $20,000 now or $22,000 in one year. When the rate of return is higher than 10%, you will have more than $22,000 at the end of the year; therefore, you should choose to receive the $20,000 today.

Decision: $20,000 Today or $22,000 One Year from Today

Rate of Return	Interest Earned on $20,000 Investment	Value at the End of One Year ($20,000 + Interest)	Preferred Option[5]
8%	$20,000 × 8% = $1,600	$21,600	$22,000 at year end
10%	$20,000 × 10% = $2,000	$22,000	indifferent
12%	$20,000 × 12% = $2,400	$22,400	$20,000 now

This scenario compares *future* values; that is, at 8% per year, $20,000 today is worth $21,600 at the end of one year. To evaluate these same options, we can compare *present* values. Present value comparisons are more helpful when a company is evaluating an investment that will generate multiple inflows and outflows over several periods.

THINK ABOUT IT 9.3

If $20,000 invested today at 8% per year yields $21,600 at the end of one year, then $21,600 received at the end of one year, at an 8% investment rate, is worth $20,000 today. How much is $22,000 received at the end of one year, at 8%, worth today—more or less than $20,000? Does it matter whether you use present or future values when determining your preference between $20,000 now and $22,000 in one year?

The process of determining how much an amount of money to be received in the future is worth today is called **discounting**. The discounted amount is the **present value** of the future amount, which is always smaller than the future value. The interest rate used in these calculations is called the **discount rate**.

Calculating Present Value

To determine the present value of any future amount, you need to know three pieces of information: (1) the future amount to be received, (2) the interest rate, and (3) when the future amount will be received. Armed with this information, you can use a financial calculator or present value tables like the Present Value of $1 Received in *n* Periods table in Appendix 9-1 to calculate the present value of a lump sum to be received in the future. Look at the table and notice that the columns represent different interest rates and the rows represent the number of periods in the future.

Let's assume you are going to receive \$22,000 in five years and you currently invest at a 10% rate of return. To use Appendix 9-1 to calculate the present value of \$22,000 received five years in the future at an interest rate of 10%, look across the period 5 row until you reach the 10% column. There you will find the number 0.6209, called the **present value factor**. To calculate the present value, multiply the \$22,000 to be received in five years by the present value factor. We use $PV_{n,i}$ as a shorthand notation to indicate a present value of a payment to be received in n years at a discount rate of i, so we would indicate this present value as $PV_{5,10\%}$.

Periods	4%	5%	6%	7%	8%	9%	10%	11%	12%	13%	14%	16%	18%	20%
1	0.9615	0.9524	0.9434	0.9346	0.9259	0.9174	0.9091	0.9009	0.8929	0.8850	0.8772	0.8821	0.8475	0.8333
2	0.9246	0.9070	0.8900	0.8734	0.8573	0.8417	0.8264	0.8116	0.7972	0.7831	0.7695	0.7432	0.7182	0.8944
3	0.8890	0.8638	0.8396	0.8163	0.7938	0.7722	0.7513	0.7312	0.7118	0.6931	0.6750	0.6407	0.6086	0.5787
4	0.8548	0.8227	0.7921	0.7629	0.7350	0.7084	0.6830	0.6587	0.6355	0.6133	0.5921	0.5523	0.5158	0.4823
5	0.8219	0.7835	0.7473	0.7130	0.6806	0.6499	0.6209	0.5935	0.5674	0.5428	0.5194	0.4761	0.4371	0.4019

$$
\begin{aligned}
PV_{5,10\%} &= \text{Future value} \times \text{Present value factor} \\
&= \$22{,}000 \times 0.6209 \\
&= \$13{,}659.80
\end{aligned}
$$

We can also think about present value from a slightly different perspective. That is, the present value is the amount you would need to invest today to receive a specific amount at a specific time in the future. In the example just given, if you invested \$13,659.80 today at 10% per year, you would have \$22,000 (rounded) at the end of five years:

Year	Beginning Balance	Annual Interest (Beg. Bal. × 10%)	Ending Balance
1	\$13,659.80	\$1,365.98	\$15,025.78
2	\$15,025.78	\$1,502.58	\$16,528.36
3	\$16,528.36	\$1,652.84	\$18,181.20
4	\$18,181.20	\$1,818.12	\$19,999.32
5	\$19,999.32	\$1,999.93	\$21,999.25

Compound Interest

In the example just given, note that the second year's interest is calculated on \$15,025.78, not on the original \$13,659.80. When the interest from year 1 is *compounded*, or built into, the principal balance, the interest is referred to as **compound interest**. The frequency with which interest is compounded can make a big difference in how fast the principal balance grows. In the example just given, interest was compounded annually. Some investments compound interest more frequently—semiannually, quarterly, or even daily.

What is the present value of \$22,000 received in five years at a 10% return if the interest is compounded semiannually instead of annually? With a few adjustments,

> **WATCH OUT!**
>
> Compounding interest more frequently than annually changes both the number of periods ***and*** the discount rate. The number of years to receive the future amount is *multiplied* by the number of times per year the interest is compounded to arrive at the number of periods for discounting. The annual interest rate is *divided* by the number of times per year the interest will be compounded to arrive at the discount rate.

we can use the same approach. Since the interest will be calculated twice a year, the number of periods changes from 5 to 10. And though the annual interest rate doesn't change, the compounding rate is divided by 2 to yield 5% twice a year.

$$
\begin{aligned}
PV_{10,5} &= \text{Future value} \times \text{Present value factor} \\
&= \$22{,}000 \times 0.6139 \\
&= \$13{,}505.80
\end{aligned}
$$

The present value is $13,505.80—lower than with annual compounding, since the interest will grow at a faster rate.

Discount Rates and Present Value

You may have noticed a relationship between the discount rate and the present value: The two are inversely related. That is, as the discount rate increases, the present value decreases. Why does this relationship hold true? Think about it this way. If you want $22,000 in five years and you can invest your funds at 10%, you will need less money today than if you can invest your funds at only 6%. That's because the amount of interest you earn at 10% is greater than the amount you earn at 6%.

Recall that we calculated the present value of $22,000 received in five years at 10% to be $13,659.80. What is the present value of this same amount if the discount rate is only 6%? The answer is $16,440.60 ($22,000 × 0.7473). So as the discount rate falls from 10% to 6%, the present value amount rises from $13,659.80 to $16,440.60.

Present Value of an Annuity

While some investment opportunities offer future payment of a single amount, or a *lump sum*, other opportunities provide a stream of annual payments. For instance, Lotto Texas® offers jackpot winners the option of receiving 30 annual payments rather than a single amount. Such a stream of equal cash flows received at set time intervals is called an **annuity**. Just as you can calculate the present value of a single future amount, you can calculate the present value of an annuity.

Calculating the Present Value of an Annuity

Let's say that instead of receiving $22,000 at the end of the five years, you will receive $22,000 at the end of each of the next five years. This five-year annuity is the same as five lump-sum payments, so you could calculate five separate present values using the Present Value of $1 table (Appendix 9-1) and then add the five amounts. That is how the Present Value of an Annuity table (Appendix 9-2) was constructed—each individual present value factor was added to determine the present value factor for the annuity. In the excerpt from the Present Value of $1 table presented earlier, for instance, if you add the five individual present value factors in the 10% column, you will get 3.7907—the same factor you will find in the Present Value of an Annuity table for five periods at 10%. To calculate the present value of an annuity, multiply the amount to be received each year by the present value factor. So a $22,000 annuity for five years at 10% would have a present value of $83,395.40 ($22,000 × 3.7907). The following table shows the present value calculation using both approaches.

Lump-Sum	Year	Payment	PV Factor$_{n,10\%}$	Present Value
	1	$22,000	0.9091	$20,000.20
	2	$22,000	0.8264	$18,180.80
	3	$22,000	0.7513	$16,528.60
	4	$22,000	0.6830	$15,026.00
	5	$22,000	0.6209	$13,659.80
	Total		3.7907	$83,395.40
Annuity				
	1–5	$22,000	3.7907	$83,395.40

WATCH OUT!

To determine the present value of an annuity, multiply the annual payment amount, ***not*** the total dollars to be received, by the present value of an annuity factor. Your answer should always be less than the total dollars to be received.

THINK ABOUT IT 9.4

Suppose an advertising campaign costs a company $10,000 for the first three years and $15,000 for years 4 and 5. What kind of cash flows are these, and how would you determine the campaign's present value?

Using Excel® to Calculate Present Values

Spreadsheet packages such as Microsoft Excel® provide specialized functions to calculate the present value of an annuity. Exhibit 9-3 shows how to use Excel's PV function to calculate the present value of the $22,000 five-year annuity. First, insert the PV function into a cell. Then enter the annual interest rate as a decimal—enter 10% as 0.1—in the rate box, the number of periods of the annuity in the Nper box, and the amount of each annuity payment in the Pmt box. Click on the OK box and the present value of the annuity is displayed in the original cell. Alternatively, you can enter the function directly into the cell by typing +PV(0.1, 5, −22000).

WATCH OUT!

If you enter the annuity amount as a positive amount, Excel assumes this is a cash outflow and the present value will be reported as a negative number. If your annuity is a cash inflow, enter the amount as a negative number and the present value will be reported as a positive number.

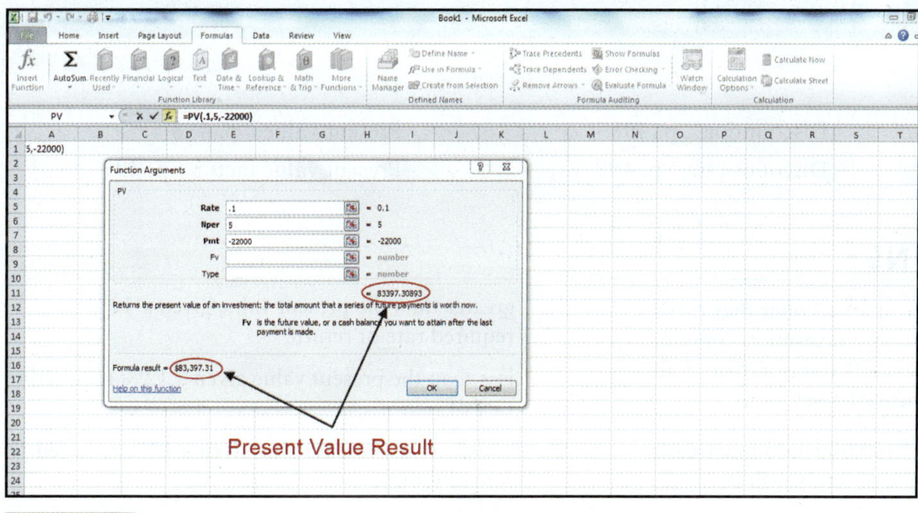

EXHIBIT 9-3 *Using Microsoft Excel's PV function to calculate the present value of an annuity.*

REALITY CHECK—*If you build it, they will stay*

© Blurra/iStockphoto

The world of professional sports is a world of big money, and sometimes this puts team owners at odds with city officials when it comes to stadium updates. Since the Raiders' and Rams' departures from Los Angeles in 1994, leaving the city without an NFL team, 18 different teams have threatened to move to Los Angeles unless their current cities work to build new stadiums. And now the Rams will be returning to Los Angeles after St. Louis failed to come forth with a new stadium to keep the team located there. Two other southern California NFL teams, the San Diego Chargers and the Oakland Raiders, are being courted to join the Rams in the new stadium.

What does it cost to build a stadium? Estimates for the Rams' new 80,000-seat stadium range from $1.86 billion to $3 billion. In an effort to keep the Chargers in San Diego, a new $1.33 billion stadium is being proposed. On a much smaller scale, Washington, D.C., is building a $286.7 million stadium for its D.C. United Major League Soccer team.

A key component in the new stadium proposal is the net present value financial model. Included in the model are annual revenue streams for ticket sales, taxes, parking fees, and other related cash flows. The model calculates the present value of the cash flows and determines a net present value for the stadium project. One plan for the San Diego stadium shows a present value of $1.4 billion for cash inflows over the stadium's 30-year life using a 4% discount rate. Using the same discount rate and a 32-year time horizon, the D.C. United stadium has a net present value of $38 million to the District.

The San Diego stadium shows a present value of $1.4 billion for cash inflows over the stadium's 30-year life.

Sources: Citizens' Stadium Advisory Group, "Site Selection and Financing Plan for a New Multi-Use Stadium in San Diego," May 18, 2015, http://www.voiceofsandiego.org/wp-content/uploads/2015/05/CSAG_Report_FINALv2_web.pdf (accessed April 26, 2016); Levi Damien, "Graphic Shows 18 Different Teams Use Los Angeles Threat as Leverage in Past 20 Years," SilverandBlackPride.com, January 7, 2015, http://www.silverandblackpride.com/2015/1/7/7511345/graphic-shows-18-different-teams-use-los-angeles-threat-as-leverage-20-years-oakland-raiders (accessed April 26, 2016); Joe Nocera, "In Losing the Rams, St. Louis Wins," *The New York Times*, January 15, 2016, http://www.nytimes.com/2016/01/16/sports/football/st-louis-should-be-glad-it-lost-the-rams.html?_r=0 (accessed April 26, 2016); Matthew Ponsford, "Los Angeles to Build World's Most Expensive Stadium Complex," January 19, 2016, CNN.com, http://www.cnn.com/2016/01/19/architecture/new-nfl-stadium-los-angeles/ (Accessed April 26, 2016).

UNIT 9.2 REVIEW

KEY TERMS

Annuity p. 500	Discounting p. 498	Present value p. 498
Compound interest p. 499	Discount rate p. 498	Present value factor p. 499

PRACTICE QUESTIONS

1. LO 2 Mary can invest money in an account that earns 6% interest per year. Given this investment option, she would prefer to have $10,000 today rather than $11,000 a year from now. True or False?

2. LO 2 The present value of $150,000 in annual cash flows given a 10% required rate of return will be
   a. greater than the present value given a 12% required rate of return.
   b. less than the present value given a 12% required rate of return.
   c. equal to the present value given a 12% required rate of return.
   d. unknown because it depends on the timing of the cash flows.

3. LO 2 Assuming an 8% discount rate, the present value of a $10,000 payment received in five years is

a. $3,194.

b. $6,768.

c. $6,806.

d. $10,000.

4. LO 2 Assuming a 14% required rate of return, the present value of a $10,000 annual cash flow to be received for the next 20 years is

a. $1,401.

b. $46,106.

c. $66,231.

d. $200,000.

UNIT 9.2 PRACTICE EXERCISE

Sweepstakes Express recently announced a $10 million sweepstakes. Assume that the winner will receive $400,000 for 19 years plus a final payment of $2,400,000 in the 20th year.

Required

a. What part of this payout is an annuity?
b. What is the present value of the entire sweepstakes payout at a discount rate of 8%?
c. If the appropriate discount rate is 14%, how much is the payout worth today?
d. If you had a choice between this payout schedule and a single payment of $5 million today, which would you prefer, assuming that you could invest the funds at 6%?
e. What other factors might influence your decision to take an immediate payout versus a 20-year payout?

SELECTED UNIT 9.2 ANSWERS

Think About It 9.3

$22,000 to be received in one year at an 8% rate is worth *more* than $20,000 received today. It makes no difference whether you compare present values or future values:

	Present Value	one year @ 8% rate	Future Value
option 1:	$20,000.00	=	$21,600
option 2:	$20,369.80	=	$22,000

Either way, option 2—$22,000 received one year from today—is the preferred financial choice.

Think About It 9.4

The $10,000 payment is a three-year annuity. The $15,000 is an annuity in years 4 and 5, so you *cannot* use a two-year annuity factor to determine its present value. You can calculate the campaign's present value in two ways:

	$\$10,000 \times PVA_{3,i}$		$\$10,000 \times PVA_{3,i}$
+	$\$\ 15,000 \times PV_{4,i}$	+	$\$15,000 \times (PVA_{5,i} - PVA_{3,i})$
+	$\$\ 15,000 \times PV_{5,i}$		
	PV of ad campaign		PV of ad campaign

Let's give it a try with a 10% discount rate:

	$10,000 × 2.4868 = $24,868.00		$10,000 × 2.4868 = $24,868.00
+	$15,000 × 0.6830 = $10,245.00	+	$15,000 × (3.7907 − 2.4868) = $19,558.50
+	$15,000 × 0.6209 = $ 9,313.50		
	$44,426.50		$44,426.50

Practice Questions

1. False
2. A
3. C
4. C

Unit 9.2 Practice Exercise

a. $400,000 per year for 19 years

b. $(\$400{,}000 \times PVA_{19,8\%}) + (\$2{,}400{,}000 \times PV_{20,8\%}) = (\$400{,}000 \times 9.6036) + (\$2{,}400{,}000 \times 0.2145)$

$= \$3{,}841{,}440 + \$514{,}800 = \$4{,}356{,}240$

c. $(\$400{,}000 \times 6.5504) + (\$2{,}400{,}000 \times 0.0728) = \$2{,}620{,}160 + \$174{,}720 = \$2{,}794{,}880$

d. Present value of $5,000,000 today = $5,000,000

Present value of payout at 6% $= (\$400{,}000 \times 11.1581) + (\$2{,}400{,}000 \times 0.3118)$

$= \$4{,}463{,}240 + \$748{,}320$

$= \$5{,}211{,}560$

Choose the annuity payout—its present value is higher than the one-time $5,000,000 payout.

e. Uncertainty about the ability of Sweepstakes Express to make payments for the next 20 years may make the immediate payout more desirable.

UNIT 9.3

Discounted Cash Flow Techniques

GUIDED UNIT PREPARATION

Answering the following questions while you read this unit will guide your understanding of the key concepts found in the unit. The questions are linked to the learning objectives presented at the beginning of the chapter.

LO 3

1. How is net present value calculated?
2. In using the net present value method, what determines whether or not a project is acceptable?
3. What happens to a project's net present value if the discount rate is increased? If the discount rate is decreased?
4. What is the difference between a project's net present value and the present value of its net future cash inflows?

LO 4

5. What formula can be used to solve for the internal rate of return when a project's cash flows are equal?
6. How is the internal rate of return related to net present value?

Capital assets generate cash flows for several years. Since a dollar today is worth more than a dollar at any time in the future, any evaluation of those cash flows should include a consideration of the time value of money. In this unit we will see how to apply three capital budgeting techniques that do just that: net present value, internal rate of return, and profitability index.

Net Present Value

In Unit 9.1 you learned about the cash flows associated with the purchase of a capital asset, some of which were cash inflows and some of which were cash outflows. The **net present value (NPV)** approach to capital budgeting requires you to calculate the present value of each cash flow and then add, or "net," those present values to arrive at the capital project's net present value. This approach to capital budgeting involves four steps:

1. Identify the amount and timing of each cash flow.
2. Determine the appropriate discount rate.
3. Calculate the present value of each cash flow.
4. Calculate the net present value of the project.

Amount and Timing of the Cash Flows

The first step in calculating the net present value of a project is to identify the amount and timing of each cash flow. Let's revisit C&C's project to manufacture baseball caps, which we examined in Unit 9.1. As Exhibit 9-2 shows, this project will require a $50,265 cash outflow in year 0 for the purchase and installation of the equipment. In each year of the equipment's ten-year life, the projected annual sales volume of 250,000 baseball caps will generate a cash inflow of $625,000 and a cash outflow of $614,600 for direct materials, direct labor, variable overhead, variable selling expenses, and fixed cash expenses. Exhibit 9-4 summarizes the cash flows associated with this project year by year.

	Year 0	Year 1	Year 2	Year 3	Year 4	Year 5	Year 6	Year 7	Year 8	Year 9	Year 10
Purchase and installation of TopCap System	$(50,265)										
Sales revenue		$625,000	$625,000	$625,000	$625,000	$625,000	$625,000	$625,000	$625,000	$625,000	$625,000
Direct materials		(500,000)	(500,000)	(500,000)	(500,000)	(500,000)	(500,000)	(500,000)	(500,000)	(500,000)	(500,000)
Direct labor		(57,600)	(57,600)	(57,600)	(57,600)	(57,600)	(57,600)	(57,600)	(57,600)	(57,600)	(57,600)
Variable overhead		(37,500)	(37,500)	(37,500)	(37,500)	(37,500)	(37,500)	(37,500)	(37,500)	(37,500)	(37,500)
Variable selling expenses		(12,500)	(12,500)	(12,500)	(12,500)	(12,500)	(12,500)	(12,500)	(12,500)	(12,500)	(12,500)
Fixed expenses		(7,000)	(7,000)	(7,000)	(7,000)	(7,000)	(7,000)	(7,000)	(7,000)	(7,000)	(7,000)
Annual net cash flow	$(50,265)	$ 10,400	$ 10,400	$ 10,400	$ 10,400	$ 10,400	$ 10,400	$ 10,400	$ 10,400	$ 10,400	$ 10,400

EXHIBIT 9-4 *TopCap System cash flows by year.*

Appropriate Discount Rate

Before you can calculate the present value of a cash flow, you must determine the appropriate discount rate to use. The appropriate discount rate varies from company to company, and for C&C's TopCap project, we will use a 12% discount rate. While the mechanics of its calculation are beyond the scope of this course, let's look at some of the issues involved in determining the discount rate.

If C&C is going to purchase the TopCap system, the company will need to come up with $50,265 to cover the purchase price and installation cost. The company doesn't have this cash on hand, so it will need to raise cash by borrowing money from the bank. Since borrowed funds require the payment of interest, the calculation of the appropriate discount rate for the project should include a component related to the interest rate on borrowed funds. Alternatively, C&C could ask the company's owners to provide additional equity funding. Investors require a rate of return on their investment, so once again, the discount rate will include a component related to the investors' expected rate of return. Therefore, in its simplest form, the discount rate is the weighted average of the company's interest rate on borrowed funds and the required return to shareholders.

Two other factors will influence the discount rate. First, finance theory states that risk and rates of return are positively correlated. That means that as the level of risk increases, the required rate of return increases with it. So if a project is a high-risk project in terms of its expected cash flows, you will need to increase the discount rate. Second, the discount rate should be increased if inflation is expected to occur over the life of the project.

THINK ABOUT IT 9.5

If you have determined the amount and timing of a project's cash flows, how can you manipulate the project's present value without substantially altering the cash flows? How can a company prevent managers from using such methods to their benefit?

Present Value of Each Cash Flow

Once the cash flows and discount rate have been determined, you will need to calculate the present value of each cash flow by multiplying each one by the appropriate present value factor. Since the cash flows for C&C's TopCap project are identical for each year, we can treat them as an annuity. The present value of the cash flows is then calculated by multiplying the $10,400 annual cash inflow by the 5.6502 present value factor for a ten-year annuity at 12%. The present value of these annual cash flows is $58,762.08. If there were additional cash flows that occurred at sporadic times, you would need to repeat this process for each cash flow amount using the appropriate factor from the Present Value of $1 table (Appendix 9-1). Since the cash payment for the acquisition and installation of the equipment occurs in year 0 (the present), the present value factor is 1.0, and the present value is $50,265.

Exhibit 9-5 summarizes these present value calculations. Note that rather than showing each individual cash flow identified in Exhibit 9-4, we have subtracted the annual operating expenses (cash outflows) from the annual revenue (cash inflows) to arrive at an annual net cash inflow of $10,400. Doing so simplifies the net present value calculation; it has no effect on the outcome, other than to reduce the number of calculations. However, if you are more comfortable showing each individual cash flow, then keep all the detail.

REALITY CHECK—*Don't discount the choice of a discount rate*

Niyazz/Shutterstock

Discount rates are used to value any number of things, including investments in equipment, future earnings for purposes of lawsuits, and property settlements in divorce proceedings and estate distributions. Given the importance of the discount rate in present value calculations, care should be exercised in selecting the rate to be used. Since discount rates reflect risk and other situational factors, no single discount rate is appropriate in every case. In fact, in presenting information in a legal proceeding, attorneys for the plaintiff and the defense will probably use different discount rates to value the same asset.

In presenting information in a legal proceeding, attorneys for the plaintiff and the defense will probably use different discount rates to value the same asset.

One choice for a discount rate is a company's cost of capital, which varies by firm and industry. Dr. Aswath Damodaran, professor of finance at New York University's Stern School of Business, has estimated the cost of capital in several industries. His January 2016 data show a range of industry rates, from financial services (non-bank and insurance) at 2.39% to tobacco at 11.82%.

The cost of capital can also vary greatly within an industry. ThatsWACC.com, which estimates companies' weighted average cost of capital, provides the following estimates for companies in the food processing industry.

Campbell Soup	4.7%
General Mills	6.5%
Hormel Foods	7.8%
Kellogg	5.9%
Kraft Heinz	4.9%
Mondelez	10.4%
J. M. Smucker	6.1%

Sources: Stephen R. Braunstein, "Eeny Meeny Miny Discount Rate," *Today's CPA,* 31, no. 3 (November/December 2003): 18–22; Aswath Damodaran, "Cost of Capital by Sector, January 2016," http://www.stern.nyu.edu/~adamodar/New_Home_Page/datacurrent.html (accessed April 29, 2016).

	Present Value	Present Value Factor	Year 0	Year 1	Year 2	Year 3	Year 4	Year 5	Year 6	Year 7	Year 8	Year 9	Year 10
Purchase and installation of TopCap System	$(50,265.00)	1.0	$(50,265)										
Annual cash flow	58,762.08	5.6502		$10,400	$10,400	$10,400	$10,400	$10,400	$10,400	$10,400	$10,400	$10,400	$10,400
Net present value	$ 8,497.08												

EXHIBIT 9-5 *Net present value of the TopCap System project.*

Net Present Value of the Project

Once you have calculated the present value of each cash flow, you must add them together to determine the net present value of the project. For C&C's TopCap project, the net present value is $8,497.08, as Exhibit 9-5 shows. If the net present value of the project is greater than or equal to zero, the project has achieved the required rate of return and should be accepted. If the net present value is less than zero, the project does not achieve the required rate of return and should be rejected. The following table summarizes the three possible outcomes of the net present value calculations and what they mean for the project.

NPV Value	What It Means	Project Acceptable?
> 0	Return on proposed project exceeds the discount rate	Yes
= 0	Return on proposed project equals the discount rate	Yes
< 0	Return on proposed project is less than the discount rate	No

Another Look at Net Present Value Calculations

The previous TopCap System example was a simple illustration, but most net present value calculations will be more complex. Consider an equipment replacement situation that O'Sullivan Printing is facing. O'Sullivan Printing prepares C&C's catalog and other print materials. O'Sullivan is considering the purchase of new printing equipment to replace some of its older equipment. The equipment costs $60,000, and the sales representative claims that the efficiency and quality of the machine will save O'Sullivan $9,000 per year in operating costs over the ten-year life of the machine, since the operating costs of the new machine are $71,000 per year compared to the old machine's operating costs of $80,000 per year. When calculating net present value, a cost savings such as this is treated like a cash inflow.

O'Sullivan's old equipment could be sold right away for $3,000 if the new equipment is purchased; if it is kept another ten years, it will have no salvage value. The new equipment is expected to be sold for $5,000 at the end of its ten-year life. Both of these cash inflows should be included in the net present value calculation.

Finally, if O'Sullivan were to keep the existing equipment, it would need a $10,000 maintenance overhaul in year 2 to keep it in good working condition. An avoided overhaul, like a cost saving, should be treated as a cash inflow to the project because buying the new equipment would prevent the company from paying for the overhaul.

The decision to replace the old equipment with the new equipment can be analyzed in two ways, both of which yield the same answer. We can calculate the cost of each decision separately—keep the old equipment or replace the old equipment with new equipment. Alternatively, we can perform an incremental analysis, focusing only on what is relevant—that is, what is avoidable—if O'Sullivan purchases the new equipment. The results of these two approaches, assuming a 12% discount rate, are shown in Exhibit 9-6.

When the two alternatives are analyzed separately, the net present value of the cost to keep and operate the old equipment is ($459,988) and the net present value of the cost to purchase and operate the new equipment is ($456,554). Thus, the net present value shows that it costs more to operate the old equipment than to purchase and operate the new equipment. The incremental approach shows that the new project has a net present value of $3,434. What are the differences between the two approaches? Under the two-alternative approach the operating costs are outflows, but under the incremental approach the difference between the two operating costs is a cost savings, or cash inflow. With two alternatives, the overhaul is an outflow for the old machine, but it is an inflow in the incremental analysis. Understanding how the cash flows are recognized is clearly an important part of both approaches. Neither approach is necessarily better than the other. If done correctly, both will result in the same decision: It makes more financial sense for O'Sullivan to buy the new equipment.

	Keep Old Equipment				Purchase New Equipment				Incremental Approach			
	Cash Flow	Time Period	Present Value Factor (i = 12%)	Present Value	Cash Flow	Time Period	Present Value Factor (i = 12%)	Present Value	Cash Flow	Time Period	Present Value Factor (i = 12%)	Present Value
Purchase price	—				$(60,000)	0	1	$ (60,000)	$(60,000)	0	1	$(60,000)
Salvage of old equipment	—				$ 3,000	0	1	$3,000	$ 3,000	0	1	$ 3,000
Operating costs	$(80,000)	1–10	5.6502	$(452,016)	$(71,000)	1–10	5.6502	$(401,164)	—			
Operating cost savings	—				—				$ 9,000	1–10	5.6502	$ 50,852
Overhaul	$(10,000)	2	0.7972	$ (7,972)	—				—			
Overhaul avoided	—				—				$ 10,000	2	0.7972	$ 7,972
Salvage of new equipment	—				$ 5,000	10	0.3220	$ 1,610	$ 5,000	10	0.3220	$ 1,610
Net present value				$(459,988)				$(456,554)				$ 3,434

EXHIBIT 9-6 *Calculating the net present value of an equipment replacement.*

Using Excel® to Calculate Net Present Value

You learned in Unit 9.2 that spreadsheet packages such as Excel can calculate the present value of an annuity. Similarly, you can use these packages to calculate the net present value of a project. We will illustrate Excel's NPV function using O'Sullivan's equipment purchase project.

Exhibit 9-7 shows a spreadsheet detailing all the cash flows of O'Sullivan's proposed purchase using the incremental approach. After constructing the spreadsheet, insert the NPV function in the desired cell to open the function's dialog box. Enter the discount rate in the rate box and the cell addresses of the annual net cash flows, rather than the amounts, in the value 1 box. Do not include the current period's cash flows in the value 1 box; however, you must edit the NPV formula to add the year 0 cash flows to the NPV function results. An advantage of this method is that it is easy to adjust the cash flow information in the worksheet as parameters change and have the net present value recalculate automatically.

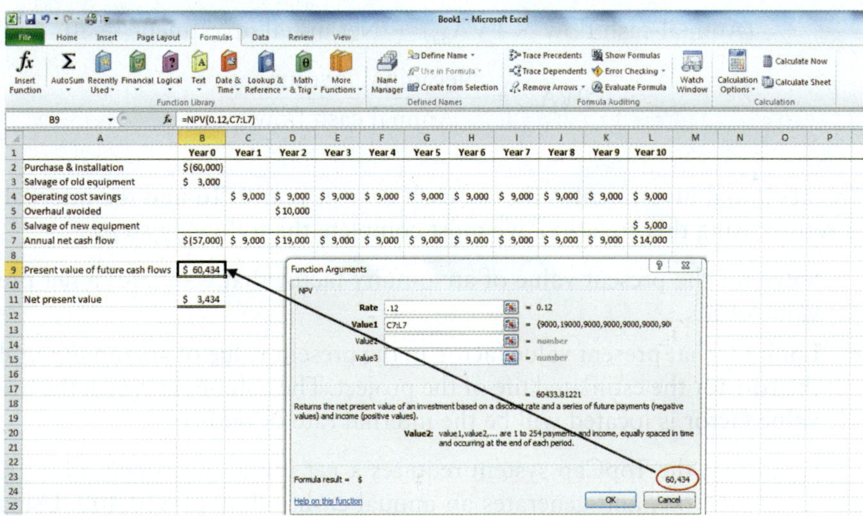

EXHIBIT 9-7 *Using Microsoft Excel's NPV function to calculate net present value.*

Assumptions of the Net Present Value Model

Like most models, the net present value model makes several assumptions. In our examples, we assumed that we knew exactly when, and in what amounts, the cash flows occurred. In reality, however, cash flows are difficult to predict with accuracy. After all, how sure can we be about an event that will happen ten years from now? And we made no allowance for inflation. We also assumed that all cash flows occurred at the end of the year. Of course, this isn't usually the case; cash flows typically occur throughout the year. But making this assumption simplifies the calculations. Finally, we assumed that as cash inflows from the project were received, they were reinvested in another project earning a return equal to the discount rate.

Internal Rate of Return

Another discounted cash flow method yields a project's **internal rate of return (IRR)**, or the actual return expected to be earned by the project. Like net present value, the internal rate of return considers the amount and timing of future cash flows. To determine whether a project is acceptable, you compare its return to the organization's discount rate, or minimum required rate of return. If the internal rate of return is greater than or equal to the company's discount rate, the project is acceptable. If the internal rate of return is less than the company's discount rate, the project should be rejected.

IRR Value	Compare to NPV	Project Acceptable?
$>$ discount rate	NPV > 0	Yes
$=$ discount rate	NPV $= 0$	Yes
$<$ discount rate	NPV < 0	No

Note that when a project's internal rate of return equals the discount rate, the net present value is zero.

Projects with Even Cash Flows

Let's see how to calculate the internal rate of return for a project with even cash flows (an annuity). Since net present value equals zero when the internal rate of return equals the discount rate, we can write the following equation, letting i equal the internal rate of return:

$$(\text{Annual cash flow} \times \text{PVA}_{n,i}) - \text{Net initial investment} = \$0$$

$$\text{PVA}_{n,i} = \frac{\text{Net initial investment}}{\text{Annual cash flow}}$$

The **net initial investment** is the net cash flow in year 0. To find the internal rate of return using this equation, we must complete the following steps:

1. Solve for the present value of an annuity factor that generates a net present value of $0.
2. Look for that present value factor, in the present value of an annuity table, in the row for the estimated life of the project. The column in which the present value factor is located will be the internal rate of return.

Recall that the TopCap system requires a net initial investment of $50,265, has a ten-year life, and generates an annual cash inflow of $10,400. Using the equation just given, we can solve for the present value factor that generates a net present value of $0.

$$(\text{Annual cash flow} \times PVA_{10,i}) - \text{Net initial investment} = \$0$$
$$(\$10{,}400 \times PVA_{10,i}) - \$50{,}265 = \$0$$
$$PVA_{10,i} = \frac{\$50{,}265}{\$10{,}400}$$
$$PVA_{10,i} = 4.8332$$

Looking across the row for ten periods in the present value of an annuity table, we find a present value factor of 4.8332 in the 16% column. Thus, the internal rate of return for the TopCap system is 16%. C&C's required rate of return is 12%, so with an internal rate of return of 16%, the project is acceptable.

Periods	4%	5%	6%	7%	8%	9%	10%	11%	12%	13%	14%	16%	18%
1	0.9615	0.9524	0.9434	0.9346	0.9259	0.9174	0.9091	0.9009	0.8929	0.8850	0.8772	0.8621	0.8475
2	1.8861	1.8594	1.8334	1.8080	1.7833	1.7591	1.7355	1.7125	1.6901	1.6681	1.6467	1.6052	1.5656
3	2.7751	2.7232	2.6730	2.6243	2.5771	2.5313	2.4868	2.4437	2.4018	2.3612	2.3216	2.2459	2.1743
4	3.6299	3.5460	3.4651	3.3872	3.3121	3.2397	3.1698	3.1024	3.0373	2.9745	2.9137	2.7982	2.6901
5	4.4518	4.3295	4.2124	4.1002	3.9927	3.8897	3.7907	3.6959	3.6048	3.5172	3.4331	3.2743	3.1272
6	5.2421	5.0757	4.9173	4.7665	4.6229	4.4859	4.3553	4.2305	4.1114	3.9975	3.8887	3.6647	3.4976
7	6.0021	5.7864	5.5824	5.3893	5.2064	5.0330	4.8684	4.7122	4.5638	4.4226	4.2883	4.0386	3.8115
8	6.7327	6.4632	6.2098	5.9713	5.7466	5.5348	5.3349	5.1461	4.9676	4.7988	4.6389	4.3436	4.0776
9	7.4353	7.1078	6.8017	6.5152	6.2469	5.9952	5.7590	5.5370	5.3282	5.1317	4.9464	4.6065	4.3030
10	8.1109	7.7217	7.3601	7.0236	6.7101	6.4177	6.1446	5.8892	5.6502	5.4262	5.2161	4.8332	4.4941

Projects with Uneven Cash Flows

Not many projects have even annual cash flows, as we saw when we analyzed O'Sullivan's decision whether to purchase new printing equipment. When the annual cash flows are uneven, you cannot use the annuity table method to calculate the internal rate of return. One option is to do a series of net present value calculations, until by trial and error you find the discount rate that results in a net present value of $0. Since we have already found that the project's net present value is greater than zero, we know that its internal rate of return must be greater than the 12% discount rate. We might begin with a 13% discount rate, which yields a net present value of $1,104 as shown in Exhibit 9-8. Since the internal rate of return results in a net present value greater than $0, we need to try a higher discount rate to lower the net present value. Trying a 14% discount rate yields a negative net present value of ($1,011). So the project must have an internal rate of return somewhere between 13% and 14%.

	Cash Flow	Time Period	13% Discount Rate	14% Discount Rate
Purchase price	$(60,000)	0	$ (60,000)	$(60,000)
Operating cost savings	9,000	1–10	48,836	46,945
Overhaul avoided	10,000	2	7,831	7,695
Salvage of old equipment	3,000	0	3,000	3,000
Salvage of new equipment	5,000	10	1,437	1,349
Net present value			$ 1,104	$ (1,011)

EXHIBIT 9-8

Trial-and-error calculation of the internal rate of return, O'Sullivan Printing.

WATCH OUT!

Do not include financing decisions like interest expense in net present value or internal rate of return calculations. The discount rate (or hurdle rate) accounts for the company's cost of financing.

Using Excel® to Calculate Internal Rate of Return

Using the trial and error approach to find an internal rate of return is cumbersome and time consuming. A much easier and faster way to calculate the internal rate of return on a project is to use Microsoft Excel's built-in IRR function. Exhibit 9-9 shows how to use the function to calculate the internal rate of return of O'Sullivan's new printing equipment. Notice that the cash flow information is identical to what we used to calculate the net present value in Exhibit 9-7. To calculate the internal rate of return, insert the IRR function and enter the cell range for the cash flows from year 0 to year 10 in the dialog box. The internal rate of return will then display in the dialog box: 13.52% in this example.

EXHIBIT 9-9

Using Microsoft Excel's IRR function to calculate internal rate of return.

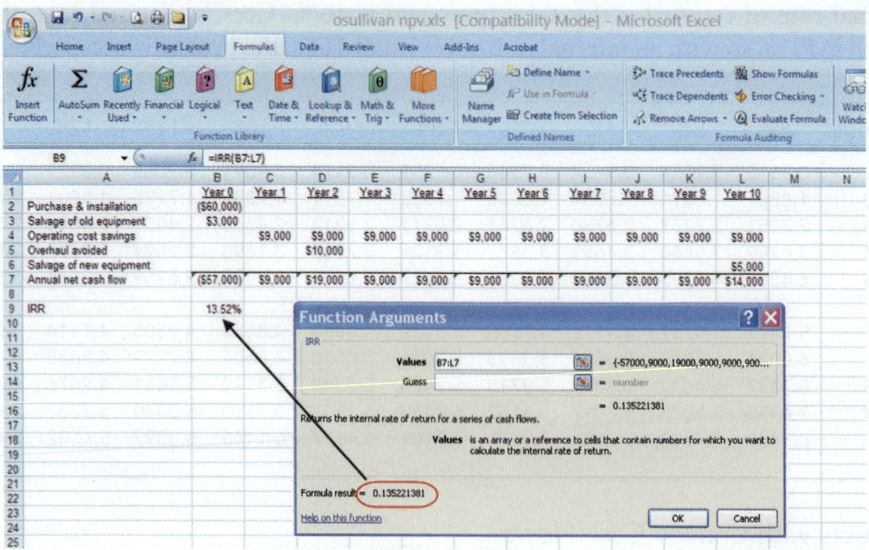

	A	B	C	D	E	F	G	H	I	J	K	L
1		Year 0	Year 1	Year 2	Year 3	Year 4	Year 5	Year 6	Year 7	Year 8	Year 9	Year 10
2	Purchase & installation	($60,000)										
3	Salvage of old equipment	$3,000										
4	Operating cost savings		$9,000	$9,000	$9,000	$9,000	$9,000	$9,000	$9,000	$9,000	$9,000	$9,000
5	Overhaul avoided			$10,000								
6	Salvage of new equipment											$5,000
7	Annual net cash flow	($57,000)	$9,000	$19,000	$9,000	$9,000	$9,000	$9,000	$9,000	$9,000	$9,000	$14,000
8												
9	IRR	13.52%										

Assumptions of the Internal Rate of Return Model

The internal rate of return model makes assumptions similar to those of the net present value model. It assumes that the amount and timing of all cash flows are known exactly and that all cash flows occur at the end of the year. The internal rate of return model also makes assumptions about the reinvestment of cash flows; however, the assumption is that as cash inflows from the project are received, they are reinvested in another project earning a return equal to the internal rate of return. While this may sound no different from the assumption made when using net present value, consider this example. A project that has a 20% internal rate of return assumes that the cash flows are reinvested at 20%. This rate may be dramatically different from the company's cost of capital, which is a more realistic rate for reinvestment of project cash flows.

Screening and Preference Decisions Using NPV and IRR

Both net present value and internal rate of return are useful tools to use when screening capital projects for acceptable returns. As you have learned, projects with a net present value greater than or equal to zero generate a return that is at least equal to the discount rate, or required rate of return. Thus, these projects pass the screening decision. Likewise, projects whose internal rate of return is greater than or equal to the hurdle rate pass the screening decision. Since the TopCap system has a positive net present value, and its 16% internal rate of return is greater than the 12% hurdle rate, the system passes both screening factors.

Once projects have passed the screening decision using one of these methods, managers generally must rank-order projects in order of preference for funding. Some projects may be mutually exclusive, such that the company will select only one project to fund. For instance, assume that C&C also considered a second baseball cap system, the FlyVisor. The FlyVisor system requires an initial investment of $80,000, has a useful life of ten years, and will produce annual cash inflows of $15,660. The present value of the FlyVisor annual cash flows is $88,482.13 ($15,660 × 5.6502), yielding a net present value of $8,482.13 and an internal rate of return of 14.5%. Chad Davis needs to select only one of those systems; there is no need to purchase both. Since both systems have essentially the same net present value, which should C&C choose to implement?

The internal rate of return is frequently used to provide a preference ranking of competing projects. The project with the highest internal rate of return is the preferred project. If funds exist to invest in additional projects, the project with the next highest internal rate of return is funded, and so on, until funds are exhausted. Therefore, Chad Davis would choose to implement the TopCap system, since its internal rate of return of 16% is higher than FlyVisor's 14.5% internal rate of return.

You might think that Chad could use net present value to make this preference ranking by selecting the project with the highest net present value. In this case, the two systems have virtually the same net present value—$8,497.08 for TopCap and $8,482.13 for FlyVisor. But the investments required by the two systems are quite different, making the choice based on net present value more complicated than it might seem.

Projects of different sizes can be evaluated using the **profitability index**, which compares the present value of the project's cash flows to the net initial investment. The profitability index is calculated using the following formula; the project with the highest profitability index is the preferred project.

$$\text{Profitability index} = \frac{\text{Present value of future cash flows}}{\text{Net initial investment}}$$

For the TopCap system, the profitability index is 1.17 $\left(\frac{\$58{,}762.08}{\$50{,}265}\right)$, which is greater than the FlyVisor system's profitability index of 1.11 $\left(\frac{\$88{,}482.13}{\$80{,}000}\right)$. Therefore, the TopCap system is the preferred project.

UNIT 9.3 REVIEW

KEY TERMS

Internal rate of return (IRR) p. 510
Net present value (NPV) p. 505
Profitability index p. 513
Net initial investment p. 510

PRACTICE QUESTIONS

1. LO 3 Lilac Designs has a capital project with a net present value of $1,090, assuming a 10% discount rate. Lilac Designs should

   a. use a higher discount rate to generate a net present value of $0.

   b. reject the project because the net present value is too low.

   c. revise the cash flows to generate a higher net present value before accepting the project.

   d. accept the project because the net present value is greater than $0.

2. LO 3 If a project has a net present value that is less than zero, then the present value of the total net cash inflows is less than the net initial investment. True or False?

3. LO 3 Chad's Chocolates is considering the purchase of a new candy press. The machine under consideration costs $17,550 and would generate $2,650 in annual savings of direct labor costs over its 20-year life. At the end of 20 years, the press could be sold for $500. Chad's required rate of return is 16%. What is the machine's net present value?

   a. $1,813

   b. $(1,813)

   c. $(1,839)

   d. $(1,339)

4. LO 3 Oakcrest Industries has the opportunity to invest $90,000 in a new packing machine that should provide annual cash operating inflows of $29,000 for six years. At the end of that period it can be sold for $10,000. Oakcrest's required rate of return is 14%. What is the machine's net present value?

   a. $27,328

   b. $22,772

   c. $61,671

   d. $18,221

5. LO 4 Hess Company is analyzing a capital budgeting decision involving the purchase of a used delivery truck for $22,000. The company's discount rate is 12%. Managers have calculated an 11% internal rate of return on the truck. In this analysis, which of the following statements will be true?

   a. The net present value of the truck is greater than zero.

   b. If the truck's annual maintenance costs increase, its internal rate of return will increase.

   c. The truck is an acceptable investment under the internal rate of return method.

   d. The present value of the future cash flows generated by the truck is less than $22,000.

6. LO 4 Which of the following statements is true of a project that has a positive net present value at a 12% required rate of return?

   a. The internal rate of return is less than 12%.

   b. The internal rate of return is greater than 12%.

   c. Actual cash flows will be 12 times the cost of the investment.

   d. None of the above are true.

7. LO 4 Chad's Chocolates is considering the purchase of a new candy press. The machine under consideration costs $17,550 and would generate $2,650 in annual savings of direct labor costs over its 20-year life. At the end of 20 years, the press could be sold for $500. Chad's required rate of return is 16%. Which of these rates is the machine's internal rate of return closest to?

   a. 11%

   b. 12%

   c. 14%

   d. 16%

8. LO 4 Chow Company is considering the purchase of a piece of equipment costing $142,500. The equipment has an eight-year useful life and will generate $30,000 in annual cash flows. The company has a 10% required rate of return and uses the straight-line depreciation method. The internal rate of return on this equipment is closest to

   a. 10%.

   b. 13%.

   c. 22%.

   d. 43%.

UNIT 9.3 PRACTICE EXERCISE

C. Wren Designs is considering the purchase of a new computer-aided drafting station to assist in the preparation of architectural plans. The company's current system is ten years old and has begun to crash at least once a day. The new system has a purchase price of $20,132 and will save the company $4,000 per year in operating expenses. The system is expected to last seven years. Wren estimates its cost of capital to be 8%.

Required

a. What is the net present value of the new computer-aided drafting station? Based on net present value, should Wren purchase the new system? Why or why not?
b. What is the new system's internal rate of return? Based on the internal rate of return, should Wren purchase the new system? Why or why not?
c. What is the system's profitability index?

SELECTED UNIT 9.3 ANSWERS

Think About It 9.5

If you lower the discount rate, the present value will increase. Companies can prevent managers from lowering the discount rate to increase a project's net present value, thus making it acceptable, by setting a company-wide minimum discount rate that all projects must meet or exceed.

Practice Questions

1. D
2. True
3. B
4. A
5. D
6. B
7. C
8. B

Unit 9.3 Practice Exercise

a. ($4,000 × 5.2064) − $20,132 = $693.60

Purchase the system, since the net present value is greater than $0.

b. $\frac{\$20{,}132}{\$4{,}000} = 5.0330 = PVA_{5,i}$

$i = 9\%$

Purchase the system, since the IRR is greater than the discount rate.

c. $\frac{\$4{,}000 \times 5.2064}{\$20{,}132} = 1.03$

UNIT 9.4

Other Capital Budgeting Techniques

GUIDED UNIT PREPARATION

Answering the following questions while you read this unit will guide your understanding of the key concepts found in the unit. The questions are linked to the learning objectives presented at the beginning of the chapter.

LO 5

1. What does the payback period measure?
2. How is the payback period calculated when a project's annual cash flows are equal? When its annual cash flows are unequal?

LO 6

3. How is the accounting rate of return calculated?
4. How does average annual income differ from cash flow?

When evaluating capital projects, most companies use net present value and/or internal rate of return. However, some use simpler methods that ignore the time value of money. In this unit, we will explore two of those techniques, the payback period and the accounting rate of return.

Payback Period

In Unit 9.1 we discussed *return of investment*—that is, getting back the amount of the original investment. The **payback period** is the time it takes, in years, for an investment to return the original amount of invested capital. The payback period is used most often as a screening tool by companies that have established a maximum acceptable payback period. As long as the payback period is less than the stated maximum, the project can move forward to the preference decision.

Projects with Even Cash Flows

The payback period of a project that produces even cash flows each year is calculated by dividing the net initial investment by the projected annual cash flow. For example, the TopCap system that C&C Sports is evaluating has a net initial investment of \$50,265 and is expected to generate \$10,400 in cash flow each year. The payback period is therefore 4.83 years.

$$\text{Payback period} = \frac{\text{Net initial investment}}{\text{Annual cash flow}}$$

$$\text{Payback period} = \frac{\$50{,}265}{\$10{,}400} = 4.83 \text{ years}$$

Projects with Uneven Cash Flows

For a project with uneven cash flows, calculating the payback period is more complicated. We must add up the annual cash flows until the cumulative total cash flow equals the net initial investment. Let's revisit O'Sullivan's decision to purchase new printing equipment. Exhibit 9-10 shows the annual and cumulative cash flows for this project.

EXHIBIT 9-10

Cumulative cash flow for O'Sullivan's new printing equipment replacement.

	A	B	C	D	E	F	G	H	I	J	K	L
1		Year 0	Year 1	Year 2	Year 3	Year 4	Year 5	Year 6	Year 7	Year 8	Year 9	Year 10
2	Purchase & installation	(\$60,000)										
3	Salvage of old equipment	\$3,000										
4	Operating cost savings		\$9,000	\$9,000	\$9,000	\$9,000	\$9,000	\$9,000	\$9,000	\$9,000	\$9,000	\$9,000
5	Overhaul avoided			\$10,000								
6	Salvage of new equipment											\$5,000
7	Annual net cash flow	(\$57,000)	\$9,000	\$19,000	\$9,000	\$9,000	\$9,000	\$9,000	\$9,000	\$9,000	\$9,000	\$14,000
8												
9	Cumulative cash flow	(\$57,000)	(\$48,000)	(\$29,000)	(\$20,000)	(\$11,000)	(\$2,000)	\$7,000	\$16,000	\$25,000	\$34,000	\$48,000
10												
11												

Notice that the cash flow information is identical to what we used to calculate the net present value in Exhibit 9-7 and internal rate of return in Exhibit 9-9. The new equipment has generated a cumulative cash flow of ($2,000) at the end of year 5 and of $7,000 at the end of year 6. Thus, the payback period is between five and six years. We need to find out when in year 6 the new equipment will have generated the remaining $2,000 needed to complete the return of investment. In calculating the payback period, cash flows are assumed to occur evenly throughout the year. To determine how long it will take to generate the remaining $2,000, then, we simply divide the amount remaining by the cash flow in year 6. Doing so, we find that it will take 0.22 years (2.6 months) to generate the required cash flow. Therefore, the payback period for this project is 5.22 years.

$$\text{Additional payback period} = \frac{\$2{,}000}{\$9{,}000} = 0.22 \text{ years}$$

$$(12 \text{ month} \times 0.22 = 2.6 \text{ months})$$

Limitations of the Payback Period

Although the payback period is a simple technique that is used by many organizations, particularly smaller ones, it is subject to some limitations. First, this method ignores the time value of money; cash that is received five years from now is valued in the same way as cash received today. Suppose C&C Sports is comparing two different machines for attaching belt loops to baseball pants (see Exhibit 9-11). Both machines cost $15,000, and both have the same three-year payback period. Looking at just the payback period, you cannot distinguish between the two investments. But machine 2 is a better investment because it returns more cash earlier in its life than machine 1. In fact, its internal rate of return is 23%, compared to machine 1's 19%. So the payback period is not a useful tool for ranking potential investments.

Year	Machine 1 Cost = $15,000		Machine 2 Cost = $15,000		
	Annual Cash Flow	Cumulative Cash Flow	Annual Cash Flow	Cumulative Cash Flow	
1	$2,000	$ (13,000)	$5,000	$ (10,000)	
2	$4,000	$ (9,000)	$8,000	$ (3,000)	
3	$9,000	$ 0	$2,000	$ 0	payback = 3 years
4	$4,000	$ 4,000	$4,000	$ 4,000	
5	$8,000	$ 12,000	$8,000	$ 12,000	

EXHIBIT 9-11

Cash flow timing during the payback period.

The second limitation of the payback period is that it ignores cash flows that occur after the payback period. Consider the two options presented in Exhibit 9-12, both of which cost $20,000. Machine 1 has a payback period of four years; machine 2, a payback period of three years. If C&C uses a three-year payback period threshold, machine 1 won't be considered, even though it delivers a sizable cash flow after the payback period. In comparison, machine 2 never generates any return on investment; it simply returns its original cost of $20,000. Machine 1 is clearly the better choice, even though it doesn't meet the payback period threshold.

	Year	Machine 1 Cost = $20,000		Machine 2 Cost = $20,000		
		Annual Cash Flow	Cumulative Cash Flow	Annual Cash Flow	Cumulative Cash Flow	
	1	$ 5,000	$(15,000)	$10,000	$(10,000)	
	2	$ 5,000	(10,000)	$ 7,000	$ (3,000)	
	3	$ 5,000	$ (5,000)	$ 3,000	$ 0	payback = 3 years
payback = 4 years	4	$ 5,000	$ 0	$ 0	$ 0	
	5	$12,000	$ 12,000	$ 0	$ 0	

EXHIBIT 9-12 *Cash flow after the payback period.*

Accounting Rate of Return

The final capital budgeting technique we will study is the **accounting rate of return**, the return generated by an investment based on its net operating income. This method differs from the other techniques we have examined in that it does not focus on cash flows. Rather, it includes non-cash expenses, such as depreciation, in the return. This method is also known as the **simple rate of return** and the **unadjusted rate of return.**

The accounting rate of return is determined by calculating the additional revenues generated by the investment and then subtracting *all* additional operating expenses to determine the incremental net operating income. The net operating income is then divided by the amount of the initial investment. If any existing equipment is sold as part of the project, the initial investment is reduced by its salvage value.

$$\frac{\text{Project revenues} - \text{Project operating expenses}}{\text{Initial investment} - \text{Salvage of old equipment}} = \text{Accounting rate of return}$$

Let's calculate the TopCap system's accounting rate of return. From Exhibit 9-2, we know that the TopCap system will generate $625,000 in revenues and $614,600 in cash expenses each year. Assuming that C&C uses straight-line depreciation, the TopCap system will generate $5,026.50 $\left(\frac{\$50,265}{10 \text{ years}}\right)$ in depreciation expense each year. Therefore, the annual net operating income for the TopCap system is $5,373.50 ($625,000 − $614,600 − $5,026.50). With the initial investment of $50,265, the TopCap system's accounting rate of return is 10.69%.

$$\frac{\$625{,}000 - \$614{,}600 - \$5{,}026.50}{\$50{,}265} = 10.69\%$$

WATCH OUT!

Remember to subtract depreciation expense in calculating the accounting rate of return if the investment is a depreciable asset.

You may be wondering how the accounting rate of return is calculated if a project does not have a constant net operating income. That's a good question because many projects will produce uneven operating income. In those cases, you can use the *average* annual net operating income over the life of the project.

Two major weaknesses of accounting rate of return are that it doesn't consider cash flows or the time value of money. Since most companies maintain accounting records based on accrual accounting rather than cash flow, this information is readily available and comparable across investments.

REALITY CHECK—*So many choices, so little money*

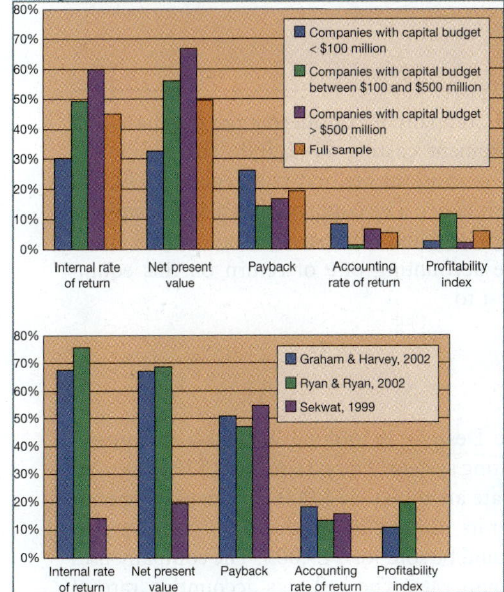

With multiple methods available for evaluating capital projects and allocating limited resources, which methods do companies actually use? Several researchers have asked that question over the past 50 years.

In early studies, the payback period was found to be the most popular capital budgeting technique; discounted cash flow methods such as net present value and internal rate of return were least popular. But preferences have changed over the years. A survey of Fortune 1000 firms found that net present value was the most frequently used technique, followed closely by the internal rate of return. The payback period was third, and the accounting rate of return a distant fourth. The study also found that as the size of the capital budget increases, so does the frequency of use of net present value and the internal rate of return. The relationship between capital budget size and frequency of use of the payback period was just the opposite: the smaller the budget, the more likely firms were to use the payback period.

A broader survey done by Graham and Harvey echoed these results. When asked which capital budgeting techniques their companies used, 74.9% of CFOs said they always or almost always used net present value. The internal rate of return was used slightly more often, with 75.7% of CFOs reporting their companies always or almost always used the technique. The payback period came in third at 56.7%.

Large companies are more likely to use net present value than small companies.

Not all organizations follow this pattern, however. Graham and Harvey found that large companies are more likely to use net present value than small companies. And a study of municipal governments in Tennessee found that 61.5% of them used the payback period in evaluating capital projects, but only 21.4% used net present value.

Sources: John Graham and Campbell Harvey, "How Do CFOs Make Capital Budgeting and Capital Structure Decisions?" *Journal of Applied Corporate Finance*, 15, no. 1 (Spring 2002): 8–23; Patricia A. Ryan and Glenn P. Ryan, "Capital Budgeting Practices of the Fortune 1000: How Have Things Changed?" *Journal of Business and Management*, 8, no. 1 (Winter 2002): 355–366; Alex Sekwat, "Capital Budgeting Practices among Tennessee Municipal Governments," *Government Finance Review*, 15, no. 3 (June 1999): 15–19.

THINK ABOUT IT 9.6

Complete the following table by answering "Yes" or "No." One cell is done for you.

	CONSIDERS TIME VALUE OF MONEY	USES CASH FLOWS	USES ACCOUNTING PROFITABILITY	CONSIDERS CASH FLOWS OVER ENTIRE LIFE OF PROJECT
Net present value	Yes			
Internal rate of return				
Profitability index				
Payback period				
Accounting rate of return				

UNIT 9.4 REVIEW

KEY TERMS

Accounting rate of return p. 518
Payback period p. 516
Simple rate of return p. 518
Unadjusted rate of return p. 518

PRACTICE QUESTIONS

1. LO 5 A proposed capital project will produce $5,000 per year in incremental cash flows over its useful life of 15 years. If the project has a payback period of five years, the cash flows received in years 6–15 will be ignored in the calculation of the payback period. True or False?
2. LO 5 Chad's Chocolates is considering the purchase of a new candy press. The machine under consideration costs $17,550 and would generate $2,650 in annual savings of direct labor costs over its 20-year life. At the end of the 20 years, the candy press could be sold for $500. Chad's uses a 16% discount rate. What is the press's payback period?

   a. 1.1 years
   b. 3.2 years
   c. 6.6 years
   d. 20 years
3. LO 5 If a proposed project has uneven annual cash flows, the payback period should be calculated using the average annual cash flow. True or False?
4. LO 6 The accounting rate of return is identical to the internal rate of return. True or False?
5. LO 6 Chow Company is considering the purchase of a piece of equipment costing $142,500. The equipment has an eight-year useful life and will generate $30,000 in annual cash flows. The company has a 10% required rate of return and uses the straight-line depreciation method. The accounting rate of return on this equipment is closest to

   a. 8.55%
   b. 10.00%
   c. 21.05%
   d. 33.55
6. LO 6 Claire Designs is looking at a new computer-assisted drafting system. The system costs $125,000 and would generate an annual $33,000 in savings of operating costs over its 12-year life. At the end of the 12 years, the system could be sold for $15,000. The company uses a 16% discount rate. The system's accounting rate of return is closest to

   a. 16%
   b. 17%
   c. 18%
   d. 19%

UNIT 9.4 PRACTICE EXERCISE

Jason's WebDesigns is owned and operated by Jason Armstrong, who has been working out of his home for the last five years. Jason has decided that it is time to establish a more professional appearance. A small building in a central business district has become available. Though it is too small for most businesses, it will offer Jason just the right amount of space to get started. The building, which has a useful life of 25 years, will cost $250,000. Jason will hire an assistant to handle his phone calls, email, invoicing, and other office tasks. The salary plus benefits that he intends to offer will total $40,000 per year. Other office operating costs should run $25,000 per year. With the extra time and visibility he gains from these changes, Jason expects to increase his revenue by $125,000 per year.

Required

a. Calculate the payback period for Jason's move to the new building.
b. Calculate the accounting rate of return for this move.

SELECTED UNIT 9.4 ANSWERS

Think About It 9.6

	CONSIDERS TIME VALUE OF MONEY	USES CASH FLOWS	USES ACCOUNTING PROFITABILITY	CONSIDERS CASH FLOWS OVER ENTIRE LIFE OF PROJECT
Net present value	Yes	Yes	No	Yes
Internal rate of return	Yes	Yes	No	Yes
Profitability index	Yes	Yes	No	Yes
Payback period	No	Yes	No	No
Accounting rate of return	No	No	Yes	No

Practice Questions

1. True
2. C
3. False
4. False
5. A
6. D

Unit 9.4 Practice Exercise

a. $\frac{\$250{,}000}{\$125{,}000 - \$40{,}000 - \$25{,}000} = 4.17 \text{ years}$

b. $\frac{\$125{,}000 - \$40{,}000 - \$25{,}000 - \$10{,}000}{\$250{,}000} = 20\%$

BUSINESS DECISION AND CONTEXT Wrap Up

Chad Davis, C&C's vice president of operations, now has the information he needs to decide whether to manufacture baseball caps. He has found that the TopCap system will generate $10,400 in additional annual cash flow over the next ten years. Based on the company's 12% discount rate, the TopCap System has a net present value of $8,497.08 and a 16% internal rate of return. Thus, it exceeds the company's minimum required rate of return of 12%. The system also has a payback period of 4.83 years and a 10.69% accounting rate of return.

Based on these criteria, Chad decides to purchase the TopCap system and add baseball caps to the company's product line. Once production has begun, Chad will revisit his estimates and compare them to actual results to determine whether this decision was a wise one.

CHAPTER SUMMARY

In this chapter you learned how to evaluate projects using capital budgeting techniques. Specifically, you should be able to meet the objectives set out at the beginning of the chapter:

1. ***Identify the cash flows associated with capital budgeting decisions. (Unit 9.1)***

   Cash flows will differ depending on the project under consideration. Common cash flows include the following:

   - Purchase price of new assets—buildings, equipment, etc. (outflow)
   - Revenues from new sales generated by the project (inflow)
   - Operating costs generated by the project (outflow)
   - Sale of old equipment (inflow)
   - Savings on operating costs generated by the project (inflow)

2. ***Explain the time value of money and calculate present values of lump sums and annuities. (Unit 9.2)***

   A dollar received today is worth more than a dollar received in the future because today's dollar can be invested to earn a return. To determine what an amount of money to be received in the future is worth today, you need to know: (1) how much money is to be received, (2) when the money is to be received, and (3) the relevant interest rate. If the money to be received in the future is a lump sum (received once), the present value is determined as follows:

$$PV_{n,i} = \text{Future amount} \times \text{Present value of \$1 factor}$$

Where: n = number of periods in the future when the amount is received

i = interest rate

$PV_{n,i}$ = present value of the amount to be received in n periods at i rate

If the money to be received in the future is an annuity (an equal series of identical payments), the present value is determined as follows:

$$PVA_{n,i} = \text{Future amount} \times \text{Present value of annuity factor}$$

Where: n = number of annuity payments

i = interest rate

$PVA_{n,i}$ = present value of an annuity to be received for n periods at i rate

3. ***Use net present value to determine the acceptability of a project. (Unit 9.3)***

The net present value of a project is the present value of its cash inflows less the present value of its cash outflows. If the net present value is greater than or equal to zero, the project is acceptable. If the net present value is less than zero, the project should be rejected.

4. ***Use the internal rate of return to determine the acceptability of a project. (Unit 9.3)***

The internal rate of return of a project is the discount rate that returns a net present value of zero. If the project includes both an investment (initial cash outflow) and an annuity (series of equal cash inflows), the internal rate of return can be found by (a) solving for the present value of an annuity factor ($PVA_{n,i}$) in the following equation and (b) locating that factor in the present value of an annuity table.

$$PVA_{n,i} = \frac{\text{Net initial investment}}{\text{Annual cash flow}}$$

If the project returns a series of uneven cash flows, the internal rate of return can be found either by trial and error or by using Microsoft Excel's IRR function.

5. ***Calculate a project's payback period. (Unit 9.4)***

The payback period shows how quickly the initial investment in a project will be recovered from the yearly cash flows. If the annual cash flows are even, the payback period can be calculated as follows:

$$\text{Payback period} = \frac{\text{Net initial investment}}{\text{Annual cash flow}}$$

If the annual cash flows are uneven, then they must be added up until they equal the net initial investment. The number of years it takes for the annual cash inflows to equal the net initial investment is the payback period. The payback period has two flaws: It ignores both the time value of money and cash flows that occur after the payback period.

6. ***Calculate a project's accounting rate of return. (Unit 9.4)***

The accounting rate of return is the only capital budgeting technique that is based on accounting income rather than cash flows. It can be calculated as follows:

$$\frac{\text{Project revenues} - \text{Project operating expenses}}{\text{Initial investment} - \text{Salvage of old equipment}} = \text{Accounting rate of return}$$

Periods	4%	5%	6%	7%	8%	9%	10%	11%	12%	13%	14%	16%	18%	20%
1	0.9615	0.9524	0.9434	0.9346	0.9259	0.9174	0.9091	0.9009	0.8929	0.8850	0.8772	0.8621	0.8475	0.8333
2	0.9246	0.9070	0.8900	0.8734	0.8573	0.8417	0.8264	0.8116	0.7972	0.7831	0.7695	0.7432	0.7182	0.6944
3	0.8890	0.8638	0.8396	0.8163	0.7938	0.7722	0.7513	0.7312	0.7118	0.6931	0.6750	0.6407	0.6086	0.5787
4	0.8548	0.8227	0.7921	0.7629	0.7350	0.7084	0.6830	0.6587	0.6355	0.6133	0.5921	0.5523	0.5158	0.4823
5	0.8219	0.7835	0.7473	0.7130	0.6806	0.6499	0.6209	0.5935	0.5674	0.5428	0.5194	0.4761	0.4371	0.4019
6	0.7903	0.7462	0.7050	0.6663	0.6302	0.5963	0.5645	0.5346	0.5066	0.4803	0.4556	0.4104	0.3704	0.3349
7	0.7599	0.7107	0.6651	0.6227	0.5835	0.5470	0.5132	0.4817	0.4523	0.4251	0.3996	0.3538	0.3139	0.2791
8	0.7307	0.6768	0.6274	0.5820	0.5403	0.5019	0.4665	0.4339	0.4039	0.3762	0.3506	0.3050	0.2660	0.2326
9	0.7026	0.6446	0.5919	0.5439	0.5002	0.4604	0.4241	0.3909	0.3606	0.3329	0.3075	0.2630	0.2255	0.1938
10	0.6756	0.6139	0.5584	0.5083	0.4632	0.4224	0.3855	0.3522	0.3220	0.2946	0.2697	0.2267	0.1911	0.1615
11	0.6496	0.5847	0.5268	0.4751	0.4289	0.3875	0.3505	0.3173	0.2875	0.2607	0.2366	0.1954	0.1619	0.1346
12	0.6246	0.5568	0.4970	0.4440	0.3971	0.3555	0.3186	0.2858	0.2567	0.2307	0.2076	0.1685	0.1372	0.1122
13	0.6006	0.5303	0.4688	0.4150	0.3677	0.3262	0.2897	0.2575	0.2292	0.2042	0.1821	0.1452	0.1163	0.0935
14	0.5775	0.5051	0.4423	0.3878	0.3405	0.2992	0.2633	0.2320	0.2046	0.1807	0.1597	0.1252	0.0985	0.0779
15	0.5553	0.4810	0.4173	0.3624	0.3152	0.2745	0.2394	0.2090	0.1827	0.1599	0.1401	0.1079	0.0835	0.0649
16	0.5339	0.4581	0.3936	0.3387	0.2919	0.2519	0.2176	0.1883	0.1631	0.1415	0.1229	0.0930	0.0708	0.0541
17	0.5134	0.4363	0.3714	0.3166	0.2703	0.2311	0.1978	0.1696	0.1456	0.1252	0.1078	0.0802	0.0600	0.0451
18	0.4936	0.4155	0.3503	0.2959	0.2502	0.2120	0.1799	0.1528	0.1300	0.1108	0.0946	0.0691	0.0508	0.0376
19	0.4746	0.3957	0.3305	0.2765	0.2317	0.1945	0.1635	0.1377	0.1161	0.0981	0.0829	0.0596	0.0431	0.0313
20	0.4564	0.3769	0.3118	0.2584	0.2145	0.1784	0.1486	0.1240	0.1037	0.0868	0.0728	0.0514	0.0365	0.0261

$$PV_{n,i} = \frac{\$1}{(1+i)^n}$$

APPENDIX 9-1 *Present value of \$1 received in* n *periods.*

Periods	4%	5%	6%	7%	8%	9%	10%	11%	12%	13%	14%	16%	18%	20%
1	0.9615	0.9524	0.9434	0.9346	0.9259	0.9174	0.9091	0.9009	0.8929	0.8850	0.8772	0.8621	0.8475	0.8333
2	1.8861	1.8594	1.8334	1.8080	1.7833	1.7591	1.7355	1.7125	1.6901	1.6681	1.6467	1.6052	1.5656	1.5278
3	2.7751	2.7232	2.6730	2.6243	2.5771	2.5313	2.4868	2.4437	2.4018	2.3612	2.3216	2.2459	2.1743	2.1065
4	3.6299	3.5460	3.4651	3.3872	3.3121	3.2397	3.1698	3.1024	3.0373	2.9745	2.9137	2.7982	2.6901	2.5887
5	4.4518	4.3295	4.2124	4.1002	3.9927	3.8897	3.7907	3.6959	3.6048	3.5172	3.4331	3.2743	3.1272	2.9906
6	5.2421	5.0757	4.9173	4.7665	4.6229	4.4859	4.3553	4.2305	4.1114	3.9975	3.8887	3.6847	3.4976	3.3255
7	6.0021	5.7864	5.5824	5.3893	5.2064	5.0330	4.8684	4.7122	4.5638	4.4226	4.2883	4.0386	3.8115	3.6046
8	6.7327	6.4632	6.2098	5.9713	5.7466	5.5348	5.3349	5.1461	4.9676	4.7988	4.6389	4.3436	4.0776	3.8372
9	7.4353	7.1078	6.8017	6.5152	6.2469	5.9952	5.7590	5.5370	5.3282	5.1317	4.9464	4.6065	4.3030	4.0310
10	8.1109	7.7217	7.3601	7.0236	6.7101	6.4177	6.1446	5.8892	5.6502	5.4262	5.2161	4.8332	4.4941	4.1925
11	8.7605	8.3064	7.8869	7.4987	7.1390	6.8052	6.4951	6.2065	5.9377	5.6869	5.4527	5.0286	4.6560	4.3271
12	9.3851	8.8633	8.3838	7.9427	7.5361	7.1607	6.8137	6.4924	6.1944	5.9176	5.6603	5.1971	4.7932	4.4392
13	9.9856	9.3936	8.8527	8.3577	7.9038	7.4869	7.1034	6.7499	6.4235	6.1218	5.8424	5.3423	4.9095	4.5327
14	10.5631	9.8986	9.2950	8.7455	8.2442	7.7862	7.3667	6.9819	6.6282	6.3025	6.0021	5.4675	5.0081	4.6106
15	11.1184	10.3797	9.7122	9.1079	8.5595	8.0607	7.6061	7.1909	6.8109	6.4624	6.1422	5.5755	5.0916	4.6755
16	11.6523	10.8378	10.1059	9.4466	8.8514	8.3126	7.8237	7.3792	6.9740	6.6039	6.2651	5.6685	5.1624	4.7296
17	12.1657	11.2741	10.4773	9.7632	9.1216	8.5436	8.0216	7.5488	7.1196	6.7291	6.3729	5.7487	5.2223	4.7746
18	12.6593	11.6896	10.8276	10.0591	9.3719	8.7556	8.2014	7.7016	7.2497	6.8399	6.4674	5.8178	5.2732	4.8122
19	13.1339	12.0853	11.1581	10.3356	9.6036	8.9501	8.3649	7.8393	7.3658	6.9380	6.5504	5.8775	5.3162	4.8435
20	13.5903	12.4622	11.4699	10.5940	9.8181	9.1285	8.5136	7.9633	7.4694	7.0248	6.6231	5.9288	5.3527	4.8696

$$PVA_{n,i} = \frac{\$1 - \dfrac{1}{(1+i)^n}}{i}$$

APPENDIX 9-2 *Present value of an annuity of \$1 per period.*

KEY TERMS

Accounting rate of return (Unit 9.4)
Annuity (Unit 9.2)
Capital asset (Unit 9.1)
Capital budgeting (Unit 9.1)
Compound interest (Unit 9.2)
Depreciable asset (Unit 9.1)
Discounting (Unit 9.2)
Discount rate (Unit 9.2)
Hurdle rate (Unit 9.1)
Internal rate of return (IRR) (Unit 9.3)
Long-lived asset (Unit 9.1)
Net initial investment (Unit 9.3)
Net present value (NPV) (Unit 9.3)
Payback period (Unit 9.4)
Preference decision (Unit 9.1)
Present value (Unit 9.2)
Present value factor (Unit 9.2)
Profitability index (Unit 9.3)
Return of investment (Unit 9.1)
Return on investment (Unit 9.1)
Screening decision (Unit 9.1)
Simple rate of return (Unit 9.4)
Unadjusted rate of return (Unit 9.4)

EXERCISES

9-1 Identifying cash flows (CMA adapted) (LO 1) Metro Industries is considering the purchase of new equipment costing $1,200,000 to replace existing equipment that will be sold for $180,000. The new equipment is expected to have a $200,000 salvage value at the end of its four-year life. During the period of its use, the equipment will allow the company to produce and sell an additional 30,000 units annually at a sales price of $20 per unit. Those units will have a variable cost of $12 per unit. The company will also incur an additional $90,000 in annual fixed costs.

Required

Identify the amount and timing of all cash flows related to the acquisition of the new equipment.

9-2 Identifying cash flows (LO 1) Mighty Vita produces a wide range of herbal supplements sold nationwide through independent distributors. In response to an increasing demand for its products, the company is considering the purchase of a new packaging machine to replace the seven-year-old machine currently in use. The new machine will cost $160,000, and installation will require an additional $15,000. The machine has a useful life of 10 years and is expected to have a salvage value of $8,000 at that time. The variable cost to operate the new machine is $10 per carton compared to the current machine's variable cost of $10.10 per carton, and Mighty Vita expects to pack 250,000 cartons each year. If the new machine is purchased, Mighty Vita will avoid a required $10,000 overhaul of the current machine in four years. The current machine has a market value of $14,000.

Required

Identify the amount and timing of all cash flows related to the acquisition of the new packaging machine.

9-3 Calculating the present value of a single amount (LO 2) Margaret wants to buy a car when she graduates from Central University four years from now. She believes that she will need $30,000 to buy the car.

Required

a. Calculate how much money Margaret must put into her savings account today to have $30,000 in four years, assuming she can earn 8% compounded annually.

b. Calculate how much money Margaret must put into her savings account today to have $30,000 in four years, assuming she can earn 8% compounded semiannually.

9-4 Calculating the present value of an annuity (LO 2) Parker is planning for his retirement this year. One option that has been presented to him is the purchase of an annuity that would provide a $60,000 payment each year for the next 15 years.

Required

Calculate how much Parker should be willing to pay for the annuity if he can invest his funds at 9%.

9-5 Calculating present values (CMA adapted) (LO 2) Review the data provided in Exercise 9-1.

Required

Calculate the present value of each cash flow assuming an 8% discount rate.

9-6 Calculating present values (LO 2) Chuck has just won the Flyball Lottery. He has two options for receiving his prize. The first option is to accept a $200,000 cash payment today. The second option is to receive $20,000 at the end of each of the next 19 years and a $50,000 lump sum payment in the twentieth year. Chuck can invest money at a 5% rate.

Required

a. Which option should Chuck choose to receive his winnings? Why?
b. If Chuck could invest money at 9%, which option should he choose? Why?

9-7 Net present value (CMA adapted) (LO 3) Review the data provided in Exercise 9-1.

Required

a. Calculate the net present value of the proposed equipment purchase. Assume that Metro uses a 12% discount rate.
b. Do you recommend that Metro Industries invest in the new equipment? Why or why not?

9-8 Net present value (LO 3) Review the data provided in Exercise 9-2.

Required

a. Calculate the net present value of the new packaging machine. Assume that Mighty Vita uses an 8% discount rate.
b. Do you recommend that Mighty Vita purchase the new machine? Why or why not?
c. Assume that Mighty Vita has adopted a new 12% discount rate. Do you recommend that Mighty Vita purchase the new machine? Why or why not?

9-9 Net present value (LO 3) Larry's Lawn Service needs to purchase a new lawnmower costing $7,756 to replace an old lawnmower that cannot be repaired. The new lawnmower is expected to have a useful life of four years, with no salvage value at the end of that period.

Required

a. If Larry's required rate of return is 11%, what level of annual cash savings must the lawnmower generate to be considered an acceptable investment under the net present value method?
b. If Larry's required rate of return is 14%, what level of annual cash savings must the lawnmower generate to be considered an acceptable investment under the net present value method?

9-10 Net present value (LO 3) The Seago Company is planning to purchase $500,000 of equipment with an estimated seven-year life and no estimated salvage value. The company has projected the following annual cash flows for the investment:

Year	Projected Cash Flows
1	$200,000
2	150,000
3	100,000
4	60,000
5	60,000
6	40,000
7	40,000
Total	$650,000

Required

Calculate the net present value of the proposed equipment purchase. Seago uses a 10% discount rate.

9-11 Internal rate of return (LO 4) Harrison Hammocks is considering the purchase of a new weaving machine to prepare fabric for its hammocks. The machine under consideration costs $88,235 and will save the company $14,000 in direct labor costs. It is expected to last 14 years.

Required

a. Calculate the internal rate of return on the weaving machine.
b. If Harrison uses a 12% hurdle rate, should the company invest in the machine? Why or why not?

9-12 Internal rate of return (LO 4) Garrett Boone, Farish Enterprises' vice president of operations, needs to replace an automatic lathe on the production line. The model he is considering has a sales price of $285,000 and will last for 9 years. It will have no salvage value at the end of its useful life. Garrett estimates the new lathe will reduce raw materials scrap by $40,000 per year. He also believes the lathe will reduce energy costs by $25,000 per year. If he purchases the new lathe, he will be able to sell the old lathe for $5,305.

Required

a. Calculate the lathe's internal rate of return.
b. If Farish Enterprises uses a 15% hurdle rate, should Garrett purchase the lathe?
c. Without doing any calculations, what do you know about the lathe's net present value?

9-13 Internal rate of return (LO 4) Boyer Cosmetics is planning to expand its product line to include stage makeup. The expansion will require the company to purchase special mixing equipment at a cost of $125,532. The equipment will have a useful life of 16 years.

Required

a. If Boyer uses a 12% hurdle rate, what is the minimum annual net cash inflow required to make this project acceptable under the internal rate of return method?
b. If Boyer estimates that the new product line will generate $16,000 in additional annual net cash inflow, is the project acceptable given the company's 12% hurdle rate? Why or why not?

9-14 Payback period (LO 5) Tom Falkland is considering refinancing his home mortgage to reduce his house payment by $125 per month. Closing costs associated with the refinancing will total $5,000. Tom will finish medical school in four years, at which time he will sell the house and move to another state.

Required

a. What is the payback period for refinancing this loan?
b. Given Tom's plans, should he refinance his mortgage at this time? Why or why not?

9-15 Payback period with even cash flows (LO 5) Wyer's Accounting Museum is exploring the purchase of a new building with a useful life of 15 years to use as its main gallery space. The building will cost $850,000. Once it has been purchased, the museum will terminate its current lease, which costs $60,000 per year. The new gallery will allow the museum to display more of its permanent collection, as well as to showcase traveling exhibits. The increased exhibit space, along with the new building's location, is expected to increase admissions revenue by $25,000 per year.

Required

Calculate the payback period for the proposed investment in the building. Assume that all cash flows occur evenly throughout the year.

9-16 Payback period with uneven cash flows (LO 5) The Seago Company is planning to purchase $500,000 of equipment with an estimated seven-year life and no estimated salvage value. The company has projected the following annual cash flows for the investment.

Year	Projected Cash Flows
1	$200,000
2	150,000
3	100,000
4	60,000
5	60,000
6	40,000
7	40,000
Total	$650,000

Required

a. Calculate the payback period for the proposed equipment purchase. Assume that all cash flows occur evenly throughout the year.
b. If Seago requires a payback period of three years or less, should the company make this investment?

9-17 Accounting rate of return (LO 6) Danny Bostic is evaluating a new ticketing system for his theater. The system will cost $275,000 and will save the theater $57,800 in annual cash operating costs. Danny expects the new system to last ten years, at which time the system will have a salvage value of $15,000. If Danny purchases the new system, he will be able to sell his existing system for $10,000.

Required

a. Calculate the accounting rate of return for the proposed ticketing system.
b. Danny Bostic wants to earn a minimum accounting rate of return of 10% on his projects. Should he invest in the new equipment? Why or why not?

9-18 Accounting rate of return (LO 6) Payton and Finley Davis run a real estate brokerage firm. They have just moved into a new building and want to add some outdoor digital signage to advertise the firm's services. The sign they are considering has two display areas that can display two different images at the same time and costs $140,000. It is expected to have a useful life of five years. In an effort to recoup the cost of the sign, Payton and Finley will rent one display panel to other tenants in the building for $36,000 a year. Electricity to power the sign is expected to be $1,000 per year.

Required

a. Calculate the annual net operating income generated by the new sign.
b. Calculate the accounting rate of return of the new sign.
c. If the sign is successful in generating new business for the firm, how will the accounting rate of return be affected?

9-19 Accounting rate of return (LO 6) Hannah's House of Music wants to purchase TransposeIt, a system that transposes any song in its database and prints sheet music in the requested key. This system allows singers to obtain sheet music in keys that are suitable to their vocal range. The software for the system costs $10,000; a new computer and a laser printer costing $3,500 will be needed to run the system. Hannah estimates that the system will generate additional annual sales revenue of $23,000 and that annual cash expenditures will be $18,115. Hannah uses straight-line depreciation. The software, computer, and printer will have a useful life of five years. The system will have no salvage value at the end of its five-year useful life.

Required

a. Calculate the annual net operating income generated by the system.
b. Calculate the accounting rate of return of the system.

PROBLEMS

9-20 Present value of an annuity (LO 2) Martha Gentry won an $18 million lottery and elected to receive her winnings in 30 equal annual installments. After receiving the first 10 installments, Martha and her husband divorced, and the remaining 20 payments became part of the property settlement. The judge who presided over the divorce proceedings awarded one-half interest in the future lottery payments to Martha and the other half to her ex-husband.

Following the divorce, Martha decided to sell her interest in the 20 remaining lottery payments to raise the cash needed to open a flower store. An investor has offered Martha $2,945,430.

Required

a. What discount rate did the investor use in calculating the purchase price?
b. If Martha can invest the money she gets at 6%, which is the better option, keeping the annuity or accepting the investor's offer? Why?
c. What needs might Martha have that would make the investor's offer the preferable option, no matter what the interest rate (within reason)?

9-21 Net present value (LO 3) AutoQuest has been selling auto parts to the general public for over 70 years. It has built a reputation for outstanding customer service, becoming the third largest auto parts retailer in the Southwest. Hoping to expand its sales to other regions, managers have decided to establish an online retail presence. Dan Jennings, CIO of AutoQuest, is charged with the task of evaluating how the company should implement this strategy.

One of the first things Dan needs to determine is how to acquire the network servers the company will need. He knows the vendor he wants to use, but he is uncertain whether he should buy or lease the servers. If he buys the servers for $4.3 million, AutoQuest will incur annual maintenance costs of $50,000 over their five-year life. If he leases the servers for five years, AutoQuest will make lease payments of $1.2 million in each of the first three years and $1 million in each of the last two years. Annual maintenance costs under the lease will be $80,000.

Required

a. Which option will cost the company less to implement, assuming a 12% discount rate?
b. What salvage value would AutoQuest need to receive on the purchased servers at the end of year 5 so that the purchase option is essentially equal to the lease option? Assume a 12% discount rate.
c. What annual cash inflow from the new online sales would be necessary for the lease option to be financially acceptable? Assume a 12% discount rate.
d. What nonfinancial issues might Dan Jennings consider in deciding whether to purchase or lease the servers?

9-22 Net present value (CIMA adapted) (LO 3) Farmville Regional Airport is modernizing its terminal facilities in anticipation of significant growth in the number of passengers using the airport. A consultant's study commissioned by the airport's board predicts that the number of passengers using the airport will increase by 10% per year for the next 4 years as a result of a "low-cost" airline opening new routes to and from the airport.

Currently, the airport terminal has only one food outlet selling sandwiches and drinks. To improve the terminal amenities available to customers, the airport board is considering opening an additional restaurant that will sell a range of hot food and drinks. The cost of outfitting the new restaurant space, which will have to be completely refurbished in four years, is $350,000. The restaurant's equipment and furnishings are expected to have a salvage value of $30,000 at the time of the refurbishment.

The consultant's study reported the following information concerning expected revenue and costs for the new restaurant:

Average revenue per customer:	$ 9
Average variable cost per customer:	$ 5
Customers per day in year 1:	500
Number of employees years 1 and 2:	4
Number of employees years 3 and 4:	5
Average annual employee salary:	$20,000
Fixed annual cash operating costs:	$70,000

Future customer demand for the new restaurant will increase by 10% each year for the next four years.

The current cold food outlet has an average contribution margin of $2.50 per customer. If the new hot food restaurant is not opened, it is expected that the cold food outlet will sell to 1,200 customers per day in year 1, with the number of customers increasing by 10% per year in the subsequent three years.

If the new hot food restaurant is opened, the consultant's report predicts the number of customers served at the cold food outlet will be 40% lower than without the restaurant in year 1. Thereafter, the number of customers would increase by 10% per year.

The airport operates 360 days per year, and the airport board uses an 8% discount rate to evaluate projects of this type.

Required

a. Calculate the annual contribution margin generated by the proposed hot food restaurant.
b. Calculate the annual impact that the proposed hot food restaurant will have on the contribution margin generated by the existing cold food outlet.
c. Calculate the net present value of opening the proposed hot food restaurant.
d. Should the airport board move forward with its plan to open the hot food restaurant? Why or why not?

9-23 Net present value, profitability index (LO 3) Bill Zimmerman is evaluating two new business opportunities. Each of the opportunities shown below has a ten-year life. Bill uses a 10% discount rate.

	Option 1	Option 2
Equipment purchase and installation	$70,000	$80,000
Annual cash flow	$28,000	$30,000
Equipment overhaul in year 3	$ 5,000	—
Equipment overhaul in year 5	—	$ 6,000

Required

a. Calculate the net present value of the two opportunities.
b. Calculate the profitability index of the two opportunities.
c. Which option should Bill choose? Why?

9-24 Internal rate of return (LO 4) TimeTrends integrated time clock and payroll system sells for $271,673. At this price, the annual cost savings that the system will generate for Building Keepers, a facilities management company, over its ten-year life will yield an internal rate of return of 13%. Building Keepers requires that all projects achieve a minimum return of 16%.

Required

What price does Building Keepers need to negotiate with TimeTrends so that the system will achieve that return?

9-25 Net present value, internal rate of return (CMA adapted) (LO 3, 4) Harker Company manufactures automobile components for the worldwide market. The company has three large production facilities in Virginia, New Jersey, and California, which have been operating for many years. Brett Harker, vice president of production, believes it is time to upgrade operations by implementing computer-integrated manufacturing (CIM) at one of the plants.

Brett has asked corporate controller Connie Carson to gather information about the costs and benefits of implementing CIM. Carson has gathered the following data:

Initial equipment cost	$6,000,000
Working capital required at start-up	$ 500,000
Salvage value of existing equipment	$ 75,000
Annual operating cost savings	$ 900,000
Salvage value of new equipment at end of its useful life	$ 100,000
Working capital released at end of its useful life	$ 500,000
Useful life of equipment	10 years

Harker Company uses a 12% discount rate.

Required

a. Calculate the net present value of Harker's proposed investment in CIM.
b. Use Excel or a similar spreadsheet application to calculate the internal rate of return on Harker's proposed investment.
c. Do you recommend that the company proceed with the purchase and implementation of CIM? Why or why not?
d. Andrew Burr, manager of the Virginia plant, has been looking over Carson's information and believes she has missed some important benefits of implementing CIM. Burr believes that implementing CIM will reduce scrap and rework costs by $100,000 per year. The CIM equipment will take up less floor space in the factory than the old equipment, freeing up 5,000 square feet of space for a planned new research facility. Initial plans called for renting additional space for the new facility, at a cost of $30 per square foot. Calculate a revised net present value and internal rate of return using this additional information. Does your recommendation change as a result of this new information? Why or why not?

9-26 Payback period, accounting rate of return (LO 5, 6) Cindy Alexander, Turner, Inc.'s vice president of marketing, has received a sales call from a vendor of customer relationship management (CRM) software. The vendor claims that the software and other data her company provides will enable Turner to target its advertising more appropriately and to identify new markets. The average improvement in sales volume from CRM is 10%, with no increase in advertising costs. The cost of the software and related services is $1,200,000. Turner depreciates software over five years. The company's current cash-basis income statement, based on sales of 60,000 units, follows.

Sales revenue		$6,000,000
Cost of goods sold (all variable)		2,700,000
Gross margin		3,300,000
Less operating expenses		
Selling expense (50% variable)	$ 900,000	
Administrative expense (all fixed)	2,000,000	2,840,000
Income		$ 460,000

Required

a. Calculate the payback period for the software if Turner, Inc. realizes the reported average improvements.

b. Compare the payback period to the useful life of the software. Is the payback period adequate?

c. Calculate the accounting rate of return the software will generate.

9-27 Net present value, internal rate of return, payback period (LO 3, 4, 5)

Jonathan Lark's lifelong dream is to own a restaurant. He owns a premium site for a restaurant across the street from the local university. Now he needs to decide what kind of restaurant to open.

Recently, Jonathan began to investigate one of the fastest-growing fast-food franchises in the country, Pepper Roni Pizza. A Pepper Roni Pizza franchise costs $40,000, an amount that is amortized over 15 years. As a franchisee, Jonathan would need to adhere to the company's building specifications. The building would cost an estimated $425,000 and would have a $60,000 salvage value at the end of its 15-year life. The restaurant equipment (fryers, steam tables, booths, counters) is sold as a package by the corporate office at a cost of $150,000, will have a salvage value of $10,000 at the end of its five-year life, and must be replaced every five years.

Jonathan estimates the annual revenue from a Pepper Roni Pizza franchise at $1,000,000. Food costs typically run 38% of revenue. Annual operating expenses, not including depreciation, total $455,000. For financial reporting purposes, Jonathan will use straight-line depreciation and amortization. Based on past experience, he uses an 18% discount rate.

Required

a. Calculate the restaurant's net present value over the franchise's 15-year life.

b. Use Excel or a similar spreadsheet application to calculate the restaurant's internal rate of return over the franchise's 15-year life.

c. Calculate the restaurant's payback period.

d. Should Jonathan open a Pepper Roni Pizza? Why or why not?

e. What potential shortcomings do you see in Jonathan's estimates? How would you recommend he adjust his analysis to address those shortcomings?

9-28 Net present value, internal rate of return, payback period (LO 3, 4, 5)

Jewel Pix currently uses a six-year-old molding machine to manufacture silver picture frames. The company paid $85,000 for the machine, which was state of the art at the time of purchase. Although the machine will likely last another ten years, it will need a $15,000 overhaul in three years. More important, it does not provide enough capacity to meet customer demand. The company currently produces and sells 10,000 frames per year, generating a total contribution margin of $50,000.

Martson Molders currently sells a molding machine that will allow Jewel Pix to increase production and sales to 15,000 frames per year. The machine, which has a ten-year life, sells for $125,000 and would cost $9,000 per year to operate. Jewel Pix's current machine costs only $7,000 per year to operate. If Jewel Pix purchases the new machine, the old machine could be sold at its book value of $4,000. The new machine is expected to have a salvage value of $9,000 at the end of its ten-year life. Jewel Pix uses straight-line depreciation.

Required

a. Calculate the new machine's net present value assuming a 14% discount rate.
b. Use Excel or a similar spreadsheet application to calculate the new machine's internal rate of return.
c. Calculate the new machine's payback period.

9-29 Net present value, internal rate of return, payback period, accounting rate of return (LO 3, 4, 5, 6) Farrior Fashions needs to replace a beltloop attacher that currently costs the company $40,000 in annual cash operating costs. This machine is of no use to another company, but it could be sold as scrap for $2,160. Managers have identified a potential replacement machine, Euromat's Model HD-435.

The HD-435 is priced at $48,720 and would cost Farrior Fashions $30,000 in annual cash operating costs. The machine has a useful life of 11 years, and it is not expected to have any salvage value at the end of that time.

Required

a. Calculate the net present value of purchasing the HD-435, assuming Farrior Fashions uses a 14% discount rate.
b. Calculate the internal rate of return on the HD-435.
c. Calculate the payback period of the HD-435.
d. Calculate the accounting rate of return on the HD-435.
e. Should Farrior Fashions purchase the HD-435? Why or why not?

C&C SPORTS CONTINUING CASE

9-30 Capital investment analysis (LO 1, 3) After one year using the TopCap system, Jonathan Smith, vice president for marketing at C&C Sports, is convinced that the company could sell even more baseball caps. Apparently, the market demand for plain caps that are suitable for logo embroidery by corporations, fraternities, and other groups is greater than current manufacturers can supply. The potential for C&C Sports to extend its sales of baseball caps beyond the athletic team market is huge.

The initial specifications for the TopCap system required three workers per eight-hour shift to make up to 1,000 caps per day. Based on initial demand forecasts, Jonathan asked Chad Davis, vice president for operations, to make 250,000 caps in the first year the product was offered. Jonathan is convinced that C&C could sell at least 500,000 caps per year with the correct investment in marketing.

Required

a. By how much would annual operating income increase if a second shift was used to produce additional caps? Refer to Exhibit 9-2 for current revenue and cost information. Assume that the relevant range for the fixed costs is 750,000 caps.
b. What additional one-time marketing cost could be justified to increase sales to meet anticipated demand? Remember that there are only 9 years of usable life remaining for the TopCap system and that C&C Sports uses a 12% discount rate.

CASES

9-31 Net present value (CMA adapted) (LO 3) "Maybe I should have stuck with teaching high school art. No matter what I try, I can't seem to turn that Roanoke plant around." That's how the meeting between Warren Wingo, CEO of clothing manufacturer Wingo Designs, and Angie Tillery, vice president of corporate lending at First National Bank, ended. Wingo and Tillery had just concluded that the Roanoke plant was draining corporate cash flow and income, and should be closed on December 31, 2018.

When he returned to his office, Wingo summoned corporate controller Ron Wright to tell him the bad news. "Ron, I wish there were some way to turn this situation around. We've had so many bad things happen lately—the fire in Lexington, the strike in Pulaski, and now this. Why didn't I stay at Cave Spring High?"

"Warren, it may not be as bad as it seems," Ron replied. "Let's put our heads together and do some investigating. We've got some great folks working here, and I bet if we asked them to think about it, they could come up with some options." With that encouragement, Warren sent Ron out to find some way of disposing of the Roanoke facility.

Early Monday morning, Ron ran into Warren's office waving a legal pad. "We've done it, Warren. We've got three good options for the Roanoke plant. One of them even has us keeping the plant." Warren listened intently as Ron laid out the three options his staff had developed:

Option 1

Sell the plant immediately to Tinsley Togs for $9,000,000.

Option 2

Lease the plant for four years to Star City Mills (one of Wingo's suppliers). Under the lease terms, Star City would pay Wingo $2,400,000 in rent each year and would grant Wingo a 10% discount on fabric purchased by another of its plants. The fabric normally sells for $2 per yard, and Wingo expects to purchase 2,370,000 yards of it each year. Star City would cover all the plant's ownership costs, including property taxes. At the end of the lease, Wingo would sell the plant for $2,000,000.

Option 3

Use the plant for four years to make souvenir 2022 Winter Olympic jackets. Fixed overhead, before equipment upgrades, is estimated at $200,000 a year. The jackets are expected to have a variable cost of $33 per unit and to sell for $42 each. Estimated unit sales are as follows; annual production would equal sales.

Year	Jacket Sales in Units
2019	200,000
2020	300,000
2021	400,000
2022	100,000

To manufacture the jackets, some of the plant's equipment would have to be replaced at an immediate cost of $1,500,000. The equipment would have a useful life of four years. Because of the upgraded equipment, Wingo could sell the plant for $3,000,000 at the end of four years.

Required

a. Calculate the cash flows for years one through four for each option.
b. Calculate the net present value of each option. Assume a 12% discount rate.
c. Use Excel or another spreadsheet application to determine the discount rate that equates options 1 and 2. Do the same for options 1 and 3.
d. What should Wingo do?

9-32 Net present value, ethics (adapted from Roland L. Madison, "Should Finance Make the Numbers 'Come Out'," Strategic Finance, 86, no. 10 (April 2005): 17–18.) (LO 3) Amy Kimbell, CPA, CMA, and a member of the Institute of Management Accountants, recently joined Magee Metals and Moldings as a senior financial analyst. One of her major responsibilities is to prepare data to support capital equipment purchases.

Magee is trying to expand its international operations. The company is currently spending $275,000 each year on international travel, an amount that is expected to increase by

20% each year for the next four years and then level off. Since none of Magee's current fleet of corporate jets has the range to fly internationally, Magee's CFO, Tony Smith, recently asked Amy to run some numbers on the purchase of a new corporate jet with an international range.

Amy determined that the jet upper managers want to buy has a purchase price of $15 million and a useful life of 15 years. Variable operating costs are an estimated $220,000 per year, based on a projected usage of 400 hours per year. Fixed operating costs are estimated at $375,000 per year, not including depreciation. When Magee employees aren't using the company's jets, they are rented to other parties at a rate of $3,500 per hour. Based on existing rental requests, Amy estimated that the new jet would be rented for 500 hours each year.

Using Magee's 12% discount rate, Amy calculated the net present value of the new jet purchase to be at most ($6,000,000). She knew there was no way the capital budget committee would approve a purchase with such a large negative net present value. When she presented her analysis to Tony, he responded. "Go back and check your work. When I ran the preliminary numbers, I found a positive net present value. You must have made a mistake." Tony suggested that she increase the useful life of the jet to 25 years, raise the salvage value by 25%, and increase the rental usage by 50%.

Amy did some additional research and determined through discussions with the jet's manufacturer that her original salvage value and estimated life were aggressive, but realistic. In fact, if the jet were used for 25 years, it would require a multimillion-dollar overhaul in year 15 to remain flightworthy. Beginning in year 11, operating costs would increase by 30%. With this new information, Amy reworked her analysis and obtained an even larger negative net present value.

When Tony saw the revised numbers, he blew up. "I told you what to do with the numbers and you did something else. Now go back and do what I said. And have the correct analysis back to me by the end of the day."

Amy returned to her office slowly, thinking about what Tony was telling her to do. She had been at Magee for only a month and really liked her job. In fact, she was looking forward to a long career at Magee.

Required

a. Should Amy make the changes Tony has requested, noting in her analysis that the CFO provided the estimates? Why or why not?

b. If Amy makes the changes Tony has requested, but doesn't want to list him as the source of the estimates, should she send an unsigned note to the chair of the capital budget committee, informing him of the problems with the analysis? Why or why not?

c. What actions should Amy take in response to Tony's final request? Support your answer by referring to the IMA's Statement of Ethical Professional Practice.

d. Tony Smith is a licensed CPA and a member of the IMA. Should Amy report his behavior to the state accounting board and the IMA? Why or why not?

ANALYTICS PROBLEM

9-33 Capital Budgeting Screening and Preference Decisions (LO 3, 4, 5)

Preston Plastics is about to wrap up its capital budgeting cycle, and department managers across the company have submitted 500 capital project requests for consideration in the next round of funding. Preston's CFO, Dan LaMontagne, is trying to decide which projects to recommend for funding to the capital projects executive committee. He has gathered all the information about each project's estimated life, initial investment, and cash flows in an Excel spreadsheet and is ready to make his decisions. Preston requires all capital projects to have a payback period of 5 years or less and uses a 12% discount rate.

Required

a. Calculate the net present value (use Excel's NPV formula with a 12% discount rate), internal rate of return (use Excel's IRR formula), payback period, and profitability index for each project and save in the worksheet.
b. How many of the submitted projects meet the payback period screening criterion? *Hint:* Use Excel's COUNTIF formula to easily calculate this number.
c. Copy the original data and your calculations from part (a) to a new worksheet. Sort the data by payback period and delete all projects that do not meet the screening criteria.
d. Preston has only $2 billion in capital funds to allocate this period. Will this be enough to fund all the requested projects that meet the payback screening criterion? What is the shortfall amount?
e. Suppose Preston chooses to fund capital projects based on net present value. How many projects will be funded? What is the total amount of capital funds that will be allocated? *Hint:* Sort the data from part (c) by net present value and calculate a running sum of project investment to help you determine which projects can be funded.
f. Suppose Preston chooses to fund capital projects based on internal rate of return. How many projects will be funded? What is the total amount of capital funds that will be allocated? *Hint:* Sort the data from part (c) by internal rate of return and calculate a running sum of project investment to help you determine which projects can be funded.
g. Suppose Preston chooses to fund capital projects based on profitability index. How many projects will be funded? What is the total amount of capital funds that will be allocated? *Hint:* Sort the data from part (c) by profitability index and calculate a running sum of project investment to help you determine which projects can be funded.
h. Which of the three metrics do you recommend that Preston use to allocate the $2 billion to fund the capital projects? Why?
i. Dan has just learned that projects 16808 and 17011 are required to meet new regulatory requirements, and therefore must be funded regardless of the metrics. How will this information change your funding recommendations?

The Excel data files for answering this problem can be found in WileyPLUS.

ENDNOTES

1. ExxonMobil paid dividends during this period, which would also be considered part of the return of investment; however, we are ignoring those dividends to simplify the illustration. You can learn more about ExxonMobil by visiting its website at http://corporate.exxonmobil.com.
2. Patrick McGeehan, "La Guardia Airport to Be Overhauled by 2021, Cuomo and Biden Say," *The New York Times*, July 27, 2015, http://www.nytimes.com/2015/07/28/nyregion/la-guardia-airport-to-be-rebuilt-by-2021-cuomo-and-biden-say.html?_r=0 (accessed April 29, 2016).
3. The Manufacturing Institute, National Association of Manufacturers, and RSM McGladrey, Inc. *The Future Success of Small and Medium Manufacturers: Challenges and Policy Issues* (2006), 42.
4. To learn more about making baseball caps, visit http://www.madehow.com/Volume-4/Baseball-Cap.html.
5. The choices are based strictly on the financial result. However, someone may prefer $20,000 today regardless of the rate of return because of the need to buy food, pay rent, and the like. At 10%, an investor may not be indifferent if he or she doesn't want to bear the risk that investment returns will decline. Investment decisions are not based solely on the financial outcome; however, if all other factors are the same, the higher return would always be preferred.

Esben Emborg/Getty Images

DECENTRALIZATION AND PERFORMANCE EVALUATION

© Africa Studio/Shutterstock

UNITS	LEARNING OBJECTIVES
UNIT 10.1 Centralized versus Decentralized Organizations	**LO 1:** Identify the difference between a cost center, a profit center, and an investment center.
UNIT 10.2 Segment Evaluation	**LO 2:** Prepare a segment margin income statement and evaluate a segment's financial performance.
UNIT 10.3 Return on Investment	**LO 3:** Evaluate an operating segment or project using return on investment.
UNIT 10.4 Residual Income and EVA®	**LO 4:** Evaluate an operating segment or project using residual income and economic value added.
APPENDIX Transfer Pricing	**LO 5:** Calculate the minimum transfer price between divisions that maximizes corporate income.

Business Decision and Context

Monica Waltrip, vice president of Centex Yarns' Nylon Fibers division, answered the telephone. It was **CEO James Cameron**. "Monica, I just got the latest corporate income statement. Your division is showing a loss for the third straight year. I think I've given you plenty of time to turn things around, so we need to meet at 1:00 to make some hard decisions about the division's viability." All Monica could manage to reply was, "I'll be there."

Monica knew she was going to be in the hot seat. Yes, the division had shown a loss on the corporate income statement for the past three years, but she and her team had worked hard to improve operations. Sales were up and the cost of goods sold was down. She needed to know why those improvements weren't making it to the bottom line, and she needed to know now. So she went to visit the **division's controller, Luke Carlson**.

"Luke, I've got to meet with James Cameron at 1:00 to discuss the future of the division. Given our three straight years of losses, I'm afraid our conversation will end with a recommendation to close the division. Can you give me anything to help argue that we should remain open?"

"Three years of losses in this economy will be hard to argue against," Luke replied, "but let me take a look at the numbers and see what I can come up with. Maybe I can pull a rabbit out of my hat."

Monica left without much optimism for the division's future. "I just wish there was some way to show James that we're contributing to the company's overall success."

> "I just wish there was some way to show James that we're contributing to the company's overall success."

she thought. "I know deep down that we are, but James isn't going to make decisions based on my gut feel."

SUPPLY CHAIN KEY PLAYERS

END CUSTOMER

UNIVERSAL SPORTS EXCHANGE

C&C SPORTS

DURABLE ZIPPER COMPANY

BRADLEY TEXTILE MILLS

CENTEX YARNS

Chief Executive Officer
James Cameron

Vice President of Nylon Fibers Division
Monica Waltrip

Nylon Fibers Division Controller
Luke Carlson

NEFF FIBER MANUFACTURING

BRUIN POLYMERS, INC.

UNIT 10.1

Centralized versus Decentralized Organizations

GUIDED UNIT PREPARATION

Answering the following questions while you read this unit will guide your understanding of the key concepts found in the unit. The questions are linked to the learning objectives presented at the beginning of the chapter.

LO 1

1. What is a decentralized organization?
2. What are the advantages of decentralization? The disadvantages?
3. What is responsibility accounting?
4. As a manager, would you support the use of responsibility accounting? Why or why not?
5. What are the three categorizations (centers) of decentralized organizations, and how are managers of those centers evaluated?

When you think of CBS Corporation, you probably think of its popular television shows, such as *NCIS, The Big Bang Theory,* and *The Amazing Race*. But CBS is much more than a collection of television shows. In fact, the company has 25 different divisions, including the CBS Television Network, CBS Television (a group of 29 television stations), Showtime, CBS Radio (a group of 117 radio stations), and publisher Simon & Schuster. Imagine how difficult it would be for the president and CEO of CBS Corporation to know all the details of running those divisions on a daily basis.

CBS has a decentralized management structure that gives decision-making authority to the divisional presidents and CEOs. In some of those divisions, decision-making authority is further delegated within the division. Simon & Schuster, for instance, has eight divisions—adult publishing; children's publishing; audio; digital; and the international divisions in the United Kingdom, Canada, India, and Australia—each of which is evaluated individually. In this unit, you will learn about the issues associated with decentralization and the reasons some companies choose to decentralize their operations.

C&C Sports has not reached a point of needing to decentralize its operations; George Douglas is able to manage the day-to-day activities. In this chapter, we will focus on Centex Yarns, the company that manufactures the yarns used to make the fabric C&C Sports uses in its jerseys, pants, and jackets. Centex Yarns has grown to the point that it has many managers throughout the organization making the day-to-day decisions, and these managers are evaluated on how well they implement the company's strategic goals and objectives.

Why Decentralization?

When Centex Yarns began business years ago, it was easy for CEO James Cameron to stay on top of everything that was going on in the company. Centex Yarns had a single product, a single plant location, and few employees. As CEO, James was responsible for making all the major decisions. This organizational structure, in which decision-making authority for the entire organization rests in the hands of one person or a small group of people in a single location, is called **centralization**.

As Centex Yarns grew by adding more product lines, more plant locations, and more employees, James found it more and more difficult to remain informed about the company's activities. Eventually he reached the point at which he did not have the information or knowledge he needed to make informed decisions. At that point, James decided to abandon his centralized organizational structure in favor of **decentralization**, in which decision-making authority is dispersed throughout the organization. In this new structure, managers of Centex Yarns' various operating units were given substantial decision-making authority.

We can think of organization structure as a continuum. On the centralized end of the continuum, operational managers have no authority to make decisions. On the decentralized end of the continuum, managers have complete control over operational decisions. Rarely does an organization operate at either end of the continuum. Each organization must choose the degree of decentralization that works best; there is no single degree of decentralization that is right for all organizations.

After an organization implements a certain level of decentralization, it is not committed to maintaining that level for the life of the organization. As Home Depot spread nationally and internationally, it recognized that a regional approach to merchandising gives store managers the ability to control their inventory to meet customers' tastes and preferences.[1] Inventory managers at corporate headquarters in Atlanta were not the best people to make inventory decisions for stores in California or Texas. Walmart has made similar moves to provide more localized inventory purchasing. Alternatively, an organization may decide to reduce the level of authority managers have enjoyed in the past. When General Motors Corp. reorganized its European operations, top managers at the Saab, Vauxhall, and Opel units lost some of their autonomy, and top officials in Zurich gained in power.[2]

Before making the decision to change the degree of decentralization, top managers must consider the advantages and disadvantages of such a move. Exhibit 10-1 summarizes the pros and cons.

EXHIBIT 10-1

Advantages and disadvantages of decentralization.

Advantages of Decentralization	Disadvantages of Decentralization
• Yields better information for operational decision making	• Allows conflict between operational decisions and corporate strategy
• Yields more timely information for operational decision making	• Duplicates work efforts across units
• Develops decision-making skills of next generation of top managers	• Reduces communication across units
• Allows top managers to focus on strategic planning and decision making	• Increases potential for errors in decisions made by inexperienced managers

Advantages of Decentralization

Why would top managers decide to increase the level of decentralized decision-making authority in their company? First, managers at the operational level of the organization have better information about the organization's day-to-day activities. They can identify problems, recognize situational changes, and respond to issues more quickly than top management. If top management makes these decisions, the operational-level manager must first gather the information and then send it up the organizational chain of command. By the time top managers have had a chance to digest the information and gain an understanding of the situation, the window for making the decision may have already closed.

Second, top managers should give attention to grooming the next generation of top managers. While some companies hire experienced managers from other organizations, many companies choose to develop their own managers internally. A decentralized organization assists in this process by giving lower-level managers practice in developing their decision-making skills. Top managers can then evaluate the results, determine managers' potential for promotion, and mentor high-potential managers.

Finally, managing an organization is a time-consuming function. If the organization is going to be successful, top managers need to focus on strategic planning activities, not on day-to-day operational issues. Decentralizing decision-making authority allows them to do just that. When operational planning and decision making are delegated to those who are closest to operations, top management is free to focus on the long term.

Disadvantages of Decentralization

Though decentralization can offer many benefits to an organization, it does have some disadvantages. Top managers generally have the clearest picture of an organization's overall strategy and goals, as well as the resources available to implement the strategy and achieve the goals. One challenge for top managers is to communicate those strategies and goals throughout all levels of the organization. If lower-level managers do not understand the company's strategies and goals, they may make decisions that are not in the best interest of the organization as a whole. For example, the company may have the goal of reducing the amount of direct labor it uses through automation. If an operational manager decides to produce a hand-made product, that decision will conflict with the organization's goals.

Another disadvantage of decentralized decision making is that two or more operational managers may evaluate and make the same decision, duplicating their efforts. The company may even end up with two identical pieces of equipment in two different departments, each of which is used only 50% of the time. Better coordination of the decision-making process might have led to the purchase of a single machine to be shared by the two departments, reducing the cost to the company.

Moreover, as decision making is spread throughout the organization, managers tend to focus on their own units and often lose contact with others in the organization. When communication is reduced, the potential for sharing ideas throughout the organization is reduced with it. Lower-level managers may not fully understand the ramifications of their localized decisions on the organization as a whole.

Finally, decision making is not an easy skill to learn. Effective decision making requires practice, which sometimes results in poor or even costly decisions. When decision making is spread to lower-level managers with no significant experience in decision making, the quality of managerial decision making may decline.

Responsibility Accounting

In a decentralized organization, upper managers need a way to evaluate the performance of the unit managers. For the evaluation to be meaningful, unit

REALITY CHECK—*Taking center stage—or not*

© Justin Guariglia/Corbis

From Alfred Sloan's days at General Motors when each division maintained its own profit and loss statement to today, companies have adopted varying degrees of decentralization. The trick is for each company to find the right degree of decentralization.

Advanced Disposal Services, Inc., the fifth largest solid waste company in the United States, has adopted a highly decentralized structure. The company, which operates more than 3,100 trucks in 16 states and the Bahamas, prides itself on making decisions locally. Its website boasts, "We're not some massive conglomerate that manages business from a remote corporate office. . . . Decisions can be made locally, quickly and implemented thoroughly."

Arnault wants division managers to run their operations as if they were family businesses.

In the world of high fashion, LVMH Moet Hennessy Louis Vuitton SA's owner Bernard Arnault promotes decentralization. He has stated, "One key element of management of a group like this is decentralization." Faced with managing 125,000 employees across 70 design houses and 6 operating groups, along with stores from New York to Mongolia, Arnault wants division managers to run their operations as if they were family businesses.

Sources: Susan Adams, "Master of the Brand: Bernard Arnault," *Forbes Asia*, December 2010, Vol. 6, Issue 14; http://www.advanceddisposal.com/about-advanced-disposal.aspx (accessed May 9, 2016); Jim Johnson, "Advanced Grows but Philosophy Remains the Same," *Waste & Recycling News*, 21612048, December 12, 2012, Vol. 18, Issue 18.

managers should be evaluated only on those items over which they have control. This type of evaluation is referred to as **responsibility accounting**.

Depending on how a unit is structured, managers may have control over costs, profits, and/or investments in operating assets. Based on which of these factors are under the unit manager's control, organizational units are categorized as cost centers, profit centers, or investment centers. Let's look at each of these categorizations in more detail.

Cost Centers

A **cost center** is an organizational unit whose manager is responsible only for the costs incurred in the unit. The goal of the cost center manager is to minimize total costs while providing an acceptable level of service or quality of product. Service departments and production departments, which typically do not generate revenues, are often considered to be cost centers. Their managers' performance is measured largely by comparing the actual costs incurred to the flexible budget—that is, to the costs that are budgeted for the actual level of production (see Unit 6.1).

Luke Carlson, controller of Centex Yarns' Nylon Fibers division, is responsible for managing the division's accounting department. Since Luke has control over the costs incurred by the department, and the accounting department does not generate revenue or invest in assets, the accounting department is a cost center. Another example of a cost center at Centex Yarns is the division's winding department, which winds yarn onto bobbins.[3] Again, this department does not generate revenue or invest in assets, so its manager focuses solely on the costs that he can control.

Profit Centers

> **WATCH OUT!**
>
> You can't classify a unit as a cost, profit, or investment center simply by looking at its name or its location on the organization chart. Managers of two similarly named units in two different organizations may have dramatically different decision-making authority. Always determine the level of decision-making authority in a unit before classifying it.

A manager who is responsible for both the revenues and the costs incurred in generating a product or service is managing a **profit center**. Though this unit is expected to generate profits, not just revenues or costs, the manager cannot commit funds to invest in assets. The manager's performance is typically measured based on the unit's overall profit compared to the flexible budget—that is, the profit that is budgeted to be earned at the unit's actual level of production.

At Centex Yarns, the Textile Yarns group, part of the Nylon Fibers division, is responsible for producing and selling nylon yarns to the textile market. Micky Yager, the group's manager, is responsible for its costs and revenues, and therefore its profit. Thus, the Textile Yarns group is considered to be a profit center.

Investment Centers

The manager of an **investment center** is expected to invest in assets that generate profits. Investment center managers have the broadest responsibility of the three types of managers. Although their performance could be evaluated using the same methods as for cost center and profit center managers, most organizations use measures such as return on investment and residual income, which consider both the unit's income and its level of assets. You will learn about these performance measures in Units 10.3 and 10.4.

Monica Waltrip, vice president of Centex Yarns' Nylon Fibers division, is responsible for the revenue generated by the division, as well as its costs. She is also responsible for securing the productive assets needed to create the nylon yarn. Since Monica has responsibility for costs, profits, and investments, the Nylon Fibers division is considered an investment center.

Exhibit 10-2 shows a partial organization chart for Centex Yarns. Notice that if you read from the bottom up, you generally move from cost centers to profit centers to investment centers. That is because, at higher levels of the organization, managers typically receive more decision-making authority than they do at lower levels.

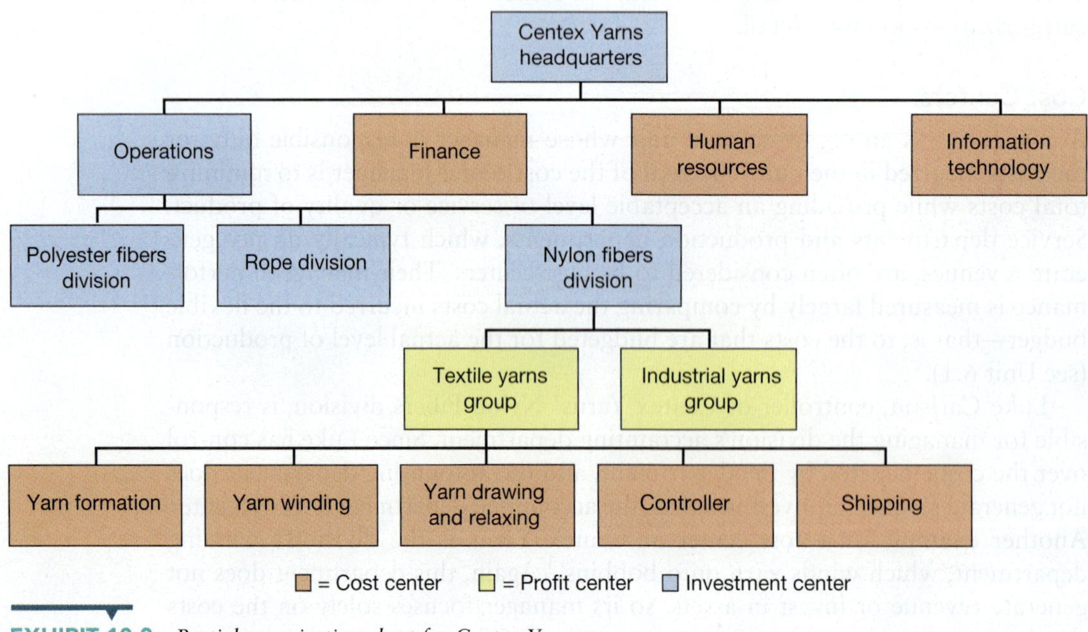

EXHIBIT 10-2 *Partial organization chart for Centex Yarns.*

THINK ABOUT IT 10.1

Barnes and Noble, Inc. is the world's largest bricks-and-mortar bookseller. You may have visited one of the company's retail stores. In addition to the Barnes and Noble retail stores, the company also operates subsidiaries such as Barnes & Noble.com; Barnes & Noble College Booksellers, LLC; NOOK Media, LLC; and Sterling Publishing Co., Inc. According to the company's 2015 annual report, Barnes and Noble operates three business segments: Retail, NOOK, and College. How do you think its subsidiaries are viewed internally—as cost centers, profit centers, or investment centers? Why?

UNIT 10.1 REVIEW

KEY TERMS

Centralization p. 539	Decentralization p. 539	Profit center p. 542
Cost center p. 541	Investment center p. 542	Responsibility accounting p. 541

PRACTICE QUESTIONS

1. LO 1 In a decentralized organization, decision-making authority
   a. rests with a single individual.
   b. is spread throughout the organization.
   c. is not an important role of the organization.
   d. always rests with cost center managers.

2. LO 1 Which of the following is *not* a disadvantage of decentralization?
   a. Operational managers may act in ways that are not in the organization's best interest if corporate goals and strategies are not communicated throughout the organization.
   b. Lack of communication throughout the organization may result in duplication of effort and decisions.
   c. Operational managers may make decisions that conflict with corporate strategy.
   d. Information needed to support decision-making activities is available to decision makers on a timely basis.

3. LO 1 A cost center manager will be held responsible for
   a. only the center's investments in assets.
   b. only the center's costs.
   c. the center's revenues, costs, and investments in assets.
   d. only the center's profits.

4. LO 1 Houck Industrial Supply has three operating divisions, each headed by a divisional vice president. The divisions operate independently, and each vice president is responsible for all aspects of the division's operation. Most likely, each division operates as a(n)
   a. cost center.
   b. profit center.
   c. investment center.
   d. subsidiary.

UNIT 10.1 PRACTICE EXERCISE

Classify each of the following organizational units as a cost center, a profit center, or an investment center. Explain the reason behind your decision.

a. **Luxury Leather Products' luggage division**—The luggage division is one of Luxury Leather Products' two divisions. It operates independently, and all business decisions are made locally in Plano, Texas.
b. **The Modern Dance Department of Mitchell International University**—The Modern Dance department is housed in the School of Fine Arts. Besides the courses it offers to its own dance majors, it offers several service courses through the Physical Education Department. Students pay a flat tuition charge to the university, regardless of the number of courses taken or the department that teaches the courses.

c. **Miles, Miles and Miles, LLP business consulting practice**—This large public accounting firm includes auditing, tax, and business consulting practices. Johnson Miles is the partner in charge of the business consulting practice. As the lead partner, Johnson makes all hiring decisions and is responsible for selling consulting services to clients. Partners' compensation is based on the profits generated by their groups.

SELECTED UNIT 10.1 ANSWERS

Think About It 10.1

Barnes and Noble's subsidiaries are likely treated as investment centers. It would be unreasonable to treat them as cost centers; because the managers are no doubt responsible for generating revenues, they should be evaluated based on the revenues and costs under their control. Would it be reasonable to assume that the managers of these divisions are responsible for investing in assets, too? Probably so. Given that the operations of these subsidiaries are so different and so complex (online selling and publishing), it is unlikely that upper management at Barnes and Noble would want to be involved in the details of those businesses in addition to running the corporate business.

Practice Questions

1. B
2. D
3. B
4. C

Unit 10.1 Practice Exercise

a. Investment center: The division makes all operating decisions, including investments in operating assets.

b. Cost center: The department is not directly responsible for generating revenue since all tuition is paid to the university regardless of the courses taken.

c. Profit center: The group's managing partner is responsible for revenues and costs.

UNIT 10.2

Segment Evaluation

GUIDED UNIT PREPARATION

Answering the following questions while you read this unit will guide your understanding of the key concepts found in the unit. The questions are linked to the learning objectives presented at the beginning of the chapter.

LO 2

1. What is a segment of an organization? Identify several segments of your university.
2. What is segment margin? How is it calculated?
3. How does segment margin differ from a segment's net operating income?
4. Why are common allocated fixed costs an issue in evaluating segment performance?
5. Once a cost has been identified as a common allocated fixed cost, can it ever be considered a traceable fixed cost? Why or why not?

In both profit and investment centers, the evaluation of a manager will include some measure of profit. Consistent with the principles of responsibility accounting, it is important that the profit calculation include only those items that are under the manager's control. In this unit, you will learn how to prepare a segment margin income statement that will assist in evaluating a segment's financial performance, and ultimately the segment manager's performance.

Defining a Segment

A **segment** of an organization is any part of the organization that management wishes to evaluate. Perry Ellis International, one of the United States' leading apparel companies, divided operations into four segments in 2015—men's sportswear and swim, women's sportswear, direct-to-consumer, and licensing—up from the two segments it reported in 2010. While the company evaluates these four segments individually, there are other ways that managers will want to divide and evaluate the company.

Within the men's sportswear and swim segment, managers may want to evaluate the performance of the Perry Ellis® or Munsingwear® product lines. Alternatively, managers may want to compare how well different distribution channels, such as luxury stores and chain stores, perform. Somewhere in the company a manager is in charge of each of those product categories and distribution channels. The point is, there are many different ways to divide an organization into segments.

Let's look at one way that Centex Yarns defines its segments. Exhibit 10-3 shows an income statement that breaks out the company's three divisions. As reported in this income statement, the Nylon Fibers division lost $100,000 during the year. This is the statement that prompted James Cameron's call to Monica Waltrip in the chapter-opening scenario. If you were in James's shoes, would you have felt compelled to make that call?

	Polyester Fibers Division	Rope Division	Nylon Fibers Division	Total
Revenue	$10,600,000	$6,725,000	$8,650,000	$25,975,000
Cost of goods sold	7,638,550	4,011,800	6,959,750	18,610,100
Gross profit	2,961,450	2,713,200	1,690,250	7,364,900
Selling & administrative expenses	2,332,450	1,309,200	1,790,250	5,431,900
Operating income	$ 629,000	$1,404,000	$ (100,000)	$ 1,933,000

EXHIBIT 10-3 *Segmented income statement for Centex Yarns.*

Segment Margin Income Statements

You should have noticed that the income statement shown in Exhibit 10-3 was presented in the functional format, not the contribution margin format. Because it does not show which expenses are fixed and which are variable, it isn't very helpful in managerial decision making. If you could recast the income statement into a contribution margin format, it would help you to assess the segment's performance. Doing so was part of the challenge facing Luke Carlson as he tried to prepare for Monica's meeting with James Cameron.

What is really needed to measure a segment's performance is an income statement that highlights all the elements under the segment manager's control. You learned how to create such a statement in Unit 8.2 by preparing a segment margin income statement. As you should recall, the segment margin income statement

REALITY CHECK—*The whole isn't always greater than the sum of its parts*

© Ruaridh Stewart/Zuma Press

Closing the Forth and Towne stores allowed Gap to focus on its other, more profitable brands.

Organizations frequently develop synergies between two or more of their operating segments. The resulting corporate value can be greater than the sum of the segment values. However, some segments may not contribute value to the organization. In that case, managers must take corrective action, even if it means closing the segment.

Gap, Inc., best known for its Gap, Banana Republic, and Old Navy brands, did just that with its Forth and Towne segment. The company opened this chain of women's specialty apparel stores to compete with stores such as Chico's, but the concept never caught on with shoppers. Closing the Forth and Towne stores allowed Gap to focus on its other, more profitable brands. Nike, Inc., focuses its efforts on athletic shoes and apparel. When the company found that its Cole Haan luxury footwear, accessories, and outerwear subsidiary took too much away from the core business, it put the company up for sale.

Retailer Stein Mart took less drastic measures in its home division when the linens segment failed to live up to expectations. Rather than remove linens from Stein Mart's stores, managers looked at ways to improve the segment's performance, including changes in packaging, selection, and pricing.

Sources: Cecile B. Corral, "Home a 'Troubled Category' and Stein Mart," *Home Textiles Today*, March 26, 2007, 18; James Covert and Amy Merrick, "Gap Reverses Pressler, Shuts a Niche Chain," *The Wall Street Journal*, February 27, 2007, http://www.wsj.com/articles/SB117250240615019352 (accessed July 20, 2016); "NIKE, Inc. Announces Sale of Cole Haan to Apax Partners," NIKE, Inc. News Release, November 16, 2012, http://news.nike.com/news/nike-inc-announces-sale-of-cole-haan-to-apax-partners (accessed July 20, 2016).

excludes all allocated costs in the calculation of the segment margin. Only the traceable fixed costs should be subtracted from the contribution margin to arrive at the segment margin. Common fixed costs should not appear in the segment analysis; rather, they should be reported only in the corporate total column. Exhibit 10-4 shows Centex Yarns' segment margin income statement.

	Polyester Fibers Division	Rope Division	Nylon Fibers Division	Total
Revenue	$ 10,600,000	$ 6,725,000	$ 8,650,000	$ 25,975,000
Less variable expenses:				
Cost of goods sold	5,543,000	2,368,000	4,414,000	12,325,000
Selling & administrative	1,334,000	649,000	890,000	2,873,000
Contribution margin	$ 3,723,000	$ 3,708,000	$ 3,346,000	$ 10,777,000
Less traceable fixed expenses:				
Cost of goods sold	1,685,000	1,382,000	2,208,000	5,275,000
Selling & administrative	236,000	174,000	273,000	683,000
Segment margin	$ 1,802,000	$ 2,152,000	$ 865,000	$ 4,819,000
Common fixed expenses				2,886,000
Net operating income				$ 1,933,000

EXHIBIT 10-4 *Segment margin income statement for Centex Yarns.*

Notice what happens to the evaluation of the Nylon Fibers division when allocated common fixed costs are removed from the analysis. This division is actually covering its variable costs plus all its traceable fixed costs, and it is contributing an additional $865,000 toward covering the company's common fixed costs. If this division were eliminated, as James Cameron is inclined to do, the company's net operating income would decrease by $865,000. So closing the division appears to be a poor decision.

> **WATCH OUT!**
>
> Several terms can be used in referring to common costs, including allocated costs and unavoidable costs. In preparing a segment margin income statement, instead of looking for a certain phrase that describes the cost (e.g., *traceable* or *common*), look for the **reason** the cost was incurred. If it was incurred specifically for the segment, then it is a traceable cost. If it was incurred to support the company as a whole, then it is a common cost.

When Traceable Fixed Costs Become Common Costs

As an organization is broken down into finer segments, costs that were traceable fixed costs at one level may become common fixed costs at a lower level. Let's look at the Nylon Fibers division in more detail. This division has two groups, Textile Yarns and Industrial Yarns. Monica Waltrip treats each group as a profit center and uses segment margin analysis to evaluate each group's financial performance. Exhibit 10-5 presents the Nylon Fibers division's segment margin income statement.

	Textile Yarns Group	Industrial Yarns Group	Nylon Fibers Division
Revenue	$6,055,000	$2,595,000	$8,650,000
Less variable expenses:			
Cost of goods sold	3,168,400	1,245,600	4,414,000
Selling & administrative	683,000	207,000	890,000
Contribution margin	2,203,600	1,142,400	3,346,000
Less traceable fixed expenses:			
Cost of goods sold	744,400	415,200	1,159,600
Selling & administrative	191,100	81,900	273,000
Segment margin	$1,268,100	$ 645,300	1,913,400
Common fixed expenses			1,048,400
Net operating income			$ 865,000

EXHIBIT 10-5 *Segment margin income statement for Centex Yarns' Nylon Fibers division.*

Notice that the $2,208,000 in traceable fixed product costs for the Nylon Fibers division shown in Exhibit 10-4 now has been divided into $1,159,600 in traceable fixed costs and $1,048,400 in common fixed costs. Apparently the managers of these two groups do not control all the fixed costs in the division. Some of those fixed costs are kept under Monica's control at the divisional level. Therefore, the group managers should not be held responsible for them.

Segment Reporting, Segment Margin, and GAAP

ASC 280, *Segment Reporting*, provides the generally accepted accounting principles that require companies to report selected information about operating segments in the annual report. But even with this pronouncement of generally accepted accounting principles, all companies do not report identical segment information.

Let's revisit Perry Ellis International's segment reporting in its 2015 10-K. Do the reported operating incomes of $20,068,000 from men's sportswear and swim and $7,649,000 from licensing equal the segment margins for those two segments? The answer is no, because the operating incomes include all the common fixed expenses. In fact, the segment information footnote includes the following statement: "The Company allocates certain selling, general and administrative expenses based primarily on the revenues generated by the segments."[4] Thus, the segment margins for the two segments are higher than the operating incomes included in the annual report.

Abbott Laboratories, a diversified healthcare company that makes pharmaceuticals and medical devices, takes a different approach in its GAAP-based segment reporting. In its 2015 10-K, the company reported segment operating income, not including some common corporate expenses. In such cases, the reported segment incomes will be closer to the segment margins.

One thing that is missing from GAAP-based segment reporting is a breakdown of variable and fixed costs. Thus, when cost behavior is important, even statements that exclude common fixed costs will not be that useful in decision making.

THINK ABOUT IT 10.2

Do you think managers would support additional segment disclosures in the annual report? Why or why not?

UNIT 10.2 REVIEW

KEY TERMS

Segment p. 545

PRACTICE QUESTIONS

1. LO 2 There is only one way to divide an organization into segments. True or False.
2. LO 2 The Kleypas Division reported a $1,000,000 net operating loss for the year. Included in that amount were $1,500,000 in common fixed corporate expenses that were allocated to divisions based on sales revenue. The division's segment margin was
   a. $500,000.
   b. $1,500,000.
   c. $(1,000,000).
   d. $(500,000).
3. LO 2 The home healthcare division of Medical Arts, Inc., generated $5,000,000 in revenues during the year. Variable expenses totaled $1,200,000, direct fixed expenses totaled $1,600,000, and common fixed expenses totaled $1,800,000. The division's segment margin for the year was
   a. $400,000.
   b. $2,200,000.
   c. $3,400,000.
   d. $3,800,000.

UNIT 10.2 PRACTICE EXERCISE

Andrew Hejtmanek, vice president of operations at Houdyshell Enterprises, received the following income statement for the company's Imaging Products division.

	X-Ray Group	MRI Group	Total
Revenue	$1,500,000	$2,800,000	$4,300,000
Less variable expenses:			
Cost of goods sold	540,000	1,800,000	2,340,000
Selling & administrative	200,000	575,000	775,000
Contribution margin	760,000	425,000	1,185,000
Less fixed expenses	350,000	800,000	1,150,000
Operating income	$ 410,000	$ (375,000)	$ 35,000

Andrew is not pleased with the division's performance, and he believes that the MRI group is responsible for its disappointing results. He wants to close the group.

Required

a. Kim Pippin, the division's controller, has determined that corporate headquarters allocated $225,000 and $500,000 in common fixed expenses, respectively, to the X-Ray and MRI groups. Prepare a segment margin income statement that will provide Andrew with a better basis for evaluating the two divisions' performance.

b. What action do you recommend that Andrew take concerning the MRI group? Why?

SELECTED UNIT 10.2 ANSWERS

Think About It 10.2

Because annual reports are distributed to shareholders and creditors, and in the case of publicly traded companies, to the public, increased disclosure would reveal more information about the business. Depending on the nature of the information, managers might be concerned that revealing the information to competitors could jeopardize business operations. On the other hand, managers of publicly traded companies might prefer to have certain information disclosed in order to demonstrate their superior performance.

Practice Questions

1. False
2. A
3. B

Unit 10.2 Practice Exercise

a.

	X-Ray Group	MRI Group	Total
Revenue	$1,500,000	$2,800,000	$4,300,000
Less variable expenses:			
Cost of goods sold	540,000	1,800,000	2,340,000
Selling & administrative	200,000	575,000	775,000
Contribution margin	760,000	425,000	1,185,000
Less traceable fixed expenses	125,000	300,000	425,000
Segment margin	$ 635,000	$ 125,000	760,000
Less common fixed expenses			725,000
Operating Income			$ 35,000

b. Andrew should not close the MRI Group. The group is generating $125,000 in segment margin, which is helping to cover the $725,000 in common fixed expenses incurred at the corporate level. Closing the MRI group would reduce total operating income by $125,000, resulting in a $90,000 loss.

UNIT 10.3

Return on Investment

GUIDED UNIT PREPARATION

Answering the following questions while you read this unit will guide your understanding of the key concepts found in the unit. The questions are linked to the learning objectives presented at the beginning of the chapter.

LO 3

1. How is return on investment (ROI) calculated?
2. What two ratios can be multiplied to calculate ROI? Define those ratios.
3. All else held equal, what three actions can a manager take to improve a division's ROI?
4. How can using ROI as an evaluation tool lead to suboptimal behavior by managers?

Once an organization has chosen to decentralize its decision making, it must develop a system of accountability to facilitate the evaluation of its decisions. For a cost center manager, that typically means an examination of actual costs against budgeted costs. For a profit center manager, the evaluation will include a review of both revenues and expenses, with a focus on operating income. An investment center manager should be evaluated based on how well assets have been used to generate income. In this unit you will learn about return on investment, a common measure used to evaluate an investment center's performance.

Return on Investment

In the early 1900s, faced with the challenge of evaluating managers in a decentralized organization, executives at the DuPont Powder Company (now E. I. du Pont de Nemours and Company, or more commonly, DuPont) were looking for new performance measures that included invested capital as well as profit. They used the measure they developed, called return on investment, to evaluate proposals to build new manufacturing facilities and to allocate corporate funds across various facilities. Return on investment is still widely used today to evaluate a broad range of investment options, from manufacturing plants to corporate training programs. It is also used to evaluate entire organizations; organizational units such as divisions, plants, and product lines; and individual investment projects. Finally, it can be used to evaluate past results or to predict future results.

Formally defined, **return on investment (ROI)** measures the rate of return generated by an investment in assets. Expressed as a percentage, it is calculated as

$$\text{ROI} = \frac{\text{Operating income}}{\text{Average operating assets}} \quad \text{or} \quad \frac{\text{Segment margin}}{\text{Average operating assets}}$$

There is some variation in the income measure used in the calculation of ROI. When an entire organization is being evaluated, operating income, or income before interest and taxes, is a common choice, since at the corporate level, all expenses are under the CEO's control. When ROI is used to evaluate a unit within the organization, the income measure needs to be one that includes only those items that are under the unit manager's control. Some unit managers use the segment margin because it represents revenues and expenses that are directly traceable to the operating unit and controllable by the unit manager. Whatever the income choice, the measure must be used consistently. Throughout the rest of the chapter, we are going to use "operating income" in future formulas, but be aware that "segment margin" can always be substituted when the calculation is for a unit rather than the entire organization.

Since the income measure used in the ROI calculation represents the results obtained for the entire year, the denominator needs to represent the assets used during the year. The most common measure chosen is a simple average of the assets used during the year, computed by adding the beginning and ending asset balances and dividing by 2:

$$\text{Average operating assets} = \frac{\text{Beginning asset balance} + \text{Ending asset balance}}{2}$$

The assets to include in this calculation are those that were actually used in operations, among them cash; accounts receivable; inventory; and property, plant, and equipment. Any asset that was not used to support operations, such as a manufacturing facility that was shut down or a piece of equipment that was no longer in use, should not be included in the asset balance.

Let's calculate the ROI for each of Centex Yarns' divisions. In the following calculations, the segment margins are drawn from Exhibit 10-4.

	Polyester Fibers Division	Rope Division	Nylon Fibers Division
Segment Margin	\$ 1,802,000	\$ 2,152,000	\$ 865,000
Average Assets	\$ 8,153,000	\$ 8,406,250	\$ 2,703,000
ROI	$\frac{\$1{,}802{,}000}{\$8{,}153{,}000} = 22.1\%$	$\frac{\$2{,}152{,}000}{\$8{,}406{,}250} = 25.6\%$	$\frac{\$\ 865{,}000}{\$2{,}703{,}000} = 32\%$

ROI is a relative measure of return. In other words, it says nothing about the *dollar amount* of return; it is simply a *rate* of return. Notice that of the three divisions, the Nylon Fibers division has the highest ROI, yet it also has the smallest segment margin and the smallest dollar amount of assets to use in generating that margin. Based solely on ROI, the Nylon Fibers division is outperforming the other two divisions. Based on segment margin alone, however, the Rope division is outperforming the other two divisions.

THINK ABOUT IT 10.3

Return on investment is based on the book value of operating assets. However, book value may not be as realistic a measure of the assets' current value as fair market value or appraised value. What effect would using fair market value instead of book value have on the return on investment?

The DuPont Model

Around 1912, Donaldson Brown, an explosives sales engineer who had transferred to DuPont's financial staff, decomposed the original ROI formula into two components, **margin** and **asset turnover**:

$$\text{ROI} = \overbrace{\frac{\text{Operating income}^*}{\text{Sales revenue}}}^{\text{Margin}} \times \overbrace{\frac{\text{Sales revenue}}{\text{Average operating assets}}}^{\text{Asset turnover}}$$

*Or segment margin.

Notice that sales revenue appears in both the denominator of the margin side of this expression and the numerator of the asset turnover side. Thus, it cancels out, leaving the original ROI formula. This expanded formula for ROI is often referred to as the **DuPont model**.[5] Exhibit 10-6 further breaks down the two components of the DuPont model, showing the different choices managers have to improve ROI.

EXHIBIT 10-6

Improving ROI through the components of the DuPont model.

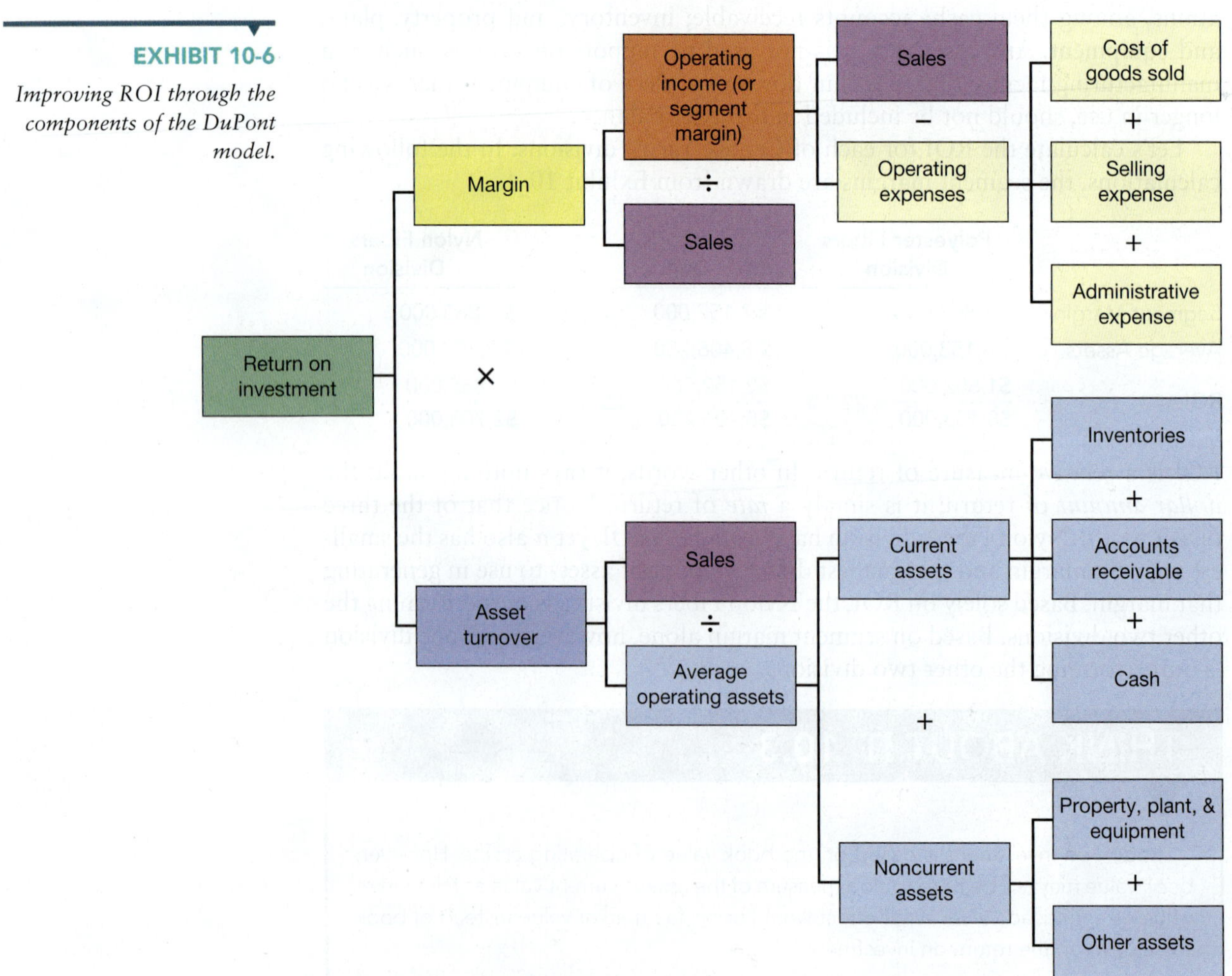

What advantage does the DuPont model offer compared to the standard ROI calculation? The answer is that the two parts can help to identify the actions required to improve an ROI. Let's consider two divisions that both have a return on investment of 20%:

	Division A	Division B
Margin	10%	4%
Asset turnover	2 times	5 times
ROI	20%	20%

Both of these divisions might want to improve their ROIs, but they would need to go about it in different ways. Division A has a relatively high margin and relatively low asset turnover. Division A's management may need to focus on improving asset turnover by increasing sales or decreasing the average level of operating assets. Division B has a low margin and a relatively high asset turnover. To improve its ROI, Division B's management may want to focus on improving margin by decreasing expenses to increase operating income. Therefore, ROI can be improved by any combination of three separate actions—increasing sales revenue, decreasing expenses, or decreasing assets.

Increase in Sales Revenue

If managers want to increase ROI, an increase in sales revenue will increase both margin and asset turnover. Suppose Monica Waltrip, vice president of Centex Yarns' Nylon Fibers division, were to increase sales volume by 10%. An increase in sales volume would increase sales revenue, variable costs, and contribution margin. Referring back to Exhibit 10-5, sales revenue would increase to \$9,515,000 (\$8,650,000 × 1.1). Total contribution margin (sales less variable costs) would increase to \$3,680,600 (\$3,346,000 × 1.1). Fixed expenses would remain constant, resulting in an increased segment margin of \$1,199,600 (\$3,680,600 – \$2,481,000) and an increased ROI of 44.39%, as follows:

	Original Data	10% Increase in Sales Volume
Margin	$\frac{\$865,000}{\$8,650,000} = 10.00\%$	$\frac{\$1,199,600}{\$9,515,000} = 12.61\%$
Asset turnover	$\frac{\$8,650,000}{\$2,703,000} = 3.2$	$\frac{\$9,515,000}{\$2,703,000} = 3.52$
ROI	10.00% × 3.2 = 32.00%	12.61% × 3.52 = 44.39%

WATCH OUT!

In calculating the effects of increased sales volume on ROI, don't forget that variable costs will increase, too. Your best bet for arriving at the increased operating income is to calculate the increase in contribution margin that will result from the increased sales. That increase drops straight to the bottom line, since fixed costs will remain constant.

Another way to increase sales revenue is to raise the selling price. Remember, though, that increasing the selling price may decrease the sales volume due to price elasticity of demand.

Decrease in Expenses

As Exhibit 10-6 shows, a decrease in operating expenses will increase operating income, and thus margin. To increase operating income, a manager can choose to reduce variable or fixed expenses. Suppose Monica Waltrip were to negotiate a new contract that lowers direct materials cost by 8%. The division's direct material cost is \$2,865,000, so an 8% reduction will save \$229,200 (\$2,865,000 × 0.08). This reduction will increase the contribution margin, and thus the segment margin, by \$229,200 to \$1,094,200 (\$865,000 + \$229,200). As Exhibit 10-6 indicates, this action will increase the division's operating income and margin, raising its ROI to 40.48%, as follows. Notice that this action does not affect asset turnover.

	Original Data	10% Decrease in Direct Materials
Margin	$\frac{\$\ 865{,}000}{\$8{,}650{,}000} = 10.00\%$	$\frac{\$1{,}094{,}200}{\$8{,}650{,}000} = 12.65\%$
Asset turnover	$\frac{\$8{,}650{,}000}{\$2{,}703{,}000} = 3.2$	$\frac{\$8{,}650{,}000}{\$2{,}703{,}000} = 3.2$
ROI	10.00% × 3.2 = 32.00%	12.65% × 3.2 = 40.48%

Decrease in Assets

The final action that will increase ROI is a reduction in the asset base, which increases the asset turnover. Suppose that Monica Waltrip were to implement a just-in-time inventory program. With more frequent deliveries of smaller quantities, Monica would be able to reduce the division's inventory balance by $203,000. After the program's implementation, the division's average assets would be reduced to $2,500,000 ($2,703,000 − $203,000). This reduction in inventory would increase the division's ROI to 34.6%, as follows, due to the increased asset turnover. Notice that this action has no effect on the division's margin.

	Original Data	$203,000 Reduction in Assets
Margin	$\frac{\$\ 865{,}000}{\$8{,}650{,}000} = 10.00\%$	$\frac{\$\ 865{,}000}{\$8{,}650{,}000} = 10.00\%$
Asset turnover	$\frac{\$8{,}650{,}000}{\$2{,}703{,}000} = 3.2$	$\frac{\$8{,}650{,}000}{\$2{,}500{,}000} = 3.46$
ROI	10.00% × 3.2 = 32.00%	10.00% × 3.46 = 34.6%

You have now learned that a company has three options for improving its ROI. Increasing sales revenue or decreasing expenses increases ROI by improving the company's margin. Reducing the amount of assets will increase ROI by reducing asset turnover.

Shortcomings of Return on Investment

Although return on investment is used widely as a performance measure, it has some shortcomings. Consider the following scenario. Centex Yarns starts a new Modal Fiber division with $1,000,000 of operating assets. In the first year of operation the division generates $200,000 in operating income. At the end of the year, Centex records depreciation of $100,000 ($1,000,000 ÷ 10-year useful life) on the assets. The new division's ROI for the year would be 21.05%, calculated as

$$\frac{\$200{,}000}{(\$1{,}000{,}000 + \$900{,}000)/2} = \frac{\$200{,}000}{\$950{,}000} = 21.05\%$$

Now assume that the second year of operation is identical to the first: $200,000 in operating income and another $100,000 in depreciation on the assets. The division's ROI for year 2 would be 23.53%, calculated as:

$$\frac{\$200{,}000}{(\$900{,}000 + \$800{,}000)/2} = \frac{\$200{,}000}{\$850{,}000} = 23.53\%$$

REALITY CHECK—*Getting a healthy ROI*

Christopher Futcher/Getty Images, Inc.

BP America estimates it achieved an overall $2.10 return on each $1 invested in the program.

A Society of Human Resources study in 2015 found that employee wellness programs are offered by 70% of U.S. employers, with another 8% of employers expected to add a program in the coming year. The thought is that improving an employee's health will reduce the employer's overall healthcare benefits costs. But does it really pay to be healthy? That's a question that many companies are asking. And with employers spending an average of $693 per employee on wellness incentives in 2015, it's a question that needs a quick answer.

Studies have shown a wide range of financial benefits of wellness programs. Research by the Rand Corporation finds that the return on investment depends on the type of wellness program—disease management programs returned $3.80 for every $1 spent, while lifestyle management programs returned only $0.50 for every dollar spent, resulting in an average return of $1.50 for every dollar spent.

However, some companies have reported significantly better results with their wellness programs. BP America launched its program in 2010 and estimates it achieved an overall $2.10 return on each $1 invested in the program over the first three years of its wellness program. So, apparently it does pay to be healthy.

Sources: Magaly Olivero, "Is Your Company's Employee Wellness Program Right for You?," *U.S. News and World Report,* August 10, 2015, http://health.usnews.com/health-news/health-wellness/articles/2015/08/10/is-your-companys-employee-wellness-program-right-for-you (accessed May 3, 2016); Rand Corporation, "Do Workplace Wellness Programs Save Employers Money?," 2014, http://www.rand.org/content/dam/rand/pubs/research_briefs/RB9700/RB9744/RAND_RB9744.pdf (accessed May 3, 2016); "BP America," http://thehealthproject.com/winner/bp-america/ (accessed May 3, 2016); Vicky Valet, "More Than Two-Thirds of U.S. Employers Currently Offer Wellness Programs, Study Says," *Forbes*, July 8, 2015, http://www.forbes.com/sites/vickyvalet/2015/07/08/more-than-two-thirds-of-u-s-employers-currently-offer-wellness-programs-study-says/#77e98f086c7b (accessed May 3, 2016).

Notice that the ROI has increased without any change in operations. Because depreciation reduces the book value of the operating assets, the return on investment automatically increases. For this reason, some managers choose to calculate the return on investment using *gross* operating assets (that is, the historical cost). In this example, using gross operating assets would yield a 20% return on investment in each of the two years ($200,000 ÷ $1,000,000).

Another disadvantage of using ROI as an evaluation tool is that it can encourage some undesirable behavior by managers. Let's assume that Monica Waltrip is investigating the purchase of $500,000 of equipment from a small competitor that is going out of business. The additional equipment will allow Centex Yarns to produce a new line of yarn that Monica estimates would generate $90,000 in additional segment margin each year. This investment has an expected ROI of 18% ($90,000 ÷ $500,000). What would happen to the Nylon Fibers division's ROI if Monica made this purchase? Because the new equipment's ROI is lower than the division's current ROI of 32%, opening the new line would decrease the division's ROI to 29.82%.

$$\frac{\$865{,}000 + \$90{,}000}{\$2{,}703{,}000 + \$500{,}000} = \frac{\$955{,}000}{\$3{,}203{,}000} = 29.82\%$$

If Monica is evaluated based on the trend of the division's ROI, she will not be inclined to move forward with the purchase of the new equipment. Yet if Centex Yarns has a minimum ROI of 15%, indicating that any return higher than 15% is desirable for the corporation as a whole, deciding not to invest in the project would not be in Centex Yarns' best interest. Although the organization as a whole would be better off if Monica purchased the equipment, the decrease in the Nylon Fibers division's ROI would reflect negatively on Monica's performance. Therefore, Monica will likely choose an action that conflicts with overall corporate objectives. Her action is an example of the negative effect that decentralization can have on overall organizational performance.

Similarly, because the replacement of assets (for example, equipment) will typically decrease asset turnover due to the increased asset balance, managers may be reluctant to replace outdated or poorly functioning equipment because of the lower ROI. Or a manager may postpone incurring a needed expense, such as preventive maintenance, because it will decrease the margin, and thus the ROI. Unfortunately, lack of preventive maintenance may actually increase costs in the future, as machines begin to malfunction. Notice that although the manager's actions may improve ROI in the short run, they may do so at the expense of the company's long-term financial health.

UNIT 10.3 REVIEW

KEY TERMS

Asset turnover p. 552
DuPont Model p. 552
Margin p. 552
Return on investment p. 550

PRACTICE QUESTIONS

1. LO 3 Which of the following actions will *not* automatically increase return on investment?

   a. Reducing variable selling and administrative expenses by 14%

   b. Selling $100,000 in unused assets at book value

   c. Selling 20,000 additional units at a profit

   d. Purchasing a $100,000 piece of equipment on sale for $75,000

2. LO 3 Ncube Gaming Systems generated operating income of $400,000 on $3,200,000 in sales. The company had $1,800,000 in assets on January 1 and $2,200,000 in assets on December 31. What was the company's return on investment for the year?

   a. 12.5%

   b. 18.2%

   c. 20.0%

   d. 22.2%

3. LO 3 Lumus Lighting's Theatrical division currently generates a 16.5% ROI. Brandon Lumus, the division's director, has just received several new contracts to provide stage lighting for shows at the Bijoux Theater. Which of the following contracts would he most likely *not* accept?

   a. A contract that generates a 22% return on investment

   b. A contract that generates $5,000 in operating income on an investment of $20,000 in lighting fixtures

   c. A contract that generates a margin of 10% and an asset turnover of 1.2

   d. All of the above

UNIT 10.3 PRACTICE EXERCISE

Minor & Neece, Ltd. operates retail clothing stores in Nashville, Knoxville, and Memphis, Tennessee. Each store is evaluated as an investment center. Selected results from the latest year are as follows:

	Nashville	Knoxville	Memphis
Sales	$5,000,000	$8,000,000	$2,000,000
Variable expenses	2,000,000	4,800,000	1,000,000
Direct fixed expenses	2,000,000	2,500,000	800,000
Average assets	4,000,000	5,000,000	1,600,000
Required rate of return	14%	14%	14%

Required

a. Calculate the margin, asset turnover, and ROI for each of the three stores.

b. The corporate office is giving the stores the option of purchasing a new inventory management system. The new system will cost the stores $100,000; they can expect a $15,000 increase in their annual segment margins, generating a 15% ROI for the investments. If store managers are evaluated based on the trend of their ROIs, which stores will invest in the new inventory management system?

SELECTED UNIT 10.3 ANSWERS

Think About It 10.3

For certain assets, such as land, fair market value increases over time. An increase in asset value without a comparable increase in sales and/or operating income will decrease return on investment. On the other hand, fair market value might decrease faster than book value, as is often the case with machinery. Without a comparable change in sales and/or operating income, return on investment will increase. In either of these cases, if management hasn't changed operations and the way that income is earned, a change in return on investment doesn't reflect actions that are under the control of management.

Practice Questions

1. D
2. C
3. C

Unit 10.3 Practice Exercise

a.

	Nashville	Knoxville	Memphis
Sales	$5,000,000	$8,000,000	$2,000,000
Variable expenses	2,000,000	4,800,000	1,000,000
Contribution margin	3,000,000	3,200,000	1,000,000
Direct fixed expenses	2,000,000	2,500,000	800,000
Segment margin	$1,000,000	$ 700,000	$ 200,000

	Nashville	Knoxville	Memphis
Margin	$\frac{\$1,000,000}{\$5,000,000} = 20\%$	$\frac{\$700,000}{\$8,000,000} = 8.75\%$	$\frac{\$200,000}{\$2,000,000} = 10\%$
Asset turnover	$\frac{\$5,000,000}{\$4,000,000} = 1.25$	$\frac{\$8,000,000}{\$5,000,000} = 1.6$	$\frac{\$2,000,000}{\$1,600,000} = 1.25$
ROI	$20\% \times 1.25 = 25\%$	$8.75\% \times 1.6 = 14\%$	$10\% \times 1.25 = 12.5\%$

b. The Knoxville and Memphis stores will invest in the new inventory management system, since its expected 15% return is higher than their current ROIs. Adding a project with a 15% return will increase their ROIs.

UNIT 10.4

Residual Income and EVA®

GUIDED UNIT PREPARATION

Answering the following questions while you read this unit will guide your understanding of the key concepts found in the unit. The questions are linked to the learning objectives presented at the beginning of the chapter.

LO 4

1. What is residual income? How is it calculated?
2. How does residual income overcome the shortcomings of ROI as a performance measurement tool?
3. What is EVA? How is it calculated?

If, from the corporate viewpoint, ROI can lead to undesirable managerial actions, is there any better way to evaluate a manager's performance? Two alternative measures, residual income and EVA®,[6] can overcome many of the problems with ROI.

Residual Income

Residual income is the income that is earned above a specified minimum level of return. As long as a project's residual income is positive, it is earning a return in excess of the corporate minimum. Residual income is calculated as

Residual income = Operating income* − (Average assets × Required minimum rate of return)

*Or segment margin.

Let's look at Centex Yarns' Nylon Fibers division again. The division has \$2,703,000 in operating assets. At a 15% required minimum rate of return, the division is expected to generate at least \$405,450 in income (\$2,703,000 × 15%). Any income above that amount is residual income. Since the division earned \$865,000 last year, its residual income is \$459,550 (\$865,000 − \$405,450). Exhibit 10-7 shows the residual income calculation for each of Centex's divisions. We have assumed in this example that all divisions have the same required rate of return, but a company may require different divisions to generate different rates of return.

EXHIBIT 10-7

Calculation of Centex Yarns' divisions' residual income.

	Polyester Fibers Division	Rope Division	Nylon Fibers Division
Assets	\$8,153,000	\$8,406,250	\$2,703,000
× Required rate of return	15%	15%	15%
Minimum required income	\$1,222,950	\$1,260,938	\$ 405,450
Segment margin	\$1,802,000	\$2,152,000	\$ 865,000
− Minimum required income	1,222,950	1,260,938	405,450
Residual income	\$ 579,050	\$ 891,062	\$ 459,550

THINK ABOUT IT 10.4

If you had been asked to guess whether the residual income for each of Centex Yarns' divisions would be positive or negative, how could you have used their returns on investment to answer the question?

How does Monica Waltrip's opportunity to purchase $500,000 of assets from a small competitor look when evaluated using residual income? Exhibit 10-8 shows the results. Notice that since the new assets' 18% ROI is higher than the corporate minimum of 15%, their residual income is positive. Notice too that the Nylon Fibers division's residual income increases with the purchase, since the assets generate a rate of return that is higher than the corporate minimum. Using residual income as an evaluation tool would encourage Monica to invest in the new equipment, and both the Nylon Fibers division and Centex Yarns will profit.

EXHIBIT 10-8

Residual income for a proposed asset purchase.

	Nylon Fibers Division Currently	Proposed Asset Purchase	Nylon Fibers Division Including New Assets
Assets	$2,703,000	$500,000	$3,203,000
× Required rate of return	15%	15%	15%
= Minimum required income	$ 405,450	$ 75,000	$ 480,450
Segment margin	$ 865,000	$ 90,000	$ 955,000
− Minimum required income	405,450	75,000	480,450
= Residual income	$ 459,550	$ 15,000	$ 474,550

Shortcomings of Residual Income

While residual income may appear to solve the problems associated with ROI, it has its own shortcomings. Because residual income is an absolute measure that is stated in absolute dollars, using it to compare divisions of different sizes is difficult.

Consider Centex Yarns' two divisions, the Polyester Fibers division and the Nylon Fibers division. As Exhibit 10-7 shows, the Polyester Fibers division had residual income of $579,050 last year, compared to the Nylon Fibers division's residual income of $459,550. At first glance, the Polyester Fibers division appears to be the better performer, but notice that the Polyester Fibers division has $8,153,000 in assets—almost four times the Nylon Fibers division's $2,703,000 in assets. Thus, we might expect that the Polyester Fibers division should show a residual income nearly four times that of the Nylon Fibers division.

In sum, in comparing the performance of multiple units, ROI is a better performance measure than residual income, since it is a relative measure. In evaluating a single unit, however, residual income is the better measure of performance.

Economic Value Added (EVA)

Another performance measure, **economic value added (EVA)**, was developed by Stern Stewart & Co., a global consulting firm, as a variation of residual income that measures "economic profit."[7] The idea behind this measure is that to create value, a firm must earn enough income to cover the cost of invested capital and to provide additional income to shareholders. As long as EVA is positive, the firm's managers have used the invested capital to create additional value for shareholders. A negative EVA indicates that the firm's managers are destroying shareholder value. EVA has been adopted by many of the world's leading companies, including Alcan Aluminum; Bausch & Lomb; The Coca-Cola Co.; Eli Lilly & Co.; JC Penney; Rubbermaid, Inc.; Siemens A.G.; and Sprint. It is calculated as

EVA = Net operating profit − [Invested capital × Weighted-average cost of capital]

Let's use Centex Yarns' Nylon Fibers division to illustrate the EVA calculation, which has four steps.

Step 1: Calculating Net Operating Profit

The first step in calculating EVA is to determine the **net operating profit**, which is operating income minus income taxes. This amount is sometimes referred to as net operating profit after taxes, or NOPAT. One of the goals of EVA is to remove what some people view as income distortions created by the application of generally accepted accounting principles (GAAP). For example, many companies incur research and development costs to provide an ongoing stream of viable products. GAAP requires that these costs be expensed as they are incurred, even though the research and development effort provides future benefits. EVA adjusts operating income to recognize the future benefits of these costs. Some EVA models make over 150 such adjustments to operating income.

The complexities of these adjustments, however, are beyond the scope of this chapter. For our purposes, we will use the reported operating profit as our EVA income measure. To obtain the *net* operating profit, we must subtract the income tax that is due on the operating profits. The Nylon Fibers division's operating profit is its controllable segment margin of $865,000. Since Centex Yarns is in the 30% tax bracket, *net* operating profit for the division is $605,500 ($865,000 × [1 − 30%]).

Step 2: Calculating Invested Capital

The Nylon Fibers division earns its net operating profit because of its investment in productive assets such as inventory and equipment. The amount of its invested capital is its total assets minus its current liabilities.

Invested capital = Total assets − Current liabilities

Why are current liabilities subtracted from total assets? Current liabilities, such as accounts payable, really do not qualify as "invested capital," since the company has received no cash from them. Being allowed to pay a bill 30 or 60 days after the purchase does not require an investment of capital by the creditor.

The Nylon Fibers division has total assets of $2,703,000 and total current liabilities of $600,000. Therefore, total invested capital is $2,103,000 ($2,703,000 − $600,000). Some companies make adjustments to invested capital similar to those made to net operating profit. For instance, many companies add the value of "off-balance sheet" assets, such as operating leases, that carry a long-term commitment. The goal of these adjustments is to determine the most accurate measure possible of invested capital. Again, these adjustments are beyond the scope of this chapter, so we will use the simple formula of total assets minus current liabilities.

Step 3: Calculating the Weighted-Average Cost of Capital

Creditors and investors provided the capital necessary for the Nylon Fibers division to conduct business and earn a profit. Needless to say, they do not provide their capital for free; they expect to earn a return on their investment. Finance theory says that the rate of return required by creditors is different from the return required by investors. The **weighted-average cost of capital (WACC)** is the combined rate of return required by all capital providers. The WACC is calculated for the company as a whole and then used in divisional calculations.

To calculate the weighted-average cost of capital, we need to know the relative percentage of capital provided by each source, as well as the required rate of return. Let's assume that creditors provide 40% of Centex Yarns' capital as debt, and investors provide 60% of the company's capital as equity. Creditors require a 6% return on their loans and investors require a 12% return. Therefore, Centex Yarns' weighted-average cost of capital is 9.6%, calculated as follows:

Source of Invested Capital	Cost of Invested Capital (A)	Share of Invested Capital (B)	Weighted-Average Cost of Capital (A × B)
Debt	6%	40%	2.4%
Equity	12%	60%	7.2%
			9.6%

$$\text{WACC} = (6\% \times 40\%) + (12\% \times 60\%) = 9.6\%$$

For most companies, the calculation of weighted-average cost of capital is more complex than this example. You will learn much more about this calculation in your corporate finance class.

Step 4: Calculating EVA

Once we have determined the net operating profit, invested capital, and weighted-average cost of capital, we can calculate EVA. The Nylon Fibers division's EVA is $403,612, calculated as

$$\text{EVA} = \text{Net operating profit} - [\text{Invested capital} \times \text{Weighted-average cost of capital}]$$

$$\text{EVA} = \$605{,}500 - [(\$2{,}703{,}000 - \$600{,}000) \times 9.6\%] = \$403{,}612$$

This positive EVA shows that the Nylon Fibers division is creating value for Centex Yarns and its investors.

EVA Compared to Residual Income

Now that you have studied both residual income and EVA, you may think they are fairly similar, and they are. You can think of EVA as residual income based on *actual* weighted-average cost of capital rather than on management's required minimum rate of return. Why does using the actual weighted-average cost of capital matter? If the required minimum rate of return differs from the weighted-average cost of capital, the amount of income required to cover the cost of the investment will also differ.

Let's consider a potential investment of $100,000 in new equipment that will generate $14,000 in annual income for the Nylon Fibers division. As Exhibit 10-9 on the next page shows, if the division is evaluated on the basis of residual income at a required minimum rate of return of 15%, the equipment will not be purchased because it generates a negative residual income. However, if the division is evaluated using EVA, at a 9.6% weighted-average cost of capital and a 30% tax rate, the piece of equipment will be purchased.[8] Even though the machine will create value for shareholders based on EVA, the 15% required minimum rate of return will lead the manager to reject the investment. EVA doesn't always lead managers to make a decision different from residual income.

WATCH OUT!

Because managerial performance is multidimensional, more than one metric is required to adequately evaluate it. Don't rely solely on residual income or EVA as an evaluation tool.

REALITY CHECK—*Finding value in compensation*

© Andy Dean Photography/ Shutterstock

In 2011, Leong's EVA bonus was $2.6 million, down from $3.6 million he earned in 2010.

One of the challenges in designing executive compensation plans is getting managers to focus on the long-term value of the company. Many bonus plans are structured in a way that encourages managers to take actions that will maximize their short-term bonus payout while placing the company in a weaker position in the long term. But companies are now incorporating economic profit measures such as EVA into bonus calculations in an attempt to lengthen managers' time horizons. In fact, a 2012 global survey conducted by PricewaterhouseCoopers found that these economic profit measures were the most widely used metrics for determining incentive compensation, with 27% of respondents reporting their use to calculate short-term incentives.

Consider CapitaLand. Located in Singapore, CapitaLand is one of Asia's largest real estate companies. One part of President and CEO Liew Mun Leong's bonus is based on the company's EVA performance. In 2011, Leong's EVA bonus was $2.6 million, down from $3.6 million he earned in 2010. In Leong's case, the bonus is credited to a bonus account, and he receives one-third of the balance each year, as long as the bonus account is positive. This means that in poor performing years when the bonus account is in a negative position, the company may "clawback" previously paid bonuses.

But executive compensation is not the only area affected by the use of economic profit measures. Kaiser Aluminum Corp. found that employees were more efficient in using inventory after it tied short-term incentives to economic profits. PepsiCo believes it can lower capital spending from 5.5% of sales to 4.5% of sales as a result of employees making better decisions based on economic profit.

Sources: Emily Chasan, "Stock Loses Some Sway on Pay," *The Wall Street Journal*, October 30, 2012; Jamie Lee, "Bonus Model for Bosses May Need Tweaking," *The Business Times*, June 8, 2012; Jamie Lee, "CapitaLand CEO Earnings 16.7% lower at $5.63m," *The Business Times*, April 5, 2012; Xin Min Wang, "EVA Promotes 'Employee Capitalism'," *The Business Times*, June 16, 2012.

EXHIBIT 10-9

Comparison of residual income and EVA.

	Residual Income	EVA
Assets	$100,000	$100,000
× Required rate of return	15%	9.6%
= Minimum required income	$ 15,000	$ 9,600
Net operating income	$ 14,000	$ 9,800[a]
− Minimum required income	15,000	9,600
= Residual income	$ (1,000)	$ 200

[a] $14,000 × (1 − 0.3)

However, it is important for managers to understand the assumptions behind each model and the inputs into each, so that they will make decisions that benefit the organization as a whole.

UNIT 10.4 REVIEW

KEY TERMS

Economic value added (EVA) p. 559
Net operating profit p. 560
Residual income p. 558
Weighted-average cost of capital (WACC) p. 561

PRACTICE QUESTIONS

1. LO 4 A project that a division manager deems unacceptable using ROI as a criterion will always be deemed unacceptable using residual income as a criterion. True or False.

2. LO 4 Pinolla Company's Southern region operates as an investment center. Bob Pinolla, the region's director, has set an 18% required minimum rate of return. Bob is considering investing in a $50,000 machine that is expected to generate $15,000 in additional operating income. What is the machine's residual income?

   a. $50,000
   b. $15,000
   c. $9,000
   d. $6,000

3. LO 4 Pinolla Company's Northern region operates as an investment center. Casey Pinolla, the region's director, has set an 18% required minimum rate of return. Casey is considering investing in a $100,000 machine that is expected to generate $30,000 in additional operating income. Pinolla's weighted-average cost of capital is 14%, and its tax rate is 25%. What is the machine's EVA?

   a. $6,000
   b. $8,500
   c. $9,000
   d. $15,000

UNIT 10.4 PRACTICE EXERCISE

Minor & Neece, Ltd., operates retail clothing stores in Nashville, Knoxville, and Memphis, Tennessee. Each store is evaluated as an investment center. Selected results from the latest year are as follows.

	Nashville	Knoxville	Memphis
Sales	$5,000,000	$8,000,000	$2,000,000
Variable expenses	2,000,000	4,800,000	1,000,000
Direct fixed expenses	2,000,000	2,500,000	800,000
Assets	4,000,000	5,000,000	1,600,000
Required rate of return	14%	14%	14%
Weighted-average cost of capital	8%	8%	8%
Tax rate	30%	30%	30%

Required

a. Calculate the residual income for each of the three stores.
b. The corporate office is giving the stores the option of purchasing a new inventory management system. The new system will cost the stores $100,000; they can expect a $15,000 increase in their annual segment margins. If store managers are evaluated based on residual income, which stores will invest in the new inventory management system?
c. What is the EVA of the new inventory management system?

SELECTED UNIT 10.4 ANSWERS

Think About It 10.4

Let's compare the calculation of the return on investment to residual income:

$$\frac{\text{Operating income}}{\text{Average assets}} = \text{Return on investment}$$

Operating income = Return on investment × Average assets

Operating income − (Return on investment × Average assets) = 0

Operating income − (Required minimum rate of return × Average assets) = Residual income

if Return on investment > Required minimum rate of return, Residual income > 0

if Return on investment < Required minimum rate of return, Residual income < 0

Since all the divisions' returns on investment are greater than Centex's required minimum rate of 15%, then all the residual incomes will be greater than zero.

PRACTICE QUESTIONS

1. False
2. D
3. B

UNIT 10.4 PRACTICE EXERCISE

a.

	Nashville	Knoxville	Memphis
Sales	$5,000,000	$8,000,000	$2,000,000
Variable expenses	2,000,000	4,800,000	1,000,000
Contribution margin	3,000,000	3,200,000	1,000,000
Direct fixed expenses	2,000,000	2,500,000	800,000
Segment margin	$1,000,000	$ 700,000	$ 200,000
Asset base	$4,000,000	$5,000,000	$1,600,000
× Required rate of return	14%	14%	14%
= Minimum required income	$560,000	$ 700,000	$ 224,000
Segment margin	$1,000,000	$ 700,000	$ 200,000
− Minimum required income	560,000	700,000	224,000
= Residual income	$ 440,000	$ 0	($ 24,000)

b.

	Nashville	Knoxville	Memphis
Asset base	$4,100,000	$5,100,000	$1,700,000
× Required rate of return	14%	14%	14%
= Minimum required income	$ 574,000	$ 714,000	$ 238,000
Segment margin	$1,015,000	$ 715,000	$ 215,000
− Minimum required income	574,000	714,000	238,000
= Residual income	$ 441,000	$ 1,000	($ 23,000)

All three stores will choose to invest in the new inventory management system, since it increases their residual income.

c. With invested capital of $100,000 and a weighted-average cost of capital of 8%, the required income is $8,000 ($100,000 × 8%). Since the new system generates $10,500 in after-tax net operating income [$15,000 × (1 − 30%)], the EVA is $2,500 for each system installed.

APPENDIX

Transfer Pricing

GUIDED UNIT PREPARATION

Answering the following questions while you read this unit will guide your understanding of the key concepts found in the unit. The questions are linked to the learning objectives presented at the beginning of the chapter.

LO 5

1. What is a transfer price?
2. What are the four ways of determining a transfer price? Explain the advantages and disadvantages of each.
3. What is the minimum acceptable transfer price for a division that has excess operating capacity?
4. What is the minimum acceptable transfer price for a division that is operating at full capacity?

When organizations choose to decentralize their operations, divisions may end up exchanging goods and services with one another rather than with external suppliers or customers. Consider Smithfield Foods, the world's largest pork producer. The company's hog production division sells its hogs to the pork division that produces the ham, bacon, and other meat products sold to consumers. Since the managers of both these divisions will be evaluated based on how well their divisions perform, they will want any transaction with another division to generate positive results.

Similar divisional transfer opportunities exist within Centex Yarns. For example, since the Rope division uses industrial yarns in some of its manufactured ropes, it could purchase those yarns from the Industrial Yarns group in the Nylon Fibers division rather than from another company. In this instance, industrial yarns are an **intermediate product**—that is, a product that is purchased for the purpose of making another product rather than for sale to an end user.

When this type of transfer occurs between the two divisions, the question arises: What price should the Industrial Yarns group charge, and what price should the Rope division be willing to pay? The price at which the exchange between divisions takes place is referred to as the **transfer price**. Although transfer prices can be determined in several ways, a manager's willingness to accept the transfer price depends on how the transfer will affect the division's bottom line and what other options are available to the manager. In this appendix, you will learn how to establish transfer prices and how those prices affect each division's financial performance.

Selecting a Transfer Price Base

Determining a transfer price is not a trivial exercise. Transfer prices can be based on any of several measures, and the choice of a transfer price can have a significant impact on managers' behavior and on taxable income. Transfer prices are an even larger issue for companies that are executing transfers internationally, as illustrated by Glaxo SmithKline's \$3.4 billion settlement and AstraZeneca's \$1 billion settlement with the Internal Revenue Service.[9]

The most unbiased transfer price is the **market-based price**, which is easily determined by monitoring similar trades that occur in the marketplace between unrelated parties. This is the price that the selling division would charge to other customers and that the buying division would pay to other suppliers. The management of Smithfield Foods believes that the transfer prices used for transactions between the hog production and pork divisions approximate the market prices paid by other hog sellers and buyers.

In the case of Centex Yarns, industrial yarns sell on the open market for an average of \$25 per reel. Given this price, it would be hard for either the Rope division manager or the Industrial Yarns group manager to argue with a transfer price of \$25 per reel. At this market-based transfer price, the Industrial Yarns group manager has an incentive to control production costs, since any difference between those costs and the transfer price will be recognized as segment profit.

Market-based prices are not always readily available, however. For instance, the intermediate product might not be actively sold. Let's assume that the Industrial Yarns group doesn't sell to any external companies, but instead provides yarns only to other Centex Yarns divisions. Without a market price to guide the transfer, what is the appropriate price for the sale of industrial yarns to the Rope division?

One alternative is a **cost-based price**, or the cost to produce the intermediate product. Hormel Foods uses this approach when it transfers products between its business segments. In Centex Yarns' case, the Industrial Yarns group's cost accounting records show that the cost of goods sold for one reel of industrial yarn is \$16. Although the Rope division might be happy to pay \$16 per reel, that

REALITY CHECK—*The taxing transfer*

© WillSelarep/iStockphoto

Intercompany transactions within multinational enterprises account for 50–60% of all global trading.

How would you like to get a billion-dollar tax bill? That's exactly what Glaxo SmithKline and AstraZeneca received when they settled transfer pricing disputes with the IRS. Many more companies could be facing a similar fate as transfer pricing rises to the top of tax authorities' list of concerns.

Recent studies indicate a growing interest in transfer pricing among taxing authorities around the world. In 1994, approximately 12 countries had transfer pricing rules; by 2012, that number had risen to more than 70. Why all the interest? In a word, globalization. Intercompany transactions within multinational enterprises account for 50–60% of all global trading. With cross-border mergers and acquisitions increasing, this percentage is likely to rise. That's a lot of transfer pricing, and tax authorities want to make sure they get their fair share of the revenue on those trades.

A simple example will illustrate what is at stake. Suppose Company A's Division W is located in a country with a 20% tax rate, while Division Y is located in a country with a 40% tax rate. Division W makes a part that costs $10 and sells for $30. Division W then transfers this part to Division Y, which sells it for $45. If the transfer price is $10, Division W makes $0 profit and pays no taxes. Division Y will make $35 in profit and will pay $14 in taxes. But if the transfer price is made at the market price of $30, Division W makes a profit of $20 and will pay $4 in taxes. Division Y will make $15 in profit and will pay $6 in taxes. So Company A is better off with the second transfer price since it minimizes taxes.

Many tax authorities believe that multinational corporations play transfer pricing games to avoid paying taxes. As a result, companies must closely monitor tax legislation in each country where they operate to make sure they can justify the transfer prices they use.

Sources: Ernst & Young *2005–2006 Global Transfer Pricing Surveys: Global Transfer Pricing Trends, Practices, and Analysis*, November 2006; KPMG, *Improving Transfer Pricing Risk Management in High-Technology Companies*, 2007; Andrew Jack, "AstraZeneca Pays $1bn in US Tax Settlement," *Financial Times*, March 28, 2011; TP Analytics Country References, http://tpa.randomanalyst.com/tp-reference/country-references/ (accessed July 20, 2016).

price would provide no profit for the Industrial Yarns group. If the Industrial Yarns group is treated as a cost center, that arrangement is acceptable. But if it is a profit center, the group's management will want to earn a profit on the sale.

To provide some level of profit to the seller, the two divisions may agree to a **cost-plus-based price**, in which some markup is added to the product's cost to arrive at the transfer price. For example, Centex Yarns management might dictate that any transfer for which no market price exists should be priced at cost plus 20%. In this case, the resulting transfer price would be $19.20 per reel ($16 per reel × 1.2).

Unlike the market-based transfer price, cost-based and cost-plus-based transfer prices do not provide any incentive to the selling division to control costs. Such a transfer price will work well for the selling division, but it is not in the best interest of the corporation as a whole if the cost to produce the intermediate product is higher than it really should be.

A final option is a **negotiated price**, or one that is agreed to by both the buying and the selling division. Unlike a dictated cost-plus price, a negotiated price leaves the decision making to the division managers. While this price might be agreeable to the individual divisions, it does not necessarily maximize income for the corporation as a whole.

Determining the Minimum Transfer Price

Transfer prices should not be set to benefit only those divisions involved in the transfer. The goal of setting a transfer price is to motivate managers to behave in the best interest of the firm as a whole. Setting a minimum transfer price using the following formula will ensure that the buying and selling divisions act not only in their own best interest, but also in that of the corporation as a whole:

Minimum transfer price = Variable cost to produce/sell + Contribution margin forgone from the transfer

You already know how to determine the variable cost to produce and sell a product. The contribution margin forgone from the transfer is the contribution margin the selling division must give up on lost sales to external companies in order to make the sale internally. Let's see how this formula works for Centex's Industrial Yarns group and Rope division. We'll use the following information about the Industrial Yarns group:

Normal selling price	$25 per reel
Variable product costs	$12 per reel
Fixed product costs	$ 4 per reel
Variable selling and administrative costs	$ 2 per reel
Production capacity	150,000 reels

As we'll see, the minimum transfer price will vary depending on whether or not the selling division has excess capacity.

Selling Division Has Excess Capacity

Suppose that the Rope Division wants to buy 10,000 reels of industrial yarn from the Industrial Yarns group and that the Industrial Yarns group currently sells 103,800 reels of industrial yarn. With a production capacity of 150,000 reels, the Industrial Yarns group has enough excess capacity to produce 46,200 additional reels (150,000 reel capacity − 103,800 reels currently in production). Therefore, the Industrial Yarns group can produce and sell the 10,000 reels to the Rope division without affecting its current sales. Since no current sales to external customers will be forfeited to meet the Rope division's needs, no contribution margin is lost on the transfer. Thus, the minimum transfer price is determined as follows:

Minimum transfer price = ($12 + $2) + $0 = $14

Will the transfer between the Industrial Yarns group and the Rope division take place at the $14 price? Let's consider their options.

Options for the Industrial Yarns Group	Options for the Rope Division
• Make the additional 10,000 reels and sell them to the Rope division for $14 per reel • Do not make and sell the additional 10,000 reels	• Purchase 10,000 reels from the Industrial Yarns group for $14 per reel • Purchase 10,000 reels from another vendor for $25 per reel • Do not purchase 10,000 reels

A transfer price of $14 will just cover the variable costs incurred by the Industrial Yarns group to make the yarn. Since the transfer of yarn at this price will not change the group's contribution margin, and thus its segment margin, the group is indifferent between selling the reels and not selling them. However, the Rope division would prefer to purchase the reels from the Industrial Yarns group at $14 rather than from an outside vendor at $25 because that option will generate a higher margin for the division. Even so, the Rope division has to be sure that, overall, buying the yarn makes sense. In addition to the variable cost of the yarn, the Rope division incurs additional variable costs of $31 per reel to produce and sell the rope, resulting in a total variable cost of $45 per reel ($14 + $31). The rope is sold for $60 per reel, resulting in a contribution margin of $15 per reel ($60 − $14 − $31 = $15). Exhibit 10-10 shows that the $14 transfer price results in the best overall outcome for the corporation.

Industrial Yarns group transfers 10,000 reels to the Rope division at $14 per reel

	Industrial Yarns Group	Rope Division	Corporate Total
Sales	10,000 × $14 = $140,000	10,000 × $60 = $600,000	$740,000
Variable costs—industrial yarn	10,000 × $14 = 140,000	10,000 × $14 = 140,000	280,000
Other variable costs	0	10,000 × $31 = 310,000	310,000
Contribution margin	$0	$150,000	$150,000

Industrial Yarns group does nothing, and Rope division buys 10,000 reels externally at $25 per reel

	Industrial Yarns Group	Rope Division	Corporate Total
Sales	$0	10,000 × $60 = $600,000	$600,000
Variable costs—industrial yarn	0	10,000 × $25 = 250,000	250,000
Other variable costs	0	10,000 × $31 = 310,000	310,000
Contribution margin	$0	$40,000	$40,000

Industrial Yarns group does nothing, and Rope division does nothing

	Industrial Yarns Group	Rope Division	Corporate Total
Sales	$0	$0	$0
Variable costs—industrial yarn	0	0	0
Other variable costs	0	0	0
Contribution margin	$0	$0	$0

EXHIBIT 10-10 *Calculation of corporate profits at a minimum transfer price of $14.*

While $14 per reel is the *minimum* transfer price acceptable to the Industrial Yarns group, the group's manager is likely to negotiate a higher price to provide some additional contribution margin. The Rope division's manager will be happy to pay anything less than the $25 per reel market price. Therefore, the actual transfer is likely to be somewhere between $14 per reel and $25 per reel.

Selling Division Has No Excess Capacity

In the last scenario, the Industrial Yarns group had plenty of excess capacity to meet the Rope division's needs. Let's assume now that the Industrial Yarns group is operating at the maximum capacity of 150,000 reels, and all those reels are currently sold to external customers at a price of $25 per reel. That means that to fill the Rope division's order for 10,000 reels, the Industrial Yarns group would need to give up some sales to external customers, resulting in a lost contribution margin of $11 per reel ($25 sales price − $14 variable cost per reel). In this case, the minimum transfer price would be:

$$\text{Minimum transfer price} = (\$12 + \$2) + (\$25 - \$14) = \$25$$

With the group's performance evaluated on the basis of its segment margin, the manager of the Industrial Yarns group is not willing to give up $110,000 in lost contribution margin ($11 per reel contribution margin × 10,000 reels). Notice that in this case, the transfer price is the same as the external market price that the Industrial Yarns group currently receives for its reels. At a minimum transfer price of $25 per reel, what options do the Industrial Yarns group and the Rope division have?

Options for the Industrial Yarns Group	Options for Rope Division
• Sell 10,000 reels to the Rope division for $25 per reel • Sell 10,000 reels to external customers for $25 per reel • Do nothing	• Purchase 10,000 reels from the Industrial Yarns group for $25 per reel • Purchase 10,000 reels from another vendor for $25 per reel • Do not purchase the 10,000 reels

Both the Industrial Yarns group and the Rope division are indifferent between an internal transfer and a transaction with an external party. Either way, the corporation will maximize its profits.

THINK ABOUT IT 10.5

The variable costs for the Industrial Yarns group include both production and selling and administrative costs. Might it be possible for variable selling and administrative costs to be lower on an internal transfer than on an external sale? If those variable costs are lower, what will happen to the minimum transfer price?

Let's look at an alternative scenario in which the Rope division's variable costs are $65 per reel when it must purchase this type of yarn from an external vendor ($25 for the yarn and $40 for other variable costs). Since the selling price for the rope is only $60, the division would lose $5 on each reel sold. Now the Rope division's manager wants the Industrial Yarns group manager to sell him 10,000 reels at $20 per reel, so he can break even. The Industrial Yarns group manager refuses because his profits will be reduced if he forfeits external sales at $25 per reel in order to make the transfer to the Rope division at only $20 per reel. To settle the standoff, James Cameron, Centex Yarns' CEO, intervenes and requires the transfer to take place at $20 per reel.

Exhibit 10-11 shows that the required transfer at $20 per reel is not the best option for the corporation, as a whole. At the appropriate minimum transfer

WATCH OUT!

Just because you can calculate the minimum transfer price doesn't mean that a transfer should take place. Sometimes is it best for a division to remain idle or to do business with an external party.

Industrial Yarns group transfers 10,000 reels to Rope division at $20 per reel

	Industrial Yarns Group	Rope Division	Corporate Total
Sales	$200,000	$600,000	$800,000
Variable costs—industrial yarn	140,000	200,000	340,000
Other variable costs	0	400,000	400,000
Contribution margin	$ 60,000	$ 0	$ 60,000

Industrial Yarns group sells 10,000 reels externally for $25 per reel, and Rope division buys 10,000 reels externally at $25 per reel

	Industrial Yarns Group	Rope Division	Corporate Total
Sales	$250,000	$600,000	$850,000
Variable costs—industrial yarn	140,000	250,000	390,000
Other variable costs	0	400,000	400,000
Contribution margin	$110,000	$ (50,000)	$ 60,000

Industrial Yarns group sells 10,000 reels externally at $25 per reel, and Rope division does nothing

	Industrial Yarns Group	Rope Division	Corporate Total
Sales	$250,000	$0	$250,000
Variable costs—industrial yarn	140,000	0	140,000
Other variable costs	0	0	0
Contribution margin	$110,000	$0	$110,000

EXHIBIT 10-11 *Calculation of corporate profits at a minimum transfer price of $20.*

price of $25 per reel, the Industrial Yarns group would be indifferent between selling externally or internally to the Rope division, but the Rope division's manager would choose to do nothing rather than show a negative profit. Therefore, the Industrial Yarns group will end up making $110,000 in contribution margin by selling externally, benefiting both itself and the corporation as a whole. Under a forced transfer at $20 per reel, the company would realize only $60,000.

APPENDIX REVIEW

KEY TERMS

Cost-based price p. 565	Intermediate product p. 565	Negotiated price p. 566
Cost-plus-based price p. 566	Market-based price p. 565	Transfer price p. 565

PRACTICE QUESTIONS

1. LO 5 There is only one acceptable transfer price to use when transferring products between operating divisions. True or False.

2. LO 5 Spillburgh Media develops media campaigns for a variety of clients. The Internet group is working on a website and needs 40 production hours to produce a video clip. Spillburgh's Video group provides these services to both in-house projects and outside clients. The Video group's variable costs are $800 per production hour; it charges outside clients $1,500 per production hour. Based on a capacity of 5,000 production hours, the Video group's fixed costs are $400 per production hour. The Video group currently has only 4,800 production hours scheduled. What is the minimum transfer price that will maximize corporate profits?

   a. $400 per production hour

   b. $800 per production hour

   c. $1,200 per production hour

   d. $1,500 per production hour

3. LO 5 Spillburgh Media develops media campaigns for a variety of clients. The Internet group is working on a website and needs 40 production hours to produce a video clip. Spillburgh's Video group provides these services to both in-house projects and outside clients. The Video group's variable costs are $800 per production hour; it charges outside clients $1,500 per production hour. Based on a capacity of 5,000 production hours, the Video group's fixed costs are $400 per production hour. The video group is currently working at full capacity. What is the minimum transfer price that will maximize corporate profits?

   a. $400 per production hour

   b. $800 per production hour

   c. $1,200 per production hour

   d. $1,500 per production hour

APPENDIX PRACTICE EXERCISE

Caffeine Connections sells a variety of exotic teas and coffees through a national network. The company operates its own roasting division, which supplies roasted coffee beans to its own wholesale division as well as to other external customers. Even though the roasting division can roast 500,000 pounds of beans each month, current market demand is only 425,000 pounds, so that is the current level of production.

The wholesale division has designed a new promotional product for which it needs 50,000 pounds of roasted coffee beans. The roasting division can supply the beans at a cost of $6.75 per pound. Of that cost, $5 per pound is variable and $1.75 is fixed. The beans could also be purchased from another roaster at $8 per pound. Both the roasting and wholesale divisions are treated as profit centers.

Required

a. If Caffeine Connections chooses to use a cost-based transfer price for the beans, what transfer price would the two divisions use? Is the transfer likely to occur? Why or why not?

b. If Caffeine Connections chooses to use a cost-plus-based transfer price for the beans, what transfer price would the two divisions use, assuming a 25% markup? Is the transfer likely to occur? Why or why not?

c. If Caffeine Connections chooses to use a market-based transfer price for the beans, what transfer price would the two divisions use? Is the transfer likely to occur? Why or why not?

d. What is the minimum transfer price for the beans?

e. What is the likely range of a negotiated transfer price?
f. If the roasting division currently roasts and sells 500,000 pounds of coffee to external customers, what is the minimum transfer price?

SELECTED APPENDIX ANSWERS

Think About It 10.5

Variable selling and administrative costs include selling commissions and customer order processing costs. When transactions occur between divisions of the same corporation, some or all of those costs may be saved. If some variable selling and administrative costs are saved, then they don't need to be included in the calculation of the minimum transfer price. In the case of Industrial Yarns group, for example, $2 of the variable costs are for selling and administrative expenses. If those costs can be saved, then the minimum transfer price will be $23, not $25. Thus, even if a company is operating at capacity, it is possible that a transfer could be made at less than the market price.

Practice Questions

1. False
2. B
3. D

Appendix Practice Exercise

a. $5 per pound based on variable cost, or $6.75 per pound based on full cost. At a price of $5 the transfer is not likely to occur because the roasting division is a profit center and this price does not provide any profit for the division. However, any price above $5 per pound contributes toward covering fixed costs and providing profit. The wholesale division would be happy with any price lower than $8.
b. $5 × 1.25 = $6.25 per pound based on variable cost, or $6.75 × 1.25 = $8.44 per pound based on full cost. At the $8.44 price the roasting division will want to make the sale but the wholesale division won't buy since it can get the product externally for $8 per pound. At $6.25 the wholesale division will want to buy, and the roasting division should want to sell to cover some of its fixed costs.
c. $8 per pound. Both divisions will be willing to make the transfer: The roasting division will earn a profit, and the wholesale division won't be paying more than the market price.
d. $5 variable cost + $0 opportunity cost = $5 per pound
e. Between $5 and $8 per pound
f. $5 variable cost + $3 opportunity cost = $8 per pound

BUSINESS DECISION AND CONTEXT Wrap Up

Monica Waltrip is now armed and ready for her meeting with James Cameron. The analysis Luke Carlson prepared confirmed her belief that the Nylon Fibers division is making a significant contribution to the financial performance of Centex Yarns.

Monica will begin her discussion with James by pointing out that the income statement he was viewing allocated common fixed costs to the three operating divisions, distorting the divisions' true contribution to corporate profits. When the divisions are evaluated based on their segment margins, it becomes clear that the Nylon Fibers division is contributing $865,000 to the company's bottom line. Closing the division would reduce overall profits by that amount. The Nylon Fibers division is also reporting a 32% return on investment—the highest ROI of the three divisions.

Once James has the appropriate tools for evaluating divisional performance, he will be in a better position to decide which divisions, if any, are candidates for closure. Those tools will also provide him with additional ways to evaluate new projects the company may be considering.

CHAPTER SUMMARY

In this chapter you learned about decentralization and various ways to evaluate divisional performance. Specifically, you should be able to meet the objectives set out at the beginning of this chapter:

1. ***Identify the difference between a cost center, a profit center, and an investment center. (Unit 10.1)***

The difference between a cost center, a profit center, and an investment center has to do with the level of decision making and control the manager has. A cost center is an organizational unit in which the manager is responsible only for the costs that are incurred. The goal of a cost center manager is to minimize costs while providing an acceptable level of service or quality of product. A profit center is an organizational unit in which the manager is responsible for both revenues and costs incurred to generate a product or service sold. This center is expected to generate profits, not just revenues or costs. An investment center is an organizational unit in which the manager is expected to invest in assets and generate profits. Investment center managers have the broadest responsibility of the three types of manager.

2. ***Prepare a segment margin income statement and evaluate a segment's financial performance. (Unit 10.2)***

In evaluating a segment's financial performance, only those revenues and costs over which the manager has control should be included. Following is an example of a segment margin income statement. Notice that the segment margin is calculated as segment revenue less variable expenses and traceable fixed expenses. Corporate expenses that support the organization as a whole are not allocated to segments. Instead, these common fixed expenses are subtracted only from the total corporate revenues.

	Segment A	Segment B	Total
Revenue	$X	$X	$X
Less variable expenses:			
Cost of goods sold	(X)	(X)	(X)
Selling & administrative	(X)	(X)	(X)
Contribution margin	X	X	X
Less traceable fixed expenses	(X)	(X)	(X)
Segment margin	$X	$X	X
Less common fixed expenses			(X)
Operating income			X

If the segment margin is positive, then the segment is making a contribution to the corporate bottom line. Dropping the segment will decrease corporate income by the amount of the segment margin. If the segment margin is negative, then it is causing the corporation to lose money. Dropping the segment will increase corporate income by the amount of the segment margin.

3. ***Evaluate an operating segment or project using return on investment. (Unit 10.3)***

Besides looking at the segment margin to evaluate segment performance, companies will calculate return on investment. The formula for return on investment (ROI) is:

$$\text{ROI} = \frac{\text{Operating income}}{\text{Average operating assets}} \quad \text{or} \quad \frac{\text{Segment margin}}{\text{Average operating assets}}$$

Return on investment is a percentage that can be compared to a corporate minimum return or to other segments' ROIs. All else held equal, the higher the ROI, the better. ROI can be broken down into two measures, margin and asset turnover, to focus on specific components in need of improvement.

Margin × Asset turnover

$$\text{ROI} = \frac{\text{Operating income*}}{\text{Sales revenue}} \times \frac{\text{Sales revenue}}{\text{Average operating assets}}$$

*Or segment margin.

4. ***Evaluate an operating segment or project using residual income and economic value added. (Unit 10.4)***

Residual income is the income that is earned above a required minimum rate of return. As long as a project's residual income is positive, it is earning a return in excess of the required minimum. Residual income is calculated as

Residual income = Operating income* − (Assets × Required minimum rate of return)

*Or segment margin.

Economic value added (EVA)® is similar to residual income. The formula for EVA is as follows:

EVA = Net operating profit − [Invested capital × Weighted-average cost of capital]

5. ***Calculate the minimum transfer price between divisions that maximizes corporate income. (Appendix)***

When two divisions want to engage in a transfer, the selling division wants the price to be as high as possible, but the buying division wants the price to be as low as possible, since both are evaluated on how well their divisions perform financially. The minimum transfer price that will result in the best outcome for the corporation as a whole is:

Minimum transfer price = Variable cost to produce/sell + Contribution margin forgone from the transfer

This transfer price doesn't guarantee that the transfer will occur. Instead, it is the price that encourages the divisional managers to act in the best interest of both their divisions and the corporation, whether that is to engage in the transfer, to transact with an external company, or to do nothing.

KEY TERMS

Asset turnover (Unit 10.3)
Centralization (Unit 10.1)
Cost-based price (Appendix)
Cost center (Unit 10.1)
Cost-plus-based price (Appendix)
Decentralization (Unit 10.1)
DuPont Model (Unit 10.3)
Economic value added (EVA®) (Unit 10.4)
Intermediate product (Appendix)
Investment center (Unit 10.1)
Margin (Unit 10.3)
Market-based price (Appendix)
Negotiated price (Appendix)
Net operating profit (Unit 10.4)
Profit center (Unit 10.1)
Residual income (Unit 10.4)
Responsibility accounting (Unit 10.1)
Return on investment (ROI) (Unit 10.3)
Segment (Unit 10.2)
Transfer price (Appendix)
Weighted-average cost of capital (WACC) (Unit 10.4)

EXERCISES

10-1 Responsibility centers (LO 1) Blakefield, Inc. has grown significantly over the past decade through innovation and acquisition. Information on several of its divisions follows.

- The OlliePods division sells children's recreational shoes. The division's president is responsible for all short-run decisions on the manufacturing and sale of the shoes.
- The Polyspreen division manufactures the main ingredient for the shoes produced by OlliePods. All Polyspreen output is transferred to the OlliePods division.
- All long-run strategic decisions for the OlliePods and Polyspreen divisions are made by the staff at corporate headquarters.
- Monk Recreation, which operates a regional chain of retail sporting goods stores, is Blakefield's newest corporate acquisition. Blakefield managers have decided to retain all Monk Recreation employees, and all decision-making responsibility related to the sporting goods stores remains with those employees.

Required

a. Classify each of the three divisions of Blakefield, Inc. as a cost center, a profit center, or an investment center.
b. What type of responsibility center is the corporate headquarters group?

10-2 Responsibility centers (LO 1) Hewett and Hefner, LLP is a regional public accounting firm with 34 offices throughout the southeastern United States. To provide employees with cost-effective continuing professional education, the company maintains an in-house education and training staff that develops and delivers one-day seminars on current topics in accounting and taxation. There is no charge to employees to attend these seminars.

Required

a. Should Hewett and Hefner, LLP treat the training department as a cost center, a profit center, or an investment center? Why?
b. Suppose Hewett and Hefner, LLP has received numerous requests from smaller firms to participate in the seminars provided by its training staff. Some of the firms are willing to pay a fee and travel to a Hewett and Hefner office to attend the seminars. Others have expressed interest in engaging Hewett and Hefner's staff to deliver customized seminars at their own offices. If management decides to allow the training staff to provide external training for a fee, how should Hewett and Hefner treat the training department? Why?

10-3 Responsibility centers (LO 1) North Town Medical Arts is a new healthcare provider in Baytown. The company operates a community hospital, an outpatient surgery center, and a medical offices building. Indicate whether each of the following responsibility centers is a cost center, a profit center, or an investment center.

- North Town Community Hospital
- Corporate human resources
- North Town Community Hospital pharmacy
- Maintenance department
- Hospital cafeteria
- Radiology department

10-4 Segment margin income statement (LO 2) Bridges Optics manufactures two products: microscopes and telescopes. Information for each product is as follows.

	Microscopes	Telescopes
Sales price	$ 40	$ 30
Sales volume	300,000	150,000
Variable cost per unit	$ 18	$ 17
Annual traceable fixed expenses	$3,800,000	$1,200,000
Annual allocated common fixed expenses	$2,400,000	$1,000,000

Required

Prepare a segment margin income statement for Bridges Optics that provides detail on both the product lines and the company as a whole.

10-5 Segment margin income statement (LO 2) Magellan & Columbus, Ltd. manufactures boats and personal watercraft. The company operates three separate divisions: yachts, sailboats, and jet skis. The company's latest income statement is presented by product line as follows:

	Yachts	Sailboats	Jet Skis	Total
Sales revenue	$60,000,000	$22,000,000	$6,000,000	$88,000,000
Variable cost of goods sold	30,000,000	12,000,000	3,500,000	45,500,000
Fixed cost of goods sold	9,000,000	5,000,000	700,000	14,700,000
Gross profit	21,000,000	5,000,000	1,800,000	27,800,000
Variable operating expenses	8,000,000	1,500,000	850,000	10,350,000
Fixed operating expenses	4,000,000	1,000,000	300,000	5,300,000
Allocated corporate costs	3,000,000	2,000,000	1,000,000	6,000,000
Operating income	$ 6,000,000	$ 500,000	$ (350,000)	$ 6,150,000

Required

a. Prepare a segment margin income statement showing each of the three divisions. Fixed cost of goods sold and fixed operating expenses can be traced to each product line.
b. Chris Columbus, CEO, is concerned about the Jet Ski division's operating loss; he wants to close the division to save money. Do you support his decision? Why or why not?

10-6 Segment margin income statement (LO 2) Kimball Equipment sells equipment to sports enthusiasts. Doug Kimball, the company's president, just received the following income statement reporting the results of the past year.

	Baseball	Soccer	Basketball	Total
Sales revenue	$1,450,000	$3,600,000	$1,380,000	$6,430,000
Variable cost of goods sold	950,000	2,340,000	960,000	4,250,000
Fixed cost of goods sold	140,000	188,000	120,000	448,000
Gross profit	360,000	1,072,000	300,000	1,732,000
Variable operating expenses	185,000	576,000	210,000	971,000
Fixed operating expenses	90,000	84,000	105,000	279,000
Common fixed costs	120,000	130,000	80,000	330,000
Operating income	($ 35,000)	$ 282,000	($ 95,000)	$ 152,000

Doug is concerned that two of the company's divisions are showing a loss, and he wonders if the company should stop selling baseball and basketball gear to concentrate solely on soccer gear.

Required

a. Prepare a segment margin income statement. Fixed cost of goods sold and fixed operating expenses can be traced to each division.
b. Should Doug close the baseball and basketball divisions? Why or why not?
c. Doug wants to change the allocation method used to allocate common fixed costs to the divisions. His plan is to allocate these costs based on sales revenue. Will this new allocation method change your decision on whether to close the baseball and basketball divisions? Why or why not?

10-7 Segment margin income statement (LO 2) Jane Baldwin, Anderson Flooring's accounting intern, has prepared the following income statement for the month of June.

	Residential	Commercial	Total
Sales revenue	$1,750,000	$3,125,000	$4,875,000
Variable expenses	1,035,000	2,520,000	3,555,000
Contribution margin	715,000	605,000	1,320,000
Fixed expenses	645,000	620,000	1,265,000
Operating income	$ 70,000	$ (15,000)	$ 55,000

In preparing the income statement, Jane was unsure what to do with $250,000 in corporate fixed expenses that cannot be traced to a particular division. Since these costs were incurred to run the business as a whole, and she believed that each division benefited equally, she just allocated half to each division.

Required

a. How do you think Jane should have handled the $250,000 in corporate fixed expenses?
b. Prepare a segment margin income statement that highlights each division's contribution to corporate profits.

10-8 Calculating return on investment (LO 3) Browning Design Works generated $300,000 in operating income on sales revenue of $2,000,000. The company had $2,200,000 in assets on January 1 and $2,800,000 in assets on December 31.

Required

a. Calculate Browning's margin.
b. Calculate Browning's asset turnover.
c. Calculate Browning's return on investment.

10-9 Calculating return on investment (LO 3) Paula Boothe, president of the Armange Corporation, has mandated a minimum 10% return on investment for any project undertaken by the company. Given the company's decentralization, Paula leaves all investment decisions to the divisional managers as long as they anticipate a minimum rate of return of at least 10%. The Energy Drinks division, under the direction of manager Martin Koch, has achieved a 14% return on investment for the past three years. This year is not expected to be different from the past three. Koch has just received a proposal to invest $1,800,000 in a new line of energy drinks that is expected to generate $216,000 in operating income.

Required

a. Calculate the return on investment expected on the new line of energy drinks.
b. If Martin Koch is evaluated based on the division's return on investment, will he choose to invest in the new line? Why or why not?
c. Would Paula Boothe prefer that Martin Koch invest in the new line? Why?

10-10 Return on investment (LO 3) Joyner Pickled Pepper Company produces pickled jalapeno pepper relish. Selected results from the most current year were as follows:

Sales revenue	$3,375,000
Operating income	540,000
Average total assets	1,687,500

Production manager Veronica Brockman is investigating the purchase of a new brining station that will increase the plant's production capacity. Based on her research, Veronica thinks the station would cost $762,500 and would increase sales revenue by $300,000 and operating profit by $66,375.

Required

a. Calculate Joyner's current margin, asset turnover, and return on investment.
b. Calculate Joyner's margin, asset turnover, and return on investment assuming the company purchases the new brining station.
c. Assume Veronica Joyner's annual bonus is based on the company's return on investment. Will Veronica support the purchase of the new brining station? Why or why not?

10-11 Return on investment (LO 3) Resilon, Inc., reported the following results for last year.

	Liles Division	Marston Division	Outland Division
Net operating income	$ 120,000	$ 45,000	$ 300,000
Sales revenue	600,000	150,000	1,200,000
Average operating assets	1,000,000	300,000	1,500,000

Required

a. Which division generates the highest margin?
b. If the divisions are evaluated based on return on investment, which division is doing the best job?

10-12 Return on investment (LO 3) Dale Decor sells home decor items through three distribution channels—retail stores, the Internet, and catalog sales. Each distribution channel is evaluated as an investment center. Selected results from the latest year are as follows:

	Retail Stores	Internet	Catalog Sales
Sales revenue	$10,000,000	$4,000,000	$3,200,000
Variable expenses	4,000,000	1,500,000	1,800,000
Direct fixed expenses	4,500,000	1,000,000	1,200,000
Average assets	8,000,000	4,000,000	2,000,000
Required rate of return	12%	12%	12%

Required

a. Calculate the margin, asset turnover, and ROI for each of the three distribution channels.
b. The corporate office is giving the managers of each channel the option of a customer relationship management system that will allow the managers to gather data about their customers and be more effective in their marketing efforts. The system will cost $800,000 and is expected to generate $160,000 in additional annual segment margin. If distribution channel managers are evaluated based on the trend of their ROIs, which managers will invest in the system? Explain your reasoning.

10-13 Return on investment (LO 3) Jordan Williams, a divisional manager, is evaluated based on return on investment. In the last quarter her division achieved a 15% margin and an 18% return on investment. The division had $4,000,000 in operating assets that quarter.

Required

a. What was the division's sales revenue for the quarter?
b. What was the division's net operating income for the quarter?

10-14 Calculating residual income (LO 4) Refer to Exercise 10-9.

Required

a. Calculate the residual income for the proposed new line of energy drinks.
b. If Martin Koch is evaluated based on residual income, will he choose to invest in the new line of energy drinks? Why or why not?

10-15 Calculating residual income (LO 4) Refer to Exercise 10-12.

Required

a. Calculate the current residual income for each distribution channel.
b. Calculate the residual income of each distribution channel assuming it purchases the new customer relationship management system.
c. Why is the residual income for each distribution channel higher in part (b) than in part (a)?

10-16 Calculating residual income (CMA adapted) (LO 4) Colleen Barry is the general manager of Whitten Industries' Industrial Products division. The division is treated as an investment center, and Colleen's performance is measured using residual income. In preparing the forecast for next year, Colleen assumes the division will generate $30 million in revenue using average operating assets of $19 million. The required minimum rate of return is 15%.

Required

a. If Colleen wants the division to achieve $2 million in residual income, what is the maximum amount of operating expenses the division can incur to achieve that target?
b. If Colleen doesn't believe she can control expenses to the level calculated in part (a), what action should she take?

10-17 Weighted-average cost of capital (LO 4) Draper Dynamics finances its operations with $30,000,000 in debt and $50,000,000 in stockholders' equity. The debt carries a 6% interest rate, and stockholders require a 12% return.

Required

What is Draper's weighted-average cost of capital?

10-18 Calculating economic value added (LO 4) Refer to Exercise 10-9. Assume that Armange Corporation's actual weighted-average cost of capital is 9% and its tax rate is 30%.

Required

a. Calculate the economic value added of the proposed new line of energy drinks.
b. If Martin Koch is evaluated based on economic value added, will he choose to invest in the new line of energy drinks? Why or why not?

10-19 Calculating return on investment, residual income, and economic value added (LO 3, 4)

	Segment A	Segment B	Segment C	Segment D	Segment E
Sales revenue	$1,000,000	$1,500,000	i.	$400,000	$310,000
Operating income	$ 100,000	f.	$ 420,000	$ 60,000	o.
Tax rate	30%	25%	20%	l.	20%
Total assets	$ 500,000	g.	$1,400,000	$500,000	$124,000
Current liabilities	$ 40,000	$ 40,000	j.	$ 40,000	$ 10,000
Corporate required return	15%	18%	16%	m.	20%
Weighted-average cost of capital	12%	14%	15%	10%	18%
Margin	a.	5%	k.	15%	2%
Asset turnover	b.	3	1.5	n.	2.5
Return on investment	c.	h.	30%	12%	p.
Residual income	d.	$ (15,000)	$ 196,000	$ 0	$ (18,600)
Economic value added	e.	$ (8,150)	$ 142,800	$ (4,000)	q.

Required

Compute the missing amounts labeled a–q.

10-20 Return on investment, residual income, and economic value added (LO 3, 4)

Isabelle Abiassi operates a popular summer camp for elementary school children. Projections for the current year are as follows:

Sales revenue	$8,000,000
Operating income	$700,000
Average assets	$4,000,000

The camp's weighted-average cost of capital is 10%, and Isabelle requires that all new investments generate a return on investment of at least 14%. The camp's current tax rate is 25%.

At last week's advisory board meeting, Isabelle told the board that she had up to $50,000 to invest in new facilities at the camp and asked them to recommend some projects. Today the board's president presented Isabelle with the following list of three potential investments to improve the camp facilities.

	Playground	Swimming Pool	Gym
Incremental operating income	$ 3,500	$ 4,800	$ 2,700
Average total assets	25,000	40,000	15,000

Required

a. Calculate the return on investment, residual income, and economic value added for each of the three projects.

b. Which of the three projects do you recommend Isabelle undertake? Why?

10-21 Calculating transfer prices (LO 5)

Martell Corporation makes power tools. The Power division makes a battery that the Small Tools division needs for a new product. The Power division's variable cost of manufacturing the component is $10 per unit. The component is also available on the open market at a price of $13 per unit. The Small Tools division needs 50,000 motors per year.

Required

a. If the Power Division has adequate excess capacity to supply the 50,000 motors, what is the minimum transfer price?

b. If the Power Division has adequate excess capacity to supply the 50,000 motors, what is the range of prices that is likely to be acceptable to both the Power division and the Small Tools division?

10-22 Calculating transfer prices (LO 5)

The Fabricating division makes a component part that the Assembly division needs for a new product. The Fabricating division's variable cost of manufacturing the component is $20 per unit. The component is also available on the open market at a price of $50 per unit. The Assembly division needs 900 units per year, and the Fabricating division has excess capacity of 1,000 units.

Required

a. Calculate the cost-based transfer price that the Fabricating division should charge the Assembly division.

b. Calculate the market-based transfer price that the Fabricating division should charge the Assembly division.

c. What arguments would the Fabricating division's manager and the Assembly division's manager make in an attempt to get the price each wants?

10-23 Calculating transfer prices (LO 5)

Division A's cost accounting records show that the cost of its product is $150 per unit—$100 in variable costs and $50 in fixed costs. The market price of the product, $160, barely covers Division A's cost of production plus its selling and administrative costs. Division A has a maximum capacity of 100,000 units; it is currently producing and selling 75,000 units. Division B makes a product that uses Division A's product and would like to purchase 10,000 units from Division A for $150. With $40 additional variable costs, Division B produces and sells the product for $225. Division A's manager is not happy with Division B's offer and is refusing to sell.

Required

Calculate the increase in corporate income in the following situations:

a. Division A sells 10,000 units to Division B for $150 each, and Division B produces and sells 10,000 units for $225.

b. Division A does not sell to Division B. Division B purchases 10,000 units from an external supplier at $160 each and produces and sells 10,000 units for $225.

10-24 Calculating transfer prices (LO 5) Oglesby Service Corporation has three divisions that are treated as profit centers. The Printing division provides services to the other two divisions, as well as to external customers. In the middle of the year, the Accounting division ran out of brochures and needed to place an order. The Printing division bid $2,500 for the order; another vendor in town bid $1,600. Although the Accounting division's manager wanted to keep the business within the corporation, the $900 difference between the bids was too high to ignore. The Printing division's manager argued that variable costs on the project were $1,700 and fixed costs were $700, so the $2,500 price only returns $100 on the job. Both managers agreed that the Printing division's products were of a greater quality than the local competitor's, but the competitor's quality was adequate for the Accounting division's purposes.

Required

Using Exhibit 10-11 as a guide, identify the options available to the Printing and Accounting divisions. Which option would provide the greatest return (or least cost) to the corporation? Support your answer with calculations.

PROBLEMS

10-25 Segment margin income statement (LO 2) Jim Coston was reviewing the latest income statement for Trenton Communications. For the second year in a row, the Audio division was showing a negative segment margin, and Jim thought it was time to close the division to increase the company's operating income. The income statement that he examined follows.

	Video Division	Audio Division	Total
Sales revenue	$5,300,000	$2,860,000	$8,160,000
Less variable expenses	3,650,000	1,645,000	5,295,000
Contribution margin	1,650,000	1,215,000	2,865,000
Less traceable fixed expenses	943,000	1,275,000	2,218,000
Segment margin	$ 707,000	$ (60,000)	647,000
Common fixed costs			555,000
Net operating income			$ 92,000

When Jim broke the news, Chloe Sams, manager of the Audio division, was upset. Chloe thought that Jim could be making a snap judgment, and suggested that he look at the division's detailed operating results. The Audio division is composed of two groups, Streaming and CD. Streaming accounts for 75% of the division's sales and contribution margin; CD accounts for the other 25%. Streaming's traceable fixed costs are $450,000; CD, $350,000.

Required

a. Prepare a segment margin income statement for the Audio division that shows the segment margin of each group.

b. Should Jim Coston close the Audio Division? Why or why not?

10-26 Segment margin income statement (LO 2) Shoe Shock Innovations manufactures athletic shoe inserts that cushion the foot and reduce the impact of exercise on the joints. The company has two divisions, Sole Inserts and Heel Inserts. A segmented income statement from last month follows.

	Sole Inserts Division	Heel Inserts Division	Total Shoe Shock
Sales revenue	$500,000	$2,500,000	$3,000,000
Less variable expenses	300,000	2,000,000	2,300,000
Contribution margin	200,000	500,000	700,000
Less traceable fixed expenses	120,000	350,000	470,000
Segment margin	$ 80,000	$ 150,000	230,000
Common fixed costs			175,000
Net operating income			$ 55,000

Chris Kelly is Shoe Shock's sales manager. Although this statement provides useful information, Chris wants to know how well the company's two distribution channels, specialty footwear stores and drug stores, are performing. Marketing data indicates that 20% of sole inserts and 75% of heel inserts are sold through specialty footwear stores. A recent analysis of corporate fixed costs revealed that 50% of all fixed costs are traceable to specialty footwear stores and 45% of all fixed costs to drug stores.

Required

a. Prepare a segment margin income statement for Shoe Shock's two distribution channels.
b. Based on your analysis, what recommendations would you make to the company?

10-27 Calculating return on investment (LO 3) Sanders Siding produces and sells two products—aluminum and vinyl. Each of these products is made in a dedicated manufacturing facility, and the product line managers are evaluated based on the product line's return on investment. The following data is from the most recent year of operations.

	Aluminum	Vinyl
Sales	$4,000,000	$3,000,000
Variable costs	1,800,000	1,800,000
Direct fixed costs	1,500,000	900,000
Average assets	2,000,000	1,200,000

Required

a. Calculate the margin, asset turnover, and return on investment for each product line.
b. Evaluate the relative performance of each product line manager.
c. Both product line managers would like to improve their respective returns on investment, and each manager has a different idea about how to accomplish this.
   1. If the aluminum product line manager was able to increase sales volume such that the new asset turnover was 2.2 times, what would be the new operating income and the new return on investment?
   2. If the vinyl product line manager was able to reduce variable costs by 8%, what would be the new operating income and the new return on investment?

10-28 Evaluating segment performance (LO 3, 4) Mims Corporation recently announced a bonus plan to reward the manager of its most profitable division. The three divisional managers are to decide which performance measure will be used to evaluate profitability. Mims Corporation requires a 10% minimum return on investment.

The following information is available for the year just ended.

Division	Gross Book Value of Assets	Divisional Operating Income
Ashton	$900,000	$99,000
Drye	820,000	94,300
Poole	480,000	57,600

Required

a. Based on return on investment, which division performed the best?
b. Based on residual income, which division performed the best?

c. Assume that Mims Corporation's weighted-average cost of capital is 8% and its tax rate is 30%. Based on economic value added, which division performed the best?

d. What measure will the division managers select? What should the upper management of Mims Corporation do?

10-29 Evaluating segment performance (LO 3, 4) Hannalinn Corporation operates three divisions—Archer, Barrett, and Corvell. Division managers are evaluated based on the division's return on investment, and historically, the Corvell division has consistently outperformed the other two divisions. Hannalinn's senior management team has recently discovered that the Corvell Division manager has chosen not to invest in projects that would have been beneficial to the organization as a whole, and they are concerned that the current practice of evaluating the division managers' performance using return on investment may have contributed to these decisions. Therefore, the senior management team is considering the use of residual income or EVA to evaluate the division managers' performance. The following data is taken from the most recent year of operations.

	Archer	Barrett	Corvell
Assets	$30,000,000	$20,000,000	$8,000,000
Current liabilities	2,250,000	750,000	325,000
Operating income	4,200,000	3,200,000	1,520,000
Minimum rate of return	14%	14%	14%
Weighted-average cost of capital	8%	8%	8%
Tax rate	30%	30%	30%

Required

a. Calculate the return on investment, residual income, and EVA for each division.

b. Comment on the expected results of switching performance evaluation methods to either residual income or EVA.

10-30 Calculating transfer prices (CMA adapted) (LO 5) Marlys Consolidated has several divisions, two of which transfer their products to other divisions. The Mining division refines toldine, which it then transfers to the Metals division. The Metals division processes the toldine into an alloy and sells it to customers at a price of $150 per barrel. Marlys currently requires the Mining division to transfer its total annual output of 400,000 barrels of toldine to the Metals division at total manufacturing cost plus 10%. Unlimited quantities of toldine can be purchased and sold on the open market at $90 per barrel. While the Mining division could sell all the toldine it produces on the open market at $90 per barrel, it would incur a variable selling cost of $5 per unit to do so.

Barker Jonas, manager of the Mining division, is unhappy with having to transfer the division's entire output of toldine to the Metals division at 110% of cost. In a meeting with the management of Marlys, he protested, "Why should my division be required to sell toldine to the Metals Division at less than market price? For the year just ended in May, Metals' contribution margin was over $19 million on sales of 400,000 barrels, while Mining's contribution on the transfer of the same number of units was just over $5 million. My division is subsidizing the profitability of the Metals division. We should be allowed to charge market price for toldine when we transfer it to the Metals division."

Detailed unit costs for both the Mining and Metals divisions follow.

	Mining Division	Metals Division
Transfer price from Mining division		$ 66
Direct material	$12	6
Direct labor	16	20
Manufacturing overhead	32	25
Total cost per barrel	$60	$117

Manufacturing overhead cost in the Mining division is 25% fixed and 75% variable. In the Metals division, it is 60% fixed and 40% variable.

Required

a. Explain why cost-based transfer prices are not appropriate as a divisional performance measure.
b. Using the market price as the transfer price, determine the contribution margins for both divisions for the last fiscal year.
c. If Marlys Consolidated were to institute negotiated transfer prices and allow divisions to buy and sell on the open market, what price range for toldine would be acceptable to both divisions? Explain your answer.
d. Which of the three types of transfer price—cost-based, market-based, or negotiated—is most likely to elicit desirable managerial behavior at Marlys Consolidated and thus benefit overall operations? Explain your answer.

10-31 Transfer pricing behavior (CMA adapted) (LO 5) Parkside, Inc. has several divisions that operate as decentralized profit centers. Parkside's Entertainment division manufactures handheld gaming systems using the products of two of Parkside's other divisions. The Plastics division manufactures plastic components, one of which is made exclusively for the Entertainment division. Other less complex components are sold on the open market. The Video Cards division sells its products, one of which is used by the Entertainment division, in a competitive market. The actual costs per unit for the products used by the Entertainment division are as follows.

	Plastic Component	Video Card
Direct materials	$1.25	$2.40
Direct labor	2.35	3.00
Variable manufacturing overhead	1.00	1.50
Fixed manufacturing overhead	0.40	2.25
Total cost	$5.00	$9.15

The Plastics division sells its commercial products at full cost plus a 25% markup. Its manager believes the proprietary plastic component that is made for the Entertainment division would sell for $6.25 per unit on the open market. The market price of the video card the Entertainment division uses is $10.98 per unit.

Required

a. If upper management requires the video card to be transferred from the Video Card division to the Entertainment division at full cost, what behavior will the transfer likely motivate in the Video Card division?
b. If the Entertainment division can purchase a large quantity of comparable video cards from an outside source at $8.70 per unit and the Video Card division has excess capacity, what transfer price should the Video Card division set? What could be the result of this action on Parkside's profit?
c. If the Plastics department negotiated a transfer price of $5.60 per unit with the Entertainment division, what behavior would the transfer be likely to motivate in both departments?

C&C SPORTS CONTINUING CASE

10-32 Return on investment (LO 3) After seeing the results of the segment analysis for the Nylon Fibers division, James Cameron wants all three divisions focusing on the correct avenues for improving division performance. Refer to Exhibit 10-4 and the related information on page 551 to answer the following questions.

Required

a. Calculate the margin and asset turnover for Centex Yarns' three divisions. Show that margin × asset turnover equals the return on investment for each division as reported in the text.
b. Compare the margin and asset turnover for the three divisions and make suggestions for increasing the return on investment of each division.

CASES

10-33 Comprehensive case (LO 2, 3, 4, 5) Thompson Manufacturing has been in business for over 50 years, making a variety of consumer electronics products. Mary Felix recently joined the business as vice president of the Conley division, one of the company's newest divisions. During her first week on the job, Mary met with CEO Mitch Thompson to discuss the division's future.

"I know we're one of the newest and smallest divisions in the company," Mary said, "but I think we're in a position to realize some dramatic growth through product line expansion. We've got a full pipeline of products under development, and I'd like to speed up development of a couple of those products. If we work hard, I think we can have the new express charger ready for release by the end of the year."

Mitch thought for a minute and then replied. "That sounds like a good idea, Mary. I just don't want you to move so fast that you don't have a good understanding of how the introduction of the new product will affect the division's performance. Remember, I'm a big fan of maintaining our return on investment."

Mary went back to her office after the meeting and began to crunch the numbers on the express charger. At a price of $10 per unit, the marketing department estimates demand for the product at 40,000 units. The division will need to purchase a new machine for $100,000 to produce the charger. Mary also estimates that the division will incur an additional $140,000 in fixed costs that are directly attributable to the charger.

One component of the charger is currently produced by Thompson's Amber division at a variable cost of $3 per unit. The component is sold to outside customers for $5 per unit. Mary had met with Caroline Smith, vice president of the Amber division, earlier in the week to discuss the possibility of the Amber division supplying the component to the Conley Division. "Sure," Caroline began, "I'd like to help you out on this. We can provide the components at our market price of $5 per unit. We have the capacity to make 150,000 of the components, and we're currently making only 135,000 for our external customers." Mary thanked Caroline for her time saying, "I'll get back to you next week."

The Conley division currently earns $250,000 on $2.5 million in sales revenue. The division has an asset base of $1,250,000. Mary knows that Mitch will not be happy if the new product reduces the division's return on investment, and she is concerned that Caroline's offer to sell the component at $5 per unit will push product costs too high to maintain the division's ROI. She thinks that if she can meet with Caroline again to explain the situation, maybe she can negotiate a lower transfer price.

Required

a. What is the Conley division's current return on investment?
b. Given the projected demand for the charger and the current cost estimates for the product, what is the maximum total variable cost that Mary can incur and still maintain the division's ROI? What would be the resulting contribution margin per unit for the charger?
c. What is the minimum transfer price that the Amber division should be willing to charge the Conley division for the 40,000 components it needs to produce the charger?
d. Regardless of your answer to part (b), assume that Mary has determined that the maximum acceptable variable cost per unit is $6 and that all but $2 of that cost will be attributable to the component transferred from the Amber division. Will Mary accept the Amber division's minimum transfer price?
e. Suppose that Mitch has decided to evaluate division vice presidents based on residual income rather than return on investment. If he requires a 14% minimum rate of return, will Mary be able to accept the Amber division's minimum transfer price? Why or why not?
f. What do you recommend?

10-34 Ethics and return on investment (LO 2, 3) "I need you to run some numbers for me," Hannah Randall, the Barstow Group's manager, said as she walked into Isaac Bradley's office. "As you know, we've been considering a new line of hair care products. It looks like we're going to need a $1 million investment to get it up and running. We're getting a great deal on the equipment because my brother-in-law, the manufacturer's sales representative, is willing to lower the sales price and sacrifice some of his commission to make the sale."

"I'll ask the marketing department for some sales estimates and develop an estimate of the additional operating income we can expect from the line," replied Isaac. "I'm sure I can have something for you tomorrow."

Isaac met with Brenda Bell, head of market research, and told her what he needed. "Isaac, I can't give you a specific sales number; our research indicates a range of possible sales," Brenda replied. "There is a 40% probability of $2 million in sales, a 50% probability of $2.5 million in sales, and a 10% probability of $3 million in sales." "Thanks, Brenda," Isaac said. "I can work with that information."

Isaac returned to his office and began to run the numbers. Based on Brenda's estimates, he decided to calculate projected operating income at each of the three possible sales levels. After consulting additional information that Hannah had provided, Isaac developed the following projected income statements.

Sales revenue	$2,000,000	$2,500,000	$3,000,000
Variable expenses	1,300,000	1,625,000	1,950,000
Contribution margin	700,000	875,000	1,050,000
Fixed expenses	700,000	700,000	700,000
Operating income	$ 0	$ 175,000	$ 350,000
ROI	0%	17.5%	35%

Isaac met with Hannah the next day to give her the numbers. "Isaac, why are you giving me three different sets of numbers?" Hannah asked after looking over the report. "I need *one* set to present to the president and get his approval to proceed with the project." Isaac explained what Brenda Bell had said about the probability of the three different sales levels.

Hannah thought for a minute and then replied, "I've been wanting to start the Hannah Hair Care line for quite some time. The division will never approve a project with an ROI that is lower than the 18% corporate minimum. I want you to prepare an analysis based on only the $3 million projected sales level. The division will approve anything with a 35% ROI."

Isaac returned to his office and began preparing the analysis Hannah had requested.

Required

a. What are the ethical issues facing Hannah, Isaac, and Brenda?
b. Should Isaac comply with Hannah's request to prepare an analysis based on only the $3 million sales estimate? Why or why not? What guidance does the IMA's Statement of Ethical Professional Practice provide to Isaac?
c. What, if any, additional actions should Isaac take at this point?

ANALYTICS PROBLEM

10-35 Evaluating projects using ROI and residual income (LO 3, 4) Preston Plastics is about to wrap up its capital budgeting cycle, and department managers across the company have submitted 500 capital project requests for consideration in the next round of funding. Preston's CFO, Dan LaMontagne, is trying to decide which projects to recommend for funding to the capital projects executive committee. He has gathered all the information about each project's estimated life, initial investment, and cash flows in an Excel spreadsheet and is ready to make his decisions. Dan's performance bonus is based on improving the company's overall ROI. The company requires a 16% minimum ROI and currently has an 18% ROI.

Required

a. Calculate the return on investment for each individual proposed project. Save your work to use in answering the remaining questions. **NOTE:** Remember that ROI is based on income, not cash flows. You will need to subtract the annual straight line depreciation from the cash flow to estimate the operating income for each project.

b. Calculate the residual income for each individual proposed project. Save your work to use in answering the remaining questions. **NOTE:** Remember that residual income is based on income, not cash flows. You will need to subtract the annual straight line depreciation from the cash flow to estimate the operating income for each project.

c. What is the overall ROI and residual income for the portfolio of proposed projects?

d. Recall that Dan's performance bonus is based on increasing the company's ROI at the end of the year. Using return on investment as the decision criterion and assuming the company has $2 billion to invest in new capital projects, what decision rule is Dan likely to use in allocating funds to new capital projects? With this rule, how many projects will Dan likely recommend for funding? What is the total amount of capital funds that will be allocated? Hint: Sort the data by return on investment and calculate a running sum of project investment to help you determine which projects can be funded.

e. Assume that Dan's performance bonus is based on increasing the company's residual income at the end of the year. Using residual income as the decision criterion and assuming the company has $2 billion to invest in new capital projects, what decision rule is Dan likely to use in allocating funds to new capital projects? With this rule, how many projects will Dan likely recommend for funding? What is the total amount of capital funds that will be allocated? Hint: Sort the data by residual income and calculate a running sum of project investment to help you determine which projects can be funded.

f. Look at project 16934. What is the funding decision for this project based on ROI? What is the funding decision based on residual income? Why do your funding decisions differ based on the evaluation criterion used?

g. Which funding criterion do you recommend Preston Plastics use to maximize corporate welfare? Why?

The Excel data files for answering this problem can be found in WileyPLUS.

ENDNOTES

1. Ann Zimmerman, "Home Depot Learns to Go Local," *The Wall Street Journal*, October 7, 2008.
2. Stephen Power, "GM Plans Major Overhaul of Business in Europe," *The Wall Street Journal*, June 17, 2004.
3. To learn more about the production of yarn, visit http://www.madehow.com/Volume-3/Yarn.html (accessed January 31, 2013).
4. 2015 Perry Ellis International Form 10-K, p. F-38.
5. For a discussion of the history of the development of the DuPont formula see Robert S. Kaplan, "The Evolution of Management Accounting," *The Accounting Review*, 59, no. 3 (July 1984): 390–418.
6. EVA® is a registered trademark of Stern Stewart & Company. You can learn more about the company by visiting its website at http://www.sternstewart.com/.

7. A comprehensive tutorial on EVA is available at http://www.investopedia.com/university/EVA/ (accessed January 31, 2013).
8. Notice that current liabilities are not subtracted from total assets in this calculation of EVA. That is because, in this example, the equipment purchase does not generate additional current liabilities.
9. Internal Revenue Service, "IRS Accepts Settlement Offer in Largest Transfer Pricing dispute," News Release IR-2006-142, September 11, 2006, http://www.irs.gov/uac/IRS-Accepts-Settlement-Offer-in-Largest-Transfer-Pricing-Dispute (accessed January 31, 2013); Andrew Jack, "AstraZeneca Pays $1bn in US Tax Settlement," *Financial Times*, March 28, 2011.

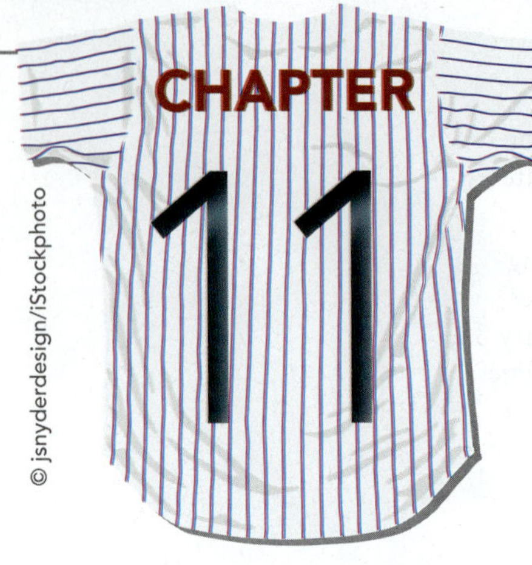

CHAPTER 11 PERFORMANCE EVALUATION REVISITED: A BALANCED APPROACH

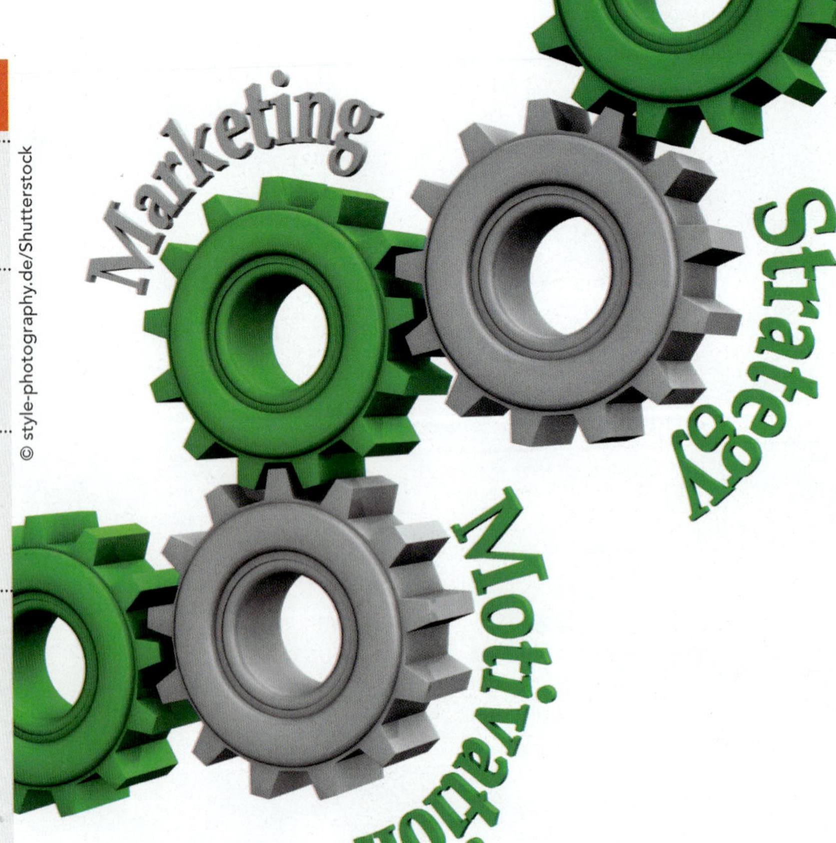

UNITS	LEARNING OBJECTIVES
UNIT 11.1 Performance Measures	**LO 1:** Identify the desirable characteristics of performance measures.
UNIT 11.2 The Balanced Scorecard	**LO 2:** Explain how to use a balanced scorecard to improve an organization's performance.
UNIT 11.3 Benchmarking	**LO 3:** Explain how to use benchmarking to improve an organization's performance.
APPENDIX Measures of Meeting Delivery Expectations	**LO 4:** Calculate delivery cycle time, manufacturing cycle time, and manufacturing cycle efficiency.

Business Decision and Context

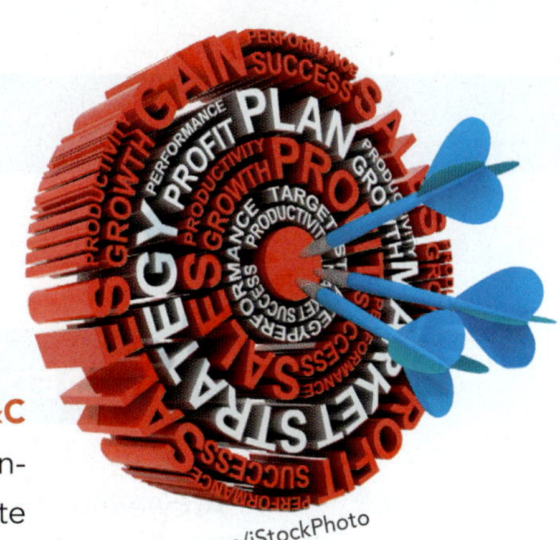

German/iStockPhoto

"It's been an interesting year," observed **George Douglas, president of C&C Sports**. "We've learned more about jacket production and the activities it consumes. We've got a plan for evaluating our batch processes to eliminate non-value-added activities. And we're going to add a new product line this year. I don't doubt that these changes will improve our profitability; however, we're just reacting to events that have gone badly. We need to identify proactive measures, so we won't find ourselves in the same predicament next year."

Chad Davis, vice president for operations, agreed. "We have a habit of waiting until we see an income statement or a bank statement to decide whether or not things are going well. That's too late to prevent anything bad from happening. If I see new workers in the sewing room, I know we're going to have problems with quality, speed, or both. What we need to do is figure out what signals good times or bad times in each of our areas and find proactive measures so we won't find ourselves in the same predicament next year."

> "What we need to do is figure out what signals good times or bad times in each of our areas and find proactive measures so we won't find ourselves in the same predicament next year."

"Not a bad idea," replied **Jonathan Smith, vice president for marketing**. "But I don't think that's enough. We need a plan that brings everything together."

"What's that going to look like?" asked Chad.

"I don't know," Jonathan said, "but it seems like the right thing to do."

Watch the Southwest Airlines video in WileyPLUS to learn more about the use of the balanced scorecard in the real world.

SUPPLY CHAIN KEY PLAYERS

END CUSTOMER

UNIVERSAL SPORTS EXCHANGE

C&C SPORTS

President
George Douglas

Vice President for Operations
Chad Davis

Vice President for Marketing
Jonathan Smith

DURABLE ZIPPER COMPANY

BRADLEY TEXTILE MILLS

CENTEX YARNS

NEFF FIBER MANUFACTURING

BRUIN POLYMERS, INC.

UNIT 11.1

Performance Measures

GUIDED UNIT PREPARATION

Answering the following questions while you read this unit will guide your understanding of the key concepts found in the unit. The questions are linked to the learning objectives presented at the beginning of the chapter.

LO 1

1. What is a lagging indicator of performance? What is a leading indicator of performance? Provide some examples of each.
2. Explain why organizations need to monitor both leading and lagging indicators.
3. What is a financial measure of performance? What is a nonfinancial measure of performance? Provide some examples of each.
4. What are SMART measures?
5. What are key performance indicators? How does a company decide which performance indicators are the key indicators?

Many of the topics presented in this book have to do with measuring and evaluating performance. Why are we revisiting performance evaluation in this chapter, then? What's left to learn? In earlier units, we focused on individual performance measures. Now we want to explore how those and other measures can be combined to create a better tool not only for measuring past performance but for driving the future achievement of an organization's strategic goals.

Lagging Indicators

Think about the performance measures you have already studied in this book—for example, the direct materials variance, return on investment, residual income, and EVA®. All these measures are quantitative, all are based on financial results, and all are calculated after the end of some period. So these are measures of *outcomes*; they answer the questions "How did (fill in the blank) do?" and "What did (fill in the blank) achieve?" Measures that can be determined only after something is finished are called **lagging indicators** of performance because their calculation "lags" the performance that is being measured, indicating whether a particular objective has or has not been met.

Let's illustrate lagging indicators with an example you are familiar with, test grades. A grade on a particular exam is a measure of what you have learned in a class. Because the grade is calculated after you have studied and taken the test, it is a lagging indicator of your preparation and knowledge. In the business world, many lagging indicators of performance are published in the financial press. For example, earnings per share, a measure that appears on every published income statement, is often used to evaluate a company's performance. In the airline industry, average on-time arrivals is an important lagging indicator.[1] And universities report four-year graduation rates and job placement statistics.

THINK ABOUT IT 11.1

List several lagging indicators that you have used to evaluate performance.

Don't think, however, that just because lagging indicators measure past performance, they have no practical use. In fact, lagging indicators can be used to predict future results. Because they provide evidence that a certain result has been obtained, the expectation is that the same result will occur again as long as conditions remain the same. If you get an A on the first exam in a course, it is reasonable to think that you can make an A on the next exam. And if your resumé (a lagging indicator of your experience) shows that you maintained a 3.2 GPA while working 25 hours per week and holding a leadership position in a service club, potential employers may reasonably expect that you can handle a job requiring time-management skills and multitasking. In the absence of such indicators, it would be difficult to convince others that you can achieve your goals.

Leading Indicators

Let's revisit the example of a test score as a lagging indicator of your achievement. Think about what goes into your preparation for a test: reading material in preparation for class, working the homework problems, attending class, and studying for the test. We could develop a measure of your performance on each of these activities: time spent preparing for class, the number of homework problems completed correctly, the number of classes attended, and time spent studying for the exam. We could think of these measures as predictors of your ultimate performance on the test. Such performance measures are called **leading indicators** of performance, because they help to predict a future result. If you complete homework problems correctly, for example, your work should lead to a higher test score. If you read only 40% of the assigned reading before class, you are likely to earn a lower test score than if you read more of it.

Leading indicators provide managers with the information they need to take timely, corrective action. If managers had to wait for lagging indicators to be calculated and reported, opportunities for improvement would pass them by. Think again about your test performance. If you waited until you got your final test grade to assess your performance, it would be too late to improve your performance in the course. However, if you monitor the number of homework problems that you solve correctly as you prepare for the test and find that you don't understand all the material, you can review it or ask your professor for help before you take the test.

When an organization relies solely on one performance measure, managers can easily be misled into thinking that all is well, when in reality, there are issues that require their corrective attention. Therefore, performance is best evaluated through multiple measures of performance. Although tracking multiple leading indicators helps managers determine whether they are on the right track, it is only when managers review the reports of actual results (lagging indicators) that they know if their efforts have been successful. Therefore, managers must use both leading and lagging indicators to adequately monitor the organization's performance.

WATCH OUT!

Identifying whether a measure is a leading or lagging indicator can be difficult because a lagging indicator of one event can be a leading indicator of another. For example, although a customer satisfaction score is a lagging indicator of the customer's experience, a trend in customer satisfaction scores can be a leading indicator of a company's financial performance. Before deciding whether a measure is a leading or lagging indicator, be sure you know what event the measure is related to.

Financial versus Nonfinancial Measures

Traditionally, organizations have measured success in financial terms. Because **financial measures** such as net income, earnings per share, and return on investment are based on information taken from accounting reports, they are quantitative and objective. However, financial measures alone do not capture all aspects of an organization's performance. **Nonfinancial measures**, which are not based on accounting results, can be either qualitative or quantitative. Qualitative indicators tend to be based on feelings or perceptions. Because they are subjective, their values may differ from person to person. Asking employees to rate the "adequacy of employee training opportunities," for instance, yields a qualitative indicator, since each employee has a unique perspective. Quantitative indicators, in contrast, are the same regardless of who is doing the measuring. Everyone who calculates "defective parts per 100 units produced" will get the same results. Exhibit 11-1 lists several commonly used nonfinancial measures.

Internal Operating Measures	Employee-oriented Measures	Customer-oriented Measures
• Production volume	• Employee satisfaction	• Market share
• Labor productivity	• Employee skills	• Time to fill customer orders
• Setup efficiency	• Employee empowerment	• Delivery performance
• Manufacturing cycle time	• Accidents per month	• Time to respond to customer problems
• Inventory levels	• Employee training	• Product flexibility
• Product defects	• Employee turnover	• Customer satisfaction
• New product introductions	• Absenteeism	• Customer acquisition
• New product design efficiency		• Customer retention

EXHIBIT 11-1 *Examples of nonfinancial measures.*

Source: Chee W. Chow and Wim A. Van der Stede, "The Use and Usefulness of Nonfinancial Performance Measures," *Management Accounting Quarterly*, 7, no. 3 (Spring 2006): 3.

A study by Deloitte LLP provides insight into the current use of nonfinancial measures. When 250 top executives and board members were asked about the importance of nonfinancial measures, 73% reported that their organizations were under increasing pressure to use such measures. Ninety-two percent believed that their organizations' strengths and weaknesses were not adequately gauged by financial measures alone (see Exhibit 11-2).

EXHIBIT 11-2

The importance of nonfinancial performance measures.

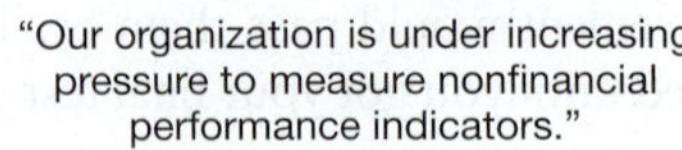

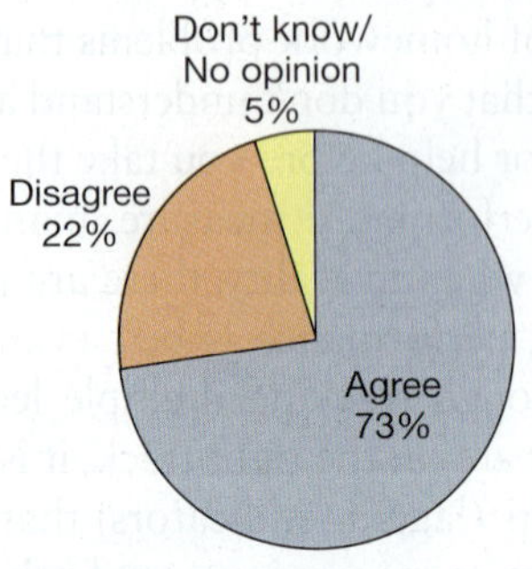

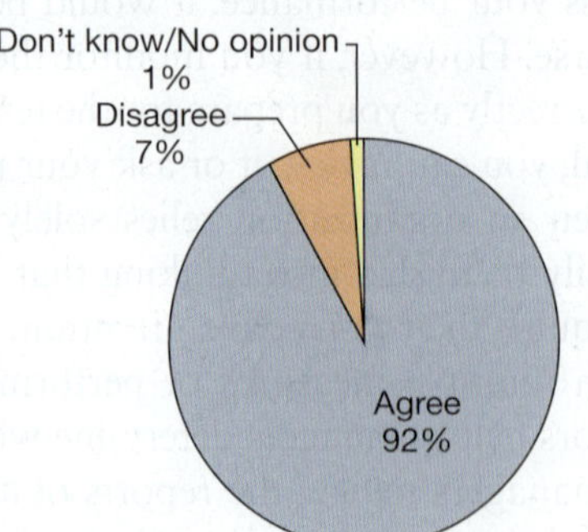

Source: Deloitte LLP, *In the Dark: What Boards and Executives Don't Know about the Health of Their Businesses*, 2007.

McDonald's 2014 Good Business Report, available on the company's website, highlights nonfinancial measures such as "% of coffee volume from verified sustainable sources" and "% of managers who feel favorable about the training they receive on the job." These nonfinancial measures focus on factors that are important to customers and employees. Certainly McDonald's trains employees, but if management doesn't bother to measure the results of the training, how will they know that it is successful?

Although executives recognize the importance of nonfinancial performance measures, companies are not particularly good at using them. In fact, as Exhibit 11-3 shows, only 35% of executives and board members surveyed by Deloitte felt their companies were excellent or good at measuring and monitoring the nonfinancial aspects of performance. In contrast, 86% felt their companies were excellent or good at measuring and monitoring financial performance. Why don't organizations use nonfinancial performance measures? As Exhibit 11-3

EXHIBIT 11-3

Companies' ability to use financial and nonfinancial performance measures.

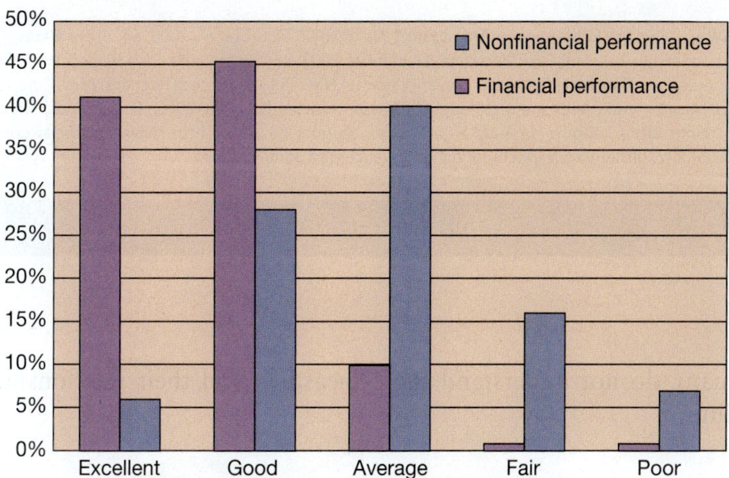

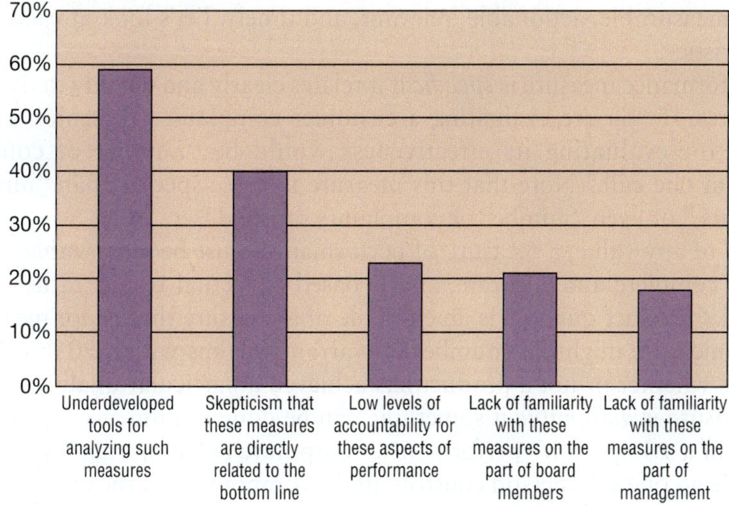

Source: Deloitte LLP, *In the Dark: What Boards and Executives Don't Know about the Health of Their Businesses*, 2007.

REALITY CHECK—*Batter up*

Robert Beck/Sports Illustrated/Getty Images

Leading indicators on the baseball field? Yes, for at least two reasons.

In Game 7 of the 2003 American League Championship Series, Red Sox pitcher Pedro Martinez neared 100 pitches for the game. And that's when his performance began to decline and the Yankees' batting average began to climb. When comparing the number of pitches Martinez threw to the opposing team's batting average, it becomes clear that the number of pitches is a leading indicator. Armed with this knowledge, managers can watch this indicator more closely when deciding if it's time to send in a relief pitcher.

More recently, Little League Baseball has identified the number of pitches thrown as a leading indicator of arm and shoulder injury. In 2007, the organization changed from innings pitched to number of pitches as the regulator for pitchers. Pitchers 10 years old and under can throw only 75 pitches a day, while 17- and 18-year-olds can throw up to 105. The number of pitches thrown also dictates how many rest days must be allowed between appearances on the mound.

Little League Baseball has identified the number of pitches thrown as a leading indicator of arm and shoulder injury.

Sources: John Alter, "Curses! Foiled again. And again." *Newsweek*, October 27, 2003, 54; Steve Bates, "Baseball Gaffe Provides Leadership Lessons," *HRMagazine*, December 2003, 16; Scott Leibs, "Measuring Up," *CFO*, June 2007, 63–66; Little League Baseball, "Little League Implements New Rule to Protect Pitchers' Arms," news release, August 25, 2006, http://www.littleleague.org/Page56025.aspx (accessed July 20, 2016); Dick Patrick, "Pitch Count, Not Innings, to Limit Little League Hurlers," *USA Today*, August 28, 2006, http://www.usatoday.com/sports/baseball/llws/2006-08-27-little-league-pitch-count_x.htm (accessed June 4, 2008).

shows, many do not understand these measures and their relationship to the bottom line.

Choosing the Right Measures

As you might imagine, countless measures could be captured and reported to managers. The best measures relate to corporate strategy and are SMART: specific, measurable, actionable, relevant, and timely. Let's look at each of these characteristics.

A performance measure is *specific* if it relates clearly and directly to the process it measures. If you are evaluating a customer complaint call center, a specific measure for evaluating its effectiveness would be "number of complaints satisfied in one call." Note that this measure is more specific than "number of complaints," or even "number of complaints satisfied."

To be of any value, a measure of performance must be *measurable*, meaning that it is complete and accurate, and is based on actual results rather than on estimates. "Product quality" is an example of a measure that is *not* measurable. A better measure might be "number of warranty claims within 90 days," which addresses whether or not a product has achieved a particular quality standard.

A measure is *actionable* if something can be done to influence its value. As a measure of a salesperson's performance, "corporate profit margin" is not actionable, since no one salesperson controls all the components of the corporate profit margin. However, a single salesperson can control—to a greater degree—"total sales revenues generated per quarter."

A measure is *relevant* if it relates to a corporate strategic objective. Collecting data and measures on items and processes that do not promote the corporate strategy is a waste of everyone's time and can deflect attention from measures that will help to improve performance. If the goal is to reduce employee turnover, for example, then total headcount is not as relevant a measure as the number of voluntary employee terminations.

Finally, to be useful, a measure must be *timely*. Managerial decisions must be made within a limited time window, so reporting a measure after that window has closed serves no purpose. As decision windows and operating cycles continue to shorten, this characteristic of a measure is becoming more important. Last year's product defect rates are of little value in assessing the production processes that are running this week. Yesterday's defect rates, or the last hour's, are much more helpful in monitoring and correcting current production processes.

Using Measures to Drive Performance

Once managers realize that leading, lagging, financial, and nonfinancial measures need to be monitored, they must identify the **key performance indicators (KPIs)** that measure successful progression toward the organization's goals. An airline will consider its on-time departure rate to be key; a construction company may choose the percentage of projects completed within 10% of budgeted cost. As Exhibit 11-4 shows, an Aberdeen Group study found that for best-in-class companies, the primary reasons for monitoring KPIs are to improve company performance and align business activities with the corporate strategy.

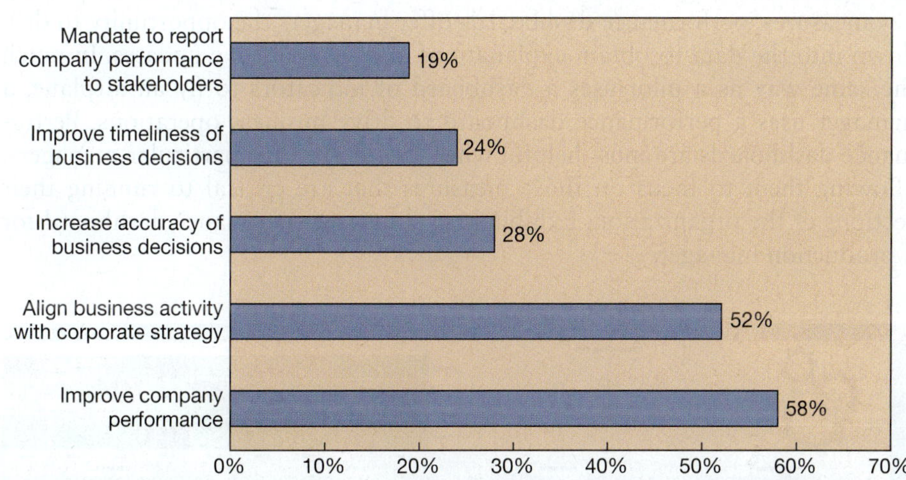

Source: David Hatch, "Smart Decisions: The Role of Key Performance Indicators," Aberdeen Group, September 2007.

EXHIBIT 11-4

Why companies use key performance indicators.

The key to using these measures to drive performance is understanding the cause-and-effect relationships they represent. Increases in customer satisfaction, for instance, should increase the sales volume and thus net income. If employees interact directly with customers, employee satisfaction and attitudes may influence customer satisfaction. A study of 800 Sears stores found that increasing employee attitude scores by 5 points led to a 1.3 point increase in customer satisfaction and a 0.5% increase in revenues.[2] Another study of 100 media companies found a direct link between employee satisfaction and customer satisfaction, and between customer satisfaction and improved financial performance.[3]

Despite these research results, the majority of companies fail to identify and measure the cause-and-effect relationships that lead to increased financial performance. In a recent study of 157 companies, only 23% of them consistently established and verified cause-and-effect relationships. On average, those firms had a 2.95% higher return on assets and a 5.14% higher return on equity than companies that failed to explore such relationships.[4]

Watch what you wish for in terms of performance measurement, however. In the early 1990s, Domino's Pizza implemented a 30-minute delivery guarantee. If their pizza wasn't at your door within 30 minutes, it was free. In trying to meet that promise, several Domino's drivers were involved in automobile accidents, and the company became embroiled in several lawsuits, one of which resulted in a $79 million award to the plaintiff. As you might guess, Domino's dropped the guarantee in late 1993.

THINK ABOUT IT 11.2

Explain the meaning of the assertion "You get what you measure" and relate it to organizational performance evaluation.

A tool some organizations use to report performance measures to managers is the **performance dashboard**, a visual display of the key measures related to an organization's operational goals and strategies. In addition to displaying key measures, performance dashboards offer managers the opportunity to drill down into the data to obtain explanations and see real-time updates. In much the same way as a pilot uses a dashboard of indicators to fly an airplane, a manager uses a performance dashboard to drive business operations. Performance dashboards are most helpful when customized for particular managers, allowing them to focus on those measures that are critical to running their sections of the organization. Exhibit 11-5 shows a performance dashboard for a production manager.

EXHIBIT 11-5

Performance dashboard for a production manager.

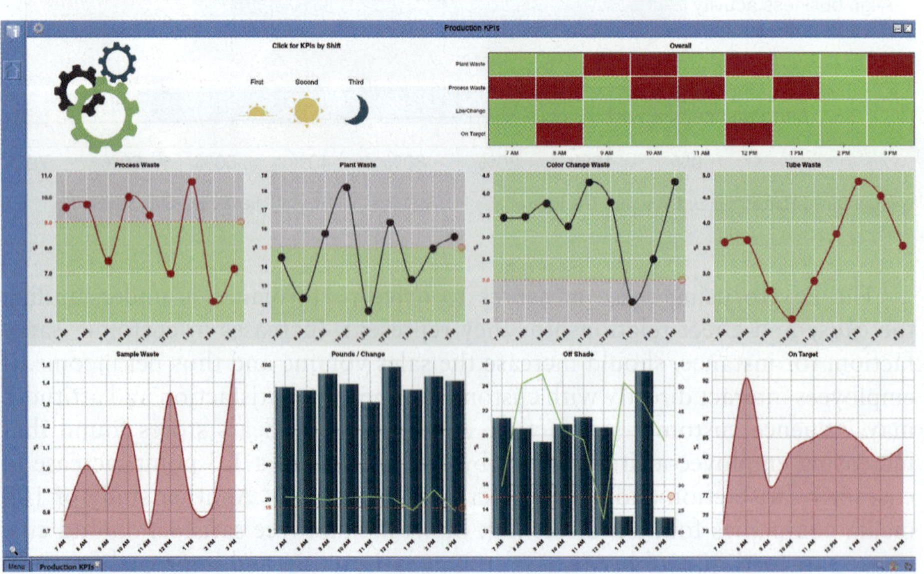

Courtesy of iDashboards.com

UNIT 11.1 REVIEW

KEY TERMS

Financial measure p. 592
Key performance indicator (KPI) p. 595
Lagging indicator p. 590
Leading indicator p. 591
Nonfinancial measure p. 592
Performance dashboard p. 596

PRACTICE QUESTIONS

1. LO 1 Lagging indicators provide evidence that a particular outcome occurred in the past. True or False?
2. LO 1 Which of the following is a leading indicator of customer satisfaction?
   a. Customer satisfaction score
   b. On-time delivery
   c. Customer profitability
   d. All are leading indicators of customer satisfaction
3. LO 1 Financial measures alone do not help managers to evaluate performance because they lag the events that produce financial results. True or False?
4. LO 1 Subjective nonfinancial measures, such as a customer satisfaction score, are considered quantitative because they are reported numerically. True or False?
5. LO 1 Which of the following statements about key performance indicators is *not* true?
   a. They help managers to focus on the measures that are most relevant to company success.
   b. They are useful only if the cause-and-effect relationships between the measures and the organization's performance are known.
   c. They are best suited to for-profit organizations, since nonprofit organizations have no financial goals.
   d. They are a mixture of financial and nonfinancial, leading and lagging indicators.

UNIT 11.1 PRACTICE EXERCISE

Taylor Construction builds custom homes in Dallas, Texas. Brandon Taylor knows that his future depends on the quality of the homes he builds and the service he provides to customers. Most new-customer sales arise from word-of-mouth advertising by former customers. Place an X in the appropriate columns to indicate whether the following measures are leading or lagging and financial or nonfinancial indicators of Taylor Construction's financial performance:

	Leading	Lagging	Financial	Nonfinancial
a. Number of customer complaints	X			X
b. Employee turnover				
c. Net profit per house constructed				
d. Turnaround time on customer design changes				
e. Hours of training per employee				
f. Average labor cost per house				
g. Dollars invested in new equipment				
h. Grade (quality) of brass fixtures				
i. Variances between budgeted and actual costs of building a house				

SELECTED UNIT 11.1 ANSWERS

Think About It 11.1

Some examples might include:

Academic performance: GPA, class rank
Car performance: Miles per gallon
Athletic team performance: Win–loss record
Baseball player performance: RBI

Think About It 11.2

It's human nature to give attention to whatever is deemed appropriate. If your instructor bases 90% of your grade on attendance, you will be sure never to miss a class. The same is true of organizations: The measures that are reported and monitored are the ones that receive the most attention from employees. If customer satisfaction is measured and reported and employee raises are based on the results, a great deal of attention is likely to be given to customers, regardless of the costs to provide that level of service. However, if cost reduction is measured and reported and employee raises are based on the results, costs are likely to be reduced, to the detriment of customers, research and development, and other aspects of the business. Using multiple measures of performance can help to ensure that improvement on one measure does not come at the expense of other aspects of performance.

Practice Questions

1. True
2. B
3. True
4. False
5. C

Unit 11.1 Practice Exercise

	Leading	Lagging	Financial	Nonfinancial
a. Number of customer complaints	X			X
b. Employee turnover	X			X
c. Net profit per house constructed		X	X	
d. Turnaround time on customer design changes	X			X
e. Hours of training per employee	X			X
f. Average labor cost per house		X	X	
g. Dollars invested in new equipment	X		X	
h. Grade (quality) of brass fixtures	X			X
i. Variances between budgeted and actual costs of building a house		X	X	

UNIT 11.2

The Balanced Scorecard

GUIDED UNIT PREPARATION

Answering the following questions while you read this unit will guide your understanding of the key concepts found in the unit. The questions are linked to the learning objectives presented at the beginning of the chapter.

LO 2

1. How does the balanced scorecard differ from just having multiple measures of performance?
2. What are the four areas of performance measurement included in the balanced scorecard?

3. Why is the use of the balanced scorecard preferable over performance measurement based solely on financial data?
4. Why is the balanced scorecard different for different companies?
5. What is a strategy map?
6. Why does attempting to improve measures such as customer satisfaction and market share not necessarily result in improved financial health for a business?

Sometimes, managers may use multiple measures to evaluate performance without getting the results they desire. The reason may be that in developing the measures, the managers failed to consider how improving performance in one area could affect performance in another. Consider coffee purveyor Starbucks. In an effort to increase its retail footprint, the company switched from neighborhood stores to uniform store design, from manual espresso machines to automatic ones, and from fresh ground coffee to packaged ground coffee. However, as CEO Howard Schultz noted in a January 2008 memo, in doing so, the company lost sight of the customer experience, and in 2007 and 2008 Dunkin' Donuts replaced Starbucks in the "Coffee and Doughnuts" top spot of Brand Keys' Annual Customer Loyalty Engagement Index.

To help managers understand the interrelationships between various areas of an organization, David Norton and Robert Kaplan developed the **balanced scorecard**, a management tool that integrates performance measures across four different perspectives to guide operations toward achieving an organization's strategy.[5] In a 2015 survey of global business executives, Bain & Company found that 38% of the firms they represented were using a balanced scorecard to monitor performance, making it the sixth most used management tool in the survey.[6]

When a company creates a balanced scorecard, managers are stating a hypothesis about the results that will occur if certain performance measures are stressed. The balanced scorecard assists in communicating the corporate strategy throughout the organization. Therefore, before a balanced scorecard can be developed, managers must be clear about the strategy they are trying to achieve. And with studies finding that between 70% and 95% of employees are unaware of or do not understand the organization's strategy, this step cannot be marginalized.[7] In addition, they must understand the cause-and-effect relationships between various measures. Once the strategy is known and the cause-and-effect relationships are understood, managers can execute the strategy. Later, we will discuss C&C Sports' strategy, but first let's review the four perspectives.

The Four Balanced Scorecard Perspectives

Traditionally, organizations have evaluated their performance using only financial measures, such as the stock price or earnings per share. Many other performance indicators should be considered, however. To address the need for multiple measures of performance, the balanced scorecard includes five to seven measures in each of four perspectives: learning and growth, internal business processes, customer, and financial. Let's look at each of these in greater detail.

Learning and Growth Perspective

The **learning and growth perspective** answers the question "Are we developing employees and providing technologies that facilitate change and improvement?"

In other words, is the organization hiring the right people, training them effectively, and giving them the technologies they need to develop and produce the products and services customers desire? This perspective is the foundation for improvement in all other areas because if employees cannot meet customers' needs, the company will not be successful in the long run.

At first glance, the learning and growth perspective may appear to be focused solely on employee training and development. That is not the case, however. Learning is more than just technical training. To be successful in developing the work force, an organization must develop and maintain a corporate culture that facilitates those activities. Such a culture might include mentoring and formal communication lines that enable workers to collaborate in solving problems.

An organization that is experiencing financial difficulty cannot afford to make drastic reductions in learning and growth activities. If the work force is not able to complete the processes that deliver goods and services to customers, the company's financial distress will only increase. Ultimately, the organization must ensure that employees are productive and are satisfied with their jobs so that they will remain with the organization.

Measures that relate to the learning and growth perspective include:

- Employee turnover rate
- Number of employees who possess relevant professional certification
- Number of suggestions generated by employees
- Training hours per employee
- Percentage of vacancies filled with internal candidates
- Employee satisfaction
- Training dollars spent per employee
- Technology spending per employee
- Revenue per employee

Internal Business Processes Perspective

The **internal business processes perspective** answers the question "Are we improving our business processes in order to deliver maximum value to our customers?" This is what the organization does to meet customer expectations, so the focus is on creating products and services that customers desire and delivering them in a timely manner. If the organization accomplishes these goals, customer satisfaction should improve, and improved financial performance should follow.

Conversely, impediments to internal business processes and mistakes in production cost time and money. Therefore, measures related to this perspective assist managers in assessing the efficiency and effectiveness of production processes. For many organizations, this perspective includes measures of research and development processes that create the products to meet customers' changing demands and counter competitors' new product introductions.

Measures that relate to the internal business processes perspective include:

- Percentage of on-time deliveries
- Time to market
- Cost per unit
- Defect rate
- Response time to customer request
- Rework hours
- Manufacturing cycle efficiency
- Number of equipment breakdowns
- Delivery cycle time

THINK ABOUT IT 11.3

What are some internal business process measures that your favorite clothing store might care about? By default, what internal business process measures might your least favorite clothing store overlook? Rather than selecting measures from the preceding table, think about what a store does to make your shopping experience either worthwhile or miserable.

Customer Perspective

The **customer perspective** answers the question "Are we meeting our customers' expectations?" When customers consider making purchases, they have expectations about quality, price, delivery speed, and service. If their expectations are not met, they will become dissatisfied and will likely seek other suppliers. If the company meets or exceeds their expectations, however, customers should be satisfied, and the company should see an increase in sales to existing and new customers. To be successful, companies should first decide which customers they want to serve (for example, early adopters versus followers, young versus old, high versus median or low income). Then they can discover what those customers want.

Measures that relate to the customer perspective include:

- Customer satisfaction index
- Number of customer complaints
- Percentage of revenue from new customers
- Number of new customers
- Customer loyalty index
- Market share
- Product return rate
- Customer attrition rate
- Customer profitability

Financial Perspective

The **financial perspective** answers the questions "Are we reaching our financial goals?" and "How do investors see us?" The achievement of financial goals is expected to follow success in the other three areas, and this perspective is ultimately where results of successful implementation of the corporate strategy will appear. Of all the measures we have discussed, managers are most comfortable with the measures related to this perspective because those are the ones most organizations have always used to measure success.

Measures that relate to the financial perspective include:

- Net income
- Residual income
- Profit margin
- Earnings per share
- EVA®
- Cash flow
- Return on investment
- Revenue growth
- Net income per employee

To recap, the measures included in each perspective should be selected based on cause-and-effect relationships, such as the ones shown in Exhibit 11-6. Until managers have the results from the measures in each perspective, these cause-and-effect relationships are just hypotheses. In a well-designed balanced

EXHIBIT 11-6

Cause-and-effect relationships in the balanced scorecard.

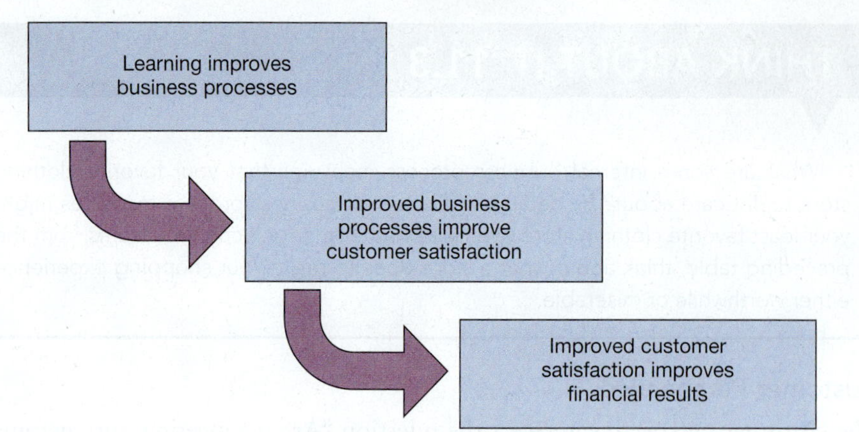

scorecard, the four perspectives are integrated, and information gleaned from measures in one area can inform another, as illustrated in Exhibit 11-7. Exhibit 11-7 also shows that the central driving force behind the balanced scorecard is the organization's strategy.

EXHIBIT 11-7

The four perspectives of the balanced scorecard.

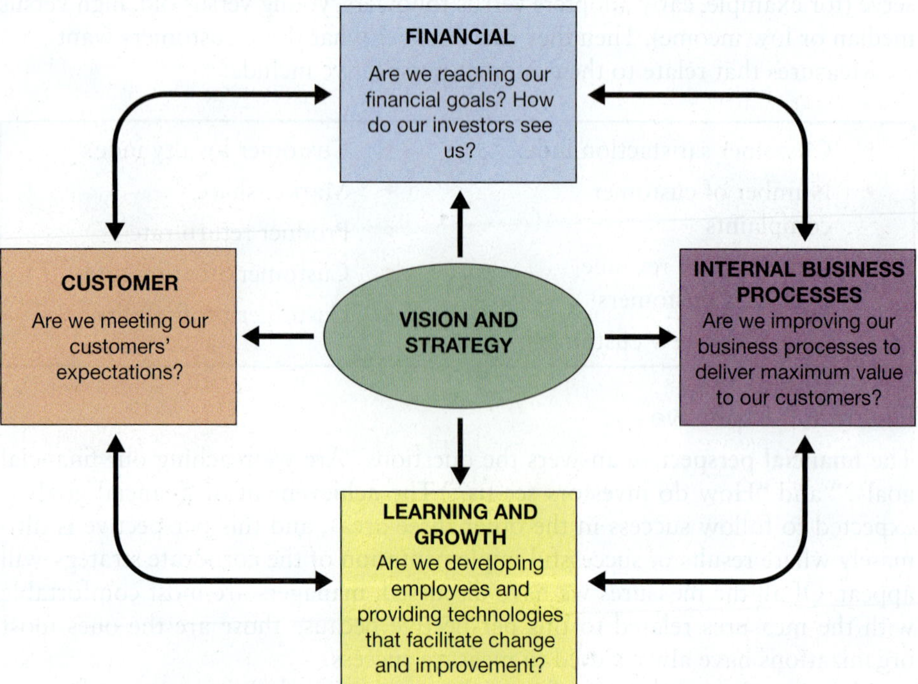

Building a Balanced Scorecard[8]

Because the organization's vision and strategy lie at the heart of the balanced scorecard, the first step in developing the scorecard is to clarify the strategic focus. As part of this process, organizations may develop a **strategy map**,[9] a pictorial representation of the cause-and-effect relationships embodied in the strategy.

Once the organization has clarified the strategy, managers will need to translate it into operational objectives and select measures that will provide evidence of their achievement. In selecting those measures, managers should limit themselves to between four and seven measures for each perspective. Otherwise, they will suffer from information overload. According to The Hackett Group, the average company reports no fewer than 132 performance measures to senior management. As Hackett's Finance Practice Leader Cody Chenault explains, "If you are tracking nine times the recommended number of metrics, you're confusing detail with accuracy, and it's going to be almost impossible to see indicators that might emerge from the data."[10]

To balance the scorecard, organizations should also select a mix of leading and lagging, qualitative and quantitative measures for each perspective. This is how "balance" is achieved in the scorecard. Don't be misled into believing that just because an organization claims to have a balanced scorecard, its scorecard is balanced. According to another study by The Hackett Group, many companies that claim to use a balanced scorecard actually devote almost 75% of their measures to the financial perspective.[11]

After selecting the appropriate measures, managers should set a target that defines "success" for each measure. For instance, they may set the target for total revenue generated from new products at 65% and the target for employee turnover at 5%. The targets will allow managers to monitor progress and identify any gaps between actual and desired performance. Exhibit 11-8 shows an excerpt from a hypothetical balanced scorecard. Note the gaps in column 4. The identification of such gaps helps managers to develop action steps that will move the organization toward the targets, thus achieving the organization's strategy.

EXHIBIT 11-8

Balanced scorecard measure targets and gap analysis.

Measure	Current Output Measure	Target	Gap (Target–Output)
Learning and Growth Perspective			
Percentage of staff holding a relevant professional certification	55%	45%	No gap
Percentage of staff who agree that "this department provides adequate opportunities for professional development"	66%	90%	24%
Percentage of staff who participate in annual goal development workshop	86%	90%	4%

Finally, scorecards should not be cast in stone. Since the selection of the objectives and measures is based on an organization's strategy, as the strategy changes, so should the scorecard. And though the balanced scorecard typically includes four perspectives, some organizations will add a fifth that highlights an additional area of strategic importance, such as supplier relations, community involvement, or environmental impact.

C&C Sports' Strategy Map

Recall that C&C Sports decided not to follow the trend of transferring manufacturing operations to China and other foreign countries where labor is cheaper. Instead, managers chose to focus on product quality, quick delivery, and fast customer response within the local market, the state of Texas. This basic strategy has not changed, even with recent ups and downs in operations.

What does C&C need to do to ensure the success of its strategy? Exhibit 11-9 shows the company's strategy map, which George Douglas and other C&C managers believe shows the cause-and-effect relationships that drive C&C's success. Remember, though, that those relationships are hypotheses. Until C&C's

EXHIBIT 11-9

C&C Sports' strategy map.

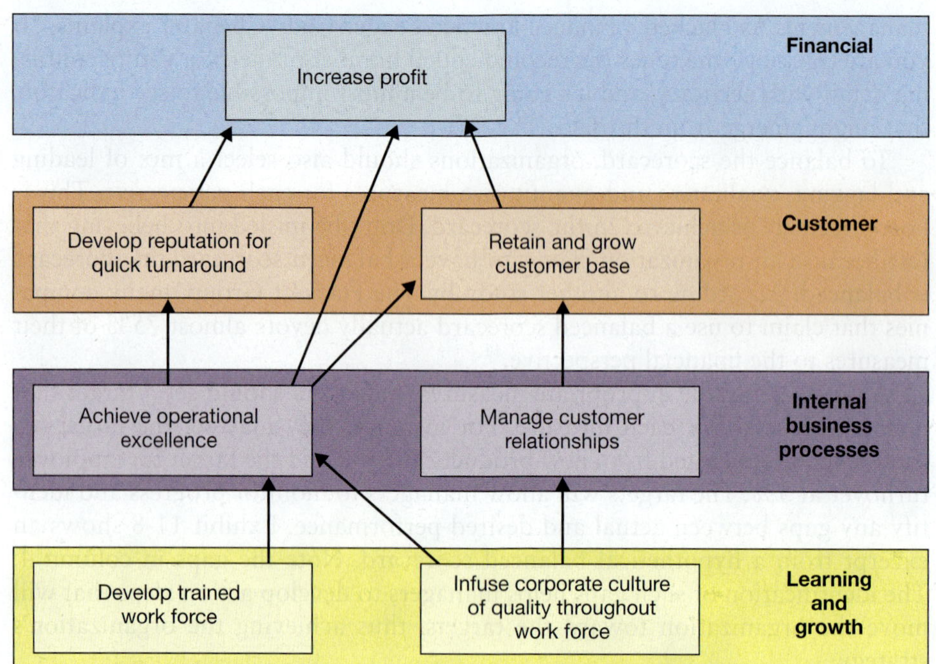

managers complete the balanced scorecard and use it to track key measures and identify the impact on other areas, they won't know whether the strategy works. If it doesn't work, they will go back to the drawing board.

In short, the balanced scorecard is not a guarantee of success. Instead, it is a system that forces managers to consider how different parts of their company affect one another. Let's examine those relationships in more detail.

Learning and Growth Perspective

The key to C&C's production of high-quality products is a trained and stable work force. In south Texas, where C&C's production facility is located, worker turnover is higher than the national average. With a modest sewing background, workers can get up to speed fairly quickly on pants and jerseys, but jackets take more time to master. Nevertheless, finding, hiring, and training new employees reduce the speed with which products can be made and increase the number of defective products. Therefore, C&C's managers need to establish programs and incentives to retain productive workers and reduce employee turnover. They also need to cross-train workers to make all the company's products with equal speed and accuracy so that, when the production mix changes, no time will be lost as workers shift from one product to another.

Internal Business Processes Perspective

If employees are well trained and turnover is low, fewer mistakes should occur in the production of pants, jerseys, and jackets. With fewer defects, complete batches should be produced at a faster pace and at a lower cost. Even without considering defects, if employees can shift quickly from one product to another, production should go more quickly, and costs should fall.

Customer Perspective

If products can be made faster and with fewer defects, customers should be happy with the results. As long as capacity is not taken up by products that later prove defective, enough capacity should be available to supply new customers, especially with award jackets. Thus, the sales department needs to work on generating sales from new customers.

REALITY CHECK—*Not your typical balanced scorecard*

Courtesy of Youth Villages

Some organizations have moved outside the box to create more "specialized" balanced scorecards.

While most people think of the traditional balance scorecard with its financial, customer, internal business processes, and learning and growth perspectives, some organizations have moved outside the box to create more "specialized" balanced scorecards.

Youth Villages is a nonprofit child welfare organization in Tennessee. When the state implemented a performance-based contracting initiative in 2006, Youth Villages developed its own balanced scorecard system that focuses on actionable outcome metrics. Following up with children *after* they leave care, Youth Villages tracks outcomes such as permanence of child placements, educational status, and interactions with the legal system. The agency has a national reputation and serves as a model for other social service providers.

Truven Health Analytics (now part of IBM Watson Health) evaluates health systems and hospitals using a balanced scorecard with five categories: inpatient outcomes, process of care, extended outcomes, efficiency, and patient experience. Using metrics such as 30-day readmission rate, risk-adjusted mortality (in-hospital), and adjusted operating profit margin, the organization identifies the 100 Top Hospitals®.

Sources: "IBM Watson Health Closes Acquisition of Truven Health Analytics," April 8, 2016, http://www-03.ibm.com/press/us/en/pressrelease/49474.wss (accessed May 10, 2016); John M. Kamensky, "Tennessee Child-Services Provider's Performance-Management System Offers Balanced Scorecard of Metrics," April 22, 2016, http://www.govtech.com/opinion/Tennesee-Child-Services-Providers-Performance-Management-System-Offers-Balanced-Scorecard-of-Metrics.html (accessed May 10, 2016); "MidMichigan Health Named One of the Nation's 15 Top Health Systems," April 25, 2016 https://www.midmichigan.org/about/news/newsroom-2016/nations-15-top-health-systems/ (accessed May 10, 2016).

Financial Perspective

If both defects and production time are reduced, the contribution margin per product should increase. If sales from new customers increase, revenues will increase. And if both the contribution margin per product and sales revenues increase, profits should increase.

C&C Sports' Balanced Scorecard

Now that C&C's managers have specified the company's strategy, they can begin to develop a balanced scorecard that is based on that strategy. For each of the four perspectives, managers must select a set of measures to use in monitoring their progress toward implementing the strategy. To facilitate the monitoring process, they should also set a goal for each measure.

Learning and Growth Perspective

With a strategy to create a cross-trained work force that can produce high-quality products, C&C's learning and growth measures should focus on the development of workers' skills. Besides training, managers will want to monitor employee turnover and retention, and their attention to quality. On the next page are the measures managers have selected for the balanced scorecard. Notice that in addition to the measures, managers specified goals for each.

Measures	Goals
Employee turnover	<5%
Employee satisfaction index	90% satisfied or very satisfied
Percentage of direct labor workers cross-trained to make all products other than chenille lettering	>80%
Number of employee-generated quality improvement suggestions	5 per quarter

Internal Business Processes Perspective

C&C's strategy requires operational excellence. Products must be defect-free and must be produced in a timely manner in order to meet promised customer delivery dates and seasonal market demands. Employees must also manage customer relationships effectively by responding to customers' inquiries in a timely manner. With those requirements in mind, managers selected the following measures and goals for the balanced scorecard.

Measures	Goals
Defect rate	<1%
Average production time	15 minutes per pants 12 minutes per jersey 90 minutes per jacket
Capacity utilization	85%
Average time of initial response to customer inquiry	20 minutes
Number of quality complaints from customers	<2 per quarter

Customer Perspective

C&C has adopted a strategy of quick delivery to customers. Translated into actions, this strategy means that C&C must meet customer delivery dates, even those in the near future. Consistently meeting customer deadlines should increase customer satisfaction. As satisfied customers share their experiences with others, new customers should switch to C&C. Managers selected the following measures and goals to monitor the customer perspective.

Measures	Goals
Customer satisfaction index	100% rating of good or excellent
On-time delivery	100%
Customer order lead time	<5 days
Sales growth to existing customers	12%
Sales growth to new customers	20%

Financial Perspective

If C&C's hypotheses about the cause-and-effect relationships identified in the strategy map are valid, achievement of the strategy should improve the company's financial performance. Managers selected the following measures and goals to track the strategy's financial success.

Measures	Goals
Profit growth	10% per year
Revenue growth	10% per year
Return on assets	9%
Return on investment	12%

C&C SPORTS' Balanced Scorecard			
Perspective	**Strategic Objective**	**Measure**	**Goal**
Financial	Increase profit	• Profit growth	• 10%
		• Revenue growth	• 10%
		• Return on assets	• 9%
		• Return on investment	• 12%
Customer	Develop reputation for quick turnaround	• On-time delivery	• 100%
		• Customer order lead time	• <5 days
	Retain and grow customer base	• Sales growth to existing customers	• 12%
		• Sales growth to new customers	• 20%
		• Customer satisfaction index	• 100% rating of good or excellent
Internal business processes	Achieve operational excellence	• Defect rate	• <1%
		• Capacity utilization	• 85%
		• Number of quality complaints from customers	• <2 per quarter
		• Average production time	• 15 minutes per pants 12 minutes per jersey 90 minutes per jacket
	Manage customer relationships	• Average time of initial response to customer inquiry	• 20 minutes
Learning and growth	Develop trained work force	• Employee turnover	• <5%
		• Employee satisfaction index	• 90% satisfied or very satisfied
		• % of cross-trained direct labor workers	• <80%
	Infuse corporate culture of quality throughout work force	• Number of employee-generated quality improvement suggestions	• 5 per quarter

EXHIBIT 11-10 *C&C Sports' balanced scorecard.*

UNIT 11.2 REVIEW

KEY TERMS

Balanced scorecard p. 599

Customer perspective p. 601

Financial perspective p. 601

Internal business processes perspective p. 600

Learning and growth perspective p. 599

Strategy map p. 602

PRACTICE QUESTIONS

1. LO 2 Which of the following is *not* one of the four perspectives included in the balanced scorecard?
   a. Internal growth
   b. Learning and growth
   c. Financial
   d. Customer
2. LO 2 The measures in the customer perspective of the balanced scorecard are always qualitative because you can't quantify how customers feel. True or False?
3. LO 2 Which of the following measures would *not* be relevant to the learning and growth perspective?
   a. Employee turnover
   b. Training hours per employee
   c. Technology investment per quarter
   d. Training hours per customer
4. LO 2 Managers construct a strategy map after they have hypothesized the cause-and-effect relationships among the four perspectives. True or False?
5. LO 2 A balanced scorecard is a hypothesis until the cause-and-effect relationships it is based on have been proven to be true. True or False?

UNIT 11.2 PRACTICE EXERCISE

Advanced Systems operates in the highly competitive software development market. The company is considered an industry leader, and its systems are often imitated by other developers. To maintain its reputation among competitors and customers, Advanced Systems needs to develop new software every 18 months. Customers are willing to switch to new software that frequently because of the productivity improvements the new software delivers and the availability of 24/7 technical support. Because this industry requires a great deal of research and development, Advanced Systems must generate enough cash from sales of existing software to fund the development of new software.

Required

Identify two measures for each of the four balanced scorecard perspectives that will help Advanced Systems to achieve its strategy.

Learning and growth perspective:
1.
2.

Internal business processes perspective:
1.
2.

Customer perspective:
1.
2.

Financial perspective:
1.
2.

SELECTED UNIT 11.2 ANSWERS

Think About It 11.3

- Product mix
- Customers per store clerk
- Time to greet/help customers
- Store cleanliness score
- Clothes displayed per square foot of space
- Average checkout time
- Out-of-stock percentage

Practice Questions

1. A
2. False
3. D
4. True
5. True

Unit 11.2 Practice Exercise

Learning and growth perspective:

1. Investment in new technology
2. Training hours per technical consultant

Internal business processes perspective:

1. Time to launch new products
2. Time to resolve customers' technical problems

Customer perspective:

1. Customer-reported productivity improvements
2. Repeat sales

Financial perspective:

1. Cash flow
2. Revenue growth

UNIT 11.3

Benchmarking

GUIDED UNIT PREPARATION

Answering the following questions while you read this unit will guide your understanding of the key concepts found in the unit. The questions are linked to the learning objectives presented at the beginning of the chapter.

LO 3

1. What is benchmarking?
2. How does an organization benefit from benchmarking with an organization outside its industry?
3. What is a best practice?
4. How are benchmarking partners protected from losing their competitive advantage during the exchange of benchmarking data?

Throughout our discussion of performance evaluation in this and other chapters, the focus has been on comparing a company's actual performance to its own internal goals or budget. Another way of evaluating a company's performance is to compare it to that of other companies. In this unit we will explore benchmarking against other companies as a way to improve a company's performance.

Over the past several years, organizations of all types have participated in benchmarking studies as a way of improving their performance. **Benchmarking** is the practice of using data from other organizations to identify the processes and practices associated with world-class performance. Such processes are referred to as best practices. In other words, **best practices** are the processes that lead to the best performance.

Benchmarking is not about trying to achieve another company's metrics, but about replicating the successful practices that led to their outstanding metrics. Ford Motor Company's benchmarking of Mazda is a good example. In the early 1980s, as part of a process improvement program, a team of Ford employees visited Mazda to examine its business processes. During that visit, the team discovered that Mazda's accounts payable department operated with only five employees, compared to Ford's 500 employees.[12] If benchmarking meant trying to match a particular metric value, Ford's managers would have concluded, "We need to reduce our accounts payable staff to five people." But Ford recognized that benchmarking means identifying and adapting *processes*, not metrics. In investigating *how* Mazda processed accounts payable, Ford discovered that Mazda did not process suppliers' invoices. Instead, Mazda paid suppliers when goods were received. In the end, Ford took what employees had learned from Mazda and redesigned the company's business processes, which eventually reduced the accounts payable staff.

In sum, benchmarking "is focused on identifying, studying, analyzing, and adapting best practices and implementing the results."[13] The best companies deliver their products and services with a high level of both quality and productivity. Exhibit 11-11 shows some potential improvement paths that companies may choose to follow. Notice that some quality improvements do not greatly influence productivity, and some productivity improvements may have little impact on quality. The goal of benchmarking is to identify those best practices that improve both quality and productivity.

EXHIBIT 11-11

Best practices of world-class companies.

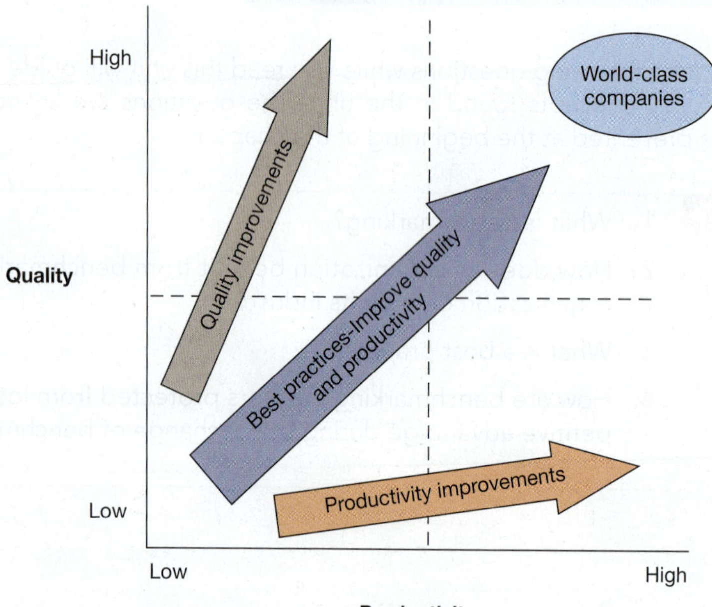

Adapted from Figure 2.11, Mark T. Czarnecki, *Benchmarking Strategies in Accounting and Finance.* The Benchmarking Network, Inc.: Houston, 1993, pp. 2–19.

THINK ABOUT IT 11.4

Why would a company that has been identified as having best practices be willing to benchmark with another company?

REALITY CHECK—*Benchmarking in health care*

Imagine that you are expecting to have major surgery and must choose which hospital to go to. Wouldn't it be helpful to have information about each hospital's record on particular types of surgery? Many people have called for such information, and now, thanks to their efforts, you can find it rather easily. For example, a quick visit to the website of the Dartmouth-Hitchcock Medical Center, based in Lebanon, New Hampshire, will provide the hospital's report card. The U.S. government has even gotten into the act, now that Medicare provides online information on the quality of hospital care.

Although this type of information sharing is often referred to as benchmarking, it tells us nothing about the processes underlying the level of care. Rather, it simply reports a metric and compares it to a national average. Knowing that a hospital's performance is higher than average doesn't mean that you will receive high-quality medical care.

Knowing that a hospital's performance is higher than average doesn't mean that you will receive high-quality medical care.

Benchmarking would tell a hospital *how* to improve the level of care. What hospitals need to do is to look for best practices that lead to higher-quality care. For example, the Nebraska Medical Center was not satisfied that patients needed to make 1.4 calls, on average, to schedule an appointment at the interventional radiology department. After investigating the issue, managers found that some patients had to make seven calls before getting an appointment. Following some process changes, the maximum number of calls required fell from seven to three, but the average number remained 1.4. That was a big improvement in the process, even though the reported measure did not change.

Source: Dartmouth-Hitchcock Medical Center website, http://www.dartmouth-hitchcock.org/quality/reports_a_to_z.html (accessed May 10, 2016); Laura Landro, "Dartmouth Offers Care-data Model," *Wall Street Journal*, April 6, 2005; Rhonda L. Rundle, "Medicare Puts Data Comparing Hospitals onto Public Website," *Wall Street Journal*, April 1, 2005; Victor E. Sower, "Benchmarking in Hospitals: More Than a Scorecard," *Quality Progress* (August 2007): 58–60.

You may think that companies benchmark only within their industry, but that is not the case. When Xerox needed to benchmark its order fulfillment processes, it studied L.L. Bean's processes, not those of another copier company. Because all companies share many of the same basic processes, it is best to benchmark against companies with the very best processes, regardless of industry. In fact, APQC developed the APQC Process Classification Framework^{SM}, which standardized the definitions of processes, to facilitate cross-industry benchmarking.[14]

Even for processes that are not identical, companies may benefit from benchmarking outside their industry. When a telephone company wanted to benchmark ways to protect its underground cable network, for instance, managers didn't turn to another telephone or utility company. Rather, they contacted a company that had underground pipelines. While the two companies came from different industries, their approaches to solving the problem of protecting underground assets were potentially similar.[15]

Is benchmarking worth the effort? While each organization must assess the potential return from a benchmarking project, APQC's *The 2016 Value of Benchmarking* indicates that benchmarking is perceived as a valuable practice. The study finds that 51% of the respondents have increased their investments in benchmarking activities over the past three years. And while 61% of the respondents don't measure the direct financial impact of their benchmarking efforts, 7% reported returns of more than $1 million from benchmarking.

Some people worry that if a company participates in benchmarking, a competitor may be able to gain an advantage. That should not be a problem if companies follow some commonsense practices. Participants should adhere to the Benchmarking Code of Conduct,[16] which provides general principles to follow during the benchmarking process. Benchmarking does *not* require an organization to share trade secrets or proprietary information. What *is* shared is information about processes and process metrics, which benefits both parties to the arrangement. Another option for collecting benchmarking data is to participate in collaborative efforts such as the APQC's Open Standards Benchmarking Collaborative[SM]. Even when best-of-class partners cannot be found, benchmarking with another organization can help to improve quality and productivity.

UNIT 11.3 REVIEW

KEY TERMS

Benchmarking p. 609
Best practices p. 609

PRACTICE QUESTIONS

1. LO 3 The easiest way to benchmark is to find publicly available ratios (for example, earnings per share) and try to achieve those standards. True or False?
2. LO 3 Which of the following kinds of companies would a grocery store *not* want to benchmark?
   a. Another grocery store
   b. A toy retailer with best practices in inventory management
   c. A hotel with best practices in employee training
   d. A grocery store might want to benchmark all these companies.
3. LO 3 If a company wants to benchmark, which partners would provide the best result?
   a. Those with best practices in quality
   b. Those with best practices in productivity
   c. Those with best practices in quality and productivity
   d. Those that have completed a benchmarking study in the past
4. LO 3 Benchmarking partners should protect their competitive advantage by benchmarking common processes, not proprietary information. True or False?

UNIT 11.3 PRACTICE EXERCISE

Bronson Methodist Hospital in Kalamazoo, Michigan, benchmarked with the Ritz-Carlton Hotel Co. and The Walt Disney Company. What processes would Bronson have in common with those nonhospital companies?

SELECTED UNIT 11.3 ANSWERS

Think About It 11.4

Even companies with best practices in one area are not likely to have best practices in all areas. A benchmarking partnership should be devised so that both partners benefit.

Practice Questions

1. False
2. D
3. C
4. True

Unit 11.3 Practice Exercise

Processes in common with the Ritz-Carlton: employee training, room service, custodial services, customer orientation
Processes in common with Disney: employee training, customer orientation

APPENDIX

Measures of Meeting Delivery Expectations

GUIDED APPENDIX PREPARATION

Answering the following questions while you read this appendix will guide your understanding of the key concepts found in the appendix. The questions are linked to the learning objectives presented at the beginning of the chapter.

LO 4

1. What is delivery cycle time?
2. What trade-offs do managers make when they reduce delivery cycle time?
3. What is manufacturing cycle time?
4. What value-added activities are included in manufacturing cycle time? What non-value-added activities are typically included in manufacturing cycle time?
5. How is manufacturing cycle efficiency calculated?
6. What number represents perfect manufacturing cycle efficiency? Is that number attainable?

Customers typically have expectations for how quickly they should receive a product they have ordered. All other things held equal, they would prefer as short a wait as possible. All things are not equal, however; different businesses must perform different tasks between an order's placement and its shipment. If delivery time is the competitive advantage a company needs, how can managers monitor a company's effectiveness with respect to delivery? Three measures can help managers to monitor their delivery processes: delivery cycle time, manufacturing cycle time, and manufacturing cycle efficiency.

Delivery Cycle Time

Delivery cycle time is the time between an order's placement and its shipment. This time varies depending on the type of business. Retailers that keep a large amount of inventory on hand need only process the order, pull the product from the shelf, and put it on the delivery truck. At the other extreme, manufacturing companies that produce to order must actually make the product before putting it on the delivery truck (see Exhibit 11-12). To be competitive, managers must keep delivery cycle time as short as possible, while still delivering the right product of the right quality. Because costs must often be incurred to reduce delivery cycle time, managers must decide whether the cost is worth the benefit.

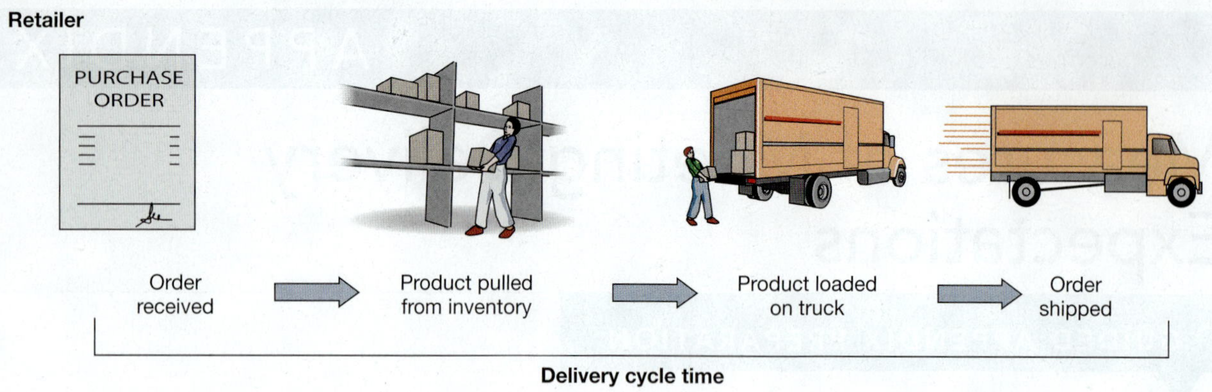

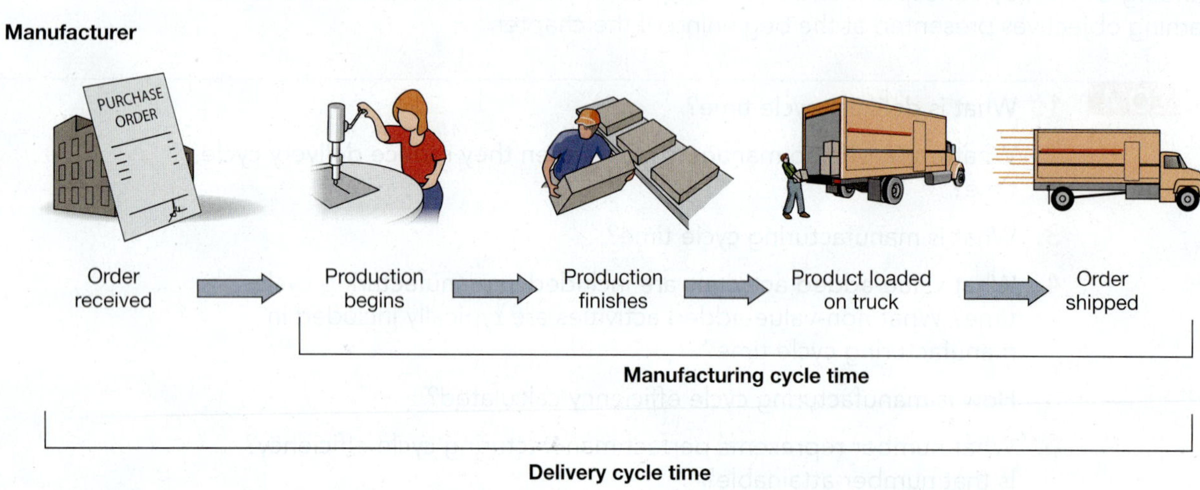

EXHIBIT 11-12 *Delivery cycle time and manufacturing cycle time for retailers versus manufacturers.*

Let's consider a step in the delivery cycle that is similar for retailers and manufacturers: the time between receipt of the order and the point when the product is pulled from inventory (for a retailer) or put into production (for a manufacturer). From a customer's perspective, this time lapse is non-value-added. It is a function of the company's order system and the number of orders that are ahead of the customer's. Even service industries experience this time lag.

Let's think about this process in a sit-down restaurant. The waiter takes your order, delivers it to the kitchen, and lets the chef know that it needs to be prepared. Often, between the time the waiter takes your order and delivers it to the chef, someone at one of his other tables asks a question, causing him to forget one of the items you ordered and increasing the time between your order's placement and its preparation. To reduce this time and increase the accuracy of orders, some restaurants have installed computers in the dining room, on which the waiter can enter the order. While this tactic shortens the wait, it doesn't prevent customers from stopping the waiter on the way to the computer. Handheld computers that allow the waiter to place your order right at your table are another possibility. That is likely to be a costly solution, which could be the reason we don't see many restaurants using them.

These days, many retailers—especially online retailers—have point-of-sale systems that communicate orders to the warehouse as soon as they are placed. Whether the orders can be pulled from the shelves immediately depends on whether the item is in stock and whether there are enough workers available to pull them. Many retailers use analytical systems that evaluate demand and the costs of carrying inventory to determine how much inventory to keep on hand.

Within a retailer's entire delivery cycle, what activities would customers consider to be value-added? The answer is very little. At most, they would include the time needed to ensure that the right product is put into the right box.

Manufacturing Cycle Time and Efficiency

Manufacturing cycle time, or **throughput time**, is the time from the start of production to the shipment of the product to the customer (see Exhibit 11-12). Once the order has been received by the production area, raw materials are sent to the factory floor and converted into the finished product, which then is either stored or placed directly onto the delivery truck. How much of this time is value-added? Only the conversion of the raw materials into the final product is value-added. Moving the materials from one stage of production to the next, waiting for a machine to become available, and inspecting the finished product are examples of activities that do not add value to the finished product.

Managers can keep track of production processes by monitoring manufacturing cycle time or by calculating *manufacturing cycle efficiency*. **Manufacturing cycle efficiency** is the ratio of value-added processing time to total manufacturing cycle time:

$$\text{Manufacturing cycle efficiency} = \frac{\text{Value-added processing time}}{\text{Total manufacturing cycle time}}$$

Perfect manufacturing cycle efficiency would yield a ratio equal to one—that is, all processing time would be value-added. While such a result is not likely to occur, managers should always strive to raise the ratio in that direction.

When Chad Davis, vice president of operations at C&C Sports, calculated the manufacturing cycle time for Midway High School's order of 200 jackets, this is what he discovered:

Operation	Hours Required
Cutting	15
Sewing/chenille lettering	285
Moving materials from one station to another	10
Waiting for an operation to begin	74
Packaging	16
	400 hours

Chad was surprised that the total manufacturing cycle time was 400 hours. Because of his focus on direct labor hours (cutting and sewing), he hadn't realized the amount of non-value-added time incurred during the process. The manufacturing cycle efficiency for this order was:

$$\frac{15 + 285}{400} = 75\%$$

That is, only 75% of the manufacturing cycle time was spent on value-added cutting and sewing activities. The other 25% was spent on non-value-added activities. The largest amount of non-value-added time was spent waiting for the jackets to move from one work station to another. Chad realized he needed to find out where the bottlenecks were so he could remove the constraints and speed up the jackets' progress through the manufacturing process.

APPENDIX REVIEW

KEY TERMS

Delivery cycle time p. 613

Manufacturing cycle time p. 615

Manufacturing cycle efficiency p. 615

Throughput time p. 615

PRACTICE QUESTIONS

1. LO 4 Which of the following is *not* included in delivery cycle time?
   a. Time spent waiting between production processes
   b. Delivery time from the warehouse to the customer
   c. Time between order receipt and order shipment
   d. Packaging time once the product has been pulled from inventory

Use the following information to answer questions 2–4:

On January 3, Stevens Manufacturing received an order for 25 toasters. Following is the timeline for processing the order:

	Days
Order processed	0.25
Wait for production to begin	2.00
Raw materials moved to assembly	0.25
Assembly	3.50
Wait for packaging	0.50
Toasters packaged	0.25
Wait for shipping	2.00
Toasters loaded and shipped	0.50
Toasters in transit to customer	5.00

2. LO 4 Calculate the delivery cycle time.
   a. 14.25 days
   b. 13.75 days
   c. 9.25 days
   d. 5 days
3. LO 4 Calculate the manufacturing cycle time.
   a. 7 days
   b. 12 days
   c. 6.75 days
   d. 3.5 days
4. LO 4 Calculate the manufacturing cycle efficiency.
   a. 100%
   b. 29%
   c. 33%
   d. 50%

APPENDIX PRACTICE EXERCISE

LaCrosse, Inc. sales manager Josh Brown has been receiving calls from customers complaining about the length of time it takes to receive an order. To help him understand the issue, he gathered the following information from DanGold Enterprises' most recent order.

	Days Required
Process customer order	0.1
Wait for direct materials to arrive	3.0
Fabrication of parts	4.0
Move order to assembly department	0.5
Wait for machine time	6.5
Assembly of parts	3.0
Move order to finishing department	0.3
Wait for machine time	3.0
Finishing of units	5.0
Move to packing department	0.5
Packing	1.5
Move to shipping department	0.2
Load delivery truck	0.5
Drive to customer	1.0
Unload delivery truck	0.5
Return to plant	1.0

Required

a. Calculate the delivery cycle time for DanGold's order.
b. Calculate the manufacturing cycle time for DanGold's order.
c. Calculate the value-added time for DanGold's order.
d. Calculate the manufacturing cycle efficiency for DanGold's order.

SELECTED APPENDIX ANSWERS

Practice Questions

1. B 2. C 3. A 4. D

Appendix Practice Exercise

a.

	Days Required
Process customer order	0.1
Wait for direct materials to arrive	3.0
Fabrication of parts	4.0
Move order to assembly department	0.5
Wait for machine time	6.5
Assembly of parts	3.0
Move order to finishing department	0.3
Wait for machine time	3.0
Finishing of units	5.0
Move to packing department	0.5
Packing of units	1.5
Move to shipping department	0.2
Load delivery truck	0.5
Delivery cycle time	28.1 days

b.

Fabrication of parts	4.0
Move order to assembly department	0.5
Wait for machine time	6.5
Assembly of parts	3.0
Move order to finishing department	0.3
Wait for machine time	3.0
Finishing of units	5.0
Move to packing department	0.5
Packing of units	1.5
Move to shipping department	0.2
Load delivery truck	0.5
Manufacturing cycle time	25.0 days

c.

Fabrication of parts	4.0
Assembly of parts	3.0
Finishing of units	5.0
Value-added time	12.0 days

d. $\frac{12 \text{ days}}{25 \text{ days}} = 48\%$

BUSINESS DECISION AND CONTEXT Wrap Up

C&C Sports' managers now have a plan to focus on the performance measures that will lead to financial success. Instead of waiting until the period is over to learn the results of operations, they will focus on leading indicators. Chad Davis, vice president of operations, will monitor measures such as employee satisfaction index, employee turnover and cross-training, as well as production measures such as average production time, defect rates, and quality complaints. Jonathan Smith, vice president of marketing, will monitor measures related to delivery time, customer retention, and customer growth. At this point, however, C&C's balanced scorecard is just a hypothesis. The leading indicators will need to be tracked, and their impact on operational, customer, and financial results determined. If the expected results do not occur, then managers will need to go back to the drawing board to identify the cause-and-effect relationships that do lead to financial success.

CHAPTER SUMMARY

In this chapter you learned how to extend performance evaluation beyond financial measures. Specifically, you learned to:

1. *Identify the desirable characteristics of performance measures. (Unit 11.1)*

Individual performance measures should not be used in isolation because no single measure can give managers all the information they need to make decisions. Managers should use a combination of leading and lagging, financial and nonfinancial measures. **Leading indicators** help to predict future results. For example, the on-time delivery percentage predicts customer satisfaction. **Lagging indicators** measure results after they occur. They answer the questions "How did ______ do?" and "What did _______ achieve?" For example, cost per square foot measures how well construction costs were controlled. Because **financial measures**, such as net income, earnings per share, and return on investment, are based on accounting results, they are primarily objective, requiring no judgment in their calculation. **Nonfinancial measures**, which are not based on accounting results, can be either qualitative (for example, employee responses to a survey) or quantitative (for example, the number of defective parts per 100). Effective performance measures are SMART: specific, measurable, actionable, relevant, and timely.

2. *Explain how to use a balanced scorecard to improve an organization's performance. (Unit 11.2)*

To achieve an organization's strategy, a balanced scorecard integrates performance measures across four perspectives:

- Learning and growth perspective: "Are we developing our employees' skills and providing them with technologies that facilitate change and improvement?"
- Internal business process perspective: "Are we improving our business processes in order to deliver maximum value to our customers?"
- Customer perspective: "Are we meeting our customers' expectations?"
- Financial perspective: "Are we reaching our financial goals?"

3. *Explain how to use benchmarking to improve an organization's performance. (Unit 11.3)*

Benchmarking is using data from other organizations to identify those processes and practices that lead to world-class performance. It involves sharing information between benchmarking partners or among organizations that belong to a benchmarking consortium.

4. *Calculate delivery cycle time, manufacturing cycle time, and manufacturing cycle efficiency. (Appendix)*

Delivery cycle time is the time from order placement to order shipment. Manufacturing cycle time is the time from the beginning of production to order shipment.

$$\text{Manufacturing cycle efficiency} = \frac{\text{Value-added processing time}}{\text{Total manufacturing cycle time}}$$

KEY TERMS

Balanced scorecard (Unit 11.2)
Benchmarking (Unit 11.3)
Best practices (Unit 11.3)
Customer perspective (Unit 11.2)

Delivery cycle time (Appendix)
Financial measure (Unit 11.1)
Financial perspective (Unit 11.2)
Internal business processes perspective (Unit 11.2)
Key performance indicator (KPI) (Unit 11.1)
Lagging indicator (Unit 11.1)
Leading indicator (Unit 11.1)
Learning and growth perspective (Unit 11.2)
Manufacturing cycle efficiency (Appendix)
Manufacturing cycle time (Appendix)
Nonfinancial measure (Unit 11.1)
Performance dashboard (Unit 11.1)
Strategy map (Unit 11.2)
Throughput time (Appendix)

EXERCISES

11-1 Leading versus lagging indicators (LO 1) In a recent annual report, Lexmark, a developer, manufacturer, and supplier of printing and imaging solutions for offices and homes, made the following statement:

> "One of the most important metrics for Lexmark is our hardware revenue growth because sales of hardware drive our future sales of supplies, which is the profit engine for Lexmark."

Required

Would Lexmark's hardware growth be considered a leading or a lagging indicator? Why?

11-2 Identifying leading versus lagging indicators and qualitative versus quantitative measures (LO 1) O'Brien's Bed and Breakfast operates a small inn in Wilmington, North Carolina. Kay O'Brien knows that customer service and customer satisfaction are the keys to staying in business. Indicate by placing an X in the appropriate column whether the following measures are leading or lagging, qualitative or quantitative indicators of customer satisfaction for O'Brien's Bed and Breakfast:

	Leading	Lagging	Qualitative	Quantitative
a. Customer satisfaction score				
b. Guest room cleanliness score				
c. Annual investment in linens				
d. Employee retention				
e. Return visits per year				
f. Time to respond to reservation requests				
g. Percentage of guest rooms ready at check-in				
h. Employee satisfaction				
i. Customer referrals per year				

11-3 Identifying performance measures; determining cause-and-effect relationships (LO 1) First State Bank offers a wide range of banking services, including checking accounts, certificates of deposit, loans, credit cards, and safety deposit boxes. Bank managers know that customer satisfaction has a direct impact on the bank's ability to retain customers and to persuade them to add accounts.

Required

Think of your experiences with your bank. What specific measures might bank managers monitor to gauge customer satisfaction and to link customer retention with account growth?

11-4 Determining cause-and-effect relationships (LO 1) Focusing managerial attention on a single metric may result in undesirable employee behavior and adverse business consequences. For each of the following scenarios, identify the undesirable results that could occur.

a. A shipping department is evaluated solely on total shipping costs incurred.
b. An airline is evaluated based on on-time departures.
c. A production line is evaluated based on the percentage of time machines are running.
d. A salesperson is evaluated based on the number of new accounts opened.

11-5 Balanced scorecard (LO 2) LowFare is a no-frills airline that provides daily shuttle service in the northeast United States. Passengers are predominantly businesspeople who travel between New York and Boston for the day.

Required

Identify one measure in each of the four perspectives of the balanced scorecard that LowFare managers should monitor. Explain your reasoning for each.

11-6 Internal business process measures (LO 2) TechGeek designs and produces high-tech gadgets that appeal to highly educated men between the ages of 25 and 50. These customers aren't as concerned about price as they are about innovation and about adopting the newest technologies before their friends do.

Required

Identify three measures in the internal business processes perspective that would provide helpful information to TechGeek's managers. Explain your reasoning for each.

11-7 Learning and growth measures (LO 2) King Designs is a leading product design firm that serves consumer products companies, primarily in the area of packaging design. King's customers are seeking product packaging solutions that are functional, innovative, and creative. A typical design team includes engineers, graphic designers, copy writers, and photographers.

Required

Identify four measures in the learning and growth perspective that would provide helpful information to management. Explain your reasoning for each choice.

11-8 Balanced scorecard measures (LO 2) Return to the practice exercise in Unit 11.1.

Required

Identify the balanced scorecard perspective for each measure in the exercise.

11-9 Performance metrics and the balanced scorecard (LO 1, 2) Southwest Airlines is known for high aircraft utilization (an average of 5.7 flights and 8.78 hours of air time per day in 2014) and quick turnaround time between flights. From 2004 to 2015, Southwest's on-time arrival rate averaged 79.8%.

Required

Explain how Southwest's monthly on-time arrival rate could be considered both a lagging and a leading indicator.

11-10 Benchmarking (LO 3) The following quotation is taken from Rockford Consulting's website (http://rockfordconsulting.com/world-class-manufacturing.htm):

> "World Class Manufacturing is a process-driven approach to improving manufacturing operations. It is often confused to mean standards of quality and image such as Rolls-Royce or Rolex."

Required

Discuss this statement with respect to what you have learned about benchmarking.

11-11 Delivery cycle time; manufacturing cycle time (LO 4) Express Copy offers walk-in copying and binding services to small businesses that cannot afford to provide those services in-house. Following is a typical schedule for a 50-copy spiral-bound job:

Activity	Minutes
Processing order	15
Waiting for copying to begin	25
Copying	20
Waiting for binding	30
Binding	10
Packing for customer	4

Required

a. Calculate the delivery cycle time.
b. Calculate the manufacturing cycle time.

11-12 Manufacturing cycle efficiency (LO 4) Barron Manufacturing spends 42 minutes per order on non-value-added activities. The total manufacturing cycle time is 2 hours.

Required

Calculate the manufacturing cycle efficiency.

11-13 Manufacturing cycle efficiency (LO 4) Peterson Papers makes personalized stationery of the highest quality. The company maintains a stock of blank note cards, calling cards, stationery, and envelopes. Customers order online, indicating the product type, personalization (monogram, name), font style, and color. The following schedule is typical of an order of 100 calling cards:

Activity	Minutes
Process order	5
Wait for production to begin	60
Pull calling cards from inventory	10
Set up machine for font style and color	5
Print calling cards	30
Inspect cards	4
Wait for packaging	9
Package cards for shipping	2
Wait for pickup by FedEx	60

Required

Calculate the manufacturing cycle efficiency.

PROBLEMS

11-14 Cause-and-effect relationships (LO 1) For years, Hampton, Inc. has enjoyed high customer satisfaction scores due to both product quality and outstanding customer service. On a scale of 0 to 4, with zero representing "unacceptable performance" and 4, "outstanding performance," customer satisfaction scores have been 3.0 or higher since the company began tracking the measure. Management also monitors the percentage of monthly sales made to customers from the prior month (that is, repeat sales) and to new customers. (Not all repeat customers purchase from Hampton every month, which accounts for the fact that these two measures do not add to 100%.)

About a year ago, the production manager tried a new supplier of raw materials, expecting no difference in quality. Although she quickly determined that the materials were not of the same high quality, some products had already been sold, and the sales staff began to receive complaints.

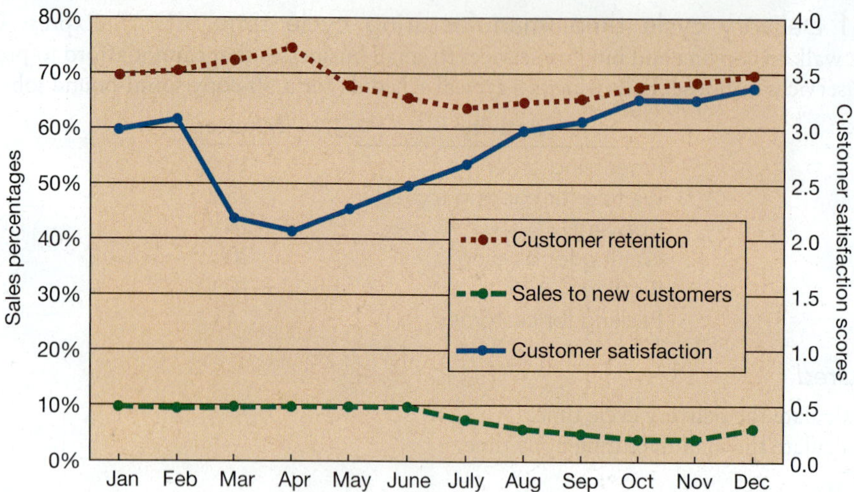

The chart above shows the relationship between customer satisfaction, customer retention (% of sales from existing customers), and sales to new customers over the last year. Sales percentages are charted on the left vertical axis and customer satisfaction scores on the right vertical axis.

Required

Explain the relationship that you believe exists between customer satisfaction, customer retention (percentage of sales from existing customers), and percentage of sales from new customers. Be sure to comment on leading and lagging relationships.

11-15 Strategy maps (LO 2) Kohl's mission, according to its website, is "to be the leading family-focused, value-oriented, specialty department store offering quality exclusive and national brand merchandise to the customer in an environment that is convenient, friendly and exciting." Neiman Marcus states in its online corporate profile that the founder's strategy was "to be recognized as the premier luxury retailer dedicated to providing our customers with distinctive merchandise and superior service."

Required

Create strategy maps for Kohl's and Neiman Marcus that take into account their two very different missions.

11-16 Nonfinancial performance metrics and the balanced scorecard (adapted from Brian Ballou, Dan L. Heitger, and Richard Tabor, "Nonfinancial Performance Measures in the Healthcare Industry," *Management Accounting Quarterly* [Fall 2003]: 11–15) **(LO 1, 2)** East Alabama Medical Center uses nonfinancial performance measures to track the following objectives:

- Maintain and improve the quality of clinical services.
- Improve patient service.
- Enhance employee recruitment and retention.

Required

a. Link each of these objectives to one of the four balanced scorecard perspectives.
b. Identify where on a balanced scorecard you would most likely find the following metrics:
    - Patient satisfaction score
    - Number of medication errors
    - Nursing turnover rate
    - Readmission rate

- Number of new hires
- Emergency room wait time before treatment
- Nurse-to-patient ratio
- Likelihood of patient recommending the hospital
- Number of patient complaints
- Employee satisfaction with incentive systems

11-17 Strategy maps and the balanced scorecard (adapted from Peter Vlant, "What Does Strategy Mapping Have to Do with HR?" *Human Capital Magazine*, June 2007) (LO 1, 2) Wesley Roberts, the Human Resources director at Elwes Limited, was concerned about the lack of commitment he perceived in many of the company employees. Employee turnover was high, as were recruitment costs. Wesley felt that if employees were more engaged, that is, committed to the mission of the company, they would not quit and performance would improve. He presented his concerns at a recent strategy development session, and the human resources group identified the following objectives:

- Implement recruitment management system.
- Train all managers in performance management.
- Achieve organization's EBIT.
- Reduce time needed to hire a candidate.
- Train all HR staff on links between employee engagement and performance management.
- Improve employee engagement.
- Contain organizational recruitment cost.
- Reduce cost to hire a candidate.
- Educate all managers on new hiring process.
- Reduce employee-initiated turnover.
- Implement performance management program.

Required

a. Using these objectives, construct a strategy map for the Human Resources department.
b. Using your strategy map, develop a balanced scorecard for the Human Resources department.

11-18 Manufacturing cycle time; manufacturing cycle efficiency (LO 4) Nelson Extruding produces containers for nurseries and landscaping businesses. The company competes based on its low-cost, high-quality products. As the company's expenses have risen, management has become concerned with the need to streamline various processes in order to reduce costs without reducing quality. The following table shows the time needed to produce a batch of 1-inch plant flats:

Activity	Time to Complete
Materials moved to production floor	30 minutes
Production in station 1	63 minutes
Materials moved to station 2	11 minutes
Wait to begin at station 2	15 minutes
Production in station 2	114 minutes
Inspection	5 minutes
Materials moved to finished goods inventory	12 minutes

Required

a. What is the manufacturing cycle time (throughput time) to produce a batch of 1-inch plant flats and prepare it for sale?
b. How much of the process time is value-added?
c. Calculate the manufacturing cycle efficiency.
d. What suggestions do you have for eliminating non-value-added time?

C&C SPORTS CONTINUING CASE

11-19 Evaluating balanced scorecard results (LO 2) After six months of using a balanced scorecard to monitor operations, Chad Davis, C&C Sports' vice president for operations, was very disappointed in the metrics in the learning and growth perspective shown below:

Measures	Goals	Actual results
Employee turnover	<5%	30%
Employee satisfaction index	90% satisfied or very satisfied	15%
% of cross-trained direct labor workers	>80%	40%
Number of employee-generated quality improvement suggestions	5 per quarter	0

The company was not even close to meeting the stated goals of any metric, and Chad realized that significant changes concerning the labor force were needed if any improvements were to be made.

Because of the seasonal nature of C&C's sales (see Exhibit 5-5) and the way Chad hires direct labor workers, he might employ as many as 75 workers during the busiest times of the year (November and December) and as few as 10 workers during the slowest times of the year (summer months). In fact, only 10 employees are guaranteed work all year long. Those 10 employees have the lowest turnover, have the highest level of satisfaction, and can produce all three products.

Required

Review Unit 5.2 to understand the current rationale for the seasonal production schedule. What trade-offs will be required if senior management determines that the current learning and growth measures are necessary to generate improvement in operations and increase net income?

CASES

11-20 Strategy maps and balanced scorecards (adapted from Susan B. Hughes, Craig B. Caldwell, Kathy Paulson Gjerde, and Pamela J. Rouse, "How Groups Produce Higher-Quality Scorecards Than Individuals," *Management Accounting Quarterly* [Summer 2005]: 34–44) **(LO 1, 2)** Eric Mathis stared at the latest operational report, trying to decipher it. As president of MetroMed, Inc., he realized that he was responsible for directing the company's progress. Yet he couldn't understand how, after six months of meeting about the company's strategic direction, its performance still seemed to be declining rather than improving.

Sherry Noel, vice president of operations, poked her head in the door. "How's it going, Eric? Did we meet our targets for last month?"

"Things could be better," Eric replied. "We spent all that time meeting about our strategic direction, and I really thought we were all in agreement on where we were heading. But now I get the monthly operating report, and it's as if no one knows what we're trying to do."

"I just read an article about something called a balanced scorecard," Sherry replied. "It's all about communicating corporate strategy throughout the organization, and then selecting the right metrics to monitor performance at achieving the strategy. Maybe we should look into it. We've already set our objectives, and I know we get lots of metrics each month in our reports."

Eric arranged a few more meetings and invited a friend with experience in developing balanced scorecards to facilitate the process. The scorecard that resulted follows:

PERSPECTIVE	OBJECTIVES	MEASURES
Financial	Achieve strong, balanced growth	• Number of new products developed • Percentage of sales by product category • Time to double sales revenue
	Generate a fair return to shareholders	• Return on equity • Earnings per share • Stock price that exceeds $30
Customer	Grow market share of existing brands	• Number of new accounts • Number of retained accounts • Increased domestic and foreign sales
	Maintain high-quality, "market leader" brand image	• Number of brands that are marketplace leaders • Number of new "icon brands" acquired • Fair pricing (price relative to competitors' prices)
Internal business processes	Improve product quality	• Defect rate • Sales growth
	Encourage innovation in terms of product and processes	• Establish inventory turnover measures • Number of new products under development • Number of continuous improvement projects • Capital budget maintained at 4.7% of sales
Learning and growth	Continue to be a values-driven company	• Number of appropriate hires • Employee turnover rate • Absenteeism rate • Training and development cost

Required

a. Prepare a strategy map to support the proposed balanced scorecard.
b. Evaluate the proposed scorecard in terms of its use of leading and lagging, financial and nonfinancial measures.
c. Evaluate the measures as they relate to the objectives. Be sure you consider the SMART criteria. What modifications would you suggest Eric make before implementing the balanced scorecard?

ANALYTICS PROBLEM

11-21 Using a Balanced Scorecard to Evaluate Initiative Success (LO 2)

(Dataset based on San Francisco International Airport 2014 and 2015 customer survey data, available at http://www.flysfo.com/media/customer-survey-data).

In an effort to attract and retain air passengers, Metropolitan International Airport has implemented several initiatives over the past year focused on improving the customer experience at airport restaurants and retail outlets (shops). Management also believed that upgrading the free WiFi network would enhance passengers' experiences at the airport. While overall customer satisfaction with the airport has been a metric included on the airport's balanced scorecard for several years, general manager Parks Gheesling has collected more detailed customer satisfaction data to help assess the initiatives' success.

Gheesling has asked you to examine the data to determine if the initiatives appear to be increasing customer satisfaction. To begin your analysis, review the information in the "Question Legend" tab of the Excel workbook to understand the data and possible passenger responses. The "Year 1" tab presents data collected before implementing the initiatives; the "Year 2" tab presents data collected after implementing the initiatives.

Required

a. What percentage of surveyed passengers purchased items from the airport stores **before** the initiatives were implemented? From the airport restaurants? Used the free WiFi? Hint: Using Excel's COUNTIF formula will help with this calculation.
b. What percentage of surveyed passengers purchased items from the airport stores **after** the initiatives were implemented? From the airport restaurants? Used the free WiFi? Hint: Using Excel's COUNTIF formula will help with this calculation.
c. What was the average customer satisfaction score for food quality **before** the initiatives were implemented? For free WiFi? For the airport as a whole? Hint: You will find Excel's AVERAGEIFS formula useful for completing this analysis.
d. What was the average customer satisfaction score for food quality **after** the initiatives were implemented? For free WiFi? For the airport as a whole? Hint: You will find Excel's AVERAGEIFS formula useful for completing this analysis.
e. Does it appear that the initiatives had the desired effect of increasing customer satisfaction? Why or why not?
f. Gheesling wonders if the initiatives may have had an effect on some passengers but not others. For instance, did the initiatives increase the satisfaction of passengers who fly more frequently but not that of less frequent flyers? To examine this possibility, repeat the above analyses after dividing the data into the TIMESFLOWN variable. Hint: You will find Excel's COUNTIF and AVERAGEIFS formulas useful for completing this analysis.
g. What other analyses would you want to perform to better understand the initiatives' impact on customer satisfaction?

The Excel data files for answering this problem can be found in WileyPLUS.

ENDNOTES

1. http://www.transtats.bts.gov/OT_Delay/OT_DelayCause1.asp.
2. Anthony J. Rucci, Steven P. Kirn, and Richard T. Quinn, "The Employee-Customer-Profit Chain at Sears," *Harvard Business Review* (January–February 1998): 82–97.
3. James Oakley, *Linking Organizational Characteristics to Employee Attitudes and Behavior—A Look at the Downstream Effects on Market Response & Financial Performance*, http://www.incentivecentral.org/pdf/employee_engagement_study.pdf (accessed September 29, 2007).
4. Christopher D. Ittner and David F. Larcker, "Coming up Short on Nonfinancial Performance Measurement," *Harvard Business Review* (November 2003): 88–95.
5. See Robert S. Kaplan and David Norton, "The Balanced Scorecard—Measures That Drive Performance," *Harvard Business Review* (January–February 1992): 71–79 and Robert S. Kaplan and David P. Norton, *The Balanced Scorecard: Translating Strategy into Action* (Boston: Harvard Business School Press, 1996).
6. Bain & Company, Darrell Rigby, and Barbara Bilodeau, *Management Tools and Trends 2015*, available at http://www.bain.com/publications/articles/management-tools-and-trends-2015.aspx (accessed May 10, 2016).
7. Robert S. Kaplan and David P. Norton, "The Office of Strategy Management," *Harvard Business Review*, October 2005, https://hbr.org/2005/10/the-office-of-strategy-management (accessed May 10, 2016); "When CEOs Talk Strategy, Is Anyone

Listening?" *Harvard Business Review*, June 2013, https://hbr.org/2013/06/when-ceos-talk-strategy-is-anyone-listening (accessed May 10, 2016).

8. For a more in-depth discussion of building a balanced scorecard, see Nils-Göran Olve, Jan Roy, and Magnus Wetter, *Performance Drivers: A Practical Guide to Using the Balanced Scorecard* (Chichester: John Wiley & Sons, 1999).
9. For more information on strategy maps, see Robert Kaplan and David Norton, "Having Trouble with Your Strategy? Then Map It," *Harvard Business Review* (September–October 2000): 167–176.
10. John Cummings, "Questioning the Balanced Scorecard," *Business Finance* (December 2004): 14.
11. David Kaplan, "Beware: The Unbalanced Scorecard," *Balanced Scorecard Report*, March 15, 2000, Harvard Business School Press Reprint #B0003E.
12. To learn more about this visit, see Chapter 2 in Michael Hammer and James Champy, *Reengineering the Corporation: A Manifesto for Business Revolution* (New York: HarperBusiness, 2001).
13. APQC, *Benchmarking: Leveraging Best-Practice Strategies*, 1999.
14. The complete classification can be found online at https://www.apqc.org/pcf (accessed July 20, 2016).
15. Anne Feltus, "Exploding the Myths of Benchmarking," *Continuous Journey: The Magazine for Continuous Improvement*, April/May 1994, 10–15.
16. The complete code of conduct is available in Institute of Management Accountants, *Statement on Management Accounting: Effective Benchmarking*, 1995, 35–36.

FINANCIAL STATEMENT ANALYSIS

UNITS	LEARNING OBJECTIVES
UNIT 12.1 Horizontal Analysis of Financial Statements	**LO 1:** Prepare a horizontal analysis of a balance sheet and income statement and use it to analyze a company's performance.
UNIT 12.2 Common-Size Financial Statements	**LO 2:** Prepare a common-size balance sheet and income statement and use them to analyze a company's performance.
UNIT 12.3 Ratio Analysis	**LO 3:** Calculate and interpret basic financial statement ratios.
UNIT 12.4 Industry Analysis	**LO 4:** Explain how to use sources of industry information to draw conclusions about a company's performance.

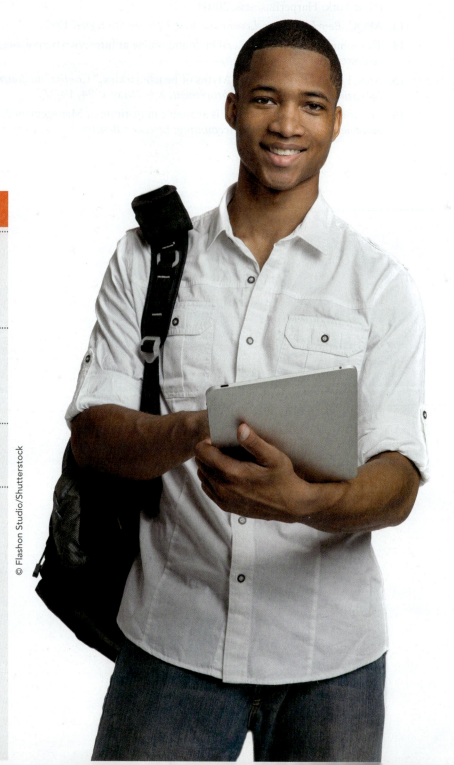

Business Decision and Context

© pictafolio/iStockphoto

George Douglas, president of C&C Sports, has been wondering about how well his company is doing. He has looked at the financial statements, but the account balances alone don't tell him much. He sees that the company's cash balance decreased dramatically over the past year, but sales revenue, accounts receivable, and inventory increased. What does all this mean? How can George assess the company's financial strengths and weaknesses so that he can predict how well the company will do in the future?

> "How can George assess the company's financial strengths and weaknesses so that he can predict how well the company will do in the future?"

George is particularly concerned about the increase in C&C's accounts receivable balance over the past year. As the company seeks to attract new customers, many of whom will want to purchase merchandise on account, he worries about granting credit to customers who may not be able to pay their bills. How can C&C's credit manager make sound decisions about new customers' credit requests?

Cedric Renn, a college senior, is considering several job offers, including one from C&C Sports, as he begins his operations management career. Several of his friends recently lost their jobs when their companies went out of business, so he is looking for an employer with a solid reputation and a bright future. How can Cedric evaluate his prospects for advancement and future employment at C&C?

Meredith Lincoln is reviewing Brazos Buttons' customer accounts. She notices that C&C Sports has applied for an increase in its credit limit. Before she grants the request, Meredith wants to make sure that C&C will be able to pay its bills on time. Where can Meredith get the information she needs to make her decision?

Here we have three decision makers grappling with three different decisions. While some of them are outside C&C Sports and others are inside the company, they can all gather information they need to support their decision making from the same place: C&C Sports' financial statements. Using financial statement analysis, George, Cedric, and Meredith can piece together a picture of C&C's financial health that is tailored to their own needs.

SUPPLY CHAIN KEY PLAYERS

END CUSTOMER

UNIVERSAL SPORTS EXCHANGE

C&C SPORTS

President
George Douglas

DURABLE ZIPPER COMPANY

BRADLEY TEXTILE MILLS

CENTEX YARNS

NEFF FIBER MANUFACTURING

BRUIN POLYMERS, INC.

UNIT 12.1

Horizontal Analysis of Financial Statements

GUIDED UNIT PREPARATION

Answering the following questions while you read this unit will guide your understanding of the key concepts found in the unit. The questions are linked to the learning objectives presented at the beginning of the chapter.

LO 1

1. What is horizontal analysis and how are the numbers calculated?
2. How is trend analysis similar to horizontal analysis?
3. What information would you hope to obtain from a trend analysis?

The account balances on the balance sheet and income statement provide a glimpse into how a company's financial position has changed from the previous year. In fact, generally accepted accounting principles (GAAP) require that companies present comparative financial statements that include both the current year and the previous year. C&C's balance sheet and income statement, presented in Exhibits T1-3 on page 37 and T1-4 on page 38, show what comparative financial statements look like. Rather than looking only at the balances reported on these statements, however, it is helpful to look at the changes in the account balances over time. This type of analysis is called **horizontal analysis**.

Preparing a Horizontal Analysis

The first step in preparing a horizontal analysis of a firm's financial statements is to gather the financial statements for at least two years. To prepare the analysis, calculate the difference between the current year's balance and the previous year's balance in each account. Then present these dollar differences in horizontal statements like those in Exhibits 12-1 and 12-2, which show a horizontal analysis of C&C Sports' balance sheet and income statement.

Let's review the calculations for C&C's Cash account. The dollar change from 2015 to 2016 was a decrease of $14,362 ($7,752 − $22,114).

Because an absolute dollar change doesn't give the whole picture, a percentage change is often included in the analysis. This percentage change, which expresses the dollar change relative to the previous year's balance, is calculated as follows:

$$\frac{\text{Current year account balance} - \text{Previous year account balance}}{\text{Previous year account balance}}$$

C&C SPORTS Balance Sheet Horizontal Analysis				
	Dec. 31, 2016	Dec. 31, 2015	$ Change	% Change
Cash	$ 7,752	$ 22,114	$ (14,362)	(64.9%)
Accounts receivable, net	623,713	583,429	40,284	6.9%
Total inventory	640,372	547,109	93,263	17.0%
Prepaid expenses	24,388	8,164	16,224	198.7%
Total current assets	1,296,225	1,160,816	135,409	11.7%
Property, plant, & equipment, net	532,858	600,647	(67,789)	(11.3%)
Other assets	41,704	35,812	5,892	16.5%
Total assets	$1,870,787	$1,797,275	$ 73,512	4.1%
Accounts payable	$ 441,602	$ 445,014	$ (3,412)	(0.8%)
Other accrued expenses	86,749	115,626	(28,877)	(25.0%)
Short-term debt	125,000	110,000	15,000	13.6%
Current maturities of long-term debt	20,000	20,000	0	0.0%
Total current liabilities	673,351	690,640	(17,289)	(2.5%)
Long-term debt	280,000	300,000	(20,000)	(6.7%)
Total liabilities	953,351	990,640	(37,289)	(3.8%)
Common stock	210,000	210,000	0	0.0%
Retained earnings	707,436	596,635	110,801	18.6%
Total stockholders' equity	917,436	806,635	110,801	13.7%
Total liabilities and stockholders' equity	$1,870,787	$1,797,275	$ 73,512	4.1%

EXHIBIT 12-1 *C&C Sports' balance sheet horizontal analysis.*

C&C SPORTS Income Statement Horizontal Analysis				
	Dec. 31, 2016	Dec. 31, 2015	$ Change	% Change
Sales revenue	$5,237,000	$4,654,000	$583,000	12.5%
Cost of goods sold	3,876,432	3,464,440	411,992	11.9%
Gross margin	1,360,568	1,189,560	171,008	14.4%
Selling & administrative expenses	1,160,566	1,067,721	92,845	8.7%
Operating income	200,002	121,839	78,163	64.2%
Interest expense	41,715	43,210	(1,495)	(3.5%)
Income before taxes	158,287	78,629	79,658	101.3%
Income tax expense	47,486	23,589	23,897	101.3%
Net income	$ 110,801	$ 55,040	55,761	101.3%

EXHIBIT 12-2 *C&C Sports' income statement horizontal analysis.*

WATCH OUT!

Refer to Exhibits 12-1 and 12-2. Note that the percentage change columns do not add up in the same way as the dollar columns. That is because each of the percentages was calculated using a different denominator.

The percentage change calculation for C&C's Cash balance from 2015 to 2016 reveals a 64.9% decrease in Cash, as follows:

$$\frac{\$7{,}752 - \$22{,}114}{\$22{,}114} = (64.9\%)$$

Similar calculations should be made for each line on the balance sheet and income statement.

Interpreting a Horizontal Analysis

The calculations are the easy part of a horizontal analysis. The challenge is to interpret the results and develop an understanding of what has happened over the period. Let's examine C&C's numbers to see what story they tell.

In looking at C&C's balance sheet (Exhibit 12-1), the first thing that jumps out is the change in cash: The company has seen its cash balance drop almost 65% in one year. Recall from the beginning of the chapter that George Douglas noticed the same thing. What might have caused this significant decrease? The best way to discover what happened to cash is to study the Statement of Cash Flows, shown in Exhibit T1-5 on page 39. From the Statement of Cash Flows we see that, although C&C's net income has increased every year, the company can't generate enough cash to cover operations. Accounts Receivable and Inventory are growing (6.9% and 17%, respectively). Although the accounts are part of the normal cash cycle, when they grow, management needs to make sure that inventory and receivables are being converted to cash in a timely manner. Another contributor to the cash decrease is the repayment of $20,000 per year in long-term debt.

Referring back to the assets portion of Exhibit 12-1, you can see that Prepaid Expenses increased a hefty 198.7%. While the dollar increase isn't large, it does contribute to C&C's cash problem. Remember, prepaid expenses represent cash paid before a benefit has been received. The decrease in Property, Plant, and Equipment is likely due to depreciation. The only caution here is for management to ensure that all equipment replacements do not occur at once, placing even more strain on C&C's cash position.

Under liabilities and equities, the decrease in Other Accrued Expenses is likely a timing difference between the dates on which payables were due last year and this year. A decrease in a payable account or another current liability account represents a drain on cash, which contributes to C&C's cash problem. Finally, Short-term Debt is increasing, likely because of the need for cash to support operations and to pay off Long-term Debt. Note that Retained Earnings has increased by the same amount as Net Income.

On the income statement (Exhibit 12-2) we see that Sales increased by a greater percentage than Cost of Goods Sold and Selling and Administrative Expenses. That positive difference allowed for the large increase in Operating Income and Net Income.

The horizontal analysis doesn't tell the complete story of C&C Sports, but it does raise important questions that C&C's management should investigate. As we continue with our analysis, we'll get a better picture of C&C's financial position.

Preparing a Trend Analysis

In another form of horizontal analysis, called **trend analysis**, each year's account balance is expressed as a percentage of the base year's (earliest year's) account balance, as follows:

$$\frac{\text{Current year account balance}}{\text{Base year account balance}}$$

Let's consider C&C's Sales Revenue for the past three years: $5,237,000, $4,654,000, and $4,668,400 in years 2016, 2015, and 2014, respectively. The earliest year in the analysis, 2014, is set as the base year, so the percentage for that year will be 100%. The trend percentages are calculated as shown in the following table:

2016	2015	2014
$\frac{\$5,237,000}{\$4,668,400} = 112.2\%$	$\frac{\$4,654,000}{\$4,668,400} = 99.7\%$	$\frac{\$4,668,400}{\$4,668,400} = 100\%$

Trend analysis will reveal more to George Douglas about operating performance to date than just one year's worth of change. Trend analysis is also useful for analyzing other information, such as supplemental information reported in corporate annual reports. For example, in its annual report, The Walt Disney Company provides data on Sales Revenue by segment. Preparing a trend analysis of this data provides information about the revenue growth in specific segments. As shown in Exhibit 12-3, the consumer products segment has experienced greater growth over the five-year period than the parks and resorts segment.

	2015	2014	2013	2012	2011	2010	2009	2008
Media networks	147%	133%	128%	123%	118%	108%	102%	100%
Parks & resorts	140%	131%	122%	112%	103%	94%	93%	100%
Studio entertainment	100%	99%	81%	79%	86%	91%	84%	100%
Consumer products	186%	165%	147%	135%	126%	111%	100%	100%
Interactive media	163%	181%	148%	118%	137%	106%	99%	100%

EXHIBIT 12-3 *Trend analysis of The Walt Disney Company's segment sales, 2008–2015.*

Source: The Walt Disney Company 2015 Annual Report; The Walt Disney Company 2012 Annual Report; The Walt Disney Company 2010 Annual Report.

Another way to use trend percentages is to compare changes in related accounts. For instance, The Walt Disney Company can compare the segment trend percentages for Revenue and Segment Profit. We would expect these accounts to move together, and any differences in the trends are due to trends in expenses. Exhibit 12-4 compares the consumer products segment's trend percentages for these two accounts from 2008 to 2015. Notice that the segment's profit increased much faster than its revenue.

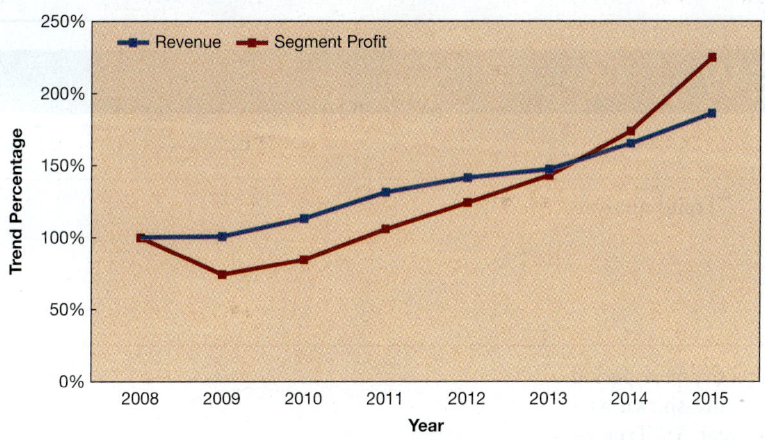

Source: The Walt Disney Company 2015 Annual Report; The Walt Disney Company 2012 Annual Report; The Walt Disney Company 2010 Annual Report.

EXHIBIT 12-4

Comparison of revenue and segment profit trends, The Walt Disney Company consumer products segment, 2008–2015.

REALITY CHECK—*How to slice an apple*

hocus-focus/iStockphoto

The iPhone had another big year in 2015; a 37% jump in the number of iPhones sold yielded a 52% increase in sales revenue for the phone and related products and services.

If you are like most students, somewhere you have a pair of earphones attached to an iPhone® or similar music device. Perhaps you even have them in right now as you are reading this chapter. No one can argue about the impact the iPhone's maker, Apple, Inc., has had on modern society with its Macintosh® computer, iPhone®, iPad®, and iTunes® website. While you may have invested in Apple's products, you could also invest in the company's stock. But before you do, you need to analyze the company's financial statements. Part of your examination should involve horizontal analysis, including an investigation of relationships among various accounts.

Apple sold 20,587,000 Mac computers in 2015, a 9% increase over 2014. Given this increase, you would expect sales revenue to increase by approximately the same amount; however, revenue from Mac computer sales increased by only 6% in 2015. While more computers were sold during the year, the average price for those computers fell by 3%. The number of iPads sold during 2015 fell by 19%, but a 5% decrease in the average unit price resulted in a 23% decrease in sales revenue.

The iPhone had another big year in 2015 with the late 2014 release of the iPhone 6 and iPhone 6 Plus; a 37% jump in the number of iPhones sold yielded a 52% increase in sales revenue for the phone and related products and services. Overall, Apple's sales revenue increased 28% in 2015.

Selling more products should also increase the cost of goods sold. Apple's cost of goods sold rose 25% in 2015, less than the increase in net revenue. This lower increase in cost of goods sold was a result of consumers shifting to higher margin products.

Bottom line: In analyzing a company's financial statements, you need to explore the expected—and sometimes unexpected—relationships that underlie them.

Source: Apple, Inc. 2015 10-K.

THINK ABOUT IT 12.1

What trend relationships should George Douglas examine to learn more about C&C Sports' cash situation?

UNIT 12.1 REVIEW

KEY TERMS

Horizontal analysis p. 630

Trend analysis p. 632

PRACTICE QUESTIONS

1. LO 1 In a trend analysis of sales over a five-year period (years 1–5), all sales account balances are shown as a percentage of the most recent year (year 5). True or False?

Use the following information to answer questions 2–5.

	2017	2016	2015
Accounts Receivable	$ 475,000	$ 400,000	$ 396,000
Sales	$3,275,000	$3,000,000	$2,800,000

2. LO 1 If you prepared a horizontal analysis for Accounts Receivable, what dollar change would be shown for 2017?

a. ($75,000)
b. $75,000
c. ($79,000)
d. $79,000

3. LO 1 If you prepared a horizontal analysis for Sales, what percentage change would be shown for 2016?

a. 17.0%
b. 9.2%
c. 7.1%
d. 6.7%

4. LO 1 A trend analysis for Accounts Receivable would show which percentages?

	2017	2016	2015
a.	119.9%	101.0%	100.0%
b.	118.8%	101.0%	100.0%
c.	100.0%	84.2%	83.4%
d.	100.0%	101.0%	100.0%

5. LO 1 Which of the following is *not* true about the changes in Accounts Receivable and Sales?

a. Accounts Receivable and Sales are increasing at different rates.
b. If Accounts Receivable increased at a faster rate than Sales, management might worry that an increasing proportion of sales are uncollectible.
c. Accounts Receivable can increase faster than Sales if management relaxes credit standards.
d. Accounts Receivable should be increasing at a slower rate than Sales so the company is sure to collect the Accounts Receivable.

UNIT 12.1 PRACTICE EXERCISE

Under Armour, Inc., included the following income statement in its 2015 Annual Report. All amounts are presented in thousands of dollars.

	Ended December 31		
	2015	2014	2013
Net revenues	$3,963,313	$3,084,370	$2,332,051
Cost of goods sold	2,057,766	1,572,164	1,195,381
Gross profit	1,905,547	1,512,206	1,136,670
Selling, general, and administrative expenses	1,497,000	1,158,251	871,572
Income from operations	408,547	353,955	265,098
Interest expense, net	14,628	5,335	2,933
Other expense, net	7,234	6,410	1,172
Income before income taxes	386,685	342,210	260,993
Provision for income taxes	154,112	134,168	98,663
Net income	$ 232,573	$ 208,042	$ 162,330

Required

1. Prepare a horizontal analysis of Under Armour's income statement.
2. Prepare a trend analysis for Net Revenues and Income from Operations. What do you conclude?

SELECTED UNIT 12.1 ANSWERS

Think About It 12.1

Since the cash issue seems to be related to the increases in Accounts Receivable and Inventory, George should compare the trends in Sales and Accounts Receivable to see whether Accounts Receivable is growing at a faster rate than Sales. He should also compare the trends in Inventory and Cost of Goods Sold to see whether Inventory is growing faster than Cost of Goods Sold.

Practice Questions

1. False
2. B
3. C
4. A
5. D

Unit 12.1 Practice Exercise

1.

	2015		2014	
	$ Change	% Change	$ Change	% Change
Net revenues	$ 878,943	28.5%	$ 752,319	32.3%
Cost of goods sold	485,602	30.9%	376,783	31.5%
Gross profit	393,341	26.0%	375,536	33.0%
Selling, general, and administrative expenses	338,749	29.2%	286,679	32.9%
Income from operations	54,592	15.4%	88,857	33.5%
Interest expense, net	9,293	174.2%	2,402	81.9%
Other expense, net	824	12.9%	5,238	446.9%
Income before income taxes	44,475	13.0%	81,217	31.1%
Provision for income taxes	19,944	14.9%	35,505	36.0%
Net income	$ 24,531	11.8%	$ 45,712	28.2%

2.

	2015	2014	2013
Net revenues	169.9%	132.3%	100.0%
Income from operations	154.1%	133.5%	100.0%

Income from operations grew at a slower rate than net revenues between 2013 and 2015. It appears that Under Armour's operating expenses grew faster than the related revenue. The faster growth in these expenses compounds the fact that Under Armour does not appear to have passed on the entire increase in cost of goods sold to customers through price increases and the increased interest expense.

UNIT 12.2

Common-Size Financial Statements

GUIDED UNIT PREPARATION

Answering the following questions while you read this unit will guide your understanding of the key concepts found in the unit. The questions are linked to the learning objectives presented at the beginning of the chapter.

LO 2

1. What are common-size financial statements? What is the base for the common-size income statement? What is the base for the common-size balance sheet?
2. What information would you hope to obtain from a set of common-size financial statements?
3. What might you conclude if the Bonds Payable percentage was increasing on the common-size balance sheet?
4. What might you conclude if the Accounts Receivable percentage for Company A on its common-size balance sheet was greater than the same percentage for Company B? Assume the companies are in the same industry.
5. What might you conclude if the Cost of Goods Sold percentage was increasing on the common-size income statement?

In Unit 12.1 you learned how to examine changes in account balances over time. While horizontal analysis is useful in analyzing a company's financial health, it doesn't tell the whole story. Another helpful approach is to examine changes in the relative size of account balances within a single statement. This type of analysis is referred to as **common-size analysis**, or **vertical analysis**.

Common-size statements are especially useful in comparing companies of different size. For example, assume you want to compare Southwest Airlines and JetBlue Airways, two low-cost airlines. At the end of 2015, JetBlue reported an asset base of $8,660 million and operating revenues of $6,416 million. That same year, Southwest Airlines reported an asset base of $21,312 million and operating revenue of $19,820 million. Obviously, the difference in the size of the two companies makes comparison based on absolute dollars meaningless. But you can compare the companies' relative performance using common-size statements.

Preparing the Common-Size Balance Sheet

In preparing a common-size balance sheet, you express all account balances as a percentage of total assets. For example, you calculate the percentage for asset accounts as:

$$\frac{\text{Individual asset account balance}}{\text{Total assets}}$$

Let's look at the Inventory account on C&C's balance sheet (see Exhibit 12-1). To compute the common-size amount for 2016, divide the Inventory account balance by Total Assets, as follows:

$$\frac{\$640{,}372}{\$1{,}870{,}787} = 34.23\%$$

Inventory represents 34.23% of C&C's assets.

While this common-size inventory amount provides some information on its own, it can provide additional information when compared to the common-size amounts for prior years. Such an analysis may reveal trends in the composition of C&C's asset base. At the end of 2015, C&C had $547,109 invested in inventory, or stated as a common-size amount, 30.44% $\left(\frac{\$547{,}109}{\$1{,}797{,}275}\right)$ of its assets.

Thus, C&C's Inventory balance increased not only in absolute size (dollars), but in relative size. This increase in inventory could be caused by overproduction or by a buildup of obsolete merchandise. Or it could indicate that management is building up an inventory buffer in anticipation of a growth in sales.

Common-size percentages for liabilities and equities are calculated in the same way as for assets, as a percentage of total assets:

$$\frac{\text{Individual liability or equity account balance}}{\text{Total assets}}$$

These percentages tell us what portion of assets is funded by certain liabilities and equity. Let's look at C&C's Accounts Payable. In 2016, accounts payable funded 23.6% of the company's total assets:

$$\frac{\$441{,}602}{\$1{,}870{,}787} = 23.6\%$$

WATCH OUT!

Unlike the percentage columns in a horizontal analysis, the columns in a common-size percentage statement *can* be totaled. However, the numbers may not add to exactly 100% due to rounding. In that case, revise your rounding to force the column to add to 100%.

This percentage was less than the 24.76% $\left(\frac{\$445{,}014}{\$1{,}797{,}275}\right)$ of assets that accounts payable funded in 2015. Exhibit 12-5 shows C&C's common-size balance sheets for 2015 and 2016.

EXHIBIT 12-5

C&C Sports' common-size balance sheet.

C&C SPORTS
Common-Size Balance Sheet
For the Years Ended December 31

	2016	2015
Cash	0.42%	1.23%
Accounts receivable, net	33.34%	32.46%
Total inventory	34.23%	30.44%
Prepaid expenses	1.30%	0.46%
Total current assets	69.29%	64.59%
Property, plant, & equipment, net	28.48%	33.42%
Other assets	2.23%	1.99%
Total assets	100.00%	100.00%
Accounts payable	23.60%	24.76%
Other accrued expenses	4.64%	6.44%
Short-term debt	6.68%	6.12%
Current maturities of long-term debt	1.07%	1.11%
Total current liabilities	35.99%	38.43%
Long-term debt	14.97%	16.69%
Total liabilities	50.96%	55.12%
Common stock	11.23%	11.68%
Retained earnings	37.81%	33.20%
Total stockholders' equity	49.04%	44.88%
Total liabilities and stockholders' equity	100.00%	100.00%

Preparing the Common-Size Income Statement

In preparing a common-size income statement, you express all revenue and expense accounts as a percentage of net sales revenue, as follows:

$$\frac{\text{Individual revenue or expense account balance}}{\text{Net sales revenue}}$$

Let's look at C&C's Cost of Goods Sold. The common-size income statement amounts for the cost of goods sold are:

2016	2015
$\frac{\$3{,}876{,}432}{\$5{,}237{,}000} = 74.02\%$	$\frac{\$3{,}464{,}440}{\$4{,}654{,}000} = 74.44\%$

WATCH OUT!

Some income statements report gross sales revenue and then deduct sales returns and allowances to arrive at net sales. If the income statement you are analyzing reports a single sales revenue amount, such as C&C's income statement in Exhibit 12-2, that is the net sales revenue to use in common-size analysis.

What does this analysis tell us? In 2015, 74.44 cents of every dollar in sales revenue was used to cover the cost of C&C's products. In 2016, slightly less than that amount (74.02 cents) was used to cover the cost of production, so C&C has reduced its cost to produce as a percentage of sales. The company may have done so by passing price increases on to customers or by controlling costs better. Either way, more of each sales dollar has become available to provide profit. Exhibit 12-6 shows C&C's common-size income statement.

C&C SPORTS Common-Size Income Statement For the Years Ended December 31	2016	2015
Sales revenue	100.00%	100.00%
Cost of goods sold	74.02%	74.44%
Gross margin	25.98%	25.56%
Selling & administrative expenses	22.16%	22.94%
Operating income	3.82%	2.62%
Interest expense	0.80%	0.93%
Income before taxes	3.02%	1.69%
Income tax expense	0.91%	0.51%
Net income	2.11%	1.18%

EXHIBIT 12-6

C&C Sports' common size income statements.

Interpreting the Common-Size Statements

Exhibit 12-5 shows that current assets increased as a percentage of total assets due largely to the increases in Accounts Receivable and Inventory. Horizontal analysis told you that these accounts had increased, along with total assets. We know that as a company grows, its account balances tend to grow with it. However, the common-size analysis reveals that Accounts Receivable and Inventory increased at a faster pace than total assets.

REALITY CHECK—*Hospitals suffer from bad debts*

© babyblueut/iStockphoto

Major U.S. hospital chains are facing an epidemic of bad debts, caused in part by the rising number of patients without health insurance.

Most people think of a hospital as a place where healing occurs. But where does a hospital go when it gets sick? Major U.S. hospital chains are facing an epidemic of bad debts, caused in part by the rising number of patients without health insurance. Some health care executives see this increase in bad debts as the most pressing financial issue facing hospitals today. As a result, some health care companies are asking patients to make payments before they are discharged, or even before they are treated.

In 2004, HCA, Inc., then the country's largest hospital chain, implemented such a program for nonemergency care. Apparently it was just what the doctor ordered. By 2015, bad debts as a percentage of revenue had fallen to 9.0% from a steep 16.2% in 2004. Tenet Healthcare Corporation saw a similar improvement, as bad debts fell from 12.1% of revenue in 2004 to 7.3% of revenue in 2015.

Sources: Dean Foust, "Weaker Vital Signs at Hospitals," *BusinessWeek*, May 3, 2004, http://www.bloomberg.com/news/articles/2004-05-02/weaker-vital-signs-at-hospitals (accessed July 20, 2016); HCA, Inc., 2015 Annual Report; Rhonda L. Rundle and Paul Davies, "Hospitals Start to Seek Payment Upfront," *The Wall Street Journal*, June 2, 2004; Bob Sechler, "Uninsured Patients Take Toll on Tenet, Triad," SmartMoney.com, October 30, 2006, http://www.smartmoney.com/onedaywonder/index.cfm?story=20061030 (accessed February 16, 2008, site now discontinued); Tenet Healthcare Corporation 2015 10-K.

Overall, current liabilities and total liabilities decreased as a percentage of total assets. That means that equity must be increasing as a percentage of total assets. By the end of 2016, approximately half of C&C's assets were funded by debt and the other half by equity.

Finally, the common-size income statement in Exhibit 12-6 reveals that C&C Sports did a better job of controlling expenses in 2016 than in 2015. However, the net income percentage is still very small, indicating that the company needs to find more ways to increase prices or reduce costs.

In today's global economy, when you assess a company's position relative to that of its competitors you may find yourself looking at financial statements denominated in a foreign currency. For example, if you are comparing Qualcomm, Nokia, and Ericsson, three companies in the mobile communications industry, you will be working with dollars ($), euros (€), and Swedish kronor (SEK). Though you really can't compare these currencies directly, Exhibit 12-7 shows how to use common-size income statements to overcome the currency problem. One note of caution, however. There may be differences in the accounting principles the companies use for reporting, and the same items may be classified differently across the three companies. That might explain Qualcomm's vastly different income from continuing operations percentage compared to Nokia's and Ericsson's.

	Qualcomm		Nokia		Ericsson	
	As Reported ($ million)	% of Sales	As Reported (EUR million)	% of Sales	As Reported (SEK million)	% of Sales
Net sales	$25,281	100.0%	€12,499	100.0%	kr 246,920	100.0%
Cost of sales	10,378	41.1%	7,046	56.4%	161,101	65.2%
Gross margin	14,903	58.9%	5,453	43.6%	85,819	34.8%
Selling & administrative expenses	2,344	9.3%	1,652	13.2%	29,285	11.9%
Research & development expenses	5,490	21.7%	2,126	17.0%	34,844	14.1%
Other operating expenses (income)	1,293	5.1%	(13)	(0.1%)	(115)	0.0%
Operating income	5,776	22.8%	1,688	13.5%	21,805	8.8%
Investment income (expense)	711	2.8%	(148)	(1.2%)	(1,933)	(0.8%)
Income before taxes	6,487	25.7%	1,540	12.3%	19,872	8.0%
Income tax expense	1,219	4.8%	346	2.8%	6,199	2.5%
Income from continuing operations	$ 5,268	20.8%	€ 1,194	9.6%	kr 13,673	5.5%

EXHIBIT 12-7 *Comparison of common-size income statements in different currencies.*

Source: Data obtained from companies' 2015 Annual Reports. Common-size percentages may not add due to rounding.

THINK ABOUT IT 12.2

Imagine you are comparing two companies, one with $1 million in assets and the other with $100,000 in assets. Both had common-size Cash percentages of 15% in year 1 and 14% in year 2. Do you consider the two changes in this account balance to be equivalent? Or do you regard the change for one company differently from the change for the other?

UNIT 12.2 REVIEW

KEY TERMS

Common-size analysis p. 637 Vertical analysis p. 637

PRACTICE QUESTIONS

1. LO 2 On a common-size balance sheet, accounts payable is shown as a percentage of

   a. total liabilities.

   b. current liabilities.

   c. total assets.

   d. total stockholders' equity.

2. LO 2 On a common-size income statement, cost of goods sold is shown as a percentage of

   a. net sales revenue.

   b. operating income.

   c. net income.

   d. gross profit.

Use the following information to answer questions 3–4.

Prepaid Expenses	$ 14,000
Total Current Assets	$195,000
Total Assets	$876,000
Bonds Payable	$125,000
Total Long-term Debt	$180,000

3. LO 2 Calculate the common-size percentage for Prepaid Expenses.

   a. 7.2%

   b. 1.6%

   c. 2.1%

   d. 5.8%

4. LO 2 Calculate the common-size percentage for Bonds Payable.

   a. 14.3%

   b. 69.4%

   c. 18.0%

   d. 55.2%

Use the following information to answer questions 5–6.

Sales	$1,500,000
Cost of Goods Sold	$ 800,000
Salaries Expense	$ 125,000
Total Operating Expenses	$ 600,000
Net Income	$ 50,000

5. LO 2 Calculate the common-size percentage for Gross Margin.

   a. 53.3%

   b. 14.0%

   c. 87.5%

   d. 46.7%

6. LO 2 Calculate the common-size percentage for Salaries Expense.

   a. 12.0%

   b. 20.8%

   c. 8.3%

   d. 15.6%

7. LO 2 If Company A's operating income percentage is higher than Company B's operating income percentage, which of the following is true?

   a. Company A is making more money than Company B.

   b. A smaller percentage of A's sales dollars are used to cover expenses.

   c. Cost of Goods Sold, as a percentage of Sales, is higher for B than for A.

   d. All of the above are true.

UNIT 12.2 PRACTICE EXERCISE

Under Armour, Inc., reported the following comparative balance sheet in its 2015 Annual Report (modified for this exercise). All amounts are presented in thousands of dollars.

	Dec. 31, 2015	Dec. 31, 2014
Cash and cash equivalents	$ 129,852	$ 593,175
Accounts receivable, net	433,638	279,835
Inventories	783,031	536,714
Other current assets	152,242	139,675
Total current assets	1,498,763	1,549,399
Property and equipment, net	538,531	305,564
Other assets	831,606	240,120
Total assets	$ 2,868,900	$ 2,095,083

	Dec. 31, 2015	Dec. 31, 2014
Accounts payable	$ 200,460	$ 210,432
Accrued expenses	192,935	147,681
Current maturities of long-term debt	42,000	28,951
Other current liabilities	43,415	34,563
Total current liabilities	478,810	421,627
Long-term debt	352,000	255,250
Other long-term liabilities	369,868	67,906
Total liabilities	1,200,678	744,783
Common Stock	72	71
Paid in capital	636,630	508,350
Retained earnings	1,076,533	856,687
Accumulated other comprehensive loss	(45,013)	(14,808)
Total stockholders' equity	1,668,222	1,350,300
Total liabilities and stockholders' equity	$ 2,868,900	$ 2,095,083

Required

1. Prepare a common-size analysis of Under Armour's balance sheet.
2. Comment on any significant percentages in the common-size statement.

SELECTED UNIT 12.2 ANSWERS

Think About It 12.2

The changes are equivalent in terms of percentages, but not in terms of dollars. Because the smaller company will likely have more difficulty than the larger one in borrowing cash or raising equity, decreases in the smaller firm's cash balance may be a greater cause for alarm than decreases in the larger firm's.

Practice Questions

1. C
2. A
3. B
4. A
5. D
6. C
7. B

Unit 12.2 Practice Exercise

1.

	Dec. 31, 2015	Dec. 31, 2014
Cash and cash equivalents	4.5%	28.3%
Accounts receivable, net	15.1%	13.4%
Inventories	27.3%	25.6%
Other current assets	5.3%	6.7%
Total current assets	52.2%	74.0%
Property and equipment, net	18.8%	14.6%
Other assets	29.0%	11.5%
Total assets	100.0%	100.0%
Accounts payable	7.0%	10.0%
Accrued expenses	6.7%	7.0%
Current maturities of long-term debt	1.5%	1.4%
Other current liabilities	1.5%	1.6%
Total current liabilities	16.7%	20.1%
Long-term debt	12.3%	12.2%
Other long-term liabilities	12.9%	3.2%
Total liabilities	41.9%	35.5%
Common stock	0.0%	0.0%
Paid in capital	22.2%	24.3%
Retained earnings	37.5%	40.9%
Accumulated other comprehensive loss	(1.6%)	(0.7%)
Total stockholders' equity	58.1%	64.5%
Total liabilities and stockholders' equity	100.0%	100.0%

2. Under Armour's asset base has changed from 2014 to 2015. The company holds a smaller percentage of its assets in the form of cash, and its relative investment in inventory has increased. The company has also made a significant increased investment in property and equipment. The growth in assets has been financed through a substantial increase in long-term debt, resulting in a more leveraged company.

UNIT 12.3

Ratio Analysis

GUIDED UNIT PREPARATION

Answering the following questions while you read this unit will guide your understanding of the key concepts found in the unit. The questions are linked to the learning objectives presented at the beginning of the chapter.

LO 4

1. What is working capital?
2. What does a current ratio of 2.0 mean?
3. Why are inventory and prepaid expenses omitted from the acid-test ratio?
4. What could cause a company's current ratio to be high but its acid-test ratio to be low?
5. Why might a high accounts receivable turnover be bad?
6. What does a high inventory turnover indicate?
7. What does a debt ratio of 0.60 indicate? What does the remaining 0.40 indicate?
8. What does a low times interest earned ratio indicate?
9. *In your own words*, what is a "return"?
10. In the return on total assets ratio, which part of the numerator is the return to shareholders and which part is the return to creditors?
11. How do you know if a company has positive financial leverage?
12. What factors could cause earnings per share to decrease?
13. Why would investors be willing to buy stock at a price that is 20 times higher than earnings per share?

We have seen in the last two units that financial statement analysis provides a wealth of information about an organization's financial health. **Ratio analysis** is another helpful tool, one that is used to examine the relationships among the financial statement accounts. To be useful, financial ratios must be based on *meaningful* relationships. For instance, the relationship between current assets and current liabilities is meaningful in assessing a company's ability to pay bills on time. However, there is no relationship between Accounts Payable and Accumulated Depreciation, so examining the ratio of those two account balances would be pointless.

In this unit, you will learn how to use several financial ratios to guide your financial statement analysis. Using ratio analysis is much like going to the doctor. The ratios provide symptoms of a company's underlying strengths and weaknesses, which then guide the diagnosis of the problem. Exhibit 12-8 summarizes the ratios discussed in this unit.

Liquidity Ratios

Liquidity is a firm's ability to pay its obligations (bills) as they come due and to meet any unforeseen needs for cash. Investigating a company's liquidity is important because a company that cannot pay its bills on time will have difficulty obtaining the resources needed to continue operating. Suppliers will grow tired of not being paid and will refuse to deliver to the company. Workers will quit if they are not paid on time. Banks will refuse to lend additional funds, and customers will seek other sources of goods when the products they desire are not available. Eventually, the firm may go out of business.

Liquidity also refers to a company's ability to convert non-cash assets into cash. Current assets such as accounts receivable and inventories are generally more liquid than long-term assets, such as property, plant, and equipment. Cash, of course, is the ultimate liquid asset.

Liquidity is important not just because a company must be able to pay its bills on time to remain in business. Companies also need the ability to take advantage of opportunities as they arise. If an investment opportunity arises that will strengthen the company's competitive position or provide significant future growth, managers will need a ready source of cash in order to make the investment.

Working Capital

Working capital is the difference between a firm's current assets and its current liabilities. Although this measure is not technically a ratio, it is a commonly used measure of liquidity. The calculation of working capital is

$$\text{Current assets} - \text{Current liabilities}$$

C&C's working capital for 2016 was $622,874 ($1,296,225 − $673,351). In 2015, C&C's working capital was $470,176.

Current Ratio

Probably the most common measure of short-term liquidity is the **current ratio**, or the ratio of current assets to current liabilities. The formula for this ratio is

$$\frac{\text{Current assets}}{\text{Current liabilities}}$$

For 2016, C&C's current ratio was 1.93 $\left(\frac{\$1{,}296{,}225}{\$673{,}351}\right)$, up from 1.68 in 2015.

Acid-Test or Quick Ratio

The assets included in the current ratio have different levels of liquidity that reflect different degrees of collectibility. Consider inventory, for instance. In the normal business cycle, goods are purchased or manufactured and then sold to

Category	Ratio	Formula	Use	For C&C Sports
Liquidity Ratios	Working capital	Current assets − Current liabilities	Measures ability to pay current liabilities	$1,296,225 − $673,351 = $622,874
	Current ratio	$\frac{\text{Current assets}}{\text{Current liabilities}}$		$\frac{\$1,296,225}{\$673,351} = 1.93$
	Acid-test (quick) ratio	$\frac{\text{Cash + Cash Equivalents + Accounts Receivable}}{\text{Current liabilities}}$		$\frac{\$7,752 + \$623,713}{\$673,351} = 0.94$
	Accounts receivable turnover	$\frac{\text{Net credit sales}}{\text{Average Accounts Receivable balance}}$	Measures ability to convert accounts receivable into cash	$\frac{\$5,237,000}{(\$623,713 + \$583,429)/2} = 8.68 \text{ times}$
	Average collection period	$\frac{\text{365 days in a year}}{\text{Accounts receivable turnover}}$		$\frac{365}{8.68} = 42.1 \text{ days}$
	Inventory turnover	$\frac{\text{Cost of goods sold}}{\text{Average inventory balance}}$	Measures ability to sell inventory	$\frac{\$3,876,432}{(\$640,372 + \$547,109)/2} = 6.53 \text{ times}$
	Average days to sell inventory	$\frac{\text{365 days in a year}}{\text{Inventory turnover}}$		$\frac{365}{6.53} = 55.9 \text{ days}$
Leverage Ratios	Debt ratio	$\frac{\text{Total liabilities}}{\text{Total assets}}$	Measures ability to meet debt obligations	$\frac{\$953,351}{\$1,870,787} = 50.96\%$
	Debt-to-equity ratio	$\frac{\text{Total liabilities}}{\text{Total stockholders' equity}}$		$\frac{\$953,351}{\$917,436} = 1.04$
	Times interest earned ratio	$\frac{\text{Earnings before interest expense and income taxes}}{\text{Interest expense}}$		$\frac{\$200,002}{\$41,715} = 4.79 \text{ times}$
Profitability Ratios	Gross margin percentage	$\frac{\text{Gross margin}}{\text{Net sales revenue}}$	Measures profitability	$\frac{\$1,360,568}{\$5,237,000} = 25.98\%$
	Return on assets	$\frac{\text{Net income + [interest expense} \times \text{(1 − tax rate)]}}{\text{Average total assets}}$		$\frac{\$110,801 + [\$41,715 \times (1 - 0.3)]}{(\$1,870,787 + \$1,797,275)/2} = 7.63\%$
	Return on common stockholders' equity	$\frac{\text{Net income − Preferred dividends}}{\text{Average common stockholders' equity}}$		$\frac{\$110,801}{(\$917,436 + \$806,635)/2} = 12.85\%$
Market Measure Ratios	Earnings per share	$\frac{\text{Net income − Preferred dividends}}{\text{Average number of shares outstanding}}$	Measures investment potential	*
	Price/earnings ratio	$\frac{\text{Market price per share}}{\text{Earnings per share}}$		*
	Dividend payout ratio	$\frac{\text{Dividends per share}}{\text{Earnings per share}}$		*

*Not applicable to C&C Sports.

EXHIBIT 12-8 *Summary of financial statement ratios.*

customers. After the sale, the account must be collected. From purchase and manufacture to collection, this cycle ranges from a few days—say, for a restaurant—to several months for a manufacturer such as Steinway, whose concert grand pianos take up to 11 months to complete.

Because of these differences in collectibility, many analysts use the acid-test or quick ratio to measure current liquidity. The **acid-test ratio** or **quick ratio** is a more stringent measure of liquidity than the current ratio. It is similar to the current ratio, except that it includes only highly liquid current assets: cash, cash equivalents such as marketable securities, and accounts receivable. Inventory and prepaid expenses are excluded.

The acid-test or quick ratio is calculated as

$$\frac{\text{Cash} + \text{Cash Equivalents} + \text{Accounts Receivable}}{\text{Current liabilities}}$$

C&C's acid-test or quick ratio for 2016 was 0.94 $\left(\frac{\$7{,}752 + \$623{,}713}{\$673{,}351}\right)$; in 2015 it was 0.88 $\left(\frac{\$22{,}114 + \$583{,}429}{\$690{,}640}\right)$.

Accounts Receivable Turnover

While the current and acid-test ratios provide information about liquidity, they do not indicate the underlying quality of current assets. To gain that kind of information, you need to look at the assets themselves.

Accounts receivable turnover is a measure of the liquidity of a company's accounts receivable. It shows how many times, on average, a company's receivables balance is "turned over," or collected, during the year. Accounts receivable turnover is calculated as

$$\frac{\text{Net Credit Sales}}{\text{Average Accounts Receivable balance}}$$

WATCH OUT!

Remember that the beginning Accounts Receivable balance for this year is the same as the ending Accounts Receivable balance for last year.

The ratio includes only credit sales because those are the ones that generate accounts receivable. However, it is difficult to separate cash sales from credit sales when looking at a published income statement. In that case, you may assume that all sales are credit sales. The ratio uses the average accounts receivable balance to compensate for changes in the balance during the year. Average accounts receivable is calculated as

$$\frac{\text{Beginning Accounts Receivable balance} + \text{Ending Accounts Receivable balance}}{2}$$

Let's look at C&C's accounts receivable turnover. Sales were $5,237,000 in 2016. With average accounts receivable of $603,571 $\left(\frac{\$623{,}713 + \$583{,}429}{2}\right)$, C&C's accounts receivable turnover for 2016 was 8.68 times $\left(\frac{\$5{,}237.000}{\$603{,}571}\right)$. A turnover of 8.68 means that accounts receivable were converted into cash 8.68 times during the year.

Average Collection Period

While accounts receivable turnover measures the quality of a company's accounts receivable, its interpretation can be a bit confusing. A related measure, **average collection period**, reveals how many days, on average, the company takes to collect cash from a credit sale. It is calculated as

$$\frac{365 \text{ days in a year}}{\text{Accounts receivable turnover}}$$

For 2016, C&C's average collection period was 42.1 days $\left(\frac{365}{8.68}\right)$, meaning that, on average, C&C collected cash from customers 42.1 days after a sale.

THINK ABOUT IT 12.3

Assume that after a review of Accounts Receivable, management determines that the credit department has not been enforcing payment terms. What can management do to encourage customers to pay faster? What might be some negative consequences of such a change?

Inventory Turnover

Inventory is commonly one of the largest current asset accounts, so examining the quality of inventory is an important part of assessing a company's liquidity.

REALITY CHECK—*Cash flow in a global supply chain*

© vuk8691/iStockphoto

It's no surprise to anyone in business today that the world is shrinking. Thomas L. Friedman turned this concept into a bestseller in his book *The World Is Flat: A Brief History of the Twenty-first Century*. Supply chains now span the globe, linking countries and currencies in a single production process.

Along with these global supply chains come cash flow implications. The longer the supply chain, the longer the time needed for cash to flow back through the chain. A supplier might have to wait for payment from a customer until the customer's customer pays up. Payments are affected not only by customers' payment cycles, but by the ability to get products through the supply chain. One slip-up by a single link in the supply chain creates a ripple effect through the rest of the chain. Why would a supplier tolerate such delays? To get the business.

One slip-up by a single link in the supply chain creates a ripple effect through the rest of the chain.

Consider the case of Pacific Writing Instruments, Inc., creators of the PenAgain™ pens (http://www.penagain.com/). Pacific found that retailers who carry the pen sometimes take 90 to 120 days to pay an invoice. That makes for a long collection period for accounts receivable. While Pacific waited for payment, the company had to order and pay for additional inventory. On large orders of over 50,000 pens, the manufacturer required an up-front payment of 30%, with the balance due 30 days after receipt. Thus, Pacific had to pay its supplier 60 to 90 days before receiving payment from its customers.

Sources: Gwendolyn Bounds, "You Got the Big Break. Now What?," *The Wall Street Journal*, November 13, 2006; Tom Diana, "Supply Chains Flow to Credit Departments," *Business Credit*, 108, no. 9 (October 2006): 48–49; Thomas L. Friedman, *The World Is Flat: A Brief History of the Twenty-first Century* (New York: Farrar, Straus and Giroux, 2005).

Inventory turnover measures how many times, on average, a company's inventory "turns over," or is sold, during the year. It is calculated as

$$\frac{\text{Cost of Goods Sold}}{\text{Average Inventory balance}}$$

This ratio uses the average Inventory balance to account for changes in the balance during the year.

Average Inventory is calculated as

$$\frac{\text{Beginning Inventory balance} + \text{Ending Inventory balance}}{2}$$

Using this formula, we find that C&C's inventory turnover for 2016 was 6.53 times $\left(\frac{\$3,876,432}{(\$640,372 + \$547,109)/2}\right)$.

Average Days to Sell Inventory

A related ratio, **average days to sell inventory**, reveals how many days elapse from the receipt of inventory to its sale to customers. This ratio is calculated as

$$\frac{\text{365 days in a year}}{\text{Inventory turnover}}$$

For 2016, C&C's average days to sell inventory was 55.9 days $\left(\frac{365}{6.53}\right)$. That means that, on average, 55.9 days passed from the time C&C received inventory, such as fabric, until the finished products were sewn and sold to customers.

Interpreting Liquidity Ratios

Now that you know how to calculate liquidity ratios, you need to interpret the picture they are providing. In doing this, you cannot choose a single ratio; rather, you have to look at the ratios together to make a useful interpretation. Let's look at C&C's liquidity ratios and assess the company's liquidity.

C&C's Liquidity Ratios	2016	2015
Working capital	$622,874	$470,176
Current ratio	1.93	1.68
Acid-test ratio	0.94	0.88
Accounts receivable turnover	8.68 times	9.85 times
Average collection period	42 days	37 days
Inventory turnover	6.53 times	6.76 times
Average days to sell inventory	55.9 days	54 days

In 2016, C&C's working capital revealed that the company had $622,874 more current assets than current liabilities, which was an improvement from the company's working capital position in 2015. This indicates that in the event of a forced liquidation of the company's assets, C&C should be able to raise more than enough cash from the sale of current assets to pay off its current liabilities. A similar picture emerges from the current ratio, which showed that in 2016, C&C had $1.93 in current assets for every $1.00 in current liabilities—almost twice as much in current assets as in current liabilities. A current ratio of 2.0 is a typical benchmark level of liquidity, although comparisons to industry standards are necessary for a complete evaluation.

Why is this type of cushion desirable? A firm that is forced to liquidate current assets to meet current liabilities will need a cushion like C&C's because it will not be able to liquidate the assets at book value. For instance, if C&C had to generate cash quickly from its accounts receivable, it would have to **factor** them (sell them) to a firm that would then be responsible for collecting the accounts. The factor would not pay 100% of the receivables' book value because there has to be some profit for the factor. So C&C might get only 90 to 95% of the receivables' book value. Similarly, a quick sale of inventory cannot be accomplished at book value. Rather, inventory will likely be sold at less than cost. Based on C&C's 2016 current ratio of 1.93, the company could factor its accounts receivable and sell its inventory for about 52% of their book value and still be able to pay off all of its current liabilities.

Exhibit 12-1 shows that prepaid expenses were included in C&C's current assets. Some analysts choose to remove prepaid current assets from the current ratio calculation because prepaid expenses generally cannot be converted to cash. Rather, these assets represent an outlay of cash for future services. If we were to exclude prepaid expenses from the calculation, C&C's current ratio would be 1.89 and 1.67 in 2016 and 2015, respectively. While the difference in calculation methods doesn't make a huge difference for C&C, the difference could be significant for a company with a high level of prepaid expenses. The acid-test ratio, while improved in 2016, still highlights that C&C had more current liabilities than highly liquid current assets. An acid-test ratio of 1.0 is typically considered the minimum level of liquidity, although comparisons to industry standards are necessary for a complete evaluation.

THINK ABOUT IT 12.4

Should C&C's management want the company's current and acid-test ratios to be as high as possible? Explain your reasoning.

The quality of assets is assessed through the turnover ratios. A higher accounts receivable turnover indicates faster cash collection and greater liquidity. But a high turnover rate may also indicate that credit terms are too tight, and the company may be losing sales from customers who cannot qualify for credit.

The average collection period should be compared to the company's credit terms. If the average collection period is 35 days and the company allows customers 30 days to pay an invoice, the collection effort is working reasonably well. But if the company gives customers only 15 days to pay, then either the collections department is not collecting receivables in a timely manner or the sales department is too lax in granting credit to customers with a poor credit history. Remember that the longer a receivable goes uncollected, the greater the chance that it will never be collected.

C&C's current credit policy is net 30, meaning that customers have 30 days to pay their bills in full. Thus, an average collection period of 42 days is too long. Remember that in our horizontal and common-size analyses we concluded that the company is having trouble collecting cash, and accounts receivable is growing faster than total assets. A collection period this slow is not helping the situation. C&C's managers need to review the accounts receivable to see which customers are taking too long to pay, and then consider changes in the company's credit policy.

Generally, a high inventory turnover rate is considered to be good. In fact, that is the goal of a just-in-time inventory system (see Chapter 1). But inventory turnover is industry-dependent. Blue Bell Creameries, an ice cream manufacturer in Brenham, Texas, has a high inventory turnover because of its use of fresh ingredients. KB Home, a U.S. homebuilder, would have a much lower inventory turnover, given the length of time required to build and sell a house.

Sometimes, high inventory turnover can signal poor inventory management. A company that carries little inventory and continually has stockouts would have a high inventory turnover, but its customer satisfaction would likely be low—a problem in the long run. Similarly, low inventory turnover can be a symptom of obsolete, slow-moving inventory or too much investment in inventory.

C&C's average days to sell inventory increased by almost two days in 2016. By combining C&C's average days to sell inventory (55.9 days) with its average collection period (42 days), we can conclude that the company takes almost 98 days to recoup the cash invested in its inventory. If George Douglas didn't know this before the analysis, he might be quite shocked when he learns the company's cash is tied up this long. No wonder C&C is having cash troubles.

The liquidity analysis for C&C Sports reveals some concerns. While the company's working capital, current ratio, and acid-test ratio all increased, indicating a stronger liquidity position, the turnover ratios and common-size statements provide a different picture. With accounts receivable taking longer to collect and inventory taking longer to sell, C&C's cash balance is declining.

Leverage Ratios

Financial leverage refers to the use of borrowed capital to finance a business or project. Most companies use a combination of debt and equity to obtain the assets needed to fund their operations. High levels of debt pose a risk for the company because debt and interest must be repaid. In comparison, equity, or common and preferred stock, does not need to be repaid, nor do dividends need to be declared. High levels of debt pose a risk for creditors, too, because they run the risk of not being repaid in the event the company fails. Why take the risk, then? All things held equal, current stockholders prefer debt financing over equity because it does not dilute their ownership in the company. If the company can earn a higher rate of return on investments in assets than the rate at which it borrows, then debt financing will generate even greater returns for the business.

Investors and creditors use several ratios to evaluate a company's level of debt. We will study three of them.

Debt Ratio

The **debt ratio** measures the ratio of liabilities to assets. Thus, it shows the proportion of assets that are financed through debt. No distinction is made between short-term debt, such as accounts payable, and long-term debt, such as notes payable. The formula for calculating the debt ratio is

$$\frac{\text{Total liabilities}}{\text{Total assets}}$$

C&C's debt ratio for 2016 was 50.96% ($953,351 ÷ $1,870,787).

Debt-to-Equity Ratio

Another way to measure a company's debt level is to calculate its debt-to-equity ratio. The **debt-to-equity ratio** measures the amount of financing provided by creditors (debt) relative to the amount provided by owners (equity). The formula for calculating the debt-to-equity ratio is

$$\frac{\text{Total liabilities}}{\text{Total stockholders' equity}}$$

C&C's debt-to-equity ratio for 2016 was 1.04 (\$953,351 ÷ \$917,436).

Times Interest Earned Ratio

Debt is not a free resource; companies must pay interest on their borrowings. Creditors make loans with the expectation that the borrowers will repay the principal on time, with interest. The liquidity ratios that we examined earlier provide one assessment of a company's ability to make these payments as they come due. The **times interest earned ratio** provides another measure of a company's ability to make interest payments out of current earnings. The formula for calculating the times interest earned ratio is

$$\frac{\text{Earnings before interest expense and income taxes}}{\text{Interest expense}}$$

C&C's times interest earned ratio for 2016 was 4.79 times (\$200,002 ÷ \$41,715).

Interpreting Leverage Ratios

Now that you know how to calculate leverage ratios, you need to interpret the picture they are providing. In doing this, you cannot choose a single ratio; rather, you have to look at the ratios together to make a useful interpretation. Let's look at C&C's leverage ratios and assess the company's debt position.

C&C's Leverage Ratios	2016	2015
Debt ratio	50.96%	55.1%
Debt-to-equity ratio	1.04	1.23
Times interest earned ratio	4.79 times	2.82 times

With a debt ratio of 50.96% at the end of 2016, almost 51% of C&C's asset base was financed through debt; the other 49% was financed through equity. This is a change from 2015, when just over 55% of the asset base was financed through debt. This means that C&C's reliance on debt financing is decreasing, and its reliance on equity financing is increasing. Creditors, like Meredith Lincoln at Brazos Buttons, prefer to see a lower debt ratio, as this indicates a lower level of risk.

One note of caution in interpreting the debt ratio: Firms may have financing arrangements, such as leases, which are structured to be off-balance sheet arrangements. For all practical purposes, these arrangements are debt, yet they are not classified as debt on the balance sheet. Walgreen's reported just \$4.1 billion in long-term debt on its 2015 balance sheet, even though the company had over \$35 billion in operating lease commitments over the next several years. In such cases, the firm may be subject to more risk than is apparent in the debt ratio.

Consistent with the debt ratio, the debt-to-equity ratio has decreased from 2015 and shows that creditors are funding a little more than half of C&C's asset base, while owners provide the remainder. Similar to the debt ratio, the higher the debt-to-equity ratio, the greater the risk to creditors.

C&C's times interest earned ratio reveals that the company could have paid almost five times the amount of interest it incurred in 2016 from its pretax earnings. This is a significant improvement from 2015's level.

Taken together, the leverage ratios show an improving leverage position for C&C Sports. The company's use of long-term debt has decreased, although the

13.6% increase in short-term debt shown by the horizontal analysis indicates that some of the long-term debt may have been replaced by short-term debt. The company is generating more than enough income to pay the interest on the debt; however, a continued decline in the company's cash balance may affect its ability to actually make the interest payments when due.

Profitability Ratios

Businesses must generate profits to ensure continuity. Thus, investors, employees, managers, and creditors all are interested in measures that indicate a company's ability to remain profitable over the long run. We will look at three profitability measures: gross margin percentage, return on assets, and return on equity.

Gross Margin Percentage

> **WATCH OUT!**
> Just as we discussed when preparing common-size income statements, when the income statement you are analyzing reports a single sales revenue amount, like C&C's income statement in Exhibit 12-2, that is the net sales revenue to use for the gross margin percentage.

The **gross margin percentage** shows how much of each sales dollar is available to cover operating expenses and provide a profit after the cost of goods sold has been covered. It is a measure of the company's ability to generate income from the sale of goods or services. The gross margin percentage is calculated as

$$\frac{\text{Gross margin}}{\text{Net sales revenue}}$$

C&C's gross margin percentage for 2016 was 25.98% $\left(\frac{\$1{,}360{,}568}{\$5{,}237{,}000}\right)$. This is the same percentage reported on C&C's common-size income statement (see Exhibit 12-6).

Return on Assets

As you may recall from your financial accounting course, assets are economic resources that have a future benefit to a company. It is this future benefit that leads a company to invest in the assets. The **return on assets** ratio measures how well assets have been employed in conducting the business.

Stockholders and creditors are interested in the return on assets, too. Stockholders expect a return in the form of income; creditors expect a return in the form of interest. The formula for the ratio considers the returns for both these sources of assets:

$$\frac{\text{Net income} + [\text{Interest expense} \times (1 - \text{tax rate})]}{\text{Average total assets}}$$

Since interest expense is subtracted from operating income to arrive at net income, it must be added back to net income to arrive at the total return to both sources of financing. Interest expense must then be multiplied by (1 − tax rate) so that both returns in the numerator will be reported on an after-tax basis. The denominator includes average total assets to account for changes in total assets during the year. Average total assets is calculated as

$$\frac{\text{Beginning total assets balance} + \text{Ending total assets balance}}{2}$$

Using this formula, we find that C&C's return on assets for 2016 was 7.63% $\left(\frac{\$110{,}801 + [41{,}715 \times (1 - 0.3)]}{(\$1{,}870{,}787 + \$1{,}797{,}275)/2}\right)$.

Return on Common Stockholders' Equity

Common stockholders (company owners) expect management to earn a reasonable return on all assets, especially those that are funded through the issue of common stock. The **return on common stockholders' equity** measures how well the funds provided by common stockholders have been used to generate a return for the company. Recall that the components of common stockholders' equity are common stock, additional paid-in capital, and retained earnings. In calculating the return on common stockholders' equity, we must first adjust net income by any preferred stock dividends declared during the period, since those dividends will reduce the amount of income available for distribution to common stockholders. The formula for the return on common stockholders' equity is

> **WATCH OUT!**
>
> If the company you are analyzing has discontinued some operations, the income statement will report "net income from continuing operations" in addition to net income. In this case, use the net income from continuing operations in the ratio calculations, since this is the amount of income that was generated by operations that will continue in the future.

$$\frac{\text{Net income} - \text{Preferred dividends}}{\text{Average common stockholders' equity}}$$

In this formula, average common stockholders' equity is used to account for changes in the equity balance during the year. Average common stockholders' equity is calculated as

$$\frac{\text{Beginning common stockholders' equity} + \text{Ending common stockholders' equity}}{2}$$

Using this formula, we find that C&C's return on common stockholders' equity for 2016 was 12.85% $\left(\frac{\$110{,}801}{(\$917{,}436 + \$806{,}635)/2}\right)$.

Interpreting Profitability Ratios

Now that you know how to calculate profitability ratios, you need to interpret the picture they are providing. In doing this, you cannot choose a single ratio; rather, you have to look at the ratios together to make a useful interpretation. Let's look at C&C's profitability ratios and assess the company's position.

C&C's Profitability Ratios	2016	2015
Gross Margin Percentage	25.98%	25.56%
Return on Assets	7.63%	6.97%
Return on Common Stockholders' Equity	12.85%	11.24%

The gross margin percentage shows that C&C retains about 26¢ of each sales dollar after covering the costs of goods sold. This amount seems low, though it needs to be compared to industry standards before reaching a conclusion. Nevertheless, C&C could increase profitability if managers could find a way to increase gross margin, either by raising prices or reducing the cost of goods sold.

Both the return on assets and return on common stockholders' equity improved from 2015 to 2016. Recall that the return on assets represents the return to both sources of asset financing—debt and equity—whereas the return on common stockholders' equity is strictly the return to common stockholders. When the return on common stockholders' equity is higher than the return on assets, we can conclude that a company is making positive use of financial leverage. That is, the company is borrowing at an average interest rate that is less than the return generated by its assets. When assets earn more than the cost to finance them, the stockholders benefit.

Market Measure Ratios

The stocks of publicly held companies like Walmart and McDonald's are traded on stock exchanges, such as the New York Stock Exchange (NYSE) and the National Association of Securities Dealers Automated Quotations (NASDAQ). Investors buy and sell shares of stock in the hope of earning a profit, as in the old "buy low, sell high" adage. They use several ratios to assess a stock's potential.

Because C&C Sports is not a publicly traded company whose stock is traded on an exchange, there is no way to assess the business using these ratios. To explore market measure ratios, we will use the example of Centex Yarns, the company that spins the yarn for the fabric C&C uses to manufacture its baseball pants and jerseys.

Earnings per Share

Earnings per share is an often-reported measure of the potential return to stockholders. In the simplest terms, it represents how much of a company's current net income could be distributed for each share of stock held by an investor. This is not a cash measure, since net income is based on accrual, rather than cash, accounting principles.

Earnings per share must be reported on the face of every income statement that is prepared in accordance with generally accepted accounting principles. The exact method of calculating this amount is beyond the scope of this discussion, but the basic calculation is

$$\frac{\text{Net income} - \text{Preferred dividends}}{\text{Average number of shares outstanding}}$$

Preferred dividends are excluded from the calculation because they are paid to preferred stockholders, not to common stockholders. Once paid, they are no longer available to the common stockholder.

For 2016, Centex Yarns reported net income of \$42,125,000 and an average 51,812,500 shares of common stock outstanding. The company paid \$550,000 in preferred dividends, yielding earnings per share of \$0.80 $\left(\frac{\$42{,}125{,}000 - \$550{,}000}{51{,}812{,}500}\right)$. Earnings per share is always rounded to the nearest cent.

Price/Earnings Ratio

Investors purchase shares of stock in the hope that their price will increase. Stock prices are bid up when the buyers believe that a company's future earnings potential is favorable. The specifics of how investors estimate a company's future earnings potential are beyond the scope of this book. One ratio that influences them, however, is the price/earnings ratio. The **price/earnings (P/E) ratio** indicates what multiple of current earnings investors are willing to pay for a share of stock. The price/earnings ratio is calculated as

$$\frac{\text{Market price per share}}{\text{Earnings per share}}$$

Recall that Centex Yarns' earnings per share for 2016 was \$0.80. On December 31, 2016, the stock was trading at \$20 per share. The company's price/earnings ratio was therefore 25 (\$20 ÷ \$0.80), which means that the stock was selling for 25 times the amount of its current earnings.

WATCH OUT!

The price/earnings ratio will change every time the stock price changes. For instance, if Centex's stock price rises to \$24 on January 15, 2017, the price/earnings ratio will increase to 30.

Dividend Payout Ratio

While investors purchase stocks for the potential return from increased share prices, they also purchase stocks for the dividend income. The **dividend payout ratio** measures how much of earnings per share is returned to common stockholders in the form of dividends. The ratio is calculated as

$$\frac{\text{Dividends per share}}{\text{Earnings per share}}$$

In 2016, Centex Yarns paid dividends of $0.12 per share, so the dividend payout ratio was 15% ($0.12 ÷ $0.80). Investors who invest mainly for future price increases prefer the dividend payout ratio to be low so that earnings can be used internally to take advantage of profitable opportunities. Investors who invest primarily for the dividend income prefer the dividend payout ratio to be high.

THINK ABOUT IT 12.5

Which type of company is likely to have a higher dividend payout, a mature company or a growth company? Which type of investor is more likely to prefer a company with a high dividend payout, a young investor or a retired investor? Why?

Interpreting Market Measure Ratios

Now that you know how to calculate market measure ratios, you need to interpret the picture they are providing. In doing this, you cannot choose a single ratio; rather, you have to look at the ratios together to make a useful interpretation. Let's look at Centex's market measure ratios and assess how the stock market views the company's potential.

Centex's Market Measure Ratios	2016	2015
Earnings per share	$0.80	$0.78
Price/earnings ratio	25 times	20 times
Dividend payout ratio	15.0%	15.4%

Centex Yarns reported an increase in earnings per share that could be the result of increased net income, decreased number of shares outstanding, or a combination of both. Either way, current shareholders benefit when earnings per share increases. The market is rewarding this increase in profitability and expected future increases in profitability with an increase in the market price.

A high price/earnings ratio indicates that investors see a high potential for earnings growth. As the price/earnings ratio increases, investors may start to worry that the stock is overpriced and may be unwilling to buy additional shares until additional evidence is available that a company will continue to be profitable. A low price/earnings ratio indicates that investors do not see much potential for future earnings growth. When the price/earnings ratio is low, investors will assess whether the stock is underperforming the market or is underpriced. If underpriced, then investors will buy the stock, driving up the price.

Centex's dividend payout ratio, at about 15%, is moderate. The company prefers to use the majority of earnings per share to reinvest in the business to increase the value of the stock.

Limitations of Financial Statement Analysis

Ratio analysis is a powerful tool for assessing the financial health of an organization, but it does have some limitations. Like the account balances used in this type of analysis, ratios yield the equivalent of a snapshot of the firm. The day after the financial statements are issued, the balances that are used in the ratios can change dramatically, altering the ratios. Assume, for example, that C&C borrowed $200,000 on a five-year note on January 2, 2017. The company's cash balance would increase to $207,752 and its long-term debt balance would increase to $480,000. Overnight, this new debt would raise the current ratio from 1.93 to 2.22, and the debt-to-equity ratio from 1.04 to 1.26. Recognize, then, that an analysis that is based on available financial statements may not reflect current reality.

The choice of accounting policies must be considered when comparing two or more companies that do not use the same accounting methods. A company that is using a first-in, first-out inventory policy can report very different inventory and cost of goods sold amounts from a company that is using a last-in, first-out inventory policy, even if there is no difference in the underlying companies' operational performance. The choice of depreciation method can also affect a company's ratios. What may look like a difference in performance may be only a difference in accounting policy.

Finally, a single ratio for a single year is not a sufficient indicator of a company's financial health. To develop an adequate understanding of a company, you need to analyze a company's results over multiple years, to discover the underlying trends. You also need to compare the company to other companies in the same industry, as well as to industry averages or standards. Such an intercompany analysis may reveal that a company that looked good in isolation does not stack up so well against its competitors, or vice versa. Only then will you know how well the company has really performed.

UNIT 12.3 REVIEW

KEY TERMS

Accounts receivable turnover p. 646
Acid-test ratio p. 646
Average collection period p. 646
Average days to sell inventory p. 648
Current ratio p. 644
Debt ratio p. 650
Debt-to-equity ratio p. 650
Dividend payout ratio p. 655
Earnings per share p. 654
Factor p. 649
Financial leverage p. 650
Gross margin percentage p. 652
Inventory turnover p. 648
Liquidity p. 644
Price/earnings (P/E) ratio p. 654
Quick ratio p. 646
Ratio analysis p. 643
Return on assets p. 652
Return on common stockholders' equity p. 653
Times interest earned ratio p. 651
Working capital p. 644

PRACTICE QUESTIONS

1. LO 3 Sand Company has an acid-test ratio of 0.60. Which of the following actions would improve the ratio?
   a. Collect accounts receivable
   b. Acquire inventory on account
   c. Sell equipment for cash
   d. Use cash to pay off a current liability

2. LO 3 Which of the following ratios helps users to assess a company's ability to meet currently maturing (short-term) obligations?
   a. Current ratio
   b. Debt-to-equity
   c. Both the current and the debt-to-equity ratios
   d. Neither the current ratio nor the debt-to-equity ratio

3. LO 3 (CMA adapted) Volpone Company reported the following sales data in its year-end financial statements.

	2017	2016
Net sales	$6,205,000	$5,175,000
Accounts receivable	350,000	320,000

Based on this data, Volpone's average collection period for 2017 is

a. 18.9 days.
c. 19.7 days.
b. 19.4 days.
d. 21.2 days.

4. LO 3 (CMA adapted) Volpone Company reported the following inventory data in its year-end financial statements.

	2017	2016
Inventory	$ 960,000	$ 780,000
Cost of goods sold	4,380,000	3,976,000

Based on this data, Volpone's average days to sell inventory for 2017 is

a. 51.2 days.
c. 71.5 days.
b. 65.0 days.
d. 72.5 days.

5. LO 3 Which of the following is *not* a reason for a decrease in accounts receivable turnover?

a. The company may have changed its credit terms.
b. Obsolete inventory is building up.
c. Customers are not paying as fast as they once did.
d. All of the above.

6. LO 3 If inventory turnover is increasing, then

a. obsolete inventory may be building up.
b. the company has increased the quantity of inventory on hand.
c. the number of days to sell inventory is decreasing.
d. all of the above.

7. LO 3 Which of the following ratios helps users to assess a company's ability to meet its long-term obligations?

a. Times interest earned
b. Return on assets
c. Both times interest earned and return on assets
d. Neither times interest earned nor return on assets

8. LO 3 Townhall Productions' dividend payout ratio is 25%. If the annual dividend is $20 per share, what is Townhall's earnings per share?

a. $4
b. $5
c. $80
d. $100

UNIT 12.3 PRACTICE EXERCISE

Refer to the income statement in Unit 12.1 Practice Exercise and the balance sheet in Unit 12.2 Practice Exercise to calculate the following ratios for the year ended December 31, 2015:

1. Current ratio
2. Acid-test (quick) ratio
3. Average collection period
4. Average days to sell inventory
5. Debt ratio
6. Debt-to-equity ratio
7. Times interest earned ratio
8. Gross margin percentage
9. Return on assets (tax rate = 35%)
10. Return on common stockholders' equity
11. Earnings per share (215,498 thousand average shares outstanding)
12. Price/earnings ratio (year-end market price $41.64)

SELECTED UNIT 12.3 ANSWERS

Think About It 12.3

Management can start charging interest to customers who don't pay within 30 days. They can also refuse to extend credit to customers who are habitually late, and offer a discount to customers who pay within 10 days. The potential consequence of a late charge and a refusal to extend credit is lost sales. C&C's management needs to determine what credit conditions competitors are offering before changing the company's credit terms. Regarding the discount, customers might pay faster, but the discount will reduce the cash C&C ultimately collects.

Think About It 12.4

Management should not want the current and acid-test ratios to be as high as possible because current assets do not generate a return (with the exception of marketable securities). Instead, excess cash should be invested in productive assets, like equipment or human capital. Current assets need to be just high enough to meet the company's short-term obligations as they come due, with a slight cushion for unexpected events.

Think About It 12.5

Mature companies are likely to have a higher dividend payout than growth companies. Growth companies need to retain their earnings to invest in operations. Retired investors are more likely to prefer companies with a high dividend payout. They are more likely than young investors to need the dividend income.

Practice Questions

1. C
2. A
3. C
4. D
5. B
6. C
7. A
8. C

Unit 12.3 Practice Exercise

1. $\dfrac{\$1,498,763}{\$478,810} = 3.13$

2. $\dfrac{\$129,852 + \$433,638}{\$478,810} = 1.18$

3. $\dfrac{\$3,963,313}{(\$433,638 + \$279,835)/2} = 11.1 \text{ times}; \quad \dfrac{365}{11.1} = 32.9 \text{ days}$

4. $\dfrac{\$2,057,766}{(\$783,031 + \$536,714)/2} = 3.1 \text{ times}; \quad \dfrac{365}{3.1} = 117.7 \text{ days}$

5. $\dfrac{\$1,200,678}{\$2,868,900} = 41.9\%$

6. $\dfrac{\$1,200,678}{\$1,668,222} = .72$

7. $\dfrac{\$232,573 + \$154,112 + \$14,628}{\$14,628} = 27.4 \text{ times}$

8. $\dfrac{\$1,905,547}{\$3,963,313} = 48.1\%$

9. $\dfrac{\$232,573 + (14,628 \times [1 - .35])}{(\$2,868,900 + \$2,095,083)/2} = 9.8\%$

10. $\dfrac{\$232,573}{(\$1,668,222 + \$1,350,300)/2} = 15.4\%$

11. $\dfrac{\$232,573}{215,498 \text{ thousand shares}} = \$1.88 \text{ per share}$

12. $\dfrac{\$35.90}{\$1.08} = 38.6$

UNIT 12.4

Industry Analysis

GUIDED UNIT PREPARATION

Answering the following questions while you read this unit will guide your understanding of the key concepts found in the unit. The questions are linked to the learning objectives presented at the beginning of the chapter.

LO 4

1. Name two sources of industry data.
2. Why are some companies hard to classify using SIC or NAICS codes?
3. What would you hope to learn by comparing a company's performance to industry data?

After completing a horizontal and vertical analysis of a company and studying its financial statement ratios, you should compare the company's results to those of other companies in the same industry. Doing so will help you understand the company's performance relative to that of its competitors. In this unit we will explore some sources of such comparative data.

Published Industry Ratio Analyses

Several sources offer information on ratio analyses of particular industries, most of which are compiled annually. The Risk Management Association publishes its *Annual Statement Studies: Financial Ratio Benchmarks*. Other pertinent publications include Dun & Bradstreet's *Industry Norms and Key Business Ratios* and the *Almanac of Business and Industrial Financial Ratios,* by Leo Troy. These publications provide financial ratios for key industries, as well as condensed common-size balance sheets and income statements. The analyses are divided into several categories based on sales revenue and total assets so that readers can select companies of comparable size.

These publications are organized by industry, as defined by either the Standard Industrial Classification (SIC) code or North American Industry Classification System (NAICS) code. The SIC system was developed in 1939 and 1940 and has been revised several times since then. It assigns a two-digit code to major industry groups and then further identifies specific industries by a four-digit code.[1] For example, Major Group 23 is "Apparel and Other Finished Products Made from Fabrics and Similar Materials," and C&C is classified under SIC code 2329 for "Men's and Boys Clothing not Elsewhere Classified."

The NAICS codes, a joint project of the United States, Canada, and Mexico, were first published in 1997. Because this system recognizes changes that have occurred in the global economy since 1940, it provides greater consistency in the classification of firms within industries. As a result, the six-digit NAICS codes are replacing SIC codes in government statistical reporting.[2] C&C Sports is

REALITY CHECK—*Growing strong farms*

© Larysa Dodz/iStockphoto

Remember when your parents told you that drinking milk would help your bones to grow strong? Well, how does the dairy farmer who produces that milk help the farm to grow strong? One tool the farmer uses is financial ratio analysis.

After a financial crisis hit the farming industry in the 1980s, the Farm Financial Standards Task Force developed a set of financial statement guidelines that included 16 key financial ratios. The guidelines provided benchmarks against which farmers could compare their own performance. For instance, the task force recommended a current ratio of between 1.5 and 2.0, a debt ratio of less than 40%, and a debt-to-equity ratio of less than 0.67.

How does today's farm compare to these guidelines? An Iowa State University report on 22 beef producers found a high degree of variability among them. Though the farms' current ratios averaged 2.1, they ranged from a low of 0.4 to a high of 8.7. Return on equity averaged 9.3%, within a range of −8.1% to 45.9%.

Two key measures for dairy farms are pounds of milk per cow and milk income per cow.

Ratio analysis isn't limited to the farmers' financial statements, however. Dairy farmers can also monitor their performance by applying ratio analysis to their operational data. Two key measures for dairy farms are pounds of milk per cow (the benchmark is at least 17,500) and milk income per cow (the benchmark is at least $2,100).

Sources: John Berry, "Calculating the 'Sweet 16' Farm Financial Measures," Penn State University College of Agricultural Sciences, http://extension.psu.edu/business/farm/management/financial-management/topics/calculating-the-sweet-16-farm-financial-measures (accessed July 14, 2016); Richard D. Duvick, "Farm Financial Records: What Is Needed and How to Get Them," *Computerized Farm Record Keeping Bulletin 890-01* (Columbus: Ohio State University), http://ohioline.osu.edu/b890/b890_20.html (accessed February 17, 2013, site now discontinued); Ralph Mayer, *Financial Benchmarks for Beef Producers*, 2001 Beef Research Report A.S. Leaflet R1752 (Ames: Iowa State University, 2001); Larry F. Tranel and Gary Frank, *Managing Dairy Farm Finances*, ISU Extension Publication LT-105 (Ames: Iowa State University, 2002).

classified under industry 315280, "Other Cut and Sew Apparel Manufacturing." Exhibit 12-9 reports selected percentages and statistics drawn on C&C's industry from Dun and Bradstreet's Key Business Ratios and Risk Management Association's *Annual Statement Studies: Financial Ratio Benchmarks*.

While it is relatively easy to determine C&C's industry under either the SIC or the NAICS system, that is not the case for many companies. Consider General Electric, which you may think is in the light bulb business. GE does make light bulbs, but the company also makes locomotives, automotive bumper systems, aircraft engines, and magnetic resonance imaging (MRI) equipment. It even has a large financing division. No single SIC or NAICS code captures General Electric's business, nor that of any other conglomerate. Even smaller companies that operate in more than one distinct industry are difficult to classify.

Industry Statistics

Developing an understanding of a company's competitive environment is an important part of a financial analysis. Numerous resources are available to assist in this task. The U.S. government is a good source of industry data, much of which is available on the Internet. For example, the U.S. Census Bureau collects a wide array of statistics and makes them available on its website, http://www.census.gov/. Using the Census Bureau's *Annual Survey of Manufactures*, C&C's managers could determine the size of their market. Since this survey does not show baseball

	2014	2013	2012	2011	2010
Select Common-Size Percentages:[1]					
Cash & equivalents	9.6%	7.2%	7.9%	8.0%	8.4%
Trade receivables, net	25.7%	24.3%	25.0%	23.1%	22.0%
Inventory	36.7%	41.0%	40.5%	41.2%	41.2%
Property and equipment	11.9%	13.2%	10.7%	11.1%	13.3%
Short-term debt	13.4%	14.3%	13.7%	13.5%	16.2%
Trade payables	16.8%	17.1%	17.1%	17.5%	15.2%
Long-term debt	6.9%	11.8%	9.6%	10.1%	12.2%
Stockholders' equity	42.3%	35.2%	40.3%	39.7%	33.2%
Gross profit	34.9%	35.2%	37.6%	37.7%	36.3%
Operating expenses	29.8%	30.9%	31.3%	31.4%	32.0%
Operating income	5.1%	4.3%	6.3%	6.3%	4.3%
Income before taxes	4.3%	3.3%	5.7%	5.7%	3.8%
Select Ratios:	2014	2013	2012	2011	2010
Current ratio	2.0	2.0	1.8	1.8	1.8
Quick ratio (Acid test)	.7	.7	.7	.7	1.0
Average collection period	38 days	37 days	36 days	38 days	38 days
Inventory turnover	4.1 times	3.5 times	3.9 times	3.5 times	4.1 times
Debt-to-equity	1.2	1.8	1.4	1.8	1.3
Return on assets[2]	5.5%	6.9%	9.1%	7.9%	9.3%
Return on stockholders' equity[2]	15.8%	18.6%	28.1%	18.9%	24.0%

[1]Risk Management Association's 2013/2014 *Annual Statement Studies: Financial Ratio Benchmarks*, NCAIS 315280.
[2]Based on income before taxes rather than net income.

EXHIBIT 12-9 *C&C sports industry data*

uniforms as a separate category, the managers must look at the market for men's and boys' team sports uniforms as a whole. As shown in Exhibit 12-10, shipments of these uniforms have been somewhat cyclical—increasing to 2003 and then falling to 2006, increasing to 2008 and then falling to 2011, and finally increasing

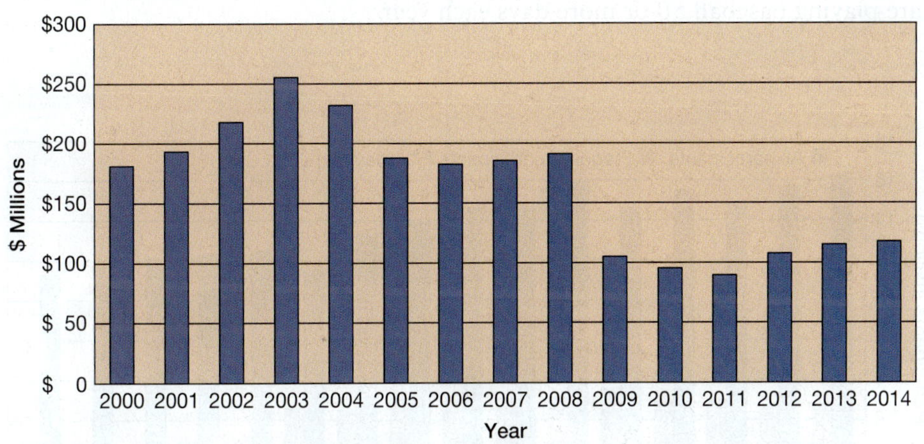

EXHIBIT 12-10

Value of U.S. men's and boys' team sports uniform shipments.

Sources: U.S. Census Bureau, *Annual Survey of Manufactures Value of Product Shipments: 2001*; U.S. Census Bureau, *Annual Survey of Manufactures Value of Product Shipments: 2004*; U.S. Census Bureau, *Annual Survey of Manufactures Value of Product Shipments: 2006*; U.S. Census Bureau, *Annual Survey of Manufactures Value of Product Shipments: 2008*; U.S. Census Bureau, *Annual Survey of Manufactures Value of Product Shipments: 2010*; U.S. Census Bureau, *Annual Survey of Manufactures Value of Shipments: 2011*; U.S. Census Bureau, *Annual Survey of Manufactures Value of Shipments: 2014*.

to 2014. The decrease in shipments in 2009 was particularly dramatic, possibly a result of the general declining economic conditions in the United States and the resulting lower consumer disposable incomes.

Industry statistics are also available from professional research and consulting organizations. Many investment firms employ analysts who specialize in a particular industry and write research reports and forecasts. IBISWorld, a leading provider of industry research and analysis reports, estimates that men's and boys' team sports uniforms account for 11.5% of the $1.1 billion Costume and Team Uniform Manufacturing industry (NAICS 31529). The market for team uniforms has been steady for the past five years, and there is little projected growth in the coming years. IBISWorld reports that manufacturers of these uniforms have largely moved manufacturing from the United States to countries that offer lower wage rates. Imports satisfied 78.3% of total U.S. demand in 2015, although this level is expected to decrease in the next few years as U.S. manufacturers increase domestic production levels. A bright spot for the team uniform industry is that many of the new high-tech specialty fabrics used in uniforms are produced primarily in the United States, which supports a healthy niche of domestic manufacturers that produce custom team uniforms using these materials.[3]

Consumers are willing to pay a higher price for a uniform that is durable and of high quality. Firms that provide a high level of customer service by producing special orders and making timely deliveries can establish a competitive advantage. While the majority of uniforms are sold through retail outlets, Internet sales are growing and becoming a more important sales channel.

Understanding the size of the potential market is important when evaluating a company's future prospects. Trade associations such as The Sports and Fitness Industry Association (SFIA) are a good source for this type of specific information. SFIA reported that in 2012 baseball was the second most popular team sport in the United States, based on total number of participants.[4] According to statistics reported by the Sports Business Research Network (SBRnet) and shown in Exhibit 12-11, the number of people playing baseball has been in gradual decline since 2004.[5] This decline has also been reflected in Little League Baseball[6] and high school baseball.[7] SBRnet also reports that 53% of baseball players in 2014 were between the ages of 7 and 17, and 49% of the players lived in a household with income of at least $75,000. The vast majority (78.6%) of players are male, and there has been recent growth in the number of people who are playing baseball 50 or more days each year.

EXHIBIT 12-11

U.S. participants in team baseball, 7 years of age or older, at least once per year.

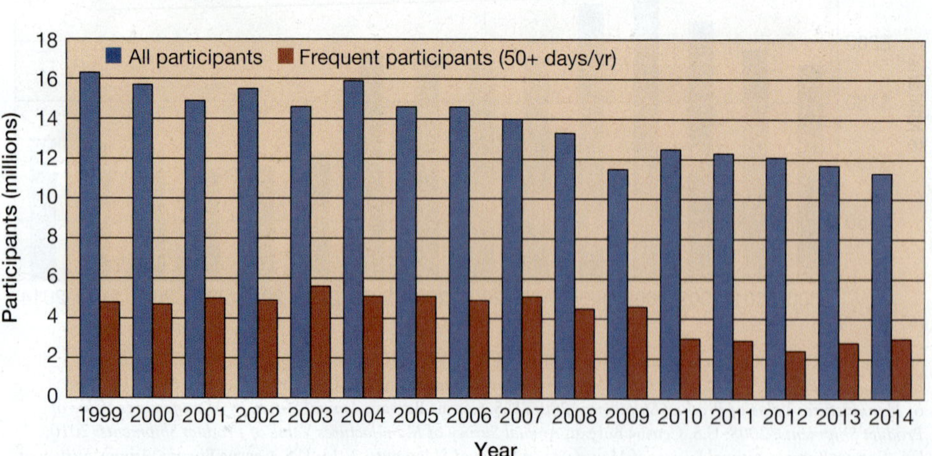

Source: Sports Business Research Network, *Baseball: Participation by Total vs. Frequent*

The final task in preparing an industry analysis is to look at the major competitors. Doing so means conducting horizontal, vertical, and ratio analyses based on their financial statements, which can be found in published annual reports or in required SEC 10-K and 10-Q filings, if the companies are traded publicly. SEC filings are available online at http://sec.gov/edgar.shtml. Other useful sources of data on competitors are Value Line, Hoover's, www.corporateinformation.com, and Mergent.

THINK ABOUT IT 12.6

C&C Sports is a small player in the athletic apparel industry. Why would C&C's president and other managers want to read published data on their industry?

UNIT 12.4 REVIEW

PRACTICE QUESTIONS

1. LO 3, 4 If Grant Company's debt-to-equity ratio is 1.3 and the industry average is 1.0, what can you conclude?
   a. Grant Company can borrow money more easily than the average company in the industry.
   b. Grant Company has more long-term debt than the average company in the industry.
   c. Grant Company is more highly leveraged than the average company in the industry.
   d. Grant Company has issued less common stock than the average company in the industry.
2. LO 4 Companies should wait for the publication of industry statistics before making major changes in their operations. True or False?

UNIT 12.4 PRACTICE EXERCISE

Compare C&C Sports' common-size financial statements (see Exhibits 12-5 and 12-6) and ratios (see Exhibit 12-8) to the industry averages in Exhibit 12-9.

Required

1. Comment on the common-size assets. For example, C&C's cash balance is much lower than the industry average. What might the differences mean for C&C?
2. Comment on the common-size liabilities and equity.
3. Comment on the common-size income statement items.
4. Comment on the financial ratios.

SELECTED UNIT 12.4 ANSWERS

Think About It 12.6

Keeping up with industry trends and data gives C&C some benchmarks for evaluating its performance. While C&C Sports might seem to be isolated in Brownsville, Texas, it is important for managers to understand their competitors and how they operate. Furthermore, trends in the demand for athletic apparel will trickle down to C&C Sports, so managers will need to be prepared to accommodate customers' needs. Because these data are not available right away—it takes time to compile and publish statistics—the sales force and upper management need to maintain close relationships with customers, who will help them to anticipate changes in demand.

Practice Questions

1. C
2. False

Unit 12.4 Practice Exercise

1. C&C holds much less cash and more accounts receivable than the average company in the industry. Inventory holdings are lower than average; property and equipment are more than twice as high as the average. The point of holding assets is to generate a return. Ratio analysis will tell us whether C&C is making good use of these assets.
2. Short-term debt is lower, and long-term debt is higher, than the industry average. If C&C is going to incur debt to support its operations, management needs to choose the type of debt that offers the most flexibility and the lowest interest rate. Since C&C's equity percentage is higher than average, we can assume that the company has a lower overall level of debt than the average firm in the industry.
3. C&C's gross profit is lower than the industry average, meaning that its cost of goods sold must be higher. To remain competitive, C&C may need to increase its gross profit percentage. On the other hand, operating expenses are lower than the industry average. C&C's operating income and income before taxes are only about half of the industry average.
4. C&C's liquidity measures are close to the industry average. Its current ratio is lower than the industry average, while its acid-test ratio is above the industry average. The company holds a higher percentage of accounts receivable than the industry average, and its average collection period is about 4 days longer than the industry average. The debt-to-equity ratio shows that C&C is less leveraged than the average firm in the industry. The two ratios in Exhibit 12-9 labeled return on assets and return on common stockholders' equity are actually calculated a little differently from the way you have learned, demonstrating that you must always know how a ratio has been calculated before making comparisons. The industry ratios should be compared to $\frac{\$158{,}287}{(\$1{,}870{,}787 + \$1{,}797{,}275)/2} = 8.63\%$ and $\frac{\$158{,}287}{(\$917{,}436 + \$806{,}635)/2} = 18.36\%$, respectively.

   Both of these ratios exceed those of the average firm in the industry.

BUSINESS DECISION AND CONTEXT Wrap Up

In the chapter opener, several stakeholders in C&C Sports had questions about the company's financial future. George Douglas, president of C&C, questioned the firm's overall performance, and specifically its credit policy. While he believes that the company is in reasonably good shape, he knows that he has to address the cash flow problems right away.

Cedric Renn wondered if C&C would have the financial stability to offer him a long-term career. He concluded that since the company is profitable and participation in team baseball has seen an uptick in recent years, he is willing to give C&C Sports serious consideration. With the increased emphasis in Internet sales for the industry as a whole, he is excited to work for a company with multiple distribution channels.

Meredith Lincoln pondered whether her company, Brazos Buttons, should increase C&C's line of credit. C&C is handling its debt obligations well right now, though the company's liquidity concerns her. Before making any final decisions, she is going to talk to Claire Elliot, C&C's vice president for finance and administration, to be sure the company has a plan in place to deal with its cash issues.

Many of these and other questions about C&C's performance can be answered using the financial statement analyses developed in this chapter. Cedric and Meredith will have only that financial information available to them, while George will have an abundance of other operational data not available to the general public. Instead of relying exclusively on the annual financial statements, George will need to look more deeply into the company's operations. However, he shouldn't lose sight of how outsiders view his company.

CHAPTER SUMMARY

In this chapter you learned how to analyze financial statements. Specifically, you should be able to meet the objectives set out at the beginning of the chapter:

1. ***Prepare a horizontal analysis of a balance sheet and income statement and use it to analyze a company's performance. (Unit 12.1)***

   A horizontal analysis shows the dollar changes in a company's account balances from one year to the next. The percentage changes are calculated using the formula:

$$\frac{\text{Current year account balance} - \text{Previous year account balance}}{\text{Previous year account balance}}$$

2. ***Prepare a common-size balance sheet and income statement and use them to analyze a company's performance. (Unit 12.2)***

   Common-size financial statements show all the company's account balances as a percentage of a particular total. On the balance sheet, all accounts are shown as a percentage of total assets. On the income statement, all accounts are shown as a percentage of net sales.

3. ***Calculate and interpret basic financial statement ratios. (Unit 12.3)***

   There are four types of financial ratios. **Liquidity ratios** measure a company's ability to manage its current assets and current liabilities. These ratios include working capital, current ratio, acid-test (quick) ratio, accounts receivable turnover, average collection period, inventory turnover, and average days to sell inventory. **Leverage ratios** measure a company's ability to meet its debt obligations. These ratios include the debt ratio, debt-to-equity ratio, and times interest earned. **Profitability ratios** measure how well a company can generate a profit or return on an investment. These ratios include gross margin, return on assets, and return on common stockholders' equity. **Market measure ratios**, which are valid only for publicly traded companies, measure how well a company's stock is performing as an investment. These ratios include earnings per share, price/earnings ratio, and dividend payout ratio. Exhibit 12-8 summarizes the financial ratios.

4. ***Explain how to use sources of industry information to draw conclusions about a company's performance. (Unit 12.4)***

   To compare a company's performance to that of competitors, you must first determine its industry category. All businesses can be categorized by industry, using either a four-digit SIC code or a six-digit NAICS code. Statistics on specific categories, including common-size statements and financial ratios, are available from various sources such as Dun & Bradstreet's *Industry Norms and Financial Ratio Benchmarks* and the Risk Management Association's *Annual Statement Studies: Financial Ratio Benchmarks.* Using ratio analysis and information acquired from these sources, you can develop a thorough knowledge of industry trends and future outlooks, which you can use to evaluate your company's performance.

KEY TERMS

Accounts receivable turnover (Unit 12.3)
Acid-test ratio (Unit 12.3)
Average collection period (Unit 12.3)
Average days to sell inventory (Unit 12.3)
Common-size analysis (Unit 12.2)
Current ratio (Unit 12.3)
Debt ratio (Unit 12.3)
Debt-to-equity ratio (Unit 12.3)
Dividend payout ratio (Unit 12.3)
Earnings per share (Unit 12.3)
Factor (Unit 12.3)
Financial leverage (Unit 12.3)
Gross margin percentage (Unit 12.3)
Horizontal analysis (Unit 12.1)
Inventory turnover (Unit 12.3)
Liquidity (Unit 12.3)
Price/earnings ratio (Unit 12.3)
Quick ratio (Unit 12.3)
Ratio analysis (Unit 12.3)
Return on assets (Unit 12.3)
Return on common stockholders' equity (Unit 12.3)
Times interest earned ratio (Unit 12.3)
Trend analysis (Unit 12.1)
Vertical analysis (Unit 12.2)
Working capital (Unit 12.3)

EXERCISES

12-1 Preparing a horizontal analysis (LO 1) The current asset portion of Darden Restaurants, Inc.'s balance sheet is as follows (in $millions).

	Fiscal Year Ended	
	May 31, 2015	**May 25, 2014**
Current assets:		
Cash and cash equivalents	$ 535.90	$ 98.30
Receivables, net	78.00	83.80
Inventories	163.90	196.80
Prepaid income taxes	18.90	10.90
Prepaid expenses and other current assets	69.40	71.70
Deferred income taxes	157.40	124.00
Assets held for sale	32.90	1,390.30
Total current assets	$1,056.40	$1,975.80

Required

Prepare a horizontal analysis of Darden Restaurants' current assets, rounding your answers to one decimal place.

12-2 Using horizontal analysis (LO 1) In a press release, Logitech, a manufacturer of computer peripherals, announced that sales revenue for the most recent fiscal year had increased 21% over the previous year. If sales revenue for the year was reported at $1.8 billion, what level of sales revenue was achieved in the previous fiscal year?

12-3 Preparing a trend analysis (LO 1) Six Flags Entertainment Corp. reported the following revenue data (in $000s) in its 2015 annual report.

Revenues	2015	2014	2013	2012	2011
Theme park admissions	$687,819	$641,535	$602,204	$576,708	$541,744
Theme park food, merchandise, and other	500,190	460,131	448,547	437,382	413,844
Sponsorship, licensing, and other fees	59,133	57,250	42,149	39,977	42,380
Accommodations	16,796	16,877	17,000	16,265	15,206

Required

Prepare a trend analysis of Six Flags' revenue sources, rounding your answers to one decimal place. Comment on any significant trends you identify.

12-4 Preparing a common-size income statement (LO 2) Chipotle Mexican Grill began with a single location in 1993 and now operates more than 1,700 restaurants. Adapted versions of the company's income statements (in $000s) are as follows:

	2015	2014
Revenue	$4,501,223	$4,108,269
Restaurant operating costs		
Food, beverage, and packaging	1,503,835	1,420,994
Labor	1,045,726	904,407
Occupancy	262,412	230,868
Other operating costs	514,963	434,244
General and administrative expenses	250,214	273,897
Depreciation and amortization	130,368	110,474
Pre-opening costs	16,922	15,609
Loss on disposal of assets	13,194	6,976
Total operating expenses	3,737,634	3,397,469
Income from operations	763,589	710,800
Interest and other income (expense), net	6,278	3,503
Income before income taxes	769,867	714,303
Provision for income taxes	294,265	268,929
Net income	$ 475,602	$ 445,374

Required

Prepare a common-size income statement for each year, rounding your answers to one decimal place. Your answers may not add perfectly due to rounding.

12-5 Common-size analysis (LO 2) Leslie's Burgers operates and franchises fast-food restaurants specializing in grilled hamburgers and chicken sandwiches. The 2015 and 2016 income statements are as follows (in $000s):

	Year Ended	
	December 31, 2016	December 31, 2015
Total revenues	$41,001	$40,183
Expenses		
Cost of restaurant sales	11,125	11,066
Restaurant operating expenses	16,898	16,726
General and administrative	6,818	5,280
Advertising	2,547	2,652
Depreciation and amortization	2,206	2,096
Impairment of long-lived assets	986	0
Total expenses	40,580	37,820
Operating income	$ 421	$ 2,363

Required

a. Prepare a common-size analysis of this section of Leslie's Burgers' income statement. Express all percentages using one decimal place. Your answers may not add perfectly due to rounding.

b. One obvious reason that operating income dropped significantly in 2016 is the impairment of long-lived assets. What other operating issues do you believe contributed to the decline in operating income?

12-6 Preparing a common-size balance sheet (LO 2) Chipotle Mexican Grill began with a single location in 1993 and now operates more than 1,700 restaurants. Adapted versions of the company's balance sheets (in $000) follow.

	Dec. 31, 2015	Dec. 31, 2014
Assets		
Current assets:		
Cash and cash equivalents	$ 248,005	$ 419,465
Accounts receivable	38,283	34,839
Inventory	15,043	15,332
Prepaid expenses and other current assets	39,965	34,795
Income tax receivable	58,152	16,488
Investments	415,199	338,592
Total current assets	814,647	859,511
Property, plant, and equipment, net	1,217,220	1,106,984
Long-term investments	622,939	496,106
Other assets	70,260	64,716
Total assets	$ 2,725,066	$2,527,317
Liabilities and shareholders' equity		
Current liabilities:		
Accounts payable	$ 85,709	$ 69,613
Accrued payroll and benefits	64,958	73,894
Accrued liabilities	129,275	102,203
Total current liabilities	279,942	245,710
Deferred liabilities	284,267	240,975
Other liabilities	32,883	28,263
Total liabilities	597,092	514,948
Shareholders' equity:		
Common stock	358	354
Additional paid-in capital	1,172,628	1,038,932
Treasury stock	(1,234,612)	(748,759)
Accumulated other comprehensive income (loss)	(8,273)	(429)
Retained earnings	2,197,873	1,722,271
Total shareholders' equity	2,127,974	2,012,369
Total liabilities and shareholders' equity	$ 2,725,066	$2,527,317

Required

Prepare a common-size balance sheet for each fiscal year, rounding all percentages to one decimal place. Your answers may not add perfectly due to rounding.

12-7 Ratio analysis (LO 3) Martha Bennett recently inherited \$100,000 from her grandmother and is evaluating several investment opportunities. One company she is looking at is Keating Genomics, a company in the health care industry. To satisfy an assignment in her managerial accounting course, Martha has decided to prepare an analysis of Keating using ratio analysis. During her analysis, she discovers that the company sold its ownership interest in MedRegs in 2016. Keating has reported the results of these operations in the income statement under discontinued operations. A portion of Keating's adapted income statement (in \$000) follows.

	2016	2015
Net income from continuing operations	\$ 899	\$4,593
Income (loss) from discontinued operations	4,482	(433)
Net income	\$5,381	\$4,160

Required

Which income amount should Martha use when she calculates ratios that involve net income? Why?

12-8 Calculating liquidity ratios (LO 3) Matthias Medical manufactures hospital beds and other institutional furniture. The company's comparative balance sheet and income statement for 2015 and 2016 follow.

Matthias Medical
Comparative Balance Sheet
As of December 31

	2016	2015
Assets		
Current assets		
Cash	\$ 382,600	\$ 417,400
Accounts receivable, net	1,065,370	776,400
Inventory	717,000	681,000
Other current assets	381,300	247,000
Total current assets	2,546,270	2,121,800
Property, plant, & equipment, net	8,678,000	8,440,100
Total assets	\$11,224,270	\$10,561,900
Liabilities and Stockholders' Equity		
Current liabilities	\$ 3,162,800	\$ 2,846,000
Long-term debt	3,702,600	3,892,600
Total liabilities	6,865,400	6,738,600
Preferred stock, \$5 par value	58,900	58,900
Common stock, \$0.25 par value	104,600	103,800
Retained earnings	4,195,370	3,660,600
Total stockholders' equity	4,358,870	3,823,300
Total liabilities and stockholders' equity	\$11,224,270	\$10,561,900

Matthias Medical
Comparative Income Statement and Statement of Retained Earnings
For the Year

	2016	2015
Sales revenue (all on account)	$10,177,200	$ 9,613,900
Cost of goods sold	5,611,600	5,298,700
Gross profit	4,565,600	4,315,200
Operating expenses	2,840,200	2,634,100
Net operating income	1,725,400	1,681,100
Interest expense	300,300	308,600
Net income before taxes	1,425,100	1,372,500
Income taxes (30%)	427,530	411,750
Net income	$ 997,570	$ 960,750
Dividends paid		
Preferred dividends	29,450	29,450
Common dividends	433,350	413,000
Total dividends paid	462,800	442,450
Net income retained	534,770	518,300
Retained earnings, beginning of year	3,660,600	3,142,300
Retained earnings, end of year	$ 4,195,370	$ 3,660,600

Required

Calculate the following liquidity ratios for 2016.

a. Working capital
b. Current ratio
c. Acid-test ratio
d. Accounts receivable turnover
e. Average collection period
f. Inventory turnover
g. Average days to sell inventory

12-9 Calculating leverage ratios (LO 3) Refer to Matthias Medical's financial statements, presented in Exercise 12-8.

Required

Calculate the following leverage ratios for 2016.

a. Debt ratio
b. Debt-to-equity ratio
c. Times interest earned ratio

12-10 Calculating profitability ratios (LO 3) Refer to Matthias Medical's financial statements, presented in Exercise 12-8.

Required

Calculate the following profitability ratios for 2016.

a. Gross margin percentage
b. Return on assets
c. Return on common stockholders' equity

12-11 Calculating market measure ratios (LO 3) Refer to Matthias Medical's financial statements, presented in Exercise 12-8.

Required

Calculate the following market measure ratios for 2016.

a. Earnings per share (average of 418,000 shares outstanding for the year)
b. Price/earnings ratio (market price of $45 at year-end)
c. Dividend payout ratio (dividends of $1.04 per common share for the year)

12-12 Industry identification (LO 4) Identify the Standard Industrial Classification (SIC) codes for the following companies using the Security and Exchange Commission's EDGAR database at: http://www.sec.gov/edgar/searchedgar/companysearch.html. Include both the name and the number for each SIC code.

a. Crocs, Inc.
b. Home Depot
c. Gap, Inc.
d. IBM
e. Ford Motor Company
f. Steinway Musical Instruments

12-13 Financial ratios and industry comparison (LO 3, 4) Kendra Massey is trying to decide how to invest a recent windfall inheritance. Because she considers herself a fashionista, her first thought was to look at two of her favorite stores, Nordstrom and Macy's. Kendra visited each company's website and calculated the following ratios based on the financial statements she found there. She also found some industry averages to use as a comparison.

	Macy's		Nordstrom		Industry Average	
	2015	2014	2015	2014	2015	2014
Current ratio	1.34	1.69	1.04	1.87	1.90	1.70
Acid-test ratio	0.29	0.53	0.27	1.12	0.50	0.60
Accounts receivable turnover	55.2 times	65.2 times	11.3 times	5.9 times	40.8 times	56.4 times
Average collection period	6.6 days	5.6 days	32.3 days	61.9 days	8.9 days	6.5 days
Inventory turnover	3.02 times	3.07 times	4.99 times	5.15 times	3.20 times	4.10 times
Average days to sell inventory	120.9 days	118.9 days	73.1 days	70.9 days	114.1 days	88.8 days

Required

a. Which of the two companies has the stronger liquidity position?
b. How do the companies' positions compare to the industry averages?

PROBLEMS

12-14 Comparing companies of different size (LO 2) Dollar Tree Stores, Inc., and Dollar General Corporation are both discount retailers. As their adapted income statements (in $ millions) show, Dollar General's sales revenue was more than double that of Dollar Tree.

	Dollar Tree	Dollar General
Sales	$6,630.5	$14,807.2
Cost of goods sold	4,252.2	10,109.3
Gross profit	2,378.3	4,697.9
Selling, general, & administrative expenses	1,596.2	3,207.1
Net operating income	782.1	1,490.8
Other expense	2.6	265.5
Income before taxes	779.5	1,225.3
Income tax expense	291.2	458.6
Net income	$ 488.3	$ 766.7

Required

a. Prepare a common-size income statement for each company. Express all percentages using one decimal place. Your answers may not add perfectly due to rounding.
b. Which company did the better job of managing expenses? How did you reach your conclusion?

12-15 Analyzing accounts receivable (LO 3) The following information (in $ millions) was taken from recent annual reports of Kellogg Company and General Mills, Inc.

	Kellogg	General Mills
Sales revenue	$13,525	$17,630
Average accounts receivable balance	$ 1,310	$ 1,435

Required

a. Calculate each company's accounts receivable turnover and average collection period.
b. Which company is doing the best job of managing accounts receivable? How did you reach your conclusion?
c. What additional information would help you in assessing the companies' accounts receivable management?

12-16 Analyzing inventory (LO 3) The following information (in $ millions) was taken from the annual reports of two companies.

	Company A	Company B
Cost of goods sold	$27,303.1	$26,558.0
Average inventory	$ 2,758.1	$ 4,949.5

Required

a. Calculate each company's inventory turnover and average days to sell inventory.
b. The two companies are Safeway, Inc., a food and drug retailer, and Caterpillar, Inc., a manufacturer of heavy construction equipment. Which of these two companies is Company A? Which is Company B? How did you arrive at each company's identity?

12-17 Accounting principle choice and ratios (LO 3) Poston, Inc., and Victor Enterprises are competitors in the toy industry. Last year the companies' operations were identical, the only difference between them being that Poston uses the last-in, first-out inventory costing method and Victor uses the first-in, first-out method. Inventory prices increased during the year. The two companies reported the following amounts in their financial statements.

	Poston, Inc.	Victor Enterprises
Sales revenue	$17,000,000	$17,000,000
Cost of goods sold	$10,000,000	$ 9,500,000
Average inventory	$ 1,000,000	$ 1,250,000

Required

a. Which company had a higher inventory turnover?
b. If all the companies' results were identical, including the number of items sold and the number remaining in inventory, why do their inventory turnover ratios differ? Should the difference influence your evaluation of the two firms?

12-18 Financial leverage (LO 3) Selected account information (in $ millions) from Target Corporation's 2015 annual report follows. While the company has authorized the issuance of 5 million shares of preferred stock, none have been issued.

	2015	2014
Income from continuing operations	$ 3,321	$ 2,449
Total assets	$40,262	$41,172
Total common shareholders' equity	$12,957	$13,997

Required

a. Calculate Target Corporation's return on assets for 2015.
b. Calculate Target Corporation's return on common stockholders' equity for 2015.
c. Is Target Corporation's financial leverage positive or negative? How do you know?

12-19 Analyzing ratios (CMA adapted) (LO 3) Baldwin Industries, a manufacturer of construction equipment, is considering the purchase of KayNet Cables, one of its suppliers. Baldwin's board of directors has given preliminary approval for the purchase, and several discussions have taken place between the management of the two companies. In preparation for the discussions, KayNet provided its financial data for the past three years and its financial forecasts for the next three years. Baldwin's controller, Nora Jaynes, has analyzed KayNet's data and prepared the following ratio analysis, which compares KayNet's performance with the industry averages.

	2016	2015	2014	Industry Average
Return on assets	13.03%	13.02%	12.98%	12.96%
Average days to sell inventory	51.16 days	47.29 days	42.15 days	44.63 days
Times interest earned ratio	3.87	3.46	3.28	3.56
Price/earnings ratio	10.96	11.23	11.39	11.54
Debt-to-equity ratio	49.66	46.32	48.24	57.14
Accounts receivable turnover	6.98	7.23	7.83	7.78
Current ratio	2.05	2.35	2.10	2.30
Gross margin	30.11	30.18	29.67	29.85

Required

a. Assess KayNet's liquidity, citing strengths or problems.
b. Assess KayNet's profitability, citing strengths or problems.
c. Assess KayNet's leverage, citing strengths or problems.
d. Assess KayNet's market position, citing strengths or problems.
e. Based on your assessment, do you recommend that Baldwin go forward with its acquisition of KayNet? Why or why not?

12-20 Financial ratios and industry comparison (LO 3, 4) Wendy's International, Inc., and McDonald's Corporation, two leading fast-food chains, are classified in SIC code 5812—Eating Places. Recent results for each company, along with industry averages, follow.

	Wendy's	McDonald's	Industry Average
Return on assets	7.7%	9.9%	6.4%
Return on common stockholders' equity	11.9%	17.7%	14.0%
Net income as a percentage of sales	7.4%	12.7%	2.9%
Debt-to-equity ratio	.67	.98	1.04

a. Which company has the stronger profitability position? Why?
b. Which company uses more debt? Why?
c. How do Wendy's and McDonald's compare to the industry averages? Based on your analysis, would you consider these two companies to be industry leaders? Why or why not?
d. The industry data reported here represent Dun and Bradstreet's industry median. Dun and Bradstreet also reports industry norms for the upper quartile (top 25%) of companies in the industry. In the top quartile, return on assets was 15.1%, return on common stockholders' equity was 34.7%, and net income as a percentage of sales was 6.1%. Do you think it would be more useful to compare Wendy's and McDonald's to these upper-quartile industry averages rather than to the median averages? Why or why not?
e. Dun and Bradstreet also provides industry data based on companies' total assets. In the industry's largest reporting companies, the median return on assets was 5.1%,

the median return on common stockholders' equity was 9.7%, the median net income as a percentage was sales of 3.6%, and the median debt-to-equity ratio was 0.93. The upper quartile values were 8.4%, 16.4%, 5.2%, and 0.65, respectively. Given that Wendy's and McDonald's are among the largest companies in this industry group, does this data change your answers to questions (c) and (d)? Why or why not?

C&C SPORTS CONTINUING CASE

12-21 Comprehensive Financial Statement Analysis (LO 1, 2, 3, 4) Using Exhibit 12-9 as a guide, compare C&C Sports' performance to the industry averages. What particular observations and recommendations do you have for George Douglas, president of C&C Sports?

CASES

12-22 Comprehensive financial statement analysis (LO 1, 2, 3) Pippin Piping Co. manufactures decorative fabric trims. The company's financial statements follow.

Pippin Piping Co.
Comparative Income Statements
For the Years Ended December 31

	2016	2015	2014
Sales revenue	$576,600	$523,000	$484,200
Cost of goods sold	291,000	259,200	234,300
Gross margin	285,600	263,800	249,900
Operating expenses	106,200	104,600	104,100
Operating income	179,400	159,200	145,800
Other revenue	22,500	15,900	23,900
Interest expense	11,200	10,500	11,900
Income before income tax	190,700	164,600	157,800
Income tax expense (40%)	76,280	65,840	63,120
Net income	$114,420	$ 98,760	$ 94,680

Pippin Piping Co.
Comparative Balance Sheets
As of December 31

	2016	2015	2014
Assets			
Cash	$ 32,000	$ 25,800	$ 20,500
Accounts receivable (net)	126,860	127,000	94,300
Inventory	60,000	80,700	56,000
Prepaid expenses	11,000	10,000	4,600
Total current assets	229,860	243,500	175,400
Property & equipment (net)	668,900	576,000	540,300
Total Assets	$898,760	$819,500	$715,700

Liabilities and Stockholders' Equity			
Accounts payable	$ 53,120	$ 81,200	$ 79,100
Accrued expenses	11,000	12,240	41,700
Total current liabilities	64,120	93,440	120,800
Long-term debt	170,000	160,000	150,000
Total liabilities	234,120	253,440	270,800
Stockholders' Equity			
Common stock, $0.50 par value	6,000	6,000	5,000
Additional paid-in capital	99,000	99,000	62,000
Retained earnings	559,640	461,060	377,900
Total stockholders' equity	664,640	566,060	444,900
Total Liabilities and Stockholders' Equity	$898,760	$819,500	$715,700

Additional information

	2016	2015	2014
Closing stock price	$ 38	$ 35	$ 30
Shares outstanding	12,000	12,000	10,000
Dividends paid per share	$ 1.32	$ 1.30	$ 1.25

Required

a. Prepare a horizontal analysis for 2016. What significant changes do you see?

b. Prepare common-size financial statements for the three years. What significant changes do you see?

c. Assess Pippin's liquidity. Has it improved or deteriorated over the three-year period? How did you reach your conclusion? (For ratios that require average balances, only calculate ratios for 2015 and 2016.)

d. Assess Pippin's leverage. Has it improved or deteriorated over the three-year period? How did you reach your conclusion? (For ratios that require average balances, only calculate ratios for 2015 and 2016.)

e. Assess Pippin's profitability. Has it improved or deteriorated over the three-year period? How did you reach your conclusion? (For ratios that require average balances, only calculate ratios for 2015 and 2016.)

f. Is Pippin's financial leverage positive or negative? How do you know?

g. How does the market view Pippin? Has the market's outlook improved or deteriorated over the three-year period? How did you reach your conclusion?

12-23 Ratio analysis (LO 3) Haver Industries is a leading consumer products company. The company's adapted comparative balance sheets and income statements (in $ millions) follow.

Haver Industries
Comparative Income Statement
For the Years Ended December 31

	2016	2015	2014	2013	2012
Net sales revenue	$68,222	$56,741	$51,407	$43,377	$40,238
Cost of goods sold	33,125	27,872	25,076	22,141	20,989
Gross profit	35,097	28,869	26,331	21,236	19,249
Research & development expenses	2,075	1,940	1,802	1,665	—
Selling, general, & administrative expenses	19,773	16,460	14,702	11,718	12,052
Nonoperating income (expense)	283	346	152	238	(211)
Interest expense	1,119	834	629	561	603
Income before taxes	12,413	9,981	9,350	7,530	6,383
Income taxes	3,729	3,058	2,869	2,344	2,031
Net income	$ 8,684	$ 6,923	$ 6,481	$ 5,186	$ 4,352
Earnings per share	$ 2.79	$ 2.70	$ 2.34	$ 1.80	$ 1.46
Dividends per share	$ 1.15	$ 1.03	$ 0.93	$ 0.82	$ 0.76

Haver Industries
Comparative Balance Sheet
As of December 31

	2016	2015	2014	2013	2012
Assets					
Cash	$ 6,693	$ 6,389	$ 4,232	$ 5,912	$ 3,427
Marketable securities	1,133	1,744	1,660	300	196
Receivables	5,725	4,185	4,062	3,038	3,090
Inventories	6,291	5,006	4,400	3,640	3,456
Other current assets	4,487	3,005	2,761	2,330	1,997
Total current assets	24,329	20,329	17,115	15,220	12,166
Property, plant, & equipment, net	18,770	14,332	14,108	13,104	13,349
Intangibles	89,027	24,163	23,900	13,507	13,430
Deposits & other assets	3,569	2,703	1,925	1,875	1,831
Total Assets	$135,695	$61,527	$57,048	$43,706	$40,776
Liabilities					
Notes payable	$ 0	$ 0	$ 6,769	$ 1,079	$ 3,113
Accounts payable	4,910	3,802	3,617	2,795	2,205
Current long-term debt	2,128	11,441	1,518	1,093	n/a
Accrued expense	4,757	2,957	2,925	2,606	2,429
Income taxes	3,360	2,265	2,554	1,879	1,438
Other current liabilities	4,830	4,574	4,764	2,906	3,519
Total current liabilities	19,985	25,039	22,147	12,358	12,704
Deferred charges	12,354	1,896	2,261	1,396	1,077
Long-term debt	35,344	12,614	12,302	11,475	11,201
Non-current capital leases	632	273	252		
Other long-term liabilities	4,472	3,230	2,808	2,291	2,088
Total liabilities	72,787	43,052	39,770	27,520	27,070
Stockholders' Equity					
Common stock	3,976	2,977	2,544	1,297	1,301
Capital surplus	57,856	3,030	2,425	2,931	2,490
Retained earnings	35,666	31,004	13,611	13,692	11,980
Treasury stock	(34,235)	(17,194)	0	0	0
Other	(355)	(1,342)	(1,302)	(1,734)	(2,065)
Total stockholders' equity	62,908	18,475	17,278	16,186	13,706
Total Liabilities & Stockholders' Equity	$135,695	$61,527	$57,048	$43,706	$40,776

Required

a. In his letters to shareholders in 2012, Haver's CEO stated that the company's goal for the next five years was to achieve 4% to 6% sales growth each year and at least 10% growth in earnings per share. Based on the results shown here, did the company meet its targets? How do you know?

b. Managing a broad collection of brands is challenging. In its 2012 annual report, Haver Industries stated that acquisitions and divestitures "are part of the Company's strategic focus on developing brands that offer the greatest potential for growth." The report went on, "This requires some difficult decisions, including a restructuring program to reduce overhead and streamline manufacturing processes." In other words, the company strives to use its assets to earn the greatest possible return. How well has the company managed its assets over the five-year period shown here?

c. Would you recommend Haver Industries shares to a friend who is interested in investing for growth potential? Why or why not?

12-24 Comprehensive financial statement analysis (LO 1, 2, 3) Koester, Inc., states in its 2016 10-K filing with the SEC, "In October 2016, two major credit rating agencies changed Koester's long-term credit rating outlook to negative and one of the credit rating agencies reduced Koester's short-term credit rating." Koester's financial statements (in $000) follow.

Koester, Inc.
Comparative Income Statement
For the Year Ended December 31

	2016	2015	2014
Sales revenue	$5,179,016	$5,102,786	$4,960,100
Cost of goods sold	2,806,148	2,692,061	2,530,617
Gross profit	2,372,868	2,410,725	2,429,483
Operating expenses	1,708,339	1,679,908	1,643,773
Operating income	664,529	730,817	785,710
Interest expense, net	42,279	58,081	61,611
Other nonoperating (income), net	(29,799)	(23,518)	(16,755)
Income before income tax	652,049	696,254	740,854
Income tax expense	235,030	123,531	203,222
Net income	$ 417,019	$ 572,723	$ 537,632

Koester, Inc.
Comparative Balance Sheet
As of December 31

	2016	2015
Assets		
Cash	$ 997,734	$1,156,835
Accounts receivable (net)	760,643	759,033
Inventory	376,897	418,633
Prepaid expenses and other current assets	277,226	302,649
Total current assets	2,412,500	2,637,150
Property, plant, & equipment (net)	547,104	586,526
Other assets	1,412,709	1,532,816
Total Assets	$4,372,313	$4,756,492
Liabilities and Stockholders' Equity		
Short-term borrowings	$ 117,994	$ 28,995
Current portion of long-term debt	100,000	189,130
Accounts payable	265,936	349,159
Accrued expenses	796,473	880,038
Income taxes payable	182,782	279,849
Total current liabilities	1,463,185	1,727,171
Long-term debt	525,000	400,000
Other	282,395	243,509
Total noncurrent liabilities	807,395	643,509
Stockholders' Equity		
Common stock, $1.00 par value	441,369	441,369
Additional paid-in capital	1,589,281	1,594,332
Treasury stock	(935,711)	(473,332)
Retained earnings	1,006,794	823,460
Total stockholders' equity	2,101,733	2,385,812
Total Liabilities and Stockholders' Equity	$4,372,313	$4,756,492

Required

a. Prepare a horizontal analysis for 2016.

b. Prepare common-size income statements for 2014, 2015, and 2016 and common-size balance sheets for 2015 and 2016.

c. Assess Koester's liquidity.
d. Assess Koester's profitability.
e. Assess Koester's leverage.
f. What data do you find that supports the credit agencies' decision to lower Koester's credit rating?

12-25 Financial ratios and ethics (CMA adapted) (LO 3) Shilstone Supply, Inc. manufactures a variety of pumps and valves that are distributed through several thousand plumbing supply houses, as well as 100 manufacturer's representatives. Due to less-than-favorable business conditions in the industry over the last several years, Shilstone's cash flow position has deteriorated. Over the past four years, the company's Accounts Receivable balance grew from 5% to 9% of assets, and its current ratio declined from 2.8 to 2.0. Over the same period, bad debts grew from 1.5% to 3% of sales. Debt covenants with Shilstone's bank require that the current ratio be above 2.1 at year-end.

Shilstone's president, Bill Rowe, recognizes the need to take action to improve the company's liquidity position. He has hired Amy Cooper, an experienced cash manager, to assess the company's situation and make recommendations for improvement. Cooper has met with Jennifer Adams, Shilstone's controller, and has gathered the following facts:

- Shilstone's products have an average contribution margin of 30%.
- Shilstone is operating at slightly less than full capacity.
- Shilstone's current credit terms are 2/12, net 45, which is in line with industry standards.
- Late notices are sent out monthly on all past due accounts, with a follow-up telephone call to delinquent accounts in excess of $8,000.
- Delinquent accounts are sent to a collection agency when they become 12 months overdue.

Based on her experience and her analysis of Shilstone's data, Cooper has classified Shilstone's customers into eight categories based on the likelihood of their accounts becoming uncollectible. She has implemented the following changes in Shilstone's credit policies to improve cash flow. Cooper believes these changes will reduce bad debts to between 1% and 1.5% of sales.

- New credit terms of 2/10, net 30 will be applied to all accounts in risk categories 1 through 5. Cooper expects these customers to accept this change without issue. The overall effect of the change should be improved accounts receivable turnover and reduced bad debts.
- Customers in risk categories 6 and 7 will be subject to stricter credit terms, such as cash on delivery. Sales to customers in risk category 8 will have to be paid in advance. While Cooper acknowledges that Shilstone will lose some sales to customers in these categories, she believes the lost sales will be concentrated in the high-risk category.
- Collection efforts will be increased to ensure better compliance with the new credit terms. Follow-up telephone calls will be made to all delinquent accounts in excess of $2,000. Accounts that are nine months overdue will be turned over to a collection agency.

Jennifer Adams is responsible for extending credit to customers and for establishing the guidelines under which the manufacturer's representatives operate. She has often relaxed the company's credit terms to meet the needs of various customers, and over time she has developed a close relationship with many of the larger customers. After reviewing Amy Cooper's suggested changes, Adams has some concerns about the effect of the new policies on some of those customers, and by extension, on Shilstone's sales. She has performed her own customer risk analysis and concluded that some of Cooper's risk classifications are inappropriate. In her view, some of the larger customers are better business risks than indicated in Cooper's analysis.

Adams has concluded that following the new policies would reduce sales by more than Cooper estimates, leading to idle manufacturing capacity. She has decided not to share her findings with Rowe or Cooper. Instead, she will continue to use her discretion in relaxing the company's credit policies, particularly as they affect larger customers.

Required

a. What are the probable effects of the new credit policies on Shilstone's liquidity position?

b. Refer to the IMA's *Statement of Ethical Professional Practice* in Exhibit 1-8. Evaluate Jennifer Adams's decision not to fully comply with the changes in credit and collection policies implemented by Amy Cooper. Refer to specific standards when making your evaluation.

c. How would you recommend that Jennifer Adams handle her disagreement with Cooper's policies?

d. Assume it is December 30, and Adams is doing a preliminary review of the company's year-end balance sheet. It appears that the current ratio will be between 2.0 and 2.1, which would likely violate the company's debt covenants. Adams knows that one of her large customers, who happens to be a category 8 risk and is teetering on the verge of bankruptcy, is trying to get enough cash together to place a significant order with Shilstone. If she relaxes the new credit policies and allows the customer to purchase on credit, the resulting account receivable will push the current ratio over the required 2.1 level, preventing Shilstone from defaulting on its bank loan. Should Adams approve the sale? Why or why not? Refer to the IMA's *Statement of Ethical Professional Practice* in making your argument.

ENDNOTES

1. A hyperlinked table of SIC codes is available at http://www.osha.gov/pls/imis/sic_manual.html.
2. A hyperlinked table of NAICS codes is available at http://www.naics.com/search.htm.
3. Max Oston, *IBISWorld Industry Report 31529: Costume & Team Uniform Manufacturing in the US*, September 2015. In the 2012 NAICS code revisions, team uniform manufacturing was reclassified from 315299 to 315280. However, industry reports still include this segment in NAICS 31529.
4. The Sports and Fitness Industry Association, *2013 Sports, Fitness and Leisure Activities Topline Participation Report.*
5. Sports Business Research Network, *Baseball: Participation by Total vs. Frequent.*
6. Marc Fisher, "Baseball is struggling to hook kids—and risks losing fans to other sports," *The Washington Post*, April 5, 2015, https://www.washingtonpost.com/sports/nationals/baseballs-trouble-with-the-youth-curve–and-what-that-means-for-the-game/2015/04/05/2da36dca-d7e8-11e4-8103-fa84725dbf9d_story.html (accessed February 16, 2016).
7. The National Federation of State High School Associations, "2014–15 High School Athletics Participation Survey," http://www.nfhs.org/ParticipationStatistics/PDF/2014-15_Participation_Survey_Results.pdf (accessed February 22, 2016).

© jsnyderdesign/iStockphoto

CHAPTER 13

STATEMENT OF CASH FLOWS

UNITS	LEARNING OBJECTIVES
UNIT 13.1 Categorizing Cash Flows	LO 1: Categorize cash activities as operating, investing, or financing.
UNIT 13.2 Cash Flows Provided by Operating Activities: The Indirect Method	LO 2: Calculate cash flows provided (used) by operating activities using the indirect method.
UNIT 13.3 Cash Flows Provided by Investing and Financing Activities	LO 3: Calculate cash flows provided (used) by investing activities. LO 4: Calculate cash flows provided (used) by financing activities.
UNIT 13.4 Constructing and Interpreting the Statement of Cash Flows	LO 5: Construct a statement of cash flows. LO 6: Analyze a statement of cash flows.
APPENDIX Cash Flows Provided by Operating Activities: The Direct Method	LO 7: Calculate cash flows provided (used) by operating activities using the direct method.

© Tsuji/iStockphoto

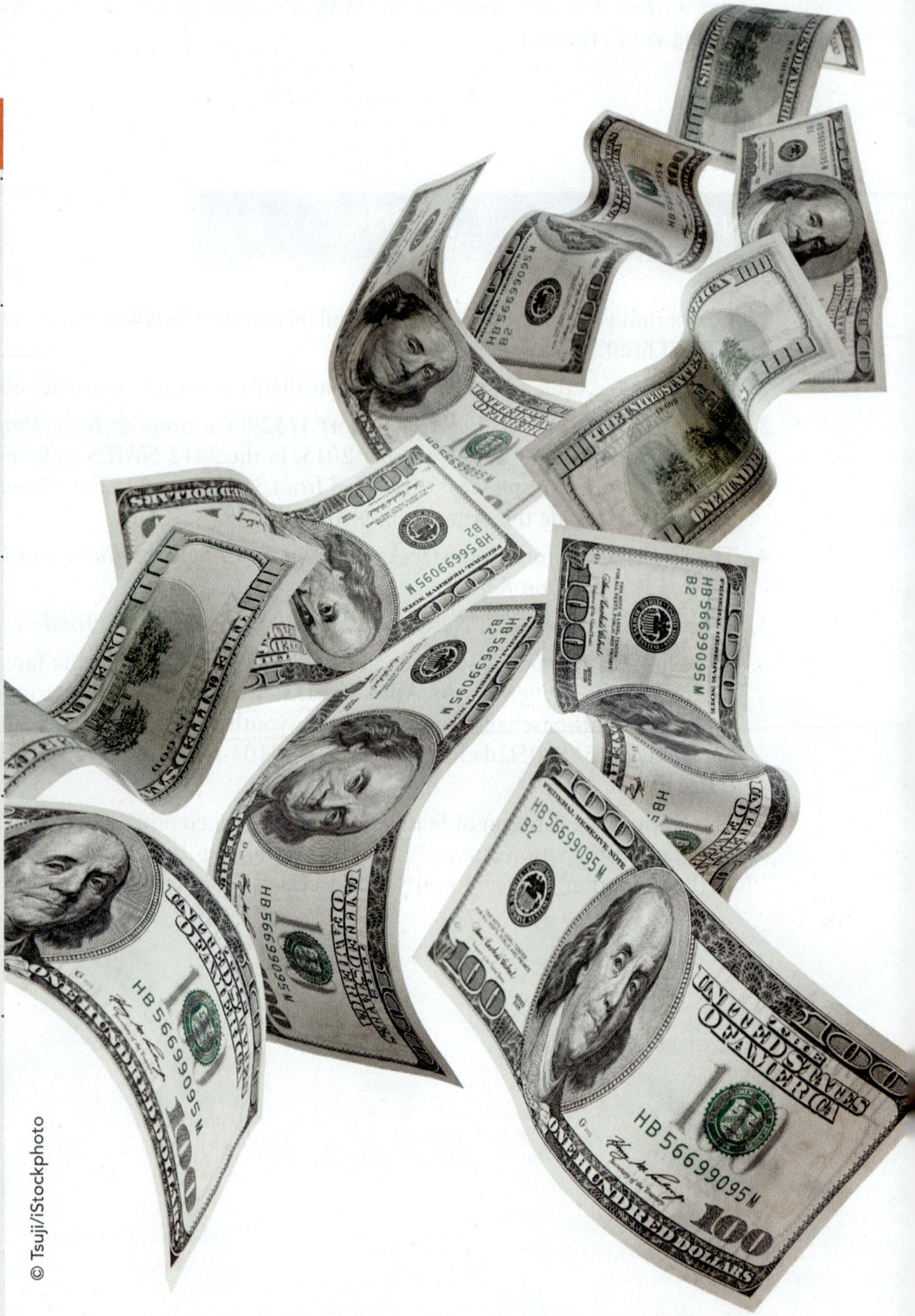

Business Decision and Context

© David Orcea/Shutterstock

"Claire, I don't understand something," said **George Douglas, C&C Sports' president**, in the weekly managers' meeting. "Our sales and income have been increasing dramatically. Interest in our baseball pants, jerseys, and award jackets is higher than ever. Every year we're profitable, but we keep having to borrow money. It doesn't make sense to me."

> "Every year we're profitable, but we keep having to borrow money. It doesn't make sense to me."

"You're right, George," replied **Claire Elliot, vice president for finance and administration at C&C Sports**. "We're profitable and we're doing a lot of business, but we have some problems with our cash flow."

"How can that be?" George asked. "Have our customers quit paying their bills?"

"No, they're still paying what they owe us," Claire responded. "It's a matter of timing. Sometimes our purchasing manager agrees to prepay a fabric purchase, for example. In that case, we spend cash before we have a pair of pants we can sell to the customer. Then, if one of our sales reps gives a customer 60 days to pay for the pants, 90 days might go by between the time we pay for the fabric and the time we get cash from the customer for the pants. The gap in timing doesn't show up on the income statement."

George thought about Claire's explanation for a minute, then asked, "What can we do to improve our cash position?"

"We need to examine how we spend and generate cash, so we'll know how our transactions with customers and creditors affect the company's cash flow," Claire responded. "We can't continue to gauge how well we're doing by looking only at our income statement. For our small company, cash flow is vital to staying in business."

SUPPLY CHAIN KEY PLAYERS

END CUSTOMER

UNIVERSAL SPORTS EXCHANGE

C&C SPORTS

President
George Douglas

Vice President for Finance and Administration
Claire Elliot

DURABLE ZIPPER COMPANY

BRADLEY TEXTILE MILLS

CENTEX YARNS

NEFF FIBER MANUFACTURING

BRUIN POLYMERS, INC.

UNIT 13.1

Categorizing Cash Flows

GUIDED UNIT PREPARATION

Answering the following questions while you read this unit will guide your understanding of the key concepts found in the unit. The questions are linked to the learning objectives presented at the beginning of the chapter.

LO 1

1. What is meant by a source of cash?
2. What is meant by a use of cash?
3. What are operating activities? Give one example.
4. What are investing activities? Give one example.
5. What are financing activities? Give one example.

You've probably heard sayings like "Money makes the world go round" and "Cash is king." These truisms mean that operating a business takes cash. Without cash, a company cannot buy inventory to sell to customers or pay employees for the work they have done. In this chapter, you will learn to determine how a company receives and spends cash by looking at the **statement of cash flows**. This statement explains the change in the Cash account balance between the beginning and end of the period by showing how cash was generated and spent.

Why would anyone be interested in examining a company's statement of cash flows? Doing so helps in evaluating the company's liquidity and in predicting its future cash flows. Both shareholders and creditors are interested in determining the likelihood that a company will be able to meet future cash obligations. They also want to know the likelihood that the company will need to secure external funding, either by taking out additional loans or by issuing new shares of stock. Finally, the statement of cash flows helps these financial statement users to understand the differences between the company's net income and the cash generated by its operations—the kind of differences Claire Elliott described in response to George Douglas's question in the opening scenario.

Why does a company's Cash account balance change? **Sources of cash** are activities that generate cash receipts, which increase the amount of cash on hand, such as collecting payments from customers or receiving interest from the bank. **Uses of cash** are activities that require cash disbursements, which decrease the amount of cash on hand, such as paying vendors for purchases and paying employees' wages. All these activities can be classified into three categories: operating activities, investing activities, and financing activities. Thus, the statement of cash flows is organized into three sections, one for each type of activity.

Look at C&C Sports' statement of cash flows in Exhibit 13-1. Notice that the statement shows cash flows provided by each of the three activity types:

EXHIBIT 13-1

C&C Sports' statement of cash flows.

C&C SPORTS
Statements of Cash Flows
For the Years Ended December 31

	2016	2015	2014
Cash flows provided by operating activities			
Net income	$110,801	$ 55,040	$ 45,244
Adjustments to reconcile net income to cash provided by operating activities			
Depreciation	67,789	66,912	70,626
Changes in operating assets and liabilities			
Accounts receivable	(40,284)	(31,466)	(21,993)
Inventories	(93,263)	(98,510)	(105,411)
Prepaid expenses/other assets	(22,116)	(14,507)	(22,116)
Accounts payable	(3,412)	9,651	8,197
Accrued liabilities	(28,877)	(8,318)	1,098
Net cash provided (used) by operating activities	$ (9,362)	$(21,198)	$(24,355)
Cash provided by investing activities	$ 0	$ 0	$ 0
Cash flows provided by financing activities			
Short-term borrowing	$ 15,000	$ 10,000	$ 10,000
Repayment of long-term debt	(20,000)	(20,000)	(20,000)
Net cash provided (used) by financing activities	$ (5,000)	$(10,000)	$(10,000)
Increase/(decrease) in cash	$ (14,362)	$(31,198)	$(34,355)
Cash at beginning of period	22,114	53,312	87,667
Cash at end of period	$ 7,752	$ 22,114	$ 53,312

operating, investing, and financing. The cash flows provided by the three types of activity add up to the total change in the Cash account. Let's examine the types of transactions included in each section. Then, in the following units, we'll see how to calculate the various cash flows.

Operating Activities

Operating activities are those activities that accomplish the company's purpose for being in business. We would expect the company's primary sources of cash to be from its basic operations—selling inventory or providing services. As customers pay for those goods and services, the company receives cash. We would expect the primary uses of cash to be payments related to the company's operations. That is, the company must pay employees, buy inventory, and cover all the other costs related to operations. The income statement reports the revenues and expenses from the company's operations.

The sources and uses of cash provided by operating activities represent the cash effect of the revenues and expenses reported on the income statement. For example, net income includes sales revenue for the period whether or not cash was collected from those sales. Cash flows from operating activities include collections from customers in the period cash is received, regardless of when the sale was made. Don't be confused by activities that sound like they involve cash but really don't. For example, ordering materials is not the same thing as paying for them.

There are two approaches to presenting cash flows provided by operating activities in the statement of cash flows: the direct method and the indirect method. The only difference between the two approaches is the manner of calculating and

REALITY CHECK—*What's in your wallet?*

© c barnesphotography/iStockphoto

How much cash is enough? If you are General Motors and trying to stave off bankruptcy, it's $11–$14 billion. Luckily, every company doesn't need that much to maintain its operations. Whatever the right amount, maintaining an adequate cash balance provides flexibility to take advantage of business opportunities when they come along.

At the end of 2015, Berkshire Hathaway reported over $71.7 billion in cash and cash equivalents. Maintaining such a high level of cash allows the company to invest in other companies, such as its 2010 acquisition of Burlington Northern Santa Fe Corporation and its 2013 acquisition of H. J. Heinz.

Apple, known for holding large amounts of cash, used $11.4 billion of its cash during fiscal 2015 to pay dividends and another $14 billion to repurchase shares of the company's stock. Even after these expenditures, the company reported over $21.1 billion in cash and cash equivalents at the end of the year.

Sources: Apple 2015 10-K; Berkshire Hathaway 2015 10-K; CNBC.com, "Berkshire Hathaway, 3G Buying Heinz for $23.3 Billion," http://www.cnbc.com/id/100442835/ (accessed February 27, 2013).

"A cash balance of over $71.7 billion allows Berkshire Hathaway to acquire other companies such as BNSF and H. J. Heinz."

WATCH OUT!

Remember that the income statement is prepared using accrual accounting. The statement of cash flows, however, shows only those transactions that affect cash. Although the operating activities shown on the statement of cash flows reflect items on the income statement, the amounts will not be identical to those on the income statement because of differences between the cash basis and the accrual basis of accounting.

reporting cash flows provided by operating activities. The **indirect method** starts with net income and adjusts for non-cash items. The **direct method** reports the specific operating activities that provided and used cash, such as inventory purchases (a use of cash) and collections from customers (a source of cash). Regardless of which method is used, the total of the cash flows provided by operating activities will be the same. Although either method can be used for financial reporting, almost all companies choose the indirect method.[1]

Investing Activities

To operate, companies must acquire productive assets such as property and equipment. C&C Sports has acquired sewing machines, a factory building, and other equipment needed to make uniforms and jackets, for example. When those assets are no longer needed, the company may sell them for cash. A company may also invest in other companies by purchasing shares of their stock or making loans to them in the form of notes receivable. Activities that affect a company's investments in assets other than current operating assets are called **investing activities**.

Financing Activities

If operating and investing activities do not provide enough cash, a company must turn to external sources of funding such as debt (both short term and long term) and equity (that is, stock) to remain in business. Activities that involve external funding are called **financing activities**. Borrowing money and selling new shares of stock are sources of cash. Repaying borrowed money, repurchasing shares of the company's own stock, and paying dividends are uses of cash.

Why should we care *how* a company generates cash? Suppose that Moad, Inc. generates cash primarily from operations, while Lankford Co. generates cash primarily by issuing long-term debt. Which company is more likely to be able to generate cash on an ongoing basis? If Lankford continues to borrow money in order to operate, at some point lenders will decide that the risk of a loan not being repaid is too high. They will stop lending money to Lankford, and the company will be forced out of business. Because Moad, Inc. generates adequate cash from operations, it has a better long-term outlook than Lankford. That is why users of financial statements care how a company generates and uses cash.

We have mentioned just a few of the activities that generate or use cash. Exhibit 13-2 lists activities commonly included in each section of the statement of cash flows.

WATCH OUT!

Payment of interest on debt and receipt of interest on investments may sound like financing and investing activities, respectively, but they are categorized as operating activities to mirror their inclusion on the income statement.

EXHIBIT 13-2

Examples of sources and uses of cash.

Activities	Source (increases cash)	Use (decreases cash)
Operating		
• Collections from customers	X	
• Payments for inventory		X
• Payments to employees		X
• Payments for operating costs such as: – Rent – Utilities – Insurance – Supplies – Interest – Income taxes		X
Investing		
• Sales of property and equipment	X	
• Payments for property and equipment		X
• Sales of investments	X	
• Payments for investments		X
• Collections of notes receivable	X	
• Loans made to customers or employees		X
Financing		
• Issue stock	X	
• Repurchasing company's own stock		X
• Issue debt	X	
• Repayment of debt		X
• Payment of dividends		X

THINK ABOUT IT 13.1

If the statement of cash flows provides information that can't be found on the income statement, why doesn't GAAP just require cash-basis accounting?

UNIT 13.1 REVIEW

KEY TERMS

Direct method p. 684
Financing activities p. 685
Indirect method p. 684
Investing activities p. 684
Operating activities p. 683
Sources of cash p. 682
Statement of cash flows p. 682
Uses of cash p. 682

PRACTICE QUESTIONS

1. LO 1 Which of the following is *not* a source of cash?
   a. Gain on sale of land
   b. Cash collections from customers
   c. Issuing new debt
   d. Issuing common stock
2. LO 1 Which of the following is a use of cash?
   a. Declaring a dividend of $3 per share
   b. Buying inventory on account
   c. Paying employees
   d. Selling an investment in another company
3. LO 1 Which of the following cash flows results from an operating activity?
   a. Making a principal payment on a loan
   b. Paying rent on a finished goods warehouse
   c. Purchasing a new delivery truck
   d. Selling a vacant lot next to the factory
4. LO 1 Which of the following cash flows results from a financing activity?
   a. Receiving a payment from a customer
   b. Receiving a stock dividend of $1.25 per share
   c. Paying quarterly employment taxes
   d. Borrowing money from the bank
5. LO 1 Which of the following cash flows results from an investing activity?
   a. Purchasing 35% of a supplier's outstanding common stock
   b. Receiving payment from a customer for last month's accounts receivable
   c. Paying quarterly income taxes
   d. Paying a vendor for last month's purchases on account

UNIT 13.1 PRACTICE EXERCISE

Classify each of the following items as a source or use of cash. Then classify each item as a cash flow provided by an operating, investing, or financing activity.

	Type of Cash Flow			Type of Activity		
	Source	Use	Not a Cash Flow	Operating	Investing	Financing
1. Apple pays cash for $1,300,000 of Intel stock						
2. John Wiley and Sons receives a $120,000 order from Barnes and Noble for 1,500 accounting textbooks						
3. The Waco office of FedEx sells an old copy machine to an employee for $100 cash						
4. Baldwin, Inc. pays $2,500 in interest due on its long-term debt						
5. Walmart pays $80,000 to OfficeMax for supplies it ordered last month						
6. Pennington College Emblems borrows $15,000 from the bank to start a new business venture						
7. Smith Automotive Manufacturers orders $500,000 of composite materials from Natural Composites, Inc.						

	Type of Cash Flow			Type of Activity		
	Source	Use	Not a Cash Flow	Operating	Investing	Financing
8. Toyota pays $6,000,000 cash for new paint sprayers that have a 10-year useful life						
9. Johnson, Inc. pays Davidson Corporation $1,000,000 for previously ordered raw materials						
10. Baylor University Press receives an order from Amazon for 500 books, accompanied by a check for the full amount of the order, $2,500						

SELECTED UNIT 13.1 ANSWERS

Think About It 13.1

The income statement represents the company's earnings, not the cash the company has collected or spent. If the statement of cash flows were to replace the income statement, there would be no accounts receivable or accounts payable on the balance sheet because we wouldn't record transactions that don't involve cash. We wouldn't know what the company was owed or what debts the company had. Similarly, because we wouldn't record assets that were purchased with debt rather than cash, we couldn't determine the company's operating assets. Using the income statement together with the statement of cash flows gives users of financial statements information about a company's earnings as well as the way it generates and uses cash.

Practice Questions

1. A
2. C
3. B
4. D
5. A

Unit 13.1 Practice Exercise Solution

	Type of Cash Flow			Type of Activity		
	Source	Use	Not a Cash Flow	Operating	Investing	Financing
1. Apple pays cash for $1,300,000 of Intel stock		X			X	
2. John Wiley and Sons receives a $120,000 order from Barnes and Noble for 1,500 accounting textbooks			X			
3. The Waco office of FedEx sells an old copy machine to an employee for $100 cash	X				X	
4. Baldwin, Inc. pays $2,500 in interest due on its long-term debt		X		X		
5. Walmart pays $80,000 to OfficeMax for supplies it ordered last month		X		X		
6. Pennington College Emblems borrows $15,000 from the bank to start a new business venture	X					X
7. Smith Automotive Manufacturers orders $500,000 of composite materials from Natural Composites, Inc.			X			
8. Toyota pays $6,000,000 cash for new paint sprayers that have a 10-year useful life		X			X	

	Type of Cash Flow			Type of Activity		
	Source	Use	Not a Cash Flow	Operating	Investing	Financing
9. Johnson, Inc. pays Davidson Corporation $1,000,000 for previously ordered raw materials		X		X		
10. Baylor University Press receives an order from Amazon for 500 books, accompanied by a check for the full amount of the order, $2,500	X			X		

UNIT 13.2

Cash Flows Provided by Operating Activities: The Indirect Method

GUIDED UNIT PREPARATION

Answering the following questions while you read this unit will guide your understanding of the key concepts found in the unit. The questions are linked to the learning objectives presented at the beginning of the chapter.

LO 2

1. Which of the two methods of calculating cash flows is preferred by the Financial Accounting Standards Board? Which of the two methods is more popular in practice?
2. In the indirect method, why are increases in current assets subtracted from net income to calculate the cash flow provided by operating activities?
3. In the indirect method, why are increases in current liabilities added to net income to calculate the cash flow provided by operating activities?

As we learned in the last unit, there are two approaches to reporting cash flows provided by operating activities: the indirect method and the direct method. Although the Financial Accounting Standards Board recommends that companies use the direct method to prepare the statement of cash flows, the 2011 edition of *Accounting Trends and Techniques* reported that 98.4% of companies surveyed used the indirect method.[2] The indirect method, which starts with net income and converts it to cash flows provided by operating activities, appeals to users of financial statements who want to know why cash differs from net income. In this unit we will focus on the indirect method; the direct method is presented in the appendix to this chapter.

Exhibit 13-3 shows how to calculate cash flows provided by operating activities using the indirect method. Notice that the calculation begins with net income; then

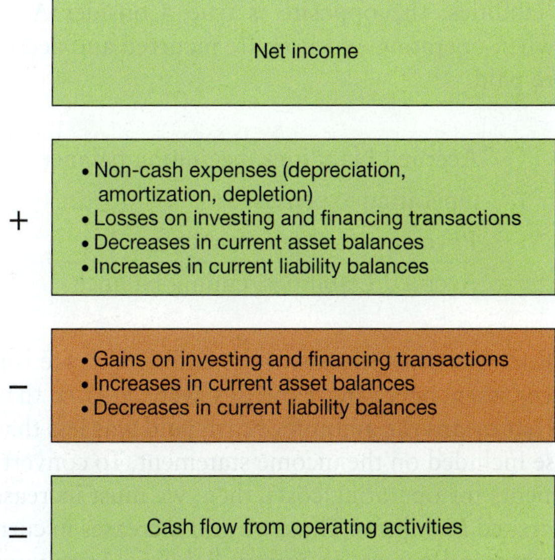

EXHIBIT 13-3

Calculation of cash flows provided by operating activities—indirect method.

non-cash expenses that were subtracted in calculating net income, such as bad debt expense, depreciation, amortization, and depletion, are added back. Although these non-cash expenses reduce income, they do not reduce the company's cash balance.

Net income must also be adjusted for gains and losses from investing and financing activities, such as sales of property, equipment, or investments and the early extinguishment of debt. Let's consider an example to see why. Suppose a company that owns some land with a book value of $80,000 sells it for $75,000. The sale will result in a $5,000 loss that must be recorded on the income statement. Net income, then, is $5,000 lower because of the sale. Because the $5,000 doesn't represent a cash transaction, however, it must be removed from net income when calculating cash flows. In converting net income to cash flows provided by operations, then, losses should be added because they were originally subtracted in calculating net income. Gains should be subtracted because they were originally added in calculating net income.

Finally, net income must be adjusted for changes in the non-cash current asset and current liability accounts.[3] How do we know whether a change should be added or subtracted? Think about how the change affects cash. Let's start with the current asset Accounts Receivable. Accounts Receivable increases by the amount of sales to customers and decreases by the amount of cash collections from customers.

Accounts Receivable, beginning balance
\+ Sales
− Collections from customers
= Accounts Receivable, ending balance

If Accounts Receivable increases (that is, if the ending balance is greater than the beginning balance), then the amount of cash collected must be less than the amount of sales included in net income. To convert from sales to collections from customers, then, we must reduce net income by the increase in Accounts Receivable:

Sales − Increase in Accounts Receivable = Collections from customers

Using the same logic, we can adjust net income for changes in each current asset balance. We subtract increases in the account balance (a use of cash) from net income. We add decreases in the account balance (a source of cash) to net income.

For current liabilities, the opposite is true. Consider Accrued Liabilities, which increases when operating expenses are incurred and decreases when operating expenses are paid.

Accrued Liabilities, beginning balance
+ Operating expenses
− Payments for operating costs
= Accrued Liabilities, ending balance

If Accrued Liabilities increases (that is, if the ending balance is greater than the beginning balance), then operating expenses were greater than payments for those expenses. That means the amount of cash paid was less than the amount of operating expense included on the income statement. To convert from operating expenses to payments for operating costs, then, we must increase net income by the increase in Accrued Liabilities. Thus, we add increases in current liabilities to net income; we subtract decreases in current liabilities from net income.

Let's work through an example to see how to calculate cash flows provided by operating activities using the indirect method. To calculate the cash flows, we will need comparative balance sheets, an income statement, and some additional information on specific transactions. Exhibits 13-4 and 13-5 show the comparative balance sheets and income statement for Prescott Company. The following information relates to transactions that occurred during the year:

- Land costing $40,000 was purchased with cash.
- Equipment with a book value of $18,000 was sold for $20,000 cash.

EXHIBIT 13-4

Prescott Company's balance sheets.

PRESCOTT COMPANY
Comparative Balance Sheets
For the Years Ended

	12/31/2016	12/31/2015	Increase/(Decrease)
Cash and cash equivalents	$ 96,600	$ 11,500	$ 85,100
Accounts receivable	23,200	11,200	12,000
Inventories	323,370	326,340	(2,970)
Total current assets	$443,170	$349,040	$ 94,130
Property and equipment, net	128,000	119,700	8,300
Total assets	$571,170	$468,740	$102,430
Accounts payable	$144,600	$162,200	$ (17,600)
Accrued liabilities	45,220	42,540	2,680
Salaries payable	1,950	1,600	350
Income taxes payable	13,200	12,000	1,200
Dividends payable	14,000	0	14,000
Total current liabilities	$218,970	$218,340	$ 630
Long-term debt	128,200	143,200	(15,000)
Total liabilities	$347,170	$361,540	$ (14,370)
Common stock	$175,000	$ 75,000	$100,000
Retained earnings	49,000	32,200	16,800
Total stockholders' equity	$224,000	$107,200	$116,800
Total liabilities and stockholders' equity	$571,170	$468,740	$102,430

PRESCOTT COMPANY Income Statement For the Year Ending December 31, 2016		
Sales		$1,050,000
Cost of goods sold		(777,000)
Gross profit		$ 273,000
Operating expenses		
Salaries	$92,400	
Depreciation	13,700	
Rent	83,000	
Interest	17,000	
Utilities	15,000	
Other	9,900	
Total operating expenses		(231,000)
Operating income		$ 42,000
Gain on sale of equipment		2,000
Income before taxes		$ 44,000
Tax expense (30%)		(13,200)
Net income		$ 30,800

EXHIBIT 13-5

Prescott Company's income statement.

- No new debt was issued.
- Common stock was issued for $100,000 cash.
- Dividends of $14,000 were declared but not paid.

Exhibit 13-6 shows Prescott's cash flows provided by operating activities using the indirect method. Notice that the exhibit begins with the net income shown on the income statement in Exhibit 13-5. Depreciation expense of $13,700 is added back, and the $2,000 gain on the sale of equipment is subtracted. The final adjustments to net income are the changes in the current asset and current liability accounts. Notice that these amounts match the changes shown in the balance sheet accounts in Exhibit 13-4. Thus, Prescott's cash flows provided by operating activities equal $20,100. The indirect method may seem complicated, but notice that the non-cash items can be found directly on the income statement, and all the changes in the current assets and liabilities are easily calculated using the balance sheet accounts.

Cash flows provided by operating activities		
Net income		$30,800
Adjustments to reconcile net income to cash provided by operating activities		
Depreciation	$13,700	
Gain on sale of equipment	(2,000)	
Changes in operating assets and liabilities		
Increase in accounts receivable	(12,000)	
Decrease in inventories	2,970	
Decrease in accounts payable	(17,600)	
Increase in accrued liabilities	2,680	
Increase in salaries payable	350	
Increase in income taxes payable	1,200	(10,700)
Net cash provided (used) by operating activities		$20,100

EXHIBIT 13-6

Prescott Company's cash flows from operations—indirect method.

REALITY CHECK—*Running out of cash?*

Valerie Macon/Getty Images Entertainment/Getty Images

Between 2006 and 2012, sales dropped by approximately 50%, and K-Swiss experienced a cash drain of over $200 million.

In 1966 a new shoe took the courts at Wimbledon when K-Swiss introduced its "Classic" model, the first leather tennis shoe. Since that time, the company has expanded its product line to include other shoes, apparel, and accessories.

But recent times have not been kind to K-Swiss. Between 2006 and 2012, sales dropped by approximately 50%, and the company experienced a cash drain of over $200 million. While the company reported $42.7 million in cash and cash equivalents at the end of 2012, this was down from $260.2 million at the end of 2006. And for each of the three years from 2010 to 2012, the company's operations used more cash than they generated.

Some analysts think that cash flows provided by operating activities is a key indicator of a company's future performance. StockDiagnostics.com founder Michael Markowski is one of them. Markowski has developed a measure called operational cash flow per share (OPS), which he believes is a leading indicator of performance that is not as easily managed as earnings per share.

With $42.7 million in the bank, isn't K-Swiss still in a good position to succeed even with the sales and cash decline? Apparently South Korean apparel distributor E.Land World Ltd. thinks so. The company agreed in January 2013 to acquire K-Swiss for $170 million.

Sources: K-Swiss 2012 10-K, K-Swiss 2009 10-K, K-Swiss 2006 10-K, http://www.kswiss.com/our-story (accessed July 14, 2016); Matt Townsend, "E.Land to Pay $170 Million for K-Swiss Shoes to Add Brands," http://www.bloomberg.com/news/2013-01-17/e-land-to-pay-170-million-for-money-losing-shoemaker-k-swiss.html (accessed February 27, 2013).

THINK ABOUT IT 13.2

Look at C&C Sports' Statement of Cash Flows in Exhibit 13-1. Compare net income to cash flows provided by operating activities. What seems to be causing C&C Sports' continual cash flow problems?

UNIT 13.2 REVIEW

PRACTICE QUESTIONS

1. LO 2 Which of the following items would be added to net income when using the indirect method of calculating cash flows provided by operating activities?
   a. A decrease in Accounts Payable
   b. A decrease in Accounts Receivable
   c. An increase in Accounts Receivable
   d. An increase in Long-Term Debt

2. LO 2 Which of the following items would be subtracted from net income when using the indirect method of calculating cash flows provided by operating activities?
   a. A gain on the sale of a piece of equipment
   b. A loss on the sale of a piece of equipment
   c. Depreciation expense
   d. A decrease in Long-Term Debt

3. LO 2 Which of the following items would not be included in the calculation of cash flows provided by operating activities using the indirect method?

   a. Net income
   b. Amortization expense
   c. An increase in Inventory
   d. Purchase of a new delivery truck

4. LO 2 During the year, Messer, Inc. purchased $500,000 in inventory from vendors and paid vendors a total of $525,000. The result was a decrease in Accounts Payable that should be subtracted from net income in determining cash flows provided by operating activities using the indirect method. True or False?

5. LO 2 During the year, Messer, Inc. paid executives bonuses of 500 shares of stock. This non-cash payment should be subtracted from net income in determining cash flows provided by operating activities using the indirect method. True or False?

UNIT 13.2 PRACTICE EXERCISE

The following balances were gathered from Newton Company's general ledger.

	December 31, 2016	December 31, 2015
Accounts Receivable	$75,581	$95,297
Inventories	213,345	117,406
Accounts Payable	60,567	75,447
Accrued Liabilities	21,885	18,113
Income Taxes Payable	2,100	3,750
Sales Revenue	7,549,515	
Cost of Goods Sold	4,529,709	
Operating Expenses	1,354,355	
Depreciation Expense	125,547	
Loss on sale of land	30,000	
Income Tax Expense	452,971	

Required

Using the indirect method, prepare the cash flows provided by operating activities section of Newton's statement of cash flows for 2016.

SELECTED UNIT 13.2 ANSWERS

Think About It 13.2

Although net income and cash flows provided by operating activities have been increasing each year, with net income more than doubling, cash flows provided by operating activities remain negative. The biggest contributors to the use of cash from operations have been the increases in Accounts Receivable and Inventories and the decreases in liabilities. Inventories in particular seem to be building up.

Practice Questions

1. B
2. A
3. D
4. True
5. False

Unit 13.2 Practice Exercise

Cash flows provided by operating activities	
Net Income	$1,056,933[a]
Adjustments to reconcile net income to cash provided by operating activities	
Depreciation	125,547
Loss on sale of land	30,000
Changes in operating assets and liabilities	
Decrease in Accounts Receivable	19,716
Increase in Inventories	(95,939)
Decrease in Accounts Payable	(14,880)
Increase in Accrued Liabilities	3,772
Decrease in Income Taxes Payable	(1,650)
Net cash provided (used) by operating activities	$1,123,499

[a] $7,549,515 − $4,529,709 − $1,354,355 − $125,547 − $30,000 − $452,971 = $1,056,933

UNIT 13.3

Cash Flows Provided by Investing and Financing Activities

GUIDED UNIT PREPARATION

Answering the following questions while you read this unit will guide your understanding of the key concepts found in the unit. The questions are linked to the learning objectives presented at the beginning of the chapter.

LO 3

1. In which asset accounts are investing activities recorded?
2. When an asset is sold for a gain, how do you determine the amount to be reported in the investing section of the statement of cash flows?

LO 4

3. In which liability and equity accounts are financing activities recorded?

As we learned in Unit 13.1, operating activities are not the sole sources and uses of a company's cash. Although those activities are certainly more important than others in generating an ongoing supply of cash, investing and financing activities also provide and consume cash.

Cash Flows Provided by Investing Activities

Recall from Unit 13.1 that investing activities involve investments in assets other than current operating assets. These activities include purchases and sales of property and equipment, loans made and collected, and purchases and sales of another company's stock. The safest way to make sure that all investing activities have been identified is to go through a company's balance sheet line by line. To calculate the cash flows provided by investing activities, let's continue with the example of the Prescott Company, introduced in Unit 13.2.

Property and Equipment

On Prescott Company's balance sheet, the first account listed after the current assets is Property and Equipment, net. The balance in this account is calculated as follows:

	Property and Equipment, net, beginning balance
+	Purchase price of assets acquired
−	Book value of assets disposed of
−	Depreciation expense
=	Property and Equipment, net, ending balance

To make sure that all cash activities involving property and equipment have been identified, we need to enumerate all the changes in this account.

In our example, Prescott paid $40,000 cash for land. This purchase is reported as a use of cash in the cash flows provided by investing activities section of the statement of cash flows. We also know that Prescott sold a piece of equipment with a book value of $18,000. Finally, we know from the income statement that $13,700 of depreciation expense was recorded. Let's plug these items into the equation for this account to make sure that all transactions have been identified:

	Property and Equipment, net, beginning balance	$119,700
+	Purchase price of assets acquired	40,000
−	Book value of assets disposed of	(18,000)
−	Depreciation expense	(13,700)
=	Property and Equipment, net, ending balance	$128,000

As you can see, the depreciation expense and the purchase and sale of property and equipment comprise all the changes in this account.

Now we need to figure out how to report these items in the investing section of the statement of cash flows. Recall that depreciation expense was added back to net income in the operating section of the statement of cash flows, so we don't need to do anything more with it. The $40,000 purchase of land is shown as a use of cash in the investing section. The sale of equipment is a source of cash, but it should be reported at the cash amount of the transaction, not the book value of the equipment. Although we already know that the equipment was sold for $20,000, let's review the transaction to see how to use book value to determine the amount reported in the statement of cash flows:

Book value of property sold	$18,000
+ Gains or − Losses	+2,000
Cash from sale of property	$20,000

Because the gain must be added to the property's book value to arrive at the cash amount, we must subtract it from net income. Refer back to the operating section of the statement of cash flows in Exhibit 13-6 to see where the gain was subtracted from net income.

WATCH OUT!

When an asset is sold at a gain or loss, remember to include two amounts on the statement of cash flows. First, subtract the gain or add the loss from the sale from net income in the operating section of the statement of cash flows. Second, report the cash amount of the sale in the investing section.

Exhibit 13-7 shows the cash flows provided by investing activities section of the statement of cash flows. Note that it reports one source of cash, the sale of equipment for $20,000, and one use of cash, the purchase of land for $40,000. The total cash flow provided by investing activities is ($20,000). It is negative because more cash was used than was generated.

EXHIBIT 13-7

Prescott Company's cash flows used by investing activities.

Cash flows provided by investing activities		
Sale of equipment	$ 20,000	
Purchase of land	(40,000)	
Net cash provided (used) by investing activities		$(20,000)

WATCH OUT!

New property and equipment is not always purchased with cash. Sometimes a company will issue debt for the purchase and pay off the balance over time. In that case, the increase does not result from a cash activity, even though the property and equipment account increases by the full purchase price. Therefore, an asset purchased by issuing debt is not reported in the investing section of the statement of cash flows. (In the problems, you will be told when assets have been purchased by a method other than cash.)

Why not just show the ($20,000) as a net use of cash from investing activities? GAAP requires that companies report these cash flows at gross, not net, amounts. That is, when a company makes an investment in an asset (a use of cash) and sells an asset (a source of cash), two lines are required on the statement of cash flows, one for the investment and one for the sale. The company cannot add purchases and sales together and report the net amount on a single line. However, combining all similar investments into a single amount, and all similar sales into another amount, is permissible.

Other Investing Assets

Although Prescott Company does not have any other investing assets, that is not always the case. Companies may also hold notes receivable, marketable securities or investments in other companies, and other assets. The following table summarizes the transactions that increase and decrease these additional investing asset accounts:

	Notes Receivable	Marketable Securities/ Investments	Other Assets
Increases	Loans made	Investments purchased/acquired	Assets purchased/ acquired
Decreases	Loans collected/ written off	Investments sold/disposed of	Assets sold/ disposed of

Increases and decreases in these accounts may or may not involve cash. For example, a firm may own stock in a company that has declared bankruptcy and gone out of business. Although the bankruptcy decreases the amount of the firm's investment in the Marketable Securities account, it is not a use of cash. The firm's financial statements should provide enough information for users to determine whether changes in these accounts were sources or uses of cash.

Cash Flows Provided by Financing Activities

Financing can be obtained through either debt (loans) or equity (stock). Financing activities include issuing and repaying debt, issuing and repurchasing stock, and paying dividends. Once again, we need to go through all the nonoperating liability and equity accounts to identify these financing activities.

Debt Financing

Debt accounts increase when new debt is issued (that is, when money is borrowed) and decrease when debt is repaid. On the balance sheet, look for accounts such as "Short-term Notes Payable," "Long-term Debt," and "Bonds Payable." Regardless of the name, the account balances are calculated as follows:

Beginning balance
+ New debt issued
− Debt repayments
= Ending balance

The balance sheet shows the beginning and ending balances in the debt account. You need only one more piece of information to make sure you have considered all possible financing activities: the amount of new debt issued or the amount of debt repaid. If either of these amounts involved a cash transaction, you must include it in the financing section of the statement of cash flows.

Let's continue with the Prescott Company example. From the information found in Exhibits 13-4 and 13-5 we know that no new debt was issued. Therefore, we can use the following equation to determine whether any debt was repaid:

Long-term Debt, beginning balance	$143,200
+ New debt issued	0
− Debt repayments	(x)
= Long-term Debt, ending balance	$128,200

Solving for x, we find that $15,000 of debt was repaid. So we must include a $15,000 use of cash in the financing section of the statement of cash flows.

Equity Financing

Companies obtain equity financing by issuing new shares of stock. Both common and preferred stock accounts increase with an issue of new stock and decrease with a retirement or repurchase of stock.[4]

Stock, beginning balance
+ New stock issued
− Stock retired/repurchased
= Stock, ending balance

The balance sheet shows the beginning and ending balances in the Stock account. You need only one more piece of information to make sure you have considered all possible financing activities: the amount of new stock issued or the amount of stock retired/repurchased. If either of these amounts involves a cash transaction, you must include it in the financing section of the statement of cash flows.

Continuing with the Prescott Company example, we know from the information provided that additional common stock was issued for $100,000 cash. This amount should be reported as a source of cash in the financing section. Let's use our equation to determine whether any stock was retired or repurchased:

Common Stock, beginning balance	$ 75,000
+ New stock issued	100,000
− Stock retired/repurchased	(x)
= Common Stock, ending balance	$175,000

Solving for x, we find that no other activities were recorded in the Common Stock account. So the only activity that must be reported on the statement of cash flows is the issue of stock.

The only other equity account we will discuss is Retained Earnings. This account increases by the amount of net income for the period and decreases by dividends declared:

Retained Earnings, beginning balance
+ Net income
− Dividends declared
= Retained Earnings, ending balance

The balance sheet shows the beginning and ending balances in Retained Earnings; the income statement shows net income. If you don't have any information about dividends, you can use this equation to determine whether dividends were declared.

From the information found in Exhibit 13-4, we know that Prescott Company declared dividends in the amount of $14,000. Let's use our equation to make sure that everything has been accounted for in the Retained Earnings account:

Retained Earnings, beginning balance	$ 32,200
+ Net income	30,800
− Dividends declared	(14,000)
= Retained Earnings, ending balance	$ 49,000

Because our equation adds up correctly, we can be sure we have accounted for all activities in this account.

Neither net income nor dividends declared is a cash flow. Thus, net income will show up on the statement of cash flows *only if* the indirect method is used. Dividends are not reported on the statement of cash flows until they have actually been paid, at which time they are reported as a use of cash in the section on financing activities.

How can you determine whether dividends were paid? If dividends were declared but the balance sheet shows no liability for dividends payable, you can assume that the dividends were paid. If the balance sheet shows a Dividends Payable account, you must analyze the account to determine whether some or all of the declared dividends were paid. The Dividends Payable account increases when a company declares a dividend and decreases when the dividend is paid:

Dividends Payable, beginning balance
+ Dividends declared
− Dividends paid
= Dividends Payable, ending balance

The balance sheet shows the beginning and ending balances in the Dividends Payable account. The Retained Earnings account indicates whether a dividend was declared. With that information, you can determine whether any dividends were paid during the year.

Continuing with the Prescott Company example, we know that $14,000 in dividends were declared. Let's use the equation to determine whether any dividends were paid:

Dividends Payable, beginning balance	$ 0
+ Dividends declared	14,000
− Dividends paid	(x)
= Dividends Payable, ending balance	$14,000

Solving for x, we can see that no dividends were paid this year.

THINK ABOUT IT 13.3

If the Retained Earnings account has not been reduced for dividends declared, can you be sure that no dividends were paid? Explain.

WATCH OUT!

The best way to make sure that you don't miss a cash flow is to explain the changes in every balance sheet account and then identify which of those changes are cash transactions.

This completes our analysis of cash flows provided by financing activities. The financing section of the statement of cash flows, shown in Exhibit 13-8, lists one source of cash, an issue of common stock for $100,000, and one use of cash, the repayment of long-term debt for $15,000. Total cash flows provided by financing activities equals $85,000.

Cash flows provided by financing activities		
Issue of common stock	$100,000	
Repayment of long-term debt	(15,000)	
Net cash provided (used) by financing activities		$85,000

EXHIBIT 13-8

Prescott Company's cash flows provided by financing activities.

UNIT 13.3 REVIEW

PRACTICE QUESTIONS

1. LO 3 During the year, Casey Machining purchased equipment for $18,000 cash and sold a piece of land with a book value of $90,000 for $80,000 cash. What were Casey's net cash flows provided by investing activities for the year?
   a. $98,000
   b. $72,000
   c. $62,000
   d. $(8,000)

2. LO 3 For the past two years, Mayfair Company's statement of cash flows has shown net cash provided by investing activities. Which of the following strategic choices could explain this result?
   a. Divestiture of a significant operating division
   b. Purchase of 29% of Fairview, Inc.'s common stock
   c. Issue 100,000 shares of preferred stock
   d. Payoff of the outstanding balance on a long-term loan

3. LO 4 Tadas & Dixon, Ltd., borrowed $100,000 from Great City National Bank on January 2. On December 31, Tadas & Dixon made its first annual principal payment of $20,000. These two transactions will be reported in the statement of cash flows as

a. two separate items in the cash flows provided by financing activities section—a source of $100,000 and a use of $20,000.

b. a single item in the cash flows provided by financing activities section—a source of $80,000.

c. two separate items in the cash flows provided by financing activities section—a source of $20,000 and a use of $100,000.

d. two separate items in the cash flows provided by investing activities section—a source of $100,000 and a use of $20,000.

4. LO 4 During 2015, Hanley Enterprises sold a piece of equipment with a book value of $50,000 for $65,000; declared preferred stock dividends of $23,000, payable on January 5, 2016; and borrowed $40,000 from Lakeside Central Bank. Hanley's cash flows provided by financing activities for 2015 was

a. $128,000.

b. $88,000.

c. $40,000.

d. $17,000.

UNIT 13.3 PRACTICE EXERCISE

Schneider Golf Resort completed the following transactions during the year:

- Purchased 50 new golf carts at a total cost of $250,000. Schneider paid $100,000 cash and issued a three-year note payable to the manufacturer for the balance.
- Borrowed $50,000 from First National Bank.
- Sold 50 used golf carts for $90,000 cash. The carts had a book value of $110,000.
- Purchased a new tractor for $25,000 cash.
- Paid $2,000 in dividends to shareholders.
- Sold 1,000 shares of Nike stock for $45 per share.

Required

Prepare Schneider Golf Resort's cash flows provided by investing activities and cash flows provided by financing activities sections of the statement of cash flows for the year.

SELECTED UNIT 13.3 ANSWERS

Think About It 13.3

No. Dividends can be paid in a year in which no dividends were declared. If that is the case, then the dividend payment represents a dividend declared in a prior period, for which a dividend payable should exist. The best way to ensure that you do not miss such dividend payments is to analyze every balance sheet account.

Practice Questions

1. C
2. A
3. A
4. C

Unit 13.3 Practice Exercise

Cash flows provided by investing activities	
Purchases of property and equipment	$(125,000)
Proceeds from sale of property and equipment	90,000
Sales of investments	45,000
Net cash provided (used) by investing activities	$ 10,000
Cash flows provided by financing activities	
Proceeds from issuance of long-term debt	50,000
Payment of dividends	(2,000)
Net cash provided (used) by financing activities	$ 48,000

UNIT 13.4

Constructing and Interpreting the Statement of Cash Flows

GUIDED UNIT PREPARATION

Answering the following questions while you read this unit will guide your understanding of the key concepts found in the unit. The questions are linked to the learning objectives presented at the beginning of the chapter.

LO 5

1. What should the cash flows from each of the three sections add up to? How do you know whether or not you have obtained the right amount?

LO 6

2. Why is it important for a company to generate cash from operating activities on a consistent basis?
3. What might a trend toward providing cash through investing activities suggest about a business?

Once you have calculated the cash flows provided by operating, investing, and financing activities, putting the statement of cash flows together is easy. As the following table shows, you just add the three cash flows to obtain the change in the cash balance. Then you add the beginning Cash balance to the change in cash to get the ending Cash balance, reported on the balance sheet. The basic form of the statement is:

	Cash flows provided (used) by operating activities
+	Cash flows provided (used) by investing activities
+	Cash flows provided (used) by financing activities
=	Change in Cash
+	Cash, beginning balance
=	Cash, ending balance

In this chapter, we calculated the cash flows for Prescott Company. Although that example doesn't include every possible type of cash flow, the techniques it illustrates can be used to calculate any other cash flows you may encounter. To make sure you have considered every cash flow, examine the changes in every balance sheet account other than cash. Exhibit 13-9 shows this process for Prescott Company.

Exhibit 13-10 shows Prescott Company's completed statement of cash flows using the indirect method. Notice that each of the three sections lists the sources

	Increase/(Decrease)	Statement of Cash Flows Treatment	
Cash and cash equivalents	$ 85,100	Change in cash	
Accounts receivable	12,000	Operating: subtracted from net income	
Inventories	(2,970)	Operating: added to net income	
Property and equipment, net	8,300	Investing: sale of equipment	$(18,000)[a]
		Investing: purchase of land	40,000
		Operating: depreciation expense added to net income	(13,700)
			$ 8,300
Accounts payable	(17,600)	Operating: subtracted from net income	
Accrued liabilities	2,680	Operating: added to net income	
Salaries payable	350	Operating: added to net income	
Income taxes payable	1,200	Operating: added to net income	
Dividends payable	14,000	Non-cash investing/financing transaction: dividend declaration	
Long-term debt	(15,000)	Financing: repayment of debt	
Common stock	100,000	Financing: issue of common stock	
Retained earnings	16,800	Operating: net income	$ 30,800
		Non-cash investing/financing transaction: dividend declaration	(14,000)
			$ 16,800

[a]Add $18,000 book value of equipment sold to the $2,000 gain on the sale of equipment to get cash proceeds from sale of $20,000, reported in the statement of cash flows.

EXHIBIT 13-9 *Tracking the changes in Prescott Company's balance sheet accounts—indirect method.*

EXHIBIT 13-10 *Prescott Company's statement of cash flows—indirect method.*

PRESCOTT COMPANY
Statement of Cash Flows—Indirect Method
For the Year Ending December 31, 2016

Cash flows provided by operating activities		
Net income		$30,800
Adjustments to net income		
Depreciation	$ 13,700	
Gain on sale of equipment	(2,000)	
Increase in accounts receivable	(12,000)	
Decrease in inventories	2,970	
Decrease in accounts payable	(17,600)	
Increase in accrued liabilities	2,680	
Increase in salaries payable	350	
Increase in income taxes payable	1,200	(10,700)
Net cash provided (used) by operating activities		20,100
Cash flows provided by investing activities		
Sale of equipment	20,000	
Purchase of land	(40,000)	
Net cash provided (used) by investing activities		(20,000)
Cash flows provided by financing activities		
Repayment of long-term debt	(15,000)	
Issue of common stock	100,000	
Net cash provided (used) by financing activities		85,000
Change in cash		$85,100
Cash, beginning balance		11,500
Cash, ending balance		$96,600
Non-cash investing and financing activities		
Declaration of dividend to be paid in 2017		$14,000

and uses of cash, as well as the total cash used or provided by those activities. Then the three section totals are added to obtain the $85,100 increase in the Cash account for the year. In the final section of the statement, the $11,500 beginning Cash balance is added to this change in cash to arrive at the $96,600 ending balance—the same as the amount reported on the balance sheet.

Although all Prescott Company's cash events have been reported on the cash flow statement, we are not finished. Significant investing and financing activities that do *not* affect cash must be reported in a separate section that follows the cash flow calculation. For Prescott Company, the only activity of this type was the declaration of dividends. Other non-cash investing and financing activities that must be reported include:

- conversion of bonds to stock
- purchase of assets using debt
- asset swaps

WATCH OUT!

The ending Cash balance that is calculated on the statement of cash flows must equal the ending Cash balance that is reported on the balance sheet. If the two amounts do not agree, you have made an error.

Analyzing the Statement of Cash Flows

As a future manager, you need to know how to interpret a statement of cash flows. The first thing you should examine is the company's ability to generate cash from operations. Over the long run, a company must generate a positive cash flow from operating activities in order to remain in business. If the cash flow from operating activities remains negative over several periods, the company will likely be forced to raise cash by borrowing, which will place additional strains on cash flow as the principal and interest payments come due.

The cash flows provided by operating activities section also provides clues to how well a company manages its assets. For example, an increase in accounts receivable may indicate increased sales, or it may indicate that customers are taking longer to pay or that managers are too lenient in granting them credit. An increase in inventory may result from a need to support an anticipated increase in sales volume, a drop in customer demand, or poor inventory management. An increase in accounts payable could signal a weakening cash position and an inability to pay accounts as they become due. Decreases in accounts payable could indicate fewer inventory purchases due to slowing or decreasing customer demand, a tightening of stringent credit policies by vendors, or inventory stockouts.

Recall that property, plant, and equipment provide the capability to produce the company's products or deliver its services. Therefore, the company should maintain an adequate level of investment in those assets. As the assets wear out or become obsolete, they should be replaced, creating a use of cash in the investing section. Purchases of equipment of roughly the same amount as depreciation expense indicate that the company is providing for continued productive capacity. The use of cash to expand a company's operations is also reported in this section. Watch for excessive sales of property, plant, and equipment combined with a lack of cash from financing activities. Such a pattern may indicate that the company is selling productive assets to raise cash to cover operating expenses because of an inability to borrow additional funds. In the long run, such actions will limit future growth.

Finally, the cash flows provided by financing activities provide insight into a company's use of debt and equity financing. If equity is the only source of financing, the company may have exhausted available lines of credit or may have been identified as a poor credit risk by lenders.

Let's examine Exhibit 13-10, which shows that Prescott Company was able to generate $20,100 in cash from operations. That amount is less than the net income Prescott generated—why? You know from having constructed the statement of cash flows that there are two primary reasons: (1) less cash was collected than the sales reported on the income statement and (2) more cash was paid for inventory than was expensed as cost of goods sold on the income statement. These are reasonable results for a company whose sales are growing.

The $20,100 that Prescott generated from operations was enough to cover the $20,000 needed for investing activities. Why do you suppose the company issued $100,000 in common stock? The beginning Cash balance of $11,500 would not have been enough to cover the $15,000 in debt that had to be repaid, but that alone would not be enough to justify a stock issue. The purchase of land suggests that the company has plans for expansion and that cash from the stock issue may be used to fund part of that expansion.

Now let's look again at C&C Sports' statement of cash flows, shown in Exhibit 13-1. Notice that it was prepared using the indirect method. As you can see, over the last three years net income has been increasing, yet the company cannot generate cash from operations. Why not? Not only are Accounts Receivable, Inventories, and Prepaid Expenses and Other Assets amounts increasing (remember that an increase in current assets decreases cash), but current operating liabilities are decreasing, using additional cash in the process.

C&C has no cash flows provided by investing activities, meaning that no assets were purchased or sold for cash. The financing section of the statement reveals that C&C is substituting short-term debt for long-term debt. The $20,000 annual repayment of long-term debt suggests that the company is following a payment schedule. Because C&C does not have enough cash to cover the long-term debt repayment, it must borrow additional cash for the short term.

Notice that C&C's managers have allowed the cash balance to drop from $87,667 at the beginning of 2014 to $7,752 at the end of 2016. While $87,667 may have been relatively high, $7,752 seems low. It is time for C&C's managers to take a hard look at their cash management techniques, credit policies, and payment practices in order to better match cash coming in with cash going out.

THINK ABOUT IT 13.4

What factors might influence how much cash managers decide to keep on hand?

UNIT 13.4 REVIEW

PRACTICE QUESTIONS

LO 5 For questions 1 through 5, find the missing amounts. Consider each column independently.

Cash provided (used) by operating activities	$ 9,000	2.	$ 1,000
Cash provided (used) by investing activities	1.	(10,000)	4.
Cash provided (used) by financing activities	11,000	5,000	(25,000)
Total change in cash	$22,000	$ (9,000)	$(16,000)
Cash balance, beginning	45,000	3.	30,000
Cash balance, ending	$67,000	$ 3,000	5.

6. LO 5 Lockhardt Industries' statement of cash flows shows no items in the financing section. That omission means that the company has no common shareholders. True or False?

7. LO 3 Nicholas Partners, Inc. purchased a building from Cameron Enterprises. To pay for the building, Nicholas issued 10,000 shares of common stock to Cameron. At the time the shares were issued, Nicholas's stock was trading for $20 per share. How will this transaction be reported on Nicholas's statement of cash flows?

   a. As a source of cash in the cash flows provided by investing activities section
   b. As a use of cash in the cash flows provided by investing activities section
   c. As a use of cash in the cash flows provided by financing activities section
   d. As a non-cash investing and financing transaction

UNIT 13.4 PRACTICE EXERCISE

Weston Todd Corporation is a manufacturer and marketer of consumer products. The company's statement of cash flows for the years 2015 and 2016 is presented below.

Weston Todd Corporation and Subsidiaries
Consolidated Statements of Cash Flows
(in millions)

	2016	2015
Cash Flows Provided by Operating Activities		
Net income	$ 364	$ (79)
Less: Cash received from contingent sales proceeds	(150)	(130)
Items not requiring (providing) cash		
Depreciation	383	403
Amortization	114	122
Other	70	622
Changes in		
Trade Accounts Receivable	23	(92)
Inventories	90	(117)
Other Current Assets	16	(36)
Accounts Payable	(126)	38
Accrued Expenses and Other	116	(125)
Net cash provided (used) by operating activities	900	606
Cash Flows Provided by Investing Activities		
Purchase of property and equipment	(357)	(454)
Purchase of software and other intangibles	(22)	(61)
Acquisitions of businesses and investments	(10)	—
Dispositions of businesses and investments	53	55
Cash received from contingent sales proceeds	150	130
Cash received from (used in) derivative transactions	(138)	96
Sales of assets	38	38
Net cash provided (used) by investing activities	(286)	(196)
Cash Flows Provided by Financing Activities		
Issuances of common stock	1	5
Purchases of common stock	(103)	(315)
Repayments of debt	(802)	(1,205)
Borrowings of debt	439	—
Payments of dividends	(302)	(296)
Net cash provided (used) by financing activities	(767)	(1,811)
Effect of changes in foreign exchange rates on cash	(172)	165
Increase (Decrease) in Cash	(325)	(1,236)
Cash balance of discontinued operations	—	3
Cash, beginning of year	1,284	2,517
Cash, end of year	$ 959	$ 1,284

Required

Comment on Weston Todd's cash flows for 2016.

SELECTED UNIT 13.4 ANSWERS

Think About It 13.4

The amount of cash to keep on hand will likely depend on how readily the company can borrow money, as well as on the interest rate at which the company can borrow. If the company has easy access to cash, then less cash will need to be kept on hand.

Practice Questions

1. $2,000
2. $(4,000)
3. $12,000
4. $8,000
5. $14,000
6. False
7. D

Unit 13.4 Practice Exercise

Weston Todd generated a positive cash flow from operations during each of the two years, and the amount of cash generated from operations increased almost 50% during 2016. In 2015, current assets increased and accounts payable decreased, while the opposite was true in 2016.

The company appears to be maintaining its productive asset base through purchases of new equipment, although the purchase of new assets declined in 2016. The company does not appear to be selling many surplus assets or business segments. Based on the line that refers to "contingent sales," however, a large sale seems to be pending.

Weston Todd has been borrowing money and is making payments on its debt. The company maintained its historical dividend payment pattern.

Overall, the company's cash position decreased during both years.

APPENDIX

Cash Flows Provided by Operating Activities: The Direct Method

GUIDED UNIT PREPARATION

Answering the following questions while you read this appendix will guide your understanding of the key concepts found in the appendix. The questions are linked to the learning objectives presented at the beginning of the chapter.

LO 7

1. Under the direct method, what are the five general categories of cash flows from operating activities?
2. How do you use the income statement and balance sheets to calculate each of the five cash flows from operating activities?

The direct method of preparing the statement of cash flows lets users know exactly how cash was generated and used in operations.[5] Specifically, cash flows from operating activities are generated by five major activities:

- Collections from customers
- Payments to suppliers
- Payments to employees
- Payments for operating costs
- Payments for income taxes

Although the results of these activities are shown on the income statement, they were reported using the accrual basis of accounting. To determine the cash effects of these activities, then, we will need to adjust the reported revenues and expenses. As long as we have the income statement and balance sheets, we have everything we need to make the adjustments.

Let's work through an example to illustrate how to calculate the five cash flows provided by operating activities. Exhibits 13-4 and 13-5 show the comparative balance sheets and income statement for Prescott Company. For each cash flow, we will use the related balance sheet accounts and the following relationship:

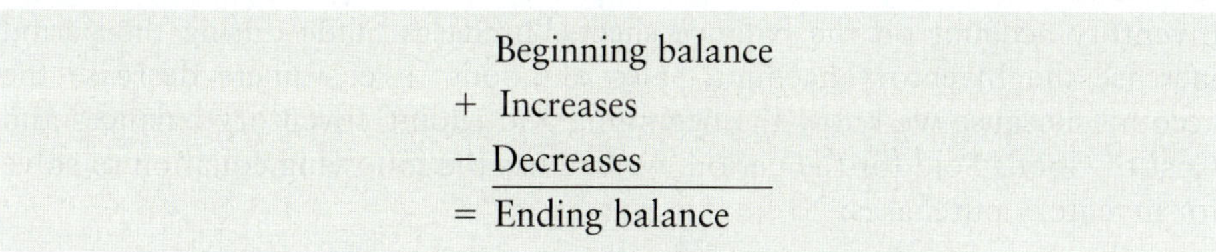

Exhibit 13-11 shows the operating section of Prescott Company's statement of cash flows as it appears when it is prepared using the direct method. Refer to this statement as we discuss each of the five cash flow calculations.

Collections from Customers

When goods or services are sold to customers, the company records sales revenue. Because customers may not pay cash at the time of the sale, however, the amount of sales revenue that is reported on the income statement does not necessarily equal the amount of cash collected from customers.

To determine how much cash was actually collected, we need to examine Accounts Receivable using the amounts shown on the comparative balance sheets. Recall that credit sales increase the balance in Accounts Receivable; cash collections decrease the balance. If we know the beginning and ending balances

Cash flows provided by operating activities		
Collections from customers	$1,038,000	
Payments to suppliers	(791,630)	
Payments to employees	(92,050)	
Payments for operating costs	(122,220)	
Payments for income taxes	(12,000)	
Net cash provided (used) by operating activities		$20,100

EXHIBIT 13-11

Prescott Company's cash flows provided by operating activities—direct method.

in Accounts Receivable, as well as the Sales Revenue for the period, we can use the following equation to solve for cash collections from customers:

Accounts Receivable, beginning balance	$ 11,200
+ Sales	1,050,000
− Collections from customers	(x)
= Accounts Receivable, ending balance	$ 23,200

Solving for x, we find that $1,038,000 was collected from customers. This amount should be reported on the statement of cash flows.

Payments to Suppliers

Just as sales revenue doesn't reflect cash collections from customers, Cost of Goods Sold, also reported on the income statement, doesn't reflect cash payments to suppliers. One reason is that inventory may be purchased in one period but not sold until a later period. Another is that, like sales, these purchases may be made on account.

To determine the actual cash payments made to suppliers, we first need to determine the amount of inventory purchased during the period using the Inventory account on the balance sheet. Purchases made during the period increase the Inventory account; sales of goods to customers decrease the account. Because we know the beginning and ending Inventory balances and Cost of Goods Sold for the period, we can use the following equation to solve for inventory purchases:

Inventory, beginning balance	$ 326,340
+ Inventory purchases	x
− Cost of Good Sold	(777,000)
= Inventory, ending balance	$ 323,370

Solving for x, we find that $774,030 was purchased from suppliers.

As we said, not all inventory purchases create a cash flow. If a company purchases inventory on account, the transaction creates an Account Payable; no cash changes hands. Thus, the purchase of inventory is not the same as a cash payment for inventory. To determine the actual amount of cash paid for inventory, we need to analyze the Accounts Payable balances on the balance sheets. Purchases of inventory on account increase the Accounts Payable balance; cash payments to vendors decrease the balance. If we know the beginning and ending Accounts Payable balances and the amount of inventory purchases, we can use the following equation to calculate cash payments for inventory:

Accounts Payable, beginning balance	$162,200
+ Inventory purchases	774,030
− Payments for inventory	(x)
= Accounts Payable, ending balance	$144,600

WATCH OUT!

Even though Payments for Inventory is found by analyzing Accounts Payable, don't forget to calculate inventory purchases first, using the Inventory account.

Solving for x, we find that $791,630 was paid to suppliers of inventory. This amount should be reported on the statement of cash flows.

Payments to Employees

Companies incur additional expenses to support their operations. As Exhibit 13-5 shows, Prescott Company incurred $231,000 in operating expenses during the year. For the statement of cash flows, we need to separate payments made to employees from payments for other operating expenses. And again, we need to convert from an accrual basis to a cash basis.

Furthermore, salaries expense shows how much expense was incurred during the year, not how much cash was actually paid to employees. To figure that out, we need to use the Salaries Payable account. If we know the beginning and ending balances in the Salaries Payable account, as well as the salaries expense reported on the income statement, we can use the following equation to calculate the actual cash payments to employees:

Salaries Payable, beginning balance	$ 1,600
+ Salaries expense,	92,400
− Payments to employees	(x)
= Salaries Payable, ending balance	$ 1,950

Solving for x, we find that $92,050 was paid to employees. This amount should be reported on the statement of cash flows.

Payments for Operating Costs

Payments for operating costs flow through the Accrued Liabilities account, which increases with operating expenses accrued and decreases with payments for operating costs. We can't use all $231,000 of operating expenses reported on the income statement, however. Although depreciation expense is considered an operating expense, it affects the Property and Equipment account (through accumulated depreciation), not the Accrued Liabilities account. Nor does depreciation expense involve a cash payment. So in analyzing the effect of operating expenses on accrued liabilities, we must exclude depreciation expense. Moreover, we have already used salaries expense in analyzing payments to employees, so we need to subtract that amount from total operating expenses as well.

Making these two adjustments leaves $124,900 in operating expenses ($231,000 total operating expense − $13,700 depreciation expense − $92,400 salaries expense). If we know the beginning and ending balances in the Accrued Liabilities account and the adjusted operating expenses for the period, we can use the following equation to solve for cash payments for operating costs:

Accrued Liabilities, beginning balance	$ 42,500
+ Operating expenses	124,900
− Payments for operating costs	(x)
= Accrued Liabilities, ending balance	$ 45,220

Solving for x, we find that $122,220 was paid for operating costs. This amount should be reported on the statement of cash flows.

THINK ABOUT IT 13.5

How could you calculate payments for operating costs if the balance sheets report both Prepaid Assets and Accrued Liabilities, but you don't know which expenses went into each account? Consider the following:

	Ending Balance	Beginning Balance
Prepaid Assets	$12,000	$ 8,000
Accrued Liabilities	$25,000	$28,000
Operating Expense	$90,000	

Calculate cash payments for operating costs.

Payments for Income Taxes

Prescott Company incurred $13,200 in income tax expense, as reported on the income statement. The accrual of the tax expense does not mean that the company has actually paid the tax, however. To determine the amount of tax paid, we need to examine the Income Taxes Payable account on the balance sheets. Income tax expense increases the Income Taxes Payable account; income tax payments decrease the balance in the account. If we know the beginning and ending balances in the Income Taxes Payable account and the income tax expense reported on the income statement, we can use the following equation to calculate cash payments for income taxes:

Income Taxes Payable, beginning balance	$12,000
+ Income tax expense	13,200
− Payments for income taxes	(x)
= Income Taxes Payable, ending balance	$13,200

Solving for x, we find that $12,000 was paid for income taxes. This amount should be reported on the statement of cash flows.

This completes the calculation of cash flows provided by operating activities. Refer again to Exhibit 13-11 to see that the five cash flows were added to arrive at the $20,100 net cash flows provided by operating activities. Compare this amount to the cash flows provided by operating activities calculated using the indirect method, as shown in Exhibit 13-6. Notice that the result is the same—$20,100 in cash flows provided by operations—even though the method used was different.

Exhibit 13-12 summarizes our analysis of the six balance sheet accounts involved in determining Prescott's cash flows provided by operating activities. Cash flows are highlighted in green; income statement items are highlighted in yellow. For quick reference, the following table lists the operating activities shown on the statement of cash flows along with the related income statement and balance sheet accounts used in the direct method.

Finally, Exhibit 13-13 shows the entire statement of cash flows prepared using the direct method. Note that the investing and financing sections, discussed in Unit 13.3, do not differ in presentation from the indirect method.

Operating accounts:

Accounts Receivable		**Inventories**		**Accounts Payable**	
Beginning balance	$ 11,200	Beginning balance	$ 326,340	Beginning balance	$ 162,200
+ Sales (Income Statement)	1,050,000	+ Purchases of Inventory	774,030	+ Purchases (from Inventory account)	774,030
− Collections from Customers	(1,038,000)	− Cost of Goods Sold (Income Statement)	(777,000)	− Payments for Inventory	(791,630)
= Ending balance	$ 23,200	= Ending balance	$ 323,370	= Ending balance	$ 144,600
Accrued Liabilities		**Salaries Payable**		**Income Taxes Payable**	
Beginning balance	$ 42,540	Beginning balance	$ 1,600	Beginning balance	$ 12,000
+ Operating Expenses[a] (Income Statement)	124,900	+ Salaries Expense (Income Statement)	92,400	+ Income Tax Expense (Income Statement)	13,200
− Payments for Operating Costs	(122,220)	− Payments to Employees	(92,050)	− Payments for Income Taxes	(12,000)
= Ending balance	$ 45,220	= Ending balance	$ 1,950	= Ending balance	$ 13,200

[a]Operating expenses less depreciation and salaries expense ($231,000 − $13,700 − 92,400 = $124,900).

EXHIBIT 13-12 *Analysis of balance sheet accounts—direct method.*

Cash Flow	Income Statement Account	Balance Sheet Account
Collections from customers	Sales	Accounts Receivable
Payments to suppliers	Cost of Goods Sold	Inventories, Accounts Payable
Payments to employees	Salaries Expense	Salaries Payable
Payments for operating costs	Operating Expenses*	Accrued Liabilities
Payments for income taxes	Income Tax Expense	Income Taxes Payable

*Adjust for depreciation and salaries expense.

EXHIBIT 13-13 *Prescott Company's statement of cash flows—direct method.*

PRESCOTT COMPANY
Statement of Cash Flows—Direct Method
For the Year Ending December 31, 2016

Cash flows provided by operating activities		
Collections from customers	$1,038,000	
Payments to suppliers	(791,630)	
Payments to employees	(92,050)	
Payments for operating costs	(122,220)	
Payments for income taxes	(12,000)	
Net cash provided (used) by operating activities		$20,100
Cash flows used by investing activities		
Sale of equipment	20,000	
Purchase of land	(40,000)	
Net cash provided (used) by investing activities		(20,000)
Cash flows provided by financing activities		
Repayment of long-term debt	(15,000)	
Issue common stock	100,000	
Net cash provided (used) by financing activities		85,000
Change in cash		85,100
Cash, beginning balance		11,500
Cash, ending balance		$96,600
Non-cash investing and financing activities		
Declaration of dividend to be paid in 2015		$14,000

APPENDIX REVIEW

PRACTICE QUESTIONS

1. LO 7 Depreciation expense is subtracted from net income in preparing the statement of cash flows using the direct method. True or False?

2. LO 7 Tomasini & Brown Enterprises reported accounts receivable of $50,000 on January 1; on December 31, the account balance was $68,000. Sales for the year totaled $482,000. The amount of collections from customers reported on the company's statement of cash flows will be

   a. $464,000. c. $500,000.
   b. $482,000. d. $532,000.

3. LO 7 Goyal, Ltd., reported accounts payable of $83,000 on January 1; on December 31, the account balance was $67,000. Inventory purchases for the year totaled $397,000. The amount of payments to suppliers reported on the company's statement of cash flows will be

   a. $381,000. c. $413,000.
   b. $397,000. d. $480,000.

4. LO 7 Treadaway Tires reported salaries payable of $18,000 on January 1; on December 31, the account balance was $20,000. Salaries expense for the year totaled $254,000. The amount of payments to employees reported on the company's statement of cash flows will be

   a. $252,000. c. $272,000.
   b. $256,000. d. $292,000.

5. LO 7 Fox & Sons Furniture reported accrued liabilities of $12,000 on January 1; on December 31, the account balance was $8,000. Operating expenses for the year totaled $277,000, which included $20,000 of depreciation expense and $80,000 of salaries expense. The amount of payments for operating costs reported on the company's statement of cash flows will be

   a. $289,000. c. $251,000.
   b. $281,000. d. $181,000.

APPENDIX PRACTICE EXERCISE

The following balances were gathered from Newton Company's general ledger.

	December 31, 2016	December 31, 2015
Accounts Receivable	$ 75,581	$ 95,297
Inventories	213,345	117,406
Accounts Payable	60,567	75,447
Accrued Liabilities	21,885	18,113
Income Taxes Payable	2,100	3,750
Sales	7,549,515	
Cost of Goods Sold	4,529,709	
Operating Expenses	1,354,355	
Depreciation Expense	125,547	
Loss on Sale of Land	30,000	
Income Tax Expense	452,971	

Required

Using the direct method, prepare the cash flows provided by operating activities section of the statement of cash flows.

SELECTED APPENDIX ANSWERS

Think About It 13.5

If all operating costs had been paid only through Prepaid Assets, you could have concluded the following:

Beginning balance	$ 8,000
+ Prepayments of costs	x
− Operating expenses accrued	(90,000)
= Ending balance	$ 12,000

Prepayments of costs would equal $94,000, or $90,000 in operating expenses plus the $4,000 increase in the Prepaid Assets account.

If all operating expenses had been paid only through Accrued Liabilities, you could have concluded the following:

Beginning balance	$28,000
+ Operating expenses accrued	90,000
− Payments of costs	(x)
= Ending balance	$25,000

Payments of costs would equal $93,000, or $90,000 in operating expenses plus the $3,000 decrease in the Accrued Liabilities account.

Because both accounts changed, you need to adjust the computation as follows:

$90,000 + increase in Prepaid Expenses + decrease in Accrued Liabilities = Payments for Operating Costs

$90,000 + 4,000 + 3,000 = $97,000

You can verify this answer by splitting the $90,000 of Operating Expenses and running part through Prepaid Expenses and part through Accrued Liabilities.

Practice Questions

1. False
2. A
3. C
4. A
5. D

Appendix Practice Exercise

Collections from customers	$ 7,569,231
Payments to suppliers	(4,640,528)
Payments for operating costs	(1,350,583)
Payments for income taxes	(454,621)
Cash provided (used) by operating activities	$ 1,123,499

Operating accounts:

Accounts Receivable

Beginning balance	$ 95,297
+ Sales (Income Statement)	7,549,515
− Collections from Customers	7,569,231
= Ending balance	$ 75,581

Accounts Payable

Beginning balance	75,447
+ Purchases of Inventory	4,625,648
− Payments to suppliers	4,640,528
= Ending balance	60,567

Income Taxes Payable

Beginning balance	3,750
+ Income Tax Expense (Income Statement)	452,971
− Payments for Income Taxes	454,621
= Ending balance	2,100

Inventories

Beginning balance	$ 117,406
+ Purchase of Inventory	4,625,648
− Cost of Goods Sold (Income Statement)	(4,529,709)
= Ending balance	$ 213,345

Accrued Liabilities

Beginning balance	18,113
+ Operating Expenses (Income Statement)	1,354,355
− Payments for Operating Costs	(1,350,583)
= Ending balance	21,885

BUSINESS DECISION AND CONTEXT Wrap Up

After examining the statement of cash flows, C&C Sports' managers now understand how the company spends and generates cash. Analyzing the statement has given them insight into the effect of their actions on the company's cash position and on its income statement. Jonathan Smith, vice president of marketing, has instructed sales representatives to offer only the standard 30-day credit terms to customers who purchase on account. Chad Davis, vice president of operations, has instructed the purchasing manager not to prepay for orders unless a substantial discount has been offered. Both vice presidents understand that they need to consult with CFO Claire Elliot to assess the cash flow implications of a departure from normal policy *before* they grant an exception. And Chad Davis will evaluate C&C's inventory practices to determine whether the company is investing too much cash in inventory.

Although CFO Claire Elliot is in charge of working with the bank on debt arrangements, she is not the only person who is responsible for the amount of cash that is available to the company. Everyone has a stake in keeping C&C Sports financially viable and should therefore be willing to take the necessary steps to improve the company's cash situation.

CHAPTER SUMMARY

1. *Categorize cash activities as operating, investing, or financing. (Unit 13.1)*

Operating activities are undertaken to accomplish the company's primary business purpose. They include selling inventory or providing services, paying employees, purchasing inventory, and paying operating costs.

Investing activities involve investments in assets other than current operating assets. These activities include buying or selling property, making or collecting loans, and buying or selling investments in other businesses.

Financing activities involve funding from external sources. They include issuing or repaying debt, issuing or retiring stock, and paying dividends.

2. *Calculate cash flows provided by operating activities using the indirect method. (Unit 13.2)*

The indirect method begins with net income, which is adjusted for non-cash expenses, losses and gains on the sale of property and investments, and the early extinguishment of debt. Adjustments are also made for increases and decreases in current assets and current liabilities. The calculation is as follows:

Net income
+ depreciation, amortization, and bad debt expense
+ losses on the sale of property and investments or on the early extinguishment of debt
− gains on the sale of property and investments or on the early extinguishment of debt
− increases in current assets
+ decreases in current assets
+ increases in current liabilities
− decreases in current liabilities
= cash flows provided (used) by operating activities

3. *Calculate cash flows provided by investing activities. (Unit 13.3)*

Once investing activities have been identified in the nonoperating asset accounts, their amounts must be added together to arrive at cash flows provided by investing activities. Only cash flows should be included, so non-cash investing activities, such as purchasing a building with debt, should not be included. Likewise, when an asset is sold, the cash amount of the sale, not the book value of the asset, should be reported.

4. *Calculate cash flows provided by financing activities. (Unit 13.3)*

Once financing activities have been identified in the nonoperating liability and equity accounts, their amounts must be added together to arrive at cash flows provided by financing activities. Only cash flows should be included, so non-cash financing activities, such as issuing debt to purchase a building, should not be included. Likewise, dividends that have been declared but not paid should not be reported as a use of cash.

5. *Construct a statement of cash flows. (Unit 13.4)*

The statement of cash flows follows this basic format:

	Cash flows provided (used) by operating activities
+	Cash flows provided (used) by investing activities
+	Cash flows provided (used) by financing activities
=	Change in Cash
+	Cash, beginning balance
=	Cash, ending balance

6. *Analyze a statement of cash flows. (Unit 13.4)*

The statement of cash flows shows how well a company generates and uses cash. When you review a statement of cash flows, ask the following questions:

- Is the company generating cash from its operations?
- What are the primary sources and uses of cash from operations?
- Do investing activities suggest that the company is expanding (purchasing assets) or retracting (selling assets)?
- Is the company continually borrowing money? If so, are the extra funds needed for asset growth or for the payment of operating costs?

7. *Calculate cash flows provided by operating activities using the direct method. (Appendix)*

The direct method calculates cash flows as follows:

	Collections from customers
−	Payments to suppliers
−	Payments to employees
−	Payments for operating expenses
−	Payments for taxes
=	Cash flows provided (used) by operating activities

KEY TERMS

Direct method (Unit 13.1)
Financing activities (Unit 13.1)
Indirect method (Unit 13.1)
Investing activities (Unit 13.1)
Operating activities (Unit 13.1)
Sources of cash (Unit 13.1)
Statement of cash flows (Unit 13.1)
Uses of cash (Unit 13.1)

EXERCISES

13-1 Identifying cash flows (LO 1) Complete the following table by identifying each item as a source or use of cash for each company named in the exercise.

	Source of Cash	Use of Cash
NBC Universal returns cash to advertisers because of ratings shortfalls.		
Deutsche Lufthansa AG purchases 19% of JetBlue Airways stock for $300 million.		
Bank of America pays shareholders a dividend of $2.12 per share.		
JP Morgan Chase receives dividends on holdings of other companies' stocks.		
Cathay Pacific Airlines pays for new airplanes.		
ExxonMobil receives payment from a major customer.		
Apple pays its income taxes.		
Facebook sells stock in its initial public offering.		
Honda Motor Co. makes a payment on its long-term debt.		

13-2 Classifying cash flows (LO 1) Complete the following table by identifying the section of the statement of cash flows that each item belongs in.

	Operating Activities	Investing Activities	Financing Activities
NBC Universal returns cash to advertisers because of ratings shortfalls.			
Deutsche Lufthansa AG purchases 19% of JetBlue Airways stock for $300 million.			
Bank of America pays shareholders a dividend of $2.12 per share.			
JP Morgan Chase receives dividends on holdings of other companies' stocks.			
Cathay Pacific Airlines pays for new airplanes.			

	Operating Activities	Investing Activities	Financing Activities
ExxonMobil receives payment from a major customer.			
Apple pays its income taxes.			
Facebook sells stock in its initial public offering.			
Honda Motor Co. makes a payment on its long-term debt.			

13-3 Classifying cash flows (LO 1) Classify each of the following items from National Beverage Corp.'s statement of cash flows as a source or use of cash, and identify the section of the statement that each appeared in.

	Source or Use	Operating Activities	Investing Activities	Financing Activities
Purchase of marketable securities				
Common stock cash dividend				
Decrease in accounts receivable				
Decrease in accounts payable				
Proceeds from disposal of property				
Sale of marketable securities				
Proceeds from the exercise of stock options				
Proceeds from the sale of assets				

13-4 Cash flows provided by operating activities—indirect method (LO 2) Perkins Co.'s current asset and liability balances for the past two years are as follows. Net income for 2016 was $1,252,000, and depreciation expense was $60,000.

	December 31, 2016	December 31, 2015
Accounts Receivable	$480,000	$380,000
Inventories	670,000	760,000
Accounts Payable	387,000	326,000
Accrued Liabilities	90,000	110,000

Required

Using the indirect method, prepare the cash flows provided by operating activities section of the statement of cash flows for 2016.

13-5 Cash flows provided by operating activities—indirect method (LO 2) Mallory Michaels, senior accountant for Trendy Fashions, has gathered the following balances from the company's general ledger:

	December 31, 2016	December 31, 2015
Accounts Receivable	$ 50,387	$ 63,531
Inventories	142,230	117,406
Prepaid Expenses	4,500	3,900
Accounts Payable	40,378	50,298
Accrued Liabilities	14,590	12,075
Income Taxes Payable	1,400	2,500
Net Income	704,621	
Depreciation Expense	83,698	
Loss on the sale of land	15,000	

Required

Using the indirect method, prepare the cash flows provided by operating activities section of the statement of cash flows for 2016.

13-6 Cash flows provided by operating activities—indirect method (LO 2) Like many companies, Roper Industries, Inc. offers stock-based compensation to some employees. Under the arrangement, employees receive stock rather than cash in payment for their services. The amount of the stock-based compensation is included in Salaries Expense for the year.

Required

Under the indirect method, how would Roper's stock-based compensation be reported on the statement of cash flows? Why?

13-7 Cash flows provided by investing activities (LO 3) Carter Hopkins Homes engaged in the following activities during the year:

- Purchased 500 shares of Google for $412,000
- Sold 1,000 shares of Starbucks for $55,000
- Purchased new equipment costing $320,000 for cash
- Sold equipment with a book value of $140,000 for $155,000

Required

Prepare the cash flows provided by investing activities section of Carter Hopkins Homes' statement of cash flows.

13-8 Cash flows provided by investing activities (LO 3) Hoffman Enterprises engaged in the following activities during the year:

- Purchased 100 shares of Monk Industries for $42,000
- Sold 50 shares of Hinson Healthcare for $9,000
- Purchased new equipment costing $80,000 for $15,000 cash and a $65,000 note payable
- Sold equipment with a book value of $50,000 for $45,000

Required

Prepare the cash flows provided by investing activities section of Hoffman Enterprises' statement of cash flows.

13-9 Cash flows provided by financing activities (LO 4) Carter Hopkins Homes engaged in the following activities during the year:

- Borrowed $600,000 from Marshall Bank
- Declared and paid dividends on common stock of $28,000
- Made a $78,000 annual principal payment on a ten-year loan from Cardinal National Bank
- Purchased 10,000 shares of Carter Hopkins Homes stock for $200,000

Required

Prepare the cash flows provided by financing activities section of Carter Hopkins Homes' statement of cash flows.

13-10 Cash flows provided by financing activities (LO 4) Hoffman Enterprises engaged in the following activities during the year:

- Borrowed $25,000 from South World Bank
- Declared and paid dividends on common stock of $27,000
- Declared preferred stock dividends of $10,000
- Repaid the $25,000 loan from South World Bank
- Borrowed $70,000 from City Financial Group

Required

Prepare the cash flows provided by financing activities section of Hoffman Enterprises' statement of cash flows.

13-11 Statement of cash flows—indirect method (LO 5) The following items were gathered from Rindt Industries' general ledger:

Sale of marketable securities	$14,000
Depreciation and amortization expense	24,262
Payment of cash dividends	3,543
Proceeds from disposal of equipment	819
Loss on disposal of equipment	150
Net income	26,043
Beginning Cash balance	19,600
Purchase of equipment	21,632
Decrease in Accounts Receivable	1,048
Proceeds from issuing common stock	2,241
Increase in Inventory	3,465
Increase in Accounts Payable	4,650
Ending Cash balance	64,173

Required

Using the indirect method, construct Rindt Industries' statement of cash flows.

13-12 Statement of cash flows—indirect method (LO 5) The following items were gathered from Carlisle Company's general ledger:

Purchase of marketable securities	$150,000
Depreciation and amortization expense	47,200
Declaration of preferred dividends	8,000
Increase in Prepaid Assets	3,500
Loss on sale of equipment	2,900
Net income	292,800
Beginning Cash balance	23,740
Repayment of bank loan	125,000
Payment for purchase of equipment	50,750
Increase in Accounts Receivable	16,760
Stock-based compensation	180,000
Proceeds from issuing common stock	25,000
Decrease in Inventory	19,200
Decrease in Accounts Payable	13,900
Ending Cash balance	230,930

Required

Using the indirect method, construct Carlisle Company's statement of cash flows.

13-13 Analyzing the statement of cash flows (LO 6) Thalina Mineral Works is one of the world's leading producers of cultured pearls. The company's condensed statement of cash flows for the years 2014–2016 follows.

	2016	2015	2014
Net cash used by operating activities	$ (937,703)	$(4,938,229)	$ (1,786,654)
Net cash used by investing activities	(336,980)	(261,468)	(333,202)
Net cash used by financing activities	(186,582)	(1,514,680)	(5,120,909)
Net change in cash and equivalents	(1,461,265)	(6,714,377)	(7,240,765)
Cash and cash equivalents at beginning of year	7,048,409	13,762,786	21,003,551
Cash and cash equivalents at end of year	$5,587,144	$ 7,048,409	$13,762,786

Required

Comment on Thalina Mineral Works' cash flows. Do you see any indicators of potential liquidity problems?

13-14 Analyzing the statement of cash flows (LO 6) Lind Industries is one of the largest manufacturers of small motors in the United States. The cash flows provided by investing activities section of the company's statement of cash flows for the years 2014–2016 follow (in $000).

	2016	2015	2014
Sale of discontinued operations, net of cash divested	—	$739,764	—
Sale of investment in unconsolidated joint venture	—	—	$ 57,767
Change in restricted cash	$(115,404)	—	—
Investments in unconsolidated joint ventures	(59,625)	(85,188)	(179,184)
Sales (purchases) of property and equipment, net	7,073	685	(17,638)
Other, net	—		772
Net cash provided (used) by investing activities—continuing operations	(167,956)	$655,261	$(138,283)
Net cash provided (used) by investing activities—discontinued operations	—	(12,112)	(4,477)
Net cash provided (used) by investing activities	$(167,956)	$643,149	$(142,760)

Required

a. How have cash flows provided by investing activities changed over the three-year period?

b. If any of these changes continue in the coming years, what concerns would you have about Lind Industries' future?

13-15 Analyzing the statement of cash flows (LO 6) Colin Confections operates convenience stores, primarily in small Southeastern towns. The cash flows provided by financing activities section of the company's statement of cash flows for the fiscal years 2014–2016 follows (in $000).

	For the Years Ended June 30		
	2016	2015	2014
Proceeds from long-term debt	—	—	$100,000
Payment of long-term debt	$(21,100)	$(31,364)	(22,814)
Proceeds from the exercise of stock options	1,346	2,104	2,941
Payment of cash dividends	(15,246)	(13,180)	(10,098)
Excess tax benefits related to stock option exercises	512	607	919
Net cash provided (used) by financing activities	$(34,488)	$(41,833)	$ 70,948

At the beginning of fiscal 2016, Colin Confections had $154,523 in cash and cash equivalents; at the end of fiscal 2016, the company had $145,695 in cash and cash equivalents.

Required

a. How have cash flows provided by financing activities changed over the three-year period?

b. Does the fact that Colin Confections reports no proceeds from long-term debt for 2015 and 2016 mean that the company has no long-term debt? Why?

c. Does it concern you that in two of the past three years, Colin Confections used more cash than was provided by financing activities? Why?

13-16 Cash received from customers (LO 7) On January 1, 2016, Glass Industries' Accounts Receivable balance was $10,000; on December 31, 2016, it was $18,000. Sales revenue for the year was $145,780.

Required

Calculate the cash received from customers in 2016.

13-17 Cash received from customers (LO 7) In its 2016 annual report, Poppie, Inc. reported Accounts Receivable of $1,453 million at the end of 2015 and $1,056 million at the end of 2016. Sales revenue for 2016 was $13,287 million.

Required

Using the direct method, what amount would Poppie, Inc. report for cash received from customers on its statement of cash flows for 2016?

13-18 Cash payments to suppliers (LO 7) At the end of 2015, Seiford Enterprises' Accounts Payable balance was $341,053; at the end of 2016, it was $160,094. Assume that the company purchased $1,951,523 of inventory during 2016 and that Cost of Goods Sold for 2016 was $1,940,562.

Required

Calculate the company's cash payments to suppliers in 2016.

13-19 Cash payments to suppliers (LO 7) On January 1, 2016, Glass Industries' Inventory balance was $20,000; on December 31, 2016, it was $18,000. The company's Accounts Payable balance was $13,500 on January 1, 2016, and $14,700 on December 31, 2016. Cost of Goods Sold for the year was $75,100.

Required

Calculate the company's cash payments to suppliers in 2016.

13-20 Cash payments to employees (LO 7) Tarpley Bakery manufactures, distributes, and markets a broad array of baked goods. In its 2016 annual report, the company reported salaries and wages payable of $64 million at the end of 2016 and $80 million at the end of 2015. Assume that the company's salaries and wages expense for 2016 was $1,640 million.

Required

Using the direct method, what amount would Tarpley Bakery report as cash payments to employees on its 2016 statement of cash flows?

13-21 Cash payments for operating costs (LO 7) In its 2016 annual report, Navya Naturals reported accrued liabilities of $10.01 million at the end of 2016 and $8.2 million at the end of 2015. The company's operating expenses for 2016 totaled $78.5 million.

Required

Using the direct method, what amount would the company report as cash payments for operating costs on its 2016 statement of cash flows?

13-22 Statement of cash flows—direct method (LO 7) The following is a list of various activities from Geiersbach Grain's latest year of operations.

Sale of marketable securities	$ 15,130
Repayment of long-term debt	19,215
Payment of cash dividends	500
Sale of equipment	20,600
Collections from customers	130,940
Payments for operating costs	27,400
Net income	37,520
Beginning Cash balance	13,645
Payments for equipment	23,670
Payments to suppliers	36,990
Proceeds from issuing common stock	1,450
Payments to employees	36,480
Payments for taxes	11,200
Ending Cash balance	26,310

Required

Using the direct method, construct Geiersbach Grains' statement of cash flows.

PROBLEMS

13-23 Statement of cash flows—indirect method (CMA adapted) (LO 2, 3, 4, 5) Kate Petusky prepared Addison Controls' balance sheet and income statement for 2016. Before she could complete the statement of cash flows, she had to leave town to attend to a family emergency. Because the full set of statements must be provided to the auditors today, Addison's president, Lance Meyers, has asked you to prepare the statement of cash flows. Meyers has provided you with the balance sheets and income statement that Petusky prepared, as well as some notes she made:

Addison Controls
Income Statement
For the Year Ended December 31, 2016

Sales revenue		$127,900
Cost of goods sold		69,800
Gross margin		58,100
Selling expense	$13,000	
Administrative expense	8,000	
Salaries expense	20,000	
Depreciation expense	1,900	
Interest expense	4,000	46,900
Income before gain and taxes		11,200
Gain on sale of land		900
Income tax expense		800
Net income		$ 11,300

Addison Controls
Comparative Balance Sheets
As of December 31

	2016	2015
Cash	$ 5,100	$ 4,300
Accounts receivable, net	6,300	5,500
Inventory	31,700	34,200
Total current assets	43,100	44,000
Property, plant, & equipment, net	211,500	215,300
Total Assets	$254,600	$259,300

	2016	2015
Accounts payable	$ 3,400	$ 5,900
Accrued expenses	2,400	2,200
Taxes payable	2,100	2,600
Bonds payable	60,000	50,000
Total liabilities	67,900	60,700
Common stock	125,000	125,000
Retained earnings	61,700	73,600
Total stockholders' equity	186,700	198,600
Total liabilities & stockholders' equity	$254,600	$259,300

- Equipment with an original cost of $35,000 was sold for $20,300. The book value of the equipment was $19,400.
- On June 1, 2016, the company purchased new equipment for cash at a cost of $17,500.
- At the end of the year the company issued bonds payable for $10,000 cash. The bonds will mature on December 31, 2020.
- The company paid $23,200 in cash dividends for the year.

Required

Using the indirect method, prepare Addison Controls' statement of cash flows for 2016.

13-24 Statement of cash flows—indirect method (CMA adapted) (LO 2, 3, 4, 5) Blake Weaver, Cook Enterprises' controller, is preparing the financial statements for 2016. He has completed the comparative balance sheets and income statement, which follow, and has gathered this additional information:

- On December 31, 2016, Cook sold a piece of equipment with an original cost of $25,000 for $30,000 cash. The equipment had a book value of $13,000.
- On February 1, 2016, Cook issued $100,000 of common stock to raise cash in anticipation of the purchase of a new building later in the year.
- On February 2, 2016, Cook took out a ten-year $75,000 long-term loan to provide the remaining funds needed to purchase the building.
- On May 15, 2016, Cook paid $150,000 for the new building.
- The company repaid $4,600 of the long-term debt before the end of the year.

Cook Enterprises
Income Statement
For the Year Ended December 31, 2016

Sales revenue		$ 1,070,000
Gain on equipment sale		17,000
Total revenue		1,087,000
Cost of goods sold		700,000
Operating expenses		
Depreciation expense	$ 30,000	
Interest expense	7,400	
Wages expenses	175,000	
Other expenses	16,000	228,400
Income before taxes		158,600
Tax expense		63,400
Net income		$ 95,200

(Continued)

Cook Enterprises
Comparative Balance Sheets
As of December 31

	2016	2015
Cash	$124,200	$ 40,400
Accounts receivable, net	287,200	269,800
Inventory	125,000	95,000
Total current assets	536,400	405,200
Property, plant, & equipment	297,000	160,000
Accumulated depreciation	90,000	60,000
Net property, plant, & equipment	207,000	100,000
Total assets	$743,400	$505,200
Accounts payable	$150,000	$175,000
Taxes payable	17,600	20,000
Mortgage payable	70,400	0
Total liabilities	238,000	195,000
Common stock	350,000	250,000
Retained earnings	155,400	60,200
Total stockholders' equity	505,400	310,200
Total liabilities & stockholders' equity	$743,400	$505,200

Required

Using the indirect method, prepare Cook Enterprises' statement of cash flows for 2016.

13-25 Analyzing the statement of cash flows (LO 6) The following statement of cash flows is adapted from Shanteza, Inc.'s 2016 annual report. Amounts are shown in millions of dollars.

	2016	2015	2014
Cash flows from operating activities			
Net income	$ 967	$ 833	$ 778
Adjustments to net income			
Depreciation and amortization	568	547	530
Other non-cash items	125	56	26
Changes in operating assets and liabilities			
Merchandise inventory	51	252	(97)
Other assets	34	18	12
Accounts payable	(4)	199	(6)
Accrued expenses and other liabilities	(235)	180	109
Income taxes payable	(94)	(4)	(102)
Net cash provided (used) by operating activities	1,412	2,081	1,250
Cash flows from investing activities			
Purchase of property and equipment	(431)	(682)	(572)
Proceeds from sale of property and equipment	1	11	22
Purchase of short-term investments	(75)	(894)	(1,460)
Maturities of short-term investments	251	1,287	1,841
Acquisition of business, net of cash acquired	(142)	—	—
Change in restricted cash	(1)	7	11
Change in other assets	(1)	(3)	8
Net cash provided (used) by investing activities	(398)	(274)	(150)

	2016	2015	2014
Cash flows from financing activities			
Payments of long-term debt	(138)	(326)	—
Purchase of treasury stock	(705)	(1,700)	(1,050)
Cash dividends paid	(243)	(252)	(265)
Other	63	165	210
Net cash provided (used) by financing activities	(1,023)	(2,113)	(1,105)
Change in cash	(9)	(306)	(5)
Cash, beginning balance	1,724	2,030	2,035
Cash, ending balance	$1,715	$ 1,724	$ 2,030

Required

Analyze Shanteza's statement of cash flows by making at least two observations about each section of the statement.

13-26 Analyzing the statement of cash flows (LO 6) Astridis, Inc. reported the following statement of cash flows in its 2016 annual report. Amounts are shown in thousands of dollars.

Astridis, Inc.
Statement of Cash Flows
For the Year Ending December 31

	2016	2015	2014
Cash flows from operating activities			
Net income	$(623,854)	$(936,248)	$(746,837)
Adjustments to net income			
Depreciation	100,670	105,749	98,555
Provision for doubtful accounts	9,082	7,613	4,011
Other non-cash items	181,206	460,013	177,536
Changes in operating assets and liabilities			
Receivables	(42,600)	(20,326)	(45,705)
Inventory	4,965	(20,246)	(6,329)
Prepaid expenses and other current assets	23,568	(61,698)	(5,372)
Accounts payable and accrued expenses	166,169	133,519	245,052
Other liabilities	62,886	85,694	125,255
Net cash provided (used) by operating activities	(117,908)	(245,930)	(153,834)
Cash flows from investing activities			
Purchases of property and equipment	(90,708)	(130,387)	(51,367)
Proceeds from sale of property and equipment	641	827	928
Purchases of investments	(4,310)	(105,279)	(173,937)
Sales of investments	40,191	255,015	48,555
Net cash provided (used) by investing activities	(54,186)	20,176	(175,821)
Cash flows from financing activities			
Proceeds from issuance of long-term debt	244,079	—	453,661
Repayment of debt	(625)	—	(57,609)
Other	4,897	25,787	75,879
Net cash provided (used) by financing activities	248,351	25,787	471,931
Change in cash	76,257	(199,967)	142,276
Cash, beginning balance	678,200	878,167	753,891
Cash, ending balance	$ 754,457	$ 678,200	$ 896,167

Required

Analyze Astridis's statement of cash flows by making at least two observations about each section of the statement.

13-27 Statement of cash flows—direct method (CMA adapted) (LO 3, 4, 5, 7) Blake Weaver, Cook Enterprises' controller, is preparing the financial statements for 2016. He has completed the comparative balance sheets and income statement, which follow, and has gathered this additional information:

- On December 31, 2016, Cook sold a piece of equipment with an original cost of $25,000 for $30,000 cash. The equipment had a book value of $13,000.
- On February 1, 2016, Cook issued $100,000 of common stock to raise cash in anticipation of the purchase of a new building later in the year.
- On February 2, 2016, Cook took out a ten-year $75,000 long-term loan to provide the remaining funds needed to purchase the building.
- On May 15, 2016, Cook paid $150,000 for the new building.
- The company repaid $4,600 of the long-term debt before the end of the year.

Cook Enterprises
Income Statement
For the Year Ended December 31, 2016

Sales revenue		$1,070,000
Gain on equipment sale		17,000
Total revenue		1,087,000
Cost of goods sold		700,000
Operating expenses		
Depreciation expense	$ 30,000	
Interest expense	7,400	
Wages expenses	175,000	
Other expenses	16,000	228,400
Income before taxes		158,600
Tax expense		63,400
Net income		$ 95,200

Cook Enterprises
Comparative Balance Sheets
As of December 31

	2016	2015
Cash	$124,200	$ 40,400
Accounts receivable, net	287,200	269,800
Inventory	125,000	95,000
Total current assets	536,400	405,200
Property, plant, & equipment	297,000	160,000
Accumulated depreciation	90,000	60,000
Net property, plant, & equipment	207,000	100,000
Total assets	$743,400	$505,200
Accounts payable	$103,000	$120,000
Wages payable	27,000	30,000
Accrued liabilities	20,000	25,000
Taxes payable	17,600	20,000
Mortgage payable	70,400	0
Total liabilities	238,000	195,000
Common stock	350,000	250,000
Retained earnings	155,400	60,200
Total stockholders' equity	505,400	310,200
Total liabilities & stockholders' equity	$743,400	$505,200

Required

Using the direct method, prepare Cook Enterprises' statement of cash flows for 2016.

13-28 Statement of cash flows—direct method (CMA adapted) (LO 3, 4, 5, 7) XLS

Kate Petusky prepared Addison Controls' balance sheet and income statement for 2016. Before she could complete the statement of cash flows, she had to leave town to attend to a family emergency. Because the full set of statements must be provided to the auditors today, Addison's president, Lance Meyers, has asked you to prepare the statement of cash flows. Meyers has provided you with the balance sheet and income statement that Petusky prepared, as well as some notes she made:

Addison Controls
Income Statement
For the Year Ended December 31, 2016

Sales revenue		$127,900
Cost of goods sold		69,800
Gross margin		58,100
Selling expense	13,000	
Administrative expense	8,000	
Salaries expense	20,000	
Depreciation expense	1,900	
Interest expense	4,000	46,900
Income before gain and taxes		11,200
Gain on sale of land		900
Income tax expense		800
Net income		$ 11,300

Addison Controls
Comparative Balance Sheets
As of December 31

	2016	**2015**
Cash	$ 5,100	$ 4,300
Accounts receivable, net	6,300	5,500
Inventory	31,700	34,200
Total current assets	43,100	44,000
Property, plant, & equipment, net	211,500	215,300
Total assets	$254,600	$259,300
Accounts payable	$ 3,400	$ 5,900
Accrued expenses	600	700
Salaries payable	1,800	1,500
Taxes payable	2,100	2,600
Note payable	60,000	50,000
Total liabilities	67,900	60,700
Common stock	125,000	125,000
Retained earnings	61,700	73,600
Total stockholders' equity	186,700	198,600
Total liabilities & stockholders' equity	$254,600	$259,300

- Equipment with an original cost of $35,000 was sold for $20,300. The book value of the equipment was $19,400.
- On June 1, 2016, the company purchased new equipment for cash at a cost of $17,500.
- At the end of the year, the company issued bonds payable for $10,000 cash. The bonds will mature on December 31, 2020.
- The company paid $23,200 in cash dividends for the year.

Required

Using the direct method, prepare Addison Control's statement of cash flows for 2016.

C&C SPORTS CONTINUING CASE

13-29 Identifying Cash Flows (LO 1) Classify each of the following items as a source or use of cash. If the item is a source or use of cash, then classify each item as a cash flow provided by an operating, investing, or financing activity.

	Type of Cash Flow			Type of Activity		
	Source	Use	Not a Cash Flow	Operating	Investing	Financing
1. C&C orders $50,000 of fabric from Bradley Textile Mills						
2. C&C pays $100,000 to Bradley Textile Mills for fabric it ordered last month						
3. C&C receives a $1,200 order from Central High School for 100 pairs of baseball pants						
4. C&C pays cash for $13,000 of Nike stock						
5. C&C pays $500 in interest due on its long-term debt						
6. C&C pays $800 cash for a new sewing machine						
7. C&C makes a $20,000 payment on its long-term debt						
8. C&C borrows $25,000 from the bank to maintain its minimum required cash balance						
9. C&C receives an order from South Avenue High School for 10 award jackets, accompanied by a check for the full amount of the order, $1,250						
10. C&C sells an old computer to an employee for $50 cash						

CASE

13-30 Statement of cash flows (LO 1, 2, 3, 4, 5, 6, 7) Vincent Fairfield, CEO of MetroAir, sat at his desk, examining the company's latest financial statements. "This just doesn't make sense to me," Vincent thought. "We're reporting $1,662,015 in net income, yet our Cash balance decreased by over $350,000. With these results, I would think the Cash balance should go up by at least $1,000,000."

MetroAir
Income Statement
For the Year Ended December 31, 2016

Sales	$78,555,000
Cost of goods sold	58,146,480
Gross profit	20,408,520
Selling expense	5,168,505
Administrative expense	3,814,660
Salaries expense	7,408,490
Depreciation expense	1,016,835
Interest expense	625,725
Income before taxes	2,374,305
Tax expense	712,290
Net income	$ 1,662,015

MetroAir
Balance Sheets
As of December 31

	2016	2015
Cash	$ 266,280	$ 631,710
Accounts receivable, net	9,355,695	8,751,435
Inventories	9,605,580	8,206,635
Other assets	691,380	359,640
Total current assets	19,918,935	17,949,420
Machinery and equipment, net	8,142,870	9,009,705
Total assets	$28,061,805	$26,959,125
Accounts payable	$ 6,624,030	$ 6,675,210
Accrued expenses	563,371	1,023,738
Salaries payable	615,940	595,380
Interest payable	58,143	55,412
Income taxes payable	63,781	59,860
Short-term debt	2,175,000	1,950,000
Total current liabilities	10,100,265	10,359,600
Long-term debt	4,200,000	4,500,000
Total liabilities	14,300,265	14,859,600
Common stock	3,150,000	3,150,000
Retained earnings	10,611,540	8,949,525
Total stockholders' equity	13,761,540	12,099,525
Total liabilities and stockholders' equity	$28,061,805	$26,959,125

Required

a. Prepare MetroAir's statement of cash flows using either the indirect or the direct method, as specified by your professor. During the year, the company purchased equipment, issued short-term debt, and retired long-term debt.
b. Prepare a memo to Vincent explaining why he should not necessarily expect an increase in cash when the company reports net income. Be specific and include any issues that should cause Vincent concern.

ENDNOTES

1. If the direct method is used, a reconciliation of net income to cash (using the indirect method) must be disclosed in the notes to the financial statements.
2. While U.S. GAAP allows companies to choose between the direct and indirect methods for reporting cash flows, International Financial Reporting Standards (IFRS) require companies to use the direct method. For more information on trends in reporting cash flows under U.S. GAAP, see AICPA, *Accounting Trends & Techniques—2011* (New York: American Institute of Certified Public Accountants, 2011).
3. Changes in short-term investments, notes receivable, and short-term debt are not included in this analysis of cash flow from operating activities because those accounts represent investing and financing activities.
4. You may recall that when a company repurchases its own stock, the stock is referred to as treasury stock.
5. While U.S. GAAP allows companies to choose between the direct and indirect methods for reporting cash flows, International Financial Reporting Standards (IFRS) require companies to use the direct method. To see an example of a published statement prepared using the direct method, visit Northrop Grumman Corporation at http://www.northropgrumman.com/ or CVS Corporation at http://www.cvscaremark.com.

Glossary

A

Absorption costing (Topic Focus 3) A product costing method that classifies direct materials, direct labor, variable overhead, and fixed overhead as product costs.

Accounting rate of return (Unit 9.4) The return generated by an investment based on its net operating income.

Accounts receivable turnover (Unit 12.3) A measure of the liquidity of a company's accounts receivable that shows how many times, on average, a company's receivables balance is "turned over," or collected, during the year.

Acid-test ratio (Unit 12.3) A measure of liquidity that includes only highly liquid current assets in its measurement; also referred to as the quick ratio.

Activity (Units 2.1, 7.1) An event that consumes resources; any repetitive event that serves as a measure of output or usage, such as sales, production, phone calls made, or miles driven.

Activity-based budgeting (Unit 7.3) The practice of using activity-based costing information and knowledge about activities and resource consumption to prepare an organization's budget.

Activity-based costing (Unit 7.1) A costing technique that assigns costs to cost objects, such as products or customers, based on the activities those cost objects require.

Activity-based management (Unit 7.3) The process of using activity-based costing information to manage a business's activities.

Activity cost pool (Unit 7.2) A group of costs combined based on their activity cost drivers and the resources to be consumed.

Activity rate (Unit 7.2) Rate calculated by dividing the total activity cost by the total activity driver volume.

Allocated cost (Unit 8.5) A cost that cannot be traced directly to a cost object but instead is incurred to support operations as a whole.

Annuity (Unit 9.2) A stream of equal cash flows received at set time intervals.

Application base (Unit 4.3) A measure of activity used to apply manufacturing overhead to the products being made. Common application bases are direct labor hours, machine hours, direct labor costs, and units of production.

Applied overhead (Unit 4.3) The amount of manufacturing overhead allocated to each job.

Asset turnover (Unit 10.3) A ratio that measures the efficiency of asset utilization; calculated by dividing sales revenue by average operating assets.

Assigned cost (Unit 8.5) A cost that cannot be directly traced to a cost object but instead is incurred to support operations as a whole.

Average collection period (Unit 12.3) The number of days, on average, the company takes to collect cash from a credit sale.

Average days to sell inventory (Unit 12.3) The average number of days that elapse from the receipt of inventory to its sale to customers.

Avoidable cost (Unit 8.1) A cost occurring only with the implementation of a particular alternative.

B

Balanced scorecard (Units 1.2, 11.2) A collection of performance measures that track an organization's progress toward achieving its goals.

Batch-level activity (Unit 7.1) An activity performed all at once on groups, or batches, of products.

Benchmarking (Unit 11.3) The practice of using data from other organizations to identify the processes and practices associated with world-class performance.

Best practices (Unit 11.3) The processes that lead to the best performance.

Bill of materials (Unit 4.3) The list and quantity of materials required to make a single unit of product.

Bottleneck process (Unit 8.4) The process that limits total output.

Bottom-up budget (Unit 5.1) A budgeting process that begins at the lowest levels of management and filters up through the organization.

Breakeven graph (Unit 3.1) A graphical representation that shows the intersection of the total revenue line and the total cost line at the sales volume where the company breaks even.

Breakeven point (Unit 3.1) The sales volume or sales revenue at which sales revenue is exactly equal to total costs, and there is no profit or loss.

Budget (Unit 5.1) An operating plan that is expressed primarily in financial terms (dollars or other currency).

Budgetary padding (Unit 5.1) The process of over- or understating budget items to make actual results look favorable when compared to the budget.

Budgetary slack (Unit 5.1) The process of over- or understating budget items to make actual results look favorable when compared to the budget.

Business process reengineering (BPR) (Unit 7.3) A managerial tool that focuses on improving the efficiency and effectiveness of an organization's business processes through radical change and redesign.

C

Capital asset (Unit 9.1) An asset that is expected to provide economic benefits for several years.

Capital budgeting (Unit 9.1) The process of evaluating an organization's investment in long-term assets.

Cash budget (Unit 5.4) A budget that helps manage cash flows by identifying budgeted cash receipts and disbursements for a period.

Cash payments for materials budget (Unit 5.4) A budget that calculates each period's cash payments for material purchases based on production schedules and payment practices.

Cash receipts budget (Unit 5.4) A budget that shows when and how much cash is expected to be collected from the sale of products or services.

Centralization (Unit 10.1) An organizational structure in which decision-making authority for the entire organization rests with the highest levels of management.

Code of conduct (Unit 1.3) A set of core values that are meant to guide employees' behavior.

Committed fixed cost (Unit 2.1) Fixed costs that cannot be changed over the short run.

Common cost (Unit 8.5) A cost that cannot be traced directly to a cost object but instead is incurred to support operations as a whole.

Common-size analysis (Unit 12.2) A financial statement analysis technique that examines the changes in the relative size of account balances within a single financial statement; also referred to as vertical analysis.

Compound interest (Unit 9.2) The interest from one period that is *compounded*, or added, to the principal balance, thus increasing the principal balance and future interest amounts.

Contribution format income statement (Unit 2.3) An income statement that classifies costs by behavior.

Contribution margin (Unit 2.3) The difference between sales and variable costs—the amount that remains to cover fixed costs and provide a profit.

Contribution margin ratio (Unit 2.3) Contribution margin divided by sales.

Controlling (Unit 1.1) One of a manager's responsibilities that requires monitoring operations to identify problems requiring corrective action.

Conversion costs (Topic Focus 2) Production costs (direct labor and manufacturing overhead) required to convert raw materials into finished goods.

Cost (Unit 2.3) The cash or other value given up to obtain goods or services with the expectation that they will generate future benefits.

Cost-based price (Chapter 10 Appendix) A transfer price that is based on the cost to produce the intermediate product.

Cost behavior (Unit 2.1) The way total costs change in response to changes in the level of activity.

Cost center (Unit 10.1) An organizational unit whose manager is responsible only for the costs incurred in the unit.

Cost of goods manufactured (Unit 4.2) The total cost of products finished during the period, whether or not they were started during the period.

Cost-plus-based price (Chapter 10 Appendix) A transfer price that is based on the cost to produce the intermediate product plus an agreed-upon markup.

Cost-plus pricing (Unit 3.4) A pricing strategy that starts with the cost to produce a product or deliver a service and adds a markup to cover the company's operating costs and contribute to profit.

Cost–volume–profit (CVP) analysis (Unit 3.2) Decision analysis tool that helps managers assess the impact of various business decisions on corporate profits.

Current ratio (Unit 12.3) Current assets divided by current liabilities.

Customer-level activity (Unit 7.1) An activity relating to specific customers (not to specific products).

Customer net profit (Topic Focus 5) A measure that determines the profit contributed by a particular customer; calculated as gross margin on products or services purchased by the customer (sales minus cost of goods sold) minus selling expenses allocated based on the customer-specific selling activities.

Customer perspective (Unit 11.2) A component of the balanced scorecard that considers the expectations of an organization's customers regarding quality, price, delivery speed, and service.

Customer profit margin (Topic Focus 5) Customer net profit divided by customer revenues; used to evaluate the profit margin generated by a particular customer.

Debt ratio (Unit 12.3) A measure of liquidity calculated by dividing total liabilities by total assets; shows the percentage of assets financed through debt.

Debt-to-equity ratio (Unit 12.3) Total liabilities divided by total stockholders' equity; shows the amount of financing provided by creditors (debt) relative to the amount provided by owners (equity).

Decentralization (Unit 10.1) An organizational structure in which decision-making authority is dispersed throughout the organization.

Decision making (Unit 1.1) The process of choosing a course of action after considering available alternatives.

Degree of operating leverage (Unit 3.2) Contribution margin divided by operating income, showing the expected magnitude of change in operating income due to a change in sales at a given level of sales.

Delivery cycle time (Chapter 11 Appendix) The time between when a customer's order is received and when it is shipped.

Depreciable asset (Unit 9.1) A capital asset other than land.

Differential (Unit 8.1) Information that differs between alternatives under consideration.

Direct costing (Topic Focus 3) A product costing method that classifies only variable production costs (direct material, direct labor, and variable manufacturing overhead) as product costs; variable costing.

Direct labor (Unit 4.1) The wages (and possibly benefits) paid to the workers who transform direct materials into a finished product.

Direct labor budget (Unit 5.3) A budget that calculates the number of direct labor hours and the total direct labor cost required to meet the budgeted level of production.

Direct labor efficiency variance (Unit 6.3) The part of the direct labor flexible budget variance that is caused by using more or fewer direct labor hours than the standard allowed for actual production; SP × (AQ − SQ).

Direct labor hours (Unit 4.1) Labor time that can be traced directly to, or easily identified with, a product.

Direct labor rate variance (Unit 6.3) The part of the direct labor flexible budget variance that results when the actual wage rate differs from the standard wage rate; AQ × (AP − SP).

Direct materials (Unit 4.1) Raw materials that can be traced directly to, or easily identified with, a product.

Direct materials price variance (Unit 6.2) The part of the direct materials flexible budget variance that results when actual materials prices differ from standard prices; AQ × (AP − SP).

Direct materials purchases budget (Unit 5.3) A budget that calculates the quantity of direct materials purchases and the total direct materials cost required to meet the budgeted level of production.

Direct materials quantity variance (Unit 6.2) The part of the direct materials flexible budget variance that is caused by using more or fewer materials than the standard quantity allowed for actual production; SP × (AQ − SQ).

Direct method (Unit 13.1) Approach to presenting cash flows provided by operating activities that reports the specific operating activities that provided and used cash.

Discounting (Unit 9.2) The process of determining how much an amount of money to be received in the future is worth today.

Discount rate (Unit 9.2) The interest rate used in calculating present value or for comparing to a project's internal rate of return.

Discretionary fixed cost (Unit 2.1) Fixed costs that can be changed over the short run.

Dividend payout ratio (Unit 12.3) Ratio measuring how much of earnings per share is returned to common stockholders in the form of dividends.

DuPont Model (Unit 10.3) Expanded formula for Return on Investment: margin × asset turnover.

Earnings per share (Unit 12.3) The portion of net income attributed to each outstanding share of common stock.

Economic value added (EVA) (Unit 10.4) A performance metric similar to residual income that measures economic profit. Calculated as net operating profit minus (invested capital × weighted-average cost of capital).

Ending inventory and cost of goods sold budget (Unit 5.3) A component of the operating budget that calculates Raw Materials, Work in Process, and Finished Goods Inventory balances and Cost of Goods Sold for the budget period based on budgeted production and sales.

Enterprise resource planning (ERP) (Unit 1.2) A system used by companies to provide information to decision makers on a companywide basis by integrating all data from the company's many business processes into a single information system.

Equivalent units (EU) (Topic Focus 2) A measure used in process costing that represents work in process (unfinished units) in terms of finished units.

Ethical behavior (Unit 1.3) Knowing right from wrong and conducting yourself accordingly so that your decisions are consistent with your own value system and the values of those affected by your decisions.

Evaluating (Unit 1.1) One of a manager's responsibilities that involves comparing actual results to planned results and assessing the performance of an individual or group of individuals who were responsible for the results.

Expense (Unit 2.3) An expired, or used up, cost.

F

Factor (Unit 12.3) Selling accounts receivable at a discounted rate to another firm that assumes responsibility for collecting the receivables.

Factory burden (Unit 4.1) The costs of production that are not direct and cannot be traced easily to a unit of product; manufacturing overhead.

Factory overhead (Unit 4.1) The costs of production that are not direct and cannot be traced easily to a unit of product; manufacturing overhead.

Factory support (Unit 4.1) The costs of production that are not direct and cannot be traced easily to a unit of product; manufacturing overhead.

Favorable variance (Unit 6.1) A variance that increases operating income relative to the budgeted amount.

Financial leverage (Unit 12.3) The use of borrowed capital to finance a business or project.

Financial measure (Unit 11.1) Quantitative and objective measures taken from accounting reports.

Financial perspective (Unit 11.2) A component of the balanced scorecard that considers an organization's financial objectives.

Financing activities (Unit 13.1) Activities that raise capital (cash) from, or repay cash to, creditors or stockholders

Finished goods inventory (Unit 4.2) An inventory account used by manufacturing firms that accumulates all production costs that have been incurred to complete products. It is equivalent to the single inventory account used by merchandising firms that buy inventory.

First-stage allocation (Unit 7.2) An activity-based costing process in which costs are assigned first to activity cost pools before being assigned to cost objects.

Fixed cost (Unit 2.1) A cost that does not change *in total* with changes in activity, but *per unit* cost varies indirectly with changes in activity.

Fixed overhead spending variance (Unit 6.4) The difference between actual fixed overhead cost and budgeted fixed overhead cost.

Fixed overhead volume variance (Topic Focus 4) The variance that results from producing/selling more or fewer units than budgeted.

Flexible budget (Unit 6.1) Used at the beginning of a period, it is a budget that calculates expected revenues and expenses over several levels of sales volume. Used at the end of a period, it is a budget that shows the revenues and expenses the company should have incurred given the actual sales volume during the period.

Flexible budget variance (Unit 6.1) The difference between the actual results and the flexible budget.

Full costing (Topic Focus 3) A product costing method that classifies direct materials, direct labor, variable overhead, and fixed overhead as product costs; absorption costing.

G

General and administrative costs (Unit 4.1) The costs associated with the general management of the company.

Generally accepted accounting principles (GAAP) (Unit 1.1) "Rules" that govern how transactions are valued and recorded and how financial information is presented.

Gross margin percentage (Unit 12.3) A measure that shows how much of each sales dollar is available to cover operating expenses and provide a profit after cost of goods sold has been covered; calculated as Gross margin ÷ Sales.

H

High-low method (Unit 2.2) A cost estimation technique that uses the equation of a line ($y = mx + b$) and a data set's highest and lowest volume points to separate a mixed cost into its fixed and variable components.

Horizontal analysis (Unit 12.1) A financial statement analysis technique that examines the changes in the account balances over time.

Hurdle rate (Unit 9.1) The minimum required rate of return of a project.

I

Ideal standard (Unit 5.2) The performance standard that implies perfection.

Incremental analysis (Unit 8.1) Calculations that show the additional impact of one alternative over another.

Indirect labor (Unit 4.1) Overhead category that includes the labor cost of all the workers who support the production process but who cannot be classified as direct labor.

Indirect materials (Unit 4.1) Overhead category that includes the supplies and materials used in production that cannot be classified as direct materials. Indirect materials may or may not be part of the final product.

Indirect method (Unit 13.1) Approach to presenting cash flows provided by operating activities that starts with net income and adjusts for non-cash items and changes in current asset and liability account balances.

Information overload (Unit 8.1) A phenomenon where an excessive amount of information available to a manager hinders decision making.

Intermediate product (Chapter 10 Appendix) A product that is a component of (direct material for) another product.

Internal business processes perspective (Unit 11.2) A component of the balanced scorecard that focuses on what organizations must do to create desired products and services and meet customers' expectations.

Internal rate of return (IRR) (Unit 9.3) The actual rate of return of a project.

Inventory turnover (Unit 12.3) A measure of the number of times, on average, a company's inventory "turns over," or is sold, during the year.

Investing activities (Unit 13.1) Activities that use or generate cash through investments in capital assets or investments in equities of other companies

Investment center (Unit 10.1) An organizational unit in which a manager has responsibility for generating revenues, controlling costs, and making investments in assets.

J

Job cost sheet (Unit 4.3) A report used in a job order costing system that accumulates and summarizes all costs incurred for a particular job.

Job order costing system (Unit 4.3) A product costing system in which the costs of products or services are accumulated by batch or customer.

Just-in-time inventory (JIT) (Unit 1.2) An inventory strategy that focuses on reducing waste and inefficiency by ordering inventory items so that they arrive just when they are needed.

K

Key performance indicator (KPI) (Unit 11.1) A performance measure that indicates whether an organization is making successful progression toward the organization's goals.

L

Lagging indicator (Unit 11.1) A performance measure that can be determined only after an event has occurred.

Leading indicator (Unit 11.1) A performance measure that helps predict a future result.

Learning and growth perspective (Unit 11.2) A component of the balanced scorecard that focuses on developing the work force and investing in technology to facilitate change and improvement within an organization.

Liquidity (Unit 12.3) A firm's ability to pay its obligations (bills) as they come due and to meet any unforeseen needs for cash.

Long-lived asset (Unit 9.1) Any asset that is expected to provide economic benefits for more than one year.

Long-term planning (Unit 1.1) A management activity that establishes the direction in which an organization wishes to go; often referred to as strategic planning.

M

Make-or-buy decision (Unit 8.3) A company's decision to make a part in-house or buy it from a supplier.

Management by exception (Unit 6.1) An evaluation method in which managers only investigate variances, favorable or unfavorable, that exceed an established threshhold.

Managerial accounting (Unit 1.1) The generation and analysis of relevant information to support managers' strategic and operational decision-making activities.

Manufacturing burden (Unit 4.1) The costs of production that are not direct and cannot be traced easily to a unit of product; manufacturing overhead.

Manufacturing costs (Unit 4.1) The costs (direct materials, direct labor, and manufacturing overhead) a company incurs to acquire raw materials and convert them to finished goods ready for sale.

Manufacturing cycle efficiency (Chapter 11 Appendix) Value-added processing time divided by total manufacturing cycle time.

Manufacturing cycle time (Chapter 11 Appendix) The elapsed time from the start of production to the shipment of the product to the customer.

Manufacturing overhead (Unit 4.1) The costs of production that are not direct and cannot be traced easily to a unit of product.

Manufacturing overhead budget (Unit 5.3) The component of the operating budget that shows the expected overhead costs for the period.

Manufacturing support (Unit 4.1) The costs of production that are not direct and cannot be traced easily to a unit of product; manufacturing overhead.

Margin (Unit 10.3) The percentage of sales revenue in excess of operating expenses; operating income ÷ sales revenue.

Margin of safety (Unit 3.1) The difference between current sales and breakeven sales.

Market-based price (Chapter 10 Appendix) A transfer price that is determined by monitoring trades that occur between unrelated parties in the marketplace.

Markup (Unit 3.4) The difference between the selling price and the cost of the product.

Master budget (Unit 5.3) A collection of operational budgets that are used to develop pro-forma (budgeted) financial statements.

Matching principle (Topic Focus 3) A fundamental concept in financial accounting that expenses should be recognized in the same period as the revenues they generate.

Materiality (Unit 6.1) An expression of the level of significance of a financial amount. If an item is material, its value is significant and should have an impact on decision making.

Materials requisition slip (Unit 4.3) A document indicating the direct materials that are to be released from the storeroom to the factory floor.

Minimum cash balance (Unit 5.4) The minimum amount of cash a firm wants to have on hand to meet unexpected cash needs, shifts in demand patterns, or certain debt requirements.

Mixed cost (Unit 2.1) A cost that has both fixed and variable components.

N

Negotiated price (Chapter 10 Appendix) A transfer price that is agreed to by both the buying and the selling divisions.

Net initial investment (Unit 9.3) The net cash outflow when a capital investment is made.

Net operating profit (Unit 10.4) An organization's operating income minus income taxes.

Net present value (NPV) (Unit 9.3) An approach to capital budgeting that requires the calculation and summation of the present values of each cash inflow and outflow.

Nonfinancial measure (Unit 11.1) Performance measure that is not based on accounting results and can be either qualitative or quantitative.

Nonmanufacturing cost (Unit 4.1) Any cost that is not a product cost.

Non-value-added activity (Unit 7.3) An activity that consumes resources but does not contribute to the value of the final product or service.

Normal costing system (Topic Focus 4) A product costing system whereby direct materials and direct labor are recorded at actual cost, and overhead is applied to products using a predetermined overhead rate.

O

Offshoring (Unit 8.3) Moving a company's business processes to a foreign country.

Operating activities (Unit 13.1) Activities that accomplish the company's core purpose for being in business.

Operating budget (Unit 5.3) A component of the master budget that provides a financial plan for operations during the budget period.

Operating leverage (Unit 3.2) The change in operating income relative to a change in sales.

Opportunity cost (Unit 8.3) The contribution margin foregone by not selecting the next-best alternative.

Organization-level activity (Unit 7.1) An activity required to provide productive capacity and to keep the business in operation.

Outsourcing (Unit 8.3) Moving the production of goods or the delivery of services from within the organization to a provider outside the organization.

Overapplied overhead (Unit 4.4) The result of applying too much overhead cost to products as they were made; applied overhead > actual overhead.

Overhead (Unit 4.1) The costs of production that are not direct and cannot be traced easily to a unit of product.

Overhead application (Unit 4.3) Dividing or allocating overhead to various products or services based on an activity driver.

P

Participative budgeting (Unit 5.1) A budgeting process whereby employees who will be held accountable for meeting the budget participate in its creation.

Payback period (Unit 9.4) The time it takes, in years, for an investment to return the original amount of invested capital.

Performance dashboard (Unit 11.1) A visual display of the key measures related to an organization's operational goals and strategies.

Period cost (Unit 4.1) Any cost that is not a product cost.

Practical standards (Unit 5.2) Standards that represent a level of performance that can be attained with reasonable effort.

Predetermined overhead rate (Unit 4.3) A rate used to allocate overhead costs to products as they are being made. It is calculated as estimated total overhead costs ÷ estimated total activity level.

Preference decision (Unit 9.1) An allocation approach whereby managers determine which projects will actually receive funds by rank-ordering them based on selected criteria, both financial and nonfinancial.

Present value (Unit 9.2) The value today of an amount to be received in the future.

Present value factor (Unit 9.2) A factor used to calculate the present value of a future amount; based on the discount rate and the number of periods until the amount is received.

Price/earnings (P/E) ratio (Unit 12.3) Performance metric indicating what multiple of current earnings investors are willing to pay for a share of stock.

Process costing system (Topic Focus 2) A costing system whereby all product costs for the period are accumulated and divided evenly over all units produced during the period.

Process improvement (Unit 7.3) The examination of business processes to identify incremental changes that may reduce operating costs.

Product cost (Unit 4.1) Any cost (direct material, direct labor, or manufacturing overhead) that a company incurs to acquire raw materials and convert them to finished goods ready for sale.

Product-level activity (Unit 7.1) An activity that supports the product lines or services a company provides.

Production budget (Unit 5.3) The budget that calculates the level of production required to meet budgeted sales and maintain desired ending levels of finished goods inventory.

Profit center (Unit 10.1) An organizational unit in which a manager is responsible for both the revenues earned and the costs incurred.

Profitability index (Unit 9.3) An evaluation tool that compares the present value of a project's cash flows to the net initial investment.

Pro-forma financial statements (Unit 5.5) Financial statements that report the organization's financial position if all the components of a budget or other estimations are achieved as planned.

Q

Quick ratio (Unit 12.3) A measure of liquidity that includes only highly liquid current assets in its measurement; also referred to as the acid-test ratio.

R

Ratio analysis (Unit 12.3) Analysis techniques used to examine the relationships among the financial statement accounts.

Raw materials inventory (Unit 4.2) The general ledger account used to accumulate raw materials purchased and used in the production process.

Regression analysis (Unit 2.2) A statistical technique that separates a mixed cost into its fixed and variable components by identifying the line of best fit for the points in a data set.

Relevant information (Unit 8.1) Information that (1) differs between the alternatives and that (2) occurs in the future; this information has an impact on decisions.

Relevant range (Unit 2.2) The normal or expected range of operating activity.

Residual income (Unit 10.4) The income that is earned above a specified minimum level of return. It is calculated as operating income minus (average assets × minimum required rate of return).

Responsibility accounting (Unit 10.1) Practice by which division managers are evaluated only on those items over which they have control.

Return of investment (Unit 9.1) The recovery of an original investment.

Return on assets (Unit 12.3) Ratio that indicates how well assets have been employed to generate income.

Return on common stockholders' equity (Unit 12.3) Ratio that indicates how well the funds provided by common stockholders have been used to generate a return for the company.

Return on investment (Units 9.1, 10.3) Any return you receive over and above the original investment. The rate of return generated by an investment in assets: Operating income ÷ Average assets.

Rolling budget (Unit 5.1) A budget that always includes 12 months of data: As one month ends, it is removed from the budget, and the entire budget rolls forward one month.

S

Sales budget (Unit 5.3) A budget that forecasts the number of units expected to be sold multiplied by the prices expected to be charged, resulting in the revenue expected to be earned.

Sales mix (Unit 3.3) The sales of each product relative to total sales.

Sales price variance (Unit 6.1) The variance resulting from the difference between the actual prices charged to customers and budgeted prices.

Sales volume variance (Unit 6.1) The variance resulting from the difference between the flexible budget and the static budget.

Scattergraph (Unit 2.2) A graph of individual data points showing total costs in relation to volume, or activity level.

Screening decision (Unit 9.1) A decision approach whereby managers compare a proposed project to a performance benchmark to determine whether the project should be considered further.

Segment (Units 8.5, 10.2) A portion of the business that managers wish to evaluate.

Segment margin (Unit 8.5) The contribution margin of a particular segment minus its direct fixed costs.

Selling and administrative expense budget (Unit 5.3) A budget that estimates when and how much selling and administrative expense will be incurred.

Selling costs (Unit 4.1) Costs that are associated with the storage, sale, and delivery of finished goods.

Short-term (operational) planning (Unit 1.1) A management activity that translates the long-term strategy into a short-term plan to be completed within the next year.

Simple rate of return (Unit 9.4) The return generated by an investment based on its net operating income; accounting rate of return.

Sources of cash (Unit 13.1) Activities that generate cash receipts, which increase the amount of cash on hand.

Standard cost (Unit 5.2) The expected cost to produce one unit of product.

Standard costing system (Topic Focus 4) A costing system whereby all inventory costs (direct materials, direct labor, and manufacturing overhead) are recorded at standard and are reconciled to actual costs by recording variances.

Standards (Unit 5.2) Expectations that specify the characteristics, rules, or guidelines that define a particular level of performance or quality.

Statement of cash flows (Unit 13.1) A statement that explains the change in the Cash account balance by showing how cash was generated and spent.

Static budget (Unit 6.1) A budget developed for a single level of expected output.

Static budget variance (Unit 6.1) The variance resulting from the difference between actual results and the static budget.

Step cost (Unit 2.1) Costs that are fixed over only a small range of activity. Once that level of activity has been exceeded, total costs increase and remain constant over another small range of activity.

Strategic planning (Unit 5.1) Very broad planning that identifies the overall focus of an organization.

Strategy map (Unit 11.2) A pictorial representation of the cause-and-effect relationships embodied in the organization's strategy.

Sunk cost (Unit 8.1) A cost that has already been incurred and cannot be changed.

Supplies Inventory (Unit 4.2) An account used to accumulate the cost of indirect materials.

Supply chain (Unit 1.2) A network of facilities that procure raw materials, transform them into intermediate goods and then into final products, and deliver the final products to customers through a distribution system.

T

Tactical planning (Unit 5.1) Development of concrete actions that turn strategic plans into reality.

Target costing (Unit 3.4) A pricing strategy that computes the desired markup and the maximum cost the company can incur to deliver a product or service at the market price.

Theory of Constraints (Unit 8.4) Theory developed to maximize the performance of a value chain by focusing on constraints that limit an organization's output.

Throughput contribution (Unit 8.4) Sales revenue minus direct materials cost.

Throughput time (Chapter 11 Appendix) The elapsed time from the start of production to the shipment of the product to the customer.

Times interest earned ratio (Unit 12.3) The measurement of a company's ability to make interest payments out of current earnings.

Time ticket (Unit 4.3) A document used to track labor costs by recording an employee's name, date, job number, and beginning and ending time on a particular job.

Top-down budget (Unit 5.1) A process by which executive managers create the budget, and that budget is then pushed down through the rest of the organization.

Total manufacturing cost (Unit 4.2) The direct materials used in production, direct labor incurred, and manufacturing overhead incurred during a particular accounting period.

Transfer price (Chapter 10 Appendix) The price at which an exchange between buying and selling divisions within the same organization takes place.

Trend analysis (Unit 12.1) A form of horizontal analysis whereby each year's account balance is expressed as a percentage of the base year's (earliest year's) account balance.

Unadjusted rate of return (Unit 9.4) The return generated by an investment based on its net operating income.

Unavoidable cost (Unit 8.1) A cost incurred under all alternatives under consideration.

Underapplied overhead (Unit 4.4) The result of charging too little overhead cost to products as they were made; applied overhead < actual overhead.

Unfavorable variance (Unit 6.1) A variance that decreases operating income relative to the budgeted amount.

Unit-level activity (Unit 7.1) An activity that benefits individual units of production.

Use of cash (Unit 13.1) Activities that require cash disbursements, which decrease the amount of cash on hand.

Value-added activity (Unit 7.3) An activity that helps create the product the customer wants to buy.

Variable cost (Unit 2.1) Any cost whose total varies in proportion to a business activity. Variable cost per unit is constant over the relevant range.

Variable costing (Topic Focus 3) A product costing method that classifies only variable production costs (direct material, direct labor, and variable manufacturing overhead) as product costs; direct costing.

Variable cost ratio (Unit 2.3) Total variable costs divided by total sales.

Variable overhead efficiency variance (Unit 6.4) The variance that captures the effect of efficient use of the activity based on the cost of variable overhead; SP × (AQ × SQ).

Variable overhead spending variance (Unit 6.4) Variance resulting from the difference between the actual cost of variable overhead items and the amount of variable overhead cost that is expected to be incurred at the actual level of activity base; Actual cost − (SP × AQ).

Variance (Unit 6.1) The difference between actual results and budgeted, or expected, results.

Vertical analysis (Unit 12.2) A financial statement analysis technique that examines the changes in the relative size of account balances within a single financial statement; also referred to as common-size analysis.

Weighted-average cost of capital (WACC) (Unit 10.4) The combined rate of return required by all capital providers.

Working capital (Unit 12.3) The difference between a firm's current assets and its current liabilities.

Work in process inventory (Unit 4.2) Inventory account that accumulates the costs of all products that have been started but are not yet complete.

X, Y, Z

Zero-based budgeting (Unit 5.1) A budgeting process under which the budget begins each year at $0 and each individual budget item must be justified.

Company Index

T

U

V

W

X

Y

Z

Subject Index

C

D

E

F

P

T

U